WITHDRAWN

LEGAL SYSTEMS
OF THE WORLD

LEARNING RESOURCE CENTER
NORTH PLATTE COMMUNITY COLLEGE

LEGAL SYSTEMS OF THE WORLD

A POLITICAL, SOCIAL, AND CULTURAL ENCYCLOPEDIA

Volume IV: S–Z

Edited by Herbert M. Kritzer

ABC CLIO

SANTA BARBARA, CALIFORNIA · DENVER, COLORADO · OXFORD, ENGLAND

Copyright © 2002 by Herbert M. Kritzer

All rights reserved. No part of this publication may be reproduced, stored in a retrieval system, or transmitted, in any form or by any means, electronic, mechanical, photocopying, recording, or otherwise, except for the inclusion of brief quotations in a review, without prior permission in writing from the publishers.
Library of Congress Cataloging-in-Publication Data

Legal systems of the world : a political, social, and cultural
encyclopedia / edited by Herbert M. Kritzer.
        p. cm.
Includes index.
    ISBN 1-57607-231-2 (hardcover : alk. paper); 1-57607-758-6 (e-book)
    1. Law—Encyclopedias. I. Kritzer, Herbert M., 1947–
    K48 .L44 2002
    340'.03—dc21
                            2002002659

"Cape Verde" originally published in the *Journal of African Law* 44, no. 1 (2000): 86–95.

Material in "Comoros" and "Djibouti" used with the kind permission of Kluwer Law International.

Material in "European Court of Justice" from Kenney, Sally J. "The European Court of Justice: Integrating Europe through Law." 81 Judicature 250–255 (1998). Reprinted in *Crime and Justice International,* November.

06   05   04   03   10   9   8   7   6   5   4   3

This book is also available on the World Wide Web as an e-book. Visit abc-clio.com for details.

ABC-CLIO, Inc.
130 Cremona Drive, P.O. Box 1911
Santa Barbara, California 93116–1911

This book is printed on acid-free paper ∞.
Manufactured in the United States of America

CONTENTS

LEGAL SYSTEMS OF THE WORLD

Volume I: A–D

Volume II: E–L

Volume III: M–R

LEGAL SYSTEMS OF THE WORLD

Volume IV

S

SAINT LUCIA
See St. Lucia

SAINT VINCENT AND THE GRENADINES

GENERAL INFORMATION

Saint Vincent is a volcanic island 18 miles long north to south and 11 miles wide. Its windward coast is lined with cliffs and rocky shores pounded by the Atlantic Ocean. The leeward coast has spectacular slopes and valleys running down to beaches lapped by the tranquil Caribbean Sea. The interior of Saint Vincent is dominated by La Soufrière, a dormant volcano that rises to 1,219 meters and last erupted in 1979.

The Grenadines comprise more than 31 islands and cays with beautiful beaches and turquoise blue waters. The larger of the Grenadine islands are Bequia, Mustique, Canouan, and Union Island. Some of the smaller islands are privately owned.

Saint Vincent and the Grenadines is blessed with a tropical climate. Temperatures range from 24° C (75° F) to 30°C (80° F). The dry season is from January to April and the rainy season from July to October. Saint Vincent and the Grenadines has a population of approximately 115,000. The country is in the Atlantic Time Zone, one hour ahead of New York City.

HISTORY

First settled by the peace-loving Ciboney around 5000 B.C.E., then by the Arawaks and the warlike Caribs, Saint Vincent has had a colorful and turbulent history. Caribs aggressively prevented European settlement on Saint Vincent until the eighteenth century.

A Dutch slave ship that wrecked off Bequia in 1675 brought the first Africans to the island. They intermarried to create the Black Caribs, whose descendants live in Saint Vincent today.

For nearly a century, the French and British fought over who would control Saint Vincent. Beginning in 1719, French settlers cultivated coffee, tobacco, indigo, cotton, and sugar on plantations worked by African slaves. In 1763 Saint Vincent was ceded to Britain. It was restored to French rule in 1779 but was regained by the British under the Treaty of Versailles in 1783. Conflict between the Black Caribs and the British continued until 1796. More than 5,000 Black Caribs were eventually deported to Roatan, an island off the coast of Honduras.

Slavery was abolished in 1834. The resulting labor shortages on the plantation attracted Portuguese immigrants in the 1840s and East Indians in the 1860s. Conditions remained harsh for both former slaves and immigrant agricultural workers, as depressed world sugar prices kept the economy stagnant until the turn of the twentieth century.

From 1763 until independence, Saint Vincent passed through various stages of colonialism under the British. A representative assembly was authorized in 1776, a Crown colony government installed in 1877, a legislative council created in 1925, and universal adult suffrage granted in 1951. On October 27, 1979, Saint Vincent and the Grenadines gained its independence from Britain.

CULTURE

The fascinating blend of African, Indian, Asian, and European influences is expressed in the lifestyle of the people, through religion, sport, music, cuisine, arts, and crafts.

In the capital, Kingstown, the colonial influence is beautifully captured in many fine churches and public buildings. The historic botanical gardens were established in 1765 and are the oldest of their kind in the Western Hemisphere. It was here that Captain Bligh first brought the breadfruit trees intended to provide food for the slaves.

West of Kingstown and more than 600 feet above the bay is Fort Charlotte. Constructed in 1806, the old barracks now houses a museum, its walls displaying a colorful pictorial history of Black Caribs.

GOVERNMENT

Saint Vincent and the Grenadines is an independent sovereign state within the British Commonwealth. Its system of government rests on a parliamentary democracy. The head of state is Britain's Queen Elizabeth II, who is represented by the governor-general and the head of government, the prime minister. The constitution is the supreme

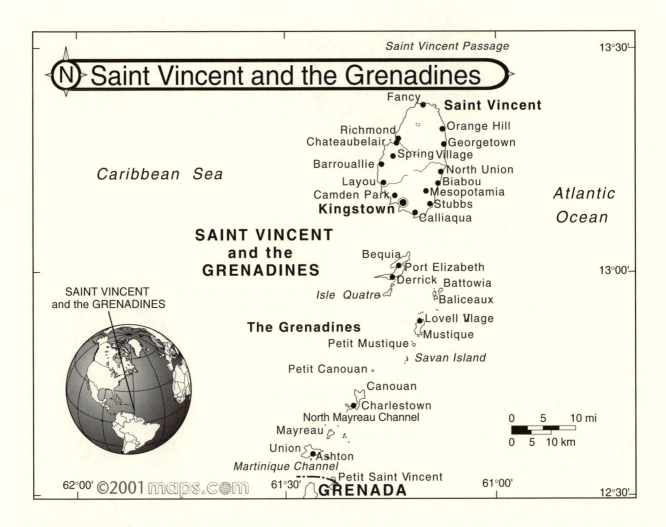

Saint Vincent Passage

13°30'

N Saint Vincent and the Grenadines

Fancy
Saint Vincent

Richmond
Chateaubelair
Orange Hill
Georgetown
Spring Village

Barrouallie
North Union

Layou
Biabou

Caribbean Sea
Camden Park
Mesopotamia

Kingstown
Stubbs
Calliaqua

Atlantic Ocean

SAINT VINCENT and the GRENADINES

Bequia
Port Elizabeth

13°00'

SAINT VINCENT and the GRENADINES
Derrick
Battowia

Isle Quatre
Baliceaux

Lovell Vlage

The Grenadines
Mustique

Petit Mustique

Savan Island

Petit Canouan

Canouan
Charlestown

North Mayreau Channel

0   5   10 mi

Mayreau

0   5   10 km

Union
Ashton

Martinique Channel
Petit Saint Vincent

62°00' ©2001 maps.com
61°30'
GRENADA
61°00'
12°30'

---

law of the land, and it embraces the concept of separation of the legislative, executive, and judiciary branches.

The parliament is a unicameral body with a fifteen-member elected house of assembly and a six-member appointed senate. Members are elected by popular vote from single-member constituencies. Following legislative elections, the leader of the majority party is usually appointed prime minister. Senators are appointed by the governor-general, four on the advice of the prime minister and two on the advice of the leader of the opposition. The parliamentary term of office is five years, although the prime minister may call elections at any time.

The executive consists of the head of government and the cabinet, which is appointed by the governor-general on the advice of the prime minister.

There is no local government in Saint Vincent and the Grenadines, and all parishes are administered by the central government.

THE JUDICIARY

Structure

As in other English-speaking Caribbean countries, the judiciary in Saint Vincent and the Grenadines is rooted in British common law. There are eleven courts in three magisterial districts. The Eastern Caribbean Supreme Court, comprising a high court and a court of appeal, is known in Saint Vincent and the Grenadines as the Supreme Court. The court of final resort is the judicial committee of Her Majesty's Privy Council in London.

Since the 1990s, however, there has been significant judicial development within the jurisdiction. Of note is the creation in 1995 of a family court, which is unusual in most jurisdictions in the Commonwealth Caribbean. This court, specializing in matters relating to families and young children, is a step above the Magistrates' Courts and has helped to reduce the burden on the magistracy. Moreover, it provides the requisite level of confidentiality and privacy that must surround these sensitive cases.

On February 2, 2001, the Honorable Chief Justice Sir Dennis Byron appointed a committee to look into the recruitment and selection of judicial officers. In March the committee submitted a report making recommendations to the various governments within the Organization of Eastern Caribbean States (OECS). Ratification is awaited by the governments of the OECS.

Legal Structure of Saint Vincent and the Grenadines Courts

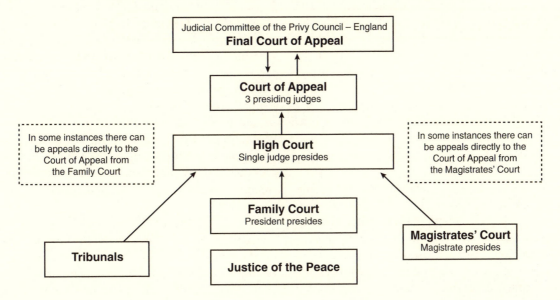

Civil Jurisdiction

Toward the end of 2000, various countries in the Organization of Eastern Caribbean States passed legislation to create in their jurisdictions the position of master and to pave the way for the Civil Procedure Rules 2000. These rules became effective beginning December 31, 2000, with a six-month transitional period ending June 30, 2001. In order to facilitate integration of the new rules in the legal system, the various bar associations in the OECS, along with the office of the chief registrar, have organized workshops to overview the new rules of the court.

It is hoped that the new rules will help reduce the backlog of civil cases, with its attendant costs and delays, and will restore public confidence in the civil justice system. At the apex of the new rules is case management, which began in earnest in January 2001. Case management allows the court to take control of the process of litigation and imposes timelines for the completion of critical phases. If its deadlines are not complied with, the court is empowered to take appropriate action against the offending party by imposing cost sanctions.

The introduction of modern technology, such as computer systems and videotape, is acknowledged to be crucial if the new rules are to be effective. To this end, the judicial body in Saint Vincent and the Grenadines has pledged its commitment to implementing technological advances and adapting them to the needs of the court.

In keeping with this continued metamorphosis, the judiciary also recognizes the need to utilize alternative dispute resolution processes. Discussions have already taken place in this regard, and implementation of such processes is imminent.

Criminal Jurisdiction

The Magistrates' Courts deal with summary offenses, while the High Court, in its criminal jurisdiction, deals with indictable offenses.

The judge at a trial on indictment is a professional judge who sits with an empaneled jury. The prosecution must be legally represented, but the accused is required to have legal counsel only in murder trials. If a defendant accused of murder lacks the means to obtain an attorney, the state will appoint and pay for one to represent him.

Criminal proceedings in Saint Vincent and the Grenadines are public, as the citizenry has an interest in seeing that the innocent are acquitted and the guilty convicted, and that offenders are properly sentenced. It is a fundamental principle of the law in Saint Vincent and the Grenadines that justice shall be administered in open court.

LEGAL PRACTICE AND TRAINING

The bar association of Saint Vincent and the Grenadines has a membership of about 120 persons. Admission to this bar is obligatory in order to be eligible to practice law. Training for the degree of bachelor of laws (LL.B.) is provided at the University of the West Indies, Cave Hill Campus, in Barbados. After graduation, candidates may sit the bar examination at the Norman Manley Law School in Jamaica or at the Sir Hugh Wooding Law School in Trinidad. Legal training in the United Kingdom is equally recognized for the law degree and the bar.

The OECS bar association also has a continuing legal education program for attorneys. Court of appeals and High Court judges also participate from time to time in continuing legal education programs, which are usually organized by the office of the chief registrar in St. Lucia.

ARBITRATION

Parties by way of a written agreement can submit disputes for resolution through arbitration. Once a dispute is formally under arbitration, any attempt by one of the parties to have the matter disposed of through the courts is typically stayed and the matter referred in accordance with the arbitration agreement.

TRIBUNALS

Various tribunals in Saint Vincent and the Grenadines perform a quasi-judicial role. The labor tribunal, however, which is frequently used to resolve employment and labor disputes, takes place in an informal setting and emphasizes mediation. Another tribunal of frequent recourse is the Public Services Commission, which mainly deals with disputes concerning public servants, civil servants, and the government.

CARIBBEAN COURT OF JUSTICE

The most herculean judicial task that the countries of the Caribbean are attempting is the creation and institution of the Caribbean Court of Justice (CCJ). The CCJ is to be established by way of an agreement signed by all Caribbean Community (CARICOM) member states. Its objective is twofold: to serve as a court of original jurisdiction in matters of international law and treaties and as the final court of appeal, replacing the Privy Council in London, in all criminal and civil matters for CARICOM member states. The creation of the CCJ is thus linked with the assertion of sovereignty and national pride among the independent nations of the Caribbean, which would no longer have to look to a foreign country, Great Britain, as the final arbiter of judicial decisions.

Several concerns have, however, been raised about the CCJ. The constitutions of the respective member states must be amended so as to give to the new court the requisite security and protection. A provision that member states may withdraw from the agreement on three years' notice has led to worry about the CCJ's stability as it is felt that three years in the life of the court is no time at all.

There are also other questions regarding costs, support by member states, and the dispersal of general information to the public. All these concerns will need to be addressed before the CCJ is introduced as the final court of justice. Indeed, Saint Vincent and the Grenadines is one of only two CARICOM member states (the other is Dominica) that have refused to sign the agreement that would allow the CCJ to replace the Privy Council.

PRISONS

In Saint Vincent and the Grenadines, it is felt that justice ends at the prison door. The rights of prisoners are seriously infringed, and overcrowding abounds. Violence is rampant in the prisons. Inmates torture each other; they are in control of the facilities, flouting prison rules and frequently rioting, for guards are insufficiently trained to maintain order. The situation has led the judges and magistrates to try to reduce the number of persons sent to prison, either by giving suspended sentences or by imposing a noncustodial sentence even in cases where justice and public safety may require a custodial sentence. This trend is a matter of much public debate and concern.

IMPACT OF THE LAW

The citizens of Saint Vincent and the Grenadines depend on the administration of justice and the rule of law for the maintenance of peace and cooperation within the society. The adoption and continued implementation of the new court rules will bring greater confidence in the judicial system, as justice will not only be done but will also manifestly be seen to be done in a timely and cost-effective manner. The trend toward alternative processes of conflict resolution, which allow people to redress grievances in a less adversarial forum than the courtroom, can only help to bolster a sense of community and togetherness among the nation's citizens.

Nicole Sylvester

See also Appellate Courts; Common Law; Constitutional Law; Judicial Selection, Methods of; Privy Council; Trial Courts

References and further reading
"Saint Vincent and the Grenadines—Government." http://www.travel.com/country/stv/gov.htm (accessed November 14, 2001).
"Saint Vincent and the Grenadines—Travel and General Information." http://svgtorism.com/info.htm (accessed November 14, 2001).
U.S. Department of State. 1998. "Background Notes: Saint Vincent and the Grenadines." http://www.state.gov/www/background_notes/stvincent_ 398_bgn.html (accessed November 14, 2001).

SAMOA

COUNTRY INFORMATION

Samoa is an independent state lying in the center of the South Pacific Ocean. It is the larger part of the Samoan archipelago that sits between 13 and 15 degrees south latitude and between 171 and 173 degrees west longitude. Samoa comprises nine islands, totaling some 1,090 square miles, dominated by the high-rise islands of Savaii (660 square miles) and Upolu (430 square miles). Samoa's exclusive economic zone extends its jurisdiction to include 200 nautical miles of ocean and seabed from the shoreline.

Samoa today, with a population of 165,000, is homogeneous in terms of its language and culture, which it shares with American Samoa, from which it was partitioned at the beginning of the twentieth century. The principal urban area of some 50,000 people is the capital of Apia on Upolu.

Agriculture forms the basis for Samoa's economy. It has been largely of subsistence type, with little money accruing to the average Samoan planter. Today, the three major cash crops are coconut (oil, cream, and copra), cocoa, and taro, which together with timber and tropical fruits constitute the main exports. Tourism is a growing income earner. In common with many other developing countries that lack mineral resources and nearby markets, Samoa finds it difficult to sustain a policy of rational economic growth against a background of limited agricultural exports and wide fluctuations in international market prices for them. The economy is assisted greatly by private remittances into Samoa from Samoans living and working in New Zealand, the United States, and elsewhere. Samoa receives financial and technical assistance from New Zealand, Australia, and other countries and from United Nations programs and agencies.

At the heart of Samoan society is the 'aiga (extended family), which, as the basic descent group, constitutes the means by which all Samoans relate to their ancestors, their matai (chiefs), their land, and their descendants. Traditional political organization is founded upon the matai system. The matai, holders of chiefly titles, are the heads of the 'aiga groups, which have rights in respect of both the title and the area of land associated with it.

The basic unit of traditional Samoan politics is the village, to which the chiefly titles of the constituent family descent groups belong. The matai meet regularly in fono (village councils), where every title has its rank. As a traditional institution of government, the village fono functions as executive, legislative, and judiciary branches. Some 250 village fono remain largely intact today. Above the 'aiga group and village, there exist large-scale district and lineage allegiances that divide supravillage-level politics into historical factions, without, however, forming the structure of a traditional national system.

HISTORY

Samoa was settled some 3,000 years ago and is, together with Tonga, at the historical base and traditional heart of the development and spread of Polynesian civilization. It was from these two archipelagos that, around 500, canoes traveled east to the Marquesas and thence to Hawai'i, Tuvalu, the Cook Islands, and New Zealand. Long periods of isolation between groups of islands fostered distinctive language and cultural development, resulting today in several Polynesian nation-states, territories, and cultures that still have much in common.

First European contact with Samoa occurred in 1721, and in 1830, the London Missionary Society introduced Christianity, to which almost all Samoans are adherents today. Throughout the latter half of the nineteenth century, the high chiefs of Samoa were embroiled in international rivalry that saw the consuls of Germany, Great Britain, and the United States endeavoring to manipulate local Samoan politics while at the same time being manipulated by them. Samoa's first constitution, which was adopted by chiefs in 1873, owed much to U.S. thinking. This and subsequent constitutions were short-lived. The desire of foreign interests was to impose a model of "king and government" unsuited to Samoan political organization at the time. Under the protection of the Treaty of Berlin of 1889, international competition was contained and culminated in the partitioning of the Samoan archipelago in 1900, when the United States took the eastern islands, and the western islands became the German colony of "Western Samoa."

Commercial interests, land claims, and the growth of a European enclave in Apia exposed Samoa to new concepts and entrenched a system of centralized legal regulation that would thereafter compete with traditional Samoan law. A feature of the German colonial administration was the introduction in 1903 of a Land and Titles Commission (later renamed a "court") to decide disputes relating to customary land and chiefly titles. After the outbreak of World War I in 1914, New Zealand occupied Western Samoa. Military administration gave way to civilian government in 1919, when New Zealand was granted a League of Nations Mandate, "C" class, for Western Samoa. Opposition to some New Zealand policies and methods of administration was expressed, over the period 1926–1936, by Samoan civil disobedience and the formation of the Mau, an organization of alternative government. After the end of World War II, Western Samoa became a United Nations (UN) Trust Territory with New Zealand as administering authority.

The period 1947–1961 saw a series of planned constitutional advances that introduced self-government and moved to independence under a constitution approved in a plebiscite of all adult Samoans. A "Westminster-style" relationship between elected legislature and executive cabinet was adopted, with an appointed but structurally independent judiciary. The UN General Assembly terminated the trusteeship, and New Zealand passed legislation ending its authority. Western Samoa became independent on January 1, 1962, and joined the Commonwealth of Nations as a full member in 1970 and the UN in 1976.

Struggles for national leadership had been frustrated in the nineteenth century, and German and New Zealand administrators discouraged the notion of a single paramount chief or monarch. In accordance with long-standing political rules, there were four *tama'aiga* titles (literally, sons of the major lineages), namely Malietoa, Tupua Tamasese, Mata'afa, and Tuimaleali'ifano. The desire for formal recognition of these paramount titles persisted, despite weakening of popular allegiance to the four historical factions referred to above. At independence, the constitution recognized Malietoa and Tupua Tamasese as the first (joint) heads of state for life, Tuimaleali'ifano was appointed to a Council of Deputies (to the heads of state), and Mata'afa continued as prime minister. Today, when the surviving head of state dies, his successor will be elected by Parliament, and the convention of electing a *tama'aiga* as prime minister has been broken.

Despite the fact that the same political party (Human Rights Protection Party) has won every general election since 1982, Samoa is a vigorous parliamentary democracy in which political influence is dispersed across villages and traditional allegiances. Under the 1962 Constitution, only *matai* could vote and be elected to forty-seven seats in Parliament. In 1990, universal suffrage was introduced, but candidature remains restricted to *matai*. It should be noted that a relatively large number (some 20,000) of adult Samoans (mainly male) are *matai*.

The length of time in office of a single political party has been conducive to certain attempts to stifle opposition, such as statutory moves to facilitate the bringing of defamation actions against the print media and attacks on the status of the controller and chief auditor, an "officer of Parliament" under the constitution. His annual report to Parliament for 1994, which was highly critical of the financial dealings of government ministers and senior officials, triggered a long-running battle between cabinet and the chief auditor, fought before a Commission of Inquiry and in the Supreme Court. In 1995 the cabinet purported to suspend the chief auditor without pay but was met by constitutional protection arguments. Government had the last say in 1997 when it used its parliamentary majority to amend the constitution to reduce the officer's term of office from "until age 60" to "three years."

Throughout its colonial and postcolonial history, Samoa has enjoyed an independent judiciary of high integrity that has not hesitated to find against the government of the day, when appropriate to do so. Inevitably, it has taken some time for the senior judiciary to become localized, but both the present chief justice and his predecessor are indigenous Samoans, and today, all members of the judiciary are of the same status.

By constitutional amendment in 1997, Parliament changed the country's name from "Western Samoa" to "Samoa" (much to the annoyance of the citizens of American Samoa).

LEGAL CONCEPTS
The sources of law discernible today are broadly threefold:

- constitutional and statutory;
- English common law (as developed in "common law" jurisdictions); and
- Samoan customary law.

The constitution allocates subject areas to types of law (e.g., *matai* titles and customary land to Samoan customary law) and determines priorities between sources of law.

The Constitution
Effective January 1, 1962, the constitution is the supreme law, rendering void any preexisting or subsequent law that is inconsistent with its terms. The constitution may normally be amended by an act that has the support of two-thirds of the total number of members of Parliament after ninety days have elapsed between second and third readings. Provisions prohibiting the alienation of customary land beyond limited lease or license may not be amended without the additional step of a referendum supported by two-thirds of votes cast.

Statute Law
The statute law component of preindependence law that was brought forward included New Zealand statutes made applicable to Samoa. Only two or three of these remain in force. All German law was repealed in 1920. Today, only Parliament makes statutes, including those providing for government expenditure, and the government enjoys regulation-making power as delegated to it by statute.

English Common Law
Prior to independence, the law of England existing on January 14, 1840 (the date New Zealand became a British colony), and the rules of English common law and equity as developed in English and New Zealand courts—except so far as inconsistent with statute or inapplicable to the circumstances of Western Samoa—were followed. The constitution brought forward this existing law, subject to its provisions, one of which was a new definition of *law*. Included in the definition of law are "the English common law and equity for the time being insofar as they are not excluded by any other law in force in Samoa." Although the common law referred to is English, the courts since independence have continued to demonstrate affinity with New Zealand and also attach particular weight to the decisions of the superior courts of Australia as well as those of the United Kingdom. In relation to fundamental rights provisions of the constitution, the courts have examined decisions of the United States. The

courts have expressed the view that "English common law" referred to a body of law originally exported from England but not necessarily applied there at the time of reception, which is when Samoa chooses to apply it. English common law may thus be developed elsewhere and borrowed later. Samoa finds other Pacific jurisdictions helpful. All courts, within the limits of their jurisdiction, administer common law and equity concurrently, and where there is conflict, the rules of equity prevail.

Samoan Custom and Usage

Express Constitutional Recognition

The constitution establishes custom and usage as a source of law in two ways. *Matai* titles and customary land are declared to be "held in accordance with Samoan custom and usage." Further, the definition of law includes "any custom or usage which has acquired the force of law in Samoa or any part thereof under the provisions of any Act or under a judgment of a Court of competent jurisdiction." The constitution also recognizes "the law relating to" Samoan custom and usage, which appears to refer to procedural rather than substantive law. It envisages legislation providing for the registration of interests and resolution of disputes, such as the Land and Titles Act of 1981, which gives effect to the constitutional requirement that there be a Land and Titles Court in relation to *matai* titles and customary land. This court's jurisdiction is exclusive. Custom that has acquired the force of law under a court judgment in this way takes priority over any English common law that is inconsistent with it. Similarly, statute may not encroach upon the domain of such substantive customary law.

Custom and Usage Defined

In the absence of a constitutional definition, the Land and Titles Act of 1981 provides a working one, "the customs and usages of Samoa accepted as being in force at the relevant time," and includes both the principles accepted "by the people of Samoa in general" and the customs and usages accepted as being in force "in respect of a particular place or matter."

Traditional Authority of Chiefs

Although the constitution makes no mention of chiefly authority as such, the "holding" of *matai* titles and customary land in accordance with custom appears to encompass the necessary attributes of such holding, including the traditional authority of chiefs in relation to such matters. Within these constitutional limitations, the *matai*'s word is law.

Authority of Village Councils

In 1990, the government decided to provide statutory support for the traditional authority of the village *fono* (councils), thus for the first time incorporating the *fono* into the formal structure of local government and the administration of justice. The legislation purports to "validate and empower" the village *fono* in the exercise of its "power and authority in accordance with the custom and usage" of the village. The village perspective, held by many *matai*, is that their authority has always existed and requires no such validation by the national legislature.

Legal Pluralism and the Duality of Legal Systems

The structural separation of court jurisdictions according to subject matter and the type of law applied does not prevent conflict between the two systems. Common law damages are occasionally claimed for harm caused by the actions of *matai* in enforcing their *fono* decisions. Such decisions may also be tested against the "fundamental rights" provisions of the constitution, such as the freedoms of religion and movement. Conflict also occurs when customary law is pleaded in the Supreme and Magistrates' Courts. Despite the popularly recognized "law and order" functions of the village councils, the absence of a statutory basis for the councils in the past denied the courts any legal justification for accepting council decisions as conclusive. Under the 1990 legislation, the courts are now required to take village punishments into account in mitigation of court penalties, but a determination of guilt or innocence by a council does not bar court action in respect of the same behavior. Similarly, the formal acceptance of the customary ritualized public *ifoga* (apology) does not preclude a civil action for damages under common law.

In short, an uneasy dichotomy exists between the conventional legal inheritance, which is concerned mainly with the areas of commercial, family, and serious criminal matters administered by the Supreme and Magistrates' Courts, and Samoan customary law applicable to 82 percent of the land area, chiefly titles and local village government, which are the responsibility of the Land and Titles Court and village *fono*. In the eyes of many citizens, uncertainties between jurisdictions leave the situation open to abuse.

CURRENT STRUCTURE

Constitutional Power and Judicial Service Commission

The constitution establishes two courts of original jurisdiction—the Supreme Court as a superior court of record, with certain constitutional functions and further jurisdiction provided by statute, and the Land and Titles Court, with such jurisdiction "in relation to *matai* titles and customary land" as is provided by statute. The constitution also establishes the Court of Appeal and such subordinate courts as are provided by statute. The Judicial

Structure of Samoan Courts

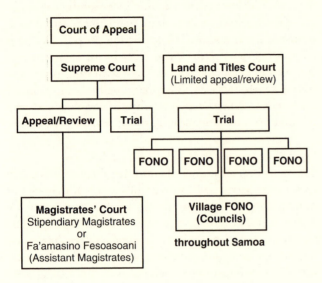

Service Commission, consisting of the chief justice, the attorney general, and a nominee of the minister of justice, is responsible for the appointment of all judicial officers other than the chief justice (who is appointed by the head of state on the advice of the prime minister) and for the dismissal of all such officers other than the chief justice and other judges of the Supreme Court. The courts of Samoa fall within the administrative responsibility of the Department of Justice.

Magistrates' Courts and Village Councils

The bulk of the formal court work is handled in the Magistrates' Courts, which have two divisions. The higher jurisdiction of the Stipendiary Magistrate (a barrister or solicitor of not less than five years' experience) includes civil matters, criminal offenses, and maintenance and affiliation proceedings. The magistrate is also the coroner, responsible for inquests and related functions consequent upon unnatural deaths. The Magistrates' Courts possess no jurisdiction in relation to customary land and *matai* titles. Currently, there are two magistrates. The lower division is presided over by one of three *fa'amasino fesoasoani* (assistant magistrates), laypersons who receive training upon appointment. They have minor jurisdictions in civil and criminal matters.

In the villages, the *fono* (councils of *matai*) deal regularly with offenses under locally prescribed village rules and generally with civil disputes and other actions that threaten village harmony. Incorporated into the formal legal structure by 1990 legislation, each council has had its power to exercise customary authority validated. It is deemed to include (but is not limited to) the imposition of fines and work orders in respect of "village misconduct," which, in addition to conduct traditionally regarded as punishable, includes breach of council rules governing hygiene and village land. The council of a village is defined as the assembly of the chiefs and orators of that village "meeting in accordance with the custom of the village." A person "adversely affected" by a *fono* decision may appeal by petition to the Land and Titles Court. This court may allow or dismiss the appeal or refer the decision back for reconsideration, but it may not vary the *fono* decision or substitute its own, nor may it entertain a further appeal after reconsideration.

Land and Titles Court: Appointments and Procedures

The Land and Titles Court is a court of record possessing exclusive jurisdiction in all matters relating to Samoan names and titles and in all claims and disputes relating to customary land. It applies Samoan custom and usage. The court consists of the president, who is the chief justice or a judge of the Supreme Court, and Samoan judges and assessors who are *matai* of character, ability, standing, and reputation appointed on the advice of the Judicial Service Commission. Samoan judges, three of whom are also *fa'amasino fesoasoani,* are appointed for three-year terms, and assessors are selected for each sitting of the court from a panel of not less than ten candidates. One or more of the Samoan judges are appointed deputy presidents. Original jurisdiction is exercised by the court, comprising the president or a deputy president and at least four Samoan judges and assessors. Appeals, with the leave of the president, are heard by the court, comprising the president and two Samoan judges appointed by him or her. There is no further appeal. Nevertheless, there remains some doubt surrounding the question whether the Supreme Court may review a decision of the Land and Titles Court on allegations of failure to observe its statute or the rules of natural justice.

A distinctive feature of this court is that its procedures are a combination of Samoan custom and court convention. Parties are required to submit written summaries of their arguments in advance, and court officials seek to mediate. When evidence is called, witnesses may not be cross-examined except by questioning from members of the court. Lawyers are not permitted to appear. The court applies custom and usage and the law relating to the application of custom and usage, and where such custom and usage do not apply, the court acts as it considers to be fair and just between the parties. The decision of the court is that of the majority of its members, and reasons for the decision are issued. The decision is final, subject to appeal to the court (reconstituted for appeals) with the leave of the president on prescribed grounds, such as new evidence, misconduct of party or witness, error of law or custom, or that the decision was manifestly against the weight of evidence. On appeal, which is by way of rehearing, the court's decision is final.

Supreme Court: Appointments and Functions

The Supreme Court comprises a chief justice, appointed by the head of state on the advice of the prime minister, and such other judges as are appointed by the head of state on the advice of the Judicial Service Commission. A judge must have been in practice as a barrister in Samoa or an approved country (New Zealand, Australia, or the United Kingdom) for at least eight years. Citizens of Samoa hold office until age sixty-two, whereas expatriate judges are appointed for a term of years. Currently, the chief justice and a second judge are citizens. The two magistrates hold warrants to act as Supreme Court judges if and when required. Judges may not be removed except by the head of state on an address supported by two-thirds of the total members of the Parliament on the grounds of stated misbehavior or infirmity of body or mind. Judicial salaries are determined by statute, and Parliament may not diminish such salaries unless as part of a general reduction of all salaries.

The Supreme Court, including any one or more of its judges, possesses "all the jurisdiction, power and authority which may be necessary to administer the laws of Samoa." The constitution gives the Supreme Court further responsibility in three areas—enforcement of the fundamental rights provisions of the constitution, interpretation of the constitution on the application of a party to any court proceedings, and interpretation of the constitution in an opinion requested by the head of state on the advice of the prime minister.

Court of Appeal

The Court of Appeal of Samoa comprises three judges, who may be the chief justice, other judges of the Supreme Court, and such other persons qualified to be Supreme Court judges who are appointed on the advice of the Judicial Service Commission. In practice, judges, lawyers, and academics from New Zealand, Australia, and other Pacific island states have been appointed to deal with cases as required. A "pool" of South Pacific judicial personnel is now established to assist Samoa and other countries of the region. The Court of Appeal hears appeals from the Supreme Court with leave and as of right, as prescribed by statute. It has no jurisdiction in relation to Land and Titles Court matters.

SPECIALIZED JUDICIAL BODIES

The most prominent example of such a body, the Land and Titles Court, has been dealt with above because of its high standing as a court of Samoa. Samoa has no army and hence no military court, but a variety of quasi-judicial bodies are appointed to determine issues relating to such matters as transportation and employee accident compensation, review of taxation commissioners' determinations, conciliation of industrial disputes, and arbi-

tration of commercial disputes. The ombudsman is an officer of Parliament appointed to investigate decisions, recommendations, or acts done or omitted within government administration. When a complaint is laid by a citizen or corporation, the ombudsman determines whether the matter under review was illegal, unreasonable, unjust, oppressive, improperly discriminatory, based on mistake of fact or law, or simply "wrong." The ombudsman has no powers of enforcement and relies upon his recommendations to cabinet and publicity surrounding his reports to Parliament.

On several occasions, the Samoan cabinet has made use of its statutory authority to establish commissions of inquiry that enjoy investigative jurisdiction, backed by powers to require the examination of witnesses and to proceed in the manner of a Supreme Court judge. In addition to investigating major accidents and disasters, Samoan commissions of inquiry have examined such matters as parliamentary salaries, superannuation, the Cocoa Board, the Health Department (twice), and the Department of Lands and Survey. Sometimes major restructuring of the administration has been recommended. In 1994, the cabinet used a commission of inquiry to attempt to mitigate the bluntness of the chief auditor's findings of corruption (see "History," above). Statutory bodies that already possess the powers of a commission of inquiry include the Accident Compensation Board, Civil Aviation Board of Inquiry, Poisons Appeal Committee, and the Law Society Council.

STAFFING

The standards of competence and integrity set by the Judicial Service Commission (see "Current Structure," above) have ensured that, by and large, Samoa has been well served by both expatriate and Samoan judges and magistrates. No special training has been involved, but in at least two respects, judges have been obliged to study their jurisdiction carefully in order to meet community expectations. First, Samoa's Constitution (in common with those of most decolonized Pacific island states) clearly asserts itself as the supreme law and requires observance of a bill of civil and political rights and freedoms. Because these two characteristics of the legal system are foreign to New Zealand academics and lawyers, and most judges and lawyers in Samoa have studied law in New Zealand and are qualified to practice there, further study of the Samoan scene is usually required before taking up duties in Samoa. Second, the chief justice or other judge who holds the office of president of the Land and Titles Court assumes great responsibilities in areas of customary law that may require further study.

Legal practitioners in Samoa may be barristers or solicitors or both. Forty-five members of the profession, who must be citizens, are engaged either in the offices of the attorney general and Justice Department or in one of the nine or ten private law firms in Apia. Because there is no law school in Samoa, practitioners have typically trained in New Zealand, but since the Law School of the University of the South Pacific began to graduate bachelors of law in 1997, a considerable number of Samoans have taken advantage of that route to practice. Professional disciplinary matters are handled pursuant to statute by the elected Law Society Council, with appeal to the Supreme Court. The Supreme Court retains its inherent supervisory role in relation to the legal profession.

IMPACT

Although the administration of justice in Samoa is regarded, in the main, as fair and efficient, it still appears to many superimposed, with the characteristics of an institution alien to Samoan society. Samoan lawyers from the regional University of the South Pacific Law School, situated in Vanuatu, are now capable of bringing to the local scene a better understanding of how introduced and customary concepts of law may be harmonized. Nevertheless, the duality of legal systems referred to above will remain a difficult and problematic feature of the Samoan legal context for decades to come. For example, central government has failed to secure the cooperation of many village councils, allowing arbitrary and sometimes illegal or unconstitutional actions on the part of these councils to go unaddressed. The courts have occasionally been called upon to uphold constitutional human rights provisions against harsh village decrees, such as the banishment of whole families, destruction of property, and interference with choice of religious observance. However, the police and other officials responsible for enforcing court orders have had great difficulty in securing obedience, and the courts are in danger of being regarded as ineffective in this area. For some thousands of Samoans, the courts will continue to be largely irrelevant in many respects.

Guy Powles

See also Barristers; Common Law; Customary Law; Lay Judiciaries; Legal Education; Legal Pluralism; Magistrates—Common Law Systems; New Zealand; Solicitors; Vanuatu
References and further reading
Anesi, Taulapapa, and Auelua Enari. 1988. "The Land and Chiefly Titles Court of Western Samoa." Pp. 107–111 in *Pacific Courts and Legal Systems.* Edited by C. G. Powles and M. Pulea. Suva: University of the South Pacific.
Davidson, J. W. 1967. *Samoa Mo Samoa: The Emergence of the Independent State of Western Samoa.* Melbourne: Oxford University Press.
Meleisea, M. 1987. *The Making of Modern Samoa: Traditional Authority and Colonial Administration.* Suva: University of the South Pacific.
Powles, C. G. 1986. "Legal Systems and Political Cultures: Competition for Dominance in Western Samoa." Pp. 191–214 in *Legal Pluralism.* Edited by Peter Sack and
Elizabeth Minchin. Canberra: Australian National University.
———. 1993. "Western Samoa." Pp. 395–430 in *South Pacific Islands Legal Systems.* Edited by Michael A. Ntumy. Honolulu: University of Hawai'i Press.
———. 1997. "Common Law at Bay? The Scope and Status of Customary Law Regimes in the South Pacific." *The Journal of Pacific Studies* 21: 61–82.
So'o, Asofou. 2000. "Civil and Political Liberty: The Case of Samoa." Pp. 133–150 in *Governance in Samoa.* Edited by Elise Huffer and Asofou So'o. Canberra: Asia Pacific Press.
University of the South Pacific School of Law. "Pacific Law Materials." http://www.vanuatu.usp.ac.fj/paclawmat/ Paclawmat_MAIN.html (cited December 20, 2001).
Va'a, Unasa L. F. 2000. "Local Government in Samoa and the Search for Balance." Pp. 151–169 in *Governance in Samoa.* Edited by Elise Huffer and Asofou So'o. Canberra: Asia Pacific Press.
Va'ai, Saleimoa. 1999. *Samoa Fa'amatai and the Rule of Law.* Apia: National University of Samoa.

SAN MARINO

COUNTRY INFORMATION

San Marino (formally, the Republic of San Marino) is the third-smallest state in Europe (only the Vatican and Monaco are smaller). Physically located south of Venice in the Italian mountain range known as the Apennines, its total area is about 61 square kilometers. As of July 2001, its estimated population was 27,336. One-third of the population lives in the town of Serravalle.

The economy of San Marino is dominated by tourism, which accounts for over 50 percent of gross domestic product (GDP); in 1999 more than 3 million tourists visited San Marino. Key industries include banking, apparel, electronics, and ceramics. In terms of employment, 60 percent of a labor force of about 18,500 are employed in services, 38 percent in industry, and 2 percent in agriculture. The agricultural sector is best known for local wines and cheeses; most food comes from agricultural areas of Italy. The per capita GDP (equivalent to approximately U.S.$32,000 in 2000) and living standards are comparable to the more prosperous regions of Italy.

San Marino is known for its commemorative stamps and collectable coins, which together generate a significant amount of government revenue. The country receives an annual subsidy from the Italian government in return for having given up certain rights.

Not surprisingly, San Marino is closely tied to Italy in terms of culture and economics. The language is Italian (the local dialect is Romannolo), and the Italian lira is legal tender. The country has three FM radio stations and one television station of its own, but the broadcast media

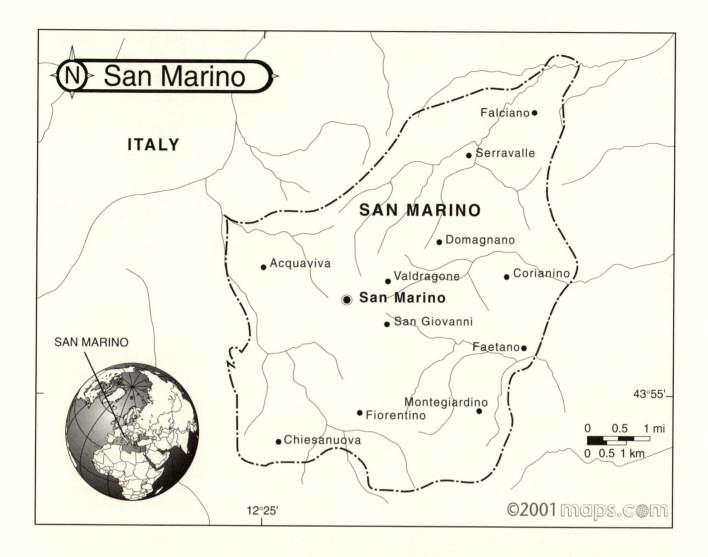

©2001 maps.com

are dominated by Italian broadcasters. The population is overwhelmingly Roman Catholic.

HISTORY

San Marino claims to be the world's oldest republic. According to tradition, it was founded in 301 by a Christian stonemason named Marinus. A republican form of government dates back to at least the thirteenth century, when a self-governing assembly known as the Arengo came into existence. That original assembly was composed of the heads of each family. A system of dual heads of state called captains regent (*capitani reggenti*) was established in 1243.

San Marino has largely escaped periods of military occupation, at least in part because of its physical isolation and the difficulty of much of its mountainous territory. Occupation occurred on only two occasions (once in 1503 and again in 1739), but neither occupation lasted for more than a brief time. San Marino's independence was recognized by the papacy in 1631; this independence was acknowledged by Napoleon in 1797 and again by the Congress of Vienna in 1815. During the nineteenth cen-

tury, San Marino became a refuge for many Italians fleeing the unrest that arose during efforts to unify Italy. San Marino survives today as a relic of the independent Italian city-states of the region's history.

Italy and San Marino signed a treaty of friendship and economic cooperation in 1862. This treaty has been revised and extended on several occasions since then. In international affairs, San Marino has followed Italy's lead, with volunteers from San Marino serving with the Italians during the two world wars (resulting in Allied bombing of San Marino in 1944). During Benito Mussolini's Fascist regime in Italy, a fascist party dominated San Marino.

Soon after World War II, the Communist Party dominated, creating some strain with the anticommunist regime in Italy. In 1957 the communists were ousted by a coalition of Christian Democrats and Social Democrats; that coalition lasted until 1973. Several different coalitions have held power since that time, always with the Christian Democrats as one coalition partner.

Women were granted the right to vote in 1960 and the right to hold public office in 1973.

GOVERNMENT

The earliest statutes in San Marino date back to 1263. The current constitution dates to 1600, although it has been modified on occasion over the last 400 years. The most recent major modification was the electoral law of 1926, which serves some of the functions of a constitution. A "manuscript of rights" was promulgated in 1974.

San Marino has a parliamentary style of government. The legislature is known as the Grand and General Council (Consiglio Grande e Generale) and has members elected by direct popular vote to serve five-year terms from geographically defined districts or townships (which correspond to the old parishes of the republic). Multiple parties (mirroring the Italian political parties) compete in the elections, ranging from the Communist Party on the left to the Christian Democratic Party on the right; in the 1998 election, the Christian Democratic Party received the largest percentage of the vote (41 percent).

Continuing the tradition established in 1243, two members of the Grand and General Council serve as cochiefs of state (capitani reggenti) for periods of six months; the reggenti come from different parties to provide a check on abuse of power. They preside over meetings of the Grand and General Council and over meetings of the ten-member cabinet (Congresso di Stato, or State Congress). The cabinet is elected by the Grand and General Council to five-year terms after each legislative election. Although formally there is no prime minister or chief executive, the secretary of state for foreign and political affairs has functioned in some ways as a prime minister.

For purposes of local government, San Marino is divided into nine districts or castles. The head of each district is called the captain of the castle and is appointed by the central government.

San Marino maintains diplomatic relations with more than 70 countries and maintains membership in many major international institutions, including the United Nations; the International Court of Justice (ICJ), although it has not accepted compulsory ICJ jurisdiction; the Council of Europe; the World Health Organization; and the United Nations Educational, Scientific, and Cultural Organization (UNESCO).

Although not a full member of the European Union (EU), San Marino has a customs union with the EU. It has adopted the euro, which replaced the lira in January 2002.

LEGAL SYSTEM

The San Marino legal system is a mixture of the very old, the somewhat old, and the relatively new. In noncriminal matters (civil and commercial law) and civil procedure, San Marino has preserved the traditional system of jus commune, which was in force in Italy and Europe prior to the development of the Napoleonic Code. Private law

Legal Structure of San Marino Courts

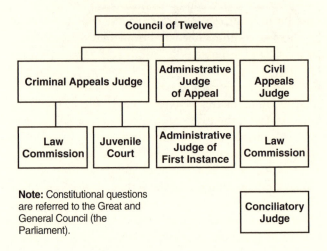

Note: Constitutional questions are referred to the Great and General Council (the Parliament).

(i.e., noncriminal law) is based on a combination of the old leges statutae (promulgated by the San Marino republic centuries ago), customary law, and Roman sources (the Justinian Code). There has been no modern effort to codify private law.

Criminal matters are dealt with under a penal code adopted in 1974 and a Code of Penal Procedure that dates from 1878 (as amended in the latter part of the twentieth century). Significant pieces of legislation were passed in the nineteenth and twentieth centuries dealing with public services, social charity, security and welfare, hygiene and health, public education, civil service, government finance, banking and commerce, bankruptcy, and property ownership and use.

Legal institutions include at least four levels of courts. Interestingly, the judges of the courts that handle the more important cases cannot, except under unusual circumstances, be citizens of San Marino. Sammarinese staff the lowest courts, handling minor cases, and the highest court, which makes final decisions on constitutional and important issues. Between these two courts, the judges are citizens of Italy, not San Marino. At the bottom of the hierarchy there are the giudice conciliatore (variously translated as conciliatory judges or justices of the peace), who handle only civil cases that do not exceed 25 million lire (about $11,600). At the top is the Council of Twelve, which is elected by the Grand and General Council for the duration of the legislature; the Council of Twelve acts as a third-instance Court of Appeals.

The general courts of first instance (trial) and second instance (first appeal) are presided over by the commissario della legga (law commissioners) and giudice delle appellazioni civili (civil appeals judges). These judges are appointed by the Grand and General Council, initially for a term of four years; their terms can be renewed (confirmed) for an undetermined period.

Noncriminal cases go initially to either a conciliatory judge or to a law commissioner, depending on the amount in controversy. Appeals from conciliatory judges go to a law commissioner, and from a law commissioner to a civil appeals judge. If decisions at the two levels considering a case conflict, then the Council of Twelve may be asked to choose between the two decisions.

In criminal matters, effective with judicial reform enacted in 1992, the case can initially be decided either by a law commissioner or by a criminal appeals judge (or, in the case of a juvenile, by a *tribunale dei minori*, or juvenile court). A criminal appeals judge handles cases in which a prison sentence of more than three years is possible. Appeal from a law commissioner (of Juvenile Court) to a criminal appeals judge is possible; no appeal, at least of sentences, is possible from a sentence imposed by a criminal appeals judge. A pardon, amnesty, or change of sentence can be given by the Grand and General Council.

There is a separate judicial hierarchy for administrative matters. Those with grievances against administrative organs of the government are heard initially by a *guidice amministrativo di primo grado* (administrative judge of first instance); appeals go to a *guidice amministrativo d'apello* (administrative judge of appeal). As with other noncriminal matters, if the judges at the first and second level disagree, the Council of Twelve has jurisdiction to resolve the conflict.

If a judge comes to have doubts whether a law or regulation is constitutional, the judge can ask for an opinion from the Grand and General Council. In such situations, the council requests the opinion of experts, and then issues its ruling. Thus, the Grand and General Council serves the role of a constitutional court to deal with the relatively rare questions that do arise.

With the exception of the Council of Twelve, all courts function with a single judge making decisions. There are no juries.

San Marino is a party to the European Convention on Human Rights (as well as other treaties dealing with human rights) and as such is subject to the European Court of Human Rights. There has been at least one judge from San Marino on that court. Through the mid-1990s the European Commission on Human Rights had received only four applications raising claims involving San Marino; none of them led to a determination that San Marino was in violation of the European Convention.

FUTURE ISSUES

San Marino has not become a full member of the European Union, opting to work with the EU in a number of ways (through a customs union, adoption of the euro, and so on) instead. Should San Marino become a full member, the legal system will need to adapt to the role played by the European Court of Justice. What specific changes, if any, such a change will require are unclear.

Herbert M. Kritzer

See also Civil Law; Italy; Roman Law
References and further reading
Astuti, Guido. 1987. "San Marino." Pp. S-13–S-15 in *International Encyclopedia of Comparative Law.* Vol. 1, *National Reports.* Edited by Viktor Knapp. Dordrecht: Martinus Nijhoff Publishers.
Chezzi, Alberto, and Luciano Ciavatta. 1995. *Investive a San Marino (Investing in San Marino).* 2d ed. Repubblica di San Marino: Maggioli Editore Rimini.
Duursma, Jorri. 1996. *Fragmentation and the International Relations of Micro-states: Self-Determination and Statehood.* New York: Cambridge University Press.
"The Legal System of the Most Serene Republic of San Marino." 1993 [1984]. Pp. 4.150.3–4.150.8 in *Modern Legal Systems Cyclopedia.* Edited by Kenneth Robert Redden. Buffalo, NY: W. S. Hein.

SANCTIONS
See Criminal Sanctions, Purposes of

SÃO TOMÉ AND PRÍNCIPE

COUNTRY INFORMATION
The twin-island republic of São Tomé and Príncipe, located in the Gulf of Guinea at 1° north and 7° east, is the second-smallest independent state in Africa, with a total area of 1,001 square kilometers and a population of 144,900 (1999 World Bank estimate). About 5,000 people live on Príncipe Island, which occupies an area of 142 square kilometers. The capital is São Tomé, with a total population of 49,930 (in 1998). According to the World Bank, the annual population growth was 2.2 percent in 2000.

The native Creole population, locally called *Forros,* is descendants of imported African slaves and Portuguese colonists and convicts, who settled the hitherto uninhabited islands in the fifteenth and sixteenth centuries. Contract workers from Angola, Mozambique, and Cape Verde, who had been recruited for the plantation economy from 1870 to 1950, formed a separate category until independence. Since then, they and their offspring have been gradually incorporated into the larger Forro community. A distinct group in the south of São Tomé island is the Angolares, descendants of runaway slaves from the sugar plantations in the sixteenth century, who had formed a maroon community and are now predominantly fishers. Apart from the official language, Portuguese, four Afro-Portuguese-Creole languages are spoken on the islands. According to official statistics, the literacy rate is 75 percent.

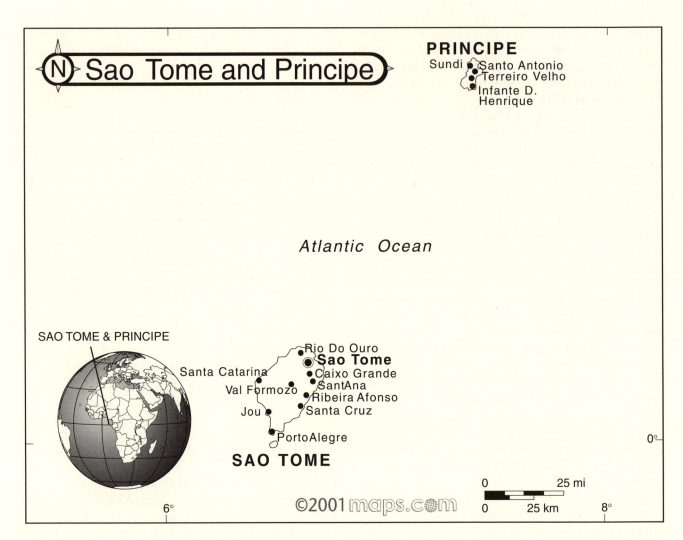

The mountainous islands are of volcanic origin. The highest mountain is the Pico de São Tomé (2,024 meters). The tropical rainforest and secondary forest cover 28 percent and 29 percent of the land, respectively. The shadow trees on the cocoa plantations account for another 32 percent of the total area. The climate is tropical, with an annual average temperature of 26.7°C and a relative humidity of 80 percent. Annual rainfall ranges from less than 1,000 millimeters in the northern lowlands to above 5,000 millimeters in the mountainous south. The rainy season lasts from September to May.

São Tomé and Príncipe is among the least developed countries and has largely been dependent on foreign aid. In 2000, agriculture and fishery accounted for 20.7 percent of the gross domestic product (GDP), industry (including construction) contributed 17.0 percent, and 62.3 percent was derived from the tertiary sector, reflecting the oversized public administration. Until recently, the island state has been a plantation economy based on cocoa. Since independence, the country's economy has been in a constant crisis. However, despite decreasing production and falling prices, cocoa has remained the dominant export product since the late nineteenth century. Due to the

failure to rehabilitate the large-scale cocoa production on plantations as part of a structural adjustment program, most plantation lands have been successively distributed to former plantation workers since 1933. While cocoa remains the main export product, potential economic growth is expected from the tourism and fishery sectors. Probable deep-water oil deposits close to the maritime borders with Nigeria are supposed to generate high incomes from 2006 onward. In March 1998, São Tomé approved a law defining the boundaries of its 370-kilometer exclusive economic zone (EEZ) that was submitted to the UN Law of the Sea Commission. In 2000, a joint exploration treaty for petroleum was signed with Nigeria.

HISTORY

The islands of São Tomé and Príncipe were discovered by Portuguese navigators around 1471, but not before 1493 did the Portuguese succeed in establishing a colony on São Tomé. A feudal lord (*donatário*) appointed by the Portuguese Crown exercised civil and criminal jurisdiction. Institutionalized African forms of political power never existed, since the islands were uninhabited when the first Portuguese arrived. Initially, the slave trade was important for the economy of the new colony; however, from 1520 on, sugarcane was the major factor in the flourishing economy. The island became the first tropical plantation economy, based on slave labor from the African mainland. Due to tropical diseases, the mortality rate among white settlers was very high. Therefore, the Portuguese encouraged mixed unions between white men and African women to populate the colony. In 1515, a royal decree manumitted these black women and their offspring. Two years later, the male slaves, who had come with the first settlers and their children, were also manumitted by royal decree. As a result, a group of free Creole blacks, the Forros, gradually emerged. In 1520, the king allowed mulattos to fulfill public functions, provided that they were married and proprietors. From 1522, a captain-general (renamed governor in 1586) became the local representative of the Portuguese king on the island. In 1525, the Crown granted city rights to São Tomé town, including the privilege to have a city council with full legal and legislative powers for the entire island.

In 1534, the Catholic Church created in São Tomé the first diocese in sub-Saharan Africa, which existed until 1677. The local Creole clergy occupied important positions within the diocese. In 1548, the king granted the city council, controlled by the great Creole planters, the right to exercise the powers of the governor whenever that office was vacant. As a result of the high mortality among officeholders, local Creoles frequently assumed the office of governor. The fragmentation of political power between the governor, the municipality, and the church; the distance from the central government in Lisbon; and the frequent power vacuum due to the early death of officeholders led to numerous conflicts. In addition, slave revolts and assaults by escaped slaves, who later became known as the Angolares, often contributed to the political instability. Moreover, in the sixteenth and seventeenth centuries, the wealth of São Tomé provoked various assaults by English, French, and Dutch fleets. However, from the first half of the seventeenth century, the sugar industry gradually declined due to the increasing competition from Brazil, the comparatively low quality of the local sugar, the threat on the Atlantic by other European powers, and frequent assaults on the plantations by the Angolares. Finally, most planters left for Brazil, and the plantation economy virtually ceased to exist. The local Creoles, who became steadily more African by blood due to the decrease of whites, cultivated some of the former plantation lands for subsistence and to provide passing ships with food. They exercised virtual control over domestic affairs. However, the local elite were involved in continuous internal power struggles. Due to the ongoing political unrest in São Tomé, the residence of the governor was transferred to Príncipe in 1753.

In 1852, the move of the capital back to São Tomé symbolized the beginning of the second colonization of the archipelago. The introduction of coffee in 1787 and cocoa in 1822, both from Brazil, had made the return of the plantation economy possible. The large-scale production of coffee and cocoa, using slave labor, began in the 1850s. The independence of Brazil in 1822 and the abolition of the slave trade in the Portuguese Empire in 1836 had contributed to the political and economic conditions for these developments. Following the abolition of slavery in the archipelago in 1875, the Portuguese planters immediately returned to the recruitment of contract workers in Angola and subsequently also in Cape Verde and Mozambique. The natives, both the Forros and the Angolares, always refused manual fieldwork on the plantations, since they considered it beneath their status as free men. When the recolonization began, many lands had been possessed by Forro owners, but in the course of the expansion of the plantations in the second half of the nineteenth century, the Portuguese planters successively dispossessed them through land purchase, fraud, and force. By the end of the century, the Portuguese held 90 percent of the land. Encouraged by booming world market prices at that time, cocoa production surpassed that of coffee, and since then, it has always remained the major export product. In 1909, cocoa production reached a peak of 30,300 tons. However, after World War I, cocoa production steadily declined due to dropping international prices, crop diseases, and increasing competition from West African smallholders. The arrival of thousands of African contract workers had changed the demographic balance to the disadvantage of the native Creoles. Until the 1940s, the contract workers outnumbered the native islanders. The colonial legislation classified the latter as citizens with formally the same legal status as the Portuguese, while the former were categorized inferior as indigenous. Only in 1961 did the Portuguese government grant formally equal status to the plantation workers.

In February 1953, it became known that Governor Carlos Gorgulho (who served in that post from 1945 to 1953) intended to resolve the labor shortage on the estates by obliging the Forros to accept plantation work. Threatened with the loss of their free status by becoming merged into a single category of black laborers together with the disdained contract workers, the natives waged a spontaneous uprising. The colonial government, supported by white volunteers and incited contract workers, put down the insurrection with great violence, killing numerous innocent and unarmed people. Later, the traumatic experience of the massacre of 1953 served to justify nationalist demands for independence. In 1960, a small group of exiled Forros founded the Comité de Libertação de São Tomé e Príncipe (CLSTP), which was based in Accra (Ghana). Following the military coup in Ghana in

1966, the CLSTP was expelled, and it virtually ceased to exist. In 1972, exiled nationalists gathered in Santa Isabel (Equatorial Guinea) to create the Movimento de Libertação de São Tomé (MLSTP) with Manual Pinto da Costa as secretary general. The political program of the MLSTP demanded immediate and total independence and the establishment of a republican, democratic, secular, anticolonial, and anti-imperialistic regime. However, prior to the military coup of April 25, 1974, in Lisbon, the MLSTP did not carry through any political action at home. Seven months after the coup, the Portuguese government recognized the MLSTP as the sole and legitimate representative of the Sãotomean people. In December, a transitional government led by the MLSTP took power. Worried by nationalist and leftist agitation, the approximately 2,000 Portuguese residents left the archipelago, depriving the new state of trained personnel in all sectors.

On July 12, 1975, São Tomé and Príncipe gained independence and constitutionally became a one-party state, modeled on the Soviet example. MLSTP leader Pinto da Costa became president of the new state. The MLSTP never officially adopted Marxism-Leninism, since in the opinion of the party, under the particular local conditions the stage of socialism had to be preceded by a transitional period of noncapitalist development. Authorized by the Constituent Assembly, whose sixteen members had been elected a few days before independence, the seven-member Political Bureau of the MLSTP approved a provisional Fundamental Law comprising twenty-two articles that had to guarantee the legal norms of the state organs until the elaboration of the Political Constitution. Right after independence, so-called party mass organizations for children, youth, and women were created, while any political organization outside the framework of the MLSTP became illegal. In November 1975, the Political Bureau and the Constituent Assembly approved the Political Constitution. Article 3 defined that the MLSTP, as the revolutionary vanguard, was the leading political force of the nation, having the duty to determine the political orientation of the state. Basic human rights were guaranteed to all citizens; however, those who favored neocolonialism, imperialism, racism, or regionalism were excluded from the exercise of these rights. The legislative power of the state was vested in the thirty-three-member Popular National Assembly (ANP), which was provisionally composed of the members of the Political Bureau of the MLSTP and another twenty-six members selected by the party. The deputies of the ANP elected the head of state for a four-year term, at the proposal of the MLSTP. The presidential resolutions had the force of law. The ANP appointed the members of the Supreme Court, again at the proposal of the MLSTP.

In December 1975, the regime established the Special Tribunal for Counter-Revolutionary Actions, presided over by a member of the MLSTP leadership, to try crimes against the internal and external security of the state. In the same year, the Portuguese plantations were nationalized and subsequently regrouped in fifteen state-owned agrarian enterprises. Other private companies were equally nationalized, and in 1979, central planning was introduced as an instrument of national development. The regime favored political relations with the socialist countries that were considered as natural allies but maintained the economic ties with the West. The first years following independence were characterized by cleavages and power struggles within the MLSTP leadership that were frequently accompanied by alleged coup attempts. As a result, the regime became steadily more repressive and authoritarian. In July 1979, the government introduced the death sentence for the crimes of being a mercenary, economic sabotage, and conspiracy with imperialism; however, that ultimate penalty has never been applied. In August of the same year, a population census, perceived by large parts of the population as an attempt to introduce forced labor on the plantations, resulted in widespread antigovernment riots. The next month, the minister of economy, Miguel Trovoada, was accused of connivance in the census turmoil and detained without charge or trial for twenty-one months before being released into exile to France. Subsequently, the regime radicalized considerably, while Pinto da Costa had reached the climax of his dictatorial powers.

In early 1980, the ANP approved an amendment of the Political Constitution that introduced the election of the delegates of the seven district assemblies by open, direct, and public vote during a mass meeting of a constituency. In turn, the district delegates had to choose the fifty-one deputies of the ANP for a five-year term. At the proposal of the MLSTP, the ANP elected the head of state, also for a five-year term. Further amendments of the constitution approved in 1982 reflected the increasing personal power of Pinto da Costa. They strengthened the position of the head of state by giving him the right to control the activities of all ministries or to assume their management.

Meanwhile, mismanagement, a lack of know-how, and malpractice had resulted in a dramatic decline of cocoa output. At the same time, attempts to diversify the economy had failed completely for the same reasons. Faced with a severe economic crisis and increasing debts, the regime decided to redefine its policies because the socialist allies were unwilling to sustain the regime. The regime returned to Western countries and the Bretton Woods institutions for aid funds. Consequently, the MLSTP government gradually liberalized the economy and shifted away from the socialist allies. Between 1986 and 1990, several contracts with foreign companies were signed for the private management of state-owned plantations, with the aim of increasing cocoa production. In 1987, an agreement on a structural adjustment program was signed with the International Monetary Fund and the World Bank. In early 1989, the regime abolished the Special Tribunal for Counter-Revolutionary Actions. In December of that year, the MLSTP held a national conference where, after three days of debating, the introduction of a multiparty democracy and a free-market economy was announced. The subsequent political transition occurred without unrest or violence and culminated in the approval of a democratic constitution by a popular referendum in August 1990. Subsequently, the MLSTP transformed itself into the neoliberal Social Democratic Party (MLSTP/PSD), and three new political parties emerged.

In the first democratic elections of January 1991, the major opposition, the Partido de Convergência Democrática—Grupo de Reflexão (PCD-GR), won a landslide victory and took over government. In March, Miguel Trovoada, who had returned from exile the previous year, was elected president in an uncontested race, since the incumbent Pinto da Costa had withdrawn his hopeless candidature. Subsequently, the struggle for power and funds placed President Trovoada in conflict with two successive PCD-GR governments. Trovoada's dismissal of two PCD-GR prime ministers in April 1992 and July 1994 created considerable political instability. The nature and ambiguities of the semipresidential constitution and the resulting overlapping competencies of the state organs were a fertile ground for the conflicts between the president and the governments. In the early elections of October 1994, the MLSTP/PSD gained a majority and returned to power. In August 1995, young officers staged a military coup and detained President Trovoada. After one week of negotiations, the constitutional order was restored when the coup plotters returned to their barracks in exchange for a general amnesty. In the presidential elections of July 1996, the incumbent Trovoada defeated his archrival Pinto da Costa in the second round by a small margin of votes. In November 1998, the MLSTP/PSD won an absolute majority in the legislative elections. In July 2001, Fradique Menezes, the candidate supported by the outgoing President Trovoada, defeated his major opponent, Pinto da Costa, by a large margin of votes in the first round. One month after his inauguration, President Menezes dismissed the MLSTP/PSD executive and formed a government of presidential initiative. Relatively free elections have been held regularly since 1991, but vote buying has increasingly become part of the process. The country's public administration has been marked by institutional weakness and sluggishness, while corruption and similar malpractice have become rampant. In São Tomé and Príncipe thus far, liberal democracy has not resulted in a sound economic policy or a prospering market economy. Attempts to increase cocoa production and to diversify agricultural exports have largely failed. Despite large amounts of foreign aid in recent years, there has only been very modest economic growth, while mass poverty and external debts have further increased since the introduction of multiparty democracy.

LEGAL CONCEPTS

Since 1980, the country has been divided into seven districts, of which six are on São Tomé; Príncipe constitutes a single district. In 1994, the island of Príncipe was granted local autonomy, with a regional assembly and a regional government. According to the law, from seven to eleven deputies are elected in each district for the district assembly (municipality), while on Príncipe, a seven-member regional assembly is elected; all serve three-year terms. The first local elections were held in December 1992, while the first regional elections on Príncipe took place in March 1995. The next local and regional elections, due in 1995 and 1998, respectively, have not been held thus far due to a lack of political will and financial constraints.

According to the constitution approved in 1990, the country maintains the former designation Democratic Republic of São Tomé and Príncipe, now defined as a democratic legal state based on the fundamental human rights. Besides the fundamental civil rights, the constitution guarantees the freedom of the press, political pluralism, private property, the freedom of strike, and the separation of powers. The death penalty is abolished. The head of state is elected directly by universal suffrage and secret vote for a five-year term and a maximum of two consecutive terms. According to the semipresidential system that is based on the Portuguese example, the president of the republic is in charge of foreign affairs and defense and can preside over the council of ministers whenever the president wants. The highest legislative state organ is the fifty-five-member National Assembly, elected according to the system of proportional representation for a four-year period. The independence of the courts is constitutionally guaranteed, and they have financial autonomy.

Since independence, São Tomé and Príncipe has maintained the Portuguese Civil Code of 1966, except for an amendment of the family law. In 1977, the government approved a new Family Law that abolishes discrimination against illegitimate children and gives the predominant customary union the same legal status as the legal marriage. The Portuguese Criminal Code of 1888 has also been largely maintained unchanged. Some alterations with regard to crimes against the state and state property were introduced during the socialist regime. The Portuguese Codes of Civil and Criminal Procedures have been taken over accordingly.

Legal Structure of São Tomé and Príncipe Courts

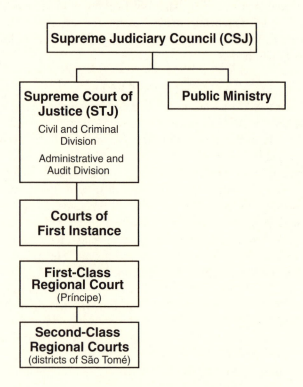

```
┌─────────────────────────────────────┐
│  Supreme Judiciary Council (CSJ)     │
└─────────────────────────────────────┘
        │
   ┌────┴──────────────────┐
┌──────────────────┐  ┌──────────────────┐
│ Supreme Court of │  │ Public Ministry  │
│ Justice (STJ)    │  └──────────────────┘
│                  │
│ Civil and Criminal│
│ Division         │
│                  │
│ Administrative and│
│ Audit Division   │
└──────────────────┘
        │
┌──────────────────┐
│   Courts of      │
│ First Instance   │
└──────────────────┘
        │
┌──────────────────┐
│  First-Class     │
│ Regional Court   │
│   (Príncipe)     │
└──────────────────┘
┌──────────────────┐
│  Second-Class    │
│ Regional Courts  │
│(districts of São Tomé)│
└──────────────────┘
```

CURRENT STRUCTURE

The Basic Law of the Judiciary System (Lei Base do Sistema Judiciário) of 1991 defines the current structure of the country's justice sector. The highest instance is the Supreme Court of Justice (STJ) in São Tomé town, composed of three judges. The president of the STJ is elected by secret vote by all judges for a four-year term and a maximum of two consecutive terms. The STJ functions with a single judge or with a plenum of three judges. There are two sections, a criminal and civil one and an administrative one. The latter is also entrusted to try fiscal cases and audit all government accounts. The STJ has both appellate and trial functions and, according to Article 111 of the constitution, controls the constitutionality of laws.

There is one court of first instance, also located in the capital, that functions with a single judge or a collective of three judges. This court also acts as a juvenile court and a labor court. In addition, there is a first-class regional court on Príncipe and second-class regional courts in each administrative district. They are in charge of minor civil, criminal, and labor cases. The attorney general (*procurador-geral da República*) represents the Public Ministry in the STJ, while the public prosecutors (*procurador da República*) appear in the court of first instance.

An eight-member Supreme Judiciary Council (Conselho Superior Judiciário, CSJ) supervises the magistrates and exercises jurisdiction over the justice functionaries.

The CSJ is headed by the president of the STJ and composed of the attorney general, one judge of the court of first instance, a delegate of the attorney general, a representative of the head of state, two members elected by the National Assembly, and one representative of the justice functionaries elected among themselves. The CSJ appoints the judges of the first instance and the delegates of the attorney general, takes disciplinary action against magistrates, and proposes to the National Assembly the names of the judges of the STJ (*juízes-conselheiros*). The members of the CSJ hold office for four-year terms.

SPECIALIZED JUDICIAL BODIES

The Special Tribunal for Counter-Revolutionary Actions existed from 1975 to 1989. The 1990 Constitution prohibits special courts exclusively designed for the trial of certain categories of crimes, except for the Military Court, which tries essentially military crimes as defined by law.

The 1991 Lei Base do Sistema Judiciáro (Basic Law of the Judiciary System) included the creation of arbitration courts to voluntarily settle conflicts involving two parties; however, such courts have not been established to date. Frequently, the police informally resolve the conflicts of contending parties.

STAFFING

The country has very few judges and no bar association. Currently, there are ten judges exercising their functions, four in the STJ and six in the court of the first instance. As long as there is no bar association, lawyers and solicitors have to register at the CSJ. As of 2001, eighteen lawyers were registered and exercised their profession.

IMPACT

Formally, the 1990 democratic constitution provides for an independent judiciary, but, in fact, judges are unlikely to be consistently impartial, given that they are submitted to bribes, political intimidation, and other types of external, subjective influences. In addition, their salaries are low, and the justice system has been affected by constant budgetary constraints, inadequate facilities, and a lack of well-trained judges, lawyers, and staff. As a result, cases only come to court after long delays, and investigations in criminal cases are hindered. In addition, the lack of human and material resources, the primacy of politics, and the complex net of personal loyalties in the intimate environment of this small and poor country have impeded the establishment of an independent and functioning judiciary. In practice, the STJ has not been in a position to exercise the function to audit all government expenditures, due to a lack of financial, technical, and human resources. A limited auditing of public finances has been exercised by the General Inspection of

Finances, but budgetary rules have frequently been violated, and financial operations have repeatedly been executed outside the official budget. The weak judiciary and the absence of an effective audit system have been major factors in the generalization of corruption in São Tomé and Príncipe.

Gerhard Seibert

See also Appellate Courts; Civil Law; Constitutional Review; Criminal Law; Family Law; Human Rights Law; Judicial Independence; Portugal

References and further reading
Garfield, Robert. 1992. *A History of São Tomé Island, 1470–1655: The Key to Guinea*. San Francisco: Mellen Research University Press.
Hodges, Tony, and Malyn Newitt. 1988. *São Tomé and Príncipe: From Plantation Colony to Microstate*. Boulder, CO, and London: Westview Press.
República Democrática de São Tomé e Príncipe. 1991. *Colecção de Legislação 1975 a 1989*. Vols. 1–6. São Tomé: Ministry of Justice and Public Administration of the RDSTP with the support of the Portuguese Ministry of Foreign Affairs.
Seibert, Gerhard. 1999. *Comrades, Clients and Cousins: Colonialism, Socialism and Democratization in São Tomé and Príncipe*. Leiden, the Netherlands: CNWS Publications.
———. 2000. "São Tomé and Príncipe." Pp. 944–959 in *Africa South of the Sahara 2001*. London: Europa Publications.
Teixeira, José Paquete d'Alva. 1995. *A evolução do sistema de controlo das despesas públicas em São Tomé e Príncipe*. São Tomé.
Tenreiro, Francisco. 1961. *A ilha de São Tomé*. Lisbon: Junta de Investigações do Ultramar.
U.S. Department of State. Bureau of Democracy, Human Rights, and Labor. 1997. *São Tomé and Príncipe: Country Report on Human Rights Practices for 1996*. Washington, DC: U.S. Department of State.

SASKATCHEWAN

GENERAL INFORMATION

Saskatchewan is a Canadian "prairie province" in western North America (latitude 49°–60° north, longitude 102°–110° west), bordering Alberta, the Northwest Territories, Manitoba, and North Dakota. It has 570,000 square kilometers (57 million hectares) of land area and approximately one million people. Known for its sun, wind, sky ("the land of the living skies"), and winters ("but it's a dry cold"), Saskatchewan's temperatures average from −30° C (winter) to +30° C (summer). Annual precipitation averages from three hundred to five hundred millimeters' rainfall and eighty to two hundred centimeters' snowfall (south to north).

Saskatchewan has several well-defined eco-regions oriented northwest-southeast: taiga shield, boreal shield, boreal plain, and prairie. The taiga shield has gray soils, open woodlands, peat bogs, and permafrost. The boreal shield has Precambrian rocks, thin glacial till, and coniferous growth. The boreal plain and prairie both have sedimentary rocks with overlying glacial deposits. The boreal plain has gray soils and mixed softwoods and hardwoods. The prairie has black and brown soils, aspen bluffs, smaller trees, and medium and short grass. Major river systems are the Churchill (north), the North and South Saskatchewan (a Cree word meaning "swift-flowing") (central), and the Qu'Appelle (south). Notable features include the Athabasca Sand Dunes (north) with rare endemic species, and the Cypress Hills (southwest) at 1,392 feet (400 meters) above the surrounding plains, with the only stand of lodgepole pines east of the Rocky Mountains (250 kilometers to the west). The province is home to 40 percent of Canada's mammalian species and is an important breeding and resting ground for many migrating birds in the Western Hemisphere.

In 1996, Saskatchewan had twenty-six million hectares of farmland (44 percent of Canada's total). Some fifty-seven thousand farms accounted for 10 percent of world wheat in trade, 11 percent of world durum production, and 7 percent of world canola production. The province produced 60 percent of Canada's wild rice and 33 percent of its barley, as well as significant livestock. It also produced 25 percent of the world's potash and 34 percent of its uranium. The province was Canada's second largest producer of oil, third of coal, and fourth of minerals, and it boasts 35.6 million hectares of forest and ninety-four thousand lakes. Forestry and fishing are additional industries, although tourism is the industry that is growing the fastest.

In 1996, of 500,000 people employed, 16 percent were in agriculture, 9 percent in tourism, 6.3 percent in manufacturing, and 3 percent in resource extraction. The province is well known as an exporter of people. The two largest cities are Regina and Saskatoon, which has approximately 200,000 people, of whom 25 percent have university degrees. Aboriginal people make up 11 percent of the population (3 percent in Canada) and are the fastest growing group. Saskatchewan has high longevity rates (78.33 years), lower-than-average smoking and cancer rates, but higher-than-average road accident, pneumonia, and multiple sclerosis rates.

Saskatchewan has the most road surface per capita of any political jurisdiction: 185,000 kilometers, of which 70,000 are paved or gravel. There are also 10,000 kilometers of railway, 19 airports, 12 ferries, 850 bridges, and 28,000 kilometers of pipeline. There are 1,560 agricultural, financial, retail, and other member-service cooperatives, and two of the province's three largest businesses are cooperatives.

EVOLUTION AND HISTORY

Archaeological digs locate human habitation at 11,500 years B.C.E. The population prior to European contact, estimated at forty thousand, consisted of indigenous tribes following seasonal game: Dene in the taiga (caribou), Cree in the boreal region (moose and small game), and Nakota on the prairie (bison).

In 1670, England's Charles II declared sovereignty over the area by purporting to grant land and governance to the Hudson's Bay Company in a royal charter. The company set up trading posts on the shores of Hudson's Bay to which Cree and Nakota brought furs. In the 1700s, both French and English traders moved inland.

Following the Treaty of Paris in 1763, England issued a royal proclamation reserving western lands to the Indians, prohibiting British subjects from buying land, and declaring that only the Crown could buy, should the Indians decide to sell. Traders, dependent on aboriginal people for guides and pemmican (dried meat and berries), brought destructive competition and disease. Fur-bearing animals were overtrapped, the bison were wiped out, and smallpox decimated aboriginal populations. Churches (Anglican, Roman Catholic, and Presbyterian) established missions to Christianize the Indians, and expeditions investigated the prairies for settlement.

In 1867, Quebec, Ontario, Nova Scotia, and New Brunswick joined to form the Dominion of Canada, a federation with Ottawa as its capital. Federal jurisdiction included national matters (for example, peace, banking, taxation, trade, and commerce), while provincial jurisdiction included local matters (for example, education, the administration of justice, property, and civil rights). The queen (Crown) was head of state, represented by the governor-general (federal) and lieutenant governor (provincial). Legislative powers were vested in the federal House of Commons (elected) and Senate (appointed), and the provincial legislative assemblies (elected). Executive powers were vested in the leaders of majority elected parties, the prime minister (federal) and premiers (provincial), who in turn appointed cabinets from elected legislators. Judicial powers were vested in (1) "Section 101" courts (established in 1875 as the Supreme Court of Canada and the Exchequer, later Federal, Court); (2) "Section 96" courts: "superior" courts of general jurisdiction established by the provinces but with federally appointed judges; and (3) "Section 92" courts: "inferior" courts of specific jurisdiction established by the provinces, with provincially appointed judges. Canada was a "responsible government," but the Judicial Committee of the Privy Council remained the final court of appeal in constitutional matters until 1949.

To deter American expansion, Canada acquired Rupert's Land from the Hudson's Bay Company in 1868 and created the Northwest Territories. In 1870, skirmishes between settlers and fur traders in the area were settled by establishing a new province (Manitoba). Contrary to federal-provincial precedent, Canada retained control of provincial lands, promising grants to Métis (French-Aboriginal) residents and negotiating "numbered" treaties with aboriginal peoples. The English-written treaties read "cede, release and surrender," but aboriginal elders understood the treaties as agreements of peace and mutual support within which they were sharing sacred trust responsibilities for the land to the depth of a plow.

In 1871, British Columbia joined Canada on the promise of a transcontinental railway. In 1872, Canada adopted the American land survey and settlement system: the Dominion Lands Act authorized a quadrilateral survey of prairie lands and offered 160-acre homesteads to any settler who would pay a $10 application fee, live on the land, and "break" it. In 1873, Canada created the Northwest Mounted Police and appointed magistrates to ensure the rule of law. It also continued to negotiate treaties with aboriginal peoples in what is now Saskatchewan: Treaty Two (1871), Treaty Four (1874), Treaty Five (1875), Treaty Six (1876), Treaty Eight (1899), and Treaty Ten (1906).

In 1883 the transcontinental railway reached the Territories, to carry settlers and manufactured goods west and prairie grain east. In 1885, Ottawa crushed an uprising sparked by Métis land issues. In 1886, Canada imposed English laws as of July 15, 1870, and a Torrens system of land registration to facilitate purchase and sale of lands by guaranteeing Crown grant titles.

In 1881, aboriginal and Métis people made up 87 percent of the prairie population, but by 1901 approximately 40 percent of the population were immigrants, including British, French, German, Mennonite, Dutch, Hutterite, Scandinavian, Ukrainian, Polish, Doukhobour, Czechoslovak, Hungarian, Romanian, and Jewish peoples. Canada confined aboriginal people to reserves while moving their children to residential schools.

In 1905, Canada created the provinces of Saskatchewan and Alberta and again retained control of lands.

By 1930, when Ottawa devolved control of lands to the prairie provinces, Saskatchewan had 930,000 people, 140,000 farms, and 900 villages along 14,500 kilometers of railway (one every 7.4 miles, on average). The 1930s, however, brought the Depression and prolonged drought. Farms were abandoned and the population fell. A "third" party emerged, the Co-operative Commonwealth Federation (CCF), later the New Democratic Party (NDP), which has remained as government or official opposition in Saskatchewan since 1944. Voting patterns reveal a persistent rural-urban split provincially and a western regional split nationally.

After World War II, farms were consolidated and the population urbanized. By century's end, farms, commu-

Structure of Saskatchewan Courts

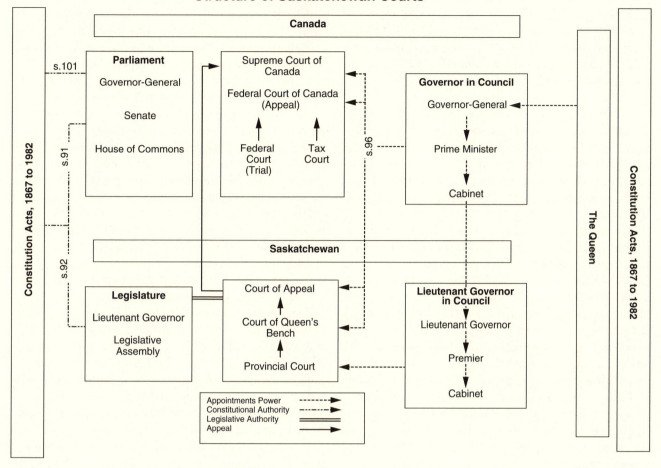

nities, and delivery points had dropped to a fraction of midcentury numbers, while farm size has increased. Habitats for wild plants and animals have been lost in up to 95 percent of parklands, 70 percent of grasslands, and 50 percent of wetlands. The prairie grizzly bear, bison, wolf, mountain lion, and wolverine are extinct; the ferret and swift fox are severely endangered.

CURRENT STRUCTURE

In 1982, Canada "patriated" its constitution. The Constitution Acts of 1867 to 1982 create a written constitution that preserves the queen as symbolic head of government, protects fundamental freedoms through a Charter of Rights and Freedoms, entrenches aboriginal and treaty rights, and subjects legislative and executive actions to judicial constitutional review.

Saskatchewan has 14 of 301 representatives in the federal House of Commons, and 6 of 105 appointees in the Senate. Its Legislative Assembly has 58 members. A third level of government (municipalities) administers local affairs under delegated authority.

The Supreme Court of Canada is the final court of appeal from all courts in Canada (see figure). The court

consists of a chief justice and eight judges appointed by the federal cabinet. Appeals are heard by leave of the court, granted according to the public importance of the legal issue. Certain criminal matters carry an automatic right of appeal. The Supreme Court also hears constitutional questions referred by the federal cabinet.

The Federal Court of Canada, with trial and appellate divisions, has jurisdiction in federal matters such as intellectual property, federal-provincial disputes, citizenship, and judicial review of federal tribunal decisions. It also has shared jurisdiction with provincial superior courts in claims by and against the Crown. The Tax Court of Canada has jurisdiction in tax and revenue matters.

Saskatchewan's Section 96 "superior" courts of general jurisdiction are the Court of Queen's Bench (trial) and Court of Appeal (appellate). The Court of Queen's Bench has the powers of common law courts as well as courts of equity. It has jurisdiction over all family matters, indictable offenses in Canada's Criminal Code, and civil matters over $5,000, as well as concurrent jurisdiction with the Provincial Court in actions for debt or damages under $5,000. The court utilizes juries at the option of the accused in criminal matters and at the expense of a requesting party in civil matters. The court consists of a chief justice and thirty-two full-time, federally appointed judges. Of these, eight are dedicated to a Unified Family Court, which consolidates jurisdiction over divorce, custody, and property settlements and offers associated support services to families.

The Court of Appeal hears appeals from any order of the Court of Queen's Bench, as well as decisions of the Provincial Court concerning indictable offenses. Argument is based on issues of law arising out of the trial record. The court also hears constitutional questions referred by the provincial cabinet. A chief justice and eight federally appointed judges hear appeals in panels of at least three judges.

Saskatchewan's Section 92 "inferior" court is the Provincial Court. The court has jurisdiction with respect to summary conviction offenses under the Criminal Code. With respect to indictable offenses, the court conducts preliminary inquiries and has jurisdiction in some offenses, such as theft under $5,000 and those in which an accused is permitted to elect trial by a Provincial Court judge. The court has jurisdiction over young offenders, except on murder charges. It has jurisdiction over regulatory offenses under Saskatchewan legislation and hears civil claims under $5,000. The court consists of a chief judge and forty-five provincially appointed judges. Appeals from Provincial Court concerning small claims and summary offenses are heard by the Court of Queen's Bench, while appeals concerning indictable offenses are heard by the Court of Appeal.

Administrative tribunals authorized by legislation and appointed by cabinets use their own procedures and expertise to resolve disputes in areas such as labor relations, liquor licensing, and human rights. Tribunal decisions are subject to judicial review. Arbitrators and mediators agreed to by the parties also settle disputes under the authority of certain legislation.

Various programs facilitate access to justice, such as legal aid for indigent people in family and criminal law matters, and court workers who assist aboriginal people. Courts, governments, and communities are working to develop meaningful programs in restorative justice, such as sentencing circles, victim-offender mediation, counseling, and prevention programs.

NOTABLE FEATURES OF LEGAL SYSTEM

Several legal regimes introduced in Saskatchewan have been adopted elsewhere. In the 1940s, the province initiated publicly funded health care (cancer treatment in 1945, hospital care in 1947, and medical care in 1964) and publicly owned and operated compulsory auto insurance (1946). Throughout the century, regimes developed to assist farmers, such as mandatory farmer-creditor mediation, homestead protection from final orders of

foreclosure, deficiency protection, statutory warranties, and restrictions on the seizure and sale of farm equipment. In 1977 the Consumer Products Warranties Act extended statutory warranties and improved consumer remedies. In 1981 the Personal Property Security Act implemented a modern, integrated, secured financing system involving a central computerized registry.

Saskatchewan also shares with other Canadian provinces legal regimes such as human rights codes, collective bargaining and worker protection systems, equal division of property upon marriage dissolution, and benefits for unmarried and same-sex couples identical to those of married couples.

The Native Law Center of Canada researches and publishes in aboriginal law and offers a summer preparatory program for aboriginal students attending Canadian law schools. Established in 1973, the program is credited with increasing the number of aboriginal lawyers in Canada from a few to several hundred.

During the 1990s, a Treaty Land Entitlement Agreement provided funds to fulfill land entitlements under the treaties, an Office of the Treaty Commissioner was established to facilitate federal-provincial-aboriginal negotiations on treaty implementation, and a Provincial Court judge was named to establish a Cree court.

In 1994, amendments to the Queen's Bench Act mandated mediation prior to examination for discovery in all civil actions suitable for mediation. Actions that remain unsettled after good-faith mediation proceed to trial. As of 2001, a new Land Titles Act is integrating land survey and land titles registries, providing Internet-based land survey examination, title registration, and an integrated spatial database (GIS).

STAFFING

The Law Society of Saskatchewan monitors the qualifications and conduct of lawyers. Admission to the bar requires successful completion of a bachelor of laws degree, twelve months' articling, and the bar course and examinations. Admission to the University of Saskatchewan College of Law requires successful completion of the LSAT examination as well as at least two years of recognized undergraduate education or equivalent experience and education as a "special student." As of June 2001, the Law Society had a membership of 1,346 practicing lawyers, of which 350 were women.

Marjorie L. Benson

With the assistance of Professor Russ Buglass (law), Dr. Ka-iu Fung (geography), and Dana Kingsbury (law)

See also Alberta; Canada; Federalism; Manitoba; North Dakota; Northern Territories of Canada
References and further reading
Archer, John. 1980. *A Saskatchewan History.* Saskatoon: Western Producer Books.

Cardinal, Harold, and Walter Hildebrandt. 2000. *Treaty Elders of Saskatchewan.* Calgary: University of Calgary Press.

Fowke, Vernon. 1946. *National Policy and the Wheat Economy.* Toronto: University of Toronto Press.

Fung, Ka-iu, Bill Barry, and Michael Wilson. 2000. *Atlas of Saskatchewan.* Saskatoon: University of Saskatchewan.

Government of Canada. "Canada's Court System." http://www.canada.justice.gc.ca (accessed May 14, 2001).

Government of Saskatchewan. "Saskatchewan Justice." http://www.saskjustice.gov.sk.ca (accessed May 14, 2001).

Henderson, J. Y., M. L. Benson, and I. M. Findlay. 2000. *Aboriginal Tenure in the Constitution of Canada.* Toronto: Carswell.

Hogg, Peter. 1997. *Constitutional Law of Canada.* 4th ed. Toronto: Carswell.

Lipset, Seymour Martin. 1968. *Agrarian Socialism: The Co-operative Commonwealth Federation in Saskatchewan: A Study in Political Sociology.* Rev. ed. New York: Anchor Books (orig. ed. University of California Press, 1950).

Native Law Center of Canada. http://www.usask.ca/nativelaw/intro.html (accessed May 14, 2001).

SAUDI ARABIA

COUNTRY INFORMATION

Saudi Arabia is a desert kingdom extending over 80 percent of the Arabian Peninsula. Most of its 868,000 square miles is arid desert, often rich in minerals but sparsely populated. Its population of perhaps 22 million (2000 estimate) is concentrated on the eastern and western coasts and in interior oases. The national population is mostly Arab and largely Sunni Muslim. Shia Muslims, less than 10 percent of the population, are concentrated in Hasa, the oil-rich eastern province. The population includes some 5 million nonnationals—temporary foreign workers drawn to jobs created by oil wealth.

The economy is dominated by oil. Oil reserves (estimated at over 260 billion barrels) are the largest in the world (one-quarter of the world's total). Saudi Arabia's gross domestic product (GDP) is roughly $170 billion (2000 estimate). Oil revenues account for the bulk of state revenues. Nearly all this oil is produced by the parastatal Saudi ARAMCO. While significant moves toward economic liberalization have occurred in recent years, the economy remains largely government owned and operated.

Oil revenues have brought Saudi Arabia prosperity and with it an expansive and expensive welfare state providing education, health care, and a myriad of services and subsidies to the national population. The Saudi economy is, however, hostage to this revenue source. Growth rates rose dramatically with the sharp rise in oil prices in the 1970s and slumped with slumping prices in the 1980s.

The Saudi government is a monarchy, ruled by descendants of its eponymous founding family, Al Saud. A member of this family and the founder of modern Saudi Arabia, King Abd al-Aziz ibn Abd al-Rahman Al Saud (known in the West as Ibn Saud), forged the peninsula's disparate provinces into a state in 1932. According to the Basic Law of 1992, the king must be a descendant of his; to date, all have been sons. The king's powers are quite broad and largely unlimited by formal institutions, although a Constitutional Council was appointed in 1992. Administratively, the country is divided into thirteen provinces, all governed by appointed members of the ruling family.

The Saudi legal system is based on Islamic law. Saudi Arabia is the birthplace of Islam and the site of its two holiest places, Mecca and Medina. Because Saudi Arabia was one of very few states in the region never colonized, its legal system has fewer of the European legal accretions found nearby, and Islamic law, reduced in most states today largely to personal status law (roughly, family and probate law), retains a central place. Since the eighteenth century, the government and religious establishment have held to the tenets of Wahhabism, which favors an emphasis on the roots of Islam: the Qur'an and Sunnah (the words and acts of the prophet Muhammad), giving less weight to the later exegesis of Islamic scholars. While historically tied to the Hanbali school of Islamic law, today's religious authorities, when augmenting the Qur'an and Sunnah, draw on all four Islamic schools. As a commitment to Islamic ideals, Saudi Arabia has no formal constitution save the Qur'an and Sunnah.

HISTORY

While the peninsula's recorded history goes back 5,000 years to the civilization of Dilmun, Saudi Arabia's legal history begins in the seventh century with the birth of Islam. The revelations of the Qur'an, believed by Muslims to be God's words, and the words and deeds of the Prophet (who, as political and religious leader of the community, first applied these ideas) form the core of Islamic law and practice.

Saudi Arabia's modern history begins in the eighteenth century with an alliance between Muhammad ibn Saud and Muhammad ibn Abd al-Wahhab, a religious leader and founder of the Wahhabi movement, which sought moral inspiration in direct study of the religious thought and practice of the Prophet and his companions. It took its intellectual bearings from the thirteenth- to fourteenth-century theologian Ibn Taymiyya, in turn influenced by the teachings of Ahmad ibn Hanbal, a ninth-century theologian and founder of the Hanbali school of Islamic law. The Saudi/Wahhabi coalition forged three successive kingdoms, culminating in the present one. Saudi Arabia began to take its modern form in the twentieth century as Ibn

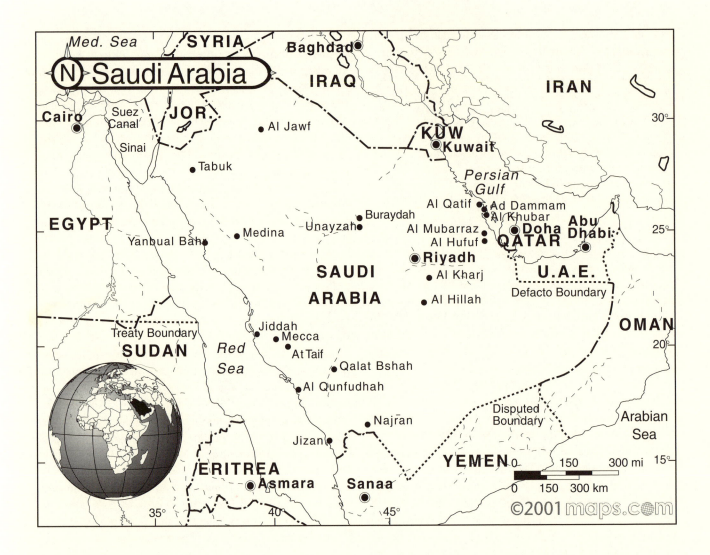

Saud unified the peninsula's disparate regions into one state, beginning in 1902 with the capture of Riyadh (today's capital), turning with the conquest of the Hijaz in 1925, and culminating in the 1932 proclamation of the Kingdom of Saudi Arabia.

Oil was discovered in the 1930s. When large-scale production began after World War II, the kingdom experienced rapid growth. With Ibn Saud's death in 1953, rule passed to his sons: Saud (r. 1953–1964), Faisal (1964–1975), Khalid (1975–1982), Fahd (1982–), and presumptively Crown Prince Abdallah. The 1990 Gulf War, bringing U.S. troops to Saudi soil, energized Islamic and liberal opposition into more active protest, prompting the 1992 creation of an appointed Consultative Council and a Basic Law that reiterated the centrality of Islamic law but also the king's independent power to issue regulations consistent with that law.

LEGAL CONCEPTS

Islamic law, or *sharia* ("path"), is the basis of Saudi law. This law is intimately bound up with Islamic political philosophy, which sees the primary role of the state as that of helping the Muslim community uphold God's moral standards, the *sharia* being the source of these standards. In this conception, the state is no neutral arena; it has an active obligation to the community to pursue good and prevent evil. Notions of both justice and legitimacy are articulated simultaneously in legal and Islamic terms.

Islamic law, divine and infallible, is rooted, first, in the Qur'an—in words Muslims believe God directly revealed to Muhammad. By laying the ethical basis for justice, the Qur'an provides both a general guide to behavior and clear and sometimes detailed guidelines to specific practices, ranging from religious duty to family and probate law, criminal law, and commercial law. The Qur'an, however, devotes only a few of its verses specifically to law and is silent on most legal issues. Like all religious texts, it must also be interpreted, and it can be interpreted in different ways. Hence, other sources were required. Consequently, in the first centuries following the Prophet's death, Islamic scholars, *ulama,* worked out agreement on additional sources of law. The second source (in importance, not scope) is the Sunnah, the acts and words of the

Prophet. Together, the Qur'an and Sunnah are the primary sources of Islamic law. A third source is consensus (*ijma'*) of the community, in practice being the community of Islamic scholars, on matters where the first two sources did not suffice. A fourth source is analogy (*qiyas*), applying principles from the Qur'an or Sunnah to new cases. The fifth source is *ijtihad*. While typically translated as "independent reasoning," ijtihad can more appropriately be viewed as the method for applying the other sources to particular legal problems. Over the first Islamic centuries, a scholarly consensus emerged on these sources as the formal basis of Islamic jurisprudence.

This framework, consisting of basic sources (the Qur'an and Sunnah) and techniques to interpret them (*qiyas, ijtihad, ijma'*), helped provide the predictable and uniform practice all legal systems require, particularly important since judges were bound neither by precedent as in common law systems (whether by decisions of other judges, even from higher courts, or by their own previous decisions) nor by code as in civil law systems (exegesis provided only guidelines, not codified law).

As the law evolved, the Islamic world expanded. With Muhammad's death in 632, a succession dispute arose. Abu Bakr became the first caliph, followed by Umar ibn al-Khattab, who began institutionalizing legal practice in the growing Muslim community. But the succession issue remained unresolved, and following the death of the last of the first four rightly guided caliphs, the community divided into Sunnis and Shias. Originally, a dispute over succession, this division evolved into a sectarian divide. While Sunnis prevailed numerically and politically in the territory that now is Saudi Arabia, as in much of the Muslim world, Shias remained a significant minority. In the Sunni world, scholarly thought eventually solidified into four schools of law associated with individual jurists (Hanbali, Hanafi, Maliki, and Shafi'i).

In the eighteenth century, the Arabian Peninsula saw the rise of the Wahhabi movement, which, taking its bearings from the writings of the Hanbali scholar Ibn Taymiyya, challenged religious scholars and judges to rely more on independent reasoning in applying the Qur'an and Sunnah. The victory of the Wahhabi movement brought this approach to the center of legal thought on the peninsula. Some substantive and procedural elements of that thinking follow.

Crimes in Islamic law fall into three categories: *hudud, qisas,* and *ta'zir. Hudud* ("limits," that is, limits set by God) crimes are crimes against God. On these, the court has, in principle, no discretion, once strict evidentiary requirements are conclusively met. These crimes are prohibited in the Qur'an or Sunnah along with specified punishments, typically corporal. They include drinking alcohol, illicit sex, false accusation of illicit sex, brigandage, rebellion, theft, and apostasy. Penalties for *hudud*

crimes are high (severing a hand for theft, flogging for fornication, stoning for adultery), but so, too, are the evidentiary standards required for conviction: Adultery, for example, requires the testimony of four upstanding male witnesses to the very act. Conviction also requires the absence of all (not merely reasonable) doubt. Thus *hudud* convictions are rare. Nonetheless, Saudi Arabia, unlike most states in the region, does sometimes enforce these penalties.

Qisas crimes are homicide and assault (acts of violence causing bodily harm). They are punishable by either retaliation (*qisas*) or, if the victim or family chooses, by a fine paid to the victim or family. In the case of murder, for example, *sharia* gives the victim's family the right to either the death penalty or financial compensation. *Ta'zir* crimes, a residual category, include crimes not covered by *hudud* and *qisas*, as well as acts that fail to meet their strict evidentiary requirements. Punishments are up to the judge, although in Saudi Arabia a body of decree law has developed. While *hudud* and *qisas* crimes typically involve nonincarcerative sanctions (corporal punishment for *hudud*, fines for *qisas*), the typical punishment for *ta'zir* crimes is prison.

In civil law, *sharia* addresses a range of issues related to personal and commercial interactions. Family law is covered in particular detail with specific rules in the Qur'an and Sunnah on inheritance, marriage and divorce, and the status of children. The *sharia* also provides many clear rules on commercial transactions, notably a prohibition on interest. Where *sharia* does not clearly address some modern business matters (a significant area, given Saudi Arabia's wealth and level of integration into the global economy), a body of government regulations has arisen, which will be addressed here.

In practice, *sharia* courts have jurisdiction over most criminal cases and over civil suits involving personal status. Three main standards of proof are used in *sharia* courts. The first is an uncoerced confession. Second is the eyewitness testimony of typically two impartial upstanding male witnesses (Quranic rules grant women's testimony half the weight of men's; women's testimony is not allowed in criminal cases). Absent the required witnesses, courts in *hudud* crimes usually require a confession for criminal conviction. All testimony must be voluntary. The third proof is an affirmation or denial by oath. While perjury certainly occurs, these oaths, sworn in court before God, are taken far more seriously than their rough Western counterparts. Parties may forgo large amounts of money by refusing to take an oath that would virtually guarantee a favorable outcome. Circumstantial evidence is accepted but reluctantly. While defendants may have an attorney (in civil but not criminal cases), the court prefers they speak for themselves. Historically, people could have a representative (usually a male relative) stand for them or assist in court, but the advocacy characteristic of Western law runs counter to Islamic legal sensibilities: Advocacy, judges believe, would slow the process and impede reconciliation. In any event, direct oral testimony is preferred, although documents are used, especially in commercial matters. While Islamic courts rely on *sharia* principles of evidence, each judge determines personally and in each case what that means. In style, these courts are informal by Western standards, and the judge enjoys broad discretion in his quest for truth. Some real judicial independence exists, although it is often exercised informally.

Legal culture is an important element in promoting fairness in the trial process, since, given its religious basis, it permeates society and so shapes to a greater degree the conduct of all participants in the process. The judicial culture takes finding the truth seriously. *Ijtihad* requires a high degree of individual conscience. Judges are seeing to God's best interests as well as to the interests of those before them, and they will be called on in the next life to account both to God and to those who passed through their courtrooms for their rulings. Some procedural protections do exist in the *sharia* courts. There is a judicial presumption of innocence. Procedural law stipulates a mandatory appeal for capital and amputation convictions. However, in criminal trials, defendants are not typically allowed an attorney (although a defendant who can afford one may be allowed to talk with the attorney before trial), again in keeping with the belief that the *sharia* provides all necessary protections—ones the judge is morally bound to zealously guard.

In criminal cases, the efficacy of these protections is hard to ascertain. Trials are rarely open to the public. The king, while bound morally and legally (albeit without positive means of constraint) by the *sharia*, is subject to no formal check (in practice, even the ruling family is typically above the law, for judges and police are often unwilling or unable to uphold their legal duties, such as issuing arrest warrants, in regard to them). Historically, the dominant sentiment in Islamic political philosophy was that the dangers of rebellion and likely consequent civil war far outweighed the dangers of submission to a bad Muslim ruler. Procedural issues, the source of most legal restraints on the state in the West, were never a primary focus of Islamic jurisprudence, which treated procedure and evidence not as separate categories, but rather in terms of their relationship to the three categories of *sharia* crime. This is not to say that such procedural checks could not be created consistent with Islamic law, just that Saudi rulers have shown little interest in doing so, favoring instead interpretations granting the state the most unrestricted authority.

In political cases, several human rights groups have documented the virtual absence of effective protections. The law allows suspects to be held in prolonged detention without access to counsel or notice to family. There is no independent judicial supervision of detention, and abuses occur. Moreover, even in *sharia* courts, convictions often turn solely on confessions obtained during an often deliberately extensive pretrial interrogation, interrogations in which pressure, physical and emotional, is often applied. Confessions must be certified by an investigating judge (who is not the trial judge), but he lacks the power to order a suspect's release. These judges sometimes warn suspects that retracting their confessions will result in further interrogation. Judges have thrown out confessions obtained through torture, but this is uncommon. Justice is often swift and final: Saudi Arabia has one of the highest execution rates in the world. The absence of formal protections falls hardest on the most powerless groups in Saudi society: women, Shias, and nonnationals.

CURRENT STRUCTURE

In the early twentieth century, the judicial system was rudimentary. The ruler appointed judges to large towns who worked with local governors to resolve cases where voluntary compliance and mediation failed. Although senior *ulama* guided judges, the only appeal was to the king. In 1925, Ibn Saud conquered the Hijaz, which had more highly developed legal institutions and was where Shafi'i and Hanafi thought dominated. Ibn Saud created a new court system in the Hijaz, but when he tried to extend this system to the rest of the country, the *ulama* balked. It was not until 1960 that his son, King Saud, was able to create a unified national judicial system. In 1970, the newly created justice ministry took over the judicial system. The 1975 Regulation on the Judiciary established the *sharia* court system's organization and jurisdiction and placed it under a Supreme Judicial Council (*majlis al-qada' al-'ala*).

Saudi Arabia has three court levels. The entry level is the Court of Urgent Matters (*mahkamat al-umur al-musta'jala*), where a single judge hears both civil and criminal cases. These courts have jurisdiction over all criminal cases, except those involving death or amputation, and over some civil cases. The next level is the Greater Court (*al-mahkama al-kubra*), which hears all cases not heard by the lower courts. This includes most civil cases (heard by a single judge) and the more serious criminal cases, the *hudud* and *qisas* cases (heard by a panel of three judges). The third court is the Appeals Court (*mahkamat al-tamiz*), in Riyadh and Mecca, which typically hears cases in three-judge panels. This court has three departments: criminal, personal status, and other. Most lower-court judgments are appealable. Sentences involving death or amputation carry an automatic appeal and are heard by a five-judge panel. As in civil law states, both prosecution and defense may appeal, although neither *sharia* nor Saudi regulation specifically allows this. The Appeals

Courts normally rule solely on lower-court proceedings. They can uphold a judgment or remand the case for re-trial to a different judge. Judicial discretion is respected; such reversals are extremely rare. At the top sits a twelve-member Supreme Judicial Council headed by the justice minister, which reviews appeals on death and amputation sentences (then ratified by the king) and matters referred to it by the king or crown prince.

Most disputes are handled outside the court system. In practice, the overwhelming majority of civil cases are settled by reconciliation. Efforts at private resolution are woven through the system and are at play long before a case approaches court. There is no such thing as a private dispute in Saudi Arabia: Family and friends actively and routinely intervene to resolve conflicts. The Qur'an encourages informal resolution. Even conflicts proceeding to trial rarely end in judgment. Most are settled, typically with the judge's active help. One important quasi-formal dispute resolution mechanism is the use of *fatwas,* religious opinions on individual matters issued by *muftis,* religious scholars who interpret Islamic law. *Fatwas* often resolve both personal and commercial disputes. Individuals solicit *fatwas* as a personal guide. Parties in a civil dispute may agree in advance to consider a *fatwa* binding. Law firms may solicit *fatwas* to predict the court's likely ruling. A Board of Senior Ulama issues *fatwas* on important public issues, generated either independently or in response to a request from the king. The Board's Standing Committee for Ifta responds to private requests.

SPECIALIZED JUDICIAL BODIES

The king has the authority under *sharia* to enact decrees as long as they do not contradict *sharia,* and he has done so. Some specialized courts (including appeals courts) deal with commercial matters and implement statutory law, for example, the Ministry of Labor and Social Affairs' Committee for the Settlement of Labor Disputes. Committees include both *sharia* lawyers and ministry-appointed members with technical and regulatory expertise.

The most important specialized court is the Board of Grievances (*diwan al-mazalim*), established in 1955. In 1982, the board's chair was given ministerial status and made answerable directly to the king. The board incorporates an old Islamic tradition of *mazalim,* the right to bring grievances to the ruler, and handles complaints against state authorities: lawsuits against government agencies and appeals of administrative decisions. The board's authority has grown over the years and now includes authority over the commercial cases (the Commerce Ministry's Committee for the Settlement of Commercial Disputes, once an important committee of this type, has had its jurisdiction transferred to the Board of Grievances) and over most non-*sharia* crimes (regulated by statute).

Since Islamic law is the sole source of legislation, these

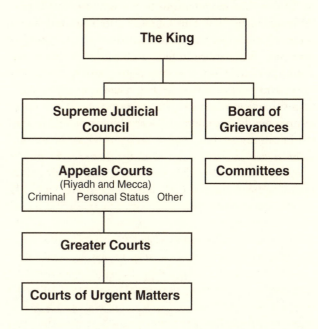

Legal Structure of Saudi Arabia Courts

- The King
  - Supreme Judicial Council
    - Appeals Courts (Riyadh and Mecca) — Criminal   Personal Status   Other
      - Greater Courts
        - Courts of Urgent Matters
  - Board of Grievances
    - Committees

courts (which are called not courts but committees) do not implement laws but rather regulations or decrees issued by the king and the Council of Ministers after consultation with high-ranking *ulama* (sometimes in the form of a *fatwa* request to the Board of Senior Ulama), who perform a kind of Islamic constitutional review. (*Muftis* also can later review the law when questions arise in application.) While the *sharia* grants rulers broad authority to enact decrees that do not contradict *sharia,* some religious opponents argue that all the non-Islamic courts should be collapsed into the *sharia* courts' jurisdiction and that regulations should always have an articulated basis in *sharia.*

STAFFING

Saudi Arabia has two bars: one for the *sharia* court, the other for the committees. Only those admitted to the local bar (restricted to male Saudi nationals) may appear in court. The king appoints and removes all judges on the recommendation of the Supreme Judicial Council. Judges must be twenty-five (older for higher courts). There is a good deal of social homogeneity to the judges, most of whom come from the central region of Qasim and have studied at the same schools. Saudi Arabia has about 650 judges, too few in number to cope with the heavy caseloads, which often results in long delays.

Historically, an Islamic judge or scholar received training in the mosque, working with respected Wahhabi mentors. Today, attorneys typically have an undergraduate degree in *sharia* from one of Saudi Arabia's three *sharia* colleges in the three Islamic universities: al-Imam Muhammad ibn Saud in Riyadh, Umm al-Qura in Mecca, and the

Islamic University in Medina. They receive training in all four schools of religious law. In the past, they were typically taught by Egyptian professors trained at al-Azhar; increasingly today, the faculty is Saudi. The High Institute of the Judiciary offers graduate-level training in *sharia*. Attorneys aspiring to work in the committees typically study in the administrative sciences colleges of regular universities, where regulatory law is the primary subject of study. They also study some *sharia*. Many study at the Institute of Public Administration (IPA), established in 1961, which trains students in regulatory law. The IPA is especially valuable for those with only *sharia*-college backgrounds. Graduates of *sharia* colleges often go to the IPA for graduate work.

IMPACT

Islamic law in Saudi Arabia permeates public and private affairs to a much greater degree than does law in the West. First, its reach is greater, comprising not just criminal and civil law, but also personal religious practice. The duties one has to God (prayer, fasting, pilgrimage) are no less a part of *sharia* than rules on theft and inheritance. Its broad moral standards cover relations with the community, with the state, and with God. In this sense, Islamic law is far more influential in Saudi Arabia than in other Muslim-populated states, where Islamic law typically enjoys the sanction of the state, with all its coercive power, only in personal status law. Second, its abstract impact is greater, since the *sharia*, being divine, is the only guide to a righteous life. People actively seek to know and obey it, even absent the danger of state enforcement. Nonetheless, in Saudi Arabia, *sharia* is law, with all its coercive force. It is not interpreted by elected leaders, and dissenting interpretations (whether from Shias, women, or Sunni Islamists) are not generally tolerated. While the system clearly functions with a good deal of popular support and hardly rests heavily on coercion, without more open debate the true level of acceptance is hard to know.

Jill Crystal

See also Islamic Law
References and further reading
The single best English-language source for the Saudi legal system is Frank Vogel's *Islamic Law and Legal System: Studies of Saudi Arabia* (Leiden and Boston: Brill Academic Publishers, 2000). Various human rights groups (Amnesty International, Middle East Watch, the Arab Organization for Human Rights) offer some coverage of court structures and processes.
Ali, Bader-El-Din. 1985 "Islamic Law and Crime: The Case of Saudi Arabia." *International Journal of Comparative and Applied Criminal Justice* 9: 45–57.
al-Sagheer, Mohamed Faleh. 1994. "Diyya Legislation in Islamic Shari'a and Its Application in the Kingdom of Saudi Arabia." Pp. 80–91 in *Alternatives to Imprisonment in Comparative Perspective.* Edited by Ugljesa Zvekic. Chicago: Nelson Hall.
Jones, Mark. 1992. "Islamic Law in Saudi Arabia: A Responsive View." *International Journal of Comparative and Applied Criminal Justice* 16: 43–56.
Moore, Richter. 1987. "Courts, Law, Justice, and Criminal Trials in Saudi Arabia." *International Journal of Comparative and Applied Criminal Justice* 11: 61–67.
Souryal, Sam. 1987. "The Religionization of a Society: The Continuing Application of Shariah Law in Saudi Arabia." *Journal for the Scientific Study of Religion* 26: 429–449.
———. 1988. "The Role of Shariah Law in Deterring Criminality in Saudi-Arabia." *International Journal of Comparative and Applied Criminal Justice* 12: 1–25.

SCOTLAND

COUNTRY INFORMATION

Scotland forms approximately the northern third of the island of Great Britain, which lies to the northwest of the continent of Europe. With adjacent inhabited islands, such as the Orkneys and Shetlands, Scotland is 30,418 square miles in area. It has a land border of about 70 miles with England, which, with Wales, forms the southern part of Britain. The climate is a temperate one but much wetter in the west than the east.

The population of Scotland is about 5 million. More than half of the people are concentrated in the flat central belt formed by the Rivers Forth and Clyde. There, most of the industry is to be found. Heavy industry, such as iron and steel making, shipbuilding, and coal mining, has largely been replaced by electronics and financial services. Tourism has the largest number of employees, many of them seasonal. To the north, the Highlands are a mainly recreational area, affording opportunities for shooting, fishing, mountaineering, and, in winter, skiing. The coastal fringe includes fishing ports, such as Peterhead and Fraserburgh, and the ancient city of Aberdeen, which, as the base for oil platforms and oil rigs in the North Sea, is the most prosperous of Scotland's largest cities, the others being Edinburgh, Glasgow, and Dundee. The language spoken by virtually all of Scotland's inhabitants is English, to which are added a number of distinctively Scottish words. However, attempts are being made to revive and even give equal status to the Celtic language of Gaelic through the media of television and radio. It has always been spoken on the islands off the west coast of Scotland.

The legal system of Scotland is, along with education and religion, the feature of Scottish culture that most sharply distinguishes it from that of its English neighbor. Its statutory law is enacted in the Parliament of the United Kingdom (UK) of Great Britain and Northern Ireland, which sits at Westminster in London, and since

1999 also in the Parliament of Scotland, which sits in Edinburgh. Law made for the purpose of achieving some reform is supplemented by law made in the highest courts, civil and criminal, as a by-product of the reasons given by judges to justify their decisions in disputed cases. Such judge-made law is to be found both where no statute law yet exists and in interpreting doubtful words in statutes.

HISTORY

The history of Scotland, insofar as it bears on the development of the country's legal system, may be taken to begin with the reign of Malcolm III (1058–1093), known as Malcolm Canmore or "Big Head." It was he who completed the process of unifying the various territorial tribes, which since the departure of the Romans around 400 C.E. had struggled for supremacy over one another and against Viking and other Norse invaders.

However, it was Norsemen—the Normans who had settled in Normandy—who were to dominate Scotland in the early Middle Ages. Many familiar Scottish surnames, such as Stewart, Bruce, Fraser, and Graham, originate in towns and villages in Normandy and were borne by leading Scots in the subsequent centuries. The Normans entered Scotland on the whole peacefully through intermarriage, after vanquishing the English at the Battle of Hastings in 1066. Malcolm's second wife, Margaret, was a powerful woman; later declared a saint, she introduced religious orders from England and France and promoted the building of churches. Their children, Alexander I (1107–1124) and David I (1124–1153), continued their civilizing influence. But they owned lands in England as well as Scotland, for which, under the principles of feudal law common to Western Europe, they had to pay homage to the English king. By the time of Edward I of England at the end of the thirteenth century, this obedience became highly controversial when Edward claimed that it meant that all Scotland was subject to his authority and that he could settle claims to its kingship. The patriot William Wallace rejected this claim and after defeating the English at Stirling Bridge was himself defeated at the Battle of Falkirk. He was executed in London in 1305, as depicted in the film *Braveheart*. Robert Bruce, a contender for the kingship, then led his people to victory over Edward II at Bannockburn in 1314. Although there were frequent battles with the English thereafter along the border between the two countries, this victory confirmed Scotland as a kingdom separate from England. Its status was reinforced by treaties, most notably the Treaty of Northampton in 1328 in which Edward III unequivocally recognized Scotland's independence. That independence had been asserted in solemn prose in an address to the pope by Scottish nobles—the Declaration of Arbroath of 1320.

Legal Institutions

During the period up to the middle of the sixteenth century, Scotland's legal institutions enjoyed intermittent development but were far short of attaining the efficiency that can confer stability on a nation. Its written law was mainly procedural, stating how rights were to be given effect and duties performed. Much of the law was customary, for example, on how property other than land was to be divided on the death of the owner. There was no distinct Parliament with a prescribed membership. Rather, the monarch summoned his nobles and senior clerics—and eventually representatives of the burghs (towns)—when he wanted advice or a favor such as a tax. At times, they would enact a statute, often reiterating for emphasis what was already law. The courts were even less satisfactory as a source of case law. Those that mattered most in giving judgments were local courts, often under the influence or control of the most powerful local magnate. The judges in the courts of the king in civil matters were simply advisers whose judgments were not published and who did not provide reasons for their opinions. Traveling royal criminal courts went around Scottish towns from time to time, dispensing justice on those accused of grave crimes such as rape and murder and especially treason. In them, the judge was called a "justiciar," and juries were used to establish the facts. In the absence of reliable civil courts, many cases were taken to the church courts, which every bishop had to provide. As well as disputes between church bodies, those courts had jurisdiction to settle matters ranging from marriage and legitimacy to succession on death and movable property. From these ecclesiastical courts, appeals went with surprising frequency to the supreme courts of the church in Rome. The law they applied was canon law, which included a strong infusion of Roman law. Thus, by that route and by the practice of future lawyers studying abroad, the law of Scotland has some important antecedents.

By the early sixteenth century, the royal central court in civil matters was sitting more regularly. Judges, both nobles and churchmen, now had some legal knowledge, and the advocates who appeared before them had had some legal training, either in the universities of Scotland at St. Andrews, Glasgow, and Aberdeen or abroad in those of France and Italy. In 1532, the central court, under the name of the Court of Session, was put on a permanent footing, financed out of church revenues and with an abbot as its first lord president and a comprehensive jurisdiction. Judges and advocates began keeping notes of cases they had participated in as a guide to future practice. These "Practicks" were copied and eventually printed. They thus became the forerunners of the law reports, an essential prerequisite of any system of judge-made law.

The use of church courts came to an end with the Reformation in 1560. Their jurisdiction over marriage (now including divorce) and succession was transferred to local and central courts. The Parliament set up a Presbyterian form of church government based on committees composed of ministers and laymen, called elders. The lowest tier, the Kirk Session, enjoyed a quasi-criminal jurisdiction over minor offenses with a moral aspect.

Unions and Conflict

A major and peaceful change in the relationship of Scotland and England occurred in 1603 when James VI of Scotland succeeded to the throne of England on the death of Queen Elizabeth. He at once moved to London and seldom returned to Scotland. For most of the seventeenth century, government was exercised in Scotland through the Scottish Privy Council. It performed both legislative and judicial functions and thus offered competition to both the Parliament and the Court of Session. During the seventeenth century, there was almost constant strife around issues of religion. James and his successors, Charles I and Charles II, wished to impose on Scotland an episcopal form of church government. By the divine right of kings that they claimed, their own nominees would be (and for short periods were) the bishops. This move was resisted in Scotland, most emphatically in the National Covenant of 1638. With its hundreds of signatures, arranged by social class, it symbolized the Scots people as united under a common religion and thus comparable to the Jews. Charles I was executed in 1649 on the orders of the English Parliament, and a republican Commonwealth was proclaimed under Oliver Cromwell. Most Scots did not recognize it. But when Charles II came to the throne in 1660, they resisted still more strongly his imposition of episcopacy, and there was much bloodshed and prosecution for treason. Charles's successor, his brother James, was a Catholic and was deposed after three years. On the invitation of some English nobles, William of Orange, his Protestant son-in-law, succeeded him, and the Scots Parliament issued a similar invitation to the throne of Scotland. The two kingdoms remained separate, sharing only a king and queen. The two law systems stayed wholly separate. However, in both countries, the terms accepted by William and his wife, Mary, were such as to ensure that sovereignty was to be shared by Parliament and monarch, and the way was paved for the future parliamentary democracy of the United Kingdom. Anne, the successor of William and Mary, had no surviving children. The two Parliaments had made different provisions for the succession. Meanwhile, the exclusion of Scots from the expanding English colonies and trade was a source of resentment to the Scots. It seemed the two countries were drifting apart.

However, in the few years before her death, Anne sought to ward off this outcome. Commissioners were appointed to negotiate the Treaty of Union (of the Parliaments). There were many interest groups that had to be won over: the judges and lawyers, the church, the burgesses of the cities and towns, the merchants. But by a judicious mixture of bribery, protective legislation, and promises, all were sufficiently persuaded for the Scots Parliament to accept an act of union in each of the three estates in which it then met—the nobles, the barons, and the burgesses. The English Parliament, with no such doubts, then ratified the treaty and passed an act to the same effect as that of the Scots. Well it might, for the two Houses of the English Parliament retained the same membership, to which were added forty-five Scots to the House of Commons and sixteen Scots peers to the House of Lords.

A United Kingdom

The union brought many advantages to Scotland. Chief among them was the access that it gave to the colonies. The importation of tobacco, sugar, rice, cotton, jute, and iron ore created new industries and raised the standard of living. In the mid-nineteenth century, it became possible to incorporate companies so that the liability of the members as shareholders was limited to the value of their shares. Farming and fishing were aided by government support. But living conditions in the cities in which the new factories sprang up deteriorated, until in the second half of the nineteenth century, water and sewage schemes were provided, hospitals were built to segregate those with infectious diseases, and police forces were created to keep order and enforce the laws. In the twentieth century, after both world wars, a great effort was made to reward the returning servicemen by creating public housing at low rents, the local authorities being the landlords under special tenancy legislation.

These measures and every other piece of legislation affecting Scotland had to be passed in the Parliament of the United Kingdom, where members from England and Wales were in the great majority. Often, too, the political complexion of the government that would promote the legislation was not that supported by a majority of voters in Scotland. By 1997, the case for a Parliament of Scotland was accepted, with power devolved from the United Kingdom Parliament. Since the European Communities Act of 1972, power has also been draining away to the European Union.

LEGAL CONCEPTS AND INSTITUTIONS

Unlike most states, the United Kingdom (and within it Scotland) has no written constitution. However, there are many unwritten but fundamental constitutional conventions—for example, that the monarch does not withhold assent from a bill passed by the House of Commons and the House of Lords. There are also statutes of a basic character, such as the Parliament Acts of 1911 and 1949 concerning the procedure for enacting a bill (a draft statute). The Acts of Union of 1707 have a unique character but in practice have been shown to be amendable like any other acts.

The Scotland Act passed by the United Kingdom Parliament in 1998 has some of the features that would be found in a written constitution for Scotland. Thus, it brings into being the Scottish Parliament and the Scottish executive and regulates the appointment of judges. It can, however, be amended by the UK Parliament—or even repealed by it.

Scottish Parliament

The Scottish Parliament is composed of 129 members (MSPs), 73 of them representing each constituency of the United Kingdom Parliament and chosen on the basis of having the most votes from the electors in a given constituency. To avoid the possibility that this will give an unfair advantage to one political party, there are a further 56 MSPs voted on to be regional members. The voting results are adjusted by a mathematical formula to correct any imbalance in party representation. The Parliament is elected for a fixed period of four years. The UK Parliament, which created the Scottish Parliament, reserved to itself certain major powers over the constitution, foreign affairs, the civil service, defense, financial and economic matters (including taxation), most matters of trade and industry, most matters of transport, employment and industrial relations, and social security and pensions. Everything else is within the law-making power of the Scottish Parliament. That includes matters of great concern to ordinary citizens, such as education, health services, housing, local government, land law, farming and fishing, and most criminal law (but not road traffic law or law on the misuse of drugs). As well as the restrictions created by reserved matters, elaborate steps have to be taken before legislation of the Scottish Parliament is enacted to ensure that that body does not exceed its competence. In practice, the governments of the United Kingdom and Scotland have so far collaborated when devolved matters of common interest require legislation (for instance, on confiscation of the proceeds of suspected drug-trafficking). The Scottish Parliament is also obliged not to enact law in breach of European Union law or the Convention Rights established under the Human Rights Act of 1998.

Scottish Executive

The government of Scotland, in respect to devolved matters, is known as the Scottish executive. It consists of the first minister, other ministers, and the law officers (who advise the executive on legal questions and head the prosecution service). They and their civil servants form the Scottish administration. The matters devolved to the executive are the same as those devolved to the Parliament.

There is, however, a list in the Scotland Act of 1998 of powers shared by ministers of the United Kingdom and of the Scottish executive. They include measures to give effect to UN Security Council decisions, funding of scientific research, mineral exploration, and road safety. In common with the Parliament, the executive must comply with European law and human rights. The executive includes a minister for justice, who is also Deputy First Minister.

Disputes concerning the operation of the Scotland Act of 1998, whether concerning the Parliament or the executive, are known as "devolution issues" and are settled through the higher courts and ultimately in a court called the Judicial Committee of the Privy Council. Its composition is created for the occasion from among those who hold or have held judicial office in one of the supreme courts of the United Kingdom.

Scotland continues to be subject to the legislation of the UK Parliament insofar as it is intended to extend to it. Thus, every year the Finance Act is drafted by the Treasury and passed with amendments by the UK Parliament. This measure provides the legal authority for the levying of taxes for the financial year throughout the United Kingdom.

CURRENT COURT SYSTEM STRUCTURE

A legal system requires means by which disputes of all kinds can be settled among individuals and corporate bodies. Thus, parents may seek a ruling on the custody of their children. One corporation may claim compensation for the late delivery of raw materials. An individual employee may sue his corporate employer for injuries sustained at work. All these are civil disputes. In addition, there must be means by which the guilt or innocence of those accused of crimes can be determined and a penalty imposed. In Scotland, as in other countries, there are civil courts for the former disputes and criminal courts for the latter. However, they overlap in a confusing way, which the accompanying figure may help to clarify. As well as making binding orders in disputes, the higher courts, in explaining and justifying their rulings, give statements of the law that, once publicized, can be used to settle similar disputes in courts of lower or the same level.

Civil Courts

The bulk of the civil work of the Scottish judicial system is performed by full-time professional judges known as sheriffs, numbering over 100, who sit in 49 sheriff courts, organized in 6 sheriffdoms, and supervised by 6 sheriffs-principal. This is the most ancient institution of Scots law and can be traced back to the reign of David I in the twelfth century. The bulk of the work of the sheriff court consists of actions for the recovery of debt, together with some more complex defended cases arising out of contract or delict (civil wrongs). Such actions are subject to no financial limits. These courts also deal with most divorces and actions on the care of children.

The Court of Session, whose origins have already been described, is both an appeal court and a court where cases are heard for the first time. It consists of thirty-two judges, twenty-four of whom hear cases for the first time, either in the form of debates on the applicable law or evidential hearings on disputes over facts. Usually, they sit alone, but in some cases of delict, the facts and any award of damages are decided by a jury of twelve laypeople. These judges also hear divorce actions, typically when a large amount of property is at stake. The other eight judges deal mainly with appeals from the sheriff courts and the Court of Session and various tribunals. They sit in two groups of four, of whom three are a quorum. The First Division of this so-called Inner House is headed by the Lord President of the whole court; the Second Division by the Lord Justice-Clerk. The judges of a division also hear petitions for the exercise of the *nobile officium*— an exceptional power to provide a remedy, where none exists, to prevent a serious injustice. In recent years, the Court of Session has greatly developed the practice of judicial review, used when it is alleged that a public authority such as a government department, a tribunal, or a local council has exceeded or misused its powers. Under certain conditions, appeals may be taken from the Inner House of the Court of Session to the House of Lords in London. Though principally a legislative body, the House of Lords has an Appellate Committee, which consists of twelve Lords of Appeal and others who have held high judicial office. By convention, at least two of the former will have been judges in Scotland. There is thus a single final court of appeal in cases originating in Scotland, England and Wales, and Northern Ireland.

Criminal Courts

Jurisdiction in criminal cases is wholly within Scotland. At the lowest level, there are district courts, where the judge is usually a justice of the peace who is not qualified in law but will have received some tuition in his or her duties. The district court tries minor cases of theft, assault, and road traffic contraventions, and it can impose a sentence of up to sixty days of imprisonment. The sheriff courts also have criminal jurisdiction, with the sheriffs either sitting alone or, in serious cases, with a jury of fifteen. In such jury trials, the normal maximum sentence is three years of imprisonment. The High Court of Justiciary tries the gravest criminal cases, such as murder, culpable homicide, rape, and large-scale drug-trafficking. It is staffed by the judges of the Court of Session, always with a jury. Three of the same judges, usually presided over by one of the two most senior judges, form an appeal court from all lower criminal courts. As well as a

guilty or not-guilty verdict, a verdict of not proven may be returned, implying that although the prosecution had not discharged its burden of proof, the judge or jury was not satisfied that the accused was wholly innocent.

SPECIALIZED JUDICIAL BODIES

To reduce congestion in the courts, many thousands of cases are dealt with every year in specialized tribunals, sitting as required and usually chaired by a legally qualified individual and two lay members. They are on the lowest rung of a judicial ladder that stretches up to the House of Lords. Among the most used and formal are the employment tribunals, which deal with claims of unfair dismissal, racial and sex discrimination, redundancy payments, and so on. Other much-used tribunals deal with issues of social security, taxation, rents, and, under the title of children's hearings, the welfare of children, including child offenders and abused children.

STAFFING THE LEGAL PROFESSION AND THE JUDICIARY

Scotland has two legal professions, the memberships of which are mutually exclusive. Advocates belong to the Faculty of Advocates and have their own library and interview rooms beside the Court of Session and High Court in Edinburgh. They number about 400, and each practices on his or her own. The more senior advocates are awarded the title of Queen's Counsel. From their ranks, judges and some sheriffs are chosen. Their main role is to represent clients in the highest courts, civil and criminal, though they are entitled to appear in any court. But they also perform much unseen work in giving opinions on the prospects of success of a court action, the options available in a dispute, or the value of a claim, and indeed they may arbitrate in a dispute. Solicitors are much more numerous, between 8,000 and 9,000. Almost all solicitors practice in partnerships, and they can be found in all Scottish cities and towns. They must be members of the Law Society of Scotland and are subject to its authority in respect to qualifications and discipline. Some appear in the sheriff and district courts. But more are involved in the buying and selling of houses, offices, and farms; advising companies; distributing the estates of deceased people; and resolving family disputes. Since 1993, solicitors who have the requisite experience and have undergone a training course and passed examinations have been allowed to represent clients in the Court of Session and High Court, but this remains an unusual occurrence.

Nearly all advocates and solicitors are graduates in law of a Scottish university. Since 1980, that education has been followed by a year's training in the university, leading to a "Diploma in Legal Practice." The graduate is then employed in a solicitor's office, working under supervision on real cases; for trainee advocates, this experi-

Legal Structure of Scotland Courts

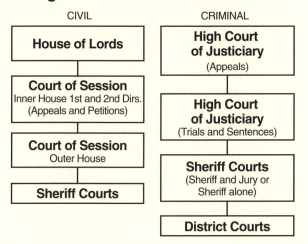

CIVIL

- **House of Lords**
- **Court of Session** Inner House 1st and 2nd Dirs. (Appeals and Petitions)
- **Court of Session** Outer House
- **Sheriff Courts**

CRIMINAL

- **High Court of Justiciary** (Appeals)
- **High Court of Justiciary** (Trials and Sentences)
- **Sheriff Courts** (Sheriff and Jury or Sheriff alone)
- **District Courts**

ence is followed by a further period of training with a practicing advocate. The Scottish Legal Aid Board provides the means for people with low incomes to receive advice and assistance on any matter of Scots law and to raise and defend meritorious court actions. Under less stringent conditions, defense lawyers can be provided for those charged with crimes and offenses.

By convention, judges of the supreme courts and the sheriffs who exercise the judicial role in the sheriff courts have long been nominated by the Lord Advocate for appointment to the bench by the monarch. However, this practice has been open to abuse, and indeed there have been cases of Lord Advocates appointing themselves to the bench. It has also seemed inappropriate that the person who is the head of the prosecution service should in any way be associated with the selection of the judges and sheriffs before whom his or her staff members appear. This criticism came to a head when a Lord Advocate was discovered to be determining the renewal of the appointment of temporary sheriffs each year. The Scottish executive now proposes the creation of a Judicial Appointments Board, chaired by a nonlawyer, to advertise vacancies, receive references, and hold interviews.

Judges and sheriffs hold office until the age of seventy; the former may have their appointments extended year by year to the age of seventy-five. The independence of judges and sheriffs is stressed, but they may be removed from office by a complex process on the grounds of "inability, neglect of duty or misbehavior." This procedure has only been used twice, both in respect to sheriffs.

IMPACT OF LAW

The rule of law is a foundation of the British way of life. Behavior contrary to law, even if not to the extent of being criminal, is condemned. The means by which law is made, principally through the UK and Scottish Parliaments, are well known, and government legislation that

was not promised in an election manifesto will be criticized on that ground. The use of law in an oppressive manner will be criticized, as well, and may even be struck down by a court.

Ian D. Willock

See also Civil Law; Criminal Law; United Kingdom

References and further reading
Ashton, Christina, and Valerie Finch. 2000. *Constitutional Law in Scotland.* Edinburgh: W. Green.
Deans, Mungo. 1995. *Scots Public Law.* Edinburgh: T and T Clark.
Page, A., C. Reid, and A. Ross. 1999. *A Guide to the Scotland Act 1998.* Edinburgh: Butterworths.
Paterson, A. A., T. St. J. N. Bates, and M. R. Poustie. 1999. *The Legal System of Scotland: Cases and Materials.* 4th ed. Edinburgh: W. Green.
Walker, David M. 2001. *The Scottish Legal System.* 8th ed. Edinburgh: W. Green.
White, Robin M., and Ian D. Willock. 1999. *The Scottish Legal System.* 2d ed. Edinburgh: Butterworths.

SENEGAL

GENERAL INFORMATION

Senegal is located at the western tip of Africa on the Atlantic coast. It has a surface area of 196,712 square kilometers. Senegal is bordered by Mauritania to the north, Mali to the east, Guinea Bissau and Guinea to the south, and the Atlantic Ocean to the west. The Gambia is a narrow enclave in the southern half of the country. It has a tropical subdesert climate, with a wet season (*hivernage*) from July to September and a long dry season. The country is flat, the only high ground being the dunes and hills on the border with Guinea. Although Senegal is desertlike in the north and the east (the Sahel), the south (the Casamance) is endowed with luxuriant vegetation. The country is split into ten administrative regions, corresponding roughly to the natural economic regions. There is no direct relation between regions and ethnicities, although some regions are dominated by a specific ethnic group (like the Diola in the southern region of Ziguinchor). In 1999 the population was estimated at 10.5 million. Two-thirds of the people live in rural areas, the majority being concentrated toward the west, near the coast. The country welcomes various ethnic groups. The main group remains the Wolofs (36 percent of the population), which share many similar cultural values with the other ethnic groups, including the Fulani and Toucouleur, Serer, Diola, and Mandingo. The most important non-Africans in Senegal are Europeans (mainly French) and Lebanese. Although the official language is French, which is dominant in government, commerce, and mass media, the constitution recognizes six indigenous languages as national languages. Islam is the chief religion, comprising

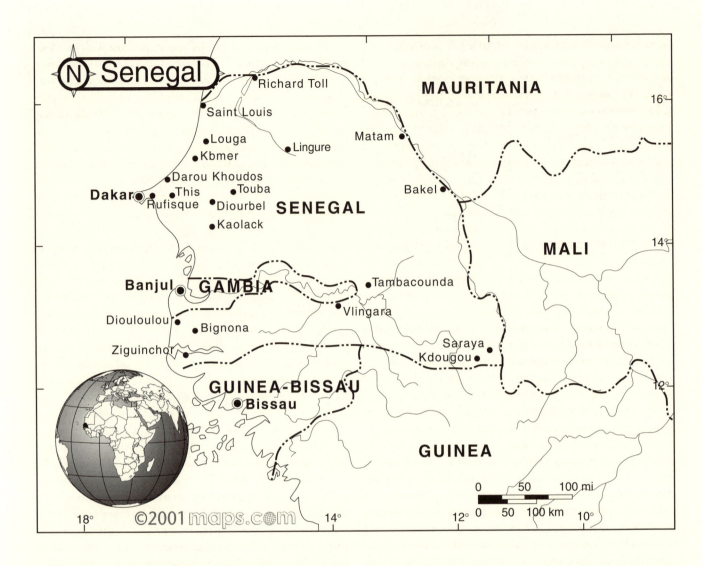

92 percent of the population. Roughly 2 percent are Christians—most of them Roman Catholics—and the remainder adhere to indigenous religions. The population is overwhelming young, 47 percent being under fifteen years of age. Agriculture (in particular nuts, rice, millet, and cotton) and fishing, and secondarily tourism, are the main resources of Senegal. As a result of a deep crisis in agriculture, there is an unstoppable move away from the countryside to the capital, Dakar. At present one out of five Senegalese lives in Dakar or its suburbs. Although the bulk of modern infrastructure is found in the capital, the city is unable to offer jobs in the formal sector to a large proportion of its residents, so that more than half of the active population works in the informal sector. The unemployment rate is estimated at 22 percent.

HISTORY

Megalithic stone circles and prehistoric potsherds and skeletons spread over the countryside indicate that the area has been inhabited for more than one thousand years. The first political entity is the Tekrour kingdom in the northern part of Senegal, which can be traced back to the ninth century C.E. In the fourteenth century, a variety of small kingdoms united and became the Dyolof kingdom, which paid tribute to the Mali Empire. The Dyolof kingdom lasted until the sixteenth century, when the constituent parts of the kingdom attained independence. In the following centuries this process of small entities uniting and splitting up continued. At the local level, people enjoyed a high degree of administrative autonomy. Political and religious power and the administration of justice were in the hands of the local kings, assisted by councils of elders and characterized by a system of checks and balances, including the possibility of deposing the king. The development of the local legal system in the area was the result of the interaction between indigenous and Islamic rules, for Islamic teachers and clerics traveled to the courts of the Wolof rulers, where they served as advisers.

The first Portuguese trading posts on the Senegalese coast were created in the fifteenth century, and from the beginning of the sixteenth century merchants from England, Holland, and France tried to establish their influence. In the mid-nineteenth century, Senegal became a permanent possession of France, which instituted a government that included representative and judiciary councils. Only in 1920 did Senegal became a political entity, when the colony and the protectorate of Senegal were joined under a single, uniform French administration. The country became an autonomous republic in 1958, still under the umbrella of France, and a year later it came together with the French Sudan (now known as Mali) to make up the Mali Federation. After the federation broke up in 1960, Senegal became an independent republic and installed Léopold Sédar Senghor as its first president.

The history of the Senegalese legal system is highly influenced by French colonial policy, which was guided by the theory of assimilation: the total integration of the Senegalese people into the French nation. This required an administrative and political system similar to the French one and the promotion of the Senegalese to French citizenship. In reality, however, the Senegalese colony was divided in two parts: the four communes (Dakar, Rufisque, Gorée, and Saint-Louis) and the protectorate. In the communes, the assimilation policy was applied. Persons born there were granted the civil rights of French citizens and ruled by French civil and penal codes. The court system for both civil and criminal matters resembled the French, with a court of appeal in Dakar and a court of cassation in Paris. In the nineteenth and early twentieth centuries, Islam became a vehicle for conveying cultural resistance to the French policy of assimilation in the communes. Muslim citizens called for the institution of Islamic courts of justice and emphasized an Islamic way of life, in particular Islamic personal law. A representative general council was created in the four communes, which had the right to elect a deputy to the French parliament. The first black African deputy to France's National Assembly, Blaise Diagne, was elected in 1914.

The rest of the country, by far its largest portion, was a protectorate under military administration. Although the inhabitants of the protectorate had French nationality, they were considered subjects (sujets) to the system of indigénat. They had no right to vote, were obliged to perform forced labor, and were entirely at the mercy of French colonial civil servants. The customary courts created for subjects had a very limited jurisdiction; most cases had to be submitted to courts presided over by the French.

In 1946, in the aftermath of World War II, the distinction between citizens and subjects was eliminated, universal suffrage was introduced, and all Senegalese, both in the protectorate and the communes, were placed under the French colonial law system.

At independence, in 1960, Senegal inherited the French civil law system. The civil, commercial, and criminal codes adopted in the first years after independence were to a great extent imitations of French codes. The

first Senegalese constitution, too, was oriented to the example of the constitution of the French Fifth Republic. The constitution provided for a president and a prime minister. The first president, Senghor, was clearly superior to the first prime minister, Mamadou Dia. As the result of a power struggle between these two politicians, the constitution was changed, in 1963, to create a pure presidential system. In 1970, a referendum sanctioned the constitutional reintroduction of the office of prime minister, whose role, nevertheless, was more modest than that stipulated in the 1960 constitution. Nominated by the president, the prime minister could be recalled either by parliament or by the president. The president also maintained some central areas of policy as his own competencies, such as foreign affairs and the formulation of his party's program. Under President Senghor, the ruling party, the Union Progressiste Sénégalaise (UPS), tended to behave as the sole party in fact. In 1976 the constitution was amended to establish a controlled multiparty system limited to three parties. These parties were supposed to represent three ideological currents: liberal democratic, the position claimed by the UPS, which became the Socialist Party; social-democratic, the line that the Parti Démocratique Sénégalais of Abdoulaye Wade was more or less forced to choose; and Marxist-Leninist, under which label the long-prohibited Parti Africain de l'Indépendance regained legal recognition. After Senghor's voluntary retreat from the presidency in 1980, his prime minister and nominated successor, Abdou Diouf, introduced on April 24, 1981, an integrated multiparty system without ideological restrictions. Only parties based on regional, ethnic, or religious cleavages were banned.

The first elections under this full-fledged multiparty system were held in 1983. Diouf entered the campaign in a weak political position. The opposition as a whole, and his principal rival, Wade, in particular, contested the legitimacy of his claim to power. An unprecedented economic crisis was exacerbated by the vicious effects of structural adjustment programs; high unemployment among people with skills and education, and increasing poverty in the cities as well as the countryside, fueled social discontent and Casamance separatist movements. Despite these circumstances, Diouf won the presidential elections, and his Socialist Party won the general election. They again won the elections in 1988, although carrying lower proportions of the vote. The opposition exacerbated the tense political situation by accusing the incumbents of electoral fraud and alleging other serious irregularities; for example, polling booths, which help maintain the secrecy of balloting, were not obligatory. Paradoxically, it was the leader of the opposition, Wade, who emerged from the elections with increased status. The volatile postelectoral climate exploded in riots under the slogan *sopi* (change). Wade was arrested and charged with responsibility for the violence. In order to defuse the tension, a roundtable conference was organized, including representatives of the regime and the opposition, and one opposition member of the opposition—contrary to every expectation, Abdoulaye Wade—accepted a post in the government. Nevertheless, the presidential elections of February 1993 brought a repeat performance: electoral fraud, violence, the arrest of opposition leaders who then joined the government after their release. Regional, municipal, and rural elections took place in November 1996, and the Socialist Party, which had been thought weakened, won easily. Similarly, the general election of May 1998 was won by the ruling party, which took 93 out of 140 seats. A total of 11 parties were represented in the new National Assembly, but once again the opposition challenged the results of the balloting, calling unsuccessfully them to be declared invalid. In response, the majority of the opposition parties boycotted the 1999 elections for the newly created Senate.

Despite a number of protests relating to the preparations, the 2000 presidential elections passed calmly. In the first round, President Diouf did not receive a majority of the vote and was forced to enter into a runoff with his eternal rival, Abdoulaye Wade. In the runoff, held on March 19, the support of several candidates who had been eliminated in the first round contributed to the election of Wade as president of the republic. For the first time since independence, through the efforts of a coalition called the Alternation Front (FAL), Senegal enjoyed a democratic transfer of power. President Wade appointed a former Socialist Party leader as prime minister and formed a government including all the parties that had supported him during the elections. He made arrangements for a referendum on a new constitution designed to provide the institutional tools required to effect the changes, the *sopi*, that had been promised to the people of Senegal. In January 2001, the new constitution was approved by the citizenry, winning endorsement on 92.5 percent of ballots; 66 percent of eligible voters cast votes. The new constitution does away with the Senate and the Economic and Social Council, established by the 1963 constitution. It also gives the president the means to dissolve the National Assembly, which he did almost immediately. As a result, after the legislative elections in April 2001, the PDS was represented in the National Assembly by 89 deputies (out of 120).

LEGAL CONCEPTS

The supreme law of Senegal is found in its constitution, which through its several revisions has always emphasized the principle of separation of powers. The principles on which the constitution rests are set forth in a preamble and in the first few articles, in which Senegal confirms its commitment to fundamental rights as defined in the 1789 Declaration of the Rights of Man and of the Citizen and in the 1948 Universal Declaration of Human Rights. Notwithstanding the protests that have followed every election, political life in Senegal is more peaceable than it is in the majority of African countries, and infringements of human rights are rare. Nevertheless, since 1980 the war between the Senegalese army and the separatists of the Casamance Movement of Democratic Forces (MFDC) has resulted in numerous violations of human rights from various quarters, violations denounced regularly by Amnesty International.

The constitution enshrines the right to form political parties and trade unions as well as the right to strike. Of the fifty-seven political parties officially registered in October 2000, fifteen stand out as entering into more or less stable political alliances according to their strategy for acquiring power. Several sector-based unions represent individual trades, and confederations of trade unions have a major influence on political and social life. Senegal is thus one of the few French-speaking African countries with a dynamic civil society.

Freedom of expression, freedom of the press, and the right of access to information are constitutionally guaranteed. For a long time, the government controlled the national television and radio stations and an official newspaper, *Le Soleil*. After the liberalization of the press two new independent daily newspapers appeared, publishing in French, like all other printed media (more than twenty publications, including a serial weekly). Alongside government radio, various private radio stations are on the air, some of them regularly broadcasting programs in the local languages. With respect to the electronic media, the High Council for Radio and Television acts as a supervisory body. The media in Senegal represent fairly well the political spectrum there. In January 2001, the government announced its intention to put an end to the state monopoly in television broadcasting by sanctioning the introduction of commercial channels.

The first article of the constitution confirms the secular character of the republic, an important statement in a country where Islamic brotherhoods often claim to have political ambitions. The religious authorities used to order their followers to vote for the PDS by pronouncing a *ndigal,* or religious instruction. The last major political *ndigal* was pronounced at the time of the 1988 elections. During the 1980s and 1990s, the Senegalese state integrated the Islamic reform and opposition movements into the political mix of the country so as to counter radical policies directed against its secular orientation. For example, the family code was revised several times without the inclusion of a greater consideration of Islamic law, and the Islamic law courts lost their jurisdictional functions.

GOVERNMENT

The president of the republic is head of the executive branch and is elected directly on the basis of universal suffrage. The elections consist of two rounds and are for a term of office of five years. A person may serve as president for a maximum of two terms. The president is the guardian of the constitution. He is responsible for the smooth running of state institutions and for the protection of national independence and territorial integrity. He determines the nation's foreign and domestic policies. He appoints the prime minister, who is the head of the government. The president of the republic can, after consultation with the prime minister and the president of the National Assembly, dissolve the National Assembly and call for new elections.

The government, under the direction of the prime minister and composed of the prime minister and the cabinet, runs and coordinates the nation's policies. It is responsible to the president of the republic and to the National Assembly.

Legislative power is invested in the National Assembly, which has sole voting responsibility for the law. Members of the National Assembly are elected directly on the basis of universal suffrage for a term of office of five years. This term of office can only be terminated by dissolution of the assembly. The National Assembly can request to hear the prime minister and other members of the government at any time in plenary session or in committee. It can also bring about the resignation of the government by passing a motion of censure. The assembly can be dissolved by the president of the republic, but not during the first two years of its term.

The Constitutional Council hears matters relating to the constitutionality of laws and international agreements, conflicts in questions of competence between the executive and the legislature, conflicts in questions of competence between the Council of State and the Court of Cassation, as well as claims of unconstitutionality submitted to the Council of State or the Court of Cassation. It has five members: a president, a vice president, and three judges. The term of office is six years, and terms are staggered so that new appointments to the council by the president are possible every two years.

The Electoral Law of 1992, the result of several months of negotiations involving most of the main political parties, was the first such law to be accepted by all parties since the introduction of a multiparty system. The Court of Appeals, which until 1993 was in charge of ensuring the legality of electoral operations, was replaced in 1997 by the Observatoire National des Elections (ONEL). In 1991, the position of political mediator was created to arbitrate between society and the state.

Like other African states, at independence Senegal inherited from its colonial government a highly centralized administrative system. Policies of national and regional development as well as administrative reforms have been implemented in order to bring the state closer to its citizens and to encourage local democracy. In 1960, the thirty existing municipalities (*communes*) became districts in their own right with full self-government. On June 30, 1966, an act was passed introducing a local administrative code. Five days later, the financial arrangements for local communities (*collectivités locales*) were fixed by decree. An act passed in April 1972 increased the number of districts to thirty-seven and established local communities in rural areas. In February 1983, Dakar was created as an urban community. In October 1992, the rural districts and communities were granted financial autonomy and legal capacity and eleven additional districts were created.

A policy of regionalization was introduced in April 1992. Regions and departments acquired the status of territorial communities with increased jurisdiction. Act 96-07, passed in March 1996, has regulated this decentralizing process of transferring competences to the regions, districts, and rural communities. Since the local elections of November 1996, Senegal has had 400 territorial communities administered by 24,000 councillors. The local representatives of the state provide supervision at each level of territorial administration. After the transfer of political power in early 2000, President Wade announced important decentralization reforms (among other things, the creation of thirty-five provinces with new borders and names to replace the existing ten regions) to be worked out by the new National Assembly, elected in April 2001. He also postponed the elections of the rural communities, which had been expected in November 2001.

JUDICIARY

The judiciary is independent from the legislative and executive branches. It consists of the Constitutional Council, the Council of State, the Court of Cassation, the Court of Audit, and the courts and tribunal. The constitution also provides for a High Court of Justice, to which the members of the executive are answerable for their actions.

Staffing

Senegal has approximately 350 judges and prosecutors, 250 barristers registered at the bar association, 27 notaries, and 30 process servers (bailiffs).

The training of lawyers in Senegal begins at the law faculties of the two universities, Cheikh Anta Diop in Dakar and Gaston Berger in Saint-Louis. Legal education at Cheikh Anta Diop, the oldest university in francophone Africa, is strongly oriented toward positive law, based on the French legal tradition. The law curriculum at Gaston Berger, established in 1989, also covers legal anthropology. In addition to the law faculties there are two specialized

Structure of Senegalese Courts

The legal institutions of Senegal: Schematic representations

A. Classification according to kind (sovereign, ordinary, or specialized)

SOVEREIGN COURTS

Court of Cassation Institutional Act 92-25 of 30 May 1992	**Court of Audit** Institutional Act 99-70 of 21 February 1999	**Constitutional Council** Institutional Act 92-23 of 30 May 1992	**Council of State** Institutional Act 96-30 of 21 October 1996

ORDINARY COURTS

Dakar Court of Appeal

Dakar	Thiés	Diourbel	Kolda	Ziguinchor	Saint-Louis	Louga

Kaolack Court of Appeal

Kaolack	Tamba	Fatick

Assize Court

Dakar, Kaolack, Saint-Louis, Ziguinchor

Legend
Courts of second instance: Courts of Appeal
Courts of first instance: Departmental Court

SPECIALIZED COURTS

Industrial Relations Tribunal Act of 1 December 1997	**Juvenile Court** Part I of Book IV of the Civil Procedure Code	**Military Court** Act 94-44 of 27 May 1994	**High Court of Justice**	**Court for the Repression of Illicit Enrichment** Act 81-54 of 10 July 1981

B. Classification of the Senegalese courts according to type of jurisdiction

Duality of type of jurisdiction	Administrative	Constitutional Council	Court of Audit	Judiciary
	Court of Cassation: Supreme Court			**Council of State: Supreme Court**

Unity of type of jurisdiction	**Court of Appeal: Court of second instance**
	Regional Court: Court of first instance (and of second instance in exceptional circumstances)
	Departmental Court: Court of first instance (for some matters only)

Legend:
Dual jurisdiction at top level
Unified jurisdiction at base
Sovereign courts that are difficult to classify according to type of jurisdiction

Structure of Senegalese Courts (continued)

C. Classification of the courts according to geographical jurisdiction

NATIONAL LEVEL

Court of Cassation Institutional Act 92-25 of 30 May 1992	Court of Audit Institutional Act 99-70 of 21 February 1999	Constitutional Council Institutional Act 92-23 of 30 May 1992	Council of State Institutional Act 96-30 of 21 October 1996	High Court of Justice

MULTIREGIONAL LEVEL

Dakar Court of Appeal	Assize Court	Kaolack Court of Appeal

REGIONAL LEVEL

(Administrative Region): The various regional courts

DEPARTMENTAL LEVEL

(Department): The various departmental courts

D. Classification of the courts according to instance

SECOND INSTANCE	Court of Appeal	Specialized Regional Court
FIRST INSTANCE	Departmental Court	Regional Court

E. Alternative methods provided by the justice system for settling disputes

Forms	Institutional framework	Legal framework
Arbitration	Common court of justice and arbitration of OHADA	c.f. Section 10 of OHADA Convention
	Dakar Arbitration Division	Dakar Arbitration Division
Bodies designed to improve access to justice system	Law centers	c.f. decree 99-1124
	Criminal mediator	c.f. Section 451 of the new Criminal Procedure Code
	Conciliator	c.f. Section 22 of decree 99-1124
Quasi-judicial bodies	Competition Commission, Order of Advocates, Order of Medical Experts, National Election Observer, National Ombudsman	

law schools, the National Administration School (École Nationale d'Administration, or ENA) for the training of civil servants and the Center for Legal Training (Centre de Formation Judiciaire, or CFJ) for the training of judges, prosecutors, and clerks. Both institutions offer two levels of training, the lower open to students with a bachelor's degree and the higher to students with a master's degree. A further option for legal education will soon be available in Porto Novo, Benin, where a regional law school, the Ecole Régionale Supérieure de Magistrature, is to be established for students from twelve francophone African countries, including Senegal. The regional school will train judges and prosecutors as well as offer specialized training in business law.

According to Act 92-26 of May 30, 1992, the career perspectives of both judges and public prosecutors are the exclusive responsibility of a special council, the Conseil Supérieur de la Magistrature, to which four members of the magistracy are elected and four members are appointed ex officio. The council is chaired by the president of the republic (or the minister of justice). Candidates for council seats must participate in a competitive examination. Lawyers who possess at least ten years' professional experience may, in exceptional cases, be nominated without taking the examination. Judges and prosecutors are appointed by the president of the republic, but only on the advice of the Conseil Supérieur. That same council acts as a court of judicial discipline in cases of alleged professional misconduct of judges and public prosecutors, and the decisions of the council cannot be appealed.

Although in principle the constitution and the law guarantee the tenure of office for judges, the reality is somewhat different. The minister of justice has the right to transfer a judge "if necessary for the public service." In such a case he makes a proposal to the council, which has only the right to fix a maximum period for the transfer. Moreover, Senegalese judges are, with very few exceptions, appointed on an interim basis and so do not enjoy tenure of office. The reason given for this situation is that the shortage of judges in Senegal means that most of them cannot be appointed according to their rank. Indeed, in most departmental courts, one judge combines the functions of president of the court, examining magistrate, and public prosecutor.

The profession of barrister is organized according to Act 84-09 of January 4, 1984. Before being admitted to the profession, a lawyer must be a trainee in a law firm for three years.

Structure

The judiciary in Senegal comprises courts of first instance, courts of second instance, specialized courts, and courts from which no decision may be appealed (sovereign courts).

The courts of first instance include the departmental, regional, and assize courts. The departmental courts are located in the principal towns of the departments and have authority over their respective departments. They are competent in civil and commercial as well as criminal matters. In the civil and commercial sphere, these courts adjudicate cases concerning movable property and real estate, landlord-tenant disputes, and the legal capacity of persons.

In personal matters or matters concerning movable property, the departmental courts are competent at first instance without appeal when cases involve amounts not in excess of 200,000 francs and are competent at first instance with the possibility of appeal if the matter does not exceed 1,000,000 francs. In residential tendency cases, the departmental courts are competent at first instance

without appeal if the rent is not in excess of 25,000 francs and competent at first instance with the possibility of appeal if the rent is at least 25,000 francs and less than 50,000 francs. In criminal cases, the departmental courts have exclusive competence with respect to petty offenses listed in Section 2 of Act 84-20, and are known as police courts.

There is a regional court in each of the ten regions of Senegal. The members of the court act either as judges or as prosecutors. The regional court is competent at first instance and in appeal proceedings. In civil and commercial matters at first instance, the regional courts are the ordinary courts for lesser indictable offenses. In administrative matters, the regional courts deal with all fiscal proceedings with the exception of applications for judicial review and appeals relating to elections. In appeal proceedings, the regional tribunals deal with all decisions from departmental courts at first instance.

Four assize courts, in Dakar, Kaolack, Saint-Louis, and Ziguinchor, meet in session every four months. Each court consists of three professional judges and four juries.

There are two courts of second instance (courts of appeal), even though the new Section 25 of Decree 84-1194 provides for the creation of four, in Dakar, Kaolack, Saint-Louis, and Ziguinchor. In 1999, there was only the court of appeal, in Dakar, competent for the whole of Senegal. Since that time, a second court of appeal has been established, in Kaolack.

The court of appeal of Dakar consists of seven chambers: two civil and commercial chambers, two social chambers, two criminal chambers, and one chamber of indictment. The court of appeal of Kaolack has four chambers. Pending the establishment of other chambers of indictment, the one at Dakar is competent to hear proceedings for its own district as well as those of Saint-Louis and of Ziguinchor. The courts of appeal hear appeals of decisions issued by regional courts and, in exceptional circumstances, departmental courts (in criminal matters and matters relating to lesser indictable offenses). Also, in exceptional circumstances the courts of appeal are competent to hear electoral matters.

Senegal's specialized courts include an industrial relations tribunal, which is competent to hear such matters as individual proceedings involving employees and employers relating to the performance of employment contracts, apprenticeship contracts, collective agreements, and arrangements relating to working conditions, health, and social security. Juvenile courts deal with criminal offenses committed by minors (Part 2, Book 3, of the criminal procedure code), and there are specialized courts treating criminal offenses committed by military personnel (Act 94-44 of May 27, 1994, relating to the military justice code). The High Court of Justice is the ultimate court for political matters. A specialized court for the repression of illicit enrichment, founded by Act 81-54 of October 7, 1981, is responsible for hearing cases involving corruption among government officials, such as the concealment and handling of stolen goods.

Upon gaining independence, Senegal established an unusual institution within a French-oriented legal system: the Supreme Court. This court was abolished in 1992 by Act 92-22. Acts concerning two sovereign courts, the Constitutional Council and the Court of Cassation, were adapted in the same year. In 1996, the act concerning the Council of State was also modified. A fourth sovereign court, the Court of Audit, was established in 1999.

The Constitutional Council was modified by Act 92-23 of May 30, 1992. It consists of five members, each elected for a single term of five years, and serves various judicial and nonjudicial functions. The council issues recommendations when the president of the republic wishes to submit new laws for a referendum, receives notifications of candidacy for the presidency of the republic, and installs the president of the republic and receives notice of his resignation. It approves or denies calls for general elections and presidential elections, and it rules on the constitutionality of laws and international engagements.

The Council of State was established by Act 96-30 of October 21, 1996. It is made up of a president, two section presidents, and four judges and auxiliary judges. Act 99-72 of February 17, 1999, provided for the appointment by decree of a law officer. The Council of State acts as a trial and appeals court when deciding applications for judicial review, the legality of actions of local communities, and electoral matters. It acts as a court of cassation when deciding on appeals against decisions of tribunals and courts in administrative matters, as well as appeals against decisions of the Court of Audit and of administrative bodies.

The Court of Cassation was established by Act 92-25, as amended on May 30, 1992. It consists of two types of legal officers, judges and prosecutors, as well as nonlegal members, including the chief registrar and associate judges. It has two major divisions, nonjudicial and judicial. The nonjudicial division consists of the Council of the Court of Cassation (made up of the president of the court, the principal state prosecutor, the presidents of the chambers, and the chief solicitor general) and the general assembly (made up of all the members of the Court of Cassation). It can engage in preliminary deliberations before the establishment of rules of procedure, and it is competent to deal with all issues brought before it by the president of the court. The judicial division consists of three chambers: criminal, civil and commercial, and social. When, after a first decision has been set aside, the same case involving the same parties is heard by the court, all three chambers meet to decide the case anew.

The mission of the Court of Cassation is threefold.

First, it decides on appeals on points of law against all decisions given in last instance, subject to the competences of the Council of State and with the exception of the decisions of the Court of Audit challenged in hearings conducted by the Council of State. Nevertheless, since the Organization for the Harmonization in Africa of Business Law (OHADA) convention came into effect in 1993, the Court of Cassation has lost some areas of jurisdiction; the Common Court of Justice and Arbitration, a community court, hears appeals against decisions given in last instance by the courts of the member states in all matters relating to questions associated with the implementation of OHADA decisions.

Second, the Court of Cassation generally does not reconsider the facts of a case but rules solely on the formal correctness of the lower court's decision. In exceptional circumstances, however, the Court of Cassation acts as a trial and appeals court for serious crimes or lesser indictable offenses committed by a legal officer. This function constitutes the second part of the court's mission. If the act is a serious crime, the chambers decide in joint session, and if the act under scrutiny is a lesser indictable offense, the criminal chamber decides alone.

Third, the Court of Cassation acts as the regulatory body for the judicial system to the extent that it is competent to deal with applications for retrial transferred from one court to another on grounds of bias, public security, the settlement of conflicts of jurisdiction between other courts, and actions for damages against a judge for a misuse of authority.

The Court of Audit was added to the legal system by Act 99-02 of January 29, 1999. The court has various organizational arrangements: the solemn plenary hearing, the full court hearing, the Court of Discipline, and the chambers. The commission for the auditing of accounts and supervision of institutions has become a chamber of the Court of Audit.

The Court of Audit carries out judicial audits of the conformity and truthfulness of receipts and expenditures described in public accounts, assesses the records of public accountants and persons whom it declares to be de facto accountants, passes judgment on faults of management, and imposes appropriate fines. The court also exercises nonjudicial supervision by auditing fund credits and securities managed by state bodies, public authorities, and public establishments; auditing the accounts and management of public sector enterprises; and ensuring that the state and its representatives are acting in accordance with the regulations of social security institutions.

IMPACT

Although officially legislation is the only source of law, the reality in Senegal (and in general in Africa) is a situation of legal pluralism in which statutory law, local law, and Islamic law are simultaneously applicable. In spite of an avalanche of postindependence state laws, most Senegalese, both in urban and in rural areas, continue to defer to local (or customary) law and Islamic law. Examples are plentiful, especially in family and probate law but also in criminal law, of the distance between the law on the books and the living law. The great majority of legal conflicts (commercial, civil, and criminal) are handled by an imam or village chief. Thus, in spite of the abolition of the colonial dual legal system, local legal norms still apply in the daily life of Senegalese. Apparently, Senegalese statutory law embodied in codes derived from French positive law is not able to address the needs of the population in virtually all realms of life. The ways in which conflicts are mediated at the local level are not based on the formal application of rules and laws but rather are found in negotiations between the parties in a legal conflict.

In order to increase access to the justice system, law centers, criminal mediators, and conciliators have been introduced. Law centers, established by decree 99-1124, fulfill five functions: provision of assistance (public counseling and information), handling of disputes and certain offenses, prevention of offenses, coordination, and counseling for people in legal difficulty. The centers were created by order of the Minister of Justice. The authority of the criminal mediators is based on authorization by the General Assembly of the Court; in urgent cases, however, provisional authority may be conferred by the public prosecutor. The role of these mediators is to look for a freely negotiated solution for the parties when there is an offense. Only the public prosecutor and the court trying a case can order the intervention of a criminal mediator. Section 22 of decree 99-1124 states that conciliators who deal with disputes should take the initiative to propose solutions. Their authority to assist parties in reaching an agreement derives from the court.

Gerti Hesseling

With the assistance of Oumar Sissokho, University Gaston Berger, Saint-Louis, Senegal.

See also Alternative Dispute Resolution; Civil Law; Constitutional Review; Customary Law; Islamic Law; Judicial Independence; Judicial Misconduct/Judicial Discipline; Legal Pluralism; Magistrates—Civil Law Systems; Mediation

References and further reading
Beck, L. 1997. "Senegal's Patrimonial Democrats: Incremental Reform and Obstacles to the Consolidation of Democracy." *Canadian Journal of African Studies* 31: 1–31.
Bendel, Brenda. 1999. "Senegal." Pp. 756–774 in *Elections in Africa: A Data Handbook.* Edited by D. Nohlen, M. Krennerich, and B. Thibaud. Oxford: Oxford University Press.
Bourel, Pierre. 1981. *Le Droit de la famille au Sénégal.* Paris: Economica.
Centre d'Etudes d'Afrique Noire (Bordeaux). http://www.cean.u-bordeaux.fr/etat/institutionnel/senegal.html (accessed March 1, 2002).
Diop, Momar Coumba, ed. 1993. *Senegal: Essays in Statecraft.* Dakar: CODESRIA.
Hesseling, Gerti. 1985. *Histoire politique du Sénégal.* Paris: Karthala.
Le Roy, Etienne. 1994. "Le Code civil au Sénégal ou le vertige d'Icare." Pp. 290–330 in *La Réception des systèmes juridiques: Implantations et destins.* Edited by J. Vanderlinden. Brussels: Bruylant.
Loimeier, Roman. 2001. *Säkularer staat und islamische Gesellchaft in Senegal.* Hamburg: Lit Verlag.
Mbaye, Kéba. 1967. *Organisation judiciaire du Sénégal.* Paris: Penant.
Nelson, Harold D. 1974. *Area Handbook for Senegal.* Washington, DC: Foreign Area Studies.
Thiam, Cheikh Tidiane. 1993. *Droit public du Sénégal: L'état et le citoyen.* Dakar: Editions du CREDILA.
Touré, Moustapha. 1975. "Histoire de l'organisation judiciaire au Sénégal: L'unification des jurisdictions et l'unité de la justice." *Revue sénégalaise du droit,* no. 7.
Vanderlinden, Jacques. 1992. *Bibliographies internationales de la doctrine juridique africaine: Sénégal.* Moncton, NB: Université de Moncton.

SEYCHELLES

COUNTRY INFORMATION

The Seychelles is one of the several island nations located in the Indian Ocean. The Indian Ocean consists of a vast region that encompasses an area of about 73.4 million square kilometers, roughly 14 percent of the earth's surface. Notably, the region played a prominent commercial role in East-West trade in the early times when colonial powers, mainly Britain and France, used its shores as trading posts and refueling stations en route to exploration/exploitation of colonies in the East before the construction of the Suez Canal in 1869.

The country of Seychelles is an island-grouped nation of 115 islands scattered over more than 1,374,000 square kilometers or 530,000 square miles in the southwest of the Indian Ocean. The actual landmass of the Seychelles' archipelagos is 445 square kilometers (172 square miles). The capital is Victoria, which also serves as its chief port located on the Mahé Island, the main and most habitable of the islands, of approximately 55 square miles holding roughly 80 percent of the population of that country. There are two main groups of islands that form the Seychelles. It has no borders with any nation and the southernmost islands are about 210 kilometers or 130 miles away from Madagascar. The climate of Seychelles is tropical but breezy with high humidity.

The people are mainly descendants of eighteenth-century French colonialists and freed African slaves. The Seychelles has a relatively homogeneous ethnic popula-

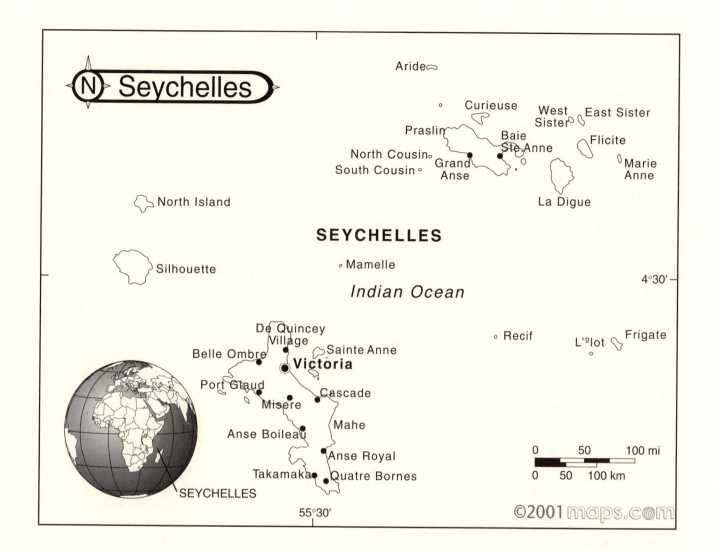

tion. The people consist of a mixture of African, Asian, and European descent. Three languages are spoken in Seychelles, namely Creole, English, and French. Education in the Seychelles is free and compulsory from kindergarten through ninth grade. There is no higher institution of learning at the university level in the island nation. Overall, the country claims an estimated literacy rate of 85 percent among adults age fifteen and above, according to a 1991 estimate and report. The government also provides free health service to all citizens.

Seychelles' economy is relatively healthy but overreliance on tourism enhances its vulnerability to external shocks, as illustrated during the Gulf War in the early 1990s. The government in recent years has diversified the economy by increasing the revenues received from fishing rights and investing in the fish-processing sector with foreign joint partners in order to move the economy away from its heavy reliance on tourism. Manufacturing is showing the potential of surpassing tourism as the most important economic activity in the island nation. With an economic rebound and an estimated gross domestic product of $590 million, as well as a real growth rate of

1.8 percent and an inflation rate of 3 percent for 1999, the economy is currently very sound.

HISTORY

Seychelles' history and its colonial legacy are intimately tied to its politics. Seychelles fashioned four constitutions in the first twenty-five years of its independence. Starting with democratic ideals, an internal self-government was granted in 1975. After independence and free elections in 1976, a military coup d'état in 1977 transformed the Seychelles into an authoritarian state dominated by military leaders, with a façade of civilian institutions, until it began its transition to democracy in the 1990s. The reinstitution of a multiparty system in 1992 and the eventual approval of a new constitution in a 1993 referendum (by a 74 percent popular vote) marked the return to democracy. Arguably, to understand Seychelles' history and politics is also to understand its struggles and, more importantly, its legal system. In spite of some gains made since independence in 1976 in the basic process of nation building and forging a civil society, the numerous coups and attempted coups during this period notwithstanding,

Seychelles today has what by many accounts amounts to an ineffective legal system.

The islands of the Seychelles were uninhabited until the French established spice plantations after 1756 to break a Dutch monopoly on the spice trade in the Far East. Before the French established plantations in 1756, Portuguese explorers had been there, and so too were the British and the Arabs. There is much speculation that early Persian and Arab seafarers made visits to these islands hundreds of years before the birth of Christ. However, with no claim of discovery, the evidence available is scanty at best. Nineteenth-century Arab charts refer to the Seychelles as *Tall Islands* and also contradict earlier Arab maps, which referred to the same islands as *Zarin*. The Portuguese claim for the discovery is credited to Vasco da Gama in 1502, but since he discovered only a portion of the islands, this conclusion is not strictly true. Finally, the British, to whom the claim of discovery of Seychelles is attributed, credit John Jourdain who arrived in 1609. Hence, the French claim in 1742, followed by Lazare Picault's subsequent renaming of Mahé in 1744, was well after the British. It would take the signing of the Treaty of Paris in 1814 for the French to cede Seychelles to Britain and hence confirm British sovereignty over the island nation.

Seychelles was administered separately as a British dependency from Mauritius. Between 1827 and 1888, an administrative and executive council was established, which for the first time allowed the involvement of the people of Seychelles in their own political affairs. Participants were drawn from a pool of candidates of the then-established Seychelles Taxpayers and Producers Association (STPA). Before the advent of political parties in 1964, the STPA (the landed strata and the principal political forces in the island nation) won most, if not all, seats to the Legislative Council. Beyond these developments, Seychelles remained a Crown colony until its independence in 1976.

The two parties created in 1964 were the Seychelles People's United Party (SPUP) led by France-Albert René and the Seychelles Democratic Party (SDP) led by James Mancham. Both were London-educated lawyers who returned to their country determined to improve its conditions. In 1967 Britain introduced universal suffrage and a partially elected governing council was seated. In 1970 a limited self-governed ministerial form of government under a chief minister was introduced and fifteen legislative seats were open for election. The SDP won ten and the SPUP five. After a constitutional conference in London in 1975, the fifteen-seat legislative assembly created in 1970 was increased to twenty-five members, with ten new members nominated by the two parties, which led to a coalition government. Seychelles gained independence on June 29, 1976; the chief of ministers and leader of the SDP, James R. Mancham, became the first president; and the leader of SPUP, France-Albert René, became the first prime minister. However, Mancham stayed in power only for a year before being ousted in a coup d'état on June 5, 1977, when he was in London at a Commonwealth conference. Prime Minister France-Albert René was sworn in as the new president, and a new government was formed.

The new constitution adopted in 1979 made the SPUP—now combined with other small parties and named the Seychelles People's Progressive Front (SPPF)—the sole party and provided for a strong executive headed by the president and a legislature of twenty-three appointed members. In the first election conducted under the new single-party constitution in June 1979, René was confirmed in office for a five-year term with 98 percent of the popular vote. This was viewed as an endorsement of his new socialist policies adopted in the years immediately following the coup d'état. He was again the sole candidate of the single-party elections in 1979, 1984, and 1989, and was again his party's candidate in the multiparty elections of 1993 and 1998. He is again a candidate at the 2001 elections taking place at this writing. Between 1979 and 1992, operating under an imposed state of emergency, with numerous coups and attempted coups threatening his regime, René won by affirmative votes ranging between 60 and 95 percent. In December 1991, his ruling SPPF party agreed to relinquish monopoly of power as the party congress approved a proposal allowing multiparty registration and the drafting of a new constitution. First, they lifted the state of emergency and then invited interest groups or parties receiving significant popular support to partake in the revision of the new constitution. Having introduced a multiparty system in 1992, the first attempt to produce a democratic constitution failed in a referendum in November 1992. Further negotiations produced a consensus that was approved in a referendum in June 1993, thus paving the way for a multiparty election in July of that year.

LEGAL CONCEPTS/FRAMEWORK

The new constitution ratified in the referendum of June 18, 1993, declared the Seychelles a democratic republic and provided a framework for a government by the rule of law. In doing so, it brought to a close the former Marxist legal framework based on a socialist political ideology. The 1993 Constitution provided for a multiparty political organization, free elections, and, unlike the past, provided for power sharing among the various institutions of the government of Seychelles. In principle, the constitution places importance on democratic values of human rights and separation of executive, legislative, and judicial functions and powers. With regard to the key institutions designed to carry out the various missions, the constitution provides for a unicameral legislature of thirty-four members (twenty-four elected and ten allotted on a proportion basis). It also provides for a president, elected by universal suffrage for three terms of five years, a Council of Ministers appointed by the president to assist in executive functions, and the judiciary, appointed by the president with recommendations from a new Constitutional Appointments Authority (CAA). The CAA is a three-member authority appointed by both the president and the leader of the opposition party for seven renewable years. Also provided in the new constitution is the office of Ombudsman, appointed by the president from a pool of candidates recommended by the CAA to investigate public officials. Last, the constitution also establishes the office of the Attorney General, appointed by the president for seven years to serve as the legal adviser to the president.

The actual legal outline that emerged out of the new democratic Constitution of 1993, at least on paper, provides more depth than the previous constitutions. At the core of the current constitution is the Seychelles' Charter on Fundamental Human Rights and Freedoms, which contains specific human rights protections. For example, it proclaims that "everyone has the right to life and no one will be deprived of life intentionally." It also states that "a law shall not provide for the sentence of death to be imposed by any court." So far there is no death penalty in Seychelles, by statute or otherwise. Also the charter provides that "every person has a right to be treated with dignity worthy of a human being and not to be subjected to torture, cruel, inhuman or degrading treatment or punishment" as well as the "right not to be held in slavery or bondage." The charter also enumerates the fundamental duties of citizens and outlines procedures for imposing a state of emergency together with other measures for "remedies." The "fundamental duty" of citizens stipulates the duty of every citizen to uphold and defend the constitution and the laws and to further the national interest and unity. Furthermore, it is also a duty to work conscientiously in a chosen profession, occupation, or trade; to contribute toward the well-being of the community; to protect preserves and improve the environment; and to strive toward the fulfillment of the aspirations of the constitution.

Provisions for invoking a state of emergency provide the president with the sole power, to the exclusion of any legislative oversight, to declare such a condition and impose it on the country. The president can proceed with a state of emergency and report to the National Assembly only if such a state of emergency exceeds seven days. With the history of prolonged states of emergency in that country before 1993, a period during which individual liberties were in jeopardy, the inclusion of this provision in the section on fundamental rights illustrates the dom-

inance of the executive authority in the constitution. Part 4 focuses on remedies and actual processes for redress, with emphasis on the constitutional court's authority in interpreting the constitution. It empanels the court interpreting the constitution not to confer on any person/group the right to engage in any activity that undermines the right or freedom in the charter. Finally, Part 5 provides guidance for appropriate judicial review in disposition of cases within the constitutional court. For instance, it forces the court to interpret the constitution only in ways that would be consistent with international obligations of Seychelles on human rights and freedoms.

With regard to the judiciary, the constitution provides for its independence; however, in practice it is reported that the judiciary is inefficient, lacks resources, and is subject to executive interference. The courts include the Magistrates' Courts, the Supreme Court, the constitutional court, and the court of appeals. Depending on the gravity of the offense, criminal cases are heard by Magistrates' Court or the Supreme Court. A jury is used in cases involving murder or treason. Trials are public, and the accused are considered innocent until proven guilty. Defendants have the constitutional right to counsel during judicial proceedings of their trial, and the rights to confront witnesses and to appeal. As structured, the courts of appeal hear appeals from the Supreme Court in both civil and criminal cases. The Supreme Court's powers, in turn, include hearing cases from the Magistrates' Court and other inferior courts of first instance. Seychelles also has another level of court known as the Family Tribunal. The constitutional court, although not part of the regular framework of the court system, can be seen as a division of the Supreme Court. Its memberships are traditionally drawn from the pool of judges on the bench in the Supreme Court. This court determines matters of a constitutional nature and considers cases that bear on civil liberties. It convenes weekly or as necessary to consider constitutional issues only. The court of appeals hears cases on appeal only from the Supreme Court and the constitutional court.

Summarily, the Seychelles' legal system consists of Magistrates' Courts (lower courts), Supreme (or trial) Court, court of appeals, and constitutional court. As dictated by its history and politics, Seychelles' legal system in practice is a blend of French and English systems and hence a confluence of common law and civil law systems. This is readily apparent in the various legal undertakings. The civil and commercial codes are French in origin. The criminal law was French until 1952 when the British system was introduced. Together these form a kaleidoscope of procedural confusion not only on which law applies in a particular situation, but which system (common law or civil law) is applicable or provides the best resolution for a case.

Structure of Seychelles Courts

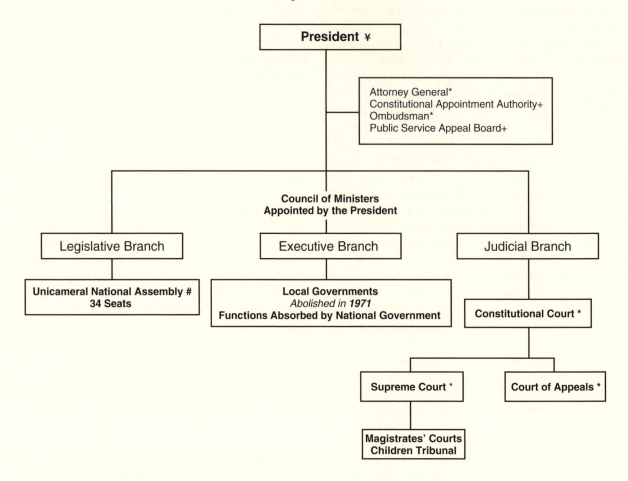

* Appointments made by the president from candidates provided by the Constitutional Appointment Authority
+ Joint appointments by the president and the leader of the opposition party
¥ The president is the chief of state and government, head of national security, which includes National Guard Force,
   Army, Presidential Protection Unit, Coast Guard, the Marines, and the Police.
Direct elections and proportional representation

CURRENT COURT SYSTEM STRUCTURE

The judicial power of Seychelles is vested in the judiciary, which will consist of (1) the Court of Appeals of Seychelles, (2) the Supreme Court of Seychelles, and (3) other subordinate courts or tribunals established pursuant to Article 1377. Furthermore, the constitution provides an independent judiciary, with constitutional immunity protecting the justices of appeal, judges, and masters of the Supreme Court from liability resulting from its proceedings or anything done or omitted in the performance of its functions. However, similar protection is also extended by legislation to the persons exercising judicial functions in the subordinate courts and tribunals. The court of appeals has special powers. It has jurisdiction to hear and determine appeals from a judgment, direction, decision, declaration, decree, writ, or order of the Supreme Court and other appellate jurisdiction as conferred upon it by the constitution or a law.

Every citizen has the right to an appeal to the court of appeals on a similar jurisdictional ground or with a writ of order of the Supreme Court. The constitution also allows the court the authority to establish its own internal rules and to regulate its proceedings related to the application of, contravention, enforcement, or interpretation of the constitution. This allows the court of appeals to give priority to constitutional issues on its docket over any other issues. The court of appeals consists of a president and two or more other justices of appeal and a judge who sits as an ex officio member of the court.

The Supreme Court authority extends to hear cases under original jurisdiction in matters relating to the application of, contravention, enforcement, or interpretation of the constitution and civil and criminal matters. It can also hear cases under its appellate jurisdiction from subordinate courts, tribunals, and adjudicating authorities. The National Assembly may also alter the Supreme

Court's jurisdiction by law. Judges of the Supreme Court may hear cases in panels of many judges or by a single judge.

In summary, Seychelles' court system is structured as follows: a three-tiered judicial system consists of Magistrates' or small claims courts, the Supreme (or trial) Court, and the court of appeals. The court of appeals hears appeals from the Supreme Court in both civil and criminal cases. The Supreme Court has original jurisdiction as well as appellate jurisdiction from cases from the magistrate and other tribunals. The system is based on English common law, with influences of the Napoleonic Code (e.g., in tort and contract matters) and customary law. Criminal cases are heard in Magistrates' Courts or the Supreme Court and here the seriousness of a charge plays a role in determining where the case ultimately begins. The right to a jury trial is limited only to cases of murder or treason. However, ordinary legal protections are extended to defendants as specified in the new constitution.

SPECIALIZED JUDICIAL BODIES

Specialized judicial bodies in the Seychelles include those inside and outside the ordinary flow of the court structure but yet performing the functions of the mainstream courts. The discussion below describes the activities of five such institutions: the Family Tribunal, the Constitutional Appointment Authority, the Ombudsman, the constitutional court, and the Public Service Appeal Board (see figure).

Family Tribunal

As a specialized court focusing on family matters, the Family Tribunal was created in 1998 by the National Assembly from a government-driven initiative started in 1995 and aimed at providing a separate institutional framework for aiding children. It has eighteen family judges who sit to hear and determine matters relating to the child care, custody, access, and maintenance of children. It functions under the control of the minister of Employment and Social Affairs who appoints the judges as prescribed by law. Currently, only paternity cases remain under the regular court's jurisdiction. The tribunal has an impressive caseload, which significantly eases caseloads at the Magistrates' and Supreme Court levels where initially such cases were filed. In 1988 alone, roughly 2,461 cases were presented to the tribunal for resolution.

Constitutional Appointments Authority

The constitution provides for the creation of a specialized body known as the Constitutional Appointments Authority (CAA). This office functions as an independent body with a constitutional mandate provided to appoint members of the judicial branch and other agencies as provided by law. The CAA consists of three members.

Two are appointed (one each) by the president and the leader of the opposition; the third member is appointed by the first two appointees and becomes the chairman of the CAA. The general requirement and qualification for CAA membership is citizenship. Furthermore, he must have held judicial office in a court of unlimited jurisdiction in Seychelles, must be a person of proven integrity and impartiality, and must have served with distinction in a high office of the government or, under the constitution, a profession or vocation. Those persons appointed will serve on the authority for a seven-year renewable term.

Ombudsman

The office of the ombudsman, by virtue of its duties and responsibilities, is a very important specialized judicial institution provided in the constitution of the Seychelles. It is vested with the same authority as a court of law. This office has the duty to initiate and investigate actions taken by public authorities in the exercise of their administrative functions. It is also charged with assisting individual complainants with respect to their legal proceedings relative to violations of the provisions of the Charter of Fundamental Human Rights and Freedoms of the Seychelles' constitution. The authority to appoint the ombudsman is given to the president and is exercised from candidates proposed by the CAA.

Public Service Appeal Board

The Public Service Appeal Board is charged with the duty to resolve disputes between public employees and public authorities only. Its membership is appointed using the same formula and processes outlined for selecting members of the CAA. It has independent authority in the performance of its service, subject to limitations prescribed by law. While it is required to hear complaints from persons aggrieved in the public service, it is exempted from hearing claims arising from positions falling under the authority of the CAA, or those committed to the president by law.

Constitutional Court

As a specialized judicial body, the constitutional court is a stand-alone institution that in many ways can be seen as a division of the Supreme Court of Seychelles. Its membership in theory is virtually the same. It determines matters of a constitutional nature relating to the application, contravention, enforcement, or interpretation of the constitution and cases bearing on civil rights and liberties provided in the constitution. It convenes weekly or as necessary to consider constitutional issues only. Its decisions can be appealed to the court of appeals, which is the court of last resort. The court of appeals convenes three times a year, for two weeks in April, August, and October, to consider appeals from the Supreme Court and the constitutional court only.

The constitutional court is not necessarily the court of last resort on constitutional issues. First, with regard to its jurisdiction, the constitution provides that not less than two judges sitting together will exercise the jurisdiction of the Supreme Court with respect to matters that invoke the constitutional court's jurisdiction. In effect, the constitution does not distinguish between the Supreme Court and the constitutional court except in the exercise of its jurisdiction on constitutional issues. That is, when the Supreme Court deals with issues of application, contravention, enforcement, or interpretation of the constitution, it must immediately transform such a proceeding to that of a constitutional court. The constitution defines a constitutional court as one where two or more judges of the Supreme Court sit for the purpose of a hearing presided over by a senior judge for the purpose of deciding a constitutional issue.

Only those who allege a violation of a constitutional right can invoke the jurisdiction of the constitutional court. However, the court may decline to hear an application where in the opinion of the court the applicant has been granted relief under any law. Generally, the court will decline an application for review except on appeal from a decision of a court below where an adequate means for redress of the alleged constitutional wrong was available under the law. Under the latter, upon ruling on the case, the court may remand the case to the appropriate court below to enter a new judgment consistent with its decision. The constitution prescribes the kinds of remedy the constitutional court can provide a petitioner who meets its jurisdictional requirements. For example, it may declare any act or omission, which is the object of the application, to be a violation of the constitution. It may also declare void any law or the provision of any law that is inconsistent with the constitution. The constitutional court also has the discretion to fashion appropriate remedy or grant any remedy that ordinarily is available to the Supreme Court against any person or authority, which is the subject of the petition or a party to any proceedings before the court. Finally, the constitution requires the constitutional court, subject to an appeal to the court of appeals, to file a copy of its decision with the president and the speaker of the assembly.

STAFFING

The staffing of the judiciary branch and other specialized judicial bodies in the Seychelles is done largely by the president, either directly with the leader of the opposition party or indirectly with the assistance of the CAA. Either way, any selection process is prescribed by a relevant section of the constitution for the appropriate judicial body or quasi-judicial body. Staffing issues also go along with other issues such as qualifications and removal from office. Sections of Seychelles' constitution speak with authority to these issues.

First, when the CAA is used, the candidates are selected following some prescribed set of constitutional requirements for qualification. With the discretion of setting their procedural criteria, the constitution requires that the CAA submit a list of candidates to the president, who then makes the final appointment to the courts. The same process is repeated for the selection of chief judges, justices, the ombudsman, and also to fill vacated positions left by judges or justices upon resignation, retirement, or death. Second, when the selection process is done directly, the president and the leader of the opposition appoint one person each and the first two candidates select a third. Should they fail to do so for any reason, they must propose a list of three candidates, at most, to the president from whom one will be appointed.

The constitution addresses issues of staffing, composition, and qualifications of judges to the court of appeals, which is the court of last resort. Specifically with regard to composition, the constitution provides that the court of appeals will consist of a president of the court of appeals and two or more other justices of appeal, as well as a judge, who is an ex officio member of the court. With regard to qualifications, discretion is provided to the Constitutional Appointment Authority. Generally, "a person is qualified for appointment as, or to discharge the functions of the President of the Court of Appeal or become a Justice of that Court if in the opinion of the CAA, that person is suitably qualified in law." The person must be "capable of effectively, competently and impartially discharging the functions of the office of Justice of Appeal or a Judge under the Constitution." A similar but slightly different outline and process are followed for staffing, composition, and qualifications of judges of the Supreme Court, the second highest court of the country.

With regard to length of time in office, the president, acting on the recommendation of the Constitutional Appointment Authority, appoints judges for seven years, subject to reappointment until the age of seventy. That applies only to citizens since the constitution limits appointment of noncitizens to the court of appeals judgeship to one term of office only, with the allowance for renewal or reappointment for more than a term in exceptional circumstances with the recommendation of the Constitutional Appointment Authority. This applies to almost all the judgeship positions in Seychelles, since almost all the sitting judges are hired from other Commonwealth countries such as Mauritius, India, Sri Lanka, Nigeria, and Zambia. A person who is appointed to the office of justice of appeal or judge may continue in office, notwithstanding any charge brought against him, during the term of the office. Reportedly, none of the justices or judges currently on the bench in the Seychelles is a citizen. However, the chief justice of the court of appeals is a naturalized citizen as required by the constitution. Employing expatriate judges in such a large pool, on the bench, brings unwelcome but just criticisms of the justice system.

The constitution also approaches the issue of vacating an office and removal differently for nationals and expatriate judges, even though there are no nationals holding judgeship positions in the country. A person holding the office of justice of appeal or judge in Seychelles will vacate that office upon death, upon being removed, or upon resigning and sending notification to that effect to the president and the Constitutional Appointment Authority. In the case of a citizen of Seychelles, she may vacate the judgeship on attaining the age of seventy, and in the case of a noncitizen, at the end of the term for which she was appointed. With regard to removal, a justice of appeal or a judge may be removed from the bench for inability to perform the functions of that office. Such inability may arise from infirmity of body or mind, or from any other cause, including misbehavior. The constitution empowers the CAA to consider the question of removing a justice of appeal before investigation and provides for the procedure it can follow.

IMPACT OF LAW

Seychelles' economy and the political and legal system have always been intertwined. It started under the 1976 independence constitution as a sovereign democratic republic, then veered to a socialist form of government in 1979, and back again to a multiparty republic in 1993. The socialist politics dictated the adoption of socialism and a socialist-type legal structure during that period. Upon initiating a new constitution and reinstituting a legal democratic framework, Seychelles held new multiparty elections in 1993. This, in a nutshell, in the last twenty-five years since independence, illustrates the several phases of constitutional change in Seychelles' experiments at self-government. To be sure, the results of these changes and their practical benefits for the country have been mixed. But again, that depends on how one sees mixed results and the respect of the rule of law. For the case of Seychelles, it matters a great deal if one understands the constitutional changes brought about during that period, not only from the perspective of the political struggles, but in light of the two prevalent political values—democracy and socialism—guiding ideas and policy decisions during that period. Remarkably, at various points of Seychelles' political struggle, both principles were emphasized as central predicates for crafting the various constitutions and moving the nation forward. While the first two constitutions of 1976 and 1977 can perhaps be seen as inconclusive because of the brevity of time they

were in force, the same cannot be said of the 1979 and 1993 Constitutions.

The 1993 Constitution provides a comprehensive Charter of Rights and gives the people fundamental protections against all types of government abuses. However, reports show that since 1994, even though the judiciary is given what amounts to judicial independence, it is subject to executive interference and influence, and is above all inefficient and lacks resources to effectively mete out justice. For unknown reasons, the ombudsman, whose office is empowered by the constitution to investigate abuses and wrongs of public officials including the president, is reluctant to pursue charges of wrongdoing or to go after abusers of individual rights. Thus, here it is clear that it is not the lack of law that is at issue, but the respect for the rule of law. The law can only gain the type of respect the society affords to its ends, and for the Seychelles, the early evidence in the post-1993 Constitution provides mixed predicators for the future. But again, it might be too early to pass judgment.

Finally, with regard to the various processes of judicial selection, it is interesting to comment on the preclearance methods used in the Seychelles. As in most countries, what is common here is how the judicial selection process itself avoids political or legislative scrutiny. Yet, it invariably seems to revolve comfortably around the president's prerogatives with a remarkable sense of ease, if not judiciousness. The notion that the inclusion of the leader of the opposition party in the process of selecting members of specialized judicial bodies makes it something more than ordinary is remarkably implied. However, no justification is provided for accepting such a view as any different than one in which the president acted alone, especially since further stages of indecision simply call for the president to act virtually alone anyway. Similarly, the review process for removal as provided by the constitution is very congested and a judge would rather resign than go through the hassle of the investigation process. Overall, it is common knowledge among public law scholars that staffing the judiciary has always been more political than rational. The difficulty, however, has always been whether to risk judicial legitimacy and erode the respect for rule of law in the long run, or garner personal short-term gains at the front end of the politics of judicial appointment. As with many other political systems, the United States included, it is obvious that Seychelles is making an attempt to juggle these two less desirable options. The consequences, however, might be too early to predict, at least from the posture presented in the 1993 Constitution.

Marc-Georges Pufong

See also Civil Law; Common Law; Constitutional Law; Criminal Law; Human Rights Law; Judicial Selection, Methods of; Marxist Jurisprudence; Napoleonic Code

References and further reading

Background Notes, Seychelles. 1980. United Department of State, Bureau of Public Affairs. Washington, DC: GPO.

Benedict, Marion, and Burton Benedict. 1982. *Men, Women, and Money in the Seychelles.* Berkeley: University of California Press.

Bunge, Frederica M., ed. 1994. *Indian Ocean: Five Island Countries, Foreign Area Studies.* American University, Washington, DC: Headquarters Department of the Army.

Chloros, A. G. 1977. *Codification in a Mixed Jurisdiction: The Civil and Commercial Law of Seychelles.* Amsterdam, NY: North Holland.

Commonwealth Observer Group. 1993. *The Presidential and National Assembly Elections in Seychelles,* July 20–23. London: Commonwealth Secretariat.

Kurian, George, ed. 1992. *Encyclopedia of the Third World.* 4th ed. New York: Facts on File, Inc.

Mancham, James R. 1983. *Paradise Raped: Life, Love, and Power in the Seychelles.* London: Methuen.

Metz, Helen Chapin, ed. 1994. *Seychelles Country Study.* Federal Research Division. Library of Congress.

Nwulia, Moses D. E. 1981. *The History of Slavery in Mauritius and the Seychelles, 1810–1875.* Rutherford, NJ: Fairleigh Dickinson University Press.

René, France Albert. 1982. *Seychelles: The New Era. Victoria: Ministry of Education and Information.* Victoria: Ministry of Education and Information.

Seychelles. National Development Plan, 1990–94. Victoria: Ministry of Planning and External Relations.

———. 2001. "The Constitution of the Republic of Seychelles." http://www.richmond.edu/~jpjones/confinder/Seychelles. html (accessed April 20, 2001).

United States. 1994. *Country Reports on Human Rights Practices for 1993.* Department of State. http://www.state.gov/www/global/human_rights/drl_reports.html (accessed January 7, 2002).

———. 2000. *Country Reports on Human Rights Practices for 1999.* Department of State. http://www.state.gov/www/global/human_rights/99hrp_index.html (accessed January 7, 2002).

———. 2001. *Country Reports on Human Rights Practices for 2000.* Department of State. http://www.state.gov/g/dr/rls/rls/hrrpt/2000/af/index.cfm? docid (accessed April 20, 2001).

SHAMING

DEFINITION

Shaming is disapproval of an illegal, immoral, or antisocial offense designed to create remorse in the person who committed the act. Distinguished by formal and informal mechanisms, and by reintegrative and disintegrative intentions, shaming can be an integral part of a system of criminal punishment.

Proponents of shaming believe that, apart from any other punishments meted out, society must make the commission of an improper act so deplorable that perpetrators will refrain from such offenses in order to avoid society's rebuke. The philosophy applies to such venues as the criminal justice system, in which members of a community are encouraged to reproach offenders, and family relations, in which a parent's disapproval is said to deter children from improper behavior.

Psychologically, shame is similar to guilt. In each a third person, group, or collective attempts to influence another's reaction to his own behavior. But where guilt admonishes an individual about how remorseful she should feel for having committed an offense, shame lets the person know that others now hold her in lower esteem as a result of the transgression. Shaming, thus, may be a potent and efficient mechanism of social control. Public bodies need not exhaust their resources to enforce community or legal norms; rather, public opinion and a sort of peer pressure encourage citizens to behave properly.

ADVANTAGES

Shaming is said to achieve restitution for social or legal offenses by encouraging offenders to apologize and make amends to their victims. Moreover, shaming plays a role in moral education, helping the offender to understand that his infraction is rejected by the community or society. Finally, proponents of shaming claim that it serves as a strong deterrent against future offenses. Because culprits may lose a degree of self-respect and public esteem for their misdeeds, they are said to refrain from future offenses that may earn them continued wrath.

PRECONDITIONS

In order to operate effectively, shaming depends on three preconditions. First, there must be a stable interaction among people, so that knowledge of both the misdeed and the community's reaction can flow back and forth between offenders and community members. Put another way, the community must know that the offender has, in fact, done something wrong, and the offender must be aware of the community's scornful reaction. This type of shared understanding is most often found in communities or societies where there is a stable interaction among members. Second, public opinion must flow freely, so that community members can share their reactions with one another. In a society of a thousand people, it does little good for a single member to shame an offender; rather, shaming is more effective when the offender faces a collective wall of community opinion. Third, shaming also depends on the offender's willingness to internalize the community norms. He must have a sense of morality and be susceptible to outside opinion or pressure, so as to be swayed by the community's moral compulsion. According to one commentator, those most open to shaming are young, anxious, verbal, intelligent, and neurotic (Wilson 1983), but the list of traits is hardly exclusive. Offenders must desire the community's respect and remain willing to change their ways in order to achieve it.

FORMAL AND INFORMAL MECHANISMS

Shaming methods vary by their connection to criminal justice processes. In some societies, shaming is an additional component of judicial punishment for criminal infractions. Apart from fines or imprisonment, defendants may be required to apologize to their victims in open court or in newspapers. The names of sex offenders may be published by the media—or even entered into Web lists—notifying the public of the particular wrongs. In North America, for example, colonial governments in the seventeenth and eighteenth centuries routinely placed miscreants on public display in stocks to suffer the community's scorn. Even today, some law enforcement agencies parade suspected perpetrators before waiting cameras as they are ushered into custody, thus creating the shame of the "perp walk." In other societies, corporal punishments are conducted in the open to maximize the public shame on the offender. In Saudi Arabia, where offenses such as theft are punishable by loss of a hand, amputations are carried out in a public square. In China, authorities publicize executions to shame the perpetrator and her family, as well as to deter would-be criminals.

But shaming can be a substitute or alternative method of enforcing community norms. Again, the prime example is the family, where parents, rather than by striking or otherwise punishing their children, may speak to them sternly to convey their displeasure over the children's misdeeds. In such cases, parents expect that their children will internalize the parents' norms and act to minimize the disapproval. Adolescent cliques use the same technique to enforce common behavior. If one member acts contrary to collective beliefs, she may be berated, "frozen out," or otherwise shamed until she changes her ways to conform with the clique's attitudes.

To be sure, adolescent dictums are a far cry from the requirements of criminal statutes, but there are reasons to encourage an informal resolution of societal infractions rather than having recourse to the cumbersome provisions of the formal criminal justice process. If an offender can be shamed into offering an apology and restitution to the victim, reconciliation is reached quickly and with minimal tension. Indeed, in many systems of customary law, judges strongly encourage defendants to acknowledge their infraction of community standards and to negotiate restitution with the victim or his family.

Even within formal or informal mechanisms of shaming, expressions of shame vary by culture. In ancient Rome, for example, offenders had their doors burned, and victims of an offense followed their perpetrators around in mourning clothes. In socialist people's courts—those found primarily in Cuba or China—ordinary citizens denounce wrongdoers in open court.

In the West, with its emphasis on individualism, informal shaming may not be as prevalent, although proponents claim that shaming may work in small or closed communities where neighbors know each other well. Nonetheless, because community pressure is most effective in collective cultures, informal shaming mechanisms are most often found in Eastern societies. In China, for example, citizens participate in neighborhood mediation committees, where the threat of public shame creates conformity to common norms. Japan, too, has community groups and community volunteers who work with offenders to help them reconnect to public standards. Cultural traditions of shaming can also play a large part in influencing public behavior. In Japan, shame is borne collectively, reaching across the offender to touch those who are closely connected to him. When a commercial aircraft crashes, the chairman of the airline may resign his position to express the company's shame. When a policeman commits a serious violation, his supervisor may quit because he feels shamed by his subordinate's misdeeds. There are even stories of Japanese parents who commit suicide when their children are arrested for heinous crimes. Nor is Japan alone. Some Muslim societies permit "honor killings," in which male members of a family kill a daughter or sister who has engaged in premarital sex, which is severely interdicted by Islam.

EFFECTIVENESS

There exists a tremendous debate about whether shaming should be reintegrative or disintegrative. Reintegration implies that the community will accept the offender once again after it has censured him and received his apology. Disintegration, however, may divide a community by failing to readmit offenders. Indeed, critics of disintegrative shaming contend that in such circumstances the shame serves only to disgrace the offender and discourage her from ever wanting to rejoin the community or society. They assert that it is important for a shaming system to disapprove of the offender's behavior, not reject him as an individual, so that the offender will accept the community's legitimacy and seek its ultimate approval. Otherwise, the offender may consider himself stigmatized by the community, and the stigma may push him into a "criminal self-concept." It might even make a "criminal subculture" or life of crime more appealing to offenders, since on some level these subcultures reject the norms of the very culture that metes out the shame.

To avoid such possibilities, advocates of shaming recommend that it focus on the offense, not the offender, that it be limited in time, and that the offender be welcomed back into the community once she has acknowledged her error and made restitution. They also warn against insisting on the severity of formal sanctions, as informal sanctions can be stronger deterrents than judicially imposed punishments. Under this theory, repute in the eyes of close friends, family, or acquaintances matters more to most people than the opinions or actions of criminal justice officials. The shame or disapproval of those who are important to us may have more effect on our behavior than sanctions imposed by a distant legal authority.

Although shaming can help enforce social norms, it carries a concomitant risk. Just as an adolescent clique may shame anyone who dares to challenge the group's values, large-scale shaming may limit diversity of opinion, becoming a mechanism by which the majority may enforce its view or beliefs against all others in the nation, community, or group. This may be the case in parts of China, where the cultural priority of collectivism over individualism may discourage citizens from challenging the social norms that are enforced. Western societies do not usually face such problems, but because shaming depends on cultural understandings of propriety, those persons with the most influence over cultural norms also enjoy the greatest power in shaping the eventual effects of shaming.

Jon B. Gould

See also China; Criminal Sanctions, Purposes of; General Deterrence; Japan; Rehabilitation; Retribution

References and further reading
Braithwaite, John. 1989. *Crime, Shame and Reintegration.* Cambridge: Cambridge University Press.
Fang, Yang, Marilyn D. McShane, and Frank P. Williams III. 1996. "Concepts and Theories in the Use of Mediation: Shaming Models in American and Chinese Cultures." In *Comparative Criminal Justice.* Edited by Charles B. Fields and Richter H. Moore, Jr. Prospect Heights, IL: Waveland Press.
Kahan, Dan M. 1996. "What Do Alternative Sanctions Mean?" *University of Chicago Law Review* 63: 591.
Wilson, James Q. 1983. *Thinking about Crime.* New York: Vintage.

SHARIA
See Islamic Law

SIERRA LEONE

COUNTRY INFORMATION
Nestled in West Africa's Atlantic bulge, Sierra Leone is about the size of South Carolina or Scotland. With Guinea to the northeast, Liberia to the southeast, and the Atlantic Ocean on the southwest, the country's 27,700 square miles (71,740 square kilometers) enclose arid regions, lowland jungles, and swampy coastlands. Buried in this differentiated landmass is an impressive array of minerals—diamonds, gold, rutile, bauxite, and iron ore. Sierra Leone has one of the finest coastlines in West Africa and one of the deepest natural harbors in the world. There are two seasons—a rainy season (from May to October) and a dry season (from November to April)—and the tropical climate is hot and very humid, with an average temperature of 80°F. Sierra Leone has a total population of approximately 5 million and is home to at least sixteen ethnic groups. Of these, the Mendes of the south and the Temnes of the north are numerically preponderant, with each accounting for at least 30 percent of the country's population. The Creoles, who live mainly in the western area and comprise no more than 3 percent of the total population, have historically exerted more influence than their numbers might suggest. The Krio language is both the native tongue of the Creoles and the country's lingua franca. English is the official language, but a variety of local languages, in addition to Krio, are also spoken. Roughly half of Sierra Leoneans adhere to indigenous religious beliefs and practices, while 30 percent are Muslim and 20 percent are Christian. The official urban-rural ratio is 35:65, but this figure does not take into account the extensive depopulation of the countryside spawned by criminal insurgency and state collapse in the 1990s. Sixty-eight percent of the people live in poverty; average life expectancy is thirty-eight years; and infant mortality hovers around 170 per 1,000 live births. Both the country's gross national product (GNP) and its GNP per capita, which stand at $0.7 billion and $140, respectively, have been on the decline since the 1980s. Sierra Leone's legal system is based on British common law, parliamentary statutes, and local customary law.

HISTORY
Portuguese explorers were the first Europeans to set foot in Sierra Leone. They named their fifteenth-century "discovery" *Sierra Lyoa* (Lion Mountain). The Portuguese, who were later joined by the British and the Dutch, were primarily interested in acquiring slaves for the plantation economies of America and the Caribbean. Relics of Sierra Leone's slave-trading past can still be found on Bunce Island, which served as a loading port for slaves en route to the Americas and the Caribbean. Descendants of Africans shipped from Bunce Island to the New World can still be found today on the coastal islands of South Carolina and Georgia.

The British government declared Freetown (the country's capital) a Crown colony in 1808, marking the beginning of the official colonial era. One of the most important developments in nineteenth-century Sierra Leone was the establishment of Fourah Bay College in 1827. As

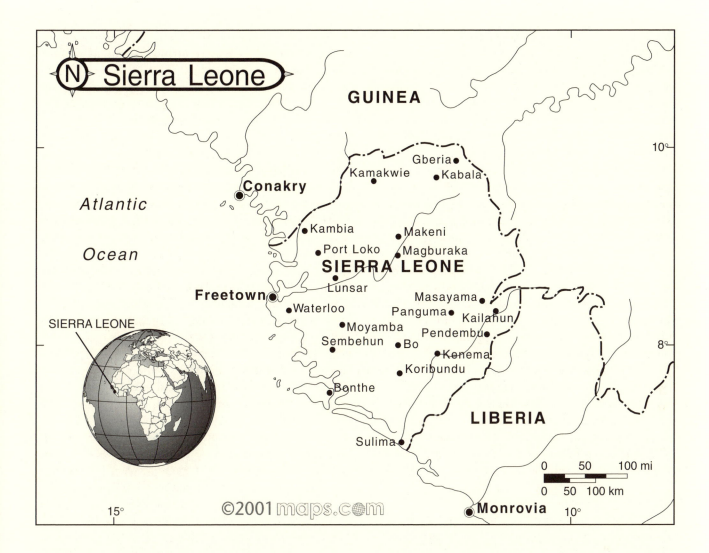

the oldest institution of higher learning in black Africa, this college trained many West Africans and earned Sierra Leone the reputation as the "Athens of West Africa."

Throughout the colonial era, a bifurcated system of administration separated the colony of Freetown from the hinterland. Declared a British protectorate in 1896, the hinterland was governed indirectly through traditional institutions that were modified to serve imperial interests. The colony, by contrast, was ruled directly by the local colonial oligarchy and municipal councils. Creoles were recognized as British subjects, whereas the inhabitants of the hinterland were relegated to the status of British protected persons. In the realm of colonial jurisprudence, Creoles were subject to the general principles of English common law, while inhabitants of the hinterland had their cases adjudicated by a three-tiered system—the court of the district commissioner, mixed courts presided over by district commissioners and paramount chiefs, and the traditional court of the paramount chief. This dualism in the theory and practice of British colonial rule left an indelible imprint on the country's political and legal landscape.

Sierra Leone gained its flag independence from Britain on April 27, 1961. The political system during the first few years of independent rule was relatively stable, open, and democratic. The country's political fortunes, however, took a dramatic turn for the worse after the death of the first prime minister, Sir Milton Margai, in 1964. Albert Margai, who succeeded his half brother as prime minister in 1964, narrowly lost a tightly contested parliamentary election in 1967 to Siaka Stevens and the All Peoples Congress (APC). The praetorian intervention of Brig. David Lansana, force commander of the Sierra Leone army and a close ally of Albert Margai, prevented a smooth and orderly transfer of power from Margai's Sierra Leone People's Party (SLPP) to the APC. Less than forty-eight hours after seizing power and declaring martial law, Lansana was toppled by Majors Blake, Jumu, and Kaisamba. This troika established the National Reformation Council (NRC) to rule the country under the leadership of Brig. Andrew Juxon-Smith. Noncommissioned officers (NCOs) of the armed forces overthrew the NRC a year later. Rather than exercise power themselves, the leaders of this subaltern coup restored constitutional democratic rule by handing over power to Siaka Stevens and the APC.

On assuming power, Stevens and the APC moved quickly to silence the political opposition and consolidate power. Sierra Leone became a one-party state in 1978, and no free and fair elections were held during the twenty-four years (1968–1992) of APC rule. Malfeasance under the APC spawned the functional contraction of the state and growing destitution among Sierra Leoneans. Several coup attempts to dislodge the APC from power failed, and the alleged coup leaders, including former APC stalwarts Brig. John Bangura, Mohamed Forna, and Ibrahim Taqi, were executed. After seventeen years at the helm, both as prime minister and president, Siaka Stevens retired in 1985 but not before handpicking one of his supplicants, Brig. Joseph Momoh, as his successor.

Momoh inherited a country that was on a downward slide. As the economy floundered and corruption mounted, domestic and external pressures to dismantle the one-party system and hold multiparty elections intensified. Momoh reluctantly bowed to these pressures in 1991 and promised to hold multiparty elections, but his deathbed conversion to democracy was overshadowed by a rebel insurgency that precipitated the APC's downfall. Junior officers of the Sierra Leone army overthrew Momoh's APC government on April 29, 1992. These officers, mostly lieutenants in their twenties, established the National Provisional Ruling Council (NPRC), which ruled the country until 1996.

NPRC corruption and its failure to end the criminal insurgency of the Revolutionary United Front (RUF) rekindled internal demands and external pressures for democratic elections. These pressures culminated in multiparty elections in 1996 and the inauguration of the second republic under the leadership of President Ahmad Tejan Kabba, winner of the 1996 presidential election. Fourteen months into the second republic, Kabba's government was violently overthrown by elements of the military underclass, who announced the formation of a ruling alliance with the RUF and the establishment of the Armed Forces Revolutionary Council (AFRC) as the country's new ruling body. Widespread rejection, both internally and externally, greeted the AFRC coup and its leaders. Most professionals, including judges, fled the country, and ten months later, in February 1998, the AFRC was chased out of Freetown by a Nigerian-led West African intervention force.

The removal of the AFRC paved the way for Kabba's reinstatement in March 1998. This was followed by the arrest and prosecution of AFRC leaders and their alleged collaborators. Twenty-four members of the armed forces (including Cpl. Tamba Gborie, who had announced the AFRC coup) were found guilty of treason by a court-martial and executed in October 1998. Foday Sankoh, the

RUF leader, was extradited to Sierra Leone from Nigeria to stand trial for a variety of offenses, including treason. Sankoh and some AFRC "collaborators" were on death row awaiting their appeal hearings when a combined force of renegade Sierra Leone army regulars and RUF irregulars invaded Freetown in January 1999. This invasion, which almost succeeded in once again toppling the government, caused the deaths of over 6,000 civilians. Thousands of homes and tenements in the east end of Freetown were razed to the ground, and many civilians, old and young, were delimbed, maimed, and scarred for life.

An embattled Kabba government emerged from the invasion convinced that it lacked the military capability to defeat criminal insurgents. Under pressure from Nigeria and the United States, Kabba signed the Lomé Peace Accord in July 1999 with Foday Sankoh, the RUF leader. This agreement granted a blanket amnesty to the RUF and rewarded its leaders with ministerial positions in the government in exchange for the RUF's agreement to disarm, demobilize, and reconstitute itself into a political party. The United Nations, which agreed to serve as moral guarantor of the agreement, subsequently assembled a peacekeeping force to replace the Nigerian-led intervention force.

The Lomé appeasement unraveled after RUF combatants began disarming UN peacekeepers, seizing their weapons and equipment. After a series of such brazen actions, which were clearly aimed at humiliating the UN force and gauging its response, the RUF abducted over 500 peacekeepers in May 2000. In clear violation of the Lomé agreement and emboldened by a UN force that was neither prepared nor willing to fight, the RUF embarked on another invasion of Freetown. But for the timely intervention of British paratroopers and marines, Freetown and its government would have fallen to the RUF in May 2000.

Since the events of May 2000, Sankoh has been in jail awaiting yet another trial, albeit this time by an international tribunal. The RUF still controls large chunks of the country, including the diamond-producing regions. Presidential and parliamentary elections scheduled for February 2001 were postponed for six months or until the security situation improved.

LEGAL CONCEPTS

The supreme law of Sierra Leone is the constitution. The present document grew out of efforts to dismantle the one-party system and was promulgated into law in July 1991. The constitution provides for a republic with sovereignty vested in the people. Libertarian rights (life, liberty, property, security of person) and freedoms (conscience, expression, assembly, association) of the individual are recognized, as are provisions regarding the fundamental principles of state policy, the representation of the people, the executive and its powers, and the composition and responsibilities of Parliament, the judiciary, and the public service commission. Although the constitution seeks to promote national integration and discourage discrimination based on place of origin, sex, religion, status, and ethnic identity, the citizenship provisions of the law are inherently sexist and racist. To qualify as a citizen of Sierra Leone, an individual's paternal grandfather must be of Negro African descent.

The constitution recognizes the president as head of state, supreme executive authority, fountain of honor and justice, commander in chief of the armed forces, guardian of the constitution, guarantor of national independence and territorial integrity, and symbol of national unity and sovereignty. To seek the presidency, one must be a citizen of Sierra Leone, at least forty years of age, a member of a political party, and qualified to be elected to Parliament. Fifty-five percent of the popular vote is required to win the presidency, and presidents cannot serve more than two five-year terms. A president can be removed from office for reasons of infirmity of mind or body. He or she can also be impeached for violating the constitution or for gross misconduct that is incompatible with the effective discharge of the duties of the president. Impeachment of the president requires a two-thirds parliamentary majority vote.

The attorney general is a member of the president's cabinet and serves as the minister of justice and principal legal adviser to the government. All offenses prosecuted under the name of the Republic of Sierra Leone are the responsibility of the attorney general. The attorney general has access to all courts, with the exception of local courts, and is assisted in his or her duties by a solicitor general and a director of public prosecutions, both of whom are appointed by the president on the recommendation of the Judicial and Legal Service Commission (JLSC).

The legislative power of the state is vested in Parliament, a body composed of seventy-two members. To be eligible for parliamentary service, one must be a nonnaturalized citizen, at least twenty-one years of age, and a registered voter who can read, speak, and write English. Members of Parliament elect a speaker, who can be either a fellow parliamentarian or a judge. Both speakers of the second republican Parliament have been judges. The first, S. M. F. Kutubu, died in office in December 2000. He was succeeded by Edmund Cowan, who defeated a parliamentarian, AO Bangura, for the post.

In addition to the constitution, the laws of Sierra Leone derive from acts of Parliament, common law, case law, and orders, rules, and regulations issued by statutory and customary authorities. Statutory laws are acts of Parliament. Case law is based on court decisions and the common law principle of stare decisis. Much of Sierra Leone's criminal law is in the form of statutes that were either inherited from Britain, such as the Offences against the Person Act of 1861, or passed by the local Parliament after independence, such as the Treason and State Offences Act of 1963. Two main branches of civil law are recognized—tort law and contract law. Customary law, whose infractions can include seducing another man's wife, is now largely incorporated into common law.

Following British common legal tradition, crimes in Sierra Leone are classified according to subject matter. There are crimes against the person, property, public morals and religion, public order, state security, and the administration of justice. Three broad categories of crimes are recognized: treason, felony, and misdemeanor. Treason is a capital offense, while felony can be a capital offense (murder, armed robbery) or a noncapital offense. Noncapital felonies (manslaughter, rape, larceny, burglary, arson, fraud, perjury, sedition) are punishable by jail terms ranging from one year to life in prison. As minor infractions of the law, misdemeanors are punishable by no more than five years in jail, fines, or both.

JUDICIARY AND COURT STRUCTURE

Sierra Leone has a dual legal structure that reflects its colonial past. There are general law courts, whose development has been shaped by British common law, and local courts, which are grounded in customary law. The general law courts of original jurisdiction are the Magistrates' Court and the High Court. In addition to its function as a court of first instance, the Magistrates' Court can hear appeals from local courts, thus helping to reconcile general law and customary law.

Sierra Leone's judiciary is headed by the chief justice, who is appointed by the president on the advice of the JLSC and with the approval of Parliament. The same process, including parliamentary approval, applies to the appointment of other superior court judges. To qualify as a superior court judge, a person must be eligible to practice as a lawyer in a court with unlimited jurisdiction in civil and criminal matters in Sierra Leone or any other country with a similar legal system. Judges hold their offices subject to good behavior and must retire at sixty-five. Removal of a judge is only allowed in cases of misconduct or infirmity of mind and body. Any such removal must be recommended by a three-member tribunal (appointed by the president) and approved by Parliament. Rather than go through the lengthy process of sacking judges, most presidents have been content to send them "on leave prior to retirement."

The superior courts of Sierra Leone are the Supreme Court, the Court of Appeal, and the High Court. The Supreme Court is the highest judicial body in the country and is composed of the chief justice and a minimum of four other justices. Supreme Court justices are usually appointed from the ranks of the Court of Appeal justices. To be appointed to the Supreme Court, a lawyer must have been in the legal profession for at least twenty years. The Supreme Court has original jurisdiction in such matters as the interpretation and enforcement of constitutional provisions and determining whether an executive action exceeded constitutional or parliamentary authority. Otherwise, the Supreme Court's role is largely appellate and supervisory. It supervises all other courts and is the final court of appeal. It can issue directions, orders, or writs—including writs of habeas corpus and orders of certiorari, mandamus, and prohibition. Failure to carry out or obey an order by the Supreme Court is a crime under the constitution. The Supreme Court normally hears about five to fifteen appeals a year.

Below the Supreme Court is the Court of Appeal, consisting of a chief justice and a minimum of seven justices. Three justices constitute a Court of Appeal for any given case, with the most senior judge presiding. Appellate justices are appointed from a pool of justices on the High Court bench. To be eligible for an appellate judgeship, a lawyer must have served in the legal profession for at least fifteen years. The primary function of the Court of Appeal is to hear and determine appeals from any judgment, decree, or order of the High Court or any justice. For most cases, the Court of Appeal is the final appellate body. Appeals to the court must be based on questions of law, fact, or both. As a review tribunal, the court's role is to determine whether a High Court correctly interpreted and applied the law in a given case. The court can dismiss an appeal, overturn a conviction, order a retrial, or impose an alternative sentence.

Next in the hierarchy of courts is the High Court, whose powers are original, appellate, and supervisory. The High Court comprises the chief justice and a minimum of nine High Court judges. The High Court's jurisdiction covers civil and criminal matters, industrial disputes, and administrative complaints. High Court cases are litigated before a judge and jury or, in exceptional cases, before a judge alone. The High Court hears appeals from the Magistrates' Courts and exercises supervisory jurisdiction over them. The appellate jurisdiction of the High Court covers the decisions of both trial courts and district appeal courts. The court can dismiss an appeal, overturn a conviction, order a retrial, or impose a substitute sentence. The court can also issue directions, writs, and orders, including writs of habeas corpus and orders of certiorari, mandamus, and prohibition. Six divisions (four criminal, two civil) of the court meet in the Law Courts Building in Freetown, and there is one resident High Court judge assigned to the southeast and one to the north. Unlike the Freetown High Courts, which meet in continuous session, High Court sessions in the provinces seldom exceed two or three a year.

The most common general law court in the provinces is the Magistrates' Court, which has limited jurisdiction and serves as a court of first instance in minor cases. Magistrates' Courts hear and dispose of minor criminal charges that carry a maximum prison term of three years. Proceedings in the Magistrates' Court are summary and do not require a jury. The court also has appellate jurisdiction in cases involving local courts. There are a total of fifteen Magistrates' Courts in the country, with eight in Freetown alone. Appeals from the Magistrates' Court are heard by the High Court.

Inferior to the general law courts are the local courts. Local courts have limited jurisdiction in minor offenses involving customary law. These courts cannot impose jail terms exceeding one year. They typically conduct preliminary hearings into felony charges, refer cases involving serious crimes to the High Court, and serve as appeal courts at the district level. Committal of cases to the High Court by local courts is usually based on prima facie evidence. While lawyers can appear before district appeal courts that review decisions of local courts, they have no right to appear before local courts. There are approximately 287 local customary courts in the country.

SPECIALIZED JUDICIAL BODIES

Military courts have played a key role in the prosecution of treasonable offenses. Courts-martial generally try cases involving military personnel. In 1971, for example, a court-martial found some senior officers guilty of treason and sentenced four of them to death. Among those sentenced to death and executed was the former armed forces commander and Stevens ally Brig. John Bangura. In more recent times, a court-martial found thirty-four soldiers guilty of treason in 1998. Twenty-four of these officers, including a woman (Maj. Kula Samba), were subsequently executed by firing squad. Two of the executed officers, Brig. Hassan Conteh and Col. Max Kanga, were former chief of defense staff and chief of army staff, respectively.

In the wake of the RUF's abduction of UN peacekeepers in May 2000, the Security Council of the United Nations reached an agreement in principle to establish a special court for Sierra Leone. The purpose of the international tribunal, which would apply both international law and Sierra Leone law, is to prosecute individuals responsible for gross human rights abuses. UN funding for this tribunal remains uncertain due to the preference of the United States for voluntary contributions, as opposed to membership assessments, to pay for the court.

STAFFING

The mass exodus of judges and prosecutors after the May 1997 AFRC coup has left the judicial branch of government undermanned. Lack of basic security remains the biggest obstacle to the administration of justice in Sierra Leone. No High Court judge, for example, has been assigned to the provinces since 1997. Despite the many problems that bedevil its legal system, Sierra Leone can still boast of having some of the finest judges and legal minds in West Africa.

Judges are selected by the president on the advice of the JLSC and subject to parliamentary approval. Members of the JLSC include the chief justice (who serves as chair), the most senior justice on the Court of Appeal, the solicitor general, one practicing attorney nominated by the Sierra Leone Bar Association and appointed by the president, the chair of the Public Service Commission, and two persons appointed from outside the legal profession by the president and approved by Parliament. In addition to its role in the appointment of judges, the JLSC appoints, promotes, and dismisses judicial and legal officers. The latter category includes the administrator and registrar general, the registrar and deputy registrar of the Supreme Court, magistrates, state counsels, and customary law officers. The majority of judges, prosecutors, and private attorneys were trained abroad, mainly in England, but the recent establishment of a law school at Fourah Bay College, University of Sierra Leone, is likely to change this pattern in the future. Although there are competent investigators in police departments, prosecutions are hampered by the absence of forensic and fingerprint experts.

IMPACT OF LAW

The complete breakdown of law and order in Sierra Leone during the second half of the 1990s has left the country's institutions in a state of disrepair and collapse. While the average Sierra Leonean is generally law-abiding, a culture of lawlessness seems to have taken hold of large segments of society, especially among the youth, since the onset of the RUF insurgency. The blanket amnesty granted to the RUF undermined the integrity of the judicial system and endangered the lives of ordinary civilians. Restoring the regulative capacity and integrity of institutions such as the judiciary would depend on the government's ability to protect its citizens and prosecute those who have committed heinous crimes against innocent civilians. Unless the protective capacity of the state is restored and the blanket amnesty granted to the RUF rescinded, lawlessness and impunity will continue to make a mockery of the country's judicial system.

Jimmy Kandeh

See also Common Law; Customary Law; Legal Pluralism
References and further reading
Daramy, Sheikh Batu. 1993. *Constitutional Developments in the Post-Colonial State of Sierra Leone.* New York: Edwin Mellen.
Thompson, Bankole. 1996. *The Constitutional History and Law of Sierra Leone.* Lanham, MD: University Press of America.

———. 1998. *The Criminal Law of Sierra Leone.* Lanham, MD: University Press of America.

SINGAPORE

COUNTRY INFORMATION

The Republic of Singapore is situated in Southeast Asia, just at the southern tip of the peninsula of Malaya in the Straits of Johor. It is bounded by the Indonesian islands of Sumatra, the Riau islands, and, to the east, the island of Borneo (or Kalimantan). Singapore lies approximately 137 kilometers north of the equator. Being in the equatorial rain forest belt, and subject to two wet monsoon seasons each year from June to September and from December to March, its climate is naturally very warm and humid for most of the year. Temperatures range from 70° F to 90° F, and the average humidity is about 84 percent, but sometimes reaches almost 100 percent. It comprises the main island of Singapore and some sixty-three offshore islands. It has a total land area of 660 square kilometers, and a population of some 3.9 million people, which includes 3.2 million citizens and permanent residents and some 0.7 million guest workers, primarily from countries in the region. The country's citizens have traditionally settled in the country from China, the Indian subcontinent, Malaysia, and Indonesia. The Malays, who are regarded as the indigent people, being the earliest settlers, form only 14 percent of the resident population, whereas the largest group are of Chinese descent, consisting of almost 77 percent of the population. The Indian group comprises almost 8 percent and others just over 1 percent of the population. The large influx of Chinese reflects the immigration patterns of the first century of the country's existence, since it was founded by Sir Thomas Stamford Raffles in 1819 as a strategically located trading station to enhance British interests in the region. Although Malay is the national language, Singapore has four official languages: English, Chinese (Mandarin), Malay, and Tamil (the main language of the Indian population). Any of the four languages may be spoken in Parliament, and all four are adequately represented in local television and radio broadcasts. However, English remains the language of administration, the law, and the courts, and is the preferred language of education in the schools and universities. It is government policy, however, that every member of an ethnic group should study English as well as his or her mother tongue, so as to be bilingual. It is a fundamental creed that Singapore should be regarded as a multiracial and multicultural society, and not as a third China. The desire of each ethnic group to maintain its own particular identity is officially respected, and no attempt is made to develop a melting pot society. It is a mul-

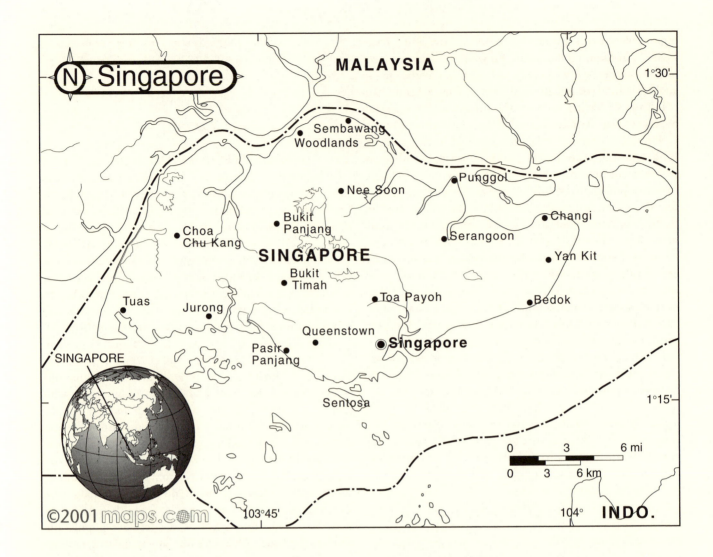

tireligious society as there is no establishment of any religion, and the constitution (Article 15) guarantees to every person the right to profess, practice, and propagate his religion. No one religion is dominant, but Singapore's main religions are Buddhism, Taoism, Islam, Christianity (including Catholicism), and Hinduism.

HISTORY

Much of Singapore's ancient history can only be traced to fragmentary written records (Turnbull 1977, 1). The first evidence of a settlement dates from the fourteenth century. A Javanese writing of 1365 named a town called Temasek (Sea Town) on Singapore island, and Singapore was claimed by the Majapahit Empire as a vassal state. Its Sanskrit name, Singapura (Lion City), was used to refer to it by the end of the fourteenth century. It is probable that a small Malay dependency of the Srivijaya Empire existed at Temasek, and many of the inhabitants were pirates in the region. About 1390, Iskandar Shah (Parameswara), a prince of Palembang, installed himself as ruler of Singapore before he was driven north, and Singapore became a vassal state of Siam (now Thailand) in the fifteenth century. Then the Malacca sultanate, founded by Iskandar, extended its authority over Singapore, until the Portuguese were said to have destroyed the sultanate's capital at Johor Lama in 1587. However, Singapore was left alone with only the presence of sea nomads and other indigenous people from the Riau-Lingga archipelago, until the reestablishment of the Johor Empire. There is little information on settlements in Singapore apart from these indigenous inhabitants and the entourage of the sultan's senior minister, the Temenggong, whose fiefdom included Singapore. When Raffles established a trading station in Singapore by an agreement on behalf of the East India Company (EIC) with the Johor sultanate in 1819, there were probably a thousand inhabitants, mostly the indigenous people, the Temenggong's entourage, and some Chinese settlers (Turnbull 1977, 5). In 1824 Singapore was ceded in perpetuity to the EIC by the sultan.

In 1826, Singapore became part of the Presidency of the Straits Settlements with Malacca and Penang, and was for many years under the jurisdiction of the British government in India. In 1867, Singapore became, with Malacca and Penang, a separate Crown colony of the

Straits Settlements. Little change took place until after World War II, when nationalism prompted the loosening of the shackles of the British Empire. In 1946, Penang and Malacca were joined to the nine Malay states in the peninsula of Malaya to form the Malayan Union, while Singapore was, with its dependencies, administered as the Colony of Singapore. Singapore received its first constitution (an order-in-council promulgated by the British government) on the recommendation of a Constitutional Commission chaired by Sir George Rendel. Singapore received its first legislative assembly, with a majority of elected members, and the first cabinet was introduced with a Council of Ministers. In 1958, the government of the United Kingdom promulgated another new constitution for Singapore, providing for full internal self-government, with a fully elected legislative assembly, but reserving control over defense and external affairs and partial control over internal security, with a power to suspend the constitution by proclamation. The elected government of 1959, with a chief minister and a constitutional head, a British governor, was drawn from the majority party then, the People's Action Party, which still remains the party in power today, after having been continuously reelected in nine successive general elections from 1963 to 1997. Constitutional talks involving the governments of the U.K., Malaya, the state of Singapore, and the Borneo territories (Sabah and Sarawak) resulted in a new Federation of Malaysia with the blessings of the U.K. government on September 16, 1963. Differences between the government of the state of Singapore and the federal government, however, resulted in Singapore being compelled to secede from the federation and become an independent and sovereign nation on August 9, 1965.

The first years of Singapore's independence were turbulent years. Not long after Singapore's independence, the U.K. government announced that it would be gradually withdrawing its armed forces stationed in Singapore and the region. Singapore, having to make its own defense arrangements, initiated a scheme of compulsory national service of two years or more for every male citizen of eighteen years of age, to make up for the lack of a military force. It still has armed forces whose members are largely reservists. As for internal security, the government decided that it would retain the Internal Security Act first enacted for the Federation of Malaysia, and which provided for detention without trial of persons suspected by the president, acting on cabinet advice, of subversive activities. This legislation was considered necessary to contain the threat of communist subversion, which had been regarded as a menace in Malaysia and Singapore from the late 1940s. Although the act has been criticized as inconsistent with the rule of law, the government has no present intention of revoking it, for it considers it necessary to deal with new forms of threats

to security, such as the incitement of racial or religious strife, which are anathema in a multiracial society. The legislature has also found it necessary to protect Singapore's sovereignty by amending the constitution (Article 6) so that any attempt by a government to relinquish sovereignty over the armed forces or police, or to form a political union with another country or territory, will require a two-thirds majority of all the electors in the state in a referendum (plebiscite). Singapore's economy depends primarily on external trade and industry, as it has few natural resources. The economy has been growing steadily, and in 1999 Singapore registered a GDP (gross domestic product) of almost S$144 billion. It is now regarded as a developed nation with large accumulated foreign reserves. Thus the legislature in 1990 provided for an elected president with, inter alia, a veto power over any future government's attempt to spend reserves not accumulated during its current term of office, in order to protect the reserves from being dissipated.

LEGAL CONCEPTS

Singapore has a common law legal system, with a written constitution that is declared to be the supreme law of the republic (Article 4). There is a bill of rights in the constitution, containing fundamental liberties such as liberty of the person, the rights to a lawyer and to know the grounds of arrest, protection against double jeopardy and retrospective criminal laws, equal protection, and the civil liberties of free speech, assembly, and association. Most rights are limited and may be restricted on specified grounds. However, two rights are absolute: freedom from slavery and the freedom of citizens from banishment.

Singapore inherited a parliamentary system of government, based on the U.K.'s so-called Westminster model. In it, there is a constitutional head of state, the president, who is required to act on the advice of the cabinet led by a prime minister (constitution, Article 21) and an elected Parliament, from whose majority party or coalition of parties the ministers are appointed by the prime minister (Article 25) and who are collectively responsible to Parliament (Article 24). The president appoints as prime minister the person who in his judgment is likely to command the confidence of the majority of the members of Parliament (Article 25). Singapore also has a written constitution, based loosely on the original state constitution of 1963, but with some concepts borrowed from the constitution of Malaysia, which had itself drawn from the experience of both the U.S. and India. It is a unitary state, with a strong central government, and by reason of its small size, with no local governments, except for town councils created with limited powers (under a Town Councils Act) to manage large new towns or residential estates. By Article 4, the constitution is stated to be the supreme law of Singapore and any law passed by the legislature inconsistent with it shall be void to the extent of the inconsistency.

The president is elected by citizens for a term of six years, and must be at least forty-five years of age, and not be a member of any political party. The qualifications are strict, and, if he has not held a specified office by which he would automatically qualify, he must be certified by a Presidential Elections Committee to have "such experience and ability in administering and managing financial affairs" as to enable him to carry out his duties and functions as president (Article 19[2][g][iv]). The primary reason for these unusual requirements was that the president had to be seen to be independent of the ruling government, and able to apply wisely his veto powers over the government's proposed expenditure of reserves accumulated by a previous government. He is also given a veto power over important or key appointments proposed by the government to protect the integrity of the public services and institutions from government cronyism. In all his duties, the constitution provides for a Council of Presidential Advisors to advise him. Apart from his veto powers, however, his role is a passive one, and he may not take the initiative in government, being a constitutional head of state, such as the queen in the U.K.

Parliament is unicameral in nature, and comprises members elected for a term of five years. Candidates must be at least twenty-one years old and not disqualified by bankruptcy or recent criminal convictions. Initially, every member was elected in a single-member constituency, as was the system in the U.K. However, recent inroads have been made by amending the constitution to embrace different kinds of members. Parliament may now be constituted from:

a. Single-member constituencies;
b. Group representation constituencies (GRCs);
c. Nominated members (NMPs); and
d. Nonconstituency members (NCMPs).

The first two categories are elected. However, single-member constituencies are few in number now, there having been only nine such constituencies in the last general election of 1997. The vast majority of members belong to GRCs or multiparty constituencies of four to six members at present. These were created to ensure the minority representation in Parliament of at least one member, being either Malay or Indian, in each. Members elected in GRCs must either all belong to one party or all be independents, and so are elected as a team. NMPs may number up to nine, and are in fact appointed by the president on nomination by a special select committee of Parliament. They must be nonpartisan and have distinguished themselves in public service, a profession, or some other field of endeavor. NCMPs are few, if any, and

are intended to supply a minimum number of opposition members from among the best losing candidates. None may be appointed if there are sufficient numbers of elected opposition members.

Parliament passes bills, which become law when they receive the assent of the president (Article 58). However, in the law-making process, every bill (with a few exceptions) must, on its final reading, be sent by the speaker to the Presidential Council for Minority Rights, who has the power to scrutinize the bill and report to Parliament if it contains what, in its opinion, is a "differentiating measure," namely one that affects a racial or religious community by being disadvantageous to them or advantageous to other communities. This provision is to ensure there is equal protection of the law in racial and religious matters. If there is no such "adverse report" received within thirty days, the bill may receive the president's assent and becomes law.

The separation of powers in the organs of government is reflected in the framework of the constitution. By Article 23, the executive authority of Singapore is vested in the president although it is exercisable by the cabinet or the prime minister. By Article 38, the legislative power is vested in the legislature, which shall consist of the Parliament and the president. In Article 93, the judicial power is vested in a Supreme Court and such subordinate courts as may be provided by written laws in force.

The Supreme Court consists of the court of appeal and the High Court (Article 94). Its jurisdiction and powers are provided for in the constitution and in the Supreme Court of Judicature Act. The court of appeal is the highest court of appeal, and hears appeals from the High Court in both civil and criminal matters. The chief justice and two judges of appeal constitute it, although a High Court judge may be appointed to sit on an appeal in the court of appeal. The High Court consists of the chief justice and the judges of the High Court. A High Court judge sits alone in all trials, even in capital cases, as juries have been abolished. A High Court hears civil and criminal cases, in its original jurisdiction in all matters where the subordinate courts do not have jurisdiction, and also hears all appeals from the subordinate courts. In addition, the High Court possesses "general supervisory and revisionary jurisdiction over all subordinate courts" (Supreme Court of Judicature Act, sec. 27) to ensure that they have acted correctly and legally. In the context of this act, subordinate court is defined (sec. 2) to include not only the five types of subordinate courts that have judicial power, but also any other court, tribunal, or quasi-judicial body from which there is a (statutory) right of appeal to the Supreme Court. Only High Court judges have the power to call for the records of inferior courts and tribunals and to issue prerogative writs or orders like certiorari, mandamus, and habeas corpus.

Legal Structure of Singapore Courts

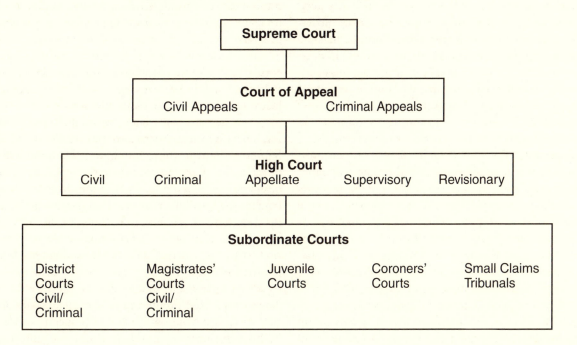

According to the Subordinate Courts Act (section 3), there are five subordinate courts. These are:

- District Courts
- Magistrates' Courts
- Juvenile Courts
- Coroners' Courts
- Small Claims Tribunals

The administrative head of the entire judiciary is the chief justice. The senior district judge is the head of the subordinate courts. Both district and magistrates' courts have jurisdiction to hear civil and criminal cases, the district court having the more extensive jurisdiction. In general, it may impose a term of imprisonment of seven years, a fine of up to S$10,000, or caning of up to twelve strokes (for male offenders). A Magistrates' Court may, however, only impose a term of two years' imprisonment, a fine of up to S$2,000, and caning of up to six strokes. In civil cases, the district court may hear disputes where the subject matter does not exceed S$250,000. A Magistrates' Court's jurisdiction is limited to a claim of S$60,000. Small claims tribunals were established in February 1985 to provide a quick and inexpensive forum for the alternative resolution of small disputes between consumers and suppliers, and to enhance access to justice. The procedure is set out in the Small Claims Tribunals Act (1996). In general, a claim must not exceed S$10,000 relating to a dispute arising from a contract for the sale of goods, a contract for the provision of services, or tortious damage to property (excluding damage from motor vehi-

cle accidents). The jurisdiction can be raised to S$20,000 if the parties agree to it in writing. The procedure for claims is kept simple, and lawyers are not permitted to represent any of the parties. A small fee is charged for lodgment of a claim. A registrar of the subordinate courts will conduct a mediation or consultation session, and if a hearing is needed, a referee will be appointed to conduct the hearing. The possibility of settlement is always explored before a hearing. Claims by tourists may be heard within twenty-four hours; otherwise hearings will be conducted within two weeks from the date of lodgment of the claim. The system has proved popular, some 40,760 claims having been lodged in the year 2000, an increase over the year 1999, when 39,117 claims were lodged (*Subordinate Courts Annual Report* 2000).

Various methods of nonlitigious settlement of disputes are now employed in the subordinate courts over a wide spectrum of matters, besides the small claims tribunals. In March 1995, the family court was set up in the subordinate courts, and is presided over by a district judge. He hears applications for divorce, ancillary applications like maintenance, custody of children, protection from domestic violence, and adoption. The family court also provides special services such as a legal clinic and a hospital referral service for applicants applying for personal protection. Parties are encouraged to resolve their disputes through mediation, including negotiation. The Primary Dispute Resolution Center has been set up in the subordinate courts, headed by a district judge. Its aim is to provide a forum for disputants to explore various options with a view to resolving their disputes without formal adjudication, and consequently more expeditiously and cheaply. The services offered by the center are court-initiated and conducted without charge. They cover mediation in civil cases, family matters, small claims, juvenile matters, and complaints to magistrates (of alleged criminal conduct). The center trains and manages a pool of volunteers, comprising specially trained court interpreters, lawyers, professional social workers, and counselors.

The Supreme Court and subordinate courts alone share judicial power, namely the power to make final and authoritative decisions involving disputes between individuals or between individuals and the state. All other courts and tribunals are not part of the system of courts with judicial power. These include courts-martial and the Military Court of Appeal, which has jurisdiction over military or armed forces personnel only, and the industrial arbitration court, which hears industrial disputes between employers and employees, and may also hear trade union representatives of employees. However, legal representation of any party is not permitted at such a hearing. There are also numerous administrative tribunals set up by statute (act of Parliament), and domestic tribunals to adjudicate on the rights of members of clubs and professional or other associations on disciplinary matters or members' disputes. They will be required merely to conduct their hearings fairly and according to the rules of natural justice, unless there are detailed procedures set out for them to follow under the statute or particular association's constitution, which will prevail. There are hearings of claims for workmen's compensation under the Workmen's Compensation Act; appeals boards (which may sit with assessors) to hear appeals by parties aggrieved by awards of compensation made for acquisition of land under the Land Acquisition Act; and a board of review under the Income Tax Act to hear appeals against assessments or other decisions of the comptroller of income tax.

There are also some specialized judicial bodies. The constitution (Article 100) provides for a constitutional tribunal to be set up consisting of not less than three Supreme Court judges to whom any matter of interpretation of the constitution may be referred for an advisory opinion. Such opinion may not be questioned in any court. So far, one such opinion had been sought, in 1995, by the previous president of Singapore. In matrimonial and related matters, as well as division of property including estates, involving Muslims, only the *sharia* court and its appeals board have jurisdiction. Under the Administration of Muslim Law Act, the *sharia* court applies Muslim law in those matters coming within its jurisdiction. Its jurisdiction is separate from, but concurrent with, that of the ordinary courts (Chan 1995).

The higher court judiciary enjoys a high degree of judicial independence. Judges of the Supreme Court possess security of tenure under the constitution, whereas subordinate court judges have the same limited tenure as other public servants who belong to the legal service as provided in the constitution. The president appoints Supreme Court judges if he, acting in his discretion, concurs with the advice of the prime minister, who is to consult the chief justice (Article 95). Once appointed, a judge remains in office until the age of sixty-five, and may not be removed except after reference for alleged misbehavior or inability to a tribunal of five judges of the Supreme Court or those who have held equivalent office in the British Commonwealth, and a report by them recommending his removal. In addition, his office may not be abolished and his remuneration cannot be altered to his disadvantage. However, the constitution provides for the appointment of judicial commissioners for such a period as the president thinks fit. This provision was intended for short-term appointments to clear the court's backlog of cases, and to alleviate the shortage of judges. There is no fixed number of judges or judicial commissioners (apart from the judges of appeal). In the year 2000, two-thirds of the High Court was composed of judges, and one-third judicial commissioners.

Singapore has a common law system with an adversary system of justice, derived from its British colonial heritage. It is generally agreed that English law (as it stood in 1826) was received in Singapore by a royal charter, known as the Second Charter of Justice. The application of English law was, however, subject to such modifications as might be necessary to suit local conditions and to prevent it operating in an unjust or oppressive manner on the inhabitants. The applicable law at the time included English statutes. However, English statutes no longer apply except as provided by the Application of English Law Act, and tend primarily to concern commercial law matters. Both common law and equity continue to apply in Singapore subject to modifications to suit local circumstances. There used to be an almost slavish reliance on English judicial precedents, partly due to the English training that lawyers here had received. However, with a far larger number of graduates from Singapore's (only) law school (founded in 1956) and an increasing body of statutes passed by the Singapore legislature, a more distinctly local jurisprudence is developing, which makes one optimistic about the development of an autochthonous Singapore legal system—indigenous and homogenous in nature—in the near future.

Lawyers serve society in a number of ways. They may be admitted to private legal practice as "advocates and solicitors," as the legal profession is a fused one. They may work in the public sector for the Singapore Legal Service in some capacity such as prosecutors, subordinate court judges, court registrars, or legal aid counsel. They may be employed as advisors in various government ministries, departments, or public corporations. They may be academic lawyers. Many work for banks and corporations. Several are qualified to be, and are engaged as, arbitrators in commercial disputes. An increasing number are involved in mediation, whether as lawyers or as mediators.

The regulation of the legal profession in Singapore is provided in the Legal Profession Act (1997). In order to practice law as an advocate and solicitor, one must be one of the following:

- a graduate of the law school of the national university of Singapore
- a graduate of one of 15 U.K. law schools
- a graduate of 1 of 4 Australian or 2 New Zealand law schools
- a Hong Kong practitioner
- a Malaysian practitioner
- a barrister or solicitor of England and Wales before a certain cutoff date (1996)

In addition, such graduates from abroad will have to read for a diploma in law at the local law school, and all would-be practitioners will do a postgraduate practical course. The Board of Legal Education created by the Legal Profession Act has power to exempt applicants from certain of the requirements. Lawyers in foreign law firms based in Singapore may not advise on Singapore law. Foreign lawyers may be admitted to appear in court in Singapore on an ad hoc basis. The requirements for practice are restrictive, not open, in the belief that it is necessary to achieve and maintain a high quality of legal services in Singapore. Having only one law school in a nation of almost 4 million, which may produce qualified persons locally, highlights the restrictions in the profession. There are at present some 4,000 lawyers in legal practice.

IMPACT OF LAW

Efficiency and credibility in the administration of justice is regarded as of fundamental importance in a country where many multinational companies and foreign investors are based. So far, Singapore has fared well in public opinion on the efficient and speedy disposal of cases, both in the subordinate courts and the Supreme Court. The courts are also widely seen as wholly free of corrupt practices. The courts have a good reputation for impartiality and transparency in the judicial process. Singapore, in relation to its system of justice and law enforcement, has also been consistently ranked favorably as a low-risk country (PERC 2000). Mediation procedures also enhance access to justice outside the conventional court system.

Singapore's adherence to the rule of law is generally good in the Southeast Asian region. The existence of de-

tention without trial and the lack of success of opposition parties to make a significant impact in general elections do not detract substantially from the rule of law. Singapore is not a signatory to the two United Nations Covenants on Human Rights, and did not implement a recommendation of the Constitutional Commission (1966) to include in the constitution a fundamental right not to be subjected to torture or inhuman or degrading treatment. Likely reasons are the reliance on capital punishment (by hanging) or corporal punishment (caning), which the courts are required to impose in a variety of offenses. Amnesty International and some other human rights agencies have voiced concern over the frequent recourse by cabinet ministers or ruling party members to bringing civil defamation suits to obtain high awards of damages against individuals from other political parties. Such recourse may tend to have a chilling effect on freedom of expression in the state.

Valentine S. Winslow

See also Administrative Tribunals; Adversarial Systems; Alternative Dispute Resolution; Appellate Courts; Capital Punishment; Common Law; Constitutionalism; Corporal Punishment; Judicial Independence; Legal Education; Mediation; Small Claims Courts; Solicitors; Trial Courts

References and further reading
Chan, Helena H. M. 1995. *The Legal System of Singapore.* Singapore: Butterworths.
Constitution of the Republic of Singapore. 1999. Reprint. Singapore: The Government Printer.
Phang Boon Leong, Andrew. 1990. *The Development of Singapore Law.* Singapore: Butterworths.
Political and Economic Risk Consultancy, Ltd. 2000. *Comparative Country Risk Report.*
Report of the Constitutional Commission. 1966. Singapore: Government Printer.
Singapore Facts and Pictures 2000. Singapore: Ministry of Information and the Arts.
Subordinate Courts Annual Report 2000. Singapore: Subordinate Courts.
Turnbull, Constance Mary. 1977. *A History of Singapore, 1819–1975.* Kuala Lumpur: Oxford University Press.
Winslow, Valentine S. 1992. "The Constitution of the Republic of Singapore." Pp. 627–654 in *Constitutional Systems in Late Twentieth Century Asia.* Edited by Lawrence W. Beer. Seattle: University of Washington Press.

SLOVAKIA

GENERAL INFORMATION

The Slovak Republic, commonly known as Slovakia, is in Central Europe, bordered by Austria, Hungary, Ukraine, Poland, and the Czech Republic. Its territory of roughly 49,000 square kilometers is composed of plains in the west and east and mountains in the north. The capital is Bratislava. Other major cities include Kosice, Banska

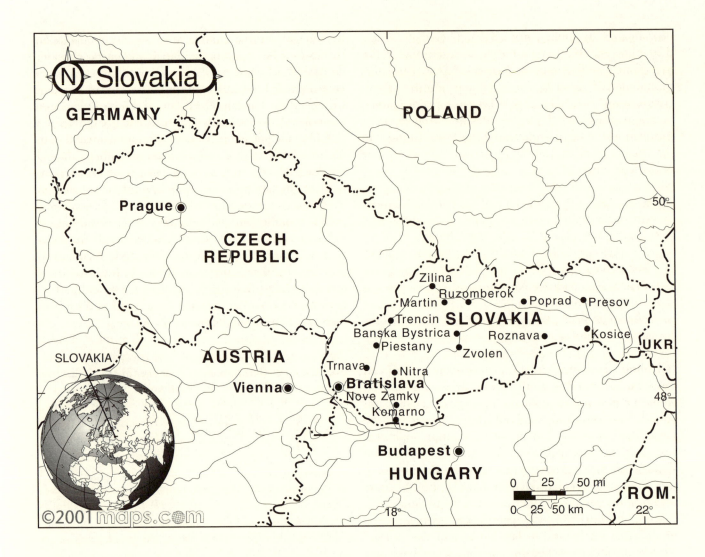

Bystrica, and Nitra. Of the country's 5.4 million inhabitants, about 85 percent are ethnic Slovaks and more than 10 percent ethnic Hungarians; the remainder of the population is made up primarily of Czechs (who are ethnically and linguistically related to Slovaks) and Roma. The largest religious group is Roman Catholics; there are also significant numbers of Protestants, Greek Catholics, Eastern Orthodox, and Jews. The official language is Slovak, but other languages, in particular Hungarian in the south, are also spoken.

Following World War II, as part of Czechoslovakia during the communist era, Slovakia experienced considerable industrialization and urbanization. In the late 1980s, the collapse of communism and the dissolution of the Soviet Union, which had provided a steady market, exposed the inefficiency of Slovakia's defense-oriented industrial base. Since 1993, as an independent state, Slovakia has continued the difficult transition from a centrally planned economy to a free-market economy. Among the problems it inherited from the communist era are derelict factories, an unconsolidated banking sector, official corruption, and considerable debt. Since 1998, the govern-

ment under Prime Minister Mikulas Dzurinda has addressed many of these problems by privatizing the banking sector, cutting the deficit, and attracting foreign investment. Nevertheless, unemployment has remained high, at about 20 percent in 2001.

HISTORY

The Slavic ancestors of present-day Slovaks settled in the very center of Europe, between the Carpathian Mountains and the Danube River, around the fifth century. In the seventh century, under Samo, they established the first important Slavic state organization. In the ninth century, Slovakia formed part of the Great Moravian Empire, which also included parts of modern Hungary, Austria, the Czech Republic, and Poland. Under the rule of the Moravian duke Rastislav, Saints Cyril and Methodius introduced Christianity. At the beginning of the tenth century, Moravia fell to the Hungarians, who created a new state, Hungary, in the Carpathian basin. For the next 900 years, Slovakia was an integral part of Hungary.

At the end of the fifteenth century, the trend of the economic growth was weakened by the expansion of the

Ottoman Empire. After the Ottoman Empire victory over Louis II of Hungary (1526), Slovakia fell under Habsburg rule and was incorporated into Habsburg's multinational central European empire. In 1536, Bratislava became the capital city of old Hungary and played an important political role, until Hungary was finally freed from the Turks in the late seventeenth century. In the eighteenth century, Maria Teresa and Joseph II formed the basis of modern state administration, a tax and transportation system, social and school reform, and finally pursued religious freedom. However, due to the intensification of Germanization policy, a Slovak national revival grew steadily in the first half of the nineteenth century. This movement, led by Ludovit Stur, formulated in 1848 a set of demands for the political and linguistic rights of Slovaks. The first Slovak representative political body—Slovak National Council—was created and its members attempted, through cooperation with Austria, to incorporate Slovakia as an autonomous country into the federal system of the Habsburg monarchy.

In 1867, to strengthen his position after several military defeats, the Habsburg emperor Francis Joseph effected a compromise with the Hungarian gentry. The Austro-Hungarian Empire was established under a common ruler, a common foreign policy, and, to some extent, common finances. However, Austria and Hungary remained independent states, each having its own parliament, administration, and judicial system based on the tradition of continental law. In 1868, the Nationalities Act, passed by the Hungarian parliament, established Hungarian as the exclusive official language of Hungary. Election laws restricted the right to vote to large property holders, who comprised only about 6 percent of the population. As a result, Slovaks were rarely elected to parliament. The Hungarian government took steps to undermine a building Slovak national movement. In 1874, it closed all three Slovak secondary schools, and in 1879, it passed a law making the Hungarian language mandatory in church-sponsored primary schools. At the beginning of the twentieth century, about 20 percent of the population emigrated to other countries, particularly the United States, which hence gave the Slovak independence movement considerable support during World War I.

As the Habsburg Empire collapsed toward the end of the war, many of its constituent nationalities agitated for independence. In May 1918, Czech and Slovak patriots signed the Pittsburgh Declaration, which provided for a common state of Czechs and Slovaks. According to the terms of the declaration, Slovakia would retain broad autonomy, with its own government institutions and with Slovak as an official language. On October 28, 1918, the Czecho-Slovak National Committee proclaimed the existence of Czech-Slovakia, with full support from the United States, England, France, and Italy. Two days later,

the Slovak National Council declared the aspiration of Slovaks to join in a common state with Czechs.

To maintain legal continuity, the new state adopted a statute making Austrian and Hungarian laws the basis of its legal order. This did not, however, create a unitary legal system, for Austrian imperial law applied in the Czech lands and the Hungarian Crown law applied in Slovakia. This legal dualism posed great difficulties, and harmonization of the legal order was achieved only much later, in the communist era, with the establishment of socialist law.

The Czechoslovak constitution of 1920 was primarily inspired by the constitutions of the European democracies, especially the French constitution. The 1920 constitution established a separation of powers in a parliamentary democracy featuring a two-chamber parliament, a weak presidency, and a cabinet responsible to the parliament. It also provided for an independent judiciary.

Relations between Czechs and Slovaks were on the one hand influenced by the concept of a common Czechoslovak nation including both Czechs and Slovaks. On the other hand, the most popular political party in Slovakia, the Slovak People's Party led by Andrej Hlinka, criticized the situation, in which the National Assembly in Prague made all key political decisions and Slovaks had no right to any form of regional self-government. The Czechoslovak republic was politically weakened in October 1938 by the terms of the Munich treaty between Germany and Great Britain, and in March 1939, when the German army marched into Prague, it ceased to exist. On March 14, the autonomous Slovak parliament proclaimed an independent Slovak state, with strong political, economic, and military dependence on Nazi Germany. A new Slovak constitution, permitting only three political parties, was founded on the principles of nation, Christianity, and estate. The Allied victory in 1945 restored Czechoslovakia to its territorial status before the Munich agreement. In 1948, after three years of conflict between democratic and communist political forces, parliamentary democracy was defeated and a Soviet-style regime was established. The 1948 constitution confirmed the leading role of the Communist Party within society and the Leninist principle of democratic centralism.

Although the 1948 constitution displayed some characteristics of constitutionalism, political terror and massive repression of political opponents de facto supported practical adoption of the law as an instrument of class struggle. According to the constitution, the state took control of all enterprises and private property was nationalized. Small farmers were forced to join collective farms. In July 1960, a new constitution was adopted that severely limited the autonomy of Slovakia. The liberal communist regime of Alexander Dubcek, who came to power in 1967, responded to voices demanding federalization of

Czechoslovakia. After the Soviet military invasion of Czechoslovakia in August 1968, nearly all of Dubcek's reforms were abolished. A new government, under Gustav Husak, tightened Communist Party control and press censorship. The only lasting outcome of the reform process was the constitutional law by which Czechoslovakia became a federal state.

During the years of normalization (1970–1989), the communist regime took various steps to eliminate Charter 77, the dissent movement within Czechoslovakia. According to the 1961 penal code, people participating in mass demonstrations could be punished by imprisonment of up to 15 years. In fact, the penal code generally provided that those who criticized the communist regime would be imprisoned. In November 1989, the fall of communism in the former Soviet bloc countries of Eastern Europe enabled the reestablishment of a democratic government and the restoration of civil rights and freedoms in Czechoslovakia. After the 1992 elections, representatives of the strongest political parties made the decision to separate Czechoslovakia into two sovereign nations. On January 1, 1993, the independent Slovak Republic came into being.

LEGAL CONCEPTS

The history and traditions of previous regimes are often incorporated into the political institutions of successor states. Builders of democracy in Slovakia did not have much to gain from the past, because Slovakia's only experience of statehood was a fascist puppet regime established with the assistance of Nazi Germany just before World War II. Therefore, Slovakia's constitutional history is based mainly on the 1960 Czechoslovak socialist constitution, combined with elements of the 1920 constitution.

The legal system of Slovakia is based on continental tradition and was consolidated after the fall of communism in the 1990s. Slovakia, like its predecessors, has drawn mainly on the Roman legal heritage, with systematic codification of the main areas of the law (civil, criminal, and commercial), which reflect the intent of the legislature. The main sources of law are normative rules of varying legal force. Judicial and administrative precedents are only de facto legal sources. The 1992 constitution is the supreme law of the land. The international treaties on human rights and political, military, or economic treaties of general character that directly confer rights or impose duties on natural or legal persons require the approval of the parliament before ratification. These international treaties then have precedence over domestic laws.

The 1992 constitution incorporated a slightly amended version of the Bill of Rights adopted by the Czech-Slovak Federal Assembly in 1991. Two predominant factors led to the institutionalization of the Bill of Rights. First, the communist regime had emphasized social rights, while constantly and systematically violating basic human rights and freedoms. These violations became the main target of the anticommunist opposition's criticism of the regime. When the dissidents came to power, they immediately adopted laws guaranteeing and protecting human rights. Second, international organizations, such as the Council of Europe and the Conference on Security and Cooperation in Europe, pressured postcommunist countries to adopt mechanisms to protect human rights as a prerequisite to membership. The fact that a quarter of the Slovak constitution deals with citizens' rights and freedoms demonstrates how important they were perceived to be.

The constitution divides rights into fundamental rights and freedoms, and economic, social, and cultural rights. The set of economic rights was primarily inspired by the former regime's concept of social rights, including the right to choose a profession, receive appropriate training, and work, as well as state guaranties of unemployment compensation, trade union membership, collective bargaining, and the right to strike. Social rights also include the right to free education and health care, and to welfare for the aged, the disabled, and single-parent families. These rights were meant to ensure that social security that had been provided by the previous regime would not disappear completely. Cultural rights include freedom of scientific research and artistic expression. In addition, the constitution protects national minorities and ethnic groups from discrimination and grants them the freedom to use their native languages.

The rights stipulated in the constitution are directly enforceable in court or through other state agencies as provided by law. Every citizen has the right to recover damages for a loss caused by an unlawful decision of a court. Social and economic rights, however, may be claimed only within the limits of the law. Consequently, the rights related to social security and welfare, including the right to strike, are not only limited but also are subject to change through legislation. Furthermore, certain basic freedoms also can be restricted, in cases specified by the law. Freedom of movement, expression, assembly, and the right to information may be restricted to protect the freedom of others, state security, law and order, health, and morality.

STRUCTURE

The 1992 constitution is the basis for the structure of the legal system. It was enacted by the parliament, called the National Council, on September 1, 1992. Slovakia is a unitary state with a parliamentary democracy, in which formal rules place parliament at the center of power, while informal rules allow the executive to take effective control of governance. The National Council is a uni-

Legal Structure of Slovakia Courts

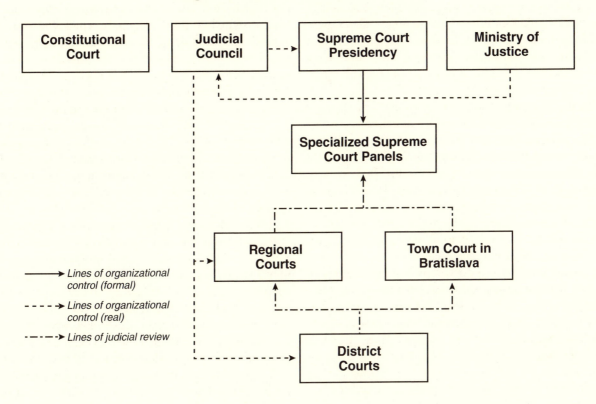

cameral chamber with 150 members, proportionally elected by universal suffrage to four-year terms. The composition of the government reflects the political representation in parliament. The government is collectively responsible, and the ministers are individually responsible, to parliament.

Bills may be proposed by deputies, parliamentary committees, and the cabinet. The National Council may pass constitutional acts with the consent of three-fifths of its members; all other laws require consent by a majority vote. The acts must be consistent with the constitution and constitutional laws. Executive decrees and ministry regulations may be issued only under explicit delegation granted by ordinary law. No other body has authority to pass laws, apart from local authorities, which may issue local ordinances. The president's role in the legislative process consists only of a right of veto, which the parliament can overturn simply by passing the bill again.

Relative to the power of parliament, the executive branch, as stipulated in the constitution, is rather weak. The cabinet is constitutionally made responsible to the legislature. Therefore, its life depends very much on the political party in power and on the extent of party discipline. The president is the head of the Slovak Republic. The president's powers are largely but not wholly ceremonial. The president appoints the prime minister, may initiate proceedings in the Constitutional Court, and

may dissolve parliament in circumstances laid down by the constitution. A 1999 constitutional amendment provides for direct election of the president. A referendum may be held on matters of local and national importance.

In the system of normative legal rules, the general binding principle prevails. A rule of a lower legal force must be consistent with the rule of a higher legal force. A legal rule can be derogated or abrogated only by another rule, provided it has the same or higher legal force. The Constitutional Court exercises judicial review over the laws, governmental regulations, generally binding regulations of ministries, and generally binding regulations of local bodies of the state administration or territorial self-administration. According to the constitution, an individual may enforce his or her rights under a fixed procedure before an independent and impartial court.

Courts with general and special jurisdiction exercise judicial power. The courts of general jurisdiction rule on civil and criminal matters, handle disputes under the commercial code, and review the legitimacy of decisions made by bodies of public administration and the legality of decisions, measures, or other actions of bodies of public authority, if laid down by law. The system of state courts consists of the Supreme Court of the Slovak Republic (*Najvyssi Sud*), regional courts (*krajske sudy*), and district courts (*okresne sudy*). Town Court in Bratislava is at the level of the regional court.

There are also military courts, military district courts, and a higher military court, which have jurisdiction over all actions of soldiers during military duty and over other organized military corps if a special law is determined for it. The military courts also have jurisdiction over some criminal actions of civilians, such as their involvement with a foreign army or forms of treason.

Slovakia has a two-instance court system. The appeal is the only regular legal remedy against judgment of the first instance. The devolutionary effect of the appeal fully applies in Slovak law, that is, the contested decision of a lower court will be resolved by the superior court. In such cases, appeals of district court decisions are referred to the regional court of territorial jurisdiction, and first-instance decisions of regional courts are resolved by the Supreme Court as the court of second instance. Decisions are made by a bench (senate) or by a single judge in certain cases specified by law. The law specifies in which cases lay judges from the general citizenry shall participate in the decision making of the senate. Lay judges are elected to four-year terms. Judges are independent and decide cases according to the constitution, constitutional law, international treaties, and statutory law. Court hearings are public, and person involved in legal proceedings have the right to use their mother tongue. Any person charged with a criminal offense is presumed innocent until proven guilty. Accused persons have the right to counsel and may choose their own counsel or request free legal assistance, as provided by law.

New procedures for alternative dispute resolution are coming along slowly. The civil procedure code enables parties to file a proposal of conciliation upon arbitration with the locally competent court. Arbitration proceedings in Slovakia have a long-standing tradition: before 1990, arbitration was the only legal means to resolve commercial disputes. Presently, however, the law has been amended to permit reaching a resolution through one or more appointed arbitrators in mutual business relations. No decisions can be made in arbitration proceedings in disputes concerning inception, change, and expiration of rights to real estate, status contests, and enforcement of decision. Alternative dispute settlements are not allowed in criminal matters.

The Constitutional Court of the Slovak Republic is an independent judicial body charged with ensuring the constitutionality of legislation, government decrees, and other generally binding legal rules and international agreements. It exercises control over the legality of legislative acts and reviews all decisions taken by administrative bodies that violate the fundamental rights and freedoms of individuals, if no other court can decide about the protection of their rights and freedoms. According to a 2001 amendment to the constitution, the court can also award financial compensation to one whose rights have been infringed.

The Constitutional Court decides jurisdictional disputes between central administrative authorities and reviews disputed decisions of central and local government authorities. In addition, it has final say in interpreting the constitution and constitutional laws and reviews decisions ordering the dissolution or suspension of a political party or political movement (when such orders are not in agreement with constitutional or other laws).

The court is composed of thirteen judges, each appointed for a twelve-year term, without possibility of reappointment. The president appoints half of the candidates nominated by parliament as judges for the court. The court can suspend the effect of challenged legal regulations if they threaten fundamental rights and freedoms or if they risk causing serious economic damage or other dangerous consequences. When the court declares a law unconstitutional, the law immediately becomes fully or partly ineffective and, after six months, invalid.

SPECIALIZED JUDICIAL BODIES

A constitutional amendment in 2001 introduced the office of ombudsman. The ombudsman, to be elected by parliament, will help protect fundamental rights and freedoms from being infringed on by the activities and decisions of public administrative bodies, in cases where such actions may be inconsistent with legal order and the rule of law. The details of the election procedure for and the scope of the ombudsman's powers have yet to be determined.

STAFFING

As of the April 2000 Ministry of Justice report on the judiciary, there were 1,240 judges in the Slovak Republic, including 77 judges of the Supreme Court, 392 judges of the regional courts, and 771 judges of the district courts. The courts were served by 624 prosecutors. In addition, 2,695 people worked as administrative staff of the courts, more than half of them serving as court clerks.

The 1992 constitution stipulated that the government propose judges for election by parliament for a four-year term, after which time the government might propose them for reelection for an unlimited tenure. This method of reelection, which exposed judges to direct political influence, was changed in 2001 by constitutional amendment. In order to strengthen the judiciary the amendment established a Judicial Council, on which it conferred the right to propose candidates for judgeships as well as to propose the removal of sitting judges, to assign judges to particular localities, and to propose candidates for nomination by the president to the chair and vice chair of the Supreme Court. The Judicial Council has eighteen members and is chaired by the head of the Supreme Court. Eight members are selected by judges, three members by parliament, three by the president, and three by the government.

To be appointed a judge, a person must be a citizen of Slovakia who is eligible for election to parliament, has attained the age of thirty, and has a law degree. A judge can be recalled upon conviction for a criminal offense, on the basis of a decision of a disciplinary senate, or if his or her eligibility for election to parliament has been terminated. A judge may not be transferred from one court to another without his or her prior consent.

The constitution provides for the right of all persons to legal assistance in proceedings held in courts and other state bodies. To implement this provision the state established various legal and other professions. The most important are advocates and commercial attorneys, who have self-administered associations that superintend the conduct of their members. The difference between advocates and commercial attorneys is that only advocates are eligible to provide legal assistance in criminal matters. In 2001, there were approximately 1,700 advocates and 1,450 commercial attorneys, the majority of them located in the capital city, Bratislava.

Persons wishing to enter a specific legal profession may become members of the appropriate association when they have met the statutory requirements and passed the prescribed examinations, including the bar examination. For example, a lawyer will be registered as an advocate upon written application and the submission of proof of fulfillment of specific requirements: full legal capacity, graduation from a law school in the Slovak Republic or from a recognized law school abroad, at least three years' practice as an advocate trainee, passage of the bar examination, and attestations of the applicant's integrity. The requirement of citizenship applies only to public notaries and judicial executors, as representatives of the authority of the state. All associations have a code of ethics as part of the charter of their profession. Violation of the code is sanctioned by disciplinary or punitive measures.

IMPACT

Adjudication plays a vital role in the process of the democratic consolidation in Slovakia. Constitutional Court decisions have helped to reveal shortcomings of the constitution and thus contributed to the formulation of amendments providing for direct election of the president and a more exact definition of the president's competencies. The 2001 amendment even revised constitutional provisions related to the Constitutional Court. From the very beginning, the Constitutional Court has enjoyed high public support and prestige among citizens. Polls have shown that from 1994 to 1999, Slovakia's citizens considered the Constitutional Court the most credible state institution, due to its performance. More important, the Constitutional Court was the only state institution that enjoyed almost equal trust among supporters of both coalition and opposition political blocks in Slovakia.

By contrast, ordinary courts tend to be excessively formal when adjudicating legal disputes. Several factors have influenced the functioning and position of the ordinary courts within Slovak society. The judiciary lacks material and human resources, there is no independent branch of justice, and through 2001 there has been no public defender of human and civil rights (ombudsman). At the same time, evidence that judges are not resistant to corruption continues to build. As a result, Slovak society is beginning to distrust the judiciary. In the January 2000 poll, only 33.7 percent of respondents said that they trusted the courts, as compared to 63.2 percent who said that they did not trust them. The continued sluggishness of the legal process is the most important obstacle in citizen-court relations. The average number of cases assigned annually to one judge in 1990 was 217.5. This figure had risen to 531.8 assigned cases in 1999. In 1990 judges settled an average of 162.9 cases per year, compared to 387.4 cases in 1999. The average duration of judicial proceedings is thirteen months for civil cases and four months for criminal proceedings.

Procedural delay is largely due to the overwhelming caseload that judges on many courts face. It is exacerbated by an unwieldy documentation system, as well as technical obstacles to the immediate circulation of documents and case files, including a dearth of senior court officials, an obsolete protocol system, and a shortage of computers. Nevertheless, from a broader perspective the legal system in Slovakia is stable and should continue to move closer to the standards of democratic states governed by the rule of law.

Erik Lastic

See also Alternative Dispute Resolution; Civil Law; Constitutional Review; Czech Republic; Judicial Review; Judicial Selection, Methods of; Law and Society Movement; Legal Professionals—Civil Law Traditions; Ottoman Empire; Parliamentary Supremacy; Roman Law; Soviet System
References and further reading
The Constitutional Court of the Slovak Republic. http://www.concourt.sk (accessed October 4, 2001).
The Government of the Slovak Republic. http://www.government.gov.sk (accessed October 4, 2001).
Gross, Grudzinska Irena, ed. 1994. *Constitutionalism and Politics*. Bratislava: Slovak Committee of the European Cultural Foundation.
Leff, Carol Skalnik. 1988. *National Conflict in Czechoslovakia: The Making and Remaking of the State, 1918–1987.* Princeton: Princeton University Press.
———. 1997. *The Czech and Slovak Republics: Nation versus State.* Oxford: Westview Press.
Liptak, Lubomir, 1997. *Slovakia in Twentieth Century.* Bratislava: Kalligram.
Mamatey, Victor, and Radomir Luza, eds. 1973. *A History of the Czechoslovak Republic, 1918–1948.* Princeton: Princeton University Press.
Meseznikov, Grigorij, Miroslav Kollar, and Tom Nicholson,

eds. 2001. *Slovakia 2000: A Global Report on the State of Society.* Bratislava: Institute for Public Affairs.

Priban, Jiri, and James Young, eds. 1999. *The Rule of Law in Central Europe.* Aldershot: Ashgate Publishing.

Wolchik, Sharon. 1991. *Czechoslovakia in Transition: Politics, Economics and Society.* London: Pinter.

SLOVENIA

COUNTRY INFORMATION

The Republic of Slovenia lies in the heart of Europe, in the junction of the Alps, the Mediterranean, and the Pannonian plains. It is one of the newborn European states, the northernmost of the six republics of the former Yugoslavia that proclaimed its independence on June 25, 1991. To the north Slovenia borders Austria, to the east Hungary, to the south Croatia, and to the west Italy and the Adriatic Sea. A relatively small country in size (20,273 square kilometers), Slovenia is the convergence point of a range of different landscapes and climates: Alpine, Mediterranean, Pannonian, and Dinaric, each of which has its own characteristics and unique features. The country population is a little under 2 million, of which nearly 90 percent are Slovenes. For historical reasons there are Slovene minorities in bordering countries Italy, Austria, and Hungary. Conversely, there are Italian and Hungarian national minorities in Slovenia. The official language is Slovene, a distinct Slavic language, spoken by only 2 million people. In areas where Italian or Hungarian minorities reside, the official language is also Italian or Hungarian. As a second language most people in Slovenia speak English, German, or Italian. The country is majority Catholic with the Evangelical church most widely spread in the eastern part of Slovenia. The capital of the country is Ljubljana (270,000 inhabitants), which is the largest city in the country as well as the political, administrative, economic, legal, educational, and cultural center of Slovenia. The country's legal system is based on European civil law and was historically strongly influenced by the Austrian-Germanic legal tradition.

HISTORY

The first state of the Slovene people was formed in 658—an Independent Duchy of Carantania. Carantania had a special and unique ceremony (which was practiced until the fifteenth century) for the enthronement of its (elected) princes: The person to be inaugurated as the new prince has to receive a slap on the face by a common person, to remind him that he serves the people (this practice was later recorded by Thomas Jefferson in his writings on the American Constitution). After the eighth century Carantania gradually came under Frankish rule. Slovenes lived under foreign rule until 1945, when they

became part of Yugoslavia as a republic, and finally became independent in 1991.

In the fourteenth century, most of the territory of Slovenia was taken over by the Habsburgs, who retained control of the area (later as the Austro-Hungarian Empire) right up to the end of the World War I. Habsburg rule had a significant social, cultural, and legal influence on the country. Law in the early Middle Ages was mainly common law, fragmented and with few written legal sources; no comprehensive court system existed. The fifteenth century brought about the rediscovery of Roman law and the first efforts of comprehensive codifications of civil and criminal law appeared. In the middle of the sixteenth century, the Reformation, mainly Lutheranism, spread across Slovene territory, helping to create the foundations of the Slovene literary language (the first Slovenian books were published in 1550). In 1698 the first Association of Lawyers was formed and ten years later first lectures in law were given in Ljubljana. A comprehensive codification of criminal substantive and procedural law (*Constitution Criminalis Theresiana*) was adopted in 1768. The code included detailed and illustrated instructions for executing torture (torture was banned only in 1776). In 1811, the first comprehensive codification of the civil code replaced the Roman law.

At the time of the Napoleonic Wars, Napoleon captured southeastern Slovene regions and created the Illyrian Provinces (1809–1813) of the French state, with Ljubljana as their capital.

The first Slovene political program, called Unified Slovenia, emerged during the European Spring of Nations in March and April 1848. After World War I, which brought heavy casualties to Slovenia, and the Austro-Hungarian defeat, Slovenia joined the Kingdom of Serbs, Croats, and Slovenes. In 1920 a new constitution, which was based on the separation of powers and included some important individual and social-economic rights of individuals, was proclaimed. However, in 1926 the king disbanded the assembly, repealed the constitution, and renamed the country the Kingdom of Yugoslavia. The majority of the Slovene nation in Yugoslavia, which was heavily centralized, had afterwards little constitutional or legal autonomy, but because of its ethnic compactness the nation actually lived a fairly autonomous existence.

During World War II, the Kingdom of Yugoslavia disintegrated, and Slovene territory was occupied by Germany, Italy, and Hungary. In 1941, the Liberation Front of the Slovene Nation was founded in Ljubljana and began armed resistance against the occupying forces. In 1943 the Communist Party took the leading role in the Liberation Front. The assembly of representatives of the Slovene nation in October 1943 decided to include Slovenia in the new Yugoslavia, and two years later the

Federal People's Republic of Yugoslavia (later renamed the Socialist Federal Republic of Yugoslavia, SFRY) was declared. Slovenia, as its constituent part, was renamed the People's Republic of Slovenia. The first constitution of new Yugoslavia was adopted in 1946 under the strong influence of the Stalinist Soviet Union. By 1947 most private property had been nationalized, a one-party (communist) system introduced, and many individual freedoms abolished in practice. After the break with the Soviet Union in 1948, Yugoslavia began introducing a much milder version of socialism, based on common ownership and self-management. The SFRY later adopted two more constitutions in a relatively short period of time—mainly in the struggle to find a proper political, economic, social, and constitutional balance that would help to consolidate the different nations and republics of Yugoslavia. The most important was the Constitution of 1974, which gave substantial political, economic, and legal autonomy to the republics. Slovenia at that time had its own National Assembly, constitution, police, court system with its own constitutional court, and jurisdiction to pass legislation in many areas. The

legal and political system was, however, not based on the separation of powers, but on the Principle of Unity of Powers (vested mainly in the National Assembly dominated by the Communist Party and the Socialist Union).

After the death of Josip Broz Tito in 1980, the economic and political situation started to become very strained, and this ultimately led, ten years later, to the end of the SFRY. Demands for democratization and resistance against the centralized Yugoslavia were sparked in 1988 by the arrest of three independent Slovene journalists and an army officer on charges of violating military secrets. All the defendants were tried by a military tribunal under unfair procedures. This incident instigated public protests on the streets of Ljubljana and opened a broad debate on legal, political, and social changes.

In 1988 the Slovenian National Assembly adopted important amendments to the republic's Constitution (among other things introducing direct elections and a multiparty system and formally abolishing the death penalty). In April 1990 the first democratic elections since World War II took place and were won by the united opposition movement. In the same year more than 88 percent of the whole electorate voted for a sovereign and independent Slovenia on a plebiscite.

The declaration of independence followed on June 25, 1991. It was proclaimed by a constitutional act, using the right to self-determination of nations expressly written in the federal constitution. The provisions of this act adopted Yugoslav legislation into a new Slovenian legal order, providing that such legislation does not contradict existing Slovenian legislation and international human rights standards; it also guaranteed respect for the rights of the national minorities living in Slovenia. The next day, the newly formed state was attacked by the Yugoslav Army. After ten days of armed conflict, a political agreement was reached and in October 1991 all Yugoslav forces withdrew from Slovenia, which was therefore spared the tragic development that followed in Croatia and Bosnia.

In December 1991 a new constitution was proclaimed. Slovenia was recognized by the countries of the European Union (EU) and the U.S. in the middle of 1992, and became a member of the UN in May 1992 and in 1993 of the Council of Europe (when it signed and ratified the European Convention on Human Rights). In 1996 Slovenia signed the EU Association Agreement. The accession process toward the EU has an immense impact on the legal system. The country had to adopt or amend numerous laws and implement regulations. It is currently envisaged that Slovenia will meet all the conditions for full membership by 2002.

LEGAL CONCEPTS

The dominant legal concept in Slovenia is strongly determined by its history, the fact that the country only in 1991 became a fully independent state, and the changes in the political and economical system during the so-called transitional period. Building a new state, restructuring the system of government, and adopting a new constitution and legislation in the areas of denationalization and commercial and criminal law—combined with privatizing public property and the accession process toward the EU—posed significant challenges to existing legal concepts. It is safe to say that by 2001 Slovenia had developed a fairly modern and comprehensive new legal framework, with a high level of actual implementation (which is/was not always the case for countries in transition). This can be partially attributed to the fact that the country, even when part of the SFRY, had a relatively developed and independent legal and economic system and was spared the economic, military, and social unrests of the extent that occurred in many emerging democracies in the beginning of the 1990s.

The supreme law of the country is the constitution, adopted in 1991. Under the constitution Slovenia is a democratic republic, governed by the rule of law and a so-

cial state. The constitution provides for a separation of legislative, executive, and judicial powers, as well as for the separation of religious groups and the state. An important emphasis of the constitution is a number of elaborated human and social rights and civil liberties (Slovenia is, for example, one of the few countries in the world where the right to an abortion is directly written into the constitution). The constitution also provides that laws and regulations must be in compliance with generally accepted principles of international law and with international agreements that bind Slovenia, and that ratified and proclaimed international agreements are directly applicable.

Slovenia is a parliamentary democracy and the Slovenian Parliament consists of two separate bodies: the National Assembly and the National Council. The National Assembly, which is the highest legislative body, is composed of ninety deputies, elected directly according to a proportionate electoral system for a period of four years. The year 2000 saw interesting political and legal controversies about the introduction of the majority electoral system—arguably aimed at the consolidation of the political parties and strengthening the government. This was resolved by an amendment to the constitution, and the proportionate electoral system stayed in force. Every person eighteen years of age and older is entitled to vote and be elected. Two seats in the assembly are reserved for the national minorities (Italian and Hungarian). Legislative initiative lies with every deputy of the assembly or the government. An instrument of the assembly quite often used (and, one could say, sometimes abused) is a parliamentary inquiry into specific matters of public interest or into abuse of public function. The assembly has the power to initiate impeachment procedures against the president of the republic, the prime minister, or individual ministers (the impeachment is finally decided by the constitutional court). The National Council, on the other hand, is a body of representatives from social, economic, professional, and local interest groups. Its forty members are elected for five years by indirect elections. Since the council has no direct legislative power, Slovenia does not have a typical bicameral Parliament, and there are ongoing discussions about the rationale of such a body in the Parliament due to its relatively limited powers.

The government, as a body of executive power and the highest body of the state administration, has sixteen members. The prime minister is nominated by the president and elected by the National Assembly. Individual ministers are nominated by the prime minister and appointed or removed by the assembly. On the motion of at least ten deputies and with an absolute majority, the assembly can take a vote of no confidence to the whole government or a specific minister. All this makes the government (which, due to the proportionate electoral system, is always a coalition of three or more parties) relatively weak. Currently, constitutional revisions are under discussion to change the system of appointment of the government (especially to limit the powers of the National Assembly regarding the appointment or removal of every individual minister).

The president of the republic is elected directly by a secret ballot of the whole electorate for a period of five years, for a maximum of two consecutive terms. According to the constitution he represents Slovenia and is the supreme commander of its armed forces. However, the president's powers are mainly symbolic and although he proclaims the laws, he does not have veto power.

The constitution states that judges shall independently exercise their duties and functions in accordance with the constitution and with the law. Extraordinary courts are prohibited by the constitution, as are military tribunals in peacetime. In addition, the constitution provides the basic principles of the organization and jurisdiction of the courts, the participation of citizens in the performance of judicial functions, the life tenure of judicial office, the election of judges, the Judicial Council, the termination and dismissal from the office of judge, the incompatibility of judicial office, and judicial immunity. While judges are elected by the National Assembly on the nomination of the Judicial Council, it almost never happens that the assembly rejects the candidate, and in general one could say that the judiciary is also in practice free of undue interference from the executive or legislative branch of government. The highest authority of judicial power for the protection of constitutionality, legality, human rights, and basic freedoms is the constitutional court. It consists of nine judges: legal experts at least forty years of age nominated by the president of the republic and elected by the National Assembly for a single nine-year term. The constitutional court is autonomous and independent, and its rulings are binding. In the last decade this court played perhaps the most central role in framing the legal and political culture in the country, deciding on the constitutionality of some controversial laws and decisions of lower courts.

The constitution also provides for the human rights ombudsman. This office is responsible for the protection of human rights and fundamental freedoms in relation to state bodies, local administrative bodies, and all those with public jurisdiction. While its office has relatively limited powers to directly influence administrative, judicial, or parliamentary proceedings, it has become an important institution with high moral authority in the area of human rights.

Slovenia also has a relatively strong tradition of so-called direct democracy. The constitution provides for a direct legislative initiative of the citizens (at least 5,000 signatures can introduce a law in the parliamentary procedure), and a referendum can be held on any issue (initiated by the Parliament or 40,000 signatures of citizens). Recently the number of referendums has increased, some very controversial, which led to a debate to limit its scope.

Legal concepts of major branches of law (criminal, civil, commercial, and so on) are based in the civil legal tradition, with codified laws. Court decisions have no formal value of a precedent (excepting the rulings of the constitutional court), but in practice the rulings and opinions of higher courts and especially of the Supreme Court de facto have such effect. Rulings of the Supreme Court and the constitutional court are also regularly published in written and electronic forms and increasingly cited in and by the courts. In addition the jurisprudence of the European Court of Human Rights is de facto binding for all Slovenian courts; the same will happen with the decisions of the European Court of Justice when Slovenia joins the EU.

Certain constitutional and legal changes have brought about significant changes in the criminal justice system. The new constitution has emphasized protection of human rights and fundamental liberties in the criminal process (miranda rights, strong limitations on pretrial detention and search and seizure powers, protection of privacy, and so on). The new criminal code and code of criminal procedure, adopted in 1995, introduced many adversarial elements into the pretrial and trial stages of procedure, and strengthened judicial control over police powers through exclusion of evidence and warrant requirements. In short, the criminal procedure can be described as typical continental European criminal procedure, a model of inquisitorial heritage. One of the main characteristics is judicial investigation in the pretrial stage of the proceedings dominated by the investigative magistrate. In principle prosecutors do not have discretion to drop prosecution; if there is probable cause, they have to prosecute. As a unique feature of the criminal system there exists a rule of evidence that prohibits all nonmaterial evidence gathered by the police from the court; only testimonial evidence gathered by the investigative magistrate can be used in court. For some time now, vivid debates have been going on in the legal community to fundamentally change the system of criminal procedure, eliminate the investigative magistrate, and empower the prosecutors to carry out investigations. Capital punishment was formally abolished in 1989, but de facto no death penalty has been carried out in Slovenia since 1957 (despite the fact that most parts of the SFRY used the death penalty until 1990).

The bulk of civil law (contracts, torts, damages, and so on) is codified in one code strongly influenced by the old Austrian codification of civil law. A new code of civil procedure, adopted in 1999, strengthen its adversarial nature and provides for different types of proceedings when dealing with classic civil cases, commercial disputes, small claims cases, trespass cases, and so on. Civil enforcement

Legal Structure of Slovenia Courts

Constitutional Court

Supreme Court

Criminal Law Chamber	Civil Law Chamber	Commercial Law Chamber
Administrative Review Chamber	Labor and Social Security Disputes Chamber	International Cooperation Division
		Registry Division

Higher Courts (General jurisdiction) (4)	Higher Court for Labor and Social Security Disputes (1)	Higher Court for Administrative Review (1)

District Courts (11)	County Courts (44)	Labor and Social Security Courts (4)	Detached Departments (3)

is entrusted to a special department of the district courts and to the court executioners (private entities with the concession of the Ministry of Justice).

The change of the self-management type of socialism to a full free-market system posed a number of challenges to the legal system. A whole set of legislation relating to corporations, mergers and acquisitions, antitrust, stock market, and so on, was adopted in the period from 1991 onward. The legal regulation of this area in many respects followed the Germanic models.

Slovenia still has to reform its labor and social security legislation, most of which still dates to the Yugoslav era. Special courts dealing with these disputes are designed to be employee-friendly (for example, litigation for employees is less expensive) and fast.

Administrative law was thoroughly reformed after 1991. Special administrative courts were created to deal primarily with the appeal of individuals against the acts of the public bodies. The administrative court in most cases hears appeals from the final decision of an administrative body. One of its separate functions is the protection of human rights violated by administrative acts; the

jurisprudence in this area, which is still relatively new, has already made an important impact.

Alternative dispute resolution is practiced for smaller criminal offenses (which are decided by nonjudicial mediation councils); there are also efforts to make it more common in civil and commercial disputes (where it is relatively rare) to alleviate the caseload of the courts.

Slovenia does not use a jury system, but the participation of laypersons in judicial adjudication is provided in criminal and (to a more limited extent) civil trials before the district courts, which are tried by mixed panels of professional judges and lay judges (for example, a presiding professional judge and two lay judges). It is interesting that lay judges (jurors) decide both facts and law, and their vote counts the same as the vote of a professional judge. In practice, however, for a number of reasons, their influence on the trial is fairly limited.

CURRENT STRUCTURE

The uniform judicial system in Slovenia includes courts of general and specialized jurisdiction.

The first-instance courts of general jurisdiction are

county courts and district courts. County courts have jurisdiction over less serious criminal cases, civil cases concerning claims for damages or property rights up to a certain value, probate and other nonlitigious matters, civil enforcement, and so on. District courts have jurisdiction over criminal and civil cases that exceed the jurisdiction of county courts, juvenile criminal cases, commercial disputes, and so on.

The appellate jurisdiction over county and district courts is assigned to four higher courts of general jurisdiction.

In addition there are two types of courts of specialized jurisdiction in Slovenia. The Court for Labor and Social Security Disputes determines labor and social security disputes (there are specialized first-instance and appeal courts in this jurisdiction). There is also an administrative court, which has the status of a higher court but is actually a first-instance court with jurisdiction over administrative disputes and protection of human rights violated by administrative acts of the government.

The highest court in Slovenia is the Supreme Court. It has appellate jurisdiction in criminal and civil cases, in commercial lawsuits, in labor and social security disputes, and in administrative review. In almost all these cases, the Supreme Court is the court of third instance. The Supreme Court has to review and decide upon all appeals that meet formal conditions; it cannot reject or grant leave to appeal. The Supreme Court is, however, not empowered to decide on the constitutionality of the legal provisions of statutes, regulations, and bylaws, or to receive individual complaints on violation of the constitution by individual acts infringing on human rights. These matters are under the jurisdiction of the Constitutional Court of Slovenia.

The prosecution service, headed by the general public prosecutor (elected by the National Assembly on the nomination of the government) is divided into three levels of jurisdiction, which correspond to the organization of the courts. Prosecutors are appointed by the government and their tenure is not limited by time. The Ministry of Justice cannot issue instructions to prosecutors in regard to individual cases.

Notaries were reestablished in 1995 (after World War II their function was taken over by the lower courts). The office of a *notary publico* is a strictly regulated semipublic office. The number of notaries, which are appointed by the minister of Justice, is at this moment limited to thirty in the whole country.

STAFFING

Legal education in Slovenia lasts four years (plus an additional year for the preparation of a final thesis). The average age of students finishing law school is twenty-four. Apart from a legal degree the prerequisite for practicing law (as a lawyer, judge, or prosecutor) is the State Juridical Exam. Before being allowed to take the exam, the candidate must undertake clerking at one of the district courts for at least one year.

Requirements to become a member of the bar are: law degree, State Juridical Exam, one year of practice as an associate attorney in a law office, and four years of working experience after the law degree. There are approximately 800 attorneys in Slovenia, mostly single practitioners with one associate. Law firms are not common. Attorneys are prohibited by law to advertise their services.

Requirements to become a judge are: citizenship, law degree, State Juridical Exam, minimum thirty years of age; work experience (for district court judge at least three years of work experience as a country court judge, a prosecutor, or attorney of law; for higher court judge a minimum six years; for Supreme Court judge a minimum fifteen years of work experience involving judicial functions or the title of university professor). Similar conditions apply to public prosecutors. All judges are elected by the National Assembly on the proposal of the Judicial Council and there is no time limit on their tenure. The Judicial Council has eleven members, five elected by the National Assembly, nominated by the president of the republic from the university law professors, attorneys of law, and other lawyers; six are elected by the judges themselves.

IMPACT

Even before the independence and democratization of Slovenia, courts were fairly independent of political influence and the public's perception of the courts was relatively positive. After the change in the system, which brought political and legal changes, the general population became increasingly aware of their legal environment and especially of their rights under the constitution and laws in general. *Rule of law* became an everyday phrase even in the language of ordinary people. In many cases relating to human rights and civil liberties, the courts justified their position as the protectors of legality and individual freedoms. However, delays in the administration of justice—especially in the area of civil lawsuits—present the most acute problem of the legal system in Slovenia today. This problem seriously undermines the credibility of the courts and the trust in the whole legal system, and poses one of the major challenges to the rule of law in the future of the Slovenian legal system.

Goran Klemencic

See also Administrative Tribunals; Civil Law; Constitutional Review; Commercial Law (International Aspects); Criminal Procedures; European Court and Commission on Human Rights; Judicial Independence; Yugoslavia: Kingdom of and Socialist Republic

References and further reading
Grad, Franc, et al. 1999. *Drzavna ureditev Slovenije.* Ljubljana: Uradni list Republike Slovenije.
Vilfan, Sergij, and Vladimir Simiè. 1996. *Pravna zgodovina Slovencev.* Ljubljana: Slovenska Matica.

SMALL CLAIMS COURTS

WHAT THEY ARE

Special judicial procedures have developed rapidly in many countries in order to overcome one of the major problems that arise in relation to the administration of civil justice: how to deal with civil actions that involve small sums of money without incurring disproportionate expense. It is no longer regarded as acceptable that a substantial proportion of all the civil actions that reach the courts generate more in legal costs than the sum of money in dispute. Therefore, civil claims up to a prescribed maximum financial limit are designated as small claims, and relatively relaxed and informal procedures have been developed in many countries in dealing with them.

Although the judicial procedures that have been developed in relation to these small claims vary widely, there are a number of common characteristics, especially the following: (1) Small claims proceedings are generally much simpler, more informal, and more relaxed than is customary in the ordinary civil courts; (2) there is a relative absence—in some countries, a complete absence—of legal representation, and the emphasis is instead placed on laypersons presenting their own cases; (3) in court, adjudicators are encouraged to offer such litigants assistance, particularly in presenting their cases and in questioning the other party; (4) adjudicators are expected to play an "interventionist" role at hearings, freely entering the arena of the dispute; (5) legal and evidential rules are relaxed, and adjudicators are granted wide latitude in determining the procedures they can adopt in reaching decisions; and (6) win or lose, the parties must pay their own legal costs.

For obvious reasons, disproportionate legal costs in civil actions are more likely to arise—and to arise at early stages in the civil justice process—when the money value of claims is low. For claims that involve relatively small sums, traditional civil court processes are simply too expensive, cumbersome, and protracted to provide a realistic means of resolution. *Proportionality* in legal costs has become the watchword in civil justice administration, and in consequence, simplified small claims procedures have become very popular in many jurisdictions. They offer an inexpensive, if unrefined, means of dealing with low-value claims. The expansion of small claims regimes has, indeed, been one of the main ways in which the authorities in many countries have sought to alleviate the crisis in their civil justice systems.

HISTORICAL BACKGROUND

The idea that ordinary civil procedures are inappropriate in dealing with actions of low monetary value is not a new one, and attempts to simplify civil court procedures as a way of handling small claims can be easily traced to the eighteenth century and beyond. But specialized small claims courts emerged only in the early part of the twentieth century, the first in Cleveland, Ohio, in 1919. Small claims courts were subsequently introduced in other parts of the United States, and the same thing has happened in other parts of the world as well. These early courts operated, it seems, largely as debt-collection agencies, with businesses using them as a relatively cheap way of recovering small debts. (In fact, this practice has been so marked that it has become customary in U.S. literature to use the word *colonize* to emphasize the extent to which commercial organizations dominate.)

It was, however, mainly in the 1960s that small claims courts began to attract much attention from policymakers, members of the general public, and legal researchers. The rise of the consumer movement, particularly in the 1960s, coupled with related concerns about access to justice, added impetus to the development of small claims initiatives not only in the United States but also in other parts of the world. In England and Wales, for instance, the massive increases in the financial limit in small claims since the mid-1990s have been seen as the most convenient and effective method by which access to the courts can be secured for ordinary people and small businesses.

MAJOR VARIANTS

Although it is easy to identify common patterns in the way that small claims are resolved in many jurisdictions, there are nonetheless wide structural and procedural variations from country to country. Some jurisdictions have, for instance, developed full-blown Small Claims Courts that have their own specialized rules, personnel, and procedures. Several other countries have, however, merely modified existing civil procedures for use in dealing with small claims. In some countries, small claims are dealt with outside the formal court system altogether—sometimes even by lay personnel—while in many others, professional judges hear all small claims.

In addition to variations of this kind, there are numerous differences in terms of the procedures adopted, the roles played by adjudicators, the length of hearings, levels of informality at hearings, the financial limits that define a small claim, and the roles played by legal representatives and by litigants. Even within the same jurisdiction, it is often evident that adjudicators adopt very disparate methods in dealing with small claims. The writer's own research on small claims in England and Wales demonstrated that the district judges who hear small claims frequently conduct hearings in very different ways even though sitting in adjacent courtrooms in the same building.

SIGNIFICANCE

It is no exaggeration to say that a silent revolution has been occurring in the civil courts in many parts of the world as increasing numbers of civil actions are being dealt with under simplified small claims procedures in order to save legal costs and reduce long delays. Small claims limits have correspondingly been raised—often very considerably—to encompass more and more civil cases. The small claims limit in England and Wales, for example, rose from £1,000 to £5,000 between 1996 and 2000, thereby transforming the position of small claims within the English civil justice system. Small claims procedures have, in consequence, moved out of the backwaters of civil justice and now provide the dominant method by which the courts resolve contested civil actions.

There is, however, a tendency to regard the expansion of small claims procedures purely as a cheap-and-cheerful mode of dealing with simple disputes that avoids heavy legal costs. But there is more to it than cost cutting. Such informal procedures are more than just a simple method of dispute resolution: They also offer a means of enhancing citizens' access to the courts. The writer's research on small claims in England and Wales has suggested that few litigants are unduly perturbed that such procedures are, in a legal sense, far from refined. Lay litigants tend not to demand a refined brand of justice, and they seem more likely to be satisfied with court decisions if they can understand them, if they accept that they have been made by an independent and authoritative adjudicator, and if they feel that they have been able to participate effectively in proceedings. Small claims procedures seem to score more highly on these criteria than do those of the ordinary civil courts.

But there is an even more important advantage with small claims that tilts the balance still further against traditional civil court procedures. This is brought about by the existence of the so-called no-costs rule that normally operates in small claims in countries such as England and Wales. The usual rule that applies in ordinary civil litigation is that losing parties are expected to pay the costs incurred by the other side. Although the United States is an exception in this regard, there is no such requirement in small claims in most other countries. Whether successful in court or not, small claims litigants have only to pay their own costs, which are unlikely to be great. This means that they avoid the serious financial risks (not to mention the distress and anxiety) that are so frequently a consequence of involvement in traditional civil court litigation. This factor makes a huge difference to litigants' perceptions of legal proceedings. Under normal court processes, the costs in civil actions can prove financially ruinous to parties, even though the sums at issue might be relatively small.

PROBLEMS WITH SMALL CLAIMS

None of the preceding discussion should be taken to imply that the financial limit in small claims should be regarded as infinitely elastic or that formal court proceedings can be replaced at an accelerating rate. We should be under no illusion: Small claims procedures, in which lay litigants present their own cases in court, provide an emphatically rough-and-ready brand of justice. Although an unrefined judicial approach might well be regarded as acceptable in disputes that involve small sums of money, the point at which simple and informal procedures become inappropriate and may produce an unjust result is quickly reached. Furthermore, certain problems have arisen in almost all jurisdictions that have devised small claims procedures. The following discussion addresses the most commonly encountered problems.

Even though informal, small claims hearings are still legal proceedings in which legal principles are applied. Lay litigants need an assurance before they attend a court hearing that their claims have legal validity. They cannot, however, be expected to assess legal validity unaided or to know how they should go about establishing a legal claim (or a defense) in court. Any observer of small claims hearings can see how strongly many litigants feel about the moral rectitude of their cases, but this applies even when a case has no legal merit whatever. It is not satisfactory simply to leave it to litigants to prepare cases in whatever way they think is appropriate and expect adjudicators to muddle through as best they can at hearings. A litigant needs preliminary legal advice, provided at a reasonable cost, about whether his or her case is likely to stand up in a court of law.

Given the wide latitude granted to adjudicators in the way they go about resolving small claims—in England and Wales, for instance, judges are allowed to adopt any method of proceeding that they consider fair—it is not surprising that their approaches vary greatly. In the writer's research, some judges said that they went "for the jugular" at small claims hearings, requiring the parties to restrict themselves to the key legal issues, regardless of what they themselves wanted to say; other judges allowed the parties to present their cases in any way they wished; still others sought mediated settlements between the parties. The judges even expressed different attitudes about how far they felt obliged to apply the ordinary law in small claims. Yet if consistency and certainty are basic requirements in a system of judicial administration, it surely cannot be right that adjudicators adopt such disparate approaches.

The role of legal representatives in small claims hearings is far from clear-cut and remains problematic. In some countries, lawyers are simply banned from small claims hearings. But even where legal representation is permitted, lawyers are likely to find themselves in a difficult position, and it may not be easy for them to adapt to the spirit of informal hearings of this kind, particularly where they have been trained in an adversarial legal tradition. Their difficulties are exacerbated by the fact that small claims adjudicators do not universally welcome the participation of legal representatives because they feel it inhibits them in playing an interventionist role. Then, too, the problems facing an adjudicator become acute where one of the parties is represented and the other is not. As small claims limits have risen, legal representation has tended to become more common. Further thought needs to be given to defining the appropriate role for lawyers to play in the expanded regime.

While the origins of small claims courts are generally traced back to the consumer movement, the point has often been made that efforts to make the civil courts more accessible to consumers have frequently backfired. In most countries, it is not consumers who make the most use of these procedures but small and medium-sized businesses. There is no doubt that informal legal procedures, although designed to assist individual litigants, can also operate to the benefit of commercial organizations, since they provide a cheap and convenient method for pursuing debtors. The consequence is that, almost everywhere, consumers are more likely to appear in court as defendants than as plaintiffs. This has happened in some jurisdictions to such an extent that it has become customary to argue that the consumer has become the victim, not the beneficiary, of the expansion of small claims. It is, indeed, for this reason that commercial organizations are prohibited in some jurisdictions from bringing cases under the small claims procedure.

Many jurisdictions have experienced serious problems in the enforcement of civil judgments, and small claims are no exception. A substantial proportion of litigants who succeed with a small claim fail to receive the payment ordered by the court. Problems of civil enforcement are deep-rooted and are not by any means confined to small claims, and it seems that the efforts made so far to overcome them have met with only limited success. Yet more than any other factor, ineffective enforcement procedures undermine the credibility and integrity of the civil courts.

ASSESSING SMALL CLAIMS PROCEDURES

One might ask whether we should be overly concerned about low-value claims. Do they really matter? When we consider "access to justice," the litmus test of any civil justice system is surely whether it provides ordinary people with satisfactory mechanisms through which they can secure redress when they run into legal difficulties. Considerable progress has been made in providing access to the civil courts to those involved in such disputes, and the adaptations that have been made to traditional litigation procedures have succeeded, at least in part, in allowing laypersons to bring their cases to the civil courts. If we are serious about access to justice, a civil justice system should involve costs and procedures that are both realistic and proportionate to the sums of money in dispute. This means that any call from legal purists for an unrealistic level of legal refinement will lead (in the absence of a massive subsidy from the state) to a situation in which only the wealthy have access to the courts. For most lay litigants, the alternative to cut-price solutions such as small claims is not a refined brand of justice: It is no access to justice at all.

John Baldwin

See also Alternative Dispute Resolution; Civil Procedure
References and further reading
Baldwin, John. 1997. *Monitoring the Rise of the Small Claims Limit: Litigants' Experiences of Different Forms of Adjudication.* London: Lord Chancellor's Department, Research Series No. 1/97.
———. 1997. *Small Claims in the County Courts.* Oxford: Clarendon Press.
National Audit Office. 1996. *Handling Small Claims in the County Courts.* London: Her Majesty's Stationery Office.
Whelan, Christopher J., ed. 1990. *Small Claims Courts: A Comparative Study.* Oxford: Clarendon Press.
Woolf, Lord. 1995. *Access to Justice: Interim Report to the Lord Chancellor's Department on the Civil Justice System in England and Wales.* London: Her Majesty's Stationery Office.

SOLICITORS

Solicitors and barristers are the established legal professionals in the United Kingdom. Traditionally, the major difference between the work of solicitors and barristers was that most solicitors had no right of audience in higher courts. Barristers are specialist advocates and advisers, and solicitors briefed barristers, that is, gave them written instructions in a case. Therefore, solicitors had direct contact with lay clients and received and held the client's money. Barristers only saw clients either to advise (i.e., in a consultant's role) or when representing them in court. They regarded solicitors as professional clients and looked to solicitors for their fees. The divided legal profession and the title of solicitor were retained by many former colonies and countries following the United Kingdom's common law tradition, including Australia, Canada, India, New Zealand, and South Africa. Many jurisdictions maintain a distinction in relation to specialist advocacy functions, but there are regulatory differences between countries and, in Canada and Australia, variations between different provinces and states.

Solicitors in the United Kingdom are controlled by the Law Society of England and Wales, the Law Society of Scotland, or the Law Society of Northern Ireland. There are 100,957 solicitors in England and Wales, of which 79,503 hold current practicing certificates (as of

July 31, 1999). In Scotland there are 10,573 solicitors, of which 8,492 hold current practicing certificates (as of October 31, 1999). In Northern Ireland there are 2,650 solicitors, of which 2,350 hold practicing certificates (as of January 5, 2000). There are differences in the three jurisdictions. For example, the Solicitors Act of 1974 (as amended) provides the statutory framework of governance and regulation for solicitors in England and Wales, but only a few sections extend to Scotland and Northern Ireland (see s. 90[4] of the SA 1974). This entry is concerned with solicitors in England and Wales.

The perception that solicitors are the lower branch of the legal profession and barristers the upper branch derives from the bar's great antiquity and its monopoly on higher court advocacy and entry to the judiciary. From the mid-sixteenth century, the bar sought to reinforce its domination by excluding attorneys and solicitors from the Inns of Court and by forbidding barristers to practice as attorneys and solicitors. By the eighteenth and nineteenth centuries, lawyers who were not barristers strove to improve their social status as gentlemen, a movement that led to the formation of the precursor of the Law Society in 1823. The current Law Society Hall, at 113 Chancery Lane, near the Supreme Court, was built by contributions from elite London solicitors and attorneys.

The organization became more inclusive by 1831, when a royal charter was granted to the Society of Attorneys, Solicitors, Proctors and Others Not Being Barristers and practicing in the Courts of Law and Equity in the United Kingdom. Members of the nascent society adopted the common title of "solicitor" so as to avoid the opprobrium attaching to attorneys. In 1845 the earlier charter, the purpose of which was to promote professional improvement and facilitate the acquisition of legal knowledge, was surrendered for a new one with wider powers. This document has since provided the constitution of the "Law Society," a title formally adopted by the Charter of 1903.

During the nineteenth century, the solicitors accrued considerable power. The Law Society drafted the Solicitors Act of 1844, which consolidated a patchwork of statutory regulation and played a significant role in promoting six other acts regulating solicitors in that century. It also played an influential role in shaping other legislation. Status was also gradually attained. In 1882 Thomas Paine became the first president of the Law Society to be knighted. In 1919 the Law Society wrested from the judiciary the power to run disciplinary proceedings and impose sanctions. In 1973 the Law Society and the General Council of the Bar of England and Wales issued a joint statement recognizing the equality of status of the branches of the profession. In the same year, the president of the Law Society was first invited to join the procession of the lord chancellor and judges that marks the start of the legal year. In 1999 the president proposed that solicitors should absorb the bar into the solicitors' regulatory regime.

Solicitors are recognized by statute as "solicitors of the Supreme Court" (Solicitors' Act 1974 s. 87[1]). The Law Society of England and Wales has a president and vice president, both elected for one year, and is governed by a council of seventy members. It has strong regional law societies with a substantial majority on the Law Society Council. The Solicitors Act of 1974 (SA) prohibits unqualified persons from acting as solicitors (SA ss. 20–23). It provides that no person shall be qualified to act as a solicitor unless he or she has been admitted as a solicitor, is on the roll of solicitors, and holds a current practicing certificate issued by the Law Society (SA 1974 s. 1). A person wishing to be admitted to the roll must also obtain a certificate from the Law Society confirming that he or she has complied with training regulations and that the society "is satisfied as to his character and suitability to be a solicitor" (SA s. 3[1][a] and [b]). The society maintains a disciplinary tribunal with a range of sanctions, including the power to strike a solicitor from the roll. It publishes guidance on conduct in *The Guide to the Professional Conduct of Solicitors.* Complaints against solicitors are investigated by a semi-independent body, the Office for the Supervision of Solicitors. Solicitors are also subject to regulations made by the Law Society Council, for example, those providing that solicitors must undergo continuing professional development.

The main route into practice as a solicitor is the successful completion of an undergraduate degree in law or a degree in a nonlaw subject and the completion of a one-year conversion course called the common professional entrance course (CPE). Although there are different routes to this point, all candidates must complete a one-year legal practice course (LPC) and a two-year training contract (formerly called "articles of clerkship") under the guidance of a solicitor approved by the Law Society for this purpose. Both a law degree and a CPE must contain seven subjects: contract, torts, criminal law, public law, land law, trusts and equity, and European Union law. Both courses must also conform to a general statement on qualifying law degrees agreed to periodically by the Law Society, the bar, and the law schools. Since 1969 the total number of solicitors holding practicing certificates has grown by 237.2 percent, at an average annual rate of 4.1 percent.

Solicitors traditionally handled a wide range of work, including conveyancing (the legal transfer of land), drafting legal documents, and conducting litigation. They were only permitted to appear as advocates in lower courts, for example, the Magistrates' Courts and county courts. Since the 1980s, government has sought to inject more competition into the legal services market. Solicitors were subjected to competition from licensed conveyancers, a new profession established under the Administration of Justice Act (1985). The Courts and Legal Services Act (1990) potentially opened up the market for advocacy and litigation services. Under the act, the Law Society was granted the right to confer rights of audience in higher courts on solicitors, provided they obtain an appropriate "higher rights qualification." Barristers were granted the right to receive instructions from other professions. This is a first step away from barristers using solicitors as intermediaries and toward barristers becoming full-service providers in competition with solicitors. The historical division in roles is, however, proving quite durable. Relatively few solicitors have obtained advocacy qualifications. Further, although the formal distinctions between solicitors and barristers are being eroded, cultural distinctions, which cast barristers as gentlemen and -women, and scholars and solicitors as businesspeople, remain significant.

While formal differences between barristers and solicitors are slowly disappearing, solicitors have become an increasingly diverse group. Of those holding current practicing certificates, 19.5 percent are employed in commerce or industry, local or central government, and a range of other organizations, an increase of approximately 9 percent since 1988. The private sector is also diverse. It comprises 8,561 solicitors' firms, of which 3,641 are sole practices, 3,509 have 2–4 partners, 972 have 5–10 partners, 316 have 11–25 partners, 99 have 26–80 partners, and 24 have 81 partners or more. These firms have 31,753 principals or partners and employ 28,364 assistant solicitors. The 24 largest firms provide employment for 17.5 percent of all private practitioners, whereas the 3,641 sole practitioners provide employment for only 9 percent.

Firms tend to specialize in different kinds of work. "High Street" firms are usually small and serve local communities, reflecting the community's circumstances and needs, or, through legal aid, they specialize in poor people's litigation. Such firms have suffered from a relative decline in income from conveyancing and legal aid. Conditional fee agreements (CFAs), under which solicitors do not charge a fee if their client loses a case but are permitted to charge an additional fee if they win, are gradually replacing legal aid. This is a significant change in litigation funding and may yet offer a more secure future for some litigation firms. At present, however, smaller outfits have found it increasingly difficult to survive. Around 25 percent of sole practitioners make a profit of £22,000 or less per annum. Accordingly, there has been a tendency for the numbers of sole practitioners to decrease and for the size of firms generally to increase.

The success of firms oriented toward business and commerce is most notable in the small numbers of large firms in metropolitan centers, particularly the City of London, which are providers of legal services to governments and globally orientated corporations. In 1997–1998 the turnover of private practice firms was £8.645 billion. Of this sum, legal aid payments to solicitors constituted 14.8 percent. Nearly 10 percent of the total, or £791 million, came from overseas earnings. This represents 5 percent of the total earned by the U.K. from business services exports. Larger firms have tended to generate higher percentage increases in gross fees, and sole practitioners have suffered reductions in real fees. In 1999 the three largest firms in the city of London grossed approximately a third of the turnover of private practice firms. Partners in some of the leading large firms earn over £1 million per annum.

As solicitors contemplate professional ascendancy, they face measures from government intended to curtail their independence, increase competition, and reduce the cost of routine legal services. In the wake of the Law Society's spirited campaign against the contraction of legal aid, the government proposed restricting expenditure of its practicing certificate income to regulation and education. The Law Society is also reducing the scope of its own activities. It recently abandoned the Solicitors' Indemnity Fund, which provided insurance coverage for negligence to the whole profession. Some solicitors, conscious of the record of delay in handling complaints, support the surrender of self-regulation. Increasing diversity in their work and rewards have undermined solicitors' homogeneity and raised questions about the capacity of the Law Society to represent all members effectively. The presidency, formerly assumed to be the right of the incumbent vice president, has been contested in recent years. On the horizon, multidisciplinary practice threatens even the largest firms with annexation by giant accountancy firms. Yet, although the position of the solicitors is in a state of flux, they will dominate the provision of legal services for the foreseeable future.

Andy Boon

See also Barristers; Commercial Law (International Aspects); England and Wales; Law Firms; Legal Aid; Legal Education; Northern Ireland; Scotland; United Kingdom

References and further reading

Abel, Richard L. 1988. *The Legal Profession in England and Wales.* Oxford: Basil Blackwell.
Boon, Andrew, and John Flood. 1999. "Trials of Strength: The Reconfiguration of Litigation as Contested Terrain." *Law and Society Review* 33, no. 3: 595–636.
Boon, Andrew, and Jennifer Levin. 1999. *The Ethics and Conduct of Lawyers in England and Wales.* Oxford: Hart Publishing.
Burrage, Michael. 1996. "From a Gentlemen's to a Public Profession: Status and Politics in the History of English Solicitors." *International Journal of the Legal Profession* 3, nos. 1–2: 45–80.

Cole, Bill. 2000. *Trends in the Solicitors' Profession: Annual Statistical Report 1999.* London: Law Society.

Holland, J. Anthony, ed. 1995. *Cordery on Solicitors.* London: Butterworths.

Kirk, Harry. 1976. *Portrait of a Profession: A History of the Solicitor's Profession, 1100 to the Present Day.* London: Oyez Publishing.

Sugarman, David. 1996. "Bourgeois Collectivism, Professional Power and the Boundaries of the State: The Private and Public Life of the Law Society, 1825 to 1914." *International Journal of the Legal Profession* 3, nos. 1–2: 81–135.

Taylor, N., ed. 1999. *The Guide to the Professional Conduct of Solicitors.* London: Law Society Publishing.

SOLOMON ISLANDS

COUNTRY INFORMATION

Solomon Islands is situated in the southwestern Pacific, about 1,796 kilometers northeast of Australia. It consists of a double chain of six large islands and several hundred smaller ones. The larger islands are Choiseul, New Georgia, Santa Isabel, Guadalcanal, Malaita, and San Cristobal. The capital is Honiara, located on Guadalcanal. The land area of 28,370 square kilometers is spread out over a sea area of approximately 1,340,000 square kilometers between the southernmost part of Papua New Guinea and the area northwest of Vanuatu. The climate is tropical.

The present population is about 328,723. Of these, about 93.4 percent are Melanesian, 4 percent Polynesian, 1.4 percent Micronesian, 0.7 percent European, and 0.2 percent Chinese. The social structure of the country is extremely complex. Culture and social organization varies from island to island and even from village to village. The official languages are English and Solomon Islands pidgin, but there are also about sixty-five vernacular languages and dialects in existence. The legal system is based on introduced common law, superimposed on indigenous customary law.

HISTORY

There is evidence of settlement in Solomon Islands dating back to 1300 to 1000 B.C.E. However, earlier settlement probably took place in about 2000 B.C.E., when explorers from Southeast Asia are believed to have arrived via Papua New Guinea. Law prior to European settlement was based on the customs of the community, pronounced orally by the chiefs. The law applied only to individual communities rather than to the country as a whole or to whole islands.

The first recorded European sighting of Solomon Islands was in 1568, when the islands were named by Spanish explorer Alvaro de Mendaña de Neira. The eighteenth and early nineteenth centuries witnessed the arrival of European settlers, who were not originally subject to any governmental control. In 1877 the British Privy Council made the Western Pacific Order in Council, authorizing the appointment of a high commissioner of the Western Pacific and establishing a High Commissioners' Court in Fiji. This court exercised jurisdiction over criminal offenses committed by British subjects in South Pacific countries, including Solomon Islands. In 1879 the high commissioner was authorized to make regulations for the government of British citizens in all countries under his jurisdiction.

In 1893, the British government declared the southern Solomon Islands a protectorate and replaced the Western Pacific Order in Council (1877) with the Pacific Order in Council (1893), which extended to indigenous inhabitants as well as British subjects. Meanwhile, Germany laid claim to the northern Solomon Islands. In 1900, Germany relinquished this claim by the second Treaty of Berlin, and the area was given protectorate status by Britain. Between 1896 and 1942, the country was administered by a resident administrator. In April 1942, Japanese forces took Guadalcanal. It was retaken by the Allies in June 1943, and the commissioner returned.

Laws of the Protectorate Period

Constituent Laws

The Pacific Order in Council (1893) provided the basis of government for the protectorate until 1974, when it was replaced by a written constitution, brought into force by the British Solomon Islands Order (1974). This constitution remained in force until independence in 1978.

Local Legislation

King's (queen's) regulations were made for the protectorate by the high commissioner of the Western Pacific between 1893 and 1960. From 1960 to 1974, ordinances were made for the protectorate by the high commissioner of the Western Pacific, with the advice and consent of the Legislative Council. From 1974 to 1978, ordinances were made by the governor of Solomon Islands, with the advice and consent of the Legislative Council.

English Legislation

Section 20 of the Pacific Order in Council (1893) applied "the substance of the law for the time being in force in England" to Solomon Islands. This stipulation was later replaced by Section 15 of the Western Pacific (Courts) Order of 1961, which applied "the statutes of general application in England on the 1st January 1961" to Solomon Islands. In addition, a number of specific acts of Parliament and subsidiary legislation of England were applied.

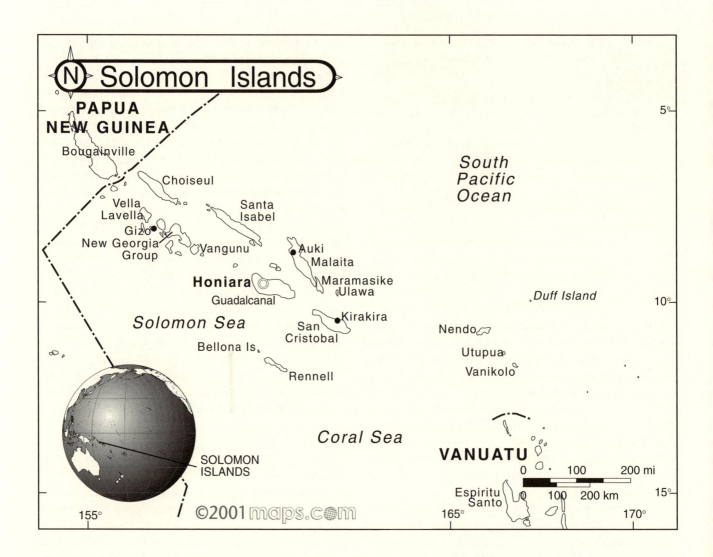

Common Law and Equity

As in the case of English legislation, the principles of common law and equity were applied to Solomon Islands by Section 20 of the Pacific Order in Council (1893), as part of "the substance of the law for the time being in force in and for England." A more specific application to Solomon Islands of common law and equity was made by Section 15 of the Western Pacific (Courts) Order of 1961, which applied to Solomon Islands "the substance of the English common law and doctrines of equity."

Customary Laws

The customary laws of Solomon Islands were not originally regarded as part of the laws of Solomon Islands, except as the basis of rights over customary land. In 1942, however, Section 10 of the Native Courts Ordinance (1942) authorized native courts to apply customary laws to minor civil and criminal proceedings involving Solomon Islanders.

In 1978, Solomon Islands gained independence and adopted a constitution, enacted as a schedule to the Solomon Islands Independence Order (1978). From about April 1998, tension began to rise between Guadalcanal people and Malaitans over land rights on Guadalcanal. This conflict came to a head in the form of the forceful eviction of approximately 20,000 Malaitan settlers from Guadalcanal. The militant Guadalcanal people became known as the Isatabu Freedom Movement. Matters escalated in January 2000, when the Malaita Eagle Force was formed in response and took up arms after raiding the police station armory in Auki, Malaita Province. This action was followed by skirmishes between the two forces and an increase in criminal activities in Honiara, which culminated in the Malaita Eagle Force and members of the police force and prison service joining together in the so-called Paramilitary Joint Operation. On June 5, 2000, the joint forces took control of the government armory. The Malaita Eagle Force then declared war against the Isatabu Freedom Movement and placed the then prime minister under house arrest. On June 28, 2000, Prime Minister Bartholomew Ulufa'alu resigned. Elections were quickly held for a new prime minister, and Manasseh Sogavare was elected and formed a new government.

On August 2, 2000, the government successfully negotiated a cease-fire agreement between the two groups. Peace negotiations commenced under the terms of the cease-fire, resulting in the signing of a peace agreement between the two factions and central and provincial governments on October 15, 2000. The agreement provided for surrender of weapons, a weapons amnesty, and a general amnesty in respect of civil liability and criminal prosecution for actions taken in connection with the armed conflict. An International Peace Monitoring Council was established to monitor, report on, and enforce the terms of the agreement. The agreement also provides for repatriation and rehabilitation of militants and demilitarization of the whole country. Governmental power was to be further devolved to Malaita and Guadalcanal Provinces, and a Constitutional Council was to be established to rewrite relevant parts of the constitution. Alterations were to be made to the National Provident Fund to allow superannuated contributions of Malaitans to be paid to a new Malaitan Provident Fund. Land and claims are to be dealt with by the appointment of a commission of enquiry to examine the acquisition of land on Guadalcanal by non-Guadalcanal people. In the meantime, a moratorium was put in place on transactions concerning Guadalcanal land. Provision was also made for improvements in infrastructure in both provinces. A Peace and Reconciliation Committee was to be established to coordinate community-based reconciliation. At the time of writing, most of these initiatives have yet to be implemented.

LEGAL CONCEPTS

Since independence, the legal system has been governed by the constitution. Section 2 provides that the constitution is the supreme law and that any inconsistent law shall be void. Solomon Islands is a sovereign democratic state and an independent member of the Commonwealth. The constitution establishes a Westminster-style system of government, with separation of powers between the executive, legislature, and judiciary. The British monarch is the head of state and is represented by the governor-general. The country is governed by a system of parliamentary democracy. The national legislature is unicameral and consists of persons elected in accordance with the constitution. There are forty-seven members, including the prime minister, who is elected by and from the body of members. Other ministers are appointed by the governor-general on the prime minister's recommendation. General elections are normally held every four years, with all citizens over eighteen being entitled to vote.

The constitution contains a fundamental rights chapter, which safeguards the rights to life, liberty, and protection from slavery and forced labor; the right to protection from inhuman treatment; the right to protection from deprivation of property; the right to protection of privacy of the home and other property; the right to protection from the law for persons charged with a criminal offense and, in more limited terms, for persons involved in civil cases; the right to freedom of conscience, expression, assembly, association, and movement; and the right to protection from discrimination on certain grounds. The constitution states that "Parliament shall make provision for the application of laws including customary laws" and that in so doing, "Parliament shall have particular regard to the customs, values, and aspirations of the people of Solomon Islands." Until such provision is made, the sources of law, other than the constitution itself, are as set out in Schedule 3 of the constitution. In descending order of importance these are:

1. Acts of Parliament of Solomon Islands
2. United Kingdom acts of general application, in force on January 1, 1961, which apply only if there is no local legislation on point
3. Customary law
4. The principles of common law and equity, provided that they are appropriate to the circumstances of Solomon Islands and are consistent with written laws or custom in force at independence

The constitution also establishes the office of ombudsman. Jurisdiction extends to investigation of conduct of government departments, statutory bodies, and provincial and local government, subject to specific exceptions. Any person or body affected may complain to the ombudsman, who has discretion whether to investigate. The ombudsman may also commence an investigation on his or her own initiative. The ombudsman must give notice to the head of the body being investigated and may require any relevant materials to be provided. Investigations are conducted in secret, and an opportunity to respond must be given to a person who may be the subject of criticism. An adverse recommendation may be made on the ground that the action is contrary to law, based wholly or partly on a mistake of fact or law, unreasonably delayed, or manifestly unreasonable.

CURRENT COURT STRUCTURE

Like many other South Pacific countries, Solomon Islands has a legacy of formal courts inherited from England. The courts operate on the basis of the common law system in which they originated. The hierarchy of the courts is a three-tiered structure, consisting of the Magistrates' Courts, the High Court, and the Court of Appeal. There are separate local courts and customary land appeal courts, empowered to deal with minor local disputes and customary land disputes.

The Court of Appeal is established pursuant to the constitution. It sits from time to time as the need arises.

Legal Structure of Solomon Islands Courts

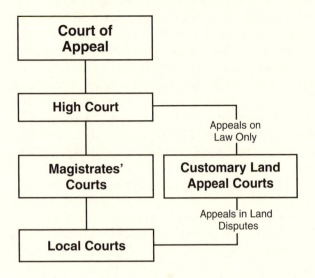

Its members are the president and justices of appeal (non-resident), together with the chief justice and the puisne (inferior) judges of the High Court. The Court of Appeal hears civil appeals as of right from the High Court sitting at first instance and, on a question of law only, from the High Court exercising appellate jurisdiction. The court hears criminal appeals from the High Court as of right against conviction on a question of law only. With leave, the Court of Appeal may also hear appeals from the High Court against conviction on a question of fact or mixed law and fact and against nonmandatory sentences.

The High Court is also established under the constitution and is governed by the High Court Act. It consists of the chief justice and a minimum of two puisne judges, assisted by a registrar of the High Court. The High Court has unlimited original jurisdiction. Subject to certain exceptions, it has jurisdiction to hear applications for declaratory judgments and other relief, based on alleged contravention of the constitution. The High Court has supervisory jurisdiction over civil proceedings in subordinate courts and also has prerogative power to deal with applications for judicial review of administrative action.

Appeals go to the High Court from the Magistrates' Court as of right in most civil and criminal cases. A decision of a Magistrates' Court may also be referred to the High Court by way of case stated. The High Court hears appeals from the Customary Land Appeal Court on questions of law other than customary law. The High Court's decision on such appeals is final. Appeals go from the Magistrates' Court to the High Court from all decisions in criminal cases.

The registrar of the High Court has jurisdiction in civil cases to deal with chambers applications, except in certain restricted cases. There is an appeal from the registrar to a single judge.

Magistrates' Courts are established by the Magistrates' Courts Act, Cap. 20. They are divided into principal magistrates' courts, magistrates' courts of the first class, and magistrates' courts of the second class. Magistrates' Courts have civil jurisdiction in claims in contract or tort, where the amount involved does not exceed Solomon Islands Dollar (SBD)1,000, or in the case of a principal magistrate, SBD2,000, and in suits between landlords and tenants for possession of any land, where the annual value or rent does not exceed the sum of SBD500, or in the case of a principal magistrate, SBD2,000. They are also empowered to make guardianship and custody orders and to grant injunctions and similar relief. The jurisdiction of second-class magistrates is limited to cases involving a maximum of SBD200. The chief justice may order an increase in the civil jurisdiction of named magistrates. This power has been used to increase the jurisdiction of three principal magistrates to SBD6,000 and to increase the jurisdiction of three named first-class magistrates to SBD2,000.

In criminal cases, a principal Magistrates' Court has jurisdiction to try all summary offenses, offenses specifically allocated to it by statute, and any offense for which the maximum penalty does not exceed fourteen years' imprisonment or a fine or both. The maximum punishment that may be imposed by a principal magistrate is five years' imprisonment or a fine of SBD1,000 or both. A first- or second-class Magistrates' Court is limited to summary trials of offenses specifically allocated to it and those for which the maximum penalty does not exceed one year's imprisonment or a fine of SBD200 or both.

The Magistrates' Court has appellate jurisdiction from a Local Court except in customary land cases, where appeal is to the Customary Land Appeal Court. It may also review Local Court proceedings.

Customary Land Appeal Courts were introduced in 1972 to deal with customary land appeals from the Local Court. They are established by chief justice's warrant under Section 255(1) of the Land and Titles Act. Each court consists of a president, vice president, and not less than three other members. Legal practitioners are not permitted to appear before a Customary Land Appeal Court.

Local courts are established by chief justice's warrant under the Local Courts Act, Cap. 19. There are at present thirty-three established courts. Each court is theoretically constituted in accordance with the law or custom of the area in which it has jurisdiction. The court may sit to hear a case, provided that at least three justices are present. Each court has a clerk appointed by the chief justice.

The Local Court has jurisdiction in minor civil disputes in which the defendant is ordinarily resident within the jurisdiction of the court, or the cause of action arose there. It also has exclusive jurisdiction to deal with customary land disputes. However, that jurisdiction may not be exercised unless the court is satisfied that all traditional means of resolving the dispute have been exhausted and that no decision wholly acceptable to both parties has been made by the chiefs. The Local Court also has jurisdiction to deal with minor criminal offenses against islanders committed within its geographical area of jurisdiction, when the offense is against another islander. The Local Court may impose a term of imprisonment not exceeding six months or a fine of up to SBD200. Further jurisdiction is conferred on local courts by statutes, for example, the Wills, Probate and Administration Act, Cap. 33.

Western-style alternative dispute resolution techniques, such as arbitration, mediation, and conciliation, have yet to make an impact in Solomon Islands, although there is an Arbitration Act in force (Cap. 2). Tribunals existing in Solomon Islands include the Trade Disputes Panel, established under the Trade Disputes Act, Cap. 75, to deal with trade disputes and complaints of unfair dismissal. The constitution also establishes the following:

a. A Public Service Commission, which deals with appointment, removal, and disciplinary control over public servants and officers
b. A Teaching Service Commission, which deals with appointment, removal, and disciplinary control over teachers
c. A Judicial and Legal Service Commission, which governs appointment, removal, and disciplinary control over public offices for which a legal qualification is required
d. A Police and Prison Service Commission, which deals with appointment to offices in the police force above the rank of inspector and has removal and disciplinary control over most offices in the force

SPECIALIZED JUDICIAL BODIES

Traditional courts, usually presided over by the village chief, or a group of chiefs if the dispute concerns more than one village, still exist in Solomon Islands, outside the formally recognized court structure and unhampered by legislative rules and procedures. Procedure differs from place to place, depending on the custom of the particular area. The decisions are not generally recorded in writing.

STAFFING

The legal profession in Solomon Islands is "fused," that is, legal practitioners act as both solicitors and barristers. The profession is governed by the Legal Practitioners Act, Cap. 16, which makes it an offense for unqualified persons to practice law. Admission to the profession is governed by the Legal Practitioners (Admission) Rules (1996), granted on the basis of five years' practice in any Commonwealth country. Provisional admission may be obtained by persons with less practical experience and by those entitled to admission in any Commonwealth or comparable jurisdiction. There are thirty-one private legal practitioners with current practicing certificates. About twenty-five of these are resident within the country and are spread out among about ten legal firms in Honiara. The professional association for lawyers is the Solomon Islands Bar Association, which currently has about thirty members.

The conduct of legal practitioners is governed by the Legal Practitioners (Professional Conduct) Rules, made under Section 21 of the act. These provide standards for the conduct and professional integrity of practitioners. For example, the rules restrict the manner in which a practitioner may advertise his or her business and prevent touting; they demand diligence in dealing with a client and impose a duty of confidentiality and avoidance of conflicts of interest. The Legal Practitioners Act permits the chief justice to appoint a disciplinary committee to investigate any complaint about the conduct of a legal practitioner.

The head of the legal profession is the attorney general, who is a public officer, appointed pursuant to Section 42 of the constitution. He or she is the principal legal adviser to the government and is appointed by the Judicial and Legal Service Commission, acting in accordance with the advice of the prime minister from among persons qualified to practice law in Solomon Islands. A solicitor general has also been appointed.

Public prosecutions are dealt with by the director of public prosecutions and legal officers acting under the director's control. The director is appointed under Section 91 of the constitution by the governor-general with the advice of the Judicial and Legal Service Commission. He or she must be qualified to practice law.

The constitution also provides for the office of public solicitor to provide legal aid, advice, and assistance to any person in need. The public solicitor is appointed under Section 92 of the constitution by the governor-general, acting in accordance with the advice of the Judicial and Legal Service Commission. He or she must be qualified to practice law. The post is currently occupied by an expatriate. The role of the public solicitor is further defined by the Public Solicitors Act, Cap. 30. This act limits the right to legal aid to those with an income below a prescribed level (currently $12,000) and provides for contributions to be made by legally aided parties who are successful in litigation.

With regard to the judiciary, the president and justices of appeal are appointed by the governor-general, acting on the advice of the Judicial and Legal Service Commission. Appointees must be qualified for appointment to the High Court. The chief justice and puisne judges (currently three) are appointed by the governor-general with the advice of the Judicial and Legal Service Commission. Applicants must be barristers or solicitors of at least five years' standing of a Commonwealth country or have held high judicial office in such a country. At the moment there are a chief justice and three puisne judges, one of whom is an expatriate. Commissioners of the High Court may be appointed to attend to urgent business.

All magistrates are appointed by the Judicial and Legal Service Commission. At the moment, there are four principal magistrates, one of whom is an expatriate, and about six first- and second-class magistrates. Four first-class magistrates have recently completed an LL.B. at the University of the South Pacific. A clerk of the court is appointed to each Magistrates' Court.

There is no provision for training lawyers or for continuing legal education or judicial training within Solomon Islands. The nearest training facilities are in Vanuatu, where the School of Law of the University of the South Pacific offers an LL.B., an LL.M., and a Ph.D., with an emphasis on South Pacific law. The Institute of Justice and Applied Legal Studies within the University of the South Pacific in Fiji offers a professional diploma in legal practice. Continuing legal education and judicial training are available in the country through short courses offered by the School of Law, and a program of judicial training is offered by the Pacific Judicial Education Programme, based at the University of the South Pacific.

IMPACT

The clear intention of the countries of the region on independence was that new laws would be made locally. Introduced English laws were only saved as a transitional step, to avoid a vacuum, while the new parliaments had the chance to enact laws suited to local circumstances. This is no doubt why a "cutoff" date was inserted, after which legislation passed overseas was not to form part of the law. However, the process of replacing English law with local legislation is very slow. In the meantime, English legislative reforms, which have taken place after the "cutoff" date, do not apply.

In 1994 a Law Reform Commission was established, but it has made little progress because it lacks resources. One of the reasons that legal reform is not regarded as a priority for funding is that the majority of people are not interested in formal law. Those living outside the capital and provincial centers are still governed by customary law and regard formal laws as alien concepts. This has resulted in a vicious circle, whereby localization and development of an indigenous jurisprudence are hampered by

lack of interest stemming from the fact that the existing legal system is foreign. An extensive program of research and legal education is required to reform the legal system and introduce changes more suitable to local circumstances.

Jennifer Corrin Care

See also Common Law; Customary Law; Indigenous and Folk Legal Systems; Legal Education; Magistrates—Common Law Systems

References and further reading
Corrin Care, J. 1997. "Developments in Solomon Islands Constitutional Law in 1997." Pp. 235–255 in *Asia-Pacific Comparative Constitutional Law Yearbook*. Edited by Cheryl Saunders and Graham Hassall. Melbourne: Centre for Comparative Constitutional Studies.
———. 1998. *Civil Procedure in the South Pacific*. Fiji Islands: IJALS.
———. 1999a. "Courts in Solomon Islands." *LAWASIA Journal* 98.
———. 1999b. "Customary Law and Human Rights in Solomon Islands—A Commentary on *Remisio Pusi v. James Leni and Others*." *Journal of Legal Pluralism* (September): 135.
———. 2000. "Customary Law and Women's Rights in Solomon Islands." *Development Bulletin* 51 (March) (ANU, Development Studies Network): 20–22.
———. 2001. *Contract Law in the South Pacific*. London: Cavendish.
Corrin Care, J., T. Newton, and D. Paterson. 1999. *Introduction to South Pacific Law*. London: Cavendish.
Narokobi, Bernard. 1983. *The Melanesian Way*. Suva: IPS, USP.
Nonggor, J. 1993. "Solomon Islands." Pp. 268–295 in *South Pacific Island Legal Systems*. Edited by Michael Ntumy. Honolulu: University of Hawai'i Press.

SOMALIA

COUNTRY INFORMATION

Composed of former Italian Somaliland and the former British Protectorate of Somaliland, the Republic of Somalia or Jamhuuriyadda Soomaaliya is strategically located on the east coast of Africa north of the equator near the Bab el Mandeb, the straits connecting the Indian Ocean to the Red Sea and Suez Canal. Bordered by Djibouti, Ethiopia, and Kenya, it has an area of 637,657 square kilometers, slightly smaller than Texas. The northern half of Somalia is hilly, while central and southern areas are flat plateau lands. The Juba and Shebelle Rivers flow across the country's south from Ethiopia to the Indian Ocean. Somalia has a hot climate, with seasonal monsoon winds, and irregular rainfall. The southwest and northeast monsoons moderate the heat from May to October and December to February respectively. The *angambili* periods between the monsoons are very hot

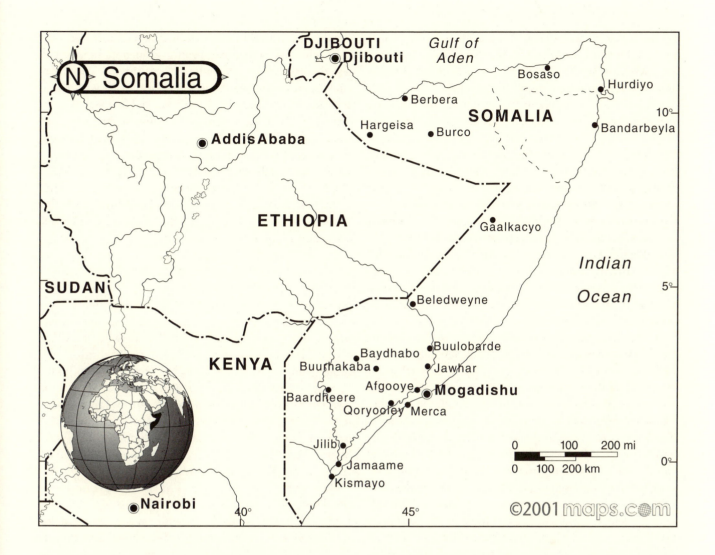

and humid. The country is subject to recurring droughts, famine, deforestation, overgrazing, soil erosion, desertification, water contamination, frequent summer dust storms, and rainy season floods.

Somalia's very young population is estimated to be 7,253,137, with a growth rate of 2.9 percent (2000). The infant mortality rate is very high and life expectancy at birth is 46.23 years. Somalia's capital, Mogadishu, is also a seaport. Other important towns are the capital of Somaliland, Hargeisa, and the ports of Kismayo, Bosasso, Brava, Berbera, and Merca. About 60 percent of all Somalis are nomadic or seminomadic pastoralists, raising cattle, camels, sheep, and goats. Another 25 percent are settled farmers, living mainly in fertile zones along the coast and between the Juba and Shebelle. Somalis are homogeneous in culture and identity. As early as the 600s, indigenous Cushitic peoples began to mingle with Arab coastal traders. A Somali culture emerged, bound by common traditions, a single language, and Sunni Islam, the faith of 99 percent of the population. More than 85 percent of the population is Somali. Speakers of Bantu languages comprise most of the remainder, along with some 35,000 Arabs, about 2,000 Italians, and 1,000 Indians and Pakistanis. The Somali language remained unwritten until October 1973, when it was declared the nation's official language and the language of instruction in all schools with an orthography using Latin letters. Arabic, English, and Italian also are widely used. Overall literacy is 24 percent, but more than twice as many men as women are able to read.

Intermittent civil war has been a feature of Somali national life since 1977. Somaliland and Puntland, the northernmost stable parts of the country, are effectively independent of Mogadishu, but not recognized by any foreign government. Beginning in 1993, UN humanitarian efforts, mainly in the south, were able to alleviate famine conditions, but when the UN withdrew in 1995, having suffered significant casualties, order still had not been restored. Differences between factions center largely around issues of justice related to previous regimes or to the factional violence of the 1990s. Established in Mogadishu in October 2000, the Transitional National Government (TNG) is struggling to establish dialogue with the Somaliland and Puntland administrations, and to deal with factional leaders in Mogadishu and the south. Its power seldom extends beyond the capital. Somalia's legal system is structured along Islamic lines with Italian and British influences dating from colonial times.

One of the world's poorest, least developed, and least stable countries, Somalia has small unexploited reserves of petroleum, natural gas, uranium, iron, tin, gypsum, bauxite, copper, and salt. Much of the country's economy has been devastated by war and drought. Its GDP is estimated to be $4.3 billion and per capita annual income is about $600 (1999). Statistics on annual growth and inflation have been unavailable for a decade. The national currency, the Somali shilling, collapsed in the mid-1980s. Somaliland has issued its own currency, the Somaliland shilling. Attempts to reestablish a monetary system in the rest of the country have been troubled by large amounts of counterfeit currency. Agriculture is the most important sector, with livestock accounting for about 59 percent of GDP and about 65 percent of export earnings. Arable land accounts for 13 percent of Somalia's area, of which only a tiny portion is cultivated. Using irrigation systems and farm machinery, the modern agricultural sector consists mainly of southern plantations growing bananas, Somalia's second most important export. Sorghum, corn, sugarcane, mangoes, sesame seeds, beans, and fish are produced for the domestic market. Aromatic woods, such as frankincense and myrrh, have also contributed to exports since ancient times. The small industrial sector, based on the processing of agricultural products, petroleum, and textiles, accounts for 10 percent of GDP, but most industries have shut down due to civil strife. Foreign aid projects have tried to establish small textile, handicraft, meat-processing, and printing industries. Electricity production is from fossil fuels only. Exports earn around $187 million (1998 estimate) and include livestock, bananas, hides, and fish. Imports costing $327 million (1998 estimate) include mostly manufactured goods, petroleum products, foodstuffs, and construction materials. Somalia's most important trade partners are Djibouti, Kenya, Belarus, India, Saudi Arabia, the UAE, Italy, Yemen, and Brazil (1997). External debt was estimated to be $2.6 billion in 1997. Receiving $191.5 million in foreign assistance in 1995, Somalia is dependant on aid and the remittances of workers abroad.

Somalia has no railways. Its road system comprises 22,100 kilometers of roads of which 2,608 kilometers are paved (1996 estimate). Throughout the late twentieth century, deepwater port facilities were built or renovated in Mogadishu, Berbera, and Kismayo by the European Union, the United States, and the World Bank. Only seven of the country's sixty-one airports have paved runways. Air transportation is provided by small air charter firms and aid agencies. There are no international flights to and from Somalia. Somalia's telecommunications system was completely destroyed or dismantled by factions in the civil war. Relief organizations depend on their own systems. Recently, cellular telephone systems have been established in Mogadishu and several other towns. Most areas are not linked to Mogadishu or Hargeisa. Broadcasting stations operate in Mogadishu and Hargeisa, including four shortwave radio stations and one television station (1997). A privately owned independent FM radio station was established in Puntland on June 17, 2001. On August 24, 2001, the Transitional National Government launched an FM station, Radio Mogadishu, the Voice of the Somali Republic. Somalia's first Internet café opened in Mogadishu in April 2001.

HISTORY

The Somali people are believed to have descended from seventh-century Koreishite immigrants from Yemen. By the late 1500s Portuguese traders ruled several coastal towns, which were subsequently taken over by the sultan of Zanzibar. Looking for good harbors, the British East India Company signed treaties with the sultan of Tajura as early as 1840. By 1886, the British had gained control over northern Somalia, which was guaranteed British protection. Until 1920, British rule was challenged by the Islamic nationalist leader Mohamed Abdullah, a popular Somali hero. In the 1880s, Italy obtained commercial rights in the area and established protectorates over the Obbia and Caluula sultanates. The Ethiopian-British Somaliland boundary was drawn in 1897. But the Ethiopian-Italian Somaliland border was never clarified. Both powers gradually extended their presence inland. In 1924, the Jubaland province of Kenya was ceded to Italy by the United Kingdom. In the late 1920s, Italian influence expanded into eastern Ethiopia's Ogaden region. Under Mussolini in 1935, Italian forces launched an offensive from their colony that led to the capture of Addis Ababa and the Italian annexation of Ethiopia. Italian troops overran British Somaliland in June 1940. The British responded quickly, expelling the Italians from the region the next year. All of Somalia was placed under British military administration, which began a transition toward self-government by establishing local courts, planning committees, and the Protectorate Advisory Council. After World War II, Italy renounced all rights to Italian Somaliland. However, in November 1949, the UN General Assembly placed Italian Somaliland under a ten-year trusteeship, with Italy as the administering authority. Meanwhile, British Somaliland moved toward self-government with legislative elections in February 1960.

British Somaliland became independent on June 26, 1960. Five days later, it joined the Italian Trust Territory of Somaliland to the south to form the Somali Republic. The legislatures of the two combined to form the National Assembly. The constitution of the Trust Territory, debated and written during the preceding three years, became the constitution of the entire nation, after a national referendum in June 1961, in which voting in former British areas was boycotted. This constitution included a bill of rights not subject to amendment and provided a unicameral National Assembly of 123 deputies elected for five years, a president elected by the National Assembly, a prime minister (named by the president), and an independent judiciary. Ex-presidents became National Assembly deputies for life. During the early postindependence period, political parties reflected clan loyalties. Pan-Somali militants pressed for unification with Somali-inhabited areas in Djibouti, Ethiopia, and Kenya.

On October 21, 1969, Maj. Gen. Mohamed Siad Barre took power in a military coup and suspended the constitution. Until 1977, his Marxist-orientated government was a close ally of the Soviet Union. Executive and legislative power was vested in a twenty-member Supreme Revolutionary Council (SRC), with Siad Barre as president. Political repression, gross human rights violations, and the manipulation of clan loyalties and regional rivalries were the hallmarks of Siad Barre's regime. The regime initiated a number of grassroots development projects. Its most impressive success was a crash program introducing an orthography for the Somali language and bringing literacy to much of the population. In the mid-1970s, the Western Somali Liberation Front began guerrilla operations in Ethiopia's Ogaden region. Fighting increased, and in July 1977 the Somali army crossed into Ethiopia to support the insurgents. Then, the Soviet Union switched sides and rescued Ethiopia with thousands of Cuban troops. Expelling the Soviets, Siad Barre was able to win backing from the United States, until criticism of his regime by the U.S. Congress led to a suspension of U.S. aid. Security forces meted out severe punishment to Mijerteen clans after a group of Mijerteen officers attempted a coup in the aftermath of the disastrous war. Wells were poisoned, cattle and camels were killed, and people were slaughtered. In response, the Somali Salvation Democratic Front (SSDF) was established by exiles in Ethiopia. In mid-1982, Ethiopian forces invaded central Somalia and the United States provided emergency airlifts to help the Somalis. Cities in the northwest were vengefully bombed. By 1988, Siad Barre was openly at war with much of his own country. The army dissolved into competing armed groups loyal to former commanders or to clan-tribal leaders. The economy was in shambles and hundreds of thousands fled. The human cost of the dictatorship was enormous and only became evident to the outside world when the regime collapsed in 1991, following armed resistance by the Somali National Movement (SNM) in the northwest, and later the United Somali Congress (USC) in the south.

For the next decade, clan militias prevented the establishment of a central government and more than twelve internationally sponsored reconciliation conferences failed. The country fell victim to rampant violence and lawlessness. Kidnappings, looting, and murder became commonplace. The infrastructure and educational system collapsed. The system determining land tenure broke down. Factional fighting between warlords Mohammed Farah Aideed, Osman Atto, and Ali Mahdi Mohammed in Mogadishu and the south left an estimated 30,000 civilians dead. Recurrent drought and flooding plague the country. At least one in nine Somalis fled to neighboring countries, with another estimated 1.7 million people displaced internally. Hundreds of thousands of displaced Somalis remain in overcrowded, disease-infested camps. Chronic insecurity impedes the delivery of aid. International efforts centered on getting food and medical assistance to Somalis, who suffered from regular famines, rather than on pursuing justice and prosecuting crimes against humanity. Seeking to safeguard relief supplies, unsuccessful peacekeeping operations were mounted by the U.S. Unified Task Force (UNITAF) from December 1992, and by the United Nations Operation in Somalia (UNOSOM) from May 1993 to March 1995. U.S. forces withdrew in 1994 after suffering losses in pitched battles in downtown Mogadishu. Largely responsible for wrecking UN efforts, Farah Aideed declared himself president in June 1995, but was killed in August 1996. His son, Hussein, succeeded him.

In May 1991, with the south consumed by factional violence, the SNM declared unilateral independence for Somaliland, based on British Somaliland's borders. Somaliland was fairly stable, with trade coming in from Saudi Arabia via the rebuilt port of Berbera. Secessionists argued that independence was justified by the atrocities inflicted on the region by Siad Barre. First Abdirahman Tur, and then former prime minister Mohammed Ibrahim Egal, were selected by elders as president and struggled for recognition. The latter was elected leader by clan elders in Boroma in 1993, and again in 1997. In the northeast, Puntland declared itself an autonomous region in 1998, at a conference in Garowe attended by delegates from the Bari, Nugal, Sool, and Sanaag regions. Unlike Somaliland, Puntland has never considered itself independent. The north is generally considered the safest part of Somalia. However, in May and June 2000, death threats and an attempted grenade attack led international aid agencies to suspend operations in Puntland.

Numerous attempts were made to bring some thirty Somali factions together. Efforts by Ethiopia, Egypt, Yemen, Kenya, and Italy failed. But in August 2000, Djibouti's president Ismael Omar Guelleh hosted talks that included former politicians, faction leaders, and military officers. These talks led to the first meeting of a 245-seat

Transitional National Assembly at Arta, Djibouti, on August 13, 2000, and the election of Abdiqassim Salad Hassan as president on August 26. Mogadishu's Islamic courts and business community, which had revived somewhat by that summer, released a joint statement supporting the assembly. But both the Somaliland and Puntland administrations boycotted these discussions, citing the fact that Salad Hassan was a former interior minister and deputy prime minister under Siad Barre, and that the assembly contained former military men who had been in command in northern territories, overseeing repressive policies. Influential leaders opposed to the Djibouti process have called for the establishment of a federal system. Salad Hassan formed the Transitional National Government (TNG) on August 30, 2000. His arrival in Mogadishu on October 14, 2000, was greeted with enthusiasm by more than 1,000 heavily armed militiamen riding on pickup trucks. However, he has been unable to assert authority beyond Mogadishu, which accommodates the majority of internally displaced persons and has been completely off limits to United Nations agencies in recent years. Nine aid workers were abducted in March 2001.

LEGAL CONCEPTS

Collective justice within a system of customary law is the guiding feature of Somali legal tradition. Somalia is divided into about 100 clans, groups of persons tracing descent from a common male ancestor, after whom the clan is named. They are usually part of larger clan-families and subdivided into smaller lineage groups. The six major clan-families are Daarood, Hawiye, Isaaq, Dir, Digil, and Rahanwayn. Clientage, the binding of large numbers of people to powerful patrons, is a trait of this system. Males in Somali society are further divided into groups who comprise members of Islamic religious brotherhoods, or *wadad*, and warriors, or *waranle*. Women have very narrow legal recognition. Every Somali also belongs to one of over a thousand *diya* groups, corresponding to lineage subdivisions. Children automatically belong to their father's group; married women remain members of their own fathers' groups. Among nomads, a *diya* group is an alliance of lineages, ranging from 200 to 5,000 males, that acts as a unit in dealings with members of other groups. In farming communities, *diya* groups are often based on villages or groups of villages numbering 5,000 to 100,000 men. These groups are concerned with the security of persons and livestock, in the case of farming communities, and with land and water rights. Traditionally, if a person was killed or injured by a member of a rival group, even in a traffic accident, the elders of the two groups would meet to discuss the matter and arrange the payment of *diya* or blood compensation, which was a group, not individual, responsibility. Warfare between

diya groups that resulted in death was compensated by payment of 100 camels for a man (50 for a woman). Settlements restored peace, while nonsettlement led to further warfare. Obligations were traditionally set down in formal *heer* agreements. During the colonial era, these agreements were filed with District Commissioners or Residents.

Prior to independence, the formal legal system of the northern region was based on English common law superimposed on Somali customary law, while that of the southern region combined Italian law and customary law. Traditional courts are councils of elders and specialists in customary law known as *wayel* and *akhyar*. In Italian Somaliland, application of Islamic *sharia* law was more common in civil and minor penal matters than in British Somaliland, where it was limited to cases pertaining to marriage, divorce, family disputes, inheritance, and some contracts. In 1964, a Consultative Commission for Integration completed work on the organization, procedures, and basic laws of a unified judicial system, embracing Islamic, British, Italian, and customary aspects, which recognized international standards. The Italian system of basing judicial decisions on the application of legal codes was retained, while English common law and doctrines of equity were applied in matters not governed by legislation. *Sharia* law was applied to most civil matters. After the 1969 coup, the Siad Barre regime assumed all judicial as well as executive and legislative powers and suspended the constitution, which was eventually replaced in 1979. In 1973 the regime introduced a unified civil code, which sharply curtailed both *sharia* and customary law and abolished traditional land, water, and grazing rights. This new code restricted *diya* payments and a subsequent amendment prohibited *diya* entirely. The attorney general, appointed by the minister of Justice and assisted by deputies, was responsible for the observance of the law and prosecution of criminal matters. This system was dismantled and the 1979 Constitution was nullified when Siad Barre was overthrown. Since 1991, traditional clan systems have reemerged and there has been little inclination to build anything resembling a formal state. Islamic courts, whose roles have blended with customary courts, adjudicate most cases, including ones involving land tenure, water and grazing rights, and the payment of *diya*. Somalia currently has no constitution. A 1979 Constitution, amended in 1990, was revoked following the overthrow of Mohammed Siad Barre in January 1991. However, the pre-1991 penal code continues to be applied in some areas.

CURRENT STRUCTURE

Somalia has had no functioning national government since the 1991 ouster of Siad Barre. Its legislature, the unicameral Golaha Shacbiga or People's Assembly, was dominated by the executive. Administratively, Somalia was subdivided into eighteen regions or *gobolka:* Awdal, Bakool, Banaadir, Bari, Bay, Galguduud, Gedo, Hiraan, Jubbada Dhexe, Jubbada Hoose, Mudug, Nugaal, Sanaag, Shabeellaha Dhexe, Shabeellah Hoose, Sool, Togdheer, and Woqooyi Galbeed. Interclan fighting for control of key economic or political prizes characterizes the present chaotic political situation. Dominated by clans vying for power, the main Somali political parties are the two factions of the United Somali Congress, the Somali National Movement, the Somali Democratic Movement, and the Somali Patriotic Movement. The Somaliland Forum is an important exile group campaigning for Somaliland independence. Universal suffrage for citizens over eighteen years of age has been effectively replaced by decisions of clan chiefs. As a result of a peace conference in Djibouti in 2000, Abdiqasim Salad Hassan was elected president by a 245-member interim National Assembly, appointed by clan chiefs. Salad Hassan then formed the Transitional National Government, recognized by most factions around Mogadishu, but not in Somaliland, Puntland, and parts of the south. He named Ali Khalif Galaid as prime minister on October 9, 2000. The National Assembly held its inaugural session in Mogadishu on November 2, 2000. Salad Hassan appointed law professor Sheikh Adan Mohamed Ibrahim as the head of a new civilian Supreme Court in January 2001. The Somali National Army, a force of about 50,000, was dissolved after Siad Barre's fall. There are no functioning central government military forces and the TNG depends on loyal clan militias. In early 2001, some 20,000 militiamen around Mogadishu were working for private sector companies or Islamic courts, a majority supporting the Transitional National Government.

Somali's first constitution provided for five levels of courts, which, from the lowest level, are: (1) *sharia* courts dealing with family and personal matters under Islamic and customary law; (2) district courts dealing with civil and criminal cases; (3) regional courts with civil and criminal sections (also dealing with military justice in Mogadishu and Hargeisa); (4) high courts of assize, with civil, criminal, and military appellate sections; and (5) a Supreme Court, for final appeals. Keeping this system at least in appearance, Siad Barre established the National Security Court to rule on cases involving attempts to destroy the independence, unity, and security of the state.

Following the breakdown of national government in 1991, this system ceased to function above its lowest level. *Sharia* courts continued to operate throughout the country and regularly extended their scope to criminal proceedings, often criticized by human rights advocates. Most convicted by these courts have had no rights to defense lawyers or appeals. Islamic courts have their own militias and prisons, which are often just steel shipping containers with a few holes punched in them to allow prisoners to breathe. In some areas, harsh punishments are meted out to offenders, including public whippings, amputations, and stoning. Criminals are sometimes turned over to their victims' families, who then exact *diya* in keeping with tradition. In January 2001, more than fifty gunmen attacked an Islamic court in south Mogadishu and released forty-eight prisoners, including five convicted murderers. The attackers were former members of the court's militia who were not paid by the TNG. Somaliland has also instituted *sharia* law and mandated separate classrooms and medical facilities for males and females, and Islamic attire for women. The Transitional National Government claimed to have nationalized Mogadishu's Islamic courts in June 2001. No longer independent entities, these courts would operate under the justice ministry and their militias would be taken over by the interior ministry and absorbed into the police force. Some judges from Islamic courts would be incorporated into the official judiciary.

Separatism has also altered Somalia profoundly. Although chaos envelops most of the country, some orderly administration has been established in the north, where clan elders in former British Somaliland established the independent Republic of Somaliland in May 1991. Not recognized by any foreign government, Somaliland maintains a stable existence due to the overwhelming dominance of one clan and the economic infrastructure left behind by British, Russian, and American military assistance programs. Also relatively stable, neighboring Puntland has criticized the TNG and has moved independently toward reconstructing representative government. A referendum in Somaliland on May 31, 2001, approved a proposed constitution for the breakaway region with 97.09 percent affirmative votes. The TNG condemned the referendum, which American and South African observers declared to be free and fair. Authorities in Puntland felt that the Somaliland vote was unwise and provocative. In August 2001, four Somaliland elders, who had claimed they were "the highest authority in Somaliland," were arrested by authorities after a half-hour gunfight.

In mid-2001 Puntland's stability was also shaken. Meeting in Garowe, Puntland's regional capital, in late July 2001, traditional elders debated the extension of the mandate of President Abdullahi Yusuf and his administration, called for new elections, and named Chief Justice Yusuf Haji Nur as acting president. Abdullahi Yusuf challenged the elders' power to resolve such a dispute and tension over control of Bosaso's seaport and airport followed. Fighting in Bosaso on August 5 left between twenty and forty dead and sixty or more wounded. The violence subsided, but subsequent conferences on the controversy were inconclusive. Around the same time, two journalists were

Structure of Somali Courts

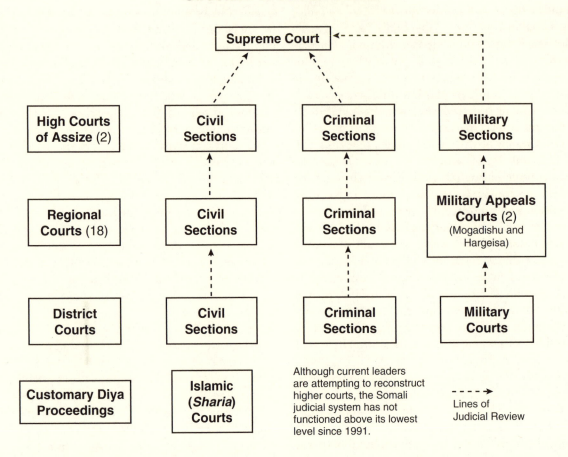

Although current leaders are attempting to reconstruct higher courts, the Somali judicial system has not functioned above its lowest level since 1991.

- - - - → Lines of Judicial Review

arrested in Bosaso, and later released after the regional prosecutor took exception to their account of a rape, because he felt it was damaging to the region's image.

In January 2001, eighty-four delegates opposed to the TNG from Bay, Bakol, Gedo, Shabeeha Hoose, Jubada Dhexe, and Juba Hoose in the south met in Baidoa to try to establish a Southern Regional Administration, modeled on Puntland and based in the port city of Kismayo, 500 kilometers south of Mogadishu. An eleven-member council, representing each of the region's major subclans, was established as a result of talks organized by the pro-TNG Juba Valley Alliance (JVA), which in 1999 forcibly expelled from Kismayo the anti-TNG Somali Reconciliation and Restoration Council (SRRC) militia, led by Gen. Muhammad Sa'id Hirsi Morgan. Poor rains heightened tensions in the agricultural south. Heavy fighting rocked Mogadishu in mid-July 2001, as militia factions loyal to Husayn Aydid and Usman Ato tried to loot a convoy of trucks carrying Saudi relief food and clashed with militias loyal to the TNG. In another incident, over twenty-five people were killed when two Abgal subclans fought in north Mogadishu. On August 7, 2001, Kismayo was recaptured from the JVA by the SRRC. Demonstrating the degree of insecurity in Somalia, the Transitional National Assembly initiated debate on a

motion to call in troops from friendly countries to help disarm the factions opposed to the TNG in August 2001. Despite numerous talks with faction leaders, Abdiqassim Salad Hassan's efforts to achieve reconciliation and political stability have hitherto met with little success and his government has been barely able to control the capital.

SPECIALIZED JUDICIAL BODIES

Somalia and its component parts have not created or been party to any specialized judicial bodies.

STAFFING

As no courts in Somalia are truly under the control of a central government, the recruitment of judges and court functionaries and the staffing of local courts are determined by clan leaders and local Islamic judges. The education of lawyers, judges, and court personnel is limited, although some have past training in either European or Islamic systems. Law enforcement also remains largely clan-based. In April 2001, a thousand former militiamen were brought to a camp in Lafole, south of Mogadishu, to begin six months' training as policemen by the TNG, which is hoping to train 5,000 militia as police officers, once funds become available. That same month, 350 police and prison service recruits began training courses in the penal code, human rights, and gender rights at Madera police training school in Somaliland. This is part of a larger UN Development Program project aimed at educating 1,000 new recruits.

IMPACT

The dissolution of central government in Somalia has meant that the impact of courts and knowledge of legal norms varies widely according to local conditions. Traditional and Islamic legal structures have offered a measure of justice in some places. But insecurity in much of Somalia has fostered widespread abuses, much suffering by civilians, and a culture of impunity, which has undermined rule of law. Various militias have been accused of arbitrary executions and other killings, torture, detention without trial, robbery, rape, and illegal checkpoints. The Mogadishu-based Isma'il Jim'ale Human Rights Centre (IJHRC), Somalia's largest human rights organization, has repeatedly expressed concern over human rights violations and conditions accompanying them. The IJHRC has close ties with international human rights groups, such as Amnesty International and Human Rights Watch. Over the years, UN special rapporteurs have visited numerous parts of the country collecting evidence of crimes against humanity. The UN Commission on Human Rights has repeatedly expressed concern at Somalia's human rights situation and lack of progress toward national reconciliation, calling on all parties to observe international law and condemning acts of violence against humanitarian workers by militias. The status of women and female genital mutilation are also major concerns.

How the traumas of the past quarter century are dealt with is crucial. Many assert that the longer human rights issues remain unaddressed, the more difficult reconciliation becomes. Heavy rains in 1997 exposed bones, clothing, and other evidence of mass death from shallow graves in Hargeisa. At the request of the UN Commission on Human Rights, an international forensic team went to Somaliland in December 1997. It concluded that the mass graves contained evidence of gross human rights abuses. Long-term psychological consequences of Somalia's past have emerged in psychiatric disturbances among survivors of atrocities and widespread feelings of guilt for failing to properly bury the dead, which would fulfill traditional obligations. Given its precarious hold, the TNG's ability to establish an effective, impartial justice system is questionable. The issue of atrocities could be politicized and used to further extremism. The ability of forensic teams to pursue investigations in more secure regions may lead to assumptions that atrocities are being recognized selectively. Alternatives would be to set up a peace and reconciliation commission, or institute an investigation by an international tribunal or UN-mandated body, technically equipped to investigate mass graves. As debates continue, vital evidence is deteriorating due to weathering. The Somaliland administration has set up the Technical Committee for the Investigation of War Crimes of the Siad Barre Regime to document and preserve the sites.

Randall Fegley

See also Civil Law; Common Law; Customary Law; Islamic Law; Italy; Qadi (Qazi) Courts; United Kingdom

References and further reading
Bureau of African Affairs. 1998. *Background Notes: Somalia.* Washington, DC: U.S. Department of State.
Bureau of Consular Affairs. 2001. *Somalia: Consular Information Sheet.* Washington, DC: U.S. Department of State.
Castagno, Margaret. 1975. *Historical Dictionary of Somalia.* Metuchen, NJ: Scarecrow Press.
Clarke, Walter, and Jeffrey Herbst, eds. 1997. *Learning from Somalia.* Boulder, CO: Westview Press.
IRIN News Briefs. Nairobi, Kenya: UN Office for the Coordination of Humanitarian Affairs/Integrated Regional Information, Networks. http://www.reliefweb.int/IRIN/index.phtml (accessed November 25, 2001).
Laitin, David, and Said Samatar. 1987. *Somalia: Nation in Search of a State.* Boulder, CO: Westview Press.
Nelson, Harold, ed. 1982. *Somalia: A Country Study.* Washington, DC: U.S. Government Printing Office.
"Somalia." 2001. *The World Factbook.* Washington, DC: CIA.
U.S. Department of State. 2001. *Somalia Country Report on Human Rights Practices, 2000.* Washington, DC: Bureau of Democracy, Human Rights and Labor, U.S. Department of State.
World Refugee Survey. 2000. Washington, DC: U.S. Committee for Refugees.

SOUTH AFRICA

COUNTRY INFORMATION

Covering 471,445 square miles (1,221,037 square kilometers) on the southern tip of the African continent, the Republic of South Africa is bounded by the Atlantic and Indian Oceans on the west, south, and east, and by Mozambique, Swaziland, Zimbabwe, Botswana, and Namibia to the north and west. The Drakensberg mountain range forms an escarpment behind which lies not only the small independent Kingdom of Lesotho in the center of South Africa, but also the interior plateau, on which lies the maize triangle and rich mineral deposits. These have driven the economic development of the country ever since the opening of the Witwatersrand gold reef in the late nineteenth century.

Today, wealth is concentrated in the province of Gauteng, which is dominated by an urban metropolis stretching from the industrial cities of the east rand through the city of Johannesburg to Pretoria, the administrative capital

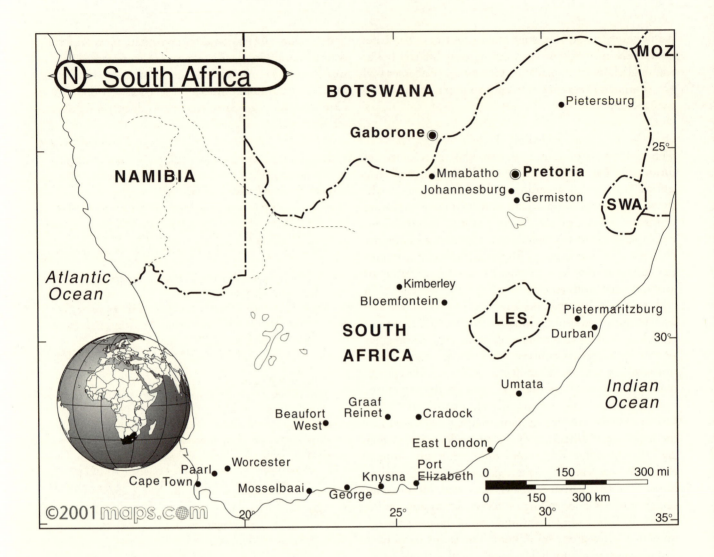

©2001 maps.com

of South Africa, in the north. In contrast, the surrounding provinces—North-West Province, Northern Province, Mpumalanga, and the Free State—are all less industrialized and much poorer. The remaining four of South Africa's nine provinces, which span South Africa's coastline from west to east, include the sparsely populated semidesert of the Northern Cape and the Western Cape, Eastern Cape, and KwaZulu-Natal—whose sunshine and beaches complement the draw of big game to make South Africa an attractive tourist destination. With climatic zones ranging from the Mediterranean climate of the southwestern Cape to subtropical KwaZulu-Natal and Mpumalanga, the country possesses a rich diversity of flora and fauna, yet with limited rainfall only about 15 percent of the land is suitable for arable agriculture.

With a population of over 40 million people speaking eleven official languages and numerous nonofficial tongues, South Africa is ethnically and culturally diverse. Despite the efforts of the apartheid regime to use this diversity to maintain a system of racial dominance, the democratic polity that emerged from the 1994 elections reflects a more historic division between those who

sought to overthrow the old regime and those who either supported it or worked within its legally inscribed system of racial and ethnic hierarchies. While a good majority of the 75 percent African majority supported the governing African National Congress in the first two democratic elections (1994 and 1999), the official opposition in Parliament appeals predominantly to the concerns of the white (14 percent), "Coloured" (8 percent), and Asian (3 percent, largely South Asian) minorities. This is despite the fact that many among these communities, including at times large sections of the Coloured and Indian communities, actively opposed apartheid and supported the ANC or other antiapartheid parties during the struggle against apartheid.

Despite the disruption of international economic sanctions and the low-intensity civil war that characterized the last decade of the apartheid regime's rule, South Africa remains one of the largest producers of minerals and is the twenty-sixth largest trading nation. It is Africa's largest and most industrially developed economy, with a sophisticated transport and telecommunications system and capacity to generate about 40 percent of the continent's electricity output. However, it also has one of the most unequal patterns of income distribution in the world, with under 6 percent of the population accounting for over 40 percent of consumption. This disparity (which still falls largely along racial lines) produces stark contrasts between highly developed suburban conveniences and completely impoverished urban and rural blight, a situation that embodies both the hope and dilemma of the challenge of development in Africa.

The collapse of apartheid-era policing in the early 1990s, greater freedom of movement, an abundance of legal and illegal weapons, as well as the exclusion of a whole generation who had forsaken limited personal opportunities to battle the old regime, spawned a violent and rising crime wave. Although the new government formally embraced the culture of rights promised by the constitutional arrangements that heralded in the postapartheid era, the impact of crime and lack of state resources led to frequent expressions of frustration against the restraints imposed by the newly adopted Bill of Rights. In fact, the decade since 1990, when the white regime first accepted the need for a democratic transition, was marked by a constant process of restructuring. From the very structure of the national state to every aspect of the legal system, there has been a series of changes that are still in the process of transforming South African society and law. Although there continues to be debate about the nature, extent, and even need for ongoing transformation, it is important to recognize that within the first decade after 1994, South Africa has successfully created a united democratic polity, adopted and followed the strictures of a justiciable constitution, and achieved significant legislative and administrative change. Although much remains to be achieved, there is little question that the last decade of the twentieth century brought dramatic and permanent change to the political and legal landscape of South Africa.

HISTORY

The development of South African law is an integral part of the history of colonialism in South Africa. Until 1994, social customs and norms constituting the law of indigenous societies, although well established and enduring in the face of occupation and dispossession, were either explicitly cast aside or ignored, except where recognized and applied as part of the colonial administration of *native* peoples. Instead, South African common law was described as a mixed system of civil and common law origin whose heritage may be traced to the Roman-Dutch law that arrived at the Cape of Good Hope in 1652 as part of the social and cultural baggage of the employees of the Dutch East India Company. Applied mainly in civil cases today, Roman-Dutch law was until the adoption of the 1993 interim constitution the source of the basic principles that the judiciary applied in interpreting and giving legal effect to the statutory enactments that comprise the dominant segment of the modern South African legal order.

The application of this uncodified variant of European civil law was, for the first 150 years of colonial history, rather limited. None of the judges were legally trained and the law library contained only ten textbooks in 1739, nearly one hundred years after the establishment of the colony. The company's control over trade and manufacture, including the importation of slaves, meant that Vryburghers—settlers whom the company had allowed to establish themselves within the colony—with claims against the company, would petition higher officials rather than bring suit in the local courts. Law at the Cape in this period largely functioned to maintain and protect company discipline, property, and morals, but slowly evolved to regulate relationships between masters and their slaves or indigenous Khoi servants.

Britain's occupation of the Cape in 1806 had little effect on the life of the colony until the introduction of a policy of vigorous anglicization that followed the arrival of British settlers in 1820. Prior to this, ad hoc changes were made to the judicial order in the colony, including introducing a court of criminal appeal (1808), circuit courts (1811), the opening of court hearings to the public (1813), and extending the powers of the courts of *landdrost en heemraden*. The new policy substituted English for Dutch as the official language and required all judicial proceedings to be conducted exclusively in English. Following the First Charter of Justice of 1827, the old Council of Justice was abolished and the Cape Supreme Court established. The Second Charter of Justice of 1832 completely transformed the local judicial establishment, professionalized the judiciary, and introduced both a code of criminal procedure and regulations for administering the estates of deceased persons, minors, and lunatics. The complete replacement of Roman-Dutch law by English common law was, however, prevented by settled principles of both colonial-era international law and English law, and the policy that colonies acquired by cession or by conquest were to retain their old law unless it was subsequently repealed. However, the influence of English common law principles was a natural consequence of sociopolitical developments in the Cape colony during the nineteenth century. British occupation and settlement, followed by the English language policy and the extension of formal equality to the Khoi and "free coloured persons," followed by the abolition of slavery, all worked to create an atmosphere in which British colonial norms became the model at the Cape. The actual mechanisms of legal reception were both formal and informal, including the adoption of the English law of evidence in 1830 and the fashioning of civil procedure along English lines. Business practice, including the use of negotiable instruments and insurance bills of lading, was influenced by English practice and reinforced by the wholesale adoption of English statutes, merely repromulgated as colonial statutes, including the Merchant Shipping Act, the Joint Stock Companies Limited Liability Act, and the Companies Act.

Although the policy of apartheid is identified with the nationalist party government that came to power in 1948, racial discrimination and segregation became embedded in South African society from the earliest days of colonial penetration. Implementing its apartheid policy after coming to power in the 1948 parliamentary elections, the nationalist government introduced a series of bills that together created an elaborate legislative scheme of statutory apartheid. To a great extent these laws attempted both to codify the existing practice of segregation and to use state power to control and shape the increasing social and political pressures that were mounting as South Africa entered the post–World War II era of anticolonial political struggles and industrialization. This statutory framework provided for the registration of citizens by race, the prohibition of interracial sex and marriage, the provision of separate unequal public facilities, and the racial segregation of the towns and cities of South Africa. While apartheid legislation eventually discriminated against black South Africans in virtually all aspects of social life, from birth to death, at the same time the government introduced a second legislative scheme to address the political pressures that were developing in this period. The Bantu Authorities Act of 1951 and the Promotion of Bantu Self-Government Act of 1959 introduced the policy of separate development under which the black majority was to be eventually divided into ten ethnic groups and granted self-government or independence within the overall framework of apartheid. At the same time the Suppression of Communism Act of 1950 began the process of political repression that culminated in this period in the Unlawful Organizations Act of 1960, which banned the African National Congress (ANC) and Pan Africanist Congress (PAC), the major black political organizations.

In the face of increasing internal resistance and international isolation, the South African government looked in the late 1970s to the political reincorporation of the Indian and Coloured communities as a means of broadening its social base. The outcome of this shift in apartheid policy was the adoption of the 1983 Constitution, which extended the franchise to Indians and Coloureds in a tricameral legislature with its jurisdiction distributed according to a vague distinction between "own" and "general" affairs. Two mechanisms ensured, however, that power remained safely in the hands of the dominant white party. First, the running of government was effectively centralized under an executive state president with extraordinary powers in both the executive and legislative arenas. Second, all significant decisions within the legislature—such as the election of president—would be automatically resolved by the 4:2:1 ratio of representatives, which ensured that even if the Indian and Coloured houses of Parliament voted in unison, the will of the white house would prevail.

The exclusion of the African majority from this scheme and resistance from within the two target communities—Indian and Coloured—meant that the 1983 Constitution was practically stillborn. The escalation of resistance and rebellion that began in late 1984 and led to the imposition of repeated states of emergency from mid-1985 sealed its fate. The ANC's publication of the *Constitutional Guidelines for a Democratic South Africa* in mid-1988 marked the first public expression by the ANC of an initiative aimed at achieving a negotiated settlement in South Africa. By publicly committing itself to the adoption of a bill of rights enforceable through the courts, the ANC assured the world of its commitment to constitutionalism. This led to the adoption of the Harare Declaration by the Organization of African Unity in August 1989. This document used the constitutional guidelines as a basis for outlining the minimum principles of a postapartheid constitution acceptable to the international community, and was later adopted by the Non-Aligned Movement and the United Nations General Assembly. Finally, the ANC proposed its own Bill of Rights for a New South Africa in 1990, with further amendments in 1991 and 1992.

LEGAL CONCEPTS

South Africa's constitution is today one of the most exemplary models of the constitutional protection of human rights, yet it is superimposed on a legal system whose sources of law were fundamentally shaped by the colonial encounter. Although South African courts formally recognize custom as a source of law, most commentators ignore its historical role in the shaping of significant legal principles, such as equality and justice, within the colonial context. For the first 150 years of colonial settlement at the Cape, agricultural production was based on slavery. At the same time the indigenous Khoisan were legally considered a free people but denied the citizenship rights held by settlers. However, with the expansion of the colony, and the company's grant of unfenced *loan farms* to European settlers, indigenous communities became squatters with no right to live on their old land. As the Khoisan herders lost their livestock and land and became servants, the custom of *apprentices* developed. This form of temporary slavery was recognized by the law in 1775 when it was declared that "all young

Africans captured in war should remain 'apprentices' from the age of eighteen months to twenty-five years old." When the northward expansion of the colony was halted by Khoisan resistance in the 1770s and 1790s, Boer commandos hunted down the Khoisan, killing them like wild game and taking their orphaned children as apprentices. Thus after nearly 150 years of colonial settlement, custom at the Cape had transformed traditional notions of equality and justice inherent in Roman-Dutch law and created a significant distinction—predicated on race—between European settlers and the indigenous Khoi Khoi, despite their formal status as free men.

The significance of statutory law in South Africa was enhanced, prior to 1994, by the doctrine of parliamentary sovereignty, which invested Parliament with *absolute power*. The perversion of this doctrine, in the context of a white minority–controlled Parliament, was further exacerbated by the dominance of the nineteenth-century philosophy of legal positivism among South African lawyers. Thus, while judges were not prohibited from rejecting interpretations of the law that violated the inherited Roman-Dutch legal tradition, their deference to the will of the sovereign and strict distinction between law and morals framed their interpretation of the law. Furthermore, this doctrine functioned as a legalistic smokescreen for the continuance of colonial rule over the black majority. The South Africa Act of 1909, the British act of Parliament that created the Union of South Africa, provided that the control and administration of native affairs throughout the union should vest in the governor-general-in-council, who should exercise all special powers in regard to native administration previously vested in the governors of the several colonies. In these colonies extraordinary powers had been conferred over native affairs. For example, in Natal the governor had taken to himself the powers of supreme chief over all natives, and the Natal Code of Native Law defined these powers, which included the exercise of all political power over natives in Natal, the right to appoint and remove chiefs, to divide and amalgamate tribes, and to punish offenders. Finally, his actions as supreme chief were not cognizable by the courts. This system was reproduced as the national model in the Native Administration Act of 1927, which declared the governor-general the supreme chief and vested him with all the powers arrogated by the Natal Code of Native Law. Thus, through statutory enactment the white minority, under the guise of the doctrine of parliamentary sovereignty, perpetuated colonial rule over the black majority by expressly abdicating its own authority over the executive in this arena and granting the executive unfettered power—free of even minimal judicial review—over the black majority.

The adoption of two new constitutions in 1993 and 1996, as the products of the democratic transition from apartheid, heralded a legal revolution revitalizing South African law. While the introduction of constitutional review and a new constitutional court are central elements of this process, these developments have also had a dramatic impact on the basic concepts underlying all aspects of the law, from criminal procedure to the notions of liberty and equality that form the background norms to any understanding of justice in the new South Africa. Most important, given the legacies of apartheid, is the constitutional embrace of a deep and substantive understanding of equality. Not only does the constitution attempt to address some of the most egregious consequences of the legally imposed inequalities of the past—such as access to landownership—it also adopts a broad definition of equality and provides for affirmative action as a mechanism to deal with this legacy. Listed among the more familiar grounds upon which discrimination is prohibited—such as race, sex, age, and ethnic origin—are pregnancy, marital status, sexual orientation, disability, and language. Furthermore, in cases of alleged discrimination on any of the listed grounds, such discrimination is assumed to be unfair. Finally, these constitutional protections are not limited to relations between the state and individuals but rather are applied to both governmental and private conduct, with the constitution mandating the legislature to enact law to prevent or prohibit unfair discrimination.

CURRENT STRUCTURE

Enshrining constitutional supremacy as one of the founding principles of the postapartheid state fundamentally transformed the legal system. The acceptance of constitutional review during the constitution-making process brought attention to the structure and staffing of the superior courts. In order to both overcome the legacy of apartheid—in which the vast majority of superior judges were conservative white males—and bolster the legitimacy of the judiciary and courts, the constitution created a new constitutional court, which would be placed above the old appellate division of the Supreme Court in decisions concerning the interpretation of the constitution and constitutional review of national legislation. With the new court came a new system of judicial appointment, including public nomination and interviews by a constitutionally established Judicial Services Commission. As part of the political negotiations it was agreed that four justices had to be drawn from among the existing judiciary while the president of the court would be appointed directly by the head of state (President Nelson Mandela) after consultation with the sitting chief justice. After a lengthy appointment process, the first eleven justices took the oath of office at the opening of the constitutional court in February 1995.

With the adoption of the "final" constitution in 1996,

Structure of South African Courts

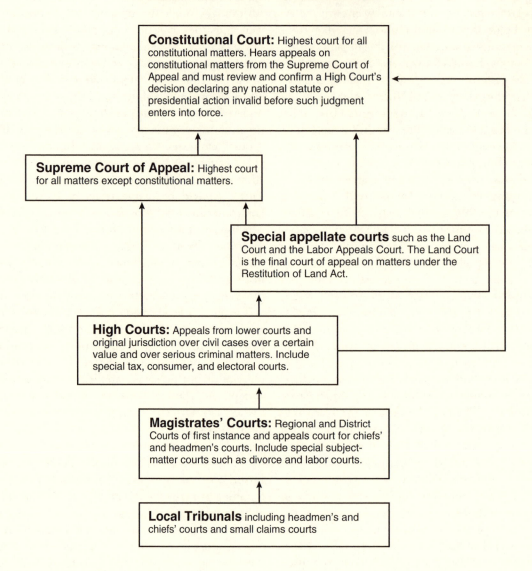

Constitutional Court: Highest court for all constitutional matters. Hears appeals on constitutional matters from the Supreme Court of Appeal and must review and confirm a High Court's decision declaring any national statute or presidential action invalid before such judgment enters into force.

Supreme Court of Appeal: Highest court for all matters except constitutional matters.

Special appellate courts such as the Land Court and the Labor Appeals Court. The Land Court is the final court of appeal on matters under the Restitution of Land Act.

High Courts: Appeals from lower courts and original jurisdiction over civil cases over a certain value and over serious criminal matters. Include special tax, consumer, and electoral courts.

Magistrates' Courts: Regional and District Courts of first instance and appeals court for chiefs' and headmen's courts. Include special subject-matter courts such as divorce and labor courts.

Local Tribunals including headmen's and chiefs' courts and small claims courts

the previous provincial supreme courts were transformed into high courts and the former appellate division of the Supreme Court has become the Supreme Court of Appeal. The constitutional court remains the court of final appeal on constitutional matters and must hear and confirm any decision to strike down an act of Parliament as unconstitutional. Although there has been some suggestion that the Supreme Court of Appeal and the constitutional court could be amalgamated into a larger supreme court with different panels to hear civil and criminal appeals as well as constitutional cases, this debate remains unresolved. Similarly, the present structure of the high courts, in which they are divided into ten divisions plus three local divisions, is likely to change to reflect the proposals of the Hoexter Commission, which is expected to suggest that the present ten divisions be reduced to nine—one for each of the nine provinces.

At the provincial level, the high courts—staffed with

approximately 183 judges—remain the superior courts and important sources of legal interpretation, taking appeals from the Magistrates' Courts and exercising direct jurisdiction over major criminal offenses and civil matters. The lower courts are the Magistrates' Courts, whose geographical jurisdiction provides one of the basic units of governance in South Africa. The 434 magisterial districts each contain a magistrates' office—staffed by a total of 1,507 magistrates, 1,649 public prosecutors, and 11,882 officials of other ranks—whose responsibilities combine both a judicial function and responsibility for aspects of state administration. The magistrate acts as the representative of all government departments that do not have a local office in the district. However, the jurisdiction of the District Magistrates' Courts is limited in criminal cases to offenses bearing prison sentences of no more than three years or a fine not exceeding R60,000. The Regional Magistrates' Courts can impose sentences not exceeding fifteen years in prison or a fine not exceeding R300,000. In addition the District Magistrates' Courts do not have jurisdiction to hear cases involving treason, murder, or rape, while the regional Magistrates' Courts have jurisdiction over all matters except treason. The civil jurisdiction of Magistrates' Courts is limited to cases worth R100,000 or below, unless the parties consent to higher jurisdiction.

In addition to the Magistrates' Courts, there are a number of specialized courts that are either constituted on an ad hoc basis within the high court—such as the special income tax courts or competition appeal courts— or have been independently constituted, such as the land claims court, the electoral court, the labor court, and the labor appeal court. At the lower level there are specialized divorce courts, small claims courts, and the courts of chiefs and headmen.

SPECIALIZED JUDICIAL BODIES

One of the important preconditions for the peaceful democratic transition in South Africa was the agreement to establish a Truth and Reconciliation Commission (TRC) in order to address gross violations of human rights and to provide amnesty for perpetrators. As a unique and historic body with a limited life span, the TRC was made up of three committees: to investigate human rights violations and conduct hearings for victims so that their experiences could be publicly acknowledged; to hold amnesty hearings at which perpetrators would have to publicly and truthfully account for their violations as a precondition to receiving amnesty; and finally a reparations committee with the task of advising the government on what reparations should be paid to victims. The amnesty hearings were presided over by a judge and two assessors (usually senior lawyers) and functioned in a quasi-judicial manner, with cross-examination and sworn testimony but no strict rules of procedure or evidence. The Committee on Human Rights Violations held its first hearing in April 1996, and by December 1997 about 20,000 victims had made statements to the TRC. The amnesty committee received 7,112 applications and by late 2000 had granted amnesty to 849 perpetrators but declined to grant amnesty to 5,392 applicants. Prosecutions of those who declined to apply or were refused have, however, been slow in coming and there has been discussion about the possibility of reopening the amnesty process, particularly for those in the former apartheid military who are yet to come forward.

STAFFING

The legal profession in South Africa was historically organized on the English model with practicing lawyers divided between advocates and attorneys. While only advocates could appear in the superior courts, only attorneys could directly represent clients. Although today there are approximately 7,932 advocates admitted to appear in the high courts as well as 13,398 registered attorneys, this distinction has been eroded by extending the right to appear to attorneys. Despite significant resistance from the profession, the Ministry of Justice has been proposing to unite the profession by eliminating the distinction between attorneys and advocates through a process of government registration for legal practitioners. Critics of these proposals are concerned that government regulation of the profession will have implications for the independence of lawyers and hence judges, who are traditionally drawn from the independent bar. Supporters point out, however, that the profession is presently dominated by white males and transformation of the profession is vital. As Justice Pius Langa of the Constitutional Court argued, "the real debate must relate to finding the best way . . . to deliver effective legal services to South Africa's diverse community."

Appointments to the judicial branch are determined by whether the appointment is to the higher courts (Supreme Courts or now high courts) or to the lower or Magistrates' Courts. While judges of the various divisions of the former Supreme Court always claimed formal independence—despite their appointment by the government—magistrates were until 1992 members of the civil service and were subject, in their appointment, assignment, and promotion, to the authority of the minister of Justice. Since 1994 all judicial appointments have been subject to processes that bring together different parts of the legal profession and government to select candidates for appointment by either the minister of Justice, in the case of magistrates, or the president, in the case of judges. Appointment of judicial officers is now provided for in the constitution: judges of the constitutional court are to be appointed by the president from a list submitted by the Judicial Service Commission (JSC), and judges of the Supreme Court of Appeal and the high courts are to be appointed by the president on the advice of the JSC. Exceptions to this process apply in the case of the president and deputy president of the constitutional court as well as the chief justice and deputy chief justice, all of whom are appointed by the president after consultation with the JSC and, in the case of the constitutional court, with the leaders of political parties represented in the National Assembly as well. Magistrates are, however, still appointed by the minister of Justice, although as a result of legislation adopted by the previous regime— concerned not to pass its own power over the magistrates on to the new government—there is now a Magistrates Commission with whom the minister must consult about appointments. More importantly, the commission and the 1992 act ensure that magistrates are far more secure in their positions and are no longer subject to the will of the government. In practice, most appointments to the higher courts still come from the ranks of advocates with the addition of a number of legal academics who previously could not be considered. As far as magistrates are concerned, there was historically no minimum legal qualification required and many magistrates were appointed from the ranks of prosecutors who began their careers in the police and studied law part-time. Now, all magistrates appointed after 1998 must have at least passed the civil service lower law examination, and the Magistrates Commission is permitted, when recommending any person for appointment as a magistrate, to give preference to those holding a law degree from a South African university or who have passed the Civil Service Higher Law Exam.

IMPACT

Debate over the impact of law in South Africa under apartheid was highlighted during the Legal Hearings of the Truth and Reconciliation Commission. On the one side there were the arguments of those who, like former chief justice Michael Corbett, continued to argue that "prior to the coming into effect of the interim Constitution on 27 April 1994, Parliament was supreme. For practical purposes it could pass any law it liked; and it did so. The courts had no power to question the validity of the laws Parliament made. Still less could they declare them invalid. The courts had no option but to apply the law as they found it, however unjust it might appear to be" (Corbett 1998, 18). On the other side, there was the counterargument made by the traditionally antiapartheid sections of the legal community, including the Black Lawyers Association, Lawyers for Human Rights, the Legal Resources Centre, and the National Association of Democratic Lawyers. These bodies argued that "lawyers and courts under apartheid, with very few and notable exceptions, had co-operated in servicing and enforcing a diabolically unjust political order" (TRC 1998, vol. 4, ch. 4, para. 18). They went on to reject parliamentary sovereignty as an adequate defense or explanation, arguing that the "validity of such a defence depended on at least a substantial degree of democracy in the political order, as well as a basic respect for the rule of law as a direct or necessary adjunct to legislative omnicompetence. Neither prerequisite was present to any significant degree in South Africa" (ibid.). Finally, they argued that "judicial independence was a myth that had been exploded in the daily experience of the courts." Although there were numerous submissions that adopted less polarized versions of these analyses, the commission's conclusions in its final report emphasized that one of the reasons for the "longevity of apartheid was the superficial adherence to 'rule by law' of the National Party whose leaders craved the aura of legitimacy that 'the law' bestowed on their

harsh injustice" (ibid. at para. 32), and that this was exacerbated by the subconscious or unwitting connivance of the courts and the legal profession in the legislative and executive pursuit of injustice.

Despite this condemnation of the law and legal profession under apartheid, the commission acknowledged the existence of both a space for resistance and active defiance by a few lawyers, including judges, teachers, and students, "who used every opportunity to speak out publicly and within the profession against the adoption and execution of rules of law that sanctioned arbitrary official conduct and injustice" (TRC 1998, vol. 4, ch. 4, para. 36). Although the commission found that participation in the system afforded credibility to the claim of an independent legal system, it concluded that the "alleviation of suffering achieved by such lawyers substantially outweighed" any harm done (para. 40).

Under apartheid, then, law served as both the edifice through which the state implemented its abhorrent policies and an arena in which space could be constantly wrestled, creating delay, frustration of, and even occasional victories over the implementation of "legal" injustice, including such systematic violations of human rights as the pass laws, forced removals, denationalization through the imposition of "homeland" independence, and the destruction of community life—all defining features of apartheid.

The introduction of a justiciable constitution in South Africa in April 1994 both demonstrated a new faith in the law and the judiciary and indicated the essential role played by the introduction of constitutionalism in enabling the democratic transition. In this regard, the incorporation of democratic constitutionalism provided an opportunity for compromise by postponing decisions on sensitive and potentially unresolvable questions. While this may be presented as a successful constitution-making strategy, it is also inherent in the nature of a justiciable constitution in that the judicial resolution of constitutional questions rarely if ever forecloses on the possibility of an alternative outcome in the future—creating a political order in which opposing parties may find their contending faiths in the constitution, and believe that their understanding may in time be vindicated.

The creation and legitimation of a constitutional court provided a unique institutional site within which the process of mediation between alternative constitutional imaginations could be sustained. It created the possibility that the judiciary in its role as primary interpreter of the constitution would be able to sustain and civilize the tensions inherent in the repeated referral and contestation of political differences. However, there has been concern among nongovernment organizations and human rights bodies that the social crisis in the country—including the continuing disparities in wealth and its racial character as well as the levels of violence and criminal activity—may put pressure on government to sidestep and hence erode some of the exemplary human rights gains of the democratic transition. In this sense, debates over the funding of the independent constitutional institutions, such as the Independent Electoral Commission, the Human Rights Commission, and the Commission on Gender Equality—constitutionally mandated bodies designed to protect and further democracy—have focused on the relationship between their fiscal dependence and a potential threat to their autonomy from the ruling party and government. Those concerned with the autonomy of these institutions have expressed their concerns in terms of both the continuing need to implement the constitution's human rights guarantees and a broader concern about the future of democracy itself. Others, including most notably the ruling ANC, argue that it is the very socioeconomic disparities and their continuing racial character that need to be addressed if the future of democracy and human rights is to be secured.

Heinz Klug

See also Botswana; Constitutional Review; Lesotho; Magistrates—Common Law Systems; Namibia; Parliamentary Supremacy; Roman Law; Swaziland; Zimbabwe

References and further reading
Abel, Richard. 1995. *Politics by Other Means: Law in the Struggle against Apartheid 1980–1994.* New York: Routledge.
Chanock, Martin. 2001. *The Making of South African Legal Culture 1902–1936: Fear, Favour and Prejudice.* Cambridge: CUP.
Corbett, Michael. 1998. "Presentation to the Truth and Reconciliation Commission." *South African Law Journal* 115: 17.
Davenport, T. R. H. 1969. "The Consolidation of a New Society: The Cape Colony." In *The Oxford History of South Africa.* Edited by Monica Wilson and Leonard Thompson. Reprinted 1975. Oxford: OUP.
Dugard, John. 1978. *Human Rights and the South African Legal Order.* Princeton: Princeton University Press.
Klug, Heinz. 2000. *Constituting Democracy: Law, Globalism and South Africa's Political Reconstruction.* Cambridge: CUP.
Lobban, Michael. 1996. *White Man's Justice: South African Political Trials in the Black Consciousness Era.* New York: Oxford University Press.
Parsons, Neil. 1993. *A New History of Southern Africa.* 2d ed. London: Macmillan.
Sachs, Albie. 1973. *Justice in South Africa.* Berkeley: University of California Press.
Truth and Reconciliation Commission (TRC). 1998. *Final Report.* 5 vols. October 29. Cape Town: Juta.
Wilson, Richard. 2001. *The Politics of Truth and Reconciliation in South Africa: Legitimizing the Post-Apartheid State.* Cambridge: CUP.
Zimmerman, Reinhard, and Daniel Visser, eds. 1996. *Southern Cross: Civil and Common Law in South Africa.* New York: Oxford University Press.

SOUTH AUSTRALIA

GENERAL INFORMATION

South Australia (SA) is situated in the lower half of central Australia and occupies 12.8 percent of the total landmass. Most (73 percent) of SA's 1.5 million people live in and around its capital city, Adelaide. South Australia is the driest state in Australia, with a Mediterranean climate in the south and a desert climate in the north. It is noted for its production of high-quality wines, which are exported all over the world.

EVOLUTION AND HISTORY

The area that became known as South Australia after 1834 had been inhabited by indigenous peoples for thousands of years. These peoples had developed complex legal systems that governed the ownership of land, the regulation of social relationships (including marriages), and the trial and punishment of those who offended against the law. The laws of each indigenous group had been handed down by word of mouth from one generation to the next through designated elders, but these indigenous legal systems were not recognized by the British immigrants who arrived in the area in 1836 to establish a convict-free "province" of England. Instead, the new settlers followed the lead of the other Australian colonies and imposed their own law on the indigenous peoples, with disastrous results for the original inhabitants. Land was appropriated to the English Crown at will by the new colonial administration and sold to immigrant settlers for residential and farming purposes.

South Australia was established as a social experiment by a group of reformers in England. Its founding philosophy was derived from the theories of Jeremy Bentham, and its composition and organization were inspired by the reformist ideas of Robert Gouger and Edward Gibbon Wakefield. Wakefield described his settlement intentions as "not to place a scattered and half barbarous colony on the coast of New Holland, but to establish . . . a wealthy civilized society" (Whitelock 2000, 3). The emphasis was, therefore, on creating a democratic society, free of the English class distinctions based on hereditary wealth as well as aristocratic and Church of England privilege. As a result of their beliefs, the founders were committed to pursuing civic and religious freedom in the new province. These aspirations were originally reflected in the South Australia Act of 1834 and a statutory division of authority between the governor and colonization commissioners under the South Australian Colonisation Act of 1834. This dividing of power was unique to the establishment of South Australia in 1836 and meant that while the governor was responsible for the administration of the province, the commissioners were in charge of the sale and distribution of land. The money raised from the sale of land was supposed to finance further controlled emigration from England and contribute to the self-support of the province.

However, the Colonisation Act was badly drafted and proved unworkable. After only six years, it was repealed, and the British Parliament enacted new arrangements for the settlement, which abolished the colonization commissioners and empowered the queen, through a legislative council composed of seven persons including the governor, to make laws. The body of law and the adversarial legal process were thus derived from England and administered through the authority of colonial governors, as they were in the other settlements in Australia.

During the 1840s, there was a growing demand for self-government in all the Australian colonies. This was granted by the English Parliament in the passing of the Australian Constitutions Act of 1850. The act allowed for the setting up of a partly elected legislative council in each colony, which could, in turn, alter the colony's constitution and establish its own responsible government. True to the founding ideals of democracy and freedom, fierce debate ensued in South Australia about the necessity for adult male suffrage for both proposed houses of Parliament. However, conservative English governors, judges, and other officials who had been appointed in Britain wanted to retain their power within a nominated legislative council. In the final outcome, adult male suffrage was only granted for the lower house. Uniquely, this included aboriginal men, who were later disenfranchised by the Australian Constitutions Act of 1901 at the time of federation. Unrestricted franchise for the upper house in South Australia was not gained until 1973.

Nevertheless, the ideals of civic and religious freedom that animated the settlement of South Australia inspired notable breaks with English legal tradition. South Australia was the first British colony to break the connection between church and state (in 1852), to allow divorce (in 1858), to extend the lower house franchise to all males (in 1855), and, at the same time, to introduce the secret ballot for elections. It also pioneered the first Children's Court in 1890, the Boards of Conciliation for industrial arbitration in 1894, and the first Workers Compensation Act in 1900.

South Australia also has a proud history of promoting equal rights and opportunities for women. Women were admitted uncontroversially to all University of Adelaide degree programs in 1880, and they graduated in the arts, medicine, mathematics, and the sciences from the 1880s on. However, it was not until 1916 that the first female law graduate in Australia, Mary Kitson, was admitted to the bar. In 1894, South Australian women were also the first in Australia to get the vote, soon after female suffrage was won in the U.S. states of Wyoming and Colorado as well as in New Zealand. At the same time, they were the first women in the world to gain the right to stand for Parliament. Kate Cocks, who was a member of the SA police force at the time, pioneered a probation system for young offenders in 1906. She also formed the Women's Police Department in 1915—the first of its kind in the world to be organized by a woman. South Australia was also the first state to appoint a woman, Roma Mitchell, as a Queen's Counsel (in 1962) and as a judge of the Supreme Court (in 1965). Dame Roma, as she became known in 1982, was the founding chairperson of the now-defunct Australian Human Rights Commission when it was established in 1981 and the first woman chancellor not only of the University of Adelaide but also of any university in the British Commonwealth. In 1991, she also became the first woman in Australia to be appointed a governor of the state.

In the twentieth century, South Australia was not always in the vanguard of law and legal system reform as it had been in the past, but it did have a strong tradition of active government promotion of the democratic process. For example, a government legal aid scheme was instituted in 1926, well ahead of similar schemes worldwide. This was followed in the 1930s by an innovative legal profession pro bono plan. In the 1960s and 1970s, too, South Australia led the rest of the country in legislative reform. It was the first state to pass land rights legislation for indigenous peoples, who now have native title to about 20 percent of the land in South Australia. It also passed legislation that prohibited racial discrimination and restored indigenous people's rights to freedom of movement. Governments also legislated for comprehensive town planning programs, consumer and environmental protection, jury service for women, abortion, and the decriminalization of homosexuality as well as sex and race antidiscrimination laws. The twentieth century also saw wide social reforms in education, health, and urban development and the relaxation of censorship laws. In the 1990s, a statutory authority to administer the courts was created and with it a case-flow management scheme that has dramatically reduced the waiting lists for court hearings and trials.

Legal aid is provided by central and suburban branches of the Legal Services Commission, which provides free telephone and face-to face legal advice as well as means-tested assistance for litigation in all jurisdictions. There are also a number of free community legal centers in suburban areas.

CURRENT STRUCTURE

There is a three-tiered court system in South Australia: the Supreme Court, the District Court, and the Magistrates' Court. There is also a range of other specialized courts, including the Youth Court; the Coroner's Court; the Environment, Resources and Development Court;

and the Industrial Relations Court of SA. A number of tribunals and boards also deal with specific statutory areas, such as the provision of liquor licenses, worker's compensation, guardianship, the conduct and discipline of legal practitioners, an employee ombudsman, public advocacy, paroles, and residential tenancies.

The Supreme Court is the highest court in the state and deals with all major civil claims and serious criminal charges. It also grants probate of wills of deceased persons and determines land and valuation matters. It has an appellate jurisdiction that hears appeals in civil and criminal cases from the lower courts, boards, and tribunals. These appeals are heard by a single judge of the Supreme Court, with the exception of appeals from the District and Supreme Courts, which are heard by a full court of three judges. Appeals from the full court are, by leave, heard by the High Court of Australia. The Supreme Court sits in Adelaide and conducts circuits in two large regional cities in South Australia.

The District Court is the principal trial court for civil, criminal, administrative, and disciplinary matters as well as criminal injuries compensation. In an approach that led the way in Australia, the District and Supreme Courts introduced a free mediation scheme in 1998 to encourage litigants to pursue alternative dispute resolution at an early stage of proceedings. The scheme has been very successful. Mediations are conducted mainly by retired judges trained in mediation techniques. The court sits in Adelaide and conducts circuits in six regional cities.

The Magistrates' Court has a civil and a criminal jurisdiction. In its criminal jurisdiction, it hears and determines charges of summary and minor indictable offenses that can be dealt with by way of a fine, imprisonment of up to two years, good behavior bonds, and community service orders. The court also conducts the preliminary examination of persons charged with indictable offenses. In its civil jurisdiction, the court hears and determines a range of civil matters, including motor vehicle injury claims up to $60,000, other claims up to $30,000, disputes between commercial landlords and tenants, and recovery of debts up to $5,000. There is also a small claims court presided over by a magistrate, which has simplified procedures for claims of up to $5,000. The Magistrates' Court also offers free mediation in minor and general civil matters. This scheme has been very successful and has attracted a good deal of interest from other jurisdictions. The court is also the only court in Australia to appoint its own panel of experts, who may sit with magistrates in civil matters to provide specialist advice or give expert testimony. The court is based in Adelaide and four suburban areas. All regional cities and country areas are serviced by magistrates on circuit from courts in Adelaide.

In recent years, the Magistrates' Court has also introduced four innovative specialist services in the areas of family violence, aboriginal justice, drugs, and for persons suffering from a mental impairment. The Family Violence Court began operating in 1997 and aims to reduce the incidence of domestic violence by directing perpetrators of violence to programs that modify behavior. In 1999, for the first time in Australia, a court intervention program was established to help minor offenders who may have intellectual impairment; with the person's consent, the program can direct these minors away from the criminal justice system and into suitable assessment and treatment programs. In June 2000, a twelve-month pilot project was pioneered in the Port Adelaide Magistrates' Court to deal with the sentencing of adult aboriginal offenders. Defendants who plead or are found guilty are

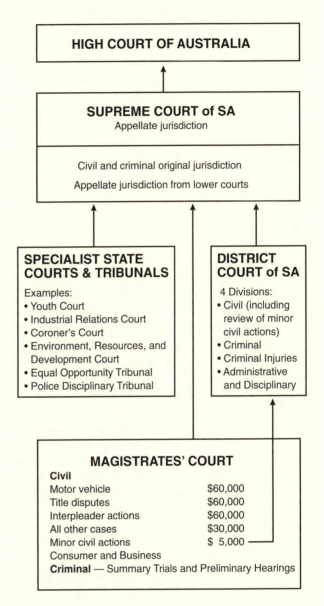

Legal Structure of South Australia Courts

HIGH COURT OF AUSTRALIA

SUPREME COURT of SA
Appellate jurisdiction

Civil and criminal original jurisdiction

Appellate jurisdiction from lower courts

SPECIALIST STATE COURTS & TRIBUNALS

Examples:
• Youth Court
• Industrial Relations Court
• Coroner's Court
• Environment, Resources, and Development Court
• Equal Opportunity Tribunal
• Police Disciplinary Tribunal

DISTRICT COURT of SA

4 Divisions:
• Civil (including review of minor civil actions)
• Criminal
• Criminal Injuries
• Administrative and Disciplinary

MAGISTRATES' COURT

Civil
Motor vehicle	$60,000
Title disputes	$60,000
Interpleader actions	$60,000
All other cases	$30,000
Minor civil actions	$ 5,000

Consumer and Business

Criminal — Summary Trials and Preliminary Hearings

given the option of being sentenced in a courtroom where a magistrate, sitting at eye level with the participants, is assisted in the sentencing process by aboriginal elders and community members as well as the defendant's family. All participants, including the defendant, may address the court on behalf of the defendant. The project provides more culturally appropriate alternatives to imprisonment and aims to encourage a fall in recidivism. The Drug Court is part of an interagency rehabilitative program for adults who are dependent on illicit substances and commit offenses to support their dependency. If offenders plead guilty to offenses that would otherwise attract a prison sentence, they can choose to be directed to treatment programs instead.

The Environment, Resources and Development Court began operations in 1994 and was, at the time, unique to South Australia. It deals with development and environmental disputes, and its proceedings are both adversarial and inquisitorial. It has powers to enforce civil and criminal breaches of the relevant legislation. It also hears appeals, applications, complaints, and building disputes brought under a number of acts. It hears matters in country areas as required.

The Youth Court is a specialist court for people under eighteen years of age. This court hears criminal, guardianship, and adoption matters and administers two diversionary schemes: the Care and Protection Unit for children considered to be at risk of physical, emotional, or psychological harm and the Young Offenders Act of 1993. This act provides for a system of informal and formal cautions (both undertaken by the police) and referral to a family conferencing team for young offenders as alternatives to appearance in the Youth Court. The diversionary schemes have gained international reputations in the field of juvenile justice. In addition, external agencies have dedicated teams who work within the court. These include police prosecutors, community police officers, legal aid solicitors, Aboriginal Legal Rights Movement solicitors, and Youth Services court liaison staff.

The Industrial Relations Court has two jurisdictions. Its general jurisdiction covers all aspects of employment law and industrial offenses. It also has jurisdiction to deal with all claims and disputes to do with, for example, occupational health and safety and worker's compensation. The court sits in Adelaide and in country areas as required.

NOTABLE FEATURES OF LAW/LEGAL SYSTEM

Unlike the situation in other Australian states, the legal profession in South Australia is fused. In 1841, members of the fledgling profession attempted to divide it into barristers and solicitors—a system under which the barristers could earn higher incomes and greater social prestige because only they could appear in the superior courts. However, this move was resisted by the chief justice at the time in the interest of providing simpler, efficient, and less costly procedures for what was then a small community. In latter-day practice, though, lawyers tend to specialize as either solicitors or barristers, especially in the superior courts. This does not, however, restrict the solicitors' rights to be heard in court.

The Torrens title system of land conveyancing originated in South Australia. Introduced into the first Parliament of 1858 by Richard Torrens, it established a government land title office where duplicates of all titles to land were kept as a guarantee of valid legal title. The system was given legal status in the Real Property Act of 1886 when, in the face of sustained opposition from many members of the legal profession who customarily made a living out of land conveyancing, the act also pioneered a new profession of accredited land brokers—who charged much less than lawyers—to conduct land transfers. The Torrens title system spread quickly to some states and other countries, including some parts of Canada and the United States. However, the system of registered land brokers, now known as conveyancers, did not follow in some states until recently.

Consistent with the constitutional doctrine of the separation of powers, the administration of the court system was placed on a statutory footing in 1993, thus making it independent of the legislative and executive arms of government. Management of the courts is now the responsibility of the State Courts Administration Council rather than, as previously, a government department that had at least the potential to compromise the independence of the judiciary. The council is composed of the chief justice, the chief judge of the District Court, the chief magistrate, and their appointed associates. No other state has yet adopted the South Australian model, which, in its implementation, was influenced by the U.S. federal court system.

The current chief justice has introduced a number of groundbreaking innovations to make the courts more accessible to the public. These include the appointment of a public information officer and an education officer, judges taking part in talk-back radio programs, and the creation of an "Ask the Judge" website for schools, whereby answers to questions are provided within forty-eight hours.

STAFFING

Lawyers are admitted to practice by the Supreme Court after they have completed a university law degree and specific practical training. They are then issued a practicing certificate by the Law Society of South Australia. They are, for the most part, employed in private legal practice, but some lawyers are also employed by the Legal Services Commission, the Aboriginal Legal Rights Movement, and government departments such as the Department of Public Prosecutions and the Attorney General's Department.

South Australia Courts Administration Authority

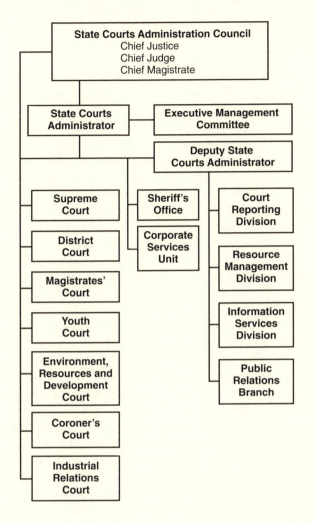

State Courts Administration Council
Chief Justice
Chief Judge
Chief Magistrate

State Courts Administrator

Executive Management Committee

Deputy State Courts Administrator

Supreme Court

District Court

Magistrates' Court

Youth Court

Environment, Resources and Development Court

Coroner's Court

Industrial Relations Court

Sheriff's Office

Corporate Services Unit

Court Reporting Division

Resource Management Division

Information Services Division

Public Relations Branch

but judges can only be removed through a vote in both houses of Parliament.

There is no formal induction process for new magistrates and judges. However, magistrates are sent to courses run by a national judicial education body in New South Wales. This body, in conjunction with an Australian or New Zealand university, also runs a five-day judicial orientation course once a year for newly appointed judges. Continuing legal education for all judicial officers is determined by the Judicial Education Committee of the Supreme Court.

RELATIONSHIP TO NATIONAL SYSTEM

The Australian colonies became a federation on January 1, 1901, when a new constitution established the commonwealth Parliament, the government, and the federal court system—in particular the High Court of Australia, which is the highest court of appeal in the country. The powers of the commonwealth are listed in the constitution and are limited. They include interstate and foreign trade, taxation, postal and telephonic services, defense, fisheries beyond the states' limit, currency and coinage, marriage and divorce, various social services, minority racial groups (including Aborigines), migration, foreign affairs, and industrial conciliation and arbitration of interstate industrial disputes. As in other Australian states, the South Australian Parliament is not restricted to a specified list of powers. There are some exclusions, however, where certain powers, such as the imposing of custom and excise duties, have been given exclusively to the commonwealth by the federal constitution. The commonwealth and the states can legislate on the same subject matter, but where there is any inconsistency commonwealth law will prevail.

Jenny Burley

Magistrates, District Court judges, and Supreme Court masters and judges are all appointed by the governor on the recommendation of the attorney general. In the case of magistrates, vacancies are advertised, and individuals who express an interest in the position are evaluated and, if appropriate, interviewed by a panel chaired by the chief magistrate. Recommendations are then made to the attorney general, who must consult with the chief justice in relation to any proposed appointment. A magistrate must have five years' standing as a legal practitioner to be eligible for appointment, a master of the Supreme Court must have seven years' standing, and a judge must have ten years' standing. Judges and masters are usually drawn from the pool of senior barristers, while magistrates are chosen from a pool of solicitors. Except for Supreme and District Court judges, who must retire at seventy years of age, all other judicial officers must retire at sixty-five. Magistrates can be removed from office if a judicial inquiry conducted by the Supreme Court finds sufficient cause,

See also Appellate Courts; Constitutionalism; Judicial Independence; Judicial Selection, Methods of; Juvenile Justice; Legal Aid; Mediation; Small Claims Courts; Trial Courts
References and further reading
Australian Bureau of Statistics. 2000. *South Australia at a Glance*, ABS Catalogue No. 1306.4. http://www.abs.gov.au (cited January 7, 2002).
Brown, Louise, Beatrix Ch. de Crespigny, Mary Harris, Kathleen K. Thomas, and Phoebe N. Matson, eds. 1936. *A Book of South Australia: Women in the First Hundred Years*. Adelaide: Rigby.
Castles, Alex C., and Michael C Harris. 1987. *Lawmakers and Wayward Whigs: Government and Law in South Australia, 1836–1986*. Adelaide: Wakefield Press.
Courts Administration Authority. 2000. *Annual Report 1999–2000*. Adelaide: Courts Administration Authority.
Pike, Douglas. 1957. *Paradise of Dissent: South Australia, 1829–1857*. London: Longmans, Green.
Selway, Bradley. 1997. *The Constitution of South Australia*. Annandale, NSW: Federation Press.
Whitelock, Derek. 2000. *Adelaide: Sense of Difference*. 3d ed. Adelaide: Arcadia.

SOUTH CAROLINA

GENERAL INFORMATION

Bounded by the Atlantic Ocean to the east and the Blue Ridge Mountains to the west, South Carolina occupies a relatively small portion of the southeastern part of the United States, ranking fortieth among the states in area and twenty-sixth in population. The region was originally inhabited by several small tribes of Native Americans; the first European explorers from Spain and France arrived in the sixteenth century but later abandoned the area. Nearly one hundred years later, in 1670, the first permanent settlements by Europeans were established by the English in areas along the coast. These settlers, primarily from the British Isles, set up plantations to grow rice and indigo. By the 1750s, the European settlers had become quite wealthy off the plantation economy. The British government encouraged settlement in the interior with migration of German and Scotch-Irish settlers from colonies farther north. This migration temporarily gave the total population a white majority, but the rise of cotton plantations resulted in African American slaves constituting a majority of the population. Following the Civil War and Reconstruction, many African Americans left the South and migrated north as the political and social climate became increasingly hostile by the turn of the century. Today, more than a fourth of South Carolina's population is African American.

Three regions characterize the political and geographic divisions in the state: the "low country," the "upcountry," and the "midlands." The low country is the coastal area surrounding the port city of Charleston, which thrived under a plantation economy in the eighteenth and nineteenth centuries. After the American Revolution, South Carolina moved its seat of government from Charleston to the new city of Columbia, located in the state's midlands, in an effort to remove power from the low country elite. The northwestern portion of the state, the upcountry, later thrived as the state's economy became dependent upon cotton. This same area would become the site for the textile industry and manufacturing in the twentieth century. Currently about one-fifth of the workforce in South Carolina is employed in manufacturing, a figure that is substantially higher than the 15 percent average for all states.

Poverty has burdened the state since the Civil War. Nearly one-fifth of the white male population died during the war, and the state's economy was destroyed. Although the expansion of military bases, changes in the textile industry, and foreign investment in manufacturing have improved economic conditions over the last thirty years, poverty has continued to be a political and social issue. At the end of the 1990s, 16 percent of the state's population fell below the poverty line, with per capita income ranking forty-second among the fifty states.

Since the founding of the nation, the political history of South Carolina has been dominated by the General Assembly. But recent changes have produced shifts in this institutional power base. In 1975, the passage of the Home Rule Act ended a system whereby the state's forty-six counties had been essentially governed by their state legislative delegations. As detailed below, the 1970s also ushered in similar changes to the state's judicial system.

EVOLUTION AND HISTORY

South Carolina has been governed by seven constitutions. Three of the seven are particularly noteworthy: the constitutions of 1790, 1868, and 1895. The state's first constitution (1790) was characterized by efforts to balance power between geographically defined political interests and to create a governmental structure that maintained legislative dominance. Under this constitution, the General Assembly was given responsibility for selecting most state and local officers, including the governor. The second major constitution was formed during Reconstruction. During that period, South Carolina, like many Southern states, convened a constitutional convention to deal with the federal government's mandate that states provide equal protection of the laws to all citizens, regardless of race. Ratified by popular vote, the 1868 Constitution extended these protections to all citizens and included several other provisions in an extensive bill of rights. For the first time, women were given the right to own property. In addition, this constitution also provided for more government officials to be elected directly by the voters.

The progressive tone of the 1868 Constitution abruptly ended when white conservatives assumed power in the 1890s. Claiming that the low country elite and the African American vote were responsible for a poor economy, these political leaders pushed for a constitutional convention that was convened in 1895. The convention yielded a constitution that, as amended, established the parameters for South Carolina's government today. Although the 1895 Constitution retained a bill of rights, many provisions reversed the protections in the 1868 Constitution that had ensured equality for African Americans. In particular, this document required separate schools for children of different races. It also prohibited interracial marriages and established literacy and property qualifications as conditions for voting. These conditions effectively disenfranchised African Americans for over a half-century until legal and political efforts dismantled segregationist laws. In the 1960s and 1970s, the civil rights movement brought about relatively peaceful change in this state.

The evolution of the state's court system paralleled its constitutional history. In the period immediately following the Revolution, the South Carolina legislature took several steps to minimize the independence of the judicial branch. Rather than centralize judicial authority, the General Assembly created specialized courts for cities and counties without consideration for an overall coherent structure. These courts multiplied through much of the nineteenth and twentieth centuries as state legislators frequently authorized judgeships to be filled by sitting or former legislators. Legislative control over judicial selection and the lack of constitutional protection for the court system strengthened the institutional power of the General Assembly. This power was dramatically illustrated in 1835 when the General Assembly abolished the Court of Appeals following a "pro-Union" judicial decision. Over time, the legislature's approach to the court system resulted in a state judiciary that lacked consistent procedures and clear jurisdictional lines. In 1970 court observers noted that there were six types of trial court in the state, but no single judicial district contained all of the six types (Hays and Mann 1992).

The push by the American Bar Association to unify state court systems made its way to South Carolina in the early 1970s. In 1972, voters approved an article of the state constitution that created a unified court system. As a result of the article, several reform efforts were implemented by the General Assembly in the mid- to late 1970s. These included the creation of a coherent family court system, the phasing out of county courts, and the consolidation of rule-making authority in the state court of last resort. Over the last several decades, the state has continued to push toward making the court system more uniform. The most recent reform included the creation of a central panel to hear appeals from several administrative agencies.

CURRENT STRUCTURE

Courts

The current judicial system is made up of the state court of last resort (the Supreme Court), an intermediate appellate court (the Court of Appeals), circuit courts, family courts, probate courts, Magistrates' Courts, and municipal courts (see figure). The chief justice of the Supreme Court is the administrative head of the unified court system and sets the terms of court and assigns judges to preside at those terms. In addition, the Supreme Court is responsible for promulgating rules that govern all courts. South Carolina's court of last resort has both appellate and original jurisdiction. It has exclusive jurisdiction to hear appeals from the circuit court in several types of cases. Included in this category are cases that involve death sentences, public utility rates, constitutional challenges to state statutes or local ordinances, public bond questions, and judgments pertaining to an election. Parties also can seek review of a decision of the Court of Appeals by filing a petition for a writ of certiorari with the Supreme Court. In its original jurisdiction, the Supreme Court may issue mandamus and other extraordinary writs, but it generally limits these actions to those cases that "involve significant public interest." The Supreme Court also may agree to answer questions of law certified to it by the highest court of another state or by a federal court.

Created in 1983 to relieve the appellate caseload of the Supreme Court, the Court of Appeals functions primarily to correct errors in cases that are appealed from the circuit court and family court. This nine-member court sits either as three panels of three judges or, on occasion, as a whole. Interestingly, preassignment to an authoring judge is made immediately after briefs are filed and panels meet to discuss cases prior to oral argument.

The circuit courts in South Carolina are the major trial courts in the judicial system. The state is divided into sixteen judicial circuits with one resident judge who maintains an office in his or her home county within each circuit. The remaining circuit judges serve on a rotating basis with terms and assignments made by the chief justice upon recommendation of the Office of Court Administration. Circuit courts are courts of general jurisdiction, hearing all cases except those for which exclusive jurisdiction is reserved to courts of limited or special jurisdiction. Each has a civil court (the Court of Common Pleas) and a criminal court (the Court of General Sessions). In addition to general trial jurisdiction, the circuit court has limited appellate jurisdiction over appeals from the probate court, Magistrates' Court, municipal court, and the Administrative Law Judge division.

As a court of special jurisdiction, the family court system has exclusive jurisdiction over all matters relating to domestic or family relationships and minors under the age of seventeen. Serious juvenile criminal charges may be transferred to the circuit court. In each judicial circuit, there are at least two judges assigned to that circuit. The remaining judges rotate from county to county; however, the more populous areas generally require more family court judges on account of high caseloads. The chief judge of the family court system is appointed by the chief justice and supervises the administrative operations of these courts.

Probate courts are somewhat different from other courts in the state, in that they are organized at the county, rather than the circuit, level. In this court, judges issue marriage licenses and hear cases involving wills, estates, and trusts. In addition, they will be involved in cases dealing with the guardianship of incompetents and will rule on involuntary commitments.

The courts of limited jurisdiction—Magistrates' Courts and municipal courts—deal with minor criminal and civil matters. More than three hundred magistrates in the state have jurisdiction over those criminal offenses

Structure of South Carolinian Courts

Supreme Court

- Exclusive jurisdiction over appeals from trial courts in cases involving death sentences, public utility rates, constitutional issues, public bonds, and elections
- Original jurisdiction in cases that "involve significant public interest"
- Certiorari from Court of Appeals
- Certified questions from federal courts and other state courts of last resort

Court of Appeals

- Appellate jurisdiction over cases from circuit court and family court in which Supreme Court has no exclusive jurisdiction

Family Court

- Exclusive jurisdiction over domestic relations and juveniles

No jury trials

Circuit Court

- Hears all cases except those for which exclusive jurisdiction is reserved to courts of limited or special jurisdiction
- Limited appellate jurisdiction over cases from probate court, magistrate court, municipal court, and the Administrative Law Judge Division

Probate Court

- Exclusive jurisdiction in mental health, estate cases

No jury trials

Magistrates' Court

- Warrants, preliminary hearings, traffic violations, misdemeanor
- Civil under $5,000

Municipal Court

- No civil jurisdiction
- Misdemeanor, preliminary hearings, traffic violations

Based on David B. Rottman et al. 2000. *State Court Organization 1998*. Washington, DC: U.S. Department of Justice, Bureau of Justice Statistics. www.ojp.usdoj.gov/bjs.

that are subject to the penalty of a fine not exceeding $500, or imprisonment not exceeding thirty days, or both. Magistrates' Courts also have civil jurisdiction when the amount in controversy does not exceed $5,000. In addition, magistrates are responsible for setting bail, conducting preliminary hearings, and issuing arrest and search warrants. In about two hundred jurisdictions, municipalities have created courts to work with Magistrates' Courts. These municipal courts do not have civil jurisdiction, but they do have authority to hear similar minor criminal cases. Together, these courts of limited jurisdic-

tion handle more than 75 percent of all litigation in the state each year (Croom and Hays 1999).

The state court system also includes several offices that support the work of the formal courts. Twenty masters-in-equity have jurisdiction in matters referred to them by the circuit courts. Their powers are the same as those of the circuit courts in nonjury cases. Masters often handle specialized cases such as mortgage foreclosures and actions to collect judgments against litigants. Appeals from decisions made by these officials are to the Supreme Court or Court of Appeals. Administrative support for the state courts is provided by the Office of Court Administration. The office compiles data on case dispositions to aid the chief justice in decisions regarding the assignment of judges. In addition, the office provides court personnel with information on legal education, procedural changes, and technology transfer.

Administrative Law

Based on the 1961 Model State Administrative Procedure Act, the South Carolina Administrative Procedure Act (SCAPA) established administrative processes that are very similar to those at the federal level. In 1993 the General Assembly amended SCAPA and created the Administrative Law Judge Division (ALJD). Although the division is an arm of the executive branch, the ALJD was established to provide a "neutral" forum for parties involved in disputes with administrative agencies. The ALJD has jurisdiction over some contested cases, appeals, and regulation hearings. In contested cases, ALJs preside as fact-finders. Although several agencies and commissions do not fall within the jurisdiction of the division (including workers' compensation and unemployment cases), the caseload of the ALJD is quite diverse. Judges in the division are expected to be generalists, so that they can hear disputes that range from denial of an alcoholic beverage permit to a challenge to a land use decision by the state's Office of Ocean and Coastal Resource Management. Generally, before obtaining ALJ review, the aggrieved party must exhaust all administrative remedies as identified by the agency and, in some cases, the relevant statutory framework. Subsequent review of ALJ decisions varies by agency, with some cases going back to the board or commission before becoming a final agency decision worthy of judicial review.

Legal Profession

Legal education in the state is limited to a single ABA-accredited law school at the University of South Carolina. Not surprisingly, graduates of this school tend to practice in the state and occupy a majority of the judicial positions. As of 2000, the South Carolina Bar had a membership of 10,063.

The Supreme Court is responsible for admitting persons to practice in the state. The court is also responsible for disciplining lawyers who engage in misconduct. Such efforts are managed by the Commission on Lawyer Conduct, a forty-four-member organization (which includes two laypersons) appointed by the Supreme Court. The court also can suspend from practice those lawyers who are incapacitated because of mental or physical condition.

Provision of Counsel for Indigent Criminal Defendants

The public defender system is a county-based system. In each county, the local bar association organizes a nonprofit ("Defender") corporation, elects members to the corporation's board of directors, and establishes a public defender office to serve the area. The Defender corporations are independent of the state, but they receive funding from the state's Office of Indigent Defense, as well as from the local county. Currently, there are thirty-nine Defender corporations serving South Carolina's forty-six counties.

STAFFING

South Carolina provides for judges to be elected by the legislature. The Supreme Court is composed of a chief justice and four associate justices who are elected by the General Assembly to ten-year terms. The terms are staggered, and a justice is not limited as to the number of terms in service. Over the court's history, most justices have also been former state legislators. The first woman to serve on the court was selected in 1988. She was installed as chief justice in 1996. A woman also currently serves as chief judge of the Court of Appeals. Like their colleagues on the Supreme Court, judges on the Court of Appeals are selected by the legislature. However, they serve shorter, staggered terms of six years. Forty-six circuit court and fifty-two family court judges are also elected by the General Assembly to staggered terms of six years. Recent criticism of legislative election as a method of judicial selection has led to the creation of a Judicial Screening Committee in the General Assembly that is charged with assessing the qualifications of judicial candidates. In addition, the General Assembly recently passed legislation that prevents the election of judicial candidates who are sitting legislators.

Other judicial positions are selected through different methods. In a somewhat populist probate court, judges are elected by the voters within each county. The only statutory requirement is that the candidate be a qualified elector of the county in which he or she resides. Masters-in-equity are appointed by the governor with the advice and consent of the General Assembly for terms of six years. Similarly, magistrates are appointed to four-year terms by the governor upon the advice and consent of the Senate. A fourth of magistrates sitting on the bench currently do not have a college degree (Croom and Hays 1999). Concern over qualifications for these positions led to the passage of a statute requiring special training and certification requirements for newly seated magistrates. Beginning in 2005, newly appointed magistrates will be required to have a four-year college degree.

NOTABLE FEATURES OF LAW AND THE LEGAL SYSTEM

As outlined above, the South Carolina legal and political system is distinctive. Unlike many other states, South Carolina's political history has been defined by legislative supremacy. Although the court unification movement that has been implemented since the 1970s has contributed to judicial independence and efficiency, the General Assembly continues to maintain control over the selection of most candidates for judicial positions. Other states in the Southeast predominantly use direct elections to select judges, but South Carolina utilizes a method of selection that is used by only one other state—Virginia.

Susan Brodie Haire

See also Judicial Selection, Methods of; Magistrates—Common Law Systems; United States—Federal System; United States—State Systems

References and further reading

Croom, Robert, and Steven W. Hays. 1999. "The Judicial System." In *Handbook for South Carolina County Officials.* Columbia, SC: Association of Counties.

Cureton, Jasper M. "Coming of Age: The South Carolina Court of Appeals." South Carolina. http://www.judicial. state.sc.us/appeals/history.cfm (accessed March 1, 2002).

Hays, Steven W., and David Mann. 1992. "South Carolina Judicial System: Continuing Reform." Pp. 102–121 in *Government in the Palmetto State: Toward the 21st Century.* Edited by Luther Carter and David Mann. Columbia, SC: Institute of Public Affairs.

Lander, Ernest M., and Robert K. Ackerman, eds. 1973. *Perspectives in South Carolina History: The First 300 Years.* Columbia: University of South Carolina Press.

South Carolina Administrative Law Judge Division Annual Report 1997–1998. http://www.law.sc.edu/alj/rpt9798.htm (accessed January 30, 2001).

South Carolina Bar. "Public Resources." http:// www.scbar.org (accessed March 1, 2002).

South Carolina Judicial Department. "Courts." http://www. judicial.state.sc.us (accessed February 1, 2001).

Swent, William B. 1996. "South Carolina's ALJ: Central Panel, Administrative Court, or a Little of Both?" *South Carolina Law Review* 48: 1.

SOUTH DAKOTA

GENERAL INFORMATION

The state of South Dakota is located in the central plains region of the United States. Its population of over 733,000 makes South Dakota only forty-fifth in the nation in population. However, South Dakota ranks sixteenth in terms of total land area. There are few large cities, the two largest being Sioux Falls and Rapid City. Only a third of South Dakotans live in metropolitan areas. The state capital is Pierre. In terms of its racial profile, South Dakota is predominantly white (90.6 percent), with the remainder of the population as follows: Native American 8 percent, Hispanic 1.2 percent, African American 0.7 percent, Asian 0.6 percent. The Native American population is largely of Sioux heritage.

The state economy remains largely dependent upon agriculture. It is first in the nation in the production of hay, second in oats, and third in both rye and flaxseed, and also among the top states for cattle and hog production. The state has been quite active recently in fostering growth in the nonagricultural sector of the economy. In 1996, manufacturing accounted for almost 15 percent of the gross state product. Businesses are being enticed to move to South Dakota by the lack of a corporate income tax. Tourism also makes a significant contribution to the state economy, with tourists particularly drawn to Mount Rushmore National Memorial, located in the Black Hills National Forest southwest of Rapid City, and Badlands National Park, located in southwestern South Dakota. The unemployment rate hovers at 3 percent while per capita income is just shy of $22,000.

EVOLUTION AND HISTORY

The geographic area covered by South Dakota was part of the northern reaches of the Louisiana Purchase of 1803. The Yankton Sioux ceded the majority of eastern South Dakota to the United States in 1858, and the Dakota Territory (including the current states of North Dakota, South Dakota, Montana, and the majority of present-day Wyoming) was officially established in 1861. The territorial government included a Supreme Court, district courts, probate courts, and justices of the peace. South Dakota was admitted to the Union as the fortieth state in November 1889 by President Benjamin Harrison, upon which the Territorial Supreme Court was dissolved.

The first constitution of South Dakota, which has not been replaced, provided for executive, legislative, and judicial branches of government. The latter included a Supreme Court, circuit courts, county courts, and justices of the peace. The three members of the Supreme Court were selected from separate judicial districts and were sworn into office on October 15, 1889. The Supreme Court was initially quartered in the county courthouse. It subsequently heard cases in the senate chamber of the state legislature before moving into a newly built capitol building in 1910, which was remodeled in 1952 and again in 1979.

Politically, the state was swayed for a short period of time from the Republican Party by the Populist movement of the late 1800s. Subsequently, a reform-minded element of the Republican Party took over, resulting in, among other things, a state hail insurance program and a state-owned and -operated coal mine. The South Dakota electorate supported Franklin Delano Roosevelt for president in 1932 and 1936 but not in 1940 or 1944. The state has moved largely in a conservative direction ever since, as evidenced by its presidential and gubernatorial voting record. Since 1940, the majority of the South Dakota electorate has voted for the Republican candidate in every presidential race, with the exception of the 1964 election when the majority of South Dakota voters supported Lyndon B. Johnson's bid for the presidency. South Dakota has also consistently voted for the Republican candidate for governor, with the exception of supporting Democrat Richard F. Kneip in the early 1970s. George McGovern represents something of an anomaly in South Dakota's general conservative trend. Opposed to the Vietnam War and an advocate of liberal social reforms, McGovern represented South Dakota as a member of the Democratic Party first in the House of Representatives (1957–1960) and then in the Senate (1963–1980). In his first presidential bid in 1972, McGovern carried only the state of Massachusetts. He made another presidential bid in 1984 but felt he would be unable to secure the Democratic nomination and, therefore, removed himself from the race. McGovern's service as a pilot in World War II, including his receipt of the Distinguished Flying Cross as well as his strong support for farm support programs, undoubtedly served as a counterweight to his generally liberal social and economic policies in the minds of conservative South Dakota voters.

CURRENT STRUCTURE

Constitution

The constitution currently in place is the original constitution adopted by South Dakota at statehood. A petition to amend the constitution must garner signatures equal to 10 percent of the vote for governor in the most recent election. Approval of an amendment requires simply a majority vote. Over the course of its history, there have been 206 amendments to the state constitution submitted, with 105 of those adopted.

Legal Profession and Legal Training

There is one American Bar Association–accredited law school in South Dakota. It is located at the University of South Dakota in Vermillion. Membership in the South Dakota bar is mandatory to practice law in South Dakota. Recent figures indicate that approximately 86 percent of those taking the South Dakota bar exam for the first time pass. The South Dakota Supreme Court is responsible for admitting attorneys to the South Dakota bar and administering attorney discipline. In this duty, the Supreme Court is assisted by the South Dakota State Bar Association and/or the circuit courts. Complaints against attorneys are filed with the State Bar Association and investigated by the seven-member Disciplinary Board of the State Bar Association. Minor offenses may be handled by the Disciplinary Board alone. More serious offenses are referred to the Supreme Court, which may opt to refer the matter to a circuit court judge who will serve as a referee and make recommendations to the Supreme Court. There are three Legal Services headquarters offices in South Dakota, plus several branch offices, providing legal services in civil matters for those meeting federal poverty guidelines. Individuals needing representation in serious criminal matters, but financially unable to retain the services of an attorney privately, have an attorney appointed for them.

Administrative Hearings

Persons disputing the decisions or actions of administrative agencies may have their initial appeal heard by a hearing officer or administrative law judge for the agency or, in some cases, the head of the agency. For example, appeals from decisions of the South Dakota Department of Social Services are heard by a hearing officer from that agency's Office of Administrative Hearings. And appeals from adverse decisions in unemployment compensation cases are heard by an administrative law judge from the unemployment insurance appeals office in the Department of Labor. Appeals from decisions of the Department of Revenue, on the other hand, go first to the secretary of that department. In each case, however, further appeals go to the circuit courts.

Judicial System

Prior to 1975, the South Dakota judiciary was characterized by confusing and duplicative jurisdictions, multiple sources of funding, and judges with uneven legal training and experience. In 1975, however, the judiciary was streamlined into the Unified Judicial System. The current South Dakota judiciary has three tiers.

Magistrates' Courts

Magistrates' Courts comprise the bottom tier of the South Dakota judiciary. They process misdemeanors (that is, crimes for which the penalty does not exceed $1,000 and/or imprisonment does not exceed one year in the county jail) and minor civil matters. Magistrates' Courts may also handle preliminary proceedings for more serious offenses. Small claims divisions of Magistrates' Courts process monetary disputes as long as the amount involved does not exceed $4,000. Among the matters Magistrates' Courts deal with are the issuance of warrants, the conduct of preliminary hearings, and the performance of marriages. Each Magistrates' Court is

Structure of South Dakotan Courts

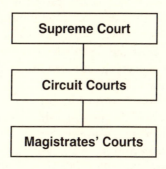

presided over by either a magistrate judge or lay magistrate. The former must be licensed attorneys, whereas the latter are only required to possess a high school diploma. Both magistrate judges and lay magistrates are selected by the presiding circuit court judge.

Circuit Courts

Circuit courts comprise the middle tier of the South Dakota judiciary. Until a very recent reorganization, there were eight judicial circuits. Currently, there are seven, each covering an aggregation of counties. The circuit courts are the trial courts of general jurisdiction, possessing original jurisdiction in all civil and criminal cases and appellate jurisdiction over Magistrates' Court decisions and administrative agencies within the state. Among the matters circuit courts deal with are probate, divorce, guardianship, civil lawsuits, and criminal proceedings. The thirty-seven circuit court judges are selected via nonpartisan elections to serve eight-year terms by the voters in their respective circuits. One circuit court judge in each circuit is selected to serve as the presiding judge by the chief justice of the South Dakota Supreme Court. In fiscal year 1999, there were 237,000 cases filed in the circuit courts, including an increase of almost 5,000 criminal cases over the prior fiscal year. Circuit court judges earn annual salaries of $86,000.

Supreme Court

The South Dakota Supreme Court sits at the apex of the judicial system. South Dakota is one of only a handful of states, including Maine, Nevada, and Wyoming, that do not have an intermediate appellate court below the Supreme Court. The Supreme Court bench consists of five members, one each from five appointment districts. The constitution permits the state legislature to increase the size of the Supreme Court bench from five to seven upon the request of the Supreme Court. The South Dakota Judicial Qualifications Commission submits a list of two or more nominees to the governor when a vacancy on the Court arises. The governor then appoints a nominee from that list to the Court. That nominee must stand for reelection on a retention ballot three years after the initial appointment and, subsequent to that, every eight years. The chief justice, the administrative head of the South Dakota judicial system, is selected by his colleagues on the Supreme Court bench to serve for a four-year term. The remaining four members of the bench are referred to as associate justices.

The chief justice is assisted in carrying out his administrative duties by the state court administrator, the clerk of the Supreme Court, and the chief of Legal Research. The state court administrator oversees the Office of Budget and Finance, the Office of Court Support Services, the director of Court Services, the Office of Personnel and Training, and the Office of Planning and Systems Development. The clerk of the Supreme Court is responsible for filing, indexing, and archiving all court records. The chief of Legal Research oversees a group of staff attorneys and the law library, as well as serves as secretary for the five-member Board of Bar Examiners. The chief justice and the Supreme Court are responsible for promulgating rules of practice and procedure as well as preparing and submitting an annual budget for the entire judicial system. This latter responsibility is especially important because all aspects of the unified court system in South Dakota are funded by the state, including the salaries for judges and all other court personnel.

While the Supreme Court has some original jurisdiction to, for example, issue writs or advise the governor regarding his executive powers, the Court primarily exercises appellate review of decisions from the circuit courts. The Court hears cases en banc; that is, the members of the Court collectively hear and dispose of each case. It most often sits in Pierre but on occasion hears cases at other locations in the state. The Supreme Court disposed of 482 cases in fiscal year 1999, relative to case filings of just under 500. South Dakota Supreme Court justices earn annual salaries of just over $92,000, a salary less than that paid to the members of state supreme courts in all but three states.

RELATIONSHIP TO THE NATIONAL SYSTEM

South Dakota has one federal district court, which has four divisions: Northern, Southern, Western, and Central. The state is located in the eighth circuit of the United States Courts of Appeals, along with Arkansas, Iowa, Minnesota, Missouri, Nebraska, and North Dakota.

Litigation begun in the state of South Dakota led to the case of *South Dakota v. Dole* (483 U.S. 203), which contributed to the court's federalism jurisprudence. South Dakota challenged congressional legislation authorizing the secretary of Transportation to withhold a percentage of a state's federal highway funds if that state permitted persons less than twenty-one years of age to drink. South Dakota's minimum drinking age law al-

lowed nineteen-year-olds to purchase beer containing up to 3.2 percent alcohol and, therefore, was subject to having some of its federal highway funds withheld. The state challenged the federal legislation as an impermissible attempt to legislate a national minimum drinking age in violation of the Twenty-first Amendment. The court declined to invalidate the legislation, finding Congress within its authority to attach a portion of federal highway funds as a means to encourage states to adopt higher minimum drinking-age laws. In doing so, it enhanced the powers of Congress vis-à-vis the states.

Wendy L. Martinek

See also Federalism; Judicial Selection, Methods of; Legal Aid; Small Claims Courts; United States—Federal System; United States—State Systems

References and further reading

Jorgensen, Delores A. 1999. *South Dakota Legal Research Guide.* Buffalo, NY: W. S. Hein and Co.

Michels, Greg. 2000. *Governments of South Dakota, 1999.* Austin, TX: Municipal Analysis Services, Inc.

Miller, John E. 2001. *South Dakota: A Journey through Time.* Sioux Falls, SD: Pine Hill Press.

Milton, John R. 1977. *South Dakota: A Bicentennial History.* New York: Norton.

Morgan, Kathleen O'Leary. 1999. *South Dakota in Perspective, 1999.* Lawrence, KS: Morgan Quitno Corporation.

Oyos, Lynwood E. 1999. *The History of the South Dakota Farmers Union.* Sioux Falls, SD: Center for Western Studies.

Reynolds, William J. 1999. *South Dakota: The Face of the Future.* Encino, CA: Cherbo Publishing Group.

South Dakota Supreme Court. 1988. *Unified Judicial System: A Guide.* Pierre: South Dakota Supreme Court.

SOUTH KOREA

GENERAL INFORMATION

South Korea is situated on the southern half of the Korean Peninsula, lying in the northeastern section of the Asian continent. The peninsula shares its northern border with China and Russia. To its east is the East Sea, beyond which neighboring Japan lies. The total land area of the peninsula, including islands, is 220,847 square kilometers, and approximately 98,480 square kilometers (44.6 percent) constitutes the territory of South Korea. Korea is a largely mountainous country, with small valleys and narrow coastal plains. South Korea's forty-seven million citizens, except for about twenty thousand Chinese, are ethnically homogeneous and belong to the Tungusic branch of the Mongoloid race. About 21 percent of the population are under the age of fifteen. The adult literacy rate is remarkable, estimated at 97.6 percent in 1999. South Korea's economy is strong in the region, with a gross domestic product (GDP) of about $457 billion in 2000. The population of the capital, Seoul, is

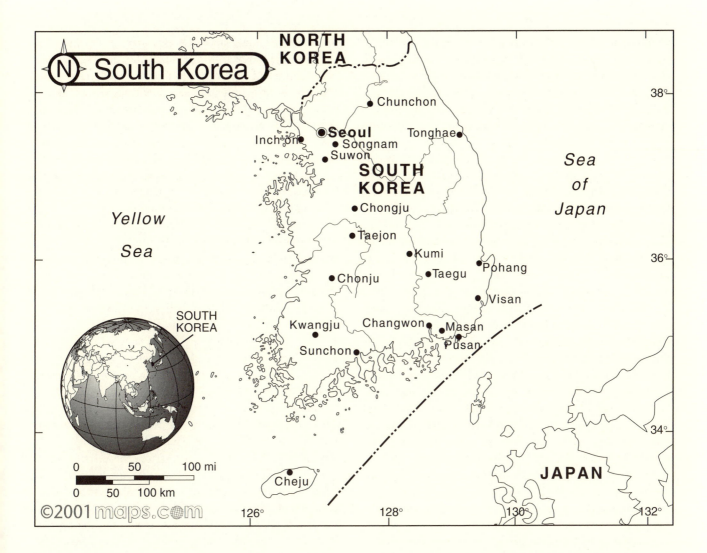

about ten million. The country is majority Buddhist, with a sizable representation of Protestant groups and Catholics. Traditional Shamanism practices are also found. The official language of the country is Korean, and the Korean language is acknowledged to belong to the Altaic family. Because of continental influences, the climate of Korea is characterized by a cold and dry winter and a hot and humid summer. The average monthly temperature in January drops below the freezing point, except along the southern coast, and the July average monthly temperature rises to about 78° F. Rainfall averages more than one hundred centimeters, and two-thirds of the precipitation falls between June and September. The country's legal system is based on European civil law.

HISTORY

A glimpse into the past reveals a long tradition of legislation in Korea. Records show that ancient Chosun, founded in 2333 B.C.E., enacted and enforced laws and regulations at a very early stage. From the fourth to the fifth centuries, the Three Kingdoms (the Koguryo Dynasty, the Baekje Dynasty, and the Shilla Dynasty) already possessed a system of acts and subordinate statutes.

The system of acts and subordinate statutes of the Koryo Dynasty (918–1392) has been passed down to the present day. At that time, Chinese legislation was recognized and supplemented to meet the needs and purposes of the Koryo period in various fields, such as the system of governmental rule, administration, taxation, criminal affairs, and civil affairs.

The Chosun Dynasty, founded at the end of the fourteenth century, inherited the legislation of the Koryo Dynasty and made elaborate improvements in order to keep pace with the changes and developments of the times. The founder of the dynasty, King Taejo, ordered a codification of laws, and in 1397 the Kyongje Yukjon (Six-Division Code for Administration) was promulgated as the result. It did not create legal norms but rather declared already in effect the legal norms that had emanated from the social reality of Korea. Afterward, three revisions of this code were produced, between 1413 and 1433. These became in turn the basis for the central legislative accomplishment of the early Chosun Dynasty, the Kyongguk Taejon (Great Code for Administering the Country), completed in 1485. The Kyongguk Taejon, the basic code of the Chosun Dynasty, was a collection of indigenous laws compiled by collecting and recording the Kyongje Yukjon, its appendix, and the various laws and decrees promulgated between the foundation of the dynasty and the compilation of this code. This rejection of Chinese law was an expression of independence, by maintaining and passing down Korea's own legal culture in the face of the danger of being overwhelmed by Chinese culture. Major supplements to the Kyongguk Taejon appeared in 1746, 1785, and 1865.

Korea's initial encounter with Western law was made under the coercion of Japan. In 1876, Korea was forced to conclude a treaty of trade and friendship with Japan, and in the following years it concluded a series of treaties with China and several Western powers. In 1894, Japan coerced a sweeping reform upon Korea in order to destroy the competing influence of China by making the Korean government over in Japan's image. The 1894 Reform resulted in the enactment of the first written constitution, granted by the king of Chosun and the introduction into Korea of a new legal system based on Western ideas and concepts, such as the rule of law, democratization of the legislative process, and the modernization of judicial procedures. In addition, the five-century-old government structure was completely swept aside, and a Japanese-style government structure was established. A cabinet with a prime minister and eight ministers with portfolios included a minister of justice, rather than a traditional minister of "punishment." In a frenzy of reform, more than 208 major laws were promulgated between July 30 and December 17. The Ministry of Justice was entrusted with the administration of courts, police, and prisons. In the spring of the following year, a second spate of reform decrees gushed forth in Korea. From April 19 to April 24, thirty-four assorted laws and edicts were promulgated. The Law of the Constitution of the Courts was promulgated as Law No. 1 on April 19, providing for a two-level system of courts. A Special Court was separately organized to deal with the criminal proceedings against a member of the royal clan.

In 1905 a treaty was concluded between Korea and Japan establishing a protectorate, and Japan obtained the right to conduct the foreign affairs of Korea. In 1910, Japan finally annexed Korea. During this period, Japanese legislation, or legislation modified to suit colonial rule, was directly applied to Korea, resulting in the virtual obliteration of all traces of the former Chosun legislation, with the exception of certain areas such as family law. Because the Japanese legislation that applied to Korea during the colonial period had itself been adopted from continental legal systems, such as those of Germany and France, Korean legislation also came within the continental legal world and thus began to rapidly approach the modernized legislation of the West. However, as a result of this process, the old legal traditions of Korea disappeared or were ignored.

When the instrument of surrender was signed by the Japanese on September 2, 1945, the Supreme Commander for the Allied Powers (SCAP) placed the residents of Korea in the territory below the 38th parallel under his jurisdiction by Proclamation No. 1, on September 7, 1945. The residents in his jurisdiction were ordered to obey all of his proclamations, ordinances, regulations, orders, and enactments. This was the beginning of the U.S. military government in Korea. U.S. troops began to land in Korea on September 8, 1945, and its commanding general assumed the role of military governor. It is difficult to enunciate clearly the judicial policy of the U.S. military government in Korea. Even in the absence of a clearly enunciated judicial and legal policy, the U.S. members of the government seem to have felt it to be their task to "instill" into the minds of the Korean lawyers "the Anglo-Saxon conception of due process of law or the rights of the individual before the courts." Although it would be more accurate to state that the military government had no clear judicial policy except to de-Japanize the Korean legal system, the military government did not even succeed in fully doing that. By the provisions of Ordinance No. 21, November 2, 1945, all laws, regulations, orders, or notices issued by any former government or having legal effect as of August 9 were continued in force unless especially repealed or modified by the military government. This meant that even the Japanese laws governing the organization of the government-general were continued. The military government finally capped its three-year rule with the Proclamation of the Rights of the Korean People on April 5, 1948, in the name of the commanding general of the U.S. forces in Korea. Eleven "inherent liberties" were enumerated in the proclamation. It included all the liberties found in the U.S. Bill of Rights.

The proclamation was certainly a great gift to the Korean legal system. The burden to implement and guarantee those "inherent rights" was now placed upon the judiciary of the new government. The military government's success in the effort to de-Japanize Korean law was rather small. With the exception of changes in the criminal procedures introduced in March 1948, the legal system remained basically Japanese, and the Japanese code remained in effect. The organization of the judiciary, the procuracy, and the bar; legal education and its curriculum; and the bar examination all remained fundamentally unchanged. As a whole, the impact of the U.S. legal system was slight. Even the changes in criminal procedures introduced by the Americans largely remained alien and irrelevant.

South Korea held elections under the supervision of the UN Temporary Commission on Korea on May 10,

1948. The new National Assembly drafted a democratic constitution, promulgated on July 17, 1948, and elected as president the conservative, U.S.-educated Syngman Rhee, who formally proclaimed the first Republic of Korea on August 15, 1948. During the 1950s, legislative activity set out to rapidly eliminate the last vestiges of Japanese legislation, and basic laws such as the criminal code, the criminal procedure code, and the civil code were newly enacted in an effort to achieve that goal. As Korea entered the 1960s, the task of removing all traces of the former Japanese legislation in the area of basic laws was completed by the enactment of the civil procedure code and the commercial code.

The 1948 Constitution was amended nine times, and mention needs to be made of some notable aspects of those amendments. The third amendment of 1960, following the fall of the Syngman Rhee government, introduced a parliamentary system. However, the fifth amendment of 1962, adopted a year after a military coup, revived the presidential system, and General Park, the leader of the coup, won the presidency. In 1972 the seventh amendment was adopted by the Emergency State Council, which vested the president with nearly unlimited power, overriding the three separate branches of government. In October 1979, President Park was assassinated, and in the following year the eighth amendment was adopted. A distinctive component of the new constitution was the explicit prohibition of constitutional amendment for extended rule. Although extension of the presidential term was possible by constitutional amendment, such a change did not apply to the president in office. The latest amendment was adopted in 1987, and pivotal in that amendment is election of a president by direct vote, which is restored after fifteen years' aberration of indirect vote. The 1987 Constitution also restored judicial review of the constitutionality of legislation. The power of constitutional review is granted to the new Constitutional Court, rather than to the Supreme Court, which exercised such a jurisdiction in the period of the Third Republic, from 1962 to 1971.

LEGAL CONCEPTS

South Korea's supreme law is found in its constitution. That document defines the territory of South Korea as the Korean Peninsula and its adjacent islands and declares a policy of peaceful unification based on the principles of freedom and democracy. The constitution provides for separation of powers into executive, legislative, and judicial branches of government. It also provides for basic and fundamental human rights, including personal liberty, freedom of speech, presumption of innocence, the right to an attorney in criminal matters, rights to health care and a good environment, guarantees of private property, and so on.

The president holds office for five years, but the term of office of the National Assembly is four years. Thus the incumbent president, Dae Jung Kim, assumed office in 1998, but a new National Assembly was sworn in in 2000. The chief justice and justices of the Supreme Court serve a six-year term, whereas all other judges serve ten-year terms. The chief justice cannot be reappointed. Legislation is passed in the National Assembly by majority vote. The president has the power of veto, but not a line-item veto. The president's veto can be overridden by the National Assembly with a two-thirds majority vote.

The president is elected by a majority of the popular votes cast. In the event that there is a tie in the presidential election, the person who receives the largest number of votes in an open session of the National Assembly attended by a majority of the total members of the National Assembly shall be elected. The constitution forbids a sitting president from being reelected. In the event the president cannot serve out his term, the prime minister or the members of the State Council, in order of priority as determined by law, take over.

The chief justice is appointed by the president with the consent of the National Assembly. The Supreme Court justices are appointed by the president on the recommendation of the chief justice and with the consent of the National Assembly.

A separate Constitutional Court consists of nine members. Three justices are nominated by the president, three by the chief justice of the Supreme Court, and three by the National Assembly. The presiding justice of the court is designated by the president with the consent of the National Assembly. The justices of the Constitutional Court serve six-year terms and may be reappointed. The Constitutional Court has jurisdiction over the following matters: the constitutionality of a law, upon the request of the courts; impeachment; dissolution of a political party; competence disputes between state agencies, between state agencies and local governments, and between local governments; and constitutional complaints as prescribed by law.

The Election Commission is an independent constitutional agency established for the purpose of managing fair elections and referenda. It has a four-tier structure that consists of the National Election Commission at the top. The National Election Commission is composed of nine commissioners, three of whom are appointed by the president, three selected by the National Assembly, and three designated by the chief justice of the Supreme Court. They serve a six-year term. By tradition, the justice of the Supreme Court is elected the chairperson.

The minister of justice, as the supreme superintendent of prosecutory affairs, directs and generally supervises public prosecutors. With respect to specific cases, however, the minister of justice directs and supervises only the prosecutor general. The prosecutor general's term of office is two years, but few prosecutor generals have served out a full term, leading to accusations that there is no true tenure or independence for that position.

By Article 6 of the constitution, treaties duly concluded and promulgated under the constitution and the generally recognized rules of international law have the same effect as domestic laws. The same article also guarantees the status of aliens as prescribed by international law and treaties. South Korea is a signatory to a number of international documents on human rights, including, among others, the Universal Declaration of Human Rights; the International Covenant on Economic, Social, and Cultural Rights; the International Covenant on Civil and Political Rights; the International Convention on the Elimination of All Forms of Racial Discrimination; the Convention on the Elimination of All Forms of Discrimination against Women; the Convention on the Rights of the Child; and the Convention against Torture and Other Cruel, Inhuman or Degrading Treatment or Punishment.

The constitution provides for the right to work. It also places the state under an obligation to enforce a minimum wage system as prescribed by law. The current minimum wage is approximately U.S.$11 per day. Special protection is constitutionally accorded to working women and working children. Workers also have a constitutional right to independent association, collective bargaining, and collective action. However, the right to collective action of workers employed by important defense industries may be either restricted or denied by law.

Criminal procedure is based on the civil law inquisitorial system, although the criminal procedure code contains some elements of the adversarial system. Only a public prosecutor may institute a public prosecution. In a case in which a criminal suspect or an accused person who has been placed under detention is not indicted as provided by law, or is acquitted by a court, that person is entitled to claim just compensation from the state.

CURRENT COURT SYSTEM STRUCTURE

The Supreme Court is the highest body within the judicial branch, serving not only as the court of last resort but also as the administrative and budgetary oversight institution for all courts. For the latter, the Court Administration Office is established under the chief justice of the Supreme Court. The Supreme Court also has exclusive jurisdiction over the validity of the election of the president or a member of the National Assembly. In addition to the Supreme Court, there are the following tribunals in South Korea:

- High Courts (primarily for review from District Courts)

- District Courts (the ordinary courts, which have both criminal and civil jurisdiction)
- Family Court (family affairs and juvenile delinquency)
- Patent Court (patent, utility model, design, and trademark issues)
- Administrative Court (provides judicial oversight to administrative decisions and dispute resolution)
- Military Courts (limited to military crimes by military personnel)

Litigants must be, in principle, represented by a qualified attorney. Exceptions are allowed—for example, in small claims, the value of which are not more than 20,000,000 Won, or approximately U.S.$15,000. When a criminal defendant is unable to secure counsel by his own efforts, the state shall assign counsel for the defendant as prescribed by law. Although attorneys have an ethical duty to represent the poor, that duty is not legally enforced. Law clinics run by universities offer popular legal advice, but they are not sufficient to meet the demand in terms of quantity and quality. The Korea Legal Aid Corporation (KLAC) was created in 1987 by a special law, and its function is to give legal aid to those who are in economic difficulty, or are not protected by the law because of ignorance of the law. Since 1987 the KLAC has provided legal aid in about 270,000 civil and family cases, and since June 1996 it has offered free legal aid in some 24,000 criminal cases involving the poor.

Article 110 of the constitution provides for military tribunals for crimes committed by military personnel. No civilian may be tried by the Military Courts, except in case of crimes as prescribed by law and in the case of the proclamation of extraordinary martial law. The Supreme Court has the final appellate jurisdiction over the Military Courts. However, military trials under an extraordinary martial law may not be appealed in certain cases prescribed by law, except in the case of a death sentence.

The High Courts were a court of first instance in administrative cases until February 28, 1998. By the Administrative Litigation Act, amended in 1994, however, Administrative Court judged in the first instance, as of March 1, 1998, such administrative cases as prescribed by the Administrative Litigation Act and those to which the Administrative Court is competent under other acts. The Supreme Court has the final appellate jurisdiction in administrative cases.

Alternative dispute resolution mechanisms are scattered in individual statutes and are voluntary or mandatory, depending on provisions therein. Voluntary dispute resolutions take one of the following three forms: mediation, conciliation, or arbitration. Parties in dispute may petition for arbitration, the outcome of which is binding on both parties. There is only one institutional arbitration body,

Legal Structure of South Korea Courts

```
                          ┌─────────────────┐
                          │  Supreme Court  │
                          └─────────────────┘

┌──────────────────────────────────────┐      ┌─────────────────┐
│             High Courts                │      │  Patent Court   │
│ Civil  Criminal  Family  Administrative│      │                 │
│              Jurisdiction              │      │                 │
└──────────────────────────────────────┘      └─────────────────┘

    ┌───────────────────────┐   ┌──────────────┐   ┌─────────────────┐
    │    District Courts     │   │ Family Court │   │ Administrative  │
    │ Civil  Criminal        │   │              │   │     Court       │
    │    Jurisdiction        │   │              │   │                 │
    └───────────────────────┘   └──────────────┘   └─────────────────┘
```

the Korean Commercial Arbitration Board, founded in 1966. South Korea, a party to the UN Convention on the Recognition and Enforcement of Foreign Arbitral Awards of 1958, will enforce arbitration awards rendered in another party's country. Parties in dispute may petition for mediation; the outcome of mediation is not binding on either party. Mediation takes one of the following forms: negotiation, independent expert appraisal, moderation, or facilitation. Voluntary conciliation and other similar dispute resolution mechanisms are provided for in many statutes: for example, the Environment Dispute Adjustment Act, the Labor Union and Labor Dispute Adjustment Act, and the Insurance Business Act. A nonexhaustive list of South Korean laws that require some form of nonjudicial dispute resolution before parties resort to arbitration or litigation includes the State Compensation Act, the Domestic Affairs Procedure Act, and the Act concerning Fairness of Subcontracting Transactions.

SPECIALIZED JUDICIAL BODIES

In May 2001, the National Assembly adopted an act establishing the National Human Rights Commission. The provisions of that act came into effect on November 25, 2001. The purpose of the National Human Rights Commission Act is to protect and promote basic and fundamental human rights through the activity of the National Human Rights Commission. The commission is composed of eleven members, four of whom are elected by the National Assembly, four designated by the president, and three designated by the chief justice of the Supreme Court. At least four of the members should be female. The adoption of the National Human Rights Commission Act was, however, not without difficulty. Many nongovernmental human rights organizations were opposed to the bill proposed by the ruling party, mainly because it did not sufficiently guarantee the independence of the proposed commission. In the end, the bill was passed by 137

to 133 votes. Article 3 of the National Human Rights Commission Act provides that the commission shall carry out its functions independently. It remains to be seen how far the independence of the commission will be realized. The National Human Rights Commission can give recommendations with regard to human rights–related legislation, institutions, and policies; investigate acts violating human rights; and survey the status of the protection of human rights, among other functions. When finding that there has been a violation of human rights, the National Human Rights Commission can recommend remedial measures, but it does not have the power to enforce them.

STAFFING

Persons who complete the two-year training program at the Judicial Research and Training Institute attached to the Supreme Court are admitted to practice after registering with the Korean Bar Association. In order to be admitted to the Judicial Research and Training Institute, one must pass the national bar examination, which is held once a year. Everyone qualifies for the national bar examination, and thus, for example, a law degree is not required of the applicant. The number of successful applicants has been fixed at several hundred, and it has increased during the past several years. Although the government recently decided to increase the number to more than one thousand, some do not see even that as sufficient to meet demand for a better legal service.

Those who graduate from the Judicial Research and Training Institute are to be appointed either judges or public prosecutors, or to become attorneys. As of 1999, there were 1,644 judges, 1,165 public prosecutors, and 4,659 attorneys. The Court Organization Act provides that judges shall not be dismissed, unless there is a decision of impeachment or punishment greater than imprisonment without prison labor. The same provision is found in the Public Prosecutor's Office Act.

About one hundred South Korean universities have a college or department of law, with about nine hundred full-time teaching staff. Of these, the Seoul National University College of Law is the largest and best. The vast majority of judges, public prosecutors, and attorneys are graduates from the Seoul National University College of Law. Of the other universities, Korea University, Yonsei University, Sungkyunkwan University, Hanyang University, and Ewha Womans University, among others, have large law faculties.

IMPACT

As in most countries, the South Korean justice administration system is one of the fundamental institutions in society. It has been said that South Koreans lack a strong spirit of compliance with law, consciousness of rights, and familiarity with the law. Some partially attribute this to Confucian tradition, Japanese colonial rule, and a troubled constitutional history. Now, however, this interpretation of the South Korean legal culture of the past has become inappropriate, with participatory civilian culture being established in the democratization process of the late 1980s. The shift from mass democracy to a participatory democracy has heightened the sense of participation and the concept of rights. The significance of law and the judicial system in South Korea will only continue to increase.

Sang-Hyun Song

See also China; Civil Law; Japan
References and further reading
Chun, Bong-Duck, William Shaw, and Dai-Kwon Choi, eds. 1980. *Traditional Korean Legal Attitudes.* Berkeley: Institute of East Asian Studies, Center for Korea Studies, University of California.
Hahm, Pyong-Choon. 1967. *The Korean Political Tradition and Law.* Seoul: Seoul Computer Press.
———. 1986. *Korean Jurisprudence, Politics and Culture.* Seoul: Yonsei University Press.
Song, Sang-Hyun, ed. 1983. *Introduction to the Law and Legal System of Korea.* Seoul: Kyung Mun Sa.
———. 1996. *Korean Law in the Global Economy.* Seoul: Bak Young Sa.
West, James M. 1991. *Education of the Legal Profession in Korea.* Seoul: International Legal Studies, Korea University.
Yoon, Dae-Kyu. 1991. *Law and Political Authority in South Korea.* Boulder, CO: Westview Press.
Yoon, Dae-Kyu, ed. 2000. *Recent Transformations in Korean Law and Society.* Seoul: Seoul National University Press.

SOVIET SYSTEM

GENERAL INFORMATION

The law and legal institutions that developed in the USSR between 1917 and 1986 represented a peculiar variant of the civil law tradition, as adapted to czarist autocratic rule in Russia and to Bolshevik (Marxian) ideas. This hybrid legal system developed first and foremost in the territory of the Soviet Union itself, and it spread after World War II to the people's democracies of Central and Eastern Europe, to China and its communist allies, and to Cuba.

HISTORY

After the Revolution of 1917, Bolshevik leaders eliminated czarist law and courts as reflecting the interests of the old regime and its ruling bourgeois class. But in developing their own law and legal institutions, they drew heavily upon the legacy of the past, bringing into Soviet law many of the concepts and procedures of czarist law, including neoinquisitorial criminal procedure. At the same time, the new codes adopted in 1922 and 1923 and the new judicial system reflected Marxist ideas and the commitment of the new leaders to a law that would serve the interests of socialism. Some Bolsheviks clung to the idea that law itself was obsolete and destined to wither away with the state, but most, like Lenin, recognized the instrumental value of law.

Soviet law in the 1920s reflected the mixed economy enshrined in 1921 by the New Economic Policy, but 1929 witnessed the end of most private business and the unleashing of a drive to collectivize land and property in the countryside. During the war against the peasantry, the observance of legal procedures declined, but the mid-1930s saw a renewed emphasis on legal forms, a more traditional legal policy (emphasizing social discipline rather than revolutionary change), and a new commitment to the centralization of power through law. Even the extrajudicial terror of 1937 through 1938 was given legal casing.

In the postwar years Soviet law became increasingly rigid and severe, such that after Stalin's death in 1953, legal reform became the order of the day. This involved, on the one hand, the curtailing of the powers of the political police (and its subordination to the political leaders) and, on the other, the rationalization, systematization, and liberalization of many areas of substantive and procedural law. At the same time, Nikita Khrushchev encouraged a revival of populist aspects of Soviet law that had fallen into disuse (including lay courts and lay participation in trials).

The spread of the Soviet legal system after World War II to the countries of socialist Eastern Europe brought with it a new diversity of legal forms (for example, of property), but the efforts of reformers in the 1960s to introduce major changes in the economic institutions of the USSR failed to gain the endorsement of the political leadership. The pressure of market forces could not be stemmed, and during the 1970s and early 1980s, a large parallel economy, operating to a large extent outside the

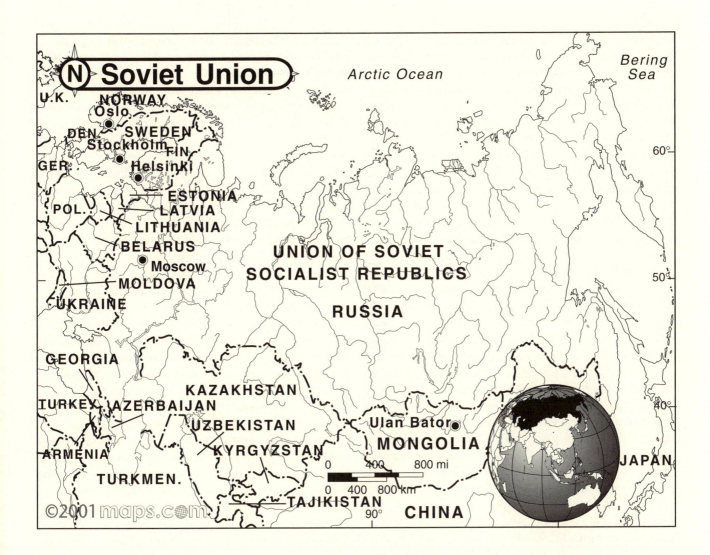

law, drew much of the public into quasi-legal or illegal forms of behavior. At the same time, the renewed severity of criminal law, its use in the persecution of political dissidents, and, from 1986, publicity about abuses of law led an increasingly educated and knowledgeable populace to support legal and judicial reform in the Gorbachev years. The reforms of 1988–1990 promised improvements in Soviet legal institutions and law within the context of Communist Party rule, but the collapse of partocracy and the disintegration of the USSR opened the door to more fundamental changes in Russian law and legal institutions.

CORE CONCEPTS

At the heart of Soviet law stood the postulate that law (*jus,* or *pravo*), like the legal enactments that constituted it (*leges,* or *zakony*), was an instrument of rule and nothing more. This naked instrumentalism reflected the influence of Russian autocratic tradition and Marxist ideology. Right up to 1917, the czar stood above the law (judicial reform notwithstanding) and felt none of the constraints supplied in other countries by an attachment to the *rechtsstaat* (let alone "rule of law"). In like manner,

the writings of Marx and Engels treated law (especially the law of property) as a tool of the ruling bourgeoisie and one that would lose its relevance in a workers' state. After the Revolution, Lenin and his colleagues recognized that law could and should serve as an instrument of rule for the socialist state, but that did not exclude the use of force (terror) in the name of protecting the new regime from its enemies.

The instrumental approach to law meant in practice that the policies of the regime shaped the meaning and application of laws, above and beyond the incorporation of policies in the laws. The dominant role of policy had a dual effect. On the one hand, the resolutions of the ruling Communist Party gained special status in practice, governing the application and interpretation of mere laws. "Party law" was to a degree analogous to "sacred law." On the other hand, to maximize flexibility in public administration and avoid restraints that laws might supply, administrative regulations or instructions (issued or changed by individual officials) acquired unusual authority, sometimes taking precedence over the laws that they were supposed to implement (especially when there were contradictions). Writ large, the reliance on instructions produced an inversion of legal hierarchy. Moreover, since many regulations remained secret, unpublished, or published for limited audiences, the content of the law in some areas (especially in matters of security and the regulation of the economy) was sometimes obscure. In addition, as another way of promoting flexibility in the administration of the law, judges were given a high degree of discretion (at least in the choice of punishments), but the exercise of this discretion was shaped by instructions in the form of the "Guiding Explanations of the Supreme Court of the USSR." Although issued by the court, these "explanations" were sanctioned by political authorities.

Another central postulate of the Soviet legal system was an emphasis on public (or state) interests over those of individuals, even in private law. Of course, the elimination by the 1930s of most private property meant that public law disputes occupied more of the playing field, and that the distinctions between public and private law were blurred. Thus, with the state as the biggest landlord in the country, conflicts over the assignment, use, and disposal of the housing stock necessarily involved public policy and the public interest. Disputes over inheritance, copyright, and torts usually remained matters of private law, but the regime's understanding of the public interest still colored the law and influenced the outcome of disputes. In the postrevolutionary period, the law of torts placed special burdens on wealthy persons when held responsible for acts or omissions ("soak the rich"), but along with other socialist features of the law, this principle fell into disuse. Later on, punitive damages had no place in Soviet law, on the grounds that they would produce unjustified gains for the recipients, though Soviet law did allow the enforcement of penalty clauses in contracts. For the whole of Soviet history, tort law included an especially demanding "duty to rescue."

Not only substantive law but also procedural law reflected the emphasis on the public interest. As we shall see, civil procedure brought a representative of the state, the procurator, into trials, and at the same time required judges to take account of interests beyond those of the parties to the case. The rules of criminal procedure as well privileged the state by avoiding for most of Soviet history the exclusion of evidence improperly obtained and by giving the investigators of crimes a second chance when they failed to produce what was needed at trial (by means of a return of the case by the judge to "supplementary investigation," rather than a verdict of acquittal).

Another characteristic of the Soviet legal system was an emphasis (in varying degrees at different times) on simplicity, populism, and the educational side of the legal process. Former lawyer that he was, Lenin had a strong dislike for the complexities of the law and what later observers would call its mystifying effects, and he sought to keep legal procedures simple and the justice system accessible. That proved a losing battle as far as procedural law was concerned, but the actual conduct of most trials retained an element of informality. At the same time, the people's courts (the lowest regular courts) were highly accessible; fees were so reasonable that access to lawyers was possible for most of the population, although the best lawyers often took supplementary payments under the table. In the 1920s, and again in the Khrushchev years, populism was the fashion of the day, and this translated into prominent roles at trial for members of the public (for example, as "public prosecutors" assisting the procurators) and the use, for simple disputes, of lay courts (the best known were the "comrades' courts"). At all periods of Soviet history, trials were meant to "educate" the public in the courtroom, and most judges took this function seriously. If a trial were taken on circuit to a factory (what was called a "show" or "demonstration trial" in the 1920s and 1930s), the educational dimension might assume excessive importance, and distort the outcome. The famous political show trials of the 1930s were contrived; not only were the charges manufactured but, in addition, the productions were guided by scripts and the accused forced to learn their lines.

Prominent among the defining features of Soviet law was its approach to property and the economy. As a consequence of collectivization and the attack on private business in the cities, private ownership of productive units was largely eliminated. In fact, the word *private* (*chastnoe*) acquired such negative overtones that the word *personal* (*lichnoe*) was used to describe what citizens could legally own (furniture, cars, and so forth). At the same time, land and natural resources also belonged exclusively to the state; citizens and legal persons could gain only limited rights of usage, and the concept of "ownership" acquired a series of gradations. The massive state-owned and -managed economy required normative regulation, but that was supplied in large part outside of the regular civil law, through a variety of laws and regulations. Taking pride of place was the "plan," especially the annual plans negotiated by each productive unit. These plans had the force of law, though many of the relationships dictated by them (for example, supply) were spelled out in contracts between different state bodies. Disputes about contract fulfillment by enterprises were heard not in the courts but by panels of the state *arbitrazh* (see below). The separation of legal regulation of the state-owned economy from the rest of civil law ran so deep that jurists more than once in Soviet history sought the establishment of "economic law" as a branch of law separate from civil law. Criminal law in the Soviet Union was also influenced by the socialist economy, first of all in the criminalization of capitalist practices (the crime of "speculation" entailed making a profit through the buying and selling of goods), and then in the use of the criminal law in the regulation of the state sector (especially holding managers and collective farm chairmen responsible for "negligence").

As in countries of the civil law tradition, Soviet law emphasized legal positivism. The main sources of law were statutes (including codes) and regulations. Officially, references to custom were considered reactionary; and references by judges to prior judicial decisions, legal doctrines, and natural law were generally avoided. At no time in Soviet history did any constitution of the USSR (1923, 1936, or 1977) become a superior source of law. While officially the supreme law, the various constitutions in fact represented in varying degrees descriptions of the system of government, programmatic statements, and public relations; none was self-executing, and there was (at least from 1930) no form of constitutional (or judicial) review until the establishment of the Committee of Constitutional Supervision on the eve of the demise of the USSR (in 1990).

Finally, the Soviet legal system was characterized by a complicated and contradictory set of attitudes about law among government officials and the public at large. Government officials displayed (with varying emphases) a mixture of excessive attachment to the letter of the law, as defined in regulations, and condescending disregard for the law. For its part, the public combined a cynicism about law, and especially the protection of rights by the courts (there was general recognition that the interests of the state came first whenever they entered a case), with a readiness to use the law whenever it might serve their particular interests (especially in matters relating to family, labor, and housing disputes). In short, Soviet law bred its own legal culture, one that reflected instrumentalism and lack of full commitment to law. That culture would present a special challenge for post-Soviet legal reform.

LEGAL PROCEDURES AND INSTITUTIONS

Soviet criminal procedure represented a version of the neoinquisitorial system. "Neoinquisitorial" refers to the system used in contemporary European countries that combines the conduct of an elaborate pretrial investigation by a supposedly impartial magistrate seeking to establish the truth and producing a full written record, with a public trial that includes oral testimony but uses the record of the investigation as evidence. While in France (for example) this "examination" is conducted by a judge on rotation (the *juge d'instruction*), in the Soviet Union from 1928 the preliminary investigation was handled by an investigator working in a prosecutorial setting (either the office of the procurator or the police). In this milieu it was difficult for the investigator to remain neutral, even if he had legal education. At the same time, decisions about such crucial matters as pretrial detention

and search and seizure were entrusted in the main to the procuracy office that would later conduct the prosecution. And, even though the pretrial investigation produced the written evidentiary basis for the trial, defense counsel had for the most part little access to case or client until the conclusion of the preliminary investigation. In short, an accusatorial bias characterized the crucial stage of preliminary investigation.

Criminal trials in the USSR followed the inquisitorial model in that the judge dominated the proceedings, taking a leading role in the process of confirming the evidence supplied in the case file introduced from the preliminary investigation. The role of defense counsel was typically limited to questioning the appropriateness of the charge and making a plea in mitigation. From the late 1940s, judges faced pressure to avoid giving acquittals and often returned cases for supplementary investigation instead. Both sides in the case had access to two forms of appeal. Through the Soviet version of cassation, either side could compel a higher court to review not only the procedures used but also the quality of the evidence. If the cassational instance supported the trial court's verdict and the sentence went into effect, the accused could request an even higher court to conduct a review in supervision, which could involve a complete reexamination of the case.

The distinguishing feature of civil procedure in the USSR was the weight given to the interests of the public in contests between private parties. This was reflected in the practice of taking note of all relevant evidence, including hearsay, and in the judge's obligation to introduce and rely upon relevant law even when not cited by one of the parties. Even more, the concern with the public interest was manifested in the participation of the procurator in civil proceedings, as the initiator of a suit on behalf of a real party, as an intervener in a case, or through a protest to a higher court of a judgment already rendered. Procuratorial involvement was mandatory for certain cases (concerning deprivation of parental rights, declaring a person missing or dead, confiscation of structures, and eviction from housing).

A vital and characteristic institution in the Soviet legal system (one usually exported to other socialist countries) was the procuracy. Descendant of a czarist forerunner established by Peter the Great to supervise compliance with law and of the post-1864 procuracy that handled criminal prosecutions, the Soviet procuracy combined legal supervisory and prosecutorial functions. Procuracy offices were responsible for supervising the legality of the work of the police, criminal investigations, prisons, and courts (even when prosecuting trials, thereby placing the procurator for some purposes above the judge), as well as for general supervision of the legality of public life. General supervision empowered procurators to conduct inquiries into the activities of any public body (especially in response to a signal), to entertain complaints from citizens about the actions of governmental officials, and to issue protests. This complaint system developed into a much used alternative to bringing complaints to a court, which until 1987 was possible only for a small number of subjects. Along with all these supervisory functions, the procuracy also handled criminal prosecutions in court and, as we have seen, played a role in civil cases as well. By the time of the post-Stalin years, the procuracy had emerged as the most powerful legal institution, and one that, in the view of post-Soviet reformers, stood in the way of the empowerment and independence of the courts.

While the courts were entrusted with criminal cases and disputes between citizens, disputes between state enterprises were handled by the state *arbitrazh*. The name notwithstanding, these panels actually adjudicated disputes and became skilled at assigning blame for failure to achieve planned targets or to fulfill delivery obligations. In the late Soviet period these panels resembled courts, and in 1991 they were transformed into the *arbitrazh* courts that handled commercial disputes in post-Soviet Russia.

LEGAL STAFF

As in civil law countries generally, there was no single legal profession in the USSR, but rather a set of legal careers, with only limited possibilities of transfer. These included investigator and procurator, judge, advocate, iurisconsult, and notary. Legal services to private citizens were supplied by advocates (organized in regional colleges) and notaries, and to enterprises and government bodies by iurisconsults (sometimes on staff). Work in the procuracy as an investigator or procurator represented a career track, as did work as a judge (sometimes preceded by a few years in the procuracy or as a legal secretary).

Throughout Soviet history political leaders tried to ensure that legal officials (such as procurators and judges) would be loyal and trustworthy servants of the regime and that lawyers (such as advocates) would serve the regime's notion of the public interest. In the years before World War II, membership in the Communist Party was a key criterion in the appointment of judges and procurators in line positions, counting for more than possession of higher legal education—that is, an undergraduate degree in law. In the early 1930s, the heyday of negative attitudes toward the law, legal education declined to the point that the whole USSR was graduating a few hundred lawyers per year. After the war, legal education came to matter more than it had before, producing a major revival of higher legal education of all forms—the regular day stream, night courses, and education by correspondence. By the 1960s, higher legal education became a requirement for newly appointed legal officials, but most new judges were still members of the party. And judges continued to depend upon party bosses for the opportunity to continue in office (party officials had a voice in the renomination of judges for periodic [unopposed] elections and for a variety of perks [including apartments]). For their part, advocates had more professional autonomy than judges, but their collegia were managed by members trusted by politicians, and the price of persistent nonconformism on the part of an advocate was potential disbarment.

IMPACT

After World War II, the international significance of the Soviet legal system grew dramatically, when that system in one form or another spread to the new people's democracies of Central and Eastern Europe and to communist regimes in Asia and Cuba. The law and legal systems of these countries soon had much in common, in the content of the law, in the procedures used, and in institutions. At the same time, there were also important differences. Poland after 1956 allowed ownership of land and small farms; Hungary from the late 1960s legalized small businesses; in the 1980s Poland developed a form of constitutional adjudication. After the Sino-Soviet split at the end of the 1960s, China ceased aping Soviet law, and its leaders emphasized differences, clinging for example to the importance of class status and the class struggle as an element in prosecution and adjudication (an idea abandoned long before in the USSR).

Wherever the Soviet legal system was implanted and lasted for a long time in a relatively pure form, that system became a fixture, making its dismantling or undoing a hard challenge. That was especially the case in the many post-Soviet states (the Baltic countries excluded) that had possessed Soviet law and legal institutions for seven decades. One postcommunist state after another struggled with such common problems as how to reform the procuracy, whether and how to rectify the accusatorial bias built into the Soviet version of the inquisitorial criminal procedure (through moves toward adversarialism?), how to make courts independent, what laws of property to introduce, how to regulate business in a fair and effective way, how to ensure implementation of civil or commercial judgments, how to organize judicial review of administrative acts, and how to institute constitutional adjudication that effectively protects individual rights. As of 2001, some postcommunist countries (such as Ukraine) have resolved few of these questions and continue, at least in practice, to operate with law and legal institutions that were largely Soviet. Others (such as Hungary) have accomplished major changes, but still see carryovers from communist times in the attitudes and relations of public officials toward legality. Even after institutions were changed, the culture associated with the Soviet legal system continued to leave its mark.

Peter H. Solomon, Jr.

See also Civil Law; Inquisitorial Procedure; Russia
References and further reading
Barry, Donald D., ed. 1992. *Toward the Rule of Law in Russia? Political and Legal Reform in the Transition Period.* Armonk, NY, and London: M. E. Sharpe.
Barry, Donald, George Ginsburgs, and Peter Maggs, eds. 1977–1979. *Soviet Law after Stalin.* 3 vols. Leyden: A. W. Sijthof.
Berman, Harold J. 1963. *Justice in the USSR: An Interpretation of Soviet Law.* Rev. ed. Cambridge: Harvard University Press.
Butler, William. 1988. *Soviet Law.* 2d ed. London: Butterworth's.
———. 1991. *Basic Documents of the Soviet Legal System.* New York: Oceana Publications (orig. pub. 1983).
Hazard, John N. 1969. *Communists and Their Law: A Search for the Common Core of the Legal Systems of the Marxian Socialist States.* Chicago and London: University of Chicago Press.
Ioffe, Olympiad S., and Peter B. Maggs. 1983. *Soviet Law in Theory and Practice.* London: Oceana Publications.
Kavass, Igor, ed. 1988. *Soviet Law in English: Research Guide and References and Further Reading, 1970–1987.* Buffalo, NY: W. S. Hein.
Solomon, Peter H., Jr. 1996. *Soviet Criminal Justice under Stalin.* Cambridge and New York: Cambridge University Press.

SPAIN

GENERAL INFORMATION

Spain is a land of enormous geographical variety. Along with Portugal, it occupies the Iberian Peninsula in southwestern Europe. Besides the mainland, contemporary Spain includes the Balearic Islands in the Mediterranean Sea, the Canary Islands in the Atlanta Ocean off the coast of Africa, and the North African enclaves of Ceuta and Melilla. Mainland Spain's 493,486 square kilometers (about 84 percent of the peninsula) presents a fascinating contrast of rugged mountains (the Pyrenees in the northwest, separating the peninsula from the rest of Europe, and the Sierra Nevada in the south), broad tableland (the central Meseta), and extensive coastland. All these geological features have had a significant impact on the country's historical and cultural development.

Spain's legal history and contemporary public affairs are best understood within the context of its social and cultural heterogeneity. Facilitated by its physical features, the concept of a "Spain of regions" reflects many centuries of often problematic relations between the dominant Castilian center and the non-Castilian peoples of the periphery. With approximately 40 million inhabitants, Spain's diverse population includes a large majority that speaks Castilian (the language generally thought of as Spanish) and smaller groups that converse in many other languages and dialects. Culturally and politically, the most important of these include Catalan, Euskera (the Basque language), and Gallego, with Valencian, Mallorcan (in the Balearic Islands), and the Andalusian dialect also worthy of note. Given such heterogeneity, Spain is best described as a multinational state. The development of its legal system parallels in many respects the social and political history of this diversified country.

Spain's uniform legal system resides well within the mainstream of European civil law traditions. Its judicial structures reflect strong centralizing tendencies in Spanish history as well as unique influences of the country's multinational nature. The transition to a democratic political system in the late 1970s and Spain's subsequent membership in the European Union are sources of more contemporary changes in the Spanish legal system.

HISTORY

While containing some pre-Roman customary, Muslim, and Germanic elements, the contemporary Spanish legal system is most strongly influenced by Roman law. The Roman Empire fully integrated Spain between 200 B.C.E. and 400 C.E. Rome's influence was nevertheless uneven. Early Rome permitted legal variation through adaptations of pre-Roman law to local circumstances. Later, during the absolutist period of the third century C.E., Rome increasingly became the primary source of law. Roman law remained dominant during the Visigoth period, but with some local adaptation regarding landownership and distribution.

The Moslem invasion of 711 C.E. set Spain on a course of history separate from other European countries. The establishment of Al-Andalus over much of the Iberian Peninsula and the subsequent centuries-long Reconquest meant that Spain was not part of the Holy Roman Empire. Under Moslem control, the peoples willing to recognize the authority of Al-Andalus retained their own laws, religions, customs, and property. Moslem tolerance for other religions permitted the application of different laws to Jews, Christians, and Moslems. The resultant legal diversification contributed to the law's becoming increasingly localized. As the Reconquest progressed, many Christian kingdoms used local laws, or *fueros,* to solidify support among the local nobility and to encourage Christian settlement in newly retaken areas. Despite variation in degrees of autonomy, many of the same monarchs increasingly came to rule these different kingdoms. More than a historical coincidence, the end of the Reconquest and the unification of Spain both occurred in 1492.

With unification of Spain under Ferdinand of Aragón and Isabella of Castile, the monarchy controlled all kingdoms in Spain, but the distinct territories retained vary-

ing degrees of autonomy, including the application of their unique legal traditions. Two broad trends characterize legal developments in Spain during the sixteenth and seventeenth centuries. First, the king's growing power, an increase in legislation by the Cortes of the many different kingdoms, especially Castile, and judicial uncertainty regarding the applicability of competing laws and legal traditions encouraged the compilation of laws and a reconciling of overlapping legal traditions. Second, rule by a unified monarchy over kingdoms with distinct constitutional orders quickly produced conflict. Philip IV's policy of imposing Castilian political institutions throughout Spain increased the king's powers at the expense of the localities. Subsequent monarchs also pursued this Castilian policy of centralization, challenging the kingdoms' unique histories, undercutting their constitutional systems, and removing conflicting sources of law. In 1379, the Cortes of Burgos established the right of local powers to delay the implementation of the central government's legal decisions if judicial conflict arose, as long as the localities recognized the king's ultimate power to legislate. Nonetheless, the territories' ability to resist Castile's cen-

tralizing tendency, and thus to protect their unique political and legal traditions, varied greatly. Some, such as the Basque provinces and Navarre, were relatively successful; consequently, their local (or foral) laws remain a part of contemporary Spain's legal system. Other regions, such as Catalonia, Valencia, Aragon, and Mallorca, saw the abolishment of their *fueros* following the Spanish War of Succession (1701–1713). Monarchical absolutism and Castilian dominance thus greatly centralized Spain's system of governance and unified much of its legal system.

The modern period of Spanish law begins with Napoleon's invasion and subsequent control of Spain in 1808. The French codified Spanish law in much the same manner that they did throughout the empire. Through the Napoleonic Code, the French Revolution's legacy that equality before the law meant that a single system of law must be applied to all was thus brought to Spain at the beginning of the nineteenth century. This codification limited judicial decisions to law and ultimately produced a nationwide systemization of penal, commercial, tax, procedural, and administrative law. However, the process of codification and recompilation was more complicated in the area of civil law. Spain's long history of foral law impeded attempts to create a unified civil code. Throughout the nineteenth century, many initiatives met strong opposition from those seeking to protect local norms and customs and force recognition of the remaining foral laws. This political stalemate was finally broken in 1880, when a reform commission was formed that included local representatives. The resultant Civil Code of 1889, clearly influenced by France's *Code Civil* of 1804, systematized Spanish civil law while preserving the use of foral laws. It remains the basis of Spanish civil law to this day.

Developments in constitutional and public law throughout the nineteenth and twentieth centuries depended heavily on Spain's uncertain political direction and its many changes of regime. Vacillation between authoritarianism and more liberal forms of government included the short-lived First Republic of 1873–1874, the conservative constitutional monarchy after 1876, the Second Republic of 1931–1939, the civil war of 1936–1939, the regime of Francisco Franco until his death in 1975, and the transition to democracy beginning in 1976. These different political regimes each affected the nature and development of Spain's legal tradition. The most recent, the post-Franco transition to democracy, is readily seen in the country's contemporary judicial system.

Spain's Constitution of 1978 ended the notion that judicial power was just another sector of public administration. In earlier, nondemocratic periods, the Spanish executive often interfered in judicial operations. Today, the Spanish judiciary is a distinct part of the state. It assumes the constitutionally based functions normally associated with developed democratic systems, including the legal exercise of public power and the protection of basic individual liberties. Beyond the constitution, several important reforms have subsequently elaborated democratic Spain's judicial and legal system. The most important was the Organic Law of Judicial Power (*Ley Orgánica del Poder Judicial,* or LOPJ) of July 1985. This fundamental law abolished the antiquated law of 1870, facilitated the development of liberal democratic principles in the judiciary, and framed several important institutional reforms regarding the application of law in Spain.

The transition to democracy also made possible Spain's entry into the European Union (EU) in 1986. As with law in many other European countries, Spanish law has increasingly become integrated into an emerging EU legal system. As part of a federalized set of legal and government processes, an additional, European-wide layer of a hierarchy of laws is now part of the Spanish system. When conflict arises, EU public law takes precedence over Spanish national law. Regarding fundamental rights, all Spanish citizens also now live under EU law, including the Convention on Human Rights.

LEGAL CONCEPTS

Two characteristics have historically distinguished the Spanish legal system from those of other European countries. First, the Roman Catholic Church's influence was quite strong during several earlier periods of Spain's political history. The Concordats of 1753, 1851, and 1953 recognized the country's Catholic nature and gave the Spanish state a strong confessional characteristic, incorporating many areas of canon law into public law. One example is family law during the Franco period, when divorce was forbidden and adultery was codified as an illegal activity in a manner consistent with canon law. In addition, the Catholic Church's central role in public life has often been given special constitutional protection. This has included defense of its sacred places of worship, subsidization through state financing, control of compulsory religious instruction in schools, and disciplinary jurisdiction regarding its own personnel. Reinforcing church-state relations, Spanish government authorities long maintained a traditional right to appoint bishops. The constitution of 1978 formally and institutionally greatly altered the church's close relationship with the Spanish state. Roman Catholicism's history and moralistic legacy nevertheless continue to influence Spain's legal system in many often subtle ways.

Second, Spain's regional diversity has also affected its legal system. As previously mentioned, a unique set of local laws, *fueros*, originated as nonwritten customary law and decisions of local authorities. Societal rather than state-based, foral laws are private, primarily customary, civil laws applied in the Basque country, Navarre, and elsewhere. As most were systematically compiled in the fourteenth and fifteenth centuries, some *fueros* managed to survive Spain's centralization under Castilian influence during the sixteenth and seventeenth centuries. Now part of contemporary Spain's legal system, they remain a legal reflection of the earlier development of separate legal traditions in Spain and reveal the distinct cultural and political history of each region.

Regionalization has also had an impact on public law in democratic Spain. The constitution of 1978 and subsequent legislative and judicial decisions have created a multinational state that seeks to balance the central state and the regions' uneven centrifugal tendencies. The resultant system of seventeen autonomous communities, achieved through three separate constitutional routes to autonomy, gives Spain a quasi-federal character. While the delineation of powers between the regions and the central state continues to evolve, each autonomous community (AC) contains public institutions such as legislatures and democratically elected governments that produce laws that apply only within that territory. Such decision making must, of course, occur in a manner consistent with the respective AC's Statute of Autonomy.

Constitutionally grounded, this system of autonomous communities significantly contributes to the making of public law in Spain.

STRUCTURE

Despite the decentralizing tendencies of the contemporary political system, the Spanish judiciary remains highly centralized and hierarchical. In a manner consistent with other European unitary systems, judicial structures extend uniformly throughout Spain. In fact, despite the turbulence of numerous regime changes, Spain's system of ordinary courts—those with general civil and criminal jurisdiction—has not changed much in the past two centuries.

The Supreme Court occupies the apex of Spain's hierarchical judicial structure. Created in 1812, it is the country's highest appellate court and holds jurisdiction throughout the country. Based in Madrid, the court is organized into five specialized chambers: civil, criminal, administrative, social, and military. Cases are brought to the different chambers by lower courts, with appeals generally based on procedural or formal issues or on arguments that a legal doctrine previously issued by the Supreme Court has been misapplied. In the former, the Supreme Court returns the case to the lower court following its decision with instructions to issue a new sentence. In the latter, the court redecides the case. In making its decisions, the Supreme Court tends to respect the general principles of Spanish civil law, leaving the making of law to the legislature. Its decisions do, however, determine a certain legal precedence within the development of Spanish legal doctrine.

Hierarchically, the National Audience (*Audiencia Nacional*) is one level below the Supreme Court in criminal, administrative, and labor cases. As a collegiate court created in 1977 and located in Madrid, the National Audience handles highly visible criminal cases of national importance, such as crimes against the highest institutions of the Spanish state, terrorism, extradition, counterfeiting, drug trafficking, and crimes committed outside Spain but within the purview of international treaties. Within these areas of criminal law, the National Audience hears appeals from the Central Courts of Instruction (*Juzgados Centrales de Instrucción*), which were also created in 1977. The Central Courts possess national jurisdiction yet serve as courts of first instance for the National Audience and the Madrid-based Central Penal Courts (*Juzgados Centrales de lo Penal*). These latter courts have national jurisdiction and hear lesser cases within the National Audience's jurisdiction. Finally, the National Audience also hears administrative appeals of cases against decisions by government ministers and their immediate subordinates.

The Superior Court of Justice (*Tribunal Superior de Justicia*) comprises Courts of First Instance for civil cases involving members of the AC parliaments or AC governmental members, as well as trademark and patent cases for AC residents. More frequently, superior courts, which replaced the earlier territorial courts and now reflect Spain's territorial division into autonomous communities, serve as appellate courts for the Provincial Audience (*Audiencia Provincial*) and, in turn, send appeals to the Supreme Court.

Courts of First Instance and Justices of the Peace constitute the entry into Spain's judicial system. The Courts of First Instance handle most civil cases and less severe criminal cases. As in many common law and European systems, Justices of the Peace exist for minor civil claims and criminal cases. These justices are nonprofessional judges in municipalities without Courts of First Instance. Appeals from both these types of courts can make their way to the Provincial Audience in that territory.

SPECIALIZED JUDICIAL BODIES

Civil law countries like Spain tend to have a separate structure of administrative courts. Such courts hear cases involving the rules, regulations, and decisions of state administrative agencies. They have the power to annul such actions as well as to act against the administrative personnel themselves. In the United States, such cases are normally adjudicated in the ordinary courts with appeals through the normal appellate structures. In France, the Council of State serves as the ultimate appellate court for its system of administrative tribunals, which are staffed by civil servants. In contrast, Spain's administrative courts are, since 1956, incorporated as special chambers within the ordinary court system, with trials taking place in the Superior Courts of Justice and the Supreme Court. Recruited as in the ordinary courts, judges are different only in that they specialize in administrative law. The growth of Spain's social welfare system and the new role of the autonomous communities in administrative matters have meant that such administrative courts have grown considerably since the country's return to democracy.

Spain's contemporary legal system maintains several special courts with jurisdiction over specific but limited subjects. For example, Social Courts (*Juzgados de lo Social*) resolve conflict over employment contracts and social security. Since 1989, the Superior Courts of Justice have dealt with cases between employers and employees outside the Social Courts' jurisdiction as well, serving as an appellate court for the Social Courts of the autonomous communities. This 1989 judicial reform was also important because it abolished the system of labor courts (*magistraturas de trabajo*), including the Central Labor Court (*Tribunal Central de Trabajo*), which had gained visibility during the transition to democracy when the labor unions played an important sociopolitical role.

Legal Structure of Spanish Courts

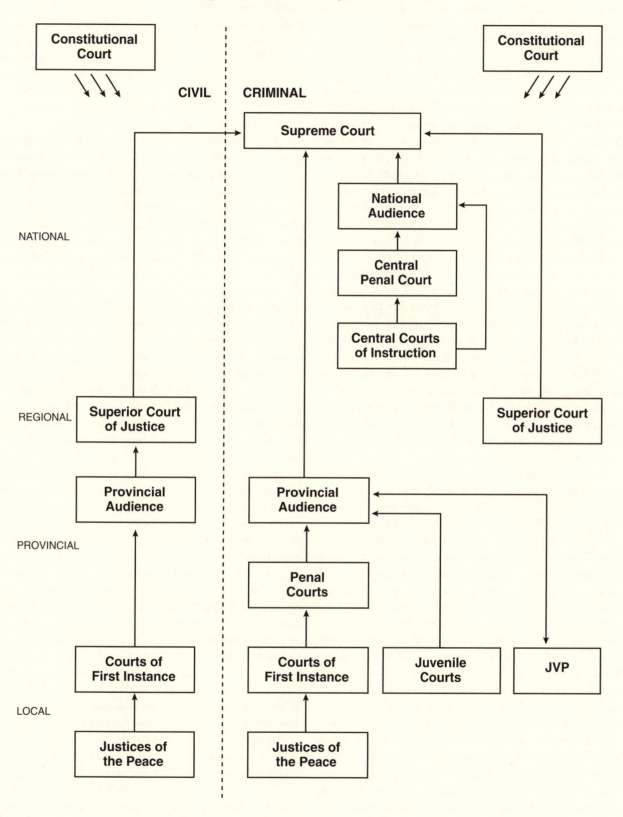

The labor courts' responsibilities of adjudicating conflict between employees and management are now handled at the AC level, with the National Audience possessing jurisdiction over national collective bargaining agreements.

The Spanish judicial system also has several special courts in the area of criminal law. These include the penal courts (*juzgados de lo penal*), the Courts for Prison Surveillance (*Juzgados de Vigilancia Penitenciaria,* or JVP), and juvenile courts (*juzgados de menores*). Created in 1988, Penal Courts are criminal courts at the provincial level. There are some 143 such courts, which can levy punishment of up to six years in prison. JPVs are criminal courts located in provincial capitals. They enforce criminal penalties involving prison time and monitor prisoner rights. As in many countries, juvenile courts in Spain adjudicate cases involving minors.

The Spanish armed forces have historically operated special military courts. During periods of authoritarian rule, these military courts were also used to combat political opposition and to suppress the civilian population. Even prior to the Franco regime, Spain's military court system often extended its jurisdiction to include civilians. Given such abuse, the Constitution of 1978 limits these courts' jurisdiction to strictly military affairs. It also prohibits the use of other special judicial institutions such as the Francoist Court of Public Order. Patently a political court, it was created in 1963 with the support of the military and with judges from the ordinary courts to combat "subversion."

Spain's Constitutional Court is the country's most important special court. While formally not part of the judicial structure, it is democratic Spain's major institutional innovation for conflict resolution of a constitutional question. Modeled after similar courts in post–World War II Germany and Italy, this special tribunal resolves disputes regarding constitutional issues of public, as opposed to private, law. Its twelve members serve nine-year terms. The Spanish government and the General Council of the Judiciary each choose two candidates. The lower chamber of the legislature, the Congress of Deputies, nominates four members. The Senate names the other four. Nominees must then receive approval from three-fifths of each house of parliament, a selection process that guarantees a majority broader than the government-opposition party division. A rotation system operates in which four new judges come onto the court every three years, with the Congress, the Senate, and the Government and the General Council of the Judiciary each taking turns in proposing their candidates. While justices must be respected jurists with at least fifteen years of experience, the selection process clearly goes beyond questions of proven individual qualifications to encompass broad institutional, political, and ideological bases.

As an autonomous institution, the Constitutional Court establishes its own budget and internal organization and operations. It elects one of its own members as president for a three-year term. It can decide to meet as a twelve-judge tribunal or plenum (which it tends to do for highly visible cases), to divide into two chambers (*salas*) with six judges each (as it normally does for *amparo* appeals, with its president and vice president each chairing a chamber), or to subdivide further into sections of three judges each for purposes of efficiency.

The Constitutional Court hears three types of cases. Questions of constitutionality involve issues dealing with statutes, general laws, and organic laws passed by the Spanish parliament or the parliaments of the autonomous communities, and executive or legislative acts such as decree-laws, legislative decrees, and internal rules of operation. The court must receive the question within three months of official publication. Questions of constitutionality arrive at the court in three ways. An unconstitutionality appeal is a direct petition seeking to have the issue declared contrary to the constitution. These petitions may originate with the prime minister, the public defender, fifty members of the Congress of Deputies, fifty senators, the executive of any of the autonomous communities, or an AC assembly. An unconstitutionality appeal does not suspend the law's application while the case is being decided unless the central government deems it necessary in cases involving autonomous community law.

Prior control is a second means to bring questions of constitutionality before Spain's Constitutional Court. Unlike unconstitutionality appeals that are raised after promulgation, prior control of unconstitutionality enables the court to intervene and consider conformity to the constitution prior to legislative enactment. Such cases tend to involve international treaties and organic laws. The court thus has responsibility for international treaties even if already approved by the country's political institutions. Prior control involving organic laws helps avoid disruption in Spain's fundamental system of governance by having to nullify laws or statutes already implemented.

A third way for questions of unconstitutionality to arrive at the Constitutional Court is via petition by a lower court judge. During a case the judge may decide, or may be solicited by either party involved, to forward to the court a question of constitutionality pertinent to the case. The trial recesses while the question is heard.

Beyond questions of unconstitutionality, the Constitutional Court hears two other types of cases. One requires it to serve as a judicial arbiter for institutional conflicts involving different components of the Spanish state. These conflicts include disputes over power and authority between institutions such as the government, the Congress of Deputies, the Senate, and the parts of the judiciary; between central state institutions and one of the autonomous communities; and between different ACs.

In such cases, the court must delimit the constitutional scope of institutional power. The Constitutional Court's role in this area has proved invaluable in the development of Spanish democracy and the application of the Constitution of 1978.

The third type of case the Constitutional Court hears is called a *recurso de amparo*. Specific to Hispanic legal traditions—and thus found in earlier Spanish constitutions as well as in some Latin American countries such as Mexico and Venezuela—the *amparo* appeal is a judicial mechanism by which fundamental individual rights can be protected against an abuse of state power. An *amparo* appeal does not challenge the constitutionality of a law or statute but instead enables private parties to seek protection against its application. Upon hearing an *amparo* appeal, the Constitutional Court may find that the application of the law is unconstitutional in the particular case. Its decision, however, does not generalize to other cases. Questions of unconstitutionality remain the primary mechanism for challenging the constitutionality of a law.

The Defender of the People (*Defensor del Pueblo*) is important to the operations of Spain's Constitutional Court as well as the overall judicial system regarding administrative matters. Like the Constitutional Court, the Office of the Defender of the People is technically not part of the Spanish legal system. It is, in fact, a high commission of the Spanish parliament, which appoints the defender. The people's defender serves as an ombudsman to protect fundamental individual rights and liberties, particularly against infringements by administrative and legislative activities.

As a watchdog of administrative activity, the defender can investigate state bureaucratic authorities and recommend changes. If these recommendations are not acted on, the state's public prosecutor (*fiscal general del estado*) can bring them directly to the attention of the relevant ministry and even to the parliament itself. In this capacity, the Defender of the People vigorously defends its right of full access to state administrative offices, and especially to obtain official documents, gather data, and conduct investigative interviews. It also has the power to file *amparo* appeals and appeals of unconstitutionality with the Constitutional Court. While both types of appeals greatly assist the defender in addressing concerns about citizens' rights, it has most heavily utilized *amparo* appeals to help individuals gain access to Spain's highest constitutional body.

STAFFING

The General Council of the Judiciary (*Consejo General del Poder Judicial*) is the Spanish judiciary's principal governing body. Deriving its authority from the Constitution of 1978, the General Council was created in 1980 to encourage judicial independence. It has twenty members, plus the president of Spain's Supreme Court, whom it elects and who in turn serves as the council's president. The Spanish parliament determines the General Council's members: the Congress of Deputies and the Senate each select from within the judicial system six active judges and four highly respected lawyers with a minimum of fifteen years' professional service. Members are chosen for five-year terms and, with the exception of the president, cannot be reelected. The three-fifths legislative majority required for election encourages partisan cooperation. Nevertheless, the appointment process has increasingly become politically problematic. One indication of this politicization is that prior to revision in 1985, twelve of the General Council's twenty members were chosen by a national electoral college of all active judges and magistrates.

The primary function of the General Council of the Judiciary is the recruitment, staffing, and appointment of Spain's judicial personnel. At the highest level, this includes the appointment of two members of the Constitutional Court as well as the president of the Supreme Court, both of whom the king must formally approve. The General Council also appoints the other Supreme Court judges, presidents of the regional Superior Courts of Justice, and those of the provincial courts. In terms of ordinary courts, the General Council takes responsibility for the training, placement, promotion, and professional discipline of judges. In this regard, it holds exclusive responsibility for the Center for Judicial Studies (*Centro de Estudios Judiciales*), which is involved in education and training. The General Council's secondary functions include maintaining an inspection system for the Spanish courts; submitting an annual report to parliament on its status and functions, including its needs regarding staffing and resources; and publishing the official records of the Supreme Court.

Judges in Spain are essentially a self-regulating group of nonpolitical, independent, and professional civil servants. They form a self-conceived elite within the Spanish legal profession. Emphasizing their official title of career judicial personnel (*funcionario de la carrera judicial*), they tend to believe they are better trained, do more important work, and have higher prestige than other civil servants. Nevertheless, their career paths are similar to those of other civil servants, and they hold the same guarantees and protections. Competitive national examinations (*oposiciones*) and a law degree from a Spanish university determine eligibility. Candidates with acceptable scores are admitted to the Center for Judicial Studies for training prior to being appointed judges in the Courts of First Instance. Promotion thereafter is determined largely by seniority.

The Spanish government, in consultation with the General Council of the Judiciary, names the public prosecutors. Like judges, they are selected from graduates of the Center for Judicial Studies, but though sharing a common educational background they have separate careers. They are responsible for protecting the rule of law, citizens' rights, and the public interest, but their most routine and visible function is the prosecution of criminal cases. Prosecutors argue the state's case, while the examining judge presents the evidence in his summary and the court's magistrates question the witnesses and control the conduct of the trial.

Spain's legal profession has three components. Following recent reforms, members of all three must hold a university law degree. First, notaries execute all transactions that require legal forms, such as contracts and property sales. Notaries are not involved in litigation or the preparation of legal cases. Second, lawyers prepare the legal cases but, in a manner similar to British solicitors, do not file or argue the cases in a court of law. Third, the procurators (*procuradores*) argue the cases in court. Attorneys in Spain must be members of a local College of Lawyers (*Colegio de Abogados*)—the equivalent of a bar association—which is found in all cities with either a Superior Court of Justice or a Provincial Audience.

IMPACT

Spain's successful transition to democracy following the death of Francisco Franco in 1975 has served as an example for other countries emerging from a period of dictatorial rule. While unique in many respects, this remarkable transformation incorporated Spain as a full and active member of the European community of liberal democratic nations. The Spanish legal system greatly facilitated this reform. Spain's legal tradition provided continuity regarding ordinary law and in the judicial application of it during the heady days of fundamental political change. Throughout the transition, the country's basic judicial structures continued to adjudicate. Thus, it is important to know that contemporary Spain's normal judicial structures and legal traditions predate the contemporary democracy. Equally important, the judiciary was quickly and successfully integrated into the democratic ethos of the new political system.

The Spanish legal system also contains several new components instituted since the transition to democracy. Many of these in turn directly affect the operation of contemporary Spanish democracy itself. New institutions such as the Constitutional Court, the National Audience and its system of lower courts, and the Defender of the People have articulated issues and provided judicial resolution in areas salient to the new democracy. They have played important roles in defending individual rights and justice, framing the evolution of a "Spain of regions," and mediating institutional conflict inherent in any new system of governance. The courts have also provided an arena to address ongoing challenges to this evolving

polity, such as terrorism, corruption, military-civilian reforms, and social, political, and legal relations between the European Union and Spain. To its credit, the Spanish legal system has continued to be perceived by most Spaniards and international observers as apolitical, fair, and independent in the exercise of its constitutionally mandated responsibilities of adjudication.

Thomas D. Lancaster

See also Basque Region; Catalonia; Civil Law; Customary Law; European Court of Justice; Federalism

References and further reading
De Esteban, Jorge, and Pedro J. González-Trevijano. 1992. *Curso de derecho constitucional español I.* Madrid: Civitas.
Herrero Herrero, César. 1996. *Introducción al nuevo código penal: Parte especial.* Madrid: Dykinson.
Heywood, Paul. 1995. "The Judiciary and the 'State of Law.'" Chapter 5 of *The Government and Politics of Spain.* New York: St. Martin's Press.
Lancaster, Thomas D., and Micheal W. Giles. 1986. "Spain." In *Legal Traditions and Systems: An International Handbook.* Edited by Alan N. Katz. New York: Greenwood.
López Guerra, Luís, et al. 1997. *Derecho Constitucional.* Vol. 2. 3d ed. Valencia: Tirant lo Blanch.
Merino-Blanco, Elena. 1996. *The Spanish Legal System.* London: Sweet and Maxwell.
Newton, Michael T., with Peter J. Donaghy. 1997. *Institutions of Modern Spain: A Political and Economic Guide.* Cambridge: Cambridge University Press.
Penalva, Pedraz, ed. 1996. *El Gobierno de la justicia: El consejo general del poder judicial.* Valladolid: Universidad de Valladolid.
Tomás y Valiente, Francisco. 1997. *Manual de historia del derecho español.* Madrid: Tecnos.
Villiers, Charlotte. 1999. *The Spanish Legal Tradition.* Brookfield: Darmouth.

THE SPANISH EMPIRE AND THE LAWS OF THE INDIES

INTRODUCTION AND CONTEXT

Believing that he had discovered a shorter route to India, Cristobal Colón (Christopher Columbus) named the world he had encountered the Indies. Even though this "new" world was eventually named America, in honor of Américo Vespucio, the cartographer who provided a map of the new regions, Spain continued to use the concept of the Indies to describe its empire in the Western Hemisphere, as well as to distinguish these territories from the mainland. The Spanish Empire developed a massive legal and administrative system to govern its domains between the early sixteenth and early nineteenth centuries. This legal and administrative system, consisting mostly of bureaucratic rules and monarchical decrees, is generally known as the Laws of the Indies. These laws were designed to provide order and administer and govern the colonies, while simultaneously consolidating Spain's control of its fragile and fragmented overseas empire. The empire further relied on a hierarchy of institutions such as the Real Consejo de Indias (Royal Council of the Indies), the *virrey* (viceroy), the *audiencias* (regional tribunals), and the office of the captain general/governor to enforce these laws.

LEGAL ANTECEDENTS

The Laws of the Indies can be understood as a continuity of pre-Hispanic legal principles rooted in Roman and Germanic traditions. Prior to the Roman presence, various tribes or ethnic communities such as Iberians, Celts, Phoenicians, Carthaginians, and Greeks populated the peninsula that we now know as Spain and Portugal. For the most part they relied on tradition and a patrimonial system as a normative source of governance.

The Roman Empire conquered these territories in 205 B.C.E. and remained in power for approximately six centuries, or until the year 414 C.E. Rome introduced its legal and administrative systems of governance in an effort to reorganize and reconfigure the peninsula. This resulted in the creation of municipalities and semiautonomous regions. Eventually Roman law permeated local institutions and coexisted with local systems of law.

Around the fourth century, several Germanic tribes invaded and began to populate the peninsula. Of these, the Visigoths became the dominant group, and eventually conquered most of the peninsula, with the notable exceptions of the northern mountainous and western coastal regions. The Visigoth reign produced a legal system known as the Fuero Juzgo that was nurtured by both the existing Roman legal system and the Germanic patrimonial traditions. By 654 the Visigoths had adopted the Fueros as the principal legal system for the governance and administration of the subjugated regions. The Fueros subsequently remained a fundamental source of law for the Spanish Empire until 1888, when Spain adopted a civil code.

In 711, Spain was conquered by the Arab Empire. The Arab Empire was governed by Muslim law, which had a religious character. The two basic sources of Muslim law were the Koran and the Sunna, compilations of secondary interpretations of law. The peninsula was governed by the Califato de Cordoba, which retained control until the reconquest in 1492. While Muslim law coexisted with the local system of law, it did not exert a dominant influence over the latter.

In 1265, in the midst of what we now call Christian Medieval Spain, Alfonso X promulgated a series of laws that provided normative guidelines for the social relations of his realm. Those laws, known as the Siete Partidas, provided the basis for a conception of civil rights in the Spanish legal system.

During the 1480s the Catholic Church, aided by various local monarchs, adopted a series of criminal and penal laws known as the Inquisition. The Inquisition provided a legal justification for the persecution and expulsion of Arabs (Moors) and Jews. By 1492 the kingdoms of Castile and Aragon had managed to oust the Arab Califa from the Iberian territories, and began the process of reconquering the peninsula. This reconquest marked both the consolidation of Spain and the beginnings of its empire.

THE ENCOUNTER

Soon after Fernando and Isabel consolidated the expulsion of the Arabs from Spain, the Crown authorized Cristobal Colón to pursue his explorations for a new route to the Indies. This authorization, known as the Capitulaciones de Santa Fé, further provided Colón with a series of legal powers, entitlements, and jurisdiction over the territories that he discovered along his voyages. The Crown generally used the system of *capitulaciones* to grant its discoverers and nobles special powers and jurisdiction over the territories that they discovered.

Soon after Colón returned from his first voyage, the church enacted the Papal Bull *Inter Cetera* (1493). This form of ecclesiastical law provided the guidelines for the propagation of the Catholic faith throughout the territories encountered by the Spanish conquistadors. Sometime between 1509 and 1513, the eminent Spanish jurist Juan López de Palacios drafted a set of laws known as the Requerimientos (Requirements). Based on the assumption that the pope could delegate temporary spiritual responsibilities to the Spanish Crown, these laws provided further guidelines for the conquest of the New World and the treatment of the non-Christian Indians and their property. In addition, these laws provided a legal foundation for the conquest of the Indies and the pursuit of a "just war" against its native inhabitants.

THE CONQUEST

The conquest of the Caribbean served as an early experiment in government and administration for the subsequent Spanish Empire. In addition to the powers granted by the Capitulaciones, the Spanish Crown used the title of the *adelantado* (a special charge or title given to representatives or delegates of the Crown) to empower its representatives in the initial conquest of the Indies. The *adelantado* was charged with organizing the conquered territories and instituting the legal and administrative policies of the Crown there. The office of the *adelantado* was first instituted in the overseas empire in 1510, when the Spanish Crown recognized Juan Ponce de León's title to govern the island of Puerto Rico.

The first formal laws regulating the conquest of territories in the Americas were known as *repartimientos* and *encomiendas*. These laws were designed to compensate the

Legal Structure of the Spanish Empire in the Americas

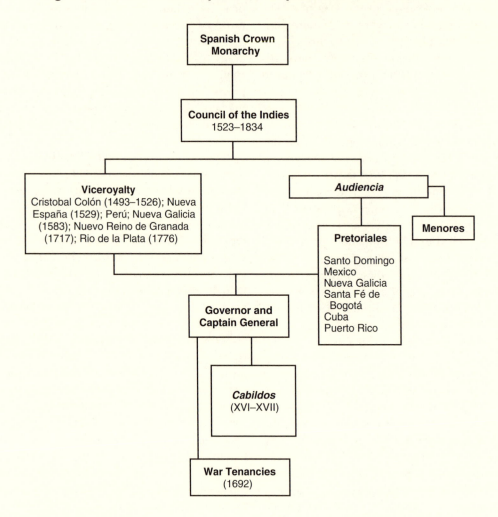

conquistadors and to provide some property rights over their allotted lands. Initially the *repartimientos* sought to regulate the distribution of groups of Indians among the Spanish colonizers, who used them as slave labor. The *encomienda* was designed as a system of administration of forced labor and the political reorganization of the Indian. In principle, these legal codes sought to humanize the *repartimientos* by further requiring that the Spanish landowners provide Indians with religious education.

In 1550 a Dominican friar named Bartolomé de Las Casas presented a case in defense of the Indians to a council of judges convened by the Crown. In his defense of the Indians against the practice of enslavement made possible by the *encomienda* system, he attacked the theories laid out by the Spanish jurist Juan Ginés de Sepúlveda. Sepúlveda had made a legal defense of the *encomienda* system that was informed by theories of a just cause of war and the inferiority of Indians. Some legal historians suggest that these debates laid the foundations for subsequent reforms in the governance and treatment of Indians during the conquest of the Indies.

The first formal institution developed for the governance and administration of the Indies was established in 1503. The Casa de la Contratación (House of Contracts) was originally charged with administration, government, and jurisdiction over commerce between Spain and its conquered territories. In 1523 it was replaced with the Real Consejo de Indias (Council of the Indies), which became the principal institution for the government and judicial administration of the Spanish Empire in the Indies and the Philippines. The Council of the Indies had the same jurisdictional authority over the Spanish Empire that the Council of Castile had over the Spanish peninsula. It was the highest legal office under the Spanish monarchy. The council was abolished by 1834 after most of the colonies had acquired independence.

THE COLONIZATION

The Spanish Crown developed an expansive and intricate system of judicial administration that lasted for more than three centuries. The governance of the Americas was entrusted in three institutions with regional jurisdiction.

These were the office of the *virrey*, the captain general/governor, and the *audiencias*. At a local level, the empire relied on presidents, governors, *corregimientos,* and *alcaldías mayores* (regional mayors).

During the colonization of the Americas, Spain created three mayor viceroys: Colón (abolished in 1526), Nueva España, and Perú. Initially Colón was given authority over any territories that he had discovered during his voyages. For the most part these included the territories circumscribing, including the islands within, the Caribbean Sea. The territory of the viceroy of Nueva España included the territories of Nueva Galicia (northern Mexico and the southern territories between Florida and California), Central America, the Antilles, and the Philippines (after 1583). The viceroy of Perú was much more expansive than the latter, including all of the southern part of the Americas, with the exception of Brazil, which was claimed by the Portuguese Empire. By the eighteenth century, Spain had added two viceroy subdivisions, the New Kingdom of Granada and Río de La Plata.

After the Council of the Indies, the *audiencias* were the most important legal institutions of the Spanish Empire. There were thirteen *audiencias* throughout the colonial period, beginning with the first, created in Santo Domingo in 1511 and lasting until 1898, when the United States ended the Spanish regime by conquering the remaining Spanish colonies in the Caribbean (Cuba and Puerto Rico) and the Pacific (the Philippines and Guam). These regional tribunals or courts of justice had jurisdiction over the most important aspects of the empire. Some of the major issues that the *audiencia* heard included appeals against government functionaries and lower tribunals, as well as civil trials and appeals before the Council of the Indies. It acted as the court of last instance in criminal trials; it had jurisdiction over ecclesiastical cases in which the church had abused its power or its agents were deemed incompetent; it was a court of first instance for any issues involving the Crown and its functionaries; it was charged with protecting the Indians; it heard all cases involving property and land disputes; and it assumed the role of general council for the regional and local authorities. In a sense, the *audiencia* assumed the role of both appellate regional courts and in some instances that of Supreme Court.

Spanish jurists recognized that it would be anachronistic to apply the Castilian law to the governance of the empire. As a result, the Crown decreed that the principles of law for the governance of the Indies would be derived from its own orders, edicts, and decrees, as well as those emanating from its institutions and other functionaries that were expressly empowered to develop legal norms that became the Laws of the Indies.

For the most part, the Spanish Empire's legal system relied on an evolving procedural hierarchy. Between 1505 and 1567, the Spanish regime relied on the following hierarchy: the Siete Partidas, the Fuero Real and the Fuero Juzgo, the Ordenamiento de Alcalá, the Laws of Toro, and the Legislation of the Indies. After 1567, Spain added another set of laws known as the Nueva Recopilación (New Compilation), which included a selection of Castilian laws that were authorized as a source of law in the administration of the Indies.

By the end of the sixteenth century and under the auspices of Philip II (1556–1598), the Crown had begun to commission various jurists to codify these laws into coherent compilations or collections that made the Laws of the Indies accessible to jurists. By 1681, Antonio de León Pinelo had organized the most important of these compilations. Modeled after the Castilian compilations in Spain, de León Pinelo's project was entitled Recopilación de las Indias (Compilation of the Indies). After pouring over 400,000 laws, de León Pinelo created a manuscript that comprised 7,308 laws, with 204 titles, in nine books.

The nine books of this compilation addressed the following issues: the Church in the Indies (ecclesiastical government); the Royal Council of the Indies and the Royal Audiencias; the military and political dominion of the government of the Indies; the discoveries, pacifications, and settlements in the realms belonging to the Spanish Empire; the provincial governments and justice; the treatment of the Indians; criminal and penal law; the royal treasury; and the regulation of trade, fleets, and the passage or voyage to the Indies. This compilation provides the most organized and insightful source of laws for the administration of the Indies during the colonization period.

DEMISE OF THE EMPIRE

The demise of the Spanish Empire and the Laws of the Indies should be situated within the context of the French and Haitian revolutions and the emergence of the civil code as a more efficient and liberal way to govern the nation. This process occurred simultaneously in at least three central places—namely, in Spain, South America, and the remaining colonies of Spain (Cuba, the Philippines, and Puerto Rico). Together, they marked the transformation of Spain from an empire to a nation, and the shift in the Spanish reliance on the Laws of the Indies to a civil code. This fragmented and violent process occurred during the nineteenth century and is generally known as the emergence of Spanish constitutionalism.

By 1808, Spanish mobs had forced the abdication of King Charles IV in favor of his son Ferdinand VII. Soon after, Napoleon Bonaparte compelled Ferdinand VII to abdicate the throne in favor of Joseph Bonaparte. Joseph immediately created the Constitution of Bayonne of 1808 to govern Spain. Subsequently, Spanish elites met in Cadiz to develop a revolutionary constitution that would challenge the Bonaparte regime. The Constitution of Cadiz of 1812 became the first constitution drafted by Spain, and it set the foundations for the development of the liberal Spanish nation informed by the principles of the French Revolution. Simultaneously, the American colonies were rebelling against the Spanish Empire. Like the Bayonne Constitution, the Cadiz Constitution sought to prevent the secessions in the Americas by incorporating all of the subjects of the Spanish realm into the nation through the recognition of liberal citizenship rights and other concessions premised on equal recognition.

In the Americas, notable figures such as Simón Bolívar had led a full-fledged war against Spain, which resulted in the emancipation of South America by 1824 and Central America by 1834. Inspired by the principles of the French Revolution and the Code Napoléon, Bolívar and other South American jurists began to abandon their reliance on the Laws of the Indies in favor of a more efficient, less complicated, and coherent civil system of law.

By 1824, Cuba, the Philippines, and Puerto Rico were the only remaining colonies loyal to Spain. The Spanish constitutions of the nineteenth century promised to create special laws for the governance of its overseas colonies. Their local governors/captains general generally governed the islands in the absence of the creation of the promised laws and the implementation of any form of constitutional protections. While the last *audiencia* had been moved to Cuba, Spain created a special *audiencia* in Puerto Rico by 1831. This *audiencia* would eventually become the Puerto Rican Supreme Court. In 1834, Spain disbanded the Council of the Indies.

It was not until the 1870s that Cuba and Puerto Rico reached some administrative unity with Spain, and their institutions and inhabitants are governed by the same national constitution. During the nineteenth century, colonial jurists generally relied on the Laws of the Indies as a source of law.

As a result of the Spanish-American War of 1898, Spain lost its remaining colonies. In the case of Guam, the Philippines, and Puerto Rico, the local system of law was quickly replaced by a common law system, which sought to Americanize the islands by harmonizing the existing Spanish legal system with the new American common law jurisprudence. While it is possible to identify remnants of the Laws of the Indies as a local source of jurisprudence in Puerto Rico as late as 1901 (*Soler v. Soler,* 2 D.P.R. 201), the United States recognized only the Spanish civil code as a legitimate source of Puerto Rican law.

Charles R. Venator Santiago

See also Spain

References and further reading
Alcalá-Zamora y Torres, Niceto. 1980. *Nuevas reflexiones sobre las leyes de Indias.* 3d ed. Mexico: Editorial Porrúa, S.A.

Carr, Raymond. 1982. *Spain, 1808–1975.* 2d ed. Oxford: Clarendon Press.

de Las Casas, Bartolomé. 1992. *In Defense of the Indians.* Translated by Stafford Poole. DeKalb: Northern Illinois University Press.

de León Pinelo, Antonio. 1992 [1681]. *Recopilación de Las Indias.* 3 vols. Edited by Ismael Sánchez Bella. Mexico: Miguel Angel Porrúa.

Espinosa Jaramillo, Gustavo. 1996. *El nuevo mundo en el derecho: Crónica legal, Siglos XVI, XVII, y XVIII.* Cali, Colombia: Universidad Santiago de Cali.

Mirow, M. C. 2000. "The Power of Codification in Latin America: Simón Bolívar and the Code Napoléon." *Tulane Journal of International and Comparative Law* 8 (spring): 83–116.

Pagden, Anthony. 1990. *Spanish Imperialism and the Political Imagination.* New Haven: Yale University Press.

Tyler, S. Lyman. 1980. *The Indian Cause in the Spanish Laws of the Indies.* Salt Lake City: American West Center, University of Utah.

Zavala, Silvio A. 1988 [1935]. *Las instituciones jurídicas en la conquista de América.* 2d ed. Mexico: Editorial Porrúa, S.A.

SPECIFIC (INDIVIDUAL) DETERRENCE

DEFINITION

Specific deterrence, sometimes called special or individual deterrence, refers to "the effect of punishment on those being punished" that is caused by the fear or cost of that punishment to the offender (Andenaes 1952, 180). More particularly, specific deterrence refers to the reduction in an individual's rate of offending because punishment raises the cost of crime relative to its benefits.

APPLICABILITY

Specific deterrence is a concept that applies to all judicial and legal systems of the industrialized world. All, or virtually all, legal systems in the modern world specify laws that prohibit behavior and criminal sanctions for those who break the law. Although these criminal sanctions may also be used to prevent crime through rehabilitation or incapacitation, specific deterrence has historically been an important justification for punishment in legal systems across the world.

VARIATIONS

It is important to first define the word *deterrence* if we are to understand specific deterrence. For criminologists, deterrence refers to preventing individuals from committing crimes by instilling in them a fear of punishment. We usually instill this fear of punishment through the imposition of a criminal sanction. The idea that individuals need to be deterred from crime has its roots in the writings of social philosophers such as Thomas Hobbes, who saw people as hedonistic beings. The idea that individuals can be deterred from crime is most strongly based, though, on the assumptions of the classical school of thought. The classical school assumes that individuals are rational, free-willed, and hedonistic. Individuals' behavior, both criminal and noncriminal, then results from decisions that they make in attempts to increase their pleasure and avoid pain. Under these assumptions, criminal behavior can be controlled with criminal sanctions if they reach a certain level of swiftness, severity, and certainty.

Specific deterrence is one of two types of deterrence. In specific deterrence, the purpose of the criminal sanction is to instill fear in an offender, thus reducing the likelihood that he or she will commit another crime. Specific deterrence can be contrasted with general deterrence, which refers to the effect of punishment on the behavior of people other than the offender. Under general deterrence, the purpose of punishing an individual offender is to illustrate to the general public the costs of crime. Deterrence theory predicts that when individuals see someone being punished for a crime, it reduces their likelihood of ever committing a crime.

Within both specific and general deterrence, it is also useful to distinguish between absolute deterrence and partial deterrence. In the context of general deterrence, absolute deterrence refers to the situation in which an individual never commits a specific offense because of fear of punishment. Absolute deterrence in the context of specific deterrence refers to the individual who, once punished, never commits that crime again. Partial deterrence, however, refers to a situation in which offenders lower the rate at which they offend.

Specific deterrence is different from other preventive effects a criminal sanction may have on an individual offender. These other preventive effects include rehabilitation, incapacitation, and aging out. Rehabilitation occurs when offenders reduce their level of offending because of a nonpunitive treatment that changed what caused these offenders to commit their crimes in the first place. Another way that a criminal sanction may affect an individual's rate of offending is incapacitation. This refers to a reduction in an offender's crime rate because he or she is prevented from committing any further crimes. Finally, aging out refers to the reduction in an individual's rate of offending simply because he or she is older. It is important to keep these differences in mind when thinking about why an individual who just got out of prison does not commit another crime. It is often difficult, however, to know which of these four preventive effects—deterrence, rehabilitation, incapacitation, or aging out—caused that offender to lower his or her rate of offending.

EVOLUTION AND CHANGE
The philosophical framework underlying deterrence, both general and specific, comes from the classical school of thought, which was established by the writings of Cesare Beccaria (1764) and Jeremy Bentham (1789). Based on the idea of offenders as rational, free-willed, and hedonistic, Bentham argued that the main justification for criminal sanctions should be general deterrence. He, along with Beccaria, argued that the most efficient method of crime control was to set sanctions at a level at which they raised the cost of crime higher than the benefits. For example, Beccaria argued that severity, promptness, and certainty characterize sanctions that will effectively reduce the rate of crime. For Beccaria, severity meant that sanctions should be proportionate to the harm done by the crime. Sanctions that were more severe than that, he argued, would cause crime as offenders tried to avoid punishment. Bentham too argued for sentences that were severe but limited in their severity. He argued that punishments should be no more severe than what is necessary to prevent the person from committing another offense. The promptness of a sanction is important because it connects the pain of the sanction with the pleasure of the crime in the offender's mind. Of the three characteristics, however, Beccaria argued that certainty is the most important. He believed that most people commit crimes not because they do not fear the punishment but because they do not think they will be caught. In fact, he believed that if we increased the certainty of punishments, we would be able to reduce the severity of punishments and still control crime. Beccaria and Bentham were both hopeful that punishing offenders in this efficient manner could work as both an individual and general deterrent to crime.

The classical school remained the dominant school of criminological thought until the late 1800s, when a second school of thought arose—positivism. Associated with the work of Cesare Lombroso in the mid- to late 1800s, positivism centers around the assumption that human behavior is determined. If human behavior is determined, positivism argues, then it is reasonable to assume that offenders are different from nonoffenders. In fact, positivism is based on a medical analogy in which offenders are "sick" and should be "treated" on an individual basis rather than punished as rational individuals who made a free-willed decision to offend. Under positivism, interest turned away from theories that saw crime as the result of choice and punishment as a way to reduce crime. It turned the attention of criminologists to the scientific search for the causes of criminal behavior and rehabilitation. It also turned penal philosophy away from deterrence as the major justification for criminal sanctions.

Positivism held sway throughout the first half of the twentieth century. In 1952, however, Norwegian penologist Johs Andenaes published an important paper on punishment as a deterrent to crime. In this piece, Andenaes brought back an interest in the preventive effect that punishment can have, both general and specific. He asked specifically what effect the threat of punishment by the state could have in controlling individuals' behavior. Using examples of various types of crimes, he illustrated the preventive effect punishment may have. The interest generated by this important work combined with a growing belief that "nothing works" when it comes to rehabilitative programs as well as rising crime rates to focus attention once again on the principles of classical criminology.

By the 1970s, interest in classical theory was turning policies more and more to deterrence and away from rehabilitation. Arguments for the usefulness of deterrence as a basis for correctional policy have only continued to grow since then. For example, proponents of deterrence argued that policies for sanctioning that are based on deterrence ideals would be both more effective at preventing crime and more just. They argued that these policies were more effective because they would mean increases in the costs of crime for offenders. They argued further that they were more just because sentences would not be allowed to vary based on offender characteristics.

In the United States, this emphasis on deterrence as the basis for correctional policy had one of its greatest proponents in James Q. Wilson (1975, 1983) in his book, *Thinking about Crime.* Proponents of deterrence as the justification for criminal sanctions, like Wilson, are distinguished by their promotion of a number of policies, including determinate sentencing, mandatory sentencing, and selective incapacitation. Determinate sentencing is one of the hallmarks of a system based on deterrence. With determinate sentencing, both offenders and the public know the cost of each crime because the legal code specifies the sanction they will receive if they break the law. Mandatory sentences, which set specific sentences for certain crimes that are mandated by law, are also a common characteristic of sanctions under legal systems that center on deterrence. They attempt to limit the use of discretion by judges, once again helping to ensure that offenders will be subject to the sanction that is their due.

One policy that is clearly based on deterrence principles is selective incapacitation. It refers to policies in which certain offenders are selected for increases in their sentence length because of their potential for committing future crimes. Those who argue for deterrence as the primary purpose of punishment support the use of selective incapacitation because of its potential for preventing crime. Its aim is to incapacitate those offenders for whom rehabilitation and deterrence have not seemed to work.

In other modern industrialized nations, the second half of the twentieth century saw a return to some of the ideas behind classical thought as well. In these nations, though, there does not appear to be as strong an emphasis on deterrence as there is in the United States. Michael Tonry (1999) notes that in these countries, an interest in justice for the offender acts as a balance to the call for crime prevention through deterrence. This countering interest in justice for the offender has led to an absence of the death penalty, lower imprisonment rates, and higher rates of the use of alternative sanctions in other industrialized nations.

Ruth Triplett

See also Capital Punishment; Corporal Punishment; Criminal Law; Criminal Sanctions, Purposes of; General Deterrence; Rehabilitation; Retribution

References and further reading

Andenaes, Johs. 1952. "General Prevention: Illusion or Reality?" *Journal of Criminal Law, Criminology and Police Science* 43: 176–198.
Beccaria, Cesare. 1963 (1764). *On Crimes and Punishments.* Indianapolis, IN: Bobbs-Merrill.
Bentham, Jeremy. 1948 (1789). *On the Principles and Morals of Legislation.* New York: Kegan Paul.
Tonry, Michael. 1999. "Parochialism in U.S. Sentencing Policy." *Crime and Delinquency* 45: 48–65.
Wilson, James Q. 1975, 1983. *Thinking about Crime.* New York: Basic Books.

SRI LANKA

COUNTRY INFORMATION

Sri Lanka (known as Ceylon until 1972) is a multiethnic and multireligious Indian Ocean island state with a population of approximately 18.5 million. Its total land area is 25,330 square miles. It is located in close proximity to the south of India, the closest points between the two countries being only 40 miles apart.

The Sinhalese, considered to be descendants of Aryan immigrants from north India, constitute three-fourths of the population. The Sinhalese are predominantly Buddhists (the remainder are Christians), living in almost all areas of the country except the northern part. The Tamils, predominantly Hindus, constitute 18 percent of the population. Large numbers of these people live in the north and northeast, with a small percentage in Colombo and a few other main towns. The Muslims (descendants of Arab traders) and Malays (largely descendants of Dutch soldiers) constitute the third-largest ethnic group and live in the east and in Colombo and other main towns. The Burghers, predominantly Christians, are the descendants of the Portuguese and the Dutch. Due to interracial marriages with the Sinhalese and the Tamils and as a result of migration to Australia, Burghers are, by and large, a relatively small community. From the nineteenth century until the mid-1920s, there was a large influx of Indian laborers, brought in to work on the tea estates. The citizenship of their descendants was the subject of

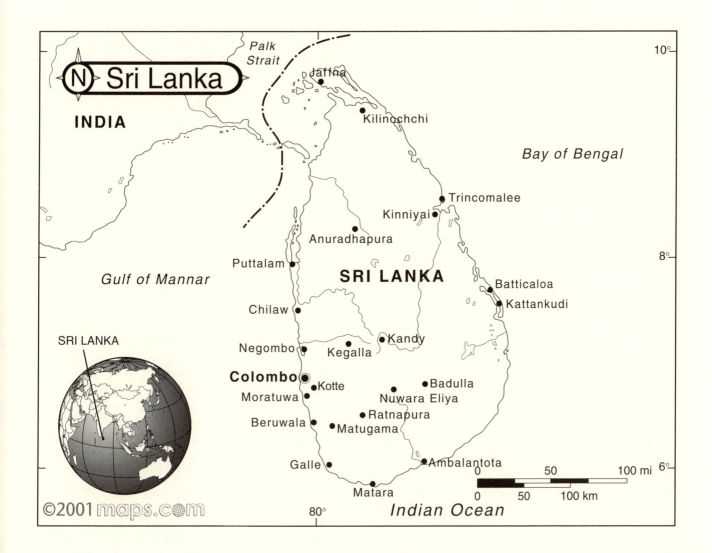

protracted negotiations between the Indian and Sri Lankan governments; while some were repatriated to India over a period of time, others were granted Sri Lankan citizenship.

HISTORY

Sri Lanka was under foreign occupation at various times in its history. Over a period of several centuries, various Indian invading forces seized control of territorial parts from time to time. The first non-Indians to capture portions of the country were the Portuguese, who arrived in 1505. The Portuguese ruled from 1505 to 1656 and were followed by the Dutch. Then, in 1796, the British arrived. The country gained independence from the British in 1948. Until a new constitution was adopted in 1972, the British monarch continued to be the head of state in Sri Lanka. The transition to independence in 1948 was without violence; the seeds of independence were, however, sowed by various nationalist movements at their origins at the beginning of the twentieth century.

Postindependent Sri Lanka witnessed communal riots between the Sinhalese and the Tamils in the late 1950s in the wake of demands for a "Sinhala only" policy. Demands for equal status and allegations of discrimination were first articulated during the period of British rule, but the colonial rulers effectively defused the tensions through direct means—for example, by providing for the representation of ethnic groups in the legislatures—and by indirect means—such as negotiations and referrals to committees. The 1983 riots were a turning point in the country's history. The demand for a "separate state" for the Tamils in the north and parts of the east of the country, which is basically a call for one-third of the territory to be declared as an independent state for one-sixth of the population, has continued. The ensuing war has exacted a heavy toll: Over 50,000 have died, and many valuable properties, including the Central Bank building and several expensive commercial aircraft belonging to Sri Lankan Airlines, have been destroyed in sporadic terrorist attacks by the militant group commonly known as the LTTE (the Liberation Tigers of Tamil Eelam) or the Tigers. An attempt by a former Indian prime minister, the late Rajiv Gandhi, to send the Indian army to maintain peace ended in disaster, with a high rate of casualties among the Indian soldiers. Later, Rajiv Gandhi himself was assassinated by a group of LTTE militants who targeted him during an election campaign in the south of India. Political assassinations in Sri Lanka go back to 1959, when Prime Minister S. W. R. D. Bandaranaike—husband of the first female prime minister in the world and the father of the current president of Sri Lanka—was shot dead by Buddhist monks, for a motive that still remains a mystery. In the early 1990s, President Ranasinghe Premadasa, who was popular for his major housing initiative for the homeless, was shot and killed by a Tamil terrorist as he was leading a political rally on May Day. Several ministers, politicians, mayors, and civil administrators have also been victims of the war. Peace negotiations under the aegis of a Norwegian diplomat proved futile, with disagreement over preconditions for peace talks. In the meantime, the LTTE has been banned from raising funds in a number of countries. Drug couriers sympathetic to the cause of the LTTE have been arrested in several nations for attempting to smuggle heroin. Tamils have been granted refugee status in European countries, and a large number of professionals have migrated to Australia, Canada, and the United States.

Many commentators have noted that peace has become a mirage in this predominantly Buddhist country. A Sinhalese youth uprising in 1971 and another in the late 1980s were crushed, with thousands losing their lives. The dominant political parties have reached a stalemate over the possibility of forming a national government that would have, as its top priority, the amicable settlement of the war.

Constitutional changes in Sri Lanka have a checkered history. The constitution under which the transition to independence was gained was perceived by many jurists as having entrenched provisions precluding any major change. Demands for an indigenous constitution that would sever all ties with the erstwhile British rulers were given effect in the early 1970s. The right of appealing to the Judicial Committee of the Privy Council was abolished in 1972, as there were concerns that any attempt to discard the existing constitution might be adjudged unconstitutional. Parliamentarians constituted themselves as members of what was termed the "Constituent Assembly" to draft and adopt the new constitution. On May 22, 1972, a new constitution was adopted. The former Ceylon thus became the Republic of Sri Lanka and decided to remain within the Commonwealth. After the general elections of 1977, measures were taken to discard the first republican constitution and to adopt another in its place. On August 31, 1978, the new constitution came into existence. It has been periodically amended but remains in force today. However, the matter of replacing this constitution has been actively considered by the present government, and a referendum to assess public opinion on this

issue was scheduled for August 2001. Granting greater regional autonomy and replacing the "executive president" system are two of the many changes envisaged.

The economy has remained relatively resilient—with a gross national product (GNP) growth rate of approximately 6 percent in the year 2000—despite adverse internal and external factors. Income from Sri Lankans working in the Middle East and from tea, rubber, and garment exports, together with earnings from tourism, have helped to sustain the economy amid the escalating costs of an eighteen-year-old war in the north and northeast of the country.

LEGAL CONCEPTS
The country's indigenous systems of law (largely uncodified) and institutional mechanisms for the adjudication of disputes underwent changes, particularly during Dutch rule in the maritime provinces and thereafter under British rule. The Charter of Justice of 1801 provided for the continuation of the laws currently applicable—namely, the Roman-Dutch law principles introduced by the Dutch, the Kandyan law that applied in the Kandyan provinces that were finally brought under British rule only in 1815, the Tesavalamai that governed the Tamils, the Muslim law, and a limited body of Buddhist and Hindu law applicable mainly to religious property and customs. The British colonial administrators and judges encountered considerable difficulty in ascertaining the applicable laws, especially in instances where Roman-Dutch law principles had been followed or were expected to be followed. On many occasions, British judges introduced English law principles on the basis that the Roman-Dutch law principle had not been introduced into the colony or, if it had been introduced, that there was ambiguity regarding its application. Systematic law reporting officially commenced only in 1896; prior to the publication of the *New Law Reports* (now replaced by the *Sri Lanka Law Reports*), some private law reports were issued, but the coverage was not comprehensive. The absence of judicial precedents, together with the uncodified state of the law, inured to the benefit of the judges, who looked for any excuse to avoid the application of Roman-Dutch law principles. This effort was not entirely successful, and consequently, a body of English law principles emerged operating alongside Roman-Dutch law principles and indigenous laws. An eminent legal historian, Tambiah Nadaraja, neatly summarized the situation when he wrote:

Today, therefore, although "the embers, to say the least, of Dutch jurisprudence are yet unextinguished," the Roman-Dutch law can at best be regarded as merely a "subsidiary common law where our own law and practice are silent." In fact, the residuary general law of modern [Sri Lanka] is a new body of law, neither pure Civil Law nor pure Common Law, which our legislators and Judges have forged on the anvil of contemporary life in [Sri Lanka] out of materials derived mainly from the Roman-Dutch and English Law; and this mixed body of law may not inappropriately be termed "an indigenous common law of [Sri Lanka], because it has largely been fashioned in this country with particular reference to the conditions here.

"One consequence of the historical circumstances which made [Sri Lanka] heir to the greatest traditions of both the Roman Civil Law and the English Common Law is the wide variety of the materials available to the makers of our law . . . we shall be entitled to say that there can be hardly any other country in the world where the Judges and the practitioners have such a vast reservoir of legal material from which they may draw." (Nadaraja 1972, 247–248)

Many statutes introduced in the nineteenth century during British rule continue to remain in force, subject to certain amendments introduced from time to time. Reference may be made in this regard to the Penal Code of 1883, the Criminal Procedure Code of 1883, the Civil Procedure Code of 1889, and the Evidence Ordinance of 1895.

In 1972, in one of the last judgments of the Judicial Committee of the Privy Council in an appeal from then Ceylon, Lord Wilberforce neatly summed up what he considered as a mutually enriching experience:

We have not only shared our Judges; we have profitably exchanged the substance of our law. The Board and the Courts of Ceylon have worked together in weaving into a consistent whole the separate strands of customary law, Roman-Dutch law, English Common Law and Equity, and modern codifications. How successful this has been is a matter for history to decide, but it is a safe assertion that each of our indigenous systems has contributed its best and that each has benefited by cross-fertilisation. (Marshall 1973)

CURRENT STRUCTURE

The highest court in Sri Lanka is the Supreme Court. It is the final court of criminal and civil appellate jurisdiction. It also has jurisdiction to determine the constitutionality of bills. Cases involving the violation of fundamental rights are heard and determined by the Supreme Court.

The Court of Appeal has the jurisdiction to grant and issue orders in the nature of writs of certiorari, habeas corpus, prohibition, mandamus, quo warranto, and so forth. It can issue injunctions and restraining orders. Elections petitions are also heard by the Court of Appeal. Finally, it hears appeals from courts of first instance, tribunals, and other institutions.

Each High Court has original criminal jurisdiction and appellate and revisionary jurisdiction in respect to the convictions, sentences, and orders of the Magistrates' Courts and Primary Courts within its jurisdiction. The High Court of Colombo is vested with exclusive admiralty jurisdiction. All major criminal trials (such as murder trials) are conducted before High Courts with a jury. The Commercial High Court of Colombo hears commercial matters over a prescribed monetary limit and intellectual property matters within the Province of Colombo. Appeals lie to the Court of Appeal.

District Courts have original civil jurisdiction. Matrimonial, testamentary, insolvency, landlord and tenant dispute cases, and the like are heard by District Court judges. Appeals lie to the Court of Appeal.

Magistrates' Courts have criminal jurisdiction in respect to prescribed matters. These courts also hear maintenance cases. Economic crimes (such as cases involving insider dealing) come within the purview of Magistrates' Courts. An appeal lies to the High Court.

Primary Courts hear civil claims below a prescribed monetary amount. These courts also hear cases relating to the enforcement of local authority bylaws, disputes affecting land, and so forth. An appeal lies to the High Court.

In commercial matters, arbitration is increasingly preferred as a precondition to litigation; there are, however, concerns that arbitration proceedings are becoming costly and protracted and increasingly dominated by lawyers who are not hesitant to raise technical objections at every conceivable opportunity.

Delays in the administration of justice, the cost of litigation, and the lack of proper record-keeping systems are major problem areas. These are being addressed through various reform measures currently being introduced. With the computerization of records and judgments there will be an improvement in the future.

SPECIALIZED JUDICIAL BODIES

The constitution provides for the establishment of the Office of the Parliamentary Commissioner for Administration (Ombudsman) to investigate and report on complaints or allegations concerning the infringement of fundamental rights and other injustices by public officers and offices of public corporations, local authorities, and similar institutions. The institution of ombudsman has not gained in popularity, as public perceptions favor recourse to the courts of law despite the associated costs and delays.

There are several commissions, such as the Human

Legal Structure of Sri Lanka Courts

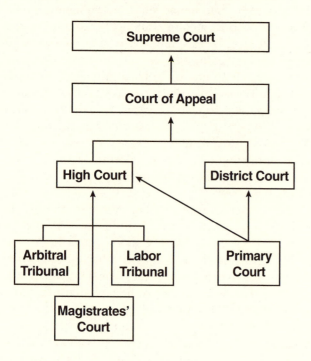

Rights Commission and the Press Council, with jurisdiction to hear and determine disputes. Bribery cases are investigated by the Commission to Investigate Allegations of Bribery or Corruption. The Criminal Justice Commission was a mechanism established in the 1970s to hear cases involving violations of the foreign-exchange laws and cases involving the 1971 youth insurrection.

The Special Presidential Commissions of Inquiry Law, enacted in 1978, has been the subject of controversy. A commission appointed under this law can recommend that any person should be made subject to civic disabilities, such as not being eligible to serve as a member of Parliament, for any act of commission or omission. Among the first whose civic rights were taken away by Parliament (in a resolution passed by not less than two-thirds of all members, including those not present) was the late Sirimavo Bandaranaike, the first female prime minister in the world. This occurred during her first term in office in the 1960s, and her minister of justice and the secretary to the Ministry of Justice also lost their civic rights.

Labour Tribunals hear and determine matters relating to the termination of services, nonpayment of wages or compensation, and industrial disputes. An aggrieved party may appeal to the High Court. There are other tribunals as well, such as the Agricultural Tribunals that conduct investigations into disputes involving cultivators.

STAFFING

The chief justice and other Supreme Court judges, the president of the Court of Appeal and other Court of Ap-

peal judges, and the High Court judges are all appointed by the president. The Judicial Service Commission, established under the constitution and comprising the chief justice and two other Supreme Court judges, appoints other judges. The independence of the higher judiciary is ensured in a number of ways, such as the special parliamentary procedure for the removal of Supreme Court and Court of Appeal judges and the prohibition on reducing the salary and other emoluments during their tenure of office. Supreme Court judges retire at sixty-five, while Court of Appeal judges retire at sixty-three. The age limit for other judicial officers is generally sixty, subject to extensions from the fifty-fifth year onward. The accompanying figure indicates the number of judges and judicial officers serving as of June 30, 2001.

Newly recruited lower-court judges and judicial officers undergo training before assuming their duties, and continuing education is now receiving more attention than at any time in the past. The Judges' Training Institute regularly organizes training courses. In addition, a relatively small number of judicial officers are sent abroad each year for training and to attend seminars and workshops. Salaries tend to be relatively low for judicial officers, thus making it difficult to attract goods lawyers, and court premises and record-keeping systems have not been improved over the years. However, under the aegis of a recent World Bank–funded project, the physical infrastructure of court premises in Colombo and selected other provinces is being developed. Court records are being computerized as well.

The Faculty of Law of the University of Colombo conducts undergraduate as well as postgraduate courses in law, leading to the LL.B., LL.M., and Ph.D. degrees. The Open University also conducts an LL.B. program. Professional courses and examinations, leading to admission as an attorney-at-law, are conducted by the Sri Lanka Law College, where the majority of the lecturers are practicing lawyers.

Until 1973, the legal profession was divided into two distinct categories, namely advocates (corresponding to barristers) and proctors (corresponding to solicitors). Requirements for admission to the Sri Lanka Law College and the syllabus followed differed depending on whether one wished to be an advocate or a proctor. In 1973, however, the legal profession was fused, with the single title attorney-at-law for all. The bar association currently has a membership of approximately 5,500, but the number of attorneys-at-law is actually much higher because membership in the association is not mandatory. A notary public is one who is entitled to execute deeds; a separate license has to be obtained for the purpose. The Supreme Court has the ultimate power to enroll as well as disbar an attorney-at-law for misconduct or similar cause.

The attorney general is appointed by the president. He

Sri Lanka Judges and Judicial Officers

Category	Number
Supreme Court Judges	11
Court of Appeal Judges	12
High Court Judges	30
District Court Judges	25
District Court and Magistrates' Court Judges Combined	29
Additional District Court Judges	27
Additional Combined Court Judges	11
Magistrates	51
Additional Magistrates	16
Primary Court Judges	11
Labor Tribunal Presidents	23

is the law officer of the state and has the right to appear before any court of law. The Attorney General's Department has full-time lawyers handling both civil and criminal cases for and on behalf of the government, as well as selected public corporations and statutory bodies. For administrative purposes, the Attorney General's Department comes under the Ministry of Justice, but unlike the justice minister, the attorney general does not change with every change of government nor does he attend cabinet meetings, unless specially invited to do so.

IMPACT

Over the years, successive governments in Sri Lanka have enacted more laws and regulations without making a fundamental assessment as to the appropriateness of the existing laws, the perceived needs, and potential directions for law reform. The government-funded Law Commission has been in existence since the 1970s, but its role in proposing the overhauling of the legal system has been marginal. The drafting of legislation is a time-consuming task due to the shortage of skilled draftspersons. There is often uncertainty as to the allocation of parliamentary time to debate important bills. Furthermore, only a few public interest groups exist, and some of them have a hidden political agenda, thus reducing the scope for an impartial and independent input.

Due to piecemeal and patchwork reforms, the statutory framework has increasingly become more complex and uncertain, and calls for the restatement of the law have gone unheeded. Meanwhile, court proceedings are expensive and protracted. A free legal aid scheme does exist, but generally the services of only junior lawyers are made available.

Uncertainty as to how the country can best resolve the war and the persistent failure to form a national government in this period of crisis have led to a situation in which priorities are misplaced. Consequently, ad hoc solutions are imposed rather than the well-structured and balanced long-term responses needed to realize the potential of law as an instrument of national development. In the 1970s and early 1980s, Sri Lanka was poised to become a Third World success story in terms of economic, social, and educational developments; today, however, there is a real threat that this possibility will become more and more a mirage.

Dayanath C. Jayasuriya

See also Common Law; Habeas Corpus, Writ of; Legal Aid; Legal Education; Legal Professionals—Civil Law Traditions; Privy Council

References and further reading
Cooray, L. J. Mark. 1972. *An Introduction to the Legal System of Ceylon.* Colombo: Lake House Investments Limited.
De Silva, Chandra Richard. 1987. *Sri Lanka: A History.* New Delhi: Vikas Publishing House Pvt Ltd.
Jayasuriya, D. C. 1982. *Mechanics of Constitutional Change: The Sri Lankan Style.* Nawala: Asian Pathfinder Publishers.
Jayasuriya, J. E. 1976. *Educational Policies and Progress during British Rule in Ceylon (1796–1948).* Colombo: Associated Educational Publishers.
Marshall, H. H. 1973. "Ceylon and the Judicial Committee." *International and Comparative Law Quarterly* 22: 155–157.
Nadaraja, Tambyah. 1972. *The Legal System of Ceylon in Its Historical Setting.* Leiden, the Netherlands: E. J. Brill.

ST. KITTS AND NEVIS

GENERAL INFORMATION

The Federation of St. Kitts and Nevis is located in that portion of the Caribbean archipelago known as the Lesser Antilles, which stretch from the islands of Trinidad and Tobago in the south to Puerto Rico in the north and which form the eastern boundary of the Caribbean Sea. The islands of St. Kitts and Nevis are situated at latitude 17°15' north, longitude 62°45' west, approximately 1,200 miles southeast of Miami, Florida. St. Kitts has a land area of 68 square miles (176 square kilometers), while Nevis is 36 square miles (93 square kilometers). Each island is dominated by a single, fairly youthful volcanic cone surrounded by fertile, gentle slopes and covered with well-manicured sugarcane fields; in St. Kitts, these fall away almost uniformly. Long stretches of golden, sandy beaches surround much of Nevis and the Southern Peninsula in St. Kitts. The climate is subtropical and maritime, while humidity is low, heavily influenced by steady northeast trade winds with an average temperature of about 81° F (27° C). Average rainfall in St. Kitts is 64 inches (1.625 millimeters) and 46 inches (1.170 millimeters) in Nevis. The two islands are separated by a two-mile channel.

The population in 2000 was approximately 40,500, with some 14,000 living in an urban setting in the federal capital, Basseterre, and the capital of Nevis, Charlestown.

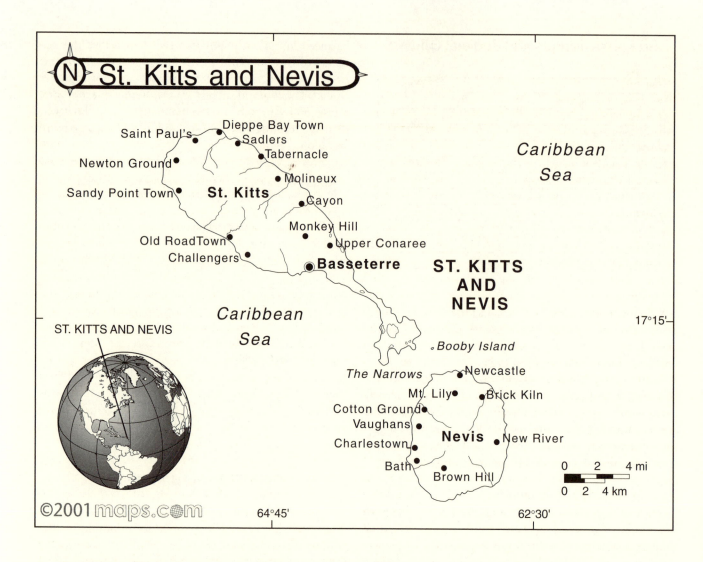

©2001 maps.com

Migration patterns during much of the twentieth century have had a stabilizing effect on population levels. About 95 percent of the country's inhabitants are of black African descent. The constitution guarantees religious freedom. The religion practiced is predominantly Christian, with mainly Protestant groups such as Anglican, Methodist, and Moravian, together with Roman Catholic, Pentecostal, and Baptist denominations.

The economy of St. Kitts and Nevis is a mixed economy based on services, tourism, agriculture, and light manufacturing. Within the past decade, a substantial increase in stay-over and cruise ship visitors from North America and Europe has led to the emergence of tourism as the primary industry, surpassing sugarcane production, which has been in decline and which had been a dominant socioeconomic force for centuries. There is a small light manufacturing sector and several enclave industries on St. Kitts, such as data processing and electronic assembly; an offshore financial services sector in Nevis is developing steadily. The labor force is made up of approximately 18,000, and in 1995 unemployment stood at 4.3 percent. The IMF reported GDP at U.S.$300 million, with per capita income at U.S.$7,000 in 1999.

The federation has an adult literacy rate of 98 percent. This may well be the result of free and compulsory education for children between the ages of five and sixteen years. There is an extensive system of public primary and secondary schools. A state-run College of Further Education offers academic and technical training to the tertiary level. There is an American offshore medical school on Nevis, as well as another on St. Kitts, which also is home to a U.S. veterinary school.

HISTORY

St. Kitts and Nevis were discovered by Christopher Columbus on November 12, 1493, and claimed for the Spanish monarchs during his second voyage to the West Indies. Columbus called St. Kitts St. Christopher, after his patron saint, but it is now more well known by its Anglicized name. Prior to his arrival, the islands had been inhabited for thousands of years by Amerindian tribes, first the Arawaks and then the Caribs, who had named St. Kitts, Liamuiga, and Nevis, Oualie. During the sixteenth century, the Spanish Crown, which laid claim to the lands in the New World, showed no interest in the small islands of the Lesser Antilles, where it was felt that there was no gold or other precious metals. In the seventeenth century, Spain's European rivals, England and France, which had sought to breach its hegemony by attacking Spanish shipping on the high seas, established agricultural settlements in the islands ignored by the Spanish.

In 1623, St. Kitts became the first such settlement in the West Indies, when an Englishman, Thomas Warner, along with fifteen men, settled on the leeward coast near the Carib Indian settlement of their chief, Tegreman. The settlers immediately planted a crop of tobacco, which was in great demand in Europe. Warner returned to England with a consignment of tobacco, seeking government and financial support, and in 1625 the English king, Charles I, issued letters patent to Warner's backers, granting the right to colonize the islands of St. Kitts, Nevis, Barbados, and Montserrat. Warner returned to St. Kitts in that year with four hundred men. In 1625, too, a small French settlement was established on the northern coast, and concerned with the ever-present threat from the Carib Indians and the Spanish, both English and French entered into a precarious but generally peaceful coexistence after massacring and enslaving the Indian population. The island was divided among the settlers, with the English occupying the middle portion and the French the two ends. From St. Kitts, Nevis was settled in 1628, and later Antigua and Montserrat, by the English, while the French settled Martinique and Guadeloupe. St. Kitts became known as the "Mother Colony" of the English and French colonies in the West Indies.

At first tobacco was grown with much success, to be replaced in the 1640s with sugarcane cultivation when competition from a better-quality tobacco on larger plantations grown in Virginia in the American colonies led to a glut and collapse of the market in Europe for the islanders. The introduction of sugarcane from Brazil brought about fundamental and far-reaching changes in the social and economic structure of the two islands. A peasant society composed of Europeans was transformed into a plantation society composed in the majority of slaves imported from Africa. Many of the small farms were amalgamated in order to meet the requirements of the sugar plantation for large acreages. Many European small proprietors and indentured servants left the island.

The colonies were established for the benefit of the "Mother Country." They were valuable properties, producing much wealth, and were used as pawns in the struggle for power between European countries during the seventeenth and eighteenth centuries. At the Treaty of Utrecht, 1713, which ended the War of the Spanish Succession, the French ceded the entire island to the English,

and reluctantly the French planters on the island gave up their prosperous plantations. Today the only relics of the French presence are a few names of towns and villages throughout St. Kitts.

Total English control meant that ultimate law-making power resided in the Imperial Parliament of the British Empire, and the management of the overseas territories was conducted through the Colonial Office in London. The English government appointed a governor to represent the interests of the Crown and to impose its will on the planters, who tried fiercely to resist the attempts at autocratic rule. The "Old Representative System" of government emerged, modeled essentially on the English Constitution, with its three estates of king, lords, and commons. The governor was the Crown's representative, while a nominated council to advise the governor was chosen from among the planters and prominent inhabitants, and a Legislative Assembly elected by property owners that made laws that had to be ratified. Local government was by and for the plantocracy, which alone possessed sufficient property to vote and hold office.

In the eighteenth century, St. Kitts had the full range of courts that existed in England. There were the Common Law Courts, Courts of Chancery, and other special courts with special jurisdiction. The legislators evidently believed that "nothing can tend more to the encouragement of trade, or more effectually promote the reputation and prosperity of the said Island, than the establishing of Courts, wherein justice may be frequently and duly administered." A Court of King's Bench and Common Pleas was established, consisting of a chief justice and four other justices' assistants. This court had wide jurisdiction in both criminal and civil matters. There was also a Court of Sessions of Peace whose jurisdiction was similar to that of the Court of Quarter Session in England. There was a Court of Chancery, with the governor being ex officio chancellor as well as vice admiral and ordinary. The Court of Ordinary adjudicated ecclesiastical matters, while the governor, in his capacity as ordinary, approved marriage licenses and letters of administration and granted the probate of wills. There was a Court Merchant, which dealt with mercantile disputes, and in civil matters there was appeal to a Court of Error, which was composed of the lieutenant governor and the council. In some cases, there was the right of appeal to the Privy Council in England. In criminal matters, appeal was normally to the governor or to the king, who could exercise the prerogative of mercy.

In 1808 there were some twenty-eight barristers listed, five of whom were king's counsel. The system of admission before the local bar was considered to be unsatisfactory, and the legislature acted. Barristers had to prove that they had been admitted to the bar at Westminster in England, or regularly kept terms at one of the Inns of Court in London for at least three years. Although there was no lack of courts and barristers, the system of justice left much to be desired. Judges were mostly prominent planters or well-known inhabitants who had no training in the law.

Sugar plantations dominated St. Kitts and Nevis, as they did many of the other islands of the English and French Caribbean, throughout the eighteenth and nineteenth centuries. Many of the vestiges of West Indian society today have their origin in the peculiarities of plantation life. The most significant were monoculture, slavery, absentee ownership, and dependence on the outside world. Sugarcane could be grown with relative ease, given fertile soil, on the same soil year after year with little skill or care, but it required considerable capital outlay in the building of a mill and boiling house used in the manufacturing process and a large, unskilled labor force, which was costly. There was an inexorable tenacity about sugar; once a mill and boiling house had been established, land bought and planted in cane, slaves acquired and trained, there was no breaking the grip of sugar on the place. Many planters returned to England to enjoy their wealth, with which they gained political influence in Parliament.

The emancipation of slaves in 1838, subsequent labor problems, and competition from other sugar-producing areas brought a century of prosperity to an end. But the plantocracy managed to survive by, among other things, consolidating landholdings, mechanizing fieldwork, adopting new processing technologies, and reducing wage payments. Unable to obtain land of their own, many underpaid former slaves elected to migrate in search of greater economic opportunities and personal freedom, thus giving rise to a migrant tradition that persists into the present. Those who stayed behind remained landless, settling in village communities on rented marginal estate land.

The passage of the Judicature Act of 1873 in Britain, to consolidate the several courts that existed there, led to a similar process in the Leeward Islands. An act to establish a Supreme Court and to define its jurisdiction, was passed in October 1873. The several courts that had existed on each island were abolished, and one court "which shall be a Court of record for the administration of justice throughout the colony of the Leeward Islands to be called the Supreme Court of the Leeward Islands," was established. In 1939 this court became the Windward and Leeward Islands Supreme Court.

On Nevis, the sugar plantation economy began to disintegrate in the early twentieth century. Many planters shifted to sea island cotton or to cattle raising. Others parceled out their land to smallholders. By the 1930s there was a substantial freeholding peasantry. On the other hand, during the first half of the twentieth century,

sugar remained the mainstay of the economy on St. Kitts, with plantations owned by absentee white and colored planters and commercial interests, and a large black labor force. By concentrating resources into the hands of a few landholders and relegating the rural working class to conditions of scarcity, deprivation, and powerlessness, the sugar plantations also engendered and perpetuated a complex social structure and set of social relations, attitudes, and behaviors that only recently have begun to unravel. Living conditions were horrible for the black working class, not only in St. Kitts but also throughout the other British colonies in the Caribbean region. Labor unrest, which began in St. Kitts in 1935 and which spread to other British colonies, led to changes by the British, especially after World War II.

On February 27, 1967, St. Kitts, Nevis, and Anguilla became the first of the Windward and Leeward Islands to become a unitary State in Association with Britain. Associated Statehood was considered a stepping-stone to full independence. The West Indies Act provided for a new constitution based on the Westminster model of government. It provided for full internal self-government. The competence of the British Parliament to legislate for its overseas territories had not been in serious doubt since the seventeenth century. This had been given legislative authority in the Colonial Laws Validity Act of 1865, which allowed for an act of Parliament to extend to any colony when made applicable by express words. While Britain remained responsible for foreign affairs and defense, the British Parliament could make only "at the request and with the consent of any associated state . . . any provision which appears necessary or expedient for the peace, order or good government of that state." A cabinet formed from the majority party in a new legislative House of Assembly was headed by a premier. Provision was made for the establishment of common courts for all the associated states.

Anguilla, which is located some 70 miles to the north of St. Kitts, was dissatisfied with the new constitutional arrangement. Its inhabitants had considered themselves to be neglected by the labor government in St. Kitts, and they lobbied for an elected local government to be put in place before Associated Statehood rather than after it, a demand that was not taken seriously by the labor government. The Anguillans rebelled, forced out the small Kittitian police contingent, and appealed to the British to take them back under their wing, which they did in 1969, though this was never recognized by the St. Kitts–based government until a change in government in 1980. Nevisian dissidents, too, were disillusioned with the government in St. Kitts and formed the Nevis Reformation Party, with their main plank being to seek secession from St. Kitts. In 1977 there was an unofficial referendum carried out in Nevis, and though it was claimed that 98 percent of those polled opted to secede from St. Kitts, the Labor Party dismissed the results.

In 1975 the plantation system was nationalized. The sugar industry had been saved by the establishment of a central factory in 1912, when individual estates had shut down antiquated mills and concentrated on cultivation. The fifty or so sugar plantations remained linked to a corporately owned central factory by a narrow-gauge railway completed in 1926. In 1952 there was record production of 51,000 tons of sugar, but since then there had been a continuous decline in production. The Sugar Estates Lands Acquisition Act was successfully challenged in court, but in the following year, the central factory was purchased and the industry came under state occupation. Public policy still saw sugar production as the mainstay of the economy.

During the 1970s, the Labor Party government sought anxiously to move "St. Kitts–Nevis–Anguilla" to full independence. They still maintained that Anguilla was part of the state. The British were willing to grant their wishes but were adamant that the St. Kitts Nevis Legislature would have "to request and consent" to devolution of Anguilla from the Associated State, a position that was unacceptable. In the general elections of 1980, the Labor Party was narrowly defeated when the Nevis Reformation Party, though overwhelmingly elected on a plank for secession, joined with the St. Kitts–based Peoples Action Movement to form a new PAM-NRP coalition government. Anguilla ceased to form part of the Associated State of St. Kitts Nevis and Anguilla when the British Parliament passed the Anguilla Act on December 19, 1980. On March 16, 1983, the House of Assembly "requested and consented" to Her Majesty in council to grant the St. Kitts and Nevis Constitution Order of 1983, conferring full responsible status within the British Commonwealth. On September 19, 1983, St. Kitts and Nevis became an independent nation.

The new government in 1980 kept St. Kitts and Nevis together. Fiscally conservative, they immediately introduced the abolition of the personal income tax. The attainment of independence and a period of economic diversification, with development of tourism, light manufacturing, and services sectors, led to strong economic growth and a significant increase in living standards. In St. Kitts, payment for, and consequential government ownership of, the sugar lands opened up opportunities for landownership and development, while the Nevis Island Administration introduced the Nevis Business Corporation (NBC) regime, followed by other offshore financial services, which have grown significantly.

LEGAL CONCEPTS

The 1983 Constitution Order revoked the 1967 Statehood Constitution and established a new constitution set out in Schedule 1 to the Order subject to Transitional Provisions set out in Schedule 2. The preamble to the constitution states that "the People of Saint Christopher and Nevis declare that the nation is established on the belief in Almighty God and the inherent dignity of each individual; assert that they are entitled to the protection of fundamental rights and freedoms; believe in the concept of true democracy with free and fair elections; desire the creation of a climate of economic well-being in the context of respect for law and order; and are committed to achieve their national objectives with a unity of purpose."

One of the many striking features in the Independence Constitution is the enshrinement of a varied nomenclature for the state. Section 1 of the constitution designates four names for the state, namely Saint Christopher and Nevis, Saint Kitts and Nevis, the Federation of Saint Christopher and Nevis, and the Federation of Saint Kitts and Nevis. "Saint" is commonly abbreviated to "St." Also, among the protection of various fundamental rights and freedoms under the constitution is that from discrimination on the grounds of sex, which established the equality of women, and birth out of wedlock. Protection of fundamental rights and many other provisions of the constitution are entrenched, meaning that they can be changed only in a referendum in which two-thirds of the voters on each island approve.

St. Kitts and Nevis is a constitutional monarchy and a member of the British Commonwealth. Constitutionally, executive authority is vested in Her Majesty, and Parliament consists of Her Majesty and a National Assembly. The role of Her Majesty is largely titular and ceremonial. The head of state is Queen Elizabeth II, who is represented by a governor-general appointed by her, on the advice of the local government. Nevis has a deputy governor-general, appointed by the governor-general. The 1983 Constitution provides for a unicameral federal legislature, the National Assembly, made up of representatives elected from both St. Kitts and Nevis in "first past the post" general elections, which must be held at least once every five years. The leader of the party with the most seats is appointed prime minister by the governor-general. Three senators are nominated, two by the governor-general acting on the advice of the prime minister, and one by the governor-general acting on the advice of the leader of the opposition in the National Assembly. The prime minister then selects a cabinet of ministers from among members of the National Assembly to form the executive.

The Federation of St. Kitts and Nevis is unique in that while St. Kitts has no local government of its own, the constitution provides for a legislature for Nevis, the Nevis Island Assembly, and an executive, known as the Nevis Island Administration and headed by a premier, chosen from among the members of the assembly elected in local government elections. The constitution grants to the Nevis Island Assembly the power to make laws called ordinances and to the administration exclusive responsibility over a wide range of matters. It provides for revenue allocation to be based on the ratio of population counted in the latest census. Perhaps what is most unusual about the constitutional arrangement is that Section 113 of the constitution allows Nevis to secede from St. Kitts following a referendum in which two-thirds of the Nevisian electorate vote for it. St. Kitts has no such right under the constitution.

While the constitution is the supreme law of the federation, it is subject to the Transitional Provisions set out in Schedule 2. These state, among other things, that all "existing laws shall be construed as may be necessary to bring them into conformity with the Constitution and the Supreme Court Order." Thus, in addition to laws passed by the local legislature, laws of the Imperial Parliament that had formed part of local law under the Colonial Laws Validity Act of 1865 remain in force until such time as they are repealed or replaced by local statute once they do not violate the provisions of the new constitution. One interesting example is the law on extradition, which is still governed by the 1871 British Extradition Act, which has never been replaced by local legislation. Two other examples of pre-1967 laws that are expressly enshrined are Transitional Provisions 9 and 10, which render entrenched the colonial laws on hanging, despite the protection from inhuman treatment as set out in Section 7 of the constitution, and the compulsory land acquisition law, unaltered in three predetermined areas.

Another "existing law" that is saved by the Transitional Provisions is the 1705 statute cited as "the Common Law (Declaration of Application) Act." Introduced in the General Assembly of the Leeward Islands meeting in Nevis to counter "contradictory judgements given in cases founded on the same Rules and Principles of Law and Reason; . . . and establishing a constant and certain Uniformity in the Proceedings of the Courts," the law declared that "the Common Law of England, as far as it stands unaltered by any written Laws of these islands, or some of them, confirmed by Your Majesty in Council, or by some Act or Acts of Parliament extending to these islands, is in force." This established St. Kitts and Nevis as a common law jurisdiction.

The West Indies Associated States Supreme Court (St. Christopher, Nevis and Anguilla) Act of 1975 supplemented the 1967 Supreme Courts Order in St. Kitts and Nevis. It should be noted that one of the Transitional Provisions of the 1983 Constitution states that the Supreme Court established by the 1967 order shall be styled the Eastern Caribbean Supreme Court. The act established that the jurisdiction of the former Supreme Court be vested in the High Court, as well as in the en-

actments of the legislature of the state and rules of court, or in default of the foregoing, by the statutes, orders, and rules governing the practice and procedure of the High Court in England. Where no law has been passed by the National Assembly of St. Kitts and Nevis, the law, procedure, and practice are those for the time being in force in England. The act also reconfirmed that the common law of England and the doctrines of equity shall be in force in the jurisdiction. Where there is a conflict or variance between the rules of common law and equity, equity prevails.

St. Kitts and Nevis is a member of the United Nations and a host of other international organizations. The federation is a signatory to the Treaty of Georgetown (1973), which formed CARICOM, a fifteen-country Caribbean Community free-trade area, and the Treaty of Basseterre (1981), which formed the Organization of East Caribbean States (OECS). While both organizations are integral to a regional integration movement, the OECS is of particular significance in that the units involved—the former Associated States, now the independent nations of Antigua and Barbuda, Dominica, Grenada, St. Lucia, St. Vincent and the Grenadines, St. Kitts and Nevis, and the British dependent territories of Anguilla, the British Virgin Islands, and Montserrat—are part of a monetary union under the East Caribbean Central Bank headquartered in St. Kitts. They have the same currency, the East Caribbean dollar (U.S.$0.37), and share the Eastern Caribbean Supreme Court, with its headquarters in St. Lucia.

CURRENT STRUCTURE

The Eastern Caribbean Supreme Court was established in 1967 by the West Indies Associated States Supreme Court Order No. 223 of 1967. It is a Superior Court of record for nine member states, the six independent (Antigua and Barbuda, Dominica, Grenada, St. Kitts and Nevis, St. Lucia, St. Vincent and the Grenadines) and the three British Overseas Territories (Anguilla, the British Virgin Islands, and Montserrat). The West Indies Associated States (Appeals to Privy Council) Order 1967 provides for a final appeal to lie to Her Majesty in Council, the Judicial Committee of the Privy Council, from decisions of the Court of Appeal given in any proceeding originating in a state in such cases as may be prescribed by or in pursuance of the constitution of that state.

The Eastern Caribbean Supreme Court consists of two divisions, a Court of Appeal and a High Court of Justice, a trial division. The judges of the Court of Appeal are the chief justice, who is head of the judiciary and president of the court, and who sits with two of the complement of three justices of appeal. The court is itinerant, traveling to each member territory, where it sits to hear appeals from the decisions of the High Court and Magistrates' Courts

Legal Structure of the Federation of St. Kitts and Nevis Courts

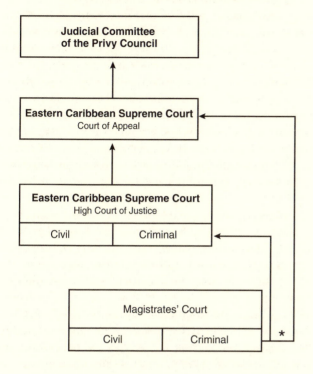

```
┌─────────────────────────────────┐
│   Judicial Committee             │
│   of the Privy Council           │
└─────────────────────────────────┘
                ▲
┌─────────────────────────────────┐
│ Eastern Caribbean Supreme Court  │◄────┐
│        Court of Appeal           │     │
└─────────────────────────────────┘     │
                ▲                        │
┌─────────────────────────────────┐     │
│ Eastern Caribbean Supreme Court  │     │
│      High Court of Justice       │     │
├───────────────┬─────────────────┤     │
│    Civil      │    Criminal      │◄──┐ │
└───────────────┴─────────────────┘   │ │
                                       │ │
    ┌─────────────────────────────────┐│ │
    │        Magistrates' Court        ││ │
    ├──────────────┬──────────────────┤│ │
    │    Civil     │    Criminal      │─┘ │
    └──────────────┴──────────────────┘ * ┘
```

*Indictable offenses commence in the Magistrates' Court for preliminary inquiry and then proceed to the High Court for trial.

in member states in both civil and criminal matters at various specified dates during the year. The court usually sits in St. Kitts and Nevis during one week in the months of April and September or October each year.

There are thirteen High Court judges, who are each assigned to, and reside in, the various member states. Each state has its own High Court, which, in addition to the High Court registry, houses the office of the local High Court judge. St. Kitts and Nevis have one High Court judge who presides over the St. Kitts Circuit and the Nevis Circuit. The trial courts sit throughout the year. Criminal Assizes convene in each jurisdiction on dates specified by statute. The High Court registry is headed by a legally trained registrar who provides the necessary administrative and legal support for the functioning of the High Court. Filing in the registries commences the proceedings in matters before the High Court in each of the nine territories.

The Supreme Court has unlimited jurisdiction in the member states, in accordance with the respective Supreme Court acts. Section 17 of the Courts Order empowers the chief justice, and two judges of the Supreme Court selected by the chief justice, to make rules of court for regulating the practice and procedure of the Court of Appeal and the High Court. New civil procedure rules,

CPR 2000, have introduced a court-driven Case Management System and the position of court master, of which there are two. Each master travels to each member state to preside over case management conferences and other procedures to assist in improving the speed and efficient discharge of civil litigation under the High Court. Also, national legislation in the countries served by the court confers rule-making authority on the chief justice in relation to matters outside the Court of Appeal and the High Court.

Judicial appointments, except that of the chief justice, who is appointed by Her Majesty by letters patent, are made by the Judicial and Legal Services Commission. The commission is also involved in the appointment of the attorney general, the director of public prosecutions, magistrates, registrars, and legal officers in the office of the attorney general. The commission also exercises a disciplinary function over all judicial and legal officer appointments. The commission is a five-person panel chaired by the chief justice, who designates a sitting Appeal or High Court judge and appoints, with the concurrence of not less than four heads of government of the participating states, a former judge. The final two members are persons discharging the functions of chairman of the Public Service Commissions of two states as designated for that time by the chief justice and are ex officio members of the commission; these are rotated after a three-year term.

To qualify for appointment as a justice of appeal, a person must be or have been a judge of a court of unlimited jurisdiction in civil and criminal matters in some part of the Commonwealth, or a court having jurisdiction in appeals from such court for an aggregate of at least five years, or a person who is qualified to practice as an advocate in such a court and has practiced for an aggregate of at least fifteen years. To qualify for appointment as a High Court judge, a person must be or have been a judge of a court of unlimited jurisdiction in civil and criminal matters in some part of the Commonwealth or a court having jurisdiction in appeals from such court, or a person who is qualified to practice as an advocate in such a court and has so practiced for an aggregate of at least ten years. To qualify for an appointment as a master, a person must be qualified to practice as an advocate and to have so practiced for an aggregate of at least ten years in a court of unlimited jurisdiction in civil and criminal matters in some part of the Commonwealth or a court having jurisdiction in appeals from such a court. A justice of appeal holds office until he attains the age of sixty-five years; a High Court judge, the age of sixty-two years. The Judicial and Legal Services Commission, acting with the concurrence of heads of government of all the states, may permit a judge to continue in his office for a period not exceeding three years. Judges have been drawn primarily from the OECS and CARICOM region, though there have been some appointments from the wider Commonwealth, such as Australia, the United Kingdom, and some African member countries.

There is a Court of Summary Jurisdiction known as the Magistrates' Court, which is constituted by the Magistrate's Code of Procedure Act. Under the 1983 Constitution, a magistrate is appointed by the governor-general on the recommendation of the Public Service Commission after consultation with the Judicial and Legal Services Commission either to the Public Service or on contract. The power to exercise disciplinary control vests in the governor-general on the recommendation of the Judicial and Legal Services Commission after consultation with the Public Service Commission. To qualify for appointment as a magistrate, a person must be qualified to practice as an advocate in the Supreme Court and to have so practiced for an aggregate of at least three years. St. Kitts is divided into two magisterial districts, with Nevis as a third. Magistrates dispense summary judgments in civil matters with limits of $5,000 for tort and $10,000 for contract, and preside over Family and Juvenile Court matters, as well as in nonindictable criminal matters. The 1986 Misuse of Drugs Act has increased significantly the jurisdiction of this court in drug matters with significant penalties. The magistrate also conducts a preliminary inquiry into indictable offenses.

There are some sixty-five attorneys called to the bar. Practitioners must have been called to the bar in England, Scotland, and Northern Ireland prior to 1980; obtain special dispensation from the chief justice on specified grounds or hold the Legal Education Certificate of a law school in Trinidad, Jamaica, or the Bahamas; and be nationals of a territory participating in the University of the West Indies.

Dennis Byron

See also Barristers; Common Law; Equity
References and further reading
Antoine, Rose-Marie. 1999. *Commonwealth Caribbean Law and Legal Systems.* London: Cavendish.
"Eastern Caribbean Supreme Court." http://www. ecsupremecourts.org.lc/ (accessed November 15, 2001).
"Government of St. Kitts and Nevis." http://www.stkittsnevis. net/ (accessed November 15, 2001).
Inniss, Sir Probyn. 1985. *Historic Basseterre.* Antigua: Antigua Printing and Publishing.
Parry, J. H., and P. M. Sherlock. 1980. *A Short History of the West Indies.* 3d ed. New York: St. Martin's Press.

ST. LUCIA

GENERAL INFORMATION

St. Lucia is found in the eastern Caribbean. It is located twenty-one miles south of Martinique and twenty-six miles northeast of St. Vincent. It forms part of the Caribbean archipelago, which starts in the north at Cuba and continues to Trinidad and Tobago in the south. St. Lucia forms part of the Windward Islands, which are themselves part of the larger grouping called the Lesser Antilles. It covers an area of 240 square miles, with a population of approximately 150,000.

The St. Lucian economy rests on three pillars: agriculture, tourism, and a fledgling manufacturing sector. In recent times a fourth pillar has emerged, a financial and services sector.

Until recently, St. Lucia's economy was based primarily on the export of bananas to the United Kingdom. However, in recent times, there has been a steady decline in the importance of the banana industry to St. Lucia's economic survival. The era of free trade and the World Trade Organization have demanded a change in trade based on preferential treatment. The tourism industry has replaced the banana industry as the main revenue-earning industry. Unquestionably, the economy is in transition.

HISTORY

The original inhabitants of the island were the Arawaks and Caribs. The exact date of the discovery of St. Lucia remains uncertain. The Dutch established a base in the south of the island in 1600. The French claimed possession of the island in 1635, and in 1651 the French West India Company established their first settlement. The French founded Soufrière as the first town, and by 1778 twelve towns had been established. After changing hands fourteen times, the island was finally ceded to Britain in 1814 by the Treaty of Paris. It became a Crown colony and was administered by the governor of Barbados from 1838 to 1885.

French culture and institutions infiltrated all aspects of St. Lucian society, and the Creole language and various institutions had French origins. The French influence still dominates all aspects of St. Lucian life and culture. Roman Catholicism is the predominant religion, although there are also Protestant faiths, such as Methodists, Anglicans, and Seventh-day Adventists. One of the more significant influences has been the Creole language, which continues to be used on the island to this day.

St. Lucia has been part of many regional groupings, the first being the Leeward Islands Group, administered by the governor of Barbados. In 1958 it became part of the West Indies Federation. The federation was short-

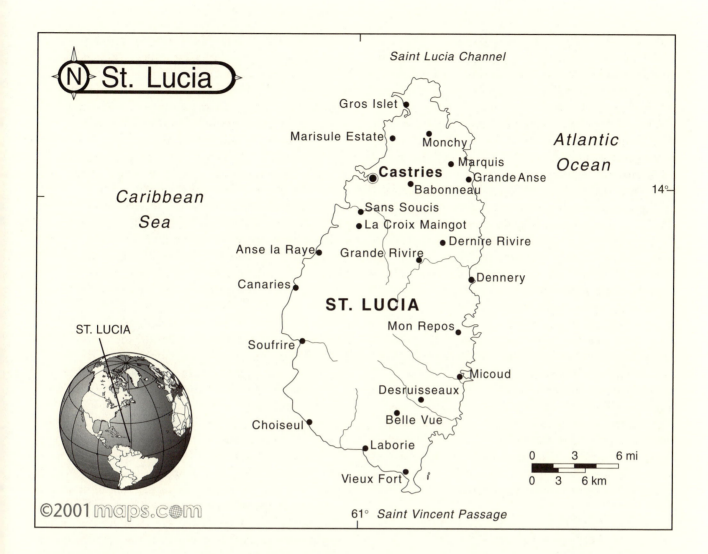

©2001 maps.com

lived and collapsed in 1962. In 1967, St. Lucia became an Associated State of the United Kingdom. This meant that St. Lucia was responsible for its internal self-government, while the United Kingdom retained responsibility for its foreign affairs. This was the first step in the process toward full self-government. Local elections held in that year gave St. Lucia its first premier, Mr. John Compton. The island progressed to full independence on February 22, 1979.

Prior to independence, St. Lucia, together with other eastern Caribbean countries, formed part of the West Indies Associated States. This organization evolved to become the Organization of Eastern Caribbean States (OECS).

The OECS promotes cooperation in many areas of common interest, such as fisheries, solid waste management, the environment, and so forth. OECS states have a common currency, the eastern Caribbean dollar, and a common judicial system. This subgrouping is part of a larger group of Caribbean countries called the Caribbean Community (CARICOM), basically an economic grouping of the English-speaking Caribbean countries. Its basic

objective is to establish a single market and economy. In that regard the Caribbean Court of Justice will be established by 2003 to determine and decide disputes arising out of the various protocols of the CARICOM treaty.

The majority of St. Lucians are of African descent; less than a tenth are of mixed European and African descent, and a much smaller percentage are Asians or Europeans.

LEGAL HISTORY

When St. Lucia was ceded to England in 1814, it had firmly rooted French traditions and institutions. The British inherited a legal system based on ancient French law, before the promulgation of the Coutume de Paris. The English passed various laws in order to effect better administration. Given the historical French heritage, it was necessary to have a system of law that would be understood by the administrators and officials, who were all English.

The local administrators turned to the Quebec Civil Code, since it was available in English. The Quebec Civil Code and the Code of Civil Procedure became part of St. Lucian law on October 20, 1879. This civil code ensured that the civil law legal system would remain part of St. Lucian law. The enactment of this civil code meant that the common law and civil law coexisted within the legal system; for all practical purposes, the legal system became a "mixed legal system."

The civil law legal system was destined to suffer. At the time of the enactment of the civil code, the French population had dwindled. The French presence in the administrative apparatus of the state was nonexistent, and the French language was no longer used, being replaced by English, although Creole lingered on. The fact that English judges and barristers dominated the St. Lucian legal system made the decline even more inevitable. The institutions that were necessary to support a civil law legal system were eventually replaced. The Anglicization of St. Lucian law did not help in this regard.

Although some changes were made to the civil code in 1927, there was a major revision in 1956. This was achieved by the St. Lucia (Revision and Reform) Ordinance, which had the consequence of importing common law aspects into the code. This was achieved either by codifying common law principles into the code or by using provisions that incorporated substantive English law. As a result, the law relating to separation agreements; the meanings assigned to adultery, cruelty, and desertion; tutorship; trusts; contracts and quasi-contracts; torts; evidence; agency; things in action; and liability for fatal accidents was imported into the civil code.

THE CONSTITUTIONAL BASIS FOR THE LEGAL SYSTEM

In 1967, St. Lucia, along with the other Organization of Eastern Caribbean States—namely Antigua, Dominica, Grenada, St. Vincent and the State of Saint Christopher, Nevis, and Anguilla—joined in a new "status of association" with the United Kingdom, in accordance with the West Indies Act of 1967. The act provided for Her Majesty by Order in Council to establish common courts for the Associated States with "such jurisdiction and powers as may be so specified or determined." The Order in Council also allowed provisions to be made for the establishment in common of a commission to appoint judges and officers of the court; for the remuneration, allowances, and pension rights of the commission, as well as the judges and officers of the court; and for defraying the expenses of the commission and the courts.

The West Indies Associated States Supreme Court Order duly followed and gave effect to Section 6 of the West Indies Act, permitting the establishment of common courts for the Associated States. Since then, this order has been given constitutional recognition and effect by two successive constitutions, the Associated State Constitution of 1967 and the Independence Constitution of 1979.

Among other things, the court order established a Supreme Court styled the "West Indies Associated States Supreme Court." The Supreme Court consists of the chief justice, who heads the judiciary, justices of appeal, High Court judges, and the recent creation of masters who are primarily responsible for procedural matters. The chief justice and usually two justices of appeal staff the Court of Appeal. The judges of the High Court include the chief justice and thirteen puisne judges. The chief justice, with the concurrence of the leaders of the member countries of the OECS, is allowed to vary the number of justices of appeal and puisne judges. Each state is empowered to confer by its constitution, or any other law, "such jurisdiction and powers" on the High Court in its territory. Likewise, the individual state is empowered by its constitution, or any other law, to assign to the Court of Appeal "such jurisdiction to hear and determine appeals and to exercise such powers as may be conferred on it." The order also made provision for the appointment and tenure of judges and acting judges, their remuneration and pension rights, and the appointment and tenure of office of a chief registrar and other officers of the court, and the Judicial and Legal Services Commission.

The most important change initiated by the Supreme Court order was the fusion of the High Court and Court of Appeal into one Supreme Court, and the confinement of all appeals to the Court of Appeal. The previous duality, which allowed the appellate jurisdiction to be shared by different appeal courts, was abolished. This new arrangement helped to facilitate greater supervisory jurisdiction over the legal system of the individual states by the Supreme Court.

It was, however, left to the constitutions of the individual states and the local legislatures to enact statutory provisions to give flesh to the Supreme Court Order of 1967. This was achieved in St. Lucia by the enactment of the West Indies Associated States Supreme Court (St. Lucia) Act. The act was extensive, comprising some 102 provisions. Part I outlined the jurisdiction and law of the High Court. Part II dealt with the jurisdiction of the Court of Appeal, criminal and admiralty appeals from the High Court, and appeals in contempt proceedings. In Part III the officers of the court were identified and their functions and duties stated. Part IV made provision for several matters of a miscellaneous character. Of these many provisions, the most important for immediate purposes are the sections that detailed the civil jurisdiction of the High Court and Court of Appeal. These impinged most directly on the island's civilian law and heritage.

The civil jurisdiction of the former Supreme Court of the Windward and Leeward Islands was vested in the High Court of the now-established West Indies Associated States Supreme Court. Indeed, many of the provisions of the predecessor court were simply reenacted. The

Legal Structure of St. Lucia Courts

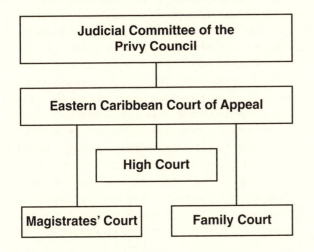

High Court was given and exercised "an original jurisdiction in all civil causes and matters whatsoever, save and except such matters as are exclusively assigned to the District courts." The High Court was allowed to maintain its jurisdiction in admiralty matters, criminal proceedings, the administration of estates, and bankruptcy proceedings "in accordance with the provision of Title IX of the Commercial Code and the rules for the time being in force in the State." The commercial code has been repealed and replaced by a new Companies Act. Additionally, the Associated State Constitution, as well as its successor, the Independence Constitution, added to the ordinary civil jurisdiction of the High Court by extending to it original jurisdiction in constitutional questions. The High Court also has original jurisdiction to hear cases involving alleged breaches of fundamental rights and freedoms.

The Court of Appeal hears appeals from all subordinate courts. Appeals from the Magistrates' Courts might be heard from "any judgement, decree, sentence or order of a Magistrate in all proceedings." In respect of the High Court presided over by a puisne judge, the Court of Appeal was given jurisdiction to hear and determine "any matter arising in any civil proceedings upon a case stated or upon a question of law reserved by the High court or by a judge." This was, however, subject to "any power conferred in that behalf by a law in operation in that state." Subject to certain exceptions, which are not material here, the Court of Appeal was allowed to "hear and determine the appeal from any judgement or Order of the High Court in all civil proceedings." For the purposes of determining any issues incidental to an appeal and the remedies, execution, and enforcement of any judgment or order made thereto, the Court of Appeal was endowed with "all the powers, authority and jurisdiction of the High Court."

The final appellate court for St. Lucia has been and continues to be the Judicial Committee of Her Majesty's Privy Council. The court comprises law lords drawn from the House of Lords and sometimes has Commonwealth judges. The constitution provides that appeals lie of right to the Privy Council in matters of great general interest or public importance, and where the Privy Council itself grants special leave. There is also an appeal as of right in constitutional and human rights cases. In 2003, St. Lucia's final court will be the Caribbean Court of Justice, which will replace the Privy Council as the final appellate court for most Caribbean jurisdictions.

MAGISTRATES' COURTS

The District Court in St. Lucia consists of five magistrates out of a complement of seven. The head of the magistracy is the chief magistrate. Two magistrates sit in the capital, Castries, and the others are located in the major towns and villages.

The District Court also comprises the Family Court and the Traffic Court. A magistrate presides in these courts. The head of the magistracy is the chief magistrate, who is responsible for the administrative aspects of the courts. The chairperson of the Family Court has the overall responsibility for hearing matters arising under the Affiliation Ordinance, chapter 8; the Separation and Maintenance Ordinance, chapter 7; and the Children and Young Persons Act of 1972.

STAFFING

The attorney general is the chief legal advisor to the government, and the constitution provides that the person in that post may either be a civil servant or a member of Parliament. The attorney general has primary responsibility for the legal affairs of the government. In the attorney general's chambers there are the solicitor general, two senior Crown counsel, and five junior Crown counsel. The director of public prosecutions (DPP) heads the Office of the Director of Public Prosecutions with the assistance of two Crown prosecutors. The DPP is appointed under the constitution by the governor-general, acting in accordance with the advice of the Judicial and Legal Services Commission. This is to ensure that the DPP is independent of the executive and the legislature. The DPP may be removed from office for inability to carry out the functions of his office or for misbehavior, once the proper procedural guarantees have been secured.

The tenures of judges and the DPP are guaranteed under the constitution. This is not the same for magistrates, however, who may be appointed under term contracts and whose security of tenure can, therefore, be more precarious. To be appointed a puisne judge or a DPP, an individual must be an attorney-at-law of at least ten years' standing.

The practice of law and legal education in St. Lucia

follow those of the other Caribbean countries. Under the treaty that established the Caribbean Council of Legal Education, prospective attorneys are required to undertake two years of training at any one of the three law schools in the region. St. Lucian students are zoned to attend the Hugh Wooding Law School. After the completion of the two years, a certificate in legal education (CLE) is awarded. A bachelor's degree in law is a prerequisite, from either the Faculty of Law, University of the West Indies, or recognized Commonwealth jurisdictions.

The Faculty of Law was opened in 1970 and is part of the University of the West Indies. The faculty has about 375 students, about 20 full-time staff, and about 8 part-time staff members. The Faculty of Law is located in Barbados at the Cave Hill Campus. The three law schools are located in Jamaica—Norman Manley Law School; Trinidad and Tobago—Hugh Wooding Law School; and the most recent, in the Bahamas—the Eugene Dupuch Law School.

Kenny Anthony
Eddy D. Ventôse

See also Civil Law; Indigenous and Folk Legal Systems; Judicial Review; Lay Judiciaries; Magistrates—Civil Law Systems; Magistrates—Common Law Systems; Privy Council
References and further reading
Anthony, Kenny D. 1984. "The Viability of the Civilist Tradition in Saint Lucia: A Tentative Appraisal." Pp. 33–75 in *Essays on the Civil Codes of Quebec and Saint Lucia.* Edited by R. A. Landry and E. Caparros. Ottawa: University of Ottawa Press.
———. 1988. "The Mixed Legal System of Saint Lucia: Its Establishment and Decline." Ph.D. thesis, University of Birmingham.
Antoine, Rose-Marie Belle. 1998. *Commonwealth Caribbean Law and Legal Systems.* London: Cavendish.
Eastern Caribbean Central Bank. 2000. *Economic and Financial Review* 20, no. 4 (December).
Eastern Caribbean Supreme Court Annual Report. August 1, 1999, to July 31, 2000.
Peters, Donald C. 1992. *The Democratic System of the Eastern Caribbean.* New York: Greenwood Press.
Williams, Eric. 1970. *From Columbus to Castro: The History of the Caribbean 1492–1969.* London: Andre Deutsch.

SUDAN

GENERAL INFORMATION

The Republic of the Sudan is the largest country in Africa, covering an area of 2,505,813 square kilometers. Its capital is Khartoum, where the Blue Nile and the White Nile join to form the River Nile. Plateaus and plains predominate, and its famous mountains are the Red Sea Mountains and the Nuba Mountains. Sudan borders Egypt to the north, Eritrea and Ethiopia to the east, the Central African Republic and Chad to the west,

Libya to the northwest, Kenya and Uganda to the south, and the Democratic Republic of the Congo to the southwest. The climate is tropical in the south and arid desert in the north. There is significant variation of temperature, from about 41°–46° C in the summer, to 6° C in the winter. The country's 34,475,690 citizens are composed of different ethnic groups: 52 percent are black African, 39 percent are Arab, 6 percent are Beja, and 3 percent are others. Some 70 percent of them are Muslim, 25 percent have indigenous beliefs, and 5 percent are Christian. Literacy among the total population is said to average 46.1 percent (male 57.7 percent, female 34.6 percent). The official language is Arabic, and among other spoken languages are Nubian, diverse dialects of Nilotic, and Sudanic languages. Agriculture employs 80 percent of the workforce. The gross domestic product is $31.2 billion.

Sudan staggered beneath a $24 billion foreign debt until the discovery of oil in the south in 1993, which has become a windfall in easing the nation's economic woes. Nevertheless, the eighteen-year civil war in the south still creates political instability. The main reasons for the war relate to conflicts between the government and rebel troops, the "Southern People's Liberation Movement," led by John Garang, over the introduction of *sharia* law (Islamic law) as the dominant law of the land. Also a matter of disagreement is the question of a fair share in natural resources and regional development, because of the redivision of the south after almost nine years (1972– 1981) of self-government. Mediation efforts exerted by the Intergovernmental Authority on Development (IGAD) and some neighboring countries so far have been unsuccessful.

The Sudanese legal system was based on English common law and Islamic law, which governed mainly Muslims' personal matters. In September 1983, however, Gaafar Numerie imposed Islamic laws, and since then *sharia* has become the dominant law of Sudan.

HISTORY

Before colonial times, the administration of justice varied from one area to another, and the grand *gadi* (judge) was in charge of deciding personal matters. When Britain and Egypt conquered the Sudan in 1898, the administration of justice became the responsibility of the two governments. The Anglo-Egyptian Agreement on the Future Administration of the Sudan set the framework for the condominium rule from January 19, 1899, to January 1, 1956. That agreement vested in the governor-general (appointed by a decree of the khedive of Egypt on the recommendation of the British government) executive, legislative, and judicial powers. The Governor-General Council was established to enact laws and to approve annual budgets. The council was made up of the governor-

general, the civil secretary, the financial secretary, the legal secretary (mainly a judge), the inspector general, the commander-in-chief of the Sudan Defense Force, and not more than four members appointed by the governor-general. Notably, the Executive Council and Legislative Assembly Ordinance of 1948 dissolved the council, established a separate Executive Council and Legislative Assembly, and allowed the Sudanese to participate in the government process. Nonetheless, the Self-Government Statute of 1953 brought out very clearly the legislative and judicial organs of the state. The legislature consisted of a bicameral Parliament and the governor-general. The executive organ consisted of a prime minister and his cabinet, and at least two of its members represent the south. The act established an independent judiciary and provided for the security of the judges' salaries and positions.

In general, the legal system was derived from a variety of sources, relating to the colonial power emphasis that laws comply with local Sudanese customs and beliefs. Hence the Civil Justice Ordinance of 1900 excluded the application of common law rules to matrimonial matters concerning Muslims and non-Muslims, who were, re-

spectively, being governed by *sharia* law and customary law. Under the Sudan Mohammedan Law Courts Organization and Civil Regulations of 1916, the ruling on *sharia* law was based on judicial circulars or the preponderant opinions of *hanafia* (members of the Muslims' Jurists School). The Chiefs Courts Act of 1932 authorized local courts to apply the prevailing customs within their jurisdiction, the ruling preserving justice, equity, and good conscience.

The courts were divided into criminal and civil courts. The Code of Criminal Procedure of 1899 established five classes of criminal court: mudir's (governor's) courts, minor district courts, and courts of magistrates of the first, second, and third classes. The Code of Criminal Procedure of 1925 maintained the Magistrates' Courts and restructured the mudir's and minor district courts to become major and minor courts, respectively. The Civil Justice Ordinance of 1900 established four classes of civil courts: the Court of Judicial Commissioner and courts of magistrates of the first, second, and third classes. By the Courts Ordinance of 1915, these classes were restructured as a High Court of Justice, province courts, and district courts of the first, second, and third grades. The criminal and civil matters were governed by common law, and the primary legal influence remained British.

When the Sudan gained independence in January 1, 1956, the adopted Transitional Constitution of 1956 reenacted most of the provisions of the Self-Government Statute and set out the functions of the executive, legislative, and judicial organs. Because of continuing political disputes, on November 17, 1958, the military seized power and governed the country by a number of constitutional decrees. By these decrees President Ibrahim Abboud exerted control over the state organs. On October 21, 1964, civilian government came to office and amended the 1956 Constitution. The 1964 Constitution created a unicameral parliament known as the Constituent Assembly, with a term of four years. Before the expiry of the first term, the Supreme Commission comprising the political parties in the coalition government dissolved the Assembly on February 7, 1968. On May 15, 1969, the military, headed by President Nimeiri (1969–1985), seized power. Nimeiri formed a legal reform commission to abrogate the common law. In 1970 the commission unveiled the Civil Code, derived mainly from the Egyptian Civil Code of 1949. The code received criticisms. First, the code's sections were derived from the Egyptian code, transplanted from the French Code, and both were entirely alien to the Sudan. Second, the code was not accompanied by a supplement to interpret its provisions. Third, it replaced the penal code, which was supported by a strong body of case law, and it disregarded the existing customary law. In 1973 the government repealed the code, returning the country's legal system to its pre-1970 common law basis. Nimeiri embarked on a political "reconciliation" with the National Islamic Front (NIF) in 1977, forming a committee to bring Sudan's laws into conformity with the *sharia*. The committee drafted seven bills: the Liquor Prohibition Bill, the Hudud (Islamic punishments) Bill, and the Zakat Fund Bill, which made mandatory the collection of a tax from Muslims for a social welfare fund administered separately from government accounts. The Islamic laws were ratified and became effective in September 1983. The excessive application of *hudud* and the application of *sharia* law on non-Muslims were criticized by secularized Muslims and Christian southerners. Following Nimeiri's overthrow in April 1985, the September 1983 laws remained dormant. The attempt by the democratic government of Sadiq al Mahdi (1985–1989) to consider abolishment of the September laws failed because of the June 30, 1989, coup d'état. In January 1991, the current regime decreed that Islamic laws would be enforced except in the three southern provinces and, to regain legitimacy, it adopted the Constitution of 1998.

LEGAL CONCEPTS

Articles 110 (m), 113, and 115 of the Constitution of 1998, respectively, provide for separation of powers; for the protection of human rights and freedoms, such as the right to life, freedom of religion, and equality; and for vesting federal organs with absolute responsibility to execute decisions relating to the control of federal lands and mineral and subterranean wealth, and channeling financial resources. Articles 36, 38 (2), and 41 of the constitution confirm that the elected president must obtain more than 50 percent of the total votes of the polling electorate, that the term of office is five years, and that the president may be reelected for only one additional term. The National Assembly is the legislative authority, and its term is four years. The Assembly consists of 360 members: 270 members elected directly from national constituencies, 61 females and state electors specially elected, and 29 members nominated through indirect elections. The General Elections Authority is an independent semijudicial body, constituted by an order of the president of the republic and approval of the National Assembly; it is responsible for all measures concerning organizing general elections and has the final decision on all disputes relating to illegal electoral practices. The authority consists of a president, having the legal status of chief justice, and two members having the same status as Supreme Court judges.

Both the 1998 Constitution and the Sudanese Judiciary Act of 1995 emphasize the importance of judicial independence and prohibit any unwarranted interference with the judicial process. The Supreme Council of the Judiciary consists of the chief justice, the chief justice deputy, two of the directors of the Administration of Justice in the states nominated by the chief justice, the minister of finance, the minister of justice, and three experienced persons of high competence to be appointed by the president. The Supreme Council recommends to the president the approval of the council's decisions concerning the appointment of judges, promotion and accountability of the chief justice deputies and Supreme Court judges, dismissal of the judges of the Court of Appeal and other lower courts, and the approval of the annual judiciary budget. The president appoints the chief justice, the chief justice deputies, the Supreme and Appeal Courts, and the judges of the courts of the first, second, and third grades.

The Constitutional Court is an independent tribunal. The president of the republic, with the approval of the National Assembly, appoints its president and six members. The Constitutional Court interprets the constitution and legal provisions upon the request of the president of the republic, the National Assembly, half the number of governors, or half the states' assemblies; it examines individuals' claims concerning the protection of their constitutional rights and freedoms, and settles conflicts between the federal and state organs over competence and any other matters prescribed by the constitution or the law. The quorum of the court's session is attained by the presence of five of its members.

The president of the republic appoints the minister of justice. The minister's responsibilities are to ensure the rule of law and prompt justice in all legal proceedings, to represent the government in all civil and criminal cases, to provide government agencies with legal services, and to register and authorize legal transactions and documents. The minister heads the Council of Legal Profession (formerly the bar association).

Sudan is a signatory of several international conventions, among which are the African Charter on Human and People's Rights; the International Covenant of Civil and Political Rights; the International Covenant of Economic, Social, and Cultural Rights; and the International Convention on the Elimination of All Forms of Racial Discrimination. There are several differences between Sudan's international human rights obligations and the human rights measures of the constitution. One such difference is that, in most human rights treaties, the conditions under which governments may derogate human rights are very narrowly enumerated: namely, human rights may be limited only when it is absolutely necessary, and several specific human rights are not derogable under any circumstances. The constitution, on the other hand, contains vague provisions stipulating that law may limit enumerated rights, and it grants the president broad powers to suspend many of the rights provided to individuals.

The Labor Act of 1997 provides several guarantees: equal pay; vacation and sick leave; and maternity leave granted after a completion of six months of service, with the full pay calculated as four weeks before delivery and four weeks after, and during maternity leave. The International Labor Organization (ILO) Governing Body received complaints from the dismantled Federation of Worker's Trade Unions of Sudan of government interference in trade union activities and violations of labor rights, such as the arrest of trade unionists and the dismissal of workers without justified reasons. The ILO-appointed committee deeply regretted the lack of response of the government to the allegations.

The principles of the Criminal Procedures Act of 1991 are the presumption of innocence, prohibition of use of force or coercion in compelling confession or testimony, and prompt and just trial. The official language of criminal procedures is Arabic, except in cases when the use of another language is needed.

The Civil Transaction Act of 1984 governs all civil matters, torts and contracts, partnerships, land, and agency and Islamic financial transactions. The act invalidated the common law tort grounds such as negligence and nuisance, and provided new grounds of tort liability based on the Islamic principle of *alkhataa,* roughly translated as "fault." Essentially, this principle obliges any person, including a minor, who acts in a way that causes harm to another to pay compensation. Equally, failure to prevent harmful acts from occurring is conduct that attracts liability under this principle. Thus the criterion here is the causation of harm, whether the tortfeasor's act is intentional or unintentional. As a result, any act causing harm is tortious and has legal consequences. Thus, theoretically and in practice, this principle is both very harsh and broad, covering all aspects of tortious acts.

Article 3 of the 1998 Constitution grants the right to litigate to all persons. However, the high legal fees constrain poor claimants from accessing justice. For example, Section 6 (7) of the orders of the Civil Procedures Act provides that "[a]ny claimant who is seeking to receive legal benefits from civil proceedings should pay the lawsuit fees." Although the claimant could file *forma pauperis,* it is argued that the discretionary nature of decisions determining who is or who is not a pauper renders the approval of pauper's application uncertain. Although the Ministry of Justice provides a proven pauper with legal aid, the scope of the present legal aid services is very limited because of a shortage of financial and human resources. The Legal Aid Office has only a few branches, in Khartoum and some other states, and has eighty-four lawyers to handle a wide range of civil, administrative, and criminal cases for the whole country. As a result, the 1997–1998 statistics revealed that Legal Aid provided services in only 275 criminal cases, twenty-three civil suits, seven family cases, and one case involving judicial review of administrative decision.

The Taxation Chamber of the Ministry of Finance and Economy is concerned with the assessment and collection of direct taxes. These taxes include business profit tax, personal income, rental income tax, capital gains, and sales tax, in addition to expatriates' contribution and development tax. The prevailing tax law is the 1986 Income Tax Act, amended in 1995. By Article 17 of that act, the minister of finance could exempt from income tax any company, whether a national or foreign company, investing in the Sudan. To encourage foreign investment, the Investment Act of 1996 offers a number of incentives to foreign investors, including an exemption from business profit tax and tax holidays ranging between five and ten years.

According to the 1999 "Report on the Judicial Institutions' Performance," courts in the Sudan finalized 386,793 out of 410,301 cases, some 93 percent, compared with 90 percent in 1998. The cutting down of the judiciary budget caused a 40 percent deficit in expenditure and affected 20 percent of resources allocated to the judges' services. The judiciary is planning to establish new courts and expand the judicial services in other provinces, to avoid chronic delays of legal proceedings.

Between 1989 and 1999, the performance of the Ministry of Justice Administrations has been as follows: the

Structure of Sudanese Courts

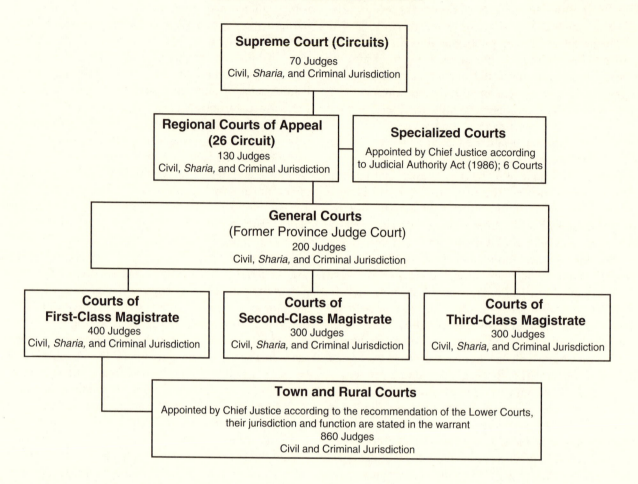

Legislation Department drafted 160 laws and 60 regulations; 7,000 cases were examined by the Civil Cases Administration; the Prevention of Unlawful Enrichment Department examined 300 complaints; 6,000 companies and 4,000 partnerships have been registered at the Companies' Registry; 460 governmental contracts were concluded; and 200 international agreements have been reviewed by the Contracts Department.

CURRENT COURT SYSTEM STRUCTURE

All higher courts in the Sudan have original and appellate jurisdiction over *sharia,* civil, and criminal matters. The courts in the Sudan are: (1) the Supreme Court, the highest body within the judicial branch; (2) the regional courts of appeal; (3) the specialized courts, appointed by the chief justice according to the Judicial Authority Act of 1986; (4) general courts, formerly known as province courts; (5) courts of first-, second-, and third-class magistrate; and (6) town and rural courts appointed by the chief justice according to the recommendation of the lower courts (they do not have jurisdiction over *sharia* matters).

Article 122 (3) of the 1998 Constitution provides that the law shall regulate the establishment of military courts and their jurisdiction over cases involving military officers.

The judiciary reviews administrative decisions. Without prejudice to that, the Public Grievances and Corrections Board is authorized to clear away grievances at the federal level and ensure efficiency in the practice of the state organs and the fairness of administrative acts, also to extend justice after the final decisions of the institutions of justice. The president of the republic, with the approval of the National Assembly, appoints the president and members of the board.

STAFFING

There are 12,023 practicing lawyers in the Sudan. Passing the bar examination is required for active practice of law. There are 70 Supreme Court judges, 130 in the appeal courts, 200 in the general courts, 400 judges of courts of first class, 300 of second class, 300 of third class, and 860 in the town and rural courts. The Ministry of Justice has 13 attorneys at senior level, 23 with the Civil Administration, 21 with the Legislation Department, 9 at the Human Rights Office, 11 at the Contracts Department, 3 legal aid officers, 13 at the Prevention of Unlawful Enrichment Department, approximately 371 at the states' offices, and 7 researchers.

The requirements for appointment as a judge stem mainly from Islamic values. These requirements include competence, integrity, honesty, and good reputation. Several reports by international authorities describe the judiciary's lack of independence and its vulnerability to political influence and pressure from the executive. Moreover, the selection of judges is based upon political allegiance rather than qualifications.

The Sudan has eight law schools, five of which are recently established. The well-established schools are the Faculty of Law, University of Khartoum; the Law School of the Nilain University (formerly the Cairo University, Khartoum Branch); and the Sharia and Islamic Studies Department at the Islamic University. No statistics are available on the number of law students and staff. The dean of the Faculty of Law, University of Khartoum, is a member of the Legal Profession Council and the Supreme Judicial Council. Newly appointed judges and attorneys are sent to the Institute of Training and Legal Reform. The institute is specialized in preparing legal reform projects and upgrading legal syllabuses for the law schools.

IMPACT OF LAW

Although the government is working on improving the legal system, the hasty introduction of the Islamic laws has had negative consequences. The sudden transformation of the legal system confused most of the judges and lawyers, who are experienced in common law, and affected the quality of judicial and legal work. The frequent changes in laws without adequate publication have created uncertainty.

Adila Abusharaf

See also Civil Procedure; Customary Law; Government Legal Departments; Human Rights Law; Islamic Law; Legal Aid; Tort Law

References and further reading
Akolain, Natalie. 1971. "Islamic and Customary Law in the Sudan: Problems of Today and Tomorrow." Pp. 279–350 in *Sudan in Africa.* Edited by Yousif F. Hassan. Khartoum: Dar ElGeel Press.
Library of Congress, Federal Research Division, Country Studies. "Sudan: Legal System." http://lcweb2.loc.gov/cgi-bin/query/r?frd/cstdy:@field(DOCID+sd0111) (accessed February 7, 2001).
Mohamed, Ramadan. 1995. *The Rules of Civil Litigation under the Civil Procedures Act of 1983.* Khartoum: Maroui Press.
Tier, Akolda. 1984. *The Legal System of the Sudan.* Khartoum: University of Khartoum Press.
United States Department of State Report, "Sudan Human Rights Practices." http://www.domini.org/openbook/sudan95.htm (accessed February 10, 2001).

SURINAME

COUNTRY INFORMATION

Suriname is located on the northern coast of South America. Guyana and French Guyana are its neighbors to the west and east, respectively, while Brazil delimits the country in the south. The capital of Suriname is Paramaribo. The land covers almost 164,000 square kilometers, and there were an estimated 431,000 inhabitants in 2000. Territories in the southeast and southwest have long been the subjects of border disputes with French Guyana and Guyana. The last dispute arose in June 2000 over the exploitation of an oil rig in the Corantijne River, the border river with Guyana. Some 92 percent of the country is covered by woodlands, and 15 percent of the land is declared as protected area. Suriname has distinct natural regions—lowland, savannahs, swamps, and highland covered with rain forest. Numerous rivers, streams, and creeks intersect the country. The Corantijne and Marowijne Rivers form the borders in the east and west. Other important rivers are the Suriname and the Coppename. The climate is tropical, with the average temperature in Paramaribo being 27°C.

The country is divided into ten districts, seven of which are located directly at the ocean border in the north. Paramaribo has about 170,000 inhabitants; other (smaller) cities are Nieuw Nickerie in the northwest and Albina in the northeast. Moengo is located in the northeast and is the center of the country's bauxite region. Life expectancy at the time of birth is 67.5 years for males and 72.7 years for females. The mean literacy rate in 1997 was 93.5 percent. The ethnic composition of the inhabitants is as follows: Hindustanis, originating from India, 37 percent; Creoles, mixed-race people of African origin, 31 percent; Javanese, from Indonesian origin, 15 percent; Bush Negroes or Maroons, descendants from runaway slaves, 10 percent; Indians, 2 percent; Chinese, 2 percent; Europeans, 2 percent; people of other origin, 1 percent. The Bush Negroes live in the interior near the rivers, and Indians are found in the coastal area and near the border with Brazil in the south.

Dutch is the official language, while the lingua franca is Srananantongo; other languages are English, Sarnami (a Surinamese Hindi-Urdu variant), Javanese, Chinese, and dialects such as Saramaccan and Paramaccan. Hinduism is the most widely practiced religion (the faith of 27.4 percent of the population); other religions include Catholicism (25.2 percent), Protestantism (22.8 percent), Islam (19.6 percent), and indigenous animistic religions (5 percent).

During the 1960s and 1970s, Suriname was considered one of the wealthiest nations of Latin America, and the level of education, employment rate, and quality of health care were considered to be far superior to those of

Suriname

Atlantic Ocean

GUYANA

Nieuw Nickerie
Paramaribo
Nieuw Amsterdam
Wageningen
Totness
Moengo
Paranam
Albina
Phedra
Apoera
Brokopondo
Matapi
Afobaka
Cayenne   5°

SURINAME

FRENCH GUYANA

VEN.

SURINAME

Cottica
Granbori

Intelewa

Kawatop

Jamaike

Papai

BRAZIL

©2001 maps.com   55°

0   50   100 mi
0 50 100 km

the neighboring states. However, through the 1980s and 1990s, the economic situation deteriorated sharply, caused by military coups, an internal war, irresponsible government spending, poor performance of most enterprises, migration of professionals, and the cessation of development funds granted by the Netherlands and the United States. Currently, almost 45 percent of all workers are on the government payroll. In 1998, the gross national product (GNP) per capita was U.S.$1,660, and average economic growth between 1990 and 1998 was 0.1 percent. Inflation was a yearly average of 138 percent over the period from 1990 to 1998, and unemployment rates were 20 percent in 1998. The country's most important export products are bauxite, crude oil, wood, shrimp and fish, rice, and bananas. Suriname's most important business partners for export are Norway, the Netherlands, the United States, France, and Japan, and the United Kingdom is becoming more important every year.

The import volume exceeded the export volume by some U.S.$50 million in 1998. Suriname imports mostly from the United States, the Netherlands, Trinidad, Japan, the United Kingdom, and Brazil. Due to the economic situation, many people, especially those who live in the interior, have taken up prospecting for gold. In fact, though gold mining has a history that goes back more than 100 years, there have never been as many people involved in this activity as there are nowadays. Small-scale mining also attracted many migrants, especially from Brazil (called *garimpeiros*). Because of the use of mercury, small-scale mining is extremely hazardous for the environment. The interior is also the scene of significant forestry activity, but logging is done by Southeast Asian companies of ill repute in their own region. Transport over land is limited to the coastal plains, where the main roads are located. Transport into the hinterland must be done by airline or by large canoes (*korjalen*). On May 19, 2000, the almost 1.5-kilometer-long Jules Albert Wijdenbosch Bridge over the Suriname River was opened, and another new bridge, over the Coppename River, is under construction. Both have to play an important role in the economic development of the district of Commewijne. Suriname has an international airport—Johan Adolf Pengel, formerly called Zanderij.

In 1995, Suriname joined the Caribbean Community

and Common Market (CARICOM) to strengthen its participation in regional economic, social, and cultural affairs. The possibility of engaging in privileged business with the European Union is provided by the African-Caribbean-Pacific-European Union Partnership Agreement, signed at Cotonou on June 23, 2000.

HISTORY

The first inhabitants of Suriname, the Amerindians, appeared in the region about 5000 B.C.E. Alonso de Ojeda, a European of Spanish descent, is generally considered to be the man who discovered Suriname in 1499. After this discovery, adventurers made frequent travels into the interior, looking for the gold of El Dorado. In 1651, Suriname was colonized by the British, and in 1667, when the British and the Dutch made the Peace of Breda, Suriname was given as a possession to the Dutch who, in turn, gave the New Netherlands and its central settlement New Amsterdam, now New York, to the British. Except for the years from 1799 to 1802 and 1804 to 1815, when it was ruled by the British, Suriname remained part of the Netherlands until it became independent in 1975.

In 1682, Suriname was sold to one private owner, to the commercial trading organization West Indian Company, and to the city of Amsterdam. From that time forward, it was rapidly transformed into a plantation-based colony. During the seventeenth and eighteenth centuries, approximately 300,000 blacks, mostly from the coasts of West Africa, were shipped as slaves to the settlement, where they were sold to the plantation owners to work on the sugar, coffee, indigo, and wood plantations. Many slaves fled the plantations and established communities in the jungle, where they permanently threatened the safety of the plantations. This situation lasted until late in the eighteenth century, when peace treaties were signed between the Maroons and the Dutch. In the 1850s, in anticipation of the abolition of slavery (which only came in 1863, some fifty years later than among other colonizing powers), contract laborers were brought to the country, mostly from China. After the abolition of slavery, people were contracted in India and Indonesia to fill the need for agricultural labor. From 1873 until 1917, some 34,000 Hindustanis emigrated to Suriname as contract laborers, and Indonesians, mostly from Java, emigrated to Suriname from 1894 until 1939. Both groups of emigrants, together with a small number of descendants of the Dutch farmers who had settled in the colony in the mid-nineteenth century, still form the backbone of the country's agriculture.

In the beginning of the twentieth century, the Aluminium Company of America (Alcoa) started to mine bauxite, which became extremely important for the aviation industry of the United States during the years of World War II. Alcoa works together with the national company Suralco. After the transfer of sovereignty over Indonesia to the Indonesians in 1949, Suriname was granted constitutional autonomy in internal affairs in 1954. (Noninternal affairs involved matters of defense and foreign affairs.) Thus, the parliamentary system was introduced with fully responsible ministers acting under the governor, who at that time was the head of the constitutional government. With regard to noninternal affairs, the governor represented the Dutch government. In 1948, universal suffrage was introduced, enabling the people to choose their representatives in the Surinaamse Staten (Parliament). At the end of the 1940s, political parties began to take shape along ethnic lines. The Creoles started the Nationale Partij Suriname (NPS, National Party of Suriname) and the Progressieve Suriname Volkspartij (PSV, Progressive Suriname People's Party). The Indonesians organized themselves in the Kaum Tani Persatuan Indonesia (KTPI, Indonesian Farmers Party), and the Hindustanis united in Verenigde Hindostaanse Partij (VHP, United Hindustan Party). In 1973, a coalition of the first three of these parties, which were all in favor of independence for the country, won the general elections. Two years later, on November 25, 1975, Suriname became constitutionally independent. The national constitution was enacted the day before. Right after independence, a stream of migrants went to the Netherlands, looking for a more secure existence than they thought the newly independent Suriname had to offer them. Johan Ferrier became the first president of the Republic of Suriname, and Henck Arron was the first prime minister.

Economic problems and internal malpractice troubled the first government. In 1980, a conflict with the army over the admissibility of a labor union led to a coup by noncommissioned officers (NCOs). On February 25, a group of sixteen NCOs, led by Sgt. Maj. Desiree Bouterse, took over power from the civilian government and removed the cabinet, while the president was left in office. The National Militaire Raad (National Military Council, NMR), formed to represent the highest power in the country, was soon internally divided, and the military commanders took over. On August 13, 1980, a state of emergency was declared by Bouterse, the constitution was suspended, and Parliament was sent home; the country was now run by military decree. The emergency state was to last until February 25, 1986. In 1982, President Henk Chin A. Sen was removed from office, and after a visit of the revolutionary leader Maurice Bishop of Grenada to Suriname, the military definitely secured their rule on December 8, 1982, when they executed fifteen prominent civilians, accusing them of conspiracy against the security of the state. As a consequence, the Netherlands unilaterally discontinued the development treaty, which provided 3.5 billion Dutch guilders to Suriname for its development process and a major source of income for the country. A process of revolutionizing started. But the revolution did not bring the expected economic and social improvements, and the population gradually lost confidence in the military.

In the second half of the 1980s, a guerrilla group in east Suriname, known as the Jungle Commando and led by a former soldier named Ronnie Brunswijk, started to attack the National Army. As a consequence of severe countermeasures taken by the army, many Bush Negroes were killed, and some 12,000 more fled to French Guyana. Unable to bring about economic reform, the army was forced to cooperate again with the old political elite. This led to a new constitution in September 1987, with general elections held two months later. Bouterse also took part in this election with his political party, the Nationale Democratische Partij (NDP, National Democratic Party). The military suffered a political defeat, and a new coalition of the NPS, VHP, and KTPI formed a government. However, in December 1990, the military forced the government under President Ramsewak Shankar to make way for them again. International pressure led to new elections in 1991, which were won by the same coalition as in 1987, who now joined forces with the Surinamese Labour Party (SPA).

This New Front government under President Ronald Venetiaan made peace with the Bush Negroes and put the army back into the barracks. In the treaty for national reconciliation and development—agreed to by the government, the Jungle Commando, and the Tucajana Amazons (an Indian paramilitary organization that was also active in the internal war of the mid-1980s)—it was stipulated that the natural resources of the country were state property and had to be deployed in the process of economic, social, and cultural development of the nation. This was followed by the express stipulation that the indigenous population of the interior part of the country was an integral part of the total population and therefore would take part in the exploitation of these natural resources and the benefits generated by them. To secure this, the government committed itself to pass real titles on land, as requested by civilians who still lived in their tribal resort. The tribal authority of these civilians was put in charge of the procedure, which had to be followed by individual members to be granted a real title for a plot in the tribal area. The same treaty stated that around the tribal community resorts, economic zones would be established where the tribal civilians could hunt, fish, and engage in forestry and small-scale mining.

In 1992, Suriname agreed on a treaty with the Netherlands to reinstall the rule of law and democracy at a fast pace. For the period until 1997, the treaty envisaged government-to-government cooperation between the Suriname Ministry of Justice and Police and the Dutch Ministry of Justice; in addition, 30 million Dutch guilders were earmarked to be spent on technical assistance, training and education, and material equipment. A number of specific legal projects were envisaged, as well, ranging from strengthening the judiciary to publishing jurisprudence and upgrading a legal library. An externally monitored structural adaptation program seemed the only way out of the economic chaos, but the Venetiaan administration was reluctant to bring in the International Monetary Fund.

Though the New Front again won in the 1996 elections, internal disagreement kept them from running government once more. Bouterse's NDP formed a new government with the help of dissidents from the VHP and the KTPI, and the NDP's Jules Wijdenbosch became president. Wijdenbosch appointed Bouterse as adviser of the state, and in the following years, the country was led to the most dramatic economic crisis ever. The Netherlands once more discontinued development aid in 1998 due to corruption, mismanagement, and the default proceedings against Bouterse, who was accused of drug-trafficking. General elections were held at an earlier date than had been formally declared, and on May 25, 2000, Wijdenbosch was completely defeated. Now the New Front—this time without the KTPI but with another party representing the Javanese population, the Pertjajah Luhur—turned out to be the winners. Once more, Ronald Venetiaan was elected as president, and in that capacity, he celebrated the twenty-fifth anniversary of the republic on November 25, 2000.

LEGAL HISTORY

After the Napoleonic times and the English interim administration, the Dutch again rose to power over the colony in 1816. Unlike the policy they pursued in the biggest colony, Indonesia, where the autochthonous population was left in their own unwritten traditional customary law, the Dutch brought Roman-Dutch law to Suriname. Dutch law was applicable in personal and family affairs; Roman law governed contracts and slaves; and for land, a special mixture of law with typical Surinamese traits was in force. Dutch and Roman law were also applied in criminal affairs. Until 1848, the Dutch king held absolute power over the colony of Suriname. With the introduction of parliamentary democracy in Holland in 1848, the minister for colonial affairs was made responsible to the Dutch parliament for the administration in Suriname. In 1868, the Surinamese Colonial Council (a parliament with partly elected representatives), in cooperation with the governor-general, was given power over local Surinamese legislation. In 1869, new codified legislation was enacted in the colony. At the same time, a civil code, a code of civil procedure, a commercial code, general provisions of legislation, a criminal code, and a code of criminal procedure were introduced.

These codes were virtually the image of the codes in use in the Netherlands, since it was policy to follow the principle of concordance, meaning that motherland and colonial codes had to be as identical as possible. From that time on, Surinamese legal order was firmly rooted in the Dutch civil law tradition, which is of old Dutch, French, and Roman law descent. When the new codification was introduced, old Dutch and Roman law was abolished. In the transitory provisions of the new codes, it was stipulated that the new law did not prejudice rights acquired under the old legislation. Though Surinamese law was, for the greater part, imported old Dutch and Roman law, this did not prevent some specific Surinamese legal phenomena from developing. The social conditions of the time, being completely different from those in eighteenth- and nineteenth-century Europe, produced, for instance, conditional property rights on plantation land, meaning that plantation holders would lose their property rights in case of a production stop. The historical title of conditional property was kept alive even after the introduction of the title of unconditional property in the Civil Code of 1869. In 1937, the colonial government announced a new policy for the allocation of agricultural plots. New allocations would be based on titles of long lease as described in the civil code. The historical title still coexists with the titles of the Civil Code.

In 1869, another civil law institution was imported in Suriname. With the introduction of the civil code, it became necessary to have civil law notaries public in the country because without them, it was impossible to perform a number of legal acts validly—testaments, donations, marital terms, and the like need authentic deeds drawn up by a notary public. Thus, the Notary Act was introduced in 1869 (it was changed in 1997 when the maximum number of notaries that could be appointed by law was increased to twenty).

The civil code saw a number of changes after 1869. The most important, introduced on March 11, 1981, at the initiative of the military authority, was probably the enabling of married women to make legal agreements without having to ask their husbands. Separate from the articles on marriage in the civil code, specific legislation was enacted in 1907 (viz. 1940) to regulate the marriage of Asians, Muhammedans (Muslims), and Hindustans.

Though the rule of concordance came to an end in 1975 with independence, the legal relationship between Suriname and the Netherlands remains a close one. Those involved in Suriname's legal education, legal system, organization of the judiciary, jurisprudence, and legal doctrine keep a close watch on the developments in the Netherlands. The major civil law change in Netherlands during the 1990s was the complete revision of the Civil Code. In January 1993, a conference was organized in Paramaribo on the desirability of a revision of the Surinamese Civil Code. After stating that the historical similarity of the Surinamese and the Dutch property law had been disrupted by the new Dutch Civil Code, that this would bring on difficulties for the study of Surinamese property law, and that such would be disadvantageous for the development of law in Suriname, it was concluded that the University of Suriname, together with external experts, would install a commission to study the feasibility of incorporation of parts of the new Dutch Civil Code into the Surinamese property law, with special attention paid to the inclusion of typical Surinamese legal concepts. However, the Surinamese Civil Code has not been changed to date.

The Commercial Code of 1869 introduced the concept of the public limited liability company, which had capital divided in transferable shares as the main form of business organization. The concept of a private limited liability company was never introduced in Suriname. The commercial code has no provisions for mergers, takeovers, or holding companies. Liquidation on bankruptcy is governed by the Bankruptcy Act of 1935. The Investment Law of 1960 provides for tax incentives, such as tax holidays. Though a draft for a new investment law has been produced—it is said to contain provisions for one investment agency for administrative affairs to reduce bureaucratic delay and an environmental paragraph—it has not been enacted yet. Civil procedure is regulated by the Code of Civil Procedure of 1935.

With the introduction of the criminal code and the code of criminal procedure in 1869, penal law became uniform for all inhabitants of Suriname. Due to their isolated situation in the interior, the Maroon communities were left to their own criminal jurisdiction for minor offenses. Since the uprooting of the Maroon communities in the 1980s and 1990s, first by the internal war and after that by the presence of large quantities of firearms, the respect for the traditional authorities started to erode. This process was accelerated still further by the arrival of migrants moving into the interior to prospect for gold, bringing with them prostitution and diseases.

LEGAL EDUCATION
AND INFORMATION STRUCTURE

Long before there was any institutionalized legal education in Suriname, admission to act in the courts was regulated by the Royal Decree of 1869, the year in which the codification was introduced. This decree ordered that any person who held a degree from a Dutch law school was capable of being admitted to the court as a practitioner. Those who did not have a Dutch degree could in substitute take an exam prepared by a special commission in Suriname. These practitioners represented the bar until the first law school was founded in 1948; this school educated both lawyers and notaries public. In 1968, the

University of Suriname came into existence and with it the Faculty of Law. Students could specialize in Surinamese law or fiscal law, or they could become notaries public. In the beginning of the 1980s, the university was renamed the Anton de Kom Universiteit of Suriname. In 1986, the organization changed, and today the Faculty of Law no longer exists as an independent unity but is part of the Faculty of Social Sciences, where students may choose to take one of six directions: law, economics, sociology, public administration, management, or the science of teaching. The education for notaries public no longer exists. In the middle of the 1980s, the Anton de Kom University entered into an agreement with the Dutch University of Amsterdam. Lecturers from Amsterdam teach short law courses in Paramaribo to inform the students on the latest developments of Dutch law. The Anton de Kom University has a modern central library with a law department. Full-time study for a law degree takes about five years. The course can also be followed on a part-time basis, which takes six and a half years. Approximately 680 students registered to study law in 1999–2000.

In 1989, a foundation for legal cooperation between Suriname and the Netherlands was established—the Stichting Juridische Samenwerking Suriname-Nederland. This foundation, funded by a Dutch mirror organization, has sponsored many activities, ranging from offering lectures and panel discussions on topics of interest to legal practitioners to organizing conferences, seminars, and postacademic courses. In order to improve on the quality and professionalism of the legal branch and the notaries public, the minister of justice and police asked the foundation in 1997 to initiate and organize vocational training for lawyers, notaries public, and law lecturers. This training is set up in cooperation with the Anton de Kom University and lawyers from the Surinamese legal practice and supported by the Dutch Bar and the Dutch Association of Notaries Public. Besides that, the foundation manages the Goncalves Law Library, develops course material for the Surinamese legal practice, and encourages law students to publish their doctoral papers by awarding a prize for the year's best paper. Student papers are an important source of legal information in Suriname because the output of legal publications by other authors is low. Access to jurisprudence is limited. From 1963 on, cases were incidentally published in the *Surinamese Jurists Periodical,* a publication of the Surinamese Jurists Association. However, this periodical was discontinued in 1985, although it appeared again in 1990. In 1992, a combination of the university, the Ministry of Justice and Police, and others joined forces to publish a yearly compilation of jurisprudence, titled *Surinaamse Jurisprudentie.* So far, compilations between 1989 and 1994 have been published. The laws of the country are published in the *Staatsblad van de Republiek Suriname (Official Gazette of the Republic of Suriname),* which is put out by the Ministry of Internal Affairs. This gazette started at independence in 1975 and was a successor to the colonial *Gouvernementsblad.* Since 1985, foreign distribution of the gazette is problematic, and no chronological lists have been produced, which makes it difficult to issue statements on the validity of any particular regulation. In 1995, the Ministry of Justice and Police published a three-volume compilation, containing almost all codes and other important regulations still in force at that time.

In the field of international law, Suriname ratified, without making any reservations, the following important international treaties, amongst others:

- The International Covenant on Civil and Political Rights, plus the Optional Protocol
- The International Covenant on Economic, Social and Cultural Rights
- The International Convention on the Elimination of All Forms of Discrimination against Women
- The American Convention on Human Rights
- The Inter-American Convention to Prevent and Punish Torture

LEGAL CONCEPTS

Suriname got its first constitution as an independent state in 1975. On one hand, this document prolonged the constitutional ideas of the period that came before. On the other hand, it closely resembled the Dutch Constitution of that time. Rumors that the constitution has been drafted in the Netherlands could therefore be true. The constitution embraced a sober catalog of fundamental human rights, as well as the separation of powers into executive, legislative, and judicial branches of government. The model of government was the Dutch version of the Westminster model, with government reigning by virtue of coalitions of parties in Parliament. The only divergence with the Dutch model was the provisions making the installation of a constitutional court possible. However, this court has never come to life.

The coup of 1980 brought a chaotic outpouring of military decrees, one after another, reflecting the situation of the power constellation of that period. In that time, Suriname became acquainted with presidents playing political roles, as long as they did so according to the wishes of the military. The transfer of power to civilians in 1987 brought about a new constitution, drafted in secrecy and lacking official clarification.

The 1987 Constitution provides for general objectives of state policy, which should convert Suriname into a welfare society of the European kind. Apparently, no one questioned the ability of the state to realize all the expectations that the constitution raised.

The economic system, according to the constitution, shall be characterized by joint, contemporaneous, and equal functioning of state enterprises, private enterprises, enterprises in which the state and private persons participate in common, and cooperative enterprises, according to rules of law applicable in that matter. It is the duty of the state to promote and to guarantee, as far as possible, all types of entrepreneurial production. The constitution also calls for a government policy aimed at raising the standard of living and the well-being of the society, based on social justice, the integral and balanced development of state and society, and an equitable distribution of the national income, directed toward a fair distribution of well-being and wealth over all strata of the population.

In international politics, the constitution provides for the rejection of any armed aggression or any form of political and economic pressure, as well as every direct or indirect intervention in the domestic affairs of other states, and promoting solidarity and collaboration with other peoples in the combat *against* colonialism, neocolonialism, racism, and genocide and *for* national liberation, peace, and social progress.

The constitution does not refer to different cultures, languages, and customs, although these differences frequently occur. Thus, the Bush Negro and Indian communities in the interior do not enjoy any special treatment. In addition, although Dutch is the language of official documents, the constitution does not mention it as an official language.

All the traditional human rights are to be found in the constitution, such as the protection of person and property; the protection against discrimination; the right to physical, mental, and moral integrity; and the protection against torture and degrading or inhuman treatment or punishment. Political freedoms such as free speech and freedom of assembly are mentioned as well. In court, one has the right to legal assistance, and the legal system must provide legal aid to the poor.

The constitution pays a great deal of attention to the rights of employees, their working conditions, the principle of equal pay for equal work, and the position of trade unions. In addition, there are many provisions formulating all kinds of state policies in a rather rhetorical way.

The National Assembly consists of fifty-one members chosen by district on the basis of general, free, and secret elections through a system of proportionate representation based on the highest number of average and preferential votes. The legislative power is exercised jointly by the National Assembly and the government. The National Assembly, among other tasks, elects the president and the vice president, provides nominations for the members of the Constitutional Court and their appointed deputies to the president, and organizes, if necessary, any people's assemblies (that is, joint gatherings of the National Assembly with the District Councils and the Local Councils).

The president is head of state of the Republic of Suriname, head of government, chair of the Council of State, and chair of the Security Council. The president is responsible to the National Assembly. The executive power is vested in the president, who has the supreme authority over the armed forces, and also directs foreign relations. According to the amendments of the Constitution of 1992, the president can be removed from office. However, in 1999, former president Wijdenbosch refused orders from the National Assembly to leave office, with an appeal based on an obscure constitutional provision calling for a people's assembly. According to the amendments of 1992, ministers are directly responsible to the president.

The Constitution of 1987 provided for the powerful Council of State. Its task was to conduct the state administration and to control the government in terms of adhering to the decisions of the National Assembly. It could suspend decisions issued by the Council of Ministers in anticipation of a decision of the president. It could also mobilize the people in case the national interest required such mobilization. Clearly, these powers were meant to guarantee the influence of the soldiers dominating the Council of State. The reforms of 1992 brought the Council of State back to the position of the revolutionary period. Today, it is no more than an advisory board for the government and the president.

The Audit Committee has to supervise reliability of the accounts of the treasury. In addition, it researches the efficiency of the use of government budgets. At least once per year, the committee has to report its findings to the National Assembly, the Council of State, and the government. The reports are made public.

The judicial power is formed by the president and the vice president of the Court of Justice, the members and the deputy members of the Court of Justice, the attorney general with the Court of Justice, and the other members of the Public Prosecutors Office and of other judicial functionaries indicated by law. The administration of justice is the responsibility of the president, the vice president, and the members and deputy members of the Court of Justice.

Elections for judges are unknown in Suriname. The members of the judicial power entrusted with the administration of justice and the attorney general with the Court of Justice are appointed by the government, after consultation with the Court of Justice. The appointments of the president, vice president, the members of the Court of Justice, and the attorney general are for life. Though the constitution provides for the establishment of a constitutional court, this institution has not yet become operational. Considering the shortage of judges (which will be discussed), this is no surprise. Another reason for the delay in installing the constitutional court may relate to the political implications involved in the appointment of the judges.

Lawsuits are not complicated in Suriname. First-instance cases are discussed in the Magistrates' Court, consisting of a single member of the Court of Justice. Cases in appeal are brought before the Court of Justice, that is, a board of some members of the court. The discussion of dissenting opinions in public is prohibited, as the principle of secrecy in consultations prevails.

In criminal cases, the public prosecution has the power to refrain from legal proceedings for policy reasons, although interested parties can make their complaints to the Court of Justice. Criminal procedures can be labeled as inquisitorial, meaning that magistrates have the right to acquire their own evidence in a case. Inquisitorial procedures differ from civil lawsuits, in which judges have to take for truth what one party says that is not denied by the other party. Thus, dossiers are built up before the trial, and the trial is mostly used to get clarification about obscurities in written documents. Juries are unknown in Surinamese criminal procedure. For criminal cases against soldiers, the legislation provides for special procedures.

Different procedures characterize the administration of justice in administrative matters. Disputes of civil servants with the state as their employer are dealt with directly by the Court of Justice without any first-instance procedure. Disputes concerning certain taxes may be under the jurisdiction of a special board of appeal. Other administrative cases, however, can be brought to court as civil lawsuits. Here, the traditional Dutch jurisprudence is applicable, based on the assumption that, as most administrative appeal procedures are inappropriate for honest procedures, the court has to administer justice.

The administration of justice in Suriname takes place as it does in many civil law countries. International human rights provisions prevail over national law. Mostly, codes of civil, commercial, and criminal law and codes for civil and criminal procedure have to be interpreted by the judge. In Suriname, as a civil law country, the principle of equity has a special connotation. It does not stand for a part of the legal doctrine as it does in common law. It has to be seen as a point of reference in case the code leaves room for argument about contract compliance. Liability for torts is, in accordance with Dutch doctrine, not limited to behavior explicitly forbidden by regulations. Every careless action in social life can lead to liability. However, claiming damages is not so popular as it is in the United States, since the compensations awarded in the courtroom are modest.

In administrative law, administrative legislation has to be applied. This legislation is, for the most part, not very elaborated in Suriname. As a consequence, the Suri-

Legal Structure of Suriname Courts

Constitutional Court
Provided for by Article 144 of the Surinamese Constitution, is not operational

Court of Justice (Paramaribo)
Also serves as tribunal for the civil service

Appeal for Magistrates' Court

Court-Martial (Paramaribo)

Magistrates' Court (Paramaribo)			Magistrates' Court (Nieuw Nickerie)
1 canton	2 canton	3 canton	1

Magistrates' Court is court of first instance

namese judge has to take refuge in principles of proper administration as they are known in Dutch handbooks (motivation of decisions, weighing of interest, keeping promises, principle of equality, and so on).

By virtue of its colonial past, Suriname's law has been compared to Dutch law in terms of its peculiarities. First, religious marriages are recognized in Surinamese law. For the moment, this concerns marriages between Hindustanis and Islamists. Requirements in terms of age are lower for religious marriages than for civil marriages, and parental consent is not needed. This has led to conversions among marriage candidates for whom a civil law marriage was out of reach. An Islamic marriage as recognized by law only partially reflects the prescriptions of Islamic belief. On the one hand, polygamy is forbidden for Islamic men. On the other, an Islamic man can end his marriage by voicing an expulsion formula against his wife. The man has only to say aloud a certain set of words in order to dissolve his marriage.

Second, the system of land tenure outside the urban zones is very complicated. Native peoples have claims on what they see as the land of their ancestors. Besides, property structures concerning former sugar plantations are unclear. Most of the original colonial land allocations have disappeared, so that contemporary dwellers (descendants of former slaves, among others) lack any written proof of their rights. Under military dictatorship, the Surinamese legislators recognized the principle of colonial domain in 1982. Plots of land were deemed state property unless others could prove prevailing rights. However, this principle has never been applied since 1982. The only solution to clarify Surinamese land law seems to be a countrywide land registration system to identify ownership in terms of the civil code. However, both urban politicians and mining companies in the interior have reasons to ignore this problem.

CURRENT STRUCTURE

The demand for justice has increased enormously since 1990. Types of crime hardly known before have emerged under military dictatorship. Human rights violations, drug-trafficking, money laundering, misuse of public funds (reports of the Audit Committee do not cause political debate), and the like became familiar phenomena in Surinamese society. Besides new types of crime, new types of conflicts between citizens arose. Scarcity on the capital market caused complaints about usury practices used by credit suppliers. Increased poverty put family relations under severe pressures, leading to an increase in family law cases.

The justice system was totally unprepared to cope with the consequences of these developments. Between 1978 and 1993, no judges were trained to enter the service. While the law provides for sixteen judges, only eleven are actually in office. Only one judge forms the court for summary proceedings in cases of emergency, which leads to delays of months. The shortage of judges also causes delays in bringing suspects before the court. Months-long waits have become a regular practice, which is a violation of international human rights standards.

Besides shortage problems, the court had to face political influence in the personal composition of the court under the former Wijdenbosch administration, at the end of the 1990s. Persistent rumors indicated that former dictator and drug baron Bouterse needed a biased court to show his innocence. This led to resistance in the circles of judges and lawyers and caused new congestion in the legal machinery.

The administration of justice is hampered by problems in terms of administrative staff, computerization, housing, available legislation, textbooks, and so on. Fortunately, the present Venetiaan II administration recognizes the problems. It can encourage the Dutch government to make development funds available to cope with these problems.

Approximately sixty lawyers are active in Suriname. The murder of the dean of the official bar association by the military in 1982 led to disputes in the lawyers' branch. Besides the bar, an alternative lawyers' association was instituted, called the Lawyers Association Suriname. Today, there is even a third organization, the Young Lawyers. Providing legal aid to the poor is not popular among lawyers, due to sparse state compensation, although one lawyer seems to be active in this field. Mediation programs as alternatives to legal dispute settlement are still unknown in Suriname. Most Surinamese jurists are members of the Surinamese Jurists Association. Because the legal branch feels the need to establish one Surinamese bar association, governed by public law and comprising all lawyers, in order to reform, among other things, the code of professional ethics and give a legal basis to the obligatory character of the vocational training for starting lawyers, a draft for a new advocates law was written in 1995 and now awaits transformation into formal legislation. The notary public branch has its own associations, while sixteen bailiffs are registered with the Court of Justice.

The Surinamese police force has a reputation for brutality in its treatment of suspects, and more than once there were accusations that it had ties with organized crime. The police narcotics department is heavily understaffed and seems to concentrate on minor figures in the drug trade. The murder of police inspector Herman Eddy Gooding in 1990 emphasized the risks of provoking major figures. Overcrowded police cells, in which suspects have to stay for months, are of concern to human rights activists. Recently, the leading Surinamese human rights organization Moiwana '86 has started courses for the police academy about international standards for human rights and police conduct. Though the military police were notorious for their role in human rights violations during times of dictatorship, they could be deployed in tasks in which the ordinary police fail. Reintroduction of investigative powers against civilians is thus in debate in government circles.

Advocates of the rule of law in Suriname hope that the decision of the court to order public prosecution in the case of the so-called December killings of 1982 will be the beginning of a new period. After all, eighteen years of silence seem to have come to an end.

H. F. Munneke
A. J. Dekker

See also Civil Law; Indigenous and Folk Legal Systems; Judicial Independence; Legal Education; Legal Professionals—Civil Law Traditions; Netherlands

References and further reading

Ardjosoediro, S., et al. 1995. *Fundamentele Surinaamse wetgeving.* 3 vols. Paramaribo: Ministerie van Justitie en Politie.

http://www.britannica.com/search?query=suriname&ct= (accessed September 12, 2001).

http://www.cia.gov/cia/publications/factbook/geos/ns.html (accessed September 12, 2001).

http://www.electionworld.org/election/suriname.htm (accessed September 12, 2001).

http://www.georgetown.edu/pdba/Constitutions/Suriname/suriname.html (accessed September 12, 2001).

Republic of Suriname, Ministry of Foreign Affairs. 1998. *Suriname in Facts and Figures.* 6th ed. Paramaribo: Corps of Honorary Consuls in Suriname.

Snijders, A. 2000. *Suriname: Mensen, politiek, economie, cultuur, milieu.* [Suriname: People, politics, economics, culture, environment]. Amsterdam and Den Haag: KIT and NOVIB.

Stichting Juridische Samenwerking Suriname-Nederland. 2000. *Vademecum voor de Rechtspraktijk 2001* [Guide for the legal practice]. Paramaribo: Stichting Juridische Samenwerking Suriname-Nederland.

SWAZILAND

GENERAL INFORMATION

Swaziland is an independent sovereign state located in southern Africa. It is a landlocked country, bordered by the Republic of South Africa to the north, west, and south and by Mozambique to the east. The geographical area of Swaziland more or less coincides with the ethnic grouping of the Swazi people. Swaziland covers an area of approximately 17,363 square kilometers, about the size of Wales. Its population is roughly 910,000.

Swaziland enjoys harmonious relations with its neighbors. It has an excellent educational system, with a number of reputable schools in the major urban areas of Manzini and Mbabane. The general infrastructure is well developed, and living conditions in the temperate climate are agreeable.

Agriculture is the major export and source of income in Swaziland. The top three exports are edible concentrates, sugar, and wood pulp. The main food crops are maize, beans, sugarcane, wheat, and sorghum. Maize dominates agriculture in Swaziland, being raised on 70 percent of the total cultivated area, followed by cotton, at 20 percent, and beans, at 3 percent. Among root crops, the most important is sweet potato, an expanding industry. Swaziland, one of the smallest countries on the continent, uses nearly all its land for agricultural purposes.

HISTORY

Swaziland is an ancient kingdom. The ruling house can trace its genealogy back for thirty generations. The great warrior king Mswati II (1840–1868) reorganized the Zulus (once part of the Swazi) and extended the power of the Swazis as far north as the Limpopo Valley.

In the mid-nineteenth century, whites began to encroach into Swazi territory. They were drawn to Swaziland for two major reasons: trade and gold. Swaziland sits astride the trade route from the Transvaal to a deepwater harbor on the Indian Ocean. In 1879, gold was discovered in Swaziland. It became one of the earliest gold-producing regions in southern Africa, with many mines operating by the 1880s. The Swazi king Mswati I was prepared to enter into transactions with whites, and the resulting land concessions became known as the paper conquest. Thus the fate of Swaziland drifted from the hands of the Swazi people into those of whites.

The first whites to enter the nation of Swaziland were the Boers, whose Dutch ancestors had settled in South Africa in the 1600s. In 1845, Boers trekked into Swaziland from Natal and founded settlements in the northeastern Highveld. The British and Portuguese later followed. A treaty concluded in 1845 between the Boers and the Portuguese defined the boundary between the two powers along the Lubombo Mountains and placed Swaziland within the Boer Republic.

The Boers were deterred from exercising sovereignty over Swaziland by the British, but Boer interest in the Swazis continued. On the coronation of King Mbandzeni in 1875 as *ngwenyama* of the Swazis, representatives of the Boer Republic of South Africa concluded a treaty with the new king. Swaziland's northern and western boundaries were set in the Pretoria Convention of 1881. The formal boundaries reduced the size of Swaziland and incorporated large portions of Swazi territory into the South African Transvaal. One positive result of the Pretoria Convention was Boer recognition of Swaziland's independence within its own boundaries. The Treaty of London of 1884 confirmed Swaziland's independence.

Although Swaziland was not a party to the treaties, Swazis were content that their independence had been promised by international treaty. Actual independence, however, was clearly dependent on the convenience of colonial powers. On July 4, 1890, the First Convention of Swaziland declared the nation's independence.

Upon gaining its long-promised independence in 1968, Swaziland not only retained its traditional monarchy but also expanded the role of the king. In addition to having the title of *ngwenyama* ("lion"), ruler of the Swazis, King Sobhuza was recognized as head of state, who could wield unchallenged political power and full executive authority. In 1973, the king repealed all independence constitutionally and assumed all judicial, executive, and legislative authority.

On the historical background of the courts in Swaziland, the protocol of 1889, which was agreed to between British government and the South African Republic, stated that in terms of the 1894 convention, the Landdrost's Court and the High Court of Swaziland were to be competent to deal with crimes committed by natives, including the paramount chief and other chiefs, who were no longer competent to exercise criminal jurisdiction. The protocol stripped away the immunities of the Swazi king, thereby reducing him to the same level as his subjects. Less than twenty years after the Pretoria Convention, Swazis had been excluded from managing their own internal affairs.

By tradition, the Swazi paramount chief had the power to establish the courts, issue warrants, define jurisdiction, and make rules of procedure. This power was subject, however, to the approval of the resident commissioner. The chief's courts had unlimited powers in civil

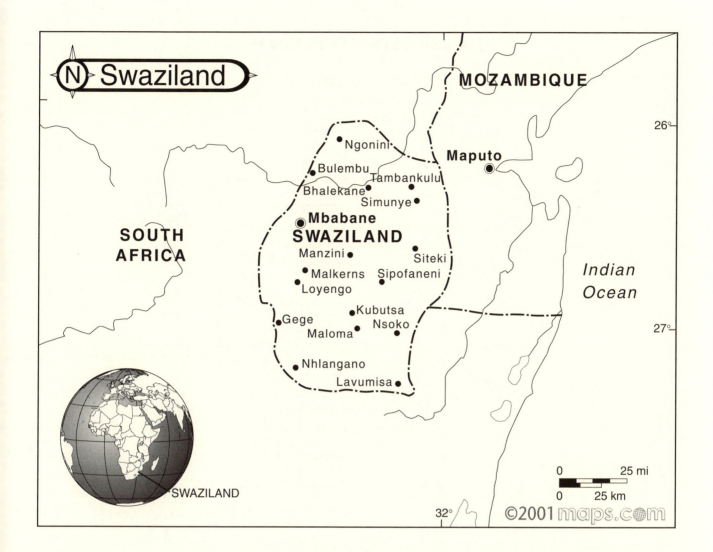

claims. District officers had the power of review only over criminal matters. The chief's jurisdiction was defined strictly in racial terms, as extending only to cases in which both parties were Swazis.

After Swaziland's independence in 1968, these traditional institutions were preserved but adapted to modern times. Appeal courts were established: the Swazi Court of Appeal, the Higher Swazi Court of Appeal, the judicial commissioner, and the High Court. These only deal with customary cases. Few changes have been made to this judicial structure, which was established under colonial rule. The present Swazi court system consists of the High Court and the subordinate courts, called Magistrates' Courts. The king may, with the concurrence of the chief justice, appoint anyone as a magistrate, and he retains the power to establish other courts as he sees fit.

LEGAL CONCEPTS

Legal concepts in Swaziland reflect the ethical principles, moral codes, and values of Swazi society. The High Court and Magistrates' Courts must apply the common law, while the Swazi courts are bound to follow customary law. The Swazi courts and their subordinate courts are bound to adhere to local law and custom insofar as they are consistent with justice and morality and with regional or national laws. They may be charged with administering the provisions of proclamations issued by the king.

The English legal tradition has been strong, especially influential in the areas of constitutional law and administrative law, including rules relating to the organization of the courts, the judiciary, and the legal profession. With regard to private law, English law has had little influence, which is seen in wills, trusts, the doctrine of estoppel, the English-inspired innovations on matrimonial property, divorce, and the freedom of testation.

Swaziland has statutory rules to regulate conflicts between domestic systems of customary law. On civil and Christian marriages, these will have little effect on the spouses' personal law (family law) in Swaziland. There is statutory choice of legal rules that preserve customary law, and the formalities for creating a marriage and divorce are governed by common law.

Like Lesotho and Botswana, Swaziland has its own indigenous laws, which are distinct from the country's

Legal Structure of Swazi Courts

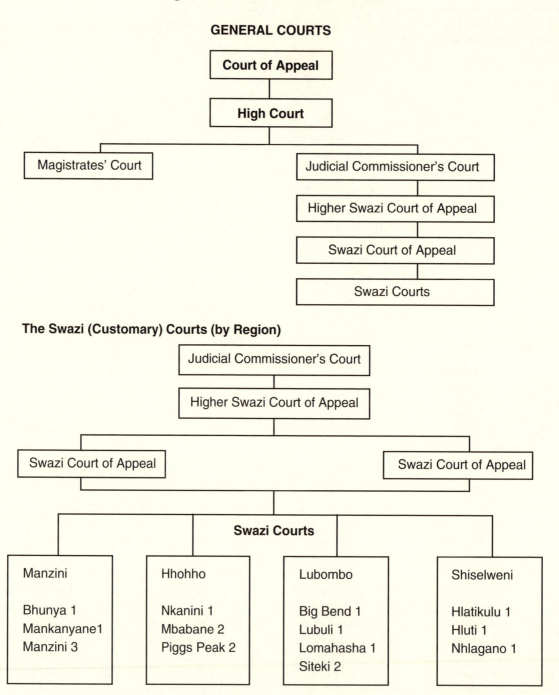

GENERAL COURTS

Court of Appeal

High Court

Magistrates' Court

Judicial Commissioner's Court

Higher Swazi Court of Appeal

Swazi Court of Appeal

Swazi Courts

The Swazi (Customary) Courts (by Region)

Judicial Commissioner's Court

Higher Swazi Court of Appeal

Swazi Court of Appeal

Swazi Court of Appeal

Swazi Courts

Manzini	Hhohho	Lubombo	Shiselweni
Bhunya 1	Nkanini 1	Big Bend 1	Hlatikulu 1
Mankanyane1	Mbabane 2	Lubuli 1	Hluti 1
Manzini 3	Piggs Peak 2	Lomahasha 1	Nhlagano 1
		Siteki 2	

general law. Indigenous law is more communal or socialist, whereas the general law is individualistic and capitalist. African ways of life are based on solidarity, which forms the basis of indigenous law. Indigenous law is is found in custom, is not divided into specializations, and lacks a developed legislative machinery or an idea of judicial precedent.

The rule of law is of paramount importance to Swazis. The actions of government agencies and officials are subject to regulation by general principles and public rules.

Equality is one of the fundamentals underlying the legal system of Swaziland, and it is reflected in the laws of the country. Swazi courts and general courts are expected to create social order through contracts and agreements.

Criminal offenses are treated as offenses against the state or the Crown, which implies that the state only is entitled to justice. Offenses committed by children are regarded as less serious than those committed by adults and thus are not considered to be crimes. The legal concepts applied in Swaziland have their basis in religion, and the king's authority is said to emanate directly from the Christian God.

CURRENT STRUCTURE

Swaziland has both statutory and nonstatutory judicial structures. Nonstatutory structures are of traditional origin and include the family, nongovernmental organizations, chief's courts, *Ndabazabantu* (described below), the church, diviners, security guards, and community police. With regard to the statutory structures they are approached and accessed according to specific needs of different individuals.

Land disputes and cases involving Swazi Nation Land are mainly heard by chief's courts, but *Ndabazabantu* and the king can also hear them. Swazi Nation Land is all land in Swaziland that is not privately owned. Land is allocated to the Municipal Council, which then divides plots and allocates them to people as residential areas. The remainder is Swazi Nation Land, which is held by the king in trust of the people.

In Swaziland the family is considered the deliverer of immediate justice. Socialization forms the basis of family relations, thus dispute resolution begins there. The decision-making body includes the head of the family (always male), his parents, his brothers, and his eldest sister. This council handles cases of a private nature, whereas cases involving public matters are heard in the Magistrates' Courts and high courts. Many Swazis are not content, however, with this structure. They would rather have the family serve as the mediator between complainants and higher judicial bodies. Moreover, the family council is male-dominated, a situation that places women's legal well-being in jeopardy.

When the family council fails to reach decisive agreement on a matter, it is referred to the chiefs. The powers and jurisdiction of chiefs are governed by the Swazi Administration Order of 1998. Cases heard typically concern minor assaults, land disputes, livestock theft, and maintenance issues. This structure is generally considered to be effective and expeditious because the chiefs are not burdened by bureaucracy.

Ndabazabantu, another nonstatutory structure, means "one who likes others' stories." The title originated in the colonial era, when the British established local administrators to adjudicate land disputes, because the colonial office had little understanding of Swazi land practices. In spite of its colonial origin, *Ndabazabantu* is an honored institution in Swaziland, and it is seen as administering justice fairly. The king appoints officers to serve as *Ndabazabantu;* the criteria for selection are unclear. This institution has no jurisdiction over criminal matters and is not empowered to impose prison sentences or fines, nor entitled to sign warrants of attachment for restitution of property in civil matters. Their areas of specialization are reconciliation and consensus matters brought by individuals, families, or chiefs. *Ndabazabantu* can also hear appeals, usually against decisions of chiefs.

Diviners, also referred to as *tangoma* or *tinyanga,* are a prominent source of justice in Swaziland. They exercise significant powers that can influence outcomes in conflicts resolved in the courts. Most people who rely on diviners are from the communal areas.

Institutions of the Christian churches are another nonjudicial structure within the current legal system of Swaziland. They have self-referential power and a passive sense of justice (the churches do not have a legally sanctioned role; they are there to correct the morals in the community).

Other nongovernmental organizations play an important role as entry points in the justice delivery system by challenging social and institutional injustices. Community police are also part of the nonstatutory structures, and they counsel couples on relationship issues.

Statutorily defined bodies include statute law courts, social welfare offices, and the police. The politically modelled, state-regulated mechanism for conflict resolution in Swaziland operates within the context of preserving the country's traditional and customary practices. Swaziland has a dual legal system, which includes Swazi law and custom, on one hand, and general law, on the other. Swazi law and custom, also known as customary law, derive from Roman common law as elaborated by the Dutch (Boers) and as modified by Swazi statutes and traditional practices. It consists of all legally binding customary practices that are not repugnant to natural law. General law in Swaziland is the common law introduced during the colonial period and has its origins in Roman-Dutch law.

This duality traces back to the British principle of indirect rule, which allowed British colonies to manage their own affairs, subject to the suspension of the colonial government. The differences between general law and Swazi law and custom (also known as customary law) have resulted in a certain amount of confusion within the legal system of Swaziland. General law is the more modern, more formalized, and less comprehensive of the two. It applies to the whole population, whereas Swazi law and custom are applicable only to so-called native Swazis. It is regarded by some, controversially, as a secondary system inferior to general law. Customary law is fixed and unchangeable, and it reflects the Swazi way of life.

In fact, Swazi law and custom and general law are not incompatible and often complement each other. Neither are they mutually exclusive, as there are some overlapping aspects between the two. The repugnancy clause of the Swazi Courts Act of 1950 regulates the operation of Swazi national courts, which are considered the inroads into customary territory. The provision makes it clear that customary law is applicable in Swaziland but is limited to matters of a Swazi nature.

The constitution remains the supreme law in Swaziland. All social institutions derive their legitimacy and powers from constitutional provisions. The present Swazi constitution, which is in the process of being rewritten, derives from a 1973 decree that maintained the superiority of general law over customary law and repealed the 1968 constitution. Roman-Dutch law remains the general law of the land and the final arbiter in all matters.

The dual system of general and customary law results in potential infringements of rights of certain persons, usually those to whom customary law applies. One solution that has been put forward is that the dual system be replaced with a uniform system of law under which the nature of a particular conflict will determine which law applies.

COURTS

Civil and criminal courts make up the adjudicating structures in Swaziland. General courts that exercise jurisdiction over all persons include the court of appeal, the high court, Magistrates' Courts, and industrial courts. In civil cases, the defendant is allowed to represent himself or herself or be represented by a lawyer if he or she can afford one. In criminal matters, the state can provide counsel who will present the defense on behalf of the accused. Customary courts, which have jurisdiction only over ethnic Swazis, comprise the Swazi National Courts, Swazi Court of Appeal, and Higher Swazi Court, and judicial commissioners make up the customary courts. At the apex of both general and customary courts is the head of state, the king, in whose name all courts administer cases. In total, thirty general courts operate in Swaziland: one court of appeal, one high court, six Magistrates' Courts, one industrial court, and twenty-one Swazi general courts.

The industrial court is a specialized judicial body concerned with issues of labor. It serves the same functions as the labor court in South Africa. The industrial court is at the same level and has the same jurisdiction as the high court, the only difference being that the industrial court deals with specific issues. An appeal can be brought to the court of appeal directly from the industrial court. This specialized court has proven to be an effective judicial body because it is not overburdened by cases, as are courts that handle a broader range of disputes.

Various legislative bodies in Swaziland regulate the making of laws. Members of the House of Assembly are elected from fifty-five constituencies. The parliament in Swaziland consists of two houses, the Senate, which has no National Council of Provinces, and the Assembly. Bills that have passed these legislatures are sent to the king for approval. The king has ultimate say in all matters of governance, and proposed legislation can become law only with his agreement. Among the statutes that

provide guidelines for the administration of justice in Swaziland is the Swazi Administration Order of 1998, which regulates the operation of Swazi national courts. These courts are empowered to exercise jurisdiction over certain matters by an act of the king in council. The Fourth National Development Plan of Swaziland outlines the purposes and functions of these structures. The Ministry of Justice, as an arm of government, comprises six departments: the Judiciary, the Law Office, the Office of Director of Public Prosecutions, the Office of Registrar General, the Deeds Office, and Correctional Services.

IMPACT

In addition to the inherent confusion in the dual justice system, as discussed earlier, the inaccessibility of the courts is a major issue in Swaziland. Most of the people who need the courts live in remote rural areas far from the urban enclaves where the courts sit, including the high court and the court of appeal, which are located in the capital city, Mbabane. Furthermore, the quality of service from Magistrates' Courts, which because of their wide jurisdiction carry a burdensome caseload, has come in for criticism. The general courts have been viewed as foreign structures, abstract and therefore unapproachable and incomprehensible. They have also been criticized for delay and inefficiency in adjudicating cases. Women are underrepresented in government generally and in the judiciary in particular. The gender disparity must be addressed so as to put capable women in the forefront and prepare them for leadership roles.

Christine Kushinga Matsvai

References and further reading
Bennett, T. W. 1985. *Application of Customary Law in Southern Africa: The Conflict of Personal Laws.* Johannesburg: Jutastat.
Nhlapo, Thandabantu. "Marriage and Divorce in Swazi Law and Custom." B.A. thesis, University of Cape Town.
Swazi: A Political Study. 1965. Pretoria: Africa Institute of South Africa.
Wanda, B. P. 1990. "The Shaping of the Modern Constitution of Swaziland: A Review of Some Social and Historical Factors." *Lesotho Law Journal* 6.
Women and Law in Southern Africa Research and Educational Trust, Swaziland. 2000. *"Charting the Maze": Women in Pursuit of Justice in Swaziland.*

SWEDEN

GENERAL INFORMATION

Geography has played a very important part in the evolution of Sweden. The country is long (approximately a thousand miles) and narrow (two to three hundred miles wide, on average). It has a land surface of 174,000 square miles, of which half is forested. Only 10 percent is cultivated. Water abounds: some 100,000 lakes, the Baltic on

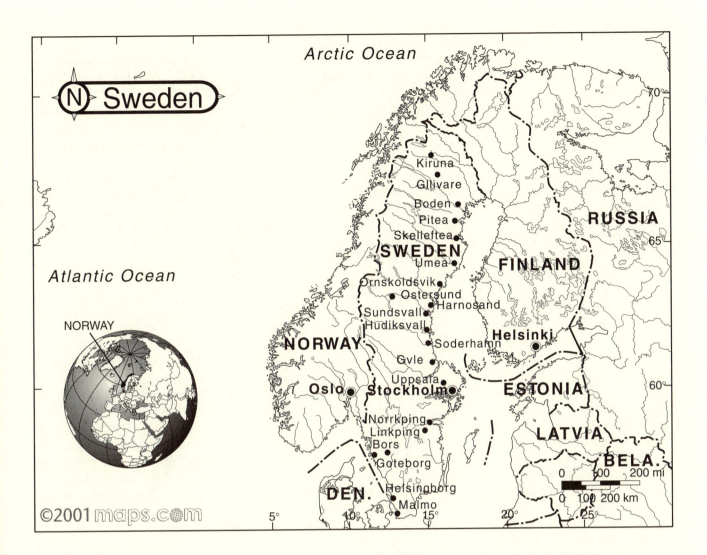

the east, and the North Sea to the west. The coastline is jagged and dotted with thousands of small islands.

Although it is the size and shape of California, Sweden more nearly resembles Alaska in latitude. Its location is tempered, however, by the warming influence of the Gulf Stream, which provides Stockholm—at the same latitude as southern Greenland—with temperatures that range from 20 to 30 degrees Fahrenheit in February and from 54 to 70 degrees in July.

The chief effect of this northern location is felt not in temperature so much as in extremes of light. Summer days are long, and winter days are short. The inhospitable location has also compelled Swedes to be adaptive and inventive, qualities often reflected in Swedish history.

The population of Sweden is 8.9 million, of whom 85 percent live in the southern half of the country. The major population clusters are Stockholm, Göteborg, and Malmö. Swedes are largely of European origin, and have close cultural and linguistic kinship with Danes, Norwegians, and Icelanders.

The relationship with Finland is more cultural than linguistic, even if there is a Swedish-speaking minority in Finland and a Finnish-speaking minority in Sweden. At one time or another, all the Nordic countries have been united with each other, if not always happily.

There is also a small Sami (Lapp) population in northern Sweden. While the Lapps are still conscious of their own identity, which is protected under Swedish law, the tendency in recent years has been toward greater assimilation.

As recently as the beginning of the 1950s, Sweden was usually characterized as a country with a highly homogeneous population. Because of labor immigration in the 1950s and the 1960s, and a flood of asylum-seekers since then, one can no longer speak of Swedish homogeneity. For example, although 85 percent of the population are still nominally members of the Swedish State Lutheran Church, there are now substantial numbers of Catholics (166,000) and Moslems (about 200,000).

By 1999, more than 400,000 foreign citizens lived in Sweden. The main groups were Finns (100,000), Bosnians (44,000), Norwegians (31,000), Iraqis (27,000), Yugoslavs (26,000), Danes (25,000), Iranians (20,000), and Turks (17,000).

Because of shifts in immigration patterns toward people of nonwestern European cultures, by the 1970s a number of tensions and problems had begun to arise. These included xenophobia, unemployment, asylum-seekers dependent on government support, and the creation of ghettoes in large urban apartment blocks.

All in all, these created situations typical of an emerging European multicultural society, in spite of the strenuous efforts of the Swedish government to provide for a smoother transition and a more tolerant atmosphere. These efforts include legislation that has criminalized racial and religious bigotry.

Sweden has a long history of respect for law. The Swedish legal tradition is sui generis. It belongs neither to the civil law nor to common law family, but contains elements of both. In its overall outlook, Sweden is probably closer to the civil law tradition, but in many respects—especially in its law of procedure and use of judicial precedent—it has moved closer to the Anglo-American approach in recent years.

HISTORY

Swedish political history begins with the settlement of several Germanic tribes in what is present-day Scandinavia. During the Viking Age, 800–1050, Swedish energies spilled abroad, mainly toward the Baltic and Russia. The Vikings did not only plunder and kill. They also were farmers and traders, who settled in many of the places they reached. Sweden was Christianized in the eleventh century. Swedish provinces had already acquired ethnic and legal identities by the thirteenth century, and by the reign of Magnus Ericsson, 1319–1364, a law code common to the entire country was created. Between 1397 and 1521, the period of the Kalmar Union, Sweden was dominated by Denmark. For about two hundred years after the middle of the fourteenth century, Swedish commerce was dominated by the German-controlled Hanseatic League. The emergence of the modern Swedish national state is a product of the successful revolt by Gustav Vasa against the Danes in 1521.

In the seventeenth and eighteenth centuries, Sweden became a Great Power, especially during the reign of Gustavas Adolphus (1611–1632). Its reach extended beyond the Nordic area into both Central and Eastern Europe.

The Swedish parliament (Riksdag) dates back to 1435. It was, however, only sporadically powerful, especially during the early eighteenth century, and the country was more often than not ruled by strong monarchs until the twentieth century.

The Constitution (Instrument of Government) of 1809 was created on the basis of separation of powers, with a powerful monarchy balanced against the Riksdag, composed of four estates (nobility, clergy, bourgeoisie, and farmers). In 1866 the Riksdag became a bicameral legislature. It became increasingly democratic during the nineteenth and twentieth centuries. The franchise was expanded, and the king gradually lost all real power; by the 1920s Sweden had become a constitutional parliamentary democracy. By the 1930s, political life was given its direction by a powerful working-class movement composed of a Social Democratic Party and its allies in the trade union movement. This Social Democratic hegemony, except for brief periods (1976–1982, 1991–1994), has been maintained since 1933, even as the Swedish population became more white-collar in its composition. The Social Democratic movement, even if it has been assisted by the non-socialist parties, has been the main architect of the Swedish Welfare State, sometimes referred to as the Swedish Model. The Swedish system, a combination of reform socialism and a market economy, was widely regarded for a long time as a "third way" between untrammeled capitalism and dogmatic Marxism.

In 1974 a new Instrument of Government was drafted; it did not represent any radical departure from the Swedish tradition, but rather an acknowledgment of changes already in practice. Sole power to make law was given to a unicameral legislature composed of 350 members elected for three-year terms. These were later changed to four-year terms, and to a membership of 349, so as to avoid in the future a repetition of the tie votes that had became common. Executive power was placed solely in the cabinet (Regeringen) and prime minister (Statsminister). The prime minister can be overthrown only by a majority of the parliament.

Organic, or constitutional, laws in Sweden are those that, unlike ordinary laws, can be repealed or modified only by extraordinary legislative measures. To amend the constitution, the Riksdag must pass two identical measures, in two separate legislative sessions, with a general election intervening.

There are provisions for referenda, which can be called when supported by a third of the members of parliament. The referenda are normally advisory only, but in constitutional questions the results of the referendum are binding if a majority of the voters opposed the proposed measure.

There are four separate documents that make up the Swedish Constitution. These are the Instrument of Government, the Act of Succession, the Freedom of the Press Act, and the Fundamental Law on Freedom of Expression.

Swedes have a long tradition of protecting civil and social rights. The Instrument of Government contains certain rights (for example, freedom of worship, prohibition against ex post facto laws, prohibition against capital or corporal punishment). These can be abridged only by changing the constitution. Other rights are enumerated (these include freedom of speech, association, and assembly) but can be regulated by the Riksdag if there are countervailing reasons.

Recent concerns for eliminating bigotry against women and minorities are reflected in the current Instrument of Government. It prohibits any laws that disfavor a person because of race, color, ethnic origin, or sex, unless those laws are part of any effort to bring about greater equality.

The Freedom of the Press Act was first passed in 1966. In its present version, it establishes the freedom for individuals to express opinions, prohibits censorship, and allows generous public access to official documents. Cases involving freedom of the press, unlike ordinary criminal actions, are tried by a jury. If the jury finds for acquittal, its verdict cannot be appealed.

The Fundamental Law on freedom of expression also enjoys constitutional status. It was adopted in 1991 and extends freedom of press guarantees to media other than printed matter. This includes radio, television, films, videos, CDs, and tapes. The major difference between this document and the Freedom of the Press Act is that prior scrutiny may be given to films and videos intended for public exhibition.

Another growing source of individual rights for Swedish citizens derives from Sweden's membership in the European Union (1995). The Swedish government, like that of all member states, is limited by the treaty of accession as well as by the legislative acts, regulations, and directives of the EU. The decisions of the European Court of Justice, when acting within its area of competence, override Swedish domestic law. Perhaps an even more important source of individual rights is that Sweden is also a signatory to the European Convention on Human Rights, which carries with it subjection to decisions of the European Court of Human Rights. These have been specifically incorporated into Swedish law.

In at least one respect—transparency of government acts—Sweden is well ahead of most European countries. The principle of public access to all official documents of both the central and local governments is fully established, both in theory and practice. Before any exception is permitted, there must be legal justification (for example, the Official Secrets Act).

During the twentieth century, Sweden has undergone a development as rapid, as complete, and as peaceful as that of any country in the world. Throughout much of the nineteenth century, Sweden was a poor country, dependent on farming, fishing, and extractive industries such as timber and iron ore. Large numbers of discontented Swedes left the country, bound especially for the United States.

From the last quarter of the nineteenth century, however, the story has been one of rapid progress. Political life was reformed and democratized. The population became more urbanized, and the economy shifted toward engineering and manufacturing, often producing export goods of very high quality. Much of the development took place on the old estate workshops (*bruk*), producing a decentralization of industrial development facilitated by abundant hydroelectric power.

By 1999 the GDP was distributed as follows: agriculture, 2 percent; industry, 28 percent; and services, 70 percent.

A productive economy, full employment, and a high level of social security became the major aims of Swedish governmental policy after the accession to power of the Social Democrats in the 1930s. The political process came to be based on a consensus brokered with opposition parties by the Social Democrats.

All this inevitably entailed the rise of a large public sector. By the 1970s the industrial emphasis was already shifting toward a more service-oriented economy, and the white collars began to outnumber the blue ones. By the end of the twentieth century, Sweden had become the global leader in the diffusion of access to information technology (IT) among its population. By 2000 more than 50 percent of Swedish houses had personal computers, more than 70 percent of the population used computers at work, and almost everyone used mobile telephones.

One important factor in Sweden's transformation from poverty to prosperity has been its foreign policy of neutrality. That policy, aided at times by good luck, has kept Sweden out of war since Napoleonic times. Neutrality, however, has not meant disarmament, pacifism, or a quiescent foreign policy. Since the end of World War II, Sweden has been an active member of the United Nations, a supporter of humanitarian rights, a provider of aid for Third World countries, and a supporter of peaceful conflict resolution. Sweden became known also for its frequent and active criticism of U.S. involvement in the Vietnam War. While membership in the EU has not meant an official end to Sweden's policy of neutrality, it has at the very least modified it.

LEGAL CONCEPTS

Widespread respect for law has helped to create a climate of agreement between elites and the public, and hence, a reduced need for the use of force as a way of bringing about compliance with the law. Other related components of this consensus include a confirmed attachment to the notion of transparency in government—aided by an energetic free press—as well as strong belief in constitutionalism, democracy, and individual rights. These would include not only the traditional individual rights (such as freedom of speech) but also newer ones—for example, group rights of women, children, and minorities.

Two other institutions that reinforce the widespread belief in legality are peculiar to Sweden, at least in their inception. These are the ombudsmen, who act as public tribunes, and the *remiss* procedure, used in the passage of important legislation.

The Office of the Parliamentary Ombudsman (Justitieombudsman, or J.O.) was created in 1809 and has been much imitated, with varying success, in other countries. At present, it consists of four ombudsmen, appointed by and responsible to the parliament. Their chief duty is to oversee the courts and the administration in order to ensure that they act within the law in individual cases. They can initiate prosecutions, and they can criticize the shortcomings of public employees, either in their annual report to the parliament or in the press.

More recently, other similar ombudsman offices have been created to represent, respectively, the interests of consumers, children, ethnic minorities, the handicapped, and, most recently, gays and lesbians. Although these newer ombudsmen are not appointed by the parliament, they function in similar ways to the traditional ombudsmen.

Another feature unique to Sweden is the *remiss* procedure for the passage of legislation, used for most if not all major laws. It is an involved, detailed, and time-consuming process. The end results, however, are laws that have been not only passed by the parliament and cabinet but also subjected to participation and consultation by opposition parties and major interest group organizations. Not all government legislation follows this path. Sometimes, in the interest of speed, legislation will be made mainly by a cabinet ministry and the parliament.

What follows is an abbreviated description of that process. The cabinet appoints a Commission of Enquiry to scrutinize a policy area (for example, a new health service) and make proposals for appropriate legislation. Commission members typically include both government and opposition M.P.s, representatives of interest groups, and some experts on the subject matter under consideration. Junior judges often act as secretaries to the commissions. The final report is printed and farmed out (*remiss* procedure) to government agencies and nongovernmental organizations for feedback.

The appropriate ministry prepares a revised bill based on the *remiss*. This goes to the parliament, which also examines and debates the bill. On occasion, it will be sent to the Law Council (Lagrådet) for an advisory predetermination of how it fits with existing Swedish law.

Because of the exhaustive process of touching all bases through which most important Swedish legislation passes, the result is a rich legislative history that can help the judges who later interpret the law. In addition, the law acquires enhanced legitimacy simply because most of the groups interested in it will have been consulted before the law assumes its final form. Furthermore, divisive issues, such as abortion, will have been put to rest in a consensus so durable that the issue is not likely to rise from the ashes to become troublesome again in the future.

Another conceptual feature of Swedish law that bears noting is that it is, by comparison with much U.S. law,

quite secular and "progressive." Cultural change is acknowledged and reflected in the law rather quickly in Sweden. For example, Sweden was among the first to pass parental leave legislation and laws removing the legal stigma of "illegitimate" birth. In 1999, Sweden passed a Registered Partnership Act, which allowed same-sex civil unions; in 1999, the Ombudsman against Discrimination on the Basis of Sexual Orientation was created. And Sweden changed the laws on prostitution in 1999; in a reversal of the usual approach, the patrons of prostitution, and not its practitioners, were subject to punishment.

While Swedish law is firmly anchored in an old national tradition, that is by no means inbred. There is much legislative harmonization with the laws of the other Nordic countries. Sweden's membership in the EU has also subjected it to supranational legal influences. Furthermore, the Swedish legislative process also regularly attempts to canvass the legal approaches of foreign countries, when relevant.

Swedish political beliefs support the idea of a strong central government with broad positive powers to undertake extensive social reform. At the apex of this system are a powerful cabinet and prime minister supported by a disciplined party system. The parties, ranging more or less from right to left, are: Moderates (Conservatives), Liberals, Center (formerly Agrarians), Christian Democrats, Greens, Social Democrats, and the Left (formerly Communist). Parties are proportionally represented in the parliament, both nationally and by election district. Parties must clear 4 percent of the national vote, or 12 percent in any one election district, in order to gain representation.

The parliament is a cross-section of Swedish occupational and professional life. Women constitute half the cabinet and almost half the parliament. By U.S. standards, the number of lawyers is few, and the number of public sector employees is large.

With such a large public sector, public administration is an important part of the Swedish political system. Any tendencies toward bureaucratic arbitrariness are countered by an insistence on the rules of law, transparency, and accountability. Not only are judges part of the civil service, but it is also true that all civil servants are expected to function like judges—that is, in accordance with legal rules known beforehand. Civil servants are free to take part in politics, even to hold office.

In spite of the unitary tendencies in Swedish government, there is a long tradition of local and regional involvement, which has grown more vigorous in recent years. The country is divided into twenty-one counties (*län*), each of which has a county administration (*länstyrelse*) and governor (*landshövding*) appointed by the central government. There is also a popularly elected county legislature (*landsting*), with considerable local

Legal Structure of Swedish Courts

Ordinary Courts

The Supreme Court (Högstdomstolen), Final court of appeal in criminal and civil cases.

6 Courts of Appeal (Hovrätter), Intermediate courts of appeal, which hear questions of law and fact.

95 District Courts (Tingsrätter), Trial courts with criminal and civil jurisdiction.

Administrative Courts

23 County administrators courts (Länsrätter), Lowest level of administrative courts, which hear complaints against administrative authorities.

4 Regional Administrative Courts of Appeal (Kammarrätter), Intermediate appellate courts, which hear appeals from provincial courts.

The Supreme Administrative Court (Regeringsrätt), Administrative court of last resort.

Special Courts

Examples include:
Labor Court
Land Courts
Insurance Courts

power. There are almost three hundred local governments (*kommun*) that have considerable power, for example, in matters relating to public schools.

CURRENT STRUCTURES

The constitution establishes an independent judiciary, totally insulated from political influence, both in the appointment of judges and in their work. Neither the Riksdag nor the cabinet can compel a court to decide a case in a certain way. There is no separate constitutional court (as in Germany). The ordinary courts do have the power of judicial review but in practice do not use it.

There are three types of courts in Sweden: the ordinary courts, with both civil and criminal jurisdiction; the administrative courts, which hear cases involving a conflict between public authorities and private citizens; and, finally, a number of special courts (for example, Labor Court).

The ordinary courts form a three-tiered system. At the lowest level are the District Courts (*tingsrätt*). There are ninety-five of these, varying in size from one or two judges to eighty (in Stockholm). These are the basic trial level for all civil and criminal cases. Civil cases are usually tried by three judges—sometimes by only one judge if the parties agree, or if the case is simplified. Most criminal and some family cases are tried by one judge and a panel of three elected lay assessors (*nämdemän*). These lay assessors, like the professional judges, rule on both questions of law and of fact.

The Courts of Appeal (*hovrätter*) are intermediate appellate courts. There are six of these; the oldest and most prestigious is the Svea Hovrätt, founded in 1614, which sits in Stockholm. If the lower court decided a case with lay assessor participation, the Court of Appeal is ordinarily made up of three judges and two lay assessors. If the lower court decision was made without lay assessors, the appellate court is made up of three or four judges alone.

The Supreme Court (*Högsta domstolen*) is at the top of the ordinary court system. It reserves the right to select cases for review, usually on the grounds of their precedental value. There are sixteen judges on the court, of which normally five hear a case. If the court is considering overruling one of its own precedents, it will sit in plenary session. Judges at this level review both questions of law and fact.

Swedish judicial procedure has been moving steadily away from the civil law approach. Since the procedural code of 1948 as amended in 1987, Swedish trials have aimed at increasing the common law preferences for immediacy, orality, and concentration. Most court judgments are based on a concentrated main oral stage in which all the evidence is heard. In civil cases, there is an earlier preparatory stage, also usually oral. In criminal cases, the main hearing is preceded by a preliminary investigation conducted by public prosecutors. In the appellate courts, there is also usually an oral main hearing, but in appropriate circumstances cases can be decided by written proceedings alone.

The winning party is usually reimbursed for litigation expenses by the losers. Legal aid is available even in civil cases. There is an income test, and an applicant may have to pay a part of the expenses according to a sliding scale. Most Swedes nowadays have litigation insurance, usually tied to their home and automobile insurance.

In criminal cases, the prosecutor has wide discretion whether to prosecute. If the decision is not to prosecute, the victim can prosecute a private case, but that rarely happens. The Swedish prosecutorial system is nationally organized into seven districts, all under the office of the prosecutor general (*Riksåklagare*).

Criminal sanctions include both imprisonment and fines. There is a reluctance to impose imprisonment, especially in the case of first offenders or juveniles. There is, however, a distinctively Swedish type of day-fine (*dagsböter*), whereby the amount is graded according to the financial position of the offender.

Sweden has a well-developed system of administrative courts. Questions with a predominantly political content can be resolved by the cabinet. Questions of a legal nature, however, are handled by a system of administrative courts. At the lowest level, there are twenty-three County Administrative Courts (*länsrätter*), which decide cases usually before a trained judge and three lay assessors. Procedure is similar to that in civil cases, albeit simpler. It also places less emphasis than does civil procedure on orality, immediacy, and concentration.

Appeals go, usually by permission, to one of four Administrative Courts of Appeal (*Kammarrätter*). Further appeals, mostly those with precedental importance, go to the Supreme Administrative Court (*Regeringsrätten*). It has seventeen members, of which two-thirds must be legally trained. Five judges constitute a quorum.

The most important center of private dispute resolution is the Stockholm Chamber of Commerce. The chamber maintains one institute for arbitration and another for mediation. Stockholm is also one of the major centers for international arbitration. During the Cold War, it offered services for arbitrating U.S.-Soviet transactions. Sweden's reputation as a neutral country no doubt fortified its position as an arbitration site. The high quality of its judiciary may also have enhanced the Swedish reputation, since there is no impediment in Sweden to judges serving as arbitrators.

The most prominent special court is the Labor Court (*Arbetsdomstol*), created in 1929. This court has helped provide the labor peace that underpinned the Swedish spirit of compromise within which the welfare state was shaped. The Labor Court has jurisdiction over all labor-management disputes, including the power to make a binding interpretation of collective bargaining agreements.

Seven members are required for a quorum. Two are appointed on the recommendation of labor and management organizations, respectively. These appointees usually have no legal training. Of the other appointees, the chairman and the deputy chairman have legal training, and the third one is chosen for special expertise in labor market matters.

Other specialized courts include the Market Court, created in 1971 after the analogy of the Labor Court. It has jurisdiction over cases involving restraints on competition. There are also the Court of Patent Appeals, Land Courts, Environmental Courts, and Maritime Law Courts.

STAFFING

Careers of lawyers and judges begin with a common training. This consists of four and a half years of law study at a Swedish university, leading to the master of law degree.

While lawyers (*advokater*) may develop specialized practices, there is no division comparable to the one in Britain between barristers and solicitors. The number of attorneys is small (about thirty-two hundred). Lawyers are not especially active or influential in Swedish political life.

Legal counsel is not required in civil trials, but it is usually employed. In criminal cases, the court will appoint defense counsel, who must be a member of the Swedish Bar Association (Sveriges Advokatsamfund). Defendants can, of course, choose their own counsel if they are financially able and so wish.

Choice of a judicial career is usually made by the end of law school. Law graduates usually serve a two-year apprenticeship as clerks at a District Court or County Administrative Court. They can then apply to become judicial trainees at a Court of Appeal or Administrative Court of Appeal. For several years, they are in training to prepare and present a variety of cases. After a probation period, they can be appointed to the bench as associate judges. After six to eight years, they can be appointed as permanent judges at the appellate level.

IMPACT

Swedes have a pronounced attachment to the rule of law. The social and political life of the country is permeated with this respect for law and legality, which even reaches into the daily routines of public administration. It is supported by a willingness of elites and public alike to follow the rules created by legislative, executive, and judicial bodies. It includes an aversion to any element of arbitrariness in the making, enforcing, or interpreting of the rules.

Judges are highly respected. They are also often used in nonjudicial capacities—that is, as clerks to commissions of inquiry. They play an indirect role in policymaking, and their putative objectivity in these capacities strongly reinforces the regard for law and for the judiciary.

Joseph Board

See also Constitutional Law; Denmark; Finland; Government Legal Departments; Judicial Independence; Norway
References and further reading
Board, Joseph B. 1988. "The Courts in Sweden." Pp. 181–198 in *The Political Role of Law Courts in Modern Democracies.* Edited by Jerold L. Waltman and Kenneth M. Holland. New York: Macmillan.

———. 1991. "Judicial Activism in Sweden." Pp. 175–188 in *Judicial Activism in Comparative Perspective.* Edited by Kenneth M. Holland. New York: St. Martin's.

"General Facts on Sweden." 1999. Swedish Institute Website: http://www.si.se.

Holmberg, Erik, and Nils Stjernquist. 1995. *Vår författning.* 12th ed. Stockholm: Norstedts juridik.

"Law and Justice in Sweden." 1999. Swedish Institute Website: http://www.si.se.

National Courts Administration (Domstolsverket). http://www.dom.se.

Runblom, Harald. 1998. "Sweden as a Multicultural Society." Swedish Institute Website: http://www.si.se.

Scott, Franklin D. 1977. *Sweden: The Nation's History.* Minneapolis: University of Minnesota Press.

Strömholm, Stig, ed. 1981. *An Introduction to Swedish Law.* Stockholm: Norstedt.

"Swedish Government." 1997. Swedish Institute Website: http://www.si.se.

"Sweden in the European Union." 1998. Swedish Institute Website: http://www.si.se.

SWISS CANTONS

LEGAL CONCEPTS

In Article 1 of the new Federal Constitution of the Swiss Confederation of April 18, 1999, the twenty-six Swiss cantons and half-cantons are enumerated. These are Zurich, Berne, Lucerne, Uri, Schwyz, Obwald, and Nidwald (half-cantons), Glarus, Zug, Fribourg, Solothurn, Basel-City, and Basel-Land (half-cantons), Schaffhausen, Appenzell Outer Rhodes, and Appenzell Inner Rhodes (half-cantons), St. Gall, Grisons, Aargau, Thurgau, Ticino, Vaud, Valais, Neuchâtel, Geneva, and Jura.

In general, the twenty-six Swiss cantons and half-cantons are not only autonomous in law, they also vary in many other points, such as size, populations, culture, and language. Although Switzerland only covers an area of about 41,300 square kilometers, the country with its twenty-six cantons and half-cantons is a colorful mix of cultures. Therefore, different regions are regarded as being comparable to different countries by many people. With respect to the language, Switzerland has four official languages (Article 4 of the Federal Constitution of the Swiss Confederation): German, French, Italian, and Romansh. German is spoken by some 64 percent of the population, 19 percent speak French, and 8 percent speak Italian. Romansh is spoken by less than 1 percent of the population, and the remaining 8 percent of the population speak other languages.

Like the American states, the Swiss cantons exist in a federal system of shared powers and overlapping responsibilities. The relationship between the confederation and the cantons and half-cantons is dominated by the principle that the cantons are sovereign insofar as their sovereignty is not limited by the Federal Constitution (Article 3). Therefore, the confederation shall accomplish the tasks that are attributed to it by the Federal Constitution. The confederation also shall assume the tasks that require uniform regulation (Article 42). This means that all the tasks that are not attributed to the confederation remain in the competence of the cantons (*see* Häfelin and Haller 2001, 299).

In Article 47, the constitution of the Swiss Confederation enacts that the confederation shall respect the autonomy of the cantons. On the other side, it is clear that the Swiss cantons and half-cantons have to respect federal law and therefore are not allowed to overrule federal law (*see* Article 49).

All Swiss cantons and half-cantons are ruled by a republican form of government with separate legislative, executive, and judicial branches (Dessemontet and Ansay 1995, 4). The Federal Constitution of the Swiss Confederation declares in Article 51 that every canton shall adopt a democratic constitution. These cantonal constitutions must be approved by the people, and must be subject to revision if required by a majority of the people. If the cantonal constitutions are not contrary to federal law, they must be guaranteed by the confederation, and the confederation shall grant this guarantee.

The cantonal constitutions commonly contain the same basic matters as the Swiss Federal Constitution. Many of them contain a catalog with the fundamental rights, such as human dignity, equality before the law, principle of good faith, right to live and personal freedom, right to privacy, freedom of religion and opinion, freedom of language, and economic freedom. All these fundamental rights are also guaranteed by the Federal Constitution of the Swiss Confederation (*see* Article 7). For this reason, the cantonal guarantees concerning fundamental rights do not have an autonomous importance anymore.

Many of the cantonal constitutions are quite new (such as the constitution of the Canton of Berne), but others find their origins in the nineteenth century. The Canton of Zurich has one of the oldest constitutions, issued on April 18, 1869. Therefore, some parts of it do not have much relevance anymore, and some parts are written in a very antiquated language. Thus, it is not surprising that, due to its old age, the constitution of the Canton of Zurich has been revised more than forty times.

Apart from the above-mentioned federal principles, the twenty-six Swiss cantons and half-cantons still retain many areas of competence. The most important of these cantonal competencies are: organization of the canton, taxes, construction, regional and local infrastructure, police, education, health, and social welfare. Although these are cantonal competencies in general, they are partly complementary to federal competencies (Jaag 1999, 3).

The organization of the cantons still differs considerably from canton to canton. With respect to the legislative, the cantonal Parliaments are unicameral and count between 50 and 200 members (for example, 180 members in the Parliament of the Canton of Zurich). In a very few cantons and half-cantons, the so-called Landsgemeinde still exist, which are people's assemblies where the voters meet to decide on various questions and for elections. The cantonal executive branch is headed by a collegial government, and—as at the federal level (*see* Article 174)—coalitions and annual change of presidency are the rule (Dessemontet and Ansay 1995, 4).

CURRENT COURT SYSTEM STRUCTURE

In Switzerland, civil and criminal law is federal. In contrast to the substantive federal law, all of the twenty-six Swiss cantons and half-cantons still have their own code of criminal and civil procedure. Although there are various similarities, these cantonal codes present a very colorful picture (Dessemontet and Ansay 1995, 241, 267). The current cantonal competence for criminal and civil (and also administrative) procedure legislation is only limited by the fundamental rights of the Federal Constitution of the Swiss Confederation, some federal laws also concerning civil and criminal procedures, and the jurisdiction of the Federal Tribunal in Lausanne.

In the beginning of the year 2000, Switzerland voted for a judicial revision. This revision is not yet in force; it will probably only come into force in 2004. One part of this revision consists in harmonizing criminal and civil procedures all over Switzerland.

The civil, criminal, and administrative courts at the trial level in Switzerland are usually cantonal (Pestalozzi and Pestalozzi 1997, 109; see diagram).

Swiss cantonal courts are generally not divided into civil and criminal courts (see figure). The twenty-six Swiss cantons and half-cantons normally operate a two-tier court structure: Each canton and half-canton has a district court (Bezirksgericht, Amtsgericht/tribunal de première instance). Normally, these district courts consist of three or five members. Their jurisdiction covers civil and criminal cases that are not specially assigned to other tribunals. In cases with lower amounts in dispute or in cases with accelerated procedures, a single judge or a commission is competent to settle the disputes (Dessemontet and Ansay 1995, 268). Cases on appeal are assigned in the first instance to the cantonal high court (Obergericht, Appellationsgericht, Kantonsgericht/tribunal cantonal, cour de justice).

Cases on appeal from the cantonal high court go then to the Swiss Federal Supreme Court (Bundesgericht/tribunal fédéral) in Lausanne (Canton of Vaud). The Swiss Federal Supreme Court normally does not consider the facts of cases, but only questions of law. Although the

Legal Structure of Swiss Cantons Courts

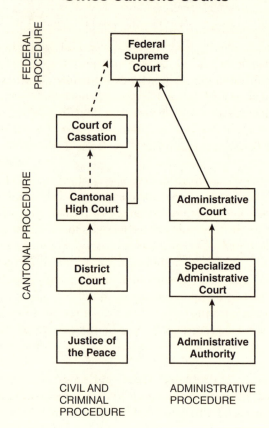

Federal Supreme Court is the court of last resort on federal constitutional matters, it may not, however, declare a federal law unconstitutional: Article 191 of the Federal Constitution of the Swiss Confederation precludes judicial control of the constitutionality of federal statutes and international law.

In the civil procedure of Swiss cantons and half-cantons, justices of the peace or mediators (*Friedensrichter, Vermittler/juge de paix*) have an important function. They try, as a first resort, to settle civil disputes between the parties by working out a draft settlement. If the conciliation fails, the justice of the peace or mediator issues a document entitling the claimant to introduce action before the competent tribunal. If there are only extremely small claims involved, the justices of the peace or mediators act as judges, which means that they have competence to find the decision (Dessemontet and Ansay 1995, 268).

Apart from the above-mentioned ordinary courts for civil and penal jurisdiction, many cantons and half-cantons have specialized courts (Dessemontet and Ansay 1995, 268):

- In four cantons (Zurich, Berne, St. Gall, Aargau), there are commercial courts for civil matters (*Handelsgericht/tribunal de commerce*). They have jurisdiction over commercial transactions of a certain importance if both parties or at least one party is listed as a firm in the commercial register. Normally they consist of two judges and three assessors, which are drawn from the local chambers of commerce.

- For labor disputes, thirteen cantons and half-cantons have specialized courts that consist of an employer representative, an employee representative, and a member of the district court acting as chairman (*Arbeitsgericht/tribunal de travail, tribunal des prud'hommes*).
- The cantons of Zurich, Fribourg, Vaud, and Geneva have a similar system for rent disputes (*Mietgericht/tribunal des baux*).
- Finally, three cantons and half-cantons (Zurich, Appenzell Inner Rhodes, St. Gall) have a court of cassation (*Kassationsgericht/court de cassation*). They are competent in cases where important rules of procedure may have been violated.

Many Swiss cantons have administrative courts (*Verwaltungsgericht/tribunal administratif*), which are separated from the ordinary courts for civil and penal jurisdiction into special courts of their own (Dessemontet and Ansay 1995, 268; see diagram). Moreover, some cantons have, apart from their general administrative courts, specialized administrative courts (*Rekurskommission/commission de recours*). They are responsible for jurisdiction in certain matters of administrative law, such as construction law, taxation law, and expropriation law (for the Canton of Zurich *see* Jaag 1999, 87).

In 1998, the twenty-six Swiss cantons and half-cantons spent 4,612 million Swiss francs for justice and police (including fire departments), which corresponds to more than 8 percent of the financial expenses of the Swiss cantons and half-cantons.

STAFFING

The admission of lawyers to the profession is controlled by each of the twenty-six cantons and half-cantons. If a lawyer has to plead in courts in other cantons and half-cantons, he has to apply to the relevant cantonal bar to seek permission. As this situation is quite impractical, especially in a small country like Switzerland, the Swiss Parliament has enacted a new law (*Bundesgesetz über die Freizügigkeit der Anwältinnen und Anwälte vom 23 Juni 2000*) permitting the free movement of Swiss attorneys and attorneys from the European Union within the twenty-six cantons and half-cantons. This legislation, which will probably come into force in the beginning of the year 2002, will allow lawyers to move freely about Switzerland without any bureaucratic restrictions.

A young lawyer who wants to become an attorney has to spend a training period of at least one year at a court or with a law firm. After completing this training period he has to pass an additional examination (*see* Article 7, *Bundesgesetz über die Freizügigkeit*). This examination is held before a cantonal committee of judges, attorneys, and law professors. Having passed this examination and after registration in a special cantonal register for attorneys, a lawyer has to be given permission to exercise his profession in any other Swiss canton and half-canton without further restrictions (*see* Article 4, *Bundesgesetz über die Freizügigkeit*; also Dessemontet and Ansay 1995, 269).

Swiss lawyers and lawyers from the European Union who want to exercise their profession in Switzerland have to respect certain professional rules for lawyers. These rules are now stated in the new federal law for lawyers (*see* Article 12, *Bundesgesetz über die Freizügigkeit*). Disciplinary proceedings against attorneys who do not or did not respect these professional rules are administered by cantonal courts or by special committees consisting of judges and attorneys.

Generally there is no need to join a cantonal bar association in order to practice in court. Nevertheless, a great number of Swiss lawyers are organized in these (normally) private bar associations. These associations have their own professional rules and their own jurisdiction.

To become a judge, a formal legal education is generally not required. Swiss judges normally join a political party, which is why the political parties play an important role in the (pre-) selection and election of judges. Cantonal judges are elected by political authorities. For lower jurisdiction (for example, district court), there generally are people's elections; judges for higher courts (for example, high court, administrative court) are elected by cantonal parliaments. Although there is no need for a formal legal education, nowadays most judges have a law school degree. However, judges with nonlegal professional backgrounds are still found in primary courts and even in cantonal tribunals of appeal (Dessemontet and Ansay 1995, 269).

Judges are supported by clerks. These clerks usually have a formal legal education and are responsible for the minutes of the proceedings and the formulation of decisions.

Thomas Wipf

See also Switzerland

References and further reading
Dessemontet, François, and Tugrul Ansay. 1995. *Introduction to Swiss Law.* 2d ed. The Hague/Boston/London: Kluwer International.
Häfelin, Ulrich, and Walter Haller. 2001. *Schweizerisches Bundesstaatsrecht.* 5th ed. Zurich: Schulthess.
Jaag, Tobias. 1999. *Verwaltungsrecht des Kantons Zürich.* 2d ed. Zurich: Schulthess.
Pestalozzi, Gmuer, and Patry Pestalozzi. 1997. *Business Law Guide to Switzerland.* 2d ed. Bicester/Oxfordshire: CCH Europe.
Statistisches Jahrbuch der Schweiz. 2001. Zurich: Institut Orell Füssl.

SWITZERLAND

GENERAL INFORMATION

Switzerland is situated in the center of Western Europe, surrounded by Germany, Austria, Liechtenstein, Italy, and France. Most of the population of 7.2 million live in the flatter regions of Switzerland, between the Alps and the Jura. Some 5.6 million inhabitants are Swiss nationals, 1.4 million foreigners. Approximately another 400,000 Swiss nationals live abroad (250,000 in other European countries, 110,000 in North or South America). The population of Switzerland is made up of persons with very different cultural backgrounds. This diversity is reflected in the religions: 46 percent are Roman Catholic, 40 percent Protestant, 7.4 percent do not belong to any religion, and the rest to various religions.

The size of Switzerland is only 41,284 square kilometers, the distance from north to south being 220 kilometers, from west to east 350 kilometers. Most of the population live in the so-called midland, a relatively small band of 50 to 100 kilometers stretching from the Lac Léman (Geneva) in the west to the Lake of Constance in the east. Within this region, almost all major cities and industrial enterprises are to be found, as well as most of the agricultural areas. Currently, two-thirds of the population live in urban areas, and a third in rural areas. The urban population covers about 17 percent of Switzerland, corresponding to a very high population density of 696 persons/square kilometer. About a fourth of Switzerland is unproductive area, mainly mountains; a third is covered by forest.

Switzerland has very few natural resources and was, for many centuries, a poor country. Today Switzerland has one of the highest incomes per capita in the world, key industries being the services sector, the chemical industry, machinery and tools, and banking. Equally important for the prosperous development of the country is the political stability and reliability of the infrastructure and all kinds of services. The unemployment rate is very low; in 1999 it was 3.2 percent, whereas the average unemployment rate within the European Union was 9.4 percent. There are hardly any strikes, and in 1999 in the whole of Switzerland, only 2,675 working days were lost due to strikes. The inflation rate is very low, usually less than or around 1 percent per year.

Switzerland belongs among the civil law systems. Its constitution reflects the strong influence of direct democracy, which in this form and extent is probably unique in the world. The different cultural influences—mainly from the French and Swiss-German speaking regions—are reflected in the legal system of Switzerland, in particular in its civil law.

HISTORY

At the beginning of August 1291, the three communities of Uri, Schwyz, and Nidwalden signed an assistance treaty in order to protect themselves against external aggression. This treaty (Bundesbrief) is regarded as the origin of the Swiss Confederation. August 1 has become the national day of Switzerland. In addition, the treaty expressed its respect for the law and stated that "we will accept no judge in our valleys who shall have obtained his office for a price, or who is not a native and resident among us" (Salamin, *Documents d'histoire suisse 1240 –1516*, 16). In the fourteenth and fifteenth centuries, ten other cantons joined this alliance. Switzerland became a substantial military power within Europe, and its soldiers were highly in demand by most European countries. In the battle of Marignano in 1515, the inevitable happened: Swiss soldiers fought both on the Italian and the opposing French side. This experience led to the concept of permanent Swiss neutrality. Also in the light of the Reformation, which split the already culturally diverse regions of the Swiss into Roman Catholics and Protestants, neutrality became an important factor for the confederation not to be torn apart in the religious wars in Europe. The deeply rooted conviction that the Swiss should not take part in any war has therefore also very important roots in internal politics. The alliance could prosper only at the price of refraining from playing an active role in future European wars. The advantage gained was a generally high political stability.

Switzerland's history has once been described as a seven hundred–year–long history of separation from the Holy Roman Empire. Even if that is not absolutely accurate—the independence of the Swiss Confederation was recognized only in the peace of Westphalia in 1648, after the Thirty Years War—it reflects in its core the fact that the small Swiss Confederation was successful in determining its own status. Decisive factors were its important military strength and the fact that it was in the interest of the major powers in Europe that this military force stayed neutral and did not take part on any side of a coalition. The permanent Swiss neutrality turned out to be a key factor in the small country's staying out of any major war; Switzerland has never seen any foreign soldiers on its territory, with the exception of the invasion by the French and Russian troops during the time of Napoléon Bonaparte in 1798.

Switzerland before 1798

Until that time, Switzerland was a loose confederation of states, the cantons. The only principal institution was the Diet (Tagsatzung). It consisted of the ambassadors of the cantons acting on strict instructions from their cantonal governments. Yet this instrument proved to be rather cumbersome. On the other hand, the cantons soon developed a skillful practice in negotiating peaceful solutions, and confederal arbitration became important in

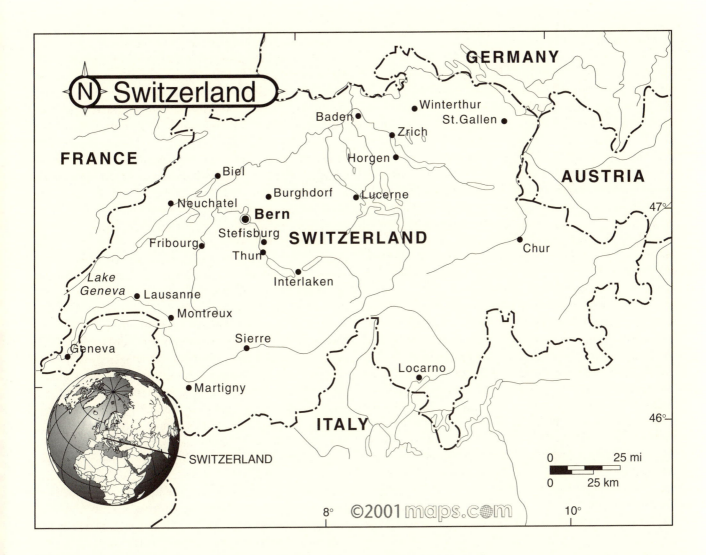

settling many internal and external conflicts. The concept of permanent neutrality and the experience of Swiss arbitrators in negotiating peaceful solutions were important factors for the many occasions in which the Swiss offered their services as mediators in international conflicts (for example, the Armistice Commission in Korea). A well-known worldwide Swiss institution is the International Committee of the Red Cross.

After a relatively short period during which the Constitution of Switzerland was modeled according to the ideas of the French Revolution as a centralized state named the Helvetic Republic, Switzerland, like most other European countries, returned to the old regime. The Congress of Vienna renewed the recognition of independence and expressly confirmed the status of permanent neutrality of Switzerland in 1815. However, in the following years, the tensions between the conservative Catholic cantons of central Switzerland and the Protestant cantons mounted: the radicals favored a strong union and a larger market with one nation; the conservative cantons disagreed. In 1847 the seven conservative cantons formed a separate alliance (Sonderbund). The

Diet declared this alliance null, and after a short internal civil war (Sonderbundskrieg), the way was open for a new constitution, which was adopted in 1848.

Constitution of 1848

The Constitution of 1848 became the basis of modern Switzerland. The confederation of states was replaced by a federal state—but with large autonomy for the then nineteen cantons and six half-cantons. For the first time, authorities for the federal state were created, in particular a bicameral parliament (the Federal Assembly) after the model of the U.S. Congress of 1787. The two chambers are the National Council (with two hundred members) and the Council of States (with forty-six members, two from each canton and one from each half-canton). The federal executive power was given to a body of seven members, the Federal Council.

At the same time, most modern democratic principles were incorporated into the constitution: separation of powers, equality before the law, enumeration of fundamental rights, representative democracy, and compulsory referendum for later amendments of the constitution.

Constitution of 1874

In 1874, after the conservative cantons realized that the new system was also to their advantage, additional powers were given to the federal state, in particular regarding the army, currency, and legislation. At the same time, safeguards for the cantons and minorities were introduced: each federal law became subject to a facultative referendum if requested by only 30,000 voters (since 1977, this has been increased to 50,000) or eight cantons. The fact that no federal law can be passed by the Federal Assembly without taking into consideration the possibility of a referendum, which is rather easily obtained, ensures that the cantons and all sorts of political parties are included to a large degree in any project of legislation. The same applies also on the cantonal level. This leads to a system of compromise and broadly accepted legislation. Indeed, the politics of direct democracy, continuous cooperation through compromise based in the Swiss constitution, led to a politically very stable system, probably not found in other democracies. The transition from a former confederation to a federal state with large autonomy for its cultural, religious, and politically diverse cantons was not a radical one, but a very cautious and pragmatic one: for example, even today the cantons dispose under their own command of army troops—a fact of no military importance at all, but a sign of the traditional respect for the cantons and an expression of the large autonomy left to them.

On January 1, 2000, the new Swiss Constitution of April 18, 1999, entered into force (see "Current Structure").

LEGAL CONCEPTS

Switzerland's legal system is based on four fundamental principles: democracy, federalism, rule of law, and social welfare.

Direct Democracy

The dominating factor in Switzerland's legal and political system is the concept of direct democracy. It is in its wide application to all levels (federal, cantons, and communities) quite exceptional. From the age of eighteen years on, every Swiss citizen is entitled to all political rights. In particular, he or she has the right to vote in elections, to be elected, and to take decisions in referendums. More so than in other states, not only any change to a provision of the constitution is subject to the approval of the people, but also any new law. This has some very characteristic consequences: new provisions can be introduced in the legal system only if a majority of the people (and not just the government) feel that it is the right time for it. Further, 100,000 voters can demand a vote on a general or specific amendment of the constitution by way of constitutional initiative. There is, strangely, no legislative initiative on the federal level; such was proposed by popular initiative in 1961 and again in 1987 by parliamentary initiative but was twice rejected. If voters want a referendum on a new provision, or a political idea, on the federal level directly, they must introduce a constitutional initiative. Inasmuch as even relatively small interest groups can collect the 100,000 signatures needed for this procedure, in Switzerland there are every year several such votes on constitutional amendments. Often these initiatives are rejected, because they are felt to be too radical, but very often a more moderate counterproposition of the Federal Assembly or Federal Council is then adopted.

Generally this system of direct democracy favors a rather conservative approach toward any changes in legislation. It means that laws often are changed only at a rather late stage, only when a majority of the Swiss voters think that they really must be changed. For example, only in the year 1971, many years after women's suffrage had been introduced in many countries, did the then still exclusively male voters of Switzerland accepted a new provision to the Swiss Constitution giving women all political rights on the federal level. By that act, one of the few obstacles to ratifying the European Convention on Human Rights (ECHR) was eliminated in Switzerland. And from the very beginning, Switzerland accepted the then-facultative provision of Article 25 of the ECHR, according to which every person under Swiss jurisdiction may bring a complaint before the European Commission on Human Rights in Strassburg (or today, after the revision of the procedures of the ECHR, file a complaint before the European Court for Human Rights against Switzerland).

Because of the influence of direct democracy, the laws have a very high legitimacy: they are applied and respected because it is the general understanding that they reflect the will of the people.

The importance of direct democracy is reflected also in the fact that on the cantonal level, judges of courts of first instance are often elected not by a cantonal parliament but in an election by the cantonal voters. In the Canton of Zurich, for example, only the judges of the second instance and of the Court of Cassation (third instance) are elected by the cantonal parliament. And on the federal level, the judges of the Federal Tribunal are elected by the Federal Assembly, yet not for a lifetime but for six-year terms. Although this may in principle raise some questions regarding the independence of judges, in practice it is hardly a problem. It has happened, though, that during the reelection process, some judges received fewer votes than others—for example, because they were considered to be too progressive by the majority of the conservative parliament. Once, such a judge was reelected only in the second round of voting by the Federal Assembly. He is today the president of the Federal Tribunal. Judges in Switzerland are usually highly respected, well trained, and well paid. However, it has also to be mentioned that in many cantons there are also laymen serving as judges in courts of first instance. This concept further reflects the will of the people to be represented directly in the courts, by persons of their kind and not just by learned jurists. Taking into account that there is no exam a judge must pass in order to assume his function, and that the requirements of modern jurisprudence are complex, it may be asked whether the system of laymen in the judicial system is not long outdated. But again, the Swiss take a pragmatic approach to such questions. Even though theoretically it might be possible to elect even a layman as judge of the Federal Tribunal, such never happens. All judges on the federal level, as well as from the second cantonal level upward, are learned jurists and usually of very high qualification. A concession is made to the political situation insofar as the judges elected also reflect the strengths of the political parties. It is felt that the democratic principle of proportionality demands that the political parties be represented proportionally in the judiciary. This may in some cases lead to a situation whereby not the best qualified person is elected, but the person proposed by the party that is "entitled" to a position in a court or in an executive body.

Rule of Law, Legality—and a Notable Exception

In order to safeguard the primacy of law and the protection of fundamental rights, the Swiss Constitution follows the principle of rule of law. The principles of separation of powers, legality, and judicial control are key elements. There is one remarkable exemption, however: the Federal Court has no authority to control the constitutionality of federal laws or international law (Article 191, Constitution of 1999). This is an intentional concession to the democratic principle. The judges shall have no power to invalidate a law that the federal parliament (with the direct or indirect approval of the Swiss voters) has adopted. In practice, this provision has little significance, inasmuch as great care is taken in preparing the laws that they are in conformity with the constitution.

In addition, the Federal Tribunal has adopted a practice according to which it interprets federal laws and international treaties in such a way as to bring them in conformity with the constitution, if ever possible. Yet, if the Federal Assembly decides willingly to derogate a federal law from the constitution, it may do so, with the sole control of a referendum of the people.

With regard to fundamental rights, it may be noted that most basic human rights have already been protected in the former Constitutions of 1848/1874, some of them by way of interpretation by the Federal Court's declaring them to be implied constitutional rights—even if they were not especially enumerated in the written constitu-

tion. After the European Convention on Human Rights entered into force for Switzerland in 1974, the Federal Court (as well as the lower instances) applied its provision directly as part of the national law. In the new Constitution of 1999, some provisions were drafted almost identically as in the ECHR.

Under the federal constitution, the cantons have every competence, every law-making power that is not expressly transferred by the constitution to the federal level. Federal law takes precedence over cantonal law and must be applied by all cantonal authorities and courts. The most important sources of codified law are the federal constitution (and the twenty-six cantonal constitutions); the Civil Code of December 10, 1907; the Code of Obligations of March 30, 1911; the Code of Execution and Bankruptcy of April 11, 1889; the Penal Code of December 21, 1937; and the Federal Law on the Organization of the Federal Courts of December 16, 1943. Whereas these federal laws are applied by all courts, the cantons have the power to organize their courts and apply their cantonal procedural laws. Therefore, in Switzerland we still find twenty-six different cantonal civil procedural laws and twenty-six penal procedural laws. In addition there are the procedural laws for civil and penal procedures before the federal authorities. This illustrates the strong position of the cantons in the judicial process—but limits the accessibility of the courts by lawyers that cannot be familiar with all these different procedural laws. Only in the year 2000 have the voters adopted a new constitutional provision according to which the procedural laws in civil and criminal matters of all cantons are to be replaced by a uniform civil procedural and penal law.

CURRENT STRUCTURE

On January 1, 2000, the new Swiss Constitution of April 18, 1999, entered into force, replacing the former Constitution of 1874. The main goal of the new constitution was to redraft the somewhat outdated wording and restructure the old Constitution of 1874, which had become a patchwork of more than one hundred amendments.

The date April 18, 1999, refers to the day when both the majority of the Swiss voters and the majority of the voters in the twenty-six cantons approved the revised constitution in a referendum. The new constitution incorporated in particular many fundamental rights that under the old constitution were guaranteed only by a long jurisprudence of the Federal Tribunal—such as personal freedom and the right of freedom of opinion. The new constitution is systematically structured and updated in such a way as to reflect all the former changes. It is from its content—not surprisingly, though—not a completely new constitution, and reflects the conservative approach within the legal and political systems of Switzerland.

Structure of Swiss Courts

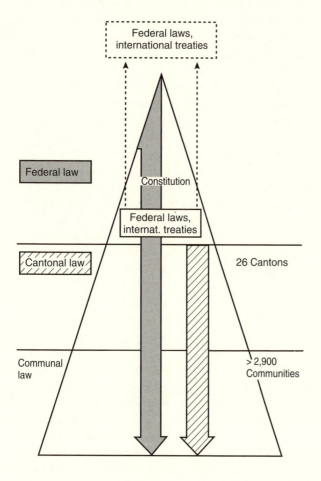

Federal laws, international treaties

Federal law

Constitution

Federal laws, internat. treaties

Cantonal law

26 Cantons

Communal law

> 2,900 Communities

The Federal Council (Conseil fédéral/Bundesrat) is the highest executive body on the federal level. Its seven members are elected by the Federal Assembly for a period of four years and represent proportionally the four major political parties. Great care is applied that the different regions and languages are represented in the Federal Council. Traditionally, two of the seven members come from the French-speaking part, and from time to time one member is elected from the Italian-speaking regions of Switzerland. Each member heads one of the seven administrative departments.

SWITZERLAND AND EUROPEAN LAW

Although located in the geographical center of the European Union, Switzerland is surprisingly not a part of the that union, mainly because the Swiss fear that too much sovereignty would be lost. One important reason may be that within the framework of the EU, there is no room for direct democracy. In 1992 the citizens of Switzerland even rejected the proposed accession to the European economic community. Nevertheless, in the intervening years, Switzerland has harmonized many of its laws in a process of so-called autonomous adoption of the laws

and regulations of the European Union. In 1999, for example, the Swiss approved the seven bilateral treaties that Switzerland has signed with the European Union and that were expected to enter into force in the year 2001 or soon thereafter. These treaties guarantee the basic freedoms valid within both the EU and Switzerland (such as freedom of circulation of persons, goods, capital, and services). Nevertheless, the question of whether Switzerland will (have to) give up more of its sovereignty in the future, and if so how much, is one of the most debated questions today in the country.

SPECIALIZED JUDICIAL BODIES

On the federal level, the most important tribunals are the Federal Tribunal and the Federal Tribunal for Social Insurance. In addition, there exists a series of highly specialized judicial bodies in the area of federal administrative law, the Federal Appeals Commissions—for example, in the area of federal tax law. Their decisions are usually subject to a recourse to the Federal Tribunal.

International arbitration plays an important role within the judicial system, and many international commercial and other disputes are settled in Switzerland. The status of a neutral country has always been an important factor in this regard.

STAFFING

In Switzerland, judges are elected, either by the citizens directly (often with first instances) or by cantonal parliament or the Federal Assembly (Federal Tribunal). Unlike lawyers admitted to the bar, judges need no legal qualification. But in reality, with the exception of judges of the peace and some judges of courts of first instance, judges are usually very well qualified and in possession of a law degree.

In the year 2000, the total number of pending cases before the Federal Tribunal in Lausanne was 6,730; 5,316 cases were decided, while at the same time 5,139 new cases were brought. The total number of judges of the Federal Tribunal was 60, plus 9 new additions in the year 2001. The total number of persons employed at the Federal Tribunal in the year 2000 was 186, of which 86 are law clerks. In the year 2001 the total number increased to 230 persons, which is necessary in order to manage the steadily increasing workload. Some 40 percent of the pending cases concerned constitutional and 23 percent administrative matters; 14 percent concerned private and 17 percent criminal law. Some 4 percent of the pending cases dealt with questions of debt collection and bankruptcy. The average time that a case was pending before the Federal Tribunal varied in the different fields—for example, in administrative suits, the average pending time was 305 days; in appeals cases in civil matters, 94 days. Some 60 percent of the cases were rendered in German, 33 percent in French, and 7 percent in Italian.

Further, the Federal Tribunal for Social Insurance, Lucerne, decided 2,242 cases with 22 judges. A total of 88 persons were employed at this specialized tribunal in the year 2000.

IMPACT

Every legal system in a modern democracy relies to a certain degree on the fact that the overwhelming majority of the population accepts the laws as just and respects the legal order. In this regard, it may be said that within Switzerland the acceptance of the decisions of the courts and also of the administrative bodies is very high. The large involvement of the voters in the law-making process and the understanding of the importance of the fundamental principles to be respected in a state of law, combined with the underlying power of the citizens to control the legal and political machinery in various ways of direct and indirect democracy, lead to a very strong acceptance of the legal system. If a decision of the Federal Tribunal is considered to be outdated, the parliament may react with the proposition of a new federal law. Or even the citizens may react by taking the initiative to change the constitution (with the help of 100,000 voters signing a popular initiative).

The high impact of the legal system and the judiciary is particularly well reflected in the way that Swiss courts and administrative bodies respect and react to the decisions of the European Court of Human Rights in Strassburg. This supranational court, which is unique in its impact on the legal order of the member states, is the last authority in interpreting the ECHR and its application by member states. Switzerland has been condemned several times by the European Court of Human Rights and has thereafter modified its internal legislation wherever it was necessary. Only once, after a reservation regarding the application of Article 6 of the ECHR on certain administrative procedures was declared null by the Strassburg organs, a debate took place in the Federal Assembly and a minority even demanded that a cancellation of the treaty be considered (ECHR Article 6 demands that there shall be full judicial control in case of any infringement of "civil rights"). The jurisprudence of the court in Strassburg made it clear that many decisions that earlier had been considered purely administrative matters fell nevertheless under the scope of that provision. Even though the fundamental rights of the ECHR are considered self-executing—and therefore under the Swiss Constitution became part of the national law and must be applied directly by all courts and administrative bodies—it is typical that most national decisions referring to the ECHR have been taken by the Federal Tribunal. This tribunal is the last instance before a complaint can be introduced against Switzerland.

Mirko Roš

See also Arbitration; Civil Law; Constitutional Law; European Court and Commission on Human Rights; International Law; Judicial Independence; Lay Judiciaries

References and further reading
Dessemontet, François, and Ansay Tugrul. 1995. *Introduction to Swiss Law.* 2d ed. The Hague: Kluwer/Schulthess. (This volume includes an extensive bibliography on further English publications on Swiss law.)
Häfelin, Ulrich, and Haller Walter. 2001. *Schweizerisches Bundesstaatsrecht.* 5th ed. Zurich: Schulthess.
Jaag, Tobias. 1999. *Verwaltungsrecht des Kantons Zürich.* 2d ed. Zurich: Schulthess.
Pestalozzi Gmuer and Patry. 1997. *Business Law Guide to Switzerland.* 2d ed. Bicester/Oxfordshire: CCH.
———. 2001. "Switzerland Law Digest."Pp. SWZ-1–SWZ-9 in *Martindale-Hubble International Law Digest 2001.* New Providence, NJ: Martindale-Hubble.
Salamin, Michel, ed. and comp. 1972. *Documents d'histoire suisse, 1240–1516.* Sierre: En dépôt à l'Imprimerie sierroise.
Wittibschlager, Martina. 2000. *Einführung in das schweizerische Recht.* München: Beck.

SYRIA

GENERAL INFORMATION

Syria is a Mediterranean country bordered by Turkey to the north, Jordan and Iraq to the south, Iraq to the east, and Lebanon, Israel, and the Mediterranean Sea to the west. Its territory encompasses 185,170 square kilometers (71,504 square miles), including 1,295 square kilometers of Israeli-occupied territory. This land can be divided into two regions: a narrow coastal plain edged with a double mountain range to the west, and a large desert plateau to the east. The climate is similarly divided, with mild, rainy winters along the coast and hot, dry summers in the desert. The common threats of nature are dust and sand storms.

With a population growth rate of 2.5 percent per annum, Syria's estimated 16,305,659 inhabitants include a mixture of Arabs (90 percent) and Kurds (9 percent), with the remainder mainly Armenians, Circassians, and Turkomans. There are 38,200 people living in the Israeli-occupied Golan Heights, including Israeli settlers. Along with its ethnic diversity Syria possesses a considerable diversity of religious views. About 74 percent of Syrians are Sunni Muslims, 12 percent Alawis, 4 percent Druze and other small Muslim sects, and 10 percent Christians. Jews are found in tiny Jewish communities. Almost 71 percent of Syrians are literate. While Arabic is the official language, minorities speak their own languages. French and English are understood but not widely spoken.

Syria's natural resources include significant amounts of petroleum and phosphate. Although water has become increasingly scarce in the Middle East, Syria has not been as severely affected by this problem as have most other countries in that region. The water supply is threatened

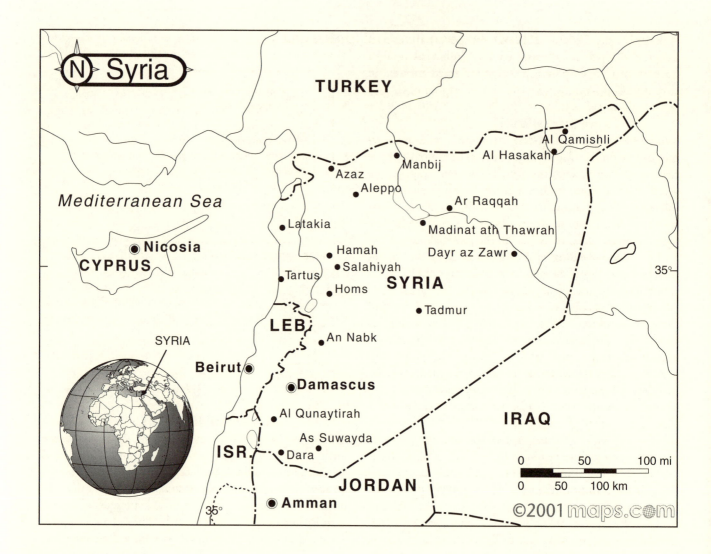

by population growth, underdeveloped distribution systems, and pollution.

The economy is state-planned and socialist. It consists of three major sectors: agriculture, industry, and services. Agriculture is underdeveloped and depends on rainfall. It contributes 29 percent to the GDP, while employing about 40 percent of the country's labor force. The industrial sector contributes 22 percent to the Syrian GDP, accounting for some 20 percent of the country's labor force; the services sector contributes 49 percent of the GDP, utilizing 40 percent of the labor force. Syrian exports are valued at about $3.3 billion, and consist chiefly of petroleum, textiles, fruit, vegetables, cotton, livestock, and phosphate. Syria's imports total $3.2 billion, most of which consist of machinery, foodstuffs, metal, textiles, and chemicals. The Syrian economy lacks a reliable infrastructure and technological base, and is unable to reach international markets. Syria's troubled economy is plagued by an unemployment rate of 13.5 percent, and it groans under a $22 billion debt. Above all, the yearly revenue of $3.5 billion compares rather unfavorably with expenditures of $4.2 billion.

HISTORY

Syria was the homeland of some of the world's oldest civilizations, dating as far back as 5000 B.C.E., and Damascus is the world's most ancient surviving capital. Syria was part of the Canaanite, Phoenician, Egyptian, Aramean, Assyrian, Babylonian, Chaldean, Persian, Greek, Roman, Nabataean, Byzantine, and Muslim civilizations. The biblical account holds that Paul was converted on the road to Damascus, and it was in Damascus that he established the first organized Christian church.

Syria has been under Muslim rule since 636 C.E. The Muslim Caliphate Omar was handed the keys to Jerusalem, and while he granted security and amnesty to Jews and Christians in Bilad Al-Sham (Syria, Jordan, Israel, Lebanon, and Palestine), soon the majority of people were Muslims.

Damascus attained its zenith when it became the capital of the Umayyad Islamic Empire, which lasted from 661 C.E. to 750 C.E.; its borders sprawled from Spain to India. Eventually the empire fell and was relegated to the status of a province under the Abbasid Empire, which took Baghdad as its capital. When the Abbasid Empire eventually fell, Damascus became a provincial capital under the Mameluke Empire. Damascus was subsequently invaded and destroyed by the Mongols in 1400. It remained a provincial capital until it came under Ottoman rule from 1517 to World War I.

When Germany, Austria, and the Ottoman Empire were defeated in 1919, the Ottoman territory came under the control of France and Great Britain under the Sikes-Picot Treaty, which divided the region, known as Bilad Al-Sham, into four political entities: Syria, Jordan, Palestine, and Lebanon. The son of Sharif Hussein, the leader of the Arab revolution against the Ottomans, became the king of Syria.

The Kingdom of Syria under King Faysal existed for only a few months before French troops clashed with Arabs in the battle of Maysalun, which cleared the way for France to occupy Syria, as the League of Nations put Syria under French mandate. King Faysal was then named king of Iraq, and Syria became a republic. The French mandate lasted until the declaration of independence on April 17, 1946.

From 1946 until 1971, Syrian politics can be described as volatile, thorny, and contentious. The government set up by the French was overthrown by a military coup in 1951. In 1954 there was a second military coup. In 1958 Syria merged with Egypt in the United Arab Republic, although the two countries lay miles apart. This combination resulted from the nationalistic views of the influential Egyptian statesman Nasser, and the Suez Canal crisis after its nationalization. The union was destroyed by another military coup in 1961. In 1963 a coup by the Ba'th Party (Arab Socialist Resurrection Party) was carried out successfully.

Syria was not to know stability, for it was convulsed by three more coups. These coups changed the people in charge, but the Ba'th Party remained in power. The last two coups resulted from the loss of the Golan Heights to Israel in the 1967 war and the controversial support for the PLO (Palestinian Liberation Organization) against Jordan in 1970. The minister of defense, General Hafiz Al-Assad, who became president and ruled until his death in 2000, led this final "bloodless" coup. During Al-Assad's presidency, political stability was maintained. Assad began the "correction movement," highly celebrated in Syria as a new wave of modernization. A new constitution was introduced in 1973 and was endorsed in a national referendum.

Since 1976, Syrian troops have been stationed in Lebanon in order to expand political influence, to support certain Lebanese groups, and to press Israel. Israeli forces besieged these troops in 1982. In that same year, the presiding regime back home in Syria was challenged by the "Muslim Brotherhood," which viewed the Ba'th Party as anti-Islam. Syria became isolated by other Arab countries because of its actions in Lebanon, and for siding with Iran in the Iran-Iraq War. It was not until Syria chose to ally itself with the Gulf War coalition against Iraq's invasion of Kuwait that it broke out of that isolation.

President Assad's son Bashar became the new president after his father's death. The constitution had to be amended to lower the minimum age allowed for a president to take office, from forty to thirty-five years of age, in order to accommodate the new president. President Bashar is a British-educated optometrist, who has taken several measures toward modernization. He has made some attempts to elevate the status of human rights and released some political prisoners. He also allowed a private banking system.

LEGAL CONCEPTS

Syria experienced a series of short-lived constitutions between independence and 1973. The constitution of 1973, however, was drafted in a Western parliamentary style, and it has proven to be more enduring. It identifies the Syrian Arab Republic as a democratic, popular, socialist, and sovereign state. It gives citizens several political and civil rights, including freedom of speech, opinion, association, and faith. Syrians also have the right to work, the right of equality of opportunity, the right to be secure in their homes, and they are guaranteed a free education. The purpose of education is to create a generation that will eventually establish the united Arab socialist nation. These rights have been suspended by emergency decrees required during the war with Israel. While the law still requires a presidential election every seven years, those elections are only symbolic.

The constitution gives the Ba'th Party, with its principles of "unity, freedom, socialism," the status of "leading party," and hence the ruling agenda and control of the military. The party advocates state ownership of industry and the redistribution of land. Consequently, there are three kinds of property ownership in Syria: property of the people (natural resources and nationalized enterprises), collective property (assets owned by popular organizations), and private property. According to the constitution, any property held privately shall be subordinated to the national economy and public interest. After the collapse of the Soviet Union, the ruling party began to abandon socialism and put more emphasis on Arab unity. Other political parties (only leftist and nationalist parties are permitted) function under the umbrella of the National Progressive Front, which is dominated by the Ba'th Party and serves as a forum to discuss the country's political agenda.

Syria is a unitary state in which all political and judicial powers are centralized. It has fourteen administrative provinces. Each of these provinces has a governor who is appointed and directed by the Ministry of Internal Affairs.

Governors are expected to work with the Local People's Councils, which are elected directly by the people, as are any municipal officials (Article 129).

The Syrian political system is based on that of the French, which is a mix of presidential and parliamentary systems. Political power is distributed among three branches: the executive (president and prime minister), legislative, and judicial. The legislature is made up of a unicameral People's Council. Its 250 members are elected by popular vote for a four-year term. Members must be at least twenty-five years old, and more than half the council must be workers or peasants. The council cannot write law; rather, it can only ratify, veto, or amend laws that are proposed by the president. According to Article 71, it assumes many political powers, such as nominating the president of the republic for the popular vote, accepting his resignation, approving the cabinet, approving the budget and international treaties, and giving general amnesty. In addition, either a two-thirds majority of the People's Council or the president of the republic can propose to amend the constitution. Yet both must approve the proposed amendment in order for it to go into effect.

The executive branch consists primarily of the president of the republic and the cabinet. The cabinet, including its head, the prime minister, is appointed by the president and must be ratified by the People's Council. The cabinet is responsible to the president, and is also subject to the council's approval. If the council does not see fit to lend its confidence, the nominees must renounce their candidacy, forcing the president to introduce another cabinet. The cabinet's function is to execute the law and to run the state bureaucracy.

The constitution gives much broader powers to the president than it does the legislature or the judiciary. He must be a citizen of good standing, an Arab Muslim, and at least thirty-five years of age. The People's Council must nominate the presidential candidate, who should also be the secretary general of the Ba'th Party, before he can be put up to popular vote. The president's term lasts seven years. If the council twice refuses a law introduced by the president, he is compelled by law to quit his efforts, unless he uses his veto power. If he uses the veto, a two-thirds majority of the People's Council is needed to overrule it. The president can dissolve the council under the condition that an election be convened within ninety days. He also has other powers, including declaring war, declaring a state of emergency, granting amnesty, and appointing vice presidents, diplomatic missions, and civilian and military personnel. Above all, he has the power to amend the constitution, with the approval of three-fourths of the People's Council. The tendency to fortify the presidency was the result of the desire for stability.

The constitution states the independence of the judicial authority (Article 131) and judges (Article 133); judges are subject only to the authority of the law. But it is clear that the president has a great deal of influence over the courts. In fact, the president is the one responsible for maintaining the state of independence for the judiciary. He has that privilege because he presides over the Higher Council of the Judiciary, which is in charge of the judges' dismissal, transfer, and appointment. In addition, courts lack independence because of a constitutional proviso that combines the membership of the Supreme Constitutional Court (SCC) with a ministerial or legislative position (Article 140). The SCC assumes the duties of electoral control and constitutional review. These duties are principally connected to the executive and legislative branches. Members from these branches who are members of the SCC are not expected to be impartial.

The Syrian legal system is a mixture of Ottoman, French, and Islamic laws. Customary law is limited to a few Bedouin tribes and religious minorities. The civil, criminal, and commercial codes promulgated in 1949 were based on the French mandate system, which had its beginnings in the Napoleon-Egyptian era. Modern Syria tried to substitute French laws for the Ottoman ones, as the latter were believed to be inefficient and ineffective, which contributed to bringing the Ottoman Empire to an end. Yet Ottoman laws still serve as one of the sources of the legal system, as stated in the constitution (Article 153).

Islamic religious courts in Syria are based on *sharia* (Muslim law), but their jurisdiction is limited to personal matters such as marriage, divorce, paternity, the custody of children, and inheritance. Personal status laws were developed by modifying the *sharia* code, clarifying the laws concerning inheritance and women. Other religious minorities are not obligated to go to Islamic courts for their personal disputes. They have special courts based upon their respective religious tenets. However, most religious minorities have used the secular civil courts.

It is estimated that a commercial or civil lawsuit spends about five years in litigation. Arbitration therefore is a favorable and legally recognized mode of redress. Only an attorney may offer representation in a court of law. The defeated party pays any costs incurred during the proceedings, although those costs may not exceed 25 percent of the dispute's worth. Syria recognizes international judicial rulings in cases of civil and commercial disputes and upon the existence of a binding treaty, unless those rulings violate Syria's public law. When there is no treaty, cases will be reexamined. Syria can agree to arbitrate only if a treaty binds it. International arbitration held in Syria is subject to Syrian law. Although Syria has rejected the International Criminal Jurisdiction, it still remains under several binding judicial treaties and is a member of the New York Convention on the Recognition and Enforcement of Foreign Arbitral Awards.

CURRENT STRUCTURE

The current Syrian judicial system has been rather unwavering since the adoption of the 1973 constitution; the last substantial change was the establishment of the Supreme Constitutional Court (SCC) in 1973. Articles 131–148 set up the basic structure of the judiciary, which includes the SCC, Courts of General Jurisdiction, Administrative Jurisdictions, and special courts. The constitution states that every defendant is innocent until proven guilty and has the right to a fair and just trial. No Syrian court uses juries. Capital punishment is still used in Syria in cases of severe crimes or sensitive national security matters. No judge is appointed for life in Syria, which fact renders judges subject to executive branch authority.

The SCC, located in Damascus, is the pinnacle of the Syrian legal system. It is composed of a chief justice and four justices. The president appoints them for a renewable four-year term. The SCC is considered the arbiter and pinnacle because of the duties it assumes. It has the power of judicial review and oversees all elections. Judicial or constitutional review occurs if the president or a quarter of the People's Council challenges the constitutionality of a law, or if the court itself has decided that a law is not constitutional. In either case, the court must decide within fifteen days, or in seven if the matter is urgent. The president may consult the court on the constitutionality of a law when it has been drafted.

The power of election control allows the court to decide on the legality of elections. If it decides that a member's election was illegal, that decision needs to be ratified by the majority of the People's Council. The SCC also has the power to try the president for any infractions of the law. It resolves jurisdictional conflicts and therefore determines the competent or appropriate court from among the different court systems. The court is forbidden to question laws approved by popular referendum.

Courts of General Jurisdiction fall into six categories, compose most of the Syrian judicial system, and lie in a hierarchy from the few most important to numerous courts of lesser importance. First is the Court of Cassation in Damascus, which is the highest court and the court of last resort. It alone has the authority to hear appeals from the lower courts and to overturn decisions by Courts of Appeal. It has jurisdictional and judicial authority over the Courts of General Jurisdiction. SCC will review decisions made by the Court of Cassation only if there is a constitutional violation. Second are the Courts of Appeal, which hear appeals of decisions rendered in previous cases. Every province has one Court of Appeal. The third category is the Tribunals of First Instance. Several of these courts can be found in every province. They are divided into different subdivisions according to the nature of the case presented. Fourth are the Tribunals of Reconciliation. There are many of these in each province,

and they take care of small civil and criminal matters. They try to mediate the issue under dispute, inasmuch as it is a minor one. If mediation fails, the case is tried according to the law. The fifth category is the Personal Status Courts. These can be found in all provinces and are concerned mainly with personal and family matters. Different religions may have different Personal Status Courts. The last category is the Courts of Minor Offenders, which deal with cases involving minors.

The Administrative Jurisdictions have judicial power over cases involving the state and its agencies. These courts deal with litigation related to administrative contracts, and try and interpret cases according to administrative laws and regulations. The High Administrative Court is the highest court concerning such matters. Administrative Courts will hear cases about fairness in appointments, promotions, early retirement, suspensions, and transfer irregularities.

SPECIALIZED JUDICIAL BODIES

State Security Courts (military tribunals) are the most important specialized courts. They enjoy special importance because Syria lives under a state of emergency. They usually consist of three military judges and have the authority to decide on cases involving national security issues, and to determine if the case poses a threat to the state. The preponderance of such cases involve armed insurrection, spying, and crimes against the armed forces and its officers.

The Economic Security Court is another special court that tries cases when economic rules are being violated, such as illegal currency exchange at the black market or smuggling. Since Syria has a state economy, this court is instrumental in maintaining the authority of the state over the economy.

Last is the Mufti Department, which gives opinions according to Islamic law. *Mufti* means to render an opinion about a disputed issue. Members of this department are knowledgeable Muslim scholars who must give the Islamic opinion upon a certain matter of public concern. The court gives consultative opinions if asked, and these opinions may be binding or not. Currently, the head of this court, the *mufti* of the republic, is a leader of the more moderate Islamic thought in Syria.

STAFFING

The High Council of the Judiciary is responsible for staffing the various courts, according to Article 131. The council is responsible for judicial appointments, dismissals, and transfers. It should be composed of senior civil judges and be chaired by the president of the republic. The president is to defend the independence of the judiciary through his role in this council. The council is to execute Article 133, which guarantees that judges

Legal Structure of Syria Courts

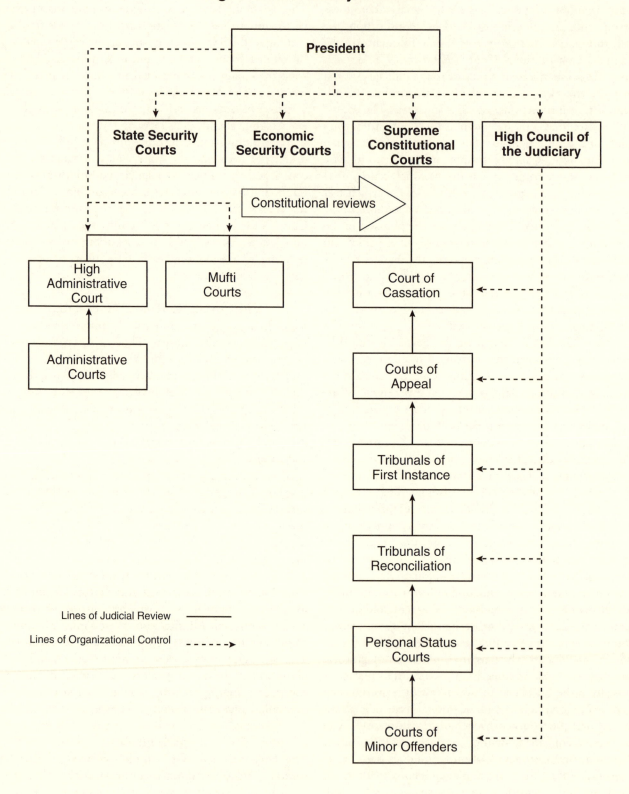

should be autonomous and subject to no authority but that of the law. The council, however, does not have the organizational capability to do this highly bureaucratic job. In practice, the minister of justice presides over the council as a representative of the president. Other members of the council are the president of the Court of Appeal, the minister's eldest deputies, the minister's assistant, the attorney general, and the president of the Judicial Inspection Department. The Ministry of Justice is important for the council to carry out its duties. It sets the agenda and develops decisions for the council. The ministry gained this position because of its administrative capability and efficiency.

Becoming a judge is a process that involves passing a series of examinations and interviews. Applicants are expected to comply with the same requirements as the public sector, not to usurp civil or political rights. They are expected to possess a law degree as well. Applicants who do well in the battery of examinations and interviews will be nominated to the job. New judges are to be trained by working with more experienced judges.

Judges suffer from the same problems as other employees in the public sector, and in Syria that especially means low salaries. Although a judge's salary is slightly above the average Syrian's, the pay is still not enough, and judges may be forced to find other work in order to subsist. Justices often lack incentive and focus because of low salaries and few employment-related benefits. As a result, the courts have lost the public trust. In addition, because the government is the major employer and the constitution grants Syrians the right to work, the judicial branch is overstaffed, which reduces efficiency.

Syrian lawyers must be members of the Syrian Bar Association (Nakabet al Muhamin). The association is managed by an elected council, which is responsible for developing the profession and elevating the status and life conditions of lawyers. Lawyers pay an obligatory yearly fee to the association to help accomplish those goals. The association has the authority to discipline lawyers and to issue penalties up to and including suspension from the profession. Any lawyer who is not a member of the association cannot practice law.

After earning a law degree, a graduate who wants to practice law must be trained for two years by another lawyer who has been practicing law for a minimum of five years. During this period, trainees are expected to maintain their membership in the bar association as lawyers under training. Trainees may appear in the courtroom under their supervising attorney's name. Upon completion of the training period, trainees are eligible to take the bar exam. Passing the exam is their license to become practicing lawyers. The exam is coordinated by the association and is generally composed of written and oral sections.

IMPACT

The judiciary in Syria does not appear to make a significant positive contribution to the good of the country. Indeed, the lack of a strong independent judiciary is a major reason for the underdeveloped political and economic conditions. The Syrian judiciary has been criticized for its rampant inefficiency, its lack of independence from the executive, and its bias toward the autocratic regime and its employees. The lack of independence, however, seems to be the unavoidable result of the constitution. Stability and streamlined presidential power, rather than checks and balances among the governmental branches, are the most important elements in the constitutional design.

Economic development and political change to restore independence and prosperity to judges are the key to a more effective judiciary. International pressure upon Syria to improve its human rights record will hasten that process.

Mohammad H. Al-Momani

See also Appellate Courts; Capital Punishment; Constitutional Law; Constitutional Review; Criminal Law; Customary Law; International Arbitration; Judicial Independence; Judicial Review; Judicial Selection, Methods of; Legal Education; Mediation

References and further reading
Abu Faris, Mohammed. 1984. *Alnidam Alkada'i fi al Islam* [*Judiciary in Islam*]. 2d ed. Jordan: Dar Al-Shorok.
Al-Gazi, Ibrahim. 1973. *Tarikh alkanon fi Wadi Alrafidain wa aldawla alromania* [*The History of Law in Alrafidain Valley and the Roman State*]. Cairo: Alazhar.
Cappelletti, Mauro. 1971. *Judicial Review in the Contemporary World.* Bobbs-Merrill.
David, Rene. 1968. *Major Legal Systems in the World Today: An Introduction to the Comparative Study of Law by Rene David and John E. C. Brierley.* London: Free Press.
Drysdale, Alasdair. 1995. *Academic American Encyclopedia.* Danbury, CT: Grolier.
Hall, Jerome. 1963. *Comparative Law and Social Theory.* Baton Rouge: Louisiana State University Press.
Hartzler, Richard H. 1976. *Justice, Legal Systems, and Social Structure.* Port Washington, NY: Kennikat Press.
Kessler, Martha, Helena Cobban, and Hisham Melhem. 1999. "What about Syria?" *Middle East Policy* 7, no. 1: 101–113.
Sadowski, Yahya. 1987. "Patronage and the Ba'th: Corruption and Control in Contemporary Syria." *Arab Studies Quarterly* 9, no. 4: 442–462.
Safra, Jacob E., Constantine S. Yannias, and James E. Goulka, eds. 1998. *Encyclopedia Britannica.* Vol. 28, pp. 361–375. Chicago.
Ziadeh, Farhat J. 1987. "Performance and Change in the Arab Legal System." *Arab Studies Quarterly* 9: 20–35.

T

TAIWAN

COUNTRY INFORMATION

Taiwan, an island in East Asia, is a province and the seat of government of the Republic of China (ROC); it is also claimed as a province by the People's Republic of China, which administers mainland China. Taiwan is separated from the mainland by the Taiwan Strait on the west and bordered on the north by the East China Sea, on the east by the Pacific Ocean, and on the south by the South China Sea. The Republic of China also administers the Penghu Islands (Pescadores), the Kinmen Islands (Quemoy) offshore from the mainland city of Xiamen, and the Matsu Islands offshore from Fuzhou, the capital of Fujian Province. Although administered by the ROC government, the Matsu and Chinmen Islands are officially part of Fujian Province. The ROC government also claims that the South China Sea—which encompasses Tungsha (the Pratas) Islands, Nansha (the Spratly) Islands, Hsisha (the Paracel) Islands, and Chungsha (the Macclesfield Bank)—is under its jurisdiction. In April 1993, the ROC Executive Yuan Council approved the Policy Guidelines for the South China Sea, which affirm the ROC's sovereignty over the islands and other islets in the South China Sea.

The total area of the islands administered by the ROC government is about 13,900 square miles. Taiwan Island accounts for about 98 percent of this. The island is shaped like a tobacco leaf, extending about 240 miles from its stem in the south to its northern tip. Most people in Taiwan are ethnic Han Chinese and were born on the mainland or have ancestors that were. They are divided into three groups based on their native Chinese dialects: Taiwanese (who speak Taiwanese, also called Min), Hakka (who speak Hakka, also called Kejia), and Mandarin. Min, Hakka, and Mandarin all belong to the Sino-Tibetan languages family. Taiwan also has a small population of Aborigines, who compose about 1.7 percent of the total population. There are nine major aboriginal tribes, each speaking a different form of Formosan, a member of the Austronesian languages family. Mandarin Chinese is Taiwan's official language.

According to statistics released by the Ministry of the Interior, the population of the ROC on Taiwan stood at 22.03 million as of August 1999. The population density of the Taiwan area was the second highest in the world after Bangladesh. The Taiwanese population is also aging: The average life expectancy was 74.58 years, with men living an average of 71.93 years and women 77.81 years. In 1998, 8.25 percent of the population were over 65 years of age and 37.59 percent were under the age of 15.

HISTORY

Taiwan's first inhabitants left no written records of their origins. Anthropological evidence suggests that Taiwan's indigenous peoples are from proto-Malayan ancestry. What is known for certain is that large tribes of indigenous peoples, plus many Han from the Chinese mainland, were already living in Taiwan when Portuguese navigators first came upon Taiwan in 1590. In 1622, the Dutch East India Company established a military base on the Pescadores Islands (Penghu). In the following year, they moved to the much larger island of Taiwan, where they established a colonial capital and ruled for the next thirty years. Dutch rule increased the amount of land under cultivation by reorganizing Chinese villages and indigenous territories. In addition to trade, Dutch missionaries were also active in converting Taiwan's population to Christianity.

While the Dutch were colonizing Taiwan, China was going through a period of strife. In 1644, the Manchus invaded China and established the Ching Dynasty. As Manchu troops poured into northern China, many Ming loyalists escaped southward. One of the most celebrated resistance fighters was Cheng Cheng-kung. Cheng made Taiwan his base to restore the Ming Dynasty. Forcing the Dutch out in 1662, he established a capital at Anping (present-day Tainan), set up schools for the young, introduced Chinese laws and customs, and built the first Confucian temple in Taiwan. Cheng's son and grandson ruled Taiwan for twenty years before surrendering control of the island to the Manchus in 1683, following military defeat. Taiwan was then ruled by the Manchus for the next 200 years.

Four ports in Taiwan were forcibly opened to foreign trade following the Treaty of Tientsin in 1858. Foreign

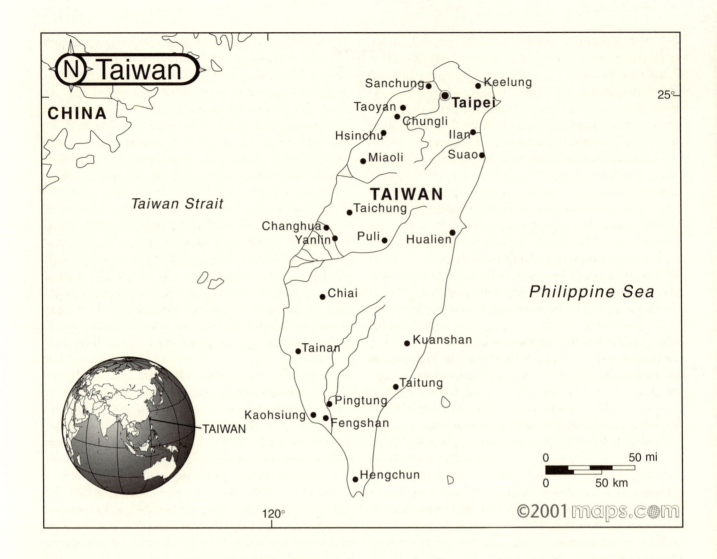

©2001 maps.com

interest in the island made the Ching court realize Taiwan's importance as a gateway to the seven provinces along China's southeastern coast. In 1885, the Ching Dynasty made Taiwan its twenty-second province. Achievements by the Ching administration were later disrupted, when Taiwan was ceded to Japan in 1895 under the terms of the Treaty of Shimonoseki. During its fifty-year rule of Taiwan (1895–1945), Japan introduced strict police controls, carried out a thorough land survey, standardized measurements and currencies, and emphasized Japanese culture and education.

Following Japan's defeat and surrender in 1945 at the end of World War II, Taiwan was retroceded to the Republic of China. However, the first years after the Japanese surrender were not smooth and resulted in one of Taiwan's greatest tragedies, the "February 28 incident" in 1947. The incident remained a taboo topic in discussion and a source of tension between Taiwanese and mainlanders until the post–martial law period of the 1990s. With the outbreak of the Korean War in late June 1950, U.S. President Harry S. Truman ordered the U.S. Seventh Fleet to protect Taiwan against attack by the Chi-

nese Communists, and the United States began to provide Taiwan with considerable economic and military assistance. This invaluable military support continued through the 1960s and 1970s.

Despite restrictions under martial law, the ROC government has long promoted local self-government. Beginning in 1950, all the chief executive and representative bodies under the provincial level were directly elected by the people, and in 1951, sixteen county and five city governments and councils were established. In June 1959, the first Taiwan Provincial Assembly was set up, extending political participation from the county to the provincial level. Following the death of Chiang Kai-shek in 1975, Yen Chia-kan briefly served as president until Chiang's son, Chiang Ching-kuo, was elected in 1978. It was under Chiang Ching-kuo's rule that full democratization began, starting with the lifting of martial law in 1987 shortly before his death in 1988. In fact, the first major opposition party, the Democratic Progressive Party (DPP), was formally established on September 28, 1986, marking the beginning of multiparty democracy in the ROC. Chiang Ching-kuo's successor, President Lee Teng-hui, continued to reform the rigid political system that had been developed after decades of civil war and martial law. Under his administration, press freedoms were guaranteed, opposition political parties developed, visits to the mainland continued, and revisions of the constitution were encouraged.

The ROC's efforts at democratization have borne fruit in recent years. Scores of new political parties have sprung up since the ban on their establishment was lifted in 1989. All members of the legislature have been chosen by direct popular election since 1992. On December 3, 1994, the governor of Taiwan Province and the mayors of the cities Taipei and Kaohsiung were directly elected for the first time. And with the first direct popular presidential election in the history of China, held on March 23, 1996, full-fledged democracy was achieved in Taiwan. The victory of the DPP's Chen Shui-bian in the second direct presidential election on March 18, 2000, was another landmark event. The peaceful transfer of power from one party to another that followed was the first ever in Chinese society.

LEGAL CONCEPTS AND GOVERNMENT BRANCHES

Taiwan has a codified civil law system. The major codes are the Civil, Criminal, Civil Procedure, and Criminal Procedure Codes. The contents of the codes were derived originally from the laws of other jurisdictions with similar codified systems (such as Germany, France, and Japan), and then infused with traditional Chinese laws.

As in most countries, the supreme law of Taiwan is its constitution. The ROC Constitution is based on principles formulated by Sun Yat-sen, the founding father of the Republic of China. His political doctrine is known as the Three Principles of the People. The Principle of Nationalism advocates not only equal treatment and sovereign status for the Republic of China in the interdependent commonwealth of nations but also equality for all ethnic groups within the nation. The Principle of Democracy assures each citizen the right to exercise the political and civil liberties due to him or her. The Principle of Democracy is the guiding doctrine behind the organization and structure of the ROC government. The Principle of Social Well-Being states that the powers granted to the government must ultimately serve the welfare of the people by building a prosperous economy and a just society. The three principles have extensively shaped current policies and legislation in areas ranging from education to land reforms, from social welfare to relations with mainland China, and, more recently, in increasingly extensive political and economic liberalization.

The ROC Constitution guarantees various rights and freedoms to all citizens. Modeled after U.S. constitutional concepts, the rights include equality, work, livelihood, and property, as well as the four political powers of suffrage, recall, initiative, and referendum. In return, the people have the duty to pay taxes and perform military service as prescribed by law. Obtaining an education is considered both a right and a duty of the people.

The people are also endowed with the basic freedoms of speech, residence, travel, assembly, confidential communication, religion, and association. Personal freedom is also guaranteed. Rights and freedoms not specified in the constitution are also protected if they do not violate social order and public interest. The law may not restrict freedoms stipulated in the constitution unless the freedoms are abused, the freedoms of others are infringed on, or public order is threatened. Even in these situations, the constitution permits restrictions on constitutional rights and freedoms only under certain circumstances. This is designed to prevent legislative bodies from making laws that overstep the limits set down in the constitution. Restrictions on constitutional freedoms are valid only if contained in legislation necessary to prevent restrictions against the freedom of others, to respond to emergencies, to maintain social order, or to enhance social interest. In any case, arrest, trial, and punishment must be implemented in strict accordance with proper legal procedures. If human rights are violated by the government, the victims are entitled to compensation by the state.

The ROC Constitution contains directives for formulating legislation and procedures addressing important government, economic, and social issues. Chapter 13 of the constitution, titled "Fundamental National Policies," contains articles on national defense, foreign policy, national economy, social security, education and culture, and frontier regions. The policies outline the government's responsibility to provide necessary support for the welfare and well-being of the people and also to foster an environment that will enable them to engage in various business and professional activities. Article 9 of the Additional Articles of the Constitution prescribes specific policy orientations on several modern issues, including scientific development, industrial upgrading, environmental and ecological protection, national health insurance, and the elimination of sexual discrimination.

On May 1, 1991, the ROC president promulgated the ten Additional Articles of the Constitution of the Republic of China that had just been passed by the First National Assembly. The articles were designed to reflect the fact that Taiwan and the Chinese mainland are administered by two separate political entities. The Additional Articles also provided the legal basis for the election of the Second National Assembly and the Second Legislative Yuan, which would be representative of Taiwan, a nationwide constituency covering the mainland, and overseas Chinese.

After the Second National Assembly assumed office on January 1, 1992, its delegates adopted Additional Articles 11 through 18. These articles were promulgated on May 28, laying the groundwork for the popular election of the president and vice president of the republic, the transformation of the Control Yuan from a parliamentary body to a quasi-judicial organ, and the implementation of provincial and local self-governance.

Then, on July 28, 1994, the Second National Assembly revised the eighteen Additional Articles, reducing the number to ten. According to the revised Additional Articles of the Constitution:

- The president (beginning with the ninth-term president since the constitution went into effect in 1947) shall be directly elected by the entire voting population in the Taiwan area.
- The presidential and vice-presidential candidates shall run on a single ticket.
- Overseas nationals may vote in the election for the president and vice president.
- The president can appoint and dismiss those officials who were appointed with the consent of the National Assembly or the Legislature without the countersignature of the president of the Executive Yuan.
- The National Assembly may have a speaker and a deputy speaker.
- The dismissal of the president of the Executive Yuan may take effect only after the new nominee to this office has been confirmed by the Legislature.

From May 5 to July 23, 1997, the Additional Articles underwent yet another amendment. The roles of the provincial government and the Control Yuan been changed drastically. Under this revision :

- The provincial government is to be streamlined, and the popular elections of the governor and members of the provincial council are suspended.
- A resolution on the impeachment of the president or vice president is no longer to be instituted by the Control Yuan but rather by the Legislative Yuan.
- The Legislative Yuan has the power to pass a no-confidence vote against the president of the Executive Yuan, while the president of the republic has the power to dissolve the Legislative Yuan.
- The president of the Executive Yuan is to be directly appointed by the president of the republic; thus, the consent of the Legislative Yuan is no longer needed.
- Educational, scientific, and cultural budgets, especially the compulsory education budget, will be given priority but are no longer restricted by Article

164 of the constitution to be at least 15 percent of the total national budget.

On September 4, 1999, the ROC Third National Assembly passed another round of constitutional amendments, which extend the current terms of deputies from May 2000 to June 2002. Under the newest revision:

- The Fourth Assembly shall have 300 delegates, who shall be elected by proportional representation based on the election of the Legislative Yuan. The seats shall be distributed among the participating parties in accordance with the proportion of votes won by the candidates nominated by each party and those members of each party running as independent candidates.
- Beginning with the Fifth National Assembly, the National Assembly shall have 150 delegates, who shall be elected by proportional representation based on the election of the Legislative Yuan.
- The delegates to the National Assembly shall serve terms of four years.
- The term of office of the Third National Assembly shall be extended to the day when the term of office of the Fourth Legislative Yuan expires.
- The terms of legislators are to be extended from the current three years to four years in the next Legislature.

The ROC Constitution also provides for dividing the government into three main levels—central, provincial/municipal, and county/city—each of which has well-defined powers. The central government consists of the Office of the President, the National Assembly, and five governing branches (called "yuan"), namely, the Executive Yuan, the Legislative Yuan, the Judicial Yuan, the Examination Yuan, and the Control Yuan.

Executive Yuan
The Executive Yuan (cabinet) has a president, usually referred to as the premier of the ROC; a vice president; a number of ministers and chairs of commissions; and five to seven ministers without portfolio. The premier is appointed by the president of the ROC.

Legislative Yuan
The Legislative Yuan (legislature) is the highest legislative organ of the state, comprising popularly elected representatives who serve for three years and are eligible for re-election. In accordance with the constitution, the legislature has the following functions and powers:

1. General legislative power: The legislature exercises legislative power on behalf of the people. The term

law as used in the constitution denotes any legislative bill passed by the legislature and promulgated by the president of the ROC

2. Confirmation of emergency orders: Emergency orders and measures proclaimed by the president in the case of an imminent threat to national security or a serious financial or economic crisis during the recess of the legislature are presented to the legislature for confirmation within ten days of issuance. Should the president issue an emergency order after dissolving the Legislative Yuan, the Legislative Yuan is to convene of its own accord within three days and has seven days to decide whether to ratify the order

3. Right to hear the president's annual national affairs report

4. Hearing reports on administration and revision of government policy

5. Examination of budgetary bills and audit reports presented from the Executive Yuan

6. Right of consent: The auditor-general in the Control Yuan is nominated and, with the consent of the Legislative Yuan, appointed by the president

7. Amendment of the constitution: On the proposal of one-fourth of the members of the Legislative Yuan and also by a resolution of three-fourths of the members present at a meeting having a quorum of three-fourths of the members of the yuan, a bill to amend the constitution may be drawn up and submitted to the National Assembly for deliberation

8. Settlement of disputes concerning self-governance: The legislature settles any disputes over items and matters of self-governance in provinces, special municipalities, counties/cities, or other administrative units

Meanwhile, in accordance with the Additional Articles of the Constitution of the ROC, the legislature has been given the additional power to institute impeachment proceedings against the president or vice president. Impeachment of the president or vice president for treason or rebellion will be initiated on the agreement of more than two-thirds of all members of the Legislative Yuan after being proposed by more than one-half of the legislators, whereupon the resolution will be submitted to the National Assembly. Should such a motion of impeachment be passed by a two-thirds majority of all delegates to the National Assembly, the party impeached will forthwith be dismissed from office.

Following amendments to the ROC Constitution on April 25, 2000, the legislature gains powers to initiate a recall of the president or vice president. Such proposals must be backed by one-fourth of the members of the Legislative Yuan, and approved by two-thirds of the lawmakers. The recall motion must then be approved by the public by means of a referendum. For the vote to be effective, at least 50 percent of eligible voters must cast ballots, and more than half of those voting must back the recall measure.

Judicial Yuan

The highest judicial body in Taiwan is the Council of Grand Justices, which reports directly to the branch of government known as the Judicial Yuan. According to Article 5 of the Additional Articles of the ROC Constitution, the Judicial Yuan is to have fifteen grand justices. The grand justices, including the president and the vice president of the Judicial Yuan to be selected from among them, will be nominated and, with the consent of the Legislative Yuan, appointed by the president of the ROC. This will take effect from the year 2003, and the provisions of Article 79 of the constitution will no longer apply. The subordinate organs of the Judicial Yuan are the Supreme Court, the High Courts, the District Courts, the Administrative Court, and the Commission on the Disciplinary Sanctions of Public Functionaries. The judiciary exercises administrative supervision of the ROC court system while enforcing compliance by ROC court personnel with constitutionally mandated structures for juridical independence from the other branches of government.

The Council of Grand Justice

The sixth Council of Grand Justices, composed of sixteen members, assumed office on October 3, 1994, following confirmation by the National Assembly. The grand justices serve nine-year terms. However, according to Article 5 of the Additional Articles promulgated in July 1997, each grand justice of the Judicial Yuan is to serve a term of eight years, regardless of the order of appointment to office, and cannot serve a consecutive term. The grand justices serving as president and vice president of the Judicial Yuan do not enjoy the guarantee of an eight-year term. Among the grand justices to be nominated by the president in the year 2003, eight members, including the president and the vice president of the Judicial Yuan, will serve for four years. The remaining grand justices will serve for eight years. The provisions of the preceding paragraph regarding term of office will not apply.

The Council of Grand Justices interprets the constitution and unifies the interpretation of laws and ordinances. Constitutional interpretations are made when there are doubts or disputes concerning: (1) the application of the constitution; (2) the constitutionality of laws, regulations, or decrees; and (3) the constitutionality of laws governing provincial or county self-governance and laws and regulations promulgated by provincial or county governments. A petition for a unified interpretation of a law or ordinance may be filed with the Council of Grand Justices if: (1) a government agency, when applying a law or ordinance, has an interpretation that is different from that already expressed by itself or another government organ, unless it is legally bound to obey the expressed opinion or has the authority to revise it; (2) an individual, a juridical person, or a political party whose rights have been infringed on and who believes that the final decision of the court of last resort was based on an interpretation of the applicable law or regulation that is different from that previously adopted in precedents by other courts; however, such requests will not be accepted if the petitioner has not yet exhausted all judicial remedies or if the opinion adopted in an earlier decision has been altered by a later one. The council meets thrice a week and holds additional meetings as necessary. Oral proceedings may be held whenever the need arises. After an interpretation of the constitution or unified interpretation of a law is made, the judiciary publishes the text of the interpretation, the reasons supporting it, and dissenting opinions, if any. The petitioner and persons concerned are also notified.

In December 1993, the judiciary formally established a Constitutional Court in accordance with Article 13 of the old version of the Additional Articles of the Constitution and the revised Organic Law of the Judicial Yuan to adjudicate cases concerning the dissolution of political parties that have violated the constitution. The Constitutional Court is composed of the grand justices and presided over by its most senior member. The Ministry of the Interior may, as the agency overseeing political parties, petition the Constitutional Court for the dissolution of a political party whose objectives and activities are found to endanger the existence of the ROC or its free and democratic constitutional order.

In addition, the Control Yuan may impeach a public functionary for malfeasance, dereliction of duty, or any other neglect of duty or if the head of any of the various branches, ministries, and commissions or the highest local administrative head requests a disciplinary measure against a public functionary for the same reasons. The Commission on the Disciplinary Sanctions of Functionaries, under the Judicial Yuan, exercises jurisdiction over such cases. The committee is composed of nine to fifteen senior members, one of whom serves as the chair. Cases are decided without any outside interference. The committee orders the impeached functionary to submit a written reply within a prescribed period of time and, when it deems necessary, may summon the functionary to appear before the committee to defend himself or herself. Such a conference is not open to the public, and its proceedings are kept strictly confidential. There are six disciplinary measures that the committee may order: dismissal, suspension from office, demotion, reduction of salary, demerit, and reprimand. Only dismissal and reprimand are applicable to political appointees.

The judicial hierarchy in the ROC consists of three levels: District Courts and their branches at the lowest level, which hear civil and criminal cases in the first instance; High Courts and their branches at the intermediate level, which hear appeals, as the court of second instance, against judgments of District Courts or their branches; and the Supreme Court at the highest appellate level, which reviews judgments by lower courts as to their compliance with or violation of pertinent laws or regulations. Thus, issues of fact are decided in the first and second instances, while only issues of law are considered in the third instance. However, there are exceptions to this "three-level and three-instance" system. Criminal cases relating to rebellion, treason, and offenses against friendly relations with foreign states are handled by High Courts as the court of first instance, and appeals may be filed with the Supreme Court.

Examination Yuan

The Examination Yuan is responsible for the examination, employment, and management of all civil service personnel in the ROC. Specifically, the Examination Yuan oversees all examination-related matters; all matters relating to qualification screening, security of tenure, pecuniary aid in case of death, and the retirement of civil servants; and all legal matters relating to the employment, discharge, performance evaluation, scale of salaries, promotion, transfer, commendation, and award of civil servants.

The examination system is applicable to all Chinese civil servants, high- or low-ranking, appointed or elected. The system is also applicable to Chinese and foreign specialized professionals and technicians. The examination function, being exercised solely by the Examination Yuan at the level of the central government, is separated from the executive power and thereby free from partisan influence.

Control Yuan

The Control Yuan is the highest control body of the state, exercising the powers of impeachment, censure, and audit. The Control Yuan was formerly a parliamentary body, with its members elected by provincial and municipal councils. However, constitutional amendments in May 1992 transformed it into a quasi-judicial organization. The new Control Yuan started operations on February 1, 1993. From July 1997 onward, its power to institute certain impeachment proceedings expired after the constitutional amendment, and the Legislative Yuan has been empowered to take over the duty.

Legal Structure of Taiwan Courts

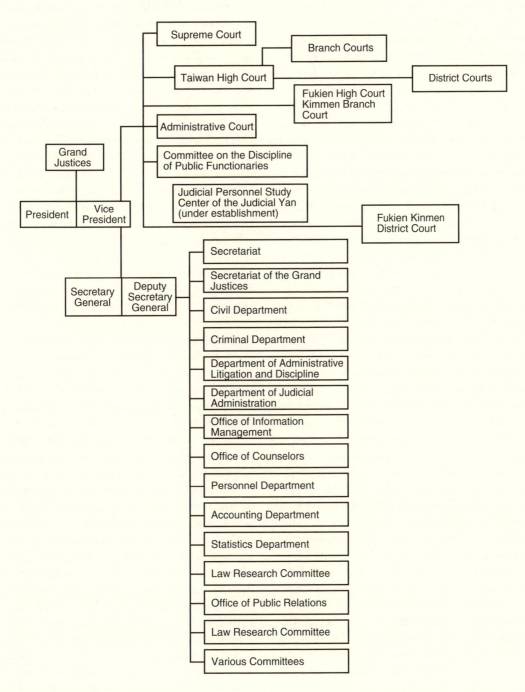

CURRENT COURT SYSTEM STRUCTURE

The judicial hierarchy in Taiwan consists of three levels: District Courts and their branches, which are at the lowest level and hear civil and criminal cases in the first instance; High Courts and their branches, which are at the intermediate level and hear appeals, as the court of second instance, against judgments of District Courts or their branches; and the Supreme Court, which is at the highest appellate level and reviews judgments by lower courts in terms of their compliance with or violation of pertinent laws or regulations. Thus, issues of fact are decided in the first and second instances, while only issues of law are considered in the third instance. However, there are exceptions to this "three-level and three-instance" system. Criminal cases relating to rebellion, treason, and offenses against friendly relations with foreign states are handled by High Courts as the court of first instance; appeals may be filed with the Supreme Court.

There are nineteen District Courts in the Taiwan area. Each has a president, appointed from among the judges, who takes charge of the administrative work of the court. Each court is divided into civil, criminal, and summary divisions. Currently, there are forty-four summary divisions in the Taiwan area to adjudicate cases that can be disposed of in a prompt and simple manner in comparison to regular proceedings. Summary proceedings are conducted by a single judge in the first instance. Appeals may be filed with the civil or criminal division of the District Court for review by a three-judge panel in the second instance. Specialized divisions may also be set up by District Courts to deal with juvenile, family, traffic, financial, and labor cases as well as motions to set aside rulings on the violations of the Statute of the Maintenance of Social Order. Cases to be tried and decided by a District Court are heard before a single judge, though more important cases may be heard before three judges sitting in council.

At present, there is one High Court in Taipei serving all of Taiwan including the Pescadores, with four Branch Courts in Taichung, Tainan, Kaohsiung, and Hualien. In the part of Fukien Province under the control of the ROC, there is the Kinmen Branch Court of the Fujian High Court, which exercises jurisdiction over cases of appeal against judgments or rulings in Kinmen County and Lienchiang County. A senior judge of the High Court is appointed to serve concurrently as president of the court, taking charge of the administrative work of the court and supervising the administrative work of its subordinate organs. The High Court is divided into civil, criminal, and specialized divisions, which deal with juvenile, traffic, and labor cases. Each division is composed of a presiding judge and associates. Cases to be tried and decided by the High Court are heard before three judges sitting in council. However, one of the judges may conduct the preliminary proceedings alone.

The High Court and its branches exercise jurisdiction over the following cases:

- Civil, criminal, and election cases of appeal against judgments of District Courts or their branches as a court of the first instance;
- Motions to set aside rulings of District Courts or their branches;
- Criminal cases relating to rebellion, treason, and offenses against friendly relations with foreign states, acting as a court of the first instance; and
- Other lawsuits prescribed by law

Although it lies under the administrative supervision of the judiciary, the entire ROC court system has juridical independence in criminal and civil matters of law. The Supreme Court is the final level of appeal in the ROC court system. The Supreme Court has a president, who is responsible for the administrative work of the court and acts concurrently as a judge. The Supreme Court is divided into seven civil divisions and ten criminal divisions. An appeal may be made to the Supreme Court only on grounds that the decision made violates a law or ordinance. Since the Supreme Court does not decide questions of fact, documentary proceedings are the rule, while oral proceedings are the exception. Cases before the Supreme Court are tried and decided by five judges sitting in council.

The Supreme Court exercises jurisdiction over the following kinds of cases:

- Appeals of judgments in civil and criminal cases rendered by High Courts or their branches as court of second instance;
- Appeals of judgments of High Courts or their branches in criminal cases as court of first instance;
- Motions to set aside rulings of High Courts or their branches in civil and criminal cases;
- Appeals of or motions to set aside rulings of District Courts or their branches as court of second instance in civil summary proceedings; and
- Cases of extraordinary appeal

The Administrative Court has a decidedly different sphere of juridical authority from that of the other courts in the system. Any person who deems that his or her rights are violated by an administrative action rendered by a government agency may institute administrative proceedings before the Administrative Court. The individual is entitled to this right if he or she objects to the decision on an administrative appeal submitted by him or her in accordance with the Law of Administrative Appeal or if no decision is rendered over three months after the submission of his or her administrative appeal or over two months of extension after the prescribed period for decision has expired. An administrative action that exceeds the legal authority of the government agency that rendered it or that results from an abuse of power is considered unlawful.

In administrative proceedings, the plaintiff is a private person and the defendant is a governmental agency, both being equally bound by the adjudication of the Administrative Court. Cases before the Administrative Court are tried and decided by five judges sitting in council. The Administrative Court decides questions of both fact and law; it may make investigations and hold oral proceedings. Since the cases have gone through appeal proceedings before the institution of administrative proceedings, adjudication by the Administrative Court is final. However, where there are legitimate grounds, retrial proceedings are permissible. Should a decision by the Administrative Court set aside or alter the original administrative action or decision, under no circumstances will such a decision be less favorable to the plaintiff than the original action or decision.

Significant reforms will be carried out to revamp the ROC judicial system and ensure fair trials. A consensus on the reform measures was reached in the National Conference on Judicial Reform held in July 1999. One of the most significant reforms to emerge from this meeting is that experts can be brought into Taiwan's courts to assist in the trying of cases that involve family affairs, juvenile crimes, labor and medical disputes, and intellectual property rights. Also, assessors may be called into court on major criminal and administrative cases. Assessors can assist presiding judges who may not necessarily be equipped with technical expertise in areas outside the legal domain. A framework for transforming the role of the judicial branch was reached. The judiciary will adopt a short-term reform plan, under which it will have civil, criminal, constitutional, and administrative courts. A long-term reform plan will eventually be implemented to seat thirteen to fifteen grand justices in the judiciary. They will be responsible for conducting civil, criminal, and administrative litigations, as well as for handling cases on disciplining public functionaries, dissolving political parties, and interpreting the constitution. This overhauling of the judiciary is expected to boost public confidence in the independence of the judicial system.

The council is the only body that may interpret the constitutionality of statutes and regulations. The highest body in the regular court system is the Supreme Court, which hears civil and criminal cases appealed to it from the courts below. Below the Supreme Court are four regional High Courts. These serve primarily as appellate courts. At the bottom of the hierarchy are eighteen District Courts, which have traffic, tax, family, and juvenile delinquency divisions. There are no juries in the Taiwanese legal system.

In keeping with the traditional aversion to litigation, Taiwan has developed an extensive system of mediation committees and commercial arbitrators to facilitate out-of-court settlements. Not surprisingly, the demand for legal services is much lower than it is in the United States. As in most countries in northeast Asia, Taiwanese lawyers must attain demanding standards, culminating in a grueling examination with an average failure rate of 85 percent.

A handful of foreign lawyers are employed by law firms in Taiwan, and a number of U.S., European, Japanese, and Canadian law firms have established branches there. Besides international trade law, foreign lawyers are required in intellectual property law, environmental law, and immigration law. Foreign lawyers and law firms are impeded by a lack of clear-cut rules governing foreign lawyers and law firms. Basically, foreign lawyers are not permitted to handle litigation for profit. Foreign law firms are similarly restricted in that they may not employ local attorneys to engage in professional activities. However, the confused state of rules governing foreign lawyers and law firms provides a degree of flexibility. Taiwan's rapidly expanding economy has created a growing demand for foreign lawyers.

Foreign lawyers employed by local law firms have had varying experiences. Some are integrated into the practice as far as possible, while others (perhaps the majority) are relegated to translation and editing. Attorneys working for foreign law firms are limited to international business, tax, and immigration law.

The Taiwan Bar Association (TBA) convened its first meeting in 1938. Today, it is bound to represent the interests of the collection of bar associations in each administrative division within Taiwan. There is one such association for each of the province's sixteen counties. According to its official literature, "the goals of the TBA encompass further reforming judicial and legal systems, enhancing the virtues and social status of lawyers, and gaining a thorough knowledge of the Chinese legal system and those of the rest of the world."

Chi-Min (Jimmy) Yu

See also China; Civil Law

References and further reading
Fa Jyh Pin. 1991. "Constitutional Developments in Taiwan: The Role of the Council of Grand Justices." *International and Comparative Law Quarterly* 40 (January): 198–209.
Gold, Thomas R. 1986. *State and Society in the Taiwan Miracle.* Armonk, NY: M. E. Sharpe.
Hsiao, Winston. 1995. "The Development of Human Rights in the Republic of China on Taiwan: Ramifications of Recent Democratic Reforms and Problems of Enforcement." *Pacific Rim Law and Policy Journal* 5 (November): 161–204.
Hungdah Chiu and Jyh-pin Fu. 1994. "Taiwan's Legal System and Legal Profession." Pp. 21–42 in *Taiwan Trade and Investment Law.* Edited by Mitchell A. Silk. Hong Kong: Oxford University Press.
"The Judicial Yuan of the Republic of China." http://www.judicial.gov.tw/E8-1-1.htm (accessed January 3, 2002).
Liu, Lawrence Shao Liang. 1991. "Judicial Review and Emerging Constitutionalism: The Uneasy Case for the Republic of China on Taiwan." *American Journal of Comparative Law* 39 (Summer): 509–558.
Tien, Hung-mao. 1989. *The Great Transition: Political and Social Change in the Republic of China.* Stanford, CA: Hoover Institution Press.
Tozzi, Piero. 1995. "Constitutional Reform on Taiwan: Fulfilling a Chinese Notion of Democratic Sovereignty?" *Fordham Law Review* 64 (December): 1193–1251.
Winn, Jane Kaufman. 1994. "Relational Practice and the Marginalization of Law: Informal Financial Practices of Small Businesses in Taiwan." *Law and Society Review* 28: 193–232.
Winn, Jane Kaufman, and Tang-chi Yeh. 1995. "Advocating Democracy: The Role of Lawyers in Taiwan's Political Transformation." *Law and Social Inquiry* 20: 561–599.

TAJIKISTAN

COUNTRY INFORMATION

A landlocked country in isolated central Asia, Tajikistan is one of the more politically and economically troubled of the former Soviet Asian Republics. Resembling a gerrymandered congressional district in the United States, Tajikistan is spread over 142,000 square kilometers and borders China in the east, Afghanistan to the south, Kyrgyzstan to the north, and Uzbekistan to the west. A mountainous country with the Pamir Mountains dominating its eastern section, Tajikistan is a haven for political and religious rebels who attack not only the Tajik government but also other central Asian states.

Tajikistan's geography has had a profound effect on its political, economic, and legal development. Several rivers flow through the country, providing water for Tajikistan and its neighbors. The Fergana Valley in the north is the most heavily populated part of Central Asia. The Amu Darya River provides most of the water for the southern part of the country. Its diversion into agricultural projects has had a dramatic effect on the ecology of Tajikistan's neighbors.

Tajikistan's mountainous terrain has limited its industrial capabilities and divided the country between east and west, north and south. The Gorno-Badakhshan Autonomous Province includes the Pamir mountain range and is known by its inhabitants as the ceiling of the world. The region supported the rebellion against the pro-communist Tajik government and suffered the consequences of being cut off from most government aid. Yet the autonomy granted the area included its own court system and the power to handle local affairs. The mountainous terrain has also contributed to the continued insurgency in the country. The combination of Tajik, Uzbek, and Russian troops have proved unable to end the military conflict. In addition, drug smugglers have taken advantage of the topography to transport their product from Afghanistan to Russia through Tajikistan.

With a population of nearly 6.5 million people, Tajikistan is composed mainly of two ethnic groups, Tajiks and Uzbeks. A small proportion of Russians, many of whom ran the Tajik political and economic system during the Soviet era, have begun emigrating back to Russia. Most of the remaining population is Sunni Muslim, with less than 10 percent practicing the Shia faith. Tajikistan's population is also young; over 40 percent of its citizens are below the age of fifteen.

Economically, Tajikistan has suffered the aftereffects of a centrally controlled command. With little industry and limited natural resources, Tajikistan is one of the poorest of the Central Asian Republics. Tajikstan's GDP of approximately $6.2 billion produces a per capita income for its citizens of $800.

HISTORY

Modern-day Tajikistan is a mountainous region of Asia originally settled by Persia. The Persian defeat by Alexander ended their control and the Chinese were the next to extend influence over the region. But the greatest change came with the Islamic invasion that produced a permanent Muslim presence in Central Asia. Islam remained the main religion even as political power was divided among the Uzbeks, the Mongols, and the Seljuk Turks. During these historical periods there was no recognized Tajik state but only a group of tribes speaking a similar language.

The Russians were the next conquerors of the area, holding it for over a century. In the 1870s, the Russian General Kaufman fought and defeated the armies of the various states, or khanates, in Central Asia. After gaining control of the territory, the czarist government did little to change the local political, economic, or social structure. Education and local affairs were left to the individual tribes as long as they did not question the Russian political or military authorities. The sole change sought by the Russians was the introduction of cotton into the Tajik region as a cash crop. Yet the Russian occupation of Central Asia attracted British interest. Great Britain feared that Russia would continue its eastward and southward march into India. The result was a series of wars in the Afghan region. Suddenly control of Central Asia became an important geostrategic goal for the European powers. But with the Russian revolution, its importance dwindled.

The rise of Soviet power centralized political authority over the region in Moscow. It was not until the collapse of the Kolchak government in Siberia in 1919 that Central Asia fell under the military power of the Soviets. Though there was armed resistance to communist authority it was overcome by the Soviets' customary brutality.

The rise of Joseph Stalin in 1924 saw a shift in Moscow's approach to its republic policy. A Georgian by birth, Stalin approved of a tightly controlled regional autonomy for the non-Russian regions. This prompted the creation of the Central Asian Republics. Initially the Uzbekistan Republic included most of the current Tajik lands. But in 1929 Tajikistan was split off and recognized as a separate Soviet socialist state. With its creation came recognition of the Tajik language and its instruction in Tajik schools.

But these limited freedoms could not compare to the strict economic and political controls put into place by Moscow. Tajikistan's lack of any industrial base or natural resources made it of little use to the central authorities. Hence central economic planners designated the republic as a major producer of cotton. With the new cash crop came large-scale public-works irrigation projects. Many of the rivers running through central Asia start in the Pamir Mountains of eastern Tajikistan. The water from

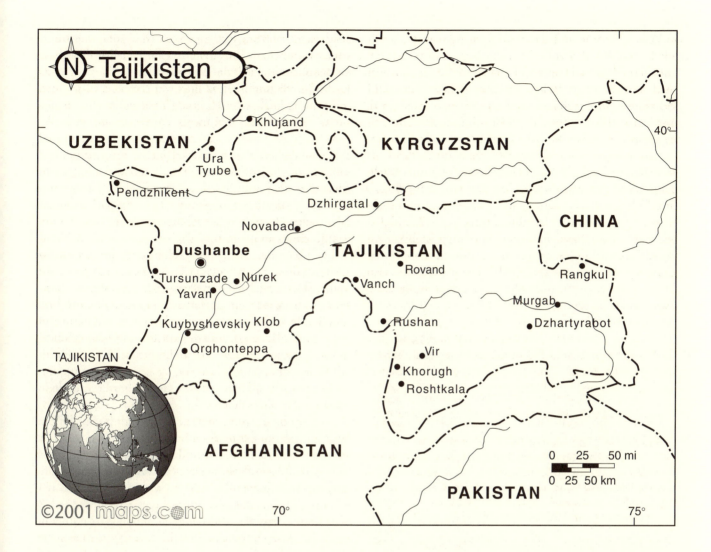

those rivers was diverted to feed the thirsty cotton plants but with devastating environmental consequences. The Aral Sea, fed by the rivers, began to dry up, and its eventual death may be the result of the Soviet desire to make Tajikistan a major cotton producer.

During the Soviet invasion of Afghanistan, Tajikistan served as the jumping-off point for the Red Army. There were attacks on Tajik targets by the Afghan rebels and the Soviets feared the Islamic insurgency would spill over into Central Asia. With Tajik independence, the country found itself buffeted by the competing Afghan groups. These groups, upon suffering defeat in their own country, would cross the Tajik border, further destabilizing the country as it tried to recover from civil war.

INDEPENDENCE AND CIVIL WAR

The formal splitting of Tajikistan from its Soviet overlord came after the collapse of the Gorbachev regime in the late summer of 1991. In September of that year the Tajik Parliament declared independence. Later it became a member of the Commonwealth of Independent States.

While Tajikistan was independent of the Soviet Union, it could not escape from the informal political structure enforced by Moscow. Much of the governmental leadership of the country originated in the Leninobad region in the north of the country. The region produced Soviet-educated leaders who adhered to a secular philosophy of government. This contrasted with the southern and eastern sections of the country, which were populated mainly by Muslims who favored a more religiously based government. These differences had a profound impact on the efforts of Tajikistan to escape its Soviet past.

As a former Soviet Republic, Tajikistan faced the difficult tasks of forming a state, developing a political system and culture, and creating institutions that would prop up a fledgling democracy. Significant legal reforms were needed, including writing a constitution that limited government and protected individual rights, composing a law code that established procedures and protections, and privatizing government property to create a stable economic system. Those goals, though, were delayed by the civil war that broke out shortly after independence. Only with a ceasefire could the government start on those difficult tasks.

After independence, Tajik society and government suffered through four years of political turmoil and military conflict as communists, reformers, and Islamic activists vied for political control of the country. Those favoring a democratic society formed a coalition government with moderate Islamists but the regime found itself under immediate attack by former communist leaders elected under the old regime. The result was political chaos descending into civil war. Street fighting, political assassinations, and a collapsed legal system followed. Russian and Uzbek troops intervened, supporting the old communist government. With the ratification of a new constitution in 1994, a measure of political stability returned. A 1996 ceasefire agreement ended the heaviest fighting but the southern and eastern reaches of the country remained in turmoil, with kidnappings and assassinations of government officials and members of international aid organizations. By 2000, Tajikistan's troubles spilled over into other states in Central Asia. Russian and Uzbek troops patrolled the Tajik and Afghan borders while an insurgency challenged the neighboring Uzbekistan and Kyrgyzstan governments.

TAJIKISTAN GOVERNMENT AND JUDICIARY

With the signing of a peace agreement and the winding down of large-scale military conflict, Tajikistan was able to compose a new constitution with new governmental institutions. The most powerful of those was that of the Tajik president, an office originally abolished after independence. The first president, Imomali Rahmonov, was elected under suspicious circumstances and with allegations of voter fraud. The office of the president includes the power to issue decrees and oversee their enforcement. The president appoints a Council of Ministers, which has the ultimate power to enforce laws but relies on the president for political support and resources. The council also works with the Supreme Assembly to compose legislation favored by the president.

The Supreme Assembly is the chief law-making body of the country. Its members are handpicked by the president and belong to his ruling party. The assembly provides unwavering support of presidential policy.

The Tajikistan judicial system is structured along lines similar to its Soviet predecessor. The highest echelons of the court system are composed of a Supreme Court, a Constitutional Court, a Supreme Economic Court, and a Military Court. Regional courts operate throughout the country and include a court for the Gorno-Badakhshan Autonomous Province and for the capital, Dushanbe. Operating below the regional courts are district and municipal courts that handle mostly criminal and civil cases.

The entire court system is centrally controlled by the president. The executive appoints judges to five-year terms of office and can remove judges for any reason.

With removal vested in the executive, judges are influenced by political pressure from both national and regional officials. This "telephone justice" includes verdicts in cases predetermined by those officials and telephoned to the judges. Refusal to abide by the political demands of the officials can lead to a judge being removed and possibly prosecuted. A regional court judge was removed after issuing a ruling in favor of one of the government's opponents. His ruling was overturned and the judge was accused of taking bribes in exchange for issuing the ruling. Such arbitrary actions send a clear signal to Tajikistan judges as to their fate if they ignore the political demands of government officials.

Each of the courts in the Tajikistan system has a different jurisdiction. The Rayon, Oblast, and municipal courts served the local population and handle most localized disputes, including misdemeanors, small civil claims, and family issues. These courts, though, function only in those areas where government control extends. In many border regions military courts run by Tajiks, Uzbeks, or Russians prosecute rebels and drug smugglers using military justice. In other areas, the rule of local warlords or tribal justice are utilized.

The regional courts operate as appellate courts for the district and municipal courts. The regional courts have the power to remove politically sensitive cases from the lower courts and serve as trial courts in those cases. Both the regional and local courts serve within the civil law system. Judges are required to interpret and apply the law and decrees handed down by the central government. Judges lack the power of judicial review and hence are unable to declare laws unconstitutional. Yet Tajikistan lacks the detailed law codes and the legal structure found in most civil law countries. Instead, the law is made through presidential decrees and hence changes with little regard to the overall structure of the code.

SUPREME AND CONSTITUTIONAL COURTS

Resembling other civil law states, Tajikistan divides the supreme judicial power between a Supreme Court and a Constitutional Court. The Supreme Court is the highest court in the regular court system. Its members, including a chairman, deputy chairman, and other justices, are appointed by the president to five-year terms. Reappointment and dismissal are at the discretion of the president. The Supreme Court hears appeals from lower courts and provides the authoritative interpretation of the law. While the Supreme Court is considered independent of political officials and the constitution criminalized any attempt to politically influence the justices, presidential control of the Court is reflected in its decisions. Specifically, in 1993 the Court ruled that four parties opposing the government were illegal even though the constitution

Legal Structure of Tajikistan Courts

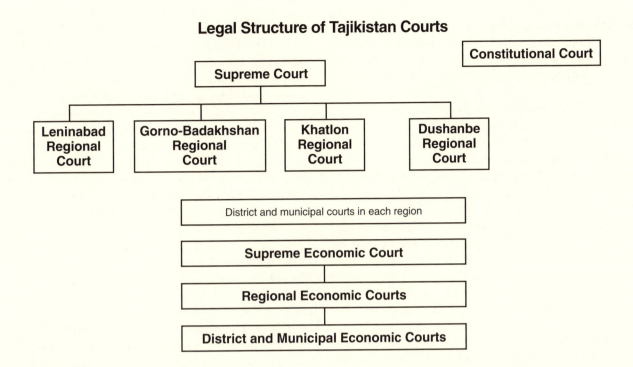

explicitly protects the right to form parties and participate in political activities.

The Constitutional Court is composed of seven justices, including one specifically appointed from the Gorno-Badakhshan region. A justice must be between the ages of thirty and sixty and have ten years of legal experience. Theoretically, the court exercises the power of judicial review and is expected to determine whether laws, decrees, and rulings by lower courts follow the many restrictions found in the constitution. Instead the court has proved to be a willing partner of the president. By 1999 it had not struck down a single executive action or legislative enactment, a fact that exhibits either legislative adherence to the constitution or the inherent weakness of the court.

With centralized control of the court system, the judiciary has become a policymaking arm of the president, granting some legitimacy to his actions and offering the facade of a legal system. In keeping with the Soviet tradition of the judiciary, the Tajikistan courts serve less as a buffer for citizens than an enforcement arm against them.

The centralization of judicial power extends to the government representative in the courts. The procurator general is the government's chief prosecutor. Appointed by the president to a five-year term, the procurator general can be removed for any reason. He also has appointment and removal power over regional and local procurators. The procurator general uses this power when conducting oversight of his subordinates in their handling of cases. As with judges, the local procurators are influenced by political concerns and are fully cognizant that a politically unpopular decision can bring removal from the top.

Among their broad powers, procurators can detain suspects for up to fifteen months. The procurator general must provide permission for detention beyond six months. The courts cannot order the procurator to release a prisoner and have no control over the procurator's decision when to go to court. In regions under military control such detention is not even checked by the procurator. Courts are not functioning and military prosecutors are responsible for holding trials.

ECONOMIC COURTS

The Tajikistan system of economic courts is separate from the regular judiciary. Economic courts are specialized in hearing only disputes involving government-owned enterprises and government agencies. The courts emphasize state power as created by presidential decree. Property rights and respect for a fixed system of law are only secondary concerns.

Tajikistan's economic courts are located throughout the country. Each large community has a court, as does each of the major regions. The Autonomous region of Gorno-Badakhshan has its own economic court, as does the capital city of Dushanbe. The Supreme Economic Court is located in the capital and hears appeals from the lower community and regional courts. The Supreme Economic Court is considered the final arbiter of economic law in the country. It is a civil law court, interpreting legislation and presidential decrees. It lacks any judicial review power and hence cannot strike down a law based on the constitution. In addition, the court can be overruled by the president, who can issue decrees overruling both court rulings and settled law. Finally, judges in the economic court systems are appointed by the president and can be removed by him for any reason. Such control limits the need for the president to overrule court decisions and ensures that most judges do not stray far from the executive's wishes.

PERSONAL AND INDIVIDUAL RIGHTS

The Tajik Constitution, much like its predecessor, promises individual rights and protection from arbitrary arrest and political suppression. The record of the Tajik government, though, is one that violates those protections. Although the 1994 Constitution replaced the Soviet-era document, much of the written law remains.

The law provides sweeping powers for the government to detain suspects. This includes a maximum fifteen-month waiting period where a defendant can be incarcerated before trial. In addition the accused are denied prompt counsel and at times denied public trials. Tajik courts also work with a presumption of guilt, requiring the defendant to prove innocence in court.

Fair trials are undermined by the political vulnerabilities of the judges. Under the control of national authorities, judges have been removed for issuing decisions detrimental to the state. A high level of political violence in sections of the country has intimidated judges, who frequently fear for their lives. The breakdown of government authority in regions of the country has led to extrajudicial actions including trading hostages between the government and its armed opponents.

PRIVATIZATION LAW

With a weakened judicial system, Tajikistan has faced difficulties in reforming its legal system. One set of reforms involved the privatization of state-owned enterprises. This much-needed reform was delayed by an absence of settled written law protecting the rights of property owners and investors.

With the power to issue decrees, the Tajik president has taken the lead in asserting property rights and privatization efforts. In a series of laws, the president stated that private and state property rights were protected under the law. At the same time privatization was hamstrung by a presidential decree requiring that the sale of any state business be approved by local and regional privatization committees. Another decree exhorted government officials to work more quickly at selling private industries to private owners.

The result of the tangled system of decrees was a delayed privatization effort bogged down by internal squabbling and a lack of any specific rule of law. The presidential decrees did not include any reform of the Soviet-era law codes that did not recognize property rights, and lacked the means for establishing corporations and joint stock ownership.

By the end of the 1990s, privatization was unevenly practiced at the regional and business levels. The capital of Dushanbe and the more economically developed Leninabad region had the most businesses under private control. The southern region and the Gorno-Badakhshan Autonomous Region had the least privatization.

But even where the efforts were the most successful, only small businesses were purchased by private interests and less then half of those businesses left government control. Larger industries, including utilities, communication, and transportation, remained under government control. The same delays found in privatization are apparent in the attempts to update the country's criminal code.

CRIMINAL CODE

Under the Soviet system, judge-made law was viewed suspiciously as courts were seen as tools of the government rather than independent institutions that served as buffers between the individual and the state. To enforce their socialist view of the economy and society, the Soviets relied upon a detailed legal code. This introduced a civil law system into a Central Asian culture that had previously relied upon tribal law and informal court structures. With each republic having a code by the time of the Soviet Union's disintegration, Tajikistan had a legal structure in place.

The Tajik criminal code resembles the detailed codes found in many civil law countries. Divided into criminal, civil, property, and state crime issues, the code includes some ominous sections that suggest methods for maintaining an authoritarian governmental system. As with the Soviet codes, the Tajik code proclaims equality under the law, guarantees rights and due process, and proclaims adherence to the rule of law. But a closer examination of the details elicits a different approach.

Composed of 405 articles, much of the code is repetition of the laws found in other European countries. But several provide the basis for the authoritarian government. Article 137 is directed against the public insult or slander of the Tajik president. Slander is defined as criticizing so as to harm the president's reputation or standing. Article 137 provides for prison sentences for those daring enough to criticize the highest levels of Tajik government.

Political activity is further limited by Article 159, prohibiting parties or organizations that infringe on citizens' rights. Article 159's broad grant of power to the government was used by the courts to ban four political parties during the political crisis of 1992 to 1993. The government interpreted citizens' rights as those furthering the safety and security of the country. Parties that challenged the government were deemed not in the citizens' best interest.

Article 330 takes repression of speech one step further. It provides criminal penalties for public insult of any official in a public speech or in the media. Violating this article can lead to an extended jail term. Its effect is to silence criticism by the media, which is already heavily regulated. Article 335 hearkens back to the old Soviet era by forbidding Tajiks from crossing the country's borders without official permission or documentation.

Overall, few changes have been made to the Tajikistan criminal code. Many of its Soviet-era provisions continue to limit individual rights. The codes are another example of a lack of change in the country's legal system.

LEGAL TRAINING

Even with the civil war, Tajikistan was able to maintain several universities and trade schools throughout the country. But the existence of these schools did not translate to a large number of degrees. There is no law school within the country, forcing students to attend universities in either the other former Soviet Republics or in the Gulf states. The Tajikistan State University is the largest secondary level school in the country and is located in the capital of Dushanbe. Because the country operates under the civil law system, lawyers seek training at law schools that teach civil law.

IMPACT OF THE LAW

Carved from the territory of its Central Asian neighbors, Tajikistan has suffered from political and economic crises since declaring independence in 1991. The civil war destroyed the nascent democracy in the country. Religious and ethnic divisions have split the country, making it all but impossible for the central government to exert control.

Although Tajikistan has broken free of Soviet institutions and political control, it has been unable to eliminate the cultural bias against the law. Executive dominance over courts has prevented an independent judiciary from taking hold. Instead, judges are functionaries of the government, caught between the president's power to remove them and the threat of political violence that permeates the country.

With limited economic or political ties to the West, the Tajik regime has little need and even less incentive to reform its legal system. Instead the law continues to be used in the Leninist tradition of maintaining the authoritarian regime. The peace agreement signed in 1996 did cause a loosening of political and legal strictures but Tajikistan remains a one-party state where the president can change the law on a whim and the constitution is enforced in the breach.

Douglas Clouatre

See also Afghanistan; Civil Law; Commercial Law (International Aspects); Kazakhstan; Soviet System

References and further reading

Akbarzadeh, Shahram. 1996. "Why Did Nationalism Fail in Tajikistan?" *Europe-Asia Studies* 48 (November): 1105–1129.
Arici, Buelent. 1997. "The State and Civil Society in Central Asia." *Perceptions* 2 (August): 132–153.
Atikin, Muriel. 1997. "Tajikistan's Civil War." *Current History* 96 (October): 336–340.
Brown, Bess. 1994. "Tajikistan to Restore Presidency." *RFE/RL Research Report* 3, no. 31 (August): 11–13.
Bushkov, Valentin, and Dmitry Mikulsky. 1996. "Tajikistan on the Brink of Collapse." *Current Digest of the Post-Soviet Press* 48 (September 11): 13–14.
Dawisha, Karen, and Bruce Parrott, eds. 1997. *Conflict, Cleavage and Change in Central Asia and the Caucasus.* New York: Cambridge University Press.
Gleason, Gregory. 1997. *The Central Asian States: Discovering Independence.* Boulder, CO: Westview Press.
Jones, Benjamin, and Leif Beck Fallisen. 1999. "The Newly Independent States: A Country-by-Country Look at How Each is Faring Today." *Europe* no. 383 (Fall): 30–35.
Martin, Keith. 1993. "Tajikistan: Civil War without End?" *RFE/RL Research Report* 2, no. 33 (August 20): 18–29.
———. 1994. "Environment: Central Asia's Forgotten Tragedy." *RFE/RL Research Report* 3, no. 29 (July): 35–48.
Smith, Graham. 1996. *The Nationalities Question in the Post-Soviet States.* New York: Longman Publishing.

TANZANIA

GEOGRAPHY

Tanzania is located on the eastern coast of Africa and covers an area of 883,749 square kilometers. It is made up of two formerly independent African states, the Republic of Tanganyika and the People's Republic of Zanzibar, which merged to form the United Republic of Tanzania (Tanzania) in April 1964. According to the 1988 census the country was expected to have a population of 32 million people by the year 2000.

The country is endowed with many unique and attractive physical features. It is the home to Africa's tallest mountain, Kilimanjaro, and to Lake Tanganyika, the second-deepest lake in the world. To the north of the country is Lake Victoria, the largest inland water body in Africa. Tanzania also has one of the most famous archeological sites in the world, the Olduvai Gorge, where archeologists found the remains of a 1.8-million-year-old Nutcracker Man (Zinjanthropus). Tanzania is bordered by the Indian Ocean on the east, and by Kenya and Uganda to the north. To the northwest are Rwanda and Burundi and to the west is the Democratic Republic of Congo. To the southwest the country borders Zambia, and Malawi and Mozambique are on its southern border.

As in many other sub-Saharan African countries, Tanzania's population is composed of many ethnic groups. It is estimated that as many as 120 distinct ethnic groups exist in the country today. The national language of Tanzania is Swahili (locally known as Kiswahili), which is also the official language of government business. English

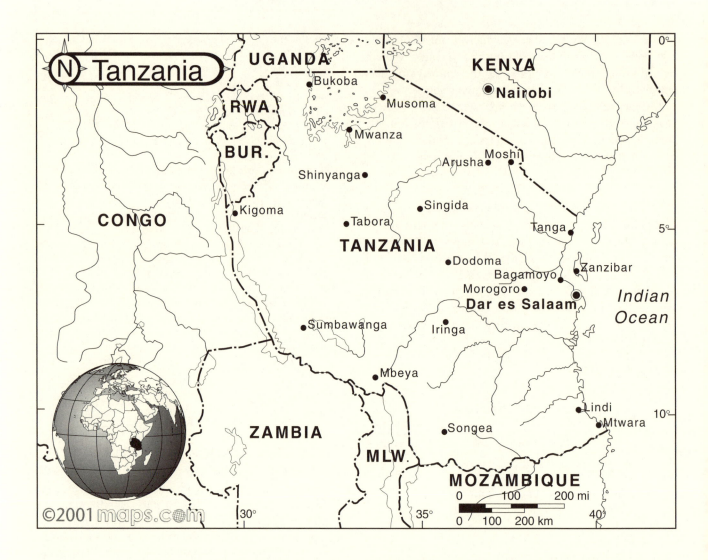

N Tanzania

UGANDA
KENYA
Bukoba
Musoma
RWA.
Nairobi
BUR.
Mwanza
Moshi
Shinyanga
Arusha
CONGO
Singida
Kigoma
Tabora
Tanga
TANZANIA
Dodoma
Zanzibar
Bagamoyo
Morogoro
Dar es Salaam
Indian Ocean
Sumbawanga
Iringa
Mbeya
Lindi
Mtwara
ZAMBIA
Songea
MLW.
MOZAMBIQUE

©2001 maps.com

is widely spoken and is the second-most-important language in the country.

POLITICAL SYSTEM

Tanzania is a presidential republic with a unique federal structure made up of Tanganyika and Zanzibar. On January 22, 1964, the then presidents of Tanganyika and Zanzibar, Julius K. Nyerere and Abedi A. Karume, respectively, declared that the two independent East African states had agreed to unite and to create a single sovereign state that was to be known as the United Republic of Tanganyika and Zanzibar. The name was changed to United Republic of Tanzania later that same year. Under the treaty referred to as the Acts of Union, the two countries agreed to surrender part of their powers and to form one sovereign state, the United Republic of Tanzania, and that there would be two governments, the government of the United Republic of Tanzania and the government of Zanzibar. The union was thus set up in such manner that Zanzibar, the smaller of the two partners, surrendered part of its sovereign powers to the United Republic and kept some within its internal authority. Tanganyika instead sur-

rendered all its authority to the union government and therefore the state of Tanganyika ceased to exist. The Acts of Union formed the basis of the Tanzania Constitution before an interim constitution was drawn in 1965.

In 1977, the country enacted its first permanent constitution, which brought about many fundamental and far-reaching changes in the country. Under the constitution, the federal government is headed by a president, elected every five years and limited to two consecutive terms. Zanzibar has its own semiautonomous government, its own president, legislature, and judiciary. The Zanzibar president is also elected for a five-year term and is limited to two consecutive terms of office. The Zanzibar government caters only to those matters that do not fall under the union (federal) jurisdiction.

TANGANYIKA UNDER COLONIALISM

Tanganyika got its political independence from Britain on December 9, 1961, and Julius K. Nyerere became its leader, first as prime minister and later as president. The 1961 independence ended almost seventy-five years of colonization in Tanganyika. Britain had officially taken over the administration of Tanganyika in 1919 as a trustee of the League of Nations. Tanganyika, which was prior to that a German colony (German East Africa), was taken over by the League of Nations under the 1919 Versailles Treaty after the defeat of Germany in World War I. It was given to Britain as a trust territory with the mandate of preparing it for independence. In 1946, after World War II, the League of Nations mandate was transferred to the United Nations.

Before the arrival of Europeans in Tanganyika the local societies were organized along ethnic or tribal communities or chiefdoms. There were no state political structures like those found in the modern-day state. Each of the many tribal organizations lived in a defined territory except for the pastoral groups, like the Masai, who were nomads. Political organizations were therefore very much fragmented and the political organization was weak and patchy. Each chieftaincy controlled its own area and no single group was powerful or sophisticated enough to consolidate the power within one centrally organized authority. The disfranchised nature of the political system contributed to the isolated, sporadic, and weak resistance against the colonial powers who began conquering Africa in the nineteenth century. There is not much record as to the political organization of those societies, but existing information reveals that the traditional societies were governed by customary rules that may be described as customary law. The laws governed all aspects of traditional African life such as communal property, rite of passage, inheritance, marriage, and crime and punishment.

The pioneers of the European arrivals to Tanganyika came as explorers and missionaries, and the earliest steps toward complete colonization took the form of agreements between the local chiefs and the colonial representatives. These were in fact treaties of subordination disguised as friendly and protective treaties. By the year 1884 Tanganyika officially became a German colony. German colonization did not face strong resistance from the local population due to the absence of a united opposition. The struggle was organized on a tribal basis and the few pockets of resistance were defeated, in part due to disorganization and inferior war technology. Between the official establishment of German rule in Tanganyika in 1884 and the defeat of Germany in World War I in 1918, there wasn't much time for the institutionalization of an efficient territorial administration and a reliable judicial system. The Germans and later on the British colonial administration engaged in what was referred to as *indirect rule,* under which the indigenous traditional African rulers were integrated into the colonial administration.

TANGANYIKA AFTER INDEPENDENCE

The independence constitution of Tanganyika of 1961 provided for the existence of a governor-general who represented the queen of England as the formal head of state. It also provided for the post of prime minister as the head of the government. An independent judiciary was also envisioned by the new constitution. The independence constitution was replaced by a republican constitution in 1962, which provided for the existence of an executive president as the head of state. The president acquired all the powers exercised by the governor-general and the prime minister, becoming head both of state and of the government. He also became the commander in chief of the army and also part of the Parliament, which meant that no law could enter into force without presidential assent. The constitution also empowered the president to dissolve the Parliament and to appoint the prime minister and other ministers. The new republican constitution did not, however, eliminate some of the characteristics of the colonial legal order. The new government left untouched some of the colonial repressive laws such as the Deportation Ordinance and the Emergency Power Ordinance. In addition, the Preventive Detention Act of 1962 was enacted. The act conferred upon the president the power to detain indefinitely and without trial any person who, in the opinion of the president, posed danger to peace and order in the country.

Following the April 1964 agreement referred to as Acts of Union between Tanganyika and Zanzibar, an interim constitution was adopted in 1965 pending the enactment of a new permanent constitution. The union between Tanganyika and Zanzibar led to the formation of a federal state where Zanzibar retained some degree of autonomy with its own presidency, legislature, and judiciary. All the powers belonging to Tanganyika were delegated to the federal government. Therefore, although some argued that the union was a voluntary act of two sovereign states, others continue to argue that it was a de jure annexation of Zanzibar by Tanganyika.

Under the Acts of Union, the two governments delegated to the federal government eleven matters that would be regulated by the federal government. These included: constitution and government of the United Republic; external affairs; defense; police; emergency powers; citizenship; immigration; external trade and borrowing; public service of the United Republic; income tax, corporation tax, customs, and excise duties; harbors, civil aviation, ports, and telegraph. The list has now grown to include more issues under federal regulation. The 1965 interim constitution declared the country a single-party state, and the new and permanent constitution enacted in 1977 further consolidated the already existing position of supremacy of the party over the state. However, between 1977 and April 2001 the constitution was amended as many as thirteen times, the most significant change being that of 1992, which repealed the constitutional provision that imposed single-party monopoly.

Independent Tanganyika inherited from the British colonial administration the English common law system, which remains as part of the British colonial legacy. The English common law system was officially introduced into Tanganyika in 1920 under the Tanganyika Order in Council of 1920. Tanganyika also experienced the dual legal system as part of the British tradition where customary law courts regulated the relationships between the natives while English common law regulated matters between British subjects and between British subjects and the natives. Following the pattern of indirect rule as established elsewhere in the British colonies and dependencies, the Native Court Ordinance was enacted in the same year, giving way to the establishment of the native courts. Under the dual legal system the native tribunals were headed by colonial administrative officers who were not obliged to possess professional legal education, nor were advocates allowed to appear before them. The decisions of the native courts were likewise appealed to the higher administrative authorities at district and territorial level.

The dual legal system existed throughout the colonial period and up until the first two years after independence. In 1963 the division of the system into two subsystems was abolished under the Magistrates' Courts Act of 1963. The new law established an integrated system that consisted of primary courts, district and resident Magistrates' Courts, and the High Court of Tanzania. The Court of Appeal of East Africa remained the highest court of appeal until the collapse of the East African Community in 1977 and the subsequent establishment of the Tanzania Court of Appeal the same year.

THE JUDICIARY

The judiciary in Tanzania is relatively independent. Nevertheless, extensive executive powers concentrated in the hands of the president as well as legislative interference casts some doubt on absolute independence of the judiciary. The president has the power to appoint judges of the high court and of the court of appeal only in consultation with the Judicial Service Commission. The president is not constitutionally bound to follow the recommendations of the commission, nor is he obliged to seek the confirmation of the legislature on such appointments. Such overwhelming powers may jeopardize the independence of such appointees. The situation may be even worse in lower courts where magistrates are appointed by the Judicial Service Commission and may be fired by the same organ. The Tanzania legislature has also at times undermined the independence of the judiciary. There have been instances, for example, when the high court declared a law to be unconstitutional only to find the legislature coming back to amend the constitution and return to the status quo. Such abuses of the Parliament's legislative powers to appease the executive does not augur well with the concept of independence of the judiciary.

Tanzania established a Law Reform Commission in 1983 whose functions were to review the existing laws and propose appropriate reforms of all the branches of law. It was entrusted with making proposals for the elimination of all anomalies and defects in the laws that were then in force. Over time, the commission has managed to review and make recommendations on various laws, some of which have been accordingly amended or repealed.

The chief justice is the head of the judiciary branch of the state. He is appointed by the president and must leave office only upon reaching retirement age or upon the recommendation of a special commission made up of judges from common law countries formed for the purpose of investigating an alleged misconduct by a judge. The chief justice is also an ex-officio member of the Judicial Service Commission. The president also appoints the other judges of the high court and of the court of appeal, who may be removed from their positions under the same procedures as the chief justice.

THE COURT SYSTEM

The Tanzania Court of Appeal was established under the Tanzania Constitution of 1977 after the breakup of the East African Community, which as a consequence caused the disintegration of the East African Court of Appeal. The court has jurisdiction to hear appeals from both sides of the United Republic of Tanzania except for matters regarding the interpretation of the Zanzibar Constitution and matters originating from the Kathi's (hereafter *qadi*) court in Zanzibar. The High Court of Tanzania was first established under the Interim Constitution of Tanzania of 1965. The court is headed by the chief justice and is composed of other judges appointed by the president. The court normally sits under one judge except for specific occasions where the law requires it to sit in full bench (three judges). In criminal cases the judge may sit with two lay assessors whose opinion is not binding on the judge. The court has unlimited jurisdiction over both criminal and civil matters. It has appellate jurisdiction over all disputes decided by the district court and the court of the resident magistrate. It also has the power to review or revise any decision of the lower courts.

The Magistrates' Courts Act requires the establishment of district Magistrates' Courts in every district in Tanzania. District courts have jurisdiction over all criminal and civil disputes in their respective districts as specified by law. In addition the chief justice is empowered to establish a court of the resident magistrate by an order published in the official Government Gazette. Such courts have jurisdiction over such areas as may be prescribed

Legal Structure of Tanzania Courts

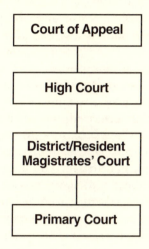

Court of Appeal

High Court

District/Resident Magistrates' Court

Primary Court

under the order. Both the district court and the court of the resident magistrate sit under one judge except as otherwise required. They have original jurisdiction over civil and criminal disputes as prescribed by the law currently in force. The district court has appellate jurisdiction over the decisions of the primary court. Decisions of the district court and of the court of the resident magistrate may be appealed to the High Court for Tanzania.

Primary courts are established under the Magistrates' Courts Act and are the lowest courts in the country. Each district must have at least one primary court. The primary court is the court of first instance and has jurisdiction over both criminal and civil disputes. It is presided over by a single magistrate sitting with two assessors whose opinion is not binding on the magistrate. The court has no appellate jurisdiction and its decisions may be subjected to review or revision by the district Magistrates' Court.

SPECIALIZED COURTS

The Military Tribunal
The military court was established by Act no. 24 of 1966 and has the mandate to try alleged violations by members of the armed forces. The decision of the tribunal may be, though very seldom is, appealed at the high court sitting in full bench (three judges) on matters of law or fact.

The Permanent Labor Tribunal
This was established under the Industrial Court Act. It deals with labor-related disputes between employers and their employees and its decision may be appealed at the high court sitting in full bench on matters of law only.

Commercial Courts
The commercial court was established under the Judicature and Application of Law Act, General notice no. 23

of 1984 (Rules of the Court). It is part of the High Court of Tanzania and its decisions may be appealed at the Court of Appeal of Tanzania.

The Juvenile Court
The juvenile court functions under the resident Magistrates' Court Act of 1984 and its decisions may be appealed at the High Court of Tanzania.

ALTERNATIVE DISPUTE RESOLUTION
The Criminal Procedure Act of 1985 allows parties to settle their dispute for nonserious offenses. The Civil Procedure Act instead allows out-of-court settlement in any dispute. In order to reduce a huge backlog of cases pending at the courts, the judiciary introduced a compulsory procedure under which the parties must seek an amicable solution to their dispute before they can file a suit at the court.

THE LEGAL PROFESSION
The rules governing the legal profession in Tanzania were introduced into the country through Indian laws. The Legal Practitioners Rules of India were made applicable in Tanganyika under the Indian Act (Application) Ordinance of 1922. The same rules were introduced in Zanzibar a year later. Some changes were made in 1955 by the Advocates Ordinance of 1955 and then by the Advocates (Amendments) Act of 1963. The rules defined, among other things, the requirements for admission into the legal profession. A person seeking admission into the legal profession was required to be a member of the bar in the United Kingdom or a solicitor of the Supreme Court of England or of a British dependent territory. The amendments made in 1963 allowed for the admission of locally trained lawyers. A Faculty of Law was established at the University of Dar es Salaam in 1963 (then part of the University of East Africa). Its aim was to cater to the great demand for lawyers immediately after independence. Students admitted at the faculty undergo three years of legal training and are thereafter required to attend a six-month internship under the supervision of experienced lawyers.

For many years the legal profession in Tanzania was under the strict control of the state in terms of training and utilization. This was mainly due to the socialist policies that the country practiced after it attained its independence. Following the abandoning of the socialist policies in the mid-1980s, the country found itself with a fairly small number of private law practitioners who could hardly satisfy the demand for lawyers, especially after economic liberalization. By 1995, the country had hardly more than 200 actively practicing lawyers. In addition to the private bar there is the Tanzania Legal Corporation (TLC), a public corporation established in

1970 with the aim of providing legal services to government-owned corporations and institutions. The lawyers belonging to the corporation enjoy more or less the same privileges as private legal practitioners. There are a few legal aid schemes such as those provided by the University of Dar es Salaam legal aid center, the state legal aid scheme, and the Tanganyika Law Society legal aid project. The legal profession is governed by different rules and regulations, some of which are imposed by statutes, others self-imposed as rules of professional codes of conduct.

ZANZIBAR

Zanzibar Islands, located twenty-five miles off the East African coast, form, since 1964, part of what is today known as the United Republic of Tanzania. Zanzibar is made up of the two major islands of Zanzibar (locally known as Unguja) and Pemba, together with a number of other smaller islands, few of which are inhabited. Zanzibar, the larger of the two main islands, covers an area of 1,554 square kilometers; Pemba covers an estimated area of 906 square kilometers. With a high birthrate and immigration from the mainland, the total population was estimated at around 800,000 by the year 2000.

Due to its geographical position, climate, and a good natural harbor, Zanzibar was in the past an important trading point and an international gateway to and from the African interior. History indicates the existence in the past of a flourishing trade in ivory, skins, slaves, ambergris, rhinoceros horns, and other items.

When the European powers were establishing colonies in Africa, Zanzibar found itself at the center of the German and British rivalry. In 1890 the sultan of Zanzibar signed an agreement with Britain to make the islands an official British protectorate. Zanzibar was under the British sphere of influence from that time on, until it achieved independence and became a constitutional monarchy on December 10, 1963. The new, independent Zanzibar government, however, had lasted for only thirty-four days when a violent revolution broke out on January 12, 1964. The new revolutionary government abolished the monarchy and declared Zanzibar a republic, nullified the constitution, abolished the parliamentary system, and banned all political parties. Three months after the revolution, on April 22, 1964, the leaders of Tanganyika and Zanzibar signed an agreement to create the United Republic of Tanganyika and Zanzibar. The newly formed united republic was later named Tanzania.

The British established in Zanzibar a dual legal system of traditional law for the natives and civil law for the British subjects and citizens of other countries. The population of Zanzibar was and still remains predominantly Muslim (approximately 97 percent) and the traditional law was by and large Islamic in character. The dual legal system existed from 1923, when the Zanzibar Courts Decree was enacted, up to 1963, when the country achieved independence. At the top of the hierarchy of the civil law system was the British court, referred to as His Majesty's High Court for Zanzibar. The native law system consisted of the Zanzibar court or His Highness the Sultan's Court for Zanzibar. The British court system applied to the British subjects in their relations among themselves and between them and the subjects of the sultan. It applied the English common law. The sultan's court dealt with the natives of Zanzibar in matters related to land, inheritance, marriages, and other related issues. Islamic law was the governing law of the court.

The new 1963 Constitution introduced a single system of administration of justice. It established the High Court of Zanzibar at the top of the court hierarchy. The constitution entered into force simultaneously with the granting of the country's independence in December 1963 but survived for only a little more than one month before the revolution took place in January 1964. The new revolutionary government annulled the existing constitution but provided for the continuation of all the previously existing laws with some modifications and exceptions and insofar as they concurred with the new republican status of the country.

The first two years of the revolution didn't bring much change and the legal system continued to operate under the common law tradition. The first changes, however, began to appear in 1966 when the Courts Decree of 1963 was repealed and replaced by the Courts Decree of 1966. More serious changes were made in 1969 under the People's Court Decree. The decree, which came into effect on January 1, 1970, provided for the establishment of the people's courts. At the top of the new system was the High Court for Zanzibar, followed by the people's district courts, and areas people's courts. Also included in the hierarchy was the qadi court, which dealt with Islamic matters. Under the decree, only the judges of the high court were required to possess professional legal education. The law required the judges to sit with two lay assessors whose opinion was not binding. Below the high court all the judges were appointed from among nonprofessionals and no particular qualification was necessary. A new constitution enacted in 1979 provided for the establishment of the Supreme Council, which played the role of an appellate body to the high court. The law again required no legal qualification for the members of the Supreme Council. The council had jurisdiction to hear appeals on manslaughter, murder, and treason cases. No advocates were allowed to appear before the council. The common law system was thus effectively turned into the people's legal system.

In 1984 a new constitution was enacted. Within the two years that followed the enactment of the new consti-

Legal Structure of Zanzibar Courts

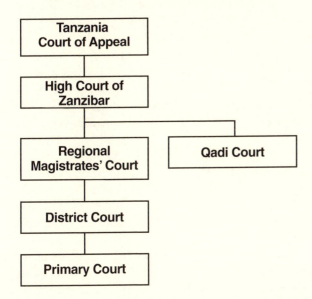

The judicial system is administered under the Chief Ministers Office. The chief justice and the judges of the high court are appointed by the president of Zanzibar and offer their oath of allegiance to the president. They are appointed for life and may leave office on retirement or upon the recommendations of a special commission formed for the purpose of inquiring into the judge's alleged misconduct. Lower courts magistrates are appointed by the Judicial Service Commission and may be removed from office upon the recommendation of the commission.

Khalfan S. Mohammed

See also Common Law; Legal Aid; Legal Pluralism
References and further reading
Allot, A. N. 1970. *Judicial and Legal Systems in Africa.* African Law Series, 2nd ed. London: Butterworths.
Ayany, S. G. 1983. *A History of Zanzibar: A Study in Constitutional Development.* Nairobi: East African Literature Bureau.
Hutchison, Thomas W. 1968. *Africa and Law. Developing Legal Systems in African Commonwealth Nations.* Madison: University of Wisconsin Press.
Maina, Chris Peter. 1990. *Human Rights in Africa.* New York: Greenwood Press.
Mtaki, C. K., and Michael Okema. 1994. *Constitutional Reform and Governance in Tanzania.* Dar es Salaam: Friedrich Noumann Foundation/University of Dar es Salaam.
Shivji, Issa G. 1990. *Tanzania: The Legal Foundations of the Union.* Dar es Salaam: Dar es Salaam University Press.
Twaib, Fauz. 1997. *The Legal Profession in Tanzania. The Law and Practice.* Dar es Salaam: Dar es Salaam University Press.

tution, major changes took place in the Zanzibar legal system. Three landmark acts were passed by the Zanzibar legislature. They included the High Court Act no. 2 of 1985, the Magistrates Act no. 3 of 1985, and the Kathi's Courts Act no. 6 of 1985. The enactment of the above three pieces of legislation marked an important turnaround in Zanzibar's legal history. It meant the abandonment of the people's courts system and the reintroduction of the common law system.

The Court of Appeal of East Africa, which was inherited by the East African countries of Kenya, Uganda, and Tanganyika and Zanzibar from the British colonial rule, ceased to exist in 1977 following the collapse of the East African Community. The Tanzania Constitution of 1977 therefore provided for the establishment of the Court of Appeal for Tanzania, and the Appellate Jurisdiction Act of 1979 extended the jurisdiction of the court of appeal to Zanzibar. The Zanzibar Constitution of 1984 further recognized the jurisdiction of the court of appeal over Zanzibar. The jurisdiction of the court of appeal over Zanzibar is, however, limited in scope. The court has no jurisdiction on cases that involve the interpretation of the Zanzibar constitution and over Islamic matters originating from the qadi court. As of 1985 the court system was composed of the following hierarchy: the Tanzania Court of Appeal, the High Court for Zanzibar, regional Magistrates' Courts, the District Magistrates' Courts, and the primary courts.

There are also qadi courts dealing with Islamic matters at the regional and district levels whose decision may be appealed at the High Court of Zanzibar. Zanzibar does not have independently existing specialized courts. The regional Magistrates' Court has the power, however, to sit as the juvenile court. A proposed industrial court has not been created.

TASMANIA

GENERAL INFORMATION

Tasmania consists of a main island and a number of smaller islands, off the southeastern corner of mainland Australia. Tasmania is the smallest Australian state. The area of the whole state is 67,800 square kilometers, making it just under one-third the size of Victoria, the second-smallest Australian state.

The population of Tasmania is predominantly of Anglo-Saxon background. Tasmania is less ethnically diverse than other Australian States. The population of Tasmania in 1999 was 471,000, and Tasmania has experienced a small decrease in recent years. The state's main centers are Hobart (the capital city, with 195,500 people), Launceston (98,500), Burnie (18,000), and Devonport (25,000).

EVOLUTION AND HISTORY

Tasmanian Aborigines lived in Tasmania for about twenty thousand years before the colonization of Tasmania by the

British Empire, and it is estimated that there were four to five thousand Tasmanian Aborigines upon the arrival of the Europeans. Aborigines fell victim to slaying and European diseases to which they had no immunity, and the last full-blooded Aborigine died during colonial times. Surviving part-blood Aborigines are integrated in the Tasmanian community and have some special land and hunting rights.

Established in 1803 as a penal colony, Tasmania is the second-oldest European settlement in Australia. Initially administered from Sydney, Van Diemen's Land (as it was then known) became a colony under its own administration in 1825 under a lieutenant governor and a legislative council of six members. Without violent insurrection, the imperial rulers steadily increased the power and membership of the legislative council.

In 1856, responsible government was established and the present bicameral Parliament met for the first time. The basic constitutional structure has remained the same since then. Women became eligible to vote in 1903, at the same time that universal adult suffrage was brought in for House of Assembly elections. Women first became eligible for election to Parliament in 1921. The first woman parliamentarian was elected in 1948. Voting became compulsory in the 1930s. The Legislative Council slowly changed from restrictive franchise to full adult suffrage in 1968.

Upon federation in 1901, Tasmania gave powers to the Commonwealth and became a state in the Australian Federation. The laws of Tasmania are controlled by the Tasmanian Parliament, unless the federal constitution prevails. The federal constitution does not, however, define the constitutional structure of Tasmanian institutions. It reserves the continued separate operation of the Tasmanian constitution and the powers of the Tasmanian government, except to the extent that power is specifically ceded to the federal government.

General law-making power in Tasmania derives from the imperial Australian Constitutions Act (No. 2) of 1850. The Tasmanian Constitution is an act of the Tasmanian Parliament: the Constitution Act 1934. As an ordinary act of Parliament, the Constitution Act can be amended by an ordinary act of Parliament, subject to only one minor exception. In accordance with the Australia Act (Request) of 1985 of the Tasmanian Parliament, both the Commonwealth and U.K. parliaments, by the Australia Act 1986, abolished the judicial, legislative, and executive connection of Tasmania with the U.K.

Although Tasmania has had three levels of government since 1901, it was not until 1988 that local government (the third tier) was recognized under the state constitution. The federal constitution still does not refer to local government. Councils are under the legislative control and executive supervision of the state government.

The twenty-nine Tasmanian municipal councils control planning and environmental outcomes, as well as development and building activity. Councils are controlled by voluntary elections by local residents. Councils provide recreation infrastructure, local roads, water, sewerage, and garbage disposal. They are increasingly providing other services as well, such as health and youth services, and are supporting local development. Councils supervise planning and resource- and land-use management.

CURRENT STRUCTURE
The Tasmanian legal system is a typical example of the English Westminster system of government: a constitutional monarchy controlled by a transparent, parliamentary democracy, and the rule of law under an independent judicial system.

As a member of the Australian Federation, Tasmania is part of the Commonwealth of Australia but remains a self-governing state with its own separate identity and its own head of state. The head of state of Tasmania is the governor.

The Tasmanian Parliament is bicameral under the Crown, its houses being the Legislative Council (or upper house) and the House of Assembly (or lower house). Parliament chooses and scrutinizes the executive government and makes state laws. The political group with a majority of members in the House of Assembly forms the executive government. Thirteen or more members make a majority. Governments may rely upon coalitions between several political parties or independents to win a majority. The size of the ministry varies but can be no more than ten.

The largest minority party in the House, the opposition, scrutinizes government action and policies and presents alternatives. The two houses of the Tasmanian Parliament have almost equal powers. The House of Assembly introduces appropriation and taxation legislation, which the Legislative Council may either accept or reject (but not amend). By convention, the House of Assembly initiates legislation and the Legislative Council acts as a house of review. There is no constitutional provision to resolve deadlocks between the two houses.

The houses act under the Tasmanian Constitution in accordance with standing orders and rules based on the practice of the English Parliament. The monarch of Australia (who is also the monarch of the United Kingdom) appoints the governor on the advice of the Tasmanian premier, the head of the executive government. The office of governor is nonpolitical and quite distinct from that of the premier.

The governor appoints the leader of the majority group in the House of Assembly as the premier, and on the premier's advice appoints ministers, assents to parliamentary bills, opens Parliament, and gives legal effect to

Structure of Tasmanian Government and Courts

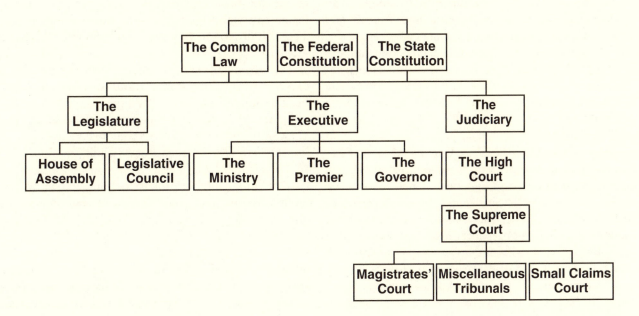

government decisions through the Executive Council. The Executive Council consists of the premier and the ministers of the government of the day.

The governor's extensive powers are exercised mainly on the advice of the premier or the Executive Council, although the governor's constitutional role is not purely formal. Sometimes governors must act on their own initiative, exercise discretion, and question legality or procedural regularity. Governors may not, however, question government policy. The governor protects the constitution, secures the orderly transition of governments, and facilitates the work of Parliament and the government.

According to the doctrine of separation of powers, Tasmania grants its judges independence following appointment. The Supreme Court acts as a court of first instance and as an appellate court (see figure). It deals only with serious offenses, and criminal trials in the Supreme Court are heard before a jury of twelve presided over by a judge. The Supreme Court has jurisdiction in all civil matters but normally deals only with disputes over sums in excess of $20,000. Civil cases are usually tried by a judge but sometimes, at the election of a party, with a jury of seven. There is a right of appeal to the Supreme Court from the decision of a Magistrates' Court and from most tribunals, although in some cases only on questions of law and not on questions of fact. A court of three or more Supreme Court judges usually hears appeals from decisions of the Supreme Court. Appeals from appellate decisions of the Supreme Court are to the High Court of Australia, from which there is no appeal.

The Tasmanian jury system is based on the English system. Most persons are eligible to serve as jurors, and

majority rather than unanimous decisions are permitted in some cases.

Judges of the Supreme Court are appointed by the governor on the advice of the government from the ranks of senior lawyers. The master of the Supreme Court exercises judicial powers as a deputy of the judges and acts as a judge in chambers. The master is appointed in the same manner and has the same tenure as a judge. The registrar of the Supreme Court is its principal administrative officer and keeps the registry of wills and estates. The sheriff of the Supreme Court enforces writs and warrants of the court and runs the selection and supervision of jurors.

The Magistrates' Court is the second tier court in the Tasmanian legal system below the Supreme Court. Magistrates determine in Courts of Petty Sessions offenses of a less serious nature, both state and federal. For trial in the Supreme Court, magistrates control the early court appearances and either check or collate evidence. The Magistrates' Court has jurisdiction over offending, neglected, needy, and uncontrollable children, and adoption. Magistrates exercise jurisdiction over civil claims of less than $20,000, or higher amounts with the consent of the parties.

The Small Claims Division of the Magistrates' Court exercises jurisdiction over some civil claims that do not exceed $3,000. Legal representation is generally not allowed in the Small Claims Division. The Small Claims Division operates under simplified and abbreviated procedures, and judgments in the Small Claims Division are enforceable like any other court order.

The Coronial Division of the Magistrates' Court investigates certain deaths, fires, and explosions, and justices of the peace perform certain basic judicial duties. The Resource Management and Planning Appeal Tribunal is an independent statutory body that conducts hearings and appeals under various planning and land use–related acts. The Resource Planning and Development Commission is an independent statutory body overseeing the state's planning system. It approves planning schemes, prepares state of the environment reports, and assesses public land-use issues and projects of state significance.

NOTABLE FEATURES OF LAW/LEGAL SYSTEM

House of Assembly elections are conducted under the unique, proportional-representation Hare-Clark system. Under that system, electors vote in order of preference for at least five candidates in five multimember electorates. Names appear on voting papers in groups according to party allegiance, with the names of the parties specified. The listing order of candidates' names within each group is rotated to minimize the effect of position on the voting paper. To be elected, a candidate must receive a quota of votes. A quota is the total first preferences cast in the electorate divided by six, plus one vote. The second preferences of the first successful candidate are transferred to other candidates after first being multiplied by a fraction called the transfer value. The transfer value is calculated as the candidate's surplus first preferences divided by his total first preferences. As each candidate wins a quota, this process is repeated until no further candidates can reach a quota. Then the candidate lowest on the poll is excluded, and the second preferences on his/her voting papers are transferred to the remaining candidates. These procedures are repeated until five candidates have been elected. Recounts, rather than by-elections, usually fill casual vacancies.

The Hare-Clark system delivers membership of the Parliament in close proportion to the votes cast. This avoids landslide victories from small margins across many single electorates decimating an opposition. The Hare-Clark system offers electors a wide choice of candidates as well as the opportunity to choose between representatives of a party grouping. It also facilitates the election of independents and micro parties.

The Legislative Council has fifteen single-member electorates using a more common preferential system of election by absolute majority through the use of the alternative vote.

STAFFING

Tasmania has a fused legal profession, with practitioners admitted both as barristers and as solicitors. Some lawyers choose to practice according to the Rules of Practice of the Bar.

As of September 2000, the private legal profession included 180 partners in forty-nine firms, and 69 sole practitioners employing a further 218 practitioners, with 11 lawyers working in community legal centers, and 10 lawyers practicing as barristers. The biggest firms in Tasmania have only 9 partners and fewer than 20 lawyers. There is no substantial presence of firms that are based interstate.

Lawyers are admitted to practice after completing a university degree course of at least four years and a legal practice diploma of six months' duration.

Under the Legal Profession Act, the Law Society acts as a regulatory and supportive body for the legal profession. A statutorily independent Disciplinary Committee convened under the Legal Profession Act disciplines lawyers found guilty of professional misconduct. A legal ombudsman monitors and reports to the attorney general on the handling of complaints about legal practitioners.

The Department of Justice and Industrial Relations is the Tasmanian government agency dealing with law and order. The Crown Law Office is the law firm of the state government. The head of the Crown Law Office is the attorney general, who is the chief law officer of the state and the principal lawyer advising government. The attorney general is a politician and a member of the government of the day. Constitutional court proceedings issue in the name of the attorney general, but the attorney general does not usually appear as counsel personally.

The Crown Law Office has three key divisions: the solicitor general, who provides legal advice to ministers, agencies, and instrumentalities of the Crown and representation in constitutional litigation in which the Crown is involved; the crown solicitor, who provides property and commercial legal services to the government; and the director of public prosecutions, who conducts criminal prosecutions, represents government agencies in courts and tribunals (including civil litigation), and represents the Crown in court appeals. The director of public prosecutions is a statutory appointment with decision-making independence, accountable to Parliament through the attorney general.

The Tasmanian ombudsman investigates complaints against Tasmanian state government departments, councils, and public authorities. The ombudsman reviews individual grievances and systemic issues of maladministration in the public sector.

RELATIONSHIP TO NATIONAL SYSTEM

Tasmania's relationship to the federal government and the other states is not structurally different from that of other states. By the terms of the constitution, Tasmania, as a small state, receives overweighted representation in the national Parliament.

Upon federation, the states sought to limit the powers of the federal government by listing a limited set of powers by subject matter. The balance of power has moved to the national government, however, assisted by federal taxation and the High Court's interpretation of the constitution. Tasmania unsuccessfully fought to defend state authority under the constitution in the *Commonwealth v. the State of Tasmania* (Tasmanian Dams Case) (1983) CLR 1, in which the High Court held that the commonwealth could prohibit construction of a dam by acting with reference to an international treaty.

Tim Tierney

See also Australia; Barristers; Common Law; Law Firms; Small Claims Courts; Solicitors

References and further reading
Bowen, Jan. 1987. *The Macquarie Easy Guide to Australian Law.* Chatswood NSW: Macquarie Library.
Chalmers, Donald C. 1989. *Legal Studies for Tasmania.* 2d ed. Sydney: Butterworths.
Derkley, H. 1994. *The Tasmanian Law Handbook.* Hobart: Hobart Community Legal Service.
Lane, P. H. 1994. *An Introduction to the Australian Constitutions.* Sydney: Law Book Company.
Tasmanian Case Law, http://www.austlii.edu.au/databases.html#tas (accessed July 10, 2001).
Tasmanian Government Home Page, http:/www.tas.gov.au (accessed July 10, 2001).
Tasmanian Legislation, http:/www.thelaw.tas.gov.au (accessed July 10, 2001).
Tasmanian Parliament, http://www.parliament.tas.gov.au/ (accessed July 10, 2001).

TENNESSEE

GENERAL INFORMATION

The state of Tennessee lies north of western Georgia, Alabama, and Mississippi; south of western Virginia and Kentucky; east of the Mississippi River (which forms its western border); and west of North Carolina. It is the thirty-fourth of fifty U.S. states by size and, with a population approaching five and a half million, the sixteenth most populous. Originally regarded as a western frontier state, Tennessee is now considered Southern.

Long a predominately rural state known for its country music and for the famous Scopes Monkey Trial of 1925, in which the state defended its ban on teaching evolution in public schools, Tennessee in recent decades has undergone rapid industrialization (including the establishment of massive auto production plants by both Nissan and Saturn) and urbanization. It is one of six states that is part of the Tennessee Valley Authority, which was instituted by the national government during Franklin Roosevelt's New Deal to control flooding and produce cheap electricity. The state's capital is Nashville, close to the center of the state.

Historically, the state has been geographically and politically divided into three major sections—East, Middle, and West—each symbolized by a star on the state flag.

Although Tennessee joined the Confederate States during the American Civil War (1861–1865), there were strong Union sentiments in the state, especially in the Eastern part. There, largely on account of the mountainous terrain, slavery never flourished, and even today the Eastern region leans to the Republican Party, whereas the other two sections lean toward the Democrats.

EVOLUTION AND HISTORY

Originally considered to be part of North Carolina, the Eastern part of Tennessee (later represented briefly in the North Carolina legislature) made an abortive attempt in the 1780s to form the state of Franklin. North Carolina subsequently ceded the area to the national government, and Tennessee became the sixteenth state in 1796, patterning its first constitution largely after that of North Carolina. During its first century of statehood, Tennesseans Andrew Jackson, James K. Polk, and Andrew Johnson all served as president of the United States. Tennesseans John Catron, Howell Jackson, Horace Lurton, and James McReyolds have served on the U.S. Supreme Court (Justice Abe Fortas was also born and educated in Tennessee), and many other Tennesseans from both the Democratic and Republican parties (including Democratic vice president Al Gore) have been prominent in American politics.

The state's first two constitutions were adopted in 1796 and 1835. The current Tennessee Constitution, the state's third, was written in convention and adopted in 1870 during Reconstruction. This constitution was not altered until 1953, but voters have subsequently adopted alterations proposed by limited constitutional conventions that met in 1953, 1954, 1959, 1972, and 1977. Voters also approved an amendment in 1982 that had been proposed by two consecutive legislative sessions. Such amendments are incorporated into the text of the constitution rather than being appended to the end of the document. Both mechanisms for adopting constitutional amendments are difficult, and court decisions usually remain the definitive interpretations of the document.

CURRENT STRUCTURE

Long known for the complexity of its judicial system, Tennessee has reformed its system in recent years, largely through legislative enactments. Tennessee continues to have a larger number of courts, often with overlapping jurisdiction, than the corresponding federal system. Like that system, Tennessee's is arranged hierarchically. The state system has four levels.

At the local level, cities and counties have created courts of limited jurisdiction. These may include juvenile courts and municipal courts (which are both generally found in larger cities), as well as general sessions courts. The latter are the most common, and are found in

Legal Structure of Tennessee Courts

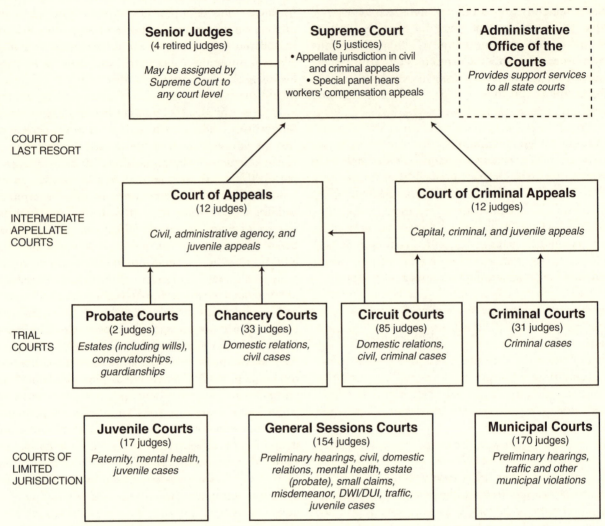

COURT OF LAST RESORT

Senior Judges
(4 retired judges)

May be assigned by Supreme Court to any court level

Supreme Court
(5 justices)
• Appellate jurisdiction in civil and criminal appeals
• Special panel hears workers' compensation appeals

Administrative Office of the Courts
Provides support services to all state courts

INTERMEDIATE APPELLATE COURTS

Court of Appeals
(12 judges)

Civil, administrative agency, and juvenile appeals

Court of Criminal Appeals
(12 judges)

Capital, criminal, and juvenile appeals

TRIAL COURTS

Probate Courts
(2 judges)

Estates (including wills), conservatorships, guardianships

Chancery Courts
(33 judges)

Domestic relations, civil cases

Circuit Courts
(85 judges)

Domestic relations, civil, criminal cases

Criminal Courts
(31 judges)

Criminal cases

COURTS OF LIMITED JURISDICTION

Juvenile Courts
(17 judges)

Paternity, mental health, juvenile cases

General Sessions Courts
(154 judges)

Preliminary hearings, civil, domestic relations, mental health, estate (probate), small claims, misdemeanor, DWI/DUI, traffic, juvenile cases

Municipal Courts
(170 judges)

Preliminary hearings, traffic and other municipal violations

Source: Vile, John R., and Mark Byrnes. 1988. *Tennessee Government and Politics.* Nashville, TN: Vanderbilt University Press.

all ninety-five Tennessee counties, although two counties in East Tennessee call them by different names. General sessions courts handle civil cases that do not exceed $10,000 or $15,000, depending on the population of the county. They may also try misdemeanor offenses or hold preliminary hearings on criminal charges. No records are made of the proceedings of general sessions courts, so any appeals from such courts must be completely reargued in the next higher court.

Courts at the next-higher level are called trial courts. Tennessee is divided into thirty-one judicial districts, each one of which contains both circuit and chancery courts. Both circuit and chancery courts handle civil cases, with circuit courts also handling criminal matters in those districts that do not (like more populous areas) have separate criminal courts. The state's two largest cities, Memphis and Nashville, both have separate pro-

bate courts to handle wills and estates. Tennessee has two intermediate appellate courts: the Court of Appeals, which hears civil and administrative agency appeals; and the Court of Criminal Appeals, which hears criminal cases. Each court has twelve judges, equally drawn from the three geographical divisions of the state. Judges typically sit in panels of three and alternate among sessions in Knoxville, Nashville, and Jackson.

The Tennessee Supreme Court is at the pinnacle of the Tennessee judicial system, and it is the only court specifically required by the state's constitution. It has five judges, no more than two of whom can be from one of the state's three main geographical divisions. The court meets in each of these geographical divisions, holding sessions in Knoxville, Nashville, and Jackson. Although most cases come to the Supreme Court through the intermediate appellate courts, it also hears some cases—including death penalty cases, in which appeal is automatic—upon direct appeal from the lower courts. An Administrative Office of the Courts, whose director is appointed by the Supreme Court, assists the Tennessee Supreme Court and the entire state court system. Supreme Court judges appoint clerks to assist them for six-year terms (clerks for the lower courts are elected to four-year terms). The state has a separate Claims Commission to hear claims against the state, but the maximum award is $300,000.

Each of Tennessee's thirty-one judicial districts has its own district attorney, with staff assistants. Since 1989, each district also has had a public defender. Such defenders earn the same salaries as their district attorney counterparts.

NOTABLE FEATURES OF LAW/LEGAL SYSTEM
Like its neighbors, Tennessee is a common law state. At least since the time of Andrew Jackson, Tennesseans have valued popular sovereignty. One arguably antiquated reflection of such confidence in the people is the state constitutional provision permitting only juries to level criminal fines of more than $50. By contrast, apart from the ratification of constitutional amendments, there is no statewide provision for an initiative, referendum, or recall election.

The Tennessee Supreme Court has led the state judiciary to greater independence. Recent decisions have been responsible for requiring equalization of state funding of public schools in urban and rural counties and of voiding the conviction of a number of defendants who were slated to get the death penalty. Controversy over one such decision led state voters to reject the confirmation of Supreme Court judge Penny White in 1996. An execution by lethal injection in 2000 was the state's first since 1960.

The state constitution prohibits Tennessee judges from presiding in cases in which they are connected to parties by either "affinity or consanguinity," or in which they have served as counsel or heard cases as lower court judges. The legislature provides for gubernatorial appointment of special judges in such cases.

State judges can be removed through either of two impeachment processes that proceed through the state legislature. In the last such case, the legislature removed Criminal Court judge Raulston Schoolfield in 1958 for misconduct in office. Since 1979, Tennessee has also had a Court of the Judiciary (whose diverse fifteen members are appointed by the Supreme Court, the Tennessee Bar Association, the governor, and the two legislative speakers) with power to investigate judges in office, sanction them, and even recommend their removal by the state legislature. Two general sessions judges and one trial judge have been removed through this procedure.

The state legislature technically has the right to abolish all state courts other than the state Supreme Court, but it cannot raise or lower the pay of judges during their terms. The Tennessee Supreme Court is the only such American court that selects the state's attorney general, who serves for an eight-year term. The director of the Tennessee Bureau of Investigation, rather than the attorney general, has power to intervene or to appoint a district attorney general pro tempore in cases in which local district attorneys are not doing their jobs. The attorney general (whose office is divided into fifteen divisions) argues appeals for the state and gives advisory opinions on constitutional matters to the governor.

Tennessee is twenty-second among the states in the number of criminal filings per 100,000 people, and its prison population and associated expenses have grown accordingly in recent years. The state is the headquarters of the Corrections Corporation of America, which runs some of the state's prisons. The state is last in the nation in the number of civil filings per capita.

In recent years, Tennessee has faced serious questions regarding the funding of state services. Although most neighboring states have lotteries or casinos, Tennessee continues to outlaw all forms of gambling. As of August 2000, the state, which relies primarily on revenues from the sales tax, had no income tax, despite lagging tax collections and efforts by successive Democratic and Republican governors to get one. Some observers think that a decision by Tennessee courts requiring further equalization in state funding of rural and urban school districts could necessitate such a tax. If adopted, the Supreme Court would ultimately have to decide whether a state income tax would be legal under the present state constitution.

STAFFING
In 1995 there were 8,314 practicing attorneys in Tennessee, ranking the state forty-first nationally by attorney-population ratio. Attorneys are required to earn a law degree and pass the state bar examination before practicing in the state. There are currently four Tennessee schools that train lawyers. The two state-supported schools are located at the University of Tennessee in Knoxville and at the University of Memphis, and offer standard three-year programs toward the juris doctor degree for college graduates. Vanderbilt University is a prestigious private school in Nashville with a similar program. The privately owned Nashville School of Law has a four-year night school to train attorneys, but its graduates are accredited only within the state. There have been many other private law schools in the state's history, when educational requirements were less standardized and rigorous. The Cumberland Law School, once one of the nation's largest, was located in Lebanon, Tennessee, just south of Nashville, before moving to Samford University in Birmingham, Alabama, in 1961.

Tennessee judges must have a law degree. Like the state's district attorneys and public defenders, both local and trial court judges in Tennessee are popularly elected for eight-year terms; they must meet certain residency requirements and must be at least thirty years of age. Judges of the Court of Appeals and the Court of Criminal Appeals are selected through a judicial nominating commission system. When vacancies occur, a fifteen-member Judicial Selection Commission (whose members are appointed to six-year terms by the speakers of both houses) submits three names to the governor, who chooses one. The nominee runs unopposed in the next August biennial election, and remains in office unless rejected by a majority of the voters. A twelve-member Judicial Evaluation Commission issues and publishes evaluations of appellate judges with a view toward aiding voters in making their decision.

Supreme Court judges are also selected, and retained or rejected, through a judicial nominating commission system, and their members serve for eight-year terms. Judges on the Supreme Court must be at least thirty-five years old, and they select their chief through the duration of the chief's term.

RELATIONSHIP TO NATIONAL SYSTEM

Three of the nation's ninety-four U.S. district courts are located within Tennessee. Cases are appealed from there to the Sixth Circuit Court of Appeals, and, ultimately, to the U.S. Supreme Court, which can also hear appeals from the state Supreme Court.

Although it did not originate in Tennessee, the historic U.S. Supreme Court decision in *Brown v. Board of Education* (1954) overturned the state's earlier system of de jure racial segregation, which had been recognized since a U.S. Supreme Court decision in 1896 and which was especially prominent in the South. Federal rulings protecting the rights of criminal defendants, invalidating most state laws regulating abortion during the first and second trimesters of pregnancy, striking down vocal prayer and Bible reading in public schools, and so forth have also affected the state.

Baker v. Carr (1962), one of the most important cases of the twentieth century, originated in Tennessee. Pointing out that Tennessee had no initiative or referendum mechanism by which to effect reform on its own, the U.S. Supreme Court decided that the state's archaic system of legislative apportionment, which allocated to rural areas of the state greater representation than population would have warranted, was justiciable. In subsequent cases impacting Tennessee and other states, the U.S. Supreme Court established the principle of "one person, one vote" for state legislative districts.

John R. Vile

See also North Carolina; United States—Federal System; United States—State Systems

References and further reading
Brake, Patricia E. 1998. *Justice in the Valley: A Bicentennial Perspective of the United States District Court for the Eastern District of Tennessee.* Franklin, TN: Hillsboro Press.
Carson, Clara N. 1999. *The Lawyer Statistical Report: The U.S. Legal Profession in 1995.* Chicago: American Bar Foundation.
Darnell, Riley C., ed. 1999. *Tennessee Blue Book, 1999–2000.* Nashville: Tennessee Secretary of State.
Ely, James, ed. Forthcoming. *"The Cornerstone of Our Government": A History of the Tennessee Supreme Court, 1796–1998.* Knoxville: University of Tennessee Press.
Greene, Lee Seifert, David H. Grubbs, and Victor C. Hobday. 1982. *Government in Tennessee.* 4th ed. Knoxville: University of Tennessee Press.
Laska, Lewis L. 1990. *The Tennessee State Constitution: A Reference Guide.* New York: Greenwood Press.
Van West, Carroll, ed. 1998. *The Tennessee Encyclopedia of History & Culture.* Nashville: Tennessee Historical Society.
Vile, John R., and Mark Byrnes, eds. 1998. *Tennessee Government and Politics: Democracy in the Volunteer State.* Nashville: Vanderbilt University Press.

TEXAS

GENERAL INFORMATION

The most notable characteristic of Texas is its size. The longest straight-line distance across the state north-south is 801 miles, while the longest east-west distance is 773 miles. Although it is often considered a state of ranches, farms, and oil wells, that image is of earlier eras. In 1940, 23 percent of the Texas population worked on farms and ranches, but in 1998 only 2 percent of the population lived there. Although the oil industry was once the dominant business force in the state, today Texas is an urban state with a highly diversified, rapidly growing economy that includes a strong high-technology segment.

In 1990, 17 million people resided in Texas. By 1998, the number of people in Texas had reached 19.76 million. Between 1990 and 1996, Texas added more people to its total population than any other state in the union. Fifty-seven percent of the population in 1998 were non-Hispanic whites, down from 61 percent in 1990. Twelve percent were African American. Twenty-nine percent were Hispanic, up from 25 percent in 1990.

EVOLUTION AND HISTORY

The current Texas constitution went into effect in 1876 and, in spite of much criticism, it has lasted far longer than any of the six other constitutions that have governed Texas. Of those early constitutions, the most important in understanding the current Texas constitution and governmental structure is the Constitution of 1869.

The Constitution of 1869 was created as a result of a Reconstruction requirement that states of the old Confederacy could not re-enter the Union until new state constitutions were adopted that gave blacks the right to vote. It also greatly increased the power of the governor. Among other things, the governor was given vast appointment powers that included the power to appoint judges. There were increased salaries for state officials and annual sessions of the legislature.

To prevent another Republican-controlled state government, which the Democrats regarded as corrupt, extravagant, and even tyrannical, the Constitution of 1876 was adopted. The framers of the 1876 Constitution wanted popular control of state government. That meant that the governor's vast appointment powers were to be limited by having public officials subject to election. Judges and other officials who had been appointed by the governor under the 1869 Constitution were now independently elected officials. State government was to be a government of limited powers. There would be a diffusion of executive powers among numerous office-holders to prevent any future governor from having the vast powers held by the previous Republican governor. Restrictions were placed on state government that would have to be modified through a complex constitutional amendment process. Lengthy, rigid, and detailed regulations were placed, not in statutes, but in the body of the constitution. The idea was that the Radical Republicans would never again be able to reign and spend in Texas. They, of course, never did, although the constitution over the years became an increasingly unwieldy document.

CURRENT STRUCTURE

Texas has a large and complex court structure. At the highest appellate level is the Texas Supreme Court, which consists of nine justices, including a chief justice (see figure). This court hears civil cases only. The term of a justice is six years—the term of all appellate judges—with at least three justices being elected every two years.

The Court of Criminal Appeals is the highest court in the state for criminal cases. This court also has nine judges, including a presiding judge. Perhaps the most important task of the Court of Criminal Appeals is to have jurisdiction over automatic appeals in death penalty cases.

Texas has fourteen other appellate courts located in various parts of the state that have both criminal and civil jurisdiction. Usually, before the Supreme Court or the Court of Criminal Appeals hears a case, the initial appeal has been heard by one of the courts of appeal. Presently there are eighty judges who serve on the fourteen courts of appeal, which range in size from three to thirteen judges. Although there are occasions when every judge on the court of appeals will hear a case, appeals at this level of court are heard mostly by panels of three judges.

The major trial courts in Texas are the district courts.

Each county has at least one district court, although rural parts of Texas may have several counties that are served by one district court. In contrast, urban counties have many district courts. These courts usually have general jurisdiction, meaning that they hear a broad range of civil and criminal cases. However, in urban counties there are some district courts with specialized jurisdiction that will hear only civil, criminal, juvenile, or family law matters. Currently, there are 396 district judges. District judges, as well as all other trial court judges, serve four-year terms.

Texas is unusual in having the office of county judge in each of its 254 counties. Not only is the county judge the chief administrative officer of county government, but, in addition, in some counties the county judge presides over the county court. Often these county courts have jurisdiction over probate cases, serious misdemeanors, and relatively minor civil cases. They may also hear appeals from municipal courts or from justice of the peace courts. However, in the more populated counties, there are county courts at law and sometimes probate courts. As a result, in the larger counties, most if not all of the county judges' judicial duties are now performed by other courts.

In larger counties, there are statutory county courts at law that are designed to aid the county court in its judicial functions. Since the county courts at law are created by statute, often at widely different times, the jurisdiction of these courts varies significantly. Usually the county courts at law hear appeals from justice of the peace and municipal courts. In civil cases, they usually hear cases involving sums greater than would be heard by a justice of the peace court, but less than would be heard by district courts. In comparison to the district courts, less serious criminal offenses would be heard by the county courts at law.

Some of the county courts at law have specialized jurisdiction; most commonly these are in the most urban counties, where some of the courts will have only civil jurisdiction and others only criminal jurisdiction. Currently there are 197 county court at law judges.

In the most urban areas of the state, the legislature has created courts known as statutory probate courts. These courts are highly specialized in that their primary activity involves probate matters, guardianship, and civil commitments. Currently, there are eighteen statutory probate court judges.

Each county in Texas has between one and eight justice of the peace precincts, depending on population. Within each precinct are either one or two justice of the peace courts. There are about nine hundred justice of the peace courts in Texas. These courts hear minor crimes that are punishable by fines. They also have jurisdiction over minor civil matters, and they function as small claims courts.

Structure of Texan Courts

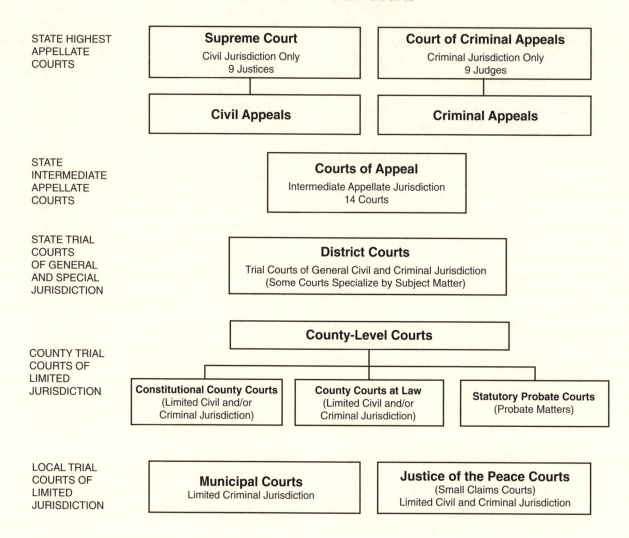

Municipal courts have been created by the legislature in each of the incorporated cities of the state. Approximately 850 cities and towns in Texas have these courts, and larger cities have multiple courts. Municipal courts have jurisdiction over violations of city ordinances and, concurrent with justice of the peace courts, have jurisdiction over misdemeanors for which the punishment is a fine. Municipal judges may issue search and arrest warrants, but they have only limited civil jurisdiction.

The Texas court system consists of a hodge-podge of courts with overlapping jurisdiction. Additionally, some courts have specialized jurisdiction, whereas others have broad authority to handle a variety of cases.

STAFFING

There are more than sixty thousand lawyers in the state, and all lawyers are required to have membership in the state bar and are subject to the bar's ethical require-

ments and continuing legal education requirements. All Texas judges must be lawyers except for justices of the peace, municipal judges, and constitutional county court judges. Seventeen percent of constitutional county court judges graduated from law school, as did 7 percent of justices of the peace and 48 percent of municipal judges. In addition to legal education, varying levels of experience are required of judges before they may serve on the bench.

Even for the appellate courts, however, the legal requirements are minimal. The only requirements are that an appellate judge must be a citizen of the United States and of Texas, at least thirty-five years of age, and a practicing lawyer or judge with at least ten years' experience. Judges in Texas have a significant amount of legal experience, considerably more than is required by the state constitution. The mean year in which Texas Supreme Court justices were licensed to practice law was 1973. It was

1975 for Court of Criminal Appeals judges and 1970 for courts of appeal judges. The mean year for all the various trial court lawyer-judges was between 1970 and 1977. Additionally, for higher courts, it was common for judges to first serve on lower courts. Seventy-eight percent of Supreme Court justices, 22 percent of Court of Criminal Appeals judges, and 29 percent of courts of appeals judges first served as judges on lower courts. The average length of service on the various courts in Texas ranges from almost six years for the Court of Criminal Appeals to ten years on municipal courts. As a practical matter, however, the main requirement for a judge in Texas has little to do with education or experience. The judge must be able to win election to the bench. Therefore, at least some political ability is the foremost requirement for judicial service in Texas. Since the governor appoints appellate judges to vacancies on the bench and also appoints trial judges to the district bench, many Texas judges owe their initial accession to the bench to gubernatorial appointment; of course, that appointment usually requires some political connections. Forty-six percent of district court judges and 40 percent of appellate judges first got their positions through gubernatorial appointment. The appointed judge must then run for election in the next election after their appointment, although initial appointment does give them the advantage of incumbency.

NOTABLE FEATURES OF LAW/LEGAL SYSTEM
All judges in Texas except municipal judges (who are usually appointed by municipal officials) are selected in partisan elections. Until 1978, this selection system did not create much concern. Texas was overwhelmingly a Democratic state, and judges were elected as Democrats. The only real competition occurred in the Democratic primary, and, with the political advantage of incumbency, judges were rarely defeated. Beginning in 1978, however, changes began to occur in Texas judicial politics. William Clements, the first Republican governor since Reconstruction, was elected. The governor has the power to appoint judges to the district and higher courts when new courts have been created, or when a judicial vacancy occurs as a result of death, resignation, or retirement. Unlike the previous Democratic governors, who appointed members of the Democratic Party, Clements began appointing Republicans. With the advantage of incumbency, some of the Republican judges began to win reelection.

Additionally, helped by the rapid growth of the Republican Party in the state, other Republicans began seeking judicial offices and winning. Thus, by the early 1980s, in statewide elections and in several counties in Texas, there began to be competition in judicial races. With that competition, incumbent judges began to be defeated, and judicial elections soon became more expensive because of the high cost of television advertising.

Judicial candidates need money, because judicial races tend to be low-visibility campaigns in which voters are unaware of the candidates and races tend to be overshadowed by the higher visibility races, such as those for governor or U.S. senator. Money was thus needed to give judicial candidates some degree of name recognition. However, it is lawyers, interest groups, and potential litigants who tend to be donors in judicial races. That has raised concerns about the neutrality of Texas judges who are deciding cases that involve the financial interests of persons who have given them campaign funds. A recent Texas poll found that 83 percent of the respondents thought that judges were strongly or somewhat influenced by contributions in their decisions; only 7 percent of respondents did not.

In spite of judicial campaigns, however, voters often know little about judicial candidates. As a result, they vote not for the best-qualified person but for the party label. As the Republican Party has become increasingly dominant in statewide races, it is the Republican label, rather than the qualifications or experience of judicial candidates, that has determined the outcome of judicial races. Yet in spite of numerous reform efforts over the years, there seems no real likelihood of change in the way Texas selects its judges.

RELATIONSHIP TO NATIONAL SYSTEM
As a state, of course, Texas's legal system is subject to the provisions of the Supremacy Clause of the U.S. Constitution. Texas's philosophy of limited government means that Texas is limited in the extent of services provided. That is especially the case in terms of services provided in its juvenile justice, mental heath, and state prison system. Federal judges have frequently been called upon to expand and improve the delivery of services by state government. The most dramatic example of the involvement of federal courts in state government occurred in *Ruiz v. Estelle*. This was a suit that declared the Texas prison system unconstitutional, put the prison system under the control of a federal judge, led to long-standing federal involvement in the prison system, and led also to massive new spending on prisons in Texas.

Overall, one must give the *Ruiz* decision a mixed evaluation. The decision did encourage the early release of prisoners, who then reentered society and committed further crimes. However, *Ruiz* also achieved its objective of encouraging increased spending on prisoners and prisons. It also changed the operation of prisons, most notably phasing out the use of building tenders, who were prisoners who functioned as guards. Perhaps most important, the *Ruiz* case moved corrections policy to the top of the state's policy agenda. But given the philosophy of limited government and state judges sensitive to their electoral future, it took federal court involvement to bring about change in the state's prison policies.

Anthony M. Champagne

See also Appellate Courts; Federalism; Judicial Selection, Methods of; Trial Courts; United States—Federal System; United States—State Systems

References and further reading

Champagne, Anthony. 1986. "The Selection and Retention of Judges in Texas." *Southwestern Law Journal* 40 (May): 53–117.

Miller, Lawrence W. 1998. "The Texas Constitution." Pp. 16–31 in *Texas Politics: A Reader.* Edited by Anthony Champagne and Edward J. Harpham. New York: W. W. Norton.

Office of Court Administration and Texas Judicial Council. 1998. *Texas Judicial System Annual Report for Fiscal Year 1998.* Austin: Office of Court Administration and Texas Judicial Council.

Ruiz v. Estelle, 503 F. Supp. 1265 (1980).

Texas Supreme Court, Texas Office of Court Administration, and State Bar of Texas. 1998. *Public Trust and Confidence in the Courts and the Legal Profession in Texas.* Austin: Office of Court Administration.

THAILAND

GENERAL INFORMATION

Thailand is situated in the heart of the Southeast Asian mainland. It covers an area of 198,115 square miles. Thailand borders the Lao People's Democratic Republic and Burma to the north, Cambodia and the Gulf of Thailand to the east, Burma and the Indian Ocean to the west, and Malaysia to the south. The country's topographic features include mountains along the northern and western borders, a central plain valley, undulating hills in the northeast, and a narrow southern peninsula between the Gulf of Thailand and the Indian Ocean. The population of Thailand is approximately 61 million, which is roughly 81 percent Thai, 11 percent ethnic Chinese, and 3 to 4 percent Malays. The remaining minorities include Cambodians, Vietnamese, Indians, and numerous hill tribes. The population in the capital city, Bangkok, alone is more than 5.6 million. Thailand is the economic leader in Southeast Asia, with a gross domestic product of $119 billion. The economy in the second quarter of the year 2000 still continued to expand at the rate of 6.6 percent.

Although 95 percent of the population is Buddhist, there is an absolute religious freedom, recognized both in the constitution and in practice. The country's legal system is civil law, influenced by European countries and Japan. In several southern provinces, Islamic law can be applied. The official language, spoken by almost all of the population, is Thai and its dialects. English, a mandatory subject in the public schools, is widely understood in Bangkok and other major cities. Thailand's climate is warm and rather humid. It has a tropical monsoon climate with little variation in temperature throughout the year. The rainy season starts in May or June and lasts until September or October. The remainder of the year is relatively dry. Temperatures are highest in March and April and lowest in December and January. The average temperature ranges from 74.66°F to 90.50°F.

HISTORY

The history of Thailand begins roughly in 1238, when King Sri Indradiya declared independence from the Khmer and established the Thai Kingdom at Sukhodaya. A stone inscription crafted during the reign of King Rama Kamhaeng explains that the king, who was the ruler of the state, acted as father of his people, upholder of the Buddhist faith, warrior, and, if necessary, adjudicator of disputes. Sukhodaya's administration was a simple form of patriarchal monarchy. The people's right and liberty were recognized.

After the decline of Sukhodaya, a new Thai kingdom emerged in 1350 at Ayudhaya. As influenced by Khmer and Hinduism, Ayudhaya's form of government was an absolute monarchy in which the king had supreme power over the land. During the Ayudhaya period, Dharmasastra was established as the highest legal authority of the realm. It was a mixture of the Code of Manu, the ancient Hindu jurisprudence, and traditional Thai custom. Its legal principles were a collection of supreme truths derived from Buddhism. The kings also issued royal ordinances, which were in conformity with Dharmasastra, to be enforced throughout the kingdom. The moral teaching of Theravada Buddhism had formed a common bond between the king and the people and had a great influence on traditional Thai law. After more than four hundred years of power, Ayudhaya was brought down by invading Burmese armies, and its capital was burned. After a single-reign capital established at Thonburi by King Taksin, a new capital was founded in 1782 at present-day Bangkok by King Rama I, the founder of the Chakri dynasty.

In the early Bangkok period, King Rama I formed a committee to restore, compile, and revise all written laws derived from Ayudhaya. Such compilation resulted in the Code of Rama I, or "The Law of Three Seals." It consisted of a treatise on jurisprudence, law of civil hierarchy, law of military, law of evidence, law of family, law of robbery, law of slavery, and property law. The "Law of Three Seals" was the highest legal authority of the country until the legal reform made during the reign of King Rama V.

In 1826, Thailand signed the Treaty of Friendship and Commerce with the United Kingdom (Bowring's Treaty). The treaty demanded that Thailand grant extraterritori-

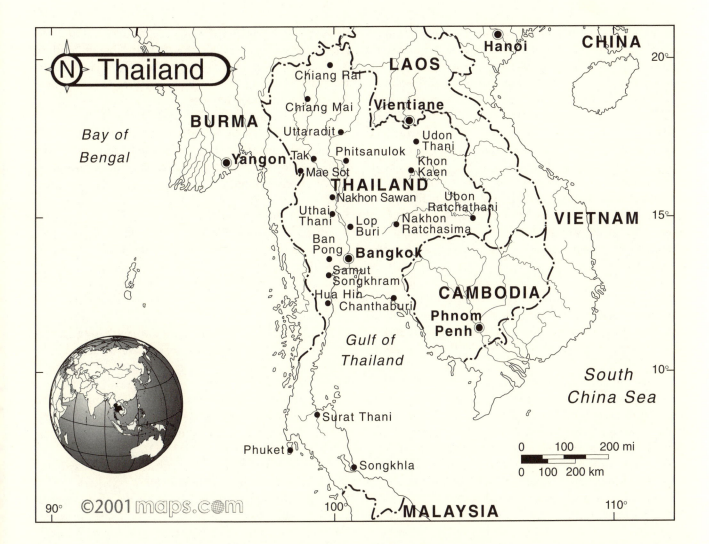

ality to British citizens and limit the import duties of all articles to a fixed rate of 3 percent. Many European countries, America, and Japan had sought similar unequal treaties. King Rama V realized that Thailand needed to modernize its legal system and the administration of the country in order to abrogate such unequal treaties and to avoid the colonization that was taking place in all surrounding countries. During his reign, King Rama V abolished slavery, established the Ministry of Justice, formed the new ministerial system, adopted the Western way of interrogating witnesses, established the first law school (in which English legal principles were taught), promulgated the first criminal code (based on the Continental French system), and drafted the Civil and Commercial Code. Technologically, too, there had been many advances—for example, railroads and trams, postage stamps, and telegraphs. The wisdom of King Rama V made Thailand the only country in Southeast Asia to avoid European colonization.

After half a century of the adoption of English legal principles, at the end of the reign of King Rama V, the government decided to create a written law after the French civil law system, because the civil law model was clear and easy to follow. A legislative council was appointed in 1897 to draft the Criminal Code. The Civil and Commercial Code, parts I and II, drafted by French legal advisors, was completed in 1923. Two years later the Civil and Commercial Code was replaced by a new draft made in line with the Japanese Civil Code, which was in turn modeled after the German Civil Code. It took quite a long time for Thailand to modernize its legal system. The Civil and Commercial Code, composed of six parts, was finally completed during the reign of King Rama VII in 1935, and it is still in force today. The Criminal Procedure Code and the Civil Procedure Code also came into effect in the same year. Bowring's Treaty was finally abrogated after seventy years, after Thailand had modernized its laws, following Western models. Other European countries also subsequently returned to Thailand the independence of the court, and Thailand was able to put an end to extraterritoriality completely by 1938.

The country's absolute monarchy came to an end during the reign of King Rama VII, on June 24, 1932, when a group of civil servants and military officers called the

People's Party staged a bloodless coup d'état and promulgated the first constitution. Since the establishment of a constitutional monarchy, the Thai people have experienced governments alternating between the democratically elected and differing degrees of military rule. Since 1932, there have been no fewer than fifty cabinets and sixteen constitutions. In October 1973, students and civilians demonstrated to demand a new constitution because the existing constitution gave enormous political dominance to the coup group led by Field Marshal Thanom Kittikajorn. Further political confusion occurred in 1992, after the military coup led by General Sunthorn Kongsompong ousted the democratically elected government and set up a National Peace Keeping Command (NPKC). The constitution provided that the prime minister need not be elected. Furthermore, any order made by the prime minister or the president of the NPKC was deemed constitutional. Thus the constitution, in effect, conferred the legislative, executive, and judicial powers on the prime minister and the NPKC. In May 1992, students and civilians protested against the proposal to nominate the vice president of the NPKC, General Suchinda Kraprayoon, as prime minister. Student protests in October 1973 and May 1992 resulted in bloodshed and the arrest of hundreds of protesters. This situation was ameliorated by the intervention of King Rama IX, within the limits of his constitutional authority. The king's moral leadership has proven immensely important in a number of national crises.

Thailand has been a functioning democracy since the general election in 1992. Prime Minister Chuan Leekpai, after winning the election in 1992, declared a political and constitutional reform to promote decentralization and to prevent corruption and vote-buying. A constituent assembly consisting of seventy-six persons elected from each province and twenty-three experts in law, political science, and public administration was formed to draft a new constitution. Public hearings were widely held during the drafting process. The constitution was finally promulgated on October 11, 1997, and described as the first "popular constitution." As prescribed by the constitution, a number of independent judicial bodies and commissions have been or are going to be established—for example, the Constitutional Court, Administrative Court, an ombudsman, the National Human Rights Commission, National Counter Corruption Commission, and the State Audit Commission. These new bodies will be an important mechanism to bring a transparency, financial accountability, and rationality to governance of the country.

LEGAL CONCEPTS

Thailand is a democratic, constitutional monarchy. The 1997 Constitution provides that the king is the head of the state, the upholder of religion, and the head of Thai armed forces. The present monarch is King Bhumibol Adulyadej, also known as King Rama IX of the Chakri Dynasty. The king has no direct political responsibility. The constitution guarantees the separation of powers among the National Assembly, the Council of Ministers, and the courts. It also provides that human dignity and the right and liberty of the people shall be protected. The Thai people enjoy, for example, equal protection under the law, presumption of innocence in criminal cases, free speech, freedom of religion, freedom of the press, the right to a twelve-year compulsory education, public health care at the state's expense, the right to access public information in possession of a state agency, the right to participate in state decision-making processes, and the right to file a complaint against state agencies. Thailand's constitution is one of Asia's most liberal codes of individual freedom.

Legislation is the primary source of law. Although the judgment of the Supreme Court is not absolutely binding, it is an extremely persuasive force. Legislation passed by the National Assembly is supplemented by royal decrees, ministerial regulations, ministerial notifications, and local government regulations. Judges are guaranteed independence in trials and adjudication. There is no jury system under Thai law.

Legislative power is vested in the National Assembly, which comprises the Senate and House of Representatives. Senators and representatives are popularly elected and hold office for six- and four-year terms, respectively. Candidates in an election for senator cannot be a member of any political party. Legislation must be approved by both houses before being presented to the king for his royal assent and promulgated in the *Royal Gazette*. Under the constitution, the king can decide whether or not to affix his signature on organic legislation, although his refusal to sign can be overridden by a two-thirds majority of both houses. In practice, the king's powers are almost exclusively pro forma in nature and exercised only with the consent of the current cabinet. The House of Representatives may pass a motion of nonconfidence against the prime minister or any minister, but, on the other hand, it may be dissolved for reelection by the king upon the cabinet's advice.

Executive power is vested in the Council of Ministers, which consists of the prime minister and thirty-five other ministers. The prime minister, who is typically the head of the political party gaining the largest vote in the general election, is appointed by the king upon nomination by no fewer than one-fifth of the members of the House of Representatives, and with the approval of more than half the members of the House. The prime minister chooses the Council of Ministers by himself. Members of the House of Representatives who are appointed prime minister or to the Council of Ministers must vacate their House seat.

Judicial power is vested in courts. Judges are appointed and removed by the king upon recommendation of the Judicial Commission. The Judicial Commission is also responsible for promoting and punishing judges of the Court of Justice. The commission consists of fifteen members: the president of the Supreme Court, four judges from the Supreme Court, four judges from the Court of Appeals, four judges from the Court of the First Instance, and two persons elected by the Senate whose professions are or have not been career judges. Political considerations play no part in the appointment, removal, or promotion of the judges. Judges are promoted according to seniority.

A separate Constitutional Court is empowered to interpret the constitution and review matters concerning the constitutionality of pending or enacted bills. Fifteen judges of the Constitutional Court are appointed by the king upon nomination by the Senate from five Supreme Court judges, two Supreme Administrative Court judges, five experts in law, and three experts in political science. All fifteen full-time judges are selected by a complicated process to ensure that they are free from conflicting political or business interests. A quorum of no fewer than nine judges will hear the case. Judges of the Constitutional Court hold office for nine years and are not eligible for renomination.

A separate Administrative Court is empowered to adjudicate disputes between state agencies and individuals on matters relating to the state agencies' performance of their official duties. Lawsuits on administrative matters can be filed to the Administrative Court of the First Instance and appealed to the Supreme Administrative Court. An Administrative Court of Appeal may be established in the future. Administrative Court judges are appointed and removed by the king upon approval of the independent Judicial Commission of the Administrative Court.

In order to guarantee citizens' rights to address corrupt or incompetent administration by state officials, three ombudsmen will be selected by the Senate to be in charge of examining such complaints. After considering a complaint, the ombudsmen will report their findings to the National Assembly. The ombudsmen may also refer the case to the Constitutional or Administrative Court.

Under the 1997 Constitution, the Constitutional Court, together with the ombudsmen and the Administrative Courts, will provide a system for judicial review of legislation and administrative actions. Interestingly, the constitution does not describe the exact jurisdictions of, or the relation among, the Constitutional Court, the Administrative Court, and the ombudsmen. Similarly, the transition between existing institutions and the new con-

stitutional institutions has not been spelled out. Those issues will have to be addressed in the organic laws.

An independent Election Commission with five members is empowered, under the constitution, to control the election, decide disputes arising out of the election, order a reelection, or announce the official result of the election. Such elections include those of members of the House of Representatives, senators, members of the local assembly, or local administrators. Members of the Election Commission are elected by the Senate upon five nominations by the Supreme Court and another five by the Selective Committee. This committee consists of the president of the Constitutional Court, the president of the Supreme Administrative Court, four rectors of state higher educational institutions, and four representatives from all political parties. Only five persons who gain the highest number of votes from the Senate become members of election committees. Members of the Election Commission hold the office for seven years and may not be reelected.

Under the 1997 Constitution, a National Human Rights Commission will be established and will have the duty of investigating human rights violations in the country and reporting their findings to the National Assembly. The commission can also propose an amendment to the legislation for the purpose of promoting human rights protection.

The constitution also creates a National Counter Corruption Commission. This independent organ has the duty of reporting to the Senate, upon an investigation of fact, that a person holding a political position, such as the prime minister, a minister, a senator, or a member of the House of Representatives, is unusually wealthy because of corruption or malfeasance. The removal of such a person will be passed by a vote of no less than three-fifths of the Senate. A request for an investigation can be made to the Senate by one-fifth of the members of either House or, alternatively, by fifty thousand eligible voters.

The attorney general is head of the Office of the Attorney General, which is an independent organ under the direct supervision of the prime minister. The Office of the Attorney General prosecutes criminal cases investigated by the police, defends government officials in criminal cases, renders legal advice, represents the government in civil cases, and provides legal aid to indigents. The attorney general and state attorneys are appointed, removed, and promoted under the consideration of the Attorney General Commission, which consists of one president elected by all eligible state attorneys, eight ex officio, three elected, and three elected senior state attorneys.

As required by the constitution, the judiciary became independent on August 20, 2000, after more than 108 years of presiding over the Ministry of Justice. With the old system, the minister of the Ministry of Justice, who is

Legal Structure of Thailand Courts

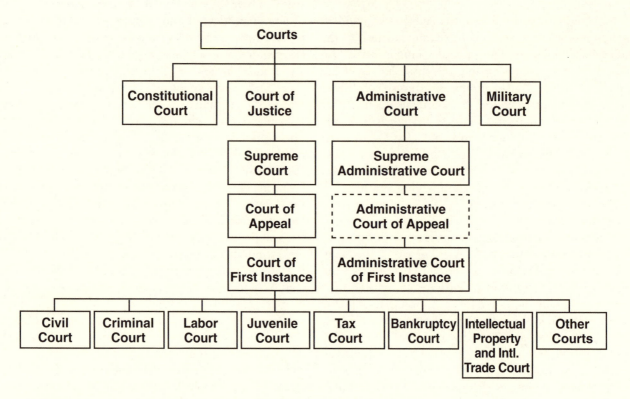

part of the executive branch, had the authority to intervene in the appointment, removal, transfer, and promotion of judges; therefore the separation of power was not genuinely guaranteed. The judiciary currently has its own autonomous Office of the Judiciary, which is responsible for the administration and budget of the Court of Justice. The president of the Supreme Court is the head of the judiciary and has the highest authority in supervising the administration of justice. After the separation, the Ministry of Justice will mainly direct the Probation Department and Legal Execution Department, among others.

CURRENT STRUCTURE

The Thai court system is complex and hybrid. The judicial branch is composed of four judicial bodies: the Constitutional Court, the Court of Justice, the Administrative Court, and the Military Court (see figure). Each court has its own jurisdiction and provides a different function under the constitution. The Constitutional Court interprets the constitution. The Administrative Court reviews administrative matters. The Military Court adjudicates criminal offense by military officials and cases in violation of military law. The Court of Justice adjudicates all civil and criminal cases. Each judicial body is independent from the others and has its own administration and budgetary institute.

The Court of Justice is made up of three tiers of courts: a Supreme Court, a Court of Appeal, and a series of lower courts usually referred to as courts of first instance. The Supreme Court is the final court of appeal in all criminal and civil cases. Five specialized courts—for example, Bankruptcy Court, Intellectual Property and International Trade Court, Labor Court, Juvenile Court, and Tax Court—preside in equal rank with other courts of first instance and adjudicate the cases within their specialized jurisdictions. Each of these courts' proceedings is expeditious. The cases are adjudicated by the joint sitting of specially trained judges and associate judges. Except for the Juvenile Court, appeals from each of these courts can be submitted directly to the Supreme Court.

Litigation in civil cases may be represented by an attorney, who obtains the license to practice law from the Law Society of Thailand. The attorney initiating the case must be delegated a power of attorney to act on his client's behalf. In criminal proceedings, the injured person may initiate the prosecution by himself, although most cases are prosecuted by the state attorney. The accused in a criminal case or the person being kept in custody, who cannot find counsel, has the right, as provided in the constitution, to receive one from the state. Legal aid for the poor can be obtained from many sources: for example, the Legal Aid Office of the Bar Association, the Council of Social Welfare of Thailand, the Law Society of Thailand, the Students' Legal Aid Programs (in the Law Faculty of Thammasat and Chulalongkorn universities), the Woman Lawyers Association, and the Office of the Attorney General.

In the four southernmost provinces of Thailand, civil proceedings among Muslims allow for a joint sitting between two state judges and one Muslim judge, to hear cases regarding matrimonial and inheritance matters. Questions on Islamic law interpreted by a Muslim judge are final.

The Military Court, although presided over by the Ministry of Defense (whose role is to oversee the administration of the court), has sole authority in the investigation, prosecution, and adjudication of crimes committed by military officials of the navy, army, and air forces. Crimes committed by military students, some civilians working for the military, and prisoners of war are also subject to the jurisdiction of the Military Court.

In response to the enormous economic growth of the late 1980s and the resultant local and international commercial disputes, the Thai Arbitration Institute (TAI) was established in 1987 under the auspices of the Ministry of Justice, whose role was to oversee the administration of arbitration under the Arbitration Act 1987. Although rarely accepted by the public in its early years, arbitration proceedings have become increasingly popular recently. The primary role of the TAI was to assist the parties with the selection of an arbitrator or conciliator, provide the physical and human resources necessary to conduct the arbitration or conciliation, and provide TAI arbitration and conciliation rules. Presently, TAI handles about 170 active cases, approximately 70 percent of which are domestic and 30 percent of which are international. The TAI's list of arbitrators contains the names of 220 eminent lawyers, as well as other professionals whose expertise includes, for example, issues of international trade, intellectual property, carriage of goods by sea, construction contract, investment, family and inheritance, real property, torts, and so forth. Parties are free to decide in which rules and language their proceeding will be conducted. The arbitration rules may be selected from, for example, Rules of the TAI, those of the International Chamber of Commerce, or those of the United Nations Commission on International Trade Law (UNCITRAL).

The Arbitration Act 1987 governs both domestic and international commercial arbitration. Only civil disputes are arbitrable. Matters under the exclusive jurisdiction of the courts—such as the civil status of a person, the validity of marriages, or bankruptcy cases—are not arbitrable.

The successful growth of arbitration in Thailand has been largely the result of the TAI's initial connection with the Ministry of Justice. However, TAI has recently been separated from the Ministry of Justice, and its name has been changed to the Dispute Resolution Office. The separation is aimed at improving and modernizing the service without any intervention by the bureaucracy. In addition, the new arbitration bill is now being drafted to be based on the UNCITRAL model law.

Apart from private dispute resolution dealing mainly with commercial issues, Thailand also has an administrative mechanism for dispute resolution called the Community Level Conciliation Program, which was established in 1984 and has been administered by the Office of the Attorney General since then. Every Provincial and Regional State Attorney Office residing all over the country provides legal training and various legal forms to the community committees, which will act as conciliators in their community; they also supervise and ensure smooth conciliation proceedings. The rule of law as well as the elements of Thai society are integrated into the conciliation proceedings to solve such disputes as breach of contract, tort, debt collection, and transfer of property, including some criminal disputes such as defamation and fraud. A total of 782 cases were conciliated in the various provinces in 1999. Conciliation results must be reported to the Office of the Attorney General. This program has proved to reduce tremendously the number of court cases at the community level.

STAFFING

As of December 2000, there were 37,170 lawyers who had registered with and obtained license to practice law from the Law Society of Thailand. Some 25,223 lawyers hold the license for life, and 11,947 lawyers have to renew their licenses every two years. There were 2,713 judges and assistant judges throughout the country as of October 2000. As of December 2000, there were 1,990 state attorneys and assistant state attorneys. Judges and state attorneys are officially retired at the age of sixty, although they are allowed to work as senior judges or senior state attorneys until the age of seventy.

To become a practicing lawyer, a graduate with a bachelor of law (LL.B.) must attend a one-year training course and successfully pass the written exam of the Law Society of Thailand. Once lawyers are registered and licensed by the Law Society of Thailand, they are entitled to practice law throughout the country. Passing the bar examination is not a requirement for obtaining a license to practice law.

The bar examination is given yearly by the Institute of Legal Education of the Thai Bar Association to law school graduates who enroll in its one-year professional course. Persons passing the examination receive the title of barrister-at-law. Only 10 percent of about five thousand candidates pass the bar examination each year. Only law school graduates who pass the bar are eligible to participate in the national examinations to become judges or state attorneys.

Candidates for the judge examination must be at least twenty-five years old and hold at least an LL.B. degree and barrister-at-law, together with two years' standing as a court registrar, deputy court registrar, legal execution officer, state attorney, practicing lawyer, or another profession specified by the Judicial Commission. The judge examination is opened once a year and regarded as the hardest legal examination in the country. Those who pass both written and oral examinations to become judges have to attend the judge-training course for one year. All judges start work as assistant judges and will be promoted according to seniority. The recruitment of state attorneys is similar to that of judges. State attorney examinations are arranged periodically by the Office of the Attorney General. Those who pass the written and oral examination will attend a one-year training course before being appointed as assistant state attorney.

Thailand has five public law schools (two of them are open institutions) and sixteen certified private law schools. All public law schools, with a total of 213 faculty members, can produce some 5,140 graduates per year. There are currently 42,568 students enrolled at the open public law schools. Private law schools have 193 faculty members, and are currently teaching some 7,797 students. Currently, graduates from public law schools make up the vast majority of the legal profession in Thailand, because most of the private law schools have just been established recently.

IMPACT OF LAW

The new constitution of Thailand enacted in October 1997 has spelled out the restructuring of law and political and legal institutions toward more decentralization, which is a precondition for popular participation in many levels. The constitution is also aimed at effectively preventing corruption and vote-buying practices, as well as reducing the hierarchical and deferential culture that has brought great difficulty to the political and legal development of Thailand. It will take a relatively long time for Thailand to ensure that all constitutional mechanisms function effectively, since the Thai people's obedience to the law and social disciplines has developed slowly. However, the emergence of globalization and the Asian financial crisis beginning in 1997 have provided impetus for change and awareness in the legal, political, social, and economic infrastructures. Apparently, about 70 percent of eligible voters throughout the country exercised their rights in the January 2001 general election, for private citizens are concerned about their well-being and wish to see sustainable development of the country. While there is no guarantee that the current reform will be visibly successful, it is to be hoped that the new constitutional framework will lead to changes for the better.

Piengpen Butkatanyoo

See also Arbitration; Civil Law; Government Legal Departments; Islamic Law; Judicial Review; Juvenile Justice; Legal Aid; Mediation; Military Justice, American (Law and Courts)

References and further reading
Asian Development Bank. "Governance in Thailand, Executive Summary." http://www.adb.org (accessed February 12, 2001).
Bowring, Sir John. 1963. *The Kingdom and People of Siam.* London: John W. Parker and Son.
Bunnag, Marut. 1981. "Access to Justice: Legal Assistance to the Poor in Thailand." Pp. 8–12 in *The Legal System of Thailand: The 7th Law Asia Conference.* August 7–12, 1981. Bangkok.
Center for Democratic Institutions. "Thai Arbitration Project." http://www.anu.edu.au (accessed February 28, 2001).
Jayanama, Direck. 1964. *The Evolution of Thai Laws.* Bonn: Royal Thai Embassy.
Kasemsup, Preedee. 1988. "Reception of Law in Thailand: A Buddhist Society." Pp. 267–299 in *The Asian Indigenous Law.* Edited by Masaji Chiba. London and New York: KPI.
Kraichitti, Sansern. 1981. "Law and Legal Profession in Thailand." Pp. 1–7 in *The Legal System of Thailand: The 7th Law Asia Conference.* August 7–12, 1981. Bangkok. Also published in *Asean Law Journal* 1, no. 1 (September 1982): 97–104.
Laird, John. 1997. *Proposals for Constitutional Reform.* Bangkok: Craftsman Press.
Lerdpaitoon, Somkid. 1998. "Mechanisms of New Constitution." *Thammasat Law Journal* 28, no. 3: 574–595.
Mewongukote, Boonsri. 1997. "Political Reform in Thailand." Pp. 126–155 in *The Proceedings of the Regional Symposium on Law, Justice and Open Society in Asia.* Edited by Piruna Tingsabadh. October 6–9, 1997. Bangkok: Institute of Comparative Law and Public Policy, Faculty of Law, Thammasat University.
Ministry of Justice. 1988. *Judicial System in Thailand.* Bangkok: Ministry of Justice.
Na Nakorn, Pinai. 1997. "History and Evolution of Constitutions in Thailand." *Administrative Law Journal* 16 (special ed.): 253–290.
National Identity Board Office of the Prime Minister. 1995. *Thailand in the 90s.* Bangkok: Amarin Printing and Publishing.

TIBET

GENERAL INFORMATION

Until 1950, Tibet was an independent country located in Central Asia, bordering on China to the east and India and Nepal to the south. This entry will discuss the original legal system of Tibet, in operation until 1959. The Tibetan plateau has been occupied by and fully incorporated into the Chinese state since 1959. For references to Tibetan law after that date, the reader should look at the entry on China.

The term *Tibet* appeared in various spellings on early maps of the Arabic explorers and is generally considered to be derived from either *sTod Bod,* which in Tibetan means "upper Tibet," or from the Indian name for Tibet, which is *bhot*. The 1.5 million square miles of the vast Tibetan plateau that the country occupied is completely surrounded by mountains and sits at an average elevation of 12,000 feet above sea level. With very little precipitation, the plateau is a high-altitude desert that is often called "the roof of the world." This desertlike environment is somewhat mollified by its latitude, between the twenty-eighth and thirty-eighth parallels. Most of the limited precipitation comes over the Himalayan Mountains on the southern border and falls on the more fertile areas of the plateau near the Tsangpo River.

Estimates of the Tibetan-speaking population prior to 1950 are subject to dispute. Various visitors have estimated that the population ranged from 2 to 6 million, mostly located in the capital city and in the south along the major river. Figures as of 1990 for the total population of ethnic Tibetans are 4.5 million on the plateau and more than 100,000 ethnic Tibetans outside of the plateau in India and Nepal. Their distinctive language, which is in the Sino-Tibetan family, is monosyllabic, with twenty-six consonants, no consonant clusters, five vowels, tones, and subject-object-verb word order. The Tibetan script was devised at the request of the first historical king, around 630 C.E. from a northern Indian script.

The nonindustrial economy was based on mixed agriculture and herding, with extensive trading along mountain routes to the neighboring countries of China and Nepal. The chief crop of the southern region was high-altitude barley with wheat, buckwheat, peas, mustard, radishes, and potatoes also important. The fields were watered by extensive irrigation systems operated by the local farmers, and the growing season varied but generally ranged from April to September. Nomadic herders, located throughout the plateau but particularly in the north and the southeastern regions, also constituted a large part of the population. Their herds were based on a buffalolike animal, the yak, domesticated in Tibet at least fifteen centuries ago and capable of surviving at elevations up to 20,000 feet. Other animals at lower altitude included sheep, cattle, and goats. The tribe was the local political unit for most nomadic groups, and it consisted of five to eighty tentholds that gathered regularly for group occasions. The nomadic population also engaged in economic activities such as traveling to markets, mining superficially and collecting salt and borax, providing transportation for travelers, hunting wild game, and gathering roots and medicinal herbs.

Marriages among the nomads were primarily monogamous, while the preferred form among the agriculturalists was fraternal polygamy, the marriage of one woman to a set of brothers. The purpose of this system has been cited as providing a stable central household for child-rearing, while male members of the household could then take on several different functional roles, such as farmer,

herder, monk, and merchant on long market trips. Some household and tenthold tasks were gender-specific, such as child-rearing, weaving, and milking, but most family members were able to exchange roles so that the family could operate as a self-sufficient unit. Thus it was not uncommon to see a woman tilling a field or shearing sheep, or a man curdling the milk in a skin bag while holding the baby.

Land in Tibet was organized into three kinds of ownership: noble estates, monastic estates, and individually held private land. At the lowest level were peasants, who had deeds to their agricultural plots. Except for the individually held private lands, most agricultural plots were organized into noble or monastic estates that then controlled part of the products of the land. Above these estates was the central government, which levied taxes on the estates and the private lands to run the bureaucracy in Lhasa, the capital city.

Tibetans are renowned for their pious devotion to a branch of Buddhism called Vajrayana. Although small numbers of Muslims and members of some other Central Asian religions lived in the larger cities, the plateau was overwhelmingly Tibetan Buddhist in religious orientation. A primary focus of the society was the maintenance of Buddhist monasteries and nunneries, which constituted an estimated 20 percent of the population before 1959. These institutions, which ranged in size from the very small to very large (one near the capital city of Lhasa housed ten thousand monks), were separate economic and social centers, employing monks or nuns in all roles from carrying water and washing the floors to translating and printing difficult texts. The monasteries were also the centers for education, the production of literature, the performance of rituals on the national and local holidays and for death ceremonies, and the training of doctors, artists, astrologers, dancers, and half of the government officials. In exchange, most families regularly contributed agricultural products, work hours, and often family members to their local monasteries and nunneries. The secular population existed in a symbiotic relationship with these religious institutions, one that has been termed the "priest-patron" relationship.

HISTORY

Archaeological and linguistic evidence indicates that what are now the Tibetan people entered the high plateau from the northeast approximately thirteen thousand years ago and migrated to the fertile southern arc. Tibetan kingdoms appear to have been established as early as 400 C.E. and are confirmed in the earliest examples of Tibetan writing, which date from around 767 C.E. The plateau was controlled by Tibetan rulers with their own legal system until the Communist Chinese entered Tibet for the last time, in 1959.

Tibetan recorded history thus begins in the empire period, which scholars date from the mid-seventh to the mid-ninth centuries C.E. During this single period of aggressive expansion, their armies spread throughout large sections of Central Asia to the northwest, and northern China and Mongolia to the northeast. Administrative records and even sections of early law codes survive from the empire period. At least three different types of rules were propounded during the first royal dynasty: the four fundamental laws prohibiting murder, thievery, lechery, and the bearing of false witness; the ten nonvirtuous acts; and the sixteen moral principles. With the murder of the last king of the Yarlung dynasty, empire-building ended and the country decentralized into many smaller states.

There are three other historical periods with an importance to the formation of the Tibetan legal system. First, in the thirteenth century, one sect of Tibetan Buddhism established a religious government in central-southern Tibet and proceeded to take control of much of the surrounding area. Although it has never been located, scholars assume that this Saskyas theocracy had a law code that it put into use. Second, following this period was the period of secular dynasties. Three distinct secular dynasties—the Phagmogru, the Rinpung, and the Tsangpa—controlled the heart of the Tibetan plateau consecutively from 1354 to 1642. This was an important period for Tibetan law, because two of the most important law codes date from this period, the Ne'udong law code of the Phagmogru (from the first half of the fifteenth century) and the Tsangpa law code (drafted sometime between 1623 and 1642). Finally, in the middle of the seventeenth century, the Mongolian Gushri Khan swept onto the plateau and installed the final Tibetan government, the Galdan Phodrang government of the Dalai Lamas. A law code was written for this period that was in effect from the mid-seventeenth century until 1959.

In 1950 the armies of Mao Tsetung and the Communist revolution swept into Tibet to take over the plateau. The Dalai Lama was left in control of his country but put under the direction of the Chinese central government. During an uneasy ten-year period, this relationship grew more and more difficult. On March 10, 1959, the Tibetan leader finally fled from a Chinese army that had invaded the capital city from the east and secretly escaped to India, where he has remained. In Dharamsala, India, the Dalai Lama heads the administration of a government-in-exile of Tibet, which oversees the affairs of more than 100,000 Tibetans in exile in India, Nepal, and abroad through a separate constitution and judicial system. The Tibetan government-in-exile runs in tandem with the Indian government a series of Tibetan settlements and schools that serve more than 100,000 refugee Tibetans. The refugee judicial system is currently being revised to include more aspects from the original Tibetan legal system, discussed

here, which existed until 1959. Tibetans continue to leave the plateau every year to seek the religious freedom not allowed in the People's Republic of China (PRC).

The plateau area is now part of the PRC and divided between the Tibet Autonomous Region (TAR) and the neighboring provinces of Quinhai, Gansu, Sichuan, and Yunnan, where several counties have been designated for ethnic Tibetans as autonomous areas. Currently, the legal system employed in the TAR is that of the Chinese central government. Negotiations between the Chinese government and the Tibetan government-in-exile have not resulted in any marked political changes or a return of the Dalai Lama to his country of birth.

LEGAL CONCEPTS

There are at least five major sources for Tibetan law and legal concepts: (1) religious source materials, such as the Vinaya law code for the monks and nuns; (2) extant official documents, which include administrative rule books, edicts, decision documents, treatises, government contracts, estate record books, tax records, and deeds to land; (3) documents issued by nongovernmental institutions, such as monastic constitutions, private leases, and private contract documents; (4) law codes; and (5) written and oral statements on the legal system in both Tibetan and other languages, such as oral statements of the operation of the legal system, letters, novels, written histories, autobiographies, and the like. From these sources, it has been possible to construct a picture of what the Tibetan legal system was like prior to 1959.

Always cited as the first and perhaps the most important source for Tibetan legal concepts is the Vinaya, or monastic code section of the Buddhist religious canon. The Buddha established legal rules to govern the members of the sangha, or the religious community, he formed by giving the circumstances, reasoning, and decision for each case that was brought before him during his long life as a religious leader. These rules were written down in the Vinaya, and they continue to govern all Buddhist monastic institutions today. Both the form of reasoning and the rules enunciated in the Vinaya have heavily influenced Tibetan society and Tibetan law. Thus, although the Vinaya applies only to monks and nuns and not to the secular population in a Buddhist country, it stands as a very strong statement of what the Buddha thought was important in terms of rules, reasoning, and procedure.

What the list of five sources above does not include is also very interesting. It does not include books on court procedure, compendiums of cases, extensive commentaries on the law codes, lists of additional statutes, books of regional variations of administrative rules, or casebooks. Tibetan law seems to have avoided such compilations, perhaps reasoning that each case was unique and that such compendiums were not valuable. The recent availability of Tibetan legal documents collected by the Chinese in 1959 will probably increase both the type and kind of sources available to us. Research into the techniques of legal document production and storage has indicated that each courtroom issued its own judgments and filed them in huge trunks that knowledgeable clerks located using a chronological indexing system. Large government record books also collected lists of real estate owners by household and date of transfer.

The fourth entry on the list was law codes. Two types of law codes of the Galdan Phodrang government of the Dalai Lamas, which ruled the plateau from the mid-seventeenth century until 1959, were generally known throughout Tibet. The first was a law code of twelve sections that dates from approximately 1650, and the second a law code of thirteen sections written in approximately 1679 by the fifth regent of the Fifth Dalai Lama. A close analysis of these important Tibetan law codes reveals that they took their structure, form, and a large part of their content from the codes of the Tsangpa secular kings of the immediately preceding period. These codes are not religious law codes, nor are they primarily criminal in nature. The code written during the time of the first regent covers a wide range of subjects and has the following subsections:

Introduction
(1) Truthful and untruthful petitions
(2) Arrest procedures
(3) Major crimes
(4) Punishments to promote mindfulness
(5) Government emissaries
(6) sTong compensation for murder
(7) Injury compensation
(8) Oathtaking
(9) Theft compensation
(10) Separation of relatives
(11) Adultery compensation
(12) Before and after midnight
Conclusion and Dedication

Other aspects of the Tibetan legal system were decidedly Buddhist in nature. Their jurisprudence involved locating the decision-making process in the minds of the participants, which emphasized the importance of consensus. The judge's decision did not necessarily mean closure of the case if the parties did not fully agree. Therefore a case was not final until an agreement between the parties had been reached, and a decided case could be reopened in the same court the next day if one's mind remained angry. Likewise, any forum the parties could agree on was generally preferred, even if the judge had no jurisdiction over the parties.

Precedent was not generally applied in the Tibetan legal system, and as a consequence, new rules were not evolved for universal application from a single case. Precedent was generally not employed because each case was unique. Karma readjusted the whole system into a previous-present-future lives perspective. All acts, both those remedied through the legal system and those that were not, were referred to as having been caused by previous bad karma or likely to result in future bad karma. Inner morality (*rang khrims*), by which the Tibetans meant a person who was governed by self-regulation and followed the moral requirements of Buddhism in all spheres of life, was the standard for assessment of character, veracity, and motivation at law. Thus "acting only for one's own benefit" or "acting without the ability to discriminate" were both references to negative motivations in the law codes of the Dalai Lamas, and they mattered in a legal suit. The ideal moral standard was represented by the Buddha himself. His right actions in his previous lives were recounted in countless stories, leaving little ambiguity for the Tibetan Buddhist about what a right-acting and right-thinking person would do under most situations.

Truth and honesty were the most universally employed terms for evaluating aspects of legal cases, and they were used to express a wide range of English terms in law, such as probity, justice, due process, and fairness. The principle of truth as consensus meant that the facts on either side had to agree, demonstrate factual consonance, not that they had to comport with the reality of the circumstances. Flexibility was evident throughout the system in choice and level of forum and type of legal procedure. Tibetans could start a case at any of a variety of levels in any of four different types of procedure, including conciliation, and then move back and forth, up and down, between levels and forums. The key element was the agreement by both parties and the decision maker to proceeding with the case to a decision. A much wider range of persons was liable for the results of criminal acts, creating a wide net of social responsibility. All the persons along the path of a transaction were presumed to have responsibility and accept liability. The Tibetans also used oracles, oaths, and dice to settle cases that were particularly intractable.

LEGAL STRUCTURE

The Tibetan government before the Chinese takeover consisted of a series of levels of administration, from the local township and district officials appointed by the central government up through the cabinet and the Office of the Dalai Lama. The Dalai Lama, who sat at the pinnacle of the government, was a monk, and all of his attendants and principal regents were monks. The judicial structure, which was tightly incorporated into the political administration, had two wings. One was ecclesiastical, for the affairs and appointments in monasteries and nunneries. Only monk officials acted as administrators and judges in this system. The other and much larger wing of the judicial system was the secular or lay side.

The first level of the secular wing was that of the household, at which many basic disputes were settled. Above the household were the levels of the local community, estate or township, and district. Each district had an assigned officer or pair of officers who also acted as magistrates for the settlement of disputes and the transaction of legal cases. Local associations could also be the site of legal decision making.

In the district office of Kyidong in 1949, for example, a monk official and a lay official acted as judges for cases with two people's representatives and two clerks. An altar with a statue of Buddha on it was placed in the center of one wall of the room, while the judges and clerks sat on pillow-mattresses with low tables in front of them. A petitioner entered the room and remained standing while being questioned. Oaths could be taken in front of the altar. Final-decision documents were drafted for the parties and had to be signed by both sides and their guarantors to try to ensure the permanence of the decision.

From the district centers, secular legal cases went either to a regional governor's office or, in the case of big districts, directly to the central bureaucracy. The cabinet was the entry point for the majority of the secular legal cases coming into any of the upper three legal levels of the government.

When the cabinet received a case, it was often referred out again to one of the other administrative departments for consideration. For example, a tax dispute from the province of Khams might be sent first to the cabinet, then referred out to the Revenue Office for a review of the tax requirements and of recent conditions in the province. The Revenue Office would then send an opinion of the case back to the cabinet, where it was reviewed. Other offices included the Office of the Army, the Storage Office, the Agricultural Office, the Armory, the New Investigation Office, the Grain Tax Office, the General Foreign Office, and the High Court. Each of these offices could act as a court for the purpose of deciding a case referred to it by the cabinet. The majority of legal cases coming into the cabinet were referred down to government departments for initial consideration and then returned to the cabinet, which would issue a decision. The cabinet could also reassign the case to a government department for decision and issuance of a decision. A much smaller number of these cases were referred up to the highest level of the government, the Office of the Dalai Lama, for consideration. Commonly, this highest level then referred the case back to the cabinet, which issued a final decision document out to the district office or the parties.

Legal Structure of Tibet

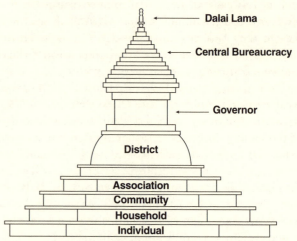

The legal units and levels of Tibet can also be understood as a three-dimensional mandala in the form of a chorten.

In one of its simple formulations, the mandala is a diagram of five deities: one in the center and four more placed at the cardinal points around the center.

SPECIALIZED JUDICIAL BODIES

The High Court of Tibet (Gsher Khrims Khang) was located in the Cathedral Complex in the center of Lhasa, along the north side of the building. It was a simple, functional, and undecorated series of rooms that housed two judges and two clerks and a caretaker when it was open during the day. Historically, the Sherkhang was famous for handling murder cases and for being the highest appeals court in Tibet. Cases came to the court by referral from the cabinet. When a murder occurred at the district level, the officers arrested the suspect, collected evidence and testimony from witnesses and participants, and then arranged to have the suspect, the documents, and the evidence taken to Lhasa. The suspect stayed in jail prior to the hearing of the case and was beaten by guards. Often both the relatives of the victim and the relatives of the suspect went to Lhasa for the case. Each was heard individually by the court after the documents were read and the evidence examined. At the conclusion of the case, the victim's relatives were always compensated according to a ranked payment system, and the murderer was usually given both physical and rehabilitation punishments; all was written down in a very detailed, point-by-point decision document.

Equivalent to the High Court but on the religious side of the judiciary was the High Ecclesiastical Court (Rtse Yig Tshang), which met in a large room in the Dalai Lama's palace. It had four judges in residence called the Four Great Monk Secretaries (*drung yig chen mo*), who presided over their assigned cases along with fifteen younger monk clerks (who wrote documents and handled files) and a caretaker (who facilitated case handling). Cases came to ecclesiastical courts from a wide variety of venues, but primarily they consisted of disputes between religious institutions or concerning the lands or affairs of religious institutions. Upon reaching the Ecclesiastical Office, a petitioner stood near the door and waited. Seeing a visitor, the office caretaker got up from his mat and went to the door to receive the written petition. This was then given to the head of the office, with a short explanation by the caretaker, and the case was taken up by the office.

One of the most famous examples of the unusual blending of religion and law in Tibet administrative institutions was the State Oracle at Nechung Monastery in Lhasa Valley, who was a very influential state advisor. When the Dalai Lama came on state business to the monastery, the monk who had been chosen as the oracle went into a trance and embodied the powerful deity Pehar. The oracle was then asked questions by the Dalai Lama and others about affairs of state and important legal cases. His answers were recorded, translated to standard Tibetan, and then considered in important regent and cabinet meetings.

STAFFING

There were two separate types of administrative officials in the government—lay officials trained in lay schools, who were drawn from the noble and clerical groups, and monk officials, who were trained from a young age to serve as monks in the administration. The result of this blending of religious and lay actors in the administration at every level was that a political or legal decision was rarely made without the influence of a monastically trained official. In the lay courts, for example, each office position had paired officials—one lay and one monastic. In 1958 the Municipal Court of Lhasa had a banc of four judges, two of whom were lay officials and two monk officials.

IMPACT

The Tibetan legal system provides a fascinating look into the operation of a pretechnological administrative court system. It was an important and fundamental aspect of Tibetan society, and most Tibetans had sections of the law code memorized. The fact that Tibet had a separate, independent, long-standing judicial system is often cited as evidence that it was a separate entity from China before the takeover in 1959. Several scholars have also stated that this legal system most coherently incorporated the fundamental ideas of Buddhism. They cite in particular the uniqueness of each case, the lack of precedent or case closure, the role of karma, and the importance placed on both parties being satisfied with the decision. While defining justice and equality in different ways, it managed to be a very successful legal system, and the government-in-exile is now incorporating many of the aspects of the original Tibetan system into their judicial processes in India.

Rebecca R. French

See also China
References and further reading
Bodde, Derk, and Clarence Morris. 1967. *Law in Imperial China—Exemplified by 190 Ch'ing Dynasty Cases.* Cambridge, MA: Harvard University Press.
French, Rebecca R. 1995. *The Golden Yoke: The Legal Cosmology of Buddhist Tibet.* Ithaca, NY: Cornell University Press.
———. 1996. "Tibetan Legal Literature: The Law Codes of the dGa' ldan pho brang." Pp. 438–457 in *Tibetan Literature: Studies in Genre.* Edited by Jose Ignacio Cabezon and Roger R. Jackson. Ithaca, NY: Snow Lion Publications.
Horner, Isaline Blew. 1938–1966. *Vinayapitaka* [*The Book of the Discipline*]. London: H. Milford, Oxford University Press.
Schuh, Dieter. 1973. *Untersuchungen zur Geschichte der tibetischen Kalenderrechnung.* Wiesbaden: F. Steiner.
———. 1976. *Urkunden und Sendschreiben aus Zentraltibet, Ladakh und Zanskar.* Vols. 1 and 2. St. Augustin: VGH, Wissenschaftsverlag.
Uray, Geza. 1960. "The Four Horns of Tibet According to the Royal Annals." *Acta Orientalia Academiae Scietarium Hungaricae* 10: 31–57.
———. 1972. "The Narrative of Legislation and Organization of the mKhas-Pa'i dGa's-sTon." *Acta Orientalia Academiae Scietarium Hungaricae* 14: 11–68.

TOGO

COUNTRY INFORMATION

Togo is a country situated slightly over the equator in West Africa. It is bordered by Burkina Faso to the north, Ghana to the west, and the Republic of Benin to the east. To the south, it has a coastal front facing the Atlantic Ocean. Situated between 6° and 11° north latitude, Togo covers an area of 56,000 square kilometers and presents a rangy shape, measuring 600 kilometers from north to south. Its population was 4.5 million as of 2000.

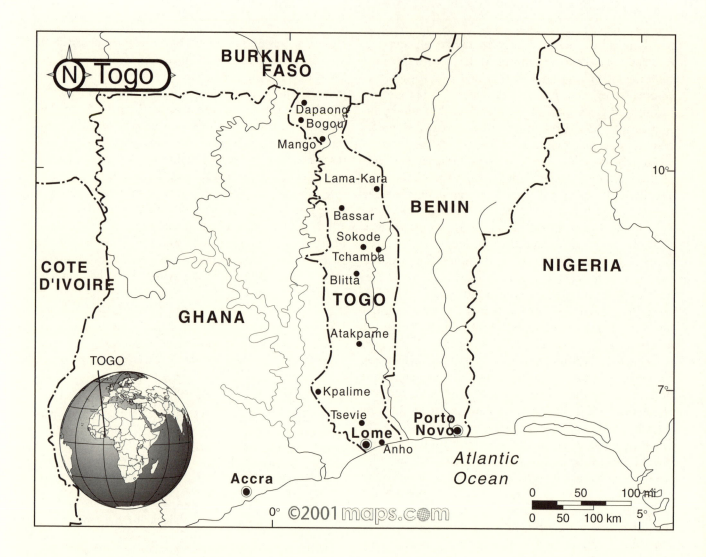

Despite it smallness, Togo has more than forty ethnic groups, the most important of which are:

- The Adja-Ewe group, which represents 44 percent of the population and is composed of Ewe, Mina, and Ouatchi; this group occupies most of the southern part of the country
- The Kabye-Tem group, which encompasses 27 percent of the population and is made up of Kabyè, Cotocoli, Losso, and Lamba; these individuals occupy the center and northeastern part of the country
- The Para-Gourma group, which makes up 16 percent of the population, consisting of Moba, Gourma, Tchamba, Bassar, and so on; this group occupies the far north and the east-central area of the country

In addition, there are a number of minority groups, such as the Akposso, Peulh and the Ana-Ifè. Officially, French is the national language, but a number of local languages are also spoken, among them Ewe, Mina, Kabye, Cotocoli, Ouatchi, and Moba.

Togo enjoys two types of climate, according to region. In the south, there are four seasons—both a short and a long rainy season, a long dry season (known as the Harmattan), and another season that has certain similarities to the monsoon season. In the northern part of Togo, there are two seasons of the Sudan-Sahelian type: a rainy season from March to November and a dry season from December to February.

The capital of Togo, Lomé, has about 1 million inhabitants and remains the economic center of the country. Lomé is one of the crossroads of the subregion of West Africa, and it serves as a transitional area between the hinterland countries (Burkina-Faso, Niger, and Mali) and the sea, thanks to its harbor. The other main towns are mostly country towns of the administrative and economic regions; they include Dapaong, Kara, Sokodé, Atakpamé, Tsévié, and Kpalimé, among others. Togo's legal system is based on a unity of juridiction.

HISTORY

Togo's legal structures and juridical concepts evolved through several broad historical stages: the precolonial period, the time of German rule, the French mandate period, and, since 1960, the postindependence era, which has witnessed dramatic political changes. Historically, the people were ruled according to the customary and traditional prescriptions of their environment. The scraps of customary law were maintained by oral tradition.

The precolonial period was defined by the traditional structures of the indigenous populations, who were ruled by three different political systems:

- The small chieftaincy among the Ewe was the prototype of the chieftaincies spread widely across the country. The Ewe chieftaincies developed from the dismantling of a great ancient kingdom, the center of which was Tado, and never succeeded in grouping themselves in vast unitary political systems. Even the Guin people's Kingdom of Glidji was better in this respect in the eighteenth and the nineteenth centuries and constituted the center of decision making for the neighboring towns. The chief and his elders were considered the competent authority to deal with all lawsuits involving land, family, marriage, divorce, and other matters.
- The great chieftaincies had great influence in the northern part of the country. The most important of the great chieftaincies' kingships were the Tem, Dagomba, Tchokossi, and Bassar. The first three of these kingships had a semi-Islamic coloration, so that rules of Muslim law were incorporated in their legal systems, particularly in regard to issues of marriage, estates (devolution of inheritance), and o forth.
- The populations with weak political systems—the Akposso, Lama-Lamba, and Moba—were the most ancient populations of the region. For long periods of time, they were isolated from external influences capable of modifying their sytem of life. The Moba group, which was a mixture of different peoples coming from the breakup of the great ancient Kingdoms of Gourm and Mossi, had strict rules of succession to the throne and rigid institutions governing family life.

The colonial administration system that was installed in the country in the nineteenth century was largely based on the ethnic backgrounds and traditional political structures of the past, for the colonializing Germans kept the old structures and used them as their administrative territorial divisions.

The Treaty of Protectorate signed at Baguida by King Mlapa I and Gustav Nachtigal on July 5, 1884, placed the Togolese territory under German protection. Thereafter, Togo was ruled partly by German law and partly by indigenous justice. In the districts of the coast, the governor dispensed justice himself. The legal penalties used were corporal punishment (whippings and drubbings), fines, imprisonment (sometimes with iron chains), hard labor, and capital punishment (execution by hanging). Concerning this last punishment, there was at the center of every town, the "Bierplatz," a hangman's tree, which dominated the administrative headquarters of the district with the purpose of discouraging and dissuading potential criminals. Hanging was reserved for those sentenced to death for committing murder. Women were not subjected to corporal punishment. Penalties were carried out in the presence of a European official and the station doctor, and the age and state of health of the accused were taken into account in applying the sentence. Fines exceeding 300 marks and imprisonment of more than six months had to have the governor's approval to be applied, and only this high civil servant could sentence the local elders. The official deemed competent in judicial matters was also deemed competent in disciplinary matters and could punish any individual whose work was found unsatisfactory due to idleness, insubordination, or negligence. This, in short, was the nature of the German juridical system in Togo before the German colonizers left the country in 1914.

In 1919, after World War I, Togo was placed under a French mandate by the League of Nations. Accordingly, French modern law was introduced in Togo during the mandate period. French rule gave much less authority or judicial competence to Togo's customary chiefs than the German system had.

Disputes and transactions between citizens throughout the whole colony of Togo were governed by the Civil Code of 1804 and the Commercial Code of 1807, respectively. The Decree of May 22, 1924, instituted the application of the French Penal Code of 1810 in Togo. That decree was abrogated by the Togolese Penal Code that was instituted by Bill No. 80-1 of August 13, 1980.

Other French laws were made applicable in Togo in other specific fields as well. From 1946, with French mandatory rule established under UN control, Togo was included in a vast movement to reform the French Constitution of 1946. By the Decree of October 25, 1946, Togo became an associated territory within the French union and had an Assembly of Representatives (ART). This assembly had thirty elected French members and twenty-four Togolese members. The Assembly of Representatives determined the same prerogatives as the General Councils of the colonies of French West Africa (AOF) and met in ordinary sessions twice in the year to discuss contributions, taxes, and duties, as well as the organization of the public services. These efforts constituted the initial stages of the bringing together of the metropolitan legislation, on one hand, and on the other hand the by-laws to the citizens of Togo and their customary law.

Gradually, a system of autonomy evolved. In drafting the Law of June 23, 1956, a statute for Togo was elaborated and submitted to the Territorial Assembly of Togo; the measure was then promulgated by decree on August 24, 1956. Thus, the autonomous Republic of Togo was declared on August 30, 1956, and on September 10, Nicolas Grunitzky was invested as prime minister. By the Decree of March 23, 1957, the regulation of internal public order was transferred to the Togolese government.

With new powers given to the autonomous government in February 1958, the assembly became the Chamber of Deputies, and the prime minister replaced the high commissioner in presiding over the cabinet. On March 29, 1958, the judicial powers were solemnly transferred to the Togolese government: Justice was henceforth dispensed on behalf of the Togolese. Independence was achieved on April 27, 1960. Thereafter, the French juridical system was gradually abrogated through the new Togolese authorities' legislative efforts, thus reducing the influence of metropolitan law. In this regard, the adoption of the Togolese Code of the Individual and the Family, by Ordinance No. 80-16 of January 31, 1980, is worth noting. The provisions of this code repealed and replaced the French Civil Code that had been applied in Togo by the Decree of May 22, 1924, mentioned above, in regard to all matters, including marriage, succession, and filiation. This law established certain local practices in regard to marriage (the option of a second marriage or polygamy), the bride-price, and the acknowledgment of marriages celebrated in church or traditionally. Similarly, the Togolese Penal Code of 1980 and the Code of Penal Procedure of 1963 replaced prior French law in regard to criminal matters.

In terms of the institutional and political structures of the country, the political history of Togo is characterized by two long periods of authoritarianism interspersed with brief periods of liberalism.

There have been six constitutional changes in Togo since independence was attained, but the current republic is only the fourth, because two of the constitutional alterations didn't involve changing the republic. The constitutional changes were as follows:

- The Constitution of April 23, 1960
- The Constitution of April 14, 1961
- The Constitution of May 11, 1963
- The Constitution of January 9, 1980
- The Constitution of October 14, 1992

In addition, a constitutional law known as Act 7 of the National Sovereign Conference provided for a transitional de facto government between September 1991 and December 1992.

These different fundamental laws reflected the politico-institutional systems that characterized the constitutional life of Togo through the postindependence period, which can be classified in the following way:

- From April 27, 1960, to April 23, 1961—a particuliamentary system with a strong propensity for presidentialism
- From April 23, 1961, to January 13, 1963—a monopartisan presidential system
- From January 13, 1963, to May 11, 1963—a pluralistic de facto civil system
- From May 11, 1963, to January 13, 1967—a pluralistic parliamentary system
- From January 13, 1967, to January 9, 1980—a de facto military-civil system
- From January 9, 1980, to August 23, 1991—a monopartisan presidential system
- From August 23, 1991, to December 31, 1992—a pluralistic de facto civil system
- From January 1, 1993, to February 20, 1994—a de facto military-civil system called "the government of crisis" that instituted a semipresidentialist system that was theoretically pluralistic
- From 1994 to the present—a pluralistic parliament with a semipresidential system.

The political life is always influenced by political parties. This led to a bipolarism shaped by the interplay of alliances, conflicts, and divisions.

Thus, from independence on, there was a confrontation between the Committee of Togolese Unity (CUT), which in 1962 became the Togolese Unity Party (PUT) of Sylvanus Olympio, on the one hand, and the coalition of the Togolese Party of Progress (PTP) of Nicolas Grunitzky and the Union of the Chiefs and People of the North (UCPN) of Derman Ayeva and Mama Fousseni—a coalition that later became the Democratic Union of the Togolese People (UDPT). Other groups included the Togolese Popular Movement (MPT) of Pedro Olympio and the Justice-Union-Vigilance-Education-Nationalism-Tenacity-Opportunism (JUVENTO) of the lawyer Anani Santos, which often clashed with the PUT in 1962.

The bipolarization of political life was revived by the democratic renewal that began in 1991 after the pluralistic party system from 1963 to 1967 and the long monopartisan rule of the Togolese People's Rally (RPT), the former single party. Thus, the presidential side, led by the RPT and a set of close political parties affiliated with or supportive of the actions of Gen. Gnassingbé Eyadema, is opposed by a bloc of many opposition parties. The most important of these opposition parties are the Union of the Forces for Change (UFC) of Gilchrist Olympio, the Committee Action for the Renewal (CAR) of the lawyer Yaovi Agboyiboa, the Party for Democracy and the Renewal (PDR) of Zarifou Ayeva, the Democratic Convention of Africa Peoples (CDPA) of Leopold Gnininvi, the Panafrican Patriotic Convergence (CPP) of Edem Kodjok, and the Alliance for Democracy and Integral Development of François Nagbandja Kampatibe.

This bipolarization, pitting the presidential side against the democratic opposition, brought about serious conflict that caused a long sociopolitical crises, the solution of which was sought successively in Colmar (France) and Ouagadougou (Burkina-Faso) at conferences between the government of Togo and all the opposition parties in Togo, and recently in the Framework Agreement of Lomé.

The recent series of negotiations to end the crisis is characterized by the signing by all the political actors of the Framework Agreement of Lomé on July 29, 1999, in order to solve the problem of the political crisis caused by the tumultuous and controversial elections of June 21, 1998. The Framework Agreement of Lomé instituted a Joint Committee for the Followup (CPS), which is charged with discussing all the latent problems inherent in the country's sociopolitical crisis since 1990. These agreements are patronized by a board of facilitators, representatives of France, Germany, the European Union, and the Francophonie to follow the process of political negotiations, one of the most important achievements of which is the Independent National Electoral Committee (CENI).

CURRENT COURT SYSTEM STRUCTURE

The Supreme Court is the highest juridiction in judicial and administrative matters. It controls the law and acts in the last resort, without any other form of appeal. It comprises two courts: the Judicial Court and the Administrative Court. Each of them is autonomous and consists of a president and his or her advisers.

The Judicial Court has four divisions: civil, commercial, criminal, and social. These bodies rule on the cases falling under their respective spheres, within the abilities allotted to the Judicial Court. Thus, Article 11 of the Organic Law No. 97–05 of March 6, 1997, holds that the Judicial Court is competent to hear:

- appeals for cassation against the decisions delivered in the last report by civil, commercial, social, or criminal jurisdictions
- Actions against the magistrates of the Court of Appeal in respect to the clauses of the Code of Civil Procedure
- Legal proceedings against magistrates of the Court of Appeal in the conditions determined by the Code of Criminal Procedure
- Requests for review of the decisions of judges (Article 124)

As for the Administrative Court, it is competent to hear:

- Recourses against the decisions delivered in matter of administrative litigation
- Resorts for abuse of power against administrative documents issued by the administration, decisions and documents issued by professional associations and private entities in charge of the management of the public utilities, and decisions and documents of bodies ruling in disciplinary matters
- Appeals for cassation against the decisions of bodies ruling in disciplinary matters
- Litigation in local elections

The complaints should be addressed within a period of eight days from the notification of the decision. In civil and commercial matters, they should be addressed within a period of two months.

For administrative procedures, the resort cannot be addressed within a period of less than three months from the legal publication of the statutory document or the notification to the person involved with the contested administrative decision.

However, when the administration does not react for more than four months after a complaint, it means the matter has been effectively discharged; the person involved in this matter can appeal again within three months.

In brief, all the parties in legal proceedings can resort to the Supreme Court except for defaulting or runaway parties. Nevertheless, despite all these measures, the only court resorted to in practice is the Judicial Court, and the Administrative Court has never been approached. Workers prefer the hierarchic recourse to the services of the Administrative Court. Finally, we can assume, on a sociological basis and according to the political context, that people are afraid to take the administration to court; it is perceived as being all-powerful, and many people are unaware that they can claim their rights from the state.

Below the Supreme Court follow in order:

- The Court of Appeal, the body of second-degree, which sits in Courts of Assizes twice per year in criminal matters
- The Court of Criminal Appeal. There are only two such courts, one in Lome and one in Kara.
- The Court of First Instance, subdivided into first-, second-, and third-class categories. These courts handle cases of land dispute, which are the most frequent, as well as disputes in matters of divorce and inheritance before the civil judge. The most common criminal cases involve fraud. In the context of the democratic process, cases involving

the violation of the press law have been treated by the first-degree judges.

• The judge of labor and the judge of the wards work directly under the Courts of First Instance.

As regards the common law, all the parties are normally represented in cases of dispute by their attorney or counsel. In criminal matters, accused individuals who are unable to afford representation are given court-appointed attorneys to present their defense.

In most cases, the parties in a dispute try hard to settle their problems out of the legal procedure. That is why bailiffs are requested for debts recovery.

LEGAL CONCEPTS

The Constitution of the Fourth Republic is the fundamental law of the country. It makes provision for the separation of powers between the executive, the legislative, and the judiciary. This fundamental text, which was adopted by referendum on September 27, 1992, and promulgated on October 14, 1992, secures all the basic liberties to the citizens. Some forty articles are devoted to human rights. Moreover, this constitution is based on principles set forth by the UN Charter of 1945, the Universal Declaration of Human Rights of 1948, the International Treaties of 1966, and the African Charter of Individual and People's Rights adopted in 1981 by the Organization of African Unity (OAU). Article 50 of the Togo Constitution finds in these documents a body of constitutional rules, as follows: "The rights and duties, stated in the Universal Declaration of Human Rights and in the international documents relating to human rights ratified by Togo are part and parcel of the present Constitution."

Thus, the Constitution of 1992 declares the following rights and freedoms: the right to live, the sacred and inviolable nature of the human being, the freedom of thought, the freedom of the press, the freedom of expression, the freedom of conscience, the right to private property, the presumption of innocence for every defendant, the right to a healthy environment, and so forth.

The highest state office is the presidency of the republic. The president is elected by direct universal suffrage for a term of five years, renewable only once. No one can serve more than two terms as president. In conformity with the spirit and the letter of Article 59 of the constitution, the head of state as of 2001, President Gnassimgbe Eyadema, in power since 1967, could not solicit another mandate at the end of his second and last exercise of power in the democratic era.

The constitution institutes a semipresidential system, with a two-headed executive (the president of the republic and the prime minister) and a unicameral Parliament elected for a five-year term. The prime minister, who is head of the government, is nominated by the head of state, the president, from among the majority party in Parliament.

The Supreme Court is the highest state jurisdiction in judicial and administrative matters. The members of the Supreme Court are appointed from among the bench by the government on the proposal of the High Counsel of the Magistrature (see Article 2 of the Organic Law No. 97–05 relative to the structure of the Supreme Court).

The constitution is secured by the Constitutional Court, which is separated from the highest jurisdiction of the country, the Supreme Court. This court became an autonomous institution in 1957. It is made up of seven members, three of whom are directly elected among lawyers and university professors of law. The other four are chosen in the following way: Two are appointed by the president of the republic and two by the prime minister, and the other two are elected by the National Assembly. Each member must have at least fifteen years in the profession. The members exercise a single term of seven years.

The submission of a case to the Constitutional Court is a privilege reserved exclusively to the president of the republic, the prime minister, the president of the National Assembly, and one-fifth of the deputies as regards the control of constitutionality. Consequently, citizens can raise issues regarding the unconstitutionality of a law before the other civil courts. In this case, the courts should stop the instance and then transmit the file to the Constitutional Court, which exercises control a posteriori. Disputes regarding elections are presented by the parties involved before the Constitutional Court.

Among its responsibilities, the Constitutional Court :

• Attends to the lawfulness of presidential elections; it hears complaints regarding the election and declares the results of the ballot
• Is in charge of election questions in general
• Is the jurisdiction that is in charge of ascertaining the definite incapacity of the president of the republic to exercise his duties (Article 65 of the constitution)
• Is the regulating instrument in terms of the functioning of the institutions and the activity of the authorities

The constitution makes provision for a High Court of Justice that is competent in judging the president and other high-ranking officials of the state for offenses committed in the exercise of their duties, particularly the offense of high treason. However, this jurisdiction has never been exercised to date for a lack of cases.

The constitution also institutes a National Commission of Human Rights (CNDH, based on the French term). It is independent and is submissive to the constitution and the law only. Made up of ten members, the CNDH is a heterogeneous institution because its members come from all sectors of the nation (the National Assembly, bar, magistrature, faculty of law, trade unions, medical association, religions, traditional authorities, human rights associations, and humanitarian groups). The CNDH deals with investigations in regards to the violation of human rights and draws the attention of the executive power to the cases raised. It intervenes to put an end to human rights violations brought to its attention.

In accordance with the constitution (Articles 50 and 140), agreements and international treaties signed in matters of human rights have more force than ordinary laws. Togo has signed the Universal Declaration of Human Rights; the International Treaty on Economic, Social and Cultural Rights; the International Treaty on Civil and Political Rights of 1966; the International Convention on the Elimination of All Forms of Racial Discrimination; the International Convention on the Elimination of All Forms of Discrimination against Women; the Convention against Torture and Other Inhuman, Cruel and Degrading Treatments; the African Charter of Individual and People's Rights of 1981 and the additional protocol which created the African Court of Individual and People's Rights; and the Convention of the United Nations on Children.

In this spirit, substantial efforts have been undertaken to protect the rights of women, particularly the adoption by the National Assembly in 1999 of a law that prohibits and punishes mutilation, especially the excision of young girls.

As regards social rights, the state acknowledges to every citizen the right to work, and it endeavors to create conditions of effective enjoyment of this right (Article 37 of the constitution). It secures equal opportunity for every citizen in terms of obtaining employment and guarantees to every worker a just and equitable remuneration. Further, no individual's rights can be infringed in his or her work on the basis of sex, origins, beliefs, or opinions. The constitution acknowledges the citizen's right to strike (Article 39) within the limits established by laws that regulate this right. The right to form trade unions is also recognized.

Finally, for each criminal instance, the right for defense is always secured, and if need be, there are officially appointed attorneys as state compulsory judicial assistance.

SPECIALIZED JUDICIAL BODIES
Togo formerly had specialized judicial bodies (or judicial bodies of exception) to deal with particular situations arising within the society—for example, embezzlement of public funds or breaches of state security and matters of subversion. This gave rise to the establishment of a special judicial body dealing with the offenses of public em-

bezzlement in the first regard and the the court-martial for judging servicemen and security agents in the second.

However, the Constitution of the Fourth Republic has formally banned the judicial bodies of exception. Such matters would instead be taken to the High Court of Justice as provided for by the fundamental law on cases concerning high-ranking civil servants.

In France, Sweden, Mali, and Burkina Faso, for instance, there are special bodies or institutions such as mediators or ombudsmen who are in charge of making sure that laws and rules related to human rights are not violated. In Togo the CNDH, which was created for that purpose, is hardly effective.

LEGAL TRAINING AND THE LEGAL CAREER
The University of Benin is the highest institution for training and research in Togo. The Faculty of Law, on the campus of Lomé, is in charge of the training the legal staff for the country. This faculty provides a basic training of four years, at the end of which successful students get their bachelor's or Master's degrees in legal studies. To the third-year student, the following options are available:

- Public law for administrative and international professions
- Judicial careers for all professions in relation to justice, such as the magistrature and professionals (attorney, bailiff, solicitor, auctioneer, and so on)
- Business law for all those who intend to manage public or private enterprises or commercial firms, organize research consultancies, or specialize in tax, financial, or economic matters

Master's degree holders have the possibility to do postgraduate courses. Three subjects are available:

- Postgraduate diploma taken before completing a Ph.D. in environmental law and policy, centered around research and higher education
- Specialized higher education diploma in business law
- Certificate of proficiency in the profession of barrister

The training of magistrates is provided by the National School of Administration for postgraduate courses. Admission to this program is determined by an entrance examination opened to those who hold a Master's in legal studies. Students receive two years of professional training, after which they are engaged as state civil servants with a special status of independence that is supposed to provide them with more autonomy than other civil servants. Much older magistrates were trained in the high schools of magistrature in France.

Structure of Togolese Courts

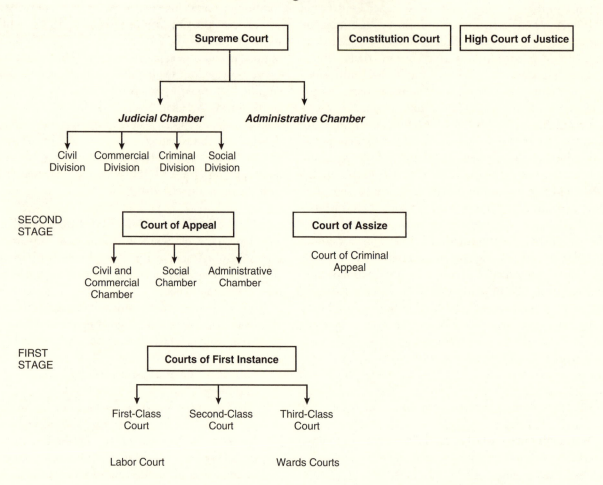

Older lawyers are also the products of the French bar. Since 1996, the Faculty of Law of Lomé has provided a postgraduate course for those who hold Master's degrees in legal studies, with an option in private law to obtain the Certificate of Proficiency for the Profession of Lawyers (CAPA, according to the French term). The CAPA replaces the annual test formerly organized by the bar of Lomé in partnership with the Faculty of Law to recruit trainee attorneys. The selected students for the CAPA program receive a pretraining course in an attorney's chambers. Then an investigation is conducted (inquiring into their morality and fitness for the exercise of the profession), after which they take an oath as trainee attorneys before the state prosecutor. The training course lasts two years. At the end of this period, the successful trainees are registered at the bar of Lomé.

Solicitors take a national training course of two years in the office of a recognized solicitor after completing their Master's in legal studies and before opening their own offices. Bailiffs receive six months of training, which gives them the right to an office after obtaining the approval of the Association of Bailiffs and the Ministries of Interior and of Justice.

IMPACT

It is rather difficult to evaluate the real impact of modern law on the social life of Togo. The statistics in this domain are practically nonexistent, as are research work and investigations. The most notorious remark is that the penetration of the juridical fact in society differs according to the part of the society that is in question. In reality, there seem to be two aspects. Essentially, the impact of law varies depending on whether the community at issue is rural or urban.

In the rural communities, customary or traditional rules are generally applied rather than modern rules deriving from the law. This is particularly true in the case of dispute between the members of the community, especially in matters such as land, marriage, and commercial disputes. However, this is not always true when the case pertains to criminal activities except for matters of theft or fraud. In matters of fraud, it is particularly the judicial authority generally represented by the police force or the gendarmerie that deals with the lawsuit.

Paradoxically, the great impact of customary and traditional rules does not particularly weaken the judicial body, as one might have thought given the eagerness for the full effectiveness of modern laws throughout the national territory.

Of course, the consequence of this situation is increased devotion to the chief and the notable of the village in judicial matters.

In the urban circles, by contrast, the predominance of the modern law is clear, though the search for compromise or consensus stemming from customary habits is not totally lost. However, this predominance is not total because there are still a great many disputes that are not inevitably subjected to the judicial process. Land and matrimonial disputes essentially constitute the vanguard in this regard. In fact, though the frequency and prevalence of the disputes in the courts are greater than in rural areas, most matrimonial disputes are still handled within the family or community circle. This situation ensues doubtlessly from the sacred nature of land and family in the customs of our societies.

Ultimately, it is difficult to evaluate the real impact of modern law on the Togolese society. However, it is essential to note the strong presence of traditional and customary law even today in Togo, where rural communities represent 65 percent of the population.

Edmond Kwam Kouassi

See also Civil Law; Customary Law; France; Legal Pluralism

References and further reading
Aboudou-Salami, M. S. 1990. "Les rapports entre les institutions de la transition démocratique du Togo." *Revue Béninoise des sciences juridiques et administratives* (spécial): 61–71.
Acoutey, M. 1989. "La 3ème république togolaise." *Revue juridique, politique et économique du Maroc* 22: 161–167.
Agbodjan, C. 1987. *Institutions politiques et organisation administrative du Togo.* Lomé, Togo: S.L.N.E.
Cornevin, R. 1960. *Le Togo—"Que sais-je."* Paris: P.U.F.
Leclerq, C. 1980. "La constitution togolaise du 13 janvier 1980." *Revue juridique et politique* 34: 817–824.
Kouassi, K. E. 1995. "Contribution à l'étude de la Constitution de la IV è république togolaise." Annales de l'Université du Bénin: Série Droit-Economie T. XIV; Lomé, Togo: Presses de l'U.B.
———. 1995. "L'évolution politique et institutionnelle du Togo de l'indépendance à nos jours." In *Common Law et Constitutions d'Afrique et d'Haïti: CICLEF, Ecole de Droit; Université de Moncton.* Nouveau-Brusvick, Canada.
Owona, J. 1980. "La constitution de la IIIè république togolaise: L'institutionnalisation du rassemblement du peuple togolais." *Revue juridique et politique* 34: 716–729.
Prouzet, M. 1976. *La république du Togo.* Paris: Berger-Levrault.
Toulabor, C. M. 1989. "Dix ans de démocratisation au Togo: les faussaires de la démocratie." *Année africaine:* 287–310.
Yagla, O. S. 1989. "La notion de Président-Guide et l'aménagement constitutionnel au Togo." *Revue juridique, politique et économique du Maroc* 22: 263–279.

TONGA

COUNTRY INFORMATION

The Kingdom of Tonga (which in the Tongan language means "south") consists of some 150 islands and islets, located in the South Pacific Ocean between 15° and 23° south latitude and 173° and 177° west longitude—about 600 kilometers south of Samoa, about the same distance southeast of Fiji, and 1,500 kilometers northeast of New Zealand.

The islands that make up the kingdom are divided into three main groups: Tongatapu group, which is the most southern; Ha'apai group, which is some 150 kilometers to the northeast; and Vava'u, the most northerly group, which lies 300 kilometers to the northeast of Tongatapu. The largest island is Tongatapu, where the capital of Nuku'alofa is situated, and about 36 other islands are inhabited. The total land area of all the islands is some 700 square kilometers.

The Tonga nation today numbers about 106,000 people, who are almost exclusively of Polynesian race and Christian religion and homogeneous in culture and language throughout the three groups of islands.

HISTORY

The first inhabitants for whom records survive appear to have been members of the Lapita people. Remnants of this people's distinctively incised pottery is found in Tonga, as in other South Pacific islands, dating from about 1000 B.C.E. The first recorded ruler of the islands was Tui Tonga (meaning "king of Tonga"), who ruled around 1000 C.E. and claimed to be the son of a union between the sun god Tongaloa and an earthly woman and thereby to have both temporal and divine spiritual powers. In later centuries, two further royal lines were formed from the Tui Tonga Dynasty. But by the early nineteenth century, a number of powerful chiefs were challenging the traditional dynasties, and the islands of Tonga disintegrated into fierce civil wars. From these emerged Taufa'ahau, who succeeded his father as ruler of Ha'apai in 1820, his brother as ruler of Vava'u in 1833, and his great-uncle as ruler of Tongatapu in 1845. Taufa'ahau had been converted to Christianity by missionaries in 1834 and had adopted the English name George out of admiration for what the missionaries told him about King George III of England, so when he succeeded his great-uncle, he took the name King Siaosi (George) Tupou. Opposition to him lingered among some chiefs of Tongatapu but was finally crushed in 1852, at which time King George Tupou could truly claim to be ruler of all Tonga. In 1865, the Tui Tonga died, and his spiritual powers were vested in King Tupou. These powers were by then insignificant, since the country had been converted to Christianity following King Tupou's leadership, but they had symbolic significance.

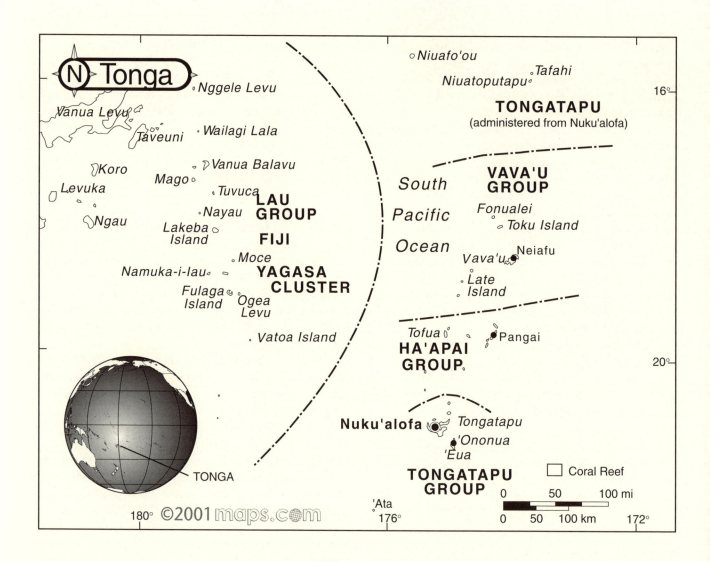

©2001 maps.com

King George Tupou proved to be not only a very skillful warrior but also a great lawgiver for his people. In Ha'apai and Vava'u in 1838, he had published a code of laws, and in 1850, he promulgated a similar code of laws for all of Tonga. He revised and renewed this code in 1862 with the assistance of a Methodist missionary, Rev. Shirley Baker, who had arrived in the kingdom in 1860 and soon became a frequent adviser to the king. One of the most significant of these laws provided for the emancipation of serfs. At this stage, the king ruled with the advice of a *fakataha,* or gathering of chiefs, but he soon resolved to adopt a form of government more similar to that of Britain, of which he had heard so much from the missionaries. In 1875, again with the assistance of Reverend Baker, he drew up a written constitution, which remains in place to this day.

King Tupou I and Rev. Shirley Baker, whom he appointed as premier after the death in 1879 of the first Tongan premier, were very anxious to obtain international recognition of the independence of Tonga. Treaties of friendship were made in 1855 with France, in 1876 with Germany, in 1879 with Britain, and in 1886 with the United States, all recognizing Tonga's independence. Most foreign traders in the country were from Britain and Germany, and in 1898, Britain and Germany agreed that Germany would yield all claims it had in Tonga to Britain in exchange for Britain's recognition of Germany's claims to Western Samoa. In 1900, a treaty of friendship was entered into between Britain and Tonga, whereby Britain was to control the foreign affairs of the country and defend it from hostile attacks, making Tonga a protected state of Britain. The treaty provided that a British consul would be appointed for Tonga and that a British consul's court would be established for the trial of foreigners in all civil proceedings and serious criminal proceedings. In 1905, in exchange for a loan to restore solvency, King Tupou II was obliged to sign a supplement to the Treaty of Friendship, which required the king to consult and accept the advice of the British consul and to obtain the consul's approval for major government appointments and changes in government appointments. Thus, Tonga was brought closely under the control of Britain.

Under the stabilizing influence of King Tupou II's daughter and successor, Queen Salote Tupou III, conditions in the kingdom and relations with Britain improved, and shortly after the accession in 1965 of her son, the current king, as King Taufa'ahau Tupou IV, the British Consul's Court was abolished, and the clauses in the Treaty of Friendship relating to foreign affairs and defense ceased to operate as of June 4, 1970. From that date forward, the Kingdom of Tonga has been an independent sovereign country.

LEGAL CONCEPTS

Constitution

After establishing himself as ruler of all Tonga in 1845 and crushing opposition in Tongatapu in 1852, King George Tupou I turned his attention to providing a legal framework for the country that would help to enable Tonga to be recognized as a civilized independent state, and he asked Reverend Baker for assistance. Charles St. Julian, the honorary consul for Hawai'i in Sydney, had earlier provided a copy of the Constitution of Hawai'i of 1852, and this was used to provide a basis for the Constitution of Tonga.

On September 16, 1875, the king presented the constitution to the assembly of chiefs, and it was approved with minor amendments and signed into law on November 4, 1875. The constitution, which contains no provisions for its suspension or repeal, has been amended on numerous occasions since 1875. In 1990, it was expressly stated to be the supreme law of the land.

Fundamental Rights

Part 1 of the Constitution of Tonga contains a number of provisions protecting fundamental rights and liberties and recognizing certain duties, modeled closely on the fundamental rights provisions of the 1852 Constitution of Hawai'i.

Rights to liberty, freedom from slavery and forced labor, equality, protection of property, protection of the law, and protection from retrospective laws are provided for; in addition, freedoms of worship, speech, the press, assembly, and petition are recognized. But there is no express recognition of freedom of movement. Two rights for foreigners were subsequently modified: The right of foreigners to apply to become naturalized citizens after two years of residence, as stipulated in the original constitution, was later amended to require 5 years of residence, and the right of foreigners to be tried by a special jury, half the members of which were resident foreigners, was removed from the constitution.

Certain duties are also provided for in the constitution: to keep the Sabbath holy, to pay taxes, to serve on juries, and to serve in the militia. In addition, the monarch is required to govern impartially on behalf of all the people, no money is to be paid out of the treasury without the prior approval of the Legislative Assembly, soldiers are subject to the laws of the land, and no government official may engage in trade or work for any other government without approval.

The Supreme Court and Court of Appeal have held that the provisions relating to fundamental rights are to be interpreted in a generous and flexible fashion, unless their wording is too precise and unambiguous to permit such interpretation (*Tuitavake v. Porter and Government of Australia* [1989] Tonga LR 14; *Vaikona v. Fuko* (No. 2) [1990] Tonga LR 68; *Fuko v. Vaikona* [1990] Tonga LR 148).

Monarch

The constitution expressly states that Tonga is a constitutional government—originally under King Tupou I, now under King Taufa'ahu Tupou IV, and ultimately under his heirs and successors in accordance with rules of succession that are delineated in great detail. The person of the monarch is declared to be sacred.

The powers of the monarch expressly stated by the constitution are: to command the armed forces, to grant pardons to convicts, to convoke the Legislative Assembly, to make treaties and receive ambassadors, to grant titles of honor and distinction, to determine the coinage, to proclaim martial law in times of civil war or war with a foreign state, to appoint and dismiss at pleasure members of the Privy Council and ministers, to assent or refuse assent at pleasure to legislation, to appoint and dismiss judges with the consent of the Privy Council, and to own all the land and to make grants of land to nobles and *matapules* (high chiefs) as hereditary estates.

The Supreme Court has held that, because the constitution states that the government is a constitutional government and establishes a Privy Council and cabinet to advise the monarch, it is to be implied that the power of the monarch to make grants of land is to be exercised only with the advice and consent of the Privy Council or cabinet, so that a grant made without such consent is unconstitutional and void (*Tuita v. Minister of Lands* [1926] II Tonga LR 18). It has not been necessary to decide whether the implication relied on in this decision is to be applied to other powers conferred on the monarch by the constitution.

Privy Council

The Privy Council, which was established to advise the monarch on his or her important functions, comprises the ministers, the governors of Ha'apai and Vava'u, and such other persons as the monarch may see fit to appoint.

The Privy Council was also given power to hear appeals from the Supreme Court in civil cases and provide advice on the remission or mitigation of services in criminal cases. In 1990, a Court of Appeal was established, and from then on, the Privy Council ceased to have appellate jurisdiction except in cases concerning estates and titles of nobles.

Since 1912, the Privy Council has had power to make ordinances, which may be suspended from operation by the chief justice until the next session of the Legislative Assembly if he considers them to be unconstitutional. No ordinances have been made since 1927.

Cabinet
The constitution originally provided for only four ministers to form the cabinet—the premier, treasurer, minister of lands, and minister of police—and it described the duties of each. Subsequent amendments have elevated the position of premier to that of prime minister, have added a minister of foreign affairs, and have authorized the monarch to appoint such other ministers as he or she pleases. All ministers are appointed by and dismissible by the monarch at pleasure, and they are required to submit an annual report to the monarch, which is to be forwarded to the Legislative Assembly. The constitution no longer describes the duties of each minister but provides generally that each minister "shall satisfy himself that all the subordinates in his department faithfully perform their duties."

Ministers, like other public officials, may be impeached before the Legislative Assembly (which is presided over, for that purpose, by the chief justice) for breaches of the laws or resolutions of the assembly, maladministration, incompetence, destruction or embezzlement of government property, or actions likely to prejudice relations with other countries. To this extent, the cabinet ministers are responsible to the Legislative Assembly, but in other respects, they are responsible only to the monarch.

Legislature
The Legislative Assembly—nine representatives of the nobles, nine representatives of the people, and the ministers who sit as nobles—is provided by the constitution with the power to pass bills, which, when assented to by the monarch, become laws. Since 1914, the Legislative Assembly has been required to sit annually. The monarch has complete discretion as to whether to grant or withhold assent to bills, and if assent is withheld, the bill cannot be discussed again until the next session of the assembly. The speaker of the Legislative Assembly has, since 1875, been appointed by the monarch.

The Legislative Assembly is required to approve the estimates of government expenditure presented by the minister of finance and to assess the amount of taxes and custom duties and fees. Most bills must have the support of a majority of all members of the Legislative Assembly before being presented to the monarch for assent, but bills relating to the monarch or the royal family or the titles and inheritances of the nobles are discussed only by nobles and are required to be approved by a majority of the nobles only.

The constitution provides that bills to amend the constitution—except the laws of liberty, succession to the throne, and the inheritances and titles of nobles and chiefs—have to be passed three times in one session and obtain the unanimous approval of the Privy Council.

Laws enacted by the Legislative Assembly and the monarch may be suspended by the chief justice until the next session of the assembly if he considers that they are at variance with the Constitution.

JUDICIAL SYSTEM
The judicial system that was originally established by the Constitution of 1875 comprised the Supreme Court, presided over by two judges sitting together, the Circuit Courts, presided over by one judge, and the Police Courts, presided over by magistrates. Since that time, the Supreme Court has remained virtually unchanged, consisting of the chief justice and such other judges as may be appointed by the monarch with the consent of the Privy Council. The one change of importance is that since 1912, at which time European judges were appointed to the court, all sittings of the Supreme Court can be presided over by one judge, instead of two. The jurisdiction of the court remains unchanged and extends to all cases in law and equity arising under the constitution and laws of the kingdom and under treaties, as well as all cases affecting public ministers and consuls and all cases of admiralty and maritime jurisdiction. In addition, the judges are required to give opinions to the monarch, cabinet, or Legislative Assembly on important questions of law and on difficult cases. Individuals charged with serious criminal offenses before the Supreme Court have the right to be tried before a jury, as do defendants in civil cases; originally, juries were composed of twelve persons, but in 1933, that number was reduced to seven. Appeals from the Supreme Court were determined by the Privy Council until 1990, when the Court of Appeal was established to hear all appeals from the Supreme Court, except those relating to the estates and titles of nobles, which continue to be determined by the Privy Council.

The Police Courts originally established by the constitution were, in 1918, renamed Magistrates' Courts. All magistrates have jurisdiction to try summarily criminal offenses for which the punishment does not exceed a $1,000 fine or three years of imprisonment, but the chief police magistrate has an extended jurisdiction over offenses in which the fine does not exceed $1,500. Likewise in civil cases, ordinary magistrates have jurisdiction to

Structure of Tongan Courts

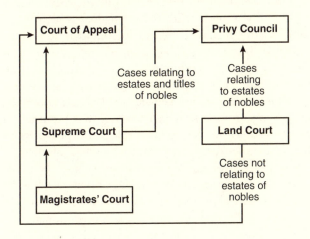

determine civil claims not exceeding $1,000, while the chief police magistrate has jurisdiction to determine civil claims not exceeding $2,000.

In 1921, the Land Court was established to hear disputes about land matters, and this court has continued to operate since then. Appeals from its decision were originally determined by the Privy Council, but since 1990, only appeals relating to the estates of nobles are so determined, the remainder being heard by the Court of Appeal.

The 1900 Treaty of Friendship between Great Britain and Tonga provided in Articles 4 and 5 for the establishment of the British Consul's Court to hear claims of a civil nature and also serious criminal charges involving British subjects and other foreigners. However, these provisions were omitted after the 1960s, and this court ceased to operate.

THE LAWS OF TONGA

The laws of Tonga consist of a mixture of locally enacted laws (that is, laws enacted by Tongan institutions) and introduced laws (that is, laws introduced from Britain). The Treaties of Friendship with Britain entered into between 1900 and 1968, which previously provided a form of law that overrode all other laws, now contain no provisions that purport to control Tonga. Since the Supplement to the Treaty of Friendship in 1905, all laws have been required to be published in Tongan and in English.

Locally Enacted Laws

Locally enacted laws fall into three categories: the constitution, legislation, and ordinances.

- The constitution (enacted in 1875 but amended on many occasions), which contains the basic framework of government and a recognition of fundamental rights and duties and is stated to be the supreme law

- Legislation, or the acts of the Legislative Assembly assented to by the monarch at his or her discretion
- Ordinances made by the monarch with the advice of the Privy Council, under a power that was introduced in 1912 but has not been exercised since 1927

It should be noted that customs are not introduced into the legal system of Tonga at all. In fact, since the Constitution of Tonga was enacted in 1875, they have had no force of law even with regard to land rights (which are regulated solely by the constitution and legislation). Tongan customs are, however, recognized by the courts and are used by them interstitially or indirectly—for example, as a factor to be considered when exercising a discretion conferred by legislation (*Hala v. R* [1992] Tonga LR 7; *Tui'iha'ateiho v. Tu'iha'ateiho* [1962–1973] Tongan LR 22) and when assessing evidence (*Nainoa v. Vaha'i* [1926] II Tongan LR 22, at 24).

Introduced Law

The British Consul's Court established in Tonga to determine civil claims and serious criminal charges against non-Tongans was authorized to apply English statutes of general application as well as English common law and equity, as far as appropriate to the circumstances of the country. But until 1966, there was no express statutory authority for the courts established by the constitution to apply English law (although Rule 9 of the Rules of the Privy Council did authorize the Privy Council to apply, where there was no rule of law available, the principles of English law as far as applicable). Despite the lack of express authorization to do so, however, the Supreme Court of Tonga seemed to have applied the principles of English common law when there was no Tonga law applicable. Thus, in *Mataele v. Niu* ([1956] 1 Tonga LR 83–84), the Supreme Court applied the principles of *Rylands v. Fletcher* ([1868] LR 3 HL 330) in civil proceedings between two Tongan neighbors for damage caused by escaping fire because "if citizens are denied the right to recover damages for civil wrongs, justice and law in the Kingdom would be brought into contempt."

Sections 3 and 4 of the Civil Law Act of 1966 now require that all courts in Tonga must apply the rules of common law and equity, as well as the statutes of general application in force in England, with three conditions: (1) if no other provision is made by or under any act or ordinance in force in the kingdom, (2) as far as the circumstances of the kingdom and its inhabitants permit, and (3) subject to such qualifications as local circumstances render necessary. The effect of this provision is that English statutes of general application, together with the principles of common law and equity, must continue to be applied unless there is a local law to the contrary but subject to any modifications rendered necessary by local circumstances.

Donald Paterson

References and further reading
Afeaki, E. 1983. "Tonga: The Last Pacific Kingdom." Pp. 57–78 in *Politics in Polynesia*. Edited by Ron Crocombe and Ali Ahmad. Suva, Fiji: University of the South Pacific.
Ghai, Yash. 1988. "Systems of Government" and "Political Consequences of Constitutions." Pp. 54–105, 350–372 in *Law, Politics and Government in the Pacific Island States*. Edited by Yash Ghai. Suva, Fiji: University of the South Pacific.
Helu, H. 1975. *The Tongan Constitution*. Nuku'alofa, Tonga: Traditions Committee.
———. 1982. "The Judiciary and Tongan Society." *Commonwealth Judicial* 4, no. 4: 11–14.
———. 1988. "Independence of Adjudicators and Judicial Decision-Making in Tonga." Pp. 48–52 in *Pacific Courts and Legal Systems*. Edited by Guy Powles and Mere Pulea. Suva, Fiji: University of the South Pacific.
Manu, T. 1988. "Lawyers in Tonga: A Personal View." Pp. 157–159 in *Pacific Courts and Legal Systems*. Edited by Guy Powles and Mere Pulea. Suva, Fiji: University of the South Pacific.
Niu, L. 1988. "The Constitution and Traditional Political System in Tonga." Pp. 305–309 in *Law, Politics and Government in the Pacific Island States*. Edited by Yash Ghai. Suva, Fiji: University of the South Pacific.
Paterson, Don. 1999. "Constitutional Law." Pp. 81–112 in *Introduction to South Pacific Law*. Edited by Jennifer Corrin Care, Tess Newton, and Don Paterson. London: Cavendish.
Powles, Guy. 1982. "Traditional Institutions in Pacific Constitutional Systems: Better Late or Never?" Pp. 345–359 in *Pacific Constitutions*. Edited by Peter Sack. Canberra: Australian National University.
———. 1988. "The Common Law as a Source of Law in the South Pacific: The Experiences of Western Samoa and Tonga." *University of Hawai'i Law Review* 10, no. 1: 105–135.
———. 1988. "Law, Courts and Legal Services." Pp. 6–36 in *Pacific Courts and Legal Systems*. Edited by Guy Powles and Mere Pulea. Suva, Fiji: University of the South Pacific.
———. 1990. "The Early Accommodation of Tongan and English Law." Pp. 145–169 in *Tongan History and Culture*. Edited by P. Herda. Canberra: Australian National University.
———. 1993. "Tonga." In *South Pacific Island Legal Systems*. Edited by Michael Ntumy. Honolulu: University of Hawai'i Press.
Rutherford, Noel, ed. 1977. *Friendly Islands: A History of Tonga*. Melbourne: Oxford University Press.
Taumoepeau, A. 1988. "The Land Court of Tonga." Pp. 133–136 in *Pacific Courts and Legal Systems*. Edited by Guy Powles and Mere Pulea. Suva, Fiji: University of the South Pacific.
Wood, Ellen. 1989. "Chief Justices of Tonga, 1905–1940." *Journal of Pacific History* 24, no. 1: 21–37.

TORT LAW

Tort law is concerned with civil wrongs. In general, where tort liability is established, the wrongdoer is required to compensate the injured person for the losses he or she sustained. Tort law is separate from criminal law and contract law, although conduct may overlap and, in some instances, may result in liability for both criminal and civil wrongdoing. In American courts, the best example is the O. J. Simpson case, in which Simpson was acquitted of murder charges but held civilly liable in a wrongful death action. In cases involving contract breaches, no tortious conduct need be established. In some cases, however, where the defendant has breached a contract, such as by supplying a defective product to a consumer, the breach may also be a tort. If so, tort law will predominate. For example, in cases involving injury caused by a defective product, tort principles will preclude the assertion of standard contracts defenses.

Tort law protects a variety of interests from unreasonable interference. It protects interests in real property, personal property, personality, and bodily integrity. It also protects certain commercial and business interests. Tort law encompasses cases where harm is caused intentionally, negligently, or recklessly. In some cases the person or entity causing harm is held strictly liable for that harm. Strict liability typically applies in cases where the person causing the harm has engaged in an unusually dangerous activity or, for social policy reasons, where it is justifiable to impose liability on the person who creates a particular risk. As a general rule, there has to be some justification for shifting the loss from one person to another through the award of damages to the injured person.

There are several approaches to tort law. One is the common law system, which includes the United States, England, Australia, and Canada. A second is the civil code system based on the French system, which adopts a single rule of liability for torts cases. A third is the German civil code system, which takes a pluralistic approach to liability through the application of specific rules for separate types of liability. Countries with roughly similar systems include Greece, Taiwan, Japan, and Thailand. A fourth includes Islamic systems, which have specific rules for specific types of interference with the interests of another. In some countries, traditional solutions provided by Islamic law may be mixed with Western legal principles, however.

There are substantial differences between common law and civil law countries, both in procedure, the payment of attorneys' fees, and available damages, all of which affect the nature and frequency of litigation. In particular, "the American legal system has fostered and encouraged the so-called 'entrepreneurial' lawyer who, with a vested interest in the litigation, pursues and vindicates client claims. This system of entrepreneurial lawyering is incompatible with civil law systems" (Mullenix 2001, 6–7).

The common law is judge-made law. It developed from a writ system in England that gave judges substantial latitude in formulating legal principles to govern claims involving a variety of injuries to persons and property. In the United States, which is a federal system of government, each of the fifty states has an independent court system that has responsibility for the formulation and application of the common law, except for Louisiana, which formulates its principles within the context of a civil code. While there are substantial similarities in the common law rules that apply in each of the states, there are also some significant differences. One example is in the area of bystander recovery for emotional distress in cases where the person who suffers emotional distress at witnessing the injury or death of a family member is not directly threatened himself or herself. There is a significant split of authority as to the best way to handle the claims. The courts have developed several different approaches to the problem. Some courts disallow recovery unless the person seeking to recover for emotional distress was in the zone of danger and threatened with physical harm. Other courts permit recovery, but only if certain guidelines are met that require the person claiming recovery to be near the scene of the accident, witness or hear the accident, and be closely related to the person who actually suffers the physical injury in the accident. There are numerous other examples of cases where there are distinctions in the scope of liability that exists for specific harms.

In the French civil code, most of the law of torts (the law of delict) is based on general principles of liability embodied in several civil code articles that have been substantially unchanged for a long period of time. The law in many countries has been influenced by the French civil code; this includes other European countries, as well as South American countries. However, there are variances in the breadth of legal liability imposed under those systems.

The general liability clause of the French civil code, Article 1382, says that "every act whatever of man which causes damage to another obliges him by whose fault the damage occurred to repair it." The code also states that "everyone is responsible not only for the damage which he has caused by his own act but also for that which he causes by his negligence or imprudence."

Because of the general nature of the code articles, much of the law is judge-made. There are three basic requirements for the imposition of liability. First, there must be damage to a protected legal interest. The concept is construed broadly enough to include injury to human feelings. Legal interests include economic loss. Second, the defendant must have engaged in culpable behavior. While there is no code definition of fault, it encompasses

cases where the defendant failed to comply with standards of conduct that he or she should have respected. Third, the conduct must have caused the damage to the plaintiff.

In Germany, the civil code does not have a single-liability rule. Instead, it establishes three separate rules. The first is where a person's injury is caused unlawfully and culpably, but only if the injury affects the person in a way that is defined in the text, including life, body, health, freedom, ownership, and any "other right." The second is where there is a violation of a statute designed to protect another person. The statutes include private and public law rules, particularly criminal rules, which are intended to protect a person or a group of persons, rather than a statute that is intended to protect the public as a whole. The third arises in cases where the person intentionally or recklessly causes harm.

While the German approach to tort law is pluralistic, it still may be differentiated from the unrestricted pluralism of common law tort law. Rather than falling under one or more general heads of liability, common law torts have been developed independently, each with its own set of rules, to deal with a variety of situations. Tort law generally involves wrongdoing or culpability based on intentional or negligent wrongdoing, although there are pockets of strict liability that apply. However, the general concept of no liability without fault has to be considered within the context of each individual tort. For example, the torts of assault and battery are intentional torts that apply where one person intentionally causes a harmful or offensive contact to another, or places that person in apprehension of such a contact. The tort of trespass to land vindicates possessory interests in property, and the tort of nuisance, the right to use and enjoyment of property. The tort of negligence encompasses a variety of wrongs, including negligent driving of an automobile, professional malpractice, and products liability cases. There are further subdivisions in which the right to recover depends on whether courts are willing to conclude that a defendant's duty extends to certain kinds of injuries.

Both common law and code systems make provision for imposition of liability on the basis of negligence, or the failure to adhere to a specified standard of care. Both systems also provide for the limitation of liability based on the balancing of interests. Some courts are more forthright in advancing social policy reasons for their decisions than others. In countries such as Israel, in which the courts play a significant role in establishing tort rules, tort law is used as an instrument for social engineering. In the United States, the courts specifically weigh and balance social policy in determining the appropriate scope of tort rules.

Tort law may be modified and supplemented, sometimes substantially, by legislation, in both common law and code systems. In the United States, in particular, common law rules are frequently amended by legislatures, sometimes to restrict the availability of tort remedies, and sometimes to provide remedies where the common law does not. Two good examples are in wrongful death cases and in cases involving the liability of sellers or providers of alcoholic beverages. At common law, the cause of action died with the person. The adoption of wrongful death statutes by the states now permits the recovery by the surviving spouse and next of kin in cases where the fault of some third person caused the death of the decedent. In cases involving the illegal sale or provision of alcohol to a person who is subsequently injured or dies in an accident, the common law rule provided that the cause of the accident was not the illegal sale of intoxicating alcohol, but rather the voluntary intoxication of the person consuming the alcohol. Many state legislatures have adopted dram shop acts, which permit limited actions by persons injured in their means of support by the illegal sale of alcohol.

In some cases, pockets of tort law may be modified so that closed compensation schemes are established, with specific rules applicable to certain types of injuries. The most common form of legislative scheme substituting for common law remedies is the workers' compensation act, which abolishes tort actions against the employer, but permits the injured employee to recover for a certain amount of economic loss suffered while working in the course and scope of employment. Many states and countries accomplished the change legislatively, although some countries have made the change through judge-made law. A second form of compensation scheme is no-fault automobile insurance, which in some American states limits the tort remedy, but does not abolish it, and provides for a form of insurance intended to compensate automobile accident victims for major elements of the economic loss they sustain in accidents. No-fault automobile insurance schemes also exist in some form in Manitoba, Saskatchewan, and Quebec. The plans are full or pure accident compensation plans that provide compensation for automobile accident injuries while abolishing the right to sue in tort for those injuries. Ontario has a modified plan that permits suit in cases involving personal injury.

More rarely, legislative compensation schemes may be substituted entirely for tort law. The best example is New Zealand's Accident Compensation scheme, which was enacted in 1972, and provides for compensation by the state on a no-fault basis for personal injuries sustained by accident. It effectively abolishes the right to sue for personal injury. Sweden has a patient insurance scheme that compensates persons who have been injured by certain medical interventions. Sweden has a patient Insurance Compensation Fund that provides compensation for those who suffer from avoidable injuries from medical care.

Tort law may also be modified by international treaty. The Warsaw Convention, adopted in 1929, imposes limitations on the liability of airlines for accidents resulting in injury, death, or property damage that occurs in international flights. The intent of the convention is to achieve uniformity in the liability rules that govern international airplane accidents. The liability limits under the convention are low, although with the Montreal Agreement, for flights that originate or end in the United States, or where the United States is a stopping place for international flights, higher limits apply. In Japan, Japanese airlines have voluntarily withdrawn from the Warsaw Convention liability limits by privately contracting for higher damage awards.

Another example of the impact of international treaties on tort liability is the European Union convention on products liability law. Products liability law is one of the most complex areas of tort law.

In 1985, the European Union adopted a Directive on Liability for Defective Products, which adopts a uniform strict liability principle for member countries, although there are certain escape clauses that permit members to deviate from certain parts of the directive. For example, the directive permits the adoption of a developmental risk defense, which insulates product manufacturers from liability in cases where the risks created by the product were not discoverable at the time the product was placed in circulation.

SUMMARY

Given the variance in approaches to tort law, it is difficult to make accurate generalizations about tort law that encompass all legal systems. If there is a common thread, it is that the compensatory aspect of tort law is typically not triggered unless the defendant has engaged in some culpable wrongdoing, or conduct that the state has decided should justify compensation. Whether liability is imposed through tort law or statutory compensation schemes, the goal of compensation has to be balanced against the need to contain liability rules within manageable limits.

Michael Steenson

See also Civil Procedure

References and further reading
Dobbs, Dan B. 2000. *The Law of Torts*. Eagan, Minnesota: West Group.
Ferrari, Franco. 1993. "Comparative Remarks on Liability for One's Own Acts." *Loyola of Los Angeles International and Comparative Law Journal* 15: 813–840.
Khare, R. S. 1999. *Perspectives on Islamic Law, Justice, and Society.* Lanham, Maryland: Rowman and Littlefield Publishing.
"Liability for One's Own Act." 1979. *XI International Encyclopedia of Comparative Law.* Ch. 2, Torts. The Hague, the Netherlands: Kluwer Law International.

Mullenix, Linda S. 2001. "Lessons from Abroad: Complexity and Convergence." *Villanova Law Review* 46, no. 1: 6–7.

Rosen, Lawrence. 2000. *The Justice of Islam: Comparative Perspectives on Islamic Law and Society*. Oxford: Oxford University Press.

Schmidt, Joel. 1998. "The Growing Body of Israeli Law: Two New Sources on the Law of Israel—A Review Essay." *New York International Law Review* 11: 97–137.

Zweigert, Konrad, and Hein Kotz. 1984. *An Introduction to Comparative Law*. 2d ed. Oxford: Oxford University Press.

TRIAL COURTS

TRIAL COURTS DEFINED

Trial courts are courts that first listen to litigants in a case and then pass judgment based on the facts, the evidence, and the law. In some systems of law, such as civil, Islamic, and hybrid law, trial courts are referred to as courts of first instance.

ORIGINS OF COURTS

Trial courts in the United States originated from practices in English courts. When the founding fathers migrated from England, they brought with them ideas on court organization and case adjudication. However, these ideas had to be refined to suit the circumstances of the new nation. Several types of courts were formed, including specialized courts such as juvenile and family courts. Due to the federal form of government in the United States, there is no unified court system, as the English have. Instead, each of the fifty states has created its own courts, which function independently of the federal courts. State courts interpret state laws, and each state organizes and determines the role of the courts within its geographic jurisdiction. The federal trial courts have their roots in Article III of the U.S. Constitution, which grants congress the power to create inferior courts. The first of these courts were established in 1789, and today, each state has at least one, as do the District of Columbia and the territories of the United States.

In England, prior to unifying the various laws in the twelfth century and enforcing them in the newly created King's Court (Curia Regis), disputes were resolved in local courts scattered throughout the country. Judges of the King's Court were selected by the king, and they had to travel nationwide to try cases or listen to appeals from the local courts. Subsequently, Equity Courts, Courts of Star Chamber, and Courts of High Commission were created. These courts were eventually disbanded, and more contemporary courts were established in a hierarchy.

In France prior to the 1800s, several types of courts existed, each handling specific types of issues: ecclesiastical courts, communal courts, seignorial courts, and par-lement/royal courts. The royal courts comprised the Court of Requests, the Chamber of Pleas, the Court of Inquest, and the Tournelle. After the Revolution in the nineteenth century and the ascendance to power of Napoleon Bonaparte, several reforms were generated, including the Civil Code and court organization. The ideas on structuring courts that were introduced by Napoleon have been preserved over time.

The Meiji Restoration in Japan substantially changed the judiciary in that country. The judicial court of 1872 created a hierarchy of courts modeled after those in France. After 1889, German influences became integral to the Japanese legal system. The Anglo-American system introduced to Japan after World War II had a significant influence on the structure of Japanese courts.

TYPES OF TRIAL COURTS

Trial courts are called by different names from country to country, but the functions of each seem to be mostly similar. In the United States, where each state has its own court system, some states have several local courts whose functions may be similar, and sometimes even within one state, the jurisdiction of similar courts may vary from county to county. Trial courts of the state system include: Courts of Limited Jurisdiction (also called District, Justice of the Peace [JP], Common Pleas, Magistrates', or Mayor's Courts). There are approximately 14,000 of these courts, with about 18,000 judicial employees (Neubauer 1999, 89). Some of these courts, especially the Justice of the Peace, are locally (not state) funded. Justice of the Peace judges are sometimes lay judges who work in small claims courts, where fines imposed do not normally exceed $2,000. There are over 15,000 JP judges, elected in their localities. Courts of General Jurisdiction are also called Superior, Circuit, or District Courts. There are about 2,600 of these courts, with about 9,000 judges (Neubauer 1999, 90). New York refers to these courts as Supreme Courts.

The U.S. federal courts, created by Congress and patterned along state courts lines, also follow a hierarchy, with the U.S. District Courts serving as trial courts for federal issues. There are ninety-four U.S. District Courts, eighty-nine of which are located within the fifty states; there is one each in Puerto Rico, Guam, the Virgin Islands, the Northern Mariana Islands, and Washington, D.C. Some states, such as California, New York, and Texas, each have four District Courts.

In England, the trial courts are the Crown Courts and the Magistrates' Courts. The Crown Courts have about 400 circuit judges and 500 part-time judges, as well as a selected number of justices from the Queen's Bench Division of the High Court (Terrill 1999, 37). The Magistrates' Courts, also called Inferior Criminal Courts, handle most criminal cases. There are about 500 such courts, and some 60 full-time, law-trained (stipendiary) magistrates and 27,500 lay magistrates try cases in these courts. Lay magistrates are not trained in the law and are not paid for their services. Serving on these courts is deemed to be prestigious, which is the motivation for serving as a magistrate. The Queen's Bench Division of the High Court has both original and appellate jurisdiction in civil cases and sometimes in criminal cases.

In France, approximately 450 Police Courts (Tribunaux de Police) are the lowest criminal courts. Other trial courts are the Correctional Courts (Tribunaux Correctionnels), which handle lesser criminal offenses, and the Assize Courts (Cour d'Assise), which handle felonies. The civil courts are those of major jurisdiction, the Trivinaux de Grande Instance, and those of minor jurisdiction, the Tribinaux d'Instance. There are approximately 181 and 473 of each, respectively.

In Saudi Arabia, *sharia* courts have general jurisdiction to hear both civil and criminal cases. Ordinary Courts (Musta'galah Courts), which are found throughout the country, are the lowest trial courts. High Courts (Kubra) have original and appellate jurisdiction over all kinds of cases.

Japan has 50 District Courts for each of the 47 districts. The biggest district, Hokkaido, has three District Courts. These courts have original jurisdiction in both civil and criminal cases. The 448 Summary Courts, which are courts of limited jurisdiction in both civil and criminal cases, are run by both trained and untrained lawyers.

In Russia, the People's Courts, also known as District or City Courts, are the main trial courts for both civil and criminal cases. Regional Courts, also known in some jurisdictions as Supreme Courts of Autonomous Republics, have both original and appellate jurisdiction in more serious civil and criminal cases.

JURISDICTION OF TRIAL COURTS

Trial Courts of Limited Jurisdiction

Courts of limited jurisdiction in the United States have authority to try minor civil cases with claims as high as $5,000 ($10,000 for Tennessee), misdemeanors, and violations, including traffic offenses. Judges in these courts usually sign search-and-arrest warrants, preside over the initial appearance of the accused, appoint counsel for indigent defendants, and conduct the preliminary hearings. Jury trials are allowed except in small traffic issues and issues for which incarceration may be less than six months. Fines and short jail sentences of up to one year may be imposed. Since most trial courts of limited jurisdiction are not courts of records (that is, transcripts of the court proceedings are not kept), when a court of general jurisdiction has to review a case from a lower court, the trial is done all over, that is, trial de novo.

In England, the Magistrates' Courts perform functions similar to those of the lower courts of limited jurisdiction in the United States, except that these courts also hear criminal cases involving juveniles and child protection issues. In civil matters, these courts have jurisdiction over child custody, adoption, and marital separation issues.

In France, these lowest courts hear civil cases in the civil tribunal, and misdemeanors and violations are heard in Police Courts. Japanese Summary Courts hear minor civil cases, misdemeanors, and violations, as do the People's Courts of Russia and the Sharia Courts of lowest jurisdiction in Saudi Arabia. In the countries discussed, only one judge usually presides over cases. In England, one professional magistrate may hear cases, but at least two lay judges must preside over a case.

Trial Courts of General Jurisdiction

U.S. courts of general jurisdiction handle all major criminal cases (felonies and some misdemeanors, such as the possession and sale of small quantities of illegal drugs) and civil cases. Civil cases handled by these courts include personal injury, domestic relations, probate, property rights, contracts, and other commercial issues, and any amount of damages may be imposed. Most criminal cases are resolved by guilty pleas, and the judge metes out the punishment. Those that go to trial may be decided by a jury or a judge (bench trial). The punishment administered in such cases ranges from one year in prison to the death penalty. There is usually one judge in each of the district courts, but in large areas, there may be more than one, in which case the judges might agree that one hears criminal cases, while the other hears civil matters.

In the federal system, the U.S. District Courts handle both civil and criminal cases. They have jurisdiction over cases involving a federal issue, that is, a constitutional problem or issue involving treaties. Civil cases relating to rights, sexual harassment, and equal employment opportunity are among the cases handled by this court. The bulk of criminal cases deal with major drug distribution and white-collar crimes. A judge or jury is the fact finder in these courts.

In England, Crown Courts handle all major criminal cases, with decisions on guilt or innocence being made either by a judge or by a jury. Civil cases are heard either in the County Court or in the High Court, depending on the amount at issue; with the exception of slander and libel cases, juries are not used in civil cases.

In France, the courts of major jurisdiction handle civil cases, criminal cases in correctional courts, and juvenile cases. A panel of three judges decides cases, and sometimes, the jury may decide. Assize Courts may also have original jurisdiction in serious felony cases. Unlike in the United States, where guilt must be proven beyond a reasonable doubt, members of the jury in France decide a case based on how convinced they are of guilt or innocence. In France, a trial is conducted pursuant to the investigatory system, whereby rigorous pretrial investigations and interrogations are carried out so as to avoid trying innocent persons. In the United States and England, trials are conducted based on the adversarial system—a process whereby both sides in a case present their testimony and evidence under the supervision of a judge.

Japanese district courts handle both civil and criminal cases. In lesser offenses, one judge is seated; in more serious offenses, a panel of three judges decides the case. There are no jury trials in Japan. Japan blends both common law and civil law practices in its trials.

General courts in Saudi Arabia hear serious civil and criminal cases. If the case is not complex, one judge decides the issue, but in serious criminal cases carrying sanctions of amputation or death, a three-judge panel is used.

Trial Courts of Specialized Jurisdiction

The jurisdiction of specialized courts is limited to the specific issues for which they were created. In the United States, there are specialized courts in both the state and federal court systems. In the state system, there are Juvenile and Domestic Relations Courts that hear cases relating to juvenile delinquency, child protection, adoptions, paternity suits, foster care placements, divorce, and separations, among others. Surrogate Courts hear cases concerning the estates of incompetent or deceased persons. Drug Courts were created in the 1980s to handle the increasing number of drug-related issues, to impress on offenders the need for treatment, and to assess any impediments to successful treatments. These courts exist in over twenty jurisdictions (Albanese 1999, 278).

In the federal system, by virtue of Article III of the U.S. Constitution, federal courts have jurisdiction to hear specific kinds of cases and issues concerning specific parties. Therefore, the difference between specialized courts and federal trial courts is that the latter has jurisdiction over all types of cases in a region, while the former has jurisdiction over all cases relating to a specific issue throughout the country. Courts created pursuant to this constitutional provision are commonly referred to as Constitutional or Article III Courts. Judges who work in these courts have lifetime tenure but may be impeached for bad behavior; also, their salaries may not be reduced. The specialized Constitutional Courts are the Court of International Trade and the Court of Appeals for the Federal Circuit. The jurisdiction of the Court of International Trade spans issues such as duties due for exported and imported goods. This court also resolves issues pertaining to the quality of commodities imported to the country. The Court of Appeals for the Federal Circuit hear appeals relating to trademarks, patents, international trade, and a variety of claims against the federal government.

Occasionally, some specialized courts may temporarily employ the services of judges from other federal courts. This trait distinguishes these types of courts from other Constitutional and Legislative Courts. Courts that fall in this category are: the Alien Terrorist Removal Court, which is responsible for determining if an alien should be repatriated for being a terrorist; the Foreign Intelligence Surveillance Court, which hears issues relating to electronic surveillance of foreign intelligence agents; and the Foreign Intelligence Surveillance Court of Review.

Legislative courts are also federal courts created by Congress based on Article I of the U.S. Constitution. Using its legislative powers, Congress has created several specialized courts. Judges who preside over these courts are appointed for a specific duration, and unlike constitutional court judges, their salaries are not protected. The legislative courts are: the Court of Federal Claims, which adjudicates cases relating to monetary claims against the federal government; the Tax Court, which handles tax disputes and may act as an appellate court over tax issues tried in district courts; the Court of Veteran Appeals, which hears appeals on benefits and loans for veterans and their survivors; and the U.S. Court of Appeals for the Armed Services, which hears appeals under the Uniform Code of Military Justice (these appeals may include queries regarding prison sentences and dishonorable discharges).

In England, courts created to handle juvenile cases are called youth courts. The Commercial Court, which is a specialized division of the Queen's Bench Division of the High Court, handles cases relating to commercial transactions.

France has two types of courts that specialize in juvenile issues. The Court of Assize for Juveniles handles cases relating to offenders ranging in age from fifteen to eighteen; while the juvenile court, which is a branch of the court of major jurisdiction, handles issues relating to juveniles under the age of eighteen. The Court of Assize for Juveniles is made up of a judge from the district court of appeals, two judges who specialize in juvenile matters, and nine jurors. The juvenile court comprises one magistrate trained in juvenile issues and two lay assessors. France also has administrative courts, which hear cases relating to violations of the rights of private persons by government agents. An example of an issue heard by this court is misleading or false information provided by a government agent to a private person about taxes or pension. These courts do not have jurisdiction over police abuse of power or over abuses by judicial officials. The Council of State (Conseil d'Etat) is the highest administrative court.

In Japan, family courts are the only specialized courts (Terrill 1999, 379). These courts, which were created in 1949, specialize in juvenile and family issues. Matrimonial issues, including equal rights of spouses, as well as juvenile cases, including crimes by minors, truancy, and related matters, are handled by the fifty family courts in the country. A judge presides in this court, and probation officers furnish the judge with relevant information about the juvenile.

The Board of Grievance in Saudi Arabia hears a variety of issues, including cases relating to the actions of private persons against government officers, issues relating to foreign business owners and the government of Saudi Arabia, and complaints concerning administrative decisions. The Committee for the Settlement of Labor Disputes is another specialized tribunal, which has exclusive jurisdiction over labor-related accidents and claims (Fields and Moore 1996, 397).

PROBLEMS OF LOWER COURTS

In the United States and certain other countries such as England and France, the sheer volume of cases handled by the trial courts causes several obvious problems, such as inadequate funding, backlog of cases, unconventional court procedures (for example, rapid disposal of cases), use of judges without legal training, and small and inconvenient facilities. Japan seems to be free of many of these problems, since it has a lower rate of litigation due to its reliance on the practice of informal social control.

Victoria M. Time

See also England and Wales; Fines; France; Incarceration; Islamic Law; Japan; Juries; Lay Judiciaries; Philippines; Plea Bargaining; Russia; Saudi Arabia; Small Claims Courts; United States—Federal System; United States—State Systems
References and further reading
Albanese, Jay S. 1999. *Criminal Justice.* Boston and London: Allyn and Bacon.
Baum, Lawrence. 1990. *American Courts: Process and Policy.* 2nd ed. Boston: Houghton Mifflin.
Calvi, J. V., and S. Coleman. 2000. *American Law and Legal Systems.* 4th ed. Upper Saddle River, NJ: Prentice-Hall.
David, René, and John E. C. Brierley. 1985. *Major Legal Systems in the World Today.* 3rd ed. London: Stevens and Sons.
Dean, Meryll. 1997. *Japanese Legal System: Text and Materials.* London: Cavendish.
Fairchild, Erika, and Harry R. Dammer. 2001. *Comparative Criminal Justice Systems.* 2nd ed. Belmont, CA: Wadsworth Publishing.
Fields, C. B., and R. H. Moore, Jr. 1996. *Comparative Criminal Justice: Traditional and Nontraditional Systems of Law and Control.* Prospect Heights, IL: Waveland Press.
Moore, R. 1987. "Courts, Law, Justice, and Criminal Trials in Saudi Arabia." *International Journal of Comparative and Applied Criminal Justice* 11, no. 1: 61–67.
Morrison, Fred L. 1973. *Courts and the Political Process in England.* Beverly Hills, CA: Sage.
Neubauer, David W. 1999. *America's Courts and the Criminal Justice System.* 6th ed. Belmont, CA, and Albany, NY: West/Wadsworth.
Posner, Richard A. 1985. *The Federal Courts: Crisis and Reform.* Cambridge, MA: Harvard University Press.
Reichel, Philip L. 1999. *Comparative Criminal Justice Systems: A Topical Approach.* 2nd ed. Upper Saddle River, NJ: Prentice-Hall.
Rudden, Bernard. 1973–1974. "Courts and Codes in England, France, and Soviet Russia." *Tulane Law Review* 48: 1010–1028.
Shelley, Louise L. 1987. "The Structure and Function of Soviet Courts." Pp. 199–216 in *The Distinctiveness of the Soviet Law.* Edited by F. J. M. Feldbrugge. Dordrecht, the Netherlands: Martinus Nijhoff.
Terrill, Richard J. 1999. *World Criminal Justice Systems.* 4th ed. Cincinnati, OH: Anderson Publishing.

TRINIDAD AND TOBAGO

COUNTRY INFORMATION

The Republic of Trinidad and Tobago (TT) lies at the southern end of the chain of West Indian islands in the Caribbean Sea, northeast of Venezuela. Tobago was united with Trinidad in 1889. Trinidad's area is approximately 4,829 square kilometers; Tobago's is about 300 square kilometers. The climate is tropical, with a dry season extending from January to May and a wet season from June to December. Both islands were European colonies from 1498—when Christopher Columbus claimed them for Spain—to 1962, when political independence was obtained from Britain. They were constituted as a republic in 1976. The 1995 population was approximately 1.3 million citizens, a colorful mix of ancestries from Asia, Africa, and Europe. The 1990 census reported these percentages: African (39.6 percent), East Indian (40.3 percent), mixed (18.4 percent), white (0.6 percent), Chinese (0.4 percent), other (0.2 percent). About 29.4 percent are Roman Catholic, 23.8 percent are Hindu, 10.9 percent are Anglican, 5.8 percent are Muslim, 3.9 percent are Presbyterian, and 25.7 percent belong to assorted other religions. English is the official language, and the country's literacy rate stands at 97.9 percent. The gross national product (GNP) per capita is about U.S.$3,770. Britain seized the islands from Spain in 1797 and introduced the country's common law–based legal system.

HISTORY

Amerindians—primarily Caribs and Arawaks—inhabited Trinidad and Tobago before the Europeans arrived. Essentially an agricultural people, the Amerindians had a simple, well-ordered family life, with some gender-based division of labor. They were governed by elders known as *caciques,* whose rule was paternal. The position of cacique was hereditary, passed on to the son of the incumbent's eldest sister. Social harmony and peaceful relations predominated. Theft seemed to have been the only punish-

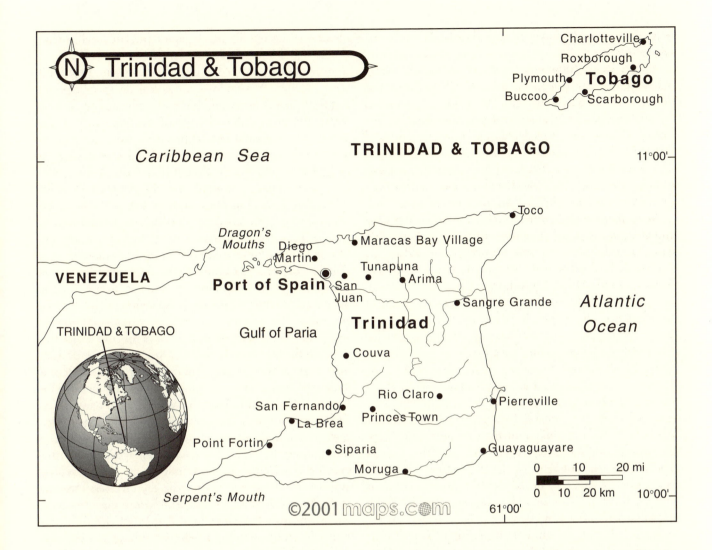

able crime, but it was considered very serious. Even petty theft was punished with death.

The country's formal legal history began with Spanish colonial rule in the late 1400s. Over roughly three centuries, Spain institutionalized a civil law system—with Spanish laws and customs as well as the Roman Catholic religion—to maintain its rule. Spanish law permitted settlers from Spain to enslave Amerindians and also authorized the sale of enslaved Amerindians to work in the gold mines of Hispaniola (the present-day Dominican Republic and Haiti). In the eighteenth century, economic production included a fledgling tobacco trade, followed by a short-lived effort to cultivate cocoa. Economic development languished because of Spain's preoccupation with the acquisition of gold and silver in Mexico and Peru. Also, its colonial bureaucracy was inadequate and inefficient. Consequently, Trinidad and Tobago remained a colonial backwater.

The Amerindian population dwindled rapidly from forced labor or their resistance to colonial domination. Their plight was successfully taken up by the Spanish missionary Bartolomé de Las Casas, who persuaded the Spanish government to end Amerindian slavery. This Amerindian gain, however, was a loss for Africans, who were substituted as enslaved workers in the colonies.

Spanish criminal and civil law was gradually ousted following the British conquest of Trinidad in 1797. By 1848, the transition to English law was complete. (Some 114 years later, a provision for the preservation of Spanish law was written into Section 19 of the 1962 Supreme Court of Judicature Act, No. 12 of 1962. But Spanish law is not used in legal or judicial practice, and no one seems to know why it was reintroduced.)

The current legal system is a product of eighteenth-century English common law, the doctrine of equity, and statute law. The English common law system was planted lock, stock, and barrel in colonial Trinidad and Tobago and subsequently adjusted by the wealthy sugar planter class, which controlled the legislature. Until 1925, the legislature was nominated by the colonial governor. After 1925, elected representatives joined nominated members on the legislative council. By 1940, elected representatives began to outnumber nominated members, and within ten years, the powers of government had passed completely into the hands of elected representatives.

Theoretically, common law should reflect the needs and conditions of the society within which it is used, but despite the political and legislative changes during the colonial period, Trinidad and Tobago's common law system continued to mirror a dated English social reality and retain its British colonial structure and legal concepts. Over the years, laws covering fiscal, economic, educational, social, political, and constitutional matters have been added to the colonial, English-based legal system.

With political independence in 1962, a written constitution was adopted, but this critical legal document was "handed down" in an order in council issued by the British queen Elizabeth II. It was not, as in the United States or South Africa, drawn up with local participation, and it did not address the particular characteristics and circumstances of the people it was intended to govern. Nevertheless, this document became fundamental law for the people of Trinidad and Tobago.

In 1962, Parliament passed 20 bills, including the Supreme Court of Judicature Act, which contained the curious provision to preserve Spanish law despite its abolition by 1848. Between 1963 and mid-1975, Parliament passed thirty or forty bills annually; among the most notable were the Emergency Powers Act, the Trinidad and Tobago Constitution Amendment Act, and the Firearms Act, all passed in 1970, and the Matrimonial Proceedings and Property Act and the Industrial Relations Act, both of which were passed in 1972.

A few efforts at reform were initiated in the postindependence period. In 1969, the Revised Statutes and the Law Commission Acts respectively authorized the creation of the Law Commission and the Statute Law Revision Commission to recommend reforms, but it was not until 1974 that commission members were appointed to begin their work. The Law Commission issued its recommendations in three working papers that addressed revisions with respect to family law, land, compensation for injuries, civil procedure, mental treatment, criminal law and procedure, married women's property, county courts, legal education, narcotics control, and the interpretation of law.

In 1971, Prime Minister Eric Williams appointed the Wooding Commission, headed by Chief Justice H. O. B. Wooding, to hold public hearings throughout the country and to propose a new draft constitution that was suited to social life in postcolonial Trinidad and Tobago. The commission's Majority Report contained many radical proposals for constitutional change, such as proportional representation and stronger local government. It was rejected by the prime minister, who instead accepted the Minority Report. A few reforms were introduced, including the 1976 Constitution, which established the

country as a republic. But by and large, the legal system, the legacy of British rule, was left intact.

Law making proceeded over the years—in a cut-and-paste manner but steadily—not within any specific philosophical legal framework but primarily in response to such economic and sociocultural developments as the growth of new industries and the rise of new religious sects. Between 1951 (when Trinidad and Tobago's legislature became an entirely elected body) and 2000, 1,980 laws were enacted, an average of 40 per year. They involved issues ranging from income taxes and fiscal matters, pensions, credit and loan institutions, housing, criminal offenses, and industrial disputes to the incorporation of numerous religions and/or religious sects, marriage and family, children, education, gambling, dangerous drugs, dangerous dogs, and, more recently, deoxyribonucleic acid (DNA), human tissue transplants, and intellectual property.

But despite the patchwork style of the legislative process, the laws passed since 1990 in particular do suggest a progressive trend toward legal change. Recent measures involve: protection of women (Domestic Violence Act, 1991 and 1999; the Maternity Protection Act, 1998), protection from discrimination (the Equal Opportunity Act, 2000), promotion of the public's right to know about the actions of government agencies and officials (the Freedom of Information Act, 1999), professional behavior and accountability by civil servants (the Integrity in Public Life Act, 2000), consumer protection (the Consumer Protection and Safety Act, 1985), extrajudicial conflict resolution (the Community Mediation Act, 1998), recognition of common law relationships (the Cohabitational Relationships Act, 1998), recognition of non-Christian marriage customs (the Hindu Marriage Act, amended 1953; the Muslim Marriage and Divorce Act, 1961; the Orisha Marriage Act, 1999), protection of workers (the Minimum Wages Act, 1976, amended in 2000; the Workmen's Compensation Act [Amendment], 1986; the Unemployment Levy Act, 1970), protection of the public health (the Pesticides and Toxic Chemicals Act, 1979; the Environmental Management Act, 2000), public assistance (the Socially Displaced Persons Act, 2000), and legal aid (the Legal Aid and Advice [Amendment] Act, 1999).

LEGAL CONCEPTS

The 1976 Constitution of the Republic of Trinidad and Tobago Act provided the foundation for the country's current legal system and continues to serve as the basis of all the country's laws and institutions and the fabric of the society. The constitution stipulated the form of government (parliamentary democracy); defined civil, political, and human rights; and specified tax and miscellaneous other revenue provisions for the government.

The constitution also authorized the establishment of an independent judiciary (one of the three arms of the state), headed by a chief justice. The other two branches of authority are the executive—the prime minister, president, and the cabinet—and a bicameral legislature containing the House of Representatives and the Senate.

Despite negotiating political independence from Britain in 1962, Trinidad and Tobago continued to honor a Westminster-style parliamentary system modeled after England's political structure, with the reigning monarch as the figurehead and an elected Parliament comprising the government and the opposition. Under the rules of this model, executive power was still vested in Britain's Queen Elizabeth II through a locally appointed governor-general who acted on her behalf. The 1976 Constitution called for the appointment of a president. It also granted the president minimal discretion and then only in a few isolated instances. True executive authority resided with an elected prime minister. The constitution prescribed considerable power to the cabinet—the prime minister and the ministers of the cabinet.

Trinidad and Tobago inherited the concept of equity—the equivalent of moral law and the associated principles of reason, logic, and justice—that England had borrowed from canon and Roman law and added to their property-based common law system. Officials considered the "equity of the case" in the English courts to circumvent the biases of judicial decision makers that favored the propertied classes—a pattern that harkened back to the feudal period. In current legal practice in Trinidad and Tobago, one application of the principles of equity requires an aggrieved person to take action quickly and to have "clean hands" when challenging a wrong. Quick and honest action is considered fair to both complainant and defendant in a court of law, as it is presumed to be more likely than delayed complaints and "tainted hands" to lead to a just and reasonable resolution.

Because of its English common law legacy, Trinidad and Tobago's legal system does not formally allow for the inclusion of wider social conditions, cultural factors, or other local or personal circumstances that may impinge on the "equity of a case" in the courts. As neither judges nor lawyers are trained in the legal dimensions of social responsibility, judicial decisions are made within a narrow legalistic framework.

The doctrine of judicial precedent is another characteristic of Trinidad and Tobago's legal system. This doctrine, also part of the British colonial legacy, requires judges to follow the rules left by their predecessors. This practice has resulted in judicial conservatism that is at odds with social change in postcolonial Trinidad and Tobago. Legal arguments and judicial rulings are frequently framed against very old, preindependence precedents from English or other British Commonwealth courts.

Since 1990 however, judicial precedents from U.S. courts have been accepted by a few Trinidad and Tobago judges.

The concept of human rights is formally recognized—but very broadly—in certain provisions of the constitution that were modeled after the Canadian Bill of Rights. For example, the constitution recognizes the right of the individual to life, liberty, security of the person, and enjoyment of property; the right not to be deprived thereof except by due process of law; and the right of the individual to equality before the law and the protection of the law. The lack of clarity of the human rights listed in the constitution leaves judges with extensive discretion in interpreting concepts such as "due process of law."

Labor rights were legally recognized by the Industrial Relations Act of 1965, which authorized the creation of the Industrial Court, to be staffed by justices. That court became the domain for all industrial disputes, trade union matters, and worker grievances. Its purpose is to arbitrate these conflicts and preserve industrial order and stability.

Parliament is second to the constitution as a major source of law in Trinidad and Tobago. It consists of an upper house of elected legislators and a lower house of senators—nominated by the government and opposition and appointed by the president. The president, who is an official selected by the prime minister in consultation with the opposition, is required to assent to legislative acts before they become law. Parliament enacts new laws and amends old laws to address changing social conditions.

The law-making process begins with the drafting of a proposal by the government to address some problem in the society. The minister whose jurisdiction includes the topic consults senior ministers on existing law in relation to the defect and submits a report to the prime minister's cabinet. If amendments to an existing law would solve the problem, there may be no further action by the ministry. If the cabinet decides that a new law is needed, the ministry prepares a brief for the cabinet, describing the history of the issue and explaining how the proposed legislation would correct the problem and help fulfill the goals of the government. After review and approval, the cabinet requests that the ministry prepare draft legislation. If the topic is controversial or has wide social implications (as, for example, the Domestic Violence Act and the death penalty do), the cabinet issues a white paper for public discussion before draft legislation is prepared.

Following cabinet approval and/or public debate and changes to the proposal, the government ministry takes it to the chief parliamentary counsel's (CPC) department for review and the preparation of a draft bill. The CPC advises the government on the legality of the proposed legislation and warns if it conflicts with another law or with the constitution. In instances of such conflict, the government solicits the support of the opposition to

Legal Structure of Trinidad and Tobago Courts

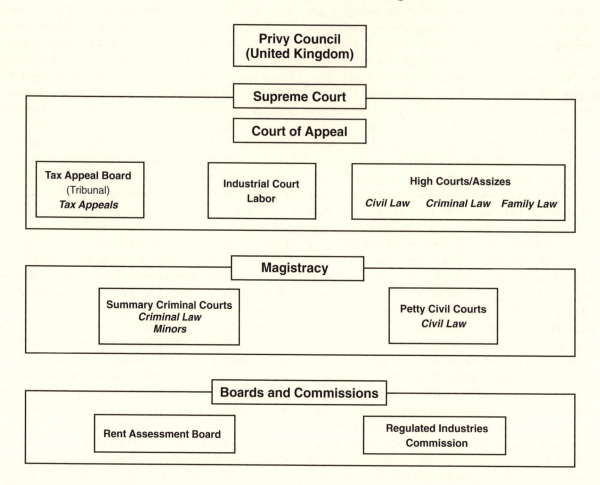

amend the bill. This version of the draft bill is reviewed by the cabinet for final approval, introduced in Parliament for debate and passage by both the upper and lower houses, and assented to by the president. However, draft bills can be initiated in either house by any member of that house.

A bill must be approved in its entirety by both houses. There are three sequential readings of all bills in each of the two houses of the Parliament. The bill is introduced at a first reading, and a full debate occurs at the second reading. At this second reading, a general committee, a select committee representing one house, or a joint select committee representing both the upper and lower houses may be constituted to consider the bill in detail and to arrive at a version that will be approved by the entire house. At the third reading, the bill is presented for passage, becoming an act. The act is then forwarded to the president for assent. At this point, it takes effect as law.

Because judges in common law systems are not entrusted with the role of interpreting the shortcomings of new laws, acts are expected to cover all possible situations and contingencies. Judges in Trinidad and Tobago (like their traditional English counterparts) typically rely on the

Parliament's literal interpretation of the law, while their counterparts in civil law countries view legislation as a guide with a series of principles for a particular area of law and therefore exercise wide latitude in their interpretation.

CURRENT STRUCTURE

The judiciary consists of the Supreme Court—which is made up of a High Court of Justice (also known as the Assizes) and a Court of Appeal (as the superior courts of record)—and the Magistracy (lower judiciary). Both the High Court and the Magistracy have original jurisdiction over criminal and civil matters. The High Court (modeled after the British High Court of Justice as set out by the United Kingdom's Supreme Court of Judicature [Consolidation] Act of 1925) has jurisdiction over indictable criminal cases, family matters involving unmarried parties, and civil matters involving sums over U.S.$250/TT$15,000. Parallel to the High Court but with their own hierarchies and budgets are the Industrial Court, for all industrial relations matters, and the Tax Appeal Board. The Court of Appeal has appellate jurisdiction over decisions from both of these entities.

The Supreme Court consists of the chief justice—who

has overall jurisdiction for the administration of justice in the country—and twenty-three High Court puisne (associate or junior) judges, three of whom, as of 2001, were women. Judges of the High Court (or puisne judges) adjudicate decisions in three divisions: criminal, civil, and family/matrimonial. In the civil division, there are open civil courts and chamber civil courts. Other senior judicial officers are the two masters of the High Court, who have the jurisdiction of judges in the chamber civil court matters (with some statutory exceptions), and the seven registrars of the Supreme Court. As of 2001, one of the masters of the High Court and five of the registrars were women. The Supreme Court is housed at four locations—Port of Spain, the capital; San Fernando, the second-largest city; the island of Tobago; and Chaguaramas, a suburban town in the northwest corner of Trinidad.

The magistracy is divided into the Courts of Summary Jurisdiction and Petty Civil Courts. Summary Criminal Court magistrates have jurisdiction in criminal matters that carry prison terms of two years and under, and they hear preliminary inquiries in indictable offenses (serious felonies with prison terms of over two years) to decide which cases are to be "held over" for trial in the High Court. Petty Civil Court magistrates deal with civil matters involving sums less than U.S.$250/TT$15,000.

In addition to the chief justice, who serves as the president of the court, the Court of Appeal includes seven justices of appeal, two of whom, as of 2001, were women. In hearing appeals, the court consists of three judges for High Court matters and two for Summary Court matters or decisions of High Court judges in chambers.

Appeals from the magistracy and the High Court are heard in the Court of Appeal. By the terms of the Supreme Court of Judicature Act—which prescribes the rules of appeal—decisions issued by the Court of Appeal can be appealed to the Privy Council in England, either as a right in certain specified instances or with permission ("leave") from the Court of Appeal or the Privy Council.

The magistracy is divided into thirteen districts. It is headed by a chief magistrate, followed by a deputy chief magistrate. The remainder of the magistracy consists of fifteen senior magistrates (eight of whom, as of 2001, were women) and twenty-six magistrates (twenty of whom, as of 2001, were women).

There are no administrative or community courts. Instead, there is an ombudsman who investigates citizens' complaints against government agencies, officials, and employees. The ombudsman's office is headed by an independent, high-level public official who is accountable to the Parliament.

STAFFING

The chief justice and the ombudsman are appointed by the president of the country after consultation with the prime minister and the leader of the opposition. The other Supreme Court judges are appointed by the president in accordance with the advice of the Judicial and Legal Service Commission (JLSC); the president must accept the commission's advice. In addition, the JLSC appoints masters of the High Court, magistrates, and all other judicial officers, including registrars, deputy registrars, assistant registrars, and the administrative secretary to the chief justice.

The JLSC comprises two ex officio members—the chief justice, who serves as chair, and the chair of the Public Service Commission (PSC)—and three members who are appointed by the president in consultation with the prime minister and the leader of the opposition. One of the appointed members must be a current or former judge. The other two must have legal qualifications, but only one lawyer in active practice may be a member. In 2001, one of the three appointed JLSC members was a woman.

Qualifications for judicial appointments are as follows: Justice of Appeal—three years as a High Court judge or fifteen years as an attorney; High Court judge—a minimum of ten years as an attorney; master of the High Court—a minimum of seven years as an attorney; and magistrate—a minimum of five years as an attorney. Additional criteria include integrity, suitable temperament, competence, and experience.

All judges, including the chief justice, are appointed with security of tenure and carry out their duties, subject to removal for incapacity or misbehavior, until the age of sixty-five. Other senior legal officers (the director of public prosecutions, the solicitor general, and the chief parliamentary counsel)—all of whom are selected by the JLSC—also hold office until the age of sixty-five. All other judicial and legal officers involved in the administration of justice hold office until the age of sixty.

There are about 1,600 attorneys in Trinidad and Tobago. About 120 work for the government, several as legal specialists in various ministries—including the attorney general and the solicitor general from the Office of the Attorney General and the director of public prosecutions. The posts of solicitor general and director of public prosecutions are often used as stepping-stones to judicial appointments. The attorney general is selected by the prime minister. He or she advises the cabinet and the government on the legal ramifications of proposed government action, law reform, and legislation. The attorney general also represents the government in court, both initiating lawsuits and defending the government from legal challenges. The solicitor general handles civil matters for the government. Duties include advising the cabinet on a variety of issues (including the negotiation of foreign loans), advising government ministries without in-house counsel and providing a second opinion on legal matters, investigating and preparing ("vetting") documents (such as deeds) for the High Court, advising the state or initiating action with respect to delinquent loans or unlawful activity against the state, and representing the attorney general on various boards (such as the Adoption Board). The director of public prosecutions generally prosecutes criminal cases for the government in the High Courts and the magistracy. He or she prepares summaries of evidence and briefs for trials and decides which cases to initiate, take over, terminate, or appeal. The chief parliamentary counsel—who is selected by the JLSC—advises the attorney general about legislation that should go before the Parliament and drafts the legislation.

Until about twenty years ago, most TT lawyers were trained at British law schools. Today, however, most students receive legal training at the Hugh Wooding Law School in Trinidad or at University of the West Indies Law School in Barbados or Jamaica.

IMPACT

There is considerable disenchantment with the legal system in Trinidad and Tobago today. The major complaint is that it fails to reflect the contemporary social reality of the nation's people. Because judges and magistrates customarily adhere to English principles and judicial precedents, their rulings ignore the social and cultural reality framing the matters before them. Critics, many of whom are practicing attorneys, describe the outdated legal system as being in a state of "fossilized inactivity and antiquity." Development of the judicial process has been at a standstill for decades despite the fact that scores of laws are passed yearly. Although many of these laws—such as the Domestic Violence Acts and the Equal Opportunity Act of 2000—address pressing local problems, enforcement is woefully wanting.

There are persistent demands for a serious overhaul of the entire system. Some critics consider the English common law system, with its reliance on British judicial precedents, to be largely irrelevant to modern social needs. The characteristic conservatism of judges is seen as an obstacle to legal reform. The neglect of legal theory building among attorneys and in the curriculum of the law schools is seen as another flaw. Moreover, official indifference to legal reforms has been disappointing. The government ignored the comprehensive series of recommendations of two Constitutional Commission reports in 1974 and 1986, which contained reforms that would have resulted in a rational legal system grounded in the contemporary social conditions of Trinidad and Tobago. Among the 1974 commission recommendations were the creation of a one-chamber legislature, a system of proportional representation, and greater emphasis on local government.

A more recent recommendation is that judges abandon 500-year-old English case law and use the latitude permitted by English common law to generate principles and judicial precedents framed within the context of modern Trinidad and Tobago's multicultural population and its particular social history. Another recommendation is to combine elements of the civil law model with the relevant parts of the common law model to create a more practical legal system like that of the United States.

There is still no clearly defined philosophy of law framing the legal system, so existing laws are a hodgepodge of borrowed legislation from Britain and the Commonwealth. There is a law school, but it produces only lawyers and little, if any, legal scholarship. There is no serious analytical literature on judicial decisions, little incisive debate among legal minds, few learned commentaries about statute law, and few textbooks. Critics are calling for immediate reform and urging judges to shed their dependence on external judicial precedents and be creative in their decision making, producing a new set of precedents grounded in local social and economic life.

A heated debate rages over the death penalty and a campaign to replace England's Privy Council with the Caribbean Court of Appeals as the highest appellate court. There are also passionate public discussions about the effectiveness of certain laws on the books, such as the Domestic Violence Act, and about the promise of new laws, such as the Equal Opportunity Act (EOA). The EOA authorizes the establishment of a panel of judges to hold hearings and adjudicate complaints of discrimination.

Limited legal aid is available to the poor or people who have modest economic means. In accordance with the Legal Aid and Advice Act, the Legal Aid and Advisory Authority was established in 1976 to extend access to attorneys for litigants with criminal, civil, or family law matters. In addition, the Hugh Wooding Law School Legal Aid Clinic was created between 1978 and 1979 for the dual purpose of providing both supervised training for advanced law students and legal assistance to poor clients.

The legal system must be reformed to make the administration of justice more efficient. To accomplish this, it has been recommended that the chief justice be given a bloc vote for operating funds and that the day-to-day administrative duties of both the chief justice and the registrar of the Supreme Court be handed over to a professional manager. Currently, trained lawyers manage and administer the judicial system.

There is no shortage of proposals for streamlining the court bureaucracy. One idea is to establish separate courts with permanent presiding judges who are experts in various areas of law, for example, a motor claims court, petty civil courts, a family court, and criminal courts. In the short term, this strategy is expected to substantially reduce the massive backlog of cases. In the long term, it may prove to be a useful reform for the efficient operation of the judicial system.

In 2000, a jurisdictional dispute erupted between the current chief justice, Michael de la Bastide, and the attorney general, Ramesh Lawrence Maharaj, over the independence of the judiciary. The attorney general claimed that he held ministerial control over the judiciary. The chief justice insisted on judicial independence and the separation of powers. The Georges Report, based on an inquiry commissioned by the Trinidad and Tobago Law Association and conducted by a highly respected Caribbean jurist, Justice Telford Georges, corroborated the chief justice's position and ruled that the judiciary was an independent institution and not part of the attorney general's portfolio.

Also, a constitutional dispute arose over executive authority illegally claimed by President A. N. R. Robinson to deny eight cabinet appointments recommended by Prime Minister Badeo Panday. In Trinidad and Tobago's Westminister-style government, the president can have influence, but it is the prime minister who has the final say in the selection of cabinet ministers: The constitution requires the president to appoint ministers "in accordance with the advice of the prime minister." Because this law is based on the assumption that the president will act on ministerial advice, not his or her preferences, there is no judicial provision for holding the president accountable for fulfilling the functions of office in compliance with the constitution.

There are some promising, albeit fledgling, efforts to promote public education about the law through publications such as Michael Theodore's *Law: The Air We Breathe* and the Attorney General Office's *The Law and You*. Members of the Trinidad and Tobago public are slowly learning about the weaknesses of the legal system and the need for major reforms. They are confronted with a number of questions: Should the Caribbean Court of Appeal replace the Privy Council? Should the death penalty be abolished? How can constitutional reform be made a reality? Can the customs and cultural legacies of the country's major ethnic groups be tapped for such reform? Providing appropriate answers to such questions in the years ahead is the challenge for the people of Trinidad and Tobago.

Cynthia Mahabir

The author would like to acknowledge the assistance of Michael Theodore, Fyard Hosein, El-Farouk Hosein, Stephanie Daly, Caroline Kangalee, Jo-Anne Connor, and Gar Smith.

See also Civil Law; Common Law; Criminal Law; Equity; Family Law; Human Rights Law; Judicial Independence; Legal Aid; Magistrates—Common Law Systems; Mediation; Privy Council; Roman Law

References and further reading
Capildeo, Suren. 1988. "The Legal System Is Dead." *Trinidad Express,* February 29.
Daly, Stephanie. 1989. "The Development of the Law Affecting East Indians in Trinidad and Tobago." *The Lawyer* 3, no. 4 (July): 15–24.
Douglas, Sir William. 1982. "The Role of the Judiciary in Shaping West Indian Law." *West Indian Law Journal* (May): 25–32.
"Dysfunctions of the Legal System." 1992. *Blast,* August 28.
Hosein, Fyard. 1990. "The Reception of Matrimonial Islamic Law in Trinidad and Tobago." *The Lawyer* 3, no. 3 (July): 5–11.
Judiciary of the Republic of Trinidad and Tobago. "Structure and Jurisdiction," "Overview of the Judiciary of Trinidad and Tobago," "Appointment to the Judiciary," "The Supreme Court of Trinidad and Tobago," "The Magistracy of Trinidad and Tobago." http://www.ttlawcourts.org/ (cited January 17, 2001).
Khan, Israel B. 1993. *Scales of Justice.* St. Augustine, Trinidad: Legal Books Ltd.
Reddy, Marlita A., ed. 1996. *Statistical Abstract of the World.* 2nd ed. Detroit, MI: Gale Publishing.
Richards, Peter. "Trinidad and Tobago: Government, Judiciary Remain at Loggerheads." *The Black World Today.* http://www.tbwt.com/ipsnews/ips1745.asp (accessed September 24, 2000).
Theodore, Michael. 1994. *Law: The Air We Breathe.* Trinidad: Caribbean Legal Publications Ltd.
University of Pennsylvania. "Basic Statistics: Country." http://litserver.literacy.upenn.edu/explorer/country_results.iphtml?ID=77 (cited February 7, 2001).
Williams, Eric. 1962. *History of the People of Trinidad and Tobago.* London: Andre Deutsch.
Wooding, Hugh O. B. 1966. "Law Reform Necessary in Trinidad and Tobago." *Canadian Bar Journal* 9: 292–298.

TUNISIA

COUNTRY INFORMATION

Tunisia's territory is considered a linking point between the two parts of the Arab world: the Machrek (the east) and the Maghreb (the west). It also divides the eastern and the western Mediterranean basins. The territory covers 164,150 square kilometers and has a coastline of 1,200 kilometers. Its population is 9,000,000, with an annual population growth of 1.3 percent. Being a coastal and relatively flat country (its highest mountain, the Ghambi, does not exceed 1,500 meters), Tunisia has witnessed many invasions and conquests. From Berber stock, like the rest of the people of the Maghreb, Tunisians have known the Phoenician conquest, the foundation of Carthage (Aristotle's Politea evoked the Carthaginian Constitution), the Roman Conquest in 145 B.C.E., as well as the advent of the Vandals in 439 C.E. and the Byzantines in 534 C.E. Arab Muslims founded Kairouan in 670 C.E., and after a harsh Berber resistance, Kairouan became the capital city of the Aghlabide Dynasty. Later, Tunisia saw the establishment of the Fatimides (909–972), Zirides (972–1160), and Hafcides (1227–1574) Dynasties, all of which were

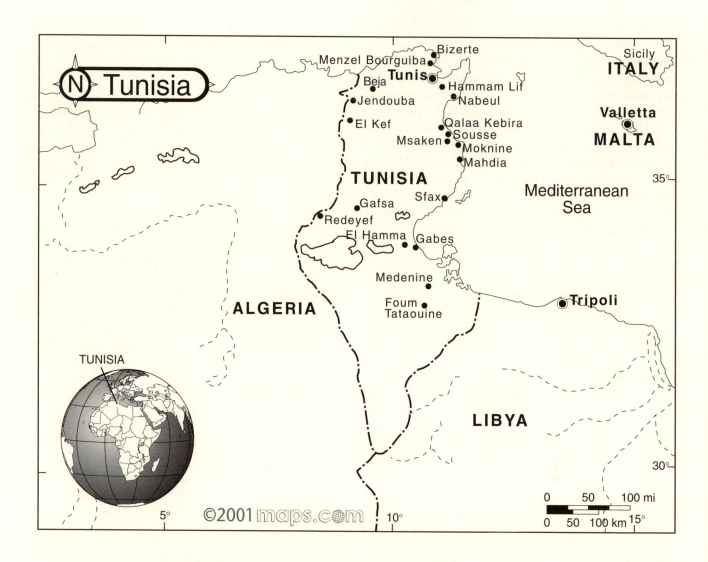

Arabo-Berber. Ottoman Turks conquered Tunisia in 1574 C.E., and a French protectorate lasted from 1881 to 1956, following which Tunisia gained independence.

Tunisian history is characterized by unrest and violence. Carthage was destroyed by the Romans in 146 B.C.E., Kairouan was destroyed by the Hilalian tribes in 1057 C.E., and the bloody and devastating revolt of Abu Yazid (nicknamed "the donkey owner") in 946 deeply affected/scarred/impacted Tunisian civic spirit.

Several times, the country also experienced religious conflicts and schisms, both Christian (Aryanism and Donatism) and Muslim (Shiism and Kharejism). But after the Zirides Dynasty, Tunisia's unity and strength increased in three ways. First, Kharejism and Shiism were displaced by Muslim Sunnism. Second, the population was almost thoroughly Arabized. And third, Christianity declined: In 1053, only 5 Christian bishops remained out of the 200 existing in the seventh century.

According to World Bank statistics, the Tunisian economy had a gross domestic product of 19,956 ($ millions) in 1998, with an annual rate of growth of 5 percent and a gross national product per capita of $2,060.

HISTORY

In terms of culture and legislation, Tunisia is the product of three influences: Malekism (one of the four schools of Sunni jurisprudence), French law, and legislation produced after independence under the republic's first president, Habib Bourguiba, who died on April 6, 2000.

The precolonial Tunisian legal system was governed by both tribal and urban customs and usages and by the Malekite Islamic law. Property law was a mixture of customary law and *sharia* (Islamic law).

Before the French protectorate, Tunisia was part of the Ottoman Empire and followed its political reforms. Thus, slavery was abolished in 1846. A constitutional charter known as the Fundamental Pact was promulgated in 1857, recognizing certain basic rights and individual freedoms. The first constitution was adopted in 1861, on the model of a constitutional monarchy. The first municipal organization created in the capital of Tunis dates back to 1860. Tunisian reforms were particularly embodied in the work of great minister Khayreddine "Aqwam al Massalik fi ma'rifati ahwâl al mamâlik" (The best ways to know the nations). From that time on, the legal culture evolved thoroughly. A completely new idea based on a secular legislating state and positivism emerged. This idea was totally different from the traditional legal culture in which the law stemmed from the sacred texts—the Koran and the Sunnah (traditions) of the Prophet—and eventually from the interpretation of legal scholars (*fuqaha*) and customs conforming with sharia.

Another important evolution occurred in terms of personal rights based on freedom and equality, ideas developed by reformers such as Ibn Abi Dhiaf, a historian and politician; Qabadu, a poet; and Khayreddine, a statesman.

But the crucial turning point in the history of the legal system dates back to the French protectorate, which was instituted by the Treaty of Kassar Saïd on May 12, 1881.

In spite of the powerful traditional state, radically new and modern political, administrative, and judicial rules and structures emerged, of which land law reform can be considered one of the most important. Inspired by the Torrens Australian system, a system of land registration was adopted in 1885.

A commission for the codification of Tunisian laws was set up in 1885. David Santillana, a native Tunisian jurist, played an active part in the codification work; Santillana, who was naturalized British and then Italian, had mastered Arabic and Islam (Ben Achour 1995, 59). A draft of a civil code was made in 1899 and translated into Arabic. After being closely examined by a group of *ulema* (Islamic legal scholars) belonging to the great Tunisian mosque Ezzitouna, it was promulgated by a statutory order of the *bey* (king) on December 15, 1906, and entitled the Code of Obligations and Contracts. This code is still in force. In the same spirit, the Code of Civil Procedure was adopted, sanctioning the existing division of courts in three branches: Sharaïc justice, secular Tunisian justice, and French justice (Charfi 1997, 109). Religious questions had their own separate orders: Hanefite and Malekite under Muslim law and rabbinic justice for disputes between Tunisian Jews. (Judicial unification did not occur until after independence, under President Bourguiba, in 1958.) The Penal Code was promulgated on July 9, 1913, and the Criminal Procedure Code on December 31, 1921. Only family law and inheritance law did not follow the new trend. Reform in these areas awaited action by President Bourguiba, who, on August 13, 1956, promulgated the Status Book (Code de Statut Personnel), which organized family and inheritance law.

Modernization, positivism, codification, and the private and public law distinction are thus the main trends of the protectorate period—trends that were continued by the state after independence.

LEGAL CONCEPTS

Within the Islamic world, Tunisia is the most developed country in the field of juridical modernity. As indicated earlier, the colonial era was a crucial transition period (except in the area of family law). But three years before adopting its constitution on June 1, 1959, Tunisia experienced a genuine revolution when Bourguiba made the bey adopt the Status Book in 1956 (Ben Achour 1992, 203–224).

The most important innovations of the Status Book were:

- The ban on polygamy in Article 18
- The free and mutual consent of spouses for marriage (previously, the wife had to be represented by her guardian)
- The repeal of repudiation and the institutionalization of judicial divorce in Article 30
- The obligation of a minimum marriage age (seventeen for a woman and twenty for a man)
- The reform of inheritance law, except for the division of/share between brother and sister (the brother inherits twice the sister's share)

Following the same impetus, Bourguiba had the statute order on adoption promulgated on March 4, 1958, despite its prohibition in Islamic law. It is worth noting that Tunisians consider the Status Book their constitution.

The state reform in the field of family law did not stop when Bourguiba was dismissed on November 7, 1987. The new government has pursued the Bourguiba policy and undertaken some other important reforms, such as providing for a divorced woman's allowance (July 5, 1993), the granting of Tunisian nationality through a Tunisian mother to a child born abroad of a foreigner father (July 13, 1993), and the granting of a patronymic name to a child born of an unknown father (October 18, 1998).

The Tunisian Constitution was promulgated on June 1, 1959. It has been modified twelve times. Several modifications are especially significant. An April 8, 1976, constitutional revision transformed the executive power by dividing it in two unequal parts: The president of the republic, on one hand, and the government (ministers and prime minister), on the other, acting under the authority of the president and appointed by him. This revision provides for a mechanism of ministerial responsibility before the Chamber of Representatives, but this has never been enforced. A July 25, 1988, revision changed rules applied for running for presidency. Henceforth, the candidate must be presented by "elected members," according to the Electoral Code, which requires that the candidacy be filed by thirty representatives or municipal council presidents. Bearing in mind that the governmental party holds an almost total monopoly on political life, this provision actually prevents any candidacy other than one from the Rassemblement Constitutionnel Democratique (RCD) governmental party. The October 24, 1999, presidential elections needed a special derogatory and exceptional constitutional revision to enable some of the recognized minority parties to run candidates for the presidency.

The constitutional revision on November 6, 1995, formalized the Constitutional Council, a body existing since 1987 whose task was to give advice on the compliance of laws with the constitution before their promulgation. Another revision, on November 2, 1998, modified Article 75 of the constitution, giving a binding character to the Constitutional Council's advice.

The main feature of an October 27, 1997, revision was to provide a framework for the legislative matters, to set up a referendum mechanism for modifying the constitution, and to provide rules that were binding on political parties.

The Tunisian Constitution is a liberal and democratic one. It adheres to the European continental concept of the "state of law" (état de droit) and relies on the following concepts and principles, which are articulated in the constitution's preamble: respect for the republican regime; for common human values of dignity, justice, and freedom; for the separation of governmental powers; for the precepts of Islam; and for the unity of the Great Maghreb (countries in northwest Africa). The constitutional provisions acknowledge the human being as inviolable (Article 5) and recognize freedom of thought, of worship, of expression, of the press, of assembly, and of association, as well as labor rights. The provisions also recognize the right to constitute political parties (Article 8), freedom of movement (Article 10), the inviolability of home and secrecy of correspondence (Article 9), the presumption of innocence and due process for the criminally accused (Article 12), a prohibition against ex post facto laws (Article 13), and the right to own property (Article 14). Tunisia has ratified the general conventions and covenants concerning human rights, specifically those on women's rights and against torture and any cruel and inhuman punishments.

The constitution also provides for the separation of governmental powers, with Chapter 2 dealing with legislative power, Chapter 3 with the executive, and Chapter 4 with the judicial. Legislators are elected through direct, free, and secret universal suffrage. The same is true for the president of the republic. The president serves a five-year term and can be reelected twice. Ben Ali came to power on November 7, 1987, under Article 57 of the constitution (relative to presidential incapacity) when then-President Bourguiba suffered from illness and old age; Article 57 provided that in cases of presidential incapacity, the prime minister would be invested with the functions of president. Ben Ali served as acting president until the presidential elections of March 1988, when he first stood for election and was elected. He was first re-elected in March 1994 and then reelected again in October 1999 after a constitutional revision. In 1999, three candidates ran for president: Ben Ali, Bel haj Amor, and Tlili. The elections results were as follows: Ben Ali, 3,269,067; Bel haj Amor, 10,492; Tlili, 7,662. Having been reelected in 1994 and then again in 1999, Ben Ali cannot, according to Article 39 of the constitution, stand for reelection in the presidential elections of 2004.

The liberal and democratic rules of the constitution have not, in practice, been effective for several reasons, the most important of which is the monopoly of political life by one party. That party, which was a de facto unique party during the Bourguiba era, became a broadly dominant one afterward. The second reason is that certain laws concerning fundamental rights and freedoms are very narrow, such as the Press Code (April 28, 1975, modified), the Public Assemblies Law (January 24,1969), and a right of association law (November 7, 1959, modified on April 2, 1992), which is obviously contrary to the constitution and provoked the resignation of two members of the Constitutional Council in 1992. The third reason concerns abuses by the political regime, which have become increasingly important and have been denounced both locally and internationally, namely, by Amnesty International, Human Rights Watch, the European Parliament, and the UN Special Reporter K. Hussein in 2000. What is held against the regime concerns harm to the physical integrity of citizens, the absence of press freedom, the unjustified withdrawals of passports, and, in general, a monolithism that weighs heavily on political life.

Tunisian law is characterized by three principal features. First, Tunisia is a quasi-exclusive statute law country. Second, Tunisian law remains strongly influenced by French law. Third, it is a very secular system, though it relies on Islamic law in the field of family law.

The Positive Structure of Law

Tunisia is a statute law country with a pyramidal legal structure. At the top is the constitution, below which are the statutes, then the presidential statute orders (decrees), and finally the ministerial orders and bylaws. The main sections of Tunisian law are in the form of codes. Some codes, such as the Obligations and Contracts Code and the Penal Code, were adopted under the French protectorate.

Since independence, other codes have been adopted. The most important are the Status Book, the Civil and Commercial Procedure Code (1959), the Commercial Code (1959), the Real Law Code (1965), the Labor Code (1966), the Criminal Procedure Code (1968), the Insurance Codes (1992), the Arbitration Code (1993), and the Urbanism Code (1994). Laws and regulations are published in the "official bulletin" (Mellouli 2000, 44, 45).

There is no judicial review of the constitutionality of

laws but merely a consultative procedure before an advisory body called the Constitutional Council, set up in 1987. The members of that council are appointed by the president of the republic. The council's advice is required in some important fields of law, such as electoral law, budget law, and laws concerning public freedoms, nationality, crimes, property, and labor.

The presidential orders (decrees) can be divided in two parts: the under-law orders (the law enforcement decrees) and the self-sustaining orders. The latter were introduced by the constitutional amendment of October 27, 1997, which shortened the field of laws to fundamental matters such as public liberties, private property, civil and commercial obligations, nationality, status of persons, determination of crimes and misdemeanours as well as the penalties imposed thereof, civil obligations, procedural rules before the courts, amnesty, and certain other matters such as taxes, public finance, and public enterprises. Article 35 of the constitution provides that: "the matters other than that belonging to the domain of laws, come within the general regulation power" (that is, the presidential power to make regulations by decrees). However, the presidential statutory orders, unlike all other executive and administrative decisions, cannot be subjected to the "abuse of power appeal" (*recours pour excès de pouvoir*) to the Administrative Tribunal.

The Influence of French Law

The Tunisian legal system is directly influenced by French law. This is true for its general concepts and principles as well as its rules and its administrative and judicial organization. The unique exception is family law. Tunisian law makes a distinction between private and public law, subjects that are taught separately at the university. Professors of law are divided into "publicists" and "privatists."

The Influence of Islamic Law

The reference to Islam is pointed out in the preamble as well as in Article 1 of the constitution. This article provides that "Tunisia is a free, independent and sovereign state. Its religion is Islam." Some other references to Islam also exist in the Obligations and Contracts Code and in the Penal Code but without an important impact.

There are two opposing opinions concerning the Status Book. For some, it is a secular law; for others, it is inspired by Islamic law. The reality is that the Status Book is neither totally secular (because of its inheritance rules) nor merely Islamic (as discussed earlier). However, it is worth noting that there is a gap between legislation and decisions in the civil courts. Whenever confronted with an issue asking for an interpretation, civil courts let themselves be guided by Islamic law. For example, they have applied the inheritance impediment for religious causes,

to annul the marriage between a Muslim woman and a non-Muslim man, and to refuse custody to a foreign mother because of the absence of legal and religious community. These positions of the Supreme Court (Cour de Cassation), based on Article 1 of the constitution, are not, however, unquestionably observed by lower tribunals. Lately, some tribunals of first instance have applied non-Islamic solutions over Islamic ones. In the same sense, the New York Convention of 1962 had prevailed against an Islamic interpretation of Article 5 of the Status Book; some actions for exequatur of foreign judgments (Moroccan, Egyptian, Saudi) concerning repudiation were dismissed because of their breach with the Tunisian public order and their violation of Article 6 (on equality) of the constitution, of the Universal Declaration of Human Rights of 1948, and of the Convention on the Elimination of All Forms of Discrimination against Women of 1979 (see, for example, the judgment of the Tribunal of First Instance of Tunis, dated June 27, 2000).

CURRENT STRUCTURE

The administrative organization of Tunisia is based on two fundamental concepts—"disconcentration" and decentralization. The disconcentrated administrative authorities are directly answerable to the central government. The decentralized authorities (such as the municipalities, which are the local territorial units) have more autonomy.

For disconcentrated administration, Tunisian territory is subdivided into twenty-four *wilaya* (departments), each headed by a *wali*. The wali is appointed by an order of the president of the republic and is in charge of the general management of the regional territory unit and of the maintenance of public order there. The wali is the head of the administrative authorities within the wilaya, namely, the *mu'tamad* (delegates) and the *omda* (subdelegates).

Unlike the disconcentrated administrations, the decentralized ones enjoy the juridical personality and are elected. There are two types of decentralized administration in Tunisia: 24 wilaya (led by a Regional Council) and 257 municipalities, which run the urban units courts organization.

Court organization is characterized by separate jurisdictions: the civil courts, the Administrative Tribunal, and, since 1996, the Council of the Conflicts of Competence. In addition, there are two financial administrative control courts: the Audit Office (Cour des Comptes) and the disciplinary financial court. Special courts also exist for political and military trials.

The court organization is based on the duality of jurisdictions. The constitution distinguishes between the "judiciary power" and the administrative jurisdiction that is embodied in the Council of State; the Council of State is itself subdivided into two branches—the Audit

Tribunal and the Administrative Tribunal—but it is solely the Administrative Tribunal that settles disputes between public authorities and private parties (firms or individual members).

As for the judiciary power, the constitution acknowledges the independence of judges, who are to obey only the law. The High Council of the Judiciary, which is presided over by the president of the republic, deals with the guarantees granted by law to the judges in issues relative to appointments, promotion, transfer, and discipline. The court organization follows a pyramidal model. At the bottom, we find the cantonal tribunal, with a single judge who decides civil cases (except those involving real estate) not exceeding 7,000 dinars (about U.S.$7,000) and also decides certain cases of inheritance and alimony. In penal cases, the cantonal tribunal's jurisdiction is limited to the minor offenses, and its decision can be appealed to the first-instance tribunal.

The April 27, 2000, reform changed first-instance tribunals into ordinary courts of general jurisdiction to handle civil, commercial, and penal trials. The same reform for felony cases also introduced a new principle of double examination (from a court of first instance to a court of appeal).

The tribunals of first instance, aside from the civil and minor offenses divisions (correctional chambers), also have commercial and felony divisions. These tribunals are composed of a labor division judge, a tutelage judge, a children's judge, enterprises judges, and a register of commerce judge.

A judgment rendered by the first-instance tribunals can be appealed by parties to the Appeal Courts (of which there are ten). The Appeal Court examines de novo the whole case. The decision of the Appeal Court, however, can be subject to review before the Court of Cassation (Supreme Court) only on a question of law. The Court of Cassation can annul the attacked judgment and then transfer the case to the same tribunal made up of other judges or to another tribunal of the same degree. In the field of land registration, there is a special court called the Tribunal Immobilier. Its decisions are without recourse to appeal.

The Administrative Tribunal is one of the two branches of the Council of State provided for in the constitution. It was actually created by the law of June 1, 1972, which was substantially modified on June 3, 1996. Since 1996, the Administrative Tribunal consists of First-Instance Divisions, Chambers of Appeal, and the Plenary Assembly acting as a Court of Cassation. The Administrative Tribunal has jurisdiction to act in administrative litigation and specifically to annul retroactively administrative decisions constituting abuses of power. Its jurisdiction also encompasses disputes concerning contracts, liability for damages, and eminent domain involving real estate.

Because of several important past conflicts between the judiciary and the Administrative Tribunal, a Council of the Conflicts of Jurisdiction was created by Law No. 38 of June 3, 1996, to resolve conflicts between two orders claiming or disclaiming jurisdiction. This council equally represents both orders.

The Audit Office (Cours des Comptes) is the second branch of the Council of State. It was created in 1968 to check the accuracy of the public territorial decentralized or disconcentrated units' accounts, the public agencies' accounts, and public enterprises' accounts. The Disciplinary Financial Court can sanction all sorts of transgression of financial law and regulations.

Certain exceptional courts also have jurisdiction over specialized matters. The High Court of Justice established by the constitution acts on "the high treason of members of government." In 1970, this court decided the former minister Ahmed Ben Salah's case and, in 1984, Driss Guiga's case in political trials that aroused public opinion. The Military Tribunal deals with offenses committed by the military or by civilians against the army. The Court of State Security, abolished in 1987, sat on trials of dissidents or trade unionists.

STAFFING

Public officers are distinguished by rank, employment, and responsibilities. Rank and employment determine one's legal career and depend on the level of studies completed, seniority, and merit. Responsibilities require government appointment, with top-ranking positions filled by the president of the republic, as in the case of the presidents of the Court of Cassation, of the Appeal Court of Tunis, of the Administrative Tribunal, of the Real Estate Tribunal, and of the Audit Office. For the other judges, the advice of their respective high councils is requested.

Judges are hired from among those who hold diplomas from the Magistrate High Institute (MHI). Graduates holding a Master's degree (after four years of university study) must then pass an exam for entry to the MHI, where they train for two years.

Future practicing attorneys must be university graduates and pass an examination to obtain the Ability for Attorney Practice Certificate, or they must hold a postgraduate diploma (two years of study after the Master's degree). Attorneys constitute a liberal profession, headed by an elected council of the bar.

Bailiffs and notaries are also considered to be judicial officers. They must be graduates and registered on the bailiffs and notaries list set by the minister of justice. Bailiffs serve summonses, give notices of protest, execute various court orders, and make affidavits. Notaries are responsible for giving advice on and drafting certain documents, such as contracts and wills, and for preparing certain legal documents that must be certified.

Law professors at the university are entitled to teach law at the university and specifically at institutions (*facultés*) of legal sciences. There are now establishments teaching law in Sousse, in Sfax, and in Jendouba. These teachers are hired through national competitive examinations and are divided into four classes: assistants, major assistants, senior lecturers, and full professors. Since 1989, teachers of law can no longer both teach and represent parties in court because of Articles 22 and 81 of the September 7, 1989, law concerning attorneys and also according to the legal statute of teachers at the university.

IMPACT

The evolution of the Tunisian social state of mind, values, and civic spirit is undoubtedly the result of the legal system. This statement is all the more true when it comes to women's rights. Today, Tunisian women are represented in almost all fields of employment and professions. In education, they hold 50 percent of the positions, and their share is growing. The role of the Status Book in this evolution has been overwhelming. So it is possible to assert today that the impact of legal modernization on the economy, services, administration, and education is permanent.

The major weakness of the system remains the weakness of the political regime itself. Quite often, the legal rules remain unapplied, while the arbitrary decision prevails. The most harmful consequence is that the citizen automatically seeks recourse through important relatives or friends to solve a problem, rather than seeking recourse through the law, having lost any trust in its value. On top of that, the slowness of the bureaucracy and trials worsens the situation.

These facts are ever present in Tunisian political life. Official speeches abound with references to the "state of law," but arbitrariness is the rule whenever it comes to political participation and freedoms. Moreover, opponents to the regime face serious threats to their physical integrity and life (for example, the attempted murder of Tunisian journalist R. Ben Fadhel in April 2000, just after the publication of his critical article in the French newspaper *Le Monde*).

The six recognized opposition parties are not creditable, and elections are not trustworthy (Ben Ali won the last elections with more than 99 percent of the votes). If Tunisia is to become a truly modern state, it must gain the most important component of modernism—freedom.

Yadh Ben Achour

See also Civil Law; Islamic Law; Legal Positivism; Notaries
References and further reading
Ben Achour, Sana. 1995. "Aux sources du droit moderne tunisien." Thesis, Faculté des Sciences Juridiques, Tunis.
Ben Achour, Yadh. 1992. *Politique, religion, et droit dans le monde arabe*. Tunis: CERES-CERP.
Charfi, Mohamed. 1997. *Introduction à l'étude du droit*. 3rd ed. Tunis: CERES.
Mellouli, Slaheddine. 2000. *Introduction à l'étude du droit*. Tunis: IORT.

TURKEY

COUNTRY INFORMATION

The Republic of Turkey, established in 1923, is the heir to the multiethnic, multireligious, and multilingual Ottoman Empire. Turkey covers an area of 814,578 square kilometers, 24,378 square kilometers of which is in Europe, the rest in Asia. Turkey has land borders with Greece, Bulgaria, Georgia, Armenia, Iran, Iraq, and Syria. The Black and Mediterranean seas form Turkey's northern and southern borders respectively, while the Aegean separates southwestern Turkey from Greece. The Bosphorus passes through Turkey's largest city, Istanbul. The capital of Turkey is Ankara, but Istanbul is the country's most important cultural and commercial center. Turkey's population is 65 million, 98 percent of whom are Muslim. Most Turks belong to the majority Sunni branch of Islam. A small minority belongs to the smaller Alavi sect of Islam. There are also communities of Jewish and Greek Orthodox, Armenian, and other Christian sects living in Turkey. The Kurds, 10–15 percent of the population, are the largest non–Turkish speaking group. Turkish law does not recognize minorities beyond those non-Muslim groups enumerated in the Lausanne Treaty of 1923. Turkey applied for membership in the European Union in 1987 and received candidate status in 1999. Full membership in the European Union is contingent upon extensive political and economic reforms. Turkey is also a member of NATO. The legal system is based on the continental European civil law tradition. The political system is republican, unitary, and secular.

HISTORY

The Ottoman legal system was based on a mixture of Islamic law (*sharia*) and customary law (*kanun*). Jewish and Christian communities living in the empire enjoyed internal legal autonomy. The administration of justice was further complicated by the grant of extraterritoriality rights to European powers. In the second half of the nineteenth century, under pressure from European powers and a small but influential group of indigenous reformers, the Ottomans attempted to modernize the political, legal, and economic structure of the empire. These attempts culminated in the proclamation of the First Ottoman Constitution in 1876. Modeled after the 1830 Belgian Constitution, the constitution and its 1908 replacement did not transform the Ottoman political system into a constitutional monarchy. However, they introduced concepts such

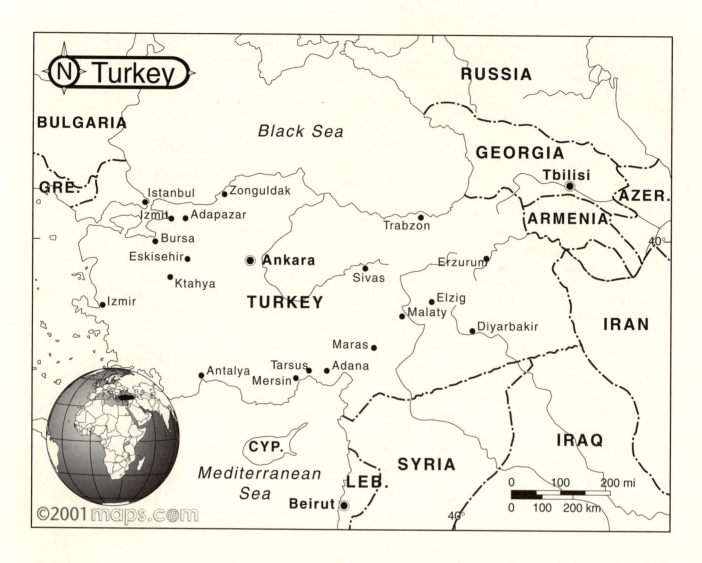

©2001 maps.com

as rule of law and constitutionalism into Turkish political discourse.

The Ottoman defeat in World War I was followed by the Turkish War of Independence (1918–1922). Led by Mustafa Kemal Ataturk and supported by a large segment of the Turkish society, the war ended with the abolition of the Ottoman Empire in October 1922 and the official proclamation of the Turkish Republic with Ataturk as its first president in 1923. During the war a legislative body with extensive executive powers known as the Turkish Grand National Assembly (GNA) had replaced the Ottoman parliament. The GNA had enacted a short constitutional document in 1921. Although not a constitution in the proper sense of the word, this document for the first time recognized the principle of national sovereignty and laid the cornerstone for the establishment of a republican form of government. A new constitution was adopted in 1924. Legislative and executive powers were deposited in an elected unicameral legislature. The legislature exercised its executive powers through the president of the republic, elected by the GNA, and a prime minister and cabinet appointed by the president. Until 1945

Ataturk's Republican Peoples' Party was the only legal party. The single-party period came to an end when President Inonu, who had replaced Ataturk after the latter's death in 1938, allowed the formation of opposition parties. Turkey's first transition to multiparty democracy began with the victory of the newly established Democratic Party (DP) in 1950. DP rule, however, became increasingly authoritarian with the passage of time. On May 27, 1960, a military coup ended Turkey's first democratic period. Turkey began its second transition to democracy in 1961 under a new constitution.

The 1961 Constitution adopted a parliamentary system of government based on a bicameral legislature and the proportional representation electoral system. The legislature exercised its executive powers through the prime minister and the cabinet. The office of the presidency became a ceremonial position. The constitution also recognized extensive civil rights and increased the autonomy and independence of the universities and the judiciary. Civil liberties, however, were curbed by constitutional amendments adopted in response to a military ultimatum in 1971. The constitution recognized the principle of judicial review and created a powerful and independent constitutional court (Anayasa Mahkemesi). It also strengthened the Council of State (Danistay) to dilute the powers of administrative agencies. Turkey's second democratic period was ended on September 12, 1980, when the Turkish military intervened to end increasing social and political unrest.

A new constitution was adopted in 1982, and power was returned to elected civilian politicians in 1983. The new constitution, drafted by a committee appointed by the military junta, was ratified in a national referendum on November 7, 1982. The 1982 Constitution maintained the parliamentary system of government but eliminated the upper house of the legislature. The members of the GNA are elected based on proportional representation with a national threshold of 10 percent of the total vote. Parliamentary elections are held at least once every five years, although early elections are common. The constitution further curbed civil liberties, decreased the autonomy of universities and the judiciary, and banned political activity by interest groups including bar associations.

An important aspect of the Turkish political system under the 1982 Constitution is the further institutionalization of the military's role in politics. The 1961 constitution and the constitutional amendments of 1971 had already taken important steps in this direction by first creating and then strengthening the National Security Council (NSC). The 1982 constitution further expanded the powers of this body. The NSC is composed of the prime minister, ministers of Defense, Internal and Foreign Affairs, the chief of general staff of the military, and the commanders of the army, navy, air force, and gendarmerie. The council meets under the chairmanship of the president of the republic. According to Article 118 of the constitution the NSC "shall submit to the Council of Ministers its views on taking decisions and ensuring necessary coordination with regard to the formulation, determination, and implementation of the national security policy of the State. The Council of Ministers shall give priority consideration to the decisions" of the NSC. Over the past two decades the NSC has emerged as a powerful decision-making institution.

A second important characteristic of the 1982 Constitution is the expanded powers of the president of the republic. The president is still elected by the GNA for a single seven-year term. The president enjoys extensive executive powers, including the power of appointment to the country's high courts and the power to ask the GNA to reconsider legislation.

Fragmentation, volatility, and weak coalition governments characterize Turkish politics. Since the early 1980s the political system has been challenged by the rise of Kurdish nationalism and political Islam. The fight against the separatist Kurdish Workers' Party (PKK) in southeast Turkey has resulted in more than 30,000 deaths and has led to a number of extrajudicial killings and disappearances. Despite the arrest and conviction of the PKK's leader in the spring of 1999, no permanent solution to the conflict has been found, nor are there any attempts at a negotiated settlement.

Political Islam is another source of conflict within the staunchly secular Turkish political system. The first legal Islamist political party was formed in 1970 and banned by the constitutional court a year later. It was then replaced by a new party, which was banned after the 1980 military coup. After the return to civilian rule in 1983, the Welfare Party became the country's main Islamist party. It emerged as the largest political party when it won 21 percent of the vote in the 1995 parliamentary elections. Eventually Welfare formed a coalition government with one of the center-right parties. This government was forced to resign in the summer of 1997 under pressure from the NSC. The Welfare party was banned by the constitutional court in January 1998. Welfare's replacement, the Virtue Party, came in third in the 1999 parliamentary elections, thus becoming the main opposition party, only to be banned by the constitutional court in June 2001. This action resulted in the formation of two new Islamist parties. The constitutional court has also banned a number of pro-Kurdish parties.

LEGAL CONCEPTS

The constitution is the main source of law, and all other codes, decrees, and regulations have to conform to it in substance and form. Sovereignty is vested in the nation without reservation or condition. The constitution defines the Turkish Republic as "a democratic, secular and social State governed by the rule of law; and bearing in mind the concepts of public peace, national solidarity and justice, respect for human rights, and loyalty to the nationalism of Ataturk."

The 1982 Constitution recognizes an impressive array of political, social, and economic rights for the individual, but it also enumerates conditions under which these rights can be limited or suspended. According to the constitution (Article 13), "Fundamental rights and freedoms may be restricted by law, in conformity with the letter and spirit of the Constitution, with the aim of safeguarding the indivisible integrity of the State with its territory and nation, national sovereignty, the republic, national security, public order, general peace, the public interest, public morals and public health, and also for specific reasons set forth in the relevant articles of the Constitution." Rights can also be restricted at times of war and during a state of emergency. This last provision has been particularly important in the Kurdish-inhabited areas where the state of emergency has been in effect for two decades.

Statutory laws, decrees, and regulations compliment

the constitution. Only the Turkish Parliament has the power to enact, amend, or repeal statues. Acts of Parliament become law after the president of the republic signs them. The president may choose to return the legislation to the Parliament for further consideration. If the Parliament readopts the legislation without amendments, the president has to sign it. The Parliament can also empower the Council of Ministers to issue decrees with the force of law. These decrees cannot go into effect without the approval of the president, a provision that is a source of friction between the president and the prime minister.

Turkish legal codes in force today have their roots in the reforms of the 1920s and are for the most part translations of various European codes. The criminal code, adopted in 1926, is a translation of the Italian code of 1889; the code of criminal procedures (1929) is a translation of the German code of 1877; and the civil code (1926) was borrowed from Switzerland. Since the first part of the nineteenth century France has been the main source of administrative law. Although these codes have been amended through the years, their basic frameworks remain the same. At the time of this writing the Parliament was considering a major overhaul of the civil code.

As in other systems based on the civil law tradition, customs and precedents have limited roles in Turkish law. Customs can be used as a source of law only if there are no applicable provisions in written laws. In theory Turkish judges are not bound by precedents. The only exceptions are the decisions of the General Assembly of the Court of Cassation (Yargitay). These decisions are binding on both lower courts and the various panels of the court of cassation. In practice, however, precedent plays a larger role than theory suggests. The parties to a conflict might be reluctant to begin proceedings when higher courts have consistently dismissed similar cases. Similarly, since the promotion of judges is in part based on the approval rate of their decisions on appeal, judges are sensitive to the rulings of higher courts.

International treaties and conventions are another source of law. In general, international treaties can only be used as a source of law if they are promulgated through an act of Parliament. Turkey is a signatory to various international conventions on human rights, most notably the European Convention for the Protection of Human Rights and Fundamental Freedoms (ECHR). Turkey ratified the ECHR in 1954, and since 1987 has recognized the competence of the European Court of Human Rights and the European Commission on Human Rights to decide cases brought by individuals alleging violations of their rights by the Turkish state. Although on numerous occasions the Turkish state has been found in violation of its obligations under ECHR and the European and UN Conventions for the Prevention of Torture (both of which were ratified by Turkey in 1988), domestic political considerations have prevented amendments of relevant laws and practices needed to bring Turkey into full compliance.

COURT SYSTEM

Articles 138 through 160 of the 1982 Constitution deal with the organization of the judiciary. Article 138 forbids any individual or institution from attempting to influence the judiciary. This article also prohibits the GNA from debating or expressing an opinion on court cases. The constitution instructs legislative and executive organs of the state to comply with the decisions of the courts.

The Turkish legal system does not recognize trial by jury. Most courts of original jurisdiction are presided over by a single judge who makes decisions using the inquisitorial system. Panels of judges make decisions at the appellate level and the constitutional court.

Security of tenure for judges and public prosecutors is constitutionally guaranteed. Decisions concerning appointments, promotion, transfers, disciplinary actions, and dismissals of judges and public prosecutors fall under the jurisdiction of the Supreme Council of Judges and Public Prosecutors. The council consists of five regular and five substitute members appointed for four-year terms by the president of the republic from among candidates nominated by the court of cassation and the Council of State. The undersecretary of the Ministry of Justice serves as an ex-officio member of the council. The council meets under the chairmanship of the minister of Justice. Bar associations and jurists have argued that the participation of the minister of Justice and his undersecretary in the deliberations of the council undermines the independence of the judiciary.

The legal system is based on a two-tier court structure consisting of the following.

High courts:
- The constitutional court (Anayasa Mahkemesi);
- The court of cassation or the Supreme Court (Yargitay);
- The Council of State (Danistay);
- The court of accounts (Sayistay);
- The military high court of appeals (Askeri Yargitay);
- High military administrative court of appeals (Askeri Yüksek İdare Mahkemesi);
- The jurisdictional conflict court (Uyusmazlik Mahkemesi).

Courts of original jurisdiction:
- Criminal courts, consisting of 906 magistrates' courts, 1003 general criminal courts, and 181 felony courts;
- Civil courts, consisting of 912 courts of peace, 1047 general civil courts, and 39 commercial courts.

Legal Structure of Turkey Courts

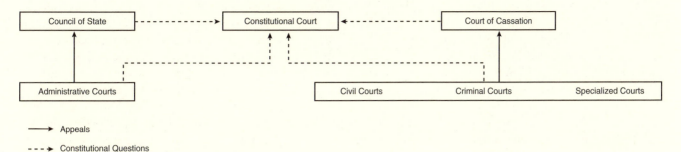

In addition the following specialized courts are operational in Turkey:

- 8 state security courts (Devlet Güvenlik Mahkemesi);
- 6 juvenile courts;
- 557 land registration offices;
- 81 labor courts.

The constitutional court examines the constitutionality of laws, governmental decrees with the force of law, and the internal regulations of the Grand National Assembly. Legislative decrees issued during states of emergency, martial law, or in wartime are not subject to review by the constitutional court. The president of the republic, the parliamentary groups of the party in power or the main opposition party, or one-fifth of the members of the GNA have standing to challenge the constitutionality of laws and decrees within sixty days after their publication in the Official Gazette. This period is ten days if the objection is procedural. The court can also accept cases referred to it by other courts if those courts determine that the case before them involves a constitutional question. The court cannot revisit a question until ten years have passed since the publication of the original decision in the Official Gazette.

The constitutional court is the venue of original jurisdiction in cases against the president of the republic, members of the Council of Ministers, presidents, members, and prosecutors of the constitutional court and other high courts, and the presidents and members of the Supreme Council of Judges and Public Prosecutors. The constitutional court is the venue for the trial of political parties and has the power to close political parties. Since 1983, the court has closed more than a dozen political parties, including the Islamist Welfare party, which at the time of its closure in January 1998 was the largest political party in the GNA.

The constitutional court consists of eleven regular and four substitute judges. Appointments to the court are made by the president of the republic from among appellate court judges nominated by the plenary assemblies of the high courts, including the military high courts. The president also appoints one member from among university professors nominated by the Higher Education Council. Three regular members and one substitute member of the court are selected from among senior civil servants and lawyers. Members of the constitutional court, like all other judges and prosecutors, retire at sixty-five. Decisions of the constitutional court are made by an absolute majority and are binding on other courts and executive and legislative organs of the state.

The court of cassation is the highest court in most criminal and civil cases. It, however, does not have jurisdiction over the decisions of military courts, which are subject to review by the military high court of cassation. The court of cassation is divided into two plenary assemblies, one dealing with civil cases and the other with criminal cases. Each assembly is further divided into a number of chambers. There are twenty-one civil and eleven criminal chambers. Each chamber is presided over by a president and four judges. If there are conflicting decisions among the chambers, the decisions will be reviewed by the appropriate plenary assembly, or by the plenary assembly of the court of cassation as a whole. Only the decisions of the plenary assemblies constitute legal precedent.

All administrative acts are subject to review by administrative courts. The decisions of civilian administrative courts can be appealed to the Council of State. The Council of State is modeled after the French Conseil d'Etat and is one of the oldest institutions of the state, dating back to the Ottoman times. The president of the republic appoints one-fourth of the members of the Council of State, and the Supreme Council of Judges and Prosecutors appoints the rest. In addition to the review of the decisions of lower administrative courts, the Council of State is also the venue for the adjudication of administrative disputes. The council also plays an advisory role to the government and can review draft legislation and regulations.

The court of accounts is basically the auditing arm of the GNA and audits various public entities. Mention should also be made of the Supreme Election Council (SEC), whose members are elected by the plenary sessions of the court of cassation and the Council of State from among their own members. SEC organizes elections and deals with issues arising from the conduct of elections. Conflicts arising from the concurring jurisdictions of different courts are resolved by the jurisdictional conflict court.

Military courts have competence to try cases against military personnel and civilians for offences connected with military service and duty, or when the offence has taken place in military areas. Decisions of military courts can be appealed to military high courts.

SPECIALIZED COURTS

One of the more controversial aspects of the Turkish court system is its reliance on state security courts (SSC). SSCs were originally organized to deal with the increasing political violence of the 1970s. The constitutional court, however, found them in violation of the 1961 Constitution's provision that prohibited the creation of extraordinary tribunals and guaranteed trial before the natural (legally designated) courts. Although the same provision exists in the 1982 Constitution, the framers of the latter constitution resurrected the SSCs under Article 143 of the constitution. According to this article, "Courts of the Security of the State shall be established to deal with offenses against the indivisible integrity of the State with its territory and nation, the free democratic order, or against the republic whose characteristics are defined in the Constitution, and offenses directly involving the internal and external security of the State." Many of the cases tried by SSCs arise from the fight against Kurdish activists and political Islam. Over the years, however, the jurisdiction of SSCs has expanded to involve a variety of cases, including organized crime, corruption, and banking. The SSCs are also the venue for the trial of writers, academicians, journalists, and political and human rights activists who are prosecuted for violating various laws that limit freedom of expression. Decisions of state security courts can be appealed to the court of cassation. SSC trials, like all other trials, are public.

Whereas trials in general courts are held before a single judge, trials in SSCs and felony courts are presided over by a panel of three judges, consisting of a president and two associate judges. SSCs also include two substitute judges, one public prosecutor, and a number of deputy public prosecutors. Until April 1999, when the constitution was amended, one associate and one substitute judge were active-duty military officers from military courts, a provision that was found to be in violation of the principle of the independence of the courts by the European Court of Human Rights.

Proceedings before SSCs have also been criticized because suspects are denied legal representation in the early stages of interrogation. Suspects in cases before general criminal courts have the right to have an attorney present at the very first interrogation. The Turkish code of criminal procedures, however, specifically exempts SSCs from this provision. Accordingly, suspects only have a right to legal representation in the second and subsequent interrogations. Lawyers practicing before SSCs often complain of harassment and inadequate access to their clients. A further complaint arises from allegations of torture, although use of torture has declined.

STAFFING

Upon graduation from a law faculty an individual can choose to enter public service or go into practice as a private lawyer. Those choosing to enter public service apply to the Ministry of Justice to take the appropriate examination. If accepted, they begin a two-year apprenticeship period. They are then appointed as full-fledged judges and prosecutors. The Supreme Council of Judges and Public Prosecutors administers personnel matters, including appointments, promotions, and disciplinary actions, concerning judges and public prosecutors of civilian courts. There are various ranks for judges and prosecutors. Only the judges and prosecutors who have achieved the highest rank (first degree) can serve on the high courts. Promotions for judges, particularly at the lower levels, are based on evaluations by superior judges and their record on appeal. This system encourages the lower-ranking judges to pay attention to precedent and prevents the promotion of maverick judges.

Court rapporteurs are responsible for preparing the documents necessary for trial, assisting the judge in finding the applicable law, and recording the trial proceedings. In cases before the constitutional court, they assist the justices by preparing detailed reports on the cases before the court.

Notaries prepare deeds and other legal documents. Although notaries have law degrees and are licensed by the Ministry of Justice, they do not receive a salary from the ministry.

Turkish law requires all private lawyers (*avukat*) to hold a law degree and to join a local bar association. In 1997 bar associations had a total membership of 39,000. Private lawyers begin their careers with a short apprenticeship in the courts, after which they can join a bar association. Those joining university teaching faculties can join the bar after attaining the rank of associate professor. After the apprenticeship period private lawyers follow a career path that is radically different from judges and prosecutors. There is almost no professional contact between the two groups outside the courtroom. Although some judges and prosecutors might choose to go into private practice after retirement, the reverse is not possible.

Bar associations have no role in the appointment of judges, including those serving on high courts. These factors help explain the extraordinarily high levels of animosity between defense lawyers and prosecutors and judges. Bar associations can take disciplinary actions against their members. However, the initiation of such action requires the permission of the minister of justice.

IMPACT OF LAW

The rule of law has been part of Turkish political discourse since the mid-nineteenth century. Most observers, including many Turkish jurists, however, would agree that Turkey's record has not been exemplary. In recent years there has been a renewed emphasis on the rule of law, and the number of extrajudicial actions has greatly declined. The courts have also been at the forefront of the fight against corruption. The Turkish judiciary is an important political actor and is one venue for the resolution of political differences. The prominent role of the courts and the prospects of joining the European Union have pushed the reform of the judicial system to the top of the political agenda.

Hootan Shambayat

See also Civil Law; European Court and Commission on Human Rights; Islamic Law; Judicial Review; Ottoman Empire

References and further reading
Ahmad, Feroz. 1993. *The Making of Modern Turkey.* London: Routledge.
Ansay, Turgul, and Don Wallace, Jr., eds. 1987. *Introduction to Turkish Law.* 3rd ed. Deventer, the Netherlands: Kluwer Law and Taxation.
Biçak, Vahit. 1996. *Improperly Obtained Evidence: A Comparison of Turkish and English Laws.* Ankara: V. Bicat.
Dodd, Clement Henry. 1990. *The Crisis of Turkish Democracy.* Huntingdon, Cambridgeshire: Eothen.
Lawyers Committee for Human Rights and Crowley Program in International Human Rights. 1999. *Obstacles to Reform: Exceptional Courts, Police Impunity & Persecution of Human Rights Defenders in Turkey.* New York: Lawyers Committee for Human Rights.
Özbudun, Ergun. 1995. *Türk Anayasa Hukuku.* Ankara: Yetkin Yayinlan.
———. 2000. *Contemporary Turkish Politics.* Boulder, CO: Lynne Reiner.
Payaslioglu, Arif. 1993. *An Introduction to Law and the Turkish Legal System.* Ankara: Yüksekögretim Kurulu Matbaasinde.
Starr, June. 1990. "Islam and the Struggle over State Law in Turkey." In *Law and Islam in the Middle East.* Edited by Daisy Hilse Dwyer. New York: Bergin and Garvey.
———. 1992. *Law as Metaphor: From Islamic Courts to the Palace of Justice.* Albany: State University of New York Press.
Zürcher, Erik J. 1993. *Turkey: A Modern History.* London: I. B. Tauris.

TURKMENISTAN

COUNTRY INFORMATION

One of the largest of the Central Asian republics, Turkmenistan has valuable natural resources, access to the Caspian Sea, and a political system more stable than those of its neighbors. Spread out over 488,000 square kilometers (190,000 square miles), Turkmenistan is the fourth largest state in the Commonwealth of Independent States behind Russia, Kazakhstan, and Ukraine. It is bordered to the south by Iran and Afghanistan, to the east by Uzbekistan, to the north by Kazakhstan, and to the west by the Caspian Sea.

Its population of 4.7 million is over 80 percent Turkmen with a smattering of Russians and Uzbeks. Turkmenistan is divided according to tribal loyalties rather than political or religious differences. The various tribes, descended from those that conquered the region over the centuries, differ in their clothes, food, and lifestyle. The once sizable Russian minority has declined since independence as the Turkmenistan government placed restrictions on the speaking of Russian in the country. Prominent Russian businessmen and officials have been deported from the country. The government has made clear its intention to separate the country from Russian influence both economic and political.

Turkmenistan is over 75 percent desert with a mountain range along the Iranian border. The desert, known as Karakum or black sands, dominates the country and makes travel difficult. At the same time it is believed to hold an immense quantity of natural gas and oil. Turkmenistan is bolstered by its extensive natural resources but has had difficulty in finding a safe and reliable method of transporting the gas to market. A pipeline through the south would run through Iran or Afghanistan, countries suffering from political instability. A proposed pipeline through southern Russia is endangered by unrest in the Russian Caucasus region and political instability in the former Soviet republics. But even with these difficulties, Turkmenistan remains one of the wealthiest countries in the region with a per capita income of $1,800. Yet economic advancement is hindered by continued adherence to a centrally planned economy. Most citizens work in the agricultural sector as the government pursues the destructive policy of growing cotton in one of the driest regions of the world.

The Turkmenistan government has also adopted a policy of separation from Russia and the Commonwealth of Independent States (CIS). Unlike its neighbors Uzbekistan and Tajikistan, the Turkmen government has refused to participate in military operations with the Russians and has rejected close economic and political ties to its neighbor to the north. This form of strict neutrality has allowed the government to play regional powers

against each other but has not led to close ties to any of its neighbors.

Turkmenistan has also had difficulty in forming a sense of nationhood among its people. The Soviet system deliberately attempted to create a republic without a national identity. The tribal loyalties within the Turkmen region also prevented a nation from developing. Instead the different tribes compete against each other and tend not to pose a threat to the central government. Such competition is part of the history of the region.

HISTORY

Much of the history of the Turkmen can be traced back to nomadic tribes originating in Mongolia. A confederation of those tribes, the Nine Oghuz, settled in modern-day Central Asia and Iran. By the tenth century one part of the confederation, the Seljuks, separated from the confederation and settled in the desert and mountainous region near the Caspian Sea. Religious differences led to another division, with the Turkmen refusing to follow Islam and splitting away from the Muslim regions.

The Mongol invasion of the area scattered the various Turkmen tribes through the desert and along the Caspian Sea. Yet the Mongols were unable to completely pacify the area. Their departure in the sixteenth century saw the Turkmen once again operate as independent tribes raiding their neighbors to the east and south. There was no identifiable Turkmen state. The neighboring Uzbek Khanate fought pitched battles with the tribes and suppressed them. Although they were able to end the military threat to their region, the Uzbeks were unable to control the desert region. That task fell to an invader from the north.

During Czar Alexander II's reign, Russian forces pushed into central Asia. Their invasion of the Turkestan territory in 1869 was bloody and successful. To combat the hit and run tactics of the Turkmen, the Russians raided settlements and massacred civilians and soldiers alike. By 1881 the Russians had destroyed organized military resistance and subdued the population. They ran the region with a military government composed of Russians and Turkmen. Yet because of its primitive communications, politics, and economy, the renamed Turkestan was ignored by the central government. This changed once the czarist regime was overthrown.

During czarist and Soviet rule, the Turkmen lived up to their reputation as rebellious and independent-minded nomads. A 1916 rebellion threatened Russian rule while a series of military clashes in the 1920s and 1930s threatened Soviet rule. It was not until the end of the 1930s that the Soviets were able to subdue the revolt, but only after the deaths of thousands of civilians in the region.

The Soviet takeover led to the Turkestan region's being granted a tightly controlled statehood and official recognition in 1924. The Turkmen Soviet Socialist Republic was formed by Joseph Stalin as a political sop to nationalistic desires. But Moscow controlled the republic by handpicking Russian and Turkmen officials to run the government. The Turkmen Republic remained relatively quiescent after the 1930s and the communist government attempted to make the desert an agricultural production center. Through widespread irrigation systems the communist regime diverted water from Central Asian rivers to grow cotton. This policy led to the slow destruction of the Aral Sea as water was siphoned from its sources. The result was agriculture at the expense of drinking water. Much of northern Turkmenistan was poisoned by runoff. These practices continued to present problems after the Soviet Union's collapse.

The Soviet government also developed the natural gas and oil resources of the area and made Turkmenistan the fourth-largest producer of natural gas and oil in the world. This made the area wealthy by Soviet standards and better able to meet the economic problems associated with independence.

The opportunity to break away from the Soviets came with the collapse of the Gorbachev government and revolts by several of the country's republics. Turkmenistan was not one of those. Instead it was the highest political leadership rather than the grass roots that drove the country toward independence. President Niyazov took the lead by calling for an independence referendum. In doing so he led the move from the Soviet system and was able to maintain his position after Turkmenistan independence.

TURKMENISTAN GOVERNMENT AND JUDICIARY

The collapse of centralized control in Moscow led Turkmenistan into declaring its independence in October 1991. The old Soviet-era constitution remained in effect until May 1992. At that time a new constitution was ratified, although its content continued the Soviet-era policy of state control of most social, economic, and political resources. Under the new constitution the Turkmenistan president was granted broad appointment, removal, and law-making powers. He has used those powers to create a cult of personality around him. The president's picture can be found all over the country, his accomplishments—both real and imagined—broadcast over state-run radio and television, and his name used only in a positive manner.

The president is aided by several institutions, all of which bow to his authority. The president appoints the Council of Ministers, which is responsible for running the government, and the prime minister, who heads the council. In addition the president can remove any minister including the prime minister for any reason. The president is elected to a five-year term of office and cannot serve more than two terms. But a 1993 referendum extended the current president's term to ten years ending in 2002.

The president's appointment power also extends to local officials. The five regions, or *velayests,* have governors, all of whom are appointed by the president. The governors in turn appoint lower-level district officials but do so with the clear understanding that the president must tacitly agree with the appointments. The president appoints all judges from the Supreme Court down to city courts. While judges have a constitutional five-year term of office, the president can remove any judge at any time for any reason.

In addition to the appointment power, the president is granted legislative power under the constitution. The president can issue edicts that have the force of law and can dissolve the National Assembly. Because the president also serves as the de facto head of the sole party in the country, he controls the nomination and election of each member of the General Assembly.

In keeping with the Soviet tradition, the Turkmenistan judiciary is centralized and under the political control of the president. As a Soviet republic, Turkmenistan had its own judiciary and prosecutor, all of whom were appointed by the Soviet government and were considered under its control. With the disintegration of the Moscow regime, the Turkmenistan government asserted control over the republic's courts.

The judiciary is the weakest branch of the Turkmenistan government. Its powers are limited in the civil law tradition to interpreting the law. But the judicial power is split between courts and political bodies that can also interpret and change the constitution.

The judiciary is divided according to jurisdiction. There are a total of sixty-one local and district courts that hear minor criminal and civil cases. Most family legal disputes are also heard in these courts. The regional courts serve an appellate function with the state and the individual able to appeal an adverse lower court decision to the regional court. All of the courts operate under the civil law system, limiting judges to interpreting and applying the law. Courts lack judicial review powers and hence cannot use the constitution as the basis for striking down a law.

The Supreme Court is the highest judicial body in the country. Composed of twenty-one judges serving five-

Legal Structure of Turkmenistan Courts

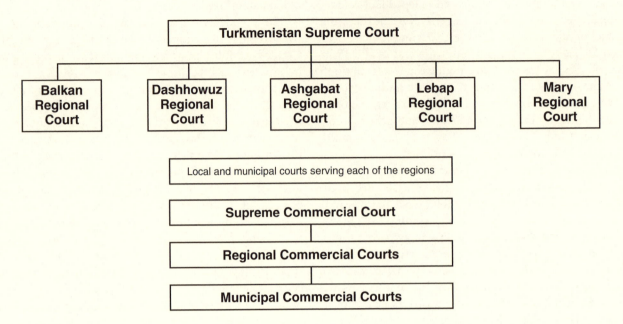

year terms, the court hears appeals from lower courts and ensures that the law is interpreted in a uniform manner. The country lacks a constitutional court, denying to the judiciary the ability to consider and rule on the constitutionality of Turkmenistan law.

Turkmenistan continued the Soviet practice of separating commercial courts from the regular court system. The commercial courts settle disputes between the government and state-owned enterprises. Commercial courts operate at the local and regional levels. The courts base their decisions on the law, interpreting the legal protections granted state-owned enterprises. Appeals of their decisions are heard by the high commercial court. Both the government and the state-owned enterprise have a right to appeal to this court. Its decisions are final, although they can be overturned by presidential decree or legislation.

The Turkmenistan constitution also weakens the courts by creating competing institutions with legislative and judicial powers. One such institution is the National Council of Turkmenistan. The council is composed of several political officials who have quasi-judicial roles. The council includes the Turkmenistan president, members of the National Assembly, members of the Supreme Court, justices from the supreme commercial court, ministers from the Council of Ministers, individuals elected from the various districts of the country, and cultural and scientific leaders. Under Article 50 of the constitution the council can decide on constitutional amendments or a new constitution, the introduction of a referendum question, determining state or district borders, declaring war, recommending certain foreign or

domestic policies, and interpreting the constitution and laws as allowed under the law. The president is the chairman of the council and has the power to call it into session as he sees fit. Because the members of the council are dependent upon the president for their authority, their independence is limited and they usually ratify presidential decisions.

The president also exerts control over the country's prosecutors. The president oversees the procurator general or national prosecutor and all regional and local procurators. In dealing with prosecutions, the president has amnesty and pardon powers and uses them when finding examples of prosecutorial abuse. President Niyazov, facing economic pressures and seeking financial aid from international organizations and the West, used his pardoning and removal power in 1997 to show his concern for human rights. Declaring that the Turkmen judicial system was beset by corruption, he fired the procurator general and several regional and local procurators. He then declared a general amnesty in which some 2,000 prisoners either were released or had their sentences reduced.

The judicial and prosecutorial powers of the government remain under presidential control. With his power to remove judges and prosecutors, the president can apply pressure on the courts and ensure that legal decisions match his political goals. Although the Turkmenistan judiciary is used to maintain the regime's powers, it has proved less able to meet the needs of a changing world. The Turkmenistan government's dependence upon personal rule has limited the development of law in the areas of privatization and individual rights.

PRIVATIZATION LAW

One of the major issues facing all of the former Soviet states is the privatization of state-run enterprises. In order to survive in a globally linked economy, these states must create a method of eliminating government control over the country's industry. Turkmenistan has faced difficulty in privatization and the development of a rule of law.

During the first years of independence the government used its oil and gas wealth to subsidize inefficient industries and to maintain public ownership of most property. But as commodity prices slumped and the economy began to contract, the Turkmen government sought to change the legal structure and its approach to property rights. But even with these demands on the law, Turkmenistan remains a country that pays mostly lip service to the rights of property owners.

Most of the farmland in the country remains in government hands. Farmers work government land under leases that prohibit them from selling their produce on the free market. Farmers have no property rights under this arrangement. In addition any farmland, either publicly or privately owned, can be seized by the government if officials perceive the land is not being used in the country's best interest. In urban areas, land ownership is restricted to business enterprises. Most individuals own no land and ownership is not explicitly protected under civil law.

The government also limits property ownership by foreign investors, requiring that all negotiations with foreign companies be conducted through the president's office, hence giving him a veto over any foreign acquisitions. Foreign investors also find that their investments are not protected under the law but rather are allowed only by the whim of the president.

A lack of codified property law has also limited privatization efforts. Most private businesses involve small enterprises that provide products and services that cannot be found in the public sector. Large state-owned businesses including manufacturers, utilities, transportation, and communication remain under the government's control. Without investment laws or joint stock ownership laws, it appears those industries will not be privatized.

The rights of individual workers are also not protected under the law. Labor unions are operated by the government and are used to determine wages. Membership in the union is required to work for state enterprises and a worker leaving a job may be prevented from moving in the country to find another position.

The main source of control over economic enterprises is the executive. The president not only negotiates most agreements with foreign investors but also can change economic laws using his power of decree. With few limits on the scope of decrees, the president can eliminate property rights with the stroke of his pen. He also has the power to force greater privatization. But because most privatization law is executive-based it has lacked clear and consistent enforcement. Starting in 1995, the president issued decrees that favored privatization. In 1998 a decree was issued mandating that a state agency oversee the privatization of most large industries in the country. The result was inaction. In 1999 the government signed agreements protecting copyrighted and patented materials in the country, yet no enforcement agency was created to implement the law. A series of decrees were issued supporting privatization and assuring foreign investors that their property would be protected, yet these decrees have not been enforced. Overall most foreign investments receive no legal protection from nationalization by the government. This forces most foreign businesses to rely on the good graces of government officials. This translates into bribes and kickbacks to those officials to allow businesses to operate.

The entire financial structure of the country remains in state hands and capital is invested on political rather than economic grounds. The economic downturn prompted the president to issue another decree limiting currency exchanges and hence making it more difficult for foreign investment to flow into the country. Such rapid and arbitrary changes in the law have spooked most foreign investors, who place their money elsewhere.

The lack of movement toward privatization of state industries is matched by a lack of progress in protecting individual rights. While the country's constitution grants extensive rights to practice religion and in freedom of speech and association, these rights have been ignored during the first decade of Turkmenistan independence.

INDIVIDUAL RIGHTS IN TURKMENISTAN

The Turkmenistan constitution includes several articles protecting individual rights, including freedom to practice religion, freedom to participate in public debate, free speech, and free association. Yet Turkmenistan has proved to be as intolerant of political dissent as its Soviet predecessors. A 1995 protest march through the capital of Ashgabat led to dozens of arrests. Those calling for change were accused of violating drug laws and of being involved with a drug-smuggling ring that sought to overthrow the government. They were convicted in closed trials and the most prominent among them were known as the Ashgabat Eight.

Their imprisonment was roundly criticized by international human rights groups and foreign governments. Such pressure in combination with the need for economic aid from the West prompted the government to create the Institute for Democracy and Human Rights. Given the task of promoting individual freedom, the institute collects complaints against government. Most deal with judges and prosecutors that abuse their power. Yet lacking enforcement powers, the institute represents only a cosmetic change in government policy. It has had even less effect on the government's treatment of religious minorities.

While the Turkmenistan constitution promised freedom of religion, the law restricts the right to practice religious beliefs. The 1996 Freedom of Conscience and Religious Organizations Law requires that all religious organizations register with the government before engaging religious worship, before distributing religious materials, or before attempting to proselytize. The 1996 law also requires a religion to provide the names of 500 members before being allowed to register. The 500 number is enforced for registration requirements at the national, regional, and local levels. Hence religions seeking to practice in the capital must identify 500 members living within that city.

The numerical requirement has led to the registration of only Sunni Muslims and the Russian Orthodox Church. These faiths are the only ones that can legally operate within Turkmenistan. Other faiths, including Jehovah's Witnesses, the Baha'i faith of Iran, and Armenian Christians have been rejected for registration or have had their registrations pulled as requirements were heightened or technicalities found to limit them.

Without being registered these groups are forced to meet clandestinely and illegally. The Turkmenistan authorities have been aggressive in breaking up meetings, seizing religious materials, and detaining followers. The government also exerts control over the religions that are allowed to practice in Turkmenistan. In many countries with large Muslim populations, Islamic law is practiced and enforced through a separate legal system. Turkmenistan allows Islamic law to be practiced under careful state regulation and control. A Turkmenistan Muslim Religious Board oversees the instruction and practice of Islam in the country. Part of its power includes the selection of all religious leaders. Composed of members handpicked by the president, the board appoints only those leaders who pose no challenge to the government.

The Ministry of Justice oversees all Islamic judges. Their official organization, the Kuziat, is registered with the ministry. Only those judges belonging to the organization can practice Islamic law in the country. Hence the government controls the practice of Islamic law and Turkmenistan continues the Soviet practice of tightly controlling the practice of religious beliefs.

In religious freedoms and political freedoms, Turkmenistan law falls far short of the goals established in the constitution. The freedoms supposedly protected in the constitution are regularly restricted. The government continues to use the Soviet-era criminal code, which further limits rights. Without significant changes in the law code or an enhancement of judicial power, individual rights will remain a distant goal.

LEGAL TRAINING

The Turkmenistan government operates a single university. The Turkmenistan State University is the sole avenue for the people to receive a university education. Legal training in the university is limited to the civil law and is conducted under the oversight of a National Council of Education. Law school is limited to only the best students, which is usually interpreted as the most politically loyal students. Because of the domination of the educational process by the national government, few students are allowed to study overseas to obtain a law degree. Staffing of the courts is also restricted in seeking those lawyers who were trained in Turkmenistan law.

IMPACT OF THE LAW

As a former Soviet Republic, Turkmenistan faced restructuring its economy, solving environmental problems, and building a political system from one that lacked the rule of law or a functional and independent judiciary. In the decade after its independence, the country proved unable to escape the legacy of Soviet rule.

Turkmenistan is the one Central Asian state that has maintained a government closely resembling its Soviet predecessor. An authoritarian presidency built on a cult of personality maintains strong economic controls and has built a government that promotes and protects presidential powers. This includes the judicial system. Judges and prosecutors are appointed by the president and can be removed for any reason. This places the judiciary under the direct control of the president.

The executive branch includes institutions that compete with the judiciary for power to interpret the constitution and the law. The National Council is controlled by the president, as he appoints its members and directs its agenda. Its legislative power is limited by presidential decrees. In issuing decrees, the president has become the key player in any legal reform in Turkmenistan. It has also given the president power over economic reforms, privatization of government-owned enterprises, and protection of individual rights. Because of the unwillingness of the president to act and the paucity of power invested in competing government institutions, change has come slowly in Turkmenistan. At the same time the legal system has allowed the president to exert even greater control over the country.

Douglas Clouatre

See also Appellate Courts; Civil Law; Kazakhstan; Kyrgyzstan; Soviet System

References and further reading

Bohr, Annette. 1996. "Turkmenistan and the Turkmen." In *The Nationalities Question in the Post-Soviet States.* Edited by Graham Smith. New York: Longman.

Curtis, Glenn E., ed. 1996. *Kazakstan, Kyrgyzstan, Tajikistan, Turkmenistan, and Uzbekistan.* Washington, DC: Library of Congress.

Dawisha, Karen, and Bruce Parrott, eds. 1997. *Conflict Cleavage and Change in Central Asia and the Caucasus.* New York: Cambridge University Press.

Gleason, Gregory. 1997. *The Central Asian States: Discovering Independence.* Boulder, CO: Westview Press.

Jones, Benjamin, and Leif Beck Fallisen. 1999. "The Newly Independent States: A Country-by-Country Look at How Each Is Faring Today." *Europe,* no. 383 (Fall): 30–35.

Nissman, David. 1994. "Turkmenistan (Un)Transformed." *Current History* (April): 183–186.

Olcott, Martha Brill. 1996. *Central Asia's New States.* Washington, DC: United States Institute of Peace Press.

Panfilov, Oleg. 1999. "The Turkmenistan Institute of Human Rights and Other Fantastic Stories from Central Asia." *Transitions* (October).

TUVALU

GEOGRAPHY AND BACKGROUND

Tuvalu is an island country located in the South Pacific between 5° and 10° south latitude and 176° and 179° east longitude. The country is made up of nine atolls, eight of which are inhabited by its population of more than 8,000 people. Tuvalu was formerly known as the Ellice Islands. As such, it came under the protection of the British monarch in September 1892. On January 12, 1916, in conjunction with the Gilbert Islands it became known as the Gilbert and Ellice Islands Colony. It was established by an Order of the Queen in Council dated July 25, 1978, with effect from October 1, 1978, as a separate colony. It then adopted the name *Tuvalu* (meaning "eight standing together").

Tuvalu thus became politically independent on October 1, 1978, but retained Britain's reigning monarch as its sovereign and head of state, with a governor-general as the monarch's representative. It has a written constitution, which has been revised once since independence (in 1986).

THE COMMON LAW SYSTEM

Tuvalu adopted the English legal system and its primary institutions when it became independent in 1978. Some of the main characteristics of the Westminster model of law include the adversarial system, the use of the English common law as a source of law, the presumption of innocence, the right to a fair trial, and the right to be represented by a lawyer. However, some fundamental features of the Westminster model were also left out. Particularly obvious is the lack of a jury as the judge of facts. In Tuvalu, as in most other South Pacific jurisdictions, the judge is the arbiter of both facts and law. As will be discussed, the Tuvalu legal system has developed quite distinct features since the country became independent in 1978.

THE SYSTEM OF CONSTITUTIONAL GOVERNMENT

Article 1 of the Constitution of Tuvalu establishes the country as an independent democratic state founded according to certain fundamental principles, including the upholding of the traditions and customs of Tuvalu society and the foundational principles of the Christian religion. It is a unitary system of government, although there are provincial governments as well within this unitary framework.

The constitution assumes the operation of a Westminster model of responsible cabinet government. It entrenches the separation of parliamentary, judicial, and executive powers. Part II of the constitution establishes a bill of rights and the supremacy of the rule of law. Part II provides for the explicit guarantee of such human rights as freedom of expression, protection of law, freedom from slavery, protection of property, freedom of movement, freedom of expression, and others.

TYPES AND SOURCES OF LAW

As declared by the Laws of Tuvalu Act of 1987, there are five sources of law in Tuvalu: the constitution, acts of Parliament, customary law, applied laws, and the common law. In addition, international law applies in Tuvalu (Ntumy 1993, 344).

Constitution

According to both the 1986 Constitution and the Laws of Tuvalu Act of 1987, the constitution is the supreme law of Tuvalu. Any law inconsistent with the constitution would thus be void to the extent of its inconsistency. Additionally, all laws must in interpreted in such a way as to conform to the constitution (Ntumy 1993, 344).

Acts of Parliament

The second source of law in Tuvalu is legislation enacted by the Tuvaluan Parliament, including subsidiary legislation made pursuant to an Act (Ntumy 1993, 344).

Customary Law

The third source of law in Tuvalu is customary law. The preamble to the constitution refers to the upholding of values, culture, and tradition of Tuvalu but does not go further to define what these terms mean. Customary law is, however, defined in the Laws of Tuvalu Act of 1987 as the customs and usage of the people of Tuvalu. Customary law is used predominantly in land matters and can be pleaded in any court except where the recognition and application of customary law would result in injustice or be contrary to the public interest.

However, important to note is that different rules apply to the recognition of customary law in criminal and

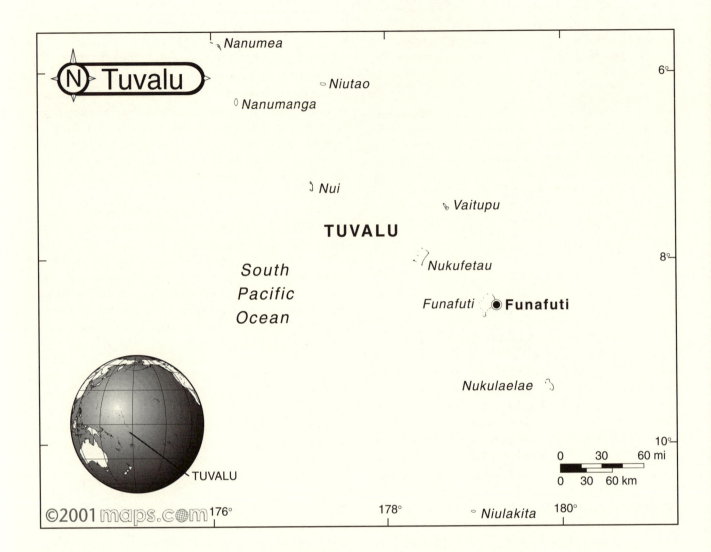

Tuvalu

Nanumea
Niutao
Nanumanga
Nui
Vaitupu
TUVALU
South
Pacific
Ocean
Nukufetau
Funafuti ● Funafuti

Nukulaelae

TUVALU

Niulakita

0   30   60 mi
0   30   60 km

©2001 maps.com   176°   178°   180°
6°
8°
10°

civil cases. In criminal law, customary law may only be taken into consideration for the following purposes:

• Ascertaining the existence of a state of mind of a person;
• Deciding the reasonableness of an act, default, or omission by a person;
• Deciding the reasonableness of an excuse;
• Deciding whether to proceed to the conviction of a guilty party; or
• Deciding the penalty to be imposed on a guilty party.

In civil matters, customary law must be considered in:

• All matters pertaining to the ownership and use by custom of land, including rights of hunting on and gathering and taking minerals from native land;
• Ownership by custom of and customary navigation and fishing rights over any part of the territorial sea, lagoon, inland waters, foreshore, and seabed;
• The ownership by custom of water, or of rights in or over water;

• The devolution of native land or rights in, over, or in connection with native land;
• Defamation;
• The legitimacy, legitimization, and adoption of children;
• The rights of married persons arising out of their marriage in relation to the termination of their marriage by nullity, divorce, or death;
• The right of a member of a family to support by other members of that family or the right to custody or guardianship of infants;
• The duties of members of a community to contribute to projects for the welfare of that community;
• Any transaction that the parties intent should be or that justice requires should be regulated wholly or partly by custom and not by any other law.

All questions about the existence or scope of custom are to be determined as questions of law. The court should first consider submissions of the parties and then consult cases, legal textbooks, or similar sources. If it still has doubts, then it is required to hold an inquiry.

Applied Laws

The fourth source of law in Tuvalu is the "applied laws," defined as "those enactments which have effect as part of the law of Tuvalu." These include British statutes, orders, and regulations. British law was first applied under the Pacific Order in Council of 1893 (UK). Then, by Section 15 of the Western Pacific (Courts) Order of 1961, British statutes of general application in force in England as of January 1, 1961, were applied to the then Ellice Islands "subject to such qualifications as local circumstances render necessary." The attorney general has power to amend such legislation to bring it to conformity with the constitution, local legislation, and customary law.

Common Law

The final source of law mentioned in the Laws of Tuvalu Act is the common law. This is taken to comprise the rules of English common law and the doctrines of equity. Where common law and equity conflict with each other, equity will prevail (Ntumy 1993, 347). This applies a standard formula for the relationship between common law and equity as found in Section 25(11) of the Judicature Act of 1873 (UK).

THE KEY STRUCTURES

Legislature

At the national level, the Parliament of Tuvalu is one of the main organs of government and law making. It consists of a single chamber with twelve elected members and a speaker, who is also elected. The normal life of Parliament is four years. The Parliament is the legislature and is vested with the power to make laws for the whole country. The law-making powers of Parliament may be delegated to any other person or authority specialized in the field where the law will apply. Parliamentarians are competent to introduce a bill in Parliament. The bill then passes through two sessions of Parliament for comments before it is assented to by the governor-general and becomes an act of Parliament (Ntumy 1993, 348).

Only citizens of Tuvalu who have attained the age of twenty-one are qualified to be elected to Parliament. The constitution disqualifies anyone who owes allegiance to a foreign power, has been declared a bankrupt, commits an offense, or holds any public office other than those specifically exempted by law.

Members of Parliament may lose their seats if Parliament is dissolved, if they are absent from sittings of Parliament, if they resign, are sentenced to death or imprisonment, or have an interest in any matter under discussion without disclosing their interest. Moreover, the constitution gives immunity to members of Parliament, hence no civil or criminal proceedings can be instituted against any member where words are spoken in Parliament or a committee of Parliament.

Executive

Like the neighboring countries with a Westminister model of government, Tuvalu also has an executive, which exercises executive authority on behalf of the government. The executive is made up of the governor-general representing the monarch in England and the cabinet headed by the prime minister.

Judiciary

The Tuvaluan court system consists of lower courts having limited jurisdiction (Island Courts, Land Courts, Magistrates' Courts) and higher courts having general trial and appellate jurisdiction.

Island and Land Courts

These bodies are found at the bottom of the Tuvaluan court system. The Islands Court Act (Cap 3) regulates the eight Land Courts. These are courts of summary jurisdiction within the islands on which they are situated. The civil jurisdiction of the courts includes divorces in which both parties are resident or normally resident in Tuvalu; actions for property, debt, or damage claims of less than A\$60; maintenance; and custody. The criminal jurisdictions of the Island Courts include offenses in which the maximum penalty is a fine of A\$100, six months of imprisonment, or both.

Civil appeals on divorce and fines of more than A\$10 go to the Magistrates' Court. Criminal appeals in respect to conviction to undergo imprisonment without fine, fines in excess of A\$10, or imprisonment of a term exceeding seven days in default of the payment go to the Magistrates' Court (Ntumy 1993, 348).

A separate system of Land Courts has been established under the Native Lands Act to determine customary land disputes. Each island has a Land Court, composed of six members. The jurisdiction covers all cases regarding rights to customary land, land boundaries, transfers of titles and customary land, and disputes on the use and possession of such land. Probate over customary wills and succession also falls within the jurisdiction of the Land Court, as do fishing rights. Appeals from this court go to a Land Court Appeals Panel, consisting of three members, and then to the Senior Magistrates' Court.

Magistrates' Court

The Magistrates' Court and the Senior Magistrates' Court were established under the Magistrates' Court Act (Cap 2), and each is headed by a senior magistrate. Currently, there is one Magistrates' Court and one Senior Magistrates' Court in Tuvalu, with just one magistrate sitting at each. The Magistrates' Courts have original jurisdiction in all civil matters except those under the jurisdiction of the Land Court or matrimonial proceedings that have already been commenced in an Island Court. In criminal matters, the Magistrates' Court has jurisdiction over any offense for which the maximum penalty does not exceed imprisonment for one year, a fine of A$200, or both. The Senior Magistrates' Court has jurisdiction over any offense for which the maximum punishment does not exceed fourteen years of imprisonment, a fine of A$1,000, or both. In addition, the Magistrates' Court also has power to review any judgments by the Island Courts (Ntumy 1993, 349).

High Court
The High Court of Tuvalu is established under Part VII of the constitution and consists of the chief justice and additional appointments made by the head of state on advice of cabinet. Sections 130–132 of the constitution prescribe the jurisdiction of the High Court to include enforcing the bill of rights, handling questions on the membership of Parliament, interpreting or applying the constitution, and hearing appeals from the lower courts.

To qualify for appointment as a High Court judge, a person must have been qualified as a barrister or a solicitor in a country with a legal system similar to Tuvalu's and must be a judge of a court of unlimited jurisdiction and appellate jurisdiction.

Court of Appeal
The Court of Appeal of Tuvalu is established under Sections 134 and 135 of the constitution. The court was to be regulated by an act of Parliament that hasn't been enacted.

Sovereign in Council
Decisions of the Court of Appeal may be appealed to the sovereign in council. However, appeals are restricted to cases involving interpretation or application of the constitution, appeals relating to the enforcement of the bill of rights; and final or interlocutory decisions of the Court of Appeal that in the opinion of the Court of Appeal are of public importance (Ntumy 1993, 351).

THE FALEKAUPULE
Falekaupule means "the Council of Elders." Traditionally, the Falekaupule institution has been the governing body of the local communities within the Tuvaluan society. The Falekaupule is responsible for the community's wellbeing. It sets local community rules, resolves disputes, and, where necessary, decides on appropriate punishment. When Tuvalu came under British control, the Local Government Act (Cap 19) was enacted to establish local government councils. These councils were distinct from the Falekaupule and assumed the traditional role of the Falekaupule. The only power the Falekaupule had was to appoint the president of the local council. In 1997, however, the Falekaupule Act was passed by Parliament to give statutory recognition to the Falekaupule and

Legal Structure of Tuvalu Courts

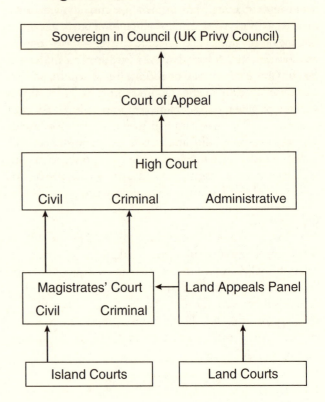

vest in them greater control over island affairs.

The Falekaupule Act now confers on the Falekaupule the functions formerly conferred on local government councils. This gives the Falekaupule greater autonomy to manage local communities. Some of the functions of the Falekaupule are provided in Schedule 3 of the Falekaupule Act. These include developing and regulating agriculture, building and town planning, education, forestry, land, relief of famine and drought, markets, public health, public order, communications, trade, and industry.

The act leaves certain powers in the hands of the minister of local government, so that there is uniformity in matters such as salaries and rates. However, in most cases, the minister's powers can only be exercised after consultation with the Falekaupule.

Since 1997, when this act came into force, the Falekaupule has achieved a marked success. It has not only helped to reduce the level of deviance in Tuvaluan society but also contributed positively to development in the fields over which it has authority. This is an institution that is unique to Tuvalu and one that has positively contributed toward law and order.

CIVIL LAW AND PROCEDURE
The civil laws of Tuvalu, like those of any other common law jurisdiction, are those not contained in the Penal Code. They involve civil offenses committed against

members of the community. The laws that regulate civil behavior in Tuvalu include torts, contracts, administrative law, constitution law, and family law. Civil claims of $500 or less can be initiated in the Magistrates' Court, while claims between $500 and $10,000 can be brought up in the Senior Magistrates' Court.

CRIMINAL LAW AND PROCEDURE

In Tuvalu, criminal conduct is defined and regulated by Cap 8 of the Laws of Tuvalu. The Penal Code prescribes criminal behavior and also safeguards individual rights. Criminal procedure is provided for in Cap 7—Criminal Procedure Code. The Criminal Procedure Code outlines the rules and procedure that have to be followed in prosecuting criminal offenses, including the suspect's right to be presumed innocent, the right against adverse inference, the right to representation, and the right to a fair trial. Where a crime is committed, the public prosecutor prosecutes the case on behalf of the state. The accused is presumed to be innocent until proven guilty beyond a reasonable doubt.

LEGAL AID

The constitution guarantees that accused persons may have the assistance of an interpreter without payment and may defend themselves at their own expense (Constitution of 1986, Section 22 [3]). Additionally, a people's lawyer is also appointed to advise the public on legal issues, as well as educate them about their rights and duties. The people's lawyer in Tuvalu was established in 1985 as a result of efforts made by the Commonwealth secretariat to assist small jurisdictions. Today, the people's lawyer is regulated under the People's Lawyers Act—Cap 3A, Laws of Tuvalu. The people's lawyer has been active in the community and made positive contributions toward reducing the volume of litigation that passes through the courts.

LAWYERS

As of 2001 there were four qualified lawyers serving a population of 12,000 Tuvaluans; that is, roughly 3,000 people per lawyer. From 1988, Australia and New Zealand began funding students to study law in Australian and New Zealand universities (Powles and Pulea 1988, 243). Since the 1994 establishment of the Law School at the University of the South Pacific in Vanuatu, most law students from Tuvalu are sent to that institution.

The attorney general, who is the principal legal adviser to the government, attends cabinet and Parliament meetings, is responsible for prosecutions, and conducts the more serious cases on behalf of the government. The attorney general is appointed according to Section 159 (4) (a) as stipulated under Section 79 of the constitution.

Phillip Tagini

See also Common Law; Customary Law
References and further reading
Findlay, M. 1996. *The Criminal Laws of the South Pacific.* Suva, Fiji: IJALS, University of the South Pacific.
Ntumy, M. 1993. *South Pacific Islands Legal Systems.* Honolulu: University of Hawai'i Press.
Powles, G., and M. Pulea, eds. 1988. *Pacific Courts and Legal Systems.* Suva, Fiji: University of the South Pacific, in association with the Faculty of Law, Monash University.

U

UGANDA

COUNTRY INFORMATION

Uganda, nicknamed the Pearl of Africa, lies in the heart of East Africa on the northern bank of Lake Victoria. It shares its borders with five countries, including Kenya to the east, Sudan to the north, the Democratic Republic of the Congo (DRC) to the west, and Rwanda and Tanzania to the south. Although covering only 93,981 square miles, Uganda's geography, climate, and vegetation are, nevertheless, diverse. Anchored by the Ruwenzori and Virunga mountains in the west and Mt. Elgon in the east, the elevated basin in between the two flanks of the Great Rift Valley is covered by tropical forest, woodland, and open savanna. The Victoria and Albert Nile rivers flow northward through Uganda and, along with other freshwater lakes and rivers, make the country one of the most fertile in eastern Africa.

Agriculture dominates Uganda's economy, with 82 percent of the populace engaged in subsistence or commercial farming. Farmers produce for domestic consumption a variety of grains, legumes, tubers, vegetables, and fruits, and there is a small but growing dairy sector. Light industry includes sugar, beer brewing, tobacco, cotton cloth, and cement. The country's primary export commodities are coffee, cotton, tea, and tobacco. The country also contains gold, cobalt, and copper deposits. The Gross Domestic Product real growth rate for 1999 was estimated at 5.5 percent.

Uganda was at the epicenter of the HIV-AIDs epidemic in the 1980s and 1990s. Infection rates peaked at roughly 30 percent. Besides hampering economic productivity, it caused severe social dislocation, most evident in the large numbers of orphaned children. Public awareness campaigns have reduced infection rates, but life expectancy at birth has fallen to forty-three years.

The population of 23,317,560 persons is ethnically diverse. The Baganda are numerically the largest group. Others include the Banyankole, Basoga, Banyoro, and the Batoro. Nilotic-Hamitic groups include the Langi, Acholi, Ateso, and Karamojong. South Asians have played a significant economic role in Uganda since the early 1900s, when the British imported them to fill the lower ranks of the colonial civil service or to trade. Uganda lacks a national language. The military uses Kiswahili, while English serves as the official language.

HISTORY

Long before 1894, when England declared Uganda a British protectorate, the kingdoms of central and western Uganda had evolved centralized states complete with administrative and judicial institutions. The Kingdom of Buganda, dominant in the region, asserted authority through a hierarchy of administrative chiefs. A deliberative assembly, the Lukiiko, advised the *kabaka* (king) and served as an appellate court to the local chiefs' courts. The replication of these administrative and judicial structures throughout Uganda served as the cornerstone of England's colonial policies. Referred to as indirect rule, the colonial government maximized its limited resources by relying on local chiefs to maintain order, collect taxes, mobilize labor for public works projects, and to administer justice.

It was in the reliance on local chiefs' courts that the British cemented customary law as the foundation of Uganda's legal system, a legacy that endures today. The British Order-in-Council of 1902 declared as law in Uganda the English common law, the doctrines of equity, statutes of general application in force in England at the time, and customary law as long it was not repugnant to natural justice, morality, and good conscience, or in conflict with written law. The order conferred on the High Court, presided over by British judges, full jurisdiction over all persons and matters. Appeals against the High Court lay before the Court of Appeal for East Africa, located in Mombassa, Kenya, and subsequently the Privy Council in London. The protectorate imported the penal code and rules of evidence used by the British in India.

In reality, the majority of cases involving Ugandans proceeded through the chiefs' courts under civil customary law. Exceptions included cases between Ugandans and non-Africans and crimes subject to capital punishment. Colonial officers resisted the High Court's involvement in native affairs, for fear that the British justices and magistrates would undermine customary law, which the former viewed as necessary to maintaining control in the

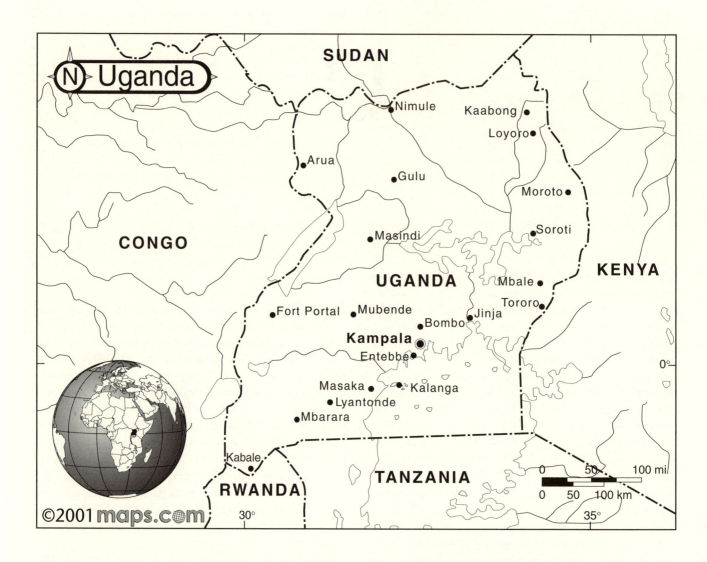

face of the economic and social dislocation caused by colonialism.

After World War II, with agitation for independence growing, the Judicial Advisers' Conference of 1953 recommended the integration of the courts and the development of a unified body of law. The African Courts Ordinance of 1957 transformed native chiefs' courts into African courts with appeals directly to the High Court, bypassing the colonial district officer. Ugandan court staff received training in English law, the Penal Code, the Criminal Procedure Code, and the Evidence Ordinance. In 1964, the Uganda Magistrates' Courts Act (MCA), substantially amended in 1970, established the chief magistrate and magistrates grades I, II, and III. The national assembly abolished appeals to the Privy Council in 1964 and to the Court of Appeals for East Africa in 1967.

With independence in 1962, Uganda was first constituted a federation with autonomy extended to the kingdoms of Ankole, Buganda, Bunyoro, and Toro. From 1962 to 1966 the king of Buganda was president of Uganda, while Milton Obote, a northerner, served as the first prime minister. In 1966 tension between the king

and Obote led the former to flee into exile. Obote abolished the kingdoms and, in 1967, enacted a republican constitution that made him the president. General Idi Amin's coup against Obote in 1971 set off fifteen years of economic chaos and civil war. In 1979 the Tanzanian Defence Forces and Ugandan exiles overthrew Idi Amin. Fraudulent elections in 1980 brought Milton Obote back to power but plunged the country into a civil war and a series of short-lived regimes. Tito Okello forced Obote into exile in 1985 but was himself overthrown by Yoweri Museveni's National Resistance Army in 1986.

Museveni has brought a more stable and prosperous climate to central and southern Uganda, but he has been unable to end the rebellions by the Lord's Resistance Army in the north and the Allied Democratic Forces in the west. Uganda has also been embroiled in the DRC, where they supported a rebel group seeking to overthrow the government of Lauren Kabila.

Uganda is a one-party state, organized around the National Resistance Movement (NRM). Political parties, including the Democratic Party and the United Peoples' Congress, exist, but their candidates cannot hold political rallies or campaign on a party platform. In June 2000, Ugandans passed a referendum to ban parties for another five years, although low voter turnout marred its legitimacy.

The cornerstone of Museveni's government has been the decentralization of authority to the districts. In 1987, under the Resistance Councils and Committees Act No. 9, the NRM established resistance councils (RC) at the village, parish, subcounty, county, and district levels. In 1988, under the Resistance Committees (Judicial Powers) Statute No. 1, RCs were granted judicial capacity. Renamed Local Councils (LC) in 1996, the Local Governments Act No. 1 of 1997 is the most recent specification of the division of authority between central and local governments. LCs exercise all political and executive powers and functions, including the provision of education, health, water, and road services; the implementation of government policy; and the monitoring of government officials. The district council is the primary planning authority and has legislative power to pass ordinances.

Until 1998, Uganda employed electoral colleges to elect the nine-member councils beyond the village level, leaving observers skeptical to claims that the LC system constituted participatory democracy. Village LCs, the only directly elected body, constituted an electoral college to elect the parish councils. Parishes, in turn, elected subcounty LCs. The pattern varied, with the subcounty councils electing the district council while the county councils were responsible for representatives to the National Resistance Council. In line with the affirmative action policies specified in the 1995 Constitution, representation on the councils is guaranteed for women, youth, and the disabled.

LEGAL CONCEPTS

The 1995 Constitution is the culmination of a five-year national debate on numerous issues, including the role of political parties, the status of women, the need for a national language, the resurrection of traditional rulers, and land reform. The Constitutional Commission invited a spectrum of individuals and organizations to submit ideas; they conducted seminars and solicited the opinions of ordinary Ugandans through community meetings. The latter exercise resulted in widespread knowledge of the constitution even in rural areas. In 1994, Ugandans went to the polls to elect a constituent assembly that debated and passed the final document.

The constitution specifies the powers and functions of the executive, legislative, and judicial branches of government; the protection of human rights, including civic, cultural, and economic rights; the structure and financing of local government; and issues of national security, including the police forces and prison services. The document also contains twenty-nine political, cultural, eco-

nomic, and environmental objectives. Amending the constitution can be accomplished by one of three methods, depending on the articles being amended: the support of two-thirds of all members in Parliament; a national referendum; or ratification by two-thirds of the members of the district councils in two-thirds of the districts.

The Ugandan Constitution is the first African constitution to extend equality to women. Article 33 grants women full and equal dignity of person with men, calls for affirmative action to redress imbalances, and prohibits any laws, cultures, customs, or traditions that undermine women's status or welfare. Article 21 outlaws discrimination on the basis of gender, race, ethnic origin, religion, or disability. The constitution, however, contains unresolved conflicts: Article 37 protects cultural rights and practices that some women consider to undermine their status and welfare.

Uganda employs multiple sources of law, including statutory, case, customary, and religious law (Mohammedan and Hindu). Criminal law is primarily statutory, but in civil suits, the Judicature Act specifies that written law, when applicable, takes precedence over customary or religious law. In divorce cases, the type of marriage determines which set of laws pertains, although the lower Magistrates' Courts tend to apply customary law to domestic cases. Likewise, the property rights of parties to land disputes depend on whether the land is registered or held under customary tenure. Where customary law prevails, courts may require witnesses to prove its authenticity.

The government's emphasis on popular justice has reinforced the significance of customary law by encouraging people to bypass the formal judiciary and to take their cases to the local council courts. Popular justice is supposed to emphasize local cultural values and community participation in justice, and to provide more accessible and efficient processes. Ethnic minorities and women, however, perceive LCs as biased institutions. Women who take marital land disputes to village or parish courts present their cases to LCs dominated by their in-laws. Obtaining a trial date often requires the payment of fees beyond those prescribed in the statute. Some LCs make it difficult to appeal their decisions in higher courts.

The judiciary is incorporating alternative dispute resolution and case management techniques to reduce processing delays and to eliminate the backlog of cases. Magistrates are authorized, under the Magistrates' Court Act, to suspend proceedings, to pursue reconciliation, or to mediate out-of-court settlements. Current efforts aim to create formal mechanisms and procedures and to eliminate procedural loopholes that allow lawyers to seek infinite adjournments in cases they anticipate losing.

Uganda has a small but growing legal and paralegal aid movement. The Ugandan Association of Women Lawyers established a local chapter of Federación Internacional de las Abogadas (FIDA) in 1974 that caters to the legal needs of women and children. They run clinics in three urban centers and train paralegals in three other districts. The Uganda Law Society oversees the Legal Aid Project, with offices in four districts. The Foundation for Human Rights Initiative trains community volunteers as paralegals to provide legal information to rural residents. To assist with the legal problems of orphans, the Makerere Law Faculty opened up a children's clinic.

CURRENT STRUCTURE

Parliament, elected every five years, has 276 members, including 214 constituency representatives, 39 women's representatives, 10 members of the Uganda People's Defence Forces, 5 representatives each for youth and the disabled, and 3 workers' representatives. The quorum to pass legislation is one-third of all members and two-thirds to override a presidential veto.

The president, who is the chief of state, head of government, and commander-in-chief of the armed forces, serves no more than two five-year terms. Parliament may initiate removal with written notice by one-third of all members to the speaker of Parliament. Grounds include abuse of office, violation of the oaths of office or the constitution, or physical or mental incapacity. The chief justice appoints a three-person tribunal of judges from the Supreme Court to investigate and report to Parliament. Two-thirds of Parliament must pass the resolution to remove. Under the 1995 constitution, the president, in consultation with the cabinet and subject to parliamentary approval, retains the right to proclaim states of emergency for periods of ninety days. The president appoints a vice president, subject to approval by a simple majority in Parliament.

The cabinet, limited to twenty-one members unless expanded by Parliament, is appointed by the president with parliamentary approval. Ministers must be members of Parliament. The prime minister assists the president with the supervision of the cabinet. The Supreme Court is the final court of appeal in Uganda (see figure). Headed by the chief justice, the court retains seven sitting justices. When presiding over appeals against the decisions of the Constitutional Court, the court sits as a full bench. Eight justices sit on Uganda's Court of Appeal, headed by the deputy chief justice. The Court of Appeal serves two functions. First, it hears appeals from the High Court. Second, it forms the Constitutional Court of five justices. The Constitutional Court has the authority to determine whether acts of Parliament, or the acts or omissions of other persons of authority, are consistent with or in contravention of the constitution.

The Constitutional Court was at the center of a recent controversy when, in October 2000, it declared null and void the Referendum and Other Provisions Act. The government had previously used a national referendum to continue the ban on political parties. The court ruled that Parliament's reliance on the voice omnibus voting method and the lack of a quorum were unconstitutional. Parliament responded by amending the constitution to make valid all acts and appointments of Parliament since its inception in 1996. The amendment also curtails the Constitutional Court's right of judicial review over parliamentary acts. The High Court, with a total of twenty-eight judges, is headed by the principal judge. Seventeen judges preside in Kampala, while the remainder are resident in six districts. The High Court is both a court of unlimited original jurisdiction and an appellate court against magistrates' decisions. In criminal cases, crimes punishable by capital punishment are heard as original cases in the High Court, including murder, rape, kidnapping with the intent to murder, and crimes against the state such as treason. Other courts include the Commercial Court, with three justices, and a Family Court, both divisions of the High Court.

There are currently twenty-four magisterial districts. The magistrature contains four levels. Chief magistrates, the highest judicial officer in the district, and magistrates grade one are law-degree holders, while magistrates grade two and three are lay members. The latter complete a one-year training program at the Law Development Center. Jurisdictions correspond to the monetary value in civil suits and the severity of punishment in criminal cases with unlimited jurisdiction in suits governed by civil customary law. Appeals against the decisions of chief magistrates lie before the High Court; appeals against grade one magistrates who act as head of station travel to the chief magistrate, otherwise to the High Court; chief magistrates hear appeals against magistrates grades two and three.

The Resistance Committees (Judicial Powers) Statute No. 1 of 1988 extended judicial capacity to village, parish, and subcounty local councils, as part of the decentralization of power and services to local governments. A quorum is five persons. LCs share concurrent jurisdiction with the lay Magistrates' Courts, and plaintiffs may choose whether to proceed before LCs or magistrates. Their jurisdiction includes debts, contracts, assault and battery, property damage, and trespass. LCs may preside over customary matters including land, the marital status of women, the paternity of children, the identification of customary heirs, the impregnation of or elopement with a girl under eighteen years of age, and customary bailment. LCs are known to go beyond their jurisdiction, however, sometimes presiding over serious criminal offenses such as murder and rape. The LCs are linked to the formal judiciary through the appeals process. Persons who elect to use the LC system must initiate their suits in the village court. Appeals move to the parish and sub-

Structure of Ugandan Courts

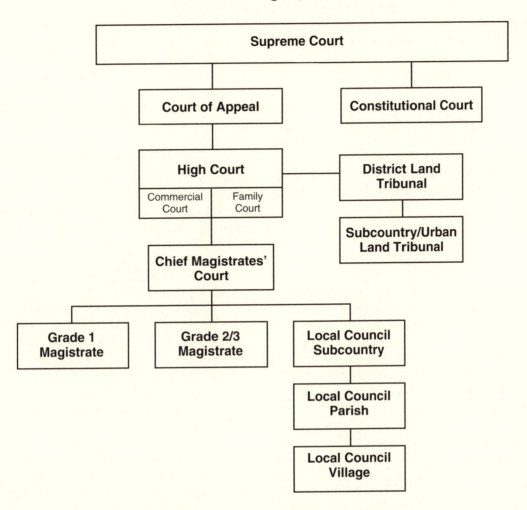

county levels before reaching the chief magistrate, who can uphold or overturn decisions or send the case back to either a magistrate or LC court for retrial.

The Land Act of 1988 created tribunals at the district and subcounty or urban levels to adjudicate property disputes. The Judicial Service Commission (JSC) appoints the three members at the lower level, while the chief justice, on the recommendation of the JSC, appoints the three members of the district tribunal, including the chair, who must meet the qualifications of a magistrate grade one. Appeals against the district board lie before the High Court. Terms are for five years. Tribunals may recommend mediation by traditional authorities or another person.

The administrator general (AG) oversees the administration of estates by vetting applications for letters of administration or probate. The AG's office issues a letter of no objection, at which point the relevant parties may apply to the courts for the granting of letters.

The criminal justice system includes the Department of Public Prosecutions, the Criminal Investigation De-

partment, and the courts. The director of Public Prosecutions must have the qualifications to be appointed to the High Court. According to the constitution, the director is not subject to the direction or control of any person or authority and serves under the same terms and conditions as judges of the High Court.

SPECIALIZED JUDICIAL BODIES

Article 51 of the constitution establishes the Uganda Human Rights Commission. It is composed of a chair person, who must be a judge of the High Court, and at least three other persons appointed by the president, with the approval of Parliament. The commission retains broad powers to investigate violations of the rights and freedoms contained in the constitution, to monitor the government's compliance with international treaties and conventions on human rights, and to educate the populace about their rights.

The Inspector General of Government (IGG), created in 1987, investigates government abuses of human rights, including arbitrary arrests and detention without trial, the denial of a fair and public trial before an impartial and independent court, torture, and corruption. Shortages of financial and human resources and the presidential appointment of the IGG undermines the independence and effectiveness of the office.

Uganda is a signatory to several international treaties on the protection of human rights. These include the Convention on the Elimination of All Forms of Discrimination against Women (CEDAW), the African Charter on Human and People's Rights, the United Nations Convention against Torture and Other Cruel, Inhuman or Degrading Treatment or Punishment, and the International Covenant on Economic, Social and Cultural Rights.

STAFFING

The JSC advises the president on appointments, exercises disciplinary measures, disseminates information to judicial officers and the public, and issues proposals for reforms. Membership includes two Supreme Court judges, one person nominated by the Public Service Commission, two advocates nominated by the Uganda Law Society, and two lay members of the public nominated by the president. The president appoints all members with the approval of Parliament. The attorney general is an ex officio member. Members serve a four-year term renewable once.

The president, with the advice of the JSC and the approval of Parliament, appoints the chief justice, the deputy chief justice, the principal judge, and justices of the Supreme Court, the Court of Appeal, and the High Court. They serve at his pleasure. Requirements range from a minimum of ten years as an advocate in a court of unlimited jurisdiction for High Court justices, to a minimum of twenty years for the chief justice. The JSC or the cabinet may recommend removal to the president, who appoints a tribunal. In the case of the chief, deputy chief, and principal justices, the tribunal comprises justices of the Supreme Court or courts of similar jurisdiction or advocates of twenty years' experience. Reasons for removal include the inability to perform official functions, misbehavior, or incompetence. The JSC oversees the recruitment of magistrates.

Court clerks are civil servants in the employment of the Public Service Commission. They receive no specialized training and can be transferred to nonjudicial postings at any time. Their salaries do not provide a living wage, leaving clerks vulnerable to corrupt practices.

The Law Development Center (LDC) serves the legal community. It offers a one-year course to law degree holders from Makerere Law Faculty, the sole law school in Uganda, in the practical skills needed to practice law. Courses are oriented toward admission to the bar, with one term spent in a clerkship. It provides training to new magistrates and has facilitated the circulation of statutes to the legal community.

Professional societies include the Uganda Law Society (ULS) with 510 members, FIDA with approximately 200 members, the National Association of Women Judges, and the Uganda Magistrates' Association. Membership in the ULS is required for advocates in private practice. The Uganda Magistrates' Association, formed in 1970, was rejuvenated in the mid-1990s.

IMPACT OF LAW

Uganda's political leaders have contributed to the public's skepticism toward the impartiality and effectiveness of the police, judiciary, and other sectors of the legal system. Milton Obote oppressed his political opposition in the 1960s with sedition charges and illegal detentions; when the courts refused to convict, the police rearrested suspects as they left the court. The low point in Uganda's legal history occurred in 1972, when Idi Amin's security agents kidnapped Benjamin Kiwanuka, the first Ugandan chief justice, from his chambers and later murdered him. When inflation eroded salaries in the 1970s to almost nothing, corruption pervaded the judiciary. This reputation has been difficult to shake.

The Museveni administration has had a contradictory effect on the law. Spurred on by donors, the government has increased the number of magistrates and judges, raised their pay scales to living wages, and instituted training programs in mediation and court administration. Donor funding has assisted with the distribution of key legislation and the constitution to magistrates, and the rebuilding of dilapidated courthouses. Even so, the government's commitment to judicial improvements is weak.

Two negative aspects merit mention. First, the slow progress of the Law Reform Commission (LRC) and Parliament to bring the laws of Uganda into conformity with the 1995 Constitution weakens the latter. The stalled Domestic Relations Bill is a good example. The LRC took several years to gather information on customary practices on marriage, divorce, and property. They released a draft version in 1997, but after the Muslim community protested the limits on polygamous marriage, Parliament shelved the bill indefinitely. Courts currently rely on outdated and discriminatory laws.

Second, Museveni undermines confidence in the law by criticizing both actors and processes. He paints a picture of rampant corruption and charges the legal process with being slow, expensive, inaccessible, and culturally inappropriate to Africa. He criticizes principles of law that provide due process protections as remnants of Uganda's colonial past, including the presumption of innocence, the right to remain silent, the right to bail, and the right to appeal (Busuttil et al. 1991, 656).

The lack of reform, training, and funding for the criminal justice system makes it one of the weakest points in the legal process. Low salaries, especially to the police force, contribute to corrupt practices and low morale. A Commission of Inquiry in the mid-1990s found prisoners waiting several years before obtaining a trial. Inadequate coordination between the Criminal Investigation Department, the state attorneys, and the courts results in lost cases. The police have few resources with which to carry out investigations, resulting in lengthy delays. They lack vehicles, forensic expertise, and other technical support. In capital cases, the state must assign and pay for legal defense; when funding runs out, trials are postponed until the next session.

Lynn Khadiagala

See also Alternative Dispute Resolution; Common Law; Customary Law; Lay Judiciaries; Legal Aid; Legal Pluralism; Magistrates—Common Law Systems

References and further reading
Busuttil, James S., Robin L. Dahlberg, Sheldon J. Oliensis, and Sidney S. Rosdeitcher. 1991. "Uganda at the Crossroads: Current Human Rights Conditions, A Report of the Committee on International Human Rights." *Record of the Association of the Bar of the City of New York* 46, no. 6: 598–673.
Hansen, Holger Bernt, and Michael Twaddle, eds. 1998. *Developing Uganda.* Oxford: James Currey.
Khadiagala, Lynn. 1999. "Law, Power, and Justice: The Adjudication of Women's Property Rights in Uganda." Ph.D. diss., University of Wisconsin.
Mamdani, Mahmood, and Joe Oloka-Onyango, eds. 1994. *Uganda: Studies in Living Conditions, Popular Movements and Constitutionalism.* Vienna: Austrian Journal of Development Studies Book Series; Kampala: Center for Basic Research.
Ministry of Justice and Constitutional Affairs. n.d. "Final Report of the *Commission of Inquiry on Judicial Reform.*" Kampala.
Mugaju, Justus, and Joe Oloka-Onyango, eds. 2000. *No-Party Democracy in Uganda: Myths and Realities.* Kampala: Fountain Publishers.
Okumu-Wengi, Jennifer. 1997. *Weeding the Millet Field: Women's Law and Grassroots Justice in Uganda.* Kampala: Uganda Law Watch Center.
Tamale, Sylvia. 1999. *When Hens Begin to Crow: Gender and Parliamentary Politics in Uganda.* Boulder, CO: Westview Press.

UKRAINE

GENERAL INFORMATION

Ukraine is a republic in Eastern Europe that consists of a vast plain bounded by the Carpathian Mountains in the west and by the Black Sea and Sea of Azov in the south. It has a total area of 603,700 square kilometers, slightly smaller than the state of Texas and about the size of France. Ukraine shares borders with Belarus, Hungary, Moldova, Poland, Romania, Russia, and Slovakia, and has 2,782 kilometers of coastline. The terrain consists mostly of fertile plains and plateaus with the Carpathian mountain range in the west and the Crimean Mountains in the extreme south. The climate is mostly temperate continental, with the southern Crimean coast hosting a more moderate climate. The western and northern portions of the country receive disproportionately high precipitation compared with the eastern and southeastern parts. Ukraine's capital is the city of Kiev.

Due largely to a stagnant economy, Ukraine's population experienced a negative annual growth rate of –0.6 percent between 1996 and 2000, having a population of 50.3 million in 2000. Except for a large Russian minority located primarily in the eastern portion and Crimea, the population is quite homogenous. Some 73 percent of the population are ethnic Ukrainian, 22 percent are Russian, and 5 percent are of other ethnicities.

Ukraine boasts a literacy rate of 98 percent. About 70 percent of the adult population possess a secondary education or higher. Although it had one of the best educational systems in the former Soviet Union, today it remains virtually owned and run by the government; it is underfunded and has a shortage of teachers, particularly in subjects that have changed since the fall of communism: economics, law, business, political science, and international relations.

Ukraine has several of the components of a major European economy: rich farmlands, a well-developed industrial base, highly trained labor, and a good educational system. However, at present the economy is in poor condition. The standard of living for most citizens has dropped more than 50 percent since independence, and years of declining GDP have led to widespread poverty. Ukraine's currency, however, the *hryvnia,* was introduced in September 1996 and has remained fairly stable, and the country experienced substantial growth in 2000.

Exports are diversified and include metals, chemicals, sugar, and semifinished goods. The annual per capita gross domestic product for 2000 was approximately $630. However, millions of employees go months without being paid, and most individuals derive a significant proportion of their income from the shadow economy. Ukraine is making a difficult transition from a centrally planned to a market-based economy. The private sector has continued to grow and now represents a substantial portion of the economy. Nevertheless, the country remains in a serious economic crisis, due to the absence of the critical level of reform needed to generate sustained economic growth. Industrial output has suffered years of sharp decline. Reform, particularly in the agricultural sector, has stagnated; however, at year's end the president signed a far-reaching decree on agricultural reform.

Ukraine's heavy industry was built on cheap oil and

gas, primarily from Russia and Turkmenistan. When Russia liberalized energy prices in the early 1990s to bring them more in line with Western prices, Ukraine's exceedingly energy inefficient industry incurred huge debts. Russia's patience with gas payment arrears may have been motivated in part by its ability to exploit its near-monopoly in supplying gas by forcing Ukraine to accept far higher gas prices than those paid by its west European customers. Although Russia lowered its prices with Ukraine in 1998, they remain substantially above world prices, a cost that Ukraine is ill equipped to afford.

Since independence Ukraine has seen deterioration in the population's health because of the substantial drop in health spending and the social dislocation related to the economic collapse. Although Ukraine has a high number of hospitals—more than twenty-seven hundred—underfunding has precipitated a drastic fall in the availability of health care. Doctors commonly supplement their salaries by charging for operations and maternity care, and drugs are often available only through private sources. To solve the funding crisis, the United Nations has recommended that the government introduce mandatory health insur-

ance. But with the pace of reform so slow, restructuring the health-care sector won't occur anytime soon.

HISTORY

Political History

Ukraine, literally translated, means "on the edge" or "borderland," and for most of its history it was a frontier region changing hands between neighboring powers. During the first millennium B.C.E., Cimmerians, Scythians, Sarmatians, and Goths were among the first identifiable groups to populate the area now known as Ukraine. In the sixth century, Slavic tribes inhabited central and eastern Ukraine. Those tribes helped found Kiev on these lucrative trade routes, and it became the capital of the powerful state of Kievan Rus, which, during the eleventh century, was geographically the largest state in Europe. But in the twelfth century, conflict between feudal lords led to the state's decline, and Mongol marauders sacked Kiev.

With the arrival of a Mongol army under a grandson of Genghis Khan in 1240, Ukraine suffered the first of a series of invasions that were to last for seven hundred years. In 1362 the Mongols were driven out by the Grand Duchy of Lithuania, which in 1569 merged with the kingdom of Poland to form the Polish-Lithuanian Commonwealth. It was during this time that Ukrainian peasants who had fled the Polish effort to force them into servitude came to be known as Cossacks and earned a reputation for their fierce martial spirit. Defying their Polish masters, the Cossacks gathered under warlike leaders called *hetmans* in the vastness of the steppe. After a revolt led by Bohdan Khmelnytsky, the Cossacks formed their own state in 1649. But in 1654—still fighting the Poles—they entered a pact with Russia, which soon exerted control. The last vestiges of Ukrainian autonomy were lost to the Russian empress, Catherine II, in 1781. Two years later she annexed Crimea, previously an Ottoman protectorate. In 1795, under pressure from more Cossack rebellions and Russian expansionism, the Polish Commonwealth collapsed, leaving western Ukraine under the control of the Austro-Hungarian Empire.

Modern Ukraine's national movement emerged in the nineteenth century. In Russian-ruled eastern Ukraine, it centered on use of the Ukrainian language, developed as a literary medium by the poet Taras Shevchenko, and banned by the Russians. In the Hapsburg-ruled West, Ukrainians were free to form their own cultural and political institutions in competition with the Poles. The movement came to a head in the chaotic aftermath of the Russian Revolution.

Between the two world wars, the territory of present-day Ukraine was split between the Soviet Union in the east and Poland, Romania, and Czechoslovakia in the west. Ukrainian nationalism persevered, and on the Polish side of the border, moderate Ukrainian parties increasingly lost ground to the Organization of Ukrainian Nationalists (OUN), a terrorist group that assassinated government officials, provoking violent reprisals. The Soviet reaction was severe, particularly under Stalin, who imposed terror campaigns that ravaged the intellectual class. He also created artificial famines as part of his forced collectivization policies, which killed millions. Estimates of the number of deaths from the 1932–1933 famine alone range from 3 to 7 million.

A new wave of terror swept Ukraine with the German invasion of 1941. While the vast majority of Ukrainians joined the Soviet Army, in the west the OUN and other nationalist groups initially supported the Nazis. But when Germany's unwillingness to back Ukrainian statehood became clear, the nationalists formed an independent partisan army, the remnants of which survived into the 1950s. During the German occupation Ukraine lost one in six of its population, nearly half of them Jews. With the Soviet Union's takeover of western Ukraine in 1945, and the transfer of Crimea to the republic in 1954, Ukraine attained its present-day borders.

Prior to 1991, Ukraine was the westernmost part of the Soviet Union and was essentially controlled from Moscow. The Russians employed central planning to manage the vast agricultural and industrial resources of the region. Although central planners were typically shortsighted, they could rely on local governors for enforcement of Soviet policy.

Ukraine declared its independence on August 24, 1991, as the Soviet Empire entered its final stages of disintegration. A local counterpart to the Soviet perestroika movement, known in Ukraine as *rukh,* emerged as a dominant revolutionary force by 1988, and since then, through the years of independence, members of this group have controlled the parliament and the executive authority.

Ethnic tensions in Crimea during 1992 prompted a number of pro-Russian political organizations to advocate secession of Crimea and annexation to Russia. In July 1992, the Crimean and Ukrainian parliaments determined that Crimea would remain under Ukrainian jurisdiction while retaining significant cultural and economic autonomy.

Leonid Kravchuk, the first president of independent Ukraine, focused on state- and nation-building, largely ignoring political and economic reform. His successor and the current president, Leonid Kuchma, launched an IMF-backed reform program following his election in 1994. However, tension between the president and the Verkhovna Rada have greatly hampered reform.

History of the Modern Legal System

The Ukrainian legal system is greatly influenced by the Russian legal tradition. Ukraine follows a civil law model of the Germanic legal family and retains certain characteristics from Soviet jurisprudence. The civil law tradition is particularly reflected in the many codes of law, legal education, and judicial formation and jurisprudence. Soviet influences are reflected in the government bureaucracy, government ownership of large industries, resistance to land reform, and institutions such as the procuracy. Since 1991, the country has embarked on a journey into democracy, which, not surprisingly, has been slow and difficult.

During Soviet rule, Communist Party officials considered the judiciary an arm of the state, and the courts often served as administrative appendages to their decisions. The populace understood this and developed a deep mistrust and lack of respect for the judiciary. Judicial jobs were taken when other jobs were not available. The Ukrainian Supreme Soviet looked toward the establishment of an independent judiciary when it proclaimed Ukraine a sovereign republic on August 24, 1991. Parliament then established a Constitutional Commission to draft a new constitution for the republic. The Constitutional Commission sought to divide the state powers into three separate branches: legislative, executive, and judicial. Yet several years after claiming independence, a completely independent judiciary does not exist.

Since declaring independence, the parliament has promulgated numerous laws in an effort to establish an independent judicial branch. The present constitution and more than twenty statutes guarantee judicial independence and autonomy. Parliament has passed legislative acts concerning the status of judges, constitutional courts, commissions of judges, advocatura, and notaries. The 1992 Law on the Status of Judges sets forth the structure of the Ukrainian judicial system, but much of the law has not yet been implemented. This law endeavors to further judicial independence by establishing procedures for the election of judges, as well as rules concerning their dismissal and suspension of judicial powers. It also establishes legal guidelines for the administration of justice and prohibits interference in this process, ensures the confidentiality of deliberations of judicial decisions, institutes penalties for contempt of court, and protects the immunity of judges. The present restructuring makes the precise status of the Ukrainian judicial system less than clear.

LEGAL CONCEPTS

The Ukrainian legal system is a combination of the continental legal system and socialist law. When the Ukrainian Supreme Council proclaimed Ukraine a sovereign republic on August 24, 1991, it envisioned adopting a new constitution in a timely fashion and forming a Western-looking democracy. It did not adopt a new constitution for nearly five years, reflecting the political tensions in the country, and its democracy remains in its fledgling stage. The new 1996 Constitution established three separate branches of government. A directly elected president heads Ukraine's executive branch and serves as chief of state. Incumbent president Leonid Kuchma was reelected after two rounds of voting in October and November 1994. A prime minister, Viktor Yushchenko, serves as head of government.

Ukraine's legislature consists of a unicameral parliament, known as the Supreme Soviet or Verkhovna Rada. The Verkhovna Rada's 450 members are elected in part according to proportional representation and partially by direct constituency mandate. While there were some irregularities during the election campaign and during the balloting, almost all observers agreed that the election results reflected the will of the electorate. Despite numerous flaws and irregularities, previous national elections in 1998 and 1994 generally had reflected the will of the electorate. The president appoints the cabinet and controls government operations.

In Ukraine the judicial branch has developed more slowly than the executive and legislative branches, partic-

ularly at the lower court levels. The primary reason for this delay has been a shortage of resources. Without the Ministry of Justice supplying the necessary resources, the judiciary is unable to operate effectively.

The Security Service of the Ukraine (SBU), the Ministry of Internal Affairs (which controls the various police forces), and the Ministry of Defense all have equal responsibility for internal security and report to the president through the cabinet. The National Bureau of Investigations, established by presidential decree in 1997 but never fully funded, was abolished in a government reorganization in December. The armed forces have largely remained outside of politics. While civilian authorities generally maintain effective control of the security forces, institutional government corruption sometimes can lead to their improper use. The SBU and other government agencies have interfered indirectly in the political process through criminal investigations of politicians, journalists, and influential businessmen. Members of the security forces have committed human rights abuses.

Ukraine's human rights record in recent years has been mixed. Although there has been limited progress in some areas, serious problems persist. According to the U.S. State Department, members of the military killed soldiers during violent hazing incidents, and there have been some reports of possibly politically motivated killings. Police and prison officials regularly beat detainees and prisoners, and there were numerous instances of torture, sometimes resulting in death. The beating of conscripts in the army by fellow soldiers was common and sometimes resulted in death. Prison conditions are harsh and life threatening. There were instances of arbitrary arrest and detention. Lengthy pretrial detention in very poor conditions was common, and detainees often spent months in pretrial detention for violations that involved little or no prison time if convicted. Long delays in trials are a problem. The government rarely punishes officials who commit abuses. The SBU, police, and prosecutor's office have drawn domestic and international criticism for their failure to take adequate action to curb institutional corruption and abuse in the government. Many high-profile corruption cases have been dropped, ostensibly because of lack of incriminating evidence. Anticorruption legislation has been enforced selectively, mostly against government opponents and low-level officials. Political interference and corruption affect the judicial process. The judiciary is overburdened, inefficient, and lacks sufficient funding and staff. These factors undermine citizens' right to a fair trial. The criminal justice system has been slow to reform because of lack of government effort and strained economic resources. The state has continued to intrude in citizens' lives and infringe on their privacy. The government partially limited and increasingly interfered with freedom of the press during 1999, most notably during the period leading up to the October presidential elections.

CONSTITUTION

The Ukrainian Constitution was adopted at the fifth session of the Verkhovna Rada on June 28, 1996. The document contains 161 articles divided between fourteen chapters, and a fifteenth chapter containing fourteen transitional provisions. The Verkhovna Rada adopted this Fundamental Law of Ukraine on behalf of the citizens of Ukraine of all nationalities to, inter alia, provide for human rights and freedoms, and to develop and strengthen a democratic, social, and law-based state. The first chapter lays out general principles for the democratic, law-based republic, which include recognizing three branches of government, the territorial sovereignty of the country, local self-government, Ukrainian as the national language, and consequences of the Chernobyl disaster.

The second chapter specifies the fundamental human and citizens' rights guaranteed under the constitution. Equality under the law is guaranteed, and discrimination based on race; color; political, religious, and other beliefs; sex; ethnic and social origin; property status; place of residence; and language are prohibited. Every person has the right to life, dignity, freedom, and personal inviolability. The right of privacy is guaranteed for mail, telephone, telegraph, and other correspondence. The constitution limits the collection, storage, use, and dissemination of confidential information about a person without that person's consent, and, where it is allowed, grants citizens the right to examine and rectify incorrect information. Everyone is guaranteed freedom of movement, expression, religion and personal philosophy, and association, including the right to take part in trade unions. Citizens have the right to elect and be elected to government positions and have access to the civil service. Everyone has the right to file individual or collective petitions; own, use, and dispose of property; and participate in entrepreneurial activity. Monopolies and unfair competition are prohibited.

The constitution guarantees certain economic rights, such as paid leave for pregnant women, safe and healthful work conditions, minimum wage, paid vacation, disability payments, unemployment insurance, health insurance, pension, legal assistance, and a standard of living that includes adequate nutrition, clothing, and housing. The constitution guarantees accessible and free preschool, secondary, vocational, and higher education, though higher education is on a competitive basis, so the right there is to compete for those openings.

Parents, under the constitution, are obligated to support their children until they reach the age of majority, and adult children are obligated to care for their parents who are incapable of work. Children born in and out of wedlock are equal before the law. The care of orphans is entrusted to the state.

Everyone has the right to a safe environment and access to information about the environment. Citizens are guaranteed protection of their intellectual property rights, and the government must protect, and take measures to return to Ukraine, cultural treasures of the nation. Everyone has the right to compensation for material and moral damages inflicted by unlawful decisions, acts, or omissions of state bodies.

A person is presumed innocent until proven guilty before a court of law, and the state must pay material and moral damages inflicted by a groundless conviction. Everyone is obligated to pay taxes as established by law and abide by the constitution and laws of Ukraine. Courts protect human and citizen rights, and everyone can appeal to the Authorized Human Rights Representative of the Verkhovna Rada and can appeal to the relevant international judicial institutions or organizations of which Ukraine is a member.

Chapter 3 covers elections and referendums, while chapter 4 creates the legislative branch, the Verkhovna Rada, which consists of 450 national deputies selected for four-year terms. Citizens of Ukraine who are twenty-one years of age, have the right to vote, and have resided in Ukraine for the past five years may be a national deputy. The powers of the Verkhovna Rada include introducing amendments to the constitution, designating referendums, adopting laws, approving the state budget, approving presidential appointments, and consenting to international treaties among other powers.

Chapter 5 creates the office of president to act as head of state. The president is elected for a five-year term through a direct popular vote. The powers of the president include conducting international relations for Ukraine; appointing the prime minister, members of the cabinet, one-third of the constitutional court, and the heads of the military and federal agencies; signing or vetoing laws; and issuing decrees. The remaining chapters address the powers of the cabinet of ministers, the procuracy, the courts, the autonomous Republic of Crimea, local governments, and the constitutional court.

CURRENT COURT SYSTEM STRUCTURE

Since independence, the Verkhovna Rada has promulgated numerous laws directly or indirectly addressing the judiciary. The new constitution maintained this priority in Transitional Provision Twelve, which granted the Supreme Court and High Arbitration Court authority to operate until legislation forming courts of general jurisdiction was passed within a mandated five years. This five-year transitional period ended on June 28, 2001, with the Verkhovna Rada's adopting a flurry of new legislation not only relating to the courts but also in the areas of civil and criminal procedure. Following heated debates and lobbying by Westerners urging the parliament to avoid a constitutional crisis, ten laws addressing the judicial system were adopted on June 27.

Ukraine's jurisprudence system is organized into three major court systems: the Constitutional Court; the courts of general jurisdiction, at the top of which stands the Supreme Court; and the Arbitration Courts, at the top of which stands the High Court of Arbitration.

Chapter 12 of Ukraine's constitution creates the Constitutional Court of Ukraine, and the Law on the Constitutional Court, which the Verkhovna Rada adopted on October 16, 1996, sets forth the functions and procedures of the court. The court is similar to the constitutional courts of western Europe in that it is a separate body from the courts of general jurisdiction and is the sole and final judicial interpreter of the constitution. Constitutional questions are therefore not heard by other courts but referred to the constitutional court. The political nature of this judicial body is recognized in how the judges are selected—six by the president of Ukraine, six by the Verkhovna, and six by the Congress of Judges—and by the fact that it is described in a different chapter of the constitution than the court system, and also by its subject matter jurisdiction.

The Constitutional Court is responsible for guaranteeing the supremacy of the constitution, and to that end it is charged with the official interpretation of the constitution, the constitutionality of the laws and acts of the Verkhovna Rada of Ukraine and of the autonomous Republic of Crimea, and the acts of the president and cabinet of ministers of Ukraine. The court also has authority to decide constitutional questions regarding international treaties and rules of procedure in presidential impeachment proceedings. The court specifically does not have jurisdiction over the legality of acts of state bodies (other than constitutional claims), the legality of acts of state bodies in Crimea or local self-government, or issues under the authority of the courts of general jurisdiction.

The following persons may initiate proceedings before the Constitutional Court: the president of Ukraine, the Supreme Court of Ukraine, a minimum of forty-five deputies of the Verkhovna, the representative on human rights of the Verkhovna Rada, the Verkhovna Rada of the Autonomous Republic of Crimea, and individuals if it involves constitutionally guaranteed rights and freedoms. The court may decline review if the petitioner does not have standing or if the court lacks subject matter jurisdiction. Decisions of the Constitutional Court are published, and the judges are appointed for a nine-year nonrenewable term.

The Constitutional Court has shown independence as it has implemented the rule of law. In the Ustymenko case (1997), the court found that the constitution guarantees citizens the right to obtain information about themselves, and to prevent unlawful retention and dissemination of that information. During the same year, the court upheld the constitution's prohibition on national deputies holding two government positions simultaneously.

In 1999 the court declared the death penalty unconstitutional and told parliament to strike it from the criminal code, as well as to pass laws to ban the practice. The court found that the absence of a constitutional provision allowing capital punishment means that there is no exception to Article 27 of the constitution, which grants the inalienable right of each human being to life. The court also relied on Article 28, which prohibits torture, and cruel or inhuman punishment.

In 2000 the Constitutional Court rejected as unconstitutional two of the six questions proposed for the April 16 national referendum, and decided that the results would be binding, not consultative in character. The case came to the court after deputies challenged the president's January 14 decree that ordered the national referendum. The court held that the first question, whether the public supports a vote of no confidence in the Verkhovna Rada, is not subject to a national referendum under the constitution. The court decided that the sixth question, regarding the right of the people to approve a constitution through a national referendum, was also unconstitutional, because it circumvents the constitution's process for amendment. On April 16 the public gave overwhelming support to the four remaining referendum proposals of creating a bicameral parliament, reducing the number of deputies in the Verkhovna Rada from 450 to 300, granting the president authority to dismiss the Verkhovna Rada if it could not develop a parliamentary majority within three months or approve a national budget within a month, and limiting lawmakers' immunity from prosecution.

The courts of general jurisdiction include municipal courts, Rayon Courts (People's Courts), Inter-Rayon Courts, oblast courts, military courts, the Supreme Court, and specialized courts, meaning Arbitration Courts that handle contractual and commercial law matters. Present restructuring makes the precise status of the Ukrainian judicial system less than clear.

The Supreme Court is the highest judicial body in the system of general courts. It has appellate jurisdiction over cases tried by lower courts but may also function as a court of first instance under specific rules. If new evidence becomes available in a case, the Supreme Court conducts a de novo review. The court has jurisdiction to adjudicate election claims when a petitioner challenges a decision of the Central Election Commission.

Ukrainian trial judges tend to be much younger than their U.S. counterparts, which reflects, in part, the civil law tradition that starts training judges during law school. They are eligible for appointment from the age of twenty-five, following a law degree and three years of work experience in the legal profession. Current practices that undermine the impartiality of judges include: judges assisting plaintiffs in gathering evidence for their case; chief judges interfering with or reviewing their colleagues' judicial decisions; and government officials and politicians exerting pressure on judges.

Although the constitution mandates an independent judiciary, Ukrainian officials face an enormous challenge to reform and create one. The courts are funded through the Ministry of Justice, arguably a constraint on independence. The local courts are woefully underfunded and face low public opinion. According to the U.S. Department of State, Ukrainian courts are subject to political interference and corruption, and are inefficient.

SPECIALIZED JUDICIAL BODIES
Although Ukraine's constitution abolished the largest network of specialized courts, the Arbitration Courts, some specialized courts remain. Like their counterparts in the United States, they are administrative courts and courts of particular expertise, such as tax courts.

LEGAL PROFESSION
The Ukrainian Bar, like the bar in all of the countries of the former Soviet Union, is organized and governed by laws adopted by the Verkhovna Rada, or by decrees issued by the president of Ukraine. The government controls most aspects of its operation.

A subset of the Ukrainian Bar, the Union of Advocates of Ukraine, has slowly emerged from its communist-era thinking to increasingly resemble a bar association more typical of Western democracies. In 1997 it began working on a draft code of ethics for advocates in Ukraine that was widely analyzed and discussed both in Ukraine and outside the country. These discussions not only resulted in a draft code but also had the effect of building political support for the final draft.

In 1999, President Kuchma issued a decree authorizing the Qualification and Disciplinary Commission of the Ukrainian Bar to adopt this code of ethics, and later that year the commission adopted the code. The Union of Advocates then accepted the responsibility for training advocates about the new code.

Because of the slowness of the Ukrainian Bar and the Union of Advocates to train lawyers in the new laws of Ukraine, nongovernmental organizations (NGOs) filled some of this void. Kharkiv-based Justo Titulo, an NGO of legal professionals, trained more than four thousand legal professionals between 1996 and 2000, running continuing legal education (CLE) programs in the major cities of Ukraine. The Union of Advocates is beginning to recognize the importance of CLE programs and now of-

Legal Structure of Ukraine Courts

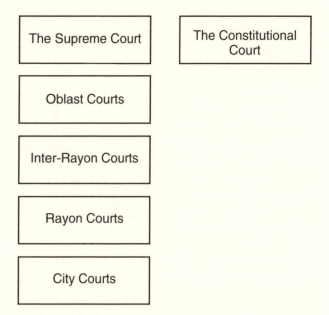

fers a program, "The Role of Lawyers in a Democratic Society," that focuses on the role of lawyers in promoting law reform and in implementing democratic principles in day-to-day life.

The Union of Advocates and legal educators in Ukraine, at the urging of the American Bar Association's Central and East European Law Initiative (CEELI), are beginning to recognize the importance of training in advocacy skills and increasing awareness of citizens to their rights in a democracy. Legal education in Ukraine has historically offered but minimal skills training. This absence from the law school curriculum was addressed in part through practicums in which students worked in the offices of various governmental agencies. However, students typically performed administrative tasks there and rarely received training in advocacy. Law schools are beginning to offer clinical legal education, to train students in the practical skills of lawyering. In 1996, Lviv State University created the first clinical legal education program in Ukraine when it began the Environmental Law Clinic with the Ecopravo-Lviv, a Ukrainian environmental NGO. The faculty of law and economics at the University of Internal Affairs, and the faculty of law at the National Academy of Law then created an environmental law clinic in Kharkiv in 1997 with Ecopravo-Kharkiv. The law faculties at Donetsk State University, Lviv Commercial Law Academy, Azov Regional Institute of Management, Taras Shevchenko National University, and Simferopol State University have now all created law clinics in which law students, under faculty supervision, provide pro bono legal assistance to clients.

The Union of Advocates has also started an Institute

of Advocacy to train lawyers in advocacy skills at both the trial and appellate levels. As citizens and corporations increasingly resort to courts to settle their disputes, advocacy skills are in demand. The institute offers practitioners and government lawyers a way to develop and hone these skills.

IMPACT OF LAW

Although slow to reform, the Verkhovna Rada did adopt a number of substantial reforms in 2001. Those reforms envision a greater role for the courts in the administration of justice and the protection of citizens' rights. For example, prior to the criminal procedure amendments, a warrant from the Procurator General's Office, the Militia, the Tax Police, or other law enforcement agencies was sufficient to search a home or arrest an individual in Ukraine. Now these acts can be performed only pursuant to a ruling of a court of law.

The Prosecutor General's Office, previously a virtual fourth branch of government wielding enormous powers to oversee the other branches, now is deprived of its universal right to oversee the observance of law in the country. Its role has been reduced to representing the state in court and ensuring the execution of laws. The new criminal code that came into effect on September 1, 2001, is in line with Western democratic principles.

Ukrainian efforts to overhaul the Soviet collective farm system have gone slowly, as those who stand to lose have effectively blocked serious land reform. On October 25, 2001, nearly all of the 113 communist members of the Verkhovna Rada stormed the podium and unfurled banners in the 450-member parliament in a protest aimed at stopping a land reform bill that would allow the state to sell its vast farmland holdings to private buyers. Ukraine, once a Soviet breadbasket but now suffering from low production, has 81.5 million acres of fertile farmland. Amid this chaos and vitriol, parliament still passed the new land code for the country that legitimized the privatization of the land covered by President Kuchma's executive order of December 1999. While Ukrainians will now have the right to own land, with all associated rights of investiture, the ability to sell and purchase parcels will be severely restricted until January 2005, when land becomes a full-fledged commodity. Even then, however, for a period of ten years, the purchase of land will be limited to one hundred hectares.

Ukrainian politicians, citizens, and international experts identify corruption as a major hindrance to the investment climate, as well as political and economic reform. Corruption also has hurt the effectiveness of efforts to combat organized crime, according to the U.S. State Department.

John C. Knechtle

See also Civil Law; Ottoman Empire; Soviet System
References and further reading
"Background Notes: Ukraine." U.S. Department of State. May 2000. www.state.gov/www/backround_notes/ukraine_0005bgn.html (accessed October 30, 2001).
Constitution of Ukraine. Adopted at the Fifth Session of the Verkhovna Rada of Ukraine on June 28, 1996. www.rada.kiev.ua/const/conengl.htm (accessed October 30, 2001).
"Freedom in the World 2000—Ukraine." Freedom House. www.freedomhouse.org/survey/2000/ (accessed September 15, 2001).
Futey, Bohdan A. "Comments on the Law on the Constitutional Court of Ukraine." *East European Constitutional Review* 6, nos. 2 and 3 (spring/summer 1997): 56–63.
"Nations in Transit 2000—Ukraine." Freedom House. www.freedomhouse.org/research/nitransit/2000/ukraine/ukraine.html (accessed September 15, 2001).
Solomon, Peter, Jr., and Todd Fogelsong. "The Two Faces of Crime in Post-Soviet Ukraine." *East European Constitutional Review* 9, no. 3 (summer 2000): 72–76.
Ukrainian Weekly. www.ukrweekly.com (accessed October 30, 2001).
Varfolomeyev, Oleg. "Another Year of Slow Transition." *Country Files: Ukraine, Transitions Online, 1999.* www.ijt.cz/coutries/uaarr99.html (accessed September 15, 2001).

UNITED ARAB EMIRATES

GENERAL INFORMATION

The United Arab Emirates (UAE) occupies the southeast corner of the Arabian Peninsula, lying between latitudes 22 and 28.5. It borders on the Arabian Gulf to the north and northwest, on Oman to the east, on Saudi Arabia to the west and southwest, and on Qatar to the northwest. UAE has a total area of 82,880 square kilometers, stretching from Abu Dhabi in the west to Fujeirah in the south. The country is largely desert, although there are mountains in north. The climate of UAE is hot and dry in desert regions, with frequent high humidity along the Gulf coast.

The UAE is a federal state, established in 1971 and made up of the emirates of Abu Dhabi, Dubai, Sharjah, Ras Al-Khaimah, Ajman, Fujeirah, and Umm Al-Qwwain.

Among the country's estimated 2.3 million people, only about 12 percent actually are UAE citizens. The remaining 88 percent are foreigners, consisting of ethnic Arabs from other Arab countries as well as non-Arabs. The religion of most citizens is Sunni Muslim. About 60 percent of the foreign population are Sunni Muslims, 20 percent Shia Muslims, and 20 percent Hindus, Christians, and others. The population of the UAE is overwhelmingly urban, with more than 90 percent of the people living in cities. The largest city, Abu Dhabi, the

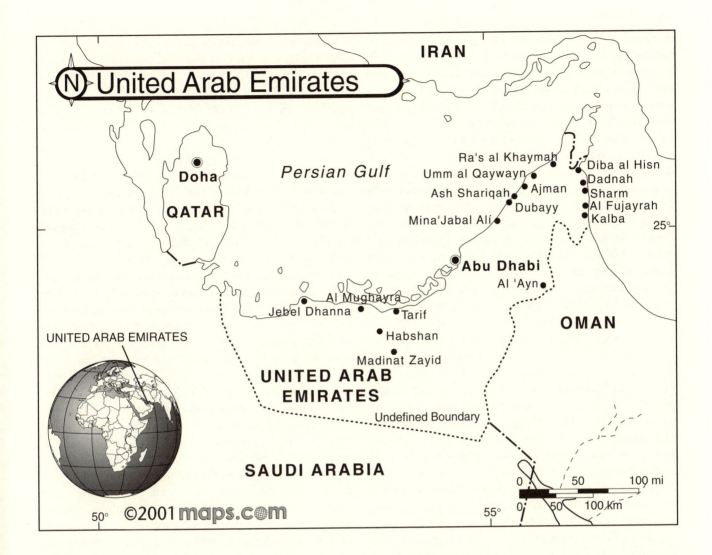

capital, has an estimated population of 500,000. The official language of the country is Arabic.

The UAE's oil resources make it one of the wealthiest countries in the world. Taking into account the small population and a Gross Domestic Product of about $41.5 billion, the population below the poverty line becomes nil. The birth rate is 18 per 1000 population, and the death rate 3.68, making the population growth rate 1.61 percent.

HISTORY

In the past, the Arabian Peninsula was not divided into several political states as is the case today. Oman occupied one of the territories in the Arabian Peninsula, which comprised Yemen, Hajaz, Hadramut, Aseer, Najed, and Al-Ehs'a. Until the eighteenth century, Oman extended from the south of the state of Qatar to the Indian Ocean and contained the Sultanate of Oman and the United Arab Emirates.

The first Arabs to settle in Oman were the Azide tribe, a subdivision of the Qahtani half of Arab genealogy, which emigrated from Yemen in the second century C.E.

and dominated the area. Subsequent Arab migration brought in people from the northern Arabian Peninsula to settle. Those people were of Adnani extraction; they represented the second of the two branches of Arab genealogy. The current native inhabitants of the area originate mainly from those two tribes.

After the emergence of the Islamic religion in the Arabian Peninsula, in the sixth century C.E., and during the Prophet Mohammed's life, the Omanis, like most Arabs, converted to Islam. Since that time the Islamic religion has become one of the two most significant factors influencing the development of the area's political and social spheres. The second significant factor that played an important role in shaping the area has been the tribal system. Although these two factors are incompatible in theory, they nonetheless interacted in the sequence of events that make up the region's history.

No sooner had Vasco De Gama discovered the route to India than Portugal realized the significance of the Gulf region, since it controlled trade routes to the Far East. In the early years of the sixteenth century, Portugal had sent armed forces to set up military forts, crushing occasional rebellions by the inhabitants in the process. The Portuguese dominated the region for the next century.

At the beginning of the seventeenth century, a combination of several factors led to a weakening of Portuguese control in the region. One of these factors was the arrival of the British after the establishment of the East India Company on December 31, 1600. They confronted the Portuguese and finally succeeded in driving them out of the region and dominating it.

By the early nineteenth century, the Arab tribes of the Omani Coast had reorganized themselves. A major force among them were the Qawasim, a maritime people who lived in Ras al-Khaimah and Sharjah emirates. The other major tribal force was the Bani Yas federation, which spread its influence in the lower Gulf and dominated the area stretching between present day Dubai and Abu Dhabi.

At the beginning of the nineteenth century, conflict arose between these two tribes and the British, who soon deployed their navy. After long and bloody clashes, Britain succeeded in forcing the Sheikhs of the emirates to accede to a maritime treaty called the General Treaty of Peace (1821); this treaty was followed by other treaties. In 1853 the British signed a maritime truce with the rulers of the emirates, and since that day they have come to be known as the Trucial Emirates.

In 1892 the British political resident in the Gulf signed another treaty with the emirates' rulers. According to this treaty, Britain handled the external affairs of the emirates and left the rulers to deal with domestic matters. As a result, the emirates lost their independence and were put under British protection.

Immediately after Britain declared its intention in 1968 of withdrawing from the area by the end of 1971, the ruler of Abu Dhabi Emirate made his historical announcement that Abu Dhabi was prepared to make a federation with any of the Gulf's emirates. The rulers of Dubai, Sharjah, Ajman, Fujeirah, and Umm Al-Qawain emirates accepted the initiative, and a constitution for the federation was drafted. On December 2, 1971, the constitution was promulgated; the UAE was officially established and became an independent federal state after the withdrawal of Britain. On November 10, 1972, Ras Al Khaimah Emirate also joined the federation. The UAE joined the Arab League in December 1971, and the United Nations in 1972.

Prior to the formation of the UAE in 1971, the emirates' legal and judicial systems went through two stages of development. The first stage lasted for a long time and ended in the late 1960s. The available literature shows that the tribal system was the predominant factor shaping the political and social life of the emirates, both before and after the establishment of the emirates as political entities in the late eighteenth and early nineteenth centuries.

Despite British domination of the region in the early nineteenth century, each emirate was nonetheless an independent state with its own independent judicial authority. These emirates were, and still are, governed by sheikhs who have usually been selected by the accord and acceptance of their family elders. Rulership, in general, is passed from father to son upon the death or the resignation of the father.

During this stage, the administrative system of the emirates was so rudimentary as virtually to be nonexistent. The emirates had no law courts or judges (except for the traditional court, or *mahkamah*), no civil service, no military force apart from the rulers' guards, and no police. Until 1950, then, the legal system was completely fashioned by traditional and tribal values.

Prior to the existence of law courts in the emirates, disputes arising among tribesmen were referred to the sheikhs of the tribe, the emirate's ruler, or to local judges, *qudah*. The judge, or *qudi,* in the towns of the emirates was not formally trained but was a learned man, or *mutawwa,* with general education and some understanding of the Holy Qur'an. Merchant and pearling communities had their own customary courts, which resolved the disputes between members of these communities.

This judicial system for settling disputes remained in effect until significant developments took place in the mid-1940s. These developments were brought about by the inflow of aliens to the emirates and the increasing connections with other countries. For example, legal rules were needed to govern the operation of British aircraft and their passengers and crew, British oil companies, merchants, and civil officials. This made it necessary for the British government to consider concluding an agreement with the emirates' rulers whereby jurisdiction over British subjects as well as foreigners would be formally ceded to Britain. As a result, in July 1945 the British political resident in Bahrain, considered the highest British authority in the area, signed an agreement with the rulers of the emirates by which they ceded to the British government jurisdiction over British subjects and all foreigners.

British jurisdiction, which diminished from 1960 onward, was ended formally in 1971 with the emergence of the UAE. Thus the UAE acquired jurisdiction over all people (nationals and foreigners) and institutions. With the British withdrawal from the area and the foundation of the UAE in 1971, local and federal authorities modeled new laws on those of Egyptian, Sudanese, and other Arabic countries, as well as on Islamic *sharia,* rather than on the British legal system.

The second stage of the development of the emirates' legal and judicial systems extended between the years of 1966 and 1971, and this stage witnessed the radical transformation of the traditional system into a modern one. This transformation resulted from the discovery of large quantities of oil in Abu Dhabi and Dubai, which boosted the economy dramatically and caused remarkable changes in the social and political life of the emirates.

After the announcement by the British government in January 1968 that its forces would withdraw completely from the Gulf by the end of 1971, the establishment and modernization of government was accelerated in all the Trucial Emirates. The rulers of the emirates were conscious of the necessity to establish new government departments to deal with matters that until then had been handled by the British, including new courts to replace the outgoing British courts, and new laws to fill the legislative vacuum in the emirates. This involved modernizing the legal system and legal institutions of individual emirates. In implementing the task of modernization, the emirates' governments prepared new legislation in the form of statutes and codes—forms of law until then unknown to the people of the emirates.

This legislation can be classified into two major groups: Abu Dhabi legislation as applied in Abu Dhabi Emirate, and Dubai legislation as applied in Dubai Emirate and other northern emirates, albeit with some modifications. The core of this legislation dealt with the establishment, organization, and administration of the judiciary.

LEGAL CONCEPTS

The UAE is a federal state, consisting of seven emirates or states. Its constitution, which is considered the state's supreme law, by implication, provides for two types of government: local governments and the central federal government. The organization and administration of the local governments was left to be dealt with at the local level by local written laws or by tribal customary laws.

The central federal government, however, is comprehensively covered by the state constitution. According to the provisions of the constitution, the government is based on the Western approach of separation of powers, in that state power is theoretically separated into three distinct authorities: executive, legislative, and judicial.

The executive authority of the UAE is composed of three branches: the Supreme Council, the presidency, and the ministers' cabinet. The Supreme Council consists of the rulers of the federation's seven emirates and is the highest authority in the state. Each ruler is entitled to one vote in Supreme Council debate.

The Supreme Council is responsible for the following matters: formation of state policies; approval of federal laws; approval of the union's annual budget; approval of international agreements and treaties; appointing the prime minister; appointing the federal Supreme Court president and judges; and accepting the resignations of such officials.

In addition to the Supreme Council, there is the executive authority, of which the president and vice president are members; they serve for five years and thereafter are eligible for reappointment. The president and vice president must be members of the Supreme Council, which elected them. In using their executive powers, they are assisted by a council of ministers made up of the prime minister, his deputies, and his ministers. Since the establishment of the UAE, the key positions in the federal government have consistently been acquired by Abu Dhabi and Dubai emirates, the presidency being held by the ruler of Abu Dhabi and the office of vice president, prime minister, and one of his deputies by Dubai Emirate.

According to the UAE Constitution, a certain degree of legislative authority is vested in the federal National Assembly. The members of the federal National Assembly are appointed by the rulers of the emirates for two-year terms. The powers of the Assembly are restricted to discussion and approval of the union's budget and of draft federal legislation presented by cabinet ministers.

The enactment of federal legislation involves the Council of Ministers, the federal National Assembly, and the federal Supreme Council. The process is as follows: the Council of Ministers drafts federal legislation, which is then passed to the National Assembly, which discusses the drafts, makes amendments, and gives its approval or disapproval. The drafts thereafter are submitted to the federal Supreme Council and the president of the union. However, the president of the union and the Supreme Council are not obliged to accept the modifications made by the National Assembly, because, according to the constitution, the president and the Supreme Council have the authority to issue federal laws without regard to the National Assembly's recommendations.

In order to facilitate the integration of the emirates, not only in legal terms but also in political and social terms, and to foster the establishment of national identity, the constitution provides for the rapid promulgation of federal laws and the replacement of local laws.

For the purpose of unifying the emirates' legal systems, sole jurisdiction for promulgating laws in the principal legal areas was, under Articles 120 and 121 of the UAE Constitution, conferred on the federal legislature. The legislature, for example, is given exclusive legislative jurisdiction in matters related to labor relations and social security; real estate and expropriation in the public interest; extradition of criminals; banks; insurance of all kinds; protection of agricultural and animal wealth; major legislation relating to penal law, civil and commercial transactions, and company law; and procedures before civil and criminal courts.

Moreover, though the constitution preserves the right of local governments to enact local laws, this right is restricted by two conditions: first, that local authorities shall not legislate in fields within the federal legislature's domain; and second, that local law shall not conflict with federal law. If such a conflict should arise, the local law in question becomes null and void. Responsibility for examining the conformity of local law to the constitution or to federal law is given to the federal judiciary, namely to the federal Supreme Court.

Provisions were made in the constitution for the establishment of the federal Supreme Court with jurisdiction in disputes of great significance, such as constitutional or political disputes between the emirates of the union or between one or more of the emirates and the federal authorities. The constitution also provides for the establishment of the federal first instance courts and for the transformation of the local judiciaries into a single federal judiciary. It should be noticed here that, according to the constitution, the transformation of local judiciaries shall be at the local governments' request.

Therefore, in 1978, when the local authorities of Abu Dhabi, Sharjah, Ajman, and Fujeirah emirates requested transferral of their local judicial authorities to federal judicial authority, the federal first instance courts were established by Federal Law No. 6\1978. Further, in 1991, the federal government accepted the request submitted by Umm Al-Qwwain Emirate concerning the transferral of its local judicial body to the federal judiciary. At present the judicial authorities of five out of the seven emirates of the UAE are federal.

In recognition of the state's legal traditions and culture, the constitution provides for an important position for Islamic Law within the state legal system. Section 2 of Article 7 states: "[T]he Islamic Law shall be a main source of legislation in the Federation."

This constitutional clause is significant in that it is considered by the federal legislature as the constitutional and philosophical basis for the Islamization programs of law. The Islamization of law, in general, means replacing laws of Western origin with governmental enactments derived from Islamic law, or at least compatible with its provisions. The Islamization of law program, which was started in the UAE in 1978, resulted in making the state legal system come into conformity with Islamic law. In some major legal areas, the Islamic jurisprudential rules were codified and enacted through federal governmental legislations, such as the case in the UAE Civil Transactions Code of 1985. Moreover, the Islamic law is considered by the Civil Transactions Code as the first supplementary source of law that shall be consulted to find the actual text of a legal rule, in cases in which the code does not contain a rule to cover the legal problem at hand. It is also provided by the code that, for the interpretation and the application of its provisions, the Islamic theory of law (*Usool al-feqh*) shall be followed.

In the criminal law area, Islamic law, in its traditional form, has been made one of the formal sources of law. Article 1 section 1 of the Federal Penal Code states that "in the Crimes of doctrinal Punishments (*Hudud*), Retaliation (*Qisas*), and blood money (*Diah*), the provisions of the Islamic Law shall be applied."

However, it should be noted here that the UAE legal system, as it stands today, contains rules of different origins: rules of Islamic law origin; and rules of Western origin, especially French origin.

CURRENT COURT SYSTEM STRUCTURE

At the present time there are two types of courts in the UAE, local courts and federal courts. The courts of two emirates out of the seven emirates constituting the federation—namely Dubai and Ras Al-Khaimah—are local courts, and the remaining emirates have federal courts.

In the past, the jurisdictions of the courts of Dubai and Ras Al-Khaimah, their constitutions, and the laws governing them were largely the same. This situation has been dramatically changed since the establishment of Dubai High Court of Cassation and Dubai Public Prosecutions Department, by the which Dubai judicial system became more advanced and highly organized in comparison to that of Ras Al-Khaimah. Indeed, the measures adopted by the Dubai local government in the last two decades concerning the modernization of its governmental departments, can be viewed as revolutionary, and resulted in making Dubai departments more advanced than other governmental departments in the UAE, including federal departments and federal courts.

Inasmuch as the jurisdiction of the High Court of Dubai is concerned with reviewing the Dubai appeal courts' judgments when petitions of cassation have been made against them, the court is considered to be the highest judicial authority in Dubai Emirate. Therefore it is safe to say that Dubai Emirate, by establishing the High Court, maintained the independence of its judiciary from the federal judiciary for the foreseeable future. The current court system of Dubai consists of the first instance courts, appeal courts, and the High Court of Cassation.

Although the local courts are under the direct supervision and control of local authorities and are independent from federal judicial authority, federal laws and legislation are the main source of law for these courts. Significant substantive as well as procedural laws applied by local courts are provided for by federal laws, such as civil transactions laws, commercial laws, civil procedures law, criminal laws, and criminal procedures law. Thus the laws applied by the local courts are in general the same as those of the federal courts.

The federal judiciary, as provided for by Federal Law No. 3/1983, consists of the Federal Public Prosecution Department and federal courts. By the promulgation of Federal Law No. 6/1978, the Federal Public Prosecution Department came into operation in the federal courts. Its jurisdictions, provided for by Article 44 of Federal Law

Legal Structure of the United Arab Emirates Courts

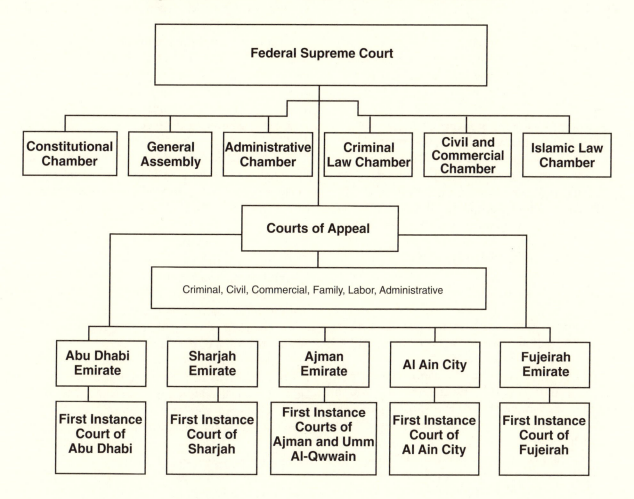

No. 10\1973, are essentially concerned with investigating criminal offenses and charging suspects.

The federal courts consist of federal first instance courts, federal appeal courts, and the federal Supreme Court. The Federal First Instance Court is a first rank court. It has jurisdictions in all cases and matters, including criminal, civil, commercial, administrative, labor, and personal status.

The federal Appeal Court has the competence to review decisions made by first instance courts, and it consists of three judges. Until very recently, there were two federal appeal courts: one is in Abu Dhabi and has jurisdiction over appeals made against decisions issued by Abu Dhabi and Al-Ain first instance courts; the other appeal court is in Sharjah City, and its jurisdictions involved appeals made against decisions issued by the first instance courts of Sharjah, Ajman, Umm Al-Qwwain, and Fujeirah emirates. By the promulgation of Federal Law Nos. 20 and 21/2000, dated September 16, 2000, the situation has changed: three other federal appeal courts came into operation in Ajman and Fujeirah emirates, in addition to Al-Ain City. The first court has jurisdiction in appeals made against

judgments issued by Ajman and Umm Al-Qwwain first instance courts, whereas the second and the third courts deal with appeals made against judgments issued by the first instance courts in Fujeirah and Al Ain, respectively.

The federal Supreme Court was established in 1973 by Federal Law No. 10\1973. As stated above, the Supreme Court is considered a federal constitutional authority, independent of central government and local authorities, and it is the highest judicial body in the UAE. The constitutional provisions concerning the appointment of the court's president and judges demonstrate the key role played by the federal Supreme Court in the UAE legal system, particularly concerning the system's independence.

The constitution determines that this court shall consist of one president and four judges, appointed by federal decree upon approval by the federal Supreme Council. Once appointed, these court judges cannot be removed from office unless they reach retirement age, are in ill health, or are appointed to other offices with their consent. They may, of course, resign.

The number of judges sitting in the Supreme Court depends on the type of legal matter that the court is dealing with. Five judges sit in the Supreme Court in cases involving the following:

1. Disputes between emirates.
2. All types of constitutional matters, whether related to the constitutional review of laws or to the interpretation of the provisions of the state constitution.
3. If any division of the Supreme Court, when hearing a dispute laid before it, finds that conflicting decisions have previously been issued by the court, relative to the dispute under consideration, or when a division decides to change a definite principle laid down by the court, it shall order the submission of the matter to a general assembly of the court consisting of all its members to decide the matter. The Supreme Court is composed of three judges when it decides on the other matters.

The Supreme Court also has a jurisdiction of reviewing the federal appeal courts' decisions when a petition of cassation has been made against them. Therefore, by virtue of this jurisdiction, the Supreme Court has become a high court of appeal (or cassation court) with the authority to examine any federal appeal court's decisions, so as to ensure that the court has applied the law correctly in a particular case (see figure).

The Supreme Court seat is in Abu Dhabi, the capital city of UAE, but the court, at its own discretion, can hold its seat in the capital of any emirate of the federation.

It is worth mentioning here that the parties involved in any civil or commercial dispute always have a right to refer their dispute to private arbitration rather than the courts. The decision reached through arbitration is legally binding, and shall be executed by the first instance court, insofar as it does not conflict with public order and morality, or with the provisions of the Federal Civil Procedures Law.

SPECIALIZED JUDICIAL BODIES
In the UAE there are no specialized judicial bodies. The ordinary courts deal with all cases and matters that might arise before them.

STAFFING
As the UAE is a federal state consisting of federal courts and local courts, the practice of law involves lawyers at the federal level and lawyers at the local level. Because of this legal structure, it is difficult to obtain statistical data on practicing lawyers at the local level. But at the federal level statistical data is available, though it is tentative. This data shows that there are 245 judges practicing in federal courts, including the federal Supreme Court. There are 104 prosecutors in the federal Public Prosecu-

tion Department, 44 state attorneys working at the legal opinion and legislative department, and 301 practicing lawyers registered at the Federal Bar Association.

With respect to the appointment of judges and prosecutors, they have to hold a bachelor's degree in law from a recognized university. In addition, they undergo further training for a period of two years in one of the two judicial institutions in the country, which provide extensive legal training covering the practical aspects of the law in the UAE.

As far as the practice of law is concerned, lawyers are also required to hold a bachelor's degree in law from a recognized university, and one year's practical training with a reputable legal firm in the country.

IMPACT OF LAW
The UAE Constitution makes provisions in Chapter 4 for fundamental and basic human rights, among these: the right of free speech, the right to an attorney in criminal cases, the right to a fair trial, presumption of innocence, the right to free education and health care, guarantees of private property, and so forth. For the implementation of these constitutional human rights, detailed federal laws have been promulgated, such as Article 4 of the Federal Criminal Procedures Law No. 35 of 1992, which provides for the right of a person accused of criminal offense punishable by capital punishment or imprisonment to be represented in the trial by a qualified private attorney paid for by the state.

The state is committed to the rule of law in government and in the protection of individual rights, as they are provided for by the constitution. It operates on the basis of separation of powers among the branches of government. The constitution guarantees rights, duties, and powers free from interference by other branches of the government. As a result, the judiciary is independent in discharging its responsibility in the administration of justice. In addition, the constitution gives individuals the right to seek the protection of the judiciary in case of a violation of the rights guaranteed under Chapter 4 of the constitution.

Butti Sultan Al-Muhairi

See also Islamic Law
References and further reading
Albaharna, Husain M. 1968. *The Legal Status of the Arabian Gulf States.* Manchester: Manchester University Press.
Anthony, June Duke, 1975. *Arab States of the Lower Gulf: People, Politics, Petroleum.* Washington, DC: Middle East Institute.
Ballantye, W. M. 1986. *Commercial Law in the Arab Middle East: The Gulf States.* London: Oceana Publications.
Heard-Bey, Frauke. 1984. *From Trucial States to United Arab Emirates.* London: Longman.
Hosani, Ali Ebrahim Al-. 1989. "Constitutional and Judicial Organization in the United Arab Emirates." Unpublished Ph.D. thesis. University of Exeter, U.K.

Mayer, Ann E. 1990. "The Shari'ah: A Methodology or a Body of Substantive Rules?" Pp. 177–198 in *Islamic Law and Jurisprudence*. Edited by Nicholas Heer. Seattle: University of Washington Press.

Miles, S. B. 1919. *The Countries and Tribes in the Persian Gulf*. 2 vols. London: Privately printed.

Owais, Hadif Rashid Al-. 1989. "The Role of the Supreme Court in the Constitutional System of the United Arab Emirates: A Comparative Study." Unpublished Ph.D. thesis. University of Durham, U.K.

Zahlan, Rosemaria Said. 1987. *The Origin of the United Arab Emirates: A Political and Social History of the Trucial States*. London: Macmillan Press.

UNITED KINGDOM

COUNTRY INFORMATION

The United Kingdom (UK) consists of Great Britain (itself composed of England, Scotland, and Wales) and Northern Ireland. The Channel Islands and the Isle of Man are not included within the United Kingdom, although in some contexts, they are deemed to be included.

The UK is located in Western Europe. The territory of Great Britain is an island surrounded by the North Atlantic Ocean to the west and north, the English Channel to the south, and the North Sea to the east. Northern Ireland consists of the northeastern sixth of the island of Ireland, which lies to the west of Great Britain. Northern Ireland shares a border with the Republic of Ireland. The total land area of the UK is 244,820 square miles. The population is approximately 59.5 million, of which approximately 85 percent are in England, 9 percent in Scotland, 2 percent in Wales, and 1.8 percent in Northern Ireland. The principal religious denominations are: Church of England (Anglican) (27 million); Roman Catholic (9 million); Muslim (1 million); Presbyterian (800,000); Methodist (760,000); Sikh (400,000); Hindu (350,000); and Jewish (270,000) (all figures are approximations). The capital is London. The principal language is English, although Gaelic, Welsh, and many other minority languages are spoken.

HISTORY

Historical continuity is also said to be a prime feature of the history of the islands that now form the UK. Thus, references continue to be made to historical sources of law and principle such as those set out in the Magna Carta of 1215, passed by the English Parliament long before the formation of the UK (Bradley and Ewing 2000). Few of the provisions of the Magna Carta remain on the statute book, but this legislation nonetheless continues to possess considerable symbolic importance. Among its most famous provisions are those providing that no man should be denied justice or punished except by the judgment of his peers and in accordance with the law of land. While there has been no conquest by an external power since the Norman Invasion in 1066, there have been periods of considerable turmoil and unrest, which have had a substantial influence on constitutional development and in particular on the relationship between the monarchy and Parliament, on the one hand, and the relationship between these institutions, located as they are in England, and Scotland, Wales, and Ireland.

In particular, in the seventeenth century, the Civil War between the Monarchists and the Parliamentarians led to the execution of King Charles I and to "experiments" in republican government through Parliament (Munro 1999, 5). When these failed, Oliver Cromwell took office as lord protector in 1653. Following his death, the Crown was restored, although its power and authority thereafter declined as Parliament became the supreme law-making authority, and executive power shifted to the ministers of the Crown, thereby establishing the foundations of the modern constitution. The shift in power from the Crown to Parliament is reflected in the terms of the Bill of Rights (1689). This provided, in particular, that the Crown could not dispense with laws and could not suspend law without the consent of Parliament (Articles 1 and 2). Nor could the Crown raise money or keep a standing army without Parliament's consent (Articles 4 and 6). The Bill of Rights also enacted the principle that there is freedom of speech in Parliament and that what is said in Parliament cannot be impeached or questioned in any court or place outside of Parliament (Article 9). At that time, there was a separate Parliament in Scotland (see later discussion), which enacted a modified version of the Bill of Rights (the Claim of Right) in 1689. Many of the provisions of the Bill of Rights and the Claim of Right still represent the law.

We shall now turn to the relationships between England, Wales, Scotland, and Northern Ireland. While it is commonly assumed that the United Kingdom contains a single jurisdiction, this is not in fact the case. Rather, three distinct legal jurisdictions exist within the UK—the jurisdictions of England and Wales (but see the discussion on devolution); Scotland; and Northern Ireland.

Scotland

Until the eleventh century, Scots law was local and based on custom. From the eleventh century on, and especially from the thirteenth century, the Scottish legal system became heavily influenced by the Roman (civilian) system and evolved a highly systematized body of principles. By the fifteenth century, Scots law was clearly different from English law, especially in the area of private law (Walker 2001). The Act of Union of 1707 (the Scots refer to it as the "Treaty") between England and Scot-

United Kingdom

land established a common Parliament and created a United Kingdom of Great Britain. Scotland, however, retained its own established Church (the Presbyterian Church of Scotland), its own court system, and its own system of local government and education (see the discussion of devolution).

One significant aspect of Scots law is the importance of the institutional writers: Craig's *Jus Ferndale* (1655); Viscount Stair's *Institutions of the Law of Scotland* (1681); Erskine's *Institute of the Law of Scotland* (1773); and Bell's *Commentaries on the Law of Scotland* (1800) and *Principles of the Law of Scotland* (1829). For criminal law, see Alison's *Principles* (1832) and *Practice of the Criminal Law of Scotland* (1833).

Wales

Wales was annexed by the Crown in 1284 but was not legally united with England until the Act of Union of 1536. Unlike Scotland, Wales possesses no independent legal jurisdiction, although the courts were not fully absorbed into the English system until 1830, when the Courts of Great Sessions of Wales were abolished.

Northern Ireland

The relationship between Ireland and Great Britain has been marked by centuries of often violent unrest, and this unrest continues in Northern Ireland, despite the peace efforts. Here, I shall only provide an outline of the formal relations.

Ireland became part of the UK by virtue of the Act of Union of 1800. Northern Ireland was separated from the rest of Ireland in 1920 under the terms of the Government of Ireland Act 1920. Following an armed uprising in southern Ireland, the Irish Free State was formed in 1922, later to become the Irish Republic. Thereafter, the United Kingdom included Great Britain and Northern Ireland. Northern Ireland had its own Parliament from 1921 to 1972, when it was supplanted by direct rule from Westminster. In turn, Westminster's rule was replaced by devolution under the Northern Ireland Act of 1998.

The Channel Islands

When the duke of Normandy became William I of England in 1066, the Channel Islands (Jersey, Guernsey, Sark, and Alderney) were part of his dukedom. When

King John lost control of Normandy, the islands remained possessions of the Crown. Jersey, the largest of the islands, has a lieutenant governor and other officers, including a bailiff, appointed by the Crown. It has a unicameral legislature that is presided over by the bailiff and consists of twelve senators elected for six years, twenty-eight deputies elected every three years, twelve constables elected by the parishes, and the law officers and dean of Jersey, who cannot vote. There is universal suffrage. Acts of Parliament only extend to Jersey if expressly stipulated or by necessary implication. While some legislation will only come into effect if the assent of the Crown is obtained, regulations of more limited effect may be enacted without this consent. The autonomy of the island is reflected in the fact that it has its own fiscal laws and has immunity from UK taxation. Guernsey's institutions closely resemble Jersey's. Sark is substantially autonomous and is owned by a feudal lord. Alderney has its own representative legislature, but in 1948, responsibility for its main services was vested in Guernsey. Appeals lie from the highest courts in the islands to the Judicial Committee of the Privy Council (JCPC).

LEGAL CONCEPTS

The constitution of the UK is not contained in a single constitutional document. For this reason, it is often misleadingly said that the United Kingdom does not have a constitution. The reality is that the UK does have a constitution, but its characteristics are to be found in a number of sources. These include acts of Parliament (such as those already mentioned), the common law as reflected in decisions of the courts, conventions (that is, prescriptive practices that are not, strictly speaking, law), and the law and custom of Parliament. Since the UK's accession to the European Economic Community (EEC) in 1972, European Community (EC) law (including the treaties establishing the community, now known as the Economic Union, or ED), the legislation enacted by the EC institutions and decisions of the European Court of Justice, are also of importance. So, too, is the law relating to the European Convention of Fundamental Freedoms and Human Rights (ECHR), particularly since the Human Rights Act of 1998 went into effect.

The constitutional system may be said to rest on the existence of a constitutional monarchy based on hereditary principles, with a supreme or sovereign Parliament. There are two Houses of Parliament—the House of Lords (or Upper House), which is unelected, and the House of Commons, consisting of 659 elected members of Parliament (MPs). Elections to the House of Commons must be held at least once every five years (according to the Parliament Act of 1911, Section 7). The main political parties in England are the Labour Party, the Conservative Party, and the Liberal Democrats. Plaid Cymru is influential is Wales, as are the Scottish National Party (SNP) in Scotland and the Ulster Unionist Party and the Nationalist/Republican Parties in Northern Ireland.

The leader of the largest party is invited by the monarch to form the government and becomes the prime minister. The prime minister appoints the ministers who form the executive government and selects those who sit in the cabinet, which he or she chairs. The principal government departments are headed by ministers, who are usually designated secretaries of state. They are assisted by noncabinet ministers, who have more specific responsibilities. Ministers answer to Parliament for the conduct of their departments, by virtue of the convention of ministerial responsibility. Most proposed legislation is sponsored and presented to Parliament by government ministers. Bills normally become acts of Parliament (primary legislation) once they have passed through both Houses of Parliament and formally received the royal assent. By virtue of the Parliament Acts of 1911 and 1949, the House of Lords has no veto power, and, subject to exceptions, its power is limited to delaying the passage of legislation by one year.

The constitutional system of the United Kingdom does not establish a formal separation of powers. Thus, for example, ministers are both members of the executive and usually members of the legislature (Parliament). The highest court within the UK is the House of Lords acting in its appellate capacity (note that in this capacity, the House acts through a committee composed of law lords); the most senior judge is the lord chancellor, who, however, rarely presides. The lord chancellor is a political appointment made by the prime minister. As well as fulfilling a judicial role, he or she is also a member of the cabinet (the executive) and chairs the deliberations of the House of Lords in its legislative capacity.

The lord chancellor also plays a key role in the appointment of the judiciary. Judges are not elected, and there is no career judiciary, as there is in many countries. The most senior judges (those who sit in the Court of Appeal and above) are formally appointed by the monarch on the recommendation of the prime minister, who will consult the lord chancellor in this regard. High Court judges are appointed by the monarch on recommendation of the lord chancellor. That individual also appoints less-senior judges, including magistrates and members of some tribunals. Over the years, there has been considerable criticism of this system of appointment, principally on the grounds that it lacks transparency. Certainly, the British judiciary has traditionally been drawn from a very narrow social class and is overwhelmingly male in composition. One reason for this is that, until recently, senior judges were drawn exclusively from the ranks of senior barristers (QCs—Queen's Counsel). A further criticism is that, despite the formal role played by the Crown, the process of appointing judges is exclusively in the hands of those who are also political members of the executive.

Structure of United Kingdom
Principal Civil Courts

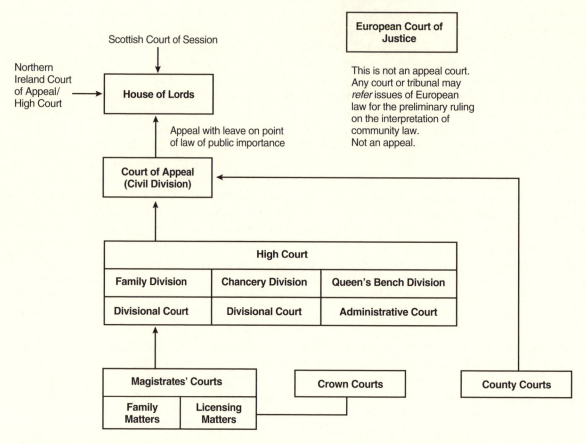

Note: The Judicial Committee of the Privy Council is the highest appeal court on devolution matters

Devolution

This system of government, as described, relates to the central institutions of government as representing the whole of the United Kingdom. In 1998, the Westminster Parliament passed three Acts of Parliament devolving powers to the three parts of the UK: the Scotland Act, the Government of Wales Act, and the Northern Ireland Act. Powers were devolved asymmetrically, Northern Ireland and Scotland have a system of legislative devolution, whereas Wales has a system of executive devolution. The newly formed Scottish Parliament and the Northern Ireland Assembly have had devolved to them extensive legislative powers over a wide range of matters (although they have no power to legislate contrary to the European Community law or the ECHR). Westminster retains the sole power to legislate on matters of national concern. The Scottish Parliament and the Northern Ireland Assembly are directly elected by a system of proportional representation once every four years. They each have their own system of government, headed by a first minister (in Northern Ireland, there is also a deputy). The devolution acts establish a system of preen-actment scrutiny, in an effort to ensure that bills are intra vires, and a court system to resolve devolution issues.

As mentioned, Wales has a system of executive devolution. The Welsh Assembly is elected by a system of proportional representation, and Wales has an executive headed by a first minister, but the assembly has no primary law-making powers. Laws continue to be made at Westminster, and the Welsh Assembly fills in the details by way of delegated legislation. Judicial review concerning Welsh devolution issues may be heard in Cardiff, thereby bringing a specific Welsh element into the normal unified legal system of England and Wales.

The Judicial Committee of the Privy Council is the highest court for devolution issues, and its decisions on these matters are binding on all other courts. Under the devolution acts, the JCPC is composed of the law lords and those judges of the High Court and Court of Appeal in England, Wales, and Northern Ireland and the Court of Session in Scotland who are privy counselors (the JCPC has a different composition when exercising its other functions). The definition of a devolution issue is

Structure of United Kingdom
Principal Criminal Courts

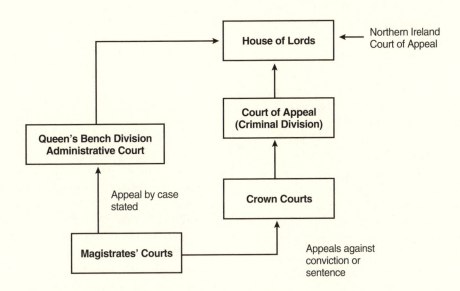

European Court of Justice

This is not an appeal court. Any court or tribunal may *refer* issues of European law for the preliminary ruling on the interpretation of community law.

House of Lords ← Northern Ireland Court of Appeal

Court of Appeal (Criminal Division)

Queen's Bench Division Administrative Court

Crown Courts

Appeal by case stated

Magistrates' Courts

Appeals against conviction or sentence

Note: No appeal from Scottish Courts to House of Lords in criminal matters. Questions in criminal trials involving devolution matters may appeal to the Judicial Committee of the Privy Council.

provided in the three devolution acts. In essence, these are issues that relate to the competence of the devolved legislature and devolved executive.

SOURCES OF LAW

Treaties

The United Kingdom adopts a dualist approach to international law, which is therefore not a direct source of law within the UK. In particular, treaty obligations only create rights and obligations within domestic law when incorporated by an act of Parliament. The European Communities Act of 1972, for example, incorporated European Community law, and the Human Rights Act of 1998 has effectively incorporated certain of the rights and freedoms set out in the ECHR.

Statutes

For most practical purposes, statute law is the principal source of law within the UK. The absence of a written

constitution, coupled with the doctrine of parliamentary supremacy, means that as a general rule, Parliament's primary legislation may make or unmake any law. While the courts may review actions of the executive and administrative authorities to ensure that they do not exceed or abuse powers conferred by the Parliament at Westminster, the courts cannot review the legality of primary legislation itself. This principle is now subject to important qualifications. First, primary legislation may be held nonapplicable on the grounds that it conflicts with norms of EC law. Second, Section 3 of the Human Rights Act of 1998 provides that "so far as it is possible to do so, [legislation] must be read and given effect in a way which is compatible" with the ECHR. If a superior court is satisfied that legislation is incompatible with the convention, it may make a "declaration of incompatibility" (Section 4(2), Human Rights Act of 1989). Such a declaration does not affect the legality of the Westminster legislation, however.

These provisions are widely seen as representing a shift of political power to the courts in the UK. While it is too early to say what the longer term effect of the Human Rights Act will be, there can be little doubt that the judiciary now plays a far more significant role in the political life of the nation than it did in 1970. Some indication of this is evident in the recent rise in the numbers of applications for judicial review, seeking to challenge decisions of public bodies. During 1981, there were 533 such cases; by 2000, the annual number had increased to 4,247 (official statistics).

Common Law

The decisions of judges over the centuries have formed a body of legal principles applicable to the UK known as the common law. The basis of the common law is the system of precedent (stare decisis). Broadly speaking, this provides that the legal aspects of decisions made by courts (the *ratio decidendi*) will normally be binding on courts of equal or lower status if the facts are similar. If the facts materially differ, the earlier decision may be distinguished. Prior to 1966, the House of Lords regarded itself as being bound by its own previous decisions. In that year, however, the house relaxed this rule. To achieve a balance between consistency and certainty, on the one hand, and flexibility, on the other, the house, while normally considering itself bound, is free to depart from previous decisions where it is just to do so. The Court of Appeal is bound by its own previous decisions (subject to specific exceptions).

Custom

While the common law may have had its basis in custom (particularly in the context of the laws relating to business and commercial practice), custom is no longer a significant general source of law in the UK. Nonetheless, specific and local customary practices may be used to support an argument in a case if certain requirements are satisfied. These include the requirements that the customary practice was exercised continuously and be shown to have existed since "time immemorial," which is taken to mean since before 1189.

The accompanying figures portray the essential structure of the civil and criminal court systems in England and Wales. They show in particular the principal avenues of appeal, including the relationship between the domestic courts and the European Court of Justice. In addition to the courts, many tribunals deal with a vast array of disputes, in particular concerning administrative justice in areas such as social security, education, immigration, employment rights, mental health law, and taxation.

Brigid Hadfield
Maurice Sunkin

See also Common Law; European Court and Commission on Human Rights; European Court of Justice; Judicial Review

References and further reading
Bailey, Stephen, and Michael Gunn. 2002. *The Modern English Legal System*. 4th ed. London: Sweet and Maxwell.
Bradley, Anthony, and Keith Ewing. 2000. *Constitutional and Administrative Law*. 12th ed. London and New York: Pearson Educational.
Cownie, Fiona, and Anthony Bradney. 2000. *The English Legal System in Context*. 2nd ed. London: Butterworths.
Dickson, Brice. 1993. *Introduction to the Legal System in Northern Ireland*. 3rd ed. Belfast: SLS.
Elliott, Catherine, and Frances Quinn. 2001. *The English Legal System*. 3rd ed. London and New York: Pearson Educational.
Munro, Colin R. 1999. *Studies in Constitutional Law*. London, Edinburgh, Dublin: Butterworths.
Partington, Martin. 2000. *Introduction to the English Legal System*. Oxford: Oxford University Press.
Walker, David M. 2001. *The Scottish Legal System*. 8th ed. London: Sweet and Maxwell.

UNITED STATES—FEDERAL SYSTEM

The colonists' declaration of independence from the British crown in 1776 did not immediately produce a government for the ages. After struggling under the state-dominated Articles of Confederation during the 1780s, key figures within the revolutionary generation sought a new form of republican rule that would place the nation's central government on more sure footing. Aware of the suspicions this newly empowered federal government might raise within the states, the drafters of the federal constitution settled on a regime of limited powers, strong enough to fend off enemies foreign and domestic but not so strong as to dominate the thirteen state governments. The delicate constitutional balance struck during the summer of 1787 featured a central government of three separate branches: the Congress, the executive, and the judiciary. In *The Federalist Papers*, no. 78, Alexander Hamilton called the federal judiciary the "least dangerous branch" of this new government. Defying such modest predictions, the federal courts in fact would come to exert more than their share of influence over the development of this growing young nation.

CONSTITUTIONAL PROVISIONS

Article III, Section 1, of the U.S. Constitution vests the judicial power of the United States "in one supreme Court, and in such lower inferior Courts as the Congress may from time to time ordain and establish." In Article 2, Section 2, the president is granted the "Power, by and with the Advice and Consent of the Senate" to appoint "Judges of the supreme court." (By contrast, the document does not require that Congress actually establish inferior courts and thus is silent as to how such inferior court judges might also be appointed.) And to ensure a

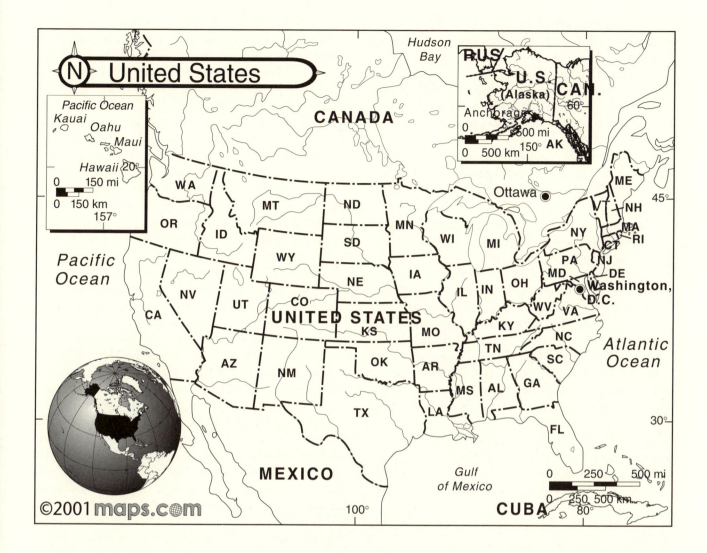

degree of independence not found in many state judiciaries of the late eighteenth century, the framers of the constitution provided that both supreme and inferior federal court judges would hold their respective offices "during good Behavior" and would receive a compensation that would "not be diminished during their Continuance in Office" (Article III, Section 1, par. 1).

The innovation of federal courts presiding in coexistence with geographically overlapping state courts was unusual for its time; no other country had ever before attempted such a dual system of judiciaries. Given the confusion that was sure to result, the constitutional language defining the scope of the federal courts' jurisdiction would play a critical role in this new judicial system's success. The Supreme Court received grants of original and appellate jurisdiction to hear cases. As provided in Article III, Section 2, the court's original jurisdiction includes cases between two or more states or between the United States and a state; cases involving foreign ambassadors, ministers, consuls, and their staffs; and cases commenced by a state against a citizen of another state or nation. Meanwhile, the court's appellate jurisdiction extended to all other cases arising under the constitution or laws of the United States; admiralty and maritime cases; cases between citizens of different states; cases between citizens of the same state claiming land under grants of different states; and cases between the citizens of a state and foreign states, citizens, or subjects. Meanwhile, Congress maintained the power to make "exceptions" to and otherwise regulate the high court's appellate jurisdiction (Article III, Section 2, par. 2).

HISTORY AND DEVELOPMENT OF THE FEDERAL COURT SYSTEM

Although the constitution established the broad contours of this new federal judicial system, it was left to Congress to flesh out how the system would actually look in practice. In the Judiciary Act of 1789, Congress established that the high court would consist of "a chief justice and five associate justices" who would meet in two sessions each year. Congress also provided for the creation of district courts and circuit courts, the latter of which bear little resemblance to modern-day circuit courts of appeals. At the system's outset, each state constituted a district, and in each district at least one district court judge presided. Three circuit courts (representing the Eastern, Southern, and Middle Circuits), were each staffed by two justices of the Supreme Court and one district court judge. Circuit courts performed trial and appellate functions in eleven of the thirteen states (the exceptions were Kentucky and Maine). (Thus, in addition to their responsibilities sitting on the nation's highest tribunal, Supreme Court justices at the beginning of the republic also "rode circuit," traveling to their assigned circuits on a regular basis.)

Although circuit courts heard some appeals directly from the district courts, they served primarily as trial courts and presided over two types of cases: (1) cases triable under federal law and not reserved by law exclusively to the district courts; and (2) diversity of citizenship cases where the amount in controversy exceeded $500. Meanwhile, the district courts enjoyed exclusive jurisdiction over matters involving low-level crimes and certain types of admiralty or seizure cases. District courts also shared jurisdiction with circuit courts over certain types of tort suits by aliens, suits against consuls, and cases in which the federal government itself brought suit for $100 or less. In truth, these lower federal courts enjoyed only a limited sphere of jurisdiction, as even "federal question" cases were heard in state courts unless Congress specifically dictated otherwise. (This asymmetrical system of lower courts would persist in various forms until 1866, when *all* district courts (including those in Kentucky and Maine) were finally brought within a federal circuit for the first time.)

The early history of the federal court system thus proved mostly uneventful, with the Supreme Court rightfully viewed as a woefully weak third branch of the federal government. The precarious position of the new central government left the high court reluctant to needlessly incur the wrath of state supreme courts, such as by aggressively reviewing their final judgments (that power had been explicitly granted to the U.S. Supreme Court by section 25 of the 1789 Judiciary Act). Additionally, the court did not exercise the controversial power to invalidate federal statutes until 1803. That year, in the landmark case of *Marbury v. Madison,* the Supreme Court struck down a provision of the 1789 Judiciary Act that (the court concluded) had unconstitutionally expanded the original jurisdiction of the court to include request for a writ of mandamus. Although *Marbury* would alter many politicians' perceptions of the court's status by establishing the court's power of judicial review, the case hardly marked a new age of judicial activism. In fact, the court would not again exercise this power of judicial review until the eve of the Civil War. Institutionally speaking, the federal judiciary was more a bystander than a participant in the political wars that raged within this new nation.

Although Congress made slight modifications to the federal circuit court system for the next fifty years, the most dramatic change would not come until much later in the nineteenth century. Critics of the system had long complained of the conflicts inherent in having Supreme Justices preside over circuit court cases and then later over those same cases on appeal. Additionally, many of the justices were excessively burdened by the travel their positions required: in the early nineteenth-century United States, journeys by public conveyances took a significant toll on justices, especially those assigned to far-off locations in the South and out West. Thus the increasingly anachronistic practice of riding circuit fell into disuse by the 1840s. In 1869 Congress responded by creating the new position of "circuit court judge," whose authority extended only to the geographical limits of the respective circuits. Even more fundamental reform took place in 1891, with the establishment of full circuit courts of appeals that had jurisdiction to hear appeals from all federal district courts located in the already existing circuits. The traditional circuit courts of original jurisdiction were finally abolished once and for all in 1911, at which point all federal trial functions were vested in the federal district courts.

Between 1866 and 1928, the boundaries of the nation's nine circuit courts were left mostly intact: new states admitted to the Union were assigned either to the Eighth or Ninth Circuit, both of which ballooned in size during that sixty-two-year period. In 1929, the Eighth Circuit was split up into the Eighth and Tenth Circuits; and in 1980 the Fifth Circuit was divided up into the Fifth and Eleventh Circuits. (Other circuit courts of appeals included the U.S. Court of Appeals for the District of Columbia Circuit and the confusingly titled U.S. Court of Appeals for the Federal Circuit, created out of a merger of the Court of Customs and Patent Appeals and the U.S. Court of Claims). Meanwhile, the far-flung Ninth Circuit, anchored by California out West, with jurisdiction over more citizens and territory than any other circuit court of appeals by far, remains virtually unchanged from its early twentieth-century form.

Unlike the Supreme Court, which was vested with constitutionally guaranteed spheres of jurisdiction, the lower federal courts enjoyed only those powers specifically conferred on them by statute. Thus district and circuit courts alike exercised only limited jurisdiction to hear cases during the late eighteenth and early nineteenth centuries. The first significant expansion in the jurisdiction of lower federal courts came with the extension of the removal statute in 1863, which allowed certain actions begun in state courts (e.g., lawsuits brought against federal officers) to be removed to the federal circuit courts. Federal laws dealing with slavery and Native American claims were also litigated in federal courts. But the true explosion of growth in federal court jurisdiction waited

Legal Structure of the U.S. Federal System Courts

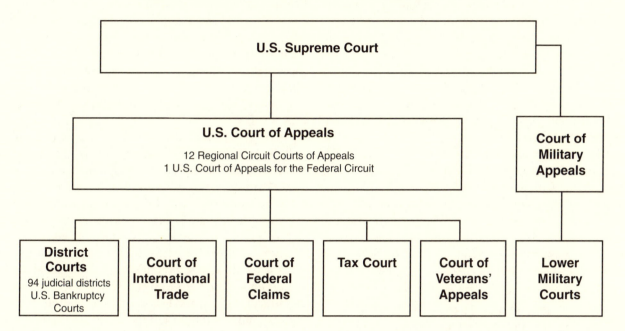

until after 1875, when Congress gave the federal courts original jurisdiction (concurrent with the state courts) in all matters exceeding $500 arising under the constitution, laws of the United States, or treaties. Subsequently, just about any person claiming a right under federal laws or the constitution was free to initiate his suit in a federal or state court. Coupled with the explosive growth of federal lawmaking by the federal government in the late eighteenth and early nineteenth centuries, the business of the federal courts began to increase significantly.

Meanwhile, as the federal court system grew by leaps and bounds, the Supreme Court's relationship with lower federal courts was destined to be transformed. In the early part of the nineteenth century, the six- and (beginning in 1807) seven-member Supreme Court occasionally exercised "supervisory powers" over inferior courts through the writs of prohibition, mandamus, certiorari (cert), and others. Although such writs were made famous in cases like *Marbury v. Madison* (in which the court considered a writ of mandamus) the high court itself firmly established that such writs could only be issued in furtherance of appellate jurisdiction specifically authorized by statute. The far more common tool for supervising lower federal courts was through a "writ of error," which was issued after the final judgment. Congress also vested in the Supreme Court the power to issue a "writ of scire facias, habeas corpus, and all other writs not specifically provided for by statute, which may be necessary." The writ of habeas corpus in particular was used widely by the court to inquire into the basis for holding certain prisoners in custody.

In addition to the Supreme Court's appellate jurisdiction over the circuit courts (exercised only when specifically authorized by statute), in 1802 Congress authorized the judges of a circuit court to certify disagreements among themselves to the U.S. Supreme Court for review as well. During the nineteenth century, a number of cases arrived at the high court by this process of certification. Other than through the writ of habeas corpus, the court was not able to hear appeals from federal criminal cases until 1889, when Congress first authorized federal defendants to take a writ of error to the Supreme Court in all capital cases. After the circuit courts of appeals were created in 1891, this jurisdiction was extended further to include all "capital" and other "infamous crimes," the latter term construed to include any offense where the defendant was sentenced to some jail time.

By the end of the nineteenth century, the large number of mandatory appeals brought to the Supreme Court—now with its modern allotment of nine members—had become an excessive burden. The first significant relief arrived in 1891, with the establishment of circuit courts of appeals authorized to take most appeals from the district or circuit courts. The decisions of the circuit courts of appeals were deemed "final" in diversity, equity, admiralty, and criminal cases, as well as in all suits brought under the revenue and patent laws. Of course, such "final decisions" could still be reviewed by the Supreme Court, but only by a "writ of certiorari." In practice, this meant the Supreme Court would only hear those classes of cases in which it felt that questions of "gravity and importance" were presented. By contrast, other types of appeals, including all those from the Supreme Court of the District of Columbia, remained mandatory. Even with these reforms, the Supreme Court was still annually placing in excess of 500 federal and state cases onto its docket well into the twentieth century.

By far the most significant reduction in the court's caseload occurred after 1925, when the "Judges' Bill" passed by Congress gave birth to the modern Supreme Court. Among the law's provisions was the extension of the writ of certiorari to many areas of appeals that had once been mandatory. Thus the circuit courts of appeals in effect became the final court of appeal, except where the Supreme Court decided in its discretion to hear the case by issuing a writ of certiorari or in certain limited areas where Congress specifically mandated an appeal to the high court. Since 1925 the Supreme Court has enjoyed nearly unlimited discretion to craft its docket from state high court and federal circuit court appeals.

KEY FEATURES OF THE MODERN FEDERAL COURT SYSTEM

Federal Jurisdiction

Although the rules of federal jurisdiction are complex, the types of cases properly admitted to the federal system generally fit into one of three categories: (1) federal question jurisdiction, which entitles federal courts to hear cases based on the constitution and the laws and treaties of the United States; (2) federal party jurisdiction, which entitles federal courts to hear cases in which the United States (or one of its agencies and officers) is a party; and (3) diversity jurisdiction, which grants citizens of two different states admission to federal courts if their lawsuit rises to the amount of $75,000 or more. (If one party is a citizen of a foreign country, he or she may also sue in federal court for the proper jurisdictional amount.) Many types of lawsuits, such as civil cases brought by the federal government, can be brought in either state or federal courts. And although most cases that fall under some form of federal jurisdiction are heard in federal court, the great majority of legal disputes in the United States are still handled in state (and local) court forums.

Judicial Selection on the Federal Courts

The formal rules for selecting federal judges vested with authority under Article III have remained essentially the same since the beginning of the republic. All justices of the U.S. Supreme Court, as well as judges of the federal circuit courts of appeals and the district courts, are nominated by the president and confirmed by a simple majority of the Senate. Because these justices and judges serve for good behavior, vacancies on federal courts occur at irregular and unpredictable intervals: when a judge resigns, retires, or dies or when Congress creates a new judgeship. (Many Article III judges who are eligible to retire decide to continue to hear cases on a full- or part-time basis as "senior judges.") By contrast, judges on "legislative courts" established by Congress pursuant to Article I may be selected in a variety of ways. For example, the president and the Senate play no role at all in the selection of bankruptcy and magistrate judges, which are appointed for limited terms by circuit court of appeals judges and district court judges, respectively.

Naturally, the level of the judicial vacancy being filled will dictate the degree of scrutiny the Senate chooses to place on a judicial nominee. A Supreme Court vacancy presents the greatest opportunity for a president to influence the judiciary, but it also presents considerable challenges. Although the Senate confirms the great majority of Supreme Court nominations made (89 percent during the twentieth century), confirmation of high court nominees is hardly automatic. Interest groups (including the organized bar) seek to influence every stage of the appointment process, and occasionally opposition to a candidate builds steadily within the Senate itself. The much-publicized rejection of Judge Robert Bork, who was President Ronald Reagan's nominee to the U.S. Supreme Court in 1987, came about once concerted interest group opposition found an audience among many liberal and moderate senators. By contrast, the numerous vacancies that arise on the federal circuit district courts are less likely to generate such high levels of opposition. Such lower court nominations are generally dictated by home-state senators (usually from the president's party), who actively sponsor their favorite candidates for such vacancies and then steer those nominees through a much less rigorous confirmation process.

Agenda Setting in the U.S. Supreme Court

The three most common ways that cases arrive at the Supreme Court are (1) pursuant to its original jurisdiction, (2) on review of the final decision of a state supreme court, and (3) on review of a final decision of a U.S. Court of Appeals. Since 1925 the U.S. Supreme Court has enjoyed wide-ranging discretion to choose cases for its docket by granting (or refusing to grant) a writ of certiorari, as its own rules make clear: "A review on writ of certiorari is not a matter of right, but of judicial discretion, and will be granted only when there are important and specific reasons therefore." A denial of a writ of certiorari by the high court normally enjoys no precedential value whatsoever for future cases.

By tradition, the court grants a writ of certiorari whenever four justices vote to hear the case. Although there are exceptions, the court normally does not provide any specific reasons for granting or denying the writ, rendering the process itself something of a mystery. Still, scholars who have studied the process identify several key factors in a cert petition that will increase the likelihood that it will be heard on the merits. When the federal government seeks review, the chances of a case being taken by the court increase significantly. Amicus briefs on certiorari filed by key interest groups may increase the likelihood that cert will be granted. A split among the circuit courts of appeal has traditionally played a key role in swaying the cert decisions of certain justices. Finally, justices may vote to grant or deny cert based on their own personal calculations of how the case will ultimately be judged on the merits. Regardless of the reasons, the court enjoys absolute discretion to either (1) hear all of the issues presented by the litigants, (2) limit review to particular questions raised, or (3) ask the parties to argue brand new questions that had never been raised by the parties themselves.

Specialized Jurisdiction Courts

The U.S. Supreme Court, the circuit courts of appeals, and the federal district courts all hear a broad range of civil and criminal cases. By contrast, so-called specialized courts in the federal judicial system focus on a relatively narrow set of issues, which theoretically allows them to provide a more uniform interpretation of certain federal programs. Specialized federal trial courts include the U.S. Tax Court; the Court of Federal Claims, charged with hearing claims against the federal government; the Court of Veterans Appeals; the Court of International Trade; the Rail Reorganization Court, and the Foreign Intelligence Surveillance Court. The federal court system also features specialized appellate courts, including the U.S. Court of Appeals for the Federal Circuit, which hears appeals from patent and trademark cases, as well as claims against the federal government; the Foreign Intelligence Surveillance Court of Review; and the U.S. Court of Military Appeals.

Critics charge that these specialized courts often develop a strong point of view about the policy issues that they address. For example, the short-lived U.S. Commerce Court—created in 1910 to hear appeals from the Interstate Commerce Commission—drew considerable criticism for heavily favoring the railroads. (Awash in political controversy practically from the outset, the court was quickly abolished by Congress in 1913). Their emphasis on a narrower set of issues may also leave specialized courts more susceptible to the pleas of interest groups that focus on parallel issue areas. The organized bar has been among the most ardent opponents of such courts, preferring generalist judges as the best means to guarantee a "diverse and independent judiciary." Such fears of a co-opted judiciary are somewhat mitigated in the case of the Rail Reorganization Court and the Foreign Intelligence Surveillance Court, each of which borrows judges from the district and circuit courts for limited-duration assignments on those two courts.

Article I Courts

Unlike Supreme Court justices and judges in "inferior courts" established under Article III, judges on courts created by Congress pursuant to its Article I powers do not enjoy either lifetime appointments or the constitutional guarantee that their salaries will not be reduced. Rather, such Article I courts—often termed "legislative courts"—provide Congress with greater flexibility to specify fixed judicial terms or provisions of removal. Congress might choose to create legislative courts within administrative agencies or elsewhere for several reasons. It might want to allow agencies that currently possess rule making and investigative powers to decide judicial controversies within their expertise. Congress might also believe such legislative courts offer advantages of cost savings and efficiency. Finally, judges who sit on legislative courts are less likely to be independent precisely because they lack life tenure and salary protections. Article I courts in existence today include the aforementioned U.S. Tax Court, Court of Federal Claims, and Court of Veterans Appeals, as well the hundreds of administrative courts and tribunals found within federal agencies such as the Social Security Administration and others. Despite being created in a wholly different manner, legislative courts for the most part resemble Article III courts in the judicial procedures they employ.

Congress's power to create legislative courts under Article I is not unlimited, however. In truth, the constitution itself offers no specific authority for granting other bodies (such as Congress) the power to decide Article III judicial matters. Accordingly, Congress has never been permitted to create legislative courts to hear all constitutional matters or to decide particular controversial cases according to Congress's specific wishes. There appear to be four situations in which legislative courts are permissible: (1) for cases in U.S. possessions and territories, (2) for military matters, (3) for civil disputes between the United States and private citizens, and (4) for certain criminal matters or public disputes among private citizens in which the legislative courts serve as effective adjuncts of an Article III court.

This last category applies to federal bankruptcy courts, whose judges are appointed for fourteen-year terms by the U.S. Courts of Appeals. Since 1984, federal bankruptcy courts have served as adjuncts of Article III courts, which (upon objection) may engage in de novo review of all bankruptcy court orders. Similarly, district court judges appoint magistrate judges for renewable eight-year terms. Magistrate judges are empowered to decide pretrial motions in civil or criminal cases upon reference by a judge; they may also try civil cases and criminal misdemeanor cases with the consent of the parties. Given the significant role that legislative courts and tribunals play in much federal litigation, it seems unlikely that the

Supreme Court would ever declare all legislative courts to be unconstitutional, the ambiguous language of the constitution notwithstanding.

Administrative Support for the Federal Courts

According to federal statute and administrative practice, each individual court is charged with appointing its own support staff, supervising its own spending and budgets, and managing its own court records. Naturally, the chief judge of each court plays an important supervisory role in this regard, but the chief clerk of each court (including the U.S. Supreme Court) is the primary administrative officer who manages the court's nonjudicial functions. Among the clerk's critical functions are communicating with the public through court notices and summons; administering the jury system; maintaining the records and docket of the court; and overseeing all courtroom support services.

In addition to coordinating important intracourt matters, the chief justice of the United States also presides over the entire federal court system through the Judicial Conference of the United States. Authorized to recommend policy reforms for federal judicial administration, the conference consists of the chief justice, the chief judge of each Circuit Court of Appeals, one district judge from each regional circuit, and the chief judge of the Court of International Trade. The Administrative Office of the U.S. Courts is a judicial branch agency responsible for carrying out policies of the Judicial Conference and its committees. The director of the Administrative Office serves as the chief administrative officer of the entire federal courts system. Within each circuit there also exists a "circuit judicial council," which monitors the administration of courts located within its geographic boundaries. Finally, the Federal Judicial Center provides training for judges and other court personnel in areas such as case management, court technology, and other aspects of court administration. It also maintains an active research agenda, studying federal court operations and forwarding reform proposals on to the Judicial Conference.

CURRENT CONTROVERSIES AND PROPOSALS FOR REFORM

Faced with the reality of ever-increasing federal caseloads and outdated modes of administering the federal courts, officials from within and without the federal judicial system have offered numerous proposals for reform that have yet to be enacted into law. Among the reforms most often discussed are those treated below.

A National Court of Appeals

In 1971, then Chief Justice Warren Burger appointed a national commission to study the Supreme Court's excessive caseload. One of the most controversial proposals offered by that commission was the creation of a National Court of Appeals, which would review all petitions for writ of certiorari and select the most worthy for the Supreme Court. As proposed, this national appeals court would also have the authority to decide cases in which there was a split among the circuits, if it determined that the case was not sufficiently important for the Supreme Court's direct review. Even fifteen years later, the national court of appeals proposal continued to enjoy the endorsement of Chief Justice William Rehnquist, among others.

Critics of the proposal charge that such an intermediate appeals court would effectively strip the Supreme Court of some of its agenda-setting authority. Some also suggest that an intermediate appeals court would lessen the prestige of the existing courts of appeals. But perhaps the most damning indictment of the national appeals court proposal is that it would fail to reduce the Supreme Court's docket, as the high court would be forced to review the decisions of this extrajudicial body, including its referral decisions. Although the proposal has drawn considerable attention over the years, it has never come close to being enacted by Congress. More recent calls for an "intercircuit tribunal" (comprising circuit court judges who would resolve circuit splits) has also made little headway. In the meantime, the Supreme Court's so-called caseload crisis appears to have resolved itself: during the late 1990s the high court decided less than ninety cases each term, less than half the number it had decided a decade earlier.

Eliminating Diversity Jurisdiction

The caseload crisis in the lower courts has also spurred reform proposals that seek to reduce the number of cases that may be filed in the first place in federal courts. For example, some reformers have called for the abolishment of diversity jurisdiction, which currently opens the federal district courts up to all civil actions between citizens of different states where the matter in controversy exceeds the statutorily required amount (currently $75,000). Although diversity jurisdiction has existed since the adoption of the Judiciary Act of 1789, controversy continues to rage over whether it serves any real purpose. The traditional theory behind such jurisdiction was that it protected out-of-state residents from the potential bias of other state courts. However, some scholars believe the real fear was that populist state legislatures might adopt antibusiness laws: federal court jurisdiction (and even more important, federal common law rules) offered businesses significant protection against such discrimination.

Critics of diversity jurisdiction argue that the fear of bias against out-of-staters in other state courts has no basis in fact. A Supreme Court decision in 1938 (*Erie Railroad Co. v. Tompkins*) required federal courts to apply state law in diversity cases, which effectively blurs the distinction between the justice accorded to out-of staters in federal and state courts. Moreover, diversity jurisdiction is expensive, unnecessarily taking up approximately a quarter of the civil docket in most district courts. Meanwhile, supporters of diversity jurisdiction—including the politically powerful American Trial Lawyers Association—counter that bias against out-of-staters does still exist and that even the perception of such bias might inhibit national commercial transactions. Less persuasively, they suggest that allowing two courts systems to look at similar issues gives rise to more ideas and perhaps leads to better decisions. To date, bills to abolish diversity jurisdiction have made little headway in Congress. As a compromise, the American Law Institute recently proposed restricting diversity jurisdiction somewhat by preventing a plaintiff from filing diversity lawsuits in a federal court located in his or her home state.

Modifying the Federal Sentencing Guidelines

Since the mid-1980s, the sentencing of those convicted of federal crimes has been governed by the federal sentencing guidelines in federal courts. Responding to concerns raised about the great variation among sentences imposed by different federal judges upon similarly situated offenders, a 1984 federal law authorizes a United Sentencing Commission to establish mandatory guidelines that federal judges must apply in sentencing. The guidelines specify narrow ranges of permissible sentences for each federal crime, with some adjustment provided for different circumstances such as the defendant's age, past criminal record, and so on.

Unfortunately, when Congress passed the Sentencing Reform Act in 1984, it did not anticipate subsequent developments such as the passage of severe mandatory penalty laws that—when coupled with sentencing guidelines—effectively stripped judges of nearly all their sentencing discretion. Critics charge that the complexity and rigidity of these guidelines conflict with the "sensitive judgment and individualization one expects Article III judges to exercise." In recent years, the American Bar Association, the American Judicature Society, and other groups have suggested ways of improving the federal guidelines, including simplifying the structure of the sentencing process, providing judges with greater discretion to depart from sentence ranges without prosecutorial consent, and encouraging the use of intermediate punishments (i.e., between prison and probation) that would accommodate society's limited resources in dealing with offenders.

Reorganization of the Ninth Circuit

The San Francisco–based U.S. Court of Appeals for the Ninth Circuit has been the subject of often intense debate in recent years. By far the largest of the thirteen federal circuits (it includes California, Arizona, Nevada, Oregon, Washington, Idaho, Montana, Alaska, and Hawai'i), the Ninth Circuit currently serves a population of more than 45 million people, 60 percent more than the next-largest circuit. Because of its gargantuan size, Congress has authorized 28 judgeships for the circuit, 11 more than any other circuit. Critics complain that the presence of so many judges undermines the predictability and consistency of Ninth Circuit case law, as well as unduly limiting the use of en banc procedures. Additionally, they note that the Ninth Circuit takes an average of fourteen months to dispose of cases, several months longer than other circuits. Recommendations for reform range from outright splitting the Ninth Circuit to restructuring the circuit into three adjudicative divisions of seven to eleven judges each (a "circuit division" of senior judges would then be available to resolve conflicts among the divisions). Defenders of the current structure counter that any such restructuring would bring its own set of problems, including (1) high start-up costs for new facilities and relocation, (2) greater inconsistencies in the law, and (3) further delay in the resolution of cases.

An Inspector General for the Federal Courts

In the mid-1990s, legislation was introduced in Congress that would have amended the Inspector General Act of 1978 to establish an Office of Inspector General in the Administrative Office of the U.S. Courts. Traditionally, inspectors general—appointed by the president with the advice of the Senate—have been charged with auditing and investigating federal agencies and, where appropriate, recommending policies that would promote the efficiency and effectiveness of each agency. Even more critical, inspectors general report directly to Congress when they discover "particularly serious or flagrant problems, abuses, or deficiencies." Supporters of such an amendment contend that other congressional forays into judicial administration threaten the independence of the judicial branch. By contrast, extension of the inspectors general statute would enhance the public's ability to monitor and understand the workings of the court without threatening judicial independence in the process. Opponents counter that establishment of an inspector general's office in this context may itself be perceived as a form of congressional intrusion on the courts. Additionally, the highly decentralized nature of the federal court system might pose too great a challenge for an inspector general exercising his or her statutory authority.

THE FUTURE OF THE FEDERAL JUDICIAL SYSTEM

Clearly, the federal court system has progressed by leaps and bounds from its modest beginnings. For the first 100 years of this nation's history, lower federal courts enjoyed only limited jurisdiction to hear cases of local or national concern; the Supreme Court thus filled its docket primarily with cases from the more influential state judiciaries. Today, lower federal courts have the power to decide the constitutionality of federal statutes, resolve other disputes over federal laws, and rule on additional categories of cases as defined by Congress. Because of its exponential growth in size and influence, the federal judicial system has been forced to address a whole new set of administrative challenges. Specifically, federal judges facing increased caseloads in a world of limited resources have been forced to rely on court support staff to assist them in processing cases. In addition to their personal chambers staff (which includes law clerks and secretaries), judges must increasingly depend on court clerks, court reporters, court librarians, pretrial services officers, probation officers, and even staff attorneys. Is the nature and quality of justice dispensed by federal courts somehow compromised by the "bureaucratization" of the federal judiciary? The challenge facing federal courts at the beginning of the twenty-first century is a significant one: how to balance the practical realities of running a large judicial bureaucracy against the concern that prosecutors, defendants, and civil litigants will be given a fair and full hearing on the merits of their claims. Reform proposals in the years to come must address what has become a vexing dilemma for the largest and most influential legal system in the United States.

David Yalof

See also Appellate Courts; Federalism; Habeas Corpus, Writ of; Judicial Review

References and further reading
Baum, Larry. 1998. *American Courts: Process and Policy.* 4th ed. Boston: Houghton-Mifflin College.
Carp, Robert, and Ronald Stidham. 1991. *The Federal Courts.* Washington, DC: Congressional Quarterly Press.
Federal Judicial Center. 1987. *Federal Courts and What They Do.* Washington, DC: Federal Judicial Center.
Hartmus, Diane. 1998. "An Inspector General for the Federal Courts." *Judicature* 81 (March–April): 188–189.
McLauchlin, William P. 1984. *Federal Court Caseloads.* New York: Praeger.
Perry, H. W. 1991. *Deciding to Decide: Agenda Setting in the United States Supreme Court.* Cambridge: Harvard University Press.
Rogers, Elizabeth. 1999. "Remedy of Last Resort: ABA Opposes Plan to Restructure 9th Circuit Court of Appeals," *American Bar Association Journal* 85: 101.
Surrency, Erwin C. 1987. *History of the Federal Courts.* New York: Oceana Publications.
Yackle, Larry W. 1994. *Reclaiming the Federal Courts.* Cambridge: Harvard University Press.

UNITED STATES—STATE SYSTEMS

HISTORY

The United States has a federal system of shared powers and overlapping responsibilities. While the federal government is supreme in specified areas, the states possess significant residual powers, which creates fundamental differences in the interpretation and application of state laws.

State constitutions commonly address the same basic matters as the federal constitution, but there are important differences in terms of length and emphasis. State constitutions are considerably longer than the U.S. Constitution. Surveying 104 of the 145 state constitutions in use since 1776, Christopher Hammons (1999) found Alabama's 1901 Constitution to be the longest, at 220,000 words. The average for all state constitutions is approximately 26,000 words, which is roughly four times longer than the U.S. Constitution, which contains 7,400 words.

Like the U.S. Constitution, state constitutions describe the basic framework of government. Framework provisions specify the powers and responsibilities of the legislative, executive, and judicial branches of government. Many state constitutions also specify fundamental civil rights that are ostensibly beyond the reach of temporary majorities and voting procedures. In general, state constitutions spend considerably more time on framework matters than the U.S. Constitution. The average state constitution contains 505 framework provisions, whereas the U.S. Constitution has only 226 such provisions (Hammons 1999).

State constitutions depart notably from the federal mold when it comes to particularistic provisions (i.e., very specific and detailed provisions). These provisions, which might best be described as superlegislation (Friedman 1988) or "constitutional legislation" (Tarr 1998), are little different from regular legislation except they are more difficult to change. Of 104 state constitutions used by the states since 1776, particularism varies from zero (New Hampshire, 1776; South Carolina, 1776; Virginia, 1776 and 1840) to 69 percent (Louisiana, 1974). The U.S. Constitution contains only 6 percent particularistic provisions, but on average, state constitutions devote 39 percent to these provisions. In sum, state constitutions are 23 times more particularistic than the U.S. Constitution (Hammons 1999).

Examples of particularistic provisions include those prohibiting the legislature from picking textbooks (Wyoming, 1890), regulating women's property (Arkansas, 1868 and 1874), limiting the governor's salary (Tennessee, 1796), appointing stockholders in particular railroad companies as railroad commissioners (Mississippi, 1890), or specifying the creation, maintenance, and names of a highway system (Minnesota, 1919) (Friedman 1988). Others include limits on net fishing in

Florida (1968), telephone regulations in Oklahoma (1907), and indemnification of peanut farmers for losses incurred as a result of *Aspergillus flavus* and freeze damage in peanuts in Alabama (1901) (Hammons 1999).

LEGAL CONCEPTS

Most legal remedies in the United States are sought in state courts (Jacobs 1996). The states remain the primary source of law in the United States, and significant authority for state courts flows from these state laws. State statutes provide the remedies that bring people to court, but given the vast differences in state constitutions, there are enormous differences in specific legal remedies from state to state. Further, each state enjoys its own common law tradition—except Louisiana, which has a civil law tradition based in the Napoleonic Code.

The federal constitution places limits on the exercise of powers by the national government. For example, Congress may act in certain delegated areas. By contrast, states within the federal system possess plenary power. In general, state legislatures have residual powers not ceded to the national government or prohibited to them by the U.S. Constitution. Ordinarily, this means that the constitutionality of a state statute concerns not whether the act is authorized by the constitution but whether the constitution prohibits the action.

Unlike the delegated powers possessed by Congress that do not require that they be exercised, state legislatures possess plenary power and state constitutions impose specific duties on state government. These responsibilities can provide a cause of action when state governments fail to meet these affirmative responsibilities. What would be rights claims under the federal constitution are commonly recast in terms of the obligations that state governments owe their citizens. Just as they create government obligations to their citizens, state constitutions also place limitations on the plenary power of their legislatures and have applied varied restrictions through history.

In recent decades, numerous court decisions have been based on state constitutions, but these cases have been largely devoid of coherent constitutional content (Gardner 1992; Kahn 1993). This failure may stem not from the judges but from the constitutions they interpret. State constitutions depart quite substantially from codifying only fundamental principles, and as a consequence, state court constitutional interpretation typically applies the particularistic provisions that are common in many state constitutions.

CURRENT COURT SYSTEM STRUCTURE

One of the most obvious features of state court systems is their complexity. No two are exactly alike. However, every state has trial courts and at least one state supreme court. Texas and Oklahoma have separate supreme courts

Table 1
THE NUMBER OF JUDGES SERVING IN STATE COURTS, 1999

State	Court of Last Resort	Intermediate Appellate Court	General Jurisdiction Trial Courts
Alabama	9	10	131
Alaska	5	3	32
Arizona	5	22	132
Arkansas	7	9	104
California	7	88	789
Colorado	7	16	111
Connecticut	7	9	174
Delaware	5	—	22
Florida	7	61	455
Georgia	7	10	169
Hawaii	5	4	27
Idaho	5	3	37
Illinois	7	42	864
Indiana	5	15	273
Iowa	9	6	348
Kansas	7	10	149
Kentucky	7	14	93
Louisiana	8	54	214
Maine	7	—	16
Maryland	7	13	132
Massachusetts	7	14	341
Michigan	7	28	210
Minnesota	7	16	252
Mississippi	9	10	48
Missouri	7	32	134
Montana	7	—	37
Nebraska	7	6	51
Nevada	5	—	46
New Hampshire	5	—	29
New Jersey	7	32	372
New Mexico	5	10	69
New York	7	51	457
North Carolina	7	12	95
North Dakota	5	—	46
Ohio	7	65	369
Oklahoma	9*	12	71
Oregon	7	10	94
Pennsylvania	7	24	366
Rhode Island	5	—	22
South Carolina	5	9	43
South Dakota	5	—	36
Tennessee	5	12	142
Texas	9**	80	395
Utah	5	7	68
Vermont	5	—	31
Virginia	7	10	144
Washington	9	20	161
West Virginia	5	—	62
Wisconsin	7	16	233
Wyoming	5	—	17

* Statistic reported for the Supreme Court; 5 justices sit on the Court of Criminal Appeals

** 9 Justices sit on both the Supreme Court and Court of Criminal Appeals

Copyright 2000–2001 Council of State Government. Reprinted with permission from *The Book of States.*

Table 2
ANNUAL SALARIES (IN DOLLARS) FOR STATE COURT JUDGES, 1999

State	Court of Last Resort	Intermediate Appellate Court	General Jurisdiction Trial Courts
Alabama	115,695	114,615	80,615
Alaska	111,562*	105,384*	103,152*
Arizona	114,257	111,536	108,816
Arkansas	108,883	105,440	93,702
California	131,085	122,893	107,390
Colorado	94,000	89,500	85,000
Connecticut	117,610	109,359	104,469
Delaware	121,200	— *	115,300
Florida	137,314	123,583	110,754
Georgia	120,000	119,246	86,125
Hawaii	93,780	89,780	86,780
Idaho	86,468	85,468	81,043
Illinois	126,579	119,133	101,876
Indiana	115,000	110,000	90,000
Iowa	103,600	99,600	94,800
Kansas	96,489	93,044	83,883
Kentucky	98,800	94,767	90,734
Louisiana	103,336	97,928	92,520
Maine	90,909	— *	85,975
Maryland	107,300	100,300	96,500
Massachusetts	107,730	99,690	95,710
Michigan	124,770	114,788	104,807
Minnesota	94,395	88,945	83,494
Mississippi	98,300	91,500	88,700
Missouri	108,783	101,591	82,961
Montana	77,092	— *	72,042
Nebraska	101,648	96,556	94,025
Nevada	85,000**	— *	79,000**
New Hampshire	95,623	— *	89,646
New Jersey	132,250	124,200	115,000
New Mexico	83,593	79,413	75,443
New York	125,000	115,500	113,000
North Carolina	100,320	96,140	90,915
North Dakota	82,164	— *	75,824
Ohio	107,350	99,950	91,950
Oklahoma	97,807	93,530	88,511
Oregon	93,600	91,500	85,300
Pennsylvania	122,864	119,016	106,704
Rhode Island	110,761	— *	99,722
South Carolina	106,713	104,045	101,377
South Dakota	78,762	— *	73,556
Tennessee	107,820	102,804	98,364
Texas	113,000	107,350	101,700
Utah	99,500	94,950	90,450
Vermont	90,584	— *	80,046
Virginia	116,526	110,700	108,175
Washington	112,078	106,537	100,995
West Virginia	85,000	— *	80,000
Wisconsin	100,690	94,804	90,661
Wyoming	85,000	—	77,000

* Location and cost of living differences; lowest listed
** Range of salaries based on experience and location; lowest listed

Copyright 2000–2001 Council of State Government.
Reprinted with permission from *The Book of States*.

for criminal and civil cases. Thirty-nine states have intermediate appellate courts. The supreme courts have appellate jurisdiction over the entire state. Trial courts, both limited and general, have original jurisdiction over geographic areas consisting of cities, counties, or circuits. In some states, intermediate appellate courts have appellate jurisdiction over an entire state; in others, their jurisdiction is limited to regions within the state.

Trial courts may be called, among other names, Superior Courts, District Courts, Circuit Courts, Courts of Common Pleas, Municipal Courts, or other names. High courts are most commonly called supreme courts. In New York, the Supreme Courts are trial courts, and the highest court is called the Court of Appeals.

SPECIALIZED JUDICIAL BODIES

Each state has commissions that interact with the state judiciary to provide formalized input and oversight on such matters as disciplinary actions involving attorneys and sitting judges and judicial selection. Additionally, at the trial court level, states increasingly are utilizing alternative dispute resolution (ADR), which may take the form of informal mediation, arbitration, private judging, or some similar arrangement (Carp and Stidham 1998). ADR may occur in lieu of or in addition to formal litigation and may be private (functioning completely independently of the courts) or court-connected.

STAFFING

Each state controls the practice of law within its borders through licensing procedures. Generally, bar membership is restricted to those who have completed a three-year course of study and passed an examination. Additionally, ethics rules and other restrictions are conditions of retaining the license to practice. Practicing law without a license is illegal in every state.

The states provide a wide array of staffers to support the judicial function, though there are considerable variations from state to state and across courts in terms of the amount of support available. Each state now has a court administrator with some supervisory capacity vis-à-vis the overall judiciary, and each court usually has a clerk of court and secretarial support; some also have law clerks.

In the United States, there is no formal training to become a judge. Judges are attorneys (with a few exceptions) who have met some minimal residency and practice requirements. Table 1 describes the total number of judges serving in each state's court of last resort, intermediate appellate court, and general jurisdiction trial courts in 1999. As the data indicate, the states vary significantly in the number of judges staffing the bench at all levels of the judiciary. General jurisdiction trial courts range in size from 16 judges (in Maine) to 864 judges (in Illinois);

Table 3
METHODS FOR SELECTING STATE COURT JUDGES: COURTS OF LAST RESORT

Partisan Elections	Nonpartisan Elections	Missouri Plan	Gubernatorial Appointment	Legislative Selection
Alabama	Georgia	Alaska	Delaware***	Connecticut
Arkansas	Idaho	Arizona	Hawaii***	Rhode Island
Illinois*	Kentucky	California	Maine	South Carolina
Mississippi	Louisiana	Colorado	Massachusetts***	Virginia
New Mexico*	Michigan	Florida	New Hampshire	
North Carolina	Minnesota	Indiana	New Jersey	
Pennsylvania*	Montana	Iowa	New York	
Tennessee	Nevada	Kansas	Vermont***	
Texas	North Dakota	Maryland		
West Virginia	Ohio**	Missouri		
Oregon	Nebraska			
Washington	Oklahoma			
Wisconsin	South Dakota			
	Utah			
	Wyoming			

*Retention after initial election
**Partisan primaries
***Governor's choices limited to list provided by Judicial Nominating Commission

Copyright 2000–2001 Council of State Government. Reprinted with permission from *The Book of States.*

intermediate appellate courts range from 3 to 88; and courts of last resort are composed of 5 to 9 members. In half of the states, courts of last resort consist of 7 members. These courts typically sit en banc.

Table 2 reports salary information for state court judges, which as the table reveals, varies substantially among the states. Moreover, salaries are higher for judges in appellate courts than in trial courts; movement up the judicial hierarchy results in increased compensation. In 1999, annual salaries for justices in state courts of last resort ranged from $77,092 (in Montana) to $137,314 (in Florida).

Each state determines how the judges of the state judiciary will be chosen. In addressing this extremely important and complex issue, the states have attempted to design selection mechanisms that balance the principles of judicial independence and electoral accountability. Judicial independence rests on the assumption that judges should be insulated, to the greatest extent possible, from external political pressures. The principle of electoral accountability, however, asserts that public officials are representatives who must justify their decisions to the voters or face removal from office.

While some states have opted for the federal model, which maximizes the degree of judicial independence by eliminating the electoral process, the large majority of states have struck the balance moretended to in favor of accountability by choosing to utilize elections, a device to promote popular control. As a result, judges in thirty-eight states must seek reelection regularly, either in partisan elections, nonpartisan elections, or retention elections.

Overall, the states have developed five basic methods for recruiting and retaining judges, which emphasize, to varying degrees, the principles of independence and accountability. First, a number of states utilize partisan elections to staff the bench. In partisan election systems, candidates seek judicial office in elections in which the candidates' partisan affiliations are listed on the ballot. Additionally, candidates in general elections typically are nominated in partisan primaries.

Second, some states use nonpartisan elections to select their judges. In nonpartisan elections, candidates appear on the ballot in general elections, without political party designations. Nonpartisan elections were designed as a reform, wherein voters are expected to substitute assessments of the candidates' qualifications for the candidates' partisan affiliations as the primary basis for casting ballots. Also, nonpartisan elections were designed to reduce the control of polical parties over the judicial selection process.

Third, the largest proportion of states currently use the Missouri (or "Merit") Plan to staff the state bench. The Missouri Plan is a combination of appointment and election and was designed to capture the best features of both. While there are significant variations from state to state in the way the Missouri Plan actually operates, the process begins with the governor appointing a judicial nominating commission, which is responsible for recommending candidates for each vacancy. As vacancies occur, the commission screens potential nominees, evaluating their suitability for judgeship. The commission then presents a list of three candidates to the governor, who must appoint one of the three to fill the vacancy. On appointment, the nominee immediately assumes office. Shortly thereafter, usually in the next general election, the candidate must win voter approval in a retention election. Retention elections ask voters to decide whether a current

Table 4
TERMS OF OFFICE (IN YEARS) FOR STATE COURT JUDGES

State	Court of Last Resort	Intermed. Appellate Court	General Jurisdiction Trial Courts	Mandatory Retirement Age
Alabama	6	6	6	70
Alaska	10	8	6	70
Arizona	6	6	4	70
Arkansas	8	8	4*	70*****
California	12	12	6	—
Colorado	10	8	6	72
Connecticut	8	8	8	70
Delaware	12	—	12	—
Florida	6	6	6	70*****
Georgia	6	6	4	75
Hawaii	10	10	10	70
Idaho	6	6	4	—
Illinois	10	10	6	—
Indiana	10	10	6	75
Iowa	8	6	6	72
Kansas	6	4	4	70*****
Kentucky	8	8	8	—
Louisiana	10	10	6	70
Maine	7	—	7	—
Maryland	10	10	15	70
Massachusetts	Life	Life	Life	70
Michigan	8	6	6	70*****
Minnesota	6	6	6	70
Mississippi	8	4	4	—
Missouri	12	12	6	70
Montana	8	—	6	—
Nebraska	6	6	6	—
Nevada	6	—	6	—
New Hampshire	Life	Life	Life	70
New Jersey	7**	7**	70	70
New Mexico	8	8	6	—
New York	14	5	14****	70
North Carolina	8	8	8	72
North Dakota	10	—	6	—
Ohio	6	6	6	70
Oklahoma	6***	6	4	—
Oregon	6	6	6	75
Pennsylvania	10	10	10	70
Rhode Island	Life	—	Life	—
South Carolina	10	6	6	72
South Dakota	8	—	8	70
Tennessee	8	8	8	—
Texas	6***	6	4	75
Utah	10	10	6	—
Vermont	6	—	6	70******
Virginia	12	8	8	70
Washington	6	6	4	75
West Virginia	12	—	8	—
Wisconsin	10	6	6	—
Wyoming	8	—	6	70

*Chancery probate court judges serve 6 year terms
**Tenure granted upon reappointment after initial term
***Terms of office are the same for the Supreme Court and Court of Criminal Appeals
****County court judges serve 10 year terms
*****Retirement is mandatory at the end of the term during which the specified age is reached

Copyright 2000–2001 Council of State Government. Reprinted with permission from *The Book of States*.

officeholder should continue in office; opposing candidates do not appear on the ballot, and the partisan affiliation of the candidate is not listed on the ballot. If voters approve, the judge begins a regular term of office, facing subsequent retention elections at the end of every term. If voters disapprove, the process begins anew.

Fourth, some states allow their governors to appoint judges, usually with the approval of the state senate. Certain of these states restrict the governor's choices to nominees approved by a judicial nominating commission. Other states allow the governor complete discretion in nominating candidates. This process most closely parallels the system used in the federal courts.

Finally, three states empower their legislatures to select judges. Each chamber of the legislature has a committee to handle judicial appointments, and nominees are approved or rejected through the normal legislative process. Choices are not subject to veto by the governor.

A number of states use several methods of selection, depending on the type of court being staffed. For instance, some states utilize partisan or nonpartisan elections for choosing trial court judges and the Missouri Plan for the court of last resort. Table 3 provides information about the method utilized by each state for selecting justices for the court of last resort. As the table reveals, nine states utilize partisan elections, thirteen states use nonpartisan elections, sixteen states employ the Missouri Plan, eight states utilize gubernatorial appointment, and four states use legislative election.

In practice, selection systems are more varied than just described. For example, judges in some states (Illinois, Louisiana, Mississippi, Kentucky, Maryland, Nebraska, Oklahoma, and South Dakota) are selected from districts, while judges in other states are elected statewide. Also, there can be substantial differences between formal selection mechanisms and informal practice. For instance, every state has a process for filling unexpected vacancies, usually by allowing the governor to appoint someone to fill the vacancy until the term expires. Because judges may resign or retire from the bench during a term if their political party controls the governorship, many judges in elective systems actually get their jobs initially through appointment rather than by winning an election. Through strategic retirements and *ad interim* appointments, the political party retains control of the office, and the appointee gains the advantage of running as an incumbent in the next regular election.

Table 4 lists terms of office for each state's court of last resort, intermediate appellate court, and general jurisdiction trial courts. The states differ substantially in the length of time judges serve at all levels of the judiciary, although appellate court judges generally enjoy longer terms than trial court judges. Also, terms for judicial of-

Table 5
METHODS FOR REMOVING STATE COURT JUDGES

State	Impeachment	Recall	Supreme Court	Legislative Address
Alabama	✓		✓	
Alaska	✓		✓	
Arizona	✓	✓	✓	
Arkansas	✓		✓	✓
California	✓	✓	✓	
Colorado	✓		✓	
Connecticut	✓		✓	✓
Delaware	✓		✓	
Florida	✓		✓	
Georgia	✓		✓	
Hawaii			✓	
Idaho	✓		✓	
Illinois	✓		✓	
Indiana			✓	
Iowa	✓		✓	
Kansas	✓		✓	
Kentucky	✓		✓	
Louisiana	✓		✓	
Maine	✓		✓	✓
Maryland	✓		✓	✓
Massachusetts	✓		✓	✓
Michigan	✓		✓	✓
Minnesota	✓		✓	
Mississippi	✓		✓	✓
Missouri			✓	
Montana	✓		✓	
Nebraska	✓		✓	
Nevada	✓	✓	✓	✓
New Hampshire	✓			✓
New Jersey	✓		✓	
New Mexico	✓		✓	
New York	✓		✓	✓
North Carolina			✓	
North Dakota	✓	✓	✓	
Ohio	✓	✓	✓	✓
Oklahoma	✓		✓	
Oregon			✓	
Pennsylvania	✓		✓	
Rhode Island	✓		✓	✓
South Carolina	✓		✓	✓
South Dakota	✓		✓	
Tennessee	✓			✓
Texas	✓		✓	✓
Utah	✓		✓	
Vermont	✓		✓	
Virginia	✓		✓	
Washington	✓		✓	
West Virginia	✓		✓	
Wisconsin	✓	✓	✓	✓
Wyoming	✓		✓	

Copyright 2000–2001 Council of State Government.
Reprinted with permission from *The Book of States*.

Table 6
TOTAL FILINGS IN STATE COURTS, 1996*

	All States
Courts of Last Resort	88,010
Intermediate Appellate Courts	198,722
General Jurisdiction Trial Courts	
Civil	10,304,491
Criminal	4,363,532
Limited Jurisdiction Trial Courts	
Civil	9,833,691
Criminal	9,659,724

Source: National Center for State Courts, 1996.
Used by permission.

* Figures for limited jurisdiction trial courts are misleading, because many states do not report caseload statistics for these courts.

fice at all levels tend to be longer than terms for most other state and federal political offices.

Across the fifty states, terms in courts of last resort range from six years to life. Terms for intermediate appellate courts and general jurisdiction trial courts range from four years to life. However, only nonelective states grant judges lifetime tenure.

Looking only at the thirty-eight states that utilize elections, the range of terms in the courts of last resort is six to twelve years. Most commonly, justices in these courts serve six-year terms, although a substantial number of states provide eight-year or ten-year terms for these offices. Only three elective states (California, Missouri, and West Virginia) elect justices for twelve-year terms.

In elective states having intermediate appellate courts, almost half (fifteen of thirty-two) designate six-year terms for these courts. Two states (Kansas and Mississippi) use a four-year term. Only one state (New York) uses a five-year term. The remaining fourteen states utilize eight-year, ten-year, or twelve-year terms.

Finally, the most common term for judges in general jurisdiction trial courts in elective states is six years. Twenty-two states use six-year terms for their major trial courts. The remaining states use terms ranging from four to fifteen years for these courts.

Table 4 also documents the extent to which the states set mandatory retirement ages for judges. As can be seen in column five, eighteen states do not place upper limits on the age of their judges, while thirty-two require retirement somewhere between ages seventy and seventy-five.

Table 5 lists the various methods used for removing judges and the states that utilize each method. As the table demonstrates, state court judges across the nation are subject to impeachment, legislative address, recall, and removal by the state supreme court. Forty-six states provide for the impeachment of their judges, sixteen states empower their legislatures to remove judges through the process of legislative address, six states allow

Table 7
Proportion of State Supreme Court Dockets Devoted to Five Issue Categories

State	Criminal	Civil – Government	Civil – Private	Juvenile	Non-adversarial	Number of Cases
Alabama	0.1650	0.1700	0.6300	0.0100	0.0250	200
Alaska	0.0280	0.4196	0.5524	0.0000	0.0000	143
Arizona	0.6667	0.1111	0.1746	0.0000	0.0476	63
Arkansas	0.4750	0.1450	0.3800	0.0000	0.0000	200
California	0.5147	0.3088	0.1765	0.0147	0.0000	68
Colorado	0.1685	0.2753	0.2079	0.0056	0.3427	178
Connecticut	0.2745	0.3529	0.3399	0.0065	0.0261	153
Delaware	0.2821	0.1282	0.5000	0.0000	0.0897	78
Florida	0.3869	0.2211	0.1256	0.0101	0.2563	199
Georgia	0.5300	0.1550	0.2900	0.0050	0.0200	200
Hawaii	0.4947	0.2316	0.2526	0.0105	0.0105	95
Idaho	0.1898	0.4234	0.3869	0.0000	0.0000	137
Illinois	0.4762	0.2000	0.3238	0.0190	0.0000	105
Indiana	0.4882	0.3706	0.1412	0.0000	0.0000	170
Iowa	0.3000	0.3000	0.3800	0.0100	0.0100	100
Kansas	0.5256	0.2628	0.2308	0.0192	0.0000	156
Kentucky	0.3034	0.4157	0.2584	0.0000	0.0225	89
Louisiana	0.2720	0.3120	0.4080	0.0080	0.0000	125
Maine	0.2050	0.2450	0.5200	0.0000	0.0300	200
Maryland	0.3529	0.2843	0.3235	0.0196	0.0196	102
Massachusetts	0.3900	0.3050	0.2650	0.0050	0.0350	200
Michigan	0.3494	0.3133	0.3373	0.0000	0.0000	83
Minnesota	0.2385	0.4231	0.3231	0.0000	0.0154	130
Mississippi	0.4150	0.2450	0.1400	0.0100	0.1900	200
Missouri	0.3293	0.4268	0.2439	0.0000	0.0000	82
Montana	0.3333	0.1970	0.4545	0.0000	0.0152	198
Nebraska	0.2200	0.2950	0.4450	0.0350	0.0050	200
Nevada	0.4405	0.2083	0.3452	0.0060	0.0000	168
New Hampshire	0.3308	0.2707	0.3684	0.0000	0.0301	133
New Jersey	0.2718	0.3592	0.3592	0.0097	0.0000	103
New Mexico	0.2338	0.3377	0.3896	0.0130	0.0260	77
New York	0.3905	0.3491	0.2367	0.0178	0.0059	169
North Carolina	0.7445	0.1533	0.0949	0.0073	0.0000	137
North Dakota	0.2700	0.2450	0.4650	0.0150	0.0050	200
Ohio	0.2010	0.6181	0.1658	0.0101	0.0050	199
Oklahoma	0.4667	0.3407	0.1926	0.0000	0.0000	135
Oregon	0.2558	0.5116	0.2326	0.0116	0.0000	86
Pennsylvania	0.3861	0.3228	0.2848	0.0000	0.0063	158
Rhode Island	0.3000	0.2950	0.3650	0.0100	0.0300	200
South Carolina	0.3421	0.3553	0.2895	0.0000	0.0132	152
South Dakota	0.2671	0.1712	0.5411	0.0068	0.0137	146
Tennessee	0.2936	0.1376	0.5321	0.0092	0.0275	109
Texas	0.4835	0.1694	0.3471	0.0000	0.0000	242
Utah	0.1919	0.3636	0.4444	0.0000	0.0000	99
Vermont	0.2500	0.3125	0.3750	0.0208	0.0417	48
Virginia	0.1504	0.1681	0.6372	0.0000	0.0442	113
Washington	0.4825	0.2719	0.2193	0.0088	0.0175	114
West Virginia	0.2450	0.2800	0.4300	0.0150	0.0300	200
Wisconsin	0.3235	0.3824	0.2059	0.0098	0.0784	102
Wyoming	0.2924	0.2807	0.4211	0.0058	0.0000	171
Total	**0.3383**	**0.2835**	**0.3380**	**0.0073**	**0.0343**	**7115**

their judges to be recalled, and virtually every state empowers its state court of last resort to remove judges.

IMPACT OF LAW

State courts address virtually every aspect of life in the United States, including matters of federal law that arise within the context of both criminal and civil disputes. Today, the states process over 99 percent of the nation's litigation (Glick 1993).

Table 6 describes the filings in state courts in 1996 by level of court. To some extent, the figures are misleading because many states fail to report caseload data for their trial courts of limited jurisdiction. As the table indicates, however, the total filings in all state courts reached over 34 million cases in 1996. Most of these involved civil rather than criminal disputes. Also, the caseloads for trial courts greatly exceeded those of the appellate courts.

Table 7 reports the proportion of cases in each state devoted to five mutually exclusive and exhaustive categories of litigation in courts of last resort in 1996. Clearly, state high courts exhibit substantial variation in the ways in which their dockets are devoted to particular types of disputes. Regarding criminal matters, the amount of docket space taken up with these decisions ranges from 2.8 percent (in Alaska) to 74.5 percent (in North Carolina), with an average of 33.8 percent. Concerning civil cases in which governmental entities are litigants, the states range from 11.1 percent (in Arkansas) to 61.8 percent (in Ohio), for an average of 28.5 percent. In civil cases involving private parties only, docket space ranges from 9.5 percent (in North Carolina) to 63.7 percent (in Virginia), for an average of 33.8 percent. Finally, dockets contain small proportions of other matters, such as juvenile cases and other nonadversarial matters. Generally, these variations suggest that state judiciaries may vary substantially in their impact on state law and the state political system.

Paul Brace
Melinda Gann Hall

See also Alternative Dispute Resolution; Appellate Courts; Arbitration; Civil Law; Common Law; Constitutional Law; Criminal Law; Criminal Procedures; Federalism; Incarceration; Judicial Review; Judicial Selection, Methods of; Law Clerks; Mediation; Merit Selection ("Missouri Plan"); Napoleonic Code; Trial Courts

References and further reading
Carp, Robert A., and Ronald Stidham. 1998. *Judicial Processes in America*. Washington, DC: Congressional Quarterly.
Council of State Governments. 1999. *Book of the States, 1998–99 Edition*. Lexington, KY: Council of State Governments.
Froman, Lewis A., Jr. 1966. "Some Effects of Interest Group Strength in State Politics." *American Political Science Review* 60, no. 4 (December): 952–962.
Hall, Melinda Gann, and Chris Bonneau. 2000. "The Wisconsin Judiciary." Pp. 114–138 in *Wisconsin Government and Politics*. Edited by Ronald E. Weber. New York: McGraw-Hill.
Hammons, Christopher W. 1999. "Was James Madison Wrong? Rethinking American Preferences for Short, Framework-Oriented Constitutions." *American Political Science Review* 93 (December): 837–849.
Gardner, James A. 1992. "The Failed Discourse on State Constitutionalism." *Michigan Law Review* 90 (February): 761–837.
Kahn, Paul W. 1993. "Interpretation and Authority in State Constitutionalism." *Harvard Law Review* 106 (March): 1147–1168.
National Center for State Courts. 1996. *A Survey of State Judicial Fringe Benefits*. 2nd ed. Chicago: American Bar Association.
———. 1997. *State Court Caseload Statistics, 1996*. Williamsburg, VA: National Center for State Courts.
———. 2000. *Survey of Judicial Salaries*. Williamsburg, VA: National Center for State Courts.

URUGUAY

GENERAL INFORMATION

Uruguay (complete formal name is Oriental Republic of Uruguay) is located in the southeastern part of South America, bordering the Atlantic Ocean to the southeast, Brazil to the east and north, Argentina to the west, and the Río de la Plata to the south. Uruguay's 72,172 square miles are almost entirely made of plains, with only a few hills rising to the east, toward the border with Brazil. Its 120-mile coastline extending both on the Rio de la Plata and the Atlantic Ocean, combined with mild temperatures in the spring and summer months of September through March, make for a most attractive chain of beaches, a center of tourism not only for Uruguayans but also for its neighbors, Argentines and Brazilians. Montevideo, the capital of Uruguay, which is the southernmost capital city in Latin America, is located on the shores of the Río de la Plata, itself bordered by beaches. Uruguay's homogeneous population of 3.2 million is 90 percent of European descent, with 6 percent mestizo and 4 percent black. By 1832, Native Indians called the Charrúas had been all but exterminated by the criollos (Spanish descendants born in the colonies). Some 91 percent of the population lives in urban areas, and the 1996 census shows a literacy rate of 96.9 percent. The 1999 Human Development Report of the UN Development Program (UNDP) places Uruguay number forty among the forty-five nations with a high human development index, behind only Chile and Argentina in Latin America. Spanish is the official language and Roman Catholicism the most practiced religion, although in later years Protestantism has been gaining increasing numbers of followers.

HISTORY

In 1516, Juan Díaz de Solís, the Spanish conquistador who had advanced farther south than any of his prede-

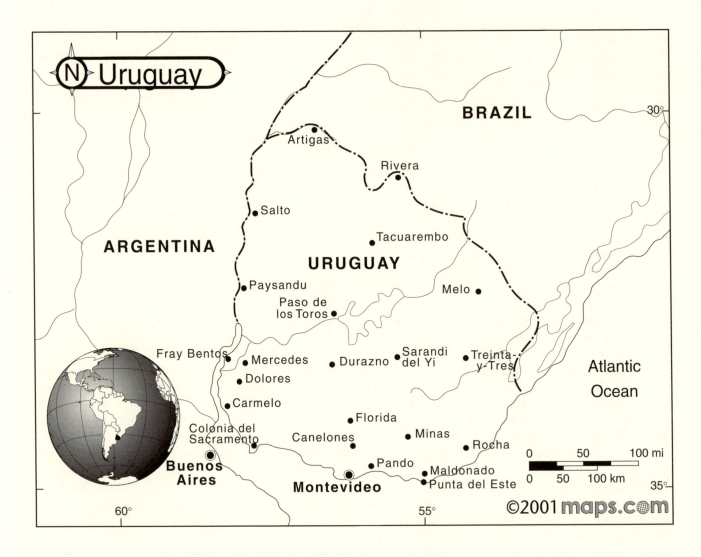

cessors, sailed the Río de la Plata westward, hoping to find a strait that would lead him across the continent. He was the first Spaniard to land in Uruguay, in a zone about seventy miles east of where Montevideo would be founded in 1726. In spite of the lack of precious metals treasured by the colonial powers of the time, the Banda Oriental, which was then the name of the colony, became important for both the Spanish and the Portuguese as the conflictive frontier between the two empires. This feud marked the history of Uruguay up to and including its independence in 1825. At the beginning of the seventeenth century, under the leadership of José Gervasio Artigas, the Banda Oriental, which was part of the Spanish viceroyalty of the Río de la Plata, with its capital in Buenos Aires, began its road to independence. Artigas proposed the declaration of independence of the provinces that formed the viceroyalty and the formation of a confederation tailored after the U.S. Constitution, to be called the United Provinces of the Río de la Plata and to provide for the political and economic autonomy of each province. In 1813 the delegates from the Banda Oriental who had Artigas's instructions for such a pro-

posal, which became known as "The Instructions of the Year Thirteen," were not allowed in the congress of all the provinces that was summoned in the centralist city of Buenos Aires, thus causing the Banda Oriental to break relations with Buenos Aires. In 1816 the Portuguese invaded the Banda Oriental, and it became the Cisplatine Province. Artigas fought the Portuguese until 1820, the year in which he fled to Paraguay, where he died in 1850. On April 19, 1825, a group of thirty-three Uruguayans, which became known as the "Thirty-Three Orientals," under the leadership of Juan Antonio Lavalleja, crossed the Río Uruguay from Argentina and, after regaining control of part of the territory, declared the independence of Uruguay on August 25, 1825.

British trade interests in the region dictated the need for a buffer state between the heirs of the colonial powers, Argentina and Brazil. With the mediation of Great Britain, the Treaty of Montevideo was signed on August 27, 1828, by which both countries renounced all territorial claims over Uruguay and began withdrawing their troops from its territory. The first constitution was adopted on July 18, 1830. It provided for a unitary republic called the República Oriental del Uruguay. As a colony, Uruguay was first ruled by the Spanish Law of the Indies, and once independent, it tailored its laws after the Napoleonic Code.

After independence and for the rest of the nineteenth century, the country was almost continuously involved in struggles between factions supported by Argentines and Brazilians. The two main political parties, which continue to exist up to our day, the Partido Nacional and the Partido Colorado, were born in the years of independence and were the main protagonists of armed conflict until the end of the century.

In 1903 and again in 1909, José Batlle y Ordoñez became president of Uruguay, implementing a series of reforms that were to define modern Uruguay. After signing peace accords with the followers of Aparicio Saravia, who had led a revolution and was killed in 1904, Batlle commenced his social and economic reforms, which made Uruguay a welfare state. Based mainly on its exports of wool and beef, Uruguay knew years of economic development and growth, accompanied by a fair distribution of the country's wealth that, until the decade of the 1950s, created a large middle class. Because of economic stagnation during the following decade, however, Uruguay—which together with Chile had enjoyed a stable and long-lasting democracy—was set upon from both the Left and the Right. During the 1960s an urban guerrilla group called Movimiento de Liberación Nacional Tupamaros sought power through the use of force and the overthrow of democratic institutions. The Uruguayan Armed Forces were first used to fight the Tupamaros but soon became the instrument utilized by the government to quell the unrest caused by declining economic conditions and resulting social injustice. In spite of the fact that by the end of the 1960s the Tupamaro movement had all but been exterminated by the armed forces, their existence, together with the alleged corruption of the political class, was used as the excuse for the military takeover of the government on June 27, 1973. The incumbent president, Juan María Bordaberry, stayed on in office, giving the coup more of a civil-military nature, which it maintained until power was returned to elected civilian officials in 1985.

During their rule, the military suspended the constitution and ran the country with what were known as the Institutional Acts, which had constitutional level. The route to the restoration of democracy began with the result of a plebiscite that the military held in November 1980. After years of a most repressive dictatorship that reached all economic and social classes, and the implementation of a dollar-pegged, export-led model of dependent development that proved disastrous to the country, the military called a plebiscite on a constitutional reform that would in fact institutionalize their presence in the government upon the country's return to democracy. By a plurality of 57.2 percent, the Uruguayan people turned down the military's proposed constitution, being the first time in the history of the world that a plebiscite organized by a dictatorship was rejected.

A second setback for the military occurred in 1982. Internal elections in the political parties were called in November of that year. Although the leftist coalition Frente Amplio and an important part of the Blanco Party were barred from participating, a sweeping majority of Uruguayans voted for factions within the Blanco and Colorado Parties, which were openly opposed to the military. The military-backed party suffered an unquestionable defeat, destroying any hopes for their political participation upon return to democracy. Faced with the reality of their disastrous economic performance and widespread rejection by the people, the military called for a dialog with the political class, in order to set a timetable for their withdrawal and a return to democracy. Negotiations concluded in August 1984 with the signature of an agreement called the Naval Club Pact, for it was signed at the Naval Club; the pact provided for elections to be held in November of that year, along with other actions toward a return to democracy. Julio María Sanguinetti of the Colorado Party was elected president in that election and was sworn into office on March 1, 1985. Since there were still some political parties and politicians barred from participating that year, the first completely free elections were held in 1989. The Blanco Party candidate, Luis Alberto Lacalle, won that election. In 1994 and again in 1999, the Colorado Party won the election, this last time under a newly revised constitution. The alternation of political parties in power through open and fair elections demonstrates that the transition to democracy is now finished. Uruguay is well along in the consolidation of its democracy, with full participation of its democratic institutions.

LEGAL CONCEPTS

Uruguay is a unitary state divided into nineteen administrative jurisdictions called departments. The Uruguayan Constitution provides for a democratic republic as the organization of the state, with the separation of powers into executive, legislative, and judicial branches of government. It also provides for fundamental human rights, including the right to life, honor, freedom, security, work, and property, as well as freedom of religion and habeas corpus. Under its provisions the law is to promote the organization of workers' unions, workers being thereby guaranteed the right to strike, and it is also to regulate the work of women and children. There is no death penalty in Uruguay and no trial by jury. The constitution, last reformed in 1997, now includes provisions for the protection of the environment.

Rules of law are hierarchically ordered in the Uruguayan legal system. The constitution is the supreme law, and the lower echelon is formed by decrees issued by the executive. Legislation is the only formal source of law. Custom becomes a source of law only when it is incorporated in an act sanctioned by the legislature; precedents are considered a guide but are not mandatory.

International treaties to which Uruguay is a signatory become mandatory only after they are incorporated as law by the Uruguayan Parliament. In the area of human rights, Uruguay is a signatory to the Universal Declaration of Human Rights; the International Pact on Economic, Social and Cultural Rights; the International Pact on Civil and Political Rights; the Inter-American Convention on Human Rights; the Convention on Elimination of All Forms of Discrimination against Women; the Convention against Torture and Other Cruel, Inhumane or Degrading Punishments or Treatments; and the Convention on the Rights of Children.

The legislative power is vested in the General Assembly, consisting of two chambers: the Chamber of Deputies and the Chamber of Senators. The first is composed of ninety-nine members elected directly by the people under a system of proportional representation that takes into account the votes cast in favor of each political party throughout the country. Each one of the nineteen departments is to have at least two representatives. The Senate is composed of thirty members elected directly by the people in a single electoral district by a system of integral proportional representation. It includes the vice president of the republic, who serves as the presiding officer of the Senate as well as of the General Assembly. In order to be a representative, one must be twenty-five years of age and a natural citizen, or have been a legal citizen for at least five years. In order to be a senator, one must be thirty years old and be a natural citizen, or have been a legal citizen for a minimum of seven years. Representatives and senators hold office for five years, and there is no limitation on re-elections. All members of the General Assembly have immunity of prosecution, but the Chamber of Representatives has the right of impeachment before the Chamber of Senators of both its members and the members of the latter. The Senate has the right to remove the accused from office, who is then subject to trial under the law by the judiciary.

The executive power is vested in the president of the republic, acting either with a minister or ministers according to the subject matter being decided upon, or with the council of ministers formed by all the ministers in the cabinet. The vice president fills the office of president in case of temporary or permanent vacancy. As provided for in the 1997 constitutional amendment, the president and the vice president are elected jointly and directly by the people by absolute majority—50 percent plus one—of the voters. Only one candidate to the presidency and to the vice presidency elected in party internal elections may run in each party ticket. If no candidate obtains the required majority in the first round, a runoff is held a month later between the top two vote-getters. A simple majority is required to be elected in this second round. The president and the vice president hold office for a period of five years, and there is no immediate re-election permitted. A period of five years must elapse before an incumbent may run again.

The Uruguayan constitution provides for a judicial power vested in the Supreme Court of Justice and other courts established by law. The Supreme Court of Justice is composed of five members, at least forty years of age, who must be natural citizens, or legal citizens for a minimum of ten years with twenty-five years of residency in the country; a graduate lawyer for more than ten years; or a lawyer who has been a judge or member of the office of the attorney general for at least eight years. They are appointed by the General Assembly with a two-thirds special majority. If within ninety days of a vacancy that majority is not attained, the judge of the appellate courts with seniority in such post is automatically appointed. At the present time there are two Supreme Court justices who became automatically appointed because of a lack of agreement among the members of Congress. Supreme Court justices serve for ten years, or until they turn seventy years of age, and may not be re-elected until a five-year lapse of the previous term. The presidency of the court rotates yearly among the five members in order of seniority as a member of the court.

CURRENT COURT SYSTEM STRUCTURE

In addition to the Supreme Court of Justice, which decides matters on last appeal and the constitutionality of the law, and also exercises the administrative and budgetary supervision of the judiciary, there are Courts of Appeals, Trial Courts, Justices of the Peace, and a Misdemeanor Court.

1. The Courts of Appeals are located in Montevideo. They have national jurisdiction and decide on appeals filed against sentences awarded by the Trial Courts. There are a total of fifteen Courts of Appeals: seven that hear appeals on civil, administrative, customs, and commercial law cases; two on family law cases; three on labor law cases; and three on criminal law cases.

2. Trial Courts (called Courts of First Instance) have departmental jurisdiction. There are a total of eighty-nine Trial Courts in Montevideo. Each hears cases in either family law—which includes cases on alimony, custody and divorce; administrative law, including all cases in which the state acts as either

Legal Structure of Uruguayan Courts

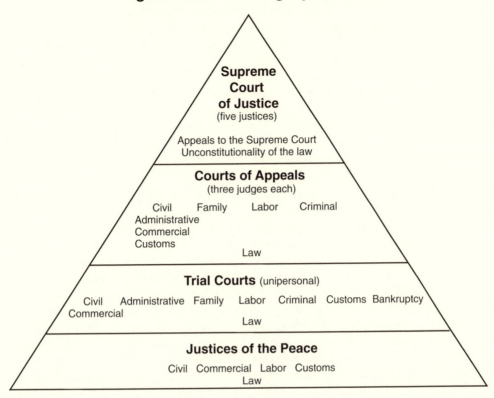

Supreme Court of Justice (five justices)

Appeals to the Supreme Court
Unconstitutionality of the law

Courts of Appeals (three judges each)

Civil   Family   Labor   Criminal
Administrative
Commercial
Customs
Law

Trial Courts (unipersonal)

Civil   Administrative   Family   Labor   Criminal   Customs   Bankruptcy
Commercial
Law

Justices of the Peace

Civil   Commercial   Labor   Customs
Law

plaintiff or defendant; civil, customs, and commercial law; and labor law—or criminal law. There are eighty-one Trial Courts in the remaining eighteen departments of the country.

3. There are 170 justices of the peace that preside over a constitutionally mandated hearing to attempt a settlement between parties prior to their bringing a case to court for trial. They are organized in four categories determined by territorial jurisdiction and amount of claims, except for family or criminal law cases, in which they have no jurisdiction. There is also a Misdemeanor Court located in Montevideo.

The judiciary also provides legal counsel free of charge to people of lower income through the Public Defenders Service. There are 180 public defenders throughout the country that serve under a director in Family, Civil, Criminal, Labor Law, and Criminal Sentences Enforcement. In criminal cases, since the Uruguayan constitution provides for mandatory defense, there is no maximum income limit to obtain free legal counsel by this service.

Mediation Centers under the direction of a coordinating board were created by the Supreme Court of Justice as a pilot project in 1995. These centers are located in the lowest income, most populated neighborhoods of Montevideo and function in the Neighborhood Health Centers. They are staffed by lawyers, social workers, public notaries, and judiciary branch civil servants doing voluntary work. The purpose of these Mediation Centers is to make for an easier access to legal counsel and provide mediation services to settle everyday disputes among neighbors and family members.

A reform to the procedural law—except for criminal procedural law—was enacted in 1989 by which the procedure by hearings was established in substitution of the all-written procedure used previously. A similar reform is being studied with regard to criminal procedural law that will be implemented in the near future.

SPECIALIZED JUDICIAL BODIES

There is an Administrative Tribunal that has jurisdiction only to hear cases in which the annulment of government administrative decisions is claimed. In order to become a member of this five-judge tribunal, a candidate must fulfill the same requirements for becoming a member of the Supreme Court of Justice. The decisions of this tribunal admit no further review. If an administrative decision is annulled, the plaintiff is entitled to compensation by the government.

A Peace Commission was installed by the executive branch in August 2000 to investigate the truth about the disappeared while in detention during the military dictatorship. Upon return of the country to democracy in 1985, Uruguayan society was faced with the most painful of its consequences—that is, the manner in which to process the human rights violations that occurred during the thirteen years of military government. The civil-military confrontation that ensued was ended by an amnesty law voted by the Uruguayan Parliament and later ratified by the civil society in a plebiscite that was held in April 1989. This amnesty waived the right of the Uruguayan state to bring the military to trial in criminal courts; however, there were several civil reparations awarded for human rights violations during those years. With the installation of the Batlle administration in March 2000, a commitment was made by the executive, for the first time since the return to democracy, to search for the truth with regard to those disappeared while in detention during the dictatorship—the outstanding issue that had never been resolved. The Peace Commission, presided over by the Archbishop of Montevideo, is formed by two lawyers, a Jesuit priest and two other prominent public figures. Its only objective is the search for the remains of those disappeared during the military government and their delivery, if possible, to their relatives. Working with information provided by Uruguayan groups and individuals, and in conjunction with the Argentine government and human rights groups, by October 2000 the commission was able to establish that there have been 120 disappeared Uruguayans, of whom 23 disappeared in Uruguay, 90 in Argentina, and the rest in Paraguay and Chile. This body will not judge, or even reveal the names of, the military personnel involved in the actions that are the subject of their investigations, but locate the remains of the disappeared and by turning them over to their relatives contribute to the final reconciliation of the Uruguayan society.

STAFFING

The judiciary branch is presently staffed with 467 judges in all echelons of the judiciary; 788 other professionals that work in the administration of justice, such as lawyers, public notaries, social workers, and psychologists; and 2,666 administrative personnel and clerks.

An aggressive program is being implemented for the advanced training of administrative personnel, and there is a Center of Judicial Studies that permanently offers courses for judges, public defenders, and other professionals working in the judiciary to improve their performance and service.

The Office of the Public Ministry is headed by the attorney general, who is appointed by the executive with the consent of the Chamber of Senators. It is staffed with thirty-three national attorneys, the same number of adjunct national attorneys, and attorney secretaries in Montevideo; thirteen are criminal prosecutors, and the rest represent the interests of the society in civil, customs, juvenile, and public finance law. There are forty-six departmental attorneys serving in the other eighteen departments of the country.

There are approximately five thousand attorneys presently practicing law in Uruguay. Once a law degree has been obtained in either the School of Law of the University of the Republic—which offers free education up to and including graduate education—or in one of three private universities, membership in the Uruguayan Bar Association is not required in order to practice law. Legal counsel is mandatory for all litigants.

IMPACT OF LAW

The Uruguayan system of justice is a traditionally recognized pillar of the Uruguayan society. Because the proposed budget for the judicial branch goes to Parliament through the executive, which may modify it, the independence of the judicial branch has been questioned as of late. In 1999 there was a constitutional amendment proposed that would allow for the Supreme Court of Justice to submit its budget directly to Parliament, but it did not obtain the required majority to be passed. In spite of the very low allocation of resources to the judicial branch, 1.4 percent of the total budget in 1999, a modernization and reform project is underway with the use of a computerized system as a base for the upgrading of all administrative services in connection with the administration of justice. Quite apart from any charges of corruption or any doubts as to the honesty of judges in Uruguay, the matter of the excessive length of time taken by trial proceedings was one of the subjects that contributed to a deteriorating image of the judicial branch and the courts. The procedural law reform that was implemented in 1989 has dramatically shortened trial length, thus contributing highly to a renewed confidence and trust in the Uruguayan judicial system.

Lilia Ferro-Clérico

See also Dispute Resolution under Regional Trade Agreements; Judicial Independence; Napoleonic Code; The Spanish Empire and the Laws of the Indies
References and further reading
Caetano, Gerardo, and José Rilla. 1996. *Historia Contemporánea del Uruguay: De la Colonia al MERCOSUR.* Montevideo: Editorial Fin de Siglo.
Constitution of the Republic of Uruguay. 1997.
Fitzgibbon, Russell H. 1956. *Uruguay: Portrait of a Democracy.* London: George Allen and Unwin.
Linz, Juan J., and Alfred Stepan. 1996. "A Risk-Prone Consolidated Democracy: Uruguay." Pp. 151–165 in *Problems of Democratic Transition and Consolidation—Southern Europe, South America and Post-Communist Europe.* Baltimore and London: Johns Hopkins University Press.
UN Human Development Report. 1999. http://www.undp.org/hdro (accessed December 16, 2001).
Véscovi, Enrique. 1968. *Introducción al Derecho.* Montevideo: Editorial Letras.

Weinstein, Martin. 1988. *Uruguay: Democracy at the Crossroads.* Boulder: Westview Press.

Zubillaga, Carlos, y otros. 1992. *Ediciones Quinto Centenario.* Vol. I: *Estudios Antropológicos.* Montevideo: Departamento de Publicaciones de la Universidad de la República.

UTAH

GENERAL INFORMATION

The state of Utah is located in the west-central United States, between Nevada and Colorado. It is 84,900 square miles in area, making it the eleventh largest state. Its estimated 2000 population was 2,233,169. More than three-quarters of the state's population lives in a narrow corridor less than one hundred miles long, along the Wasatch Mountain range. More than two-thirds of the population belongs to the Church of Jesus Christ of Latter-day Saints (Mormons), whose members came to settle the area in 1847.

EVOLUTION AND HISTORY

Beginning in 1849, Utah citizens wrote six constitutions and applied unsuccessfully for statehood six times before Congress finally accepted the constitution of 1895 and admitted Utah to the Union in 1896. Resistance to Utah statehood was fueled by continuing tensions in Utah between Mormons and non-Mormons, including many leaders of the federal territorial government, and by nationwide suspicion of the Mormon practice of polygamy, which was not abandoned by church leadership until 1890.

Mormon doctrine holds that the framers of the U.S. Constitution were divinely inspired. Nonetheless, church members lost faith in civil law after it failed to protect them in violent clashes with neighbors in Ohio, Missouri, and Illinois before the migration to Utah, and later vigorously prosecuted them for their religious practice of polygamy. Church doctrine also preached the importance of settling disputes among the Saints via negotiation and brotherly love, rather than adversarially.

Consequently, in Utah Territory the Mormon Church developed an elaborate system of ecclesiastical courts that served its community in both secular and religious disputes. Members were forbidden to take civil disputes with other Mormons into the territorial courts, although they did recognize its jurisdiction in criminal matters and disputes between Mormons and non-Mormons. Legal doctrines developed that differed significantly from the common law prevailing elsewhere in the United States in property, contract, and domestic relations law. For example, divorces were more easily obtained in church courts at the time than in civil courts.

The Constitution of 1895 was written to put the new state's history of religious conflict behind it and hasten its move into the national economy, however, so it included few features peculiar to Utah (but see Notable Features, below). Drafters borrowed provisions from the constitutions of Washington, California, Wyoming, and New York, among others. It joined Colorado and Wyoming in granting women the right to vote and hold office, a right women had enjoyed for seventeen years under the territorial government, until the federal Edmunds-Tucker Act took it away in 1887 to increase pressure on polygamists.

As of 1996, Utah was one of only nineteen states still operating under their original constitutions. After defeating a proposal for a constitutional convention in the mid-1960s, Utah created, first temporarily and later permanently, a Constitutional Revision Commission, which has successfully promoted significant reforms of the legislative, executive, and judicial articles, among others.

CURRENT LEGAL STRUCTURE

Courts

The Utah judiciary consists of a Supreme Court, Court of Appeals, a general jurisdiction trial court called the District Court, a limited jurisdiction Juvenile Court, and a court not of record, the Justice Court (see figure). The system is now considerably simpler and more centralized than it had been in earlier years, with administration largely consolidated at the state level.

The Supreme Court consists of five justices. The justices elect their own chief justice for a term of four years. The court's jurisdiction includes appellate review of first degree and capital felony cases, and all civil cases except domestic relations from the District Court. It can, however, transfer any of these cases back to the Court of Appeals except the capital cases and certain issues concerning voting, elections, removal of public officers, and legislative subpoenas. The Supreme Court also has appellate jurisdiction over cases from the Court of Appeals and formal adjudicative proceedings of several state agencies: the Public Service Commission; the Tax Commission; the School and Institutional Trust Lands Board; the Board of Oil, Gas, and Mining; the State Engineer; and the Division of Forestry, Fire and State Lands. It also reviews proceedings of the Judicial Conduct Commission.

The Court of Appeals has appellate jurisdiction over formal adjudications of other administrative agencies, domestic relations, and less serious criminal cases of the District Court, and all cases from the Juvenile Court. An unusual feature is that the Court of Appeals also receives transfers of other civil cases from the Supreme Court, an arrangement designed to balance the workload across the courts and provide variety for the Court of Appeals judges. The majority of civil cases are transferred in this fashion. The Court of Appeals has seven judges, who sit in panels of three. It does not sit en banc. The judges elect a colleague as chief judge for a two-year term. The Court of Appeals was created in 1986 by legislation designed to implement the 1985 revision of the judicial article of the constitution, and it seated its first judges in 1987.

The District Court includes seventy full-time judges and seven commissioners across eight judicial districts, who have original jurisdiction to try all civil cases and all criminal felonies and some misdemeanors. They hold trials de novo for cases appealed from the small claims department or Justice Court. Court commissioners assist district judges by making recommendations in domestic relations cases and involuntary civil commitments.

The Juvenile Court consists of twenty-five judges and one commissioner, who serve in the state's eight judicial districts. The Juvenile Court hears cases against offenders under eighteen years of age and cases involving child abuse, neglect, or dependency. It has the power to terminate parental rights and to determine child custody, support, and visitation in some circumstances. If a minor is charged as an adult, the Juvenile Court conducts the preliminary hearing. The Juvenile Court also administers a probation department.

The justice courts hear class B and C misdemeanors, infractions, violations of ordinances, and small claims. Unlike the other courts, which are administered statewide, justice courts are established and staffed by cities and counties. Litigants often appear pro se. Approximately 150 cities and counties have created justice courts, which are staffed by approximately 130 judges, some serving more than one court.

Administrative Law

Utah has a centralized Division of Administrative Rules, but a decentralized system for administrative adjudication. Each state or local agency hires its own administrative law judges. Utah's rule-making process forbids the adoption of rules with changes after the proposed rules were published. If substantive changes are made, the rules must be republished before adoption.

Legal Profession

As of October 2000 there were 5,440 active attorneys licensed with the state bar. Public legal representation is administered by each jurisdiction. Appointed city attorneys handle civil law work, infractions, and misdemeanors for municipalities. Elected county attorneys (the "district" attorneys in Salt Lake County) handle misdemeanors in unincorporated areas, all felonies, and the counties' civil work. Statutory authorization exists for multicounty district attorneys, but this has been little used.

The elected state attorney general has statewide criminal trial jurisdiction but usually just assists the county or

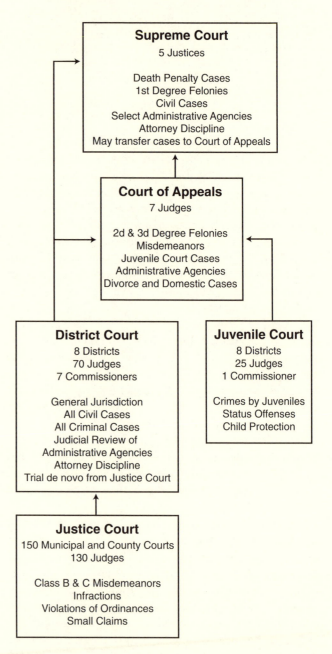

Legal Structure of Utah Courts

Supreme Court

5 Justices

Death Penalty Cases
1st Degree Felonies
Civil Cases
Select Administrative Agencies
Attorney Discipline
May transfer cases to Court of Appeals

Court of Appeals

7 Judges

2d & 3d Degree Felonies
Misdemeanors
Juvenile Court Cases
Administrative Agencies
Divorce and Domestic Cases

District Court

8 Districts
70 Judges
7 Commissioners

General Jurisdiction
All Civil Cases
All Criminal Cases
Judicial Review of
Administrative Agencies
Attorney Discipline
Trial de novo from Justice Court

Juvenile Court

8 Districts
25 Judges
1 Commissioner

Crimes by Juveniles
Status Offenses
Child Protection

Justice Court

150 Municipal and County Courts
130 Judges

Class B & C Misdemeanors
Infractions
Violations of Ordinances
Small Claims

district attorneys upon request. The attorney general manages all criminal appeals. In addition, the attorney general's office represents state agencies and has special units that prosecute financial crimes and consumer fraud and provide support and training for child abuse and domestic violence prosecution.

Criminal defense for indigents is provided by court-appointed attorneys or, in larger cities, by private firms contracted to provide the service. Counties and cities bear the costs of appointed counsel.

The state contains two law schools, one at the University of Utah and one at Brigham Young University. Neither provides for degrees earned through evening classes.

NOTABLE FEATURES

The Utah judiciary is notable for an unusually strong delegation of policy-making authority to a Judicial Council. The council has constitutional authority to adopt uniform rules and staffing levels for the courts statewide. Since 1989 the council has also administered a judicial performance evaluation system for the judges in courts of record (see Staffing).

The council consists of the chief justice of the Supreme Court, who chairs it, one other Supreme Court justice, one judge from the Court of Appeals, five District Court judges, two Juvenile Court judges, three Justice Court judges, and a representative from the state bar. The state court administrator staffs the council. In addition, each level of court has its own board, to which the judges of that level choose members who serve as a liaison between the judges and the Judicial Council, and who pass administrative rules for that court compatible with guidelines of the Judicial Council.

Utah is also among the few states that retain a level of courts with lay judges, the justice courts. These courts date back to the original state constitution of 1896 and retain enough political clout to have survived the rewriting of the judicial article in 1985. They now have a statutory requirement of thirty hours annually of judicial education, but the constitution forbids a requirement that they be admitted to practice law.

Because of its unique history and its prolonged struggle to be admitted as a state, unusually strong provisions for separation of church and state are included in the state constitution. In addition to clauses similar to those in the federal constitution, Article I, Section 4, states: "There shall be no union of Church and State, nor shall any church dominate the State or interfere with its functions. No public money or property shall be appropriated for or applied to any religious worship, exercise or instruction, or for the support of any ecclesiastical establishment." Article III, Section 1, states: "Perfect toleration of religious sentiment is guaranteed. No inhabitant of this State shall ever be molested in person or property on account of his or her mode of religious worship; but polygamous or plural marriages are forever prohibited." Nonetheless, these clauses have not precluded occasional legal and political conflicts over church and state, usually but not always featuring Mormons and non-Mormons on opposite sides.

STAFFING

When Utah revised the judicial article of its constitution in 1985, it changed the process of staffing the judiciary. Previously, Juvenile Court judges had been reappointed by the governor every six years, and judges of the Supreme Court and District Court ran in nonpartisan elections. Under the new constitutional article the state adopted the merit system for the judges of all courts except the justice courts. Merit nominating commissions present slates of candidates to the governor, who appoints the judge subject to senate confirmation by a majority vote. Judges face the voters in retention elections in the first general election after they have served for three years, then every six years for judges on the Juvenile Court and District Court and Court of Appeals and every ten years for Supreme Court justices.

Each of the eight judicial districts in the state has its own nominating commission for trial court judges, and another nominating commission screens candidates for the appellate courts. The Appellate Court Nominating Commission consists of seven members appointed by the governor for four-year terms, with the chief justice sitting ex officio. No more than four members may be from the same political party. No more than four appointees may be members of the Utah State Bar. The governor must appoint two commissioners from a list of six persons nominated by the Utah State Bar. Commissioners may not succeed themselves. The composition of the trial court nominating commissions is the same, except that the number of nominees from the Utah State Bar for two seats on the commissions varies with the population of the judicial district.

The governor obtained the power to appoint all members of the commissions in 1995 following the Appellate Court Nominating Commission's failure to nominate a candidate that he preferred for the Supreme Court. The number of candidates the Appellate Court Nominating Commission must send to the governor increased to at least five, and no more than seven candidates for appellate vacancies. Trial court commissions are to submit five names to the governor for any vacancy if there were fifteen or more applicants for the vacancy and if five applicants receive the requisite number of votes, which is four if all seven commissioners are voting (or fewer if some commissioners are not present). The commissions must submit at least three names. The statute also includes rules forbidding the commissions from disqualifying an applicant if he or she had unsuccessfully applied previously.

Once judges reach the bench, the Judicial Council plays a role in their retention. The Judicial Council is required to certify that judges standing for retention election have met a set of eligibility criteria. These include standards for caseload management, compliance with the Code of Judicial Administration and the Code of Judicial Conduct, physical and mental fitness, compliance with judicial education standards, and satisfactory scores on judicial performance surveys conducted among attorneys and jurors. Judges are legally permitted to file for retention election in the absence of certification by the Judicial Council, but this has not happened in a court of record and has happened only once in the Justice Court.

Attorney surveys for judges on the courts of record are completed twice between retention elections for judges with six-year terms and three times for those with ten-year terms. Juror surveys are conducted only for District Court judges. The questionnaires ask respondents about the judges' integrity, knowledge of the law, ability to communicate, preparation, attentiveness, dignity, control over proceedings, and punctuality. Results of the certification process for judges in the courts of record, including survey results reported in 1 percent increments, are published in a voter information guide produced and distributed by the lieutenant governor's office.

The staffing of the justice courts is quite different from that of the courts of record. County judges are initially appointed by county officials and then stand for retention election every four years. All county Justice Court judges run for retention in the same year. Municipal judges are appointed by city officials and then may be reappointed by the same officials every four years. The Justice Court judges are subject to the same certification criteria as judges in the courts of record, but the collection of survey data to supplement the judges' affidavits of compliance has not at present been funded.

RELATIONSHIP TO NATIONAL SYSTEM
In the federal judiciary, Utah comprises a single U.S. District Court. Its decisions are appealed to the Tenth Circuit Court of Appeals. As of 2000, the District of Utah is authorized for five district judgeships.

Probably the most famous U.S. Supreme Court case originating in Utah is *Reynolds v. U.S.,* 98 U.S. 145 (1879). In its first case interpreting the Free Exercise of Religion clause, the court ruled that polygamy was a crime, not a religious practice, upholding the federal statute against plural marriages in Utah Territory. The case established a narrow interpretation of the Free Exercise Clause as protecting religious belief but not practice, which has since been modified.

Susan M. Olson

See also Juvenile Justice; Lay Judiciaries; Merit Selection ("Missouri Plan"); Pro Se Cases; United States—Federal System; United States—State Systems

References and further reading
Firmage, Edwin Brown, and Richard Collin Mangrum. 1988. *Zion in the Courts: A Legal History of the Church of Jesus Christ of Latter-Day Saints, 1830–1900.* Urbana: University of Illinois Press.
Utah State Courts, http://courtlink.utcourts.gov/.
White, Jean Bickmore. 1996. *Charter for Statehood: The Story of Utah's State Constitution.* Salt Lake City: University of Utah Press.

UZBEKISTAN

COUNTRY INFORMATION
Uzbekistan, formerly the Uzbek Soviet Socialist Republic of the USSR, is located in Central Asia, bordering Kazakhstan to the west and north, Kyrgyzstan to the east, Tajikistan to the southeast, and Afghanistan and Turkmenistan to the south. It includes Karakalpakstan Autonomous Republic, which occupies almost 40 percent of the territory. Uzbekistan's land surface is 172,750 square miles and its population 23,206,000. Tashkent is the capital city with a population of 2,100,000 (1994). Bukhara (228,000) and Samarkand (388,000) are the country's most famous historical and cultural centers. The Turan plain and its flat, dry lowlands occupy four-fifths of the country's territory, whereas its north-central part, Kyzylkum, is one of the largest deserts in the world. Two large and historical rivers, the Amu Darya and Syr Darya, fertilize the soil in the eastern one-fourth of the republic, where lies most of the arable land (9 percent of total surface). The Aral Sea (with a 420 kilometer shoreline), where these rivers flow, has been heavily tapped for irrigation and has declined sharply in recent decades, altering severely the ecosystem in the area and causing one of the major ecological and economic problems that face the country. The situation is deteriorating from concentration of chemical pesticides, industrial wastes, and agricultural chemicals. The climate is extremely dry, desert continental with extreme variation in temperature throughout the year, ranging from about 21.2° F to 89.6° F.

Uzbekistan is the world's third largest cotton exporter. Its GDP was estimated in 1999 at $59.3 billion (GDP per capita $2,500 (1999 est.)). The government began a timid economic reform in 1994 by introducing some privatizations, but without, however, bringing structural changes to a heavily state controlled economy. The country faces a growing national debt ($3.2 billion (1998 est.)) and significant inflation (29 percent estimated for 1999).

The majority of the population (over 70 percent) are Uzbeks, the rest being Russian (7 percent), Tajiks (5 percent), Kazakhs (4 percent), and Karakalpaks (2 percent). The latter live mostly in Karakalpakstan Autonomous Republic. The majority of the population speaks Uzbek, a Turkic language. Russian is the second spoken language.

The country is traditionally Islamic. The famous *madrasahs* (Islamic theological schools of Bukhara, Khiva, and Samarkand) have not ceased to function even during the Soviet era. Still, the republic is a secular state and there are not signs of inherent Islamic fundamentalism, although there are concerns for the action of Islamic militant groups from Tajikistan and Afghanistan. The majority of the population is Sunni Muslim, whereas most of the Russians are Orthodox Christians.

HISTORY

An autonomous Uzbek state was not formed until the Soviet era in 1924. However, the history of the Uzbeks begins in the thirteenth century, when the country formed part of the Mongol Empire, and more especially its western part (the Golden Horde). In the sixteenth century the Uzbek tribal federation ousted the earlier empire founded by Tamerlane, reaching almost the present borders of the country. However, it does not seem that an Uzbek nationhood as such existed at this time, as the social and political life was organized around the tribe or clan. These seminomadic tribes continued their traditional way of life until the Soviet era.

In the centuries that followed, the land has been ruled by the khanates of Bukhara, Khiva, and Kokand, which became vassal states of Russia during the czarist expansion between 1855 and 1873. In 1916 Uzbeks revolted against the czarist authorities and after the October Revolution of 1917 many joined the Bolsheviks, although the Soviet power was resisted by the nationalist *basmachis*. In 1924 the Uzbek Soviet Socialist Republic was formed, including the former Turkistan Autonomous Soviet Socialist Republic and Khiva and Bukhara People's Soviet Republics.

Although the Uzbek authorities remained loyal to Moscow until the end of the Soviet Union and the vast majority of population voted against the dissolution of the USSR, Uzbekistan became the first Central Asian Republic to declare that its own legislation had sovereignty over that of the federal Soviet (June 1990). The republic achieved full independence in 1991, after the official dissolution of the USSR, and became a member of the Commonwealth of Independent States.

The leader of post-Soviet Uzbekistan is President Islom Karimov, who won 86 percent of the vote as sole candidate in December 1991 and 200 seats out of 205 in the December 1994 election. In 1995 Karimov's tenure as president was by referendum extended by 99.6 percent of total vote to the year 2000, when he was reelected for a new five-year term. Karimov rules the country with a strong hand. He has banned the major opposition parties, including the Tajik political and social organizations. He has also closed the Tajik University at Samarkand. The media are placed under strict state control and recent efforts toward a moderate economic liberalization have not been accompanied by analog steps toward political democratization.

LEGAL CONCEPTS

The country's legal system is still marked by the legacy of Soviet-era law, although recently an effort to modernize and westernize the legislation is taking place. Laws passed in 1992 provided for property and land ownership, banking, and privatization. The new post-communist constitution of 1992 provides for separation of powers into executive, legislative, and judiciary. It ensures the protection of fundamental human rights, including the rights to life, to freedom and personal inviolability, the presumption of innocence, the prohibition of torture, the freedom of speech and conscience (arts. 24–31). Political rights, including the rights to participation, to demonstrations, to associate in trade unions and political parties, and to submit applications, are also protected (arts. 32–35). Following the tradition of the Soviet constitutions, social rights, such as the rights to work, to paid vacation, to social assistance, to medical care, to education, and to cultural achievements also enjoy constitutional protection (arts. 36–41). Each person is guaranteed judicial protection of her or his rights and freedoms, as well as the right to appeal in a court of law the unlawful acts of state agencies, officials, and social associations.

However, constitutional protection remains often merely nominal. For instance, although censorship is not officially allowed, despite the existence of 450 newspapers and 115 periodicals, practically all opposition movements and independent media are essentially banned. Amnesty International, Human Rights Watch, and the United States Department of State consistently have identified the human rights situation as among the worst in the former Soviet Union.

EXECUTIVE AND LEGISLATIVE BRANCHES

According to the constitution, the country is a secular, democratic presidential republic. The Supreme Soviet was replaced by a Supreme Assembly, the 250-seat Oliy Majlis, which was first elected in early 1995 and is considered to be the supreme organ of the state. The deputies are elected from territorial electoral districts in multiparty elections for terms of five years. Citizens of the Republic of Uzbekistan who have reached the age of twenty-five years possess the right to be elected. The present parliament was elected in December 1999.

The president of the Republic of Uzbekistan is the head of state and of the executive branch and he is elected for a term of five years by direct elections. He appoints the prime minister and full cabinet of ministers, presides over the cabinet of ministers, and is commander in chief of the armed forces. He may declare a state of emergency or of war and he has also the right to introduce draft legislation in the Parliament. He issues decrees, resolutions, and orders that have obligatory force over the entire territory of the republic. It is self-evident that the actual political power is concentrated in the presidency, which exerts an effectively authoritarian rule. He has the power to dissolve the Parliament, with the concurrence of the constitutional court, in effect neutralizing the Oly Majlis's veto power over presiden-

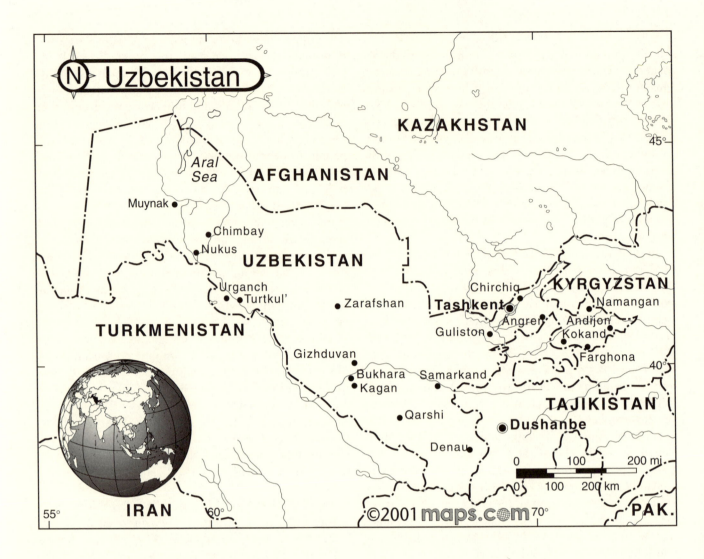

tial nominations (still very theoretical, as all political parties in the present legislature are supporting President Karimov).

The country is divided into twelve provinces and the autonomous Karakalpakstan republic. The Republic of Karakalpakstan has its own constitution, which may not contradict the Constitution of the Republic of Uzbekistan. It elects its own legislature and, in theory, has the right to secession on the basis of a general referendum of the people of Karakalpakstan. Its chairman is the republic's head of state and a deputy chairman of the national Parliament.

The Councils of People's Deputies (former Soviets) are the representative agencies of power in regions, districts, and cities (except cities subordinate to districts, or districts that are part of cities); are headed by governors; and, proceeding from the interests of the state and citizens, decide issues ascribed to their jurisdiction.

The chief executive of each province is the *hakim,* who is appointed by the president.

Although the constitution nominally adheres to political pluralism, the political atmosphere is not favorable to multipartism. A new law on political parties was introduced in 1997, prohibiting parties with ethnic or religious bases or those advocating subversion of the constitution. The dominant party is the People's Democratic Party (former Communist Party). Other parties are the Adolat (Justice), the Democratic National Rebirth Party (Milly Tiklanish), the Fatherland Progress Party, and the Social Democratic Party. The opposition parties Birlik (Unity) Movement, the Islamic Rebirth Party, and the Erk (Freedom) Democratic Party were banned in 1992; Erk was reinstated in 1994. The parties represented in the present Parliament unanimously support President Karimov.

THE JUDICIARY

The judicial system consists of a Constitutional Court of the Republic of Uzbekistan, a Supreme Court of the Republic of Uzbekistan, a High Commercial Court of the Republic of Uzbekistan, a Supreme Court of the Republic of Karakalpakstan, and a Commercial Court of the Republic of Karakalpakstan, all elected for terms of five years, as well as regional, Tashkent City, district, city, and commercial courts, all appointed for terms of five years. The establishment of emergency courts is not allowed. Judges at all levels are appointed by the president and approved by the Oly Majlis. They must have high legal education and their selection is ensured by qualification commissions. Similar commissions have competence jurisdiction over assessing the qualification of lawyers.

According to the constitution, judges are independent, subordinate only to the law. Any sort of interference in the work of judges in carrying out justice is forbidden and they enjoy immunity. Before the end of their terms of office, they are dismissed for reasons indicated by law.

All defendants are nominally ensured the right to defense. The right to professional legal assistance is, theoretically, guaranteed at any stage of an investigation or judicial proceeding. The bar acts to provide legal assistance to citizens, enterprises, institutions, and organizations.

The Constitutional Court of the Republic of Uzbekistan reviews cases concerning the constitutionality of legislative and executive acts. It is composed by specialists in the fields of political science and law, and consists of a chair, assistant chair, and the judges of the constitutional court, including a representative of the Republic of Karakalpakstan. The court exerts control of constitutionality of the laws and of the accordance of the Constitution of the Republic of Karakalpakstan with the Constitution of the Republic of Uzbekistan and provides interpretation of the norms of the constitution and laws.

The Supreme Court of the Republic of Uzbekistan is the highest judicial branch agency in the spheres of civil, criminal, and administrative legal proceedings. The Court exerts supervision over the Supreme Court of the Republic of Karakalpakstan and regional, city, and district courts.

Economic conflicts arising between enterprises, institutions, and organizations in the economic sphere, in the process of economic management, based on various forms of property, or between business people are resolved by the high commercial court and other commercial courts, within the confines of their jurisdiction.

The prokuratura (Procuracy), an institution of Soviet inspiration, oversees uniform compliance with the law on the territory of the republic. The procurators are simultaneously the state's chief prosecuting officials and the chief investigators of criminal cases. The head of the prokuratura is the procurator general of the Republic of Uzbekistan, who is the highest law enforcement official in the country. Procurators of regions, districts, and cities are appointed by the procurator general. The procurator of the Republic of Karakalpakstan is appointed by the highest representative agency of the Republic of Karakalpakstan with the agreement of the procurator general of the Republic of Uzbekistan. The term of office of the procurators is five years.

The Institute of the Authorized Person for Human Rights (ombudsman) was implemented at the First Session of Oliy Majlis, by the Decree of May 6, 1995. Its activities are regulated by the Law on the Authorized Person of the Oliy Majlis for Human Rights (Ombudsman) (April 24, 1997). The ombudsman is a deputy of the Oliy Majlis, appointed by Parliament for a term of five years. He is supposed to act as an impartial defender of human rights, examining pleas and investigating cases on violations made by individual organizations and officials. He is entitled to request the appropriate sanctions and to elaborate programs for the promotion of the observation of human rights. A ten-member Commission on the Observation of Constitutional Rights and Freedoms was also established, in order to provide assistance to the ombudsman.

Despite the efforts of modernization of the economy and the political system, the current political structures ensure the dominating influence of the executive power in the economy and the political process. It is true that, beginning with the 1991 Law on Privatization, a number of laws and decrees have provided the policy framework for a market economy. Still, the privatization process is relatively slow, concerning principally the housing, retail trade, and services and light industry sectors. As a result of the failure of reforms to bring about necessary structural changes, the IMF suspended the country's arrangements in late 1996.

On the political ground the regime remains highly centralist and autocratic, the power personified round President Islam Karimov, the former local Communist party leader. The government justifies its restraining policies by emphasizing the need for stability against Islamic extremism, especially after a number of terrorist bombings (February 1999). As a result, the most important opposition parties are still illegal and their activities prohibited. However, despite the Islamic resurgence common to this area (about half of ethnic Uzbek respondents professed belief in Islam when asked to identify their religious faith), practice of the main precepts of Islam is weak.

Despite the extensive constitutional protections, according to international human rights organizations (Amnesty International, Human Rights Watch), the regime is actively suppressing the rights of political movements and continues to ban unsanctioned public meetings and demonstrations and to arrest opposition figures.

George Katrougalos

See also Administrative Law; Administrative Tribunals; Civil Law; Commercial Law (International Aspects); Constitutional Law; Constitutional Review; Criminal Law; Human Rights Law; Judicial Review; Legal Professionals—Civil Law Traditions; Private Law; Public Law; Soviet System

References and further reading
Akiner, Shirin, ed. 1992. *Economic and Political Trends in Central Asia.* New York: Routledge and Kegan Paul.
Curtis, Glenn E., ed. 1996. Uzbekistan, Federal Research Division, a country study, Library of Congress, March.
Ferdinand, Peter. 1994. *The New States of Central Asia and Their Neighbours.* New York: Council on Foreign Relations Press.

Mandelbaum, Michael, ed. 1994. *Central Asia and the World: Kazakhstan, Uzbekistan, Tajikistan, Kyrgyzstan, and Turkmenistan.* New York: Council on Foreign Relations Press.
Undeland, Charles, and Nicholas Platt. 1994. *The Central Asian Republics: Fragments of Empire, Magnets of Wealth.* New York: Asia Society.
United States. Central Intelligence Agency. 2000. *The World Factbook 2000.* Washington, DC: GPO.

V

VANUATU

COUNTRY INFORMATION

Vanuatu, formerly called New Hebrides, is an archipelago of about eighty islands, roughly in the shape of the letter Y, which is located between 12° and 21° south latitude and 166° and 171° east longitude. It lies about 400 kilometers east-northeast of New Caledonia and about 800 kilometers southeast of Solomon Islands and is about one-third of the way between the Fiji Islands and the northwest coastline of Queensland, Australia.

The population is estimated to be about 190,000, of which about 94 percent are Melanesian ni-Vanuatu, 2 percent European, and 2 percent Chinese and Vietnamese. Approximately 85 percent of the people live in rural areas, and 15 percent are in the capital, Port Vila, and other urban areas.

HISTORY

The islands of the archipelago were inhabited about 3000 B.C.E. by groups of Melanesians proceeding probably from Southeast Asia. In the early seventeenth century, the islands were discovered by Europeans—a Spanish expedition that attempted unsuccessfully to establish a settlement—but it was not until the mid-eighteenth century that they were revisited by Europeans: in the 1760s, the French explorer Antoine de Bougainville and then, about ten years later, the English explorer Capt. James Cook, who named them New Hebrides after the islands lying off the west coast of Scotland.

During the nineteenth century, the islands were visited by traders, including the notorious "blackbirders," transporters of indentured laborers to Fiji and Queensland, and also by missionaries and later by merchants and planters who bought land and settled to establish stores and plantations. From the 1870s on, there was an increasing presence of French and British settlers, and hostilities began to break out between them and the indigenous New Hebrideans. The locals/natives at that time were living in many separate tribes, without any tribal grouping or heirarchy and without any paramount chiefs or rulers. Britain and France were increasingly called on to protect their citizens in conflicts with New He-

brideans, and in 1887, they signed a convention that established the Joint Naval Commission to patrol the islands, protect British and French citizens, and maintain order. This measure proved inadequate, and in 1906, a further convention was signed between Britain and France declaring New Hebrides to be a "joint sphere of influence" in which the subjects of each country (and those of other countries who opted to do so) would be regulated by British and French laws, respectively, while the British high commissioner of the western Pacific in Fiji and the French high commissioner in New Caledonia and their respective delegates, the resident commissioners in New Hebrides, would jointly make laws for New Hebrideans and all residents in the country. Three separate court systems were to apply the three separate legal systems: British national courts, French national courts, and Condominium joint courts. In 1914, a more detailed protocol to replace the convention was signed shortly before the outbreak of World War I and ratified in 1922.

The Convention of 1906 and the Protocol of 1922 regulated the government and legal systems of the country until the 1970s, when agitation against foreign rule became widespread. The advisory council, which had been set up in 1957 to advise the resident commissioners, was replaced in 1975 by a representative assembly, which was mainly elected. In 1978, a government of national unity was formed, which established the Constitutional Drafting Committee to prepare a draft constitution for approval by Britain and France. The document was approved with some amendments at a constitutional conference in September 1979, and on July 30, 1980, the country attained independence under the new name of Vanuatu, which means "everlasting country."

CONSTITUTION

The constitution, which has been amended on three occasions—in 1980, 1981, and 1983—is divided into fifteen chapters, the first of which makes it clear that Vanuatu is a sovereign democratic state, that the constitution is the supreme law, and that the national language is Bislama, although the official languages also include English and French, the two languages of instruction.

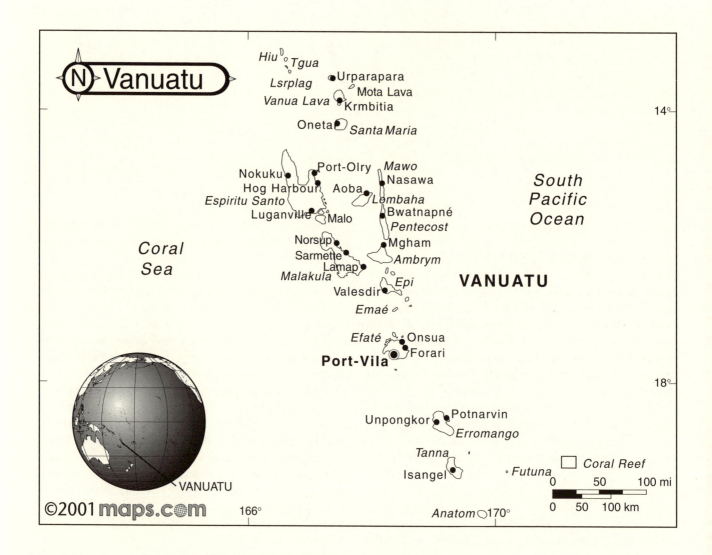

Neither the constitution nor the Interpretation Act, Cap 132, contains any principles or rules for the way in which the provisions of the constitution should be interpreted, but this issue received extensive consideration in 1997 by the Supreme Court, which ruled: "The Court when interpreting the Constitution must adopt a broad-oriented and purposive approach directed towards advancing the constitutional objectives taking due account to the country [sic] circumstances and resources" (*Virelala v. The Ombudsman* [unreported] Civ Cas 4/1997 [22 September 1997], at p16).

As noted, the constitution is stated to be the supreme law, and on several occasions, legislation has been held to be void because of inconsistency with the constitution (*Sope v. Attorney-General* [1980–1988] 1 Van LR 411; *Attorney-General v. President Timakata* [1989–1994] 2 Van LR 679; *Virelala v. Ombudsman* [unreported] Civ Cas 4/1997 [22 September 1977]).

FUNDAMENTAL RIGHTS AND DUTIES

Article 5 of the constitution recognizes fundamental rights and freedoms in a manner and in terms modeled on the Bill of Rights Act of 1960, Cap 44, of Canada, and Chapter 1 of the Constitution of Trinidad and Tobago. Article 5(1) of the constitution provides that all persons are entitled—without discrimination on grounds of race, place of origin, religious or traditional beliefs, political opinions, language, or sex—to certain rights and freedoms, including life; liberty; security of the person; protection of the law (which is spelled out in more detail in Article 5[2]); freedom from inhuman treatment and forced labor; freedom of conscience and worship; freedom of expression; freedom of assembly and association; freedom of movement; protection for the privacy of the home and other property and from unjust deprivation of property; and equal treatment under the law and administrative action.

All these rights and freedoms are stated in Article 5(1) to be subject to certain limitations, which are also described in terms of great generality: respect for the rights and freedoms of others; the legitimate public interest in defense, safety, public order, welfare, and health; and restrictions imposed by the law on noncitizens.

The Supreme Court and the Court of Appeal discussed the provisions relating to fundamental rights and freedoms fully in *President Timakata v. Attorney-General* ([1989–1994] 2 Van LR 575; 679), and held that these provisions were to be given a flexible and generous interpretation. There is no reported case, however, in which the court has been required to discuss in any detail the interaction between the fundamental rights and freedoms as generally described an Article 5(1) of the constitution and the three broad limitations placed on these rights and freedoms in that same article.

Part 2 of Chapter 2 of the constitution provides in Article 7 that every person has certain fundamental duties that are, however, nonjusticiable: to respect and act in the spirit of the constitution; to participate actively in the development of the national community; to participate fully in the government of the republic; to protect the republic and safeguard the wealth, resources, and environment; to work in socially useful employment; to respect the rights and freedoms of others and to cooperate fully with them; to contribute as required by law, according to one's means, to the revenues required by the republic; in the case of a parent, to support, assist, and educate all his or her children, legitimate and illegitimate; and in the case of a child, to respect his or her parents.

NATIONAL COUNCIL OF CHIEFS

Although the National Council of Chiefs, called Malvatumauri, is given a prominent position in the constitution, appearing between the chapters relating to the Parliament and the head of state, it is actually given very few powers. The National Council of Chiefs is required only to be consulted by Parliament when it provides a national land law, which has not yet happened. The council may also be consulted on any question relating to tradition and custom in connection with any bill before Parliament, but it very rarely has been so consulted because there have been few bills that have raised such questions. The National Council of Chiefs has a general competence to discuss all matters relating to custom and tradition and make recommendations for the preservation and promotion of ni-Vanuatu culture and languages, but it has not made much impact on the public consciousness with regard to such matters.

A representative of the National Council of Chiefs is required to be a member of the Judicial Service Commission, and the chairman of the National Council of Chiefs is required to be consulted on the appointment of an ombudsman. Rather curiously, however, the council is not required to be involved in any way in the appointment of the president.

The constitution requires that the members of the council must be elected by their peers sitting in District Councils of Chiefs; furthermore, the elections are to be organized by the Electoral Commission. In recent years, there have been disputes about the elections in some districts, which has hampered the work of the National Council of Chiefs.

HEAD OF STATE

The head of state, called the president, is elected for a period of five years by secret ballot by two-thirds of an electoral college consisting of members of Parliament and the chairs of the local government councils. Only indigenous ni-Vanuatu citizens are qualified to be elected as president. Such an election must take place within three weeks after a vacancy in the office occurs or, if Parliament is dissolved, within three weeks of the first meeting of the new Parliament.

A president may be removed from office only for gross misconduct or incapacity by the vote of at least two-thirds of the electoral college of members of Parliament and chairs of the local government councils when at least three-quarters of the members, including at least a compararable share of the chairs of the local government councils, are present.

The functions of the president are basically ceremonial. The president is required to symbolize the unity of the nation but has few specific functions, and most of these the president is either required to perform without any discretion or else is required to perform in his discretion but in accordance with advice. The only powers that the president is authorized to exercise solely on his own initiative, without either advice or consultation, are: the appointment of an acting prime minister if the current prime minister dies and there is no deputy prime minister; the appointment of the chair of the Public Service Commission from among the members of the commission; and the referral to the Supreme Court of a bill passed by Parliament or a regulation if he believes that it is inconsistent with a provision of the constitution. The president has exercised this power of referral of bills to the Supreme Court on several occasions (*Re President's Reference, President v. Attorney-General* [1993] LRC [Const] 141; *President Timakata v. Attorney-General* [1989–94] 2 Van LR 575, 679; *Re President's Referral, President v. Attorney General* [1998] Civ Cas 169/1997).

PRIME MINISTER AND COUNCIL OF MINISTERS

The executive power of the republic is vested in the prime minister and the Council of Ministers and is required to be exercised in accordance with the constitution or a law.

The prime minister is to be elected by Parliament from among its members, and the prime minister must appoint ministers from among such members; in addition, the prime minister can assign and remove their responsibilities, but the total number of ministers is not to exceed a quarter of the members of Parliament. Members of Parliament appointed as ministers retain their membership in Parliament.

The Council of Ministers is collectively responsible to Parliament, which may pass a motion of no confidence with at least one week's written notice. If the motion is successful, the prime minister and other ministers must resign, although they may continue to exercise their functions until a new prime minister is elected. The Council of Ministers also ceases to hold office whenever the prime minister resigns or dies, but its members continue to exercise their functions until a new prime minister is elected. Ministers also cease to hold office (1) if, after a general election, Parliament meets to elect a new prime minister, (2) if they cease to be members of Parliament for any reason other than a dissolution of Parliament, or (3) if elected as president of the republic or as speaker of Parliament.

In times of emergency when the republic is at war or the president has declared a state of emergency, the Council of Ministers may make regulations for dealing with the public emergency. Such regulations are required to be reasonably necessary in the circumstances of the emergency and justifiable in a democratic society. They may also override the fundamental rights and freedoms recognized by the constitution, except that no regulation may derogate from the right to life and to freedom from inhuman treatment and forced labor or make provision for the detention of persons, except enemy aliens, for more than one month without trial. Any citizen aggrieved by a violation of such a regulation may apply to the Supreme Court, which may determine the validity of the regulation. This power was exercised when riots occurred in January 1998 outside the offices of the Vanuatu National Provident Fund and there was widespread looting in the capital, Port Vila.

LEGISLATURE

The legislature of Vanuatu is the single-chambered Parliament, which consists of the total number of members elected by constituencies as determined by the Electoral Commission. At the general elections in 1998, there were fifty-two members of Parliament elected from seventeen constituencies. The electoral system is required by the constitution to have an element of proportional representation so as to ensure fair representation of different political groups and opinions. This element is provided by the multimember constituencies, which at present number eleven out of the seventeen constituencies.

The details of the electoral system are provided by the Representation of the People Act, Cap 146, and under that act, citizens over the age of eighteen are entitled to vote and citizens over the age of twenty-five are entitled to stand for election, except the president, members of the judiciary and the police, public servants, teachers,

members of the National Councils of Chiefs, and members of the Citizenship Commission. Disputes as to whether a person has been validly elected as a member of Parliament are determined by the Supreme Court, and there is no provision for an appeal from its decision.

Parliament has been given power by Article 16(1) of the constitution to make laws for the peace, order, and good government of Vanuatu, and bills for laws may be introduced by any member of Parliament. A bill relating to the registration of electors for elections for Parliament, the National Council of Chiefs, local government councils, or municipal councils must be referred to the Electoral Commission and the principal electoral officer for comment before being introduced into Parliament. A bill to amend the constitution and also a motion to dissolve Parliament requires a two-thirds majority of all members of Parliament, and a bill relating to the status of the three languages (Bislama, English, and French), the electoral system, or the Parliamentary system must not only be passed by two-thirds of Parliament but must also be supported in a national referendum. No motion for levying or increasing taxes or for the expenditure of public funds can be introduced unless it is supported by the government. The constitution requires that Parliament must meet twice a year in ordinary session, but it may also meet in extraordinary session if requested by a majority of its members, the speaker, or the prime minister.

Treaties negotiated by the government are required by Article 26 of the constitution to be ratified by Parliament if they concern international organizations, peace, or trade or if they expend public funds, affect the status of people, require amendment of the laws of Vanuatu, or provide for the transfer, exchange, or annexing of territory.

The government is required to submit a bill for a budget to Parliament for its approval, and no taxation shall be imposed or altered and no expenditure of public funds shall be incurred except by or under a law passed by Parliament. Parliament is also required to provide for the office of auditor general, whose function is to audit and report to Parliament and the government on the public accounts of Vanuatu.

Parliament may pass a motion of no confidence in the prime minister after giving one week's notice to the speaker, and if the motion, which must be signed by one-sixth of the members of Parliament, is supported by an absolute majority of the members of Parliament, the prime minister and other ministers must cease to hold office, although they can continue to exercise their functions until a new prime minister is elected.

The term of Parliament itself is four years from the date of election unless it is dissolved before that time either by the president on the advice of the Council of Ministers or by a resolution of the Parliament supported by an absolute majority of the members at a special sitting, of which one week's notice has been given and at which at least three-quarters of the members are present.

COURTS

Prior to independence in 1980, the New Hebrides had a quite complicated judicial system. There were British courts for British citizens and those foreign residents, termed "optants," who opted to be regulated by British laws, French courts for French citizens and optants, and native courts for New Hebrideans. In addition, there were Courts of First Instance and a Joint Court for matters involving different nationalities and offenses under the protocol or the joint regulations applying to all people in the country. After independence, this multiplicity of courts was swept away, and in their place, four courts have been established that have jurisdiction over all persons in Vanuatu: Island Courts, Magistrates' Courts, the Supreme Court, and the Court of Appeal.

Island Courts are composed of three or more justices who are knowledgeable in custom and of whom at least one is a custom chief, appointed by the president on the advice of the Judicial Services Commission. They sit in eight of the more populous islands and have jurisdiction to determine disputes relating to customary land and minor civil and criminal matters. When hearing land disputes, an Island Court must be presided over by a magistrate, who records the decision of the court. Island Courts are required to apply the customary law prevailing within their territorial jurisdictions insofar as it is not in conflict with the written law and is not contrary to justice, morality, and good order. Appeals from Island Courts on customary land matters lie to the Supreme Court, but appeals on other matters lie to the Magistrates' Courts.

Magistrates' Courts are presided over by a magistrate and are located in the two principal towns. An ordinary magistrate has jurisdiction to try summarily criminal offenses punishable by not less than two years of imprisonment; a senior magistrate has jurisdiction to try summarily criminal offenses punishable by not less than five years of imprisonment. All Magistrates' Courts have jurisdiction to conduct preliminary inquiries in criminal cases that are to be tried by the Supreme Court to see that there is sufficient evidence to justify the charge. They have jurisdiction in civil proceedings to determine civil claims not exceeding VT2,000,000, as well as undefended proceedings for divorce or judicial separation and claims for maintenance not exceeding VT1,200,000 per year. Magistrates' Courts also hear appeals from Island Courts, except with regard to customary land, and when hearing such appeals, they must sit with two or more assessors who are knowledgeable in custom.

The Supreme Court has unlimited jurisdiction in civil and criminal matters and is stated by the constitution to

Structure of Vanuatu Courts

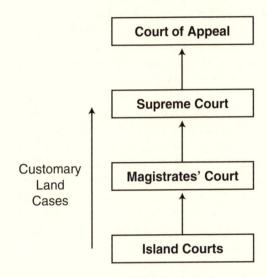

consist of the chief justice and three other judges. In fact, however, the Supreme Court has quite frequently had less than three other judges. When hearing appeals from land cases, the court is required to be assisted by at least two assessors knowledgeable in custom. The Supreme Court has jurisdiction to hear appeals from Magistrates' Courts and also from Island Courts, but only in customary land cases. As indicated earlier, it also has jurisdiction to determine applications for the enforcement of fundamental rights and freedoms, disputes about elections, presidential referrals of bills or regulations, and challenges to the validity of emergency regulations made by the Council of Ministers.

The Court of Appeal has wide jurisdiction to hear appeals from decisions of the Supreme Court, exercising original and appellate jurisdiction in civil cases and in criminal cases. From some decisions of the Supreme Court, however, there is no appeal to the Court of Appeal—particularly decisions enforcing fundamental rights and freedoms, decisions on election disputes, and decisions on appeals from Island Courts regarding customary land.

LAWS OF VANUATU

The laws of Vanuatu consist of a mixture of introduced and locally made laws, deriving partly from the period of the Condominium and from the time since independence was attained in 1980.

Introduced Laws

During Condominium times, certain British statutes and the principles of English common law and equity were applied to British citizens and optants, certain French laws were applied to French citizens and optants, and joint regulations made by the high commissioners or, more usually, the resident commissioners applied to everybody, including New Hebrideans.

At the time of independence, the British and French laws and the joint regulations, which were in force at the time of independence, were, unless incompatible with the independent status of Vanuatu, continued in force by the constitution until repealed by Parliament. However, the constitution was unclear on the issue of whether the national laws would continue to apply only to those persons who were previously subject to them (British subjects and optants or French subjects and optants) or whether the British and French laws were to apply to everybody after independence; also unclear was what would happen if these laws were in conflict. The Supreme Court has held on several occasions that since independence, both British and French laws apply to everybody in Vanuatu (*SELB Pacific Ltd v. Mouton* [unreported] Civ Cas 42/1994 [30 May 1996]; *Banga v. Waiwo* [unreported] App Cas 1/1996 [17 June 1996]). In neither case did the court have to consider what should happen if there was a conflict between the British and French laws.

Local Laws

According to Article 95(1) of the constitution, joint regulations made by the British and French resident commissioners before independence were to continue in operation after independence until otherwise provided by Parliament but subject to such adaptations as might be necessary to bring them into conformity with the constitution.

Acts of Parliament enacted by that body since 1980 and subsidiary legislation authorized by such acts make up a very significant proportion of the current laws of Vanuatu.

Customary law is also stated by Article 95(3) of the constitution to continue to have effect as part of the law of the republic, and the constitution makes it very clear in Articles 71 to 73 that custom is to provide the basis for ownership and use of land in Vanuatu; moreover, only indigenous citizens who have acquired land in accordance with a recognized system of land tenure shall have perpetual ownership of land. Apart from ownership and use of land, however, the constitution does not indicate to what matters or what persons customary law is to apply. Nor has legislation done so, and the courts have not been called on to determine the exact scope of application of customary law.

Donald Paterson

References and further reading
Bulu, Hamlinson. 1986. "Law and Custom in Vanuatu." *Queensland Institute of Technology Law Journal* 2: 129–131.
———. 1988. "The Judiciary and the Court System in Vanuatu." Pp. 229–232 in *Pacific Courts and Legal Systems.* Edited by Guy C. Powles and Mere Pulea. Suva, Fiji: University of the South Pacific.
Corrin Care, Jennifer. 1985. "Sources of Law under the Constitution of Vanuatu." *Queensland Institute of Technology Law Journal* 1: 225–233.
Lynch, C. Joseph. 1981. "The Constitution of Vanuatu." *Parliamentarian* 62: 46–53.
Paterson, Don. 1986. "Vanuatu Penal Code." *Queensland Institute of Technology Law Journal* 2: 119–127.
———. 1993. "Vanuatu." Pp. 365–394 in *South Pacific Islands Legal Systems.* Edited by Michael Ntumy. Honolulu: University of Hawai'i Press.
———. 1999. "Constitutional Law." Pp. 81–112 in *Introduction to South Pacific Law.* Edited by Jennifer Corrin Care, Tess Newton, and Don Paterson. London: Cavendish Publishing.
Weisbrot, David. 1989. "Custom, Pluralism and Realism in Vanuatu: Legal Development and the Role of Customary Law." *Pacific Studies* 13: 65–97.

VATICAN

GENERAL INFORMATION

The Stato della Città del Vaticano ("State of the Vatican City"), more commonly known as the Vatican City, is the smallest sovereign state in the world. It consists of 108.7 acres and is home to fewer than one thousand people. Located at the end of a broad boulevard called Via della Conciliazione in Rome, the Vatican City provides the geographical home for the spiritual head of the Roman Catholic Church, the Holy See.

As defined by canon law, the official law of the Catholic Church, the Holy See consists of the pope, the Office of the Secretariat of State, and rest of the Roman Curia. The secretariat and the rest of the Curia are the sizable bureaucracy that assists the pope in overseeing the Roman Catholic Church. The Curia includes nine congregations, eleven councils, three canon law tribunals, and several other auxiliary organizations, including *L'Osservatore Romano* (the Vatican newspaper). The pope employs approximately twenty-four hundred people, the majority of whom are Italian. Therefore the predominant culture and working language of Vatican City are Italian. Even so, the workforce is highly diversified, inasmuch as it draws people from around the world.

A confusion of terms clouds the differences between the Holy See, the leadership of the Catholic Church, and the Vatican City, as a territorial state. In some instances, however, the ambiguity between the Holy See and the Vatican City provides necessary political cover in domestic politics. Two examples demonstrate this point. First, in *Americans United for Separation of Church and State v. Reagan,* 786 F. 2d 194 (3rd Cir. 1986), a U.S. court dismissed a challenge to the Reagan administration's imple-

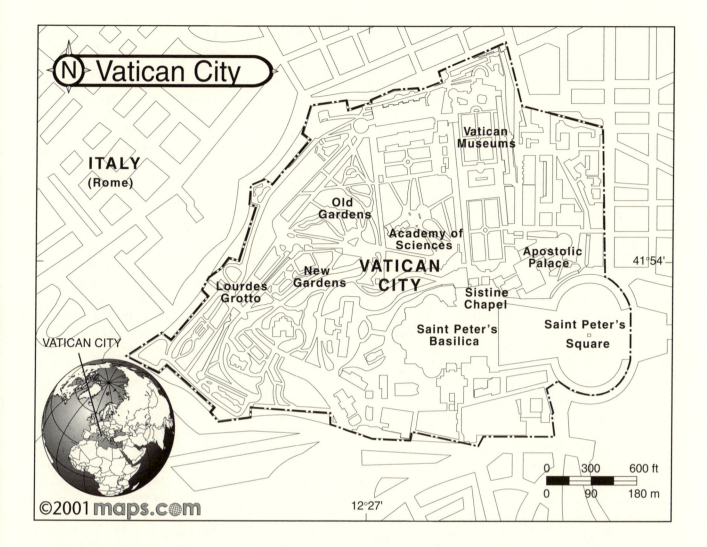

©2001 maps.com

mentation of diplomatic relations with the Holy See. The court asserted that because the Holy See is a territorial sovereign, along with being a religious organization, the court did not need to address the question of whether the U.S. president may constitutionally establish diplomatic relations with a church. A second set of examples are papal trips. John Paul II, who became pope in 1978, was able to officially travel to countries that do not recognize the Catholic Church, such as communist Poland and to Greece, as a territorial ruler, not as a religious leader.

HISTORY

The pope personifies the Holy See. He is both a spiritual leader and the territorial ruler of the Vatican City. This dual nature continues a long history of popes ruling large parts of present-day Italy. While the popes have always led the Catholic Church, their territorial powers have waxed and waned. Popes have asserted that territorial sovereignty is necessary for their religious mission. The Vatican City exists solely as a territorial base for the Holy See. While the history of the Vatican City began in 1929, the history of the Holy See's efforts vis-à-vis territory began much earlier.

From 800 to 1870, popes ruled the Papal States, which at one time covered 16,000 square miles. The French Revolution of 1789 ushered in almost one hundred years of steady decline in the material fortunes of the Holy See. Twice between 1808 and 1870, foreign armies forced the reigning pope from Rome. The first exile was between 1809 and 1814, when Napoleon's troops took Pius VII (pope from 1800 to 1823) prisoner. The second was between 1848 and 1850, when the Italian army forced Pius IX (pope from 1846 to 1878) from Rome. At various times throughout the nineteenth century, Spanish, Austrian, French, and Italian troops have occupied parts of the Papal States. Eventually Italian forces conquered the Papal States during Italian unification, the *risorgimento* ("resurgence"). In 1870, Italy conquered the remaining area of the Papal States and then, after a plebiscite, annexed them.

The pope, however, refused to recognize the Kingdom of Italy and its control over the Papal States. The pope demanded a return of at least some of the Holy See's territory. The Italian government responded to this demand by issuing the Law of Guarantees on May 13, 1871. The law recognized the Holy See's rights of immunity, of inviolability, and of extraterritoriality, the right to have violations of these rights punished under Italian law, and the right to exchange diplomatic representatives. In addition, the law provided a subsidy to the Holy See. Despite all this, the Italian government wanted to make it clear that it ruled all of Italy, including what had been the Papal States, which made the Italian concessions unacceptable to the pope.

The "Roman Question" is the name of the controversy between the Holy See and the Italian government from 1870 to 1929 over the status of the former Papal States. The Holy See and the Italian government each refused to recognize the sovereignty of the other, and each considered the other to be interfering in its internal concerns.

In 1929, Mussolini's government and the Holy See sought a solution to the Roman Question, for very different reasons. Mussolini wanted a settlement in order to cultivate support in the traditional elements of Italian society and to seek support from the Roman Catholic Church. Pius XI (pope from 1922 to 1939) sought the settlement in order to provide political protection through absolute territorial sovereignty for the Catholic Church. Negotiations between the parties resulted in the Lateran Treaty.

Signed on February 11, 1929, the Lateran Treaty is a bilateral treaty between the Holy See and Italy. Pursuant to the treaty, Italy ceded to the Holy See 108.7 acres, which became the new state of the Vatican City. Italy recognized the sovereignty of the Holy See. In turn, the Holy See recognized the Italian government.

While the Holy See claims sovereignty because of its religious nature, the territory of the Vatican City provides a legal fig leaf for its international independence. The Holy See uses this independence and is extremely active diplomatically. The Holy See is a member of UNESCO, the World Health Organization, the International Labor Organization, the Council of Europe, and the World Trade Organization. The Holy See is also a permanent observer at the United Nations and listed as a state in numerous conventions and programs there. As of 2000, the Holy See has diplomatic relations with 174 countries.

While the pope is the absolute monarch of the Vatican City, he has delegated the management of its day-to-day activities to the Pontifical Commission for the Vatican City State. The commission consists of cardinals appointed by the pope for five-year terms. The president of the commission holds executive power, although he must consult with the whole commission in matters of major importance and, in matters of substantial importance, consult with the secretariat of state. The president typically turns over basic everyday management to a special delegate. Like many states, the Vatican City finances a postal service, telephone service, maintenance, refuse collection, fire protection, a police force, and a small army.

The Vatican City's police force is the Corpo di Vigilanze, and the army is the Papal Swiss Guard. The police force has 120 members and is indistinguishable from any modern police force. The Swiss Guard, however, is very distinguishable from a modern army. With just over a hundred members, the Swiss Guard is the official guard of the pope. They wear blue and yellow uniforms that, according to legend, Michelangelo designed. Both of these forces symbolize the territorial independence of the Vatican City, as does its legal system.

LEGAL CONCEPTS

Three key concepts form the basis of the Vatican City's legal system. First and foremost is the religious nature of the pope as leader of the Roman Catholic Church. Canon law, the internal law of the Catholic Church, has a very significant effect on the lives of those who live or work in the Vatican City. The legal system of the Vatican City borrows much of its personnel from the canon law system. Not only is the Vatican City legal system secondary to the canon law system, it, like the whole structure of the Vatican City, is secondary to the religious nature of the Holy See.

The second key concept is that the pope is an elected absolute monarch. The Vatican City has a constitution: Pius XI enacted the first Fundamental Law in 1929, and John Paul II recently enacted a new Fundamental Law that took effect on February 22, 2001. Even so, both laws dictate that the pope has full legislative, executive, and judicial authority. Popes have delegated their judicial authority to a court system, but that does not diminish the fact that the pope may completely bypass the system at any time.

Finally, the Vatican City relies to a great extent on the Italian legal system. The structure of the Vatican City's legal system is the same as that of the Italian system. Vatican City courts may apply Italian law in situations in which there is no controlling Vatican City law. At the request of the Vatican City, Italy will prosecute individuals for criminal acts committed on the Vatican City's territory. Italy also grants the pope the same legal protection as the Italian leader. This grant gave Italy the authority to prosecute Mehmet Ali Agca, who attempted to assassinate the pope in 1981. Finally, Italy provides police protection in St. Peter's Square, which is Vatican City territory and open to the public.

CURRENT STRUCTURE

The pope is an elected monarch. The citizens of the Vatican City, however, do not elect the pope. The College of Cardinals, whom the pope appoints, elects the new pope after the death of the former pope. Upon the death of a pope, all the cardinals gather in Rome for an election.

The maximum number of cardinal electors must not exceed 120, although John Paul II has regularly named more than 120 cardinals. Only those cardinals under the age of eighty may participate in a papal election. A valid election requires a two-thirds majority. However, after three days, if the cardinals have not elected a new pope, the balloting continues on a majority basis. Once elected, the pope automatically becomes the monarch of the Vatican City.

As the monarch, the pope has full judicial authority and may intervene in any case at any time. Even so, popes have established a working court system for the Vatican City. The present system is the result of several reorganizations. Pius XI established the system with his promulgation of the Fundamental Law on June 7, 1929. He and subsequent popes have reorganized the system three times since then, in 1932, 1946, and 1987. The pope reorganizes the system on his own authority by the publication of a *Motu Proprio* (literally, "of his own accord"), an apostolic letter. The most recent reorganization was on November 21, 1987, when John Paul II issued his *Motu Proprio* entitled *Quo civium iura*. Prior to *Quo civium iura*, the Vatican City's court system interrelated much more closely with the canon law system. Under the old system, the dean of the Rota, which is the court of appeals in the canon law system, also served as the president of the Vatican City's Court of Appeals. In addition, the other two judges of the Court of Appeals had to be Rota judges. Under the new system, there are no requirements for this relationship. Even so, in practice, Court of Appeals judges are often Rota judges as well.

The reorganized judicial system, much like the old one, follows the Italian model of a four-level system of courts. The first level is the sole judge (*giudice unico*), who presides over a limited-jurisdiction court. This judge is similar to a *pretore* in the Italian legal system and has jurisdiction over small claims, routine judicial matters, and minor criminal cases. In the judicial year 1998–1999, the sole judge took 658 judicial acts, most of which were decisions on traffic tickets and the validation of marriages (*L'Attività* 1999, 1473). The sole judge must be a citizen of the Vatican City and may serve simultaneously as a judge on the next level of courts.

The second level is the Tribunal (Tribunale), which is composed of a president and two other judges who act as a college of three. The pope appoints these judges. Considering that the Tribunal is a court of general jurisdiction, it handles relatively few cases: only thirteen in 1998–1999 (*L'Attività* 1999, 1473). This court level is more important, because it is on this level in which the primary promoter of justice (*promotore di giustizia*) works.

The pope appoints the promoter, who is the "guardian of the law" and acts as a prosecuting attorney would in the U.S. system. Unlike a U.S. prosecutor, however, the

Legal Structure of Vatican City Courts

corte di cassazione   **Supreme Court of Appeals**   Three members, all cardinals and members of Apostolic Signatura

corte d'appello   **Court of Appeals**   Four members   Appellate court and responsible for attorney discipline   Additionally responsible for appeals from the Vatican's employee discipline commissions

tribunale   **Tribunal**   Three judges   Court of general jurisdiction and first instance   Responsible for the Promoter of Justice

giudice unico   **Sole Judge**   Court of limited jurisdiction   Small claims, traffic tickets, validation of marriages, etc.

promoter has responsibilities for acting in civil cases as well. The promoter represents the Vatican City's legal system to the Italian legal system in civil actions. Similar to his U.S. counterpart, the promoter's main responsibilities are in criminal cases. In 1998–1999, the Vatican City police force sent the promoter 114 criminal matters, of which he referred 79 to the Italian authorities (*L'Attività* 1999, 1474).

The third level is the Court of Appeals (Corte d'Appello). The Court of Appeals has a president and three other judges, all nominated by the pope for five-year terms. Most of the judges on the Court of Appeals are also judges on the Roman Rota. The Court of Appeals handles only a few cases: in the most recent year for which figures are available, the court had only four cases on its docket (*L'Attività* 1999, 1474). Along with its appellate duties, the Court of Appeals has two other responsibilities. It provides lawyer discipline and hears appeals from the Vatican City's Disciplinary Commission and the Office of Work of the Apostolic See regarding employment issues.

The fourth and final level of the court system is the Supreme Court of Appeals (Corte di Cassazione). The Supreme Court is a three-member court. The president, who is a cardinal, is the prefect of the Apostolic Signatura, the highest canon law court in the Catholic Church. Two other cardinals, who are also members of the Apostolic Signatura, join the president to make up the Supreme Court. The Supreme Court hears appeals from the Court of Appeals and has original jurisdiction over those penal matters against cardinals and bishops that the pope does not handle personally.

STAFFING

The Vatican City does not have any facilities for the training of lawyers. Instead, it relies on canon lawyers. The lawyers in cases before the first two levels of courts must meet three requirements. First, they must be on the official list, which the president of the Tribunal maintains. Second, they must be members of the Order of Rotal Lawyers—that is, they must be eligible to practice before the Rota. Finally, they must have a degree in civil law.

The Court of Appeals has a slightly more expanded pool of lawyers. The president of the Court of Appeals may enroll a lawyer with a special competency. In addition, for a single case, the president may also appoint lawyers who are not officially enrolled.

Practice before the Supreme Court is much more limited. Only lawyers who are consistorial advocates and people who have taught civil or ecclesiastical law at a university may practice before the Supreme Court.

IMPACT

The impact of the Vatican City's legal system is minimal, given the nature of the Vatican City as a state. Since the Vatican City is a means to further the religious mission of the Holy See in the world, its legal system serves more as a symbol of the sovereign independence of the Holy See than as a functioning legal system.

Robert B. Shelledy

See also Canon Law; Italy
References and further reading
Annuario pontificio per l'anno 2000. Citta del Vaticano: Tipografia Poliglotta Vaticana.
"Governatorate: Tribunali." 1999. Pp. 1473–1474 in *L'Attività della Santa Sede.* Rome: Tipografia poliglotta vaticana.
Holy See. "The Official Web Site of the Vatican: The Holy See." www.vatican.va (accessed May 11, 2001).
Hyginus, E., Cardinale. 1976. *The Holy See and the International Order.* Toronto: Macmillian of Canada.
Reese, Thomas J. 1996. *Inside the Vatican: The Politics and Organization of the Catholic Church.* Cambridge: Harvard University Press.

VENEZUELA

GENERAL INFORMATION

Venezuela is located on the northern coast of South America, bordering Colombia on the west, Guyana on the east, and Brazil on the south. Within the country's 352,143 square miles are four main geographic areas: the northwest lowlands around Lake Maracaibo; the mountain range from the Andes in the west and along the Caribbean Sea; the central plains; and the tropical highlands of the east and the far south. The climate ranges from humid in the south and east to alpine in the west. The rainy season is from July through December, with torrential rains often causing destructive flooding along the coast.

About 68 percent of the country's 23 million people are a mixture of black and white, with ethnicity seen as a continuum of skin color rather than as distinct categories. About 21 percent of the population is unmixed white—many of Portuguese, Italian, and Arab descent—and about 10 percent unmixed black. Only about 1 percent of the population is indigenous, and most of them, such as the Gaujiro around Maracaibo and the Yanomami in the Amazon, live in isolated areas. About 70 percent of the population is under thirty years of age. The country is composed of twenty-two states and the Federal District, which includes the city of Caracas and its 2 million residents. The majority of the population is Catholic, but there are growing Evangelical and Pentecostal movements.

The economy is dependent on petroleum, which accounts for about 90 percent of export revenue and more than 50 percent of GDP. Another 40 percent of GDP comes from iron and natural gas, and less than 6 percent from agriculture.

HISTORY

Venezuela's legal history is characterized by efforts to create stability. After the 1810–1821 war of independence against Spain, the nation of Gran Colombia was ruled by the revolutionary leader Simon Bolívar. The 1819 Constitution created a judiciary headed by a Supreme Court, whose five members were appointed jointly by the president and Congress. In 1830 the state fragmented into the countries of Ecuador, Colombia, and Venezuela. The 1830 Venezuelan Constitution created a federal structure and kept the Supreme Court's structure, but subsequent years of civil strife did not allow the judiciary to play a significant role.

Nineteenth-century Venezuela was characterized by interprovincial conflict among caudillos (provincial strongmen) and between the Liberal and Conservative Parties. Economic development was stunted by internal violence and dependence on agricultural products prone to large price fluctuations. The Conservative Oligarchy ruled from 1830 until 1848, when a liberal coalition took power and instituted reforms such as debt relief and the abolition of slavery, which inflamed conflict that culminated in the 1859–1863 Federal Wars. Police agencies grew during this era, expanding from colonial militias, state police, and proindependence forces. Criminal laws

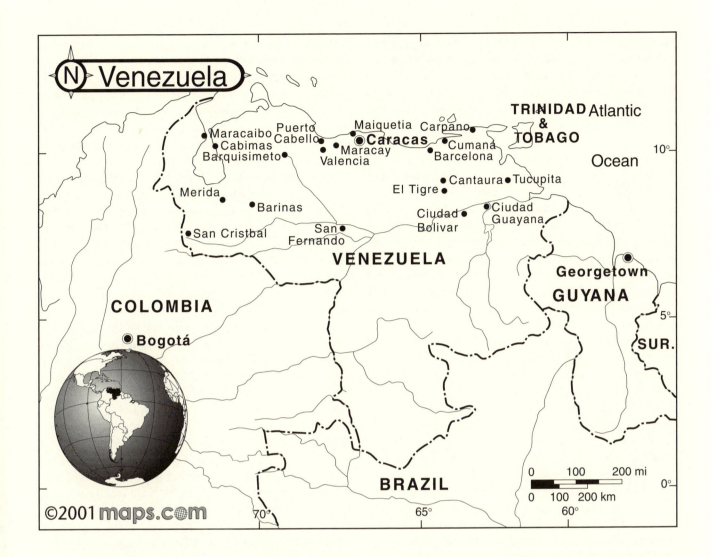

were based on a distinction between "minor" policing of community standards, headed by civilian governors, and "major" policing of the political order, headed by military commanders.

Under Antonio Guzmán Blanco, order was restored by the 1864 Constitution, which gave formal autonomy to the twenty states but in practice maintained centralization. The constitution replaced the Supreme Court with the High Federal Court (Alta Corte Federal), composed of five judges elected by Congress from a list submitted by state legislatures. Although each state had the same civil and criminal laws, the constitution made each state judiciary fully independent, which limited the Alta Corte's impact. But an appeals process was established in 1876, and the 1881 Constitution created a Corte de Casación to hear appeals from the states. Public Ministry services began in 1826, with public prosecutors (*fiscales*) appointed in each state. An 1847 law prohibited the executive from naming or removing most *fiscales,* and the 1897 penal code made the Public Ministry permanent. The first civil and commercial codes were established in 1862.

Under Guzmán, an expanding central state distributed resources to caudillos through the Regional Development Juntas, who "elected" the president through the Federal Council. The 1881 Constitution replaced most direct popular elections with indirect votes and reduced the number of states. In the 1892 "Legal Revolution," Guzmán's successor, Joaquín Crespo, reinstated the secret direct vote and the twenty-state composition. But increasing centralization led to armed opposition against Crespo and the seizure of power by Cipriano Castro in 1899. Castro accelerated centralization, undercut caudillos and traditional parties through appointment of governors and local officials, increased the executive power in the 1901 Constitution, and in the 1904 Constitution combined the two national courts into the Corte Federal y de Casación.

In 1908 an anti-Castro revolt brought Juan Vicente Gómez to power, who the following year promulgated a constitution that restored the twenty-state system. Although the regime wrote new constitutions in 1914, 1922 (which created two vice presidents, roles filled by Gómez's brother and Gómez's son), 1925, 1928, 1929, and 1931, the judiciary remained decentralized. Gómez did centralize taxation and build up the military, while Congress was subservient to the president and all opposition was swiftly repressed. Gómez's laissez-faire economic policies left little funding for social services, but when oil was discovered in the 1920s the state expanded. The oil industry also generated citizen organizing, which led to antigovernment protests in 1928 and 1929 and the development of the Acción Democrática (AD) political party.

Such opposition helped lead to liberalization after Gómez died in 1935. Eleazar López Contreras, Gómez's minister of war and successor, instituted the February Program of new social and educational services but maintained prohibition of rival political groups. The government also professionalized the police, but within a military framework and with extensive detention and investigatory authorities. López was succeeded in 1941 by Isaías Medina Angarita, whose 1945 constitution nationalized the judiciary by giving the federal government authority over the administration of justice throughout the country. He also expanded political freedoms, allowing AD to increase membership from around 75,000 in 1941 to nearly 500,000 in 1948.

In 1945 a succession crisis prompted a coup by an AD-military alliance. AD leader Rómulo Betancourt served as provisional president, ruling primarily by decree, hurrying in poorly drafted reforms, filling the courts with his allies, and creating the controversial anticorruption Tribunals of Administrative Responsibility. In 1947 the country's first ever universal elections brought the other AD leader, Rómulo Gallegos, to power. Gallegos established seven more state institutions, which tightened state control of the economy and expanded AD patronage. A 1947 Constitution limited the president to one term, guaranteed universal suffrage, ensured citizen welfare and labor rights, and re-established a Supreme Court with judicial review power. Another constitutional clause, however, allowed the president to detain any person suspected of antigovernment conspiracy. In 1948 the National Organic Law of the Judiciary replaced all of the states' organic laws on their respective judicial branches.

But AD rule threatened the church, landowners, and the armed forces, culminating in a 1948 military coup. The 1948–1958 regime of Marcos Pérez Jiménez used the National Security Agency to quell opposition, and gave many of the judiciary's powers to police forces. The regime also continued state growth, which increased citizen dependence on government jobs and resources. The regime also created the Ministry of Justice in 1950 and gave it authority over the judiciary, including that of designating all of the country's judges.

Upon the collapse of the military regime in 1958, the three political parties—AD, COPEI (Comité de Organización Política Electoral Independiente), and URD (Unión Repúblicana Democrática)—swiftly consolidated power with the 1958 Pact of Punto Fijo, an agreement among them to abide by elections, create a powerful executive, divide up government positions and resources, and agree on basic economic policies. Three years later a "rigid" constitution was enacted and became the nation's supreme law. It allowed the parties to choose electoral candidates, gave the president wide-ranging authority (such as the power of appointing state governors), granted the national government competency over all laws and judicial affairs, and, along with the Organic Law of the Judiciary, gave the judiciary judicial review and other authorities. The government replaced the National Security Agency with the judicial police (PTJ) in 1962, but, amid a leftist rebellion and increases in crime, maintained a strict law enforcement approach.

Subsequently, the ruling parties built up their patronage, dominated local affairs, and presided over unprecedented economic prosperity. But this political structure came crashing down in the 1980s under the weight of dropping oil prices, uncontrolled spending, mounting debts, and an inefficient public administration. Upstart parties began to gain strength, and reforms such as direct election of governors failed to halt the fall in the government's support. In February 1989, the unexpected introduction of austerity measures by newly elected president Carlos Andrés Pérez, who had been president from 1974 to 1979 and associated with that flush era, sparked violent widespread riots known as the *Caracazo*. Three years later, resentment within the military led to two nearly successful coup attempts. Pervasive corruption—from police bribes on the street to Pérez's impeachment over a $17 million discretionary fund—also became a source of opposition. Living standards rapidly fell: acute poverty jumped from 22.5 percent to 54 percent of the population between 1981 and 1987, and hunger increased fourfold between 1979 and 1999. Official unemployment reached nearly 20 percent and underemployment more than 40 percent. Through elections in the 1990s, citizens gradually dismantled the democracy of Punto Fijo. This was followed by the 1993 election of Rafael Caldera as president of a breakaway coalition, the end of AD's and COPEI's congressional majority in 1995, and the 1998 presidential election victory of army colonel Hugo Chávez, who had led the first failed coup six years earlier.

LEGAL CONCEPTS

Venezuela's contemporary legal system centers around the concepts of democratic government, the use of national resources, citizen rights, and a questioning of the laws and institutions designed to enforce them. By the 1990s all of the country's major institutions besides the church retained the confidence of less than 40 percent of the population. In a 1995 poll, 92 percent of respondents said that they did not believe that the nation's leaders or institutions could solve the country's crisis. The judiciary ranked particularly low. In a 1996 poll, the judiciary continued to be the second least trusted institution in the country, and in a 1997 poll only 37 percent expressed confidence in the judiciary.

The 1961 Constitution created a balance of powers between the executive, legislative, and judicial branches. The judiciary, with its power of judicial review, controls the constitutionality of law in two ways. First, through "diffuse" control, any judge can declare a law unconstitutional and thus inapplicable in a concrete case. Second, the Supreme Court has authority to annul unconstitutional laws, with effects *erga omnes*. This power applies to all laws, including state and municipal laws and executive regulations.

The executive directs foreign affairs, appoints and removes national ministers, declares states of emergency, issues regulations for the laws' execution, and runs most financial matters. The legislature is made up of the unicameral National Assembly, replacing the 1961 Constitution's bicameral Congress composed of the Senate and the House of Deputies. The Assembly has the power to make law, legislate on all national issues, and regulate all areas of public administration. National legislation may originate from any one of the three branches or from a petition of at least twenty thousand voters. When approved by one chamber after at least two debates, a bill passes to the other. After full congressional approval, the president has ten days to promulgate the law or ask for a reconsideration of any of its provisions. With a two-thirds vote, Congress can override the president's request. If it does not, the bill becomes law with a simple plurality following the president's request. The only exception is if the president's objection is based upon a charge of unconstitutionality, in which case the Supreme Court has ten days to make a ruling. If it does not make a ruling or rejects the president's charge, the law is enacted. Although the Congress retains these powers, the 1989 decentralization law transferred many administrative and law-making powers to the states and municipalities.

Despite this balance, the executive branch has dominated politics through patronage, the use of state wealth, and domination over the law. What with the primary allegiance of most legislators and judges belonging to their parties, checks and balances do not function as intended. Along with overspending of oil earnings, political patronage also created an inefficient state of nearly two million employees. Chronic suspensions also weakened the 1961 Constitution. The constitution gave the president the power to declare a suspension in cases of emergency, which must be revoked by the executive or Congress upon the emergency's cessation. Altogether, basic provisions of the 1961 Constitution were suspended twelve times, mainly in the 1960s and the 1990s. Although a suspension can be challenged in any court through a "popular action" or judicial review, it was not until 1995 that the Supreme Court heard and rejected a "popular action" asserting that the suspension was disproportionate to the "emergency." But causing more opposition among Venezuelans than party power, a bloated state, and constitutional suspensions was the use of national resources. Venezuelan social and economic policy has long been based on "sowing the oil" into a massive state, able to provide for all needed social services and economic supports. When the crisis of the 1980s ended that possibility, Venezuelans came to believe that the constitution allowed vested interests to waste and steal the nation's wealth.

Chávez's 1998 election, therefore, reflected a consensus that democracy had been hijacked by the parties and that the state was not using its oil wealth for the people. But while the 1999 Constitution reaffirms democracy, it weakens the balance of power by strengthening a president intent on restructuring the economic and political system. It increased the presidential term from five to six years, with the possibility for immediate re-election, and gives the executive the authority to dissolve Congress under certain circumstances. The new constitution also changed Congress to a unicameral National Assembly and replaced the Supreme Court with the more amenable Tribunal Supremo de Justicia. The Constituent Assembly, which drew up the constitution and was dominated by Chávez allies, also seized and exercised key judicial functions, such as the power to investigate and dismiss judges.

At the same time, Venezuelans have a strong commitment to democratic rights. As a result, the 1961 Constitution included many civil and political rights, but party controls and increasing attention to economic rights led to significant additions in the 1999 version. Reflecting the new government's economic policy, the constitution guarantees a "just distribution of wealth" and confiscation of illicitly acquired state goods. It also adds new protections such as the rights to accurate information and a "private life," as well as a prohibition against the "use of firearms and toxic substances" to control protests. It expands social rights by naming officials to protect children and youth, ensuring that retiree pensions are above the minimum wage, and guaranteeing rights to "dignified, secure, comfortable" housing. New labor rights include strong union rights, the right to loans, and against unjustified dismissal. In addition the constitution obliges the state to promote cultural expression, full access to education, the rights of indigenous peoples, and active environmental protection.

Civil rights law has also been a key aspect of the legal system, as the country's eight national and hundreds of municipal police forces stepped up practices such as arbitrary arrests. When such actions failed to halt crime, a series of congressional bills in the 1980s attempted to improve interagency coordination. In addition, the combination of judicial inefficiency and increasing incarceration made the country's penitentiary system among the world's most violent and inhumane. Most prisons operate at up to four times capacity; the average number of killings has shot up from around eighty in the late 1980s to more than four hundred in the late 1990s, and over 70 percent of inmates are unsentenced. Policy and legal responses have been largely ad hoc, such as dismantling certain facilities and bringing in the National Guard.

The rights of criminal defendants, who make up about 85 percent of all detainees, are routinely violated. Public defenders are poorly paid, have little job security, are subject to little oversight, and have far too many cases. Defenders had an annual average of less than sixty-nine cases in 1979 but more than four hundred by 1995. About two-thirds of detainees never meet with their defenders, and 16 percent meet only once. The law mandates a maximum of 46 days between arrest and the declaration, yet the average is 285 days. Legal efforts to improve the penal process have had limited impact. The 1993 Law of Penal Process, the 1992 Bail Law, and the 1980 Law of Submission to Trial and Conditional Release, along with prisoner work laws and alternative dispute resolution procedures, began to reduce the prison population. Assistance Centers set up under the 1980 law, for example, helped nearly 130,000 persons. But these programs soon became underfunded and inconsistently applied. Bail laws exclude the majority of detainees, such as those held for drug violations, while a lack of personnel prevents the majority of prisoners eligible for release from actually being freed. The legal clinics run by the Justice Ministry, municipal and state governments, universities, bar associations, and unions have been only marginally helpful.

Greater attention to civil rights has led to a gradual movement in the courts away from their traditional civil law emphasis on code over precedent and toward a more mixed system. New penal procedures, for example, follow adversarial rather than the long-standing inquisitorial process.

CURRENT STRUCTURE

Venezuela's unitary judicial system is headed by a Supreme Tribunal of Justice, which is divided into chambers in the following areas: Constitutional, Political Administrative, Electoral, Civil Appeals, Penal Appeals, and Social Appeals for agrarian, labor, and juvenile law. The High Court has wide powers, including original jurisdiction over cases in which a government is party, disputes between courts, and most appeals.

The rest of the judiciary is divided into ordinary and special courts. The ordinary courts are composed of criminal courts, civil courts governed by a civil code, and commercial courts governed by a commercial code that includes special commercial jurisdictions.

Special courts include agrarian courts, labor courts, juvenile courts, and tax courts. Administrative acts are controlled by an additional court jurisdiction: the Political Administrative Chamber of the Supreme Tribunal, the First Court on judicial review of administrative action, and fifteen superior courts on judicial review of administrative action. Administrative cases may also be handled by some specialized courts, such as the tax courts. Public Patrimony Courts were established in 1982 to handle high-level embezzlement and corruption, but they have passed down very few sentences. While regular courts may try corruption cases at the first level, this court has second-instance jurisdiction and serves as a trial court for high-level officials. Military laws and courts, governed by the Code of Military Justice, are one of the most important special jurisdictions. It had expanded during the democratic era through constitutional suspensions, laws such as the 1976 Security and Defense Law and the 1984 Drug Law, and widening application to civilians, such as charging political demonstrators with "military rebellion." While the military has increased its political role under Chávez, the 1999 Constitution mandates that the competency of military courts be limited strictly to crimes of a military nature and that rights violations against military officials be processed in civilian courts.

Almost every court jurisdiction is divided into four levels: parish courts, district or department courts, courts of the first instance, and Superior Courts, with competence depending on the amount involved or the importance of the issue. In general, all rulings may be appealed to a higher court but cannot be heard by more than two instances. Only decisions made in the second instance by a superior court can be appealed to the Supreme Court.

The newest and most innovative part of the judicial system is the Justicia de Paz (Justice of the Peace) Network, a system of popularly elected neighborhood judges empowered to settle the many disputes that do not make it to the courts. The Justicia de Paz was first created by the 1819 Gran Colombia Constitution but gradually fell out of use until the 1980s crisis led to its promotion as a way to relieve stress on the judiciary and as a method of justice appropriate to each community. It was re-established in 1993, and the high level of popular support for it was quickly apparent when the first judges received up to three times the number of votes received by municipal officials in the same elections. In their first year of functioning, the Justicia de Paz resolved thirty-five hundred disputes, about 60 percent of which involved acts of violence.

SPECIALIZED JUDICIAL BODIES

The most significant specialized judicial body in modern Venezuela has been the Judicial Council (Consejo de la Judicatura), with authority over the selection and discipline of judges as well as the management of its finances.

Legal Structure of Venezuela Courts

Regular Courts

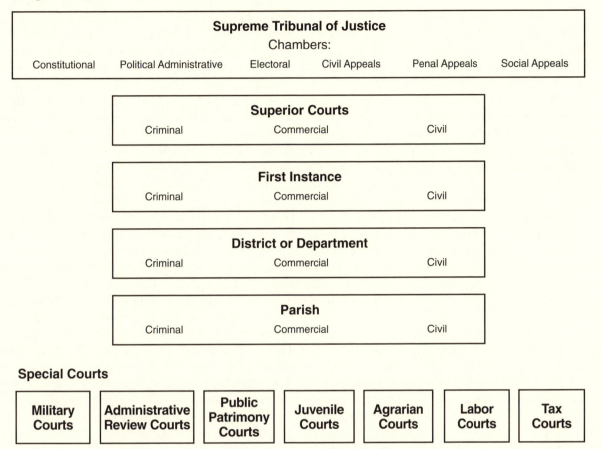

Supreme Tribunal of Justice
Chambers:

| Constitutional | Political Administrative | Electoral | Civil Appeals | Penal Appeals | Social Appeals |

Superior Courts

| Criminal | Commercial | Civil |

First Instance

| Criminal | Commercial | Civil |

District or Department

| Criminal | Commercial | Civil |

Parish

| Criminal | Commercial | Civil |

Special Courts

| Military Courts | Administrative Review Courts | Public Patrimony Courts | Juvenile Courts | Agrarian Courts | Labor Courts | Tax Courts |

Although the council was part of the 1961 Constitution, the AD government did not want a "neutral" body choosing judges and so did not legislate the required organic ("enabling") law until 1969, following the election of a COPEI president. Retaining its congressional majority, AD now wanted to limit the new executive's power over the judiciary. From the start, however, the council got bogged down in bureaucracy and politics. Complaints received by the council are reviewed by an inspector, who, if finding wrongdoing, begins a disciplinary process. But in practice most of the initial processing went to separating substantive from spurious accusations, and when investigations were actually initiated, rules such as requiring unanimity in most decisions allowed the government's appointees to protect judges affiliated with it. As a result, of the 148 judges investigated between 1971 and 1980, only 12 were dismissed. The council's ineffectiveness led to a new organic law in 1988, which reduced the council's size and strengthened its powers. The council subsequently promoted judicial reform with a $30 million World Bank grant and attacked favoritism with oversight measures such as the 1991 creation of a General Council of Judges in each juridical jurisdiction. But politicization

and bureaucracy continued. Most judges are selected through public forums in which council members review candidates' records, but Congress is not obliged to accept these nominees and may vote in secret. In addition, as accusations grew to a height of three thousand, hundreds of charges got stuck in the courts and many dismissed judges were reinstated. The council came to an end in the 1999 Constitution, which replaced it with the far more limited Executive Judicial Office within the Supreme Tribunal of Justice.

With the end of the council, responsibility for oversight on law and rights has shifted to the new "fourth branch" of government composed of the Public Ministry, the Controller General, and the Defensoría del Pueblo. A strengthened Public Ministry will continue representing the state in legal issues, with actions such as filing lawsuits to enforce the civil, penal, and administrative responsibility of state officials, and bringing penal action in cases in which a petition by the injured party is not necessary. But its former role of overseeing the state will be taken over by the newly created Defensoría del Pueblo, an independent ombudsman agency that has the power to receive citizen rights complaints, help ensure a fair administration of justice, and help guarantee a rule of law within state agencies.

STAFFING

The courts are headed by judges chosen through processes outlined in the 1980 Judicial Career Law and in the constitution. To be on the Supreme Tribunal, candidates must have a respected record and have practiced law for at least fifteen years, have an advanced degree in law, or have worked in the judiciary for at least fifteen years. *Fiscales* must have the same qualifications. Those nominated to the Superior Court or to first instance courts must be distinguished in their profession, as evidenced by academic writings and teaching, or with at least ten years' experience in the judiciary or six years as a public defender or prosecutor. Candidates for the bench at the district or municipal level must be twenty-five years of age, have a law degree, have practiced law or studied postgraduate law, or have served as a court secretary for at least two years. Candidates for all levels, in addition, must complete a training course in the Judicial School (Escuela de la Judicatura).

The actual selection process has been the responsibility of the Judicial Council. Selection decisions are made by a panel through public forums called *concursos de oposición*. For Supreme or Superior Court nominees, the panel is composed of two members of the Supreme Court chamber in the area of law to which the nominee is being considered, a member of the Judicial Council, and a scholar in the area of the law. For nominees to all other courts, the panel is composed of a Judicial Council member, an Appeals Court judge selected by the Supreme Court president, and a legal scholar. The forums consist of three stages: an initial review of credentials and merits, a written analysis of past experience, and an oral evaluation of theoretical disposition. The intrusion of political interests, however, has led to a weakening of these forums. Most court nominees have been selected through prior agreements between the two main political parties, making the forums little more than a formality. In response, the Chávez constitution has given the council's powers and responsibilities to the Supreme Tribunal of Justice. Until the enacting legislation is finalized, selection is conducted by the Commission of the Functioning and Restructuring of the Judiciary, appointed by the National Assembly.

Along with judges, within the courts there are judge-appointed secretaries, responsible for the management of each court and the processing of documents, and bailiffs, responsible for communications. Also at the disposition of the courts are forensic doctors appointed by the executive branch. Outside the courts are many other legal professions typical of a civil law system. In addition to public prosecutors and public defenders there are advocates and notaries. The advocate, roughly equivalent to an attorney-at-law in the United States, advises clients, represents them in court, and usually helps them with their other legal matters. Advocates work out of their own individual law offices, but are being gradually supplanted in Venezuela by larger law firms. The notary, finally, carries out three important areas of the legal process: drafting important legal documents such as contracts, authenticating instruments to affirm that they are accurate and legal; and producing copies of the original documents, which they retain as part of the public record. Unlike advocates, notaries are appointed and must serve all those seeking their services.

Lawyers long have been central in politics, helping to structure early governments. But when oil exports increased in the 1950s lawyers served a pivotal role for multinational corporations seeking concessions and setting up operations. In interpreting the country's laws, this generation of lawyers also became politically influential and branched out into related areas of the law, such as contracts and nationalization. Since the 1980s, however, Venezuela has an overabundance of lawyers, educated in the country's public and private university law programs. The increasing number of private schools, which have come under criticism for poor standards, are the main source for the growing number of lawyers. But even in the top law schools, which tend to be public, professors are poorly paid and do not teach full-time. To practice, a graduate must be accepted by the state's Academy of Lawyers, which is the bar association.

IMPACT

The biggest impact of the law has been through the judiciary's malfunctioning and the law's inability to stem violent crime. Above all, the Venezuelan judiciary has been inefficient, bureaucratic, biased, and inaccessible. Since 1958 judicial officials have complained of interference by the executive and the parties, a lack of cooperation by the police and prosecutors, the failure to reform or introduce many basic laws, the need for administrative modernization, and the ever-increasing influence in the courts by economic interests and law firms. Changes were implemented as criticisms grew in the 1980s, but most were overwhelmed by strikes of judicial employees, neglect of the Judicial Career Law, inadequate funds, low salaries, a lack of planning, and continuing politicization. A Judicial School was opened in 1982, but a lack of funding and party commitment forced it to shut down and re-open with only short preparatory courses. The judicial budget itself was highly politicized. Based on Supreme Court requests, the executive presents an initial budget to the House of Deputies, which makes recommendations but cannot allocate extra funds without special petitions. In most years, the final budget is about two-thirds of the

Supreme Court's initial request. As a result, deficits are high and most courts lack necessities such as computers and telephone lines. Compounding this problem is a chronic lack of judges. In 1958 there were approximately seven hundred judges for a population of about 7 million; in 1994 there were just fourteen hundred judges for a population of more than 22 million. The average time for a criminal trial is 4.5 years. Such bottlenecks have led to increased use of the emergency *amparo* and habeas corpus recourses, which further overloads the courts. Judicial functioning is also affected by the burgeoning number of "temporary" and "auxiliary" judges who stay long past their sixty-day limit and currently constitute more than half of all judges.

Several important reforms, though, have been enacted. In 1998, Congress unanimously approved a new penal code that switches the criminal trials from an inquisitorial to an accusatorial process, ends the secrecy of the initial stages of criminal investigation, and will have many courts presided over not by a set of three judges but by one judge and two citizens. Addressing budgetary shortfalls, the 1999 Constitution guarantees the judiciary 2 percent of the annual national budget. This provision will reduce politicization but will not help judicial functioning without a growing budget and better management.

The other major impact of the law is through crime and criminal law. Continuing patterns from the 1980s, Venezuela's murder rate rose by 73 percent, assaults by 16 percent, and robberies by 26 percent between 1990 and 1995. The country has Latin America's fourth highest murder rate, and Caracas's rate of 60 murders per 100,000 people is one of the world's highest urban rates. But just as high as society's fear of crime is its lack of confidence in the state's ability to reduce it. In a poll in Maracaibo, the country's second largest city, 89 percent of respondents feared being victims of crime. And though 91 percent did not "feel secure" with the police and 86 percent felt that police hurt innocent people, 60 percent favored more violence to combat crime and 47 percent favored the police killing delinquents. Throughout the country, in fact, increasingly vocal sectors have been championing their "rights" to self-protection, whose extreme version has been vigilantism. Reports indicate increases in killings of suspected criminals by both mobs and organized groups, from a few in 1995 to one nearly every few days in 2000. In a 1995 national poll, 57 percent of respondents favored the practice. The debate over balancing constitutional rights and criminal policy has also centered around controversial laws such as the 1939 Law of Vagabonds and Crooks (Ley de Vagos y Maleantes [LVM]). Exempt from penal law's due process guarantees and a presumption of innocence, the LVM allowed the detention and incarceration by nonjudicial officials of persons who have not committed crimes but were

deemed a "threat to society." Political officials supported the LVM because it helped free criminal policy from the inefficient judiciary, and after the Supreme Court struck it down in 1997, many proposed similar laws, while the police have increased the use of other detention regulations to make up for its absence.

Mark Ungar

See also Alternative Dispute Resolution; Constitutional Law; Criminal Law; Criminal Procedures; Habeas Corpus, Writ of; Human Rights Law; Incarceration; Inquisatorial Procedure; Judicial Independence; Judicial Review; Legal Aid; Legal Education; Neighborhood Justice Centers

References and further reading
Comisión Andina de Juristas. "Jurisdicción Constitucional." http://www.cajpe.org.pe (accessed October 11, 2000).
Ewell, Judith. 1984. *Venezuela: A Century of Change.* Stanford: Stanford University Press.
Gil Yepes, José Antonio. 1981. *The Challenge of Venezuelan Democracy.* New Brunswick, NJ: Transaction Books.
Goodman, Louis, et al. 1995. *Lessons of the Venezuelan Experience.* Washington, DC: Woodrow Wilson Center Press.
Hillman, Richard. 1994. *Democracy for the Privileged: Crisis and Transition in Venezuela.* Boulder, CO: Lynne Rienner.
Kornblith, Miriam. 1991. "The Politics of Constitution Making: Constitutions and Democracy in Venezuela." *Journal of Latin American Studies* 23: 61–84.
Latin American Network Information Center. "Venezuela." http://lanic.utexas.edu/ (accessed October 6, 2000).
Lawyers Committee for Human Rights and Programa Venezolano de Eduación-Acción en Derechos Humanos (PROVEA). 1996. *Halfway to Reform: The World Bank and the Venezuelan Justice System.* New York: Lawyers Committee for Human Rights.
Martz, John, and David Myers. 1986. *Venezuela: The Democratic Experience.* New York: Praeger.
McCoy, Jennifer, Andrés Serbin, William C. Smith, and Andrés Stambouli, eds. 1995. *Venezuelan Democracy under Stress.* Miami: University of Miami.
Morón, Guillermo. 1964. *A History of Venezuela.* London: George Allen and Unwin.

VERMONT

GENERAL INFORMATION

Vermont, a state in New England, in the easternmost region of the United States, is the second smallest state in population and the eighth smallest in area. Its population in the year 2000 was 608,827, and its area is 9,615 square miles. Vermont was originally inhabited by the Abenaki Indians, few of whom survive today. Subsequent settlers were French, Dutch, and finally British, who gained control of the region in 1763. Vermonters are generally representative of Protestant New England, but other ethnic groups have immigrated, such as French-Canadians in the north, Italians and Spanish in the center, Welsh in the west, and Poles and Irish in the south.

Vermont is one of the most rural states in the United States. More than two-thirds of its population lives in small towns. Dairy farming dominates its agriculture. Industries include granite quarrying, printing, paper products, and small-scale manufacturing. Vermont, with its strict environmental laws, old-fashioned small-town atmosphere, and traditional way of life, attracts visitors throughout the year.

Once a stronghold of small-government conservatism, Vermont has radically changed its character since the 1960s. By the end of the century it had become one of the most liberal states in the country. Despite strong opposition from its conservative minority, Vermont's tradition of local governmental control has given way to a larger, more centralized government. Nevertheless, public officials remain accessible, and citizens retain considerable opportunity to participate in government through public deliberations.

EVOLUTION AND HISTORY

In colonial times, Vermont settlers were subject to conflicting territorial claims by both New Hampshire and New York, which resulted in the annulment by each state of land grants to Vermont settlers by the other state. Vermonters declared their independence in 1777 but could not join the Union as a separate state because of the conflicting claims. From 1777 to 1791, Vermont was an independent republic, but it finally joined the union when New Hampshire and New York abandoned their claims to Vermont territory.

The Vermont Constitution of 1777 was very radical compared with the constitutions of the thirteen original states. It was the first state constitution to adopt universal male suffrage without regard to property ownership, and it was the first that explicitly outlawed slavery. It incorporated a series of rights similar to those later placed in the U.S. Constitution. Private property could not be taken for public use without compensation. People had a right to hold themselves, their houses, papers and possessions free from search and seizure, and warrants required the support of oaths or affirmations. Nobody could be deprived of liberty except by law and the judgment of his peers. Those accused of crimes had a right to know the nature of the charges against them, to be heard in speedy public trials before impartial juries, to confront witnesses, and not to be compelled to give evidence against themselves. They had the right to bail, and excessive bail was prohibited. Trial by jury was guaranteed for civil as well as criminal cases. Debtors could not be held in prison after delivering their assets to their creditors. All people were guaranteed freedom of religion, the right of assembly, and the right to petition the legislature. The constitution also guaranteed that those "scrupulous of bearing arms" could not be compelled to do so, provided they paid an equivalent for the defense of the state. These rights were preserved in the later Vermont Constitution of 1786, and in the final Vermont Constitution of 1793, which remains in force today, with amendments.

The Vermont constitutions of 1777, 1786, and 1793 established a Supreme Court, and additional lower courts in every county of the state, with powers exercised in the British legal tradition. Initially, the Supreme Court was only an appeals court, although its justices also rode circuit around the state to preside individually over county courts. Eventually, the state created additional judges. By 1908, the legislature had established two distinct bodies: a Supreme Court whose members sat solely in that capacity, and a Superior Court whose judges presided over courts in each county.

For most of Vermont's history, Supreme Court justices and Superior Court judges were elected or re-elected by the Vermont Legislature every one or two years. Assistant judges, also known as "side judges," joined Superior Court judges in presiding over their courts, and were elected by the people every two years. There were also justices of the peace in every organized municipality, elected by the people every two years, who heard small criminal and civil cases. Eventually municipal courts, superior to the justices of the peace, were created in the larger cities. Their judges were appointed every two years by the governor. Probate matters were heard by probate judges elected locally by the voters, also every two years.

By the late 1950s, the state recognized that the growing complexity of Vermont society and Vermont legislation required more specialized courts and a unified judicial system. In 1957 the legislature established police courts in certain regions to handle traffic violations, and in 1967 it established district judgeships to hear criminal matters. In 1974, Vermont adopted a constitutional amendment calling for "A Supreme Court, a Superior Court, and such other subordinate courts as the General Assembly may . . . ordain and establish," and giving the Supreme Court "administrative control of all the courts of the state, and disciplinary authority concerning all judicial officers and attorneys at law in the state." In the 1970s the Supreme Court brought a degree of coherence to Vermont's legal system by promulgating rules of civil, criminal, appellate, and probate procedure, as well as rules of evidence and family proceedings.

The Vermont courts, like federal courts, engage in judicial review. A recent controversial decision by the Vermont Supreme Court, *Brigham v. State of Vermont* (1997), voided Vermont's decentralized and uneven educational funding system, thereby paving the way for equalized and centralized funding. The ruling countered Vermont's tradition of decentralized government and local control. Another controversial decision was *Baker v. State of Vermont* (1999), which declared unconstitutional

Legal Structure of Vermont Courts

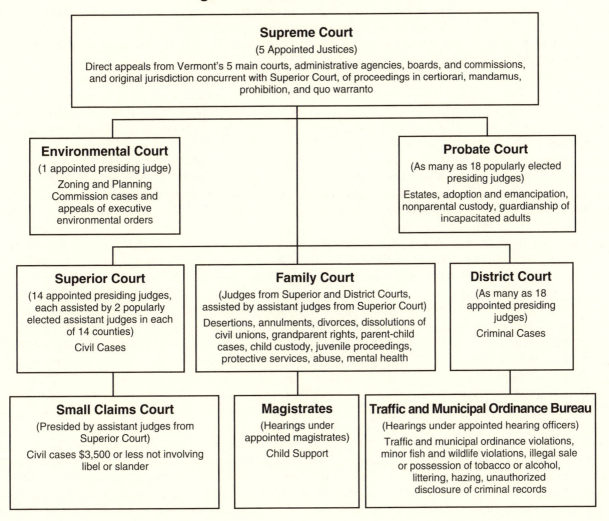

Supreme Court

(5 Appointed Justices)

Direct appeals from Vermont's 5 main courts, administrative agencies, boards, and commissions, and original jurisdiction concurrent with Superior Court, of proceedings in certiorari, mandamus, prohibition, and quo warranto

Environmental Court

(1 appointed presiding judge)

Zoning and Planning Commission cases and appeals of executive environmental orders

Probate Court

(As many as 18 popularly elected presiding judges)

Estates, adoption and emancipation, nonparental custody, guardianship of incapacitated adults

Superior Court

(14 appointed presiding judges, each assisted by 2 popularly elected assistant judges in each of 14 counties)

Civil Cases

Family Court

(Judges from Superior and District Courts, assisted by assistant judges from Superior Court)

Desertions, annulments, divorces, dissolutions of civil unions, grandparent rights, parent-child cases, child custody, juvenile proceedings, protective services, abuse, mental health

District Court

(As many as 18 appointed presiding judges)

Criminal Cases

Small Claims Court

(Presided by assistant judges from Superior Court)

Civil cases $3,500 or less not involving libel or slander

Magistrates

(Hearings under appointed magistrates)

Child Support

Traffic and Municipal Ordinance Bureau

(Hearings under appointed hearing officers)

Traffic and municipal ordinance violations, minor fish and wildlife violations, illegal sale or possession of tobacco or alcohol, littering, hazing, unauthorized disclosure of criminal records

---

the granting of state benefits to traditional married couples without granting them to others engaged in domestic unions. The ruling led to Vermont's civil unions law, which many see as tantamount to establishing homosexual marriage.

CURRENT STRUCTURE

Today the Vermont judiciary is a unified body headed by a five-member Supreme Court, and, immediately below it, a Superior Court with fourteen judges who preside over Superior Court sessions in the fourteen Vermont counties (see figure).

The Superior Court has jurisdiction over most civil cases. The assistant judges, or "side judges," join the presiding Superior Court judge to determine the facts in cases in which jury trials are waived. Matters of law are determined by the presiding judge. Assistant judges sitting alone hear small claims disputes involving no more than $3,500 that do not involve libel or slander. Superior Court judges hear appeals from small claims hearings,

but further appeal to the Supreme Court is at the Supreme Court's discretion.

Also immediately below the Supreme Court there is a single District Court with as many as eighteen judges who hold sessions in towns throughout the state as designated by the Supreme Court. Vermont statutes give the District Court jurisdiction over most criminal cases, and over cases involving state civil sanctions. Immediately below the District Court there is a Traffic and Municipal Ordinance Bureau in which hearing officers decide cases involving traffic, civil ordinances, minor fish and wildlife violations, the illegal sale or possession of tobacco or alcohol, littering, hazing, and unauthorized disclosure of criminal records. Appeals from the bureau go to the District Court, and further appeal to the Supreme Court is at the Supreme Court's discretion.

Vermont has other specialized courts immediately under the Supreme Court. The Environmental Court has one judge with statewide jurisdiction who holds hearings throughout the state. He hears cases regarding the enforcement and review of administrative orders issued by the secretary of the Vermont Agency of Natural Resources. The court also hears appeals of zoning and planning decisions of Vermont cities and towns.

There is a Family Court in each of Vermont's fourteen counties. Family Court cases are decided by a presiding Family Court judge, who is either a Superior Court judge, a District Court judge, or the Environmental Court judge, assisted by the two county Superior Court assistant judges, who, subject to their availability, join the presiding Family Court judge to determine matters of fact. Family Courts hear cases of desertion, annulment, divorce, dissolution of civil unions, parent-child cases, grandparent rights, child custody, juvenile proceedings, protective services, mental health and retardation, abuse, and enforcement of support. Child support matters themselves are heard by Family Court magistrates whose decisions may be appealed to the presiding Family Court judge. There are no jury trials in Vermont Family Courts.

There is a Probate Court in each county of Vermont, and there can be as many as eighteen Probate Court judges in Vermont. The probate courts have jurisdiction over the administration and settlement of estates, adoption and emancipation of minors, guardianship of incapacitated persons, custody of minors to someone other than a parent, and the establishment and correction of vital records.

The Supreme Court appoints one of its own, or another judge, to function as Vermont's administrative judge who assigns Superior, District, and Family Court cases to Superior and District Court judges and, if available, to the Environmental Court judge. He may also assign members of the Vermont bar to serve temporarily as acting judges in Superior, District, or Family Court, as acting magistrates in Family Court, or as hearing officers in the Traffic and Municipal Ordinance Bureau. The administration of the individual courts is carried out by county clerks for Superior Court, and clerks or court managers for other courts, all of whom are state employees.

The Vermont Supreme Court has exclusive jurisdiction over appeals from all Vermont courts, administrative agencies, boards, commissions, and officers, except that appeals from the Traffic and Municipal Ordinance Bureau go to District Court, appeals from Family Court magistrates go to Family Court, and appeals from Small Claims Court go to Superior Court. The Supreme Court has original jurisdiction, concurrent with Superior Court, of proceedings in certiorari, mandamus, prohibition, and quo warranto.

Vermont's justices of the peace, who historically carried out limited judicial functions in civil and criminal matters, lost their judicial power in 1974. Currently they sit on local boards of civil authority, perform marriages, and register voters.

Criminal prosecutions in Vermont are carried out by state's attorneys in each county. There is a state attorney general who represents Vermont in all civil and criminal matters and has the general supervision of criminal prosecution throughout the state. His powers are the same throughout the state as those of state's attorneys, whom he may consult and advise as he sees fit.

Vermont has a defender general whose office represents those without resources, to pay for their criminal defense. The defender general may enter into contracts with private attorneys to represent needy defendants.

NOTABLE FEATURES
OF VERMONT'S LEGAL SYSTEM

Through the renomination or re-election process, the Vermont judiciary has always been strongly bound to the legislature, or to the executive, or to local voters, indicating an aversion to a completely independent judiciary traceable to popular distrust stemming from the failure of the judiciaries in New Hampshire and New York to uphold land grants made by each other to Vermont settlers during the late 1700s.

Vermont's institution of popularly elected assistant judges, who join presiding judges in Superior and Family Court to determine factual matters, is a distinctive aspect of the Vermont legal system that reflects a distrust of the judiciary and a traditional New England instinct for checks and balances in government. It is also notable that there is no requirement that assistant judges, probate judges, and state prosecutors, all of whom are elected by the people, be or have been practicing attorneys, nor possess legal training, although abbreviated training is given to those assistant judges who preside alone in small claims hearings. State's attorneys and the attorney general also need not be trained in law or be practicing attorneys.

Vermont allows aspiring attorneys to learn their trade by "reading" the law as clerks to established lawyers. After a certain number of years as a clerk, one may practice law even without a degree, provided he passes the bar exam. Even a practicing attorney from another state who passes the Vermont bar exam, or who after five years' experience elsewhere is appointed to the Vermont bar, must work for a time as a law clerk before he can practice law on his own.

Unlike many states, Vermont guarantees a trial by jury for all offenses, even misdemeanors, unless a jury trial is waived. A guilty finding in the Traffic and Municipal Ordinance Bureau, where there are no juries, gives one a guaranteed right of retrial by jury on appeal to District Court. Vermont is one of the few states that require a unanimous verdict by twelve jurors for any jury trial.

STAFFING

Consistent with Vermont's aversion to a too-independent judiciary, there are no lifetime appointments to the Vermont courts. Today, Vermont's Supreme Court justices,

Superior Court judges, District Court judges, the Environmental Judge, and Family Court magistrates are appointed by the governor for six-year terms, with the consent of the Vermont Senate, from a list of practicing attorneys recommended by Vermont's Judicial Nominating Board. The board consists of two members named by the governor; three by the Vermont Senate from among its members; three by the Vermont House of Representatives from among its members; and three by Vermont's attorneys.

At the end of their terms, Supreme Court justices, Superior Court judges, District Court judges, and the Environmental Court judge may be retained for succeeding terms in office on the recommendation of a retention committee of four members of the Vermont Senate and four members of the Vermont House, and confirmed by a vote of the whole Vermont General Assembly (Senate and House combined). Family Court magistrates may be reappointed by the governor with the consent of the Senate, without review by the retention committee.

Probate Court judges, and assistant judges in Superior Court, are elected by the people for four-year terms. Hearing officers in the Traffic and Municipal Ordinance Bureau are attorneys appointed for limited periods by Vermont's administrative judge from members of the Vermont Bar. Judges, magistrates, and hearings officers must step down at seventy years of age, or immediately thereafter at the end of their terms.

State's attorneys in each county are elected by the people for two-year terms. The state attorney general is elected statewide, also for a two-year term. The Vermont defender general must be an experienced Vermont attorney and is named by the governor to a four-year term with the consent of the Senate.

The only law school in the state is the Vermont Law School, a private institution that opened in the 1970s, considered by many to be the best law school in the United States in environmental law. There were approximately twenty-one hundred practicing lawyers in Vermont in 1996, up from about five hundred in 1967.

Christopher David Costanzo

See also Lay Judiciaries; United States—Federal System; United States—State Systems

References and further reading
Baldamo, Michael. 1992. *The Republic of Vermont 1777–1791: A Short History.* Montpelier: Woodchuck Press.
Doyle, William. 1996. *The Vermont Political Tradition: And Those Who Helped Make It.* Barre: Northlight Studio Press.
Nuquist, Andrew E., and Edith W. Nuquist. 1966. *Vermont's State Government and Administration: An Historical and Descriptive Study of the Living Past.* Burlington: University of Vermont.
Sherman, Michael, ed. 1999. *Vermont State Government since 1965.* Burlington: University of Vermont.

VICTORIA, STATE OF

GENERAL INFORMATION

The State of Victoria lies at the southeastern tip of the Australian mainland. Victoria has a population of approximately 4.8 million, around 3.5 million of whom live within the metropolitan area of its capital, Melbourne. Around 25 percent of Australia's total population live in Victoria. The state's landmass is 87,884 square miles, which constitutes 3 percent of the total landmass of the continent of Australia.

EVOLUTION AND HISTORY

The State of Victoria was initially a British colony and formerly part of the colony of New South Wales, known as the District of Port Phillip. By the Australian Constitutions Act 1850 (Imp), the British Parliament provided for the separation of the district and creation of the new colony, which occurred on July 1, 1851. When the colony separated, its legal system was a consolidation of many of the various forums available in England at the time.

Due to the Australian Courts Act 1828 (Imp), the governing laws at the time of separation were those that were in force in England on July 28, 1828, insofar as they were applicable to the conditions of the colony. The Victorian Parliament had power to pass laws contrary to these, except where Imperial laws were specifically directed to the colonies, which laws had paramount force. In 1980 the Victorian Parliament passed the Imperial Acts Application Act, which repealed most English legislation otherwise applicable in Victoria not having paramount force. It was not until British and Australian Parliaments passed the Australia Acts in 1986 that Victoria could legislate contrary to Imperial acts.

In 1852, the Victorian Parliament established the Supreme Court of Victoria and later the county court. Appeals from the Supreme Court could be heard by the Privy Council in England. With the passage of the Judicature Act 1883, judges of the Supreme Court were entitled to apply the rules of common law and equity concurrently in any proceeding.

At federation of the six colonies into six states of Australia on January 1, 1901, the colony became the State of Victoria. An Australian constitution was adopted, which gave defined legislative powers to the national government and left the residual powers to the states. The High Court of Australia was established as the ultimate court in Australia, subject to appeals to the Privy Council in London. Appeals from all Australian courts to the Privy Council were finally abolished in 1986.

CURRENT STRUCTURE

Supreme Court

The superior court of Victoria is the Supreme Court. The Court comprises the trial division and the court of appeal. Membership of the Court includes the chief justice, the president of the court of appeal, appeal judges, judges, and masters. The trial division comprises:

- Common law division,
- Commercial and equity division, and
- Criminal division.

Each civil division includes a number of specialist lists into which certain proceedings are tracked.

The Supreme Court has unlimited jurisdiction. In commercial and civil matters, the court generally hears disputes that are extraordinarily complicated or involve claims for greater than AUD$200,000, or that relate to property of such value. Civil trials may be heard by judge alone or by judge and jury of six laypeople. Juries in civil proceedings can be empanelled only in cases claiming damages for defamation or in personal injury cases. A civil jury can be empanelled at the request of either party or at the insistence of the judge.

The criminal division tries cases of murder, attempted murder, treason, and murder-related offences. Criminal trials are heard by a judge and jury of twelve laypeople. A judge in the trial division can also hear appeals from the Magistrates' Court and children's court on questions of law, which the judge may then remit for rehearing.

In jury trials, the judge determines questions of law and directs the jury accordingly, while the jury determines questions of fact, the guilt or innocence of the accused, and the amount of damages in civil trials. The Supreme Court also deals with applications for injunctions and for the grant of probate. Many procedural and interlocutory matters are heard and determined before the masters, who are judicial officers, or by a judge in the practice court.

The court of appeal was established in 1995, replacing the full court structure. Its membership includes the chief justice, the president of the court of appeal, and the judges of appeal. An appeal bench is constituted by any three of these officers, but may include a judge from the trial division. The court can hear appeals from:

- The trial division of the Supreme Court,
- The county court,
- The president or a vice president of the Victorian Civil and Administrative Tribunal, and
- The president of the children's court.

County Court

The county court of Victoria is an intermediate trial court that hears and determines civil and criminal matters, as well as certain appeals by way of rehearings from the Magistrates' Court. Proceedings in the court are streamed into lists such as the business list and the damages list.

The court has unlimited jurisdiction in personal injury matters, though in other civil or commercial matters its jurisdiction is limited to claims for AUD$200,000 or less, or that relate to property of such value. The court hears all serious criminal matters save those heard in the Supreme Court, including drug trafficking, sexual offences, serious assault, and fraud. Civil and criminal trials can be heard by judge and jury in the same manner as in the Supreme Court.

In all instances where a civil jury is empanelled, the jury determines the questions of liability and the quantum of damages. However, in claims under the statutory no-fault compensation schemes for injuries in the workplace and in transport accidents, a threshold test of "serious injury" must be passed before a common law claim can be heard and determined by a jury. A judge alone determines initially whether a serious injury has occurred. Then the jury can determine questions of liability and damages. Many claims for personal injury are heard and determined by judge and jury.

The Magistrates' Court

The Magistrates' Court of Victoria is a local court that regularly sits in over fifty locations around the state. A magistrate acts in much the same way as a judge of the more superior courts, and hears and determines *without* a jury minor criminal and traffic matters, known as summary offences. The magistrate can also summarily hear and determine certain more serious indictable offences such as burglary and theft with the consent of the defendant. The potential penalties are less than those that a judge of a superior court could impose. Should a person plead not guilty to an indictable offence that will *not* be tried summarily, a magistrate will preside over a committal hearing, to determine whether the evidence justifies that person's committal for later trial in a superior court.

In civil and commercial matters, magistrates have jurisdiction to hear claims for anything under AUD$40,000. A claim for less than AUD$5,000 will be heard by arbitration, conducted with less formality. The court has broad jurisdiction to deal with many matters including:

- A limited workers compensation jurisdiction,
- Certain maintenance and child contact claims under the Commonwealth Family Law Act 1975, and
- Intervention orders to prevent contact between family members.

Magistrates also sit as members of the Victims of

Crime Assistance Tribunal, designed to provide victims of crime with both financial assistance for expenses incurred as a direct result of a criminal act, and compensation for criminal injuries.

Coroner's Court

The State Coroner's Office and the coroner's court investigate and determine the causes of reportable deaths and of fires that are of public significance, with an emphasis on making recommendations for the future prevention of death and injury.

Investigations are conducted with assistance from the Victorian Institute of Forensic Medicine, headed by a professor of Medicine of Monash University. The institute is home to the National Coroner's Information System database, an Internet-based data storage and retrieval system for coronial cases across Australia.

The Children's Court

The Children's Court of Victoria is presided over by a county court judge and magistrates. It is divided into a family division and a criminal division. The criminal division deals with offences committed by children aged between ten and less than seventeen at time of commission. The court hears all criminal matters other than murder, attempted murder, manslaughter, and related offences, which are heard in the Supreme Court. The penalties range from undertakings and bonds to youth supervision, attendance, and training center orders. The family division deals with child protection. If a child is in need of protection, the court can make a range of orders from a parental undertaking to interim accommodation or permanent custody to the government.

Victorian Civil and Administrative Tribunal

The Victorian Civil and Administrative Tribunal (VCAT) is divided into a civil division and an administrative division, each of which is divided into a number of lists.

The administrative division reviews administrative decisions made by Victorian government agencies, and resolves disputes relating to areas such as:

• The Freedom of Information Act,
• The Victorian no-fault transport accident compensation scheme,
• Land valuations for local government rating or compulsory acquisition,
• Licensing or registration of businesses and occupations,
• Local planning, and
• State taxation.

The civil division resolves disputes in areas such as:

• Discrimination under the Equal Opportunity Act,
• Consumer and fair trading claims and consumer credit,
• Domestic building,
• Residential and retail tenancies, and
• Guardianship matters.

The VCAT comprises a president—who is a judge of the Supreme Court, vice presidents—who are judges of the county court, and senior and ordinary members. The VCAT has discretion to adapt its procedures and determine how it conducts hearings. Although it must follow the rules of natural justice, it can operate in a highly inquisitorial fashion. Many senior and ordinary members are lay members with expert qualifications in areas other than law. All lists have provision for compulsory mediation prior to hearing. The right of appeal is limited to the Supreme Court on a point of law only.

NOTABLE FEATURES OF LAW AND LEGAL SYSTEM

The Supreme Court, county court, and VCAT maintain tight control of proceedings from the time a proceeding is commenced. Case-flow management has reduced the delays between the commencement of proceedings and final hearing. Through the use of specialist lists, judicial case management, and directions hearings, cases claiming similar remedies or based on similar causes of action are dealt with consistently, and persistent procedural problems are more readily identified and resolved. The courts can order the parties to engage in a pretrial mediation, with or without their consent. The Supreme, county, and Magistrates' Courts also have power to transfer proceedings between themselves as appropriate.

The Supreme Court and county court go on circuit several times each year, where they conduct judicial business in rural towns outside metropolitan Melbourne, to cater for the 1.3 million people who live in regional Victoria.

Computer technology is increasingly used in the running of hearings in the VCAT, the coroner's court, and in major Supreme Court commercial trials. Court materials and pleadings, transcripts, as well as other relevant data, can be available online and in real time to both the court and the litigants during the course of a hearing. Electronic filing of initiating processes is available in the Magistrates' Court and the VCAT.

Procedures for representative or group proceedings—class actions—have been available in the Supreme Court since 1984. By reducing the need for groups of litigants to make separate yet identical claims, or run test cases, these procedures now provide a fairer, more efficient and cost-effective procedure for mass litigation.

Structure of Victorian Courts

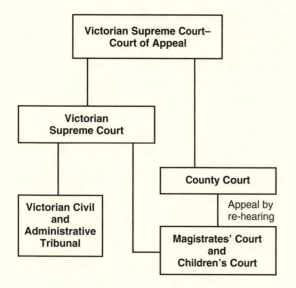

The Legal Aid Commission of Victoria is a government organization that provides government funding for indigent defendants in criminal proceedings and litigants in some family law proceedings. Community Legal Centers, located in metropolitan and regional areas, also provide volunteer legal services for litigants across Victoria.

LEGAL PRACTITIONERS

To become a legal practitioner in Victoria, a person must:

- Complete a law degree at an accredited university,
- Undertake either a six-month course in practical legal training or articles of clerkship for one year with an experienced practicing solicitor, and
- Apply for approval to the Board of Examiners, who determine whether or not the applicant is qualified, of good fame and character, and a fit and proper person to be admitted to practice.

An applicant will then be admitted by the Supreme Court to practice as a barrister and solicitor in all courts in Victoria and will be admitted to practice in federal courts. Reciprocal arrangements are in place to enable admission in other states on separate applications.

Although legal practitioners are admitted to practice as both barristers and solicitors, in practice they generally specialize in one or the other. Barristers are practitioners who specialize in advocacy and specialist litigation advice. They generally practice as members of the Victorian Bar, and work as sole practitioners.

Solicitors usually practice in partnerships and do a wide range of legal work. Their professional body is the Law Institute of Victoria.

Complaints against solicitors are made to the Law Institute. Complaints against barristers are made to the Victorian Bar Council. Complaints may also be referred to the independent legal ombudsman, who has operated in Victoria since 1996.

Victorian judges, magistrates, and tribunal members are appointed by the government. Judges and magistrates are appointed from the ranks of lawyers. In the case of superior courts, appointments are usually of senior barristers or judicial officers from lower courts. Magistrates generally, and county and Supreme Court judges, must be lawyers admitted to practice in Victoria of not less than five, seven, and eight years' standing respectively, and must retire at age seventy. Judicial officers in Victoria may be removed from office if it is determined that they are not of good behavior, by motion of both houses of the Victorian Parliament. All members of VCAT are appointed for a period of five years.

RELATIONSHIP TO NATIONAL SYSTEM

A right of appeal exists from a decision of the Victorian Court of Appeal to the High Court of Australia. Special leave to appeal must be granted by the High Court. There is a national federal court that exercises original federal jurisdiction. By agreement the Federal Parliament sometimes vests federal jurisdiction in the Victorian courts, especially in areas of federal criminal law and some areas of commercial and corporations law. In cases where a Victorian court is exercising federal jurisdiction, the parties may have rights of appeal to the federal court or High Court of Australia.

Should inconsistencies arise between Victorian and federal legislation, then the federal laws will prevail to the extent of the inconsistency, pursuant to section 109 of the Commonwealth Constitution.

Jim Kennan
Randall Kune

See also Administrative Tribunals; Barristers; Common Law; Federalism; Government Legal Departments; Lay Judiciaries; Legal Aid; Magistrates—Common Law Systems; Mediation; Privy Council; Small Claims Courts; Solicitors

References and further reading
County Court of Victoria. http://www.countycourt.vic.gov.au (accessed September 6, 2001).
Law Institute of Victoria. http://www.liv.asn.au (accessed September 6, 2001).
Magistrates' Court. http://www.magistratescourt.vic.gov.au (accessed September 6, 2001).
Parkinson, Patrick. 2001. *Tradition and Change in Australian Law.* Sydney: LBC Information Services.
Supreme Court of Victoria. http://www.supremecourt.vic.gov.au (accessed September 6, 2001).
Victoria Law Foundation. http://www.viclf.asn.au (accessed September 6, 2001).
Victorian Civil and Administrative Tribunal. http://www.vcat.vic.gov.au (accessed September 6, 2001).

Victorian Government. http://www.vic.gov.au (accessed September 6, 2001).

Victorian Law Reform Commission. http://www.lawreform.vic.gov.au (accessed September 6, 2001).

Williams, Neil J. 2000. *Civil Procedure Victoria*. Melbourne: Butterworths.

VIETNAM

COUNTRY INFORMATION

The Socialist Republic of Vietnam (Vietnam, or SRV) is located on the eastern side of the land area of Southeast Asia, south of the People's Republic of China, northwest of the Philippines, and east of Laos and Cambodia. Since the political reunification in 1976, the nation's capital and political center is Hanoi, which has a population of about 2.6 million. Vietnam's economic and commercial center is Ho Chi Minh City (Saigon), with a 1999 population of about 5 million. The other large cities are Haiphong (1.6 million), Da Nang, and Hue.

In 1999 Vietnam had a population of about 77.3 million and an annual population growth rate of 1.37 percent. The infant mortality rate stood at 34.84/1,000, with life expectancy for females at seventy years and for males at almost sixty-five.

Although the Vietnamese (Kinh) ethnic group is predominant, accounting for 85–90 percent of the population, a number of other ethnic groups also inhabit Vietnam. They include Chinese (3 percent, or about 2.3 million), Hmong, Thai, Khmer, Cham, and minority ethnic groups based in the mountains. Religions active in Vietnam include Buddhism, Hoa Hao, Cao Dai, Christian (predominantly Roman Catholic, some Protestant), animism, and Islam. In addition to Vietnamese, which is the official and widely spoken language, some English, French, Chinese, Khmer, and ethnic languages are spoken in different parts of Vietnam.

HISTORY

Resistance to foreign rule and struggles for internal unity are key themes in Vietnamese history. China ruled Vietnam for about 1,000 years until the tenth century, and in modern times Vietnam has both resisted Chinese authority and adapted to the strong influence of Vietnam's large and powerful neighbor to the north as well. A native dynasty ended direct Chinese rule in 939, and over the next centuries the Kinh expanded their influence southward through areas settled by Cham and others.

French colonial rule began in 1858. After full control was established by 1885, French authority was exercised through a colony in the south and a French protectorate in northern and central Vietnam. In the early decades of the twentieth century, nationalist and communist movements, in many cases led by intellectuals, attempted to challenge French rule. That process continued during World War II, when Japan occupied Vietnam. The Ho Chi Minh–led Viet Minh coalition played a leading role in the anti-French and anti-Japanese struggles, though by no means were they the only such actors. Seizing power in 1945, the Vietnamese Party of Labor led by Ho and its allies declared Vietnam's independence and the founding of the Democratic Republic of Vietnam on September 2, 1945, in Ba Dinh Square in Hanoi.

A guerilla war followed Vietnam's declaration of independence and the failure of the French to depart. After French forces were defeated in the 1954 battle of Dien Bien Phu, the Geneva conference (attended by France, Britain, China, the Soviet Union, and the United States) partitioned Vietnam, ostensibly temporarily, with Ho Chi Minh's forces in power in the north with Hanoi as their capital. An anticommunist government took power in the south, strongly supported by the United States and other Western governments.

In northern Vietnam, the Vietnamese Party of Labor undertook strong agrarian reforms and collectivization in the mid- and late 1950s, seeking to establish a socialist state based on Soviet and Chinese models. Intellectuals' criticisms of the rapid transition to collectivization and the lack of democratic processes were suppressed in the late 1950s.

The party also reenergized and supported guerilla activities in central and southern Vietnam aimed at weakening the southern government. Those hostilities led to war in which the United States played a substantial role, sending hundreds of thousands of soldiers to support the southern government. The war devastated much of Vietnam. After the Tet Offensive of 1968, the northern and southern governments, Viet Cong, and the United States began peace talks, which culminated in the Paris Accords of January 1973 and the withdrawal of American troops. In April 1975, northern forces took Saigon, and in July 1976 the Socialist Republic of Vietnam, absorbing south Vietnam, was established.

After reunification, and under the direction of party leader Le Duan, hardline policies were imposed. These included dispersal of private markets, confiscation of privately owned lands, and agricultural collectivization. Southern officials, military officers, and many intellectuals were sent to reeducation camps. In 1978, Vietnamese forces were sent into Cambodia to remove the Khmer Rouge from power.

Although some minor reforms were initiated in the early 1980s, hardline policies relying heavily on central planning and political coercion persisted until the Vietnamese Communist Party's Sixth Congress in 1986. Then, faced with a worsening economic situation, the failures of central planning, international isolation, Chinese

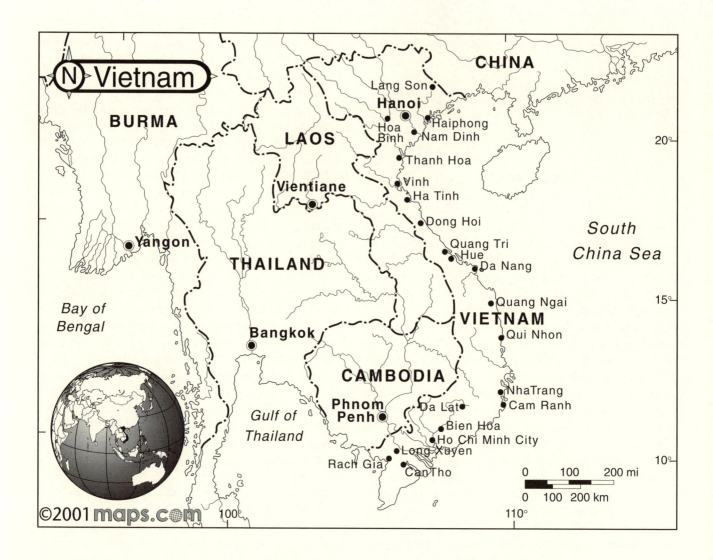

reforms, and the beginnings of change elsewhere in the socialist world, Vietnam embarked on a series of reform steps that came to be known as *doi moi,* or renovation. Implemented in the late 1980s and in the 1990s, these reforms have eased central planning, relaxed social and economic life, returned agriculture to family farming, freed many prices, and began a complex process of legal and industrial reforms.

Legal reforms in Vietnam have supported the economic liberalization of the *doi moi* period. They have included legal provisions freeing agricultural pricing, supporting family farming and contractual systems, beginning to strengthen the economic autonomy of large, state-owned industrial enterprises, starting the sensitive and complex process of strengthening cooperative and private economic sectors, and strengthening courts, legislatures, and prosecutors' offices. Early legal reforms culminated in the adoption of a new Vietnamese Constitution in April 1992 that enshrined both the central role of the Vietnamese Communist Party and reform, and sought to strengthen key political entities and policies as well as key legal institutions.

LEGAL CONCEPTS

Vietnamese law as we see it today is a product of multiple influences. Chinese rule, French rule, strong Soviet and Chinese influence, and now Western influence through donor-assisted legal reform efforts have all made their mark on the Vietnamese legal system. Four traditions—Confucian and legalist, French colonial, socialist Soviet and Chinese, and Western market-oriented—have been primary influences in the development of modern Vietnamese law.

As Professor Hue-Tam Ho Tai has indicated, the Confucian-legalist tradition in Vietnam encouraged the power of the state, and emphasized the encouragement of virtue, governance by trained people of virtue, and (in the legalist tradition) the promulgation and implementation of laws and the construction of legal institutions under state authority. In this tradition law was a punitive process and a unitary state did not neatly divide itself into the Western forms of executive, judiciary, and legislature. Those distinctions would come later, though in somewhat different forms than in the West.

French colonial influences on Vietnamese law included strengthening the role of separate court and executive bureaucracies, and the application of French law in the southern part of Vietnam, where a formal colony was established. French colonial law joined with traditional Vietnamese law to control dissent, to strengthen the hand of a central state apparatus, and to solidify the role of law as a controller of activities rather than a guarantor of rights.

The socialist Soviet and Chinese influences on Vietnamese law have given us the basic structure we see today in the Vietnamese legal system. In the 1950s, Vietnam adopted the Communist Party–dominated legal structures originally established in the Soviet Union. In this structuring—which did not conflict with Confucian-legalist and French colonial emphases on legal control and the role of the state—the Vietnamese, like the Chinese and originally the Soviet Union, relied heavily on the theory of the instrumental, subordinate role of law under party rule developed by the Soviet legal theorist and prosecutor Andrei Vishinsky that dominated socialist legal theory for decades. This structure emphasized dominant party authority and weak legislatures and courts, often (and on political issues, always) doing the direct bidding of party authorities.

Thus, socialist law antecedents and Confucian-legalist traditions combined to strengthen the guiding position of the party and state vis-à-vis the legal system, a party and state that was embodied not only with power and revolutionary legitimacy but, in its own terms, with virtue as well. Thus law in modern Vietnam has represented and served to strengthen the virtuous, controlling, punitive, and redemptive role of the state. Rights, to the degree that any have been recognized, have been granted by the state.

These strands also bring an emphasis on both punitive sanctions and on individual redemption into the modern Vietnamese legal system. While punishment is currently central to Vietnamese criminal law and other elements of the legal system, redemption has never been far from the surface, at least in rhetorical terms.

Another theme still deeply resonant today is the strength of foreign models, at least at the central level, and the complex process of reception and adaptation by the Vietnamese. Foreign legal models have had an immense effect on the development of Vietnamese law, but at each stage Vietnamese receivers of foreign legal models have made modifications, sometimes minor and sometimes significant.

Finally, and perhaps in seeming contradiction to the themes already discussed, local customs and traditions have survived and, in some periods of liberalization (such as the current period of *doi moi* [renovation]), have thrived in certain localities. More informal local systems of law and justice have intertwined with the formal mod-

els borrowed from abroad and put in place at the level of central and provincial governments, and this melding of the informal and formal, the traditional and the structured, is maintained today as well.

Today Vietnam is undergoing a new stage in legal development, one marked by the donor-driven and private market–driven entry of Western, liberal, market-oriented legal concepts and codes, and a complex process of reception and adaptation by Vietnamese policymakers, drafters, government officials, and legislators. In Vietnam, Western legal, market-oriented models emphasize private economic rights, the role of contract, formal dispute resolution through strengthened court systems, a more significant role for formal legislation and rule making in determining legal rights, and the commodification of community assets.

CURRENT STRUCTURE

The Vietnamese Communist Party and government have pursued a careful strategy of party-led legal reform since late 1986, reforms intended not to establish a pluralistic political system but to serve and strengthen party-led economic reform. Thus the core goal of strengthening the role of law, legal institutions, and legislation is to support the party and state's policies of liberalized, yet controlled, economic development.

The Constitution and the Role of the Party

The current structure of Vietnamese polity and the Vietnamese legal system is delineated in the constitution promulgated in 1992, which was partly patterned on the 1982 Chinese Constitution. In the 1992 Constitution, the Vietnamese Communist Party is defined as "the force leading the State and society." Within the Communist Party, the Central Committee serves as the highest formal decision-making body. On a day-to-day basis, the party is led by its Political Bureau.

A number of internal working institutions of the party are centrally concerned with legal and security issues. These include, most particularly, the Central Internal Affairs Commission and the Central Committee for Protection of Public Security. Other party groups whose work touches on legal issues include the Central Inspection Committee, General Office of the Central Committee, Central Organization Commission, and the Central Internal Political Defense Commission.

The constitution also explicitly recognizes the extensive economic reforms underway in Vietnam and the multisector commodity economy now developing. The constitution has provided for public, collective, and private ownership of resources, allowed private use (though not ownership) of land, and sought to encourage foreign investment.

Legal Structure in Vietnam

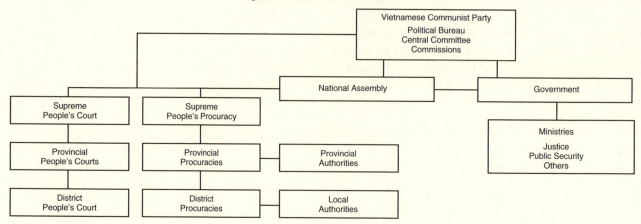

The National Assembly

The 1992 Constitution also confirmed the role of the National Assembly (Quoc hoi) as Vietnam's highest legislative body. The unicameral National Assembly is gradually increasing its role in debate, amendment, and oversight of legislation. The pace of legislative activity (and legislative and oversight debate) has accelerated rapidly in recent years. The assembly has constitutional and legislative powers and (along with its Standing Committee) is responsible for drafting and adopting national legislation.

The National Assembly also elects Vietnam's president and vice president, the prime minister, the president of the Supreme People's Court, and the procurator-general of the Supreme People's Procuracy. The assembly also plays a constitutionally defined oversight role in state budgets, financial and monetary policies, taxation and other significant aspects of domestic and foreign policy, as well as oversight of the judicial system and the procuracy. In general terms, the National Assembly and its members are gradually becoming more active policy participants in Vietnamese public life and civil governance, and increasingly active in undertaking their oversight roles.

The National Assembly consists of 450 members, who are directly elected for five-year terms, and meets twice a year for about thirty days in each session. In the last elections in 1997, 666 candidates stood for the 450 seats. Of the 450 deputies elected, 384 were members of the Communist Party and 26 percent were women. Oversight activities of the National Assembly are carried out through an Ethnic Council and committees with responsibility for law; economy and budget; science, technology, and environment; foreign affairs; security and national defense; culture; education and youth; and social affairs. A Standing Committee is empowered to issue ordinances and interpret the constitution in between National Assembly sessions, and to coordinate the work of the Ethnic Council and the National Assembly committees. The Office of the National Assembly coordinates the assembly's day-to-day work and is responsible for research and provision of legislative and policy information to National Assembly members.

The key issue facing the Vietnamese National Assembly is the problem of authority in a party-dominated system—whether the assembly will be able to continue to increase its role as Vietnamese society becomes more complex and the reform process continues.

The Government

The 1992 Constitution abolished the former collective Council of Ministers, and replaced the council with a system of government ministers led by a prime minister, with specified and expanded powers. The prime minister is assisted by several deputy prime ministers, and most of the work of the government is carried out through a number of ministries and ministry-led institutions.

Government institutions with a central role in law and legal implementation include the Ministry of Justice, Ministry of Public Security, the ministries of Trade and Planning and Investment (in economic and trade affairs), the Ministry of Foreign Affairs (in the international law arena).

The Ministry of Justice, which has a key role in legal planning, drafting, and implementation within the government, engages in vetting the drafts of legislation prepared by other ministries and agencies, directly drafts some legislation, administers the national system of attorney and notary licensing and examination as well as several law schools, and, with local authorities, administers the judicial system at local levels. The Ministry of Public Security is responsible for internal security, including national and local police forces, prisons, criminal and some political investigations, and certain investigations and interrogations of foreign nations. Uniformed police forces operate under the authority and direction of the Ministry of Public Security, but with their own hierarchy and organization. Local police forces also report to local authorities.

The 1992 Constitution also created the position of head of state (president), with specified powers in military and foreign affairs and in recommending senior appointments and dismissals.

The Judiciary

The 1992 Constitution also delineated the roles of the judiciary. The Vietnamese judiciary is structured in three levels headed by the Supreme People's Court in Hanoi. The Supreme Court includes the Council of Judges (the highest adjudication arm of the court system), appeals divisions handling appeals from province and province-level courts, and criminal, civil, economic, administrative, and labor tribunals. A central military court undertakes review of judgments in the military system.

The second level of the judicial hierarchy includes provincial people's courts that hear appellate and first instance cases. Six hundred district people's courts complete the system at the third level, hearing first instance cases of lower jurisdiction in rural districts (*huyen*), provincial capitals, larger towns, or urban districts (*quan*).

Judicial administration is bifurcated: At the central level, the Supreme People's Court is responsible for its own judicial work and for the administrative and organization of its activities. The Supreme Court is responsible for the judicial work (*cong tac xet xu*) of the provincial and district courts, and the Ministry of Justice is responsible for organization, budgets, and staff. This bifurcated system is the product of a long history of transfers of responsibility for judicial and administrative oversight of the provincial and district courts between the Supreme Court and the Ministry of Justice, mandated through successive legal policy shifts.

Judicial independence is the key long-term issue facing the Vietnamese judiciary. In the shorter term, increasing the capacity of judges and other actors in the Vietnamese court system to fairly and rapidly handle a caseload of growing size and complexity is a key problem.

The Procuracy (State Prosecutors)

The Supreme People's Procuracy (based in Hanoi) and the provincial and local procuracies are responsible for prosecution of criminal acts as well as for supervision of implementation of law by ministries and government agencies, supervising the investigation, arrest, and detention processes for criminal suspects, and related functions.

The Supreme People's Procuracy is headed by a procurator general and several deputies and includes appeals, military, research, and other prosecutorial units. At the intermediate level, procuracy offices are located at province-level units. Below those, 600 district procuracies complete the system at the local level. Local procuracies report through provincial procuracies to the Supreme People's Procuracy in Hanoi as well as to local people's councils. A parallel system of military procuracies is jointly administered by the Supreme People's Procuracy and the Ministry of Defence.

Sources of Law in Vietnam

The sources of law in Vietnam are complex. In a system in which central power (as stipulated in the constitution) is held by a communist party, party documents are one key source of policy and lead to the drafting of laws implementing those policies. These documents may be issued by the Central Committee, its Political Bureau, and various party commissions and other working bodies.

Laws and ordinances for national implementation are adopted by the National Assembly and its Standing Committee and made available in a legislative gazette. Legal documents are also issued by the government for national implementation, as well as by the several dozen government ministries and ministry-level institutions for implementation within their sphere of work and beyond. Legal documents include decrees, implementing regulations, and documents in a number of other forms, also made available through a government gazette. Provincial governments issue directives of various kinds, which may at times serve in effect to expand, restrict, or otherwise derogate from centrally administered laws and policies.

SPECIALIZED JUDICIAL BODIES

Military courts and prosecutorial offices (procuracies) have been established under the Vietnamese army to handle cases in which the defendant is an army soldier or staff member or in other cases stipulated by law. Appeals from the military courts are heard by the Central Military Court, a specialized tribunal within the Supreme People's Court. The Central Military Procuracy, located within the Supreme People's Procuracy in Hanoi, hears disputes and appeals relating to military prosecutorial functions and legal supervision within the Vietnamese armed forces.

Vietnam's legal system does not provide for specialized constitutional, human rights, or other courts.

STAFFING

The Vietnamese National Assembly has 450 deputies and several hundred staff, most based in Hanoi. In 1996, the latest year for which complete statistics are available, the Supreme People's Court included about 75 judges and more than 325 legal specialists, court clerks, and other personnel in Hanoi, Ho Chi Minh City, and Da Nang.

Provincial and district people's courts had an authorized complement of 7,747 judges; 4,458 of those judicial positions were filled. Until recently judges at the lower levels were selected largely from the ranks of decommissioned military personnel. In more recent years judicial qualifications have been strengthened through national legislation and entry testing has begun to be used for judicial selection. Judges, who are generally appointed for five-year terms, are now required to have legal experience and to undergo regular upgrading and retraining. Supreme Court judges and other personnel are drawn from provincial courts and from selection in the legal communities of Hanoi, Ho Chi Minh City, and other large cities.

In 1996, the Supreme People's Procuracy was staffed by 150 procurators and other legal specialists and more than 200 other staff, based in Hanoi, Ho Chi Minh City, and Da Nang. About 1,500 procurators staffed the provincial procuracies, and about 3,000 served at the district level. At the provincial and district levels of the judicial and procuratorial systems, about 40 percent of professional legal staff were women as of 1996.

Vietnamese attorneys are tested and admitted to the bar through bar examinations that occur after the five-year legal education curriculum or equivalent training. The Vietnamese Lawyers Association gathers the several thousand Vietnamese lawyers for training activities at the local, provincial, and national levels and seeks to represent them in discussions on legislation and other matters of interest to the bar. A separate bar association linking lawyers trained earlier in southern Vietnamese and French law schools still exists in Ho Chi Minh City and some other southern and central provinces.

In recent years most admittees to the Vietnamese bar have been trained within Vietnam, but in Hanoi and Ho Chi Minh City there are still a small number of attorneys who received their training in France or the United States. A somewhat larger number of lawyers and government legal officials were trained in the former Soviet Union, Russia, and eastern and central Europe.

Legal education is conducted through five-year undergraduate (LL.B.) and graduate (LL.M.) programs at law schools in Hanoi (including the Hanoi Law University and the Hanoi University Faculty of Law), and at law faculties in Ho Chi Minh City and Hue. Legal research is centered at the Institute of State and Law in the National Center for Social Sciences and Humanities (Hanoi), the Institute of Legal Research in the Ministry of Justice (Hanoi), the various law faculties, and a small legal research staff at the Ho Chi Minh City Institute of Social Sciences.

IMPACT

Vietnamese legal reforms since late 1986 have resulted in the drafting and promulgation of a great number of new laws and regulations to serve and strengthen economic reforms. The reforms have also strengthened legislative and judicial capacity, without necessarily strengthening the political force of the legislature or judiciary in significant ways. The pace of legislative development has not yet been matched by similar effectiveness in implementation of law; legal implementation is among the weaker areas in the new legal system under construction. New law schools have been opened and existing law schools and legal research institutions strengthened to meet the perceived needs for new lawyers, judges, prosecutors, and other legal personnel.

Some efforts have been made to strengthen and professionalize the judicial system, headed by the Supreme People's Court, and the system of state prosecutors, headed by the Supreme People's Procuracy, while maintaining firm party leadership and control over these and other institutions of legal policy, implementation, and adjudication.

These efforts have been directed toward controlled economic reform and toward maintaining social stability, two clear goals of the Vietnamese party and government's legal reform program. In both these aims the legal reform program has had significant impact on Vietnamese society. In increasing citizen participation, strengthening and defending citizens' rights, and combating bureaucracy and corruption, Vietnam's legal reforms have had somewhat less success in the fifteen years since the *doi moi* (renovation) era began.

Mark Sidel

See also China; Constitutionalism; Government Legal Departments; Indigenous and Folk Legal Systems; Marxist Jurisprudence; Soviet System

References and further reading

The Constitutions of Vietnam (1946–1959–1980–1992). 1995. Hanoi: The Gioi.

Fforde, Adam, and Stefan de Vylder. 1996. *From Plan to Market: The Economic Transition in Vietnam*. Boulder, CO: Westview.

Jamieson, Neil. 1994. *Understanding Vietnam*. Berkeley: University of California Press.

Legal Support Projects and Coordination. www.undp.org.vn (accessed Oct. 3, 2001).

Ministry of Foreign Affairs. www.mofa.gov.vn (accessed Oct. 3, 2001).

National Assembly of Vietnam. www.na.gov.vn (accessed Oct. 3, 2001).

Nicholson, Penelope. 1998. "Vietnamese Legal Institutions in Comparative Perspective: Contemporary Constitutions and Courts Considered." Pp. 300–329 in *Law, Capitalism and Power in Asia: The Role of Law and Legal Institutions*. Edited by Kanishka Jayasuriya. London: Routledge.

Rose, Carol. 1998. "The 'New' Law and Development Movement in the Post Cold War Era: A Vietnamese Case Study." *Law and Society Review* 32: 93–140.

Sidel, Mark. 1997. "Vietnam: The Ambiguities of State-directed Legal Reform." Pp. 356–389 in *Asian Legal Systems*. Edited by Poh-Ling Tan. Sydney: Butterworths.

Thayer, Carl, and David Marr, eds. 1993. *Vietnam and the Rule of Law*. Canberra: Australian National University.

Vien, Nguyen Khac. 1993. *Vietnam: A Long History.* Hanoi: The Gioi Publishers.

Vietnam Law Database. www.vietlaw.gov.vn (accessed Oct. 3, 2001).

Vietnamese Communist Party. www.cpv.org.vn (accessed Oct. 3, 2001).

VIRGIN ISLANDS, U.S.

GENERAL INFORMATION

The U.S. Virgin Islands consists of approximately fifty islands of various sizes located in the Caribbean, southeast of Florida, Cuba, and Haiti and to the east of Puerto Rico. The three major islands are St. Croix, St. John, and St. Thomas, with the territorial capital of Charlotte Amalie located on St. Thomas. The total land area of the U.S. Virgin Islands is approximately 130 square miles, with St. Croix, St. John, and St. Thomas being 84, 20, and 32 square miles in area, respectively. The British Virgin Islands, a British colony, is located nearby to the north and east of the U.S. Virgin Islands; St. John is a mere half mile away from the British Virgin Island's Great Thatch Island. Collectively, the Virgin Islands comprise the easternmost reach of the Greater Antilles.

The vast majority of the population is descended from African slaves, brought to the West Indies to work on sugarcane plantations before the slave trade was abolished in the mid-1800s. St. Thomas has a unique population segment composed of those with ancestors among the French Huguenots who arrived about 100 years ago. The population of the U.S. Virgin Islands in 1995 was just over 100,100, compared with a U.S. population of over 250 million. Only about half of the residents of the U.S. Virgin Islands were born there. Accordingly, population growth is influenced more by immigration patterns than by birth and death rates. The predominant language is English.

Almost a third of the population lives below the poverty line; however, the U.S. Virgin Islands has one of the highest per capita incomes in the Caribbean (approximately $12,700). The territorial economy is almost exclusively dependent on tourism and federal aid. The islands have little in the way of mineral resources, continually contend with freshwater shortages, and must import considerable amounts of foodstuffs. Almost 9,000 people were employed in the tourist industry in 1995, with over 1.7 million tourists spending $821 million. There are a few small industries on the islands, including rum distilling and textile manufacturing. The island of St. Croix benefits economically from a large oil refinery operating there.

EVOLUTION AND HISTORY

Prior to U.S. control of the territory, settlers from Denmark colonized much of the current U.S. Virgin Islands.

Danes first claimed St. Thomas and then St. John, and finally, they purchased St. Croix from the French. During the Danish colonial era, the islands were known as the Danish West Indies. While the United States expressed some interest in acquiring part of the Danish West Indies as early as the Civil War, it did not purchase the islands until 1916, with formal transfer from Danish to U.S. control taking place in 1917. World War II served as the impetus for vigorous and renewed U.S. interest, for the United States was eager to gain a foothold in the neighboring but unstable area and wished to prevent Germany from securing a useful base for future operations there. Prior to the sale, the Danish government in the Virgin Islands held a plebiscite and found the majority of the residents at that time favored U.S. acquisition.

On its purchase for $25 million, the U.S. Virgin Islands became a U.S. territory. For the first fifteen years after the transition, the territory was governed by the U.S. navy, with Rear Adm. James H. Oliver appointed by the president to serve as the first governor. Governance was subsequently passed on to the Department of the Interior, where it continues to reside. To facilitate the transition from Danish to U.S. control, much of the governmental structure and legal code remained unchanged. The system of territorial courts in place under Danish rule was left intact, with appeals that would previously have been reviewable in Danish courts now reviewable by the Third Circuit of the U.S. Courts of Appeals. In 1936, Congress passed the Organic Act, which provided for one municipal council for the islands of St. John and St. Thomas and another for the island of St. Croix. The act also established a territorial-wide council. These councils were abolished with the passage of the 1954 Revised Organic Act, which established separate executive, legislative, and judicial branches as part of a central government. The governor of the U.S. Virgin Islands, however, continued to be appointed by the president, with the approval of the Senate. This arrangement was changed in 1970 when popular election of the islands' governor and lieutenant governor commenced.

LEGAL PROFESSION AND LEGAL TRAINING

There are no American Bar Association–approved law schools located in the U.S. Virgin Islands. Attorneys are admitted to practice before the bar of the U.S. Virgin Islands by the Territorial Court. The Commission on Judicial Disabilities, a creation of the U.S. Virgin Islands legislature, is responsible for investigating complaints against Territorial Court judges.

THE JUDICIAL SYSTEM

The U.S. Virgin Islands Department of Justice resides in the executive branch of the government of the Virgin Islands. It functions as a source of legal advice for executive

Legal Structure of U.S. Virgin Islands Courts

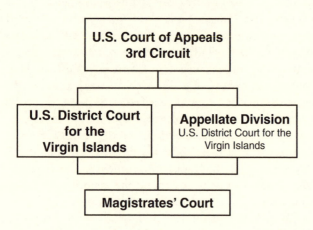

departments, boards, and agencies. In addition to prosecuting offenses against the laws of the Virgin Islands in the Territorial Court, the Virgin Islands Department of Justice represents all executive departments, boards, agencies, and officers of the government in administrative proceedings and court litigation to which they are a party.

The 1954 Revised Organic Act of the Virgin Islands vests the judicial power of the Virgin Islands in the District Court of the Virgin Islands in addition to those courts established by local law. The Territorial Court of the Virgin Islands exists pursuant to this authorization.

The Territorial Court of the Virgin Islands

The Territorial Court of the Virgin Islands is staffed by eight judges who are appointed by the governor, with the consent of the Virgin Islands legislature. Four judges are selected from the St. John–St. Thomas District and four from the St. Croix District. Each judge serves a six-year term of office, and the governor appoints one of the eight judges to serve as the presiding judge of the Territorial Court. The presiding judge is also the Territorial Court's chief administrative officer, responsible for supervising the observance of rules of practice and procedure. The Territorial Court exercises original jurisdiction over a variety of matters, including criminal violations, violations of executive regulations, administration of estate relations, divorce, and adoption petitions. Its jurisdiction is exclusive for minor civil and criminal matters and concurrent with that of the District Court for the U.S. Virgin Islands for more serious civil and criminal actions. The Territorial Court has the authority to create divisions as necessary to expedite the handling of its workload. It currently has criminal, civil, traffic, family, small claims, probate, and probations divisions.

The District Court of the U.S. Virgin Islands

The District Court of the U.S. Virgin Islands is staffed via presidential appointment, with confirmation by the U.S. Senate. The judges appointed to the District Court serve ten-year terms of office. There are two District Court judges, one each for the Division of St. Thomas–St. John and the Division of St. Croix. The most senior of the two in terms of continuous service serves as the chief judge of the District Court.

The District Court of the Virgin Islands possesses the same jurisdiction as a U.S. District Court and bankruptcy court. The District Court exercises both original and appellate jurisdiction. Its original jurisdiction is largely concurrent with that of the Territorial Court but is exclusive with respect to criminal and civil proceedings regarding income tax laws not enacted by the legislature of the Virgin Islands. The District Court's appellate jurisdiction is exercised by its Appellate Division and includes civil, juvenile, domestic relations, and criminal cases decided in the Territorial Court. A case appealed to the Appellate Division is heard by a panel of three judges. The chief judge of the District Court serves on the Appellate Division and appoints two other judges to serve with him or her.

RELATIONSHIP TO THE NATIONAL SYSTEM

The fact that the U.S. Virgin Islands are a U.S. territory rather than one of the states places its judicial system in a unique relationship with that of the federal government. First, those judges serving on the District Court for the U.S. Virgin Islands do not enjoy lifetime tenure, as do federal District Court judges serving in the states. Second, appeals from the Territorial Court are heard by the Appellate Division of the District Court or the District Court itself rather than by an indigenous court of last resort analogous to a state supreme court. Subsequent appeals are heard by the Third Circuit of the Courts of Appeals, which also includes the states of Delaware, New Jersey, and Pennsylvania. At least some of the Third Circuit's rulings regarding the distribution of judicial power in the U.S. Virgin Islands have favored the authority of the Territorial Court over the District Court. For example, in 1995, the Third Circuit held that an appeal to the District Court on a matter outside that court's jurisdiction must be dismissed rather than transferred to the Territorial Court (*The Moravian School Advisory Board v. Rawlins,* 70 F. 3d 270, 3rd Cir. [1995]).

Wendy L. Martinek

See also Appellate Courts; Small Claims Courts; United States—Federal System; United States—State Systems

References and further reading
Boyer, William W. 1983. *America's Virgin Islands: A History of Human Rights and Wrongs.* Durham, NC: Carolina Academic Press.
Division of Libraries, Archives and Museums. 1992. *Virgin Islands of the United States Blue Book.* 4th ed. Charlotte Amalie, Virgin Islands: Division of Libraries, Archives and Museums.

Evans, Luther H. 1975. *The Virgin Islands from Naval Base to New Deal.* Westport, CT: Greenwood Publishing Group.

O'Neal, Eugenia. 2001. *From the Field to the Legislature: History of Women in the Virgin Islands.* Westport, CT: Greenwood Publishing Group.

Vidal, Gore. 1998. *Virgin Islands—A Dependency of United States: Essays 1992–1997.* New York: Little, Brown.

VIRGINIA

GENERAL INFORMATION

The Commonwealth of Virginia, nicknamed "Old Dominion," is one of fifty states in the United States. It is triangular in shape and is the southernmost state of the mid-Atlantic region. Virginia is bounded on the east by the Atlantic Ocean and the Chesapeake Bay, on the north by West Virginia, Maryland, and the District of Columbia, on the south by Tennessee and North Carolina, and on the west by the state of Kentucky. The total area of Virginia measures 40,767 square miles (or 105,716 square kilometers), including 976 square miles of inland water. These measurements rank Virginia as the thirty-sixth largest state in the United States. As of 1995, Virginia's population was estimated at 6,580,000, which at the time made it the twelfth most populated state in the nation.

The Commonwealth of Virginia was one of Great Britain's original thirteen colonies in America. The first settlers of the Virginia Company of London arrived in Jamestown in 1607 after a failed attempt to settle the area the previous year. The purposes of the original settlement included building a merchant fleet, training mariners, and exploring for resources and new goods to trade in Europe. Among the most important crops in Virginia was tobacco. Later, in 1624, Virginia was made the first royal colony of England. In the century and a half that followed, its population expanded westward and northward.

Virginia gained in political power through the pre-revolutionary period and is today known for taking the lead in the crises that brought about the Revolutionary War. These included the Stamp Act Resolutions of 1765, the boycott of British goods in 1769, the first Continental Conference in 1774, and the Declaration of Independence in 1776. Until the Revolution, the Commonwealth of Virginia's population was divided evenly between colonists and slaves. Slavery was the primary source of labor for agriculture, including the production of tobacco.

Virginia also played a very important part in the American Civil War. It seceded from the Union in 1761, and its capital, Richmond, later became the capital of the new Confederacy. In 1763, Virginia lost a third of its state in the formation of the new state of West Virginia.

Virginia was also the site of numerous important battles of the Civil War, as well as the final surrender of Confederate troops by Gen. Robert E. Lee at the Appomattox Courthouse in 1865.

After Reconstruction and through the twentieth century, Virginia diversified its economy to include manufacturing, a diverse range of agriculture, and tourism. One line of manufacturing involved implements of war. The southeast shores of Virginia boomed during and after World War II in the Norfolk and Hampton Roads area, where naval ship building and military bases became a large part of the economy. The fact that it bordered on the District of Columbia also provided economic benefits. Today, this area of Virginia is one of the fastest-growing areas of the state, in part because of the high-tech industry located there.

EVOLUTION AND HISTORY

The legal and political system of the Commonwealth of Virginia has been heavily influenced by its British colonial roots as well as its nineteenth-century history with the Confederacy. The colonial form of government in Virginia impacted the organization of state politics just as it did the federal government of the United States. In addition, since the capital of the Confederate States of America was located in Virginia, its politics and legal system were further influenced by the remnants of the Confederacy as well as the state's evolution through Reconstruction. Just as Virginia's legal culture and law were impacted by slavery, so were its laws in the post-Reconstruction era (for example, segregation and Jim Crow laws).

Most important, however, was the era of the Byrd political machine that began in the 1920s. Sen. Harry Byrd crafted one of the most famous political machines in U.S. history by intimately tying together local and state interests via such political structures as the State Compensation Board. This board impacted political appointments, state budgets, and the salaries of local political actors, including judges and court clerks. One impact of this at the local level was that circuit court judges were given the power to make important local appointments, while their salary structures and elections were controlled at the state level. Judges, interestingly enough, were (and still are) elected by the Virginia State Legislature for fixed terms. This, then, allowed the Byrd machine to control judgeships from the State Assembly in the form of patronage. During the twentieth century, Virginia politics were dominated by Democrats, and so was the selection of state judges.

Virginia's judicial system is one of the oldest in the United States, and its organization is said to have influenced that of the U.S. Supreme Court. An act of the General Assembly in 1779 created four superior courts in Virginia, one of which was the Supreme Court of Appeals. These courts were staffed by judges from the courts existing in Virginia prior to the Revolutionary War—the Chancery, the Admiralty, and the General Courts. An act of the assembly in 1788 formally separated the Supreme Court of Appeals from the other courts, and this court was staffed with five judges. The Virginia Reform Convention of 1850–1851 led to yet another set of reforms, which divided the judiciary into five geographic sections, led to the popular election of the judges for terms of twelve years, set requirements for office, and required the issuance of judicial opinions as justifications for decisions. After the Civil War, the Constitution of 1870 changed the selection of judges for the high court by reestablishing selection by a vote of both Houses of the General Assembly.

In 1968, a legislative commission to study the need for court reform in Virginia was created. Based on its studies and the work of its chair, Justice Lawrence W. L'Anson, the Virginia Assembly passed a number of its recommendations in 1972 and 1973. Among these were centralizing the court system by merging all city courts into the circuit court framework, reorganizing courts not of record into a unified district court system, and including justices of the peace into a more formal magistrate system. In 1970, the State Constitution altered the name of the Supreme Court of Appeals to the Supreme Court of Virginia. One recommendation of the commission was not passed until a decade later. The State had a two-tiered judicial system until 1983, when the General Assembly created an intermediate appellate court known as the Court of Appeals of Virginia. This court began operation in 1985 after a decade of study on its needs for the effective administration of justice. Finally, in 1987, a thirty-four-member commission was formed by Chief Justice Harry Carrico and charged with making recommendations on the future of Virginia's judicial system. Its report was released in 1989, with recommendations such as merging district and circuit courts into a single trial court system, increasing citizen access to courts via legal aid, and offering a wider range of dispute resolution services including community justice (for example, alternative dispute resolution).

CURRENT STRUCTURE

The Legal Profession and Legal Training

The Virginia legal profession is regulated by the Virginia State Bar Association. As of January 2001, the bar reported a membership of 42,395 attorneys. Like most states, admission to the profession is regulated and requires a J.D. from an American Bar Association–approved law school and passing marks on the Virginia State Bar Examination. There is a procedure for admission to the state bar based on years of experience in legal practice. Legal training in the state of Virginia is offered at George Mason University, the College of William and Mary, Regent University, the University of Virginia, the University of Richmond, and Washington and Lee University. The Appalachian Law School, in southwest Virginia, was in the process of accreditation at the time this article was written.

Legal Aid and Criminal Defense Services

Criminal defendants who are deemed indigent are generally appointed legal counsel by the court, from among local attorneys in private practice. To date, there is no formal system of state-provided legal aid in the state. However, a state commission recently recommended the expansion of legal aid services in both criminal and civil cases, as well as the expansion of pro bono legal work by members of the bar. A number of nonprofit legal aid organizations (for example, Virginia Legal Aid Society) around the state provide legal assistance for poor clients in civil matters.

Administrative Hearings

Administrative legal disputes are primarily handled within agencies by administrative law judges or by their agents (such as deputy commissioners). For instance, in worker's compensation claims or appeals, evidentiary hearings and hearings on record are heard by deputy commissioners, who issue opinions. These can then be appealed to the full Worker's Compensation Commission for a decision on appeal and to judicial review before the Virginia Court of Appeals if the commission's decision is unsatisfactory. Appeals are handled in a similar manner for welfare benefits. Individuals first go through an informal conference, at which decisions are made on the benefit claim. Hearings can also be requested before the agency before turning to judicial review.

The Commonwealth of Virginia does not have a central panel system wherein disputes are handled by a separate state agency. There is one exception, however, for disputes involving state employees. Employee grievances and disputes are handled by the Department of Employee Dispute Resolution (EDR). The EDR has the mission of providing counseling, mediation, and training to deal with the disputes of state employees. This agency focuses on the prevention of workplace disputes, as well as counseling and mediation services for the resolution of such disputes.

Finally, interagency disputes are typically handled informally through negotiation among state cabinet officials. Of course, these disputes can enter the court system if they are not negotiated through some form of alternative dispute resolution.

Judicial System

The Virginia judicial system is composed of the Supreme Court of Virginia, the Virginia Court of Appeals, and circuit courts at the trial level. In addition, there are other trial courts, including general district courts, juvenile and domestic relations district courts, and Magistrates' Courts. These courts are generally arranged in a "top-down" fashion, with the Supreme Court being the highest court in Virginia (see figure).

Magistrates were formally created by an act of the State Assembly in 1974. Most duties of the magistrate were formerly those of the justices of the peace in the Commonwealth of Virginia. Today, magistrates exist in the thirty-two judicial districts within the state and generally serve as part of an independent and unbiased system for handling disputes brought by law enforcement and citizens. While most do not have law degrees, they are formally trained to handle such important tasks as issuing search warrants, arrest warrants, and subpoenas; holding bail hearings; issuing temporary protective orders; and accepting prepayment for minor fines and misdemeanors. Their authority rests within their assigned judicial district, and appeals of their decisions typically go to the trial courts of general jurisdiction known as Circuit Courts.

Most citizens in the Commonwealth of Virginia come into contact with the courts of limited jurisdiction, which are the General District Courts and the Juvenile and Domestic Relations District Courts. General District Courts are found in all Virginia cities and counties. In some cities and counties, these courts are combined; in others, they are separated for purposes of efficiency. As of the 1990s, there were 204 General District, Juvenile, and Domestic Relations Courts in Virginia. General District Courts typically handle traffic violations, criminal misdemeanor cases, civil matters, and some preliminary hearings for felony criminal cases. In civil matters, they have exclusive jurisdiction over cases valued under $3,000, and they share jurisdiction over cases from $3,000–$15,000 with the Circuit Courts. General District Court matters are typically heard before a single judge and may be appealed to the Circuit Courts for a jury trial.

The Juvenile and Domestic Relations District Courts handle criminal matters involving minors and family issues. These courts, like the General District Courts, are found in all Virginia cities and counties. They handle all juvenile cases in which an individual below the age of eighteen has committed a criminal felony, misdemeanor, or traffic offense. They also handle juvenile delinquency and status offenses, which are crimes for only minors. These courts also handle family complaints, such as those involving child custody, visitation, support, family abuse, or other crimes and misdemeanors within families.

There are over 122 Circuit Courts in 31 circuits throughout Virginia. These are the courts of general jurisdiction in the state and provide jury trials for criminal, civil, and domestic cases. Circuit Courts have the broad-est authority in the Commonwealth of Virginia. They hear all civil matter involving values above $15,000 and share jurisdiction with District Courts over cases from $3,000 to $15,000. They also hear some domestic relation cases, such as divorces, and all criminal felony cases. Circuit Courts also hear appeals from General District, Juvenile and Domestic Relations, and Magistrates' Courts.

The prosecution of criminal defendants is done at the local level by Commonwealth attorneys. Commonwealth attorneys are hired by the state, and they sit in state circuits; their salaries are set by the State Compensation Board and the State Assembly. The Commonwealth attorney system is managed by the State Attorney General's Office. Criminal defendants provide for their own representation unless they are indigent. If shown to be indigent, an individual is typically appointed counsel by the judge, who chooses from among members of the local bar.

The Virginia Court of Appeals is the middle appellate court in the Commonwealth of Virginia. Interestingly, the creation of this court was first considered along with other court reforms in the 1970s, but legislation to create the Court of Appeals was not actually enacted by the State Assembly until 1983. The Virginia Court of Appeals is staffed by eleven judges who typically sit in three-judge panels. These panels are spread out in four locations across the state. Each panel has some discretion over the appeals heard and appeals granted, as well as in deciding other cases that are assigned to them. The Court of Appeal may sit en banc when there is dissent in a panel and the aggrieved party requests an en banc hearing if two other judges agree to the request. They may also sit en banc when a judge feels that a panel's decision is in conflict with a previous precedent or when a majority of the judges agree to sit en banc after a vote on a motion. The Virginia Court of Appeals has mandatory jurisdiction over some civil, administrative agency, and original proceeding cases. They have discretionary jurisdiction in noncapital criminal cases. Those who lose in the Virginia Court of Appeals are granted the opportunity to appeal to the Supreme Court of Virginia.

Finally, the Supreme Court of Virginia is the court of last resort in the Commonwealth. It is staffed by seven justices who sit en banc and in panels. The chief justice is selected by members of the Supreme Court. The court has mandatory jurisdiction in capital, State Corporation Commission, and attorney disbarment cases. The justices have discretionary jurisdiction in civil cases, other criminal cases, some administrative agency cases, juvenile cases, some disciplinary cases, original proceedings, and interlocutory decision cases. The court's original jurisdiction is limited to cases of habeas corpus, mandamus, and prohibition.

The Constitution of Virginia makes the chief justice of the Supreme Court the chief administrator of Virginia's

Legal Structure of Virginia Courts

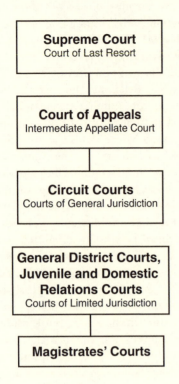

Supreme Court
Court of Last Resort

Court of Appeals
Intermediate Appellate Court

Circuit Courts
Courts of General Jurisdiction

General District Courts, Juvenile and Domestic Relations Courts
Courts of Limited Jurisdiction

Magistrates' Courts

entire court system. As such, he or she oversees and manages the funding and budgeting of the system. Among other responsibilities, the chief justice temporarily assigns or reassigns circuit judges to other circuits, appoints retired judges to fill in for circuits with heavy caseloads, and presides over committees that deal with issues of court administration.

STAFFING

The staffing of judges in the Commonwealth of Virginia is one of the more unique processes of its type in the United States. While most states employ judicial election, appointment, or merit systems, Virginia's judges are selected for fixed terms by the State Assembly. The fact that Virginia politics was long dominated by Democrats ensured that judicial candidates were selected and controlled by the Democratic Party in Virginia. Only recently has the Virginia State Assembly fallen into the control of Republicans. It remains to be seen what reforms will take place under the new leadership of the assembly. In Virginia, General District Court judges and

Juvenile and Domestic Relations Court judges are elected by the State Assembly for six-year terms. Circuit Court judges are elected by the State Assembly for eight-year terms. The judges of the Virginia Court of Appeals are also elected by the State Assembly for eight-year terms. The chief judge of the Court of Appeals is elected by a majority vote of the judges of the Court of Appeals to serve a term of four years. The present Supreme Court of Virginia is made up of seven justices elected by a majority vote of both houses of the General Assembly for a term of twelve years. By constitution and statute, the chief justice is the senior justice in terms of years of service on the court.

Magistrate judges are selected differently than other state judges. In their previous history as justices of the peace, magistrates were elected by the citizens of Virginia. However, they are appointed today by the chief Circuit Court judges for four-year terms and may be reappointed. Unlike other judges in the state (who must be members of the bar), anyone who is a U.S. citizens and a resident of the judicial district in which he or she seeks appointment is eligible to become a magistrate, unless precluded from appointment because of a statutory conflict of interest, such as having a spouse who is a law enforcement officer.

Roger E. Hartley

See also Adminstrative Law; Alternative Dispute Resolution; Family Law; Federalism; Judicial Review; Judicial Selection, Methods of; Juvenile Justice; Magistrates—Common Law Systems; Mediation; Prosecuting Authorities; Small Claims Courts; United States—Federal System; United States—State Systems

References and further reading
Carrico, Carrico. 1990. "State Judiciary News: Virginia." *State Court Journal* 14: 28–31.
Morris, Thomas R., and Larry J. Sabato. 1990. *Virginia Government and Politics.* 3rd ed. Richmond: Virginia Chamber of Commerce and Center for Public Service at the University of Virginia.
"State of Virginia." http://www.virginia.com (cited August 28, 2001).
Stumpf, Harry P., and John H. Culver. 1992. *The Politics of State Courts.* New York: Longman.
"Virginia State Bar." http://www.vsb.org (cited August 28, 2001).
"Virginia's Judicial System." http://www.courts.state.va.us (cited August 28, 2001).

WAR CRIMES TRIBUNALS

MISSION

International War Crimes Tribunals have been established on an ad hoc basis in response to violations of the laws of war and other serious violations of international humanitarian law. Although some initiatives have been taken to establish a permanent international criminal tribunal for the trial of war crimes and other serious offenses, to date no permanent international criminal court has been established, although it appears likely that one will be created in the near future.

HISTORY

Following World War I, a fifteen-member commission appointed by the Allies recommended to the Paris Peace Conference that "violations of the laws and customs of war and the laws of humanity" be punished. The Treaty of Versailles provided for the trial of the kaiser "for a supreme offense against international morality and the sanctity of treaties," and for trial of Germans accused of violating the laws and customs of war before allied tribunals. However, the Allies did not hold any trials and the kaiser was never put on trial. Instead, a dozen defendants accused of war crimes were prosecuted before the German Supreme Court in Leipzig but were given minimal sentences.

The Nuremberg tribunals established after World War II is the most significant war crimes tribunal in history. Under the Allies' November 1943 Moscow Declaration, minor Nazi war criminals were to be judged and punished in the countries where they committed their crimes, while the major war criminals would be tried and punished by joint decision of the governments of the Allies. On August 8, 1945, the Allies signed the London Agreement by which they adopted the Charter of the International Military Tribunal (IMT), setting for the jurisdiction substantive law and procedure governing the Nuremberg Tribunal.

The International Military Tribunal for the Far East, commonly known as the Tokyo Tribunal, was created by order of General Douglas MacArthur. The jurisdiction, powers, and procedures were similar to the Nuremberg Tribunal.

Following these tribunals, no international war crimes tribunals were established until the 1990s. In response to evidence of serious violations of international humanitarian law taking place in the conflict in the former Yugoslavia, the International Criminal Tribunal for the former Yugoslavia (ICTY) was established by a Security Council Resolution on May 25, 1993. The jurisdiction of the court is limited to serious violations of international humanitarian law committed in the former Yugoslavia since 1991 and includes war crimes, genocide, and other crimes against humanity.

The International Criminal Tribunal for Rwanda (ICTR) is similar to the Yugoslav War Crimes Tribunal. It was established by the Security Council of the United Nations to prosecute persons responsible for genocide and other serious violations of international humanitarian law committed in the territory of Rwanda between January 1, 1994, and December 31, 1994. It may also prosecute Rwandan citizens charged with such crimes committed in the territory of neighboring states during the same period.

The United Nations has been involved with efforts to create an international criminal court almost from its inception. In 1948 the General Assembly requested the International Law Commission to examine the establishment of an international criminal court with jurisdiction over genocide and other crimes. These efforts, however, fell casualty to the Cold War, and efforts to create such a court were held in abeyance.

In 1989, Trinidad and Tobago, concerned about problems of narcotics trafficking and terrorism, raised the issue before the United Nations. The International Law Commission, as mandated by the United Nations General Assembly, issued a draft statute for an international criminal court in 1994 and a diplomatic convention was convened in Rome in 1998 to adopt a statute for the creation of an international criminal court (*see* International Criminal Court). On July 17, 1998, the UN diplomatic conference adopted the statute for a permanent international criminal court (ICC) by a vote of 120 in favor, 7 against, and 21 abstentions. The international criminal court will come into existence when sixty states ratify the statute.

LEGAL PRINCIPLES

The judgment of the IMT stated that the IMT Charter establishing the Nuremberg Tribunal "was the exercise of the sovereign legislative power by the countries to which the German Reich unconditionally surrendered." The charter granted the tribunal jurisdiction over individuals who, as individuals or as members of organizations, committed crimes against peace, war crimes, or crimes against humanity. In addition, responsibility was imposed on leaders, organizers, instigators, and accomplices for all acts performed in execution of a common plan or conspiracy. The jurisdiction of the tribunal was limited to those war criminals whose crimes had no particular location and did not prejudice the jurisdiction of any of the national or occupation courts.

The jurisdiction, powers, and procedures of the Tokyo Tribunal were essentially similar to the Nuremberg Tribunal.

Despite the efforts to create a fair and impartial tribunal, the Nuremberg Tribunal was criticized. It was argued that the trials violated the principle against ex post facto laws particularly with respect to the charges pertaining to crimes against the peace. Additionally, it was argued that the tribunals tried only the vanquished and that the judges, all allied nationals, were not impartial. Similar criticisms were directed to the Tokyo Tribunals.

The Yugoslav and Rwanda Tribunals were created by a resolution of the Security Council acting under Chapter VII of the Charter United Nations and sets forth the substantive jurisdiction of the courts. Rules of Procedure were adopted by the judges of tribunal pursuant to the statute. Some states have voiced criticism of the courts, arguing that the creation of the courts exceeded the power of the Security Council.

MEMBERSHIP AND PARTICIPATION

The IMT at Nuremberg established the principle of individual responsibility for acts committed by persons against their own nationals and foreigners during wartime. The major leaders of the Axis efforts were brought to trial and sentences including death were imposed.

The ICTY and ICTR were created by a resolution of the United Nations Security Council and bind all member states of the United Nations. Their jurisdiction extends to natural persons, and states are required to cooperate with the tribunals in the investigation and prosecution of persons accused of committing serious violation of international humanitarian law.

PROCEDURE

The charter establishing the Nuremberg Tribunal also established the procedures to be followed. Proceedings were initiated by indictment against defendants who had been designated by the Committee of the Chief Prosecutors as major war criminals. Procedure before the Nuremberg Tribunal war was based on the Anglo American adversarial system, and defendants were granted specified rights, including the right to counsel, to testify on their own behalf, to present evidence, and to cross-examine witnesses. Trials in absentia were authorized and the death penalty could be and was imposed.

The ICTY is situated in the Hague and enjoys primacy over national courts. The statute prohibits double jeopardy, except that the tribunal may try a person who has been tried by a national court where the relevant act was characterized as an ordinary crime or where the national court proceedings were not impartial or independent, were designed to shield the accused from international criminal responsibility, or were not diligently prosecuted. The statute requires that trials be fair and expeditious and guarantees suspects and the accused internationally recognized rights. Thus, the accused is presumed innocent and among the rights guaranteed are the right to be informed promptly and in detail of the charges against him, to have adequate time and facilities for preparation of a defense, and to communicate with counsel of his own choosing, to have legal counsel provided if he cannot afford it, to be tried without undue delay; to cross-examine witnesses; to remain silent; and to obtain disclosure of certain evidence.

The ICTY is composed of three organs, the prosecutor, the Chambers, and the Registry. The prosecution acts independently as a separate organ of the tribunal to investigate the crimes within the tribunal's jurisdiction, prepare charges, and prosecute accused persons. She may request a state to arrest a suspect provisionally and to seize evidence. Upon sufficient evidence of reasonable grounds to believe that the suspect committed a crime, the indictment is submitted to a trial chamber judge, who, if he concurs, confirms the indictment and may issue any necessary orders, including order for the arrest, surrender, and transfer of the accused.

The defendant then enters a plea and the parties may make preliminary or other motions, including dismissal for lack of jurisdiction and exclusion of evidence.

Trials begin with optional opening statements followed by presentation of the evidence. Witnesses are examined by the parties, though judges may call witnesses and pose questions. In addition to the parties, the tribunal may invite or permit any state, organization, or person to appear before it and make submissions. After presentation of the evidence, the parties may present closing arguments.

Although a trial in absentia is not permitted, if the custody of the accused cannot be obtained, the prosecutor may nevertheless present the case to the trial chamber and if the chamber finds that there are reasonable grounds to find that the defendant committed the crime, an international arrest warrant can be issued. Penalties include imprisonment.

Upon conviction, penalties of imprisonment restriction can be imposed but the death penalty cannot be imposed. Both the defendant and the prosecution can appeal judgment.

The Rwanda War Crimes Tribunal is appended to the Yugoslavia Tribunal, and its statute is closely based on the latter's. It is situated in Arusha, Tanzania. Like the ICTY it is technically a subsidiary, though independent, organ of the Security Council. Its organization is identical to that of the Yugoslav Tribunal, with separate prosecutorial, judicial, and administrative organs. Although its trial chambers are separate from those of ICTY, the organization and procedure of the trial chambers are basically identical, and the two tribunals share a common appellate chamber, as well as a common prosecutor and some common prosecutorial staff.

The Rwanda Tribunal's jurisdiction extends to genocide, crimes against humanity, and war crimes. Jurisdiction is concurrent with national courts, although the tribunal has primacy over national courts. The statute's provisions on individual responsibility, defenses, immunities, and double jeopardy are identical to those in the ICTY statute.

In accordance with the tribunal's statute, the ICTR's judges adopted the Rules of Procedure and Evidence of the ICTY, with only minor changes. Both the ICTY rules and the ICTR rules have been revised on several occasions to enhance efficiency and reflect tribunal practice.

STAFFING

The Nuremberg tribunal consisted of four judges, one appointed by each of the Allied powers, Great Britain, France, the Soviet Union, and the United States. The chief prosecutor was Justice Robert H. Jackson.

The Tokyo Tribunal consisted of eleven judges, from eleven countries, Australia, Canada, China, France, Great Britain, India, the Netherlands, New Zealand, the Philippines, the Soviet Union, and the United States, all appointed by General MacArthur.

The Yugoslav War Crimes Tribunal is composed of sixteen permanent independent judges and a maximum of nine ad litem independent judges. No two judges may be nationals of the same state. Each trial chamber is composed of three permanent judges and a maximum of six ad litem judges. The appeals chamber is composed of seven permanent judges, two of whom are appointed from the International Tribunal for Rwanda. The qualifications of the judges are set forth in Article 13 of the International Tribunal Statute and require that:

The permanent and ad litem judges shall be persons of high moral character, impartiality and integrity

who possess the qualifications required in their respective countries for appointment to the highest judicial offices. In the overall composition of the Chambers and sections of the Trial Chambers, due account shall be taken of the experience of the judges in criminal law, international law, including international humanitarian law and human rights law.

Judges of the ICTY and ICTR are nominated by member states of the United Nations. The General Assembly then elects the permanent judges from a list of candidates submitted by the Security Council for a term of four years and there are no term limitations for reelection.

The permanent judges of the International Tribunal elect a president from among their number. The president is a member of the appeals chamber and assigns four others to work with the appeals chamber and nine to work with the trial chamber. The permanent judges of each trial chamber elect a presiding judge from among their number, who oversees the work of the trial chamber as a whole.

The prosecutor is appointed by Security Council on nomination by the secretary-general for a four-year term and can be reelected. The prosecutor must be "of high moral character and possess the highest level of competence and experience in the conduct of investigations and prosecutions of criminal cases."

CASELOAD

The Nuremberg Tribunal initially indicted twenty-four defendants and ultimately tried twenty-two of them, one in absentia. Of the twenty-two tried, the tribunal convicted nineteen defendants. In addition, several thousand Nazi war criminals were tried before national courts or before tribunals administered by the Allies after the war.

The Tokyo Tribunal tried twenty-eight Japanese leaders, and of these convicted twenty-five. In addition, Allied tribunals tried over 5,000 other Japanese for war crimes.

The ICTY obtained its first conviction in May 1997. Dusko Tadic was found guilty of eleven of thirty-one counts, although the appeals chamber overruled on several counts.

As of September 2001, forty-six accused war criminals were in custody in the ICTY. Four cases are awaiting judgments and thirteen cases are at the pretrial stage. There have been thirteen concluded cases, five convictions, two acquittals, three cases where charges were dismissed, two deaths of natural causes (one while in detention unit, the other on a provisional release), and one suicide.

In May 1999 the tribunal issued indictments against Slobodan Milosevic, former president of the Federal Republic of Yugoslavia, and other high-ranking officials. In

July 2001, former president Milosevic was taken into custody for trial by the ICTY.

The first indictments of the ICTR were issued in November 1995. The ICTR has focused on those individuals most responsible for the violations of international humanitarian law. More than fifty persons have been indicted by the ICTR. Many are in custody in Arusha, though several others are being held in other countries pending transfer to Arusha. The defendants come from a wide range of social and professional groups, including political, media, and business leaders. The tens of thousands of lower level criminals will be addressed by the Rwandan courts.

In January 1997, the ICTR commenced its first trial, against Jean-Paul Akayesu and in September 1998, a trial chamber convicted Akayesu of genocide and crimes against humanity—the first genocide verdict ever issued by an international court—and sentenced him to life in prison. The Akayesu verdict was also significant because it recognized rape as an act of genocide.

IMPACT

The post–World War II tribunals were important not only because they brought to justice those accused of the most heinous crimes but also because they served an educational purpose, bringing to widespread public attention the atrocities committed by the Axis powers during World War II. In addition, several important principles called the Nuremberg Principles emerged and were adopted by the General Assembly of the United Nations on December 11, 1946. These included: the principle that an individual could be held responsible for violating international law, that reliance on domestic law does not excuse an individual of responsibility, that heads of state are not immune from prosecution, and that following superior orders is not a defense.

The acceptance of the Nuremberg Principles was the first step in the development of international human rights law. These principles were elaborated on and embodied in the International Human Rights Conventions that followed. The international community affirmed that how a nation treated its own nationals is of concern to the international community and that governments would be held accountable.

Further, the principle of individual responsibility for violation of international law has been developed and strengthened by the ad hoc tribunals established in Nuremberg, the former Yugoslavia, and Rwanda. While efforts to create a permanent international criminal court continue, there is a growing consensus in the international community that a mechanism is needed to ensure that those responsible for the most serious international crimes are brought to justice.

Elizabeth F. Defeis

See also Human Rights Law; International Criminal Court

References and further reading

Aldrich, George H. 1996. "Jurisdiction of the International Criminal Tribunal for the Former Yugoslavia." *American Journal of International Law* 64: 90.

Bassiouni, M. Cherif. 1999. *Crimes Against Humanity in International Criminal Law*. 2nd ed. The Hague: Kluwer Law International.

Bassiouni, M. Cherif, ed. 1999. *International Criminal Law*. 3 vols., 2nd ed. Ardsley, NY: Transnational Publishers.

Bassiouni, M. Cherif, and Peter Manikas. 1996. *The Law of the International Criminal Tribunal for the Former Yugoslavia*. Irvington-on-Hudson, NY: Transnational Publishers.

Dinstein, Yoram, and Mala Tabory, eds. *War Crimes in International Law*. The Hague: Martinus Nijhoff.

Ferencz, Benjamin B. 1980. *An International Criminal Court: A Step Toward World Peace*. 2 vols. New York: Oceana Publications.

Green, L.C. 1985. *Essays on the Modern Law of War*. Ardsley, NY: Transnational Publishers.

MacKinnon, Catherine A. 1994. "Rape, Genocide, and Women's Human Rights." *Harvard Women's Law Journal* 5: 17.

Meron, Theodor. 1993. "Rape as a Crime under International Humanitarian Law." *American Journal of International Law* 424: 87.

Mueller, Gerhard O. W., and Edward M. Wise, eds. 1965. *International Criminal Law*. London: Sweet and Maxewell.

Taylor, Telford. 1992. *The Anatomy of the Nuremberg Trials*. New York: Alfred A. Knopf.

WASHINGTON

GENERAL INFORMATION

Washington, the northwesternmost of the contiguous United States, has a population of 5.76 million and occupies some 67,000 square miles, ranking fifteenth and twentieth nationally in those respective categories. Although the capitol is located in Olympia, the population center, and thus much of the political sway, resides in King County. Nearly 83 percent of the people in the state live within a metropolitan area, most of those in the Seattle-Tacoma-Everett metropolitan area, which surrounds Puget Sound. Other major metropolitan areas include Vancouver, in the southwestern part of the state, on the Columbia River across from Portland, Oregon; Bellingham, lying north of Seattle toward the Canadian border; Yakima and the tri-cities area (Pasco, Kennewick, and Richland) in the center of the state; and Spokane, the state's second largest city, lying far to the east along the border with Idaho.

The most prominent natural feature in Washington is the Cascades, a mountain range that trends north to south and splits the state geographically, economically, and culturally. The east side of the state tends to be rural, agricultural, and politically conservative. The west side tends to be urban, industrial, and politically liberal.

Economic growth in Washington has generally outpaced the national average since 1980. In 1998 the median household income in the state was $47,421, the fifth highest in the nation, and only 8.9 percent of the population was below the poverty line, making it the sixth lowest in that category. The state's economy is quite diversified. Extractive industries such as timber, fishing, and agriculture, led by companies such as Weyerhaeuser, once dominated, but by the 1960s a large manufacturing sector had emerged, led by the aerospace industry, including such companies as Boeing. The state has also experienced the growth of a strong tertiary sector, comprising such companies such as Starbucks and Nordstroms in the retail area and Microsoft and other dot-coms in high technology.

In racial demographics Washington is roughly 83 percent white, 6 percent Asian-American, 6 percent Hispanic-American, 3 percent African-American, and 2 percent Native American. The absence of a single large minority population, in conjunction with the state's robust economy, has helped Washington avoid much of the racial tensions experienced by other states. Nonetheless, several issues involving the working conditions of migrant farm workers and the authority of Native American tribes to regulate alcohol, gambling, and other activities on tribal lands have percolated through the courts.

EVOLUTION AND HISTORY

Washington's legal system can be traced back well before the ratification of statehood in 1889. From 1848 to 1853, Washington was a part of the Oregon Territory. At that time, three justices, each appointed by the president, served both as circuit judges, presiding over cases in three large districts, and as Supreme Court justices, hearing appeals from the same cases over which they had originally presided. When Washington achieved separate territorial status in 1853 it adopted essentially the same structure, adding a fourth district in 1884.

The state constitutional convention in 1889, heavily influenced by the Populist movement of the late nineteenth century, adopted openness provisions governing state institutions, restrictions on corporate power, and provisions for the popular election and recall of all major government officers, including judges and justices of the state Supreme Court. Delegates to the convention were also strongly influenced by the efforts of other states. They possessed a working knowledge of several other state constitutions, and the judicial article of Washington's constitution was modeled almost in its entirety after those of California and Oregon.

In addition to trial courts, the Washington constitution created a single appellate-level court. The first Supreme Court of Washington consisted of five members elected by voters of the state. The court's membership needed to be expanded twice (to seven justices in 1905 and nine in 1909) in order to help alleviate crowded dockets. Between 1909 and 1969, the court heard most cases by department—that is, by the Chief Justice together with four associate justices. In 1969 the Court of Appeals was established by constitutional amendment. Adding a second level of appellate court dramatically reduced the Supreme Court's caseload, and since that time all cases before the court are heard en banc.

STRUCTURE AND STAFFING

Legal Profession and Legal Training
In October 2000, there were 18,812 attorneys licensed to practice in Washington. The state had one lawyer for every 306 residents, compared to an average of one lawyer for every 276 persons nationally. More than two-thirds of Washington lawyers, approximately 69 percent, are men, and the profession is overwhelmingly white (92 percent). Approximately three-quarters are in private practice and one-quarter work in the public sector. Professional training takes place at three law schools in the state: one public, the University of Washington in Seattle, and two private, Seattle University and, in Spokane, Gonzaga University.

Administrative Hearings
Washington was among the leading states in adopting a central panel system for adjudicating administrative law cases. The Office of Administrative Hearings (OAH) was created by state statute in 1982, and administrative law judges, which had formerly been housed in various state agencies and departments, were relocated and centralized in that office. As in other states using the central panel system, this reform eliminates the awkwardness of having an agency use its own hearings examiner to conduct the review of its own decisions.

There are some seventy administrative law judges in the state, located in nine field offices in six separate cities (Everett, Olympia, Seattle, Spokane, Vancouver, and Yakima). The OAH is headed by a chief administrative law judge (ALJ) and two deputy chiefs. Each field office has a senior ALJ who serves as administrative chief for the office.

The OAH handles approximately 48,000 administrative cases a year. Hearings range from hourlong unemployment insurance cases, with pro se claimants and employers, to multiweek special education hearings with several parties and attorneys. Hearings are scheduled more promptly than through the judicial system, take less time, and are less formal. Typical cases involve citizen appeals of decisions by an administrative agency. Administrative judges take testimony from parties and witnesses, develop an administrative record, and then issue a decision (with findings of fact and conclusions of law) that affirms, modifies, or reverses the original decision of the administrative agency. Appeals from administrative courts go first to commissioner review boards located in the agency from which the dispute originally arose, and from there to the superior court.

The greatest volume of cases heard by the OAH are unemployment insurance cases involving disputes with the Employment Security Department (more than 27,000 cases a year) and public assistance benefits and child support cases against the Department of Social and Health Services (more than 20,000 cases a year). In addition, the OAH conducts large numbers of cases for the superintendent of public instruction, the Liquor Control Board, the Department of Licensing, and the Department of Labor and Industries.

The chief administrative law judge is appointed by the governor and confirmed by the state legislature. The chief is responsible for administering the OAH, hiring support personnel, and selecting other administrative law judges, including the senior judges in each field office.

Judicial System

The Washington court system is a fairly representative example of the unified (or "reformed") court systems now present in a majority of the states. Modeled after the federal court system, the Washington judicial system consists of four hierarchical levels, including trial courts of limited and general jurisdictions as well as two levels of appellate courts (see figure).

Courts of limited jurisdiction comprise district courts and municipal courts. District courts are county courts, and there is at least one in each county. The forty-nine district courts are established in sixty-one separate locations in the state, with at least one court in each of the thirty-nine counties. Municipal courts are established by city ordinance. Cities electing not to establish a municipal court may contract with the district court for services. There are 127 municipal courts in the state and more than 100 municipal court judges.

District and municipal courts have concurrent jurisdiction with superior courts over misdemeanor and gross misdemeanor violations and civil cases under $50,000. They have exclusive jurisdiction over minor infractions. These courts receive more than 2 million new case filings annually, of which roughly three-fourths are parking or traffic violations.

District court judges are chosen in nonpartisan elections to serve four-year terms. Municipal court judges may be elected or appointed, depending on the statutory provisions under which their seats were established. (Generally they are appointed unless they are full-time judges, in which case they are usually elected.) Judges of

Legal Structure of Washington State Courts

State Supreme Court
(1 court, 9 justices)

Court of Appeals
(3 divisions, 20 judges)

Superior Courts
(30 courts)

Courts of Limited Jurisdiction	Administrative Law Courts
(49 districts, 127 municipal courts)	(9 field offices, 70 judges)

courts of limited jurisdiction belong to the District and Municipal Court Judges' Association, created by state statute to make recommendations concerning the operation of courts served by its members. Courts of limited jurisdiction are funded out of county and municipal budgets and are served by administrative support staff under the direction of the presiding judge.

Superior courts in Washington State are the court of general jurisdiction. These courts have exclusive jurisdiction for felony matters, real property rights, domestic relations, estate, mental illness, juvenile, and civil cases over $50,000. Juvenile courts are a division of the superior courts, established by separate statute to deal with violations by youths under the age of eighteen. The superior courts also hear appeals from courts of limited jurisdiction, and, in cases originally heard by a non-attorney judge, appeals can be heard de novo. Nearly 275,000 cases are filed annually in superior courts, roughly 100,000 of which are civil suits, nearly 40,000 criminal prosecutions, and the remainder domestic relations and juvenile cases.

Superior courts are grouped into single- or multicounty districts. There are thirty such districts in the state. Counties with large populations usually constitute one district, while in less populous areas a district may comprise of two or more counties. A superior court is located in each county. In rural districts, judges rotate between counties as needed.

Superior court judges are elected to four-year terms. Vacancies between elections are filled by appointment of the governor, and a newly appointed judge serves until the next general election. A presiding judge in each county or judicial district handles specific administrative functions and acts as spokesperson for the court. Superior court judges belong to an organization, established by statute, called the Superior Court Judges' Association. Specific committees of the association work to improve the court system and to communicate with other court levels, the legislature, bar associations, the media, and the public.

Each county courthouse has its own courtroom and staff, which usually includes a bailiff, a clerk, a court reporter, and oftentimes a court administrator, who is responsible for assisting the presiding judge in budget planning for the court, assignment of cases, and implementation of general court policies. Superior courts may also employ up to three court commissioners. Commissioners, who must be attorneys licensed to practice in Washington, work under the direction of a judge and may hear uncontested matters such as probate cases, marriage dissolutions, and other judicial duties as required by the judge.

The *Court of Appeals* was created by constitutional amendment in 1969. The court hears all appeals from the trial court level that do not fall within the Supreme Court's jurisdiction. A nondiscretionary appellate court, it must accept most appeals that are filed with it. The nearly 4,000 appeals the court receives annually are roughly evenly split between criminal and civil matters.

The Court of Appeals has authority to reverse, remand, modify, or affirm the decisions of lower courts. It is divided into three geographic divisions, each of which sits in three judge panels, except in rare instances when there is an en banc hearing. Division I encompasses the six northwestern counties, Division II the thirteen southwestern counties, and Division III covers the remaining twenty counties east of the Cascades.

The twenty judges on the Court of Appeals serve staggered six-year terms. Each division is divided into three geographic districts, and a specific number of judges must be elected from each. Vacancies are filled by the governor, and an appointee serves until the next general election. A presiding chief judge for all three divisions is elected for a one-year term. Duties of the presiding chief judge include coordination of business matters among the three divisions. In addition, each division elects its own chief judge to handle its own administrative details. The court's support personnel includes a clerk who serves as the chief administrative officer for each division, court commissioners, law clerks, and other secretarial and administrative staff.

The *Supreme Court* is the state's highest appellate court. It has original jurisdiction over petitions against state officers and appellate jurisdiction in nearly all other matters. It may directly review a trial court decision if the action involves a state officer, if the trial court has ruled a statute or ordinance unconstitutional, if conflicting statutes or rules of law are involved, or if the issue is of broad public interest and requires prompt determination. In addition, all cases in which the death penalty has been imposed are reviewed directly by the Supreme Court. In all other cases, review of Court of Appeals decisions is at the Supreme Court's discretion.

Motions before the Supreme Court, and petitions for review of Court of Appeals decisions, are heard by five-member departments of the court. A less-than-unanimous vote on a petition requires that the entire court consider the matter. The Supreme Court typically receives more than 1,400 new cases each year, of which it disposes of roughly 120–140 with written opinions. All nine justices sit en banc to hear and dispose of cases argued on its appeal docket. Each case is decided on the basis of the record, plus written and oral arguments.

The Supreme Court has constitutional authority to make rules for all the state's courts. Local courts may make their own rules of procedure, but these must conform with those established by the Supreme Court. In addition, the Supreme Court is responsible for operation of the state judicial system and has supervisory responsibility over certain activities of the Washington State Bar Association, including attorney discipline.

The nine Supreme Court justices are elected to staggered six-year terms. The only requirement for office is that the prospective justice be admitted to the practice of law in Washington State. Vacancies are filled by appointment of the governor until the next general election. Since 1950, more than three-fourths of the justices have come to the court initially by appointment. The justice with the shortest elected term to serve usually acts as the chief justice. The chief justice is the court's executive officer and the chief administrative officer of the court system. Other court personnel are appointed by the Supreme Court and include a court bailiff, a clerk of the court, a court commissioner, a reporter of decisions, law clerks, and a law librarian.

A *court administrator,* also appointed by the Supreme Court, is responsible for executing the policy and rules in the state's judicial system. With assistance from staff, the administrator compiles court statistics and reports; develops and promotes modern judicial management procedures; studies and analyzes information relating to the operation and administration of state courts; and provides substantive and procedural information to members of the judicial community, the bar, other branches of government, and the general public.

The *Commission on Judicial Conduct* was established by a constitutional amendment in 1989. Its membership consists of two lawyers selected by the state bar association, three judges selected by various levels of the judiciary, and six nonlawyer citizens appointed by the governor.

Any person, organization, or association may submit written or oral allegations of judicial misconduct to the commission. Because the commission has no authority to modify judicial decisions, objections to a particular official judicial action will not normally trigger commission action. The commission's power is limited to two areas:

misconduct, as defined by the Code of Judicial Conduct, and disability that is, or is likely to become, serious enough to interfere with a judge's official duties. If misconduct is found, the commission may admonish, reprimand, or censure the judge, or may recommend to the Supreme Court that the judge be suspended or removed. Like trials, commission fact-finding hearings are held in public. The Supreme Court has appellate review of the commission's decisions. In the case of a commission recommendation, the court makes the final decision after reviewing the commission's record and taking argument on the matter. In one case, the commission's censure of a sitting Supreme Court justice for addressing a pro-life rally was reversed by the Supreme Court.

RELATION TO THE NATIONAL SYSTEM
Washington is within the jurisdiction of the Ninth Circuit Court of Appeals, which sits in San Francisco. It contains two federal districts: the Western District, sitting in Seattle, and the Eastern District, in Spokane. Over the years, numerous jurists and lawyers from Washington have been appointed to the federal bench, including William O. Douglas, who, though born in Connecticut, was hailed as a "westerner" when President Franklin Roosevelt appointed him to the U.S. Supreme Court in 1939 because he had been raised in Yakima and had attended Whitworth College in eastern Washington. Douglas retired from the Court in 1973, after thirty-six years of service, longer than any justice before or since.

Washington has served as a launching ground for many important U.S. Supreme Court decisions, including *West Coast Hotel v. Parrish* (1937), in which the Court upheld a state minimum wage law and reversed the controversial "liberty to contract" jurisprudence of the early twentieth century, and *Washington v. Glucksberg* (1997), in which it upheld a state law against physician-assisted suicide.

Cornell W. Clayton

See also Administrative Tribunals; Appellate Courts; Judicial Selection, Methods of; Juvenile Justice; Trial Courts; United States—Federal System; United States—State Systems
References and further reading
Rupp, John N. 1983. "An Essay in History (1933–1983, the First Fifty Years of the Washington State Bar Association)." *Washington State Bar News,* June 1983, pp. 27–37.
Sheldon, Charles H. 1988. *A Century of Judging: A Political History of the Washington Supreme Court.* Seattle: University of Washington Press.
———. "Politicians in Robes: Judges and the Washington Court System." In David Nice, John Pierce, and Charles Sheldon, eds., *Government and Politics in the Evergreen State.* Pullman: Washington State University Press.
———. 1992. *The Washington High Bench: A Biographical History of the State Supreme Court, 1889–1991.* Pullman: Washington State University Press.
Washington State Courts. *Brief History of the Washington*

Supreme Court. http://www.courts.wa.gov/education/history/supreme.cfm (July 2000).
———. 1997. *A Citizen's Guide to the Washington Courts,* 7th ed. Olympia.
———. *Report of the Courts of Washington 1999.* http://www.courts.wa.gov/press/1999.cfm (July 2000).

WASHINGTON, D.C.
See District of Columbia

WEST VIRGINIA

GENERAL INFORMATION
The state of West Virginia, admitted to the United States in 1863 by its separation from the state of Virginia, is located in a rugged mountain and plateau region of the eastern United States. The economy has long depended on industries related to resource extraction, such as coal mining, timbering, glass-making, chemical production, and steelmaking. Because of the erosion of employment in these industries, the state has among the highest unemployment rates and lowest average per capita income in the country. The state's 1.8 million people are overwhelmingly white (97 percent) and rural (58 percent), or resident in communities with fewer than sixty thousand inhabitants (42 percent). Compared with other American states, West Virginia's population is the oldest, is much less healthy, suffers occupational injuries more frequently, has fewer college graduates, and has among the lowest crime rates.

EVOLUTION AND HISTORY
Article VIII of the state's Constitution of 1872, as amended by the Judicial Reorganization Amendment of 1974, defines the organization of West Virginia courts. The amendment established a "unitary" judicial system (see figure) to consider cases in law and equity arising under state law. The 1974 amendment eliminated justices of the peace, specialized courts, and county courts, and assigned oversight and procedural rule-making power to the Supreme Court of Appeals. In 1986, the legislature created a family law master system. In 1999 the legislature renamed this system Family Courts, expanded the contempt powers of the masters, and provided for the partisan election of masters.

CURRENT STRUCTURE: THE JUDICIAL BRANCH

The Supreme Court of Appeals
The Supreme Court of Appeals is the state's only appellate court. The court's five justices have complete discre-

tion over the cases on the court's docket. Petitions for review reach the court from the circuit courts as criminal appeals (constituting 6.6 percent of petitions filed in 1999) or civil appeals (constituting 15.7 percent), as habeas corpus and other original jurisdiction petitions (12.3 percent), from the Workers' Compensation Appeal Board (65.2 percent), from the Judicial Hearing Board (0.1 percent), from the State Bar Disciplinary Board (0.1 percent), or on remand or certification from federal courts (0.1 percent). The court has faced an increasing number of petitions for review. The number of petitions both filed and granted tripled between 1983 and 1999. In 1999 the justices disposed of 324 cases by opinion and 830 workers' compensation cases by memorandum order.

Several practices distinguish the Supreme Court of Appeals from other appellate courts. First, the justices try to be open to parties. Therefore, after a party has petitioned the court and a response is filed, the justices conduct, at the appellant's request, a "motion" hearing early in one of the court's three yearly terms. At the hearing, which lasts ten minutes, the justices inquire into the reasons why appellant's counsel, or a pro se petitioner, requests review. Second, the justices have devised procedures for handling the large volume of petitions. Writ clerks, who are staff attorneys, prepare memoranda on petitions not considered at motions hearings and for all workers' compensation petitions. With the exception of workers' compensation cases, the writ clerks report to the justice's conference room to address questions about the memoranda. Third, the court has distinctive operational practices. The vote to grant review to a petitioner occurs at the justices' conference in reverse order of seniority on the court. At the Thursday conference, the discussion of cases argued opens with the justice assigned the case, proceeds to the other justices, and then a vote is taken in reverse order of seniority. The writing of opinions of the court rotates sequentially among justices in the majority; however, justices will occasionally trade their assignments. Finally, the court rotates the chief justiceship each year on the basis of seniority of service.

Judicial Administration
With the assistance of its Administrative Office, the court develops policies for the management of the state's courts. These policies establish, for all state courts, fiscal and staff management practices and procedural rules.

Oversight of the Bar
The state legislature has assigned oversight of the West Virginia State Bar to the court. An "integrated" bar (that is, membership in the state bar in mandatory) with 3,975 members (in 2000), the state bar's tasks include the supervision of legal ethics, the proposal of legal reforms, the management of mandatory continuing legal education,

and control of free civil legal assistance and pro bono referral programs. The Board of Law Examiners, appointed by the justices, supervises admission to law practice. Approximately 70 percent of the state's lawyers are graduates of the West Virginia University College of Law, the state's only law school. The court has established rules for admission to legal practice and rules of professional conduct. The Board of Governors of the state bar appoints a Lawyer Disciplinary Counsel to investigate complaints against lawyers and a Lawyer Disciplinary Board to either dismiss the complaint or refer the case to the Supreme Court of Appeals, which can reprimand, suspend, admonish, or disbar a lawyer.

Policy Role
In performing its duties, the Supreme Court of Appeals can reinforce or legitimate, incrementally adjust, or innovate public policies and help set the political agenda. The justices' most common choices generate policy reinforcement. Examples of reinforcement include the correction of what the justices call "screw ups," or obvious legal mistakes, and "home cooking," or bias in favor of a local litigant. Occasionally the court incrementally modifies state statutes. For example, the court has clarified statutes on the assignment of real property and on financial contributions for child support. The court has sometimes engaged in innovative policy making. For example, the justices adopted a modified comparative negligence doctrine for the remedy of personal injury claims that has affected recovery of damages in auto accidents. The court also innovated a new products liability law by adopting a rule of strict liability. Finally, but very rarely, the court has engaged in setting the policy agenda. For example, its decisions have placed state and local school finance and prison operations on the legislative and gubernatorial agendas.

Circuit Courts
Circuit courts, the trial courts of general jurisdiction, possess jurisdiction in equity and over all criminal, civil, and juvenile cases at law, with the exception of civil cases with less than $300 at issue. The Reorganization Amendment of 1974 permitted the legislature to determine the number of circuits and circuit judges. The legislature has fixed the current number of circuit judges at sixty-two and the number of circuits at thirty-one. Although court is held in every county, fourteen circuits include more than one county. The Supreme Court of Appeals can reassign judges and magistrates from one circuit to another, or can assign senior (semiretired) circuit and Supreme Court of Appeals judges to reduce caseloads. The circuit court uses a twelve-member jury in criminal cases and a six-member jury in civil actions. Verdicts must be unanimous. In the fiscal year 1998–1999, cir-

cuit courts disposed of 56,811 cases without trial (6,965 criminal, 43,810 civil, 6,036 juvenile) and held 2,020 bench trials and 527 jury trials.

Magistrates' Courts

Magistrates' Courts have countywide jurisdiction over criminal misdemeanors and can hold preliminary examinations and set bail in felony cases. They can hear civil claims with up to $5,000 in dispute. The legislature requires magistrates to complete a course of instruction after their election and to attend continuing education sessions, or be subject to penalties imposed through the state's system of judicial discipline. Today, the constitution apportions two magistrates to each county and provides the more populous counties additional magistrates through an apportionment process. In 2000 there were 157 magistrates. These courts can use six-member juries to hear criminal misdemeanors and civil claims of more than $20. Verdicts must be unanimous. However, most of the cases on magistrates' dockets are settled out of court. In 1999 Magistrates' Courts disposed of 334,056 cases without trial (270,285 criminal, 34,141 civil, 30,080 special proceedings) and held 34,444 bench trials and 316 jury trials.

Family Courts

The legislature created family courts to fulfill the state's responsibilities under the federal Child Support Enforcement Amendments of 1984. The thirty-three masters who staff the twenty-four family court circuits receive matters affecting the assignment of child custody and disputes about child custody, parental visitation rights, child support payments, and paternity. All masters must be attorneys with at least five years at the bar. A plaintiff or a child advocate from the children's support enforcement section of the state's Department of Human Services may file a family law case. To investigate the case, family law masters possess subpoena powers. They can mediate a case or hold an adversarial hearing. After a hearing, the master normally advises counsel or the child advocate to draft an order consistent with the findings the master announces at the hearing. The master reviews the draft order, modifies it as necessary, and sends it to the parties for the filing of objections. After ten days, the recommended order is sent to the circuit judge for modification or enforcement. Since 1999 the masters have had civil contempt powers to enforce child custody, child support, child visitation, and spousal support orders.

Municipal Courts

The Reorganization Amendment allowed cities and towns to establish municipal courts with jurisdiction over municipal ordinances. There are currently 122 municipal courts. One judge selected by a city or town council serves each court.

Administrative Support for the Judiciary

Several offices provide administrative support for the judiciary. The Administrative Office of the Supreme Court of Appeals manages the court's personnel and finances, prepares the budget for all courts, drafts procedural rules, oversees judicial branch finances, and develops and implements judicial branch personnel policies. Official court reporters are employees of the Supreme Court of Appeals. The clerk of courts, an elected county post, manages case filings and records and collects circuit court fees. Circuit judges can appoint commissioners in chancery and general receivers, jury commissioners, mental hygiene commissioners (who preside over mental commitment and related conservatorship hearings), juvenile referees, and Magistrates' Court staff.

Judicial Discipline

The Supreme Court of Appeals can censure or temporarily suspend any justice, judge, or magistrate for violation of ethical rules, or retire judges who are physically or mentally incapacitated. Recommendations for disciplinary action begin with complaints received by the Judicial Investigation Commission. After consideration of the evidence gathered by its counsel, the commission can file a complaint with the Judicial Hearing Board. If the complaint cannot be resolved by prehearing settlement, the Hearing Board will hold a hearing. If it finds a violation, it can recommend the judge's public or private reprimand, temporary suspension from duties, a fine of up to $5,000, or, if the judge is incapacitated, retirement. The Supreme Court of Appeals then decides whether to enforce the Judicial Hearing Board's recommendation.

CURRENT STRUCTURE: EXECUTIVE BRANCH JUDICIAL FUNCTIONS

The Attorney General

The attorney general, elected to a four-year term, is responsible for representation of the state in federal and state appellate cases to which the state is a party or amicus curiae, the representation of the state when it is a party to civil litigation, and the enforcement of civil rights, consumer protection, and antitrust laws. The office has no role in most other civil and criminal cases.

Administrative Agencies

The delegation of the disposition of selected conflicts to state administrative agencies also occurs in West Virginia. Despite a state administrative procedure act, each agency employs unique procedures. At least three patterns of activity are common. First, several executive branch agencies, such as the Public Service Commission, provide alternative dispute resolution services. Second, some agencies, such as the Department of Natural Resources,

Legal Structure of West Virginia Courts

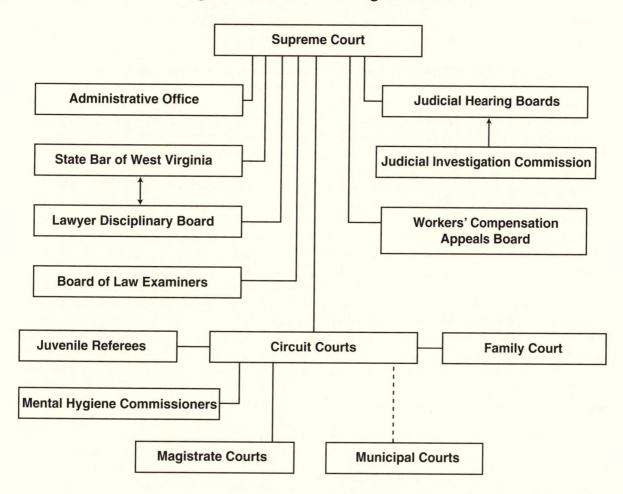

permit staff to perform adjustment of conflicts at the location of a complaint or incident. Third, with extraordinarily contested matters, adjudication occurs before administrative law judges or an agency panel.

Criminal Prosecution and Defense
In criminal cases, fifty-five full and part-time prosecuting attorneys prosecute criminal cases in the circuit and Magistrates' Courts. Elected on a partisan ballot for four-year terms in each county, prosecuting attorneys are not regulated by any executive branch official. They do not follow any statewide procedures, and they have no institutionalized communication with prosecuting attorneys in other counties. In the counties with a larger volume of criminal cases, the prosecuting attorneys have employed full-time and part-time assistants.

Criminal defense counsel for indigent persons is provided either by public defenders or by judicially appointed attorneys. Established in 1989, Public Defender Services, a state agency, has gradually expanded its provision of counsel for indigents to a majority of the state's counties. When counsel is unavailable from Public De-

fender Services, circuit judges appoint an indigent's defense counsel. However, Public Defender Services compensates judicially appointed defense counsel.

STAFFING
West Virginia's judiciary is elected by partisan ballot. The justices of the Supreme Court of Appeals serve staggered twelve-year terms. Circuit judges serve eight-year terms, with all circuit judges being selected in the same election year. Magistrates and family law masters (beginning in 2002) serve four-year terms. The governor temporarily appoints persons to judicial branch vacancies. At the next general election the voters elect a person to fill the vacancy. Supreme Court of Appeals justices must have been admitted to the practice of law for ten years prior to election, and circuit court judges must have been admitted to practice for five years. Magistrates are not required to possess a law degree. West Virginia's judiciary has been overwhelmingly white and male.

The Supreme Court of Appeals financially supports the training of circuit judges in various out-of-state programs. Also, each year the court requires circuit judges to attend two state judicial conferences that address changes in state law, court procedures, and other timely topics. Magistrates and family law masters must attend yearly training sessions or face disciplinary action.

RELATIONSHIP TO THE NATIONAL SYSTEM

The U.S. Supreme Court has very infrequently overturned Supreme Court of Appeals decisions, and the federal district courts in the Northern and Southern Districts of the state function independently of state courts. Conversely, the Supreme Court of Appeals has made incremental changes in federal rulings. Examples include the court's development of tests to determine if state tax law has contravened the U.S. Supreme Court's interpretation of the commerce clause of the U.S. Constitution, and the expansion of standards set by the U.S. Supreme Court in cases involving privileges and immunities, the right to petition without fear of defamation suits, exclusionary rule standards, and custodial interrogations. The Supreme Court of Appeals independently has used state constitutional provisions to recognize rights to the equal funding of public education, proportionality in the sentencing of habitual offenders, and media access to pretrial hearings.

Richard A. Brisbin, Jr.

See also Appellate Courts; Prosecuting Authorities; Trial Courts; United States—Federal System; United States—State Systems

References and further reading
Brisbin, Richard A., Jr. 1993. "The West Virginia Judiciary." Pp. 59–125 in *West Virginia Government: The Legislative, Executive, and Judiciary.* Edited by Christopher Z. Mooney. Morgantown: West Virginia University, Institute for Public Affairs.
Kilwein, John C. 1999. "The West Virginia Judicial System at the Crossroads of Change." *West Virginia Public Affairs Reporter* 16, no. 4: 2–8.
State of West Virginia. "West Virginia Supreme Court of Appeals." http://www.state.wv.us/wvsca/ (accessed August 1, 2000).

WESTERN AUSTRALIA

GENERAL INFORMATION

The state of Western Australia, with an area of 2,529,880 square kilometers, occupies almost one-third of the total Australian land mass. Stretching along the entire western coastline of the continent and inland to the Northern Territory and South Australian borders, Western Australia features a diverse range of landscapes and ecologies from coastal plains and desert to agricultural, wetland, and forested regions.

Although it occupies such a large area, Western Australia has a relatively small population. The 1998 national census reported the population of the state at 1,831,000,

with all but 489,100 residing in the small coastal capital of Perth. The once robust aboriginal population of the state is now estimated at only 56,205, and it is more highly concentrated in the northern half of the state. In recent years Western Australia has reported a population decline in rural areas, particularly in its mining districts. Despite this decline, mining, along with agriculture, remains the economic mainstay of the state. Western Australia is the largest producer of both energy and metallic minerals in the country, and it holds a 39 percent share of the world's diamond production.

EVOLUTION AND HISTORY

Western Australia was founded as a British colony on June 1, 1829. This date is confirmed retrospectively by the Interpretation Act of 1984 (WA) as being the relevant date for the reception of English imperial statute law in Western Australia. It is often also invoked as the relevant date for the reception of the English common law. However, the common law should properly be regarded as operative from June 18, 1829; that was the date that lieutenant-governor James Stirling issued a proclamation declaring the new colony as subject to English law. In December of 1829 the governor appointed eight free settlers as justices of the peace to adjudicate upon both criminal and civil matters within the colony. These justices, together with a legally trained chairman, staffed the first criminal court of the colony, modeled on the English Court of Quarter Sessions. In 1832 the colony's newly established Legislative Council passed a statute to create the Civil Court of Western Australia and relieve the justices of the peace from their unofficial civil law responsibility. These courts operated until the creation of the current Supreme Court of Western Australia in 1861; the Supreme Court assumed responsibility for the civil, criminal, and equitable jurisdictions of the colony. In 1863 a Court for Divorce and Matrimonial Causes was established. Western Australia was the only Australian colony to establish a discrete body to administer this jurisdiction, which is seen as a precursor to its current and uniquely independent Family Court.

As was the case with the other Australian states, the English Privy Council remained in Western Australia's court hierarchy until its abolition by the Australia Acts of 1986. These acts also secured the state's complete legislative independence from England. Western Australia has a bicameral legislature, and its constitution provides for parliamentary responsible government.

CURRENT STRUCTURE: THE JUDICIAL BRANCH

The Supreme Court
The Supreme Court of Western Australia, established in 1861, is the state's superior court of record (see figure).

Legal Structure of Western Australia Courts

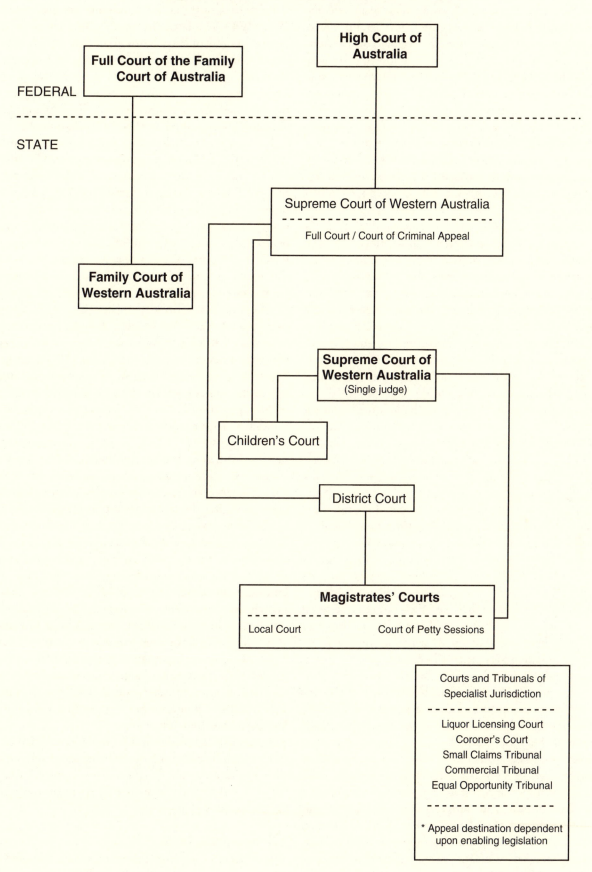

High Court of Australia

Full Court of the Family Court of Australia

FEDERAL

- -

STATE

Supreme Court of Western Australia
- -
Full Court / Court of Criminal Appeal

Family Court of Western Australia

Supreme Court of Western Australia (Single judge)

Children's Court

District Court

Magistrates' Courts
- -
Local Court   Court of Petty Sessions

Courts and Tribunals of Specialist Jurisdiction
- - - - - - - - - - - - - - - - - - -
Liquor Licensing Court
Coroner's Court
Small Claims Tribunal
Commercial Tribunal
Equal Opportunity Tribunal

- - - - - - - - - - - - - - - - - - -

* Appeal destination dependent upon enabling legislation

The court is constituted under the Supreme Court Act of 1935 (WA) and exercises civil, criminal, probate, and appellate jurisdictions. The Supreme Court is also vested with federal jurisdiction under the federal constitution. The bench of the court is currently composed of sixteen justices and a chief justice. Unlike its counterpart in New South Wales, the Supreme Court of Western Australia is not broken into divisions. Thus its judicial members rotate on a regular basis, each sitting in different jurisdictions within the court. Because of the size of the state, judges are required to conduct circuit court sittings in eleven regional centers. Most of the business of these sittings is criminal, although there is the occasional small civil matter.

Civil matters are dealt with by a single judge, although in rare cases (such as with certain defamation actions) a judge may empanel a civil jury. Some preliminary issues and calculation of costs are handled by masters of the court. The Supreme Court may grant remedies at common law or equity as well as make other consequential orders. The amount of money that may be claimed in a civil action in the Supreme Court is unlimited.

In the criminal jurisdiction, the Supreme Court deals with the trial of offenses carrying a penalty of life imprisonment. By definition, these are the most serious of the indictable offenses provided for in the Criminal Code of 1913 (WA) ("the Criminal Code") and include the offenses of willful murder, murder, and armed robbery. Until relatively recently, all indictable offenses were dealt with by judge and jury. Jury trials in Western Australia generally require a unanimous verdict. However, excepting in cases of willful murder and murder, if the jury cannot return a unanimous verdict after three hours' deliberation, the judge may direct the jury that the court will accept a majority verdict of ten or more of its members (see Juries Act of 1957 [WA] S.41). In 1994, amendments to the criminal code were passed allowing a defendant charged with an indictable offense to elect between trial by jury or trial by judge alone. Most elections in favor of judge alone trials have been cases in which the evidence or defense is particularly technical or upsetting, or in which the defendant feels that the jurors may otherwise be prejudiced. Although there is no requirement under law for the defendant to give reasons for the election, a trial by judge alone may be granted only with the consent of the prosecution.

The appellate jurisdiction of the Supreme Court is found in Section 20 of the Supreme Court Act of 1935 (WA). It is important to note that there is no common law right of appeal in Western Australia, and such appeals are governed by the legislation under which the original decision was made. Supreme Court appeals may be conveniently divided into four categories: civil (before the full court of the Supreme Court), criminal (before the

Court of Criminal Appeal), industrial (before the Industrial Appeal Court), and appeals under the Justices Act of 1902 (WA). The latter are appeals from the lower level criminal Court of Petty Sessions and are conducted by a single judge of the Supreme Court. Curiously, these appeals fall within the civil jurisdiction of the Supreme Court. Decisions of a single appellate judge may be further appealed to the full court of the Supreme Court ("the full court") in cases where leave is granted.

Decisions by a single judge of the District or Supreme Court in the civil jurisdiction may be appealed to the full court. The Supreme Court Act of 1935 (WA) dictates that the full court be constituted by a bench of any two or more judges drawn from the bench of the Supreme Court, though in practice the number of judges presiding over a full court appeal is almost always three. There is no formal time limit placed upon oral submissions before the full court, and written reasons for the decision of the court are published.

The Court of Criminal Appeal (CCA) hears appeals from trials by jury or by judge alone, conducted in the Supreme, District, or Children's courts. The CCA is constituted by a bench of at least three judges drawn from the Supreme Court. Appeals against conviction or sentence (or both) are made under the criminal code on grounds including error of law or fact. A successful appeal against conviction requires that the error have resulted in a miscarriage of justice rendering the verdict unsafe or unsatisfactory. In these circumstances the CCA may order a retrial, direct a full acquittal, or substitute a conviction for a lesser offense. In successful appeals against sentence, the court may alter the sentence. Appeals made by the director of public prosecutions on behalf of the Crown are also heard by the CCA. Such appeals are generally made against the leniency of sentence and are governed by the criminal code. Prior to the listing of an appeal, the appellant must appear before a single judge of the CCA on several motion days to settle the contents of the appeal book and define the grounds of the appeal. This "case management" approach has proved effective in limiting delays in the hearing of criminal appeals, particularly those conducted by self-represented appellants.

The Industrial Appeal Court (IAC) is constituted by a bench of three judges; it hears appeals from decisions of the Industrial Relations Commission (WA). Unlike the other appellate jurisdictions of the Supreme Court, the IAC may be constituted only by judges of the Supreme Court who are specially commissioned for the purpose. At present there are four such judges, one of whom is designated as president.

The District Court

The District Court, constituted under the District Court of Western Australia Act of 1969 (WA), is the state's intermediate court. The court is constituted by twenty judges and a chief judge. The District Court is required to conduct both civil and criminal circuit court sittings in regional centers on a regular basis. In its civil jurisdiction the District Court may deal with cases involving claims of up to $250,000, with unlimited jurisdiction for damages for personal injury. The criminal jurisdiction of the court covers any indictable offense carrying the penalty of imprisonment for a term of years. As with the Supreme Court, criminal trials in the District Court are conducted by a judge and jury of twelve or, in certain circumstances, by a judge alone. The appellate jurisdiction of the District Court is limited to civil cases on appeal from the Local Court and from specified tribunals.

The Children's Court

The current Children's Court is constituted under the Children's Court of Western Australia Act of 1988 (WA), although separate juvenile courts have existed within the state since 1907. The court is staffed by a president (drawn from the judicial bench of the District Court) and a number of magistrates. The court exercises jurisdiction in cases dealing with offenses committed by juveniles under the age of eighteen years. There is no restriction upon the type of offense that may be dealt with by the court. Trials are conducted without juries, though a juvenile defendant may elect to be tried in the Supreme or District Court before a jury. Under the criminal code, a minor under the age of ten is not criminally responsible.

Magistrates' Courts

The Magistrates' Courts are the lower level of court in the state and are staffed by thirty-five stipendiary magistrates, a chief, and a deputy chief magistrate. There are registries in six urban and twenty-two regional centers throughout the state. Magistrates are required to conduct circuit courts at all regional registries on a regular basis. The Magistrates' Courts are named in direct reference to the jurisdiction in which they are convened: the Local Court (civil jurisdiction) and the Court of Petty Sessions (criminal jurisdiction). Each jurisdiction has a different enabling act. In its civil guise as the Local Court, a magistrate may deal with claims for the recovery of a debt up to $25,000. The court has a small claims division with a limit of $3,000 and a residential tenancy disputes division. The criminal Court of Petty Sessions deals with summary (or less serious) offenses or certain indictable offenses in which an accused has elected to have the matter dealt with summarily. The Justices Act of 1902 (WA) allows for either a single magistrate or two justices of the peace to preside over matters in the Court of Petty Sessions. The Court of Petty Sessions also conducts committal proceedings on indictment for referral to superior courts.

Family Court of Western Australia

The Family Court is vested with both state and federal jurisdiction and adjudicates upon matters such as distribution of marital property, divorce, and custody of children. The court is staffed by judges and magistrates, and although it is uniquely state run, its operating costs are paid from federal funds.

Other State Courts and Tribunals

The state convenes a Liquor Licensing Court and a Coroner's Court. Significant state tribunals include the Small Claims Tribunal, Commercial Tribunal, and the Equal Opportunity Tribunal. There are also boards reviewing parole, supervised release orders, mentally impaired defendants, guardianship and administration, appeal costs, and assessment of criminal injuries compensation. These boards and tribunals often possess adjudicative functions, are less formal than courts, and are politically independent.

CURRENT STRUCTURE: EXECUTIVE BRANCH JUDICIAL FUNCTIONS

The Attorney General and Solicitor General

The attorney general is a political position appointed by the premier from within the governing party's ranks. The attorney general is the first law officer of the state and the minister responsible for the administration of justice within the state. The solicitor general is an independent office, the principal legal adviser to the attorney-general and the government.

Administrative Agencies

The Ministry of Justice provides the main administrative support to courts, boards, and tribunals. Its functions include the provision of public trustee and victim services. The ministry is also responsible for the operation of offender management services and prisons.

Criminal Prosecution and Defense

The Office of the Director of Public Prosecutions conducts criminal prosecutions and appeals in the District and Supreme courts and committal proceedings in the Court of Petty Sessions. Trials of summary offenses in the Court of Petty Sessions are usually conducted by a police prosecutor.

The Legal Aid Commission of Western Australia is an independent statutory body that offers free (or nominal fee) criminal defense and family law advice to needy members of the community. Full-time duty lawyers are available at most Magistrates' and children's courts. The Aboriginal Legal Service assists defendants of indigenous descent.

STAFFING

Judiciary

Judges of the District and Supreme courts are generally recruited from the senior or Queen's Counsel ranks of the state bar. Judges are appointed to office by the attorney general in consultation with the chief justice, members of the judiciary, and representatives of the state bar association and law society. While the selection of judges is predominantly political, all effort is made thereafter to ensure the independence of the judiciary. Thus the tenure of judges is not limited by a term of years but ceases upon the attainment of the age of seventy. The bench of the Supreme Court is not widely representative of the community, being mainly staffed by middle-class Anglo-Saxon males. However, the lower and intermediate courts of the state have claim to a slightly more gender-representative bench, and at least one indigenous member.

Legal Profession

There are three university law schools in the state offering degrees of three years (for graduates of other disciplines) or four years (for students undertaking a bachelor of laws without a previous degree). Law graduates must complete one year of supervised articled clerkship, usually in a law firm, and a twenty-five-day training program conducted by the Legal Practice Board before becoming eligible for admission. A newly admitted barrister and solicitor of the state Supreme Court must then undertake a further year of restricted practice before becoming a fully qualified legal practitioner. Although the legal profession of the state is not split—such that those doing the work of solicitors may also act as advocates in court—there exists an independent bar within the state, the members of which undertake most of the superior and appellate court advocacy. Lawyers are subject to requirements of continuing legal education and must attend a required number of professional practice and ethics courses each year.

Discipline

While the Law Society of Western Australia maintains the professional conduct rules of the legal profession, formal responsibility for the discipline of legal practitioners lies with the Legal Practice Board and its related disciplinary tribunal.

RELATIONSHIP TO THE NATIONAL SYSTEM

The Supreme Court of Western Australia is bound by the authoritative precedent of the High Court of Australia. In limited circumstances, where special leave is granted by the High Court, an appellant may appeal a decision of the full court or the Court of Criminal Appeal to the High Court of Australia. Appeals from the state Family Court are heard by the full bench of the Family Court of Australia.

Tatum L. Hands

See also Australia; Common Law; Constitutionalism; Equity; Judicial Independence; Magistrates—Common Law Systems; New South Wales; Northern Territory of Australia; Privy Council; Queensland; South Australia; Tasmania; Victoria, State of

References and further reading

Australian Bureau of Statistics. "Australia Now—A Statistical Profile." http://www.abs.gov.au/ausstats/ABS%40.nsf/94713ad445ff1425ca25682000192af2!OpenView (accessed July 28, 2000).

Battye, James S. 1924. *Western Australia: A History from Its Discovery to the Inauguration of the Commonwealth.* Oxford: Clarendon Press.

Bennett, John M., and Alex C. Castles. 1979. *A Source Book of Australian Legal History: Source Materials from the Eighteenth to the Twentieth Centuries.* Sydney: Law Book Company.

Castles, Alex C. 1982. *An Australian Legal History.* Sydney: Law Book Company.

Law Reform Commission of Western Australia. 1999. *Review of the Criminal and Civil Justice System: Final Report.* Perth: State Law Publisher.

Ministry of Justice. "Courts and Their Jurisdictions." http://www.justice.wa.gov.au/division/courts/jurisd.htm (accessed October 8, 2000).

Parkinson, Patrick. 1994. *Tradition and Change in Australian Law.* Sydney: Law Book Company.

Russell, Enid M. 1980. *A History of the Law in Western Australia and Its Development from 1829–1979.* Perth: University of Western Australia Press.

WISCONSIN

GENERAL INFORMATION

Wisconsin is a U.S. state located in the upper Great Lakes region. Covering just over 56,000 square miles, Wisconsin borders Minnesota to the west, Lake Michigan to the east, Lake Superior and the Upper Peninsula of Michigan to the north, and Illinois and Iowa to the south and southwest. Wisconsin's estimated 2000 population was nearly 5.5 million residents, many of whom are clustered around the cities of Milwaukee, Madison, Racine, and Green Bay.

Wisconsin's early history as a territory and state was shaped by the lure of inexpensive frontier property for fur-trading, mining, agriculture, and lumbering, as well as the settlement patterns of New England Yankees and European immigrants (especially Germans and Norwegians) seeking economic and religious freedom. Like many other Midwestern states, Wisconsin began to develop an industrial base in the late nineteenth century, attended by rapid urban growth. Along with industrialization came a strong progressivist tradition of advocacy for labor and other left-liberal causes in the state, personified by Robert M. "Fighting Bob" LaFollette's long career as a U.S. representative, state governor, and U.S. senator until his death in 1925. The late 1930s, however, marked the beginning of twenty years of Republican Party ascendancy, including the rise and fall of Wisconsin senator Joseph McCarthy, who made his name as a controversial leader of anticommunists during the Red Scare of the 1950s. From the 1960s to the present, the two major parties have competed on roughly equal terms.

EVOLUTION AND HISTORY

The land encompassing modern-day Wisconsin was included in the French sphere of influence until the region was ceded to the British following the French and Indian War in 1763. After the British relinquished control of the area to the United States in the wake of the War of 1812, Wisconsin was governed by the Northwest Ordinance of 1787, an interstate compact passed by the Continental Congress that set the basic rules for governing territories north of the Ohio River. At different points in time, Wisconsin was considered a part of other Northwest Territories in the United States—Indiana, Illinois, and Michigan—until in 1836 it achieved its own territorial status as the other areas joined the Union as full-fledged states.

In the summer of 1846, the U.S. Congress authorized the inhabitants of the Wisconsin Territory to form their own state. Members of Congress from northern states recognized that Wisconsin, as part of the Northwest Territories, would be admitted as a free state, thus counterbalancing the admittance of Florida and Texas as slave states in 1845. Moreover, the city of Milwaukee was developing as a major port of entry on Lake Michigan, and its sizable population rivaled Chicago at the time. The moment seemed ripe for statehood.

In response to Congress's authorization, the people of the territory immediately convened a constitutional convention in Madison, the present-day capital, to consider statehood and begin to develop fundamental law. The convention drafted the first constitutional proposal by the end of 1846 and submitted it for voter approval on April 6, 1847. The voters rejected the proposal by a 60–40 percent margin because of several controversial provisions in the draft. Chief among these provisions were a ban on the establishment of most banks in the state, the exemption of substantial amounts of real property from execution for debts, and guarantees that women could control the property they brought into a marriage.

A second convention submitted its draft of a revised constitution on March 13, 1848. The proposal easily passed a territorywide vote the following month. The second convention integrated several features of the federal constitution and the old Northwest Ordinance, including a basic institutional structure of separated powers and guarantees of various civil liberties (for example, habeas corpus, jury trials, religious freedom, and certain rights of property and inheritance). On May 29, 1848, Congress admitted Wisconsin to the Union as the thirtieth state. Its constitution, which recently celebrated its sesquicentennial, ranks as the sixth oldest state constitution in continuous use in the United States.

The judicial system was originally composed of five districts, and the judges presiding over these districts would meet en banc as an appellate tribunal to hear challenges from their own trial courts. The motivation for this arrangement was apparently efficiency and cost-consciousness, but soon the legislature saw the need for an independently organized Supreme Court. In 1853, Wisconsin established its Supreme Court by seating three justices through a statewide election. A constitutional amendment in 1903 expanded the size of the court to its current number of seven members.

The Wisconsin state legislature created many lower courts over the years in a rather haphazard way, leaving little uniformity across counties and several instances of courts with overlapping jurisdictions. Complicating matters further were hundreds of justices of the peace who enforced local ordinances. In 1959, the state legislature initiated a reorganization effort that abolished special statutory courts and justices of the peace and instituted standards for a uniform system of jurisdiction and procedure in the counties. This effort was part of a broader movement among the states to unify fragmented and highly decentralized judicial systems. In addition, to ease the workload of the Supreme Court, Wisconsin established an intermediate Court of Appeals by constitutional amendment in 1978.

CURRENT STRUCTURE

Wisconsin's constitutional framework of state government includes three branches: legislature, executive, and judicial. As is the case in the U.S. national government and most other states, the legislature is bicameral (a senate and assembly). The governor heads an extensive executive branch, which includes five other elected constitutional officers and several dozen administrative departments and independent agencies. The judicial branch is composed of the Wisconsin Supreme Court, the Court of Appeals, and circuit and municipal courts, as well as associated administrative and regulatory departments (see figure).

The Wisconsin legislature has authorized local level municipal courts to exercise original jurisdiction for violations of municipal ordinances. Most municipal court cases involve traffic matters, including first-time drunken driving offenses, as well as truancy, underage drinking,

Legal Structure of Wisconsin Courts

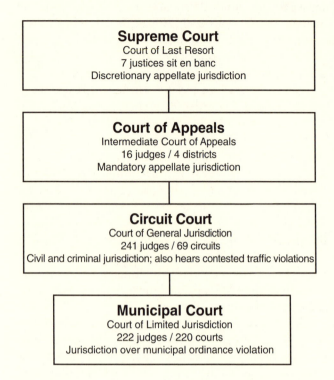

Supreme Court
Court of Last Resort
7 justices sit en banc
Discretionary appellate jurisdiction

Court of Appeals
Intermediate Court of Appeals
16 judges / 4 districts
Mandatory appellate jurisdiction

Circuit Court
Court of General Jurisdiction
241 judges / 69 circuits
Civil and criminal jurisdiction; also hears contested traffic violations

Municipal Court
Court of Limited Jurisdiction
222 judges / 220 courts
Jurisdiction over municipal ordinance violation

some minor drug offenses, and curfew violations. As of May 2000, there were 220 municipal courts in the state of Wisconsin.

Wisconsin's circuit courts act as the trial courts of general jurisdiction in the state. The circuit courts have original jurisdiction in virtually all major criminal and civil matters, as well as appellate jurisdiction over municipal court decisions. There are more than 240 circuit judgeships in the state, divided among 69 judicial circuits that are generally coextensive with county lines. Many of the more populous circuits with heavy caseloads have multiple branches, each with its own judge. For administrative purposes, each circuit belongs to one of ten districts, each supervised by a chief judge. The chief judge, whom the supreme court appoints from among the district's judges, supervises personnel and manages caseflow in the district.

With the exception of one prosecutorial unit encompassing two counties, each county has its own district attorney with prosecutorial authority (there are a total of seventy-one district attorneys in the state). Wisconsin also maintains a public defender's office, an independent state agency that provides legal representation to the indigent in criminal and certain civil matters. The office serves well over 100,000 clients a year, mostly by staff attorneys (the office contracts with private attorneys to handle about 35 percent of its caseload). In addition, the national government's Legal Services Corporation funds four separate advocacy organizations for Wisconsin's poorest citizens: Wisconsin Judicare, which serves poor clients in thirty-three counties and has a particular outreach to Wisconsin's Native American population; Legal Action of Wisconsin, which provides services through offices in Milwaukee, Madison, Racine, and Kenosha; Legal Services of Northeastern Wisconsin; and Western Wisconsin Legal Services. The LSC's Wisconsin budget for 2001 was $4.6 million.

The intermediate Court of Appeals hears cases from the lower courts. The sixteen judges on the Court of Appeals are spread over four appellate districts and sit in three-judge panels for most cases. The court has mandatory jurisdiction in civil, criminal, and administrative agency cases.

The Wisconsin Supreme Court, which sits in Madison, is the court of last resort in the state and exercises largely appellate jurisdiction over a wide range of subject matter, including appeals in civil, criminal, and administrative law cases. No appeals come to the Supreme Court as a matter of right; the court has complete discretion in case selection. The court will hear an appeal if at least three out of seven justices vote to do so. Its decisions-on-the-merits are published in *Wisconsin Reports.*

The chief justice of the Wisconsin Supreme Court has special duties as the administrative head of the state's judicial system. With the assistance of the director of state courts, the chief justice performs a general oversight function and can redirect resources to courts that have vacancies or have become overwhelmed by busy dockets.

It should also be noted that administrative law challenges are often heard in quasi-judicial settings in Wisconsin. Initial challenges to administrative rulings are considered by boards within particular agencies or by the Division of Hearings and Appeals, a quasi-judicial body associated with the Wisconsin Department of Administration. These decisions can be appealed to the Court of Appeals.

NOTABLE FEATURES OF LAW/LEGAL SYSTEM
The drafters of Wisconsin's Constitution engaged in the common practice of selective borrowing from familiar constitutional models at the time. The document's basic structure of separated institutional powers is, of course, modeled after the U.S. Constitution. The drafters were also doubtless aware of the various state constitutions being drafted throughout the mid- to late-1840s (that is, New York, Iowa, and Texas), and the imprint of Jacksonian populism was left on certain provisions, including short terms of office for elected officials (for example, two years for governor in 1848, subsequently changed to four).

The state has been at the forefront of many political issues that intersect with constitutional law. After statehood, Wisconsin consistently opposed the extension of slavery into U.S. territories, and granted suffrage to African American men in 1849. Wisconsin is also among the minority of states (twelve out of fifty) to abolish the death penalty, which it did by statute in 1853—the second state (after Michigan) to do so. Beginning in the 1920s, the state developed an active role in the development of labor law, and many labor disputes originating in Wisconsin have ultimately made their way to the U.S. Supreme Court. More recently, the state has experimented with school vouchers, welfare reform, and criminal sentencing guideline revisions, all of which have met with challenges in state or federal courts.

Wisconsin's treatment of Native Americans is another notable aspect of its legal history. Wisconsin is home to a Native American population that is not only among the largest in states east of the Mississippi but is also marked by a diversity of tribal and linguistic groupings. Early in Wisconsin history, this diversity made collective action against European settlement difficult. The fur trade and subsequent settlement displaced many tribes; those who remained were soon integrated into the federal reservation system. Reflecting broader trends, Wisconsin's tribes today have turned to gaming to reinvigorate chronically impoverished reservations, a source of endless controversy in the state legislature, courts, and political culture. The state has eleven tribal courts that serve the Native American population over a range of subject matter that varies from court to court.

STAFFING

The seven justices on the Supreme Court are elected to a ten-year term on a nonpartisan, statewide ballot. Court of appeals and circuit court judges serve six-year terms after election on nonpartisan ballots in their respective districts. (The governor appoints judges to fill vacancies between elections.) Municipal judges are also elected in nonpartisan, districtwide elections, but local governing authorities fix the term of office at two or four years. Each court may use reserve judges—often retired judges appointed by the chief justice—to fill temporary vacancies or ease caseloads. In like manner, Wisconsin's district attorneys are elected to two-year terms.

The primary mandated qualification for a Supreme Court, Court of Appeals, or Circuit Court judgeship is that a candidate must have been licensed to practice law in Wisconsin at least five years prior to taking office. There is no such statutory requirement for municipal judges—indeed, more than half of these sitting judges had no formal legal training in 2000—but local governments may at their discretion require municipal judges to be attorneys.

Of the 12,217 lawyers in Wisconsin in 1995, 8,565 were in private practice. The ratio of lawyers to the population was 416 to 1, which ranks Wisconsin thirty-seventh among all fifty states and the District of Columbia. There are two ABA-approved law schools in the state: the University of Wisconsin Law School, a public institution located at the flagship state university in Madison, and Marquette University Law School, a division of a private Catholic university in Milwaukee. Under a unique "diploma privilege" arrangement, graduates of these two law schools are not required to take a bar examination to practice in the state. Others are admitted to the Wisconsin bar through either an examination or certification that they have practiced in another state.

The Board of Bar Examiners, a regulatory agency of the Wisconsin Supreme Court, has oversight over admittance to the state bar. The Board of Attorney's Professional Responsibility, the Judicial Commission, and the Judicial Education Committee attend to issues of lawyer and judicial misconduct and continuing legal education in the state.

RELATIONSHIP TO NATIONAL SYSTEM

Consistent with the U.S. system of dual sovereignty, the Wisconsin Supreme Court has final authority to review court challenges under the Wisconsin Constitution and other cases arising in the state, except those cases addressing federal issues. In the federal system, Wisconsin is served by Eastern and Western district courts, and it shares the 7th Circuit Court of Appeals with Illinois and Indiana.

Legal disputes originating in the state have often taken on national importance. In *Ableman v. Booth* (1858), the Wisconsin Supreme Court held that the Fugitive Slave Act, which required runaway slaves who sought refuge in free states to be returned to their owners, was unconstitutional. The U.S. Supreme Court eventually reversed the decision, but it was an important display of antislavery sentiment and defiance toward the federal government early in the state's history. The U.S. Supreme Court's review of several Wisconsin labor law cases, as well as its religious freedom decision in *Wisconsin v. Yoder* in 1972 (holding that the free exercise clause of the U.S. Constitution protects the Amish practice of removing their children from school after the eighth grade), were integral elements of constitutional development.

Kevin den Dulk

See also Illinois; Michigan; Native American Law, Traditional; United States—Federal System; United States—State Systems
References and further reading
Barish, Lawrence S., and Patricia E. Meloy, eds. 1999. *Wisconsin Blue Book, 1999–2000.* Madison: Wisconsin Department of Administration.
Carson, Clara N. 1999. *The Lawyer Statistical Report: The U.S. Legal Profession in 1995.* Chicago: American Bar Foundation.
Rottman, David B., et al. 2000. *State Court Organization 1998.* Washington, DC: Bureau of Justice Statistics.
"Symposium: Celebrating Wisconsin's Constitution 150 Years Later." 1998. *Wisconsin Law Review* (1998): 661–903.

WORLD TRADE ORGANIZATION

MISSION

The central mission of the World Trade Organization (WTO) is to facilitate the negotiation, monitoring, and enforcement of interstate agreements aimed at "the substantial reduction of tariffs and other barriers to trade and . . . the elimination of discriminatory treatment in international trade relations" (article 1 of the Agreement Establishing the WTO). The WTO promotes negotiation by offering appropriate periodic forums. It carries out its monitoring function through the WTO Trade Policy Review Mechanism, which evaluates individual members' trade policies, and council and committee systems, which oversee implementation of each of the WTO's substantive agreements. Enforcement is the purview of the WTO's Dispute Settlement Body, which oversees the formation of dispute settlement panels, the adoption of dispute settlement reports, and the authorization of sanctions.

HISTORY

The WTO was formed on January 1, 1995, pursuant to an agreement signed on April 15, 1994, in Marrakesh, Morocco. It is the successor to a de facto organization arising from the General Agreement on Tariffs and Trade (GATT). The GATT was intended to be a substantive agreement, not an international organization. Its origins date back to the end of World War II, when British and U.S. officials met to negotiate a new international economic architecture to govern international economic relations. Initially, these negotiators envisaged forming a triad of institutions: the International Monetary Fund (IMF), the International Bank for Reconstruction and Development (IBRD), and the International Trade Organization (ITO). The IMF and IBRD were both formed in 1945 and were to address international monetary policy and the financing of postwar economic reconstruction. Negotiations for the creation of the ITO were concluded in 1948 in Havana, Cuba, upon signature of the Havana Charter. The U.S. Congress, however, never ratified the charter, which it believed was too broad and interventionist in scope (covering competition, employment, and development) and riddled with loopholes that undermined the United States' goal of creating a more liberal trading order. Eight of the twenty-three original contracting parties nonetheless agreed to apply GATT as a "provisional" agreement, effective January 1, 1948, until it could be folded into the ITO. But because the ITO was never formed, the GATT became a specialized agency of the United Nations, headquartered in Geneva, Switzerland, with a permanent secretariat. There have been eight GATT negotiating rounds, through which tariff rates have been progressively lowered. This process culminated in the Uruguay Round (1986–1994) and the formation of the WTO, with GATT membership steadily rising over the years.

The WTO system represents four major developments from its GATT predecessor. First, the WTO is formally recognized as an international organization. It now has a legal status independent of the United Nations. Second, the Uruguay Round of trade negotiations resulted in a significant expansion in the scope of world trading rules under a single institutional package. It comprised fifteen substantive agreements, including those covering intellectual property rights (Agreement on Trade-Related Aspects of Intellectual Property Rights, or TRIPS), services (General Agreement on Trade in Services, or GATS), agriculture, textiles, technical and sanitary standards, customs valuation, rules of origin, import licensing, antidumping, subsidies, and safeguards. WTO members agree to be bound by all these agreements as a condition of membership. This package of agreements constituted a tradeoff between the interestes of developed and developing countries, as developing countries agreed to binding rules on services and intellectual property protection in exchange for a commitment from the United States and the European Union (EU) to liberalize their textile and agricultural sectors. By the WTO's third ministerial meeting in Seattle (December 1999), however, most developing countries argued that the bargain had been unequal, for U.S. and EU textile and agricultural markets remained relatively protected.

Third, a few of these agreements changed the traditional orientation from the GATT's focus on negative integration (what governments must not do, such as discriminate against foreign goods) to a focus on positive integration (what governments must do, such as protect and enforce intellectual property rights and ensure competition in service sectors listed in a party's GATS schedule). Fourth, the parties to the WTO agreed to a uniform and more legalized dispute settlement system.

LEGAL PRINCIPLES

The core principles of GATT law are nondiscrimination (articles 1 and 3, which require most-favored-nation treatment of all members' products and national treatment of members' "like" products), the respect of bound maximum tariffs (article 2 and its schedules), and a prohibition on the use of quantitative restrictions (article 11). These principles are subject to certain exceptions, such as those needed to protect national security, health, public morals, natural resources, the national economy (including temporary restraint on imports that might cause serious injury to an industry), the formation of free trade agreements and customs unions (such as the North American Free Trade Agreement and the European Union), and certain provisions pertaining to developing countries. The TRIPS agreement adds intellectual property protection to these core principles.

The views of GATT members on the nature of the GATT's dispute settlement system were divided and often inconsistent. Europeans tended to take a more pragmatic approach, arguing that the GATT system should be seen as a conciliatory diplomatic process to maintain a balance of trade concessions. The United States tended to take a more legalistic approach, maintaining that the GATT was a system of rules to be enforced by judicial panels. This latter view largely prevailed with the advent of the WTO dispute settlement system, under which defendants may no longer block the formation of panels or the adoption of panel reports, and the time periods for decisions were tightened. Once adopted, WTO panel and Appellate Body decisions are binding, and if the losing party does not comply, then the complainant may retaliate by withdrawing equivalent trade concessions. The decisions do not have the force of stare decisis (binding precedent) but are taken into account, where relevant, in subsequent disputes. The Appellate Body has ruled that panels must take account of the rules of interpretation set forth in the 1969 Vienna Convention on the Law of Treaties when applying WTO agreements, thereby somewhat integrating public international law into WTO judicial practice.

MEMBERSHIP AND PARTICIPATION

As of July 26, 2001, there were 142 members of the World Trade Organization, all of which were countries other than the European Community countries and Hong Kong, which has a separate customs territory from that of the People's Republic of China. There were around thirty applicants in line to become members, including China and the Russian Federation. Only WTO members have the right to speak, present papers, and vote at WTO meetings. Similarly, only WTO members may initiate claims before the WTO Dispute Settlement Body. The WTO has, however, invited other international organizations to attend meetings as observers. A representative of the IMF sits at all meetings of the WTO Committee on Balance of Payments Restrictions. The WTO Appellate Body has accepted, and has held that panels may accept, *amicus curiae* briefs from private parties, including affected industries and not-for-profit nongovernmental organizations. As of July 2001, however, panel and Appellate Body proceedings remained closed to the general public, although the United States has proposed that they be opened.

PROCEDURE

Members of the WTO commit to refer all disputes under WTO rules to the Dispute Settlement Body (DSB), in accordance with article 23 of the Dispute Settlement Understanding. The DSB, which consists of all WTO members, meets approximately once every two

The Dispute Resolution Process of the WTO

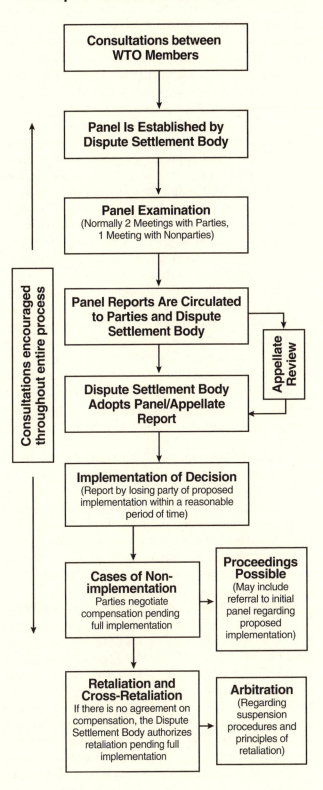

weeks. It automatically convenes dispute settlement panels, adopts panel and Appellate Body reports, and authorizes retaliation for failure to comply with a report unless all members of the DSB decide otherwise by consensus. This is a reversal of the former GATT consensus rule, pursuant to which any party, including the defendant, could block the formation of a panel or the adoption of a panel report.

Only WTO members may file claims before the DSB. First, they formally request "consultations" with another contracting party in respect of the relevant WTO agreements. If the parties fail to settle their dispute within sixty days, then the complainant may request the formation of a dispute settlement panel. The panel normally is to be formed within thirty days following the request and to render its decision from six to nine months following its formation. The parties first exchange submissions and then respectively present their case and defense, which is followed by a second round of submissions and presentations (and sometimes a third round). Third parties, defined as those WTO members with a "substantial interest" in the case (which includes a systemic interest), may also present their views. The panel may seek advice from outside experts, in particular where a case raises scientific or other technical issues. Panels and the Appellate Body have agreed that private lawyers may present party positions in the hearings, another change from former GATT practice.

The panel first submits the factual section of its report, followed by a full interim report, to the parties for comment. The period of party review is not to exceed two weeks, after which the panel issues its final report, which is circulated three weeks later to all WTO members. Panel reports are then adopted by the DSB, unless one of the parties appeals the decision to the Appellate Body or the DSB decides by consensus against adoption. The Appellate Body is then to render its decision from sixty to ninety days (although it has exceeded this time period). The decision, together with the panel report (as it may have been modified), is again automatically adopted by the DSB unless the DSB decides by consensus against adoption. The losing party must state within thirty days of adoption whether it intends to implement the report's findings and announce the "reasonable" time in which it intends to do so (interpreted by the Appellate Body, in the *Japan-Alcoholic Beverages* case, as fifteen months). If the losing party fails to implement the decision within this period, it must compensate the complainant by granting new trade concessions equal in amount to the withdrawn concessions. If the parties fail to agree on mutually satisfactory compensation, then the complainant may ask the DSB for permission to retaliate against the losing party by suspending trade concessions in an equivalent amount. If the parties disagree on the amount of re-

taliation, it is determined through arbitration (typically by the original panel). This occurred for the first time in 2000 in two cases, *European Communities-Bananas* and *European Communities-Meat Hormones*.

STAFFING

Delegates from the WTO members are elected to chair the Dispute Settlement Body, the General Counsel's Office, and subsidiary councils and committees of the DSB. These delegates preside over all meetings under their charge. In addition, the WTO has a permanent secretariat, headed by the WTO director-general, who is supported by four deputies and a staff of approximately 500 persons. The secretariat is divided into divisions, including a legal division responsible for assisting with the panel process and a smaller Appellate Body division responsible for assisting the seven members of the Appellate Body.

The WTO dispute settlement system consists of three levels, each of which involves different personnel. First, parties engage in bilateral consultations, during which they may (but rarely do) request the good offices, conciliation, or mediation services of the director-general. Second, where consultations do not resolve disputes, ad hoc panels are formed consisting of three panelists. These panelists are selected by mutual agreement of the parties to the dispute, failing which either party may request the director-general to designate them. Third, any party to a dispute may appeal a panel decision to the Appellate Body, which in turn designates three of its seven members to the case.

Although many panelists have served on more than one panel, few have served frequently. Over 85 percent of panelists have been government officials, typically delegates to the WTO from third countries deemed to be neutral; often they lack legal training. Some commentators maintain that members of the secretariat's Legal Division typically have greater knowledge of WTO case law than do panelists and, as a result, may exercise significant influence in panel proceedings and decisions. Others state that panels have become significantly more professional than in the past and that secretariat influence is exaggerated. Pursuant to the Dispute Settlement Understanding, the secretariat has compiled a roster of nongovernmental panelists to be considered for panels, on the basis of recommendations from WTO members. Academics have sometimes been selected as panelists, but they remain a minority presence.

CASELOAD

More than 650 complaints have been filed since the formation of the GATT in 1948. This is more than six times the number of cases brought before the International Court of Justice since its conception. Moreover, the rate of litigation has significantly increased since the WTO's formation, reflecting increased cross-border trade during the 1990s, expanded WTO membership, and the broadened scope of WTO legal obligations. During the first six years and four months of the WTO, 234 complaints were brought on 180 distinct matters, resulting in 51 adopted panel and Appellate Body reports. Since 1948, almost two-thirds of all formal requests for consultations have been settled before the issuance of a panel report, typically confirming or granting alternative trade concessions. The United States is by far the most active participant in the WTO-GATT system, being a complainant or defendant in over 50 percent of all cases since 1948, followed by the European Union, which was a party in over one-third of all cases.

IMPACT

The law of the GATT and the WTO has facilitated cross-border trade, complementing the impact of reduced transportation and communication costs in a globalizing economy. Between 1948 and 1998, cross-border trade expanded almost three times as fast as world production. A relatively effective WTO-GATT dispute settlement system may have contributed to this increase, for governments are more likely to agree to reciprocal trade concessions if they believe that bargains will be kept. Overall, parties have complied with most GATT and WTO panel decisions and have settled the majority of disputes in the regime's shadow. Supporters of the system maintain that it has resulted in significant increases in productivity, economic growth, and global wealth, making more products available at lower cost throughout the world. Critics, in contrast, maintain that unless accompanied by domestic social safety nets and other social policies, WTO-facilitated trade liberalization policies lead to widening income disparity and decreased bargaining power of labor vis-à-vis capital. Many critics are wary of the influence of large U.S. and EU corporate interests, in particular in relation to the TRIPS Agreement.

Gregory C. Shaffer

See also Dispute Resolution under Regional Trade Agreements; European Union

References and further reading
Bhala, Raj, and Kevin Kennedy. 1998. *World Trade Law.* Charlottesville: Lexis Law Publishing.
Croome, John. 1999. *Reshaping the World Trading System: A History of the Uruguay Round.* Boston: Kluwer Law International.
Dam, Kenneth. 1970. *The GATT: Law and International Economic Organization.* Chicago: University of Chicago Press.
Gilpin, Robert. 1987. *The Political Economy of International Relations.* Princeton: Princeton University Press.
Hudec, Robert. 1993. *Enforcing International Trade Law: The Evolution of the Modern GATT Legal System.* Salem, NH: Butterworth Legal Publishers.
Jackson, John Howard. 1998. *The World Trade Organization: Constitution and Jurisprudence.* London: Royal Institute of Internal Affairs.
———. 1997. *The World Trading System: Law and Policy of International Economic Relations.* Cambridge: MIT Press.
Petersmann, Ernst-Ulrich. 1997. *The GATT/WTO Dispute Settlement System: International Law, International Organizations, and Dispute Settlement.* Boston: Kluwer Law International.
Rodrik, Dani. 1997. *Has Globalization Gone Too Far?* Washington, DC: Institute of International Economics.
World Trade Organization. Annual Report. 1998,1999, and 2000.
———. "Dispute Settlement List of Panel and Appellate Body Reports." http://www.wto.org/english/tratop_e/dispu_e/distab_e.htm (cited September 1, 2000).

WRIT OF CERTIORARI
See Certiorari, Writ of

WRIT OF HABEAS CORPUS
See Habeas Corpus, Writ of

WYOMING

GENERAL INFORMATION

The state of Wyoming is located in the northern Rocky Mountains. While it is the ninth largest state in the union in area (97,818 square miles), it simultaneously ranks last among the states in the number of inhabitants (493,782 in 2000). Its low population density of 5.0 persons per square mile also makes it one of the most sparsely settled states, with small towns under thirty thousand residents the prevalent form of political community. With a racial makeup that is 94.2 percent white, the state's largest minorities are Hispanics (5.7 percent) and American Indians (2.1 percent). Nearly half of the land in Wyoming is owned by the federal government in the form of national parks, forests, grasslands, recreation areas, monuments, and lands under the jurisdiction of the Bureau of Land Management.

In a climate that is generally harsh, cold, and arid, Wyoming's economy has for the past fifty years been highly dependent on extractive industries (coal, oil and gas, and soda ash) and the fluctuating prices of these commodities on the world market. Many of the companies involved are controlled by out-of-state corporations, and that, when combined with the considerable presence of the federal government in the state, gives rise to talk of Wyoming's "colonial" economy. Although ranching and farming have long underscored the image of the cowboy in the state's popular culture, the role of agriculture in Wyoming's economy has declined in recent decades to the point where it produces just 4 percent of the state's gross state product, and most jobs are in the governmental and service sectors. Meanwhile, economic diversification, such as through tourism and light manufacturing, has become the watchword of the state's political and business leadership. The chief sources of revenue for financing the activities of state and local government are sales, property, and mineral severance taxes, interest earned from investment of state monies, and transfers of funds from the federal government.

Although the political culture of the state is in many ways a smaller-scale version of the national picture, there are important differences in emphasis. Wyoming's is more conservative, resting upon a bedrock of egalitarian individualism. Wyomingites cherish the rights of persons to work out their own destiny, free of regulation by government directive, especially from Washington. By and large, they prefer self-reliance and minimal government, oppose tax increases, and are suspicious of new policy initiatives. Distrust of the federal government as wasteful and run for the benefit of a few special interests is pervasive. Traditional democratic values, such as popular participation in government and majority rule, are prized, but at the same time there is a general attitude of live-and-let-live as far as minorities, dissidents, and eccentrics are concerned. This political culture has largely benefited the Republican Party, which historically has dominated state and local politics in Wyoming.

EVOLUTION AND HISTORY OF THE WYOMING LEGAL AND JUDICIAL SYSTEM

The preceding sketch of Wyoming's geography, economy, and political culture is important in understanding the development of its legal and judicial system. If the legal aspect of a society's framework of law and government is its constitution, Wyoming's fundamental legal charter is the Constitution of 1890. Adopted in convention in Cheyenne after only twenty-five days of deliberation (during which lawyers played a dominant role), it has survived for more than one hundred years as the state's only constitution in a nation of states where discard and total revision of state charters has been commonplace. The stability that marks the Wyoming Constitution has much to do with the fact that it is *practical*—that is, a collection of principles and structures gathered from earlier documents of its kind (mainly from existing state constitutions) that had proved workable in environments similar to that of Wyoming. Even provisions that were innovative, such as female suffrage and vesting ownership of surface waters in the state, were linked to the Wyoming environment, in which female settlers were few and water resources scarce.

This durability notwithstanding, the state constitution has changed as Wyoming society has undergone its own slow transformation, from a thinly populated, agricultural, frontier community to a more populous, more urbanized, and more dependent one on the cusp of the twenty-first century. Some constitutional change has been formal: seventy-five separate amendments to the original document have been adopted, the majority of them during the past forty years. Not the least significant of these formal changes concern the courts and how judges are selected, retained, and disciplined. Other important amendments provided for home rule for cities and towns, added an optional twenty-day budget session to the legislature, enabled the state to build (with federal grant money) an economic infrastructure of highways, water projects, and airports, and enlarged the taxing and borrowing powers of state and local government to finance a burgeoning public education system. As has been true of constitutional development on the national level, the legislature's expansive reinterpretations of its police and taxing authority have been a means of enabling the state to come to grips with the economic dislocations caused by boom and bust energy development during the 1970s. Finally, in a state court system not particularly noted for judicial activism, recent court interpretations of state constitutional provisions dealing with legislative responsibility for funding public schools have demonstrated how the third branch of state government also can be a powerful instrument of constitutional change.

The forces making for evolution in the midst of stability have clearly affected Wyoming's judicial system (see figure). The delegates to the constitutional convention of 1889 had the model of the territorial courts before them and saw little need for extended debate about the shape and authority of the new state court system; the only serious issue in this regard was whether there should be a separate and independent supreme court or one composed of three district judges (thus saving money). The convention voted for the former, and the result, set out in Article 5 of the constitution, was the ordinary court arrangement of a supreme court composed of three justices, district (major trial) courts, justice of the peace courts for each county, and such courts as the legislature might create for municipalities. Judges were to be elected by the voters of their jurisdiction, and judges of the higher courts had to be "learned in the law"—that is, admitted to the practice of law. There was no age at which judges were forced to retire. With only minor alterations, this system continued for more than half a century until 1948, when Article 5 was amended to permit the legislature to create juvenile and domestic relations courts. Then, between 1967 and 1996, came a series of amendments designed to "modernize" the court system by removing justice of the peace courts from the constitution

Significant Events in the Evolution of the Wyoming Legal and Judicial Systems

December 10, 1869   Wyoming becomes the first territory or state to extend the right to vote to women.

July 10, 1890   Wyoming admitted to the Union as the 44th State.

December 12, 1910   Willis A. Van Devanter named by President Taft to U.S. Supreme Court; only member ever appointed from Wyoming. Served twenty-six years.

December 14, 1914   First woman admitted to the practice of law in Wyoming (Dr. Grace R. Hebard).

January 28, 1915   Organizational meeting of the Wyoming State Bar in Cheyenne.

September 21, 1920   University of Wyoming College of Law opens its doors. First graduating class in 1923 (three students).

November 5, 1955   First University of Wyoming College of Law graduate appointed to the Wyoming Supreme Court (Glenn Parker).

February 28, 1961   Wyoming Legislature adopts the Uniform Commercial Code (Title 34.1 of the Wyoming Statutes Annotated, 1999 ed.).

October 4, 1982   First woman appointed to a district court judgeship in the state (Elizabeth A. Kail).

November 25, 1998   First woman appointed as attorney general of Wyoming (Gay V. Woodhouse).

June 6, 2000   First woman named to the Wyoming Supreme Court (Marilyn S. Kite).

September 15, 2000   First woman elected president of the Wyoming State Bar (Catherine MacPherson).

and leaving them to the will of the legislature (1967), authorizing the legislature to set the number of justices on the Supreme Court at between three and five (1972), abolishing popular election of all full-time judges, substituting instead a Missouri-type system of judicial selection and retention, and establishing procedures for disciplining misbehaving judges (1972, 1976, and 1996), and fixing a compulsory judicial retirement age at seventy (1972). This burst of activity during the past few decades was matched in the legislature, where the minor state tribunals and court centralization issues have been the focus of much experimentation and political struggle. In 1971 the legislature, in an effort to enhance the quality of justice in the minor courts, created a system of county courts with wider civil and criminal jurisdiction than justice of the peace courts, in which the judges would be full-time with salaries paid by the state, and would have to be lawyers. This system was mandatory for counties with populations of thirty thousand or more, while other counties could join in if they chose. The county courts, which by 2000 covered fifteen of the state's twenty-three counties, were in turn replaced by the present circuit court arrangement as a result of action by the legislature during its 2000 session. Recently, the legislature has also made important strides in improving judicial salaries and benefits, and in vesting substantial

Legal Structure of Wyoming Courts

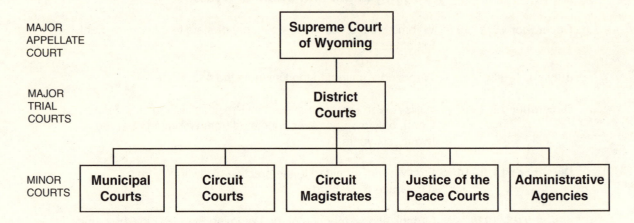

administrative supervision of the entire court system in the Wyoming Supreme Court. This latter has not occurred without resistance, however, on the part of those who see it as an encroachment upon judicial independence and the freedom of the lower courts to be more responsive to matters of local concern. The Wyoming Supreme Court itself has devoted considerable time and energy to issuing rules of procedure for the lower courts and rules of conduct governing Wyoming's approximately 1,300 lawyers and 111 judges. (Wyoming's bar was integrated in 1941, meaning that lawyers who wish to practice law in the state must become members of the Wyoming State Bar, organized in 1915.)

CURRENT STRUCTURE

The pyramidal shape of organization so characteristic of the court structures of other states is also found in Wyoming, but in a comparatively simpler form. The base of the pyramid consists of the numerous local and state courts, which deal with minor or less serious cases, defined by the legislature in terms of the body of law and the potential punishment involved (criminal cases), and the relief requested and the amount of money at stake (civil cases). Thus the eighty municipal courts in Wyoming are concerned only with infractions of city or town ordinances, while the new circuit courts and circuit court magistrates, and the dwindling number of justice of the peace courts, exercise a limited original civil (including small claims) and criminal (misdemeanor) jurisdiction in cases involving state law. "Teen courts" for handling minor offenses committed by young persons between the ages of thirteen and seventeen were authorized by the legislature in 1996. "Drug courts," supported by federal grants, have also been introduced into the state. Essentially alternative-sentencing procedures, both of these specialized judicial programs are matters of local option. In the Court Consolidation Act of 2000, the leg-

islature granted the Supreme Court substantial authority to even out the workloads of circuit court judges by reassigning them around the state as needed. The same law provided strong financial incentives for counties with justices of the peace to supplant them with circuit court systems (see figure).

More serious criminal and civil cases (such as felonies and title to land) are normally tried in one of the nine district courts, each of which has original general jurisdiction over cases arising out of the one to four counties that compose their district. These courts also handle juvenile, paternity, adoption, guardianship, divorce, and probate cases. The few appeals that come from the lower tribunals within their geographic boundaries are heard in these courts. Persons adversely affected by the rules or final decisions of administrative agencies of the state are entitled to judicial review in the district courts. There being no intermediate appellate court in Wyoming, all decisions of the district courts may be appealed directly to the Wyoming Supreme Court, which also has a limited amount of original jurisdiction (which is infrequently exercised). Trial courts are presided over by a single judge, while the Supreme Court hears appeals with all five of the justices participating. A chief justice is chosen by the other members of the court for a two-year term, rotating among themselves. In addition to its various administrative responsibilities, noted above, the Wyoming Supreme Court's primary function is to serve as final interpreter of the constitution and laws of the state. Only cases turning on questions of federal law may be appealed out of the state court system to the U.S. Supreme Court.

STAFFING

Whenever a vacancy occurs on the Supreme Court, a district court, or a circuit court, it is filled according to the four-stage Missouri Plan method of judicial selection and retention: (1) The Wyoming Judicial Nominating Commission, composed of the chief justice, three lawyers elected by the state bar organization, and three non-lawyers appointed by the governor, nominates three qualified lawyers to fill the vacancy; (2) the list of three nominees is then transmitted to the governor, who is obliged to appoint to the vacancy one person from the list, and that person serves in office for at least a year; and then (3) at the next general election that person must be retained for a full term of office (eight years for a Supreme Court justice, six years for a District Court judge, four years for a circuit judge) by the electorate of that jurisdiction, voting on a nonpartisan, noncompetitive ballot; and who (4) when that term is up must, to remain in office, be again retained by the voters for another full term of office. In this system, recruitment of judges has fallen largely to the Judicial Nominating Commission, which encourages interested lawyers to apply for the judicial post or recommend the names of others. The commission places announcements to this effect in local newspapers and on local radio and television stations, and notifies each member of the state bar. Detailed questionnaires are sent to potential candidates. On the basis of the information supplied by the applicants and other sources, letters of reference, and personal interviews, the commission then draws up its list of three nominees for the post.

Circuit Court magistrates are chosen for terms of four years by the boards of county commissioners from lists of names prepared by the district and circuit judges of a particular district; they also must run for retention in office. Justices of the peace are elected by the voters of the county to four-year terms of office. Municipal judges are appointed by the city or town mayor with the consent of the council. Their terms are as set by municipal ordinance.

Michael J. Horan

See also Merit Selection ("Missouri Plan"); United States—Federal System; United States—State Systems

References and further reading
Horan, Michael J. 1991. "The Wyoming Constitution: A Centennial Assessment." *Land and Water Law Review* 26: 13–31.
Hubbell, Larry, ed. 2000. *The Equality State: Government and Politics in Wyoming.* 4th ed. Dubuque, IA: Eddie Bowers.
Journal and Debates of the Constitutional Convention of the State of Wyoming (1889). 1893. Cheyenne: Daily Sun, Book and Job Printing Co.
Keiter, Robert B. 1986. "An Essay on Wyoming Constitutional Interpretation." *Land and Water Review* 21: 527–546.
Keiter, Robert B., and Tim Newcomb. 1993. *The Wyoming State Constitution: A Reference Guide.* Westport, CT: Greenwood Press.
Larson, T. A. 1978. *History of Wyoming.* 2d ed. Lincoln: University of Nebraska Press.

YEMEN

COUNTRY INFORMATION

Yemen is located in the southern part of the Arabian Peninsula and is surrounded by Saudi Arabia on the north, Oman on the east, and the Red Sea on the south and the west. It occupies an area of 203,796 square miles. With the exception of its mountainous western ranges, where rainfall is frequent, the rest of the country is hot and arid.

Though Yemen's history goes back thousands of years ago, its modern history can be traced to the nineteenth century, when North Yemen was under the Ottoman Empire and South Yemen was colonized by Britain (in 1839). In 1934, North Yemen became independent and in September 1962 a number of military officers deposed Imam Badr, thus ending the theocratic monarchic rule and creating in its place the Yemen Arab Republic (YAR). South Yemen gained its independence from Britain in 1967 and the country came to be known as the People's Democratic Republic of Yemen and was ruled by the Marxist-oriented Yemen Socialist Party.

After the turbulent history of the 1970s and the 1980s, the North and South Yemen governments agreed on a draft unity constitution in November 1989, and on May 22, 1990, the two countries were unified and a constitution was proclaimed. The new constitution affirmed Yemen's commitment to free elections, a multiparty political system, the right to own private property, equality under the law, and respect of basic human rights. Since the unification of the two parts of Yemen, the government has allowed a certain degree of democratization—including periodic parliamentary elections, the licensing of political parties, and universal suffrage for all Yemeni men and women who have reached the age of eighteen. Indeed, parliamentary elections were held in 1993, 1997, and 2001.

In addition to the ruling party—General People's Congress (GPC), which is headed by President Ali Abdullah Saleh—Yemen has two main parties: the Islah and the Yemen Socialist Party (YSP), and a number of small Arab-Nationalist parties. Islah has Islamic orientation and aspires to apply Islamic legal principles. Before 1990, the Yemen Socialist Party ruled South Yemen, and between 1990 and the outbreak of the civil war in 1994, the YSP was a partner in the government. Since 1994, however, the party has stayed away from Yemeni political life, and boycotted the 1997 and the 2001 parliamentary elections.

With regard to Yemen's demographic attributes, the World Bank Report for 2000 estimated Yemen's population at 16.5 million Muslim Arabs. The country's annual population growth rate is approximately 3.5 percent. The World Bank Report projected that the literacy rate among the Yemenis was 45 percent and that 57.4 percent of Yemenis between the ages of six and fifteen were attending school. Only 33.9 percent of the Yemeni females, however, were attending school, as compared to 79.4 percent of males. It also reported that the infant mortality rate was 38 per 1,000 births ,and that life expectancy was fifty-two years.

According to the 2001 Economic Freedom Index and the 2000 World Bank Report, Yemen's GDP was $4.8 billion and the per capita GDP was $275. Agriculture accounts for 22 percent of GNP, industry for 7 percent, construction for 20 percent, and services for 51 percent. The majority of the Yemeni workers—or 53 percent—work in agriculture, 17 percent in public services, 4 percent in manufacturing, and 7 percent in construction. Unemployment in Yemen is estimated at 40 percent, and is especially high in the southern parts of the country.

Yemen's economy is primarily agrarian and consists of qat, coffee, cotton, fruits, vegetables, cereals, livestock and poultry, tobacco, and honey. The industrial sector comprises petroleum production and refining, mining, food processing, and building materials. The Economic Freedom Index estimates Yemen's annual exports to be about $1.94 billion and to consist of crude petroleum, refined oil products, fish, fruit, vegetables, coffee, and plastic pipes; and its imports to be about $1.88 billion, comprised of cereals, feed grains, machinery, and transportation equipment. Yemen's trading partners include the United States, Western Europe, China, South Korea, Japan, and Saudi Arabia.

The Economic Freedom Index ranks Yemen's economy as partly free and describes banking and the financial sector as underdeveloped and lacking popular confi-

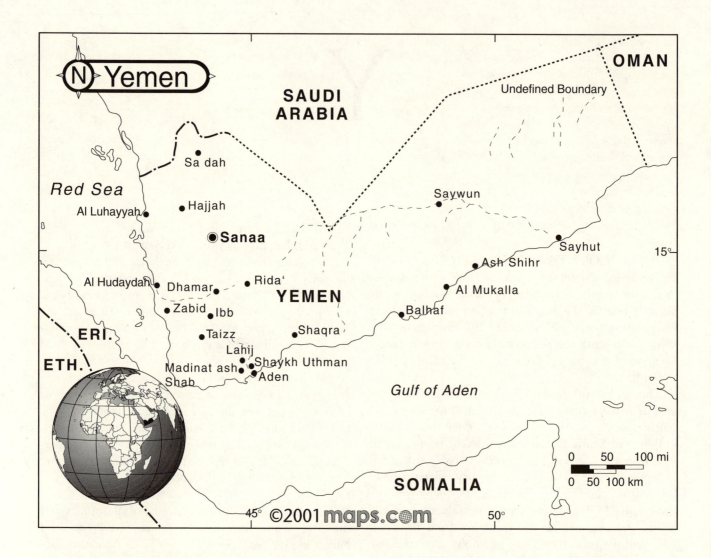

dence. It estimates that tariffs on imported goods range from 5 percent to 25 percent, and that the government's expenditures and consumption are 47 percent and 21.9 percent, respectively, of GDP. In its effort to draw more foreign investment, Yemen has modernized its investment laws and restructured its economy. Following the 1997 agreement with the International Monetary Fund (IMF), Yemen initiated a structural adjustment program to reform the financial and monetary system, balance the budget, remove governmental subsidies, deregulate the currency, and reform the civil service. In return, Yemen received IMF and World Bank credits and loans and a debt relief from the Paris Club and Russia.

Despite these economic and financial reforms, the opportunities for foreign investment continue to be hampered by bureaucratic inefficiency and corruption, the widespread black market, and the failure of the commercial courts to enforce their rulings over commercial disputes. The government's efforts to integrate the economies of both parts of Yemen were also hindered in the early 1990s by the significant drop in the remittances from the Yemeni workers following the Gulf War, the re-

duction in foreign assistance, and the outbreak of the 1994 civil war.

THE CONSTITUTIONAL FOUNDATION OF YEMEN'S POLITICAL SYSTEM

The Unity Constitution, which was ratified by the Yemeni people in May 1991 and amended in 1994, outlines the guiding principles for Yemen's political system. Articles 2 and 3 of the Unity Constitution declare Islam as the official religion of the state and Islamic *sharia* (jurisprudence) as the primary source of law. The provisions of Article 4, however, limit the impact of Islam upon Yemen's government. The article highlights the doctrine of popular sovereignty and insists that the people are the "source of all powers," and that they exercise this power through the election of their representatives to the Parliament, the local councils, the office of the president, and the independence of the judiciary.

The constitution divides the government into three separate branches: the legislative, the executive, and the judiciary. Article 40–81 delineates the powers of the Parliament and defines the relationship between the executive and legislative branches of the government. These articles give the Parliament the power to enact laws, define the country's economic and social policy, pass the budget, and ratify treaties. They also confer upon the Parliament the power to investigate the executive departments, hold the prime minister and his ministers singularly and collectively accountable, and withhold the vote of confidence from the government. By a two-thirds majority vote, the Parliament also has the power to indict the president.

Despite its constitutional power to initiate legislation, the Parliament has rarely exercised this power. It has confined itself to debating and amending governmental policy proposals, criticizing unpopular governmental policies—such as the lifting of food subsidies, and questioning ministers over policies and proposed legislation.

The 301 members of the Parliament are all elected directly by the people once every four years through a secret ballot. The constitution divides the country into electoral districts and assigns a parliamentary seat for each district. It gives the right to vote to all Yemenis who have reached the age of eighteen regardless of their gender. Candidates to the House of Representatives should be at least twenty-five years old, literate, and have a good reputation.

The constitution vests the executive power in the president of the republic, the prime minister, and his council of ministers. It stipulates that the president should be forty years old, not married to a foreign woman, and be elected by popular vote for a five-year renewable term from at least two candidates endorsed by the Parliament. The constitution gives the president the powers to conduct Yemen's foreign policy—including the power of diplomatic recognition of other states and appointing and receiving ambassadors, the power to execute the parliamentary laws and legislations and, with the approval of the Parliament, the power to declare national emergency. He also has the power to prepare the budget, draw the economic plans for the country, draft bills, maintain internal and external security, and protect the rights of the citizens. The president has the authority to dissolve the Parliament after a popular referendum, to introduce legislation, and to promulgate laws by decree when the Parliament is not in session (provided that these executive decrees are confirmed by the Parliament once it convenes). He also appoints the prime minister and, according to Article 145, the prime minister and his Council of Ministers are collectively responsible before the president and the Parliament. The constitution bans the president, the prime minister, and the ministers from engaging in business or receiving any salary from any other office to avoid any conflict of interests.

The Yemeni Unity Constitution contains a number of articles that guarantee basic civil liberties and rights to its citizens. Article 26 stipulates that the citizens have the right to participate in the political, economic, social, and cultural aspects of life, and that they enjoy the freedoms of thought and expression in accordance with the law. According to Article 27, the Yemeni citizens are equal before the law regardless of their gender, color, ethnic origin, language, occupation, social status, or religion. Articles 35 and 36 safeguard the citizens' homes, mail, telephones, places of worship, and educational institutions against any infringement by the government. Likewise, Articles 37, 38, and 39 guarantee Yemeni citizens the freedoms of education, travel, movement, and association.

The United States Human Rights Reports and the Freedom House Index on Political and Civil Rights observe that, while the Yemeni government in general does not place too many restrictions on these rights, in practice the government limits the freedoms of press, expression, petition, and assembly. For instance, the 1990 Press Law makes "the humiliation" of state institutions—including the office of the president, the cabinet, and the Parliament—and the printing of "false information against public order and interest" a crime punishable under the law. In 1998, the government amended the 1990 Press Law, requiring the owners of printed media to annually renew their license and to have a minimum operating capital of $4,375. The government owns the television and radio stations, and screens news broadcasts—often excluding items critical of its policies. Likewise, the Ministry of Information controls most printing presses and subsidizes progovernment newspapers. Though the government does not exercise press censorship, the journalists observe self-restraint, and often avoid the criticism of domestic and foreign policies and governmental corruption.

Despite the fact that the constitution does not limit the freedom of peaceful assembly, the government bans and disperses some demonstrations—presumably to avoid the outbreak of violence. At the same time that the constitution guarantees the people freedom of political association—including the right to form political parties, it excludes the formation of parties that are anti-Islamic, contradict the goals of the Yemeni revolution, or disregard Yemen's international obligations. The 1995 Labor Law extends to the Yemeni men and women the right to form unions, bargain collectively, and to strike. This right, however, can be exercised only after the failure of arbitration and mediation, and after it is approved by a majority of the workers. The law does not allow politically motivated strikes and discourages the civil servants and the public sector workers from joining unions.

THE FOUNDATIONS
OF YEMEN'S JUDICIAL SYSTEM

Prior to their unification, North and South Yemen had different legal systems. While North Yemen's judicial philosophy was heavily influenced by the legal traditions of the Ottoman Empire, Islamic *sharia,* and tribal traditions (Urf), South Yemen's legal system drew strongly upon the British legal system or common law, which was inherited, from the colonial period. Both of these distinct legal traditions are reflected in the Unity Constitution and the penal criminal code. The two legal documents contain major common law principles and emphasize that Islamic *sharia* is a primary source of law in the country. Since the end of the civil war in 1994, North Yemen's legal traditions have become increasingly dominant in former South Yemen.

The impact of the common law legal tradition can be observed in several articles dealing with the rights of a criminal defendant. Articles 31–34 contain several common law principles governing the rights of the accused. Article 31, for example, outlaws the imposition of retroactive punishments and stipulates that a criminal defendant is innocent until proven guilty. Article 32 guarantees the citizens their personal freedom and safety against any arbitrary search, arrest, or detention without a court or prosecutor order. Other provisions of Article 32 prohibit physical and psychological torture of the defendants and protect their right to remain silent and to have access to legal council. They do not allow the police to detain suspects beyond twenty-four hours without court notification of the reasons behind the arrest. The law insists that the members of the security forces who violate this provision will be punished. Article 33 forbids the use of cruel means in carrying out the punishments.

The Criminal Procedural Law no. 13/1994 also reaffirmed the rights of the criminal defendant against state tyranny. This law makes it clear that the application of the penal law is not retroactive, and that the accused is innocent until proven guilty. It also reiterated the principles of fair trial, equality before the law, and the right of the accused for legal council. Law 13 also reaffirmed the constitutional requirements that no arrest can be made without a court order, no verdict of guilt can be reached if there is any reasonable doubt, and no torture is to be used to obtain confessions from the accused.

Despite these constitutional guarantees, the United States Human Rights Report for Yemen observes that the police frequently violate the citizens' civil liberties and rights and that prolonged pretrial detention, judicial corruption and inefficiency, and executive interference in courts' rulings compromise the principles of equality before the law and due process. It remarks that the police regularly monitor citizens' activities—including their mail and telephones, search their homes without court order, and mistreat suspects. The report points to other police violations—including extrajudicial killing, the torture of and arbitrary arrest and lengthy detention of citizens without any charge, and the occasional detention of a relative while the suspect is at large. It stated that the

government has failed to curb police abuses of the citizen's rights and end societal discrimination against people with disability, racial and ethnic minorities, and women, or to extend its authority to the rest of the country. This has resulted in tribal violence and the killing of innocent citizens and foreigners. It also stated that the government does not honor the constitutional requirement to provide poor criminal defendants with defense attorneys. The report also gave a poor rating to Yemen's prisons—describing them as overcrowded and lacking adequate food and health care.

THE CONSTITUTIONAL BASES FOR THE INDEPENDENCE OF THE JUDICIARY

The 1990 Unity Constitution—which was amended in 1994, and the Judicial Authority Law no. 1/1991 contain several provisions that define the nature and the structure of the judicial branch. Article 120 of the constitution guarantees the independence of the judiciary and ascertains that judges are not subject to any authority except that of the law. Also that, once appointed, judges serve in good behavior until they retire at age sixty-five. The article gives the judiciary financial and administrative autonomy and prohibits the government from interfering in the judicial branch. It stipulates, "Interference in the administration of justice is a crime punished in accordance with the law." The Judicial Authority Law instructs that the judges and the public prosecutors can only be dismissed in accordance with the law, and that they may not be transferred to nonjudicial posts without their consent and the approval of the Supreme Judicial Council.

Section 57 of the Judicial Authority Law specifies the qualifications of candidates aspiring to become judges. It requires that individuals appointed to the judicial bench should: be "of sound mind," be thirty years old, be a graduate of the Supreme Judicial Institute, have a good reputation, and not have been convicted of any crime. Section 58 of the Judicial Authority Law explains the criteria for promotion of judges. There are nine civil service grades, and for a judge to be promoted from one grade to the next, he or she should have spent a minimum of two years in each grade. Seniority is a primary criterion for promotion. Judges with the most seniority in the district courts may be promoted to fill a vacancy in one of the appeals courts, whereas the most senior judges on the appeals courts may be appointed to the Supreme Court.

The constitution requires that the judges conduct trials and render their verdicts in public. It does, however, give the courts the power to hold closed trials for reasons of public security and morality. The constitution does not provide for trial by jury, but rather entrusts the judge with the task of trying the case, questioning witnesses and the accused, and issuing the court ruling. The Judicial Authority Law gives the defense attorneys the right to counsel their clients and cross-examine witnesses. It also guarantees the independence of the public prosecutors and regards them as an integral part of the judicial branch. Despite their independence, the prosecutors see themselves as an extension of the police.

THE STRUCTURE OF YEMEN'S COURTS

The Unity Constitution did not elaborate upon the structure of the court system in Yemen. Article 124 called for the creation of a Supreme Court and assigned for it judicial review and appellate jurisdiction, and the establishment of inferior courts as specified by the law. The 1991 Judicial Authority Law created Yemen's current courts structure and defined their jurisdiction. The law established three levels of courts to serve the different parts of the country. It set up the district courts or the first instance courts and gave them trial jurisdiction over civil, commercial, criminal, family, and administrative cases. In addition, the law created five commercial district courts and assigned for them exclusive commercial jurisdiction. Depending on the monetary value of the case, a single judge or a full court of three judges may hear the case. The Supreme Judicial Council determines the number of district courts, their location, their territorial jurisdiction, and the number of judges to serve on each court.

The rulings of the district court may be appealed to the court of appeal in its geographic region. There are eighteen courts of appeal in Yemen, divided among the eighteen provinces. Though the number of divisions within each appeals court varies in accordance with the volume and nature of cases within the province, in general the courts of appeal are subdivided into four courts to hear appeals over civil, criminal, family, and commercial cases. Each appeals court is presided over by a bench of three judges. The total number of appeals courts judges is 132. The Supreme Judicial Council determines the number of divisions within each appeals court and the number of judges serving on each court.

Yemen has one court of last resort known as the Supreme Court. Article 124 defines the Supreme Court's jurisdiction and gives it the power of judicial review to rule on the constitutionality of laws and regulations, resolve conflict over the proper jurisdictions of lower courts, and rule over conflicting precedents of inferior courts. The article also empowers the Supreme Court to investigate the legality of the parliamentary elections and to review civil, criminal, and commercial appeals. The Supreme Court also has the power to rule on administrative disputes and disciplinary cases, and to try cases involving the president, the vice president, the speaker of Parliament, the prime minister, and his Council of Ministers.

Yemen's Supreme Court has a very complex structure, as it has fifty serving judges, including the chief justice and his two deputies, and is subdivided into eight sub-

Legal Structure of Yemen Courts

Supreme Court

Has original jurisdiction including the trial of the president, the vice president, the prime minister and his council of ministers, and the speaker of Parliament.
Has appellate jurisdiction over civil, criminal, and commercial cases.
Has rule over conflicting precedents of inferior courts and the legality of parliamentary elections and administrative disputes.

Court of Appeals

Made up of 18 courts.
Has appellate jurisdiction over civil, criminal, family, and commercial cases.
Each court is composed of a bench of three judges.

District Courts
First Instance Courts

Have trial jurisdiction over civil, commercial, criminal, family, and administrative cases.

courts. These include the constitutional, the appeals and scrutiny, the criminal, the military, the civil, the family, the commercial, and the administrative divisions. With the exception of the constitutional division, which has seven judges and is headed by the chief justice, each of the remaining seven divisions comprises a bench of five judges who reviews appeals from the lower courts. The constitutional subdivision has the power of judicial review and decides cases involving contestation of parliamentary and presidential elections and cases involving the most senior members of the government. The appeal and scrutiny subcourt looks into the procedural requirements concerning all appeals and refers them to the appropriate division. The criminal and military subdivision courts have power to review appeals from the lower courts, revise sentences involving capital punishment, or the infliction of Islamic penalties such as the severance of limbs.

A number of organs oversee the work of the judicial branch. Article 123 of the constitution called for the creation of the Supreme Judicial Council to supervise the judiciary. The Judicial Authority Law no. 1/1991 gave the council far-reaching administrative powers over the Supreme Court, courts of appeal, district courts, the Public Prosecutor's Office, the Ministry of Justice, the Judicial Inspection Authority, and the Supreme Judicial Institute. The council has the power of appointment, promotion, dismissal, discipline, transfer, and the retirement of judges. It also draws the budget for the judicial branch and deliberates the bills and policies regarding the working and development of the judiciary. In addition, the council determines the number of judges, the jurisdiction, and the subdivisions of the Supreme Court, the courts of appeal, and the number of first instance courts, their location, and their territorial jurisdiction. The law stipulates that the members of the Supreme Judicial Council include the president of the republic, the chief justice of the Supreme Court and his two deputies, the attorney general, the minister of justice and his deputy, the chairman of the Judicial Inspection Commission, and three senior Supreme Court judges.

In performing its functions, the Supreme Judicial Council relies upon the support of the Ministry of Justice and the Judicial Inspection Authority. The Ministry of Justice has limited administrative authority over the judicial branch. Its main responsibility is to maintain the court facilities and the training of judges and court personnel. It is the Judicial Inspection Authority, however, which is primarily responsible for the annual assessment and evaluation of the work and professional performance and conduct of judges, the drafting of disciplinary cases against judges, and the consideration of requests for the extradition of criminals. In coordination with the minister of Justice and the president of the Supreme Court, the Judicial Inspection Authority submits to the Supreme Judicial Council the recommendation for promotions of judges, their transfers, retirement, or removal from office. The authority initiates investigation and disciplinary action against a judge if there is evidence of neglect of duty, including repeated delay of holding hearings, the taking of bribes, and disclosing state secrets. The disciplinary act may include counseling of the concerned judge, admonishing the judge, withholding of his or her allowance, temporary suspension, delaying a promotion, transfer to a nonjudicial job, or removal from office.

In addition to regular courts, Yemen has a very long tradition of tribal adjudication, which carries the same legal weight of court rulings. Because of the tribal and traditional nature of the Yemeni society, especially in North Yemen, many citizens seek tribal adjudication. It is estimated that about 70 percent of disputes in Yemen are settled through tribal adjudication. The Arbitration Act of 1992 recognizes the tribal nature of the society and accommodates tribal arbitration. The tribal elders, acting as a council of adjudication, settle disputes among tribe members. For the tribe notables to arbitrate a dispute,

however, they have to be approached by parties to the dispute.

Aside from the widespread use of tribal arbitration, the legal profession in Yemen suffers from the underdeveloped nature of commercial law. Likewise, lawyers and judges are not trained to handle international business transactions. Moreover, Yemen has two different legal backgrounds: Ottoman legal tradition and the English common Law.

The legal education in Yemen also suffers from serious problems. The main law school in Yemen is located at the University of San'a, where most of the Yemeni lawyers receive their law degree. The teaching method, curriculum, the law libraries, and the textbooks, however, are inadequate and outdated and do not measure up to the standards in neighboring Arab countries. Likewise, the law students have little opportunity for internships and practical training. Soon after their graduation, the lawyers must be registered with Yemen's bar association and obtain a license to appear before the court. The ability of the lawyer to defend cases before different levels of courts depends upon years of experience and the granting of a special permission from the bar association. Though recently law firms and partnerships were introduced to Yemen, still the overwhelming majority of the lawyers practice law individually.

CONCLUDING REMARKS

Although the constitution stresses the judicial, financial, and administrative independence of Yemen's courts and judges, in practice the judiciary is weak and is dependent upon the executive branch, and the executive frequently interferes in the discourse of the courts. Executive control over the judicial branch is exercised through the Supreme Judicial Council, which has the power of appointment, transfer, and suspension of judges. The independence of the judiciary is compromised by the fact that political consideration plays a role in the appointment, promotion, and dismissal of judges, and that judges issuing rulings against the government are harassed, transferred, or even removed from office. The judges are also dependent upon the government for training and development and for enforcing the court's rulings.

Many of the problems of Yemen's judicial system are also a direct result of the quality of legal education. The instructional material at Yemen's law schools and the Supreme Judicial Institute are dated, and the curriculum has not been modernized since the 1960s. Rather than training judges on how to hear witnesses and deal with evidence, the teaching methods focus heavily on memorization of old legal texts and, until recently, judicial training was not part of the curriculum and the judges did not have to take refresher courses. Moreover, the low salary of judges ($300 per month), the poor working conditions, and the low level of respect that the Yemeni people have for their judges keep proficient lawyers away from becoming judges, and are behind the acceptance of bribes by some judges and prosecutors. Other judges allow social, family, and governmental connections to influence courts' rulings rather than applying justice. Likewise, Yemen's courts' staff is not well trained and is paid low salaries. In return for cash, court clerks may hide some files, advance others on a court's calendar, and completely destroy other files.

Several international assistance programs in the late 1990s were submitted to the Yemeni government to reform the judicial and court system. In 1998, the World Bank signed a loan agreement of $2.5 million to train 700 judges, and the European community undertook the modernization of Yemen's legal system over a period of two years. The goals of these international initiatives include the modernization of the judicial system, the improvement of the country's legal libraries, training of the public prosecutors, and raising public consciousness and appreciation of the rule of law. Other goals aim at familiarizing the Yemeni judges with modern business and commercial law, the offering of courses on legal issues, and the training of judges in legal reasoning. Still other international legal assistance reform programs aim at increasing courts' efficiency, reducing court delays, instituting fairness in the administration of justice, and providing the judges and law students with the highest standards of personal and professional conduct. Other recommendations proposed the use of modern alternative dispute resolution methods such as private arbitration, mediation, and establishment of small claims courts to increase the efficiency of the courts.

Emile Sahliyeh

See also Appellate Courts; Commercial Law (International Aspects); Common Law; Constitutional Review; Criminal Law; Family Law; Islamic Law; Judicial Independence; Judicial Selection, Methods of; Ottoman Empire; Qadi (Qazi) Courts; Trial Courts

References and further reading
Al-Hubaishi, Husain, Former Minister of Legal Affairs. *Arbitration: Partial Remedy to Judicial Ills?* http://www. yementimes.com/99/iss05/l&d.htm (accessed November 25, 2001).
Auchterlonie, Paul. 1998. "Yemen." Santa Barbara, CA: ABC-CLIO Press. http://www.bartleby.com/151/a47.html (accessed November 25, 2001).
Burrowes, Robert D. 1995. *Historical Dictionary of Yemen.* Lanham, MD: Scarecrow Press.
Halliday, Fred. 2000. *Nation and Religion in the Middle East.* Boulder, CO: Lynne Riener Publishers.
Heritage Foundation. Index of Economic Freedom. http:// database.townhall.com/heritage/index/country.cfm?ID=159 (accessed November 25, 2001).
Law Library of Congress. http://memory.loc.gov/glin/ yemen.html (accessed November 25, 2001).
Pridham, B. R. 1984. *Contemporary Yemen: Politics and Historical Background.* New York: St. Martin's Press.
Republic of Yemen. Comprehensive Development Review—Phase I. Judicial and Legal System Building Block, January 24, 2000. Legal Department.
Stookey, Robert W. 1978. *Yemen: The Politics of the Yemen Arab Republic.* Boulder, CO: Westview Press.
U.S. Department of Labor, Bureau of Democracy, Human Rights, and Labor. http://www.usis.usemb.se/human/ human1999/yemen.html (accessed November 25, 2001).
U.S. Department of State. http://www.state.gov/www/ background_notes/yemen_1096_bgn.html (accessed November 25, 2001).
Wenner, Manfred W. 1967. *Modern Yemen, 1918–1966.* Baltimore, MD: Johns Hopkins Press.
World Bank. http://wbln0018.worldbank.org/mna/mena.nsf/ (accessed November 25, 2001).
"Yemen Judicial System." http://www.gpc.org.ye/jud00003. htm (accessed February 1, 2002).

YUGOSLAVIA: KINGDOM OF AND SOCIALIST REPUBLIC

GENERAL INFORMATION

There have been three quite different Yugoslavias in the central Balkans. This article deals with the first and second countries of that name, the Kingdom of Yugoslavia (1918–1941) and socialist Yugoslavia (1945–1991). (The third Yugoslavia, the Federal Republic of Yugoslavia, is covered under Yugoslavia: Serbia and Montenegro)

The Kingdom of Yugoslavia

The first Yugoslavia (1918–1941) was formed after World War I by uniting the prewar independent states of Serbia and Montenegro with regions of the former Austro-Hungarian Empire in which South Slavic languages were spoken by most of the population: Croatia, Bosnia, and Slovenia. Kosovo, with a large Albanian population, and parts of Macedonia had already been incorporated into Serbia in 1913, after the Balkan wars. The new state was originally called the Kingdom of Serbs, Croats, and Slovenes, a constitutional monarchy under the reign of the Serbian Karadjordjevic dynasty. A highly centralized form of government was created under the Constitution of 1921, adopted over the opposition of the Croatian political parties. These parties continued to oppose the central government, demanding autonomy and a federal system, until June 1928, when the leader of the main Croatian party was fatally shot while in the Parliament. The Croatian parties then withdrew from Parliament, organizing a separatist regime in Zagreb. In January 1929, King Alexander Karadjordjevic suspended the 1921 Constitution, disbanded Parliament, banned political parties, and assumed dictatorial control over the country. Soon

thereafter the name of the state was changed to Yugoslavia, "Land of the South Slavs," in an attempt to assert a common identity for all citizens.

The dictatorship was officially ended in September 1931, but the king retained such powers as to effectively maintain his dictatorial rule. King Alexander was assassinated in 1934, leaving a minor son as heir, but governmental power was exercised by a three-person regency headed by a cousin of the king, Prince Paul. In 1939, continued Croatian opposition to the Serbian-controlled government forced the regent to concede autonomy to the Croats under a federal system. Whether the kingdom would have remained viable became a moot point when, in April 1941, Nazi Germany invaded Yugoslavia, conquering the country in ten days and dismembering it. The young king, Peter II, assumed the throne but was forced days later to flee the country, never to return. Most of the country was ruled by occupying forces from the Axis powers: Germany, Italy, Bulgaria, and Hungary. An "Independent State of Croatia," incorporating Croatia and Bosnia-Herzegovina, was set up by the occupiers and implemented a policy of genocide against Serbs, Jews, and Gypsies.

World War II in Yugoslavia was a complex mixture of brutal occupation by the Axis powers, opposition to that occupation by royalist forces and by communists under the leadership of Marshall Tito, ethnic cleansing by the government of the "Independent State of Croatia," opposition to the Croat state by royalists and communists, and conflicts between the royalists, the communists, the Croatian state, and some smaller forces, all of which entered at times into either alliances or at least tacit truces with the Axis occupiers. As the Axis powers lost the war, the communists turned against royalist and Croat forces with increasing success, so that by 1945 the communists under Tito controlled most of the territory of prewar Yugoslavia.

Socialist Yugoslavia

In late 1944 the communists concluded a formal alliance with the exiled royal government. In March 1945 a government was proclaimed by this alliance, with Tito as premier and communists in most key positions. This government abolished the monarchy in August 1945, setting the stage for elections to a constituent assembly in November 1945. Moderate political parties were either banned from running at all or obstructed in their campaigns by the communists, so that the latter gained 80 percent of the vote. On November 29, 1945, the communist-controlled constituent assembly proclaimed the Federal Peoples Republic of Yugoslavia, which was recognized shortly thereafter by all major governments.

The constituent assembly enacted a constitution in 1946, patterned after the Soviet Constitution of 1936. However, after Tito broke from Stalin in 1948, this constitution was seen as outmoded. A "Constitutional Law" of 1953 reorganized the state except for the judiciary (see below); but the judiciary was also reorganized by a law "with constitutional effect" in 1954. In 1963 a new constitution was enacted, changing the name of the state to the Socialist Federal Republic of Yugoslavia in an effort to distinguish the country from the "Peoples Republics" of the Warsaw Pact, as Yugoslavia, along with India and Egypt, formed the Nonaligned Movement.

From 1969 to 1971 a number of amendments to the 1963 Constitution were adopted, aimed at developing the practice of "workers' self-management" as the basis of state, economy, and society. In 1974 a completely new constitution was passed to enact this vision, radically decentralizing the state. The 1974 Constitution, with 406 articles, was by far the longest constitution in the world, and it was accompanied by the nearly as long Law on Associated Labor, which attempted to regulate the new system of socialist self-management, discussed below. As part of the effort to organize the state on the principles of self-management, the federation was confederalized, with the Parliament based solely on the principle of representation of the constituent units of the federation: six "Socialist Republics" (Bosnia, Croatia, Macedonia, Montenegro, Serbia, Slovenia) and two "Socialist Autonomous Provinces" (Kosovo and Vojvodina), formally components of the Socialist Republic of Serbia but, in practice, independent polities within the federation. There was no chamber representing the people directly, as in the U.S. House of Representatives or the Indian Lok Sabha. In addition, adoption of legislation required acceptance by the representatives of all federal units, effectively giving each component of the federation a veto power over legislation.

As socialism withered in Europe, efforts were made to reform the Yugoslav system. Constitutional amendments in 1988 removed most of the structure of self-management socialism from the economic system. However, attempts to transform the unworkable de facto confederacy into a workable federation were blocked, first by Slovenia, then by Serbia and Croatia, as ruling elites saw the preservation of their own power as lying in the negation of federal authority. By 1989 the last vestige of federal authority, the Constitutional Court of Yugoslavia, was destroyed as Slovenia refused to follow a decision of that court and as the federal government, fearful of starting a civil war, refused to enforce it. With no institutions for the resolution of disputes between republics, the only method remaining was war. With the proclamations of independence by Slovenia and Croatia on June 24, 1991, the Socialist Federal Republic of Yugoslavia began its process of disintegration, with wars in Slovenia (June–July 1991), Croatia (June–December 1991 and May–August 1995), Bosnia (April 1992–November 1995), Kosovo (February 1998–June 1999), and Macedonia (2001).

LEGAL CONCEPTS

The first Yugoslavia joined territories that had been under Ottoman law (Serbia until 1830, Bosnia until 1878, Macedonia and Kosovo until 1913) with those that had been under Austro-Hungarian law (Bosnia after 1878, Croatia, Slovenia). The pre-Yugoslavia Serbian government had looked to continental Europe for legal models, mainly to Austria; the first Serbian Civil Code (1844) was patterned after the Austrian Civil Code of 1811. However, the Serbian Commercial Code of 1860 was patterned after French law. After World War I, Serbian lawyers looked to France for inspiration, though Croatian and Slovenian legal scholars and practitioners continued to be drawn to Austrian and German legal theory and practice. There were local innovations, mainly in the realm of family law. The Serbian Civil Code accommodated the traditional extended family of the south Slavs (the *zadruga*). In pre-Yugoslavia Bosnia, Muslim family law was recognized, and this continued in the first Yugoslavia.

Socialist Yugoslavia, like other socialist states, attempted to create a legal system based on Marxist principles rather than capitalist ones. While the models for socialist law were originally sought in Soviet legislation, after the break with Stalin in 1948, Yugoslavia began to develop its own variant of socialist law. The key concepts were self-management (*samoupravljanje*) and social property (*drus˘tvena svojina*). In Yugoslav theory, the flaw of Soviet-style communism was to be found in ownership and management of the means of production by the state rather than by the workers. The institutions of social property and self-management were meant to overcome this flaw.

Yugoslav law recognized three categories of property. Private property included the right of private ownership of a dwelling, of farmland under twenty hectares, and of a small business enterprise. State property was also recognized, such as the government buildings or the army's equipment. However, the major means of production were held to be social property, owned collectively by "the working class and all working people."

Self-management was the system by which these owners managed social property. Workers were organized into

Basic Organizations of Associated Labor (BOAL), each of which was a unit the work-product of which could be assigned value either on the market or within a larger organization. BOALs were combined into Composite Organizations of Associated Labor (COAL)—in effect, the traditional firm. However, all income produced by the members of a COAL belonged to its constituent BOALs. BOALs and COALs were run by Workers' Assemblies (all of the workers in the BOAL) headed by elected Workers' Councils. These organs were required to meet frequently to make business decisions. In theory, the members of the Workers' Council were freely elected; in practice, the leadership was selected by the League of Communists. That Yugoslavia had a League of Communists rather than a Communist Party was itself a reflection of self-management ideology, although in popular speech one spoke of the party (*partija*), not a league (*savez*).

By the early 1980s it was recognized that this system was inefficient, and it was largely eliminated in 1988–1989. However, postsocialist transformations of social property, like those of state property elsewhere in formerly socialist Europe, overwhelmingly benefited ruling elites.

JUDICIAL STRUCTURE

Socialist Yugoslavia had regular courts of general jurisdiction, military courts, commercial courts, arbitration courts, and "conciliation councils," a form of voluntary mediation. The 1963 Constitution added constitutional courts, the first in socialist Europe. The 1974 Constitution termed regular courts, military courts, and economic courts "instruments of state power," while creating "self-management courts" from the arbitration and mediation institutions of the earlier system, along with new "courts of associated labor" for disputes involving self-management relations. The self-management courts were meant to have decisions made by workers, not legal professionals, but in practice, legal professionals made most of the decisions in self-management courts, too.

Until the adoption of the 1974 Constitution, the Yugoslav judicial system was centralized. Courts could be created only by the federal authorities, and there was a federal Supreme Court to impart uniformity to decisions. The constitutional courts created in 1963 were also centralized, headed by a Constitutional Court of Yugoslavia. However, the 1974 Constitution, which confederalized the federation, also confederalized the judicial system, creating supreme courts in each federal unit. While there was a Federal Court, it had very limited jurisdiction, essentially only over cases involving relations within the federation; it did not have jurisdiction over most legal issues, since those issues remained under republican jurisdiction. Each constituent unit of the federation, after 1974, had its own constitution, its own courts of first in-

stance and appeal, a Supreme Court, and its own constitutional court. Similarly, each constituent unit of the federation had its own courts of associated labor, at first instance and appellate levels. There was no federal court of associated labor. The Constitutional Court of Yugoslavia, with judges from each republic, remained; however, in late 1989, Slovenia succeeded in denying the authority of this court, which thus became irrelevant.

STAFFING

The University of Belgrade law faculty is one of the three original faculties composing the university at its founding in 1908. In the 1970s about 7 percent of undergraduate degrees awarded in Serbia were in law, and 8,973 law degrees were granted in Serbia in 1980. While each such graduate is a lawyer (*pravnik*), however, few become attorneys (*advokati*), those who practice law by arguing cases before the courts: only 990 in 1980. Unlike in the other socialist countries of eastern Europe, the legal profession was never socialized in Yugoslavia, so that the attorneys were either solo practitioners or members of small firms. An aspirant to the status of attorney had to pass a bar exam.

Judges were law graduates who had taken courses aimed at prospective judges and passed a judicial exam. The judicial service was controlled by the government. As in the rest of continental Europe, the prosecutorial service was a branch of the judiciary. Through the 1980s, the position of judge was one of the most prestigious occupations in Yugoslavia. A judge would serve for life or until retirement or resignation, except in rare cases in which a judge was removed for political reasons. Trial courts sat in panels, with the professional judge joined by two lay assessors. As in most of the rest of Europe, these lay assessors were usually passive observers, letting decisions be made by the professional judge.

Judges of the Courts of Associated Labor at the trial level were mainly not judicial professionals, although a group of professional judges supervised the work of these courts. In addition, each three-judge panel of a Court of Associated Labor of first instance was "assisted" by a "secretary of the panel," almost always a young law faculty graduate studying for the judicial exam. These "secretaries" would advise the lay judges on the correct way in which to conduct a hearing and would draft the opinions of the panel.

IMPACT

Socialist Yugoslavia had a period of revolutionary justice immediately following World War II, at the time of the consolidation of the socialist system and state. However, by the mid-1960s, the legal system was a regular part of the social and political systems, in most ways comparable to that of other civil law systems. Even the so-called self-management courts created by the 1974 constitution functioned essentially as regular courts.

In essence, with the adoption of the 1974 constitution Yugoslavia became a confederation unified by the League of Communists of Yugoslavia, rather than by a set of institutions designed to structure a workable federation. With the demise of communism conceptually, and of the League of Communists as an institution, the confederal nature of the system rendered it unable to respond to challenges from republics increasingly hostile to each other. In the end, Yugoslavia's constitutional and legal systems proved not only inadequate for a federation, but dysfunctional.

Robert M. Hayden

See also Alternative Dispute Resolution; Bosnia and Herzegovina; Civil Law; Constitutional Review; Croatia; Federalism; India; Lay Judiciaries; Macedonia; Marxist Jurisprudence; Slovenia; Soviet System; Yugoslavia: Serbia and Montenegro

References and further reading
Chloros, A. G. 1970. *Yugoslav Civil Law: History, Family, Property.* Oxford: Oxford University Press.
Hayden, Robert M. 1990. *Social Courts in Theory and Practice: Yugoslav Workers Courts in Comparative Perspective.* Philadelphia: University of Pennsylvania Press.
———. 1999. *Blueprints for a House Divided: The Constitutional Logic of the Yugoslav Conflicts.* Ann Arbor: University of Michigan Press.
Rusinow, Dennison. 1978. *The Yugoslav Experiment, 1948–1974.* Berkeley: University of California Press.

YUGOSLAVIA: SERBIA AND MONTENEGRO

COUNTRY INFORMATION

The Federal Republic of Yugoslavia (FRY), comprised of two of the six constituent republics of the former Socialist Federal Republic of Yugoslavia (SFRY), was officially renamed Serbia and Montenegro in 2003. The SFRY, formed in 1946, broke up between 1991 and 1992, with the secession of the four republics of Slovenia, Croatia, Macedonia, and Bosnia and Herzegovina. Serbia and Montenegro proclaimed the formation of the FRY in April 1992.

The FRY is located in southeastern Europe, bordering Hungary to the north, Romania to the northeast, Bulgaria to the east, the Former Yugoslav Republic of Macedonia and Albania to the south, the Adriatic Sea to the southwest, and Croatia and Bosnia and Herzegovina to the west. The area of the FRY is approximately 39,500 square miles. Montenegro is a mountainous region of some 5,400 square miles, with 125 miles of coastline on the Adriatic Sea. Serbia, with a territory of 34,100 square miles, has many hills and mountains, as well as a fertile plain in the north. The territory of Serbia includes two

regions that are designated as autonomous provinces under the Constitution of Serbia: Kosovo and Metohija (4,200 square miles) in the south and Vojvodina (8,300 square miles) in the north. Although officially part of the FRY, Kosovo has been under the administration of the United Nations since June 1999.

Recent estimates place the population of the FRY at approximately 10,650,000 people, with some 9,970,000 residing in Serbia and 680,000 in Montenegro. Approximately 2 million people live in Kosovo, and approximately 2 million are in Vojvodina. Ethnic patterns in the FRY are complex. Most people consider themselves to be Serbs or Montenegrins. In Serbia proper (excluding Kosovo and Vojvodina), Serbs make up approximately 80 percent of the population. In addition, many minority ethnic groups reside in the FRY, including a substantial Albanian population (approximately 16 percent), Bosnians, Hungarians, Roma, and Romanians. Most of the people in Kosovo are of Albanian ethnicity, and the population of Vojvodina is quite diverse, with large percentages of Serbs and Hungarians. The official language of the FRY is Serbian, although the FRY Constitution provides that in regions inhabited by national minorities, the languages of those minorities shall also be used in a manner prescribed by law.

The capital of the FRY is Belgrade, which is also the capital of Serbia, while the Constitution of Montenegro establishes the city of Cetinje as the republic's capital and the city of Podgorica as its administrative center.

HISTORY

During the Middle Ages, several south Slavic governmental entities emerged in the region, including the nucleus of what became the extensive Serbian Empire in the first half of the fourteenth century. Later in the fourteenth century, the Ottoman Turks began to conquer much of southeastern Europe. The Ottoman Empire controlled most of the territory of present-day FRY until well into the nineteenth century, although the people of Montenegro maintained a considerable degree of independence. Serbs in Belgrade and its surrounding area obtained substantial autonomy in 1830, and the independent Kingdom of Serbia came into existence in 1878, the same year in which Montenegro also became an independent monarchy. In the Balkan wars of 1912 and 1913, Serbia and Montenegro were part of an alliance that successfully drove the Ottoman Empire from much of its remaining territory in Europe, and Serbia realized major territorial gains including the region of Kosovo.

Following World War I, Serbia and Montenegro entered into the newly created Kingdom of Serbs, Croats, and Slovenes. In 1929, the country's name was changed to the Kingdom of Yugoslavia. In 1946, after devastating warfare, including bitter civil conflict, the SFRY was formed under the leadership of the Communist Party of Yugoslavia and Josip Broz (Tito), who led the country until his death in 1980. Until 1989, the Communist Party (officially the Yugoslav League of Communists) and its branches in the republics were the only legal political parties in the SFRY. The party was dissolved in 1990.

In 1987, Slobodan Milosevic, who became president of Serbia in 1989 and president of the FRY in 1996, assumed leadership of the Serbian Communist Party. He was forced from office in October 2000 amid mass demonstrations following a contested election in which his opponent for the presidency, Vojislav Kostunica, was the apparent winner. Kostunica became the new FRY president, and a broad eighteen-party coalition, the Democratic Opposition of Serbia, assumed political power in Serbia.

The years of Milosevic's rule were marked by the promotion of fervent Serbian nationalism, the consolidation of political power by the Socialist Party of Serbia (SPS), the isolation of the FRY from the international community, and severe economic difficulties, exacerbated by economic sanctions imposed by the United Nations in the 1990s. Among the events of this period were the stripping in 1989 and 1990 of the autonomy of Kosovo and Vojvodina within Serbia; the wars associated with the breakup of the SFRY in Slovenia, Croatia, and Bosnia and Herzegovina; the conclusion of the Dayton Accords of 1995 to which the FRY is a party; the growing threats by Montenegro to leave the FRY; the beginnings of an armed rebellion by ethnic Albanians in Kosovo in the late 1990s and the Serbian government's suppression of that rebellion; the NATO bombing campaign of March-June 2000; the installation of UN administration in Kosovo in June 2000; Milosevic's departure from power and the SPS's loss of its political dominance in October 2000; and the transfer of Milosevic to The Hague in June 2001 to stand trial before the UN International Criminal Tribunal for former Yugoslavia. Since October 2000, steps have been taken to end the FRY's isolation, such as its admission to the United Nations on November 1, 2000.

LEGAL CONCEPTS

The institutions and normative structure of the FRY's legal system are grounded in the European continental civil law tradition. In medieval Serbia, legal development, including the promulgation of a code by Tsar Stefan Dushan in the mid-fourteenth century, was influenced by Byzantine models based on Roman law. During the formative development of the legal systems in Serbia and Montenegro in the nineteenth and early twentieth centuries, jurists borrowed extensively from continental models, particularly those of Austria and France. Elements of socialist law were introduced during the SFRY period.

In 1992, the FRY inherited the basic structure and laws of the SFRY system, which, for the most part, have remained unchanged. However, during the 1990s, the administration and functioning of the legal system, particularly the appointment and dismissal of judges, was subject to considerable intervention by political forces. Since the removal from power of the SPS in October 2000, many proposals have been advanced to reform fundamental aspects of the legal system.

The FRY is a federal state, with a federal constitution adopted on April 27, 1992. Serbia and Montenegro also have their own constitutions, promulgated on September 28, 1990, and October 12, 1992, respectively. The constitutions of the constituent republics must not conflict with the FRY Constitution; however, Serbia and Montenegro are granted considerable autonomy within the constitutional system. The region of Kosovo, meanwhile, has been outside the FRY legal system since June 1999. The UN administration in Kosovo seeks to establish an autonomous legal system.

The constitutions of the FRY, Serbia, and Montenegro are similar in format and subjects addressed. All of them contain extensive catalogs of human rights, which correspond closely to those in the European Convention for the Protection of Human Rights and Fundamental Freedoms (ECHR) and other international human rights instruments. According to the FRY Constitution, all governmental acts, including legislation, must conform to the constitution.

Each of the constitutions separates governmental power into legislative, executive, and judicial branches, as well as establishing an independent office of public prosecutor. Consistent with the FRY's grounding in the European civil law tradition, the constitutions provide that legislative acts are the supreme source of law, although they must conform to constitutional norms. Judicial precedent is not formally recognized as a source of law, although in practice judges give it considerable persuasive authority. Legislative acts include the provisions of international agreements to which the FRY is a party, although the FRY Constitution is not clear as to whether those provisions are superior to legislation in the event of a conflict.

The legislative bodies established under the three constitutions have the exclusive power to enact legislation. The federal legislature is the Federal Assembly, which has two houses: the Chamber of Citizens, in which 138 deputies are elected by the people of Serbia and 30 by the people of Montenegro, and the Chamber of Republics, in which both republics are equally represented. Deputies to both houses, who are directly elected by the people, serve four-year terms. The legislatures of Serbia and Montenegro are unicameral. In addition to law making, the legislative bodies play a crucial role in the appointment and dismissal of many other public officials, including those occupying key positions in the legal system.

Much of the legislation in the FRY has been enacted by the constituent republics. Although the FRY constitution sets forth a number of fields in which the Federal Assembly is competent to act, it allows the republics to legislate in these areas if the Federal Assembly does not do so. Consequently, many important laws, such as the criminal codes, are republican statutes. None of the legislative bodies has enacted a civil code; therefore, the topics typically addressed in such codes are distributed among a number of separate legislative acts.

Each executive branch in the FRY and the constituent republics is composed of a president, who is directly elected, and a government led by a prime minister nominated by the president and approved by the legislature. The FRY president, who is also the head of state, serves for a term of four years, while the presidents of the constituent republics serve for five years. The FRY government, which includes the prime minister, is elected by the legislature for a four-year term; however, the FRY Constitution also provides that the legislature may terminate the mandate of the government any time during that term by a vote of no confidence. A vote of no confidence requires a majority approval of the deputies in both legislative chambers.

Within the governmental sphere, state agencies discharge a range of functions, including the enactment of generally applicable legal acts when such powers have been delegated by the legislature, as well as the resolution of individual administrative matters. The FRY inherited from the SFRY an extensive body of procedural and substantive administrative law. Generally, final administrative determinations are subject to review by the courts.

As to the judicial branch, most courts are found in the republican judicial systems, which are comprised of courts of general jurisdiction, constitutional courts, and commercial courts. The only federal courts are the Federal Court, the Federal Constitutional Court, and military tribunals.

The constitutions prescribe that the office of public prosecutor must be independent of the other branches of government. The FRY and both republics have an office of public prosecutor. Under the FRY Criminal Procedure Code, the public prosecutors' exercise of discretion is strictly limited: They are obliged to initiate criminal prosecution if proof exists that a criminal offense has been committed.

The systems of criminal and civil procedure provide evidence of the FRY's roots in the continental European tradition. The Code of Criminal Procedure and the Civil Procedure Act, both inherited from the SFRY, are federal legislation. Both laws prescribe an active role for the judiciary. In criminal procedure, for example, all acts of legal force during the pretrial stage are made by an investigating judge, who thereby is expected to exercise oversight over the acts of the prosecutor and the police during the investigation of the crime. Judges also play the dominant role in the trial phase, directing the presentation of evidence and examining witnesses and the accused. Although in some criminal cases laypersons (called "lay assessors") participate along with judges in making decisions at trial, the FRY legal system does not provide for juries comprised entirely of laypersons. Meanwhile, the procedural codes also present features that represent a departure from traditional civil law systems, such as the principle that court judgments must be decided on the basis of evidence presented in concentrated, oral proceedings, rather than exclusively by means of documentary production.

CURRENT COURT SYSTEM STRUCTURE

Administration of the judicial systems is the responsibility of the ministries of justice of the FRY and the constituent republics. As a result, the courts themselves do not make the determinations as to their budgetary and staffing needs.

At the federal level, the responsibilities of the Federal Court include acting as a final appellate court for decisions made by republican courts regarding enforcement of federal legislation, determining the legality of administrative regulations adopted by federal authorities, and deciding on conflicts of jurisdiction between courts of two member republics as well as between military tribunals and other courts. The Federal Constitutional Court has exclusive competence to decide questions about the conformity of governmental acts, including the constitutions of the member republics and federal and republican legislation, with the FRY Constitution and to rule unconstitutional acts unenforceable. In this regard, the court is empowered to rule on complaints by individuals that a governmental act has violated their constitutional rights. The military tribunals decide cases concerning criminal charges against military personnel, as well as certain offenses, such as those that jeopardize the defense of the state or are directed against the military service, allegedly committed by civilians.

The structures of the court systems of the constituent republics closely resemble each other. Both republics have constitutional courts with exclusive competence to decide constitutional questions, three-tiered courts of general jurisdiction that preside over criminal, civil, and appeals from decisions of administrative agencies, and commercial courts. Separate administrative courts do not exist in the FRY. Like the Federal Constitutional Court, the Serbian Constitutional Court, which has nine justices, and Montenegrin Constitutional Court, with five justices, are empowered to rule on complaints by individuals that

Legal Structure of Yugoslavia Courts

FEDERAL COURTS

Federal Constitutional Court	Federal Court	Military Tribunals

COURTS OF THE REPUBLIC OF MONTENEGRO

Constitutional Court	**Courts of General Jurisdiction** Supreme Court Higher Courts Primary Courts	**Commercial Courts** Higher Commercial Court First-Instance Courts

COURTS OF THE REPUBLIC OF SERBIA

Constitutional Court	**Courts of General Jurisdiction** Supreme Court District Courts Municipal Courts	**Commercial Courts** Higher Commercial Court First-Instance Courts

governmental acts have violated their rights under the respective constitutions. The middle-tier courts of general jurisdiction (District Courts in Serbia, Higher Courts in Montenegro) hear appeals from decisions of the lowest-level courts (Municipal Courts in Serbia, Primary Courts in Montenegro), except where the laws prescribe that the middle-tier courts act as courts of first instance, such as in trials concerning serious criminal offenses. Both republics have Supreme Courts, which act as the final appellate body on matters arising under republican laws. The commercial (or "economic") courts are two-tiered, with first instance courts and a Higher Commercial Court in each republic. The commercial courts decide disputes arising from the activities of business organizations, including claims of criminal violations brought by public prosecutors.

A system of private arbitration in disputes involving foreign businesses is made available by the Yugoslav Chamber of Commerce and Industry, which since 1947 has administered the Foreign Trade Court of Arbitration in Belgrade. The Court of Arbitration's rules, adopted in 1997, provide that the parties to a dispute may elect to be governed by the procedural rules of the United Nations Commission for International Trade Law (UNICITRAL) and the substantive law of any country of their choosing.

The laws of the FRY also provide for judicial recognition and enforcement of foreign arbitration awards. The FRY is a party to the New York Convention on the Enforcement of Foreign Arbitration Awards of June 20, 1958, pursuant to which the states that are party to it promise to recognize and enforce foreign arbitration awards unless they have certain procedural infirmities or their recognition and enforcement would be contrary to public policy.

SPECIALIZED JUDICIAL BODIES

In March 2001, FRY President Vojislav Kostunica announced the formation of a nineteen-member Truth and Reconciliation Commission for an investigation into the events of the preceding decade, including allegations of mass human rights violations. At the time of this writing, the commission has not begun to function, and numerous questions concerning its mandate and powers await resolution.

Meanwhile, although it is outside the structure of the FRY legal system, the country's relationship to the UN International Criminal Tribunal for former Yugoslavia in The Hague has been a subject of great controversy.

STAFFING

A key characteristic of the FRY legal system is that the appointment and dismissal of all judges, at both the federal and republican levels, is performed by the respective legislative bodies. The only exception to this system is found in the military tribunals, whose judges and prosecutors are appointed and dismissed by the FRY president. Nominations for judicial appointments are generally made to the respective legislatures by the ministries of justice; however, in the case of constitutional court justices, the FRY and republican presidents make the nominations.

All judges in the courts of general jurisdiction are granted life tenure under the Serbian and Montenegrin Constitutions, subject to mandatory retirement as specified by law. Justices of the Serbian Constitutional Court also have life tenure (also subject to mandatory retirement), while their counterparts on the Montenegrin Constitutional Court serve for nine-year, nonrenewable terms. At the federal level, justices on the eleven-member Federal Court and seven-member Federal Constitutional Court serve for nine-year, renewable terms.

Along with the preceding provisions regarding life tenure or fixed terms of service, however, the constitutions also provide for dismissal of judges by the respective legislative bodies. Justices on the constitutional courts may be dismissed only if they are permanently incapable of performing their duties or are found guilty of criminal offenses that render them unfit to perform their duties. All other judges may be dismissed not only on the same grounds but also if they have performed their duties unprofessionally (or in the case of Federal Court Justices, in an "incompetent manner") or unconscientiously.

The provisions for dismissal of judges received broad application during the political turmoil in Serbia in 1999–2001. First, in 1999–2000, dozens of judges were dismissed for their perceived opposition to policies of the Milosevic regime. Then, in February 2001, the Serbian legislature dismissed a large number of Milosevic-era judges and prosecutors and reappointed the former president of the Supreme Court, who had been among those dismissed in 2000.

The public prosecutor in Serbia is also granted life tenure. The public prosecutor in Montenegro is appointed for a five-year, renewable term, while the federal public prosecutor serves a four-year, renewable term. The federal public prosecutor may also be subject to dismissal by the Federal Assembly on the same grounds as those that apply to justices of the Federal Court.

Entry into the private practice of law in the FRY is governed by a federal statute enacted in 1998. To become a licensed attorney (*advokat*), a candidate must hold a law degree, complete between two to four years of practical postgraduation training, and pass an admission examination. Six universities in the FRY grant law degrees. A qualified advokat may appear before any court in the FRY. Under certain conditions, including reciprocity, a foreign citizen who is licensed to practice law in his or her own country may be granted the opportunity to practice in the FRY. Unlike many continental European countries, the FRY does not establish notaries as a discrete legal profession; instead, the tasks of document authentication and similar functions are handled by court personnel.

Membership in a local or regional bar association is compulsory for attorneys. Bar associations maintain the list of licensed attorneys in their area and establish and enforce rules of professional conduct. The largest bar association, in the city of Belgrade, has approximately 3,000 members, among whom 2,300 are attorneys and 700 are legal assistants.

IMPACT OF LAW

A number of current developments in the FRY are expected to have an impact on the legal system in the near future. These include an intense debate over the necessity for, and direction of, fundamental reforms.

Since 1990, the legal system in the FRY has suffered a considerable loss in public esteem. Public disillusionment stems from the absence of judicial independence and frequency of arbitrary decisionmaking, resulting from the legacy of political interference in the selection and dismissal of judges. In addition, the courts are viewed as ineffective: For example, it is claimed that the police regularly have ignored court rulings.

Within the judiciary, morale has been low, due to low salaries, political influence, and general lack of respect. The period since 1990 has been marked by widespread turnovers in judicial personnel. Many judges have left for private practice, often replaced by persons selected on the basis of their affiliation to the ruling party.

The identification and implementation of measures to address these problems is a matter of intense debate. According to some critics, the goal of judicial independence will not be achieved unless the nomination, selection, and dismissal of judges is removed from the Ministries of Justice and the political arena and transferred to autonomous professional institutions. Reformers also seek improvements in the work and living conditions of the judiciary, claiming that salaries for judges and court personnel must be increased in order to improve retention and ward off the attractions of bribery or granting of special privileges. In addition, courtrooms and offices are poorly maintained and lack equipment. A related goal of reformers is the articulation and professional enforcement of judicial ethics. In April 2001, the Association of Judges of Serbia adopted a new Code of Judicial Ethics.

The laws themselves are also undergoing scrutiny. In particular, attention has been focused on criminal procedure, including the allocation of responsibilities and authority among investigating judges, prosecutors, and the police during the pretrial phase. Among the reformers' goals are protections for the independence of prosecutors, reduction of the powers and autonomy of the police, and creation of the institution of ombudsperson.

One of the consequences of the FRY's isolation has been the estrangement of its lawyers and judges from systems of cooperation among European legal systems since 1990. Steps are being taken to reverse this process: The FRY was admitted to the Organization for Security and Cooperation in Europe in November 2000 and granted guest status in the Parliamentary Assembly of the forth-three-state Council of Europe two months later. If the FRY is eventually admitted to full membership to the Council of Europe, it will become a party to the ECHR and therefore subject to the jurisdiction of the European Court of Human Rights. Finally, it can be expected that the ongoing threat of Montenegro's secession and the evolution of the UN-administered legal system in Kosovo will have significant impact on developments in the FRY.

In all, the short but turbulent history of the FRY legal system has been marked by the close interaction of law and politics. To what extent anticipated changes will occur—and the direction they will take—will depend in large part on political developments.

Peter Krug

See also Administrative Law; Arbitration; Civil Law; Constitutional Review; Criminal Procedures; European Court and Commission of Human Rights; Federalism; Judicial Independence; Judicial Selection, Methods of; Legal Professionals—Civil Law Traditions; Ottoman Empire; Prosecuting Authorities; War Crimes Tribunals

References and further reading

Bar Association of Serbia, http://www.advokatska-komora.co.yu/index-e.htm (cited June 21, 2001).
Belgrade Centre for Human Rights. "Human Rights in Yugoslavia 2000: Legal Provisions, Practice and Legal Consciousness in the Federal Republic of Yugoslavia Compared to International Human Rights Standards." http://bgcentar.org.yu (cited July 21, 2001).
Belgrade University, Faculty of Law. http://www.ius.bg.ac.yu/eng.html (cited June 21, 2001).
Government of the Republic of Serbia. "SerbiaInfo." http://www.serbia-info.com (cited September 9, 2001).
Lorenz, F. M. 2000. "The Rule of Law in Kosovo: Problems and Prospects." *Criminal Law Forum* 11: 127–142.
Lukic, Radomir V. 1995. "The Head of State in the Constitutional System of the Federal Republic of Yugoslavia." *Yugoslav Law* 22, no. 3: 61–90.
Montenet [subjects, including "Law," related to Montenegro]. http://www.montenet.org/ (cited June 21, 2001).
Organization for Security and Cooperation in Europe, Mission to the Federal Republic of Yugoslavia. "Report on the Judicial Reform Workshop, 9 April 2001." http://www.osce.org/yugoslavia/index.php3 (cited June 21, 2001).
Stojanovic, Zoran, Obrad Peric, and Djordje Ignjatovic. 1999. "Yugoslavia." *International Encyclopaedia of Laws*. Vol. 4, *Criminal Law*. Edited by L. DuPont and C. Fijnaut; General editor R. Blanpain. The Hague, London, and Boston: Kluwer Law International.
Yugoslav Association of Constitutional Law. 1995. *National Reports for the Fourth World Congress of the International Association of Constitutional Law*. Beograd: Yugoslav Association of Constitutional Law.

YUKON

See Northern Territories of Canada

Z

ZAMBIA

POLITICAL HISTORY OF ZAMBIA

Zambia has a land area of 756,309 square kilometers and a population of 9 million. It became a British protectorate through a series of concessions concluded between African Chiefs and European traders. In 1889, Rhodes secured a charter incorporating the British South Africa Company granting it powers to enter into treaties and concessions with African chiefs. The northwestern part of the country was acquired through various treaties and concessions made with Lewanika, the king of Barotseland, by officials of the company. In 1889, the Barotseland and North-Western Rhodesia Order in Council was passed and it defined the country's boundaries and provided for its administration by the company. The northeastern part of what is now Zambia was acquired through concessions made between African chiefs and Sharpe and Thompson as agents of the company. By 1900, the North-Eastern Rhodesia Order in Council was enacted, and it gave the company statutory powers of administration over that part of the country.

From 1900 to 1911, the northeastern and northwestern parts of the country were administered separately. However, as time passed, it became increasingly apparent that the two territories could be more effectively administered as a single territory. On May 4, 1911, the two territories were amalgamated by the 1911 Northern Rhodesia Order in Council. Its provisions were brought into operation by the Northern Rhodesia Proclamation of August 17, 1911. The country remained under company rule, subject to ultimate British control. Company rule was terminated in 1924 by the Northern Rhodesia Order in Council of February 1, 1924. The British government assumed responsibility for the administration of the territory, while the status of Northern Rhodesia became that of a protectorate, a situation that obtained until August 1, 1953, when the territory was made part of the British Central African Federation. The federation was dissolved on December 31, 1963, and on October 24, 1964, Northern Rhodesia became the independent state of Zambia.

Zambia is a major producer of copper. Mining was in existence long before the advent of colonial rule. From about the eighteenth century, the inhabitants of Zambia and Katanga exported smelted copper in the form of bangles or crosses to ports on both the Atlantic and the Indian Ocean coasts of Africa. They used iron for their tools, but copper was particularly important for ornaments and as a means of exchange. The discovery of the mines by white prospectors was facilitated by earlier native workings. This is an undulating area, roughly 114 kilometers in length by 48 kilometers in width. To a lesser extent than copper, Zambia produces other minerals. These include zinc, lead, silver, coal, cobalt, and amethyst. The Zambian mining industry is of tremendous importance to the country's economy. At independence in 1964, the economic structure of Zambia, like other countries in the region that are rich in mineral resources, was based on the export of raw materials, mainly its minerals. Even today, the predominant factor in the Zambian economy is the mining and processing of copper. The Zambian economy is a classic example of a dual economy in which a highly sophisticated technology-based sector exists side by side with a subsistence sector. It has a small manufacturing sector and a huge agricultural potential. Zambia is also one of the most urbanized countries in Africa. Statistics show that rural population numbers are only marginally higher than that of the towns and cities. The rural sector, comprising 60 percent of the total population, is characterized by low output and productivity and poor standards of living.

CONSTITUTIONS OF ZAMBIA

Until the very end of the colonial history of Northern Rhodesia, democratic self-government did not exist. There was no consitution in any meaningful sense. There was, however, a series of structural arrangements decreed by the British government, which were loosely termed constitutions. Enacted through orders in council, these arrangements were designed to promote governance with the active cooperation of the white settlers and acceptance by the Africans. Although a limited African franchise first appeared in 1958, becoming substantial in 1962, full suffrage only arrived in January 1964. The final Order-in-Council came later in that year. Accompanied by an Act of Independence by the

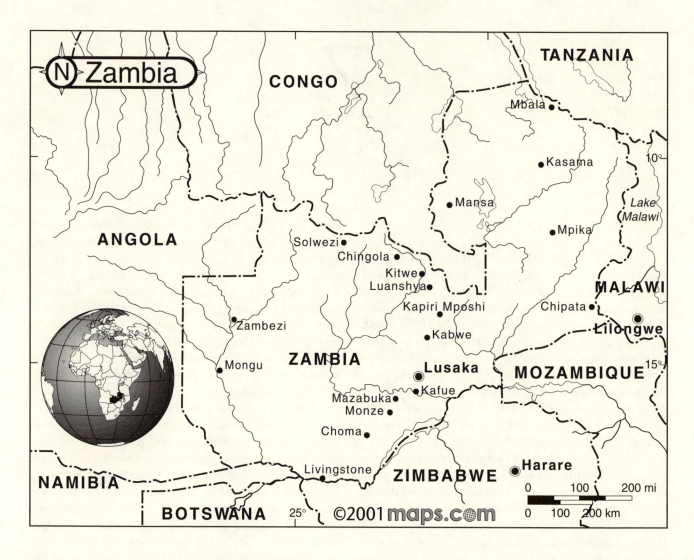

British Parliament, the Order's Schedule II set forth the Constitution of Zambia. Like its colonial predecessors, this 1964 document detailed the structure of government. Commonly, independence constitutions in British colonial Africa have borne the imprint of the Westminster model of representative government, but there are differences among them. In some, a nonexecutive president substituted for the monarch as head of state. In others, including that in Zambia, the president was also the chief executive.

The qualifications for the presidency were straightforward: Zambian citizenship, attainment of the age of thirty, and qualification as a voter in elections to the National Assembly. The constitution vested broad executive power in the president. The president is assisted by a cabinet. While the office of minister was created by Parliament, appointment of ministers from among members of the National Assembly was vested in the president. The 1964 Constitution vested all legislative powers in Parliament, which consisted of the president and the National Assembly. To be elected to Parliament, a person had to be a Zambian citizen and have attained the age of twenty-

one. Parliament was presided over by a speaker elected by the National Assembly from its membership or from those qualified to be elected to that body. The legislative power of Parliament was exercised through bills passed by the National Assembly and assented to by the president. Today, the National Assembly consists of 150 elected members and 8 nominated members. The normal duration of Parliament is a period of five years from the date of its seating, but it may be dissolved earlier by the president. A bill passed by the assembly is presented to the president for his or her assent, but if he or she withholds his or her assent, the bill is to be returned to the assembly. It cannot be presented again unless a motion is adopted by not less than two-thirds of all members of the assembly, within a period of six months of its being returned, to the effect that the bill should again be presented for assent. On its second presentation, the president is required to assent to the bill, unless he or she decides to dissolve Parliament. The constitution provided for a House of Chiefs, mainly a deliberative body. It could consider and discuss any bill introduced or proposed to be introduced in the National Assembly or any other matter referred to the house by the president. It had no legislative powers and, as such, could not enact or block legislation.

The 1964 Constitution contained an extensive bill of rights. Under it, every person in Zambia, regardless of race, place of origin, political opinions, color, creed or sex, was entitled to fundamental rights and freedoms of the individual. The rights enumerated in the constitution were life; liberty; security of the person and the protection of the law; freedom of conscience, expression, assembly, and association; freedom for the privacy of the home and other property; and freedom from deprivation of property without compensation. These rights were, however, by no means absolute. They were subject to detailed limitations, popularly referred to as "saving provisions," contained in the very articles granting the individual rights. Designed to ensure that the enjoyment of the rights and freedoms by any individual did not prejudice the rights and freedoms of others or the public interest, in practice these limitations were used by government to tamper with individual rights. Subject to these limitations, the fundamental rights were judicially enforceable. Any person who alleged that any of his or her rights as protected by the constitution were being infringed could apply to the High Court for redress.

In 1972, the government in power announced that it had decided to turn Zambia into a one-party state. This move was stated to be in the interest of unity and economic development, but the context of the decision strongly suggested that it was really a response to mounting divisions within the ruling party, which were perceived as threatening its hold on power. The one-party state constitution came into being on August 25, 1973. The 1964 Constitution was repealed and replaced by the 1973 Constitution, whose preamble declared Zambia a one-party state. It recognized the protection of life, liberty, and property and the freedom of conscience, expression, and association within the context of the national constitution. The provisions of the constitution relating to the executive, the judiciary, and Parliament remained substantially the same as those contained in the 1964 Constitution. The executive arrangement changed in that the secretary general of the party, in line with the new political order, became the deputy leader of the nation and acted in the absence of the president. The constitution created the office of the prime minister to be leader of government business in Parliament. It also declared the United National Independence Party as the one and only political party allowed to exist and operate in the country. It became illegal to form or attempt to form any other political party or organization and illegal to belong to any political party other than UNIP. One notable improvement in the 1973 Constitution over its predecessor was the introduction of the office of the investigator general

to inquire into the conduct of any person in the public service with respect to the exercise of authority or abuse thereof.

The years of the one-party state were difficult ones for Zambia. Throughout the period, from 1973 to 1991, the economy of the country continued to stagnate, with attendant unhappiness of many segments of society. As the decade of the 1980s drew to a close, demands for an end to the one-party state became more insistent. The government succumbed to pressure and amended the 1973 Constitution to permit formation of other parties. After the work of a constitutional review commission and much negotiation, an agreement was reached to reformulate the 1973 Constitution and adopt the 1991 Constitution in order to facilitate the reintroduction of multiparty politics. The 1991 Constitution, like its predecessor, provided for the protection of fundamental rights and freedoms of the individual, but it retained the limitations contained in the 1973 Constitution. Barely two months after the enactment of the 1991 Constitution, elections were held that ushered in a multiparty system of government.

In 1996, the government amended the 1991 Constitution in a manner that strengthened the government's hold on power. The government action was widely condemned. In effect, it created a new constitution through an act of Parliament made possible by its overwhelming majority. The 1964, 1991, and 1996 Constitutions provided that the constitution may be amended by means of an act of Parliament supported on the second reading and third reading of the bill by not less than two-thirds of all the members of the National Assembly. However, in the case of the amendment of certain specially entrenched provisions of the constitution, such a bill is also required to be approved by the people in a referendum.

SOURCES OF LAW
The sources of Zambian law in general are African customary law, the common law of England, and the various laws, both colonial and postindependence, enacted by Parliament.

Customary Law
The first law that ever existed in Zambia was the indigenous law of the tribes. It is generally referred to as customary law, and the great majority of Zambians still conduct most of their personal activities in accordance with and subject to it. It should be appreciated that the use of the term *customary law* does not indicate that there is a single uniform set of customs prevailing throughout the country. Rather, it is used as a blanket description covering many different systems. These systems are largely tribal in origin, and they usually operate only within the area occupied by the tribe and cover disputes in which at

least one of the parties to the dispute is a member of the tribe. There are local variations within such areas, but, by and large, the broad principles in all the various systems are the same. Today, to a large extent, customary law is only relevant in the area of personal law, in regard to matters such as marriage, inheritance, and traditional authority; it has little if any application to commercial, contracts, constitutional, or criminal law.

The Common Law

Like most other former British dependencies, Zambia is a common law jurisdiction. This description is supported by the history of the country as well as by current statutory guidelines and judicial declarations. The common law system of judicial administration was first introduced by the British in 1889. The Royal Charter of October 29, 1889, incorporating the British South Africa Company, which also entrusted the administration of Zambia to the company, authorized it to administer justice. In the Barotseland–North Western Rhodesia Order in Council of 1899, the main purpose of which was to establish an elaborate judicial system in the part of the territory to which it pertained, it was stated that English law was to apply except where otherwise stated in the order. The North-Eastern Rhodesia Order in Council of 1900 made similar provisions for the rest of Northern Rhodesia not covered by the Barotseland Order in Council of 1899.

Several other statutes refer to the law of England, but by far the most important is chapter 4 of the present laws of Zambia. This piece of legislation, the title of which is the English Law Extent of Application Act, provides that (1) the common law, (2) the doctrines of equity, (3) the statutes that were in force in England on August 17, 1911, and (4) any later English statutes applied to Zambia shall be in force in the republic. For a statute of fundamental significance, chapter 4 is uncomfortably vague. There is doubt about the significance of the 1911 date, about precisely which pre-1911 English statutes are applicable, about what *doctrines of equity* means, and most of all about whether it embraces the law as developed in common law jurisdictions other than England.

It is possible to argue that the law referred to can only include English common law, not that developed by any other common law jurisdiction. The history of the enactment supports this view. The title of the act, as well as the side notes to it, also support the view that it refers exclusively to England. This construction is also favored by the preliminary definition given in the interpretation and general provision of the statutes. So far, the practice of Zambian courts is to refer to English cases and decisions from other common law jurisdictions when there is an absence of Zambian authorities and develop the law against the background of the local social conditions. As a result, the development of Zambian law has been influenced by decisions of English-speaking courts from many parts of the world.

THE JUDICIAL SYSTEM

Local Courts

At the lowest level of the Zambian judicial system are the Local Courts, as established under the Local Courts Act of 1966. The Local Courts are divided into grades, and their jurisdiction is limited according to the grade that the court warrant assigns to them. There is a monetary limitation in terms of the value of the matters that can be brought before these courts. This does not appear to apply to inheritance or matrimonial claims under customary law. Local Courts are primarily authorized to apply and enforce customary law and bylaws and regulations promulgated under the Local Government Act. In addition, they may apply and enforce such written laws as are specified by relevant statutory instruments. As to criminal jurisdiction, local courts may try specified offenses under written laws but not crimes under customary laws. The Local Courts Act also specifies limits on the territorial jurisdiction of a local court. As to most civil matters, the courts may hear a case if the defendant has resided within the courts' jurisdiction or if the cause of action arose within the courts' jurisdiction. The main workload of the Local Courts is the law relating to nonstatutory marriages, that is, marriages under contracted customary law. Typically the issues that arise include divorce, reconciliation, custody of children, payment of *lobolo* (bride wealth), pregnancy suits, compensation for adultery, and devolution of property of persons who die without leaving a will.

Subordinate Courts

At the next higher level, Zambia has Subordinate Courts, presided over by magistrates appointed by the Judicial Service Commission. The jurisdiction of the Subordinate Court depends on its class rating and the type of magistrate sitting. For example, a Subordinate Court designated class I, with a professional resident magistrate, may hear claims in personal suits arising from a tort, a contract, or both, if the amount in controversy does not exceed a prescribed value. If a senior resident magistrate is presiding, the limit rises to a specified amount. The jurisdiction varies between classes, not only in amount but also as to types of action that can be tried. Only a first- or second-class Subordinate Court may entertain an application for an ejectment order; enforcement of attachments is reserved to first- and second-class courts; and while all Subordinate Courts may hear certain actions grounded in marriage and family law, certain other types of cases in those areas are restricted to the higher Subordinate Courts. Somewhat unexpectedly, the Criminal Procedure

Code also grants to Subordinate Courts a limited type of civil jurisdiction for awarding a judgment for the value of property illegally obtained by a public employee.

Criminal jurisdiction also varies according to the type of magistrate and class of court. The primary restrictions are stated in terms of sentencing limits. For example, a class I magistrate may impose sentences of imprisonment up to ten years in length, while lower-ranking magistrates may impose sentences of up to five years of imprisonment. These sections not only limit the sentencing power of the courts, they also restrict the types of offenses that the court may try. If a minimum sentence imposed by statute exceeds the maximum sentencing power of a court, it has been held that the court lacks jurisdiction to try the offense. The Criminal Procedure Code also prescribes limits beyond which, even though the magistrate has power to sentence an offender, a sentence given must be referred to the High Court for confirmation. Similar provisions appear regarding the imposition of fines. These provisions do not affect the jurisdictional power of the court to hear the offense; they merely affect sentencing and the execution of the sentence. The Criminal Procedure Code provides for the chief justice, by designating particular offenses, to exclude them from a Subordinate Court's jurisdiction, or reserve them for trial only by a senior magistrate. Murder and treason are statutorily barred from trial before a Subordinate Court, unless special authority is given by the High Court for such a trial.

The Subordinate Courts Act says that each court may normally exercise its jurisdiction only in the area for which it is constituted. The High Court Act, notwithstanding that restriction in the Subordinate Courts Act, allows the High Court to transfer a case to a Subordinate Court, regardless of its district, from the High Court or another Subordinate Court. The same section of the High Court Act, however, also says that such a transfer does not enlarge the civil jurisdiction limits placed on Subordinate Courts by Part III of the Subordinate Courts Act, which speaks of subject matter, and territorial jurisdiction. These restrictions do not appear to apply to the transfer of criminal cases across district lines. As to civil cases, the High Court must have intended to retain only the subject matter restrictions in Part III of the Subordinate Courts Act, although the language is not clear because the retention of the territorial restrictions would defeat the entire transfer provision. This interpretation—that the reference to Part III only means the subject matter provisions—is consistent as well with the liberality of Order XIV of the Subordinate Courts (Civil Jurisdiction) Rules, which allows for trials conducted in the nonpreferred venue under certain circumstances. These rules suggest generally that a civil case should be brought when one or more of the defendants resides or carries on business, or, if the case arises from a contract, where the con-

tract ought to have been performed. A suit commenced in the wrong district, however, may continue and be tried unless either the magistrate directs that it cease or a defendant objects, in which case the High Court may order a transfer.

Presumably, as it contains no exclusionary clause to the contrary, Section 4 of the Subordinate Courts Act also applies to criminal jurisdiction in Subordinate Courts. The Criminal Procedure Code, also controlling the exercise of criminal jurisdiction, expresses further preferences for the district in which trial should be held. In most circumstances, the law prefers a district in which the offense was wholly or partly committed, in which the consequences of the offense ensued, through which the accused passed if the offense occurred on a train, or in which the accused is apprehended, is in custody, or answers a summons. Rules regarding the transfer of cases between Subordinate Courts and the enlargement of jurisdiction authorized by the High Court also imply that these rules are more than mere venue preference and amount to normal jurisdictional limits. A magistrate may not transfer a case to another Subordinate Court lacking jurisdiction under these rules and must send an accused found in his or her district to a court in whose district the offense is alleged to have occurred. The fact that the High Court is specifically empowered to authorize a court to try a case otherwise outside its territorial limits also suggests that these restrictions amount to normal jurisdictional limits.

High Court

The Constitution Act and the High Court Act provide for the existence of the High Court of Judicature in Zambia. The president, acting in accordance with the advice of the judicial service commission, appoints the judges of the High Court, subject to ratification by the National Assembly. The constitution gives the High Court, except for matters reserved to the Industrial Relations Court, "unlimited jurisdiction to hear and determine any civil or criminal proceedings under any law, and such jurisdiction and powers as may be conferred on it by this Constitution or any other law." The High Court Act adds that, within specified limits, the High Court may also exercise "all the jurisdiction, powers and authorities vested in the High Court of Justice in England."

In addition to these broadly stated powers, various other laws and provisions in the constitution specify particular types of actions the High Court may hear. The High Court Act states that the court has jurisdiction for "judicial hearing and determination of matters in difference, the administration of or control of property or persons" and appointing or controlling guardians or keepers of persons of unsound minds and others "unable to govern themselves or their estates." The court is also given broad jurisdiction in the areas of probate and marriage law. The High Court may hear claims involving alleged past, present, and future violations of civil rights; even if such issues arise before a Subordinate Court, the matter will likely be transferred to the High Court. The court may also determine challenges to National Assembly elections, from which determination no appeal lies. The Criminal Procedure Code provides the High Court with original jurisdiction to grant an award in favor of the attorney general for the value of property illegally obtained by a public service employee, although enforcement must be ordered under other authority. The criminal jurisdiction of the High Court is also stated in broad terms. The Criminal Procedure Code says that, subject to other provisions therein, the court may try any offense under the Penal Code and any other written law. Normally, a preliminary inquiry in a Subordinate Court may precede a High Court trial, but the chief justice, by issuing a statutory order, or the director of public prosecutions, by issuing a certificate, may bring a class of cases or a particular case before the High Court for summary adjudication without a preliminary inquiry. Certain offenses, generally the more serious ones, can be tried only in the High Court. Even if a particular case can be tried in a Subordinate Court, the court may commit the accused for a trial before the High Court. Or the High Court may direct that a case before a Subordinate Court be transferred to the High Court. In addition, the High Court hears appeals from the Subordinate Courts.

Supreme Court

The Supreme Court of Zambia, created by Article 91(2) of the constitution, is the final court of appeal for Zambia. The chief justice and the deputy chief justice are members of the Supreme Court. Subject to ratification by the National Assembly, the president appoints the judges of the Supreme Court, unlike the lower court judges, without consultation with the Judicial Service Commission. The Supreme Court of Zambia Act, No. 41 of 1973, grants appellate and original jurisdiction to the Supreme Court. It states: "[The] court shall have jurisdiction, to hear and determine appeals in civil and criminal matters as provided in this Act and such other appellate or original jurisdiction as may be conferred upon it by or under the Constitution or any other law." While this section allows granting of original jurisdiction, the Supreme Court acts under present law, primarily as the final court of appeal in Zambia.

Industrial Relations Court

The Industrial Relations Court has jurisdiction over employment and industrial disputes. In some respects, this court is a quasi-judicial body because not all its members hold judicial qualifications. In this regard, only the chair-

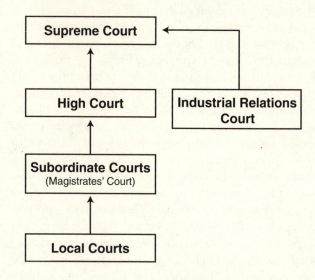

Legal Structure of Zambia Courts

person and the deputy chairperson are required to hold judicial qualifications. The members of the court are appointed by the president. The court is the country's primary labor court. The court has power, authority, and jurisdiction to examine and approve collective agreements; to inquire into and make awards and decisions in any collective disputes; to inquire into and make awards and decisions in any matters relating to industrial relations that may be referred to it; to interpret the terms of awards and agreements; and to generally inquire into and adjudicate on any matter affecting the rights, obligations, and privileges of employees, employers, and representative organizations.

Human Rights Commission

The Human Rights Act of 1996 established the Human Rights Commission. The functions of the commission are to: investigate human rights violations; investigate any maladministration of justice; propose effective measures to prevent human rights abuse; visit prisons and places of detention or related facilities with a view to assessing and inspecting conditions of the persons held in such places and making recommendations to redress existing problems; and establish a continuing program of research, education, information, and rehabilitation of victims of human rights abuses to enhance the respect for and protection of human rights. The commission has power to investigate any human rights abuses on its own initiative or on receipt of a complaint or allegation by an aggrieved person, an association, or an individual acting on behalf of an aggrieved person. The commission makes written reports of its findings and is empowered to make such recommendations as it considers necessary to the appropriate authority.

LEGAL PROFESSION

The most striking feature of the preindependence legal education in Zambia was the absence of national educational facilities. The only way to train as a lawyer was to journey to London, join an Inn of Court, and acquire English professional qualifications. There was no significant movement in terms of creating local facilities until 1961. A report on legal education of that year recommended the establishment of local training facilities. The program of local legal education commenced at the University of Zambia in 1967. The university offers the LL.B. degree. However, possession of a law degree does not of itself constitute qualification for practicing as a lawyer. Completion of a one-year period of practical training offered by the Institute for Advanced Legal Studies is required.

The legal framework governing the training and practice of the law in Zambia is the Legal Practitioners Act. An applicant for admission to practice law must produce proof that he or she is over twenty-one years of age and is a fit and proper person to be admitted to practice. The applicant should possess an LL.B. degree from the University of Zambia or another recognized university (that is, one whose degree has been recognized by the University of Zambia as equivalent to the University of Zambia LL.B. degree) and must have passed the legal qualifying examinations conducted by the Institute for Advanced Legal Studies. All practicing lawyers are required to belong to the Law Association of Zambia. The association is in charge of disciplinary matters regarding the conduct of lawyers and the profession. To engage in practice, a lawyer must obtain a practicing certificate annually from the Law Association. This requirement is intended to give the association the authority and financial ability (derived from the fees charged) to control the way lawyers handle client affairs and thus fulfill its role of professional guardianship of its members. Lawyers can appear before all courts in Zambia, with the exception of the Local Courts.

Muna Ndulo

See also Common Law; Customary Law; Indigenous and Folk Legal Systems; Legal Pluralism; Magistrates—Common Law Systems

References and further reading
Colson, Elizabeth. 1957. *Seven Tribes of Northern Rhodesia.* Manchester, England: Manchester University Press.
Ghan, Lewis H. 1958. *The Birth of a Plural Society: The Development of Northern Rhodesia under the British South Africa Company, 1894–1914.* Westport, CT: Greenwood Press.
Gluckman, Max. 1955. *The Judicial Process among the Barotse of Northern Rhodesia.* Manchester, England: Manchester University Press.
Hall, Richard Hall. 1964. *Zambia.* London: Pall Mall Press.
Mainga, Muntumba. 1973. *Bulozi under the Luyana Kings.* London: Longmans, London.
Mwanakatwe, John. 1993. *End of Kaunda Era.* Lusaka, Zambia: Muiltimedia Publication.
Ndulo, Muna. 1984. *Law in Zambia.* Nairobi: East African Publishing House.
———. 1987. *Mining Rights in Zambia.* Lusaka, Zambia: NECZAM.
Ndulo, Muna, and Robert Kent. 1996. "Constitutionalism in Zambia: Past Present and the Future." *Journal of African Law* 40: 257.
Rotberg, Robert. 1965. *The Rise of Nationalism in Central Africa.* Cambridge, MA: Harvard University Press.
Wills, Alfred John. 1973. *An Introduction to the History of Central Africa.* London: Oxford University Press.

ZANZIBAR
See Tanzania

ZIMBABWE

GENERAL INFORMATION

The Republic of Zimbabwe is a landlocked southern African state bordering Zambia to the north, Mozambique to the east, South Africa to the south, and Botswana to the west. Within its 390,245 square kilometers (152,439 square miles) lie outstanding natural features such as the Victoria Falls, Great Zimbabwe (from which the country takes its name), the Eastern Highlands, and Hwange National Park. It also shares the great man-made Lake Kariba with its northern neighbor Zambia.

The country's population of some 12 million is made up predominantly of two groups, the Mashona (some 75 percent) and the Matabele (some 21 percent). There are also small, but economically important, European and Indian populations. Life expectancy is fifty-one years, although that is falling, due largely to the ongoing AIDS pandemic.

The capital city is Harare; the other major urban centers are Bulawayo, Chitungwiza, Mutare, and Gweru. Some 35 percent of the population live in the urban centers.

At independence in 1980, Zimbabwe inherited an economy that was more industrialized than most in Africa. Its economy remains heavily reliant on crops such as tobacco, cotton, and sugar cane, and on related industries such as textiles and sugar production. Mining, particularly gold, is also significant. Recent years have seen a disastrous economic decline caused by a series of factors, including falling prices for its exports, turmoil in the agricultural sector because of the invasion of many white-owned commercial farms by so-called "war veterans" from the independence struggle, high inflation, and loss of investor confidence arising from uncertainty over domestic policies. Significant military involvement in the Democratic Republic of Congo has also significantly

©2001 maps.com

added to the economic woes. Zimbabwe is currently in arrears to internal and external creditors, leading to the suspension of international aid. This has aggravated the foreign exchange shortage in the country, making key imports, especially fuel, in short supply.

English, Shona, and Ndebele are the main languages, although there are several other indigenous languages. English is the official language of the higher courts.

The climate is temperate, with daytime temperatures averaging between 25° C and 30° C over most of the country for much of the year. Zimbabwe enjoys a dry season from around April to October and a rainy season from around November to March.

The country's legal system is largely based on Roman-Dutch law, although common law has relevance in some areas (including criminal and civil procedure and evidence). Customary law is important, particularly as regards family law and succession.

HISTORY

Zimbabwe, formerly Southern Rhodesia, was originally inhabited by descendants of the great southern migration that peopled most of southern and central Africa. A highly organized Shona-speaking state developed with a tradition of self-government and independence going back to the Kingdom of Monomotapa (Munhumutapa) and centered around Great Zimbabwe. About 1830 the Matabele, an offshoot of the Zulu nation, established a centralized state in the southwest of modern-day Zimbabwe with Bulawayo as its capital. By 1888, Lobengula, the Ndebele king, claimed sovereignty over all the territory that now forms Zimbabwe.

In October 1889, Cecil Rhodes obtained a Royal Charter setting up the British South African Company (BSAC). In 1890, Mashonaland was occupied by BSAC forces, which founded the capital in Salisbury (now Harare), and in the following year the territory was declared a British protectorate. In 1893 hostilities between the company and the Ndebele led to the occupation of Matabeleland. Lobengula was forced to flee, and reports of his death led to the British declaring the Matabele kingdom at an end. As a result, land and cattle were seized by the company. In 1895 the entire territory was named Rhodesia. The first *Chimurenga* war took place between 1896 and 1897. This was a nationwide rebellion against the occupation, although there were essentially separate revolts in Matabeleland and Mashonaland. With considerable difficulty the company regained control of the country, but the war was highly influential in the later freedom struggle.

Until 1923 the Colony of Rhodesia, as it became known in 1898, was administered by the BSAC. In a 1922 referendum on a new constitutional structure, the majority of voters (8,744 to 5,989) opted for "responsible government" rather than incorporation into the Union of South Africa. It is unlikely that the number of African voters exceeded 90 (out of an estimated population of around 900,000). Accordingly, under the Southern Rhodesia Letters Patent (1923), the country became a self-governing colony. Thus the overwhelming black majority found themselves governed under the loosest of imperial supervision by ministers responsible to a legislature elected by the white settlers and under the day-to-day control of an administration staffed by locally recruited Europeans.

The issue of land ownership, which still remains a matter of bitter dispute, has its roots in the expropriation from the indigenous people without compensation of 39 million hectares of land (96 million acres) by the BSAC. In 1930 the Land Apportionment Act then formally introduced the principle of racial discrimination into land allocation by, among other things, assigning 50.8 percent of the land to the sole occupation of Europeans. It meant that at independence in 1980, the most productive land remained in the hands of Europeans, and those interests were protected by complex provisions against compulsory land acquisition for a minimum of ten years in the independence constitution.

In 1947, Benjamin Burombo organized the African Workers' Voice Association, which was an important forerunner to the African nationalist groups. The organization was banned in 1952, but in 1957 the first nationalist party, the African National Congress, was formed with Joshua Nkomo as its president. The organization was later banned, as were its successors, the National Democratic Party and the Zimbabwe African Peoples Union (ZAPU). Following dissatisfaction with the policies of ZAPU, in 1963 the Zimbabwe African National Union (ZANU) was founded. Dedicated to national independence and liberation through the armed struggle, it launched the second *Chimurenga* war, although it was not until 1980 that this led finally to independence.

In 1961 a new constitution provided for considerable internal sovereignty and included for the first time a justiciable Declaration of Rights. However the document was fatally flawed, in that while the franchise provisions supposedly enshrined the principle of unimpeded progress to majority rule, in practice the educational and economic requirements for voting all but guaranteed a permanently subordinate role for Africans. During this period the Rhodesian government had enacted increasingly repressive security legislation. In particular, in 1960 the Law and Order (Maintenance) Act gave the government such wide and ill-defined security powers that its enactment led to the resignation of the federal chief justice, Sir Robert Tredgold, who foresaw (correctly) that it would compel the courts to become party to widespread injustice. Following the declaration of a state of emergency in 1965, the Emergency Powers Act also came into effect, which ensured the establishment of an executive dictatorship both up to independence and beyond.

Lengthy discussions between the Rhodesian and British governments over the granting of independence by Britain broke down, and on November 11, 1965, the Rhodesian prime minister, Ian Smith, and his ministers purported both to issue a Unilateral Declaration of Independence and to adopt the 1965 "Constitution of Rhodesia." The British government responded by making drastic changes to the 1961 Constitution and declaring void and of no effect any law passed or executive action performed by the illegal regime. At first the position of the judiciary was unaffected, in that the judges were regarded as continuing in office under the 1961 Constitution. Indeed, the 1965 document purported to continue their appointments without any requirement for them to take an oath acknowledging the illegal regime. It was not until the case of *Madzimbamuto v. Lardner-Burke* (1969) AC 645 that matters came to a head. Here the Judicial Committee of the Privy Council upheld the right of the United Kingdom Parliament to exercise unfettered legislative power over Southern Rhodesia and to deny all legal validity to the actions of the Smith regime. As a result, a majority of the Rhodesian judiciary acknowledged the Smith regime as the lawful government in the country and recognized the 1965 document as the only valid constitution. In 1970 the regime purported to adopt the republican constitution of Rhodesia, which precluded any prospect of majority rule.

In the 1970s the armed struggle was intensified within the country by both ZANLA (the armed wing of ZANU) and ZIPRA (the armed wing of ZAPU). Continuing international efforts to secure a settlement failed, but with the increasing success of the armed struggle, in 1978 the Rhodesian government was forced to seek an "internal settlement" with a number of compliant African leaders. As a result a new constitution for the renamed Zimbabwe-Rhodesia was introduced. The internal settlement failed largely because it did not put an end to the war, in which the Patriotic Front (the coalition of ZANU and ZAPU) was clearly winning, and because it did not receive any international recognition.

As a result, in 1979 an all-party constitutional conference was held at Lancaster House in London at which an independence constitution, based on the Westminster model, was agreed. The leaders of the Patriotic Front were virtually forced to accept its terms, including the very restrictive land acquisition provisions. Even so, the most remarkable feature of the Lancaster House conference was that it produced a settlement that led to a peaceful transition to majority rule. The parties forming the Patriotic Front fought the elections separately with ZANU(PF) (as the former ZANU became known), winning a comfortable majority over PF-ZAPU and forming the first government in April 1980, with Robert Mugabe, the leader of ZANU(PF), as prime minister.

Shortly after independence, political and military violence erupted in Matabeleland, alleged by the government to be the work of so-called "dissidents." Emergency powers were widely used, including the widespread use of both preventive detention laws and restrictions on movement. A specifically antidissident force, the 5 Brigade, was also dispatched by the government to deal with the unrest. Known as *Gukurahundi,* it was responsible for perpetrating a wide range of human rights abuses against the local civilian population. In reality the problem was largely a political one, and it was ended in 1987 by a Unity Agreement, which led to PF-ZAPU's being swallowed up by ZANU(PF), thus giving the ruling party an overwhelming parliamentary majority. It was not until the late 1990s that a viable new political party, the Movement for Democratic Change, appeared on the scene to seriously challenge the dominance of ZANU(PF).

In 1999 there was a government-sponsored attempt to adopt a new "Democratic" constitution. The process emanated from the National Constitutional Assembly, which was made up of a number of civil society organizations. Clearly wishing to control the whole process, the government then established its own Constitutional Commission, with the majority of members being its own supporters. This produced a draft constitution, but that was subsequently subject to significant alterations by the president: in particular, a provision for the compulsory acquisition of land without compensation was introduced. However, the document was rejected in a national referendum in February 2000 by 54 percent of the voters. This rejection sparked off a furious reaction from government. Within days, large-scale invasions of white-owned commercial farms began, spearheaded by so-called war veterans who are fanatically loyal to Mugabe, as well as vitriolic attacks on the MDC and whites.

In the June 2000 parliamentary elections, ZANU(PF) won a narrow victory, winning 62 seats as against 57 for MDC and 1 by another party. With another 20 members being appointed by the president and another 10 chosen by traditional chiefs, the ruling party continues to enjoy a comfortable majority in the 150-seat legislature. How-

ever it has lost its two-thirds majority and is now unable to force through any constitutional amendments or vote to retain a state of emergency without the support of the MDC.

Land resettlement remains at the heart of the crisis in the country. There is essentially no opposition to land resettlement, for it is widely recognized that an equitable system of land ownership and utilization is a fundamental prerequisite for sustainable peace and development. Rather it is the extralegal methods that have been taken to acquire land. Among other things, this has led to judges being subject to extreme pressure from government ministers, ZANU(PF), and war veterans, particularly as a result of a series of rulings by the Supreme Court that the procedure for land acquisition was unconstitutional.

LEGAL CONCEPTS

The supreme law is the 1979 Constitution of Zimbabwe. It provides that, subject to any law relating to African customary law, the law to be administered by the courts is that in force in the Colony of the Cape of Good Hope on June 10, 1891, as modified by subsequent legislation.

The 1979 Constitution provided for a prime minister as head of government, a largely ceremonial president, a bicameral Parliament, an independent judiciary, and an entrenched and justiciable Declaration of Rights. It also contained specially entrenched provisions providing for separate parliamentary representation for minorities for the first seven years, and an effective prohibition on compulsory land acquisition for the first ten years. The falling away of the specially entrenched clauses and the overwhelming parliamentary majority of ZANU(PF) led to a whole series of radical amendments to the document, the net effect of which was to considerably enhance presidential power.

The Executive

The president is the head of state and head of government and serves a term of six years. There are currently two vice presidents who are tasked with assisting the president in the exercise of the executive functions. Election of the president requires a simple majority of the popular votes cast. There is no restriction on the number of terms a sitting president may serve, and the current incumbent, Robert Mugabe, has held office since 1987 (having previously served as prime minister from independence in 1980). In the event of the president's being unable to complete a term of office, a vice president assumes the office.

The cabinet consists of the president, vice presidents, and such ministers as the president may appoint. The attorney general is the principal law officer. Under the 1979 Constitution the office-holder was independent of the executive, but following a 1989 constitutional amendment the office was removed from the Public Service; appointment is now being made by the president after consultation with the Judicial Service Commission. The incumbent is specifically designated the principal legal adviser to the government, is an ex officio member of the cabinet, and has the right to sit in on and address the House of Assembly (but has no right to vote in either). The incumbent has no security of tenure.

The Legislature

The legislature consists of the president and Parliament. Parliament comprises 150 members who fall into four categories: (1) 120 popularly elected members, based on the first past the post system; (2) eight provincial governors, appointed by the president ex officio; (3) ten chiefs; and (4) twelve others appointed by the president.

Any bill passed by Parliament requires presidential assent. If that is withheld, Parliament may re-present the bill if supported by a two-thirds majority of all members. In that case the president must then give assent, unless he/she dissolves Parliament. The only occasion when presidential assent was withheld occurred in 1999, when the president refused to assent to the Public Order and Safety Bill, which would have finally repealed the Law and Order (Maintenance) Act. Parliamentarians then resolved to allow the bill to lapse. A bill seeking to amend the constitution requires the affirmative votes of not less than two-thirds of the total membership of Parliament at the final vote.

The Judiciary

The constitution provides for judicial independence, and states that "in the exercise of his [or her] judicial authority, a member of the judiciary shall not be subject to the direction or control of any person or authority, except to the extent that a written law may place him [or her] under the direction or control of another member of the judiciary." The term *judiciary* covers the chief justice, the judges of the Supreme Court and High Court, and "persons presiding over other courts . . . that are established by [statute]."

The makeup of the higher judiciary in Zimbabwe is unusual. At independence in 1980 the General Division of the High Court (now the High Court) consisted of the chief justice, nine puisne judges, and one acting judge. The Appellate Division of the High Court (now the Supreme Court) consisted of the chief justice, the judge president, and one full-time judge of appeal. All the judges were white. As part of the process of reconciliation, the new government left in office all the members of the judiciary who had served the white minority government. By 1986 all bar one had left office, and today all judges of the High Court and Supreme Court and magistrates have been appointed to their present positions since 1980.

The racial composition of the Supreme Court, in particular, is quite unusual. In a country in which the vast majority of the population is black, the Supreme Court (as of April 2001) consists of one white, three blacks, and one Indian. Indeed, until the controversial departure of Chief Justice Gubbay in March 2001, pending retirement, the Supreme Court had never had a majority of black judges. The High Court has a total of twenty-two judges, of whom four are white, two are Indians, and one colored. There are five female judges, all in the High Court (there has never been a female in the Supreme Court). All the judges are Zimbabwean citizens, although that is not a specific requirement for appointment. There are some two hundred full-time magistrates in the country, the majority of whom are men. There are two white magistrates and one Indian.

Local courts, which apply customary law, are divided into primary courts and community courts. Primary courts are presided over by a headman who is appointed by the designated minister, who must invite the local chief to nominate a suitable person, and, "unless there are good reasons to the contrary," the minister must appoint the nominee. Community courts are presided over by a chief. Chiefs are appointed by the president to preside over a community of persons who, according to customary law, fall under the jurisdiction of a chief.

The chief justice, who is head of the judiciary, and other judges of the Supreme Court and High Court, are appointed by the president after consultation with the Judicial Service Commission (JSC). If any appointment is not consistent with the recommendation of the JSC, the president must inform Parliament as soon as is practicable, although the legislature has no power to overturn the decision. To date this has never happened.

The JSC currently consists of the chief justice, judge president, attorney general, chairman of the Public Service Commission, and two senior and experienced legal practitioners from the private sector. In practice it has worked reasonably well, although presidential influence on membership remains strong.

Qualifications for appointment to the Supreme Court or High Court are that a person either (1) is or has been a judge of a court having unlimited jurisdiction in civil or criminal matters in a country in which the common law is Roman-Dutch (in practice, South Africa or Sri Lanka) or English, and English is an official language, or (2) is or has been for not less than seven years qualified to practice as a legal practitioner in Zimbabwe, or in a country in which the common law is Roman-Dutch and English is an official language, or if the candidate is a citizen of Zimbabwe, in a country in which the common law is English and English is an official language. Since 1980 virtually all judges have been appointed on permanent terms—that is, until the age of sixty-five years (or seventy years at the election of the individual judge and subject to a satisfactory medical report).

The constitution of Zimbabwe provides that the remuneration of judges be charged upon and paid out of the Consolidated Revenue Fund. Their salaries and allowances cannot be reduced during their period in office. Magistrates are part of the Public Service, and their pay and conditions are determined by their Grade in the civil service.

Members of the judiciary still generally enjoy considerable respect within society, but, as noted earlier, Supreme Court judges in particular have recently been subject to considerable public criticism from government, the ruling party, and war veterans' organizations following a series of rulings on legislation relating to land acquisition.

The attraction of becoming a judge is also tempered by their relatively poor pay and conditions. While efforts to improve conditions of service have been made, the income of a judge is about on par with that of a junior partner in a law firm (although it is above that for a senior law professor). With an annual inflation rate of upwards of 50 percent and the significant continued increasing of fees by legal practitioners, the gap between incomes is steadily widening, and, accordingly, the attraction of the bench among leading practitioners is diminishing. The effect is for judicial appointments to be increasingly made from the ranks of the senior magistracy and the attorney general's chambers. This has the effect of reducing the scope of legal experience on the part of many judges. As regards magistrates, their pay is less attractive than that of the judges, and they enjoy few other benefits. Upon retirement, judges and magistrates receive a reasonable pension and other benefits. Overall, the present level of pay and benefits remains a barrier to efforts to attract the most successful and able legal practitioners to the bench. However, this does not call into question the integrity and competence of those actually appointed.

The assignment of cases is under the overall control of the chief justice, although in practice High Court cases are normally assigned by the judge president. In the Supreme Court, in practice the judgment in cases involving fundamental rights is normally written by the chief justice. In the vast majority of cases, the other judges merely concur with the judgment, and it is unusual to find a dissenting opinion.

The High Court has a permanent presence in Harare and Bulawayo and holds circuit sessions in three other locations. Magistrates are assigned their postings by the chief magistrate. These largely depend on the type of court and the seniority of the magistrate.

A judge of the High Court or Supreme Court may resign at any time by notice in writing to the president. The office of a judge of either court cannot be abolished during the judge's tenure of office without that judge's consent. The procedure for removal is complex and has never been used since independence. A judge of the High Court or Supreme Court can be removed from office only on the (unfortunately wide-ranging and vague) grounds of inability to discharge the functions of office, whether arising from infirmity of mind or body or any other cause, or for misbehavior. If the president considers that the question of the removal from office of the chief justice ought to be investigated, the president must appoint a tribunal of inquiry. For other judges of the High Court and Supreme Court, the process is instigated by the chief justice, who advises the president to establish a tribunal of inquiry. The tribunal consists of three or more members selected by the president among (1) persons who have held office as a judge of the Supreme Court of High Court; (2) persons who hold or have held office as a judge having unlimited jurisdiction in civil or criminal matters in a country in which the common law is Roman-Dutch or English, and English is an official language; and (3) legal practitioners of not less than seven years' standing drawn from a list of not less than three nominated by the Law Society of Zimbabwe. The tribunal recommends to the president whether or not the question of the removal of the judge from office should be referred to the Judicial Service Commission. If it is recommended, the president must refer the matter and must then remove the judge from office if the JSC so advises. There is no formal procedure for the taking of disciplinary action against judges that does not involve the possibility of removal. In practice, the matter is dealt with through an internal, informal procedure.

Magistrates are appointed by the Public Service Commission after consultation with the Judicial Service Commission. Qualifications for appointment depend upon the level of seniority. For those at the lower levels (ordinary or senior magistrate), there are no specific qualifications for appointment: acceptable qualifications are an administrative matter to be decided upon by the Judicial Service Commission. For more senior appointments, legal qualifications similar to those of a judge are required.

The Judicial College of Zimbabwe was established by statute in 1998/1999. It provides training for judges, magistrates, prosecutors, other officers of court, police and prison officers, and persons concerned in the administration of justice and the law. This emphasizes that strengthening the judiciary requires an holistic approach that involves providing ongoing training for all those involved in the judicial system. The college is mandated to develop skills and knowledge in, for example, forensic matters, penology, and court procedures.

Office of the Ombudsman

The constitution also provides for an ombudsman who is empowered to investigate: (1) action taken by any officer, person, or authority in the exercise of the administrative functions of that officer or authority in any case in which it is alleged that a person has suffered injustice in consequence of that action, and it does not appear that there is any remedy reasonably available by way of proceedings in a court or on appeal from a court; or (2) allegations that any provision of the Declaration of Rights has been contravened by any officer, person, or authority. Officers and authorities excluded from investigation include the president, the Cabinet Office, the attorney general, and judicial officers. The ombudsman has wide-ranging investigative powers and, if a complaint is upheld, may make recommendations for the injustice to be rectified. If that is not done, the ombudsman may make a special report to the president and the House of Assembly.

In practice, the ombudsman has made little impact and, in particular, has seemingly not investigated the serious human rights abuses allegedly perpetrated by government officials over recent years.

International Human Rights Instruments

Zimbabwe is a party to some of the major international human rights instruments, including the International Covenant on Civil and Political Rights (but not to either of the Optional Protocols), the Convention on the Elimination of All Forms of Discrimination against Women (CEDAW), and the Convention on the Rights of the Child. Significantly, it is not a party to the UN Convention against Torture. It is a party to the African Charter on Human and People's Rights and the African Charter on the Rights and Welfare of the Child, and a signatory to the International Criminal Court Statute. Recent statutes have enacted the Chemical Weapons and Genocide Conventions into domestic law.

Criminal Law and Procedure

Criminal law is largely based upon principles of Roman-Dutch law and remains uncodified. As regards criminal procedure, the principal enactment is the Criminal Procedure and Evidence Act (Chapter 9:07). There are, however, numerous other enactments dealing with specific aspects of the criminal process. These include modern statutes dealing with extradition, mutual legal assistance, and proceeds of crime. The constitution also contains important protections for those accused of a criminal offense, including the right to legal assistance, the presumption of innocence, and the right to confront witnesses. In practice, Zimbabwean law on criminal procedure and evidence largely follows the law of England and Wales.

The procedure is strictly adversarial. Trial by jury was abolished in 1973. Instead, the use of assessors is common. In criminal trials before the High Court, the judge must sit with two assessors who have either experience in the administration of justice or experience or skill in any matter that may have to be considered at the trial; or (in the case of the trial of a juvenile) experience or skill in dealing with juveniles; or any other experience or qualification that in the opinion of the chief justice or judge president renders that person suitable to act as an assessor. The choice of assessors is normally made by the registrar of the High Court. Assessors together with the judge decide questions of fact, and the majority view prevails. In Magistrates' Courts, in certain limited circumstances up to two assessors may be appointed to assist the magistrate in deciding issues of fact. While there is no formal system of plea bargaining, it is not unusual for legal practitioners to offer a plea of guilty by their client to a less serious offense than that originally charged.

The constitution provides all accused persons with a right to the legal representation of their choice, but at their own expense. This means that, in practice, the lack of an effective legal aid system results in the majority of indigent defendants appearing unrepresented. Only those charged with an offense that carries the death penalty are entitled to be represented pro bono. The death penalty is carried out from time to time.

The attorney general is responsible for undertaking (or discontinuing) criminal proceedings. Prosecutions at the Magistrates' Court level are normally undertaken by public prosecutors who are the representatives of the attorney general. Most prosecutors are members of the Public Service, although police officers are also appointed to the position. Most are not admitted as legal practitioners. The attorney general can also require the commissioner of police to investigate and report on any matter which, in the attorney general's opinion, relates to a criminal offense, and the commissioner must comply. An order of mandamus will also be issued if the police fail to carry out a criminal investigation in a timely fashion.

Civil Law

Customary law applies (subject to financial limits) in any case in which the parties have expressly agreed that it should apply, or it appears "just and proper that it should apply," in regard to the nature of the case and the surrounding circumstances. In other cases (except as regards the Small Claims Court), the law is that provided for in the Civil Evidence Act, which came into effect in 1992. In cases where the rules of evidence are not provided for in the act, the applicable law is that of similar cases in England.

Labor Matters

In 1992 the government requested the assistance of the ILO in revising its labor legislation. The ILO later produced a draft bill, and that was widely circulated among interested parties. As a result, the Labour Relations Amendment Bill is currently going through Parliament. Of particular interest is that it incorporates a number of

ILO conventions not yet ratified by Zimbabwe and establishes a new Labour Court that will have exclusive original jurisdiction in respect of any labor dispute.

Legal Education and the Legal Profession

Legal education is conducted in the faculty of law, University of Zimbabwe in Harare. The faculty offers a four-year bachelor of laws honor degree, holders of which are automatically entitled to register as legal practitioners. Some sixty students per year graduate with this qualification. Entering the legal profession as such is seen as being extremely desirable. Competition for entry into the law faculty at the University of Zimbabwe (the sole law school in the country) remains intense, and only those with the highest academic qualifications can expect to be admitted.

The Law Society of Zimbabwe represents the interests of the six hundred or so registered legal practitioners in the country. The legal profession is fused, although there are two de facto bars practicing out of chambers in Harare. On a number of occasions the Law Society has issued public statements critical of the government, the most recent having been in 2001 concerning the threat to judicial independence.

CURRENT COURT SYSTEM

The Supreme Court is the apex court and comprises the chief justice and four other justices of appeal. Much of its work consists of hearing appeals from the High Court and Magistrates' Courts. It also enjoys original jurisdiction to hear and determine issues relating to constitutional rights. In such cases a full bench of five judges is required. Its decisions on the protection of constitutional rights has rightly earned the court international renown.

The High Court comprises the chief justice (although in practice the chief justice seldom, if ever, takes part in its proceedings), the judge president (who is in charge of the court), and other High Court judges. The court has original jurisdiction to hear all criminal cases and civil cases. It also has power to review all proceedings and decisions of inferior courts, tribunals, and administrative authorities, and hears appeals from the Magistrates' Courts and local courts.

Magistrates' Courts hear both civil and criminal cases. They are headed by the chief magistrate, under whom are (in order of seniority) regional magistrates, provincial magistrates, senior magistrates, and magistrates.

Local courts consist of primary courts and community courts. The former are presided over by a headman and the latter by a chief. Both the law applied and the procedure and the rules of evidence are regulated by customary law, and the proceedings must "be conducted in as simple and informal a manner as is reasonably possible." Legal representation is not permitted. Appeals lie from a primary court to a community court and thence to a provincial Magistrates' Court, where the appeal takes the form of a rehearing. A final appeal lies to the High Court.

Small claims courts deal with civil matters in which the claim is subject to a maximum financial limit. Only natural persons may institute proceedings, and a corporate body may be a party to the proceedings only as a defendant or respondent. All parties to the proceedings must appear in person and cannot be represented or assisted by any other person. Small claims courts are not bound by strict rules of evidence. The judgment of the court is final, although proceedings may be brought in the High Court for judicial review.

Children's courts (previously known as juvenile courts) are staffed by magistrates and assessors. They deal with matters involving issues such as sentencing in criminal cases and adoption. There are other special courts, such as the Administrative Court (which deals, for example, with land and planning matters) and the Labour Relations Tribunal.

Courts-martial are established under the Defence Act (Chapter 11.02). They may try members of the defense forces and have no jurisdiction over civilians (except, in certain circumstances, those who have recently left the defense forces). It can hear cases involving offenses peculiar to the defense forces, as well as "ordinary" criminal offenses other than treason, murder, and rape. There is a right of appeal against conviction to the Court-Martial Appeal Court, which must consist of not fewer than two Supreme Court judges appointed by the chief justice.

THE IMPACT OF LAW

Since independence in 1980, the courts have played a vital role in maintaining the rule of law. Up to 1990 this was particularly important in the field of judicial review (especially relating to the use by the government and its agents of emergency powers) and the upholding of constitutional rights. The judiciary is now widely seen as being a bulwark against a seemingly increasingly oppressive government. Following the rejection of the government-sponsored draft constitution in February 2000, maintaining the rule of law has become increasingly difficult, with politically inspired violence—intimidation of the electorate by "supporters" of the ruling party in particular—and the invasion of commercial farms by so-called war veterans with the apparent blessing of government being the order of the day.

Tensions stemming from decisions of the Supreme Court, in particular, over the legality of the procedure for land acquisition became acute in 2000, during the course of which the president and senior government ministers refused to comply with a series of court orders; in 2001 intense pressure was brought by the government, the ruling party, and war veterans organizations upon the senior

Supreme Court judges to resign. In March 2001 the chief justice finally agreed to go.

Another significant problem remains the use of amnesty laws and presidential pardon powers, which have been used on several occasions since 1980. Perhaps the best known is the amnesty granted following the human rights violations in Matabeleland and the Midlands during the 1980s. The true extent of the violations, most of which were perpetrated by the army and other organs of government, were revealed only with the publication by two local NGOs—the Catholic Commission for Justice and Peace in Zimbabwe and the Legal Resources Foundation—of their devastating report *Breaking the Silence: Building True Peace.* Presidential desire to protect government supporters from the law was also illustrated in 2000. The period between January and July 2000, when the referendum and general election took place, was characterized by serious violence against persons and property, and by human rights violations. However, in October 2000 the president made the Clemency Order No. 1 of 2000, which granted a free pardon to every person liable to criminal prosecution for any "politically motivated" crime committed between January 1, 2000, and July 31, 2000. This encompassed offenses including culpable homicide, serious assaults, arson and other malicious damage to property, extortion, intimidation, and kidnapping.

Following the June 2000 parliamentary elections, the MDC brought election petitions before the courts, challenging the election results in thirty-seven constituencies. In response, the president sought to use statutory powers in the hearing of the cases on the grounds that "these suits are frivolous and vexatious" and were "sponsored by external interests whose motives and intentions are inimical to the political stability of Zimbabwe" (Election Act [Modification][No.3] Notice 2000). These powers were later struck down by the Supreme Court as being unconstitutional.

Until 1990 the retention of the state of emergency first introduced by the Smith regime in 1965 also led to a weakening of the rule of law, especially through the use of wide-ranging emergency regulations that affected virtually every area of public life. Today there remains concern over the continued use of preindependence security powers, especially those contained in the Law and Order (Maintenance) Act, to stifle dissent. In addition, the wishes of the president are regularly invoked by the use of the Presidential Powers (Temporary Powers) Act, which came into operation in 1986. This empowers the president to make regulations dealing with "situations that have arisen or are likely to arise and that require to be dealt with as a matter of urgency . . . such that it is inexpedient to await the passage through Parliament of an Act," to deal with the situation. Such regulations prevail over any other laws (except emergency powers regulations and the constitution) and may be used to modify existing legislation. The regulations remain in force for up to six months. Regulations have covered a whole range of areas, including, in recent years, restrictions on establishing a private cellular telephone network, amending income tax legislation, preventing the operation of a private radio station, and providing for compulsory land acquisition without compensation.

Overall, it is difficult to be optimistic over future legal developments in the country.

John Hatchard

References and further reading
www.allafrica.com/zimbabwe.
Catholic Commission for Justice and Peace in Zimbabwe. 1997. *Breaking the Silence: Building True Peace.* Harare: Legal Resources Foundation.
www.channelafrica.org/currenta.shtml.
Feltoe, G. 1998. *A Guide to Civil Procedure in the Magistrates Court.* Harare: Legal Resources Foundation.
www.fingaz.co.zw.
Hatchard, John. 1993. *Individual Freedoms and State Security in the African Context: The Case of Zimbabwe.* London: James Currey.
Palley, Claire. 1966. *Constitutional History and Law of Southern Rhodesia.* Oxford: Clarendon.
Ried-Rowland, J. 1997. *Criminal Procedure in Zimbabwe.* Harare: Legal Resources Foundation.
www.samara.co.zw.

ENTRIES BY TYPE

ALTERNATIVE SYSTEMS
Alternative Dispute Resolution
International Arbitration
Jewish Law
Mediation
Neighborhood Justice Centers

COUNTRIES
Afghanistan
Albania
Algeria
Ancient Athens
Andorra
Angola
Antigua and Barbuda
Argentina
Armenia
Australia
Austria
Azerbaijan
Bahamas
Bahrain
Bangladesh
Barbados
Belarus
Belgium
Belize
Benin
Bhutan
Bolivia
Bosnia and Herzegovina
Botswana
Brazil
Brunei
Bulgaria
Burkina Faso
Burma
Burundi
Cambodia
Cameroon
Canada
Cape Verde
Central African Republic
Chad
Chile
China
Colombia

Comoros
Confederate States of America
Congo, Democratic Republic of (Kinshasa)
Congo, Republic of
Costa Rica
Côte d'Ivoire
Croatia
Cuba
Cyprus
Czech Republic
Denmark
Djibouti
Dominica
Dominican Republic
Ecuador
Egypt
El Salvador
England and Wales
Equatorial Guinea
Eritrea
Estonia
Ethiopia
Fiji
Finland
France
Gabon
Gambia
Georgia (Country)
Germany
Ghana
Greece
Grenada
Guatemala
Guinea
Guinea-Bissau
Guyana
Haiti
Honduras
Hungary
Iceland
India
Indonesia
Iran
Iraq
Ireland
Israel

Italy
Ivory Coast. *See* Côte d'Ivoire
Jamaica
Japan
Jordan
Kazakhastan
Kenya
Kiribati
Korea, North. *See* North Korea
Korea, South. *See* South Korea
Kuwait
Kyrgyzstan
Laos
Latvia
Lebanon
Lesotho
Liberia
Libya
Liechtenstein
Lithuania
Luxembourg
Macedonia
Madagascar
Malawi
Malaysia
Maldives
Mali
Malta
Marshall Islands
Mauritania
Mauritius
Mexico
Micronesia, Federated States of
Moldova
Monaco
Mongolia
Morocco
Mozambique
Myanmar. *See* Burma
Namibia
Nauru
Nepal
Netherlands
New Zealand
Nicaragua
Niger
Nigeria

North Korea
Northern Ireland
Norway
Oman
Ottoman Empire
Pakistan
Palau
Palestine
Panama
Papua New Guinea
Paraguay
Peru
Philippines
Poland
Portugal
Puerto Rico
Qatar
Romania
Russia
Rwanda
Saint Vincent and the Grenadines
Samoa
San Marino
São Tomé and Príncipe
Saudi Arabia
Scotland
Senegal
Seychelles
Sierra Leone
Singapore
Slovakia
Slovenia
Solomon Islands
Somalia
South Africa
South Korea
Spain
The Spanish Empire and the Laws
    of the Indies
Sri Lanka
St. Kitts and Nevis
St. Lucia
Sudan
Suriname
Swaziland
Sweden
Switzerland
Syria
Taiwan
Tajikistan
Tanzania
Thailand
Tibet
Togo
Tonga
Trinidad and Tobago
Tunisia
Turkey

Turkmenistan
Tuvalu
Uganda
Ukraine
United Arab Emirates
United Kingdom
United States—State Systems
United States—Federal System
Uruguay
Uzbekistan
Vanuatu
Vatican
Venezuela
Vietnam
Yemen
Yugoslavia: Kingdom of and Socialist
    Republic
Yugoslavia: Serbia and Montenegro
Zambia
Zanzibar. See Tanzania
Zimbabwe

GENERAL SYSTEMS
Adversarial System
Buddhist Law
Canon Law
Civil Law
Common Law
Customary Law
Gypsy Law
Indigenous and Folk Legal Systems
Inquisitorial Procedure
Islamic Law
Napoleonic Code
Native American Law, Traditional
Roman Law
Sharia. See Islamic Law
Soviet System

JURISPRUDENCE SYSTEMS
Critical Legal Studies
Feminist Jurisprudence
Law and Economics
Law and Society Movement
Legal Behavioralism
Legal Positivism
Legal Realism
Marxist Jurisprudence
Natural Law

KEY CONCEPTS
Administrative Law
Capital Punishment
Cause Lawyering
Civil Procedure
Commercial Law (International
    Aspects)
Constitutional Law

Constitutional Review
Constitutionalism
Consumer Law
Corporal Punishment
Criminal Procedures
Criminal Sanctions, Purposes of
Deterrence. See General Deterrence;
    Specific (Individual) Deterrence
Environmental Law
Equity
Family Law
Federalism
General Deterrence
Habeas Corpus, Writ of
Human Rights Law
Incarceration
Individual Deterrence. See Specific
    (Individual) Deterrence
International Law
Labor Law
Legal Pluralism
Parliamentary Supremacy
Private Law
Pro Se Cases
Probate/Succession Law
Protection of Society
Public Law
Rehabilitation
Retribution
Sanctions. See Criminal Sanctions,
    Purposes of
Shaming
Specific (Individual) Deterrence
Tort Law

KEY ELEMENTS
Administrative Tribunals
Advocates—Civil Law Systems. See
    Legal Professionals—Civil Law
    Traditions
Arbitration
Barristers
Certiorari, Writ of
Citizens Advice Bureaux
Contract Law
Criminal Law
Fines
Government Legal Departments
Judges, Nonjudicial Activities of
Judicial Independence
Judicial Misconduct/Judicial Discipline
Judicial Review
Judicial Selection, Methods of
Juries
Jury Selection (voir dire)
Juvenile Justice
Law Clerks
Law Firms

Lay Judiciaries
Legal Aid
Legal Education
Legal Professionals—Civil Law
  Traditions
Magistrates—Civil Law Systems
Magistrates—Common Law Systems
Merit Selection ("Missouri Plan")
Military Justice, American (Law
  and Courts)
Missouri Plan. *See* Merit Selection
  ("Missouri Plan")
Moots
Nominating Commission Plan. *See*
  Merit Selection ("Missouri Plan")
Notaries
Paralegal
Plea Bargaining
Privy Council
Prosecuting Authorities
Qadi (Qazi) Courts
Small Claims Courts
Solicitors
Trial Courts

SUBNATIONAL SYTEMS
Alabama
Alaska
Alberta
Appellate Courts
Arizona
Arkansas
Australian Capital Territory
Basque Region
British Columbia
California
Canada, Northern. *See* Northern
  Territories of Canada
Catalonia
Channel Islands
Colorado
Connecticut
Delaware
District of Columbia
Florida
Georgia (State)

Guam
Hawai'i
Hong Kong
Idaho
Illinois
Indiana
Iowa
Kansas
Kentucky
Louisiana
Maine
Manitoba
Maryland
Massachusetts
Michigan
Minnesota
Mississippi
Missouri
Montana
Nebraska
Netherlands Antilles and Aruba
Nevada
New Brunswick
New Hampshire
New Jersey
New Mexico
New South Wales
New York
Newfoundland and Labrador
North Carolina
North Dakota
Northern Territories of Canada
Northern Territory of Australia
Northwest Territories. *See* Northern
  Territories of Canada
Nova Scotia
Nanavut. *See* Northern Territories of
  Canada
Ohio
Oklahoma
Ontario
Oregon
Pennsylvania
Prince Edward Island
Quebec
Queensland

Rhode Island
Saskatchewan
South Australia
South Carolina
South Dakota
Swiss Cantons
Tasmania
Tennessee
Texas
Utah
Vermont
Victoria, State of
Virgin Islands, U.S.
Virginia
Washington
Washington, D.C. *See* District of
  Columbia
West Virginia
Western Australia
Wisconsin
Wyoming
Yukon. *See* Northern Territories of
  Canada

TRANSNATIONAL SYSTEMS
African Court/Commission on Human
  and Peoples' Rights
APEC. *See* Dispute Resolution under
  Regional Trade Agreements
Dispute Resolution under Regional
  Trade Agreements
European Court and Commission on
  Human Rights
European Court of Justice ·
Inter-American Commission and Court
  on Human Rights
International Court of Justice
International Criminal Court
International Tribunal for the Law of
  the Sea
Mercosur. *See* Dispute Resolution under
  Regional Trade Agreements
NAFTA. *See* Dispute Resolution under
  Regional Trade Agreements
War Crimes Tribunals
World Trade Organization

GLOSSARY

Adat law—A form of customary law

As of right—When a court is obligated to consider a case or matter (contrast to "by leave"), most often with regard to appeals

By leave—When a court has discretion whether to consider a case or matter (contrast to "as of right"), most often with regard to appeals

By way of case stated—A term used to describe a particular process whereby the relevant facts in a case are sent for the opinion or judgment of another court

Case law—Legal principles established through the decisions of courts (contrast to statutes)

Cassation—A form of appeal in which the only issue(s) considered is whether the lower court has correctly interpreted and applied the law

Code of Hammurabi—A law code created by Hammurabi, King of Babylonia from 1895–1950 B.C.E.; this is one of the earliest, if not the earliest, legal codes still extant

Codification—Setting down a set of legal principles in the form of a code passed by a legislative body

Condominium—Joint administration of a territory by two or more countries, as Vanuatu under Britain and France from 1906 to 1980

Confederal—Government in the form of a confederation which is a loose version of the more familiar federal system. In a confederal system, the individual units retain a high degree of sovereignty

Court of record—The court that establishes the initial factual record of a case; typically a trial court or a court of first instance

Difference theory—A theory that explains differences in social positioning or power of various groups (e.g., men and women) as based on perceived differences in the fundamental nature of the members of the groups involved

Dominance theory—A theory from social science that considers the ways that psychological, intergroup, and institutional processes interact with one another to produce and maintain group-based, hierarchical social structures. This theory has been used by some scholars to explain the patriarchal nature of much of western society and culture.

Due process—A concept that law and legal processes should be administered with care that the processes adhere to fundamental rules and norms of fairness

En banc—A situation involving a multi-judge (collegial) court where all members of the court sit together to hear and decide cases; this may either be the standard procedure for the court (e.g., the U.S. Supreme Court), or something that is done under special circumstances (e.g., the U.S. Courts of Appeals)

Ex post facto—After the fact; an "ex post facto" law is one that makes some behavior illegal and then applies that standard to actions that occurred prior to the passage of the law

Exequatur—The procedure by which a civil authority or civil ruler grants binding force to an ecclesiastical enactment with the authority's or ruler's territory

De facto—In fact; in reality whether supposed to be the case or not (contrast to "de jure")

First instance—The court that first considers a case; a trial court

Form contracts—Contracts of a standard form that are presented on a take it or leave it basis (as in a car rental contract)

General jurisdiction—Courts with a "general jurisdiction" are empowered to hear any case brought to it except for cases specifically excluded from its jurisdiction (compare to "limited jurisdiction" or "specialized jurisdiction")

Grand Kadi—A person learned in Islamic law. *See* Qadi (Qazi) Courts entry.

Greco-Roman law—The law of ancient Greece and ancient Rome

d'Hondt system—A method of allocating seats in a proportional representation system in which party's vote total is divided by a certain figure that increases as it wins more seats. As the divisor becomes bigger, the party's total in succeeding rounds gets smaller, allowing parties with lower initial totals to win seats.

De jure—Specifically established by law (compare to "de facto")

Leave of the court—Permission granted by the court, typically to bring an appeal

Legal persons—Any entity granted the legal status of a person; corporations are "legal persons" for many purposes. *See also* Physical persons.

Lex mercatoria—The law of the merchant; a body of commercial law that is often seen as governing international commercial transactions

lex non scripta—The unwritten law

Limited jurisdiction—Courts with a "limited jurisdiction" are empowered to hear only cases of a specific type or size or magnitude (compare to "general jurisdiction" and "specialized jurisdiction")

Mala in se—Evil in itself; an offense *malum in se* is one that is naturally evil, as murder, theft, and the like

Mens rea—The intent to commit an action; most crime requires a *mens rea* in addition to the action itself, although certain acts are considered to inherently carry *mens rea*

de novo—To hear a case or matter anew. A form of appeal in which the case is presented to the higher court by the parties rather than starting with the record from a lower court.

Nuisance (state and local principle)—Anything a person does that annoys or disturbs another person in the second person's use, possession, or enjoyment of that person's property

Original jurisdiction—The court having "original jurisdiction" is the court that first hears a matter. Typically this is the trial court (essentially synonymous with "first instance").

Parentelic method—A method of determining how to pass on property after death that is common in civil law systems

Pareto-optimal solutions—A solution to a situation of strategic interaction or conflict in which it is not possible to further improve the situation of one side without harming the situation of the other

Pari materia—In connection with the same subject (e.g., "these two regulations are *in pari material* because the regulate the same activity)

Personal status—A body of law dealing with the rights and responsibilities of people depending on their relationship to others or their social position in society (e.g., as children, as husbands, as parents, as wives)

Physical persons—Actual people (in contrast to "legal persons," which need not be actual people but are treated as such by a law or regulation)

Prison rates—The proportion of a population that is incarcerated

Pro bono—Legal work done without charge by a lawyer as a public service

Procuracy—The public prosecutor

Rule of law—The concept that a government is limited by legal norms or a written constitution

Sainte-Lague formula—One of a number of formulae that can be used to allocate seats under party list systems of proportional representation. The formula, devised in 1910 by the French mathematician Sainte-Lague; involves dividing each party's vote by a series of divisors (1,3,5,7,9 etc.) and allocating seats to parties on the basis of the highest quotients. Sainte-Lague divisors (rather than a straight numeric sequence of 1,2,3,4,5) tend to favor minor parties over major parties by making it harder for major parties to win each additional seat.

Search and seizure—An area of law dealing with the power of the police to search persons and property, and to seize items found during a search

Separation of powers—A political system that separates executive, legislative, and judicial powers of government into separate branches. Some systems combine two, or even all three, powers into single institutions. In the United States, many administrative agencies actually exercise at least first level judicial powers, and many administrative agencies also exercise what amount to legislative powers in promulgating detailed legal regulations. In other systems, the absence of a separation of powers, particularly between the executive and the legislative, is more explicit, as in the Westminster-style parliamentary system.

Special leave—Leave of a court (see above) granted under special circumstances

Specialized jurisdiction—A form of limited jurisdiction in which a court is empowered to hear only cases of a specific type, such as probate court, or traffic court, or labor court (compare to "general jurisdiction" and "limited jurisdiction")

Stare decisis—Adherence to precedent

Subjects—Geographic units to which political and legal rights attach

Summary jurisdiction—A form of jurisdiction of a court dealing with very minor matters that the court can dispose of through relatively informal procedures, often without maintaining any record of the disposition

Takings (as in takings clause)—The power of the government to appropriate property for public purposes

Taxation of costs—A procedure for determining the appropriate amount of legal fees; procedures for taxation of costs are commonly used in legal systems employing a "loser pays" rule in litigation

Transparency—The concept that actions of government and decision processes should be clear and open to easy scrutiny by the public

Ultra vires—"Beyond the power"; if a legislative action is "ultra vires" it exceeds the power granted to the legislative body

Westminster-style government—The form of parliamentary government associated with Great Britain

CONTRIBUTORS

Masaki Abe
Osaka City University
Osaka, Japan
Japan

Dauda Abubakar
University of Maiduguri
Maiduguri, Borno State, Nigeria
Nigeria

Adila Abusharaf
University of Toronto
Toronto, Ontario, Canada
Sudan

Erin Ackerman
Johns Hopkins University
Baltimore, Maryland
Public Law

David Adamany
Temple University
Philadelphia, Pennsylvania
Michigan

Danny M. Adkison
Oklahoma State University
Stillwater, Oklahoma
Oklahoma

Alvaro Aguilar-Alfu
Fabrega, Barsallo, Molino & Mulino
Panama City, Panama
Panama

Sharhabeel Al Zaeem
Sharhabeel Al Zaeem & Associates
Gaza City, Gaza Strip, Palestinian
   Authority
Palestine

M. Shah Alam
University of Chittagong
Chittagong, Bangladesh
Bangladesh

Mohammad Al-Momani
University of North Texas
Denton, Texas
Syria

Butti S. Al-Muhairi
United Arab Emirates University
Sharjah, United Arab Emirates
United Arab Emirates

Seth S. Andersen
American Bar Association
Chicago, Illinois
Merit Selection ("Missouri Plan")

John L. Anderson
University of Nebraska at Kearney
Kearney, Nebraska
Nebraska

Anne N. Angwenyi
Environmental Law Institute
Washington, DC
Kenya

Kenny Anthony
Prime Minister of St. Lucia
Castries, St. Lucia, West Indies
St. Lucia

Rose-Marie B. Antoine
University of the West Indies
Bridgetown, Barbados, West Indies
Bahamas
Barbados

Nicholas Aroney
The University of Queensland
St. Lucia, Queensland, Australia
Queensland

Allan Ashman
American Judicature Society
Chicago, Illinois
Judicial Selection, Methods of

Mary Atwell
Radford University
Radford, Virginia
General Deterrence

Judith Baer
Texas A&M University
College Station, Texas
Feminist Jurisprudence

John Baldwin
University of Birmingham
Birmingham, United Kingdom
Citizens Advice Bureaux
Small Claims Courts

Scott W. Barclay
University at Albany–State University of
   New York
Albany, New York
Australia

G. Bayasgalan
Ministry of Justice and Home Affairs of
   Mongolia
Ulaanbaatar, Mongolia
Mongolia

Maureen Anne Bell
Independent Scholar
Orlando, Florida
Gypsy Law

Yadh Ben Achour
University of Tunis
La Marsa, Tunisia
Tunisia

Sara C. Benesh
University of Wisconsin–Milwaukee
Milwaukee, Wisconsin
Louisiana

Marjorie L. Benson
University of Saskatchewan
Saskatoon, Saskatchewa, Canada
Saskatchewan

Rodrigo Bermeo
Bermeo and Bermeo Law Firm
Quito, Ecuador
Ecuador

Rodolphe Biffot
The University of Queensland
Brisbane, Queensland, Australia
Gabon

Elizabeth Anona Bishop
The American University in Cairo
Cairo, Egypt
Egypt

Botond Bitskey
Office of the President of the
    Hungarian Republic, Head of
    Constitutional and Legal
    Department
Budapest, Hungary
Hungary

Ann Black
University of Queensland
Brisbane, Queensland, Australia
Brunei

Helle Blomquist
Copenhagen University
Copenhagen, Denmark
Denmark

Joseph Board
Union College
Schenectady, New York
Sweden

Michael Bogdan
University of Lund
Lund, Sweden
Cape Verde
Comoros
Djibouti

Johanna Bond
Georgetown University Law Center,
    Visiting Professor
Washington, DC
Nepal

Andy Boon
University of Westminster School
    of Law
London, United Kingdom
Solicitors

Gregory R. Bordelon
Louisiana State University Law Center
Baton Rouge, Louisiana
Napoleonic Code

Matthew H. Bosworth
Winona State University
Winona, Minnesota
North Dakota

Lauren Bowen
John Carroll University
University Heights, Ohio
Ohio

Michael W. Bowers
University of Nevada, Las Vegas
Las Vegas, Nevada
Nevada

Paul Brace
Rice University
Houston, Texas
United States—State Systems

Stephen G. Bragaw
Sweet Briar College
Amherst, Virginia
Native American Law, Traditional

Saul Brenner
University of North Carolina, Charlotte
Charlotte, North Carolina
Certiorari, Writ of

Beau Breslin
Skidmore College
Saratoga Springs, New York
Lesotho

John W. Bridge
University of Exeter
Exeter, United Kingdom
Mauritius

Richard A. Brisbin, Jr.
West Virginia University
Morgantown, West Virginia
West Virginia

Joan Brockman
Simon Fraser University
Burnaby, British Columbia, Canada
British Columbia

Sonya Brown
University of Wisconsin
Madison, Wisconsin
International Court of Justice

Carl Bruch
Environmental Law Institute
Washington, DC
Kenya

David M. Bulger
University of Prince Edward Island
Charlottetown, Prince Edward Island,
    Canada
Prince Edward Island

Jenny Burley
Flinders University
Adelaide, South Australia, Australia
South Australia

Charles Burton
Brock University
St. Catharines, Ontario, Canada
China

Piengpen Butkatanyoo
Wisconsin Law School
Madison, Wisconsin
Thailand

Dennis Byron
Chief Justice, Eastern Caribbean
    Supreme Court
Castries, Saint Lucia, West Indies
St. Kitts and Nevis

Bradley C. Canon
University of Kentucky
Lexington, Kentucky
Kentucky

Henry F. Carey
Georgia State University
Atlanta, Georgia
Adversarial System
Guyana
Jewish Law

Lidia Casas
Universidad Diego Portales
Santiago, Chile
Chile

Anthony M. Champagne
University of Texas at Dallas
Richardson, Texas
Texas

Ross E. Cheit
Brown University
Providence, Rhode Island
Rhode Island

Paul Chen
University of Southern California
Los Angeles, California
California

Hiram E. Chodosh
Case Western Reserve University
Cleveland, Ohio
Indonesia
Pakistan
Palestine

David S. Clark
Willamette University College of Law
Salem, Oregon
Germany

Cornell W. Clayton
Washington State University
Pullman, Washington
Government Legal Departments
Washington

Douglas Clouatre
Kennesaw State University
Kennesaw, Georgia
Cyprus
Grenada
Haiti
Iran
Kuwait
Liberia
Lithuania
Madagascar
Mali
Morocco
Oman
Paraguay
Qatar
Tajikistan
Turkmenistan

Jennifer Corrin Care
University of Queensland
Brisbane, Queensland, Australia
Fiji
Solomon Islands

Christopher David Costanzo
International Intelligence and Security
    Consultant
Randolph, Vermont
Vermont

Buket Ö. Cox
Independent Scholar
Istanbul, Turkey
Ottoman Empire

Bruce Cronin
University of Wisconsin
Madison, Wisconsin
International Law

Jill Crystal
Auburn University
Auburn, Alabama
Saudi Arabia

Jefferson Cumberbatch
University of the West Indies
Bridgetown, Barbados, West Indies
Antigua and Barbuda

Cristina Nogueira da Silva
Universidade Nova de Lisboa
Lisbon, Portugal
Portugal

Kenneth G. Dau-Schmidt
Indiana University
Bloomington, Indiana
Law and Economics
White & Case LLP
Hanoi, Vietnam
Bhutan

Maria Elisabetta de Franciscis
Università Degli Studi di Napoli
    Federico II
Napoli, Italy
Italy

Simon Deakin
University of Cambridge
Cambridge, United Kingdom
Labor Law

Elizabeth F. Defeis
Seton Hall University
Newark, New Jersey
Armenia
War Crimes Tribunals

A. J. Dekker
Leiden University Faculty of Law
Leiden, The Netherlands
Netherlands Antilles and Aruba
Suriname

Kevin den Dulk
Grand Valley State University
Allendale, Michigan
Wisconsin

Sinclair Dinnen
Australian National University
Canberra, Australian Capital Territory,
    Australia
Papua New Guinea

Ali G. Dizboni
University of Montreal
Montreal, Quebec, Canada
Afghanistan

Michael Dodson
Texas Christian University
Ft. Worth, Texas
El Salvador

Lauren Dundes
McDaniel College
Westminster, Maryland
Corporal Punishment

Christopher Dunn
Memorial University of Newfoundland
St. John's, Newfoundland, Canada
Newfoundland and Labrador

Ralph Durham
Kennesaw State University
Kennesaw, Georgia
Chad

Charles R. Epp
University of Kansas
Lawrence, Kansas
Kansas

Lyda Favali
Universita' di Torino
Torino, Italy
Eritrea

Randall Fegley
Pennsylvania State University
University Park, Pennsylvania
Central African Republic
Equatorial Guinea
Somalia

William F. Felice
Eckerd College
St. Petersburg, Florida
International Tribunal for the Law
    of the Sea

Lilia Ferro-Clérico
University of Uruguay
Montevideo, Uruguay
Uruguay

Bonnie S. Fisher
University of Cincinnati
Cincinnati, Ohio
Rehabilitation

Roy B. Flemming
Texas A&M University
College Station, Texas
Canada

John Flood
University of Westminster
London, United Kingdom
Barristers

Charles Manga Fombad
University of Botswana
Gaborone, Botswana
Cameroon

Craig Forrest
University of Queensland
St.Lucia, Australia
Mozambique

James C. Foster
Oregon State University
Corvallis, Oregon
Legal Education
Oregon

Gerrit Franssen
Centrum voor Rechtssociologie
Antwerpen, Belgium
Belgium

Rebecca R. French
Buffalo School of Law: State University
    of New York
Buffalo, NY
Tibet

Bertram C. Frey
United States Environmental Protection
    Agency
Chicago, Illinois
Environmental Law

Katalin Füzér
University of Pennsylvania
Philadelphia, Pennsylvania
Hungary

Michael Gallagher
Estonian Law Centre, Advisor
Tartu, Estonia
Estonia

Miriam Gani
Australian National University
Canberra, Australian Capital Territory,
    Australia
Australia

Bryant Garth
American Bar Foundation
Chicago, Illinois
International Arbitration

Noel Gbaguidi
Université de Cotonou
Cotonou, Bénin
Benin

Robert P. George
Princeton University
Princeton, New Jersey
Legal Positivism

Tracey E. George
Northwestern University School of Law
Chicago, Illinois
Contract Law

Joshua Getzler
St Hugh's College & Law Faculty,
    University of Oxford
Oxford, United Kingdom
Equity

Steven Gibens
Centrum voor Rechtssociologie
Antwerpen, Belgium
Belgium

James N. Gilbert
University of Nebraska at Kearney
Kearney, Nebraska
Fines

Mark Gillen
University of Victoria
Victoria, British Columbia, Canada
Malaysia

Georgia Brown Gillett
University of Miami
Coral Gables, Florida
Belize

Jonathan Goldberg-Hiller
University of Hawai'i
Honolulu, Hawai'i
Hawai'i

Mark Goodale
Emory University
Atlanta, Georgia
Customary Law
Moots
Romania

Michael Wallace Gordon
University of Florida
Gainesville, Florida
Common Law

Karen Gottlieb
Court Consultant
Nederland, Colorado
Channel Islands
Colorado

Jon B. Gould
George Mason University
Fairfax, Virginia
Bosnia and Herzegovina
Shaming

Mark A. Graber
University of Maryland
College Park, Maryland
Constitutional Review

Kevin R. Gray
Fellow in International Law and
    Human Rights, British Institute of
    International and Comparative Law
London, United Kingdom
*Dispute Resolution under Regional Trade
    Agreements: NAFTA*

Marla N. Greenstein
Alaska Commission on Judicial
    Conduct
Anchorage, Alaska
Alaska

Anne Griffiths
University of Edinburgh
Edinburgh, Scotland
Botswana

Joanna L. Grossman
Hofstra Law School
Hempstead, New York
Probate/Succession Law

Joel B. Grossman
The Johns Hopkins University
Baltimore, Maryland
Constitutional Law
Public Law

Gerard Gryski
Auburn University
Auburn, Alabama
Alabama

Carlo Guarnieri
University of Bologna
Bologna, Italy
Magistrates—Civil Law Systems

Helgi Gunnlaugsson
University of Iceland
Reykjavik, Iceland
Iceland

Brigid Hadfield
University of Essex
Colchester, United Kingdom
United Kingdom

Johann J. Hagen
Universität Salzburg
Salzburg, Austria
Austria

Timothy M. Hagle
University of Iowa
Iowa City, Iowa
Iowa

Susan Brodie Haire
University of Georgia
Athens, Georgia
South Carolina

Melinda Gann Hall
Michigan State University
East Lansing, Michigan
United States—State Systems

Linn Hammergren
World Bank
Washington, DC
Peru

Roger Handberg
University of Central Florida
Orlando, Florida
Costa Rica

Tatum L. Hands
University of Western Australia
Nedlands, Western Australia, Australia
Western Australia

Valerie Hans
University of Delaware
Newark, Delaware
Jury Selection (voir dire)

Katy Harriger
Wake Forest University
Winston-Salem, North Carolina
Prosecuting Authorities

Christine B. Harrington
New York University
New York, New York
Administrative Law
Neighborhood Justice Centers

Roger E. Hartley
University of Arizona
Tucson, Arizona
Pro Se Cases
Virginia

John Hatchard
University of London
London, United Kingdom
Zimbabwe

Steven H. Hatting
University of St. Thomas
St. Paul, Minnesota
Minnesota

Melissa Haussman
Suffolk University
Boston, Massachusetts
Privy Council

Robert M. Hayden
University of Pittsburgh
Pittsburgh, Pennsylvania
*Yugoslavia: Kingdom of and Socialist
    Republic*

Roger Haydock
William Mitchell College of Law
St. Paul, Minnesota
Arbitration

Stacia L. Haynie
Louisiana State University
Baton Rouge, Louisiana
Philippines

Kathryn Hendley
University of Wisconsin
Madison, Wisconsin
Russia

Steven E. Hendrix
International Human Rights Law
    Institute, De Paul University College
    of Law
Chicago, Illinois
Bolivia
Guatemala

Gerti Hesseling
African Studies Centre
Leiden, The Netherlands
Senegal

M. H. Hoeflich
University of Kansas
Lawrence, Kansas
Roman Law

Sean O. Hogan
University of Illinois at Springfield
Springfield, Illinois
Delaware

Kenneth Holland
University of Memphis
Memphis, Tennessee
Confederate States of America
Judges, Nonjudicial Activities of

Michael J. Horan
University of Wyoming
Laramie, Wyoming
Wyoming

Bob Hughes
University of the South Pacific
Port Vila, Vanuatu
Micronesia, Federated States of
Tuvalu

Patricia Hughes
University of Calgary
Calgary, Alberta, Canada
New Brunswick

Alan Hunt
Carleton University
Ottawa, Ontario, Canada
Marxist Jurisprudence

Eugene Huskey
Stetson University
Deland, Florida
Kyrgyzstan

Fiona Hussin
Northern Territory University
Darwin, Northern Territory, Australia
Northern Territory of Australia

Andrew Huxley
School of Oriental and African Studies
London, United Kingdom
Buddhist Law

Gulnara Iskakova
American University in Kyrgyzstan,
    Program in Law
Bishkek, Kyrgyzstan
Kyrgyzstan

Donald W. Jackson
Texas Christian University
Ft. Worth, Texas
*European Court and Commission on
    Human Rights*
*Inter-American Commission and Court
    on Human Rights*

Fatou Jagne
Institute for Human Rights and
    Development in Africa
Banjul, The Gambia
Gambia

Dayanath C. Jayasuriya
Attorney at Law
Nawala, Sri Lanka
Criminal Procedures
Sri Lanka

Aberra Jembere
Addis Ababa University
Addis Ababa, Ethiopia
Ethiopia

Tassaduq Hussain Jilani
Judge Lahore High Court Lahore
Lahore, Punjab Pakistan
Pakistan

David Johnson
University College of Cape Breton
Sydney, Nova Scotia, Canada
Nova Scotia

Ronald C. Kahn
Oberlin College
Oberlin, Ohio
Parliamentary Supremacy

Pascal K. Kambale
The Kinshasa Bar Association; Human
    Rights Watch
Kinshasa, Democratic Republic
    of Congo
*Congo, Democratic Republic of
    (Kinshasa)*

Jimmy Kandeh
University of Richmond
Richmond, Virginia
Sierra Leone

Ibrahima Kane
Independent Scholar
London, United Kingdom
Guinea

Mariana Karagiozova-Finkova
Sofia University Law School
Sofia, Bulgaria
Bulgaria

George Katrougalos
Athens, Greece
Greece
Uzbekistan

Kristin Kelly
University of Connecticut
Storrs, Connecticut
Connecticut

Jim Kennan
Independent Scholar
Melbourne, Victoria, Australia
Victoria, State of

Sheila Suess Kennedy
IUPUI
Indianapolis, Indiana
Indiana

Sally J. Kenney
University of Minnesota
Minneapolis, Minnesota
European Court of Justice

Roger P. Kerans
Supreme Court of the Yukon
Whitehorse, Yukon Territory, Canada
Counsel, Borden Ladner Gervais Law
    Offices
Calgary, Alberta, Canada
Northern Territories of Canada

Lynn Khadiagala
American University
Washington, DC
Uganda

Goran Klemencic
University of Ljubljana
Ljubljana, Slovenia
Slovenia

Heinz Klug
University of Wisconsin
Madison, Wisconsin
South Africa

John C. Knechtle
Florida Coastal School of Law
Jacksonville, Florida
Belarus
Georgia (Country)
Ukraine

Nora Knudsen
University of Buenos Aires School
    of Law
Laguna Beach, California
Argentina

Joel F. Knutson
American Judicature Society
Chicago, Illinois
Merit Selection ("Missouri Plan")

Yasantha Kodagoda
Senior State Counsel
Colombo, Sri Lanka
Criminal Procedures

Frank Kopecky
University of Illinois at Springfield
Springfield, Illinois
Paralegal
Juvenile Justice

Edmond Kwam Kouassi
University of Togo
Boston, Massachusetts
Togo

Daniel Kramer
College of Staten Island, CUNY
Staten Island, New York
New York

William P. Kratzke
University of Memphis
Memphis, Tennessee
Moldova

Jayanth K. Krishnan
William Mitchell College of Law
St. Paul, Minnesota
India

Daniel Krislov
University of New Hampshire
Durham, New Hampshire
New Hampshire

Herbert M. Kritzer
University of Wisconsin–Madison
Madison, Wisconsin
San Marino

Peter Krug
University of Oklahoma College of Law
Norman, Oklahoma
Macedonia
Yugoslavia: Serbia and Montenegro

Randall Kune
Barrister
Melbourne, Australia
Victoria, State of

Thomas D. Lancaster
Emory University
Atlanta, Georgia
Basque Region
Spain

Laura Langer
University of Arizona
Tucson, Arizona
Arizona

Drew Noble Lanier
University of Central Florida
Orlando, Florida
Florida

Erik Lastic
Comenius University
Bratislava, Slovakia
Slovakia

Alain A. Levasseur
Louisiana State University Law Center
Baton Rouge, Louisiana
Napoleonic Code

Nicholas J. O. Liverpool
P.O. Box 233
Goodwill, Commonwealth of
    Dominica, West Indies
Dominica

Augustin Loada
University of Ouagadougou
Ouagadougou, Burkina Faso
Burkina Faso

Peter Longo
University of Nebraska–Kearney
Kearney, Nebraska
Nebraska

James J. Lopach
University of Montana
Missoula, Montana
Montana

Aaron R. S. Lorenz
University of Massachusetts, Amherst
Amherst, Massachusetts
Jamaica
Massachusetts

Rett R. Ludwikowski
The Catholic University of America
Washington, DC
Poland

Iurie P. Lungu
Advocate, LLP, member
Chisinau, Moldova
Moldova

Jonathan Lurie
Rutgers University
Newark, New Jersey
*Military Justice, American (Law and
    Courts)*

Mona Lynch
San Jose State University
San Jose, California
Capital Punishment

Miguel Poiares Maduro
Universidade Nova de Lisboa
Lisboa, Portugal
Portugal

Cynthia Mahabir
University of California, Berkeley
Berkeley, California
Trinidad and Tobago

Marcus Mahmood
Loyola University–New Orleans
New Orleans, Louisiana
Legal Behavioralism

Richard Mahoney
University of Otago
Dunedin, New Zealand
New Zealand

Sylvia Maier
Georgia Institute of Technology
Atlanta, Georgia
Czech Republic
Malta

Richard J. Maiman
University of Southern Maine
Portland, Maine
Maine

Susan J. Marsnik
University of St. Thomas
St. Paul, Minnesota
Commercial Law (International Aspects)

Wendy L. Martinek
Binghamton University–State
    University of New York
Binghamton, New York
Guam
South Dakota
Virgin Islands, U.S.

Muhammad Khalid Masud
International Institute for the Study of
    Islam in the Modern World
Leiden, The Netherlands
Qadi (Qazi) Courts

Christine Kushinga Matsvai
University of Cape Town
Cape Town, South Africa
Swaziland

Mike McConville
City University, Hong Kong
Hong Kong
University of Warwick
Coventry, United Kingdom
Plea Bargaining

Peter McCormick
University of Lethbridge
Lethbridge, Alberta, Canada
Alberta
Manitoba

Michael D. McGowan
St. Thomas University
Fredericton, New Brunswick, Canada
Canon Law

Wayne V. McIntosh
University of Maryland at College Park
College Park, Maryland
District of Columbia
Maryland

Stephen E. Meili
University of Wisconsin Law School
Madison, Wisconsin
Consumer Law

Albert P. Melone
Southern Illinois University Carbondale
Carbondale, Illinois
Bulgaria

Carrie Menkel-Meadow
Georgetown University Law Center
Washington, DC
Alternative Dispute Resolution
Mediation

Brent Mescall
Borden Ladner Gervais LLP
Calgary, Alberta, Canada
Northern Territories of Canada

Alexandre Miguel Mestre
Confederação dos Agricultores de
    Portugal
Lisboa, Portugal
Angola

Karim Mezran
John Cabot University
Rome, Italy
Libya

Sharon Levrant Miceli
University of Cincinnati
Cincinnati, Ohio
Rehabilitation

Raymond Michalowski
Northern Arizona University
Flagstaff, Arizona
Cuba

Mark C. Miller
Clark University
Worcester, Massachusetts
Luxembourg
Norway

David C. Mirhady
Simon Fraser University
Burnaby, British Columbia, Canada
Ancient Athens

Stephanie Mizrahi
Washington State University
Pullman, Washington
Idaho

Khalfan S. Mohammed
Indiana University
Bloomington, Indiana
Tanzania

Kathleen M. Moore
University of Connecticut, Storrs
Storrs, Connecticut
Islamic Law

Matthew J. Moore
Johns Hopkins University
Baltimore, Maryland
Constitutional Law

Martha I. Morgan
University of Alabama
Tuscaloosa, Alabama
Colombia

H. F. Munneke
Universiteit Leiden
Leiden, The Netherlands
Netherlands Antilles and Aruba
Suriname

Fiona Murray
Solicitor
Melbourne, Australia
Monaco

Rachel Murray
Birkbeck College, University of London
London, United Kingdom
Guinea-Bissau

A. Peter Mutharika
Washington University School of Law
St. Louis, Missouri
Malawi

Tun Myint
Indiana University
Bloomington, Indiana
Burma

Muna Ndulo
Cornell University
Ithaca, New York
Zambia

Lisa Nelson
University of Pittsburgh
Pittsburgh, Pennsylvania
Pennsylvania

Charles Ntampaka
University of Notre Dame de la Paix
Namur, Belgium
Burundi
Rwanda

Richard T. Oakes
Hamline University School of Law
St. Paul, Minnesota
Albania

Rory O'Connell
Queen's University of Belfast
Belfast, Northern Ireland
Ireland
Natural Law

Vittorio Olgiati
University of Urbino
Urbino, Italy
Notaries

Robert E. Oliphant
William Mitchell College of Law
St. Paul, Minnesota
Family Law

Susan M. Olson
University of Utah
Salt Lake City, Utah
Utah

Timothy J. O'Neill
Southwestern University
Georgetown, Texas
Hong Kong

William R. Pace
Executive Director: World Federalist
    Movement
NGO Coalition for the International
    Criminal Court
New York, New York
International Criminal Court

Janine Alisa Parry
University of Arkansas
Fayetteville, Arkansas
Arkansas

Paul A. Passavant
Hobart and William Smith Colleges
Geneva, New York
Critical Legal Studies

Donald Paterson
University of the South Pacific
Port Vila, Vanuatu
Tonga
Vanuatu

Anthony G. Pazzanita
Independent Scholar
Wellesley Hills, Massachusetts
Algeria
Mauritania

Rogelio Pérez-Perdomo
Instituto de Estudios Superiores de
    Administracion
Caracas, Venezuela
Legal Professionals—Civil Law Traditions

Marta Poblet
Universitat Autònoma de Barcelona
Barcelona, Spain
Andorra
Catalonia

Adrian Popovici
Universite de Montreal, Pavillon
    Maximilien-Caron
Montreal, Quebec, Canada
Quebec

Guy Powles
Monash University
Victoria, Australia
Samoa

William Prillaman
Senior Latin American analyst, U.S.
    Government
Washington, DC
Honduras

Doris Marie Provine
Arizona State University
Tempe, Arizona
France
Lay Judiciaries

Marc-Georges Pufong
Valdosta State University
Valdosta, Georgia
Seychelles

Mere Pulea
University of the South Pacific
Suva, Fiji Islands
Kiribati

Steven Puro
Saint Louis University
St. Louis, Missouri
Magistrates—Common Law Systems
Missouri

Hassan Ali Radhi
Hassan Radhi & Associates
Manama, Bahrain
Bahrain

Kirk A. Randazzo
Michigan State University
East Lansing, Michigan
Appellate Courts

Malia Reddick
American Judicature Society
Chicago, Illinois
Judicial Selection, Methods of

Alison Dundes Renteln
University of Southern California
Los Angeles, California
Human Rights Law
Indigenous and Folk Legal Systems

Harold O. M. Rocha
University of Iowa College of Law
Iowa City, Iowa
Nicaragua

Ralf Rogowski
University of Warwick
Coventry, United Kingdom
Civil Law

Mirko Roš
Stiffler & Nater
Zurich, Switzerland
Switzerland

Keith S. Rosenn
University of Miami Law School
Coral Gables, Florida
Brazil

Carlo Rossetti
University of Parma
Parma, Italy
Inquisitorial Procedure

Emile Sahliyeh
University of North Texas
Denton, Texas
Jordan
Lebanon
Yemen

Helen Sakellariou
Lawyer
Athens, Greece
Greece

Shannon A. Santana
University of Cincinnati
Cincinnati, Ohio
Rehabilitation

Charles R. Venator Santiago
University of Massachusetts
Amherst, Massachusetts
Puerto Rico
*The Spanish Empire and the Laws of the
    Indies*

Georges Santoni-Recio
Russin Vecchi & Heredia Bonetti
Santo Domingo, Dominican Republic
Dominican Republic

Sara Schatz
University of Florida
Gainesville, Florida
Mexico

Stuart Scheingold
University of Washington
Seattle, Washington
Cause Lawyering

Jennifer Schense
NGO Coalition for the International
    Criminal Court
New York, New York
International Criminal Court

William D. Schreckhise
University of Arkansas
Fayetteville, Arkansas
Arkansas

Howard Schweber
University of Wisconsin
Madison, Wisconsin
Constitutionalism
Federalism
Private Law

Gerhard Seibert
Centro de Estudos Africanos e Asiáticos
    (CEAA), Instituto de Investigação
    Científica Tropical (IICT)
Lisbon, Portugal
São Tomé and Príncipe

Melanie R. Senior
Cinque Morrow Solicitors
Ballarat, Victoria Australia
Australian Capital Territory

Gregory C. Shaffer
University of Wisconsin
Madison, Wisconsin
World Trade Organization

Hootan Shambayati
Bilkent University
Ankara, Turkey
Turkey

Reginald Sheehan
Michigan State University
East Lansing, Michigan
Appellate Courts
New South Wales

Robert B. Shelledy
University of Wisconsin–Madison
Madison, Wisconsin
Vatican

Mark Sidel
University of Iowa
Iowa City, Iowa
Laos
Vietnam

Susan Silbey
Massachusetts Institute of Technology
Cambridge, Massachusetts
Law and Society Movement

Sangeeta Sinha
University of North Texas
Denton, Texas
Kazakhastan

Peter H. Solomon, Jr.
University of Toronto
Toronto, Ontario, Canada
Soviet System

Sang-Hyun Song
Seoul National University
Seoul, Korea
South Korea

Lorne Sossin
University of Toronto
Toronto, Ontario, Canada
Ontario

Vijayashri Sripati
Vaish Associates
New Delhi, India
Maldives

Gilbert K. St. Clair
University of New Mexico
Albuquerque, New Mexico
New Mexico

Michael Steenson
William Mitchell College of Law
St. Paul, Minnesota
Tort Law

Susan M. Sterett
University of Denver
Denver, Colorado
Administrative Tribunals
England and Wales

Maurice Sunkin
University of Essex
Colchester, United Kingdom
Judicial Review
United Kingdom

Nicole Sylvester
O.R. Sylvester and Co.
Kingstown, St. Vincent, West Indies
Saint Vincent and the Grenadines

Phillip Tagini
University of the South Pacific
Port Vila, Vanuatu
Micronesia, Federated States of
Nauru
Palau
Tuvalu

Susette M. Talarico
University of Georgia
Athens, Georgia
Georgia (State)

Michal Tamir
Hebrew University of Jerusalem
Tel-Aviv, Israel
Israel

Moses K. Tesi
Middle Tennessee State University
Murfreesboro, Tennessee
Congo, Republic of
Côte d'Ivoire
Namibia

Peter Tesi
University of Virginia Law School
Charlottesville, Virginia
Niger

Amy Thistlethwaite
Northern Kentucky University
Highland Heights, Kentucky
Protection of Society

Thomas H. Thornburg
University of North Carolina at Chapel
  Hill
Chapel Hill, North Carolina
North Carolina

Warwick J. Tie
Massey University
Auckland, New Zealand
Legal Pluralism

Tim Tierney
Baker Tierney & Wilson, Lawyers
Huonville, Tasmania Australia
Tasmania

Victoria M. Time
Old Dominion University
Norfolk, Virginia
Criminal Law
Trial Courts

Pekka Timonen
Ministry of Trade and Industry
Helsinki, Finland
Finland

Yolisaguyau Tom'tavala
University of the South Pacific
Port Vila, Vanuatu
Marshall Islands

Bora Touch
Legal Aid Commission of New South
  Wales, Australia
Haymarket, New South Wales, Australia
Cambodia

Ruth Triplett
Old Dominion University
Norfolk, Virginia
Criminal Sanctions, Purposes of
Specific (Individual) Deterrence

Dalia Tsuk
University of Arizona
Tucson, Arizona
Legal Realism

Keith Uff
University of Birmingham
Birmingham, United Kingdom
Civil Procedure

Mark Ungar
Brooklyn College, City University of
    New York
Brooklyn, New York
Venezuela

Alan Uzelac
Faculty of Law
Zagreb, Croatia
Croatia

Leilani Va'a
Apia, Samoa
Kiribati

Koen Van Aeken
Centrum voor Rechtssociologie
Antwerpen, Belgium
Belgium

Jerry Van Hoy
The University of Toledo
Toledo, Ohio
Law Firms

Peter J. van Koppen
Netherlands Institute for the Study of
    Criminality and Law Enforcements
    (NSCR)
Leiden, The Netherlands
University of Antwerp, Belgium
Antwerp, Belgium
Netherlands

Francis Van Loon
University of Antwerp
Antwerp, Belgium
Belgium

Eddy D. Ventôse
University of the West Indies
Bridgetown, Barbados
St. Lucia

Agri Verrija
Hamline University
St. Paul, Minnesota
Albania

Neil Vidmar
Duke Law School
Durham, North Carolina
Juries

John R. Vile
Middle Tennessee State University
Murfreesboro, Tennessee
Tennessee

Alejandro Villegas-Jaramillo
Counsel to the Ministry of Foreign
    Commerce, Republic of Colombia
Bogota, Colombia
Dispute Resolution under Regional Trade
    Agreements: Mercosur

Mary L. Volcansek
Texas Christian University
Fort Worth, Texas
Judicial Misconduct/Judicial Discipline

Ernst J. Walch
Walch & Schurti, Vaduz, Liechtenstein
Vaduz, Liechtenstein
Liechtenstein

Diane E. Wall
Mississippi State University
Mississippi State, Mississippi
Mississippi

Pinky S. Wassenberg
University of Illinois, Springfield
Springfield, Illinois
Illinois

Russell L. Weaver
University of Louisville
Louisville, Kentucky
Belarus

John B. Wefing
Seton Hall University School of Law
Newark, New Jersey
New Jersey

David Weiden
United States Naval Academy
Annapolis, Maryland
Northern Ireland
Law Clerks

Claude E. Welch
Buffalo State College, State University
    of New York
Buffalo, New York
African Court/Commission on Human
    and Peoples' Rights

Christopher A. Whann
University Without Walls
Lesotho

Donald E. Wilkes, Jr.
UGA School of Law
Athens, Georgia
Habeas Corpus, Writ of

Joy A. Willis
Michigan State University
East Lansing, Michigan
New South Wales

Ian D. Willock
University of Dundee
Dundee, United Kingdom
Scotland

Bruce M. Wilson
University of Central Florida
Orlando, Florida
Costa Rica

V. S. Winslow
National University of Singapore
Singapore
Singapore

Thomas Wipf
Stiffler and Nater
Zurich, Switzerland
Swiss Cantons

Gordon R. Woodman
University of Birmingham
Birmingham, Britain
Ghana

John Wooldredge
University of Cincinnati
Cincinnati, Ohio
Incarceration
Retribution

David Yalof
University of Connecticut
Storrs, Connecticut
Connecticut
United States—Federal System

Akiko Yanai
APEC Study Center, Institute of
    Developing Economies (IDE)
Chiba, Japan
Dispute Resolution under Regional Trade
    Agreements: APEC

Dae-Kyu Yoon
Kyungnam University
Masan, Korea
North Korea

Chi-Min (Jimmy) Yu
Soochow Law School
Taipei, Taiwan, Republic of China
Taiwan

Mamoon Amin Zaki
Lemoyne Owen College
Memphis, Tennessee
Iraq

Frances Kahn Zemans
Justice System Consultant
Chicago, Illinois
Azerbaijan
Judicial Independence

Frederick Zemans
Osgoode Hall Law School of York
    University
Toronto, Ontario, Canada
Legal Aid

Zigurds L. Zile
University of Wisconsin–Madison
Madison, Wisconsin
Latvia

Gary Zuk
Auburn University
Auburn, Alabama
Alabama

INDEX

Arms, right to bear, 702
Arranged marriages, 524
Arron, Henck, 1549
Arroyo, Gloria Macapagal, 1297–1298
Articling, 882, 1238
Aruba, 1114, **1122–1127**
Asante population, 590–592
ASEAN. *See* Association of Southeast Asian
    Nations
Asia-Pacific Economic Cooperation (APEC),
    426–428
Asian Development Bank, 1056
Al-Assad, Hafiz, 1577
ASSANDEP. *See* Association des Anciens
    Détenus Politiques et Victimes de la
    Répression
Assassinations
    Anwar Sadat, 463
    Congo's Ngouabi, 341
    Dominican Republic's Trujillo, 452
    Jesuits in El Salvador, 473
    Rajiv Gandhi, 1527–1528
Assembly of States Parties, 724–725
Assembly of the Germans, 1068
Assize Courts (France), 1642
Associated Statehood, 1534
Association des Anciens Détenus Politiques et
    Victimes de la Répression (ASSANDEP),
    161
Association of Southeast Asian Nations
    (ASEAN), 427, 1056
Asunción Treaty, 433, 435
Ataturk, Mustafa Kemal, 1658
Athens. *See* Ancient Athens
Atolls (Maldives regional units), 964, 965
Attendant circumstances, 379
Attorney General; Unity Dow v. The, 187
Attorneys
    certiorari, 283
    duties and specialties, 131–132
    prosecuting authorities, 1334–1335
    See also Barristers; Law firms; Legal
        professionals—Civil law traditions;
        individual countries, states, provinces,
        and territories
Attorneys general, 23
    Antigua and Barbuda, 57
    Bahamas, 109
    Belize, 151–152, 153
    Channel Islands, 289–290
    Colombia's Fiscalia General, 313
    Fiji, 537
    government legal departments, 596
    Guatemala, 616
    Kenya, 825–826
    Lesotho, 898
    Nigeria, 1178
    Trinidad and Tobago, 1651
    West Australia, 1779
Audiencias (Spanish legal institutions), 64, 311,
    1523
Audit commissions and courts, 159
    Moldova, 1049
    Morocco, 1073
    Netherlands Antilles, 1125
    Senegal, 1431
    Suriname, 1553

Austin, John, 729
Australia, 60, **82–89**
    adversarial legal system, 8
    APEC membership, 426, 427
    bluefin tuna case, 732
    common law distribution, 322–323
    constitution without constitutionalism, 356
    equity, 498
    general deterrence, 568
    habeas corpus, 646
    international commercial law, 320
    jury system, 802
    legal aid services, 879–880
    legal education, 882
    nonjudicial activities of judges, 789
    occupation of Nauru, 1100
    paralegals, 1276
    parliamentary supremacy, 1280–1281
    plea bargaining, 1301
    Privy Council, 1325
    spread of jury system, 802
    tort law, 1638
    Victoria, 1749–1753
    West Australia, 1776–1780
    See also individual states and territories
Australia Act (1986), 1358
Australian Antarctic Territory, 82
Australian Capital Territory (ACT), 82, **89–91**
Australian Constitutions Act (1850), 1492
Australian Courts Act (1828), 84
Austria, **91–97**
    EU, membership in, 520
    impact on Liechtenstein legal system, 913
    ITLOS and, 731
    jury system, 802
    plea bargaining, 1302
Austro-Hungarian Empire, 391
    Czech Republic, 410–411
    Hungary, 671
    Romania, 1373
    Slovakia, 1455
    Slovenia, 1460
Autarky, North Korean, 1192
Authoritarian regimes
    Burma, 222–223
    Cambodia, 240–243
    judicial independence, 791
    judicial misconduct and discipline, 795
    Latvia, 853
    Lesotho, 896
    Liberia, 903
    Mexico, 1014
    Nigeria, 1177
    Philippines, 1297
    Turkmenistan, 1665–1668
    Uzbekistan, 1725–1727
    Vietnam, 1755–1756
Authoritarianism, constitutional, 1297
Autogolpe (self-coup), 1289, 1291, 1294
Automobile insurance, 589
Autonomous institutions (AI), 368
Avocats (attorneys), 306
    Côte d'Ivoire, 374
    Luxembourg, 929
    Romania, 1376
Avoués (French legal practitioners), 306
Awate, Idris Hamid, 501

Ayala Lasso, Jose, 667
Aylwin, Patricio, 293, 294
Ayora, Isidro, 457–458
Azerbaijan, 77, **97–103**
Aztec culture, 1012–1013
Azzali, Assoumani, 325

Baca, Joseph, 1143
Bafour people, 994
Bahamas, **105–111**, 646, 1325
Bahingantahes, Council of, 232–233
Bahrain, **111–116**
Baidy, Osmane, 997–998
Bailiffs, 150, 289, 1382
Baker v. Carr, 1610
Bakke, Alan, 239
Bakongo kingdom, 340
Balaguer, Joaquin, 452
Baldwin, Mathias, 1032
Balearic Islands, 1513
Balopi Commission, 182
Baltic republics
    Estonia, 504–509
    Latvia, 851–856
    Lithuania, 916–920
Balzac v. People of Puerto Rico, 1343
Banana presidents, 657
Banda, Hastings K., 950
Bandaranaike, S.W.R.D., 1528
Bangladesh, **116–124**, 523, 646, 755, 799, 1337
Banking sector, 58
    Andorra, 49–50
    Bahamas, 107–108, 110
    Brunei's interest-free system, 204
    Estonia, 509
    Liechtenstein, 911
    Monaco, 1051
    offshore banking, 111, 128, 287–290, 1126
Bankruptcy court (Minnesota), 1035
Bannister, Saxe, 1145
Bantu Authorities Act (1951), 1486
Baojia system, 299
Bar, structure and governance, 130–131
Bar associations. *See* Legal profession;
    individual countries, states, provinces, and
    territories
Bar Council, 130–131
Bar vocation course, 131
Barbados, 110, **125–130**, 268, 715, 802,
    1325, 1533
Barbarian peoples, 390–391
Barbie, Klaus, 171
Barbuda. *See* Antigua and Barbuda
Barrios, Justo Rufino, 614
Barristers, 7, **130–132**, 1468
    British Columbia, 198
    England and Wales, 478–479
    fused legal professions, 1494, 1606
    legal education, 882–883
    Mauritius, 1003–1004
    Northern Ireland, 1202–1203
    Solomon Islands, 1475
    South Australia's fused system, 1494
Barth, Heinrich, 1170
Basel Convention on the Control of
    Transboundary Movements of Hazardous
    Wastes and Their Disposal, 485

Base-superstructure notion, 985
Basic Laws
    Germany, 582, 584
    Hong Kong, 662
    Israel, 348, 354, 758, 759
Basque Region and people, **132–136,** 682, 1217
Basse-Navarre area, 132
Bastarache; Commonwealth v., 992
Basutoland, 896
Ba'th Party, 743, 744, 998, 1577
Bathurst Trade Union, 562
Batista, Fulgencio, 397
Bay of Pigs invasion, 397
Beccaria, Cesare, 385, 567–568, 1365, 1525
Becker, Gary, 857–859
Begbie, Matthew Baillie, 196
Begriffsjurisprudenz (jurisprudence based on
    logic), 1323
Behavioralism, legal, 859–860, **880–882**
Belarus, **136–144**
Belaunde, Fernando, 1289
Belgian Congo. *See* Burundi; Congo,
    Democratic Republic of
Belgium, **144–150**
    colonization of Burundi, 227–228
    colonization of Congo, 332–338
    EU, membership in, 520
    judicial selection, 799
    jury system, 802
    Luxembourg and, 927
    use of Napoleonic Code, 1092
    Rwanda as protectorate, 1383–1384,
        1386–1387
Belize, **151–154,** 799, 1325
Bello, Andrés, 459
Belton v. Gebhart, 418
Bemba, Jean-Pierre, 278
Ben Bella, Ahmed, 36, 37
Bench memos, 864
Benedict XIV, Pope, 260
Benedict XV, Pope, 260
Benelux Economic Union, 927
Bengal. *See* Bangladesh
Benin, **154–162**
Bent, Ellis, 1144–1145
Bentham, Jeremy, 206, 323, 477, 567–568,
    857, 1491, 1525
Bentley, Arthur, 881
Berber courts, 1072
Berber courts (Morocco), 1070–1071
Berber people
    Algeria, 35, 36–37, 39
    Libya, 905, 907
    Mauritania, 994
    Morocco, 1070–1071
Beretitenti (Kiribati president), 829, 831, 832
Berle, Adolf, 893, 894
Berlin Conference (1885), 332–333, 340, 404
Berman, Harold J., 139
Bermuda, 802, 1325
Bernasconi; R v., 1208
Bet din (rabbinic courts), 781
Bharatiya Janata Party (India), 695
Bhutan, **162–168**
Biblical law, 780–782, 1068
    See also Canon law

Bicameral legislatures
    Chile, 293
    Colombia, 312
    Czech Republic, 412
    Egypt, 463
    Fiji, 534
    Gabon, 561
    Lesotho, 898
    Namibia, 1086
    Tasmania, 1604–1605
    See also individual countries, states,
        provinces, and territories
Bidwell; Downes v., 1343
Bigamy, 524
Bigge, John Thomas, 1145
Biggers, Neal Jr., 1039
Biodiversity, 485, 975
Bird, Rose, 238
Birth control bans, 348, 351
Bishop, Joel Prentiss, 525
Bishop, Maurice, 607, 609, 1549
Biya, Paul, 247
Black, Donald, 881
Black, Hugo, 888
Black markets, 179–180, 400–401
Blacks. *See* Civil rights; Discrimination, racial;
    Segregation, racial
Blackstone, William, 525, 1322
Blair, John, 789
Blanco, Jorge, 452
Bloc de constitutionnalité, 552
Block contracting, 879
*Board of Regents of the University of Oklahoma;
    Sipuel v.,* 1228
Boer War, 181, 1556
Boganda, Barthelemy, 277
Bogdo Khan, 1059
Bogle, Paul, 769
Bogor Declaration (1994). *See* Dispute
    Mediation Service
Boies, David, 273
Bokassa, Jean-Bedel, 278, 280
Boko. *See* Equatorial Guinea
Bolanos, Enrique, 1165
Bolívar, Simón, 170, 311, 312, 1524
Bolivia, **169–175,** 795, 1092, 1273
Bonaire, 1122
Bonaparte, Joseph, 1523–1524
Bonaparte, Napoleon. *See* Napoleon
Bongo, Omar (formerly Albert-Bernard), 559,
    560–561
Boniface, Pope, 260
Border disputes, 722, 1547
Boren; Craig v., 1228
Bork, Robert, 888–889
Bose Levu Vakaturaga, 534
Bosnia and Herzegovina, **175–180,** 517
Boston Massacre (1770), 991
Botswana, 18, **180–187,** 722
Bougainville, 1264, 1267
Boumedienne, Houari, 36, 37, 38
Bowers v. Hardwick, 820
Bowring's Treaty (1826), 1614–1615
Boyars, 1044
Boyle, James, 388
Brandeis, Louis, 894
Brandeis Brief, 894

Brasilia Protocol (1991), 433–434
Braveheart (film), 1419
Brazil, **188–196**
    judicial selection, 799
    jury system, 802
    Mercosur membership, 433
    War of Triple Alliance, 1273
    women's rights, 526
Brazza, Pierre de, 340
Brennan, William, 2–3
Brenner, Saul, 282
Bretton Woods Institutions. *See* International
    Monetary Fund; World Bank
Bride burning, 523
Britain
    Anglo-Iraqi treaty, 742
    and The Bahamas, 105–106
    Bechuanaland Protectorate, 181–182
    Channel Islands, 287–290
    in Chinese history, 297–298
    commercial presence in Bahrain, 112
    common law origins and procedures,
        322–324
    conquest of the Sudan, 1542–1543
    federalism, 526
    in Jamaica, 767–768
    juvenile courts, 1643
    labor law, 843–844, 845
    Maldives as protected autonomous zone,
        964
    nonjudicial activities of judges, 788–789
    Pinochet's detention in, 293
    protection of Brunei, 201
    spread of jury system, 802
    tort law, 1638–1639
    Transjordan, establishment of, 783
    trial courts, 1641–1642
    unequal treaty with Thailand, 1614–1615
    unwritten constitution, 348, 354–355
    See also Colonies, British; England and
        Wales; Protectorates, British; Scotland;
        United Kingdom
British Antarctic Territory, 1325
British Columbia, **196–199,** 252
British East India Company, 694, 1109, 1478
British Guiana. *See* Guyana
British Honduras. *See* Belize
British Indian Ocean Territory, 1325
British mandate, 755–756
British North American Acts, 254, 1160–1161
British Residential System, 201
British South African Company (BSAC), 1816
British Virgin Islands, 445, 1325
Brotherhoods (Basque region), 133
Brougham, Henry, 1324
Brown v. Board of Education, 418, 809, 1610
Brunei, **199–205,** 363, 426, 646
Bryan, William Jennings, 1227–1228
BSAC. *See* British South African Company
Buddhist law, **205–208**
    Bangladesh, 116–117
    Bhutan, 162–168
    Burma, 223–224
    Indonesia, 705
    Mongolia, 1059
    Tibet, 1621–1625
Buick Motor Co.; MacPherson v., 1150

Bulgaria, **208–215**, 1302
Bulge, Battle of the, 927
Bundesrat (German federal council), 584
Bundesregierung (German federal government), 584–585
Bundestag (German federal parliament), 584
Bureau of Prisons, 597
Burger, Warren, 2
Bürgerliche Gesetzbuch (BGB), 305, 306
Burhanuddin Rabbani, 12, 13
Burkina Faso, **215–222**, 970
Burma, 207, **222–227**
Burmese Way to Socialism, 226
Burnham, Forbes, 638
Burns, John, 655
Burombo, Benjamin, 1817
Burundi, **227–233**
Bushell's Case (1670), 801
Business sector. *See* Corporate sector
Byi (Kyrgyz hereditary judges), 838–838
Byrd, Harry, 1761
Byzantine Empire, 1243
    Cyprus, 404
    Greece, 600
    inquisitorial procedure, 710
    Iran, 737
    and Russian legal system, 815

Cabildos (local council government), 310–311
CABx. *See* Citizens advice bureaux
Cadiz, Constitution of (1812), 1523–1524
Caenegem, R. C. van, 307
CAF. *See* Central American Federation
Cahill, Thomas, 780–782
Cairo Regional Center for International Commercial Arbitration, 718
Calabresi, Guido, 857–858
Calderón Guardia, Rafael Angel, 366
California, **235–239**, 646, 800
Calmar Union, 421
Cambodia, 207, **240–245**, 381
Cameroon, **245–252**, 492
Camouco (Panamanian fishing vessel), 732
Camp David Accord (1977), 757
Campbell, John A., 789
Canada, **252–259**
    APEC membership, 426
    acquisition of British Columbia, 196–197
    common law distribution, 322–323
    constitution without constitutionalism, 356
    constitutional review, 352
    corporal punishment, 363
    equity, 498
    general deterrence, 568
    habeas corpus, 646
    imposing fines, 538–539
    judicial selection, 799
    jury system, 802, 804
    legal aid services, 879–880
    legal education, 882
    NAFTA, 429–432
    nonjudicial activities of judges, 789
    plea bargaining, 1301
    prison population, 1339
    Privy Council, 1325
    rehabilitation, 1362–1363
    Supreme Court clerks, 863, 864

tort law, 1638
    See also individual provinces and territories
Canada Act (1982), 1236
Canadian Association of Provincial Judges, 258
Canadian Charter of Rights and Freedoms, 33, 254–255
Canadian Human Rights Act, 256–257
Canadian Judicial Council, 258
Canadian Venture Exchange (CDNX), 199
Canal Zone (Panama), 1260
Canary Islands, 1513
Canon law, **259–261**, 1734–1738
    Chile's family issues, 291
    Code of Canon Law, 260, 261
    Denmark, 421
    Eritrea, 502
    Ethiopia, 512
    Germany, 582
    in Lebanon, 872
    and Napoleonic code, 1090
    Roman law and, 1370
Cantonal courts (Switzerland), 1567–1569
Cantwell v. Connecticut, 345–346
Cape Verde, **262–267**, 630–631, 731
Capital punishment, **267–269**, 1339
    abolitionists, 169
    Antigua and Barbuda, 58
    Austro-Hungarian Empire, 410
    Bhutan's elimination of, 164
    Brunei, 202
    California, 238
    Cape Verde, 264
    Caribbean nations, 58, 110, 771–772, 1650
    China's Supreme People's Court, 300
    classification of crimes, 377
    Comoros, 326
    constitutional permissibility of, 127
    as cruel and unusual punishment, 379–380
    Djibouti, 441
    Equatorial Guinea, 491–492
    Guyana's withdrawal from International Covenant on Civil and Political Rights, 641
    gypsy law, 643
    human rights law and, 154, 667
    Iraq's hard line on, 744–745
    Malaysia, 960
    Massachusetts, 992
    Monaco, 1051
    Mozambique, 1077
    Nebraska, 1107
    Nepal, 1112
    Singapore, 1453
    Slovenia, 1463
    Uganda, 1675
    Ukraine, 1686
Cappelletti, Mauro, 796, 797
Captains regent (San Marino heads of state), 1401, 1402
CAR. *See* Central African Republic
Cardozo, Benjamin N., 1150
Carias Andino, Tibucio, 657
Carib people, 605, 606, 1391, 1532–1533, 1538
Caribbean Basin Initiative (CBI-II), 450
Caribbean Community (CARICOM), 56, 1326–1327

Bahamas, 105
Barbados, 125–130
Guyana, 638
Saint Kitts and Nevis, 1536
Saint Lucia, 1539
Saint Vincent and the Grenadines, 1394
Suriname, 1548–1549
Caribbean conquest, 1521–1522
Caribbean Court of Appeals, 638
Caribbean Court of Justice (CCJ), 154, 771–772, 1326, 1394. *See also* Eastern Caribbean Court system
Caribbean Rights group, 129
CARICOM. *See* Caribbean Community
Caroline Islands, 1024, 1251
Carr; Baker v., 1610
Carter, Walter S., 865
Case law
    African nations, 593, 1677
    Bangladesh, 119–120
    Caribbean nations, 107, 126
    England and Wales, 476
    folk law, study of, 703–704
    Japanese law, 775
    Marshall Islands, 981
Case-method approach, to legal education, 883
Cassation courts, 80
    Bahrain, 114, 115
    Belgium, 148–149
    Bulgaria, 212
    Burkina Faso, 219
    Ethiopia, 513
    France, 59–60, 552
    Gabon, 560
    Haiti, 649
    Italy, 763
    Luxembourg, 928
    Senegal, 1431
    Soviet system, 1511
    Turkey, 1661
Caste system, 693, 1109
Castilian law, 133
Castro, Fidel, 171, 397
Catalonia, 47–50, 132–136, **270–272**
Catholic Church, 259–261
    Belarus, 138
    canon law, 259–261
    divorce in Chile, 291
    abuses in Guatemala, 620
    inquisitorial procedure, 710–714
    Irish rights, 747
    legal professionals, 891
    Malta, 973
    Northern Ireland, 1197
    São Tomé and Príncipe, 1405
    Spanish Inquisition, 1521
    Spanish law, 1515
    See also Vatican
Caucuses, 733
Causation, 379
Cause lawyering, **272–275**
Cayman Islands, 1325
CDNX. *See* Canadian Venture Exchange
Ceausescu, Nicolae, 1372, 1373
Cedras, Raul, 649, 651
CEELI. *See* American Bar Association Central and East European Legal Initiative

ABOUT THE EDITOR

Herbert M. Kritzer is professor of Political Science and Law at the University of Wisconsin–Madison and director of the undergraduate program in Legal Studies and the Criminal Justice Certificate Program. He holds a B.A. in sociology from Haverford College (1969) and a Ph.D. in political science from the University of North Carolina (1974). He has conducted extensive empirical research on the American civil justice system, as well as research on other common law systems. He is the author of *The Justice Broker* (Oxford University Press, 1990), *Let's Make a Deal* (University of Wisconsin Press, 1991), and *Legal Advocates: Lawyers and Nonlawyers at Work* (University of Michigan Press, 1998), and is coauthor of *Courts, Law and Politics in Comparative Perspective* (Yale University Press, 1996). Over the last five years he has conducted research on the U.S. civil justice system dealing with the impact of Rule 11 sanctions, alternative forms of advocacy and representation, and the adult guardianship process in Wisconsin; research with a cross-national element has included writing on the English Rule, propensity to sue, and the politics in the English judicial system. He is currently completing a book manuscript based on a major, multifaceted study of contingency fee legal practice in the United States. He is also working on a study of decision making by the United States Supreme Court focusing on ways that law can be systematically incorporated in empirical models of the justices' voting decisions.